The
Church
of England

Year Book

125th Edition

2009

CHURCH HOUSE
PUBLISHING

Church House Publishing
Church House
Great Smith Street
London
SW1P 3AZ

ISBN 978-0-7151-1033-1
ISSN 0069 3987

Typeset by RefineCatch Ltd,
Bungay, Suffolk

Cover Design by Visible Edge

Printed in the UK by CPI
William Clowes Beccles NR34 7TL

The Church of England Year Book
The official Year Book of the
Church of England

*125th edition © The Archbishops'
Council 2008*

Contents

INDEX TO ADVERTISEMENTS

*The inclusion of an advertisement is for purposes of information and is not to be taken as
implying acceptance of the objects of the advertiser by the publisher.*

The Kingdom of God belongs to such as these...

The Children's Society is a leading children's charity committed to making childhood better for all children in the UK. Founded in 1881 as The Church of England Central Home for Waifs and Strays by Sunday school teacher, Edward Rudolf, our Christian values have remained the same for over 127 years. We believe in creating a society, which models the values of the Kingdom of God: love, justice and forgiveness.

There are a number of ways to work in partnership with The Children's Society, such as working together to directly support children and young people in your diocese, parish or school, using our worship resources, fundraising and volunteering or through awareness raising and prayer.

The Children's Society works together with The Church of England Children's Work Advisers and the Liturgical Commission to produce a number of liturgical resources to support you in your ministry:

- **Christingle** – Advent, Christmas and Ephipany seasons
- **Leaves of Life** – Eastertide
- **Halloween Choice** – Season of All Saints in October

For further information on free support resources and how to get involved visit **www.childrenssociety.org.uk** or call our Supporter Action Line on **0845 300 1148.**

Together we can make childhood better for all children

Charity Registration No. 221124 | Photograph posed by models for The Children's Society © Laurence Dutton

St Paul's Cathedral

SUNDAY SERVICES

0800 **Holy Communion**

1015 **Sung Mattins**

1130 **Sung Eucharist**

1515 **Evensong**

1800 **Evening Service**

On other days of the week the Eucharist is celebrated at 0800 and 1230.

Evensong is usually sung at 1700.

On Feast Days and at other times service times may be subject to change.

Updated information is available on the Cathedral website **www.stpauls.co.uk**

For service and visitor information call 020 7236 4128.

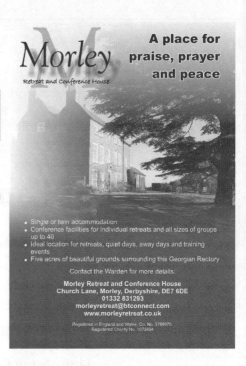

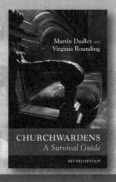

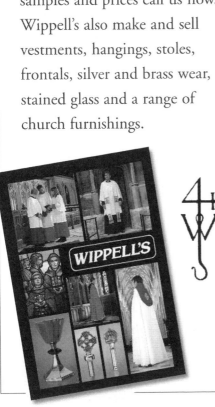

**Corporation of the
Sons of the Clergy**

**The Friends of the
Clergy Corporation**

Charities working together to support the clergy

The two leading clergy charities now work together in their grant administration and operate a unified grant-making system. Applications are considered by a common body of trustees, who are responsible for the affairs of both corporations. It is only necessary to complete a single application form and this is used by both organisations when considering an applicant's needs.

Grants are available for a wide range of purposes, including:

- ◆ **school clothing and school trips**
- ◆ **clerical clothing, holidays and resettlement**
- ◆ **heating and home maintenance for the retired**
- ◆ **bereavement expenses and expenses arising
from separation and divorce**

We can also help in cases of emergency, illness and misfortune. Our combined grants during 2007 of some £1.75m formed the largest source of charitable assistance to the clergy family nationwide.

We are now planning improvements to our services for beneficiaries, which means that more than ever help is needed in the form of donations and legacies.

For more information please contact us at:

**1 Dean Trench Street, London SW1P 3HB Tel: 020 7799 3696
Email: enquiries@clergycharities.org.uk
www.clergycharities.org.uk**

Charity No. 207736   Both registered in England and Wales   Charity No. 264724

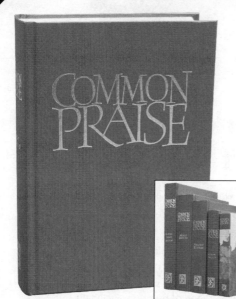

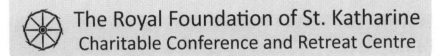

The Royal Foundation of St. Katharine
Charitable Conference and Retreat Centre

We are available for use by churches and charities and associated individuals from home and overseas.

We offer an attractive setting and modern facilities for Meetings, Conferences, Seminars, Receptions, Retreats and Quiet Days in the centre of London between the City and Canary Wharf.

» A range of meeting rooms with capacities of up to 70 people
» Residential accommodation for up to 44 people
» Free WiFi and full conference support facilities
» Wholesome food freshly prepared
» Daily worship in re-ordered chapel
» Disabled access and car parking for up to 20 cars
» Easily accessible by tube, rail and road
» Clergy save 10% on Bed and Breakfast

Go to **www.rfsk.org.uk** or call **0845 409 0138** for more information.
(2p/min from BT landline)

The Master's House

The Royal Foundation of St. Katharine   2 Butcher Row, London, E14 8DS
Tel 0845 409 0138   Email info@rfsk.org.uk   Web www.rfsk.org.uk
Registered Charity No. 223849

⊕ CHURCH HOUSE PUBLISHING

The official publisher of the Church of England

Church House Publishing equips the Church of England's local ministers and active churchgoers for worship, ministry and mission.

Alongside liturgy and reference resources – such as this Year Book – we provide practical and inspiring tools for:

- promoting mission and church growth
- ministry at major life events
- celebrating Christian seasons and festivals
- nurturing faith and discipleship with all ages.

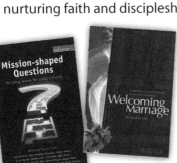

A YEAR IN REVIEW

NOVEMBER

In a House of Lords speech, the Archbishop of York criticized the 'unhealthy seam of rampant individualism' of human fertilization proposals, calling upon the Government to abandon its plans to remove the requirement for a father in IVF treatment.

The Archbishop called for fair trade in a lecture entitled 'Freedom is Coming' as part of the Wilberforce Events at Hull City Hall. Reflecting on a recent visit to the West Indies, Dr Sentamu compared the historical scene with forms of slavery today. As the Bicentenary year of the Act for the Abolition of the Slave Trade comes to a close, an ecumenical conference for church youth workers considered how the legacies of slavery in all its forms can still impact minority ethnic young people today.

The Church proposed an independent ombudsman to stop supermarkets squeezing farmers. The pursuit of cheap food coupled with the buying power of the big supermarkets was putting farming livelihoods at risk, the Church told the Competition Commission, while putting forward recommendations to consumers, supermarkets and Government. Another submission told the Government that it needs to produce a better case if it wishes to extend the time suspected terrorists can be detained without charge.

In a memorandum to the responsible parliamentary committee, the Church of England and the Catholic Bishops' Conference of England and Wales commented on the proposed amendment to the Public Order Act 1986 to create a new offence of incitement to hatred on grounds of sexual orientation. Focusing on the use of threatening behaviour or words that are used with the intention of stirring up hatred goes a considerable way towards meeting the Churches' concerns, they said.

Church Statistics 2005/6 showed increased giving and vocations. This was the first year that the statistics were available only on the Web, and not printed. A major survey found that a majority of those who did not see themselves as Christians rejected the idea that Church schools created divisions between different sections of society.

The Church started running subsidized study tours of the Holy Land to counter a marked drop in the number of pilgrimages being organized by dioceses and parishes.

The Archbishop of Canterbury paid tribute to the founder of the Samaritans, Prebendary Chad Varah, whose death was announced on 8 November.

Appointment The Very Revd David Richardson was appointed the Archbishop's Representative to the Holy See and Director of the Anglican Centre in Rome.

DECEMBER

In his Christmas sermon in Canterbury Cathedral, the Archbishop of Canterbury said, 'The joy of Christmas teaches us that God's relationship with the human race is primarily one of love for his creation.' Dr Williams added that 'our capacity to avoid this reality contributes to our confusion'. Contributing to *Pause for Thought* on Terry Wogan (BBC Radio 2), the Archbishop said, 'We sing quite a bit about "Tidings of comfort and joy" at this time of year. But it would be a pity if we felt Christmas ought to be a time when we turned our faces away from uncomfortable things in our society. Surely it ought to be a time when we summon up courage to confront a few issues – simply because it's a time when we are more conscious than ever of the good things that have been given to us, material good things to celebrate with, and also, if you're a Christian, the biggest gift of all, the birth of Jesus.'

The Archbishop of York cut up his 'dog collar' on live television, calling on the people of Britain to unite in their opposition to the Government of Robert Mugabe – to 'pray, march and protest' – and to come together to act on Darfur. In his Christmas sermon at York Minster, Dr Sentamu said that 'the message of Christmas challenges our complacency, our prejudices, and our misconceptions about God and humanity'. In a *Daily Telegraph* article, the Archbishop said: 'From an obsession with fame to child-trafficking and corrupt regimes, it is time to take responsibility for the problems of the twenty-first century.'

The Archbishop of Canterbury gave a wide-ranging lecture at the Building Bridges Conference in Singapore on the theme of why social cohesion needs religion, and discussing the position of the 'absolute truths' of faith over and above political power, and how this plays out in a society where several faiths co-exist.

A model Protocol for the Review of past child protection cases was published, following the earlier announcement of the Review's key principles.

The new Learning and Skills Council Handbook and Guidance on Multi-Faith Chaplaincy in Colleges of Further Education was launched as a joint project with the National Council of Faiths and Beliefs in FE, involving participation from multi-faith teams across the country.

The ecumenical Church Investors Group launched its own web site, not only setting out the ethical investment approach of members but also including responses to some recent controversial issues, so that members of a range of denominations can now see how their Churches are putting Christian principles into investment practice.

JANUARY

The Archbishop of Canterbury launched the official programme for the Lambeth Conference 2008: Equipping Bishops for Mission, at Lambeth Palace.

In response to reports that some Anglican church services in Harare had been disrupted by state officials, the Archbishop of Canterbury condemned unequivocally the use of Zimbabwe state machinery to intimidate opponents of the deposed bishop of Harare, Nolbert Kunonga.

The Archbishops of Canterbury and York submitted a Church of England Response to the draft Anglican Covenant.

The Archbishop of York presented gifts from Yorkshire to the Pope as part of the Week of Prayer for Christian Unity celebrations. In addition to praying, preaching and presiding with Christian communities from all denominations in Rome, Dr Sentamu met Pope Benedict XVI, Cardinal Walter Kasper, the Vatican's head of inter-church relations, Archbishop Pius Ncube, the former Archbishop of Bulawayo in Zimbabwe, and British Ambassadors to the Vatican and Italy.

In his James Callaghan Memorial lecture, 'Religious Hatred and Religious Offence', the Archbishop of Canterbury outlined the problems with the present blasphemy laws, but also looked at the problems that society could face without protection for the sacred from religious offence.

The Church compiled a Post-Christmas Debt Check for consumers worried about how much their wallets had been hit by Christmas and New Year spending.

Attendance figures for 2006 showed changing trends in churchgoing, with larger congregations at Christmas and Easter, but smaller Sunday congregations.

The Church of England's National Church Institutions were awarded the *Two*

Ticks disability symbol by Jobcentre Plus in recognition of their commitment to good practice in employing people with disabilities.

Appointment The Revd Dr Gary Wilton was appointed to the newly created post of Church of England's Representative to the EU Institutions.

FEBRUARY

In a lecture at the Royal Courts of Justice, the Archbishop of Canterbury said that UK law needed to continue to find accommodation with religious legal codes such as the Islamic system of Sharia if community cohesion and development are to be achieved.

The Archbishops of Canterbury and York called for 'good neighbours' – online and offline – to try out daily Lent suggestions to help create a safer and more pleasant environment in the real world.

The Archbishop of Canterbury criticized the 'indefensible' treatment of young people in prison, and called upon the government to look critically at the use of strip-searching and prison segregation units for children in the criminal justice system.

The General Synod met at Church House, Westminster. In his Presidential Address the Archbishop reflected on developments in Zimbabwe, on the forthcoming Lambeth Conference and on his lecture on religious legal codes such as Shariah and the reception this had received from the media. He received a standing ovation from the Synod. Major debates on detention without charge, mental health issues and casinos were also on the agenda. There was a large programme of legislative business, the most substantial item being the Revision Stage of the Clergy Terms of Service legislation. Synod had further opportunity to debate the Anglican Communion Covenant and Senior Church (Crown) Appointments, following earlier debates in July 2007, and there was also a focus on Anglican-Roman Catholic dialogue.

The Church welcomed the Government's decision not to license a regional supercasino. It also encouraged Culture Secretary Andy Burnham MP to issue a warning to the industry that he will enforce a statutory levy to fund research into and treatment of problem gambling.

Appointment Canon Robert Paterson, Chaplain and Researcher to the Archbishop of York, was appointed Bishop of Sodor and Man.

MARCH

The Church reaffirmed its belief that forced marriage is wrong both morally and legally. Responding to a Home Office consultation on 'marriage to partners from overseas', the Rt Revd Tom Butler, Bishop of Southwark, said the Mission and Public Affairs Council strongly affirmed that principle, as reflected in the consultation document, and agreed that the minimum age that someone could sponsor a marriage partner from abroad or be sponsored as a spouse should be raised to 21 years.

Responding to a statement from Secretary of State for Children, Schools and Families, Ed Balls, the Rt Revd Stephen Venner, Bishop of Dover and acting Chair of the Board of Education, said: 'The Church of England welcomes the Minister's intention to tighten up on rules to ensure schools meet the requirements of the Admissions Code 2007.'

The Church launched an easy-to-use interactive online resource for working out a household spending budget, with helpful prayers for guidance, emphasizing that the Bible teaches us to be content with what we have, rather than find satisfaction from over-spending.

A pioneering partnership between the Archbishops' Council and the University of Chester came to fruition when the first cohort of Deaf students were presented with their certificates. The Church Colleges Certificate in Christian Ministry – taught and assessed in British Sign Language (BSL) – is the first of its kind in the United Kingdom, with all the teaching delivered in BSL by 'Signs of God', an organization which specializes in promoting the use of BSL in Christian settings.

The Church welcomed the transitional relief arrangement announced in the Budget for Gift Aid claims by charities over the following three years. In the Budget speech, the Chancellor, Alistair Darling, announced a transitional rate of relief of 22 per cent from 2008/09 to 2010/11.

The Archbishop of Canterbury expressed his deep shock and sorrow at the kidnap and subsequent murder of Paulos Faraj Rahho, the Chaldean Archbishop of Mosul. 'Our prayers are daily with the people of Iraq, especially with the vulnerable Christian community, and particularly today with the Chaldeans and Archbishop Paulos' family'. Dr Williams also paid tribute to Chiara Lubich, founder of the Focolare Movement, whose death was announced on 14 March.

Appointments Canon Dr Christopher Cocksworth, Principal of Ridley Hall, Cambridge, was appointed Bishop of Coventry; the Revd Christopher Edmondson, Warden of Lee Abbey, as Bishop of Bolton; and the Ven. Mark Davies, Archdeacon of Rochdale, as Bishop of Middleton.

APRIL

The Archbishop of Canterbury called on the government to do more to protect the poorest and most vulnerable from the likely consequences of an economic downturn. Speaking in a House of Lords debate which he had sponsored, Dr Williams highlighted the fact that government targets on alleviating poverty, particularly child poverty, risked not being met and warned that in a period of economic decline the poorest in society, who carry a higher proportion of personal debt, were most at risk.

In response to reports of violence and threats towards Christians involved in the debate on human sexuality, the Archbishop strongly condemned violence against lesbian and gay people. The Church of England and the Methodist Church published a special resource designed to help churches support people who have suffered from the trauma of abuse, wherever this has occurred.

The Archbishops of Canterbury and York issued a joint statement concerning the deteriorating situation of ordinary people in Zimbabwe. After giving joint interviews, both Archbishops called for a day of prayer.

The House of Bishops' Theological Group and the Faith and Order Advisory Group produced a set of reflections on the address given in 2006 by Cardinal Walter Kasper to the Bishops of the Church of England on the proposal to ordain women as bishops.

The EU Budget, in not matching up to the EU's objectives, had failed to provide sufficiently for the European Common Good, concluded the Church of England House of Bishops' Europe Panel in a submission to the European Commission's Budget Review exercise calling for a greener Budget.

The Bishops of Birmingham and Leicester and the Dean of Peterborough were among senior clergy prepared to roll up their sleeves and cassocks on Maundy Thursday to clean and polish the shoes of dozens of office workers in towns and cities across the country – set 'to shine to reflect the love of God'.

Appointments The Bishop of Blackburn, the Rt Revd Nicholas Reade, was appointed Chairman of the Church's Committee for Ministry Among Deaf and Disabled

People. The Revd Robert Atwell, Vicar of Primrose Hill St Mary with Avenue Road St Paul, was appointed Bishop of Stockport.

MAY
The Archbishop of Canterbury sent an open Pentecost Letter to the bishops of the Anglican Communion in advance of the Lambeth Conference.

The Archbishop of Canterbury and the Archbishop of Cape Town met Ban Ki-moon, the Secretary General of the United Nations, and expressed their grave concern about the increasing violence of what appeared to be a sustained campaign against the Anglican Church in Zimbabwe, and called on the UN for mediation and protection.

The Archbishop of Canterbury and the Bishop of London, the Rt Revd Richard Chartres, welcomed leaders from business, government and civil society to Lambeth Palace for a climate change round table.

The Archbishop convened the seventh Building Bridges Seminar in Rome. This unique annual series brings together a range of internationally recognized Christian and Muslim scholars for an intensive study of relevant Biblical and Qur'anic texts. Dr Williams described his private meeting with Pope Benedict XVI in the Vatican as 'friendly and informal'. Dr Williams also gave a lecture at the London School of Economics entitled 'Religious Faith and Human Rights'.

The Church secured new funding options to help meet the challenge of training future clergy, with the vital role of Christian ministers in building social capital and community cohesion within England and Wales recognized in provisional arrangements to secure the future of funding for clergy training.

The Church welcomed the Competition Commission's decision to seek undertakings from grocery retailers to establish a Groceries Supply Code of Practice Ombudsman.

The Church described projections and comparisons published by Christian Research in its *Religious Trends* publication as 'flawed and dangerously misleading'.

JUNE
The Archbishop of Canterbury and other Church leaders called upon Christians throughout England to use the period from 1 September until 4 October as an opportunity to put the environment at the heart of their worship, and make 'Time for God's creation'. The Archbishop of York launched a scathing attack on the consumerist values of society in a speech to the Institute of Jewish Policy Research on the role of religion in politics.

The Archbishop of Canterbury convened an ecumenical gathering to discuss ways in which Christian–Muslim engagement might be strengthened and deepened 'for the sake of peace in our common home'. Dr Williams also hosted religious leaders of different faiths to discuss the power of multi-religious cooperation to combat poverty and achieve the United Nations Millennium Development Goals.

The Archbishops of Canterbury and of York issued a joint statement regarding events at St Bartholomew-the-Great: 'Those clergy who disagree with the Church's teaching are at liberty to seek to persuade others within the Church of the reasons why they believe, in the light of Scripture, tradition and reason that it should be changed. But they are not at liberty simply to disregard it.'

The Government is 'moral without a compass' said an independent report into Church and Welfare. The report by the Von Hügel Institute concluded that the government was 'planning blind and failing parts of civil society' when it comes to faith communities in general and aspects of charity law and social policy in particular.

The Rt Revd Nigel McCulloch, Bishop of Manchester, and the Rt Revd John Arnold, Auxiliary RC Bishop of Westminster, warned of the risk of a digital broadcasting 'Tower of Babel': without strong and vibrant public service content, broadcasting after digital switchover could sow confusion and mistrust rather than aid public enlightenment and social cohesion.

The Church expressed a number of concerns about the Charity Commission's latest draft guidance on public benefit and the advancement of religion while welcoming the progress the draft represents in recognizing the contribution of religious bodies to the public benefit.

Appointments The Rt Revd Timothy Thornton, Bishop of Sherborne, was appointed Bishop of Truro. The Ven. David Thomson, Archdeacon of Carlisle, was appointed Bishop of Huntingdon.

JULY

Women bishops, climate change and church tourism were just some of the major debates on the agenda at the General Synod when it met at York University. In his Presidential Address, the Archbishop of York called on the Church to 'reach out to young people involved in knife crime'.

Around 650 Anglican bishops from all over the world arrived in Canterbury for the Lambeth Conference 2008: Equipping Bishops for Mission. The Archbishop of Canterbury announced plans to mount an unprecedented mass walk of bishops and other faith leaders through central London during the forthcoming Lambeth Conference to demonstrate the Anglican Communion's determination to help end extreme poverty across the globe, and to challenge global governments on tackling poverty.

Young people who think they may be being called into ordained ministry were at the centre of a national 'Call Waiting' campaign launched by the Archbishop of Canterbury (www.callwaiting.org.uk/home.aspx).

The House of Bishops Europe Panel called on government to take the numbers experiencing fuel poverty into account when setting policy on increasing renewable energy generation.

AUGUST

The Lambeth Conference closed with a service in Canterbury Cathedral, and a concluding Presidential Address and sermon to the Conference by the Archbishop of Canterbury. Dr Williams wrote a Pastoral Letter to the bishops of the Anglican Communion, setting out his personal reflections on the Conference. The Church Commissioners and the Archbishops' Council each agreed to make available to the Lambeth Conference Company interest-free loan facilities of up to £600,000 to enable the Company to honour its commitments while fundraising efforts continued.

The Archbishop of Canterbury and the Bishop of London, the Rt Revd Richard Chartres, commended a new guide from the Church of England which offers church leaders a template for a year-long programme of practical action to reduce their congregations' carbon footprints, as energy prices head upwards. The book, *Don't Stop at the Lights*, included sermon ideas and extensive bible study notes drawing on ancient theological themes which aim to reconnect the Church to the natural world and the roots of its faith.

Religious Education grew in popularity among GCSE students again in 2008 with a tenth annual increase in GCSE Religious Education entrants, and results more successful than ever. Among subjects with more than 100,000 entrants, RE has remained at the top of the charts for increasing entrants, with a 4.7 per cent increase since last year. For the fifth year in a row the number of students taking Religious Studies A-level rose, with an increase of 5.9 per cent since 2007. The Church had posted prayers on its web site for all those receiving exam results at the beginning of the summer and considering their future options.

SEPTEMBER

On the eve of the United Nations General Assembly meeting on Millennium Development Goals in New York, the Archbishop of Canterbury underlined the commitment of the Anglican Church to continue to work for the eradication of poverty, calling for greater cooperation to meet the MDGs.

Speaking in Westminster Central Hall at an event organized by Youth for Christ, the Archbishop of York highlighted the work of Christian organizations, saying they were making a vital contribution in local communities and were often at the forefront of the provision of community services.

The Archbishop of Canterbury met the Chief Rabbis of Israel, Chief Rabbi Shlomo Amar and Chief Rabbi Yonah Metzger, at Lambeth Palace. The Archbishop was supported by the Rt Revd Michael Jackson, Bishop of Clogher and Co-Chair of the Anglican Jewish Commission, and the Rt Revd Suheil Dawani, Anglican Bishop in Jerusalem.

A new prayer was published on the Church of England web site aiming to help people caught up in the difficult prevailing financial situation. The prayer was one of a range of resources available in an online initiative backed by the Archbishop of Canterbury. Dr Williams said: 'At this time of international financial turbulence, it is important that the Church should be offering the opportunity for prayer and reflection.' The Archbishop of York spoke of his outrage at those responsible for short selling shares in HBOS, labelling those responsible as 'bank robbers' and 'asset strippers'.

The Bishop of Middleton launched the first ever national 'heroic job poll' in Manchester. Children of all ages were invited to vote for the job they considered the UK's most heroic from a list of 25, including taxi drivers, supermarket workers, journalists, doctors and parents. The national Hero Poll was part of the HalloweenChoice.org campaign, working to shift the celebration of Hallowe'en away from the anti-social supermarket-produced version of the festival, into a more fun event.

The Church of England developed a new section of its web site (www.cofe. anglican.org/darwin/) to mark the approaching bicentenary of Charles Darwin's birth in 1809, and the 150th anniversary of the publication of *On the Origin of Species* in 1859. As media interest grows in the bicentenary, the pages analyse Darwin's faith and his relationship with the Church of England. A new essay by the Revd Dr Malcolm Brown, Director of Mission and Public Affairs, gave a personal view of Darwin's contribution to science, while warning of social misapplications of his theories.

Thousands of people accepted an invitation to go 'back to church' on 28 September (www.backtochurch.co.uk/). More than 30,000 people of all ages enjoyed a range of special services led by 3,000 local churches across the country following a coordinated effort to encourage them to offer an extra-special welcome to newcomers and 'returners'.

The Archbishop of Canterbury sent a greeting to Jewish leaders and communities for the festival of Rosh Hashanah, marking the start of the Jewish New Year. He also expressed profound distress at the extreme violence in Orissa following the murder of Hindu leader, Swami Lakshmananda Saraswati.

Appointments The Revd Andrew Watson, Vicar of East Twickenham St Stephen, was appointed Bishop of Aston.

OCTOBER

A survey found that the majority of the population – including those who did not see themselves as Christian – agreed that parents should be able to choose a state-run school for their child based on their own religious, moral or philosophical considerations. But the poll also revealed that the Church still had to work on demonstrating fair admissions procedures in its popular schools.

Separate research by the Archbishops' Council's Weddings Project (www.your churchwedding.org/) showed that couples preparing for their wedding day wanted the vows to be at the heart of their planning more than anything else; and research among newly weds revealed that nine out of ten rated their church wedding experience as good to excellent. Clergy, including the Bishop of Leicester, chatted and offered advice to thousands of brides to be at the National Wedding Show at the NEC in Birmingham as part of the Church's continuing wedding-welcome. The change in the law on 1 October meant couples would be able to choose from many more churches across England.

The Church took the unprecedented step of taking out advertising space in a newspaper to soothe commuters travelling into work as schools and workplaces got back to the daily grind after the summer holiday season.

The Archbishop of Canterbury joined Susan Hitch on BBC Radio 3 Literary Proms to examine conflicting ideas about spiritual regeneration and existentialism as embodied in the characters of his literary hero, the Russian novelist Fyodor Dostoevsky, the subject of his new book, *Dostoevsky: Language, Faith and Fiction*.

Dr Williams gave the opening address at a conference he convened, entitled 'A Common Word and Future Christian–Muslim Engagement'. The conference, timed to coincide with the anniversary of the release of the open letter *A Common Word between Us and You* from 138 Islamic scholars, clerics and intellectuals, aimed to continue the dialogue between the two faiths, by reflecting on this letter and the Archbishop's letter, *A Common Word for the Common Good*. The Archbishop also sent his greetings to Muslim communities for the festival of Eid ul Fitr, marking the end of Ramadhan.

Appointment The Revd Dr Steven Croft, Archbishops' Missioner and Leader of the Fresh Expressions team, was appointed Bishop of Sheffield.

CALENDAR 2009–2010

According to the Calendar, Lectionary and Collects authorized pursuant to Canon B 2 of the Canons of the Church of England for use from 30 November 1997 until further resolution of the General Synod of the Church of England.

Key
BOLD UPPER CASE – Principal Feasts and other Principal Holy Days
Bold Roman – Sundays and Festivals
Roman – Lesser Festivals
Small Italic – Commemorations
Italic – Other Observances

JANUARY (Year B)
1 **The Naming and Circumcision of Jesus**
2 Basil the Great and Gregory of Nazianzus, bishops, teachers of the faith, 379 and 389
Seraphim, monk of Sarov, spiritual guide, 1833
Vedanayagam Samuel Azariah, bishop in South India, evangelist, 1945
4 **The Second Sunday of Christmas**
6 **THE EPIPHANY**
10 *William Laud, Archbishop of Canterbury, 1645*
11 **The Baptism of Christ** – *The First Sunday of Epiphany*
12 Aelred of Hexham, Abbot of Rievaulx, 1167
Benedict Biscop, Abbot of Wearmouth, scholar, 689
13 Hilary, Bishop of Poitiers, teacher of the faith, 367
17 Antony of Egypt, hermit, abbot, 356
Charles Gore, bishop, founder of the Community of the Resurrection, 1932
18 **The Second Sunday of Epiphany**
18–25 Week of Prayer for Christian Unity
19 Wulfstan, Bishop of Worcester, 1095
20 *Richard Rolle of Hampole, Spiritual Writer, 1349*
21 *Agnes, child martyr at Rome, 304*
22 *Vincent of Saragossa, deacon, first Martyr of Spain, 304*
24 Francis de Sales, Bishop of Geneva, teacher of the faith, 1622
25 **The Conversion of Paul** – *The Third Sunday of Epiphany*
26 Timothy and Titus, companions of Paul
28 Thomas Aquinas, priest, philosopher, teacher of the faith, 1274
30 Charles, king and martyr, 1649
31 *John Bosco, priest, founder of the Salesian Teaching Order, 1888*

FEBRUARY
1 **The Fourth Sunday of Epiphany**
2 **THE PRESENTATION OF CHRIST IN THE TEMPLE** (Candlemas)
3 Anskar, Archbishop of Hamburg, missionary in Denmark and Sweden, 865
4 *Gilbert of Sempringham, founder of the Gilbertine Order, 1189*
6 *The Martyrs of Japan, 1597*
8 **The Third Sunday before Lent**
10 *Scholastica, sister of Benedict, Abbess of Plombariola, c.543*

14 Cyril and Methodius, missionaries to the Slavs, 869 and 885
Valentine, martyr at Rome, c.269
15 **The Second Sunday before Lent**
17 Janani Luwum, Archbishop of Uganda, martyr, 1977
22 **The Sunday next before Lent**
23 Polycarp, Bishop of Smyrna, martyr, c.155
25 **ASH WEDNESDAY**
27 George Herbert, priest, poet, 1633

MARCH
1 **The First Sunday of Lent**
2 Chad, Bishop of Lichfield, missionary, 672
7 Perpetua, Felicity and their Companions, martyrs at Carthage, 203
8 **The Second Sunday of Lent**
15 **The Third Sunday of Lent**
17 Patrick, bishop, missionary, patron of Ireland, c.460
18 *Cyril, Bishop of Jerusalem, teacher of the faith, 386*
19 **Joseph of Nazareth**
20 Cuthbert, Bishop of Lindisfarne, missionary, 687
21 Thomas Cranmer, Archbishop of Canterbury, Reformation martyr, 1556
22 **The Fourth Sunday of Lent** – *Mothering Sunday*
24 *Walter Hilton of Thurgarton, Augustinian canon, mystic, 1396*
Oscar Romero, Archbishop of San Salvador, martyr, 1980
25 **THE ANNUNCIATION OF OUR LORD TO THE BLESSED VIRGIN MARY**
26 *Harriet Monsell, founder of the Community of St John the Baptist, 1883*
29 **The Fifth Sunday of Lent**
31 *John Donne, priest, poet, 1631*

APRIL
1 *Frederick Denison Maurice, priest, teacher of the faith, 1872*
5 **Palm Sunday**
6 Monday of Holy Week
7 Tuesday of Holy Week
8 Wednesday of Holy Week
9 **Maundy Thursday**
10 **Good Friday**
11 Easter Eve

12 **EASTER DAY**
13 Monday of Easter Week
14 Tuesday of Easter Week
15 Wednesday of Easter Week
16 Thursday of Easter Week
17 Friday of Easter Week
18 Saturday of Easter Week
19 **The Second Sunday of Easter**
21 Anselm, Abbot of Le Bec, Archbishop of Canterbury, teacher of the faith, 1109
23 **George, martyr, patron of England, c.304**
24 *Mellitus, Bishop of London, first bishop at St Paul's, 624*
25 **Mark the Evangelist**
26 **The Third Sunday of Easter**
27 *Christina Rossetti, poet, 1894*
28 *Peter Chanel, missionary in the South Pacific, martyr, 1841*
29 Catherine of Siena, teacher of the faith, 1380
30 *Pandita Mary Ramabai, translator, 1922*

MAY
1 **Philip and James, Apostles**
2 Athanasius, Bishop of Alexandria, teacher of the faith, 373
3 **The Fourth Sunday of Easter**
4 English saints and martyrs of the Reformation era
8 Julian of Norwich, spiritual writer, c.1417
10 **The Fifth Sunday of Easter**
14 **Matthias the Apostle**
16 *Caroline Chisholm, social reformer, 1877*
17 **The Sixth Sunday of Easter**
19 Dunstan, Archbishop of Canterbury, restorer of monastic life, 988
20 Alcuin of York, deacon, Abbot of Tours, 804
21 **ASCENSION DAY**
24 **The Seventh Sunday of Easter**
25 The Venerable Bede, monk at Jarrow, scholar, historian, 735
26 Augustine, first Archbishop of Canterbury, 605
   John Calvin, reformer 1564
   Philip Neri, founder of the Oratorians, spiritual guide, 1595
28 *Lanfranc, Prior of Le Bec, Archbishop of Canterbury, scholar, 1089*
30 Josephine Butler, social reformer, 1906
   Joan of Arc, visionary, 1431
   Apolo Kivebulaya, priest, evangelist in Central Africa, 1933
31 **PENTECOST (Whit Sunday)**

JUNE
1 **The Visit of the Blessed Virgin Mary to Elizabeth** (*transferred*)
3 *The Martyrs of Uganda, 1885–7 and 1977*
4 *Petroc, Abbot of Padstow, 6th century*
5 Boniface (Wynfrith) of Crediton, bishop, apostle of Germany, martyr, 754
6 *Ini Kopuria, founder of the Melanesian Brotherhood, 1945*
7 **TRINITY SUNDAY**
8 Thomas Ken, Bishop of Bath and Wells, nonjuror, hymn writer, 1711

9 Columba, Abbot of Iona, missionary, 597
   Ephrem of Syria, deacon, hymn writer, teacher of the faith, 373
11 **Barnabas the Apostle**
14 **The First Sunday after Trinity**
15 *Evelyn Underhill, spiritual writer, 1941*
16 Richard, Bishop of Chichester, 1253
   Joseph Butler, Bishop of Durham, philosopher, 1752
17 *Samuel and Henrietta Barnett, social reformers, 1913 and 1936*
18 *Bernard Mizeki, apostle of the MaShona, martyr, 1896*
19 *Sundar Singh of India, sadhu (holy man), evangelist, teacher of the faith, 1929*
21 **The Second Sunday after Trinity**
22 Alban, first martyr of Britain, c.250
23 Etheldreda, Abbess of Ely, c.678
24 **The Birth of John the Baptist**
27 *Cyril, Bishop of Alexandria, teacher of the faith, 444*
28 **The Third Sunday after Trinity**
29 **Peter and Paul, Apostles** *or* **Peter the Apostle**

JULY
1 *Henry, John and Henry Venn the younger, priests, evangelical divines, 1797, 1813 and 1873*
3 **Thomas the Apostle**
5 **The Fourth Sunday after Trinity**
6 *Thomas More, scholar, and John Fisher, Bishop of Rochester, Reformation martyrs, 1535*
11 Benedict of Nursia, Abbot of Monte Cassino, father of western monasticism, c.550
12 **The Fifth Sunday after Trinity**
14 John Keble, priest, Tractarian, poet, 1866
15 Swithun, Bishop of Winchester, c.862
   Bonaventure, friar, bishop, teacher of the faith, 1274
16 *Osmund, Bishop of Salisbury, 1099*
18 *Elizabeth Ferard, first deaconess of the Church of England, founder of the Community of St Andrew, 1883*
19 **The Sixth Sunday after Trinity**
20 *Margaret of Antioch, martyr, 4th century*
   Bartolomé de las Casas, apostle to the Indies, 1566
22 **Mary Magdalene**
23 *Bridget of Sweden, Abbess of Vadstena, 1373*
25 **James the Apostle**
26 **The Seventh Sunday after Trinity**
27 *Brooke Foss Westcott, Bishop of Durham, teacher of the faith, 1901*
29 Mary, Martha and Lazarus, Companions of Our Lord
30 William Wilberforce, social reformer, 1833
31 *Ignatius of Loyola, founder of the Society of Jesus, 1556*

AUGUST
2 **The Eighth Sunday after Trinity**
4 *Jean-Baptiste Vianney, Curé d'Ars, spiritual guide, 1859*
5 Oswald, King of Northumbria, martyr, 642
6 **The Transfiguration of Our Lord**
7 *John Mason Neale, priest, hymn writer, 1866*
8 Dominic, priest, founder of the Order of Preachers, 1221
9 **The Ninth Sunday after Trinity**
10 Laurence, deacon at Rome, martyr, 258
11 Clare of Assisi, founder of the Minoresses (Poor Clares), 1253

John Henry Newman, priest, Tractarian, 1890
13 Jeremy Taylor, Bishop of Down and Connor, teacher of the faith, 1667
   Florence Nightingale, nurse, social reformer, 1910
   Octavia Hill, social reformer, 1912
14 *Maximilian Kolbe, friar, martyr, 1941*
15 **The Blessed Virgin Mary**
16 **The Tenth Sunday after Trinity**
20 Bernard, Abbot of Clairvaux, teacher of the faith, 1153
   William and Catherine Booth, founders of the Salvation Army, 1912 and 1890
23 **The Eleventh Sunday after Trinity**
24 **Bartholomew the Apostle**
27 Monica, mother of Augustine of Hippo, 387
28 Augustine, Bishop of Hippo, teacher of the faith, 430
29 The Beheading of John the Baptist
30 **The Twelfth Sunday after Trinity**
31 Aidan, Bishop of Lindisfarne, missionary, 651

SEPTEMBER
 1 *Giles of Provence, hermit, c.710*
 2 *The Martyrs of Papua New Guinea, 1901 and 1942*
 3 Gregory the Great, Bishop of Rome, teacher of the faith, 604
 4 *Birinus, Bishop of Dorchester (Oxon), apostle of Wessex, 650*
 6 **The Thirteenth Sunday after Trinity**
 8 The Birth of the Blessed Virgin Mary
 9 *Charles Fuge Lowder, priest, 1880*
13 **The Fourteenth Sunday after Trinity**
14 **Holy Cross Day**
15 Cyprian, Bishop of Carthage, martyr, 258
16 Ninian, Bishop of Galloway, apostle of the Picts, c.432
   Edward Bouverie Pusey, priest, tractarian, 1882
17 Hildegard, Abbess of Bingen, visionary, 1179
19 *Theodore of Tarsus, Archbishop of Canterbury, 690*
20 **The Fifteenth Sunday after Trinity**
21 **Matthew, Apostle and Evangelist**
25 Lancelot Andrewes, Bishop of Winchester, spiritual writer, 1626
   Sergei of Radonezh, Russian monastic reformer, teacher of the faith, 1392
26 *Wilson Carlile, founder of the Church Army, 1942*
27 **The Sixteenth Sunday after Trinity**
29 **Michael and All Angels**
30 *Jerome, translator of the Scriptures, teacher of the faith, 420*

OCTOBER
 1 *Remigius, Bishop of Rheims, apostle of the Franks, 533*
   Anthony Ashley Cooper, Earl of Shaftesbury, social reformer, 1885
 4 **The Seventeenth Sunday after Trinity**
 6 William Tyndale, translator of the Scriptures, Reformation martyr, 1536
 9 *Denys, Bishop of Paris, and his companions, martyrs, c.250*
   Robert Grosseteste, Bishop of Lincoln, philosopher, scientist, 1253
10 Paulinus, Bishop of York, missionary, 644
   Thomas Traherne, poet, spiritual writer, 1674

11 **The Eighteenth Sunday after Trinity**
12 Wilfrid of Ripon, bishop, missionary, 709
   Elizabeth Fry, prison reformer, 1845
   Edith Cavell, nurse, 1915
13 Edward the Confessor, King of England, 1066
15 Teresa of Avila, teacher of the faith, 1582
16 *Nicholas Ridley, Bishop of London, and Hugh Latimer, Bishop of Worcester, Reformation martyrs, 1555*
17 Ignatius, Bishop of Antioch, martyr, c.107
18 **Luke the Evangelist** *or* **The Nineteenth Sunday after Trinity**
19 Henry Martyn, translator of the Scriptures, missionary in India and Persia, 1812
25 **The Last Sunday after Trinity** – *Bible Sunday*
28 **Simon and Jude, Apostles**
29 James Hannington, Bishop of Eastern Equatorial Africa, martyr in Uganda, 1885
31 *Martin Luther, reformer, 1546*

NOVEMBER
 1 **ALL SAINTS' DAY** *or* **The Fourth Sunday before Advent**
 2 Commemoration of the Faithful Departed (All Souls' Day)
 3 Richard Hooker, priest, Anglican apologist, teacher of the faith, 1600
   Martin of Porres, friar, 1639
 6 *Leonard, hermit, 6th century*
   William Temple, Archbishop of Canterbury, teacher of the faith, 1944
 7 Willibrord of York, bishop, apostle of Frisia, 739
 8 **The Third Sunday before Advent** – *Remembrance Sunday*
 9 *Margery Kempe, mystic, c.1440*
10 Leo the Great, Bishop of Rome, teacher of the faith, 461
11 Martin, Bishop of Tours, c.397
13 Charles Simeon, priest, evangelical divine, 1836
14 *Samuel Seabury, first Anglican bishop in North America, 1796*
15 **The Second Sunday before Advent**
16 Margaret, Queen of Scotland, philanthropist, reformer of the Church, 1093
   Edmund Rich of Abingdon, Archbishop of Canterbury, 1240
17 Hugh, Bishop of Lincoln, 1200
18 Elizabeth of Hungary, Princess of Thuringia, philanthropist, 1231
19 Hilda, Abbess of Whitby, 680
   Mechtild, béguine of Magdeburg, mystic, 1280
20 Edmund, King of the East Angles, martyr, 870
   Priscilla Lydia Sellon, a restorer of the religious life in the Church of England, 1876
22 **Christ the King** – *The Sunday next before Advent*
23 Clement, Bishop of Rome, martyr, c.100
25 *Catherine of Alexandria, martyr, 4th century*
   Isaac Watts, hymn writer, 1748
29 **The First Sunday of Advent** – *Year C begins today*
30 **Andrew the Apostle**

DECEMBER

1 *Charles de Foucauld, hermit in the Sahara, 1916*
3 *Francis Xavier, missionary, apostle of the Indies, 1552*
4 *John of Damascus, monk, teacher of the faith, c.749*
   Nicholas Ferrar, deacon, founder of the Little Gidding Community, 1637
6 **The Second Sunday of Advent**
7 Ambrose, Bishop of Milan, teacher of the faith, 397
8 The Conception of the Blessed Virgin Mary
13 **The Third Sunday of Advent**
14 John of the Cross, poet, teacher of the faith, 1591
17 *O Sapientia*
   Eglantyne Jebb, social reformer, founder of 'Save The Children', 1928
20 **The Fourth Sunday of Advent**
24 Christmas Eve
25 **CHRISTMAS DAY**
26 **Stephen, deacon, first martyr**
27 **John, Apostle and Evangelist** *or* **The First Sunday of Christmas**
28 **The Holy Innocents**
29 Thomas Becket, Archbishop of Canterbury, martyr, 1170
31 *John Wyclif, reformer, 1384*

JANUARY 2010

1 **The Naming and Circumcision of Jesus**
2 Basil the Great and Gregory of Nazianzus, bishops, teachers of the faith, 379 and 389
   Seraphim, monk of Sarov, spiritual guide, 1833
   Vedanayagam Samuel Azariah, bishop in South India, evangelist, 1945
3 **The Second Sunday of Christmas**
6 **THE EPIPHANY**
10 **The Baptism of Christ** – The First Sunday of Epiphany
12 Aelred of Hexham, Abbot of Rievaulx, 1167
   Benedict Biscop, Abbot of Wearmouth, scholar, 689
13 Hilary, Bishop of Poitiers, teacher of the faith, 367

Kentigern (Mungo), missionary Bishop in Strathclyde and Cumbria, 603
George Fox, founder of the Society of Friends (the Quakers), 1691
17 **The Second Sunday of Epiphany**
18–25 Week of Prayer for Christian Unity
19 Wulfstan, Bishop of Worcester, 1095
20 *Richard Rolle of Hampole, spiritual writer, 1349*
21 Agnes, child martyr at Rome, 304
22 *Vincent of Saragossa, deacon, first martyr of Spain, 304*
24 **The Third Sunday of Epiphany**
25 **The Conversion of Paul**
26 Timothy and Titus, companions of Paul
28 Thomas Aquinas, priest, philosopher, teacher of the faith, 1274
30 Charles, king and martyr, 1649
31 **The Fourth Sunday of Epiphany**

Other dates

8 February	Education Sunday
6 February	Accession Day
22 February	Unemployment Sunday
9 February	General Synod meets until 13 February
10 May	Christian Aid Week until 16th
7 June	Church Urban Fund Sunday
10 July	General Synod meets in York until 14th
12 July	Day of Prayer for Vocations to Religious Life
12 July	Sea Sunday
13 September	Racial Justice Sunday
4 October	Animal Welfare Sunday
18 October	Hospital Sunday
18 October	One World Week until 25th
24 October	United Nations Day
16 November	General Synod meets until 18th (if required)
15 November	Prisoners Sunday
1 December	World AIDS Day
6 December	Human Rights Day

SELECTED CHURCH STATISTICS

The Church of England today

The Church of England plays a vital role in the life of the nation, proclaiming the Christian gospel in words and actions and providing services of Christian worship and praise.

Its network of parishes covers the country, bringing a vital Christian dimension to the nation as well as strengthening community life in numerous urban, suburban and rural settings. Its cathedrals are centres of spirituality and service, and its network of chaplaincies across continental Europe meets important local needs.

The Church of England plays an active role in national life with its members involved in a wide range of public bodies. Twenty-six bishops are members of the House of Lords and are engaged in debates about legislation and national and international affairs.

The Church of England is part of the worldwide Anglican Communion.

There are a number of interviews relating to the Church of England on Premier Christian Radio, under the title 'Work in Progress'.

Key facts about the Church of England

Church attendance and visits
- **1.7 million** people take part in a Church of England service each month, a level that has been maintained since the turn of the millennium. Around one million participate each Sunday.
- Almost **3 million** participate in a Church of England service on Christmas Day or Christmas Eve. **Thirty nine per cent** of the population attend a church service around Christmas, rising to 43 per cent among households with children and, nationally, 23 per cent among those of non-Christian faiths.
- In 2007, **43 per cent** of adults attended a church or place of worship for a memorial service for someone who has died and **20 per cent** were seeking a quiet space. Both these proportions are increases on 37 per cent and 19 per cent respectively in 2003 and 29 per cent and 12 per cent respectively in 2001.
- **Eighty-five per cent** of the population visit a church or place of worship in the course of a year, for reasons ranging from participating in worship to attending social events or simply wanting a quiet space.
- Every year, around **12 million** people visit Church of England cathedrals, including almost **300,000** pupils on school visits. Three of England's top five historic 'visitor attractions' are York Minster, Canterbury Cathedral and Westminster Abbey.

Education
- **Seven in ten** (70 per cent) of the population agree that Church of England schools have a positive role in educating the nation's children.
- **One in four** primary schools and **one in 16** secondary schools in England are Church of England schools. Approaching **one million pupils** are educated in more than 4,600 Church of England schools.

Ministers
- At the end of 2007, there were **20,355** ministers licensed by Church of England dioceses, including clergy, Readers and Church Army officers: one minister for every 2,500 people in England. The total does not include almost **1,600** chaplains to prisons, hospitals, the armed forces and in education, nor around **7,000** retired ministers with permission to officiate.

Community involvement
- **More people do unpaid work for church organizations than any other organization.** Eight per cent of adults undertake voluntary work for church organizations while 16 per cent belong to religious or church organizations.
- A quarter of regular churchgoers (among both Anglicans and other Christians separately) are involved in voluntary community service outside the church. Churchgoers overall contribute **23.2 million hours** voluntary service each month in their local communities outside the church.

- The Church of England provides activities outside church worship in the local community for **over half a million (515,000) children and young people** (aged under 16 years) and 38,000 young people (aged 16 to 25 years). **More than 136,000 volunteers** run children/young people activity groups sponsored by the Church of England outside church worship.

Church buildings
- **Nearly half the population** (46 per cent) think that central taxation, local taxation, the National Lottery or English Heritage should be 'primarily' responsible for providing money to maintain churches and chapels. In fact, these churches and cathedrals are largely supported by the efforts and financial support of local communities. Often, they are the focus of community life and service.
- There are 14,500 places of worship in England listed for their special architectural or historic interest, **85 per cent of which belong to and are maintained by the Church of England.**
- Necessary repairs to all listed places of worship in England have been valued at £925m over the next five years, or £185m a year.

Sources: *Church Statistics* 2003/4, 2004/5 and 2006/7.
    Opinion Research Business national polls 2000 to 2007.
    English Heritage and Church of England Cathedral and Church Buildings Division joint research.
    Church Life Survey 2001.

Tables

The following pages contain a selection of tables as available at the Church of England web site, www.cofe.anglican.org

Table K
New measures of church attendance have been employed:

Average weekly attendance – the average number of attenders at church services throughout the week typically over a four-week period in October.

Average Sunday attendance – the average number of attenders at Sunday church services typically over a four-week period in October.

Tables N to T
The following definitions apply:

Income

Unrestricted income	income that may be used by the PCC for general church expenses.
Restricted income	income which may not be used for any purpose other than as specified by the donor. (Income which a PCC designates for a specified purpose is considered to be unrestricted, since the PCC and not the donor is determining how it is to be used.)
Recurring income	includes direct giving, other voluntary income and any other recurring income. It may be unrestricted or restricted.
One-off income	includes non-recurring grants, legacies, special appeals, insurance claims and the sale of fixed assets. It may be unrestricted or restricted.
Total voluntary income	direct giving plus income tax on gift aid plus other voluntary income.
Total direct giving	planned giving plus church collections and boxes.
Other voluntary income	all other voluntary income for ordinary expenditure excluding direct giving and income tax on gift aid, e.g. fund-raising events, net profit on magazine/bookstall, sundry donations.

Expenditure
Total charitable donations includes payments to:

the recognized missionary societies, or other overseas missions, diocesan associations, Diocesan Mission Councils; Christian organizations primarily concerned with relief and development; home missions and other Church societies and organizations (including the Church Urban Fund); other charities – payments to other charities which are secularly based.

Recurring expenditure	includes donations to charities, parish share/quota, clergy expenses, church running costs, costs relating to trading, salaries and support costs.
Capital expenditure	includes major repairs, redecoration and new building work.

Notes on tables N to T
1. Figures for cathedrals are not included.
2. *i.e. adjusted by the Retail Price Index to reflect 2006 purchasing power.
3. The Diocese in Europe is not included in these tables.
Please also note that:
1. Whilst many figures in these tables have been rounded, totals, percentages and averages were

calculated before rounding. Hence row and column totals will not always agree exactly with the sum of the stated amounts.

2. Among the 13,000 parishes of the Church of England there are around 600 Local Ecumenical Projects in roughly half of which there is a congregation and a ministry shared between the Church of England and certain other churches. In such circumstances it is not always possible (or indeed desirable) to isolate the Anglican component of the congregation. The parochial statistics will therefore include a small element which may appear also in the statistics of other churches.

3. Where figures are not available for any reason, 'N/A' appears in these tables.

A   Church of England Licensed Ministries 2007

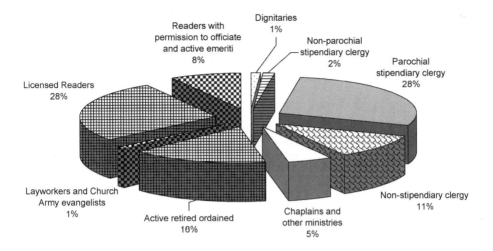

Licensed stipendiary clergy	8,808	Active retired ordained	4,600
Licensed non-stipendiary clergy incl. OLM	3,198	Licensed Readers	7,962
Chaplains and other ministries	1,569	Readers with permission to officiate and active emeriti	2,382
Licensed layworkers and Church Army evangelists	387		

Definitions

The figures for stipendiary clergy (full-time, part-time and including those outside the clergy share system) and for lay workers above are based on statistics derived from the central Church payroll. Details of chaplains and other ministers working outside the parish framework, and of non-stipendiary clergy, are based on statistics derived from the database used to compile *Crockford's Clerical Directory*. Where possible, they have been cross-referenced with material produced by organizing bodies (Church Army, the Home Office for prison chaplains, and the Hospital Chaplaincies Council for hospital chaplains).

The figure shown for active retired ordained clergy is an estimate of the number of licensed retired clergy who take an active part in ministry. It is based on the number of retired clergy known to have either permission to officiate, licence to officiate or actual appointments. Pension Board records indicate a total of 8,883 retired stipendiary clergy.

B Summary of Diocesan Licensed Ministers 2007

Ref. No.	Diocese		Full-time stipendiary clergy			Part-time stipendiary clergy			Non-stipendiary clergy		
			men	women	Total	men	women	Total	men	women	Total
1	Bath & Wells	C	170	41	211	13	8	21	42	33	75
2	Birmingham	C	133	43	176	3	2	5	20	21	41
3	Blackburn	Y	181	18	199	1	3	4	23	23	46
4	Bradford	Y	82	15	97	5	5	10	21	17	38
5	Bristol	C	104	26	130	2	4	6	25	19	44
6	Canterbury	C	115	25	140	4	1	5	25	30	55
7	Carlisle	Y	117	25	142	2	3	5	22	22	44
8	Chelmsford	C	321	70	391	4	5	9	48	46	94
9	Chester	Y	205	40	245	9	6	15	30	34	64
10	Chichester	C	284	18	302	4	2	6	49	32	81
11	Coventry	C	97	18	115	3	3	6	10	21	31
12	Derby	C	130	26	156	0	0	0	21	22	43
13	Durham	Y	154	38	192	7	2	9	25	23	48
14	Ely	C	111	32	143	5	4	9	27	26	53
15	Exeter	C	196	29	225	14	11	25	38	28	66
16	Gloucester	C	113	25	138	4	4	8	40	35	75
17	Guildford	C	144	28	172	1	8	9	33	41	74
18	Hereford	C	69	25	94	0	2	2	13	25	38
19	Leicester	C	104	31	135	3	2	5	20	25	45
20	Lichfield	C	254	47	301	3	7	10	24	32	56
21	Lincoln	C	148	38	186	2	1	3	14	22	36
22	Liverpool	Y	161	47	208	1	1	2	16	10	26
23	London	C	444	73	517	5	7	12	130	51	181
24	Manchester	Y	200	49	249	2	3	5	31	17	48
25	Newcastle	Y	109	29	138	1	2	3	13	19	32
26	Norwich	C	157	38	195	4	6	10	20	18	38
27	Oxford	C	284	87	371	4	3	7	109	87	196
28	Peterborough	C	124	28	152	2	3	5	18	12	30
29	Portsmouth	C	93	14	107	0	2	2	15	36	51
30	Ripon & Leeds	Y	92	34	126	3	1	4	20	16	36
31	Rochester	C	185	35	220	3	8	11	23	32	55
32	St Albans	C	197	61	258	3	5	8	45	49	94
33	St Edms & Ipswich	C	114	25	139	2	6	8	17	21	38
34	Salisbury	C	166	42	208	0	2	2	29	42	71
35	Sheffield	Y	126	35	161	0	5	5	15	8	23
36	Sodor & Man	Y	16	1	17	1	0	1	7	1	8
37	Southwark	C	270	80	350	4	6	10	71	74	145
38	Southwell	Y	113	38	151	1	2	3	16	25	41
39	Truro	C	91	18	109	2	0	2	18	23	41
40	Wakefield	Y	112	39	151	1	2	3	20	21	41
41	Winchester	C	185	20	205	3	3	6	38	38	76
42	Worcester	C	111	33	144	1	1	2	8	21	29
43	York	Y	191	47	238	5	4	9	49	35	84
44	Europe	C	107	12	119	0	0	0	43	14	57
Totals Province of Canterbury (C)			**5,021**	**1,088**	**6,109**	**98**	**116**	**214**	**1,033**	**976**	**2,009**
Totals Province of York (Y)			**1,859**	**455**	**2,314**	**39**	**39**	**78**	**308**	**271**	**579**
Totals CHURCH OF ENGLAND			**6,880**	**1,543**	**8,423**	**137**	**155**	**292**	**1,341**	**1,247**	**2,588**

Notes:

1 . The above figures include only those ministers who were working within the diocesan framework as at 31st December 2007.

2 . The Archbishop of Canterbury and ordained members of his staff at Lambeth Palace are classed as extra-diocesan and are not included in these figures.

Selected Church Statistics

Ordained local ministers			Total clergy (stipendiary, NSM and OLM)	Readers and Church Army	Total clergy, readers and Church Army	Diocese ref. no.
men	women	Total				
0	0	0	307	297	**604**	*1*
0	0	0	222	176	**398**	*2*
0	0	0	249	172	**421**	*3*
0	0	0	145	110	**255**	*4*
5	4	9	189	188	**377**	*5*
13	12	25	225	128	**353**	*6*
2	2	4	195	134	**329**	*7*
0	0	0	494	366	**860**	*8*
0	0	0	324	373	**697**	*9*
0	0	0	389	209	**598**	*10*
3	4	7	159	165	**324**	*11*
0	0	0	199	239	**438**	*12*
2	0	2	251	148	**399**	*13*
0	0	0	205	161	**366**	*14*
0	0	0	316	199	**515**	*15*
5	7	12	233	158	**391**	*16*
27	26	53	308	130	**438**	*17*
5	8	13	147	84	**231**	*18*
0	0	0	185	159	**344**	*19*
30	25	55	422	311	**733**	*20*
11	12	23	248	213	**461**	*21*
12	14	26	262	318	**580**	*22*
0	0	0	710	220	**930**	*23*
36	36	72	374	158	**532**	*24*
10	6	16	189	111	**300**	*25*
21	26	47	290	207	**497**	*26*
20	33	53	627	238	**865**	*27*
0	0	0	187	174	**361**	*28*
0	0	0	160	91	**251**	*29*
0	0	0	166	104	**270**	*30*
0	0	0	286	262	**548**	*31*
0	0	0	360	231	**591**	*32*
19	30	49	234	164	**398**	*33*
23	31	54	335	122	**457**	*34*
0	0	0	189	197	**386**	*35*
2	0	2	28	29	**57**	*36*
26	27	53	558	203	**761**	*37*
0	0		195	325	**520**	*38*
6	4	10	162	83	**245**	*39*
9	16	25	220	108	**328**	*40*
0	0	0	287	297	**584**	*41*
0	0	0	175	127	**302**	*42*
0	0	0	331	243	**574**	*43*
0	0	0	176	60	**236**	*44*
214	**249**	**463**	**8,795**	**5,662**	**14,457**	
73	**74**	**147**	**3,118**	**2,530**	**5,648**	
287	**323**	**610**	**11,913**	**8,192**	**20,105**	

3 . Reader and Church Army figures do not include PTO and emeriti

C Licensed Readers and Church Army 2007

Ref. No.	Diocese		Reader admissions during year		Licensed readers as at 31 December 2007[1]				Readers in training at 31 December 2007[1]		Church Army (lay evangelists) at 31 December 2007	
			men	women	men		women		men	women	men	women
1	Bath & Wells	C	4	7	143	(60)	151	(24)	7	9	3	0
2	Birmingham	C	4	9	82	(21)	92	(17)	11	17	2	0
3	Blackburn	Y	4	5	84	(37)	86	(15)	2	12	2	0
4	Bradford	Y	3	1	49	(19)	56	(9)	3	7	4	1
5	Bristol	C	10	18	77	(23)	110	(27)	7	1	0	0
6	Canterbury	C	1	1	46	(37)	76	(17)	7	8	5	1
7	Carlisle *	Y	3	4	74	(8)	58	(4)	4	9	2	0
8	Chelmsford	C	4	15	178	(45)	182	(30)	3	18	4	2
9	Chester	Y	6	11	189	(113)	178	(16)	22	19	4	2
10	Chichester	C	8	4	121	(60)	81	(23)	12	5	7	0
11	Coventry	C	3	6	80	(26)	80	(7)	11	11	3	2
12	Derby	C	2	7	122	(38)	112	(26)	5	8	4	1
13	Durham	Y	1	2	62	(31)	83	(17)	6	12	1	2
14	Ely	C	3	4	80	(28)	78	(9)	8	10	3	0
15	Exeter	C	7	8	104	(42)	88	(37)	9	15	5	2
16	Gloucester	C	2	3	85	(29)	71	(23)	9	11	1	1
17	Guildford	C	2	3	76	(39)	48	(21)	15	12	4	2
18	Hereford	C	3	2	42	(12)	38	(9)	1	5	2	2
19	Leicester	C	2	6	89	(23)	66	(12)	8	15	2	2
20	Lichfield	C	8	18	154	(59)	147	(42)	13	27	8	2
21	Lincoln	C	3	13	82	(27)	125	(11)	6	7	6	0
22	Liverpool	Y	9	13	156	(35)	152	(16)	16	26	7	3
23	London	C	9	7	110	(28)	101	(23)	15	20	5	4
24	Manchester **	Y	4	8	90	(50)	61	(10)	4	21	6	2
25	Newcastle	Y	1	5	49	(31)	58	(17)	4	9	2	2
26	Norwich	C	5	9	95	(51)	105	(35)	6	14	5	2
27	Oxford	C	3	4	126	(47)	104	(31)	9	20	6	2
28	Peterborough	C	7	4	103	(26)	66	(10)	6	14	4	1
29	Portsmouth	C	0	0	46	(20)	45	(23)	6	14	0	0
30	Ripon & Leeds	Y	3	2	47	(21)	50	(21)	12	9	4	3
31	Rochester	C	6	5	132	(72)	124	(36)	14	17	4	2
32	St Albans	C	7	4	121	(43)	104	(31)	23	28	4	2
33	St Edms & Ipswich	C	0	2	84	(28)	76	(28)	5	4	3	1
34	Salisbury	C	0	2	76	(54)	45	(26)	4	10	1	0
35	Sheffield	Y	4	1	95	(14)	77	(17)	6	10	14	11
36	Sodor & Man	Y	1	1	15	(7)	14	(0)	2	1	0	0
37	Southwark	C	4	6	106	(49)	91	(34)	12	26	3	3
38	Southwell & Nottingham	Y	8	11	152	(20)	165	(13)	8	10	7	1
39	Truro	C	2	3	47	(22)	35	(13)	9	8	0	1
40	Wakefield	Y	3	6	45	(32)	60	(15)	5	11	3	0
41	Winchester	C	5	8	168	(12)	122	(43)	15	22	5	2
42	Worcester	C	1	7	59	(21)	66	(10)	6	11	2	0
43	York	Y	5	10	107	(41)	128	(14)	9	18	6	2
44	Europe	C	-	-	32	(15)	27	(4)	17	8	1	0
	Totals Province of Canterbury (C)		115	185	2,866	(1,057)	2,656	(682)	279	395	102	37
	Totals Province of York (Y)		55	80	1,214	(459)	1,226	(184)	103	174	62	29
	Totals CHURCH OF ENGLAND		170	265	4,080	(1,516)	3,882	(866)	382	569	164	66
	Comparable figures for 2006											
	Totals Province of Canterbury (C)		117	173	2,935	(1,028)	2,600	(602)	314	442	107	39
	Totals Province of York (Y)		55	80	1,252	(402)	1,226	(175)	130	194	59	25
	Totals CHURCH OF ENGLAND		172	253	4,187	(1,430)	3,826	(777)	444	636	166	64

Notes: Figures in brackets refer to the additional number of Readers with Permission to Officiate and active Emeriti
[1] Figures revised since the publication of 'The Annual Report of the Central Readers Council of the Church of England 2007'
* Readers data from 2006   ** Readers data from 2005
There are a further four Church Army evangelists who are nationally deployed
Ordained Church Army evangelists are counted in the 'Chaplaincy and other ministries' table

D Distribution of FTE Stipendiary Diocesan clergy 2007

Actual and according to the clergy deployment formula

Ref. No.	Diocese	December 31st 2007		Number over under (-) share	Percent over under (-) share
		Actual	Share		
1	Bath and Wells	222	200	22	10.8%
2	Birmingham	179	177	2	1.1%
3	Blackburn	201	202	-1	-0.7%
4	Bradford	103	104	-1	-1.4%
5	Bristol	134	133	1	0.4%
6	Canterbury	143	155	-12	-8.0%
7	Carlisle	144	134	10	7.6%
8	Chelmsford	396	391	5	1.2%
9	Chester	251	248	3	1.3%
10	Chichester	305	276	29	10.4%
11	Coventry	119	126	-7	-5.9%
12	Derby	156	163	-7	-4.3%
13	Durham	196.5	202	-5.5	-2.7%
14	Ely	148	138	10	6.9%
15	Exeter	231	233	-2	-1.0%
16	Gloucester	142	140	2	1.6%
17	Guildford	177	155	22	14.1%
18	Hereford	95	112	-17	-15.0%
19	Leicester	137.5	149	-11.5	-7.7%
20	Lichfield	306	316	-10	-3.1%
21	Lincoln	188	222	-34	-15.4%
22	Liverpool	209	208	1	0.3%
23	London	522	497	25	5.1%
24	Manchester	251.5	263	-11.5	-4.4%
25	Newcastle	139.5	140	-0.5	-0.4%
26	Norwich	201	195	6	2.9%
27	Oxford	374.5	385	-10.5	-2.7%
28	Peterborough	155	155	0	-0.1%
29	Portsmouth	108	110	-2	-1.6%
30	Ripon and Leeds	128	139	-11	-7.9%
31	Rochester	226	187	39	20.9%
32	St. Albans	262	263	-1	-0.4%
33	St. Edms and Ipswich	143	152	-9	-5.8%
34	Salisbury	209	214	-5	-2.3%
35	Sheffield	164	163	1	0.5%
36	Sodor and Man	17.5	18	-0.5	-2.8%
37	Southwark	355	325	30	9.3%
38	Southwell	152.5	163	-10.5	-6.4%
39	Truro	110	116	-6	-5.0%
40	Wakefield	152.5	156	-3.5	-2.2%
41	Winchester	208	221	-13	-5.7%
42	Worcester	145	136	9	6.6%
43	York	243	265	-22	-8.4%
	Province of Canterbury	**6,095**	**6,042**	**53**	**0.9%**
	Province of York	**2,352**	**2,405**	**-53**	**-2.2%**
	CHURCH OF ENGLAND	**8,447**	**8,447**	**0**	**0.0%**

Note: The 'Actual' is the number of full-time stipendiary clergy plus the whole-time equivalen
of the part-time clergy. Shares are allocated as whole posts. Some actual halves are showr
to remove rounding errors.

E Ordinations 1994–2007

Proportion of ordinations by gender 1997, 2002 and 2007

1997 (total = 379): Stip. men 49%, Non-stip. women 18%, Non-stip. men 18%, Stip. women 15%

2002 (total = 540): Stip. men 37%, Stip. women 21%, Non-stip. men 13%, Non-stip. women 19%, OLM men 6%, OLM women 4%

2007 (total = 552): Stip. men 29%, Stip. women 18%, Non-stip. men 17%, Non-stip. women 23%, OLM men 7%, OLM women 6%

	1994	1995	1996	1997	1998	1999	2000	2001	2002	2003	2004	2005	2006	2007
Stipendiary men	244	245	201	186	174	199	223	190	199	181	143	158	128	162
Stipendiary women	72	65	67	57	67	78	90	105	112	120	92	103	98	102
Non-stipendiary men	55	30	46	69	73	61	81	65	67	55	63	81	82	92
Non-stipendiary women	34	42	59	67	87	76	107	89	104	77	93	108	118	128
OLM men					27	40	25	27	34	24	31	31	24	36
OLM women					40	27	43	20	24	36	47	31	31	32
TOTAL	405	382	373	379	468	481	569	496	540	493	469	512	481	552

Notes:

1. Stipendiary figures are compiled from information supplied by the Church Commissioners.

2. Non-stipendiary and OLM figures are compiled from information supplied by the Ministry Division.

3. Stipendiary figures for 2005 and 2006 have been revised to treat ordinations to part-time ministry as whole ordinations, not full-time equivalents.

E (cont'd) Ordinations & reader admissions 1994 to 2007

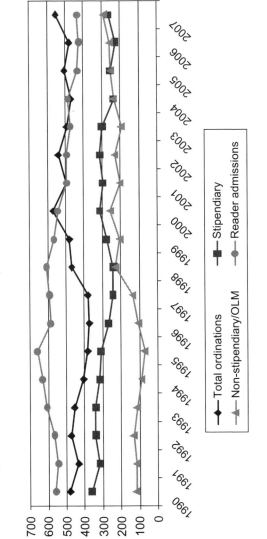

Legend:
- Total ordinations
- Non-stipendiary/OLM
- Stipendiary
- Reader admissions

Notes:

1. Stipendiary figures are compiled from information supplied by the Church Commissioners.

2. Non-stipendiary and OLM figures are compiled from information supplied by the Ministry Division.

3. Readers figures are compiled from information supplied by the dioceses

F   Parochial Baptisms and Thanksgivings 2006

Ref. No.	Diocese	Live births	Infants under one year of age	Baptisms Infant baptism rates per 1,000 live births	Children aged 1 to 12 years	All other persons	Thanksgivings Infants	Child	Baptisms and Thanksgivings Total
1	Bath & Wells	9,758	1,900	195	770	170	55	35	2,930
2	Birmingham	21,133	1,350	64	860	190	60	25	2,485
3	Blackburn	15,567	2,840	182	980	160	70	30	4,080
4	Bradford	10,127	980	97	300	70	85	15	1,450
5	Bristol	11,317	1,380	122	610	120	75	20	2,205
6	Canterbury	9,861	1,680	170	960	230	70	40	2,980
7	Carlisle	4,870	1,830	376	340	70	25	0	2,265
8	Chelmsford	38,932	3,140	81	1,770	540	320	150	5,920
9	Chester	18,006	3,500	194	1,180	190	235	70	5,175
10	Chichester	16,526	2,570	156	1,200	260	110	40	4,180
11	Coventry	9,769	1,210	124	570	200	110	60	2,150
12	Derby	11,517	1,750	152	590	130	105	30	2,605
13	Durham	16,732	3,790	227	950	170	160	20	5,090
14	Ely	7,786	1,250	161	550	140	70	25	2,035
15	Exeter	11,095	2,190	197	910	220	60	35	3,415
16	Gloucester	6,658	1,330	200	620	220	80	15	2,265
17	Guildford	11,707	1,830	156	940	180	55	15	3,020
18	Hereford	3,065	980	320	240	80	25	5	1,330
19	Leicester	11,404	1,190	104	530	180	20	10	1,930
20	Lichfield	24,119	4,210	175	1,730	410	260	75	6,685
21	Lincoln	10,463	3,060	292	860	180	40	5	4,145
22	Liverpool	17,824	3,200	180	1,310	220	105	45	4,880
23	London	58,089	2,780	48	1,920	710	100	45	5,555
24	Manchester	27,691	3,410	123	1,420	290	255	85	5,460
25	Newcastle	8,498	1,650	194	460	100	15	0	2,225
26	Norwich	8,694	1,510	174	590	130	30	10	2,270
27	Oxford	28,671	4,160	145	1,830	430	155	65	6,640
28	Peterborough	10,914	1,480	136	720	160	40	15	2,415
29	Portsmouth	8,107	1,130	139	570	130	35	15	1,880
30	Ripon & Leeds	9,437	1,490	158	500	120	35	5	2,150
31	Rochester	15,383	1,820	118	1,090	250	345	95	3,600
32	St. Albans	22,762	2,460	108	1,290	340	85	15	4,190
33	St. Edms & Ipswich	6,921	1,180	170	510	150	40	20	1,900
34	Salisbury	8,915	2,050	230	840	170	70	25	3,155
35	Sheffield	14,378	2,580	179	910	270	370	80	4,210
36	Sodor & Man	905	210	232	70	10	0	0	290
37	Southwark	40,208	2,420	60	1,660	430	110	45	4,665
38	Southwell & Nottingham	12,327	1,500	122	700	220	50	15	2,485
39	Truro	5,181	1,030	199	340	80	15	10	1,475
40	Wakefield	14,024	2,190	156	920	220	200	35	3,565
41	Winchester	14,230	2,770	195	1,080	240	90	15	4,195
42	Worcester	9,327	1,850	198	710	160	95	40	2,855
43	York	15,536	3,690	238	1,100	290	155	40	5,275
44	Europe		360	-	170	90	25	10	655
	Totals Province of Canterbury	452,514	58,020	128	27,030	6,920	2,750	1,010	95,730
	Totals Province of York	185,924	32,860	177	11,140	2,400	1,760	440	48,600
	Totals CHURCH OF ENGLAND	638,438	90,880	142	38,170	9,320	4,510	1,450	144,330
	Comparable figures for 2005:								
	Totals Province of Canterbury	435,679	60,000	138	27,500	6,900	2,900	1,100	98,400
	Totals Province of York	179,868	33,000	183	11,100	2,300	2,000	600	48,900
	Totals CHURCH OF ENGLAND	615,547	93,000	151	38,600	9,100	4,900	1,700	147,300

Notes   Figures for cathedrals are included.
Live births per diocese are estimates based on statistics obtained from the Office for National Statistics (ONS).

Selected Church Statistics

G Parochial Marriages and Funerals 2006

Ref. No.	Diocese	Marriages	Blessings of civil marriage	Total	Held in church	Held in crematoria /cemeteries	Total	Number of deaths	% with C of E funeral
		Marriages			**Funerals**				
1	Bath & Wells	1,460	120	1,580	2,520	1,940	4,460	8,644	52%
2	Birmingham	1,080	40	1,120	1,390	4,080	5,470	12,954	42%
3	Blackburn	1,120	90	1,210	2,370	2,390	4,760	13,690	35%
4	Bradford	570	30	600	940	1,010	1,950	6,237	31%
5	Bristol	950	70	1,020	1,170	1,840	3,010	8,011	38%
6	Canterbury	1,240	100	1,340	1,500	2,670	4,170	9,096	46%
7	Carlisle	800	80	880	1,950	1,050	3,000	5,323	56%
8	Chelmsford	2,450	180	2,630	3,120	5,970	9,090	24,599	37%
9	Chester	1,720	60	1,780	3,670	2,940	6,610	15,790	42%
10	Chichester	1,760	180	1,940	2,520	3,930	6,450	17,585	37%
11	Coventry	970	80	1,050	1,900	1,510	3,410	7,499	45%
12	Derby	1,160	90	1,250	2,690	1,920	4,610	10,177	45%
13	Durham	1,180	60	1,240	3,990	2,630	6,620	15,401	43%
14	Ely	870	70	940	1,630	1,320	2,950	5,815	51%
15	Exeter	1,490	180	1,670	2,930	2,380	5,310	12,074	44%
16	Gloucester	960	90	1,050	1,860	1,220	3,080	6,056	51%
17	Guildford	1,240	70	1,310	1,360	1,860	3,220	8,018	40%
18	Hereford	660	60	720	1,370	690	2,060	3,298	62%
19	Leicester	1,030	70	1,100	2,070	1,260	3,330	8,236	40%
20	Lichfield	2,330	150	2,480	5,930	4,560	10,490	20,180	52%
21	Lincoln	1,530	110	1,640	2,820	2,280	5,100	10,786	47%
22	Liverpool	1,190	70	1,260	3,760	2,050	5,810	15,705	37%
23	London	1,580	190	1,770	1,510	3,130	4,640	22,984	20%
24	Manchester	1,390	90	1,480	2,680	3,430	6,110	19,156	32%
25	Newcastle	650	80	730	1,230	2,070	3,300	8,196	40%
26	Norwich	1,150	90	1,240	2,500	2,670	5,170	9,299	56%
27	Oxford	2,840	240	3,080	3,710	4,340	8,050	16,446	49%
28	Peterborough	1,030	100	1,130	1,640	970	2,610	7,091	37%
29	Portsmouth	920	80	1,000	1,200	1,910	3,110	7,335	42%
30	Ripon & Leeds	850	80	930	1,400	1,320	2,720	7,178	38%
31	Rochester	1,130	100	1,230	1,620	4,130	5,750	10,513	55%
32	St. Albans	1,720	120	1,840	2,600	3,810	6,410	14,208	45%
33	St. Edms & Ipswich	980	90	1,070	1,920	1,260	3,180	5,954	53%
34	Salisbury	1,420	140	1,560	2,370	1,620	3,990	9,187	43%
35	Sheffield	1,230	90	1,320	2,810	3,700	6,510	11,520	57%
36	Sodor & Man	130	20	150	260	180	440	768	57%
37	Southwark	1,550	100	1,650	1,300	3,900	5,200	17,650	29%
38	Southwell & Nottingham	1,260	90	1,350	2,390	2,390	4,780	10,100	47%
39	Truro	860	90	950	1,600	680	2,280	5,686	40%
40	Wakefield	1,000	70	1,070	2,230	2,030	4,260	10,543	40%
41	Winchester	1,830	160	1,990	2,330	2,340	4,670	11,601	40%
42	Worcester	1,170	80	1,250	2,030	1,870	3,900	7,950	49%
43	York	1,690	130	1,820	3,200	3,280	6,480	14,146	46%
44	Europe	200	370	570	240	510	750		-
	Totals Province of Canterbury	39,560	3,610	43,170	63,350	72,570	135,920	318,932	43%
	Totals Province of York	14,780	1,040	15,820	32,880	30,470	63,350	153,751	41%
	Totals CHURCH OF ENGLAND	54,340	4,650	58,990	96,230	103,040	199,270	472,683	42%
	Comparable figures for 2005:								
	Totals Province of Canterbury	41,470	4,020	45,490	65,380	75,650	141,010	325,150	43%
	Totals Province of York	15,740	1,120	16,860	34,070	32,160	66,270	156,594	42%
	Totals CHURCH OF ENGLAND	57,210	5,140	62,350	99,450	107,810	207,280	481,744	43%

Notes: Figures for cathedrals are included.
The number of deaths are estimates based on statistics obtained from the Office for National Statistics (ONS)

H   Confirmations 2006

Ref. No.	Diocese	Services	Males	Females	Totals
1	Bath and Wells	47	251	363	614
2	Birmingham	53	159	276	435
3	Blackburn	77	648	832	1480
4	Bradford	33	82	121	203
5	Bristol	26	147	208	355
6	Canterbury	38	229	488	717
7	Carlisle	63	167	263	430
8	Chelmsford	85	432	771	1203
9	Chester	93	294	485	779
10	Chichester	93	462	582	1044
11	Coventry	10	139	212	351
12	Derby	42	184	292	476
13	Durham	47	210	331	541
14	Ely	44	143	219	362
15	Exeter	60	270	400	670
16	Gloucester	32	104	216	320
17	Guildford	41	299	458	757
18	Hereford	37	136	171	307
19	Leicester	10	133	202	335
20	Lichfield	112	448	667	1115
21	Lincoln	47	207	320	527
22	Liverpool	84	428	723	1151
23	London	229	790	1172	1962
24	Manchester	91	518	809	1327
25	Newcastle	57	107	190	297
26	Norwich	38	149	213	362
27	Oxford	138	717	842	1559
28	Peterborough	46	255	308	563
29	Portsmouth	13	86	122	208
30	Ripon & Leeds	58	193	281	474
31	Rochester	81	383	630	1013
32	St. Albans	76	374	545	919
33	St. Edms & Ipswich	35	137	228	365
34	Salisbury	32	358	419	777
35	Sheffield	40	162	282	444
36	Sodor and Man	11	28	36	64
37	Southwark	89	547	883	1430
38	Southwell	23	167	289	456
39	Truro	53	111	183	294
40	Wakefield	75	148	243	391
41	Winchester	100	371	431	802
42	Worcester	47	157	249	406
43	York	125	283	479	762
44	Europe	46	155	178	333
Totals Province of Canterbury		**1800**	**8333**	**12248**	**20581**
Totals Province of York		**877**	**3435**	**5364**	**8799**
Totals CHURCH OF ENGLAND		**2677**	**11768**	**17612**	**29380**
Comparable figures for 2005:					
Totals Province of Canterbury		1744	8266	12608	20874
Totals Province of York		827	3587	5372	8959
Totals CHURCH OF ENGLAND		2571	11853	17980	29833

Note: Confirmations in the Armed Forces are not included.

I Parochial Church Electoral Rolls

Ref. No.	Diocese	2006	2005	2002[1]	1996[1]	1990[1]
				Church Electoral Rolls		
1	Bath & Wells	39,500	39,000	38,000	42,700	47,300
2	Birmingham	19,100	18,900	18,200	19,300	19,900
3	Blackburn	35,800	35,800	34,300	37,400	47,000
4	Bradford	12,100	12,200	12,300	12,700	14,900
5	Bristol	17,000	17,000	16,600	19,000	22,200
6	Canterbury	22,900	22,300	21,000	21,000	21,000
7	Carlisle	21,800	22,000	21,600	24,900	25,700
8	Chelmsford	51,100	50,100	48,600	50,800	51,100
9	Chester	49,400	48,700	45,700	48,600	50,500
10	Chichester	56,700	55,700	51,800	58,200	62,700
11	Coventry	17,300	16,900	16,300	17,700	19,800
12	Derby	20,600	20,100	20,700	20,100	24,100
13	Durham	23,500	24,900	24,000	27,400	30,900
14	Ely	18,500	19,500	19,100	20,900	23,800
15	Exeter	32,100	32,200	30,500	33,900	38,000
16	Gloucester	22,500	24,100	23,600	26,300	28,400
17	Guildford	30,500	30,800	29,500	30,600	33,100
18	Hereford	18,100	18,600	18,100	18,900	20,000
19	Leicester	17,900	17,700	17,000	16,100	19,300
20	Lichfield	48,200	47,800	45,000	52,200	58,400
21	Lincoln	27,400	28,600	27,800	31,300	35,900
22	Liverpool	29,300	29,800	28,800	32,500	36,900
23	London	63,800	69,400	59,600	52,500	45,100
24	Manchester	35,700	35,800	34,500	38,000	39,300
25	Newcastle	17,000	16,900	16,700	17,500	19,500
26	Norwich	23,600	23,400	23,900	25,900	31,100
27	Oxford	57,900	57,400	54,600	60,600	58,700
28	Peterborough	19,000	18,800	18,000	19,500	21,700
29	Portsmouth	18,500	18,300	17,500	18,000	19,500
30	Ripon & Leeds	17,700	18,200	17,600	19,300	24,600
31	Rochester	31,600	31,700	29,900	31,300	34,100
32	St. Albans	42,100	41,800	39,400	43,100	50,000
33	St. Edms & Ipswich	25,200	24,700	24,100	25,300	26,900
34	Salisbury	43,600	45,100	42,500	45,900	48,200
35	Sheffield	20,600	20,000	18,600	20,700	22,600
36	Sodor & Man	2,800	2,700	2,400	2,800	3,300
37	Southwark	46,200	47,300	44,200	45,400	46,100
38	Southwell & Nottingham	19,500	19,200	18,300	18,700	20,800
39	Truro	17,500	17,000	16,900	17,600	21,900
40	Wakefield	21,600	21,700	20,300	23,200	24,900
41	Winchester	41,200	39,800	38,500	42,100	44,400
42	Worcester	20,400	20,400	20,300	22,400	21,200
43	York	37,900	35,900	35,000	38,200	41,100
44	Europe	10,800	10,400	9,300	N/A	N/A
	Totals Province of Canterbury	**921,000**	**925,000**	**880,300**	**929,000**	**994,000**
	Totals Province of York	**345,000**	**344,000**	**330,000**	**362,000**	**402,000**
	Totals CHURCH OF ENGLAND	**1,266,000**	**1,269,000**	**1,210,000**	**1,290,400**	**1,396,000**

Notes: 1. Electoral Rolls are revised annually and new rolls are compiled every six years. Thus in 1990, 1996 and 2002 new electoral rolls were compiled.
2. Figures for cathedrals are included from 2002 onwards.
3. *N/A* These figures are not available so national electoral roll totals for 1990 and 1996 do not include the Diocese of Europe.

J   Average Weekly Attendances 2006 and 2005
adults, children and young people

| Ref. No. | Diocese | Total Attendances (Adults, children and young people) | | | | | |
| | | Average Weekly | | Average Sunday | | Usual Sunday | |
		2006	2005	2006	2005	2006	2005
1	Bath & Wells	28,100	25,500	24,400	22,400	22,200	22,300
2	Birmingham	20,100	20,200	17,200	17,100	16,100	15,600
3	Blackburn	32,400	34,300	27,000	28,100	23,200	23,800
4	Bradford	11,900	12,300	9,700	10,400	8,900	9,000
5	Bristol	17,600	18,600	15,700	15,700	13,500	14,100
6	Canterbury	24,300	25,800	20,300	20,900	18,000	18,000
7	Carlisle	17,100	17,400	14,500	14,600	11,500	11,800
8	Chelmsford	42,700	43,200	38,500	38,300	34,000	33,800
9	Chester	40,100	38,800	32,900	32,500	28,100	28,200
10	Chichester	46,800	47,500	39,600	39,300	36,000	35,900
11	Coventry	16,800	17,300	14,300	15,100	13,200	13,300
12	Derby	18,800	21,000	16,400	19,200	14,400	14,800
13	Durham	20,800	23,200	17,800	19,300	15,400	16,300
14	Ely	18,300	18,800	15,600	16,900	13,500	14,900
15	Exeter	27,900	28,100	24,500	24,100	23,900	23,600
16	Gloucester	22,800	20,600	19,400	17,100	16,500	18,700
17	Guildford	29,200	28,700	25,300	24,900	23,100	23,000
18	Hereford	12,800	12,800	11,100	11,100	8,500	8,700
19	Leicester	16,500	17,700	14,600	15,200	12,900	13,100
20	Lichfield	39,000	39,700	30,300	31,800	28,500	28,500
21	Lincoln	24,700	25,500	20,000	20,500	15,700	16,200
22	Liverpool	29,400	30,200	25,600	25,400	21,700	22,500
23	London	80,600	79,300	62,200	62,200	57,400	57,500
24	Manchester	34,900	34,500	29,400	29,000	25,900	26,000
25	Newcastle	15,200	15,600	12,600	13,300	11,100	11,600
26	Norwich	22,100	22,700	19,600	19,900	16,800	17,100
27	Oxford	59,000	60,600	50,800	52,900	44,800	46,500
28	Peterborough	20,800	21,500	17,500	18,100	15,400	15,400
29	Portsmouth	15,200	14,800	13,300	13,400	12,300	12,400
30	Ripon & Leeds	16,200	17,000	13,700	13,900	11,900	12,200
31	Rochester	31,100	32,000	26,300	27,300	23,800	24,400
32	St. Albans	39,400	38,700	31,000	31,500	27,400	27,700
33	St. Edms & Ipswich	20,700	20,800	19,000	18,200	16,300	15,900
34	Salisbury	34,700	32,500	28,600	27,800	24,700	24,100
35	Sheffield	19,100	20,700	15,600	17,200	13,500	14,700
36	Sodor & Man	2,800	2,700	2,300	2,300	1,800	1,800
37	Southwark	43,000	43,900	38,600	39,500	36,400	34,700
38	Southwell & Nottingham	18,700	18,800	15,800	16,000	14,000	14,200
39	Truro	14,500	14,500	12,000	12,300	10,800	10,500
40	Wakefield	18,600	18,200	16,200	15,500	13,500	13,300
41	Winchester	36,000	35,400	30,200	30,500	27,400	28,000
42	Worcester	17,800	17,600	14,200	14,700	12,300	12,700
43	York	32,600	32,400	27,300	26,000	23,700	22,700
44	Europe	12,100	12,300	11,500	11,400	10,800	10,900
	Totals Province of Canterbury	854,000	858,000	722,000	730,000	646,000	652,000
	Totals Province of York	310,000	316,000	261,000	264,000	224,000	228,000
	Totals CHURCH OF ENGLAND	1,163,000	1,174,000	983,000	993,000	871,000	880,000

Notes: 1. Children and young people are for the majority of dioceses defined as under the age of 16 years.
2. Figures for cathedrals are included.

Selected Church Statistics

K All Age Church Attendance 2000 to 2006

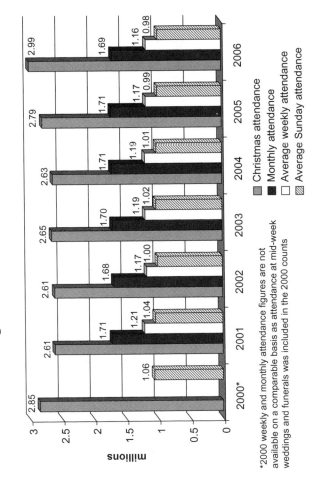

*2000 weekly and monthly attendance figures are not available on a comparable basis as attendance at mid-week weddings and funerals was included in the 2000 counts

- Christmas attendance
- Monthly attendance
- Average weekly attendance
- Average Sunday attendance

Parochial church attendance 2000 to 2006

L Weekly Church Attendance

| | Weekly attendance | | | | | | | | |
| | Adult | | | Children and young people | | | All age | | |
Year	Highest attendance 000s	Average attendance 000s	Lowest attendance 000s	Highest attendance 000s	Average attendance 000s	Lowest attendance 000s	Highest attendance 000s	Average attendance 000s	Lowest attendance 000s
2000 *	1,451	1,031	742	455	243	120	1,855	1,274	885
2001	1,332	976	727	416	229	113	1,708	1,205	862
2002	1,296	941	693	424	229	111	1,682	1,170	825
2003	1,312	957	714	430	230	110	1,704	1,187	844
2004	1,308	951	706	437	235	111	1,707	1,186	839
2005	1,302	942	696	444	232	107	1,706	1,174	823
2006	1,294	937	690	442	228	103	1,694	1,163	812

M Sunday Church Attendance

| | Sunday attendance | | | | | | | | |
| | Adult | | | Children and young people | | | All age | | |
Year	Highest attendance 000s	Average attendance 000s	Lowest attendance 000s	Highest attendance 000s	Average attendance 000s	Lowest attendance 000s	Highest attendance 000s	Average attendance 000s	Lowest attendance 000s
2000	1,191	878	660	300	180	103	1,464	1,058	781
2001	1,170	868	657	285	173	99	1,425	1,041	774
2002	1,143	838	623	278	167	94	1,395	1,005	733
2003	1,156	853	645	272	164	92	1,401	1,017	755
2004	1,147	846	638	272	164	91	1,394	1,010	746
2005	1,136	836	629	264	158	87	1,374	993	733
2006	1,123	828	622	262	155	84	1,361	983	722

Notes: 1. Figures for cathedrals are included.
2. Children and young people are under 16 years of age while adults are 16 years of age or over.
3. From 2000 church attendance figures are calculated typically from a four-week count in October.
4. * In 2000 attendance at midweek weddings and funerals was included.
5. An approximation to monthly attendance can be taken from the highest weekly attendance counted over a typical month.

Selected Financial Comparisons 1964 to 2006

N Tax-efficient planned giving to Parochial Church Councils: contributors, amounts and average weekly rates

		Actual		In real terms of 2006*	
	Subscribers	Tax-efficient** planned giving, net, £ 000s	Weekly average per subscriber	Tax-efficient** planned giving, net, £ 000s	Weekly average per subscriber
Year	000s		£		£
1964	126	2,113	0.32	29,478	4.50
1970	168	3,325	0.38	35,604	4.08
1980	362	17,692	0.94	52,388	2.78
1990	405	71,130	3.38	111,743	5.31
1995	404	111,045	5.28	147,539	7.02
1996	404	118,111	5.62	153,227	7.29
1997	401	124,439	5.96	156,517	7.50
1998	399	132,114	6.37	160,662	7.75
1999	412	145,752	6.86	174,568	8.22
2000	451	157,922	6.73	183,701	7.83
2001	491	179,669	7.03	205,262	8.03
2002	504	189,904	7.25	213,507	8.15
2003	513	201,272	7.55	219,923	8.25
2004	517	215,085	8.00	228,218	8.49
2005	523	224,636	8.26	231,773	8.52
2006	527	236,625	8.64	236,625	8.64

O Weekly average tax-efficient planned giving per subscriber 1990 to 2006**

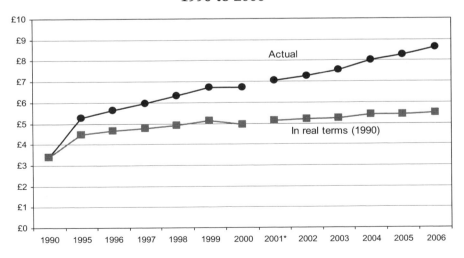

Notes: 1. * i.e. adjusted by the Retail Price Index to reflect 2006 purchasing power.

2. ** 2001 onwards include unrestricted and restricted giving, earlier years are primarily unrestricted tax-efficient planned giving.

P Direct Unrestricted Giving to Parochial Church Councils

| | Actual | | In real terms of 2006** | |
| | Total direct giving £ 000s | Weekly average per Electoral Roll member £ | Total direct giving £ 000s | Weekly average per Electoral Roll member £ |
Year				
1964	14,961	0.11	208,716	1.49
1970	15,847	0.12	169,691	1.29
1980	51,521	0.55	152,561	1.62
*1990	141,076	1.94	221,627	3.05
1995	197,163	2.58	261,958	3.43
*1996	205,417	3.06	266,491	3.97
1997	215,599	3.15	271,176	3.96
1998	244,338	3.51	297,135	4.27
1999	253,000	3.61	303,019	4.32
2000	268,541	3.78	312,378	4.40
2001	282,244	3.98	322,448	4.55
*2002	296,382	4.75	333,220	5.34
2003	306,667	4.81	335,084	5.26
2004	323,403	5.00	343,150	5.31
2005	335,095	5.08	345,741	5.24
2006	348,716	5.34	348,716	5.34

Q Total Unrestricted Voluntary and Recurring Income of PCCs

Year	Total voluntary income £ 000s Actual	Weekly average per Electoral Roll member £ Actual	Total voluntary income £ 000s In real terms (2006)	Weekly average per Electoral Roll member £ In real terms (2006)	Recurring income Actual £000s	Recurring income In real terms (2006) £000s
1964	20,033	0.14	279,474	1.95	22,108	308,422
1970	22,110	0.17	236,756	1.82	26,396	282,651
1980	72,798	0.77	215,565	2.28	85,880	254,302
*1990	195,193	2.69	306,643	4.23	237,385	372,926
1995	275,388	3.61	365,891	4.80	327,531	435,170
*1996	288,358	4.30	374,091	5.58	344,897	447,440
1997	305,345	4.46	384,056	5.61	374,324	470,816
1998	314,933	4.52	382,985	5.50	403,801	491,056
1999	326,377	4.66	390,903	5.58	418,557	501,307
2000	346,856	4.88	403,477	5.68	442,477	514,708
2001	365,851	5.16	417,965	5.90	462,664	528,568
*2002	385,861	6.18	433,820	6.95	486,597	547,077
2003	401,600	6.30	438,814	6.88	506,838	553,804
2004	423,452	6.55	449,308	6.95	538,031	570,883
2005	440,574	6.68	454,571	6.89	561,141	578,969
2006	459,800	7.04	459,800	7.04	585,399	585,399

Notes: 1. Figures for cathedrals and their daughter churches are not included.
2. Explanations of composite items and totals are given in the Definitions.
3. * Electoral Rolls are revised annually and new rolls are compiled every six years. Thus in 1990, 1996 and 2002 new electoral rolls were compiled.
4. ** i.e. adjusted by the Retail Price Index to reflect 2006 purchasing power.
5. The Diocese in Europe is not included in these tables.

R Total income of Parochial Church Councils
1998 to 2006, £ millions

Year	Unrestricted			Restricted			Total (unrestricted & restricted)		
	Recurring	One-off	Total	Recurring	One-off	Total	Recurring	One-off	Total
1998	404	36	440	54	63	117	457	100	557
1999	419	37	456	55	69	123	473	106	579
2000	442	39	482	57	86	143	499	126	625
2001	463	40	503	61	88	149	523	128	652
2002	487	46	533	61	81	142	547	128	675
2003	507	54	561	63	92	155	570	146	716
2004	538	53	591	67	101	168	605	154	759
2005	561	55	616	73	103	176	635	158	792
2006	585	59	644	75	107	182	661	166	826

S Chart of Income from 1998 to 2006

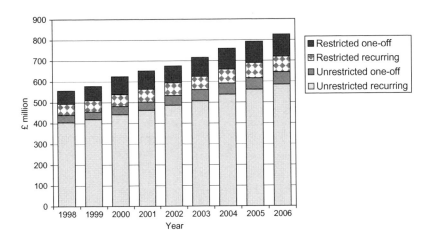

T Total Expenditure of Parochial Church Councils
1998 to 2006, £ millions

Year	Recurring expenditure	Capital expenditure	Total expenditure
1998	415	103	518
1999	437	127	564
2000	458	145	603
2001	483	145	628
2002	514	149	663
2003	535	162	697
2004	568	159	726
2005	601	178	779
2006	618	175	792

TABLE OF PAROCHIAL FEES From 1 January 2009 Prepared by the Archbishops' Council under the Ecclesiastical Fees Measure 1986 Authorised by the Parochial Fees Order 2008, subject to confirmation by Parliament	Fee Payable Towards Stipend of Incumbent (See Note 2)	Fee Payable To Parochial Church Council	Total Fee payable
BAPTISMS	£	£	£
Certificate issued at time of baptism	12.00	—	12.00
Short certificate of baptism given under Section 2, Baptismal Registers Measure 1961	9.00	—	9.00
MARRIAGES			
Publication of banns of marriage	15.00	7.00	22.00
Certificate of banns issued at time of publication	12.00	—	12.00
Marriage service (Marriage certificate – See Note 6)	123.00	131.00	254.00
FUNERALS AND BURIALS			
Service in church			
Funeral service in church	54.00	45.00	99.00
Burial in churchyard following on from service in church	—	190.00	190.00
Burial in cemetery or cremation following on from service in church (See Note 3(ii))	—	—	NIL
Burial of body in churchyard on separate occasion (See Note 3(iii))	36.00	190.00	226.00
Burial of cremated remains in churchyard on separate occasion	36.00	77.00	113.00
Burial in cemetery on separate occasion (See Note 3(ii))	36.00	—	36.00
No service in church			
Service in crematorium or cemetery (See Note 3(ii))	99.00	—	99.00
Burial of body in churchyard (See Note 3(iv))	36.00	190.00	226.00
Burial of cremated remains in churchyard (See Note 3(iv))	36.00	77.00	113.00
Certificate issued at time of burial (See Note 3(v))	12.00	—	12.00
MONUMENTS IN CHURCHYARDS			
Permitted in accordance with the rules, regulations or directions made by the Chancellor of the diocese, including those relating to a particular churchyard or part of a churchyard (but excluding a monument authorized by a particular faculty, the fee for which is set by the Chancellor)			
Small cross of wood	9.00	12.00	21.00
Small vase not exceeding 305mm × 203mm × 203mm (approx. 12" × 8" × 8")	36.00	44.00	80.00
Tablet, plaque or other marker commemorating a person whose remains have been cremated	36.00	44.00	80.00
Any other monument	51.00	101.00	152.00
(the above fees to include the original inscription)			
Additional inscription on existing monument (See Note 4)	36.00	—	36.00
SEARCHES IN CHURCH REGISTERS			
Searching registers of marriages for period before 1 July 1837 (See Note 5)			
(for up to one hour)	12.00	7.00	19.00
(for each subsequent hour or part of an hour)	9.00	7.00	16.00
Searching registers of baptisms or burials (See Note 5) (including the provision of one copy of any entry therein) (for up to one hour)	12.00	7.00	19.00
(for each subsequent hour or part of an hour)	9.00	7.00	16.00
Each additional copy of an entry in a register of baptisms or burials	12.00	7.00	19.00
Inspection of instrument of apportionment or agreement for exchange of land for tithes deposited under the Tithe Act 1836	9.00	—	9.00
Furnishing copies of above (for every 72 words)	9.00	—	9.00
EXTRAS The fees shown in this table are the statutory fees payable. It is stressed that the figures do not include any charges for extras such as music (e.g. organist, choir), bells, and flowers, which are fixed by the Parochial Church Council.	Published by Ministry Division The Archbishops' Council Church House, Great Smith Street, London SW1P 3AZ		

Selected Church Statistics

NOTES

1 DEFINITIONS
'Burial' includes deposit in a vault or brick grave and the interment or deposit of cremated remains.
'Churchyard' includes the curtilage of a church and a burial ground of a church whether or not immediately adjoining such church.
(NOTE: This includes any area used for the interment of cremated remains within such a curtilage or burial ground, whether consecrated or not.)
'Cemetery' means a burial ground maintained by a burial authority.
'Monument' includes headstone, cross, kerb, border, vase, chain, railing, tablet, plaque, marker, flatstone, tombstone or monument or tomb of any other kind.

2 INCUMBENT'S FEE
Incumbents declare their fees to the Diocese, which takes them into account in determining the stipend paid to the incumbent.

3 FUNERALS AND BURIALS
(i)   No fee is payable in respect of a burial of a still-born infant, or for the funeral or burial of an infant dying within one year after birth.
(ii) The fees prescribed by this table for a funeral service in any cemetery or crematorium are mandatory except where a cemetery or crematorium authority has itself fixed different charges for these services, in which case the authority's charges apply.
(iii) The fee for a burial in a churchyard on a separate occasion applies when burial does not follow on from a service in church.
(iv) If a full funeral service is held at the graveside in a churchyard, the incumbent's fee is increased to that payable where the service is held in church.
(v)   The certificate issued at the time of burial is a copy of the entry in the register of burials kept under the Parochial Registers and Records Measure 1978.

4 MONUMENTS IN CHURCHYARDS
The fee for an additional inscription on a small cross of wood, a small vase, shall not exceed the current fee payable to the incumbent for the erection of such a monument.

5 SEARCHES IN CHURCH REGISTERS
The search fee relates to a particular search where the approximate date of the baptism, marriage or burial is known. The fee for a more general search of a church register would be negotiable.

6 FEE FOR MARRIAGE CERTIFICATE
The following fees are currently payable to the incumbent under the Registration of Births, Deaths and Marriages (Fees) Order 2002: certificate of marriage at registration £3.50; subsequently £7.00.
These fees may be increased from 1 April 2009.

Dioceses **PART 1**

PART 1 CONTENTS

Every effort has been made to ensure that all details are accurate at the time of going to press.

Provinces of Canterbury and York

The dioceses in the respective Provinces of Canterbury and York are as below:

The Province of Canterbury Bath and Wells, Birmingham, Bristol, Canterbury, Chelmsford, Chichester, Coventry, Derby, Ely, Europe, Exeter, Gloucester, Guildford, Hereford, Leicester, Lichfield, Lincoln, London, Norwich, Oxford, Peterborough, Portsmouth, Rochester, St Albans, St Edmundsbury and Ipswich, Salisbury, Southwark, Truro, Winchester, Worcester.

The Province of York Blackburn, Bradford, Carlisle, Chester, Durham, Liverpool, Manchester, Newcastle, Ripon and Leeds, Sheffield, Sodor and Man, Southwell and Nottingham, Wakefield, York.

The entry for each diocese is preceded by a territorial description and a few vital statistics.

Population Derived from the 2006 mid-year estimates published by the Office for National Statistics (source: ONS web site www.statistics.gov.uk). Calculations are based on diocesan proportions of Ward and Civil Parish populations.

Area in square miles, as calculated from material supplied by the Office of National Statistics and the Church Commissioners.

Stipendiary clergy Full-time parochial clergy, men and women, working within the diocesan framework in parishes as at 31 December 2007 and counted under the current deployment formula.

Benefices Figures as at December 2007, compiled from information provided by the Church Commissioners. The figure does not include cathedrals or conventional districts.

Parishes / **Churches** as listed at 31 December 2007 (with later additions) in the Parish Register maintained by the Research and Statistics Department of the Archbishops' Council.

In most cases, the Diocesan Secretary/Chief Executive is also the Secretary of the Diocesan Synod.

PROVINCIAL LAY OFFICERS

Canterbury
Dean of the Court of Arches Rt Worshipful Sheila Cameron QC

Vicar-General Rt Worshipful Timothy Briden

Joint Registrars Canon John Rees, 16 Beaumont St, Oxford OX1 2LZ   *Tel:* 01865 297200
Fax: 01865 726274
email: jrees@winkworths.co.uk

Mr Stephen Slack, The Legal Office, Church House, Great Smith St, London SW1P 3AZ
Tel: 020 7898 1366
email: stephen.slack@c-of-e.org.uk

York
Official Principal and Auditor of Chancery Court of York Rt Worshipful Sheila Cameron QC

Vicar-General of the Province and Official Principal of the Consistory Court Vacancy

Registrar of Province Mr Lionel Lennox, Provincial Registry, Stamford House, Piccadilly, York YO1 9PP   *Tel:* 01904 623487
Fax: 01904 561470
email: lpml@denisontill.com

Registrar (Provincial Elections) Mr Stephen Slack (*as above*)

Archbishop of Canterbury's Personal Staff

Lambeth Palace, London SE1 7JU
Tel: 020 7898 1200   *Fax:* 020 7261 9836
Web: www.archbishopofcanterbury.org

CHIEF OF STAFF
Mr Christopher Smith

Archbishop's Personal Assistant
Mrs Sarah Walker

Secretary for Public Affairs
Mr Tim Livesey

Deputy Secretary for Public Affairs
Vacancy

Press Secretary
Ms Marie Papworth

Press Officer
Mr David Brownlie-Marshall

Patronage Secretary
Mr Derek Fullarton

Premises and Administration Secretary
Mr Andrew Nunn

Secretary for Anglican Communion Affairs
Vacancy

Secretary for International and Inter-religious Relations
Canon Anthony Ball

Secretary for International Development
Vacancy

Anglican Communion Liaison Officer
Miss Fiona Millican

Archbishop's Chaplain and Ecumenical Officer
Canon Jonathan Goodall

Secretary for Inter Faith Relations and National Inter Faith Adviser
Canon Guy Wilkinson

Archbishops' Missioner and Team Leader of Fresh Expressions
Revd Dr Steven Croft

Steward
Mr Robin Elks

Finance Officer
Miss Rebecca Pashley

Archbishop of York's Personal Staff

Bishopthorpe Palace, Bishopthorpe, York YO23 2GE
Tel: 01904 707021   *Fax:* 01904 709204
email: office@archbishopofyork.org
Web: www.archbishopofyork.org

Chief of Staff
Revd Malcolm Macnaughton

Chaplain/Researcher to the Archbishop
Revd Dr Daphne Green
email: daphne.green@archbishopofyork.org

Executive Officer/Researcher
Mrs Margaret Pattinson
email: margaret.pattinson@archbishopofyork.org

Director of Communications
Revd Arun Arora

Domestic Chaplain
Revd Brunel James

Senior Secretary
Miss Alison Cundiff

DIOCESE OF BATH AND WELLS

Founded in 909. Somerset; north Somerset; Bath;
north-east Somerset; a few parishes in Dorset.

Population 892,000   Area 1,614 sq m
Full-time Stipendiary Parochial Clergy 198   Benefices 200
Parishes 467   Churches 566
www. bathwells.anglican.org
Overseas link dioceses: Lusaka, Central Zambia, Northern Zambia
and Eastern Zambia.

BISHOP (78th)
Rt Revd Peter Price, The Palace, Wells BA5 2PD
[2002]   *Tel:* 01749 672341
                                Fax: 01749 679355
email: bishop@bathwells.anglican.org

SUFFRAGAN BISHOP
TAUNTON Rt Revd Peter Maurice, The Palace,
Wells BA5 2PD (*Office*) [2006]   *Tel:* 01749 672341
                                   Fax: 01749 679355
email: bishop.taunton@bathwells.anglican.org
Bishops' Senior Chaplain and Adviser Preb Stephen
Lynas (*same address, tel and fax nos*)
        email: chaplain@bathwells.anglican.org
Bishop's Domestic Chaplain Revd Julia Hedley
(*same address, tel and fax nos*)
        email: julia.hedley@bathwells.anglican.org

ASSISTANT BISHOPS
Rt Revd Richard Third, 25 Church Close,
Martock, Yeovil TA12 6DS   *Tel:* 01935 825519
Rt Revd William Persson, Ryalls Cottage, Burton
St, Marnhull, Sturminster Newton DT10 1PS
                                Tel: 01258 820452
Rt Revd Paul Barber, Hillside, 41 Somerton Rd,
Street BA16 0DR   *Tel:* 01458 442916
Rt Revd Barry Rogerson, Flat 2, 30 Albert Rd,
Clevedon BS21 7RR   *Tel:* 01275 541964
        email: barry.rogerson@blueyonder.co.uk
Rt Revd Roger Sainsbury, Abbey Lodge, Battery
Lane, Portishead BS20 7JD   *Tel:* 01275 847082
        email: bishoproger.abbey@btopenworld.com
Rt Revd Andrew Burnham, Bishop's House,
Church Lane, Dry Sandford, Abingdon OX13 6JP
                                Tel: 01865 390746
        email: bishop.andrew@ebbsfleet.org.uk

**CATHEDRAL CHURCH OF ST ANDREW
IN WELLS**
Dean of Wells Very Revd John Clarke, The Dean's
Lodging, 25 The Liberty, Wells BA5 2SZ [2004]
                                Tel: 01749 670278
        email: dean@wellscathedral.uk.net
Cathedral Offices Chain Gate, Cathedral Green,
Wells BA5 2UE   *Tel:* 01749 674483
                 Fax: 01749 832210
        email: office@wellscathedral.uk.net
        Web: www.wellscathedral.org.uk

Canons Residentiary
Chancellor Canon Andrew Featherstone, 8 The
Liberty, Wells BA5 2SU [2005]
                                Tel: 01749 679587
        email: andrew.featherstone@btinternet.com
Precentor Canon Patrick Woodhouse, 4 The
Liberty, Wells BA5 2SU [2000]
                                Tel: 01749 673188
        email: pwoodhouse@liberty4.fsnet.co.uk
Treasurer Canon Russell Bowman-Eadie, 2 The
Liberty, Wells BA5 2SU [2002]
                                Tel: 01749 674702
email:
        russell.bowman-eadie@bathwells.anglican.org
Archdeacon Ven Nicola Sullivan, 6 The Liberty,
Wells BA5 2SU [2007]   *Tel:* 01749 685147
        email: adwells@bathwells.anglican.org
Lay Members
Cathedral Administrator Preb John Roberts,
Cathedral Offices
        email: administrator@wellscathedral.uk.net
Preb Helen Ball, Cathedral Offices
Preb Elsa van der Zee, Cathedral Offices
Registrar Preb Mr Tim Berry, Diocesan Registry,
14 Market Place, Wells BA5 2RE
                                Tel: 01749 674747
                                Fax: 01749 834060
        email: tim.berry@harris-harris.co.uk
Cathedral Organist Mr Matthew Owens (*based at
Cathedral Offices*)
        email: musicoffice@wellscathedral.uk.net

ARCHDEACONS
WELLS Ven Nicola Sullivan, 6 The Liberty, Wells
BA5 2SU [2007]   *Tel:* 01749 685147
                  Fax: 01749 679755
        email: adwells@bathwells.anglican.org
BATH Ven Andy Piggott, 56 Grange Rd, Saltford,
Bristol BS31 3AG [2005]   *Tel:* 01225 873609
                           Fax: 01225 874110
        email: adbath@bathwells.anglican.org
TAUNTON Ven John Reed, 4 Westerkirk Gate,
Staplegrove, Taunton TA2 6BQ [1999]
                                Tel: 01823 323838
                                Fax: 01823 325420
        email: adtaunton@bathwells.anglican.org

CONVOCATION (MEMBERS OF THE HOUSE OF CLERGY OF THE GENERAL SYNOD)
Proctors for Clergy
Revd Paul Langham
Revd Jonathan Lloyd
Preb Stephen Lynas
Revd Colin Randall

MEMBERS OF THE HOUSE OF LAITY OF THE GENERAL SYNOD
Mr Edward Armitstead
Mr Tim Hind
Mr Peter LeRoy
Preb Mrs Diana Taylor
Miss Fay Wilson Rudd
Mr Richard Moon

DIOCESAN OFFICERS
Dioc Secretary Mr Nicholas Denison, Dioc Office, The Old Deanery, Wells BA5 2UG
Tel: 01749 685109
Fax: 01749 674240
email: nick.denison@bathwells.anglican.org
Chancellor of Diocese The Worshipful Timothy Briden, 1 Temple Gardens, Temple, London EC4Y 9BB
Registrar of Diocese and Bishop's Legal Secretary Preb Mr Tim Berry, Diocesan Registry, 14 Market Place, Wells BA5 2RE *Tel:* 01749 674747
Fax: 01749 834060
email: tim.berry@harris-harris.co.uk

DIOCESAN ORGANIZATIONS
Diocesan Office The Old Deanery, Wells BA5 2UG
Tel: 01749 670777
Fax: 01749 674240
email: general@bathwells.anglican.org

ADMINISTRATION
Dioc Synod (Chairman, House of Clergy) Preb Colin Randall, The Rectory, 72 High St, Wellington TA21 8RF *Tel:* 01823 662248
email: colinms.randall@virgin.net
(Chairman, House of Laity) Preb Mrs Diana Taylor, Volis Farm, Hestercombe, Taunton TA2 8HS
Tel: 01823 451545
Fax: 01823 451701
email: diana.taylor0@farmersweekly.net
(Secretary) Mr Nicholas Denison, Dioc Office *(as above)*
Board of Finance (Chairman) Dr Wyn Williams, Rhos Colwyn, Welsh St Donats, Cowbridge, Vale of Glamorgan CF71 7SS *Tel:* 01446 771243
email: wyn.dil@talktalk.net
(Secretary) Mr Nicholas Denison, Dioc Office
Finance Group Mr Nicholas Denison *(as above)*
Board of Patronage Mr Philip Nokes, Dioc Office
Tel: 01749 685108
email: philip.nokes@bathwells.anglican.org
Pastoral Committee Mr Philip Nokes *(as above)*
Redundant Churches Uses Committee Mr Philip Nokes *(as above)*
Designated Officer Mr Philip Nokes *(as above)*

Deputy Dioc Secretary Mr Philip Nokes *(as above)*
Financial Director Mr Nick May, Dioc Office
Tel: 01749 685112
email: nick.may@bathwells.anglican.org
Property Officer Mrs Penny Cooke, Dioc Office
Tel: 01749 685143
email: penny.cooke@bathwells.anglican.org
Dioc Surveyor Mr Paul Toseland, Dioc Office
Tel: 01749 685142
email: paul.toseland@bathwells.anglican.org

CHURCHES
Advisory Committee for the Care of Churches (Chairman) Mr Hugh Playfair, Blackford House, Blackford, Yeovil BA22 7EE *Tel:* 01963 440611
(Secretary) Preb Mr Tim Berry, Dioc Registry, 14 Market Place, Wells BA5 2RE
Tel: 01749 674747
Fax: 01749 834060
email: tim.berry@harris-harris.co.uk
(Assistant Secretary) Mrs Sarah Davis, Dioc Registry *(as above)*
email: sarah.davis@harris-harris.co.uk
Association of Change Ringers Revd Tim Hawkings, The Rectory, Cheddar Rd, Axbridge BS26 2DL *Tel:* 01934 732261
email: timhawkings@fish.co.uk

EDUCATION
Board of Education Diocesan Office, The Old Deanery, Wells BA5 2UG *Tel:* 01749 670777
Fax: 01749 674240
email: education@bathwells.anglican.org
Dioc Director of Education Mrs Maureen Bollard, Dioc Office *Tel:* 01749 685124
email: maureen.bollard@bathwells.anglican.org
School Improvement Advisers
Mrs Pauline Dodds, Dioc Office
Tel: 01749 865138
email: pauline.dodds@bathwells.anglican.org
Mr David Williams, Dioc Office
Tel: 01759 685123
email: david.williams@bathwells.anglican.org
School Development Adviser Mrs Tess Robinson, Dioc Office *Tel:* 01749 685132
email: tess.robinson@bathwells.anglican.org
School Development Officer Mrs Suzanne McDonald, Dioc Office *Tel:* 01759 685123
email: suzanne.mcdonald@bathwells.anglican.org
Co-ordinator for Work with Parishes, Deaneries and LMGs/Parish Adviser for Young People Mr Tony Cook, Dioc Office *Tel:* 01749 685133
email: tony.cook@bathwells.anglican.org
Parish Adviser for Children Mrs Jane Tibbs, Dioc Office *Tel:* 01749 685118
email: jane.tibbs@bathwells.anglican.org
Parish Adviser for Young Adults Mrs Bridget Down, Dioc Office *Tel:* 01749 685118
email: bridget.down@bathwells.anglican.org
Child Protection Officer Ms Fiona Gardner, Dioc Office *Tel:* 01749 685135
email: fiona.gardner@bathwells.anglican.org

MINISTRY FORUM

Chairman The Bishop of Taunton
Director of Continuing Ministerial Development Canon Russell Bowman-Eadie, Dioc Office
Tel: 01749 685107
email: russell.bowman-eadie@bathwells.anglican.org
Director of Ordinands Preb Peter Rapsey, Vicarage, Church Lane, Evercreech BA4 6HU
Tel: 01749 830322
email: peter.rapsey@btinternet.com
Dean of Women Clergy Preb Dr Catherine Wright, Rectory, West Monkton, Taunton TA2 8QT
Tel: 01823 412226
email: cjwright@onetel.com
Vocations Adviser Preb Dr Catherine Wright (*as above*)
Warden of Readers Ven John Reed, 4 Westerkirk Gate, Staplegrove, Taunton TA2 6BQ
Tel: 01823 323838
Fax: 01823 325420
email: adtaunton@bathwells.anglican.org
Director of Reader Studies Preb Graham Dodds, Dioc Office
Tel: 01749 685114
email: graham.dodds@bathwells.anglican.org
Chaplain to the Deaf Mrs Pamela Grottick, St Nicholas Cottage, Newtown, West Pennard, Glastonbury BA6 8NL
Tel: 01458 830085
email: pamg@wpci.org.uk

SCHOOL OF FORMATION

Principal Preb Graham Dodds, Dioc Office

MISSION FORUM

Chairman The Archdeacon of Bath
Executive Officer/Dioc Missioner Canon Roger Medley, Dioc Office
Tel: 01749 685128
email: roger.medley@bathwells.anglican.org
Ecumenical Officer Revd Nick Williams, Dioc Office
Tel: 01749 685125
email: nick.williams@bathwells.anglican.org
Adviser for the Ministry of Health and Healing Revd Matthew Thomson, Vicarage, Station Rd, Congresbury, Bristol BS49 5DX
Tel: 01934 833126
Fax: 01934 856173
email: revmattthomson@hotmail.com
Rural Life Adviser Revd Robert Widdowson, Rectory, Fosse Rd, Oakhill, Radstock BA3 5HU
Tel and Fax: 01749 841688
email: ruralrobert@fsmail.net
World Mission Adviser and Exec Secretary Zambia Link Mrs Jenny Humphreys, Dioc Office
Tel: 01749 685105
email: jenny.humphreys@bathwells.anglican.org

PARISH RESOURCES GROUP

Chairman The Archdeacon of Bath
Parish Resources Adviser Mrs Lesley Strutt, Dioc Office
Tel: 01749 685113
email: lesley.strutt@bathwells.anglican.org

BISHOP'S LITURGY GROUP

Chairman Revd Robin Lodge, Vicarage, Church St, Highbridge TA9 3HS
Tel: 01278 783671
email: robin.lodge1@btinternet.com

PRESS AND PUBLICATIONS

Diocesan Communications Offices (Press and Media)/Bishops' Press Officer Preb John Andrews
Tel: 01934 830208
07976 554962 (Mobile)
email: john.andrews@bathwells.anglican.org
Diocesan Communications Officer (Internal) Mrs Helen Hawthorne, Dioc Office
Tel: 01749 685145
email: helen.hawthorne@bathwells.anglican.org
Editor of 'The Grapevine' (Dioc Newspaper) Mrs Celia Andrews
Tel: 01934 830208
email: bandwnewspaper@aol.com
Editor of Directory/Database Manager Mrs Gill Davey, Dioc Office
Tel: 01749 685101
email: gill.davey@bathwells.anglican.org

WIDOWS' OFFICER

Revd Dan Richards, 1 Quaperlake St, Bruton BA10 0HA
Tel: 01749 812386
email: revdanrich@mbzonline.net

RETREAT HOUSE

Abbey House, Glastonbury (*Warden* David Hill)
Tel: 01458 831112
Fax: 01458 831893
email: info@abbeyhouse.org

DIOCESAN RECORD OFFICE

Somerset County Record Office, Obridge Rd, Taunton, Som. TA2 7PU *County and Diocesan Archivist* Mr Tom Mayberry
Tel: 01823 278805
Fax: 01823 325402

DIOCESAN RESOURCE CENTRE

Old Deanery, Wells BA5 2UG
Tel: 01749 685129
Fax: 01749 674240

RURAL DEANS
ARCHDEACONRY OF WELLS

Axbridge Vacancy
Bruton Revd Hugh Allen, Rectory, Cucklington, Wincanton BA9 9PY
Tel: 01747 841416
email: hallenarkwood@yahoo.co.uk
Cary Revd Hugh Allen (*as above*)
Frome Revd David Barge, St Mary's House, 40 Innox Hill, Frome, BA11 2LN
Tel: 01373 455996
email: dbarge@btinternet.com
Glastonbury Revd John Greed, The Rectory, Vestry Close, Street BA16 0HX
Tel: 01458 442671
email: john.greed@tiscali.co.uk
Ivelchester Revd Peter Thomas, Rectory, Cat St, Chiselborough, Stoke-sub-Hamdon TA14 6TT
Tel: 01935 881202
email: PThomas@aol.com

Yeovil Revd Anthony Perris, St James Vicarage, 1 Old School Close, Yeovil BA21 3UB
Tel: 01935 429398
email: antonyperris@yahoo.com
Shepton Mallet Canon Tony Birbeck, Beeches, Cannards Grave Rd, Shepton Mallet BA4 4LX
Tel: 01749 330382
email: tonybirkbeck@hotmail.co.uk

ARCHDEACONRY OF BATH

Bath Revd Patrick Whitworth, Rectory, Weston, Bath BA1 4BU
Tel: 01225 421159
email: pwhitworth@metronet.co.uk
Chew Magna Preb Jan Knott, Rectory, Church Lane, Farmborough, Bath BA3 1AN
Tel: 01761 479311
email: jpknott@btinternet.com
Locking Revd Richard Taylor, The Rectory, Cecil Rd, Weston Super Mare BS23 2NF
Tel: 01934 623399
Midsomer Norton Revd Christopher Hare, Rectory, South Rd, Timsbury BA2 0EJ
Tel: 01761 479660
email: chrishare@stmarystimsbury.org

Portishead Revd Ian Hubbard, Rectory, 1 Well Lane, Yatton, Bristol BS49 4HT
Tel: 01934 832184
email: ian@hubbardi.freeserve.co.uk

ARCHDEACONRY OF TAUNTON

Sedgemoor Revd Sue Rose, New Rectory, Cliff Rd, North Petherton TA6 6NY   *Tel:* 01278 662429
email: rev.suerose@virgin.net
Crewkerne and Ilminster Revd Andrew Tatham, Rectory, Broadway, Ilminster TA19 9RE
Tel: 01460 52559
email: aftatham@ukonline.co.uk
Exmoor Preb John Thorogood, Vicarage, Dulverton TA22 9DW   *Tel:* 01398 323425
email: johnthevicar@toucansurf.com
Quantock Revd Stephen Campbell, Hodderscombe Lodge, Holford, Bridgwater TA5 1SA   *Tel:* 01278 741329
email: stephencampbell0@tiscali.co.uk
Taunton Revd Sue Tucker, Vicarage, Bishops Hull Hill, Taunton TA1 5EB   *Tel:* 01823 333032
email: suetucker99@btinternet.com
Tone Revd Christopher Rowley, Vicarage, 62 Rockwell Green, Wellington TA21 9BX
Tel: 01823 662742
email: christopherrowley@uwclub.net

DIOCESE OF BIRMINGHAM

Founded in 1905. Birmingham; Sandwell, except for an area
in the north (LICHFIELD); Solihull, except for an area in the east
(COVENTRY); an area of Warwickshire; a few parishes in Worcestershire.

Population 1,424,000   Area 292 sq m
Full-time Stipendiary Parochial Clergy 158   Benefices 141
Parishes 155   Churches 193
www.birmingham.anglican.org
Overseas link dioceses: Lake Malawi, Southern Malawi, Northern Malawi (Malawi).

BISHOP (9th)
Rt Revd David Andrew Urquhart, Bishop's Croft,
Old Church Rd, Harborne, Birmingham, B17 0BG
[2006]   *Tel:* 0121 427 1163
                                                Fax: 0121 426 1322
        email: bishop@birmingham.anglican.org
Domestic Chaplain Canon Andrew Gorham, East
Wing, Bishop's Croft, Old Church Rd,
Birmingham B17 0BE
                        Tel: 0121 427 2295 (Home)
                              0121 427 1163 (Office)
email:
        bishopschaplain@birmingham.anglican.org

SUFFRAGAN BISHOP
ASTON Rt Revd Andrew Watson [2008],
16 Coleshill St, Sutton, Coldfield B72 1SH
                        Tel: 0121 426 0448 (Office)
                              Fax: 0121 428 1114
    email: bishopofaston@birmingham.anglican.org

HONORARY ASSISTANT BISHOPS
Rt Revd Anthony Charles Dumper, 117 Berberry
Close, Bournville, Birmingham B30 1TB [1993]
                                      Tel: 0121 458 3011
Rt Revd Michael Humphrey Dickens Whinney, 3
Moor Green Lane, Moseley, Birmingham B13
8NE [1989]   *Tel:* 0121 249 2856
Rt Revd Peter Hall, 27 Jacey Rd, Edgbaston,
Birmingham B16 0LL [1998]   *Tel:* 0121 455 9240
Rt Revd Maurice Walker Sinclair, 55 Selly Wick
Drive, Selly Park, Birmingham B29 7JQ [2002]
                                      Tel: 0121 4712617
    email: mauricewsinclair@blueyonder.co.uk
Rt Revd Mark Santer, 81 Clarence Rd, Moseley,
Birmingham B13 9UH [2003]
Rt Revd Iraj Mottadeheh, 2 Highland Rd,
Newport TF10 7AE [2005]   *Tel:* 01952 813615

CATHEDRAL CHURCH OF ST PHILIP
Dean Very Revd Robert Wilkes, 120 Oakfield Rd,
Selly Park, Birmingham B29 7ED [2006]
                                      Tel: 0121 472 1342
        email: dean@birminghamcathedral.com
Cathedral Office Birmingham Cathedral, Colmore
Row, Birmingham B3 2QB   *Tel:* 0121 262 1840
                              Fax: 0121 262 1860
    email: enquiries@birminghamcathedral.com

Assistant Dean Revd Canon Peter Howell-Jones,
172 Station Rd, Sutton Coldfield B73 5LE [2005]
                                      Tel: 0121 321 2493
    email: assistantdean@birminghamcathedral.com
Canons Residentiary
Canon Missioner Canon Nigel Hand, 12 Nursery
Drive, Handsworth, Birmingham B20 2SW [2008]
                                      Tel: 0121 262 1840
email:
        canonmissioner@birminghamcathedral.com
Canon Liturgist Revd Canon Janet Chapman,
Nursery Drive, Handsworth, Birmingham
B20 2SW   *Tel:* 0121 262 1840
email: canonliturgist@birminghamcathedral.com
Administrator and Chapter Clerk Vacancy,
Cathedral Office
    email: administrator@birminghamcathedral.com
Director of Music Mr Marcus Huxley, Cathedral
Office   *Tel:* 0121 262 1846
        email: music@birminghamcathedral.com

ARCHDEACONS
ASTON Ven Dr Brian Russell, c/o Dioc Office
[2005]   *Tel:* 0121 426 0400
                                  Fax: 0121 428 1114
            email: archdeaconofaston@
                      birmingham.anglican.org
BIRMINGHAM Ven Hayward Osborne, c/o Dioc
Office [2001]   *Tel:* 0121 426 0441
                                  Fax: 0121 428 1114
email:
    archdeaconofbham@birmingham.anglican.org

CONVOCATION (MEMBERS OF THE HOUSE OF CLERGY OF THE GENERAL SYNOD)
Proctors for Clergy
Revd Peter French
Canon John Hughes
Ven Hayward Osborne

MEMBERS OF THE HOUSE OF LAITY OF THE GENERAL SYNOD
Canon Dr Paula Gooder
Dr Rachel Jepson
Canon Dr Terry Slater

DIOCESAN OFFICERS

Dioc Secretary Mr Jim Drennan, 175 Harborne Park Rd, Harborne, Birmingham B17 0BH
Tel: 0121 426 0400
Fax: 0121 428 1114
email: j.d.drennan@birmingham.anglican.org
Chancellor of Diocese His Honour Judge Martin Cardinal, c/o Diocesan Registrar, Martineau, No. 1 Colmore Square, Birmingham B4 6AA
Registrar of Diocese and Bishop's Legal Secretary Mr Hugh Carslake, Martineau, No. 1 Colmore Square, Birmingham B4 6AA
Tel: 0870 763 2000
Fax: 0870 763 2001
email: lawyers@martineau-uk.com
Web: www.martineau-uk.co.uk
Dioc Surveyor Mr Alan Broadway, Dioc Office

DIOCESAN ORGANIZATIONS

Diocesan Office 175 Harborne Park Rd, Harborne, Birmingham B17 0BH   *Tel:* 0121 426 0400
Fax: 0121 428 1114
Web: www.birmingham.anglican.org

ADMINISTRATION

Dioc Synod (Chair, House of Clergy) Canon Peter Howell-Jones, 172 Station Rd, Sutton Coldfield B73 5LE   *Tel:* 0121 321 2493 (Home)
0121 262 1840 (Office)
email: assistantdean@birminghamcathedral.com
(Chair, House of Laity) Mr Stephen Fraser, 47 Wroxton Rd, Yardley, Birmingham B26 1SH
email: stevef_bham@btinternet.com
(Secretary) Mr Jim Drennan, Dioc Office
Board of Finance (Chair) Vacancy
(Secretary) Mr Jim Drennan *(as above)*
Deputy Secretary (Finance) Canon Paul Wilson, Dioc Office
Parsonages Committee Mr Jim Drennan *(as above)*
Dioc Trustees (Secretary) Canon Paul Wilson *(as above)*
Pastoral Committee Mr Jim Drennan, Dioc Office
Designated Officer Mr Hugh Carslake, Martineau *(as above)*   *Tel:* 0870 763 2000
Fax: 0870 763 2001
email: lawyers@martineau-uk.com

CHURCHES

Advisory Committee for the Care of Churches (Chair) Vacancy, c/o Dioc Office; *(Secretary)* Mr Tim Clayton, Dioc Office
email: t.clayton@birmingham.anglican.org

EDUCATION

Dioc Director of Education Miss Mary Edwards, Dioc Office
email: m.edwards@birmingham.anglican.org
Schools Support Officer Revd Peter French, Dioc Office
email: p.french@birmingham.anglican.org
RE Adviser Mrs Jill Stolberg, Dioc Office
email: j.stolberg@birmingham.anglican.org

MINISTRY

Director of Ordinands and Women's Ministry Canon Faith Claringbull, Dioc Office
email: f.claringbull@birmingham.anglican.org

FORUM FOR MINISTRIES

Chair Ven Dr Brian Russell, Dioc Office
Bishop's Adviser for Continuing Clergy Ministerial Education Revd Mark Pryce, Dioc Office
email: m.pryce@birmingham.anglican.org
Bishop's Adviser for Lay Adult Education and Training Revd Liz Howlett, Dioc Office
email: l.howlett@birmingham.anglican.org
Bishop's Adviser for Minority Ethnic Anglicans Dr Mukti Barton, Dioc Office
email: m.barton@birmingham.anglican.org
Bishop's Adviser for Children's Ministry Ms Claire Wesley, Dioc Office
email: claire@birmingham.anglican.org
Bishop's Adviser for Youth Ministry Miss Helen Tomblin, Dioc Office
email: helen@birmingham.anglican.org
Dioc Music Adviser Mr Mick Perrier, Dioc Office
email: mick@mperrier.freeserve.co.uk
Readers' Board (Secretary) Mr Michael Lynch, 57 Fairholme Rd, Hodge Hill, Birmingham B36 8HN
Tel: 0121 242 0534
email: mike4jeannie@blueyonder.co.uk

LITURGICAL

Bishop's Liturgical Advisory Committee Chair Revd Peter Babington, Parish Office, St Francis Centre, Sycamore Rd, Bournville, Birmingham B30 2AA
Tel: 0121 472 7215
email: pb@fish.co.uk

FORUM FOR MISSION AND EVANGELISM

Acting Chair The Bishop of Birmingham
Bishop's Director for Mission Canon Peter Howell-Jones, Birmingham Cathedral, Colmore Row, Birmingham B3 2QB   *Tel:* 0121 262 1840
Fax: 0121 262 1860
email: assistantdean@birminghamcathedral.com
Ecumenical Officer with Responsibility for LEPs Revd David James, 160a New Road, Rubery, Birmingham B45 9JA   *Tel:* 0121 460 1278
email: david.james5@btinternet.com
Bishop's Adviser for Stewardship Vacancy

HEALTHCARE CHAPLAINCIES

Bishop's Adviser Ven Hayward Osborne, Dioc Office

PRESS AND PUBLICATIONS

Bishop's Director of Communications Mrs Jessica Foster, Dioc Office   *Tel:* 0121 426 0438 (Office)
07973 173195 (Mobile)
email: jessica@birmingham.angilcan.org
Editor of Dioc Newsletter Mrs Jessica Foster
Editor of Dioc Directory Mrs Jessica Foster
Assistant to the Director of Communications Mrs Cara Butowski   *Tel:* 0121 426 0439
email: c.butowski@birmingham.anglican.org

INDUSTRIAL RELATIONS
Industrial Chaplain (CIGB) Mrs Barbara Hayes, Dioc Office   *Tel:* 0121 426 0425
          email: b.hayes@birmingham.anglican.org
DIOCESAN RECORD OFFICES
Birmingham Reference Library, Birmingham B3 3HQ, Archives Dept Central Library, *Head of Archives* Ms Sian Roberts, *Tel:* 0121 303 4217 (*For parish records in the City and Diocese of Birmingham*)
          email: archives@birmingham.gov.uk
Warwick County Record Office, Priory Park, Cape Rd, Warwick CV34 4JS, *County Archivist* Ms Caroline Sampson, *Tel:* 01926 738959 (*For parish records in the Metropolitan Borough of Solihull, together with those still in the County of Warwick*)
          email: recordoffice@warwickshire.gov.uk
Sandwell Community History and Archives Service, Smethwick Library, High St, Smethwick, Warley, W Midlands B66 1AB *Borough Archivist* Sarah Chubb, *Tel:* 0121 558 2561 (*For parish records in the Warley deanery*)
          email: archives.service@sandwell.gov.uk

FORUM FOR CHURCH AND WORLD
Chair Vacancy, Dioc Office

CHRISTIAN STEWARDSHIP
see Forum for Mission and Evangelism

FORUM FOR COMMUNITY REGENERATION
Chair Rt Revd Peter Hall
Vice-Chair Mr Frank Joyce, Dioc Office
Director Fred Rattley, Dioc Office
                         Tel: 0121 426 0442
          email: f.rattley@birmingham.anglican.org

COMMUNITY PROJECTS COMMITTEE
Chair Revd Simon Thorburn

AREA DEANS
ARCHDEACONRY OF ASTON
Aston Revd Andrew Jolley, Aston Vicarage, Sycamore Rd, Aston, Birmingham B6 5UH
                         Tel: 0121 327 5856
          email: andy@astonnechellscofe.org.uk
Coleshill Revd Brian Castle, Vicarage, Haywood Rd, Tile Cross, Birmingham B33 0LH
                         Tel: 0121 779 2739
          email: revbcastle@aol.com

Polesworth Revd Michael Harris, Vicarage, 224 Tamworth Rd, Amington, Tamworth B77 3DE
                         Tel: 01827 62573
          email: mike.harris26@ntlworld.com
Solihull Canon Michael Parker, Vicarage, 1811 Warwick Rd, Knowle, Solihull B93 0DS
                         Tel: 01564 773666
          email: vicar@knowleparishchurch.org.uk
Sutton Coldfield Revd Dr Matthew Rhodes, Rectory, Glebe Fields, Curdworth, Sutton Coldfield B76 9ES   *Tel:* 01675 470384
          email: catmat30@hotmail.com
Yardley and Bordesley Revd Peter Smith, Vicarage, Burney Lane, Alum Rock, Birmingham B8 2AS
                         Tel: 0121 783 7455
          email: peter@ccbl.org.uk

ARCHDEACONRY OF BIRMINGHAM
Central Birmingham Revd Andrew Lenox-Conyngham, 28 Bradshaw Close, Park Central, Attwood Green, Birmingham B15 2DD
                         Tel: 0121 666 6089
          email: lenox@birm.eclipse.co.uk
Edgbaston Revd Christopher Turner, Rectory, 773 Hagley Rd West, Quinton, Birmingham B32 1AJ
                         Tel: 0121 422 2031
          email: christurner@therectory.uklinux.net
Handsworth Revd Helen Hingley, 147 Hamstead Rd, Great Barr, Birmingham B43 5BB
                         Tel: 0121 358 1286
          email: h.hingley@btinternet.com
King's Norton Revd Colin Corke, 220 Longbridge Lane, Longbridge, Birmingham B31 4JT
                         Tel: 0121 475 3484
          email: colin@ado67.freeserve.co.uk
Moseley Revd Peter Babington, Parish Office, St Francis Centre, Sycamore Rd, Bournville, Birmingham B30 2AA *Tel:* 0121 472 7215 (Office)
                 Tel: 0121 472 1209 (Home)
          email: pb@fish.co.uk
Shirley Revd David Warbrick, Vicarage, Nuthurst Lane, Hockley Heath, Solihull B94 5RP
                         Tel: 01564 783121
          email: david.warbrick@googlemail.com
Warley Revd Anthony Perry, Vicarage, 27 Poplar Ave, Edgbaston, Birmingham B17 8EG
                         Tel: 0121 429 2165
          email: trinity20@btopenworld.com

DIOCESE OF BLACKBURN

Founded in 1926. Lancashire, except for areas in the east (BRADFORD) and in the south (LIVERPOOL, MANCHESTER); a few parishes in Wigan.

Population 1,303,000   Area 878 sq m
Full-time Stipendiary Parochial Clergy 187   Benefices 189
Parishes 226   Churches 281
www.blackburn.anglican.org
Overseas link dioceses: Free State (South Africa),
Braunschweig (Germany) (Evangelical Lutheran Landeskirche).

BISHOP (8th)
Rt Revd Nicholas Reade, Bishop's House, Ribchester Rd, Clayton-le-Dale, Blackburn BB1 9EF [2004]   *Tel:* 01254 248234
Fax: 01254 246668
email: bishop@bishopofblackburn.org.uk
Domestic Chaplain Revd David Arnold, Bishop's House
email: chaplain@bishopofblackburn.org.uk
Bishop's Secretary Mrs Sue Taylor, Bishop's House
email: secretary@bishopofblackburn.org.uk
Assistant Secretary Mrs Hilary Wilby, Bishop's House
email: asstsecretary@bishopofblackburn.org.uk

SUFFRAGAN BISHOPS
LANCASTER Rt Revd Geoffrey S. Pearson, Shireshead Vicarage, Whinney Brow, Forton, Preston PR3 0AE [2006]   *Tel:* 01524 799900
Fax: 01524 799901
email: bishoplancaster@btconnect.com
BURNLEY Rt Revd John Goddard, Dean House, 449 Padiham Rd, Burnley BB12 6TE [2000]
Tel: 01282 470360
Fax: 01282 470361
email: bishop.burnley@ntlworld.com

HONORARY ASSISTANT BISHOPS
Rt Revd Gordon Bates, Caedman House, 2 Loyne Park, Whittington, Carnforth LA6 2NX
Tel: 01524 848492
Rt Revd Michael Vickers, 2 Collingham Park, Lancaster LA1 4PD   *Tel:* 01524 848492
Rt Revd Alan Winstanley, Vicarage, Preston Rd, Whittle-le-Woods, Chorley PR6 7PS
Tel: 01257 241291
Rt Revd and Rt Hon Lord Hope of Thornes, 2 Aspinall Rise, Hellifield, Skipton BD23 4JT

CATHEDRAL CHURCH OF ST MARY THE VIRGIN
Dean Very Revd Christopher Armstrong, The Deanery, Preston New Rd, Blackburn BB2 6PS [2001]   *Tel:* 01254 52502 (Home)
email: dean@blackburn.anglican.org

Cathedral Office Cathedral Close, Blackburn BB1 5AA   *Tel:* 01254 503090 (Office)
Fax: 01254 689666
email: cathedral@blackburn.anglican.org
Canons Residentiary
Sacrist Canon Andrew Hindley, 22 Billinge Ave, Blackburn BB2 6SD [1996]
Tel: 01254 261152 (Home)
01254 503099 (Office)
email: andrew.hindley@blackburn.anglican.org
Chancellor Canon Christopher Chivers, 1 St Francis Rd, Feniscliffe, Blackburn BB2 2TZ [2005]
Tel: 01254 200720 (Home)
01254 503090 ext. 443 (Office)
email: chris.chivers@blackburn.anglican.org
Canon Susan Penfold, The Vicarage, Church Lane, Great Harwood BB6 7PU
Tel: 01254 884039 (Home)
01254 503090 ext. 245 (Office)
email: sue.penfold@blackburn.anglican.org
Administrator Canon Michael Wedgeworth, Cathedral Close, Blackburn BB1 5AA
Tel: 01254 503090 ext. 240 (Office)
email:
michael.wedgeworth@blackburn.anglican.org
Director of Music Mr Richard Tanner, 8 West Park Rd, Blackburn BB2 6DG *Tel:* 01254 56752 (Home)
01254 503090 ext. 251 (Office)
email: richard.tanner@blackburn.anglican.org

ARCHDEACONS
BLACKBURN Ven John Hawley, 19 Clarence Park, Blackburn BB2 7FA [2002]   *Tel:* 01254 262571
Fax: 01254 263394
email: archdeacon.blackburn@milestonet.co.uk
LANCASTER Ven Peter Ballard, Wheatfield, 7 Dallas Rd, Lancaster LA1 1TN [2006]
Tel: 01524 503070
email: peter.j.ballard@btinternet.com

CONVOCATION (MEMBERS OF THE HOUSE OF CLERGY OF THE GENERAL SYNOD)
Proctors for Clergy
Canon Peter Ballard
Revd Paul Benfield
Revd Dr Jim Garrard
Canon John Hall

MEMBERS OF THE HOUSE OF LAITY OF THE GENERAL SYNOD
Mr Joseph Brookfield
Mr Gerald Burrows
Mr Tim Cox
Mrs Vivienne Goddard
Prof Helen Leathard
Mrs Alison Wynne

DIOCESAN OFFICERS
Dioc Secretary Mr Graeme Pollard, Church House, Cathedral Close, Blackburn BB1 5AA
Tel: 01254 503070
Fax: 01254 667309
email: graeme.pollard@blackburn.anglican.org
Chancellor of Diocese His Honour Judge John Bullimore, Rectory, 14 Grange Drive, Emley, Huddersfield HD8 9SF
Tel: 01484 849161
Registrar of Diocese and Bishop's Legal Secretary Mr Thomas Hoyle, Diocesan Registry, Cathedral Close, Blackburn BB1 5AA
Tel: 01254 503070
Fax: 01254 667309
email: registry@blackburn.anglican.org

DIOCESAN ORGANIZATIONS
Diocesan Office Church House, Cathedral Close, Blackburn BB1 5AA
Tel: 01254 503070
Fax: 01254 667309
email: diocese@blackburn.anglican.org

ADMINISTRATION
Dioc Synod (Chairman, House of Clergy) Canon John Hall, The Vicarage, 49 Mount Road, Fleetwood FY7 6QZ *email:* johnbloem@aol.com
(Chairman, House of Laity) Mrs Elizabeth Dobie, 383 Manchester Rd, Burnley BB12 4HP
Tel: 01282 453327
(Secretary) Mr Graeme Pollard, Church House *(as above)*
Board of Finance (Chairman) Mr John Dell, 66 Moseley Rd, Burnley BB11 2RF
(Secretary) Mr Graeme Pollard *(as above)*
Property Committee (Chairman) Revd Andrew Sage; *(Secretary)* Mr Graeme Pollard *(as above)*
Pastoral Committee Mr Graeme Pollard *(as above)*
Designated Officer Mr Thomas Hoyle, Dioc Registry, Cathedral Close, Blackburn BB1 5AA
Tel: 01254 503070
Resources Officer Ms Mary Smith, Church House *(as above)*

CHURCHES
Advisory Committee for the Care of Churches (Chairman) Canon Roy McCullough, Vicarage, Church Brow, Walton-le-Dale, Preston PR5 4BH
Tel: 01772 880233
(Secretary) Mr Graeme Pollard *(as above)*

EDUCATION
Board of Education (Dioc Director) Ven Peter Ballard, Church House
email: education@blackburn.anglican.org

Principal Adviser Lisa Fenton, Church House
email: lisa.fenton@blackburn.anglican.org
Youth Officers Mr Craig Abbott and Miss Susie Mapledoram, Church House
email: craig.abbott@blackburn.anglican.org
susie.mapledoram@blackburn.anglican.org
Children's Work Adviser Mrs Susan Witts, Church House
email: susan.witts@blackburn.anglican.org

MINISTRY
Director of Ordinands Revd Dr John Darch, 24 Bosburn Drive, Mellor Brook, Blackburn BB2 7PA
Tel: 01254 813544
Director of Training Canon Dr Susan Penfold, Church House
email: sue.penfold@blackburn.anglican.org
Director of IME 1–4 Revd Dr John Darch *(as above)*
Adviser in Women's Ministry Revd Rachel Watts, St James' Vicarage, Briercliffe, Burnley BB10 2HU
Tel: 01282 423700
Mothers' Union Mrs P. Rothwell, 7 Aldon Grove, Longton, Preston PR4 5PJ
Tel: 01772 614045
Warden of Readers Revd Dr Jim Garrard, Vicarage, Commons Lane, Balderstone, Blackburn BB2 7LL
Tel: 01254 812232
email: jamesgarrard@4-mat.net
Warden of Pastoral Auxiliaries Revd Dave Thompson, 45 Abingdon Drive, Ashton-on-Ribble, Preston PR2 1EY
Tel: 01772 729197

LITURGICAL
Chairman Very Revd Christopher Armstrong *(as above)*
Secretary Revd Michael Gisbourne, St Thomas' Vicarage, Church St, Garstang, Preston PR3 1PA
Tel: 01995 602162
email: revgis@fish.co.uk

MISSIONARY AND ECUMENICAL
Board for Mission and Unity (Chairman) Bishop of Lancaster
Director for Mission and Evangelism Vacancy
Ecumenical Officer Revd Mike Hartley, Vicarage, Church Rd, Warton, Preston PR4 1BD
Tel: 01772 632227

PRESS AND PUBLICATIONS
Dioc Communications Officer Mr Martyn Halsall, Vicarage, Bridekirk, Cockermouth CA13 0PE
Tel and Fax: 01900 824555
07790 253909 (Mobile)
email: martyn.halsall@ukonline.co.uk

DIOCESAN RECORD OFFICES
Diocesan Registry, Cathedral Close, Blackburn BB1 5AB
Tel: 01254 503070
Lancashire Record Office, Bow Lane, Preston PR1 8ND *County Archivist* Mr Bruce Jackson
Tel: 01772 254868

SOCIAL RESPONSIBILITY

Director of Social Responsibility Mr Neil Carter, St Mary's House, Cathedral Close, Blackburn BB1 5AA   *Tel:* 01254 675872
          email: neil.carter@blackburn.anglican.org
Officer for People with Sensory, Physical and Learning Difficulties Ms Sheron Hall, Church House
Racial Justice and Cohesion Officer Revd Ed Saville, The Vicarage, 5 Reedley Farm Close, Reedley, Burnley BB10 2RB   *Tel:* 01282 613235
          email: e.saville@btinternet.com
Rural Areas Officer Revd Tim Horobin, 79 Main St, Warton, Carnforth LA5 9PJ
          Tel: 01524 733037
Urban Areas Officer The Archdeacon of Blackburn (*as above*)

AREA DEANS
ARCHDEACONRY OF BLACKBURN

Accrington Revd Roger Smith, St James' Vicarage, Church Lane, Haslingden, Rossendale BB4 5QZ   *Tel:* 01706 215533
          email: Rsmith9456@aol.com
Blackburn with Darwen Revd Andrew Raynes, Christ Church with St Matthew's Vicarage, Brandy House Brow, Blackburn BB2 3EY
          Tel: 01254 56292
Burnley Revd Lawrence Laycock, Vicarage, Gorple Rd, Worsthorne, Burnley BB10 3NN
          Tel: 01282 428478
Chorley Revd Michael Everitt, Rectory, 13 Rectory Lane, Standish, Wigan WN6 0XA
          Tel: 01257 421396
          email: rector@standish.org.uk

Leyland Revd Chris Nelson, St Mary's Vicarage, 14 Cop Lane, Penwortham, Preston PR1 0SR
          Tel: 01772 743143
          email: kitnel@btinternet.com
Pendle Revd Tony Rindl, Vicarage, Skipton Rd, Foulridge, Colne BB8 7NP *Tel:* 01282 870959
          email: rindl-@fish.co.uk
Whalley Revd John Hartley, St Peter's Vicarage, 49a Ribchester Rd, Blackburn BB1 9HU
          Tel: 01254 248072

ARCHDEACONRY OF LANCASTER

Blackpool Revd Canon Dr Simon Cox, All Hallows Rectory, 86 All Hallows Rd, Bispham, Blackpool FY2 0AY   *Tel:* 01253 351886
          email: drsjcox@yahoo.co.uk
Garstang Revd Andrew Wilkinson, Vicarage, Vicarage Lane, Churchtown, Garstang, Preston PR3 0HW   *Tel and Fax:* 01995 602294
          email: vic.garstang@virgin.net
Kirkham Revd Damian Porter, St Anne's Vicarage, 4 Oxford Rd, St Anne's on Sea FY8 2SE
          Tel: 01253 722725
          email: fatherd@btinternet.com
Lancaster Revd Phil Hudd, Christ Church Vicarage, 1 East Rd, Lancaster LA1 3EE
          Tel: 01524 34430
          email: phil@gorhudd.freeserve.co.uk
Poulton Revd Paul Clemence, St John's Vicarage, 35 Station Rd, Thornton-Cleveleys FY5 5HY
          Tel: 01253 825107
Preston Revd Chris Entwistle, Vicarage, 240 Tulketh Rd, Ashton-on-Ribble, Preston PR2 1ES
          Tel: 01772 726848
Tunstall Vacancy

DIOCESE OF BRADFORD

Founded in 1919. Bradford; the western quarter of North Yorkshire; areas of east Lancashire, south-east Cumbria and Leeds.

Population 675,000   Area 920 sq m
Full-time Stipendiary Parochial Clergy 85   Benefices 106
Parishes 128   Churches 164
www.bradford.anglican.org
Overseas link dioceses: South Western Virginia, Khartoum
and other northern dioceses (Sudan), Erfurt (Germany).

DIOCESES

BISHOP (9th)
Rt Revd Dr David Charles James, Bishopscroft, Ashwell Rd, Bradford BD9 4AU [2002]
Tel: 01274 545414
Fax: 01274 544831
email: bishop@bradford.anglican.org
[David Bradford]
Bishop's Chaplain Canon Denise Poole, Bishopscroft (*as above*)

HONORARY ASSISTANT BISHOP
Rt Revd Martyn William Jarrett, 3 North Lane, Roundhay, Leeds LS8 2QJ   *Tel:* 0113 265 4280
Fax: 0113 265 4281
email:
bishop-of-beverley@3-north-lane.fsnet.co.uk
Rt Revd Ian Harland, White House, 11 South St, Gargrave BD23 3RT   *Tel:* 01756 748623
email: sue@harland1.fsnet.co.uk
Rt Revd Colin Buchanan, 21 The Drive, Alwoodley, Leeds LS17 7QB [2004]   *Tel:* 0113 267 7721
Rt Revd and Rt Hon David M. Hope, 2 Aspinall Rise, Hellifield BD23 4JT [2005]

CATHEDRAL CHURCH OF ST PETER
Dean Very Revd Dr David Ison, The Deanery, 1 Cathedral Close, Bradford BD1 4EG [2005]
Tel: 01274 777722 (Office)
01274 777727 (Home)
Fax: 01274 777730
email: dean@bradford.anglican.org
Canons Residentiary
Canon Frances Ward, 3 Cathedral Close, Bradford BD1 4EG [2006]
Tel: 01274 777733 (Office)
01274 777731 (Home)
Fax: 01274 777733
email: fefward@btinternet.com
Canon Andrew Williams, 2 Cathedral Close, Bradford BD1 4EG [2006]
Tel: 01274 777721 (Office)
01274 777728 (Home)
Fax: 01274 777730
email: andy.williams@
cathedral.bradford.anglican.org
Cathedral Office 1 Stott Hill, Bradford BD1 4EH
Tel: 01274 777720
email: secretary@cathedral.bradford.anglican.org

Administrator Mr Chris Aldred, Bradford Cathedral, 1 Stott Hill, Bradford BD1 4EH
Tel: 01274 777720 (Office)
01274 777726 (Direct Line)
Fax: 01274 777730
email:
administrator@cathedral.bradford.anglican.org
Education Officer Mrs Caroline Moore, Bradford Cathedral, 1 Stott Hill, Bradford BD1 4EH
Tel: 01274 777734
Fax: 01274 777730
email: caroline.moore@
cathedral.bradford.anglican.org
Cathedral Organist Mr Andrew Teague, Bradford Cathedral, 1 Stott Hill, Bradford BD1 4EH
Tel: 01274 777725
Fax: 01274 777730
email: choirmaster@
cathedral.bradford.anglican.org

ARCHDEACONS
CRAVEN Ven Paul Slater, Woodlands, Netherghyll Lane, Cononley, Keighley BD20 8PB [2005]
Tel: 01535 635113 (Home)
01535 650533 (Office)
email: paulj.slater@dial.pipex.com
BRADFORD Ven Dr David Lee, 14 Park Cliffe Rd, Undercliffe, Bradford BD2 4NS [2004]
Tel: 01274 200698
Fax: 01274 200698
email: david.lee@bradford.anglican.org

CONVOCATION (MEMBERS OF THE HOUSE OF CLERGY OF THE GENERAL SYNOD)
Proctors for Clergy
Revd Paul Ayers
Revd Dr John Hartley
Revd Ruth Yeoman

MEMBERS OF THE HOUSE OF LAITY OF THE GENERAL SYNOD
Ms Sallie Bassham
Mrs Janet Bower
Mrs Zahida Mallard

Bradford   **15**

DIOCESAN OFFICERS
Dioc Secretary Mr Malcolm Halliday, Kadugli House, Elmsley St, Steeton, Keighley BD20 6SE
Tel: 01535 650522
Fax: 01535 650550
email: malcolm@kadugli.org.uk
Human Resources Manager Mrs Debbie Child, Kadugli House (*deputizes for Dioc Secretary*)
Tel: 01535 650521
Fax: 01535 650550
email: debbie@kadugli.org.uk
Chancellor of Diocese His Honour John de G. Walford, Ingerthorpe Cottage, Thwaites Lane, Markington HG3 3PF   *Tel:* 01765 677449
Registrar of Diocese and Bishop's Legal Secretary Mr Peter William Foskett, Diocesan Registry, 14 Piccadilly, Bradford BD1 3LX   *Tel:* 01274 202132
Fax: 01274 202107
email: peter.foskett@gordonsllp.com
Dioc Insurance Adviser Mr John Watts, Towergate Risk Solutions, Towergate House, Five Airport West, Lancaster Way, Yeadon, Leeds LS19 7ZA
Tel: 0113 391 9317
Fax: 0113 391 9334
Child Protection Adviser Mrs Jenny Price, Church House, 1 South Parade, Wakefield WF1 1LP
Tel: 01924 371802
email: jenny.price@bradford.anglican.org
Vulnerable Adults Protection Adviser Dr Tony Welsteed   *Tel:* 01274 587558

DIOCESAN ORGANIZATIONS
Diocesan Office Kadugli House, Elmsley St Steeton, Keighley BD20 6SE   *Tel:* 01535 650555
Fax: 01535 650550
email: office@kadugli.org.uk

ADMINISTRATION
Dioc Synod (*Chairman, House of Clergy*) Canon John Nowell, Vicarage, Baildon, Shipley BD17 6BY   *Tel and Fax:* 01274 594941
email: johndavidnowell@aol.com
(*Chairman, House of Laity*) Mr Ian Hamilton, 6 Garrs End Lane, Grassington, Skipton BD23 5BB   *Tel:* 01756 752197
email: ifh@girston.demon.co.uk
(*Secretary*) Mr Malcolm Halliday, Dioc Office
Board of Finance (*Chairman*) Mr Tony Hesselwood, 38 Bromley Rd, Shipley, Bradford BD18 4DT   *Tel:* 01274 586613
email: hesselwood@btinternet.com
(*Secretary*) Mr Malcolm Halliday (*as above*)
(*Accountant*) Mr Peter Capel-Cure, Dioc Office
Tel: 01535 650525
Property Committee (*Secretary*) Mr Malcolm Halliday (*as above*)
Property Officer Mr David Meadows, Dioc Office
Tel: 01535 650524
email: david@kadugli.org.uk
Pastoral Committee (*Chairman*) Mr Raymond Edwards, Crosslands, Stanbury, Keighley BD22 0HB   *Tel:* 01535 642883
Designated Officer Mr Malcolm Halliday (*as above*)

Diocesan Advisory Committee (*Chairman*) Canon John Nowell (*as above*)
(*Secretary*) Mrs Sylvia Johnson, Dioc Office
Tel: 01535 650523
email: Sylvia@kadugli.org.uk
Redundant Churches Uses Committee (*Chairman*) Canon John Nowell (*as above*)
(*Secretary*) Mrs Sylvia Johnson (*as above*)

CHURCH IN THE WORLD
Bishop's Officer Canon Sam Randall, Vicarage, Morton Lane, East Morton, Keighley BD20 5RS
Tel: 01274 561640
email: sam.randall@bradford.anglican.org
Interfaith Adviser Dr Philip Lewis, 9 Garden Lane, Heaton, Bradford BD9 5QJ
Tel: 01274 543891
Ecumenical Officer Revd Peter Mott, Rectory, 13 Westview Grove, Keighley BD20 6JJ
Tel: 01535 601499
email: peter.mott@live.co.uk
Social Responsibility see Bishop's Officer
Urban Adviser see Bishop's Officer
World Church Links
Northern Sudan Ven Dr David Lee (*as above*)
Southwestern Virginia Mrs Jill Wright, 15 Walker Close, Glusburn, Keighley BD20 8PW
Tel: 01535 634526
email: jill@woodchipcomputers.co.uk
Erfurt Vacancy

COMMUNICATIONS
Chairman Mr Michael Moss, 4 Ashfield Rd, Shipley BD18 4JX   *Tel:* 01274 823133
email: mikemoss@blueyonder.co.uk
Media Relations Officer Ms Alison Bogle, 59 Hookstone Drive, Harrogate HG2 8PR
Tel: 01423 812995
07768 110175 (Mobile)
email: alison@bogle.force9.co.uk
Dioc News/Diocesan Office (*as above*)
Newsround Mr David Markham, 29 Ashley Rd, Bingley BD16 1DZ   *Tel:* 01274 567180
Webkeeper Mr Chris Wright, 15 Walker Close, Glusburn, Keighley BD20 8PW
Tel: 01535 636981
email: chris@woodchipcomputers.co.uk

EDUCATION
Chairman Mrs Diana Chambers, Romille Lodge, 4 Ridgeway, Skipton BD23 1LX
Tel: 01756 798389
Director of Education Revd Clive Sedgewick, Windsor House, Cornwall Rd, Harrogate HG1 2PW   *Tel:* 01423 817553
Fax: 01423 817051
07903 326053 (Mobile)
email: clives@brleducationteam.org.uk

MINISTRY AND MISSION
Bishop's Officer Ven Paul Slater (*as above*)
Administrator Mrs Suzanne Evans, Dioc Office
Tel: 01535 650532
email: suzanne@kadugli.org.uk

Director of In-Service Training see Bishop's Officer

Director of Post-Ordination Training Revd Andrew Tawn, Rectory, Low Mill Lane, Addingham. Ilkley LS29 0QP   *Tel:* 01943 830276

Director of Ordinands Revd Ann Turner, Rectory, Broughton, Skipton BD23 3AN
Tel: 01282 842332
email: ann.turner@bradford.anglican.org

Associate Directors of Ordinands Revd Michael Burley, Vicarage, 21 Southfield Rd, Burley-in-Wharfedale, Ilkley LS29 7PB   *Tel:* 01943 863216
email: michael.burley@btinternet.com

Revd Ruth Yeoman, Vicarage, 12 Fairfax Gardens, Menston, Ilkley LS29 6ET   *Tel:* 01943 877739
email: vicar@stjohnmenston.org.uk

Development, Resources and Stewardship for Parishes Mr Uell Kennedy, Dioc Office
Tel: 01535 650531
email: uell@kadugli.org.uk

Ministry Development Officer Revd John Daniels, Vicarage, 21 Shires Lane, Embsay, Skipton BD23 6SB   *Tel:* 01756 798057
email: john.daniels@bradford.anglican.org

Adult Education Canon Steve Allen, 48 Toller Grove, Heaton, Bradford BD9 5NP
Tel: 01274 482059
email: steve.allen@bradford.anglican.org

Training Canon Steve Allen (*Lay*); Bishop's Officer (*Clergy*)

Evangelism Revd Robin Gamble, Vicarage, 470 Leeds Rd, Thackley, Bradford BD10 9AA
Tel: 01274 623300
email: robin.gamble@bradford.anglican.org

Warden of Readers Revd Paul Booth, 3 Gilstead Court, Gilstead, Bingley BD16 3LA
Tel and *Fax:* 01274 551071
email: paul.booth@bradford.anglican.org

Retired Clergy and Widows Officer (Bradford Archdeaconry) Canon Donald Brown, 3 Northfield Gardens, Wibsey, Bradford BD6 1LQ
Tel: 01274 671869

(*Craven Archdeaconry*) Canon John Bearpark, 31 Northfields Crescent, Settle BD24 9JP
Tel: 01729 822712

Children's Work Ven Dr David Lee (*as above*)

Healing Revd David Swales, St James' Vicarage, 1056 Bolton Rd, Bradford BD2 4LH
Tel: 01274 637193
email: david.swales@blueyonder.co.uk

Revd Gill Mack, Vicarage, Shire Lane, Hurst Green, Clitheroe BB7 9QR   *Tel:* 01254 826686
email: gillmack@tiscali.co.uk

Liturgy Chairman Dr Chris Clough, Brier Meade, 4 Scarborough Rd, Shipley BD18 3DR
Tel: 01274 778053
email: c.m.i.clough@blueyonder.co.uk

Stewardship and Funding see Development Officer

Youth Bradford Ms June Hopkinson, 20 Ravenscliffe Rd, Calverley, Leeds LS28 5RZ

Tel: 01274 310234
email: junehopkinson@ntlworld.com
Craven Mr Steve Grasham, 12 Railway St, Beechcliffe, Keighley BD20 6AQ   *Tel:* 01535 609293
email: steve.grasham@btinternet.com

DIOCESAN RECORD OFFICES
Diocesan Records Officers Mrs Mary Creaser, Rose Cottage, Austwick, Lancaster LA2 8BH
Tel: 01524 251536
email: mary.creaser@bradford.anglican.org
Mrs Margaret Barker, 2 Farnham Close, Baildon, Shipley BD17 6SF   *Tel:* 01274 595750
West Yorkshire Archives Service, 15 Canal Rd, Bradford BD1 4AT *Archivist* Ms Letitia Lawson, *Tel:* 01274 735099 (*For parishes in Bradford Metropolitan District*)
Archives Dept, Central Library, Northgate House, Halifax HX1 1UN *Archivist* Ms P. Sewell, *Tel:* 01422 392636 (*For parishes in Calderdale Metropolitan District*)
Record Office, County Offices, Kendal LA9 4RQ *County Archivist* Ms A. Rowe, County Record Office, The Castle, Carlisle CA3 8UR, *Tel:* 01228 23455 (*For parishes in the County of Cumbria*)
County Record Office, Bow Lane, Preston PR1 2RE *County Archivist* Mr B. Jackson, *Tel:* 01772 533039 (*For parishes in the County of Lancashire*)
Archives Dept, Leeds District Archives, Chapeltown Rd, Sheepscar, Leeds LS7 3AP *Archivist* S. Davidson, *Tel:* 0113 214 5814 (*For parishes in Leeds Metropolitan District*)
County Record Office, County Hall, Northallerton DL7 8AF *County Archivist* Mr M. K. Sweetmore, *Tel:* 01609 777585 (*For parishes in the County of North Yorkshire*)

RURAL DEANS
ARCHDEACONRY OF BRADFORD
Airedale Revd Derek Jackson, Woodlands, 26 Falcon Rd, Bingley BD16 4DW *Tel:* 01274 563113
email: derekjackson2901@hotmail.com
Bowling and Horton Canon Paul Bilton, St Wilfrid's Vicarage, St Wilfrid's Rd, Lidget Green, Bradford BD7 2LU   *Tel:* 01274 572504
email: paul@bunghiu.freeserve.co.uk
Calverley Revd Paul Walker, St Cuthbert's Vicarage, 71 Wrose Rd, Bradford BD2 1LN
Tel: 01274 611631
email: paulwalker@stcuthbertswrose.org.uk
Otley Vacancy

ARCHDEACONRY OF CRAVEN
Bowland Revd Roger Wood, Vicarage, Stainforth, Settle BD24 9PG   *Tel:* 01729 823010
email: roger.wood@bradford.anglican.org
Ewecross Revd Ian Greenhalgh, Vicarage, Austwick, Lancaster LA2 8BE *Tel:* 01524 251313
email: ian.greenhalgh@bradford.anglican.org
Skipton Revd Ann Turner, Rectory, Broughton, Skipton BD23 3AN   *Tel:* 01282 842332
South Craven Revd Peter Greenwood, Vicarage, Briggate, Silsden BD20 9JS   *Tel:* 01535 652204
email: greenwood@macace.net

DIOCESE OF BRISTOL

Founded in 1542. Bristol; the southern two-thirds of South Gloucestershire; the northern quarter of Wiltshire, except for two parishes in the north (GLOUCESTER); Swindon, except for a few parishes in the north (GLOUCESTER) and in the south (SALISBURY); a few parishes in Gloucestershire.

Population 920,000   Area 474 sq m
Full-time Stipendiary Parochial Clergy 113   Benefices 108
Parishes 164   Churches 205
www.bristol.anglican.org
Overseas link province: Uganda.

BISHOP (55th)
Rt Revd Michael Hill, Wethered House, 11 The Avenue, Clifton, Bristol BS8 3HG [2003]
Tel: 0117 973 0222
Fax: 0117 923 9670
email: bishop@bristoldiocese.org

SUFFRAGAN BISHOP
SWINDON Rt Revd Dr Lee Rayfield, Mark House, Field Rise, Swindon SN1 4HP [2005]
Tel: 01793 538654
Fax: 01793 525181
email: bishop.swindon@bristoldiocese.org

CATHEDRAL CHURCH OF THE HOLY AND UNDIVIDED TRINITY
Dean Very Revd Robert Grimley, The Deanery, 20 Charlotte St, Bristol BS1 5PZ [1997]
Tel: 0117 926 2443
email: dean@bristol.anglican.org
Cathedral Office Bristol Cathedral, Abbey Gatehouse, College Green, Bristol BS1 5TJ
Tel: 0117 926 4879
Fax: 0117 925 3678
email: reception@bristol-cathedral.co.uk
Canons Residentiary
Theologian Canon Douglas Holt, 9 Leigh Rd, Clifton, Bristol BS8 2DA [1998] *Tel:* 0117 973 7427
email: douglas.holt@bristoldiocese.org
City Canon Canon Timothy Higgins, c/o Cathedral Office [2006]   *Tel:* 0117 927 7977
email: canon@bristol-cathedral.co.uk
Precentor Canon Wendy Wilby, 55 Salisbury Rd, Redland, Bristol BS6 7AS [2006]
Tel: 0117 904 6903
email: precentor@bristol-cathedral.co.uk
Capitular Canons
Canon Stuart Burnett, Canon Joy Coupe, Canon Jim Harris, Revd Canon Robin Protheroe, Canon Caro Barker-Bennett
Minor Canons
Revd Catherine Coster, Revd John Lewis, Revd Gwyn Owen, Revd Dr Berj Topalian
Chapter Clerk Mr Andrew Phillips, Cathedral Office   *Tel:* 0117 946 8172
email: andrew.phillips@bristol-cathedral.co.uk

Cathedral Organist Mr Mark Lee, Cathedral Office
Tel: 0117 946 8177
email: organist@bristol-cathedral.co.uk

ARCHDEACONS
BRISTOL Ven Tim McClure, 10 Great Brockeridge, Westbury-on-Trym, Bristol BS9 3TY [1999]
Tel: 0117 962 1433
Fax: 0117 962 9438
email: tim.mcclure@bristoldiocese.org
MALMESBURY Ven Alan Hawker, Church Paddock, Church Lane, Kington Langley, Chippenham SN15 5NR [1999]
Tel: 01249 750085
Fax: 01249 750086
email: alan.hawker@bristol5.gotadsl.co.uk

CONVOCATION (MEMBERS OF THE HOUSE OF CLERGY OF THE GENERAL SYNOD)
Proctors for Clergy
The Archdeacon of Malmesbury
Canon Douglas Holt
Revd Dr Paul Roberts

MEMBERS OF THE HOUSE OF LAITY OF THE GENERAL SYNOD
Prof Glynn Harrison
Miss Jacqueline Humphreys
Mrs Kim Curle

DIOCESAN OFFICERS
Dioc Secretary Mrs Lesley Farrall, Diocesan Church House, 23 Great George St, Bristol BS1 5QZ   *Tel:* 0117 906 0100
Fax: 0117 925 0460
email: lesley.farrall@bristoldiocese.org
Chancellor of Diocese Dr James Behrens, Searle Court, 6 New Square, London WC2A 3QS
Tel: 020 7242 6105
Registrar of Diocese and Bishop's Legal Secretary Mr Tim Berry, Harris and Harris, 14 Market Place, Wells BA5 2RE   *Tel:* 01749 674747
Fax: 01749 676585
email: tim.berry@harris-harris.co.uk

DIOCESAN ORGANIZATIONS

Diocesan Office Diocesan Church House, 23 Great George St, Bristol BS1 5QZ   *Tel:* 0117 906 0100
Fax: 0117 925 0460
email: any.name@bristoldiocese.org

ADMINISTRATION

Assistant Dioc Secretary Mrs Sally Moody, Dioc Church House
Dioc Synod (Chairman, House of Clergy) Canon Peter Bailey, Vicarage, Walsingham Rd, St Andrews, Bristol BS6 5BT   *Tel:* 0117 924 8683
(Chairman, House of Laity) Prof. Gordon Stirrat, Malpas Lodge, 24 Henbury Rd, Bristol BS9 3HJ
Tel: 0117 950 5310
Board of Finance (Chairman) Mr David Froude, c/o Dioc Church House; *(Secretary)* Mrs Lesley Farrall, Dioc Church House
Finance Manager Mr David Hargrave, Dioc Church House
Pastoral Committee (Secretary) Mrs Lesley Farrall *(as above)*
Dioc Electoral Registration Officer Mrs Lesley Farrall *(as above)*
Designated Officer Mr Tim Berry, Harris and Harris, 14 Market Place, Wells BA5 2RE
Tel: 01749 674747
Fax: 01749 676585

CHURCHES

Advisory Committee for the Care of Churches (Chairman) Revd James Wilson, St Gregory's Vicarage, Filton Rd, Horfield, Bristol BS7 0PD
Tel: 0117 969 2839
email: revjameswilson@aol.com
(Secretary) Mr Tim Berry
(Asst Secretary) Mrs Jane Holmes, c/o Harris and Harris, 14 Market Place, Wells BA5 2RE
Tel: 01749 674747
Fax: 01749 676585

EDUCATION

Board of Education (Director) Mrs J. Waters-Dewhurst, All Saints RE Centre, 1 All Saints Court, Bristol BS1 1JN   *Tel:* 0117 927 7454
Fax: 0117 925 0404
email: allsaints@bristoldiocese.org

DIOCESAN LAY MINISTERS' COUNCIL

Secretary Mrs Anne Iles, 119 Monks Park Ave, Horfield, Bristol BS7 0UA   *Tel:* 0117 969 2371

DIOCESAN ECUMENICAL AND GLOBAL DEVELOPMENT OFFICER

Revd Chris Dobson, Dioc Church House

MISSION AND MINISTRY DEVELOPMENT

Director Canon Douglas Holt, Dioc Church House
Adviser for Collaborative Ministry Mr George Rendell, Dioc Church House
Adviser in Evangelism Revd Paul Rush, 5 Gold View, Rushy Platt, Swindon SN5 8ZG
Tel: 01793 872853
email: rev.paul.rush@ntlworld.com

Adviser for Initial Minsterial Education Revd Derek Chedzey, Dioc Church House
Adviser on Pastoral Care for Clergy and their Families Canon Stuart Taylor, Dioc Church House
Adviser for Licensed Ministry Revd Samantha Rushton, Dioc Church House
Asst Adviser for Licensed Ministry Canon Ray Brazier   *Tel:* 0117 952 3209
email: rayvb@tiscali.co.uk
Adviser for Licensed Lay Ministry Training (Reader) Mrs Anne-Claar Thomasson Rosingh, Dioc Church House
Child Protection Officer Mrs Carolyn Buckeridge
Tel: 0844 892 0104
Dean of Women's Ministry Canon Christine Froude, St Mary's Vicarage, 8 Priory Gardens, Shirehampton, Bristol BS11 0BZ
Tel: 0117 985 5450
email: christinefroude@lineone.net
Chair, Bishop's Advisory Group on Healing Revd Ian Wills, Soundwell Vicarage, 46 Sweets Rd, Soundwell, Bristol BS15 1XQ   *Tel:* 0117 967 1511
email: ian.wills@bristoldiocese.org
Chair, Diocesan Worship and Liturgy Committee Revd Mark Pilgrim, St Peter's Vicarage, 17 The Drive, Henleaze, Bristol BS9 4LD
Tel: 0117 962 0636
email: markpilgrimis@aol.com
Administrators Miss Rachel Williams, Mrs Stella O'Brien, Mr Ben Scotcher, Dioc Church House

PRESS, PUBLICITY AND PUBLICATIONS

Communications Officer and Press Officer Mr John Lloyd   *Tel:* 07973 419628 (Mobile)
email: johnlloyd@mediamatters.info
Editor of Dioc Directory Mr Nigel Sherratt, Dioc Church House

DIOCESAN RECORD OFFICES

Bristol Record Office, 'B' Bond, Smeaton Rd, Bristol BS1 6XN *County Archivist* Mr J. S. Williams, *Tel:* 0117 922 4224 *(For parish records in the archdeaconry of Bristol)*
Wiltshire and Swindon History Centre, Cocklebury Rd, Chippenham SN15 3QN *County Archivist* Mr John Darcy, *Tel:* 01249 705500 *(For parish records in the archdeaconry of Malmesbury)*

DIOCESAN RESOURCE CENTRE

All Saints Centre, 1 All Saints Court, Bristol BS1 1JN   *Tel:* 0117 927 7454
Fax: 0117 925 0404
email: allsaints@bristoldiocese.org

THE CHURCHES' COUNCIL FOR INDUSTRY AND SOCIAL RESPONSIBILITY

Director Revd Jon Doble, 162 Pennywell Rd, Bristol BS5 0TX   *Tel:* 0117 955 7430
Fax: 0117 955 7436
email: jon@ccisr.org.uk

The Pilgrim Centre, Regents Circus, Swindon SN1 1PX   *Tel and Fax:* 01793 491454
          email: isrswindon@btconnect.com
Administrators Mrs Alison Paginton, Mrs Christine Durant (Swindon, part-time), Mrs Vena Prater (part-time)
Industrial Chaplains Revd Heather Pencavel (part-time), Revd Tim Harrison, Revd Malcolm Warren
Chaplain for Economic Life (Swindon) Revd Angela Overton-Benge
Social Responsibility Officer (Swindon and Wiltshire) Revd Dr Simon Topping
Church and Society Officer Mr David Maggs
Inter-Faith Adviser Revd Cassandra Howes
Church Urban Fund Officer Revd Stephen Skinner
Senior Chaplain Avon and Somerset Constabulary Pastor Andy Paget (part-time)
Senior Chaplain Wiltshire Constabulary Revd Dr Richard Armitage (part-time)
Chaplain to the City Centre (Bristol) Canon Timothy Higgins (part-time)
Chaplain to Bristol Retail Centre Revd Bob Mills
Marriage and Family Life Adviser Mrs Alison Paginton
Community Ministry Adviser Mrs Sandra O'Shea
Regeneration Officer Dr Simon Bale
South West Regional Affairs Officer Revd Heather Pencavel (part-time)
Major Emergency Plan Administrator Mrs Sheila Tubey (volunteer)

AREA DEANS
ARCHDEACONRY OF BRISTOL
Bristol South Revd Gwyn Owen, Vicarage, Goslet Rd, Stockwood, Bristol BS14 8SP
          Tel: 01275 831138
          email: christtheservant@blueyonder.co.uk
Bristol West Revd Mark Pilgrim, St Peter's Vicarage, 17 The Drive, Henleaze, Bristol BS9 4LD   *Tel:* 0117 962 0636
          email: markpilgrimis@aol.com
City Revd Debbie Frazer, St Luke's Vicarage, 60 Barton Hill Rd, Bristol BS5 0AW
          Tel: 0117 955 5947
          email: rev.d.frazer@btinternet.com

ARCHDEACONRY OF MALMESBURY
Chippenham Revd Simon Tyndall, The Rectory, 9 Greenway Park, Chippenham SN15 1QG
          Tel and Fax: 01249 657216
          email: simon@tyndall.plus.com
Kingswood and South Gloucestershire Revd David Adams, Vicarage, 85 Bath Rd, Longwell Green, Bristol BS30 9DF   *Tel:* 0117 932 3714
          email: djaadams@surfaid.org
North Wiltshire Canon Andrew Evans, Rectory, 1 Rectory Close, Stanton St Quintin, Chippenham SN14 6DT   *Tel:* 01666 837187
          email: andrew@evansa63.fsnet.co.uk
Swindon Canon Rob Burles, Rectory, Verwood Close, Park North, Swindon SN34 2LE
          Tel: 01793 611473
          Fax: 01793 574924
          email: rob@burles.org.uk

DIOCESE OF CANTERBURY

Founded in 597. Kent east of the Medway, excluding
the Medway Towns (ROCHESTER).

Population 858,000   Area 970 sq m
Full-time Stipendiary Parochial Clergy 126   Benefices 155
Parishes 262   Churches 329
www.canterbury.anglican.org
Overseas link dioceses: Antananarivo, Antsiranana,
Toamasina, Mahajanga (Madagascar), Arras (Normandy), Basel.

ARCHBISHOP (104th)
Most Revd and Rt Hon Rowan Douglas Williams, *Primate of all England and Metropolitan,* Lambeth Palace, London SE1 7JU *Tel:* 020 7898 1200; *Fax:* 020 7261 9836 and Old Palace, Canterbury, Kent CT1 2EE [2003]
[Rowan Cantuar:]
Dioc Chaplain Revd Martin Short

Matters relating to the Diocese of Canterbury should be referred to the **Bishop of Dover** *(see below)*
For the **Archbishop of Canterbury's Personal Staff** *see page 4*

SUFFRAGAN BISHOPS
DOVER Rt Revd Stephen Squires Venner [1999] *Office* The Bishop's Office, Old Palace, The Precincts, Canterbury CT1 2EE   *Tel:* 01227 459382
Fax: 01227 784985
email: bishop@bishcant.org
Home Upway, 52 St Martin's Hill, Canterbury CT1 1PR
Chaplain: Revd Martin Short
Hon Chaplain Canon Ronald Diss
MAIDSTONE Rt Revd Graham Alan Cray, Bishop's House, Pett Lane, Charing, Ashford TN27 0DL [2001]   *Tel:* 01233 712950
Fax: 01233 713543
email: bishop@bishmaid.org

PROVINCIAL EPISCOPAL VISITORS
EBBSFLEET Rt Revd Andrew Burnham, Bishop's House, Dry Sandford, Abingdon OX13 6JP
Tel: 01865 390746
email: bishop.andrew@ebbsfleet.org.uk
RICHBOROUGH Rt Revd Keith Newton, 6 Mellis Gardens, Woodford Green IG8 0BH
Tel and *Fax:* 020 8505 7259
email: pev@btinternet.com

HONORARY ASSISTANT BISHOPS
Rt Revd Michael Gear, 10 Acott Fields, Yalding, Maidstone ME18 6DQ   *Tel:* 01622 817388
email: bp_mikegear@yahoo.com
Rt Revd Anthony Michael Turnbull, 67 Strand St, Sandwich CT13 9HN   *Tel:* 01304 611389
email: bstmt@btopenworld.com

CATHEDRAL AND METROPOLITICAL CHURCH OF CHRIST
Dean Very Revd Robert Willis, The Deanery, The Precincts, Canterbury CT1 2EP [2001]
Tel: 01227 865200 (Office)
email: dean@canterbury-cathedral.org
Cathedral Office Cathedral House, 11 The Precincts, Canterbury CT1 2EH
Tel: 01227 762862
Fax: 01227 865222

Canons Residentiary
Canon Treasurer and Director of Education Canon Dr Edward Condry, 15 The Precincts, Canterbury CT1 2EP [2002]   *Tel:* 01227 865228
email: edwardc@canterbury-cathedral.org
Canon Librarian and Director of Post Ordination Training Canon Christopher Irvine, 19 The Precincts, Canterbury CT1 2EP [2007]
Tel: 01227 865226
email: canon.irvine@canterbury-cathedral.org
Canon Pastor Canon Clare Edwards, 22 The Precincts, Canterbury CT1 2EP [2004]
Tel: 01227 865227
email: canonclare@canterbury-cathedral.org
Archdeacon Ven Sheila Watson, 29 The Precincts, Canterbury CT1 2EP [2007]   *Tel:* 01227 865238
Fax: 01227 785209
email: archdeacon@canterbury-cathedral.org
Precentor and Sacrist Revd Jeremy Frost, 5 The Precincts, Canterbury CT1 2EE [2004]
Tel: 01227 865225
email: frostj@canterbury-cathedral.org
Receiver General Brigadier M. J. Meardon, Cathedral House   *Tel:* 01227 865212
email: ReceiverGeneral@canterbury-cathedral.org
Cathedral organist Dr David Flood, 6 The Precincts, Canterbury CT1 2EE   *Tel:* 01227 865242
email: organist@canterbury-cathedral.org

ARCHDEACONS
CANTERBURY Ven Sheila Watson, 29 The Precincts, Canterbury CT1 2EP [2007]   *Tel:* 01227 865238
Fax: 01227 785209
email: archdeacon@canterbury-cathedral.org
MAIDSTONE Ven Philip Down, The Old Rectory, The Street, Pluckley TN27 0QT [2002]
Tel: 01233 840291
Fax: 01233 840759
email: pdown@archdeacmaid.org

CONVOCATION (MEMBERS OF THE HOUSE OF CLERGY OF THE GENERAL SYNOD)
Dignitaries in Convocation
The Dean of Canterbury
Proctors for Clergy
Canon Gill Calver
Ven Philip Down
Canon Mark Roberts
Revd Simon Tillotson

MEMBERS OF THE HOUSE OF LAITY OF THE GENERAL SYNOD
Mrs Naomi Lumutenga
Mrs Caroline Spencer
Mrs Margaret Tilley

DIOCESAN OFFICERS
Dioc Secretary Mr Julian Hills, Diocesan House, Lady Wootton's Green, Canterbury CT1 1NQ
Tel: 01227 459401
Fax: 01227 787073
email: jhills@diocant.org
Commissary General His Honour Judge Richard Walker, Trafalgar House, Gordon Rd, Whitfield, Dover CT16 3PN
Tel: 01304 873344
Fax: 01304 873355
Dioc Registrar and Legal Adviser to the Diocese Dr Richard Sturt (*same address*)

DIOCESAN ORGANIZATIONS
Diocesan Office Diocesan House, Lady Wootton's Green, Canterbury CT1 1NQ
Tel: 01227 459401
Fax: 01227 450964
email: reception@diocant.org

ADMINISTRATION
Dioc Synod (*Chairman, House of Clergy*) Canon Mark Roberts, Rectory, Knightrider St, Sandwich CT13 9ER
Tel: 01304 613138
email: revdmarkroberts@supanet.com
(*Chairman, House of Laity*) Mrs Caroline Spencer
email: c.spencer@canterbury.ac.uk
(*Secretary*) Mr Julian Hills, Dioc House
Board of Finance (*Chairman*) Mr Raymond Harris
(*Secretary*) Mr Julian Hills (*as above*)
Designated Officer Ms Gillian Marsh, Dioc House
Dioc Accountant Mr Rob Trice, Dioc House
Director of Property Services Mr Philip Bell, Old Palace, The Precincts, Canterbury CT1 2EE
Tel: 01227 478390

CHURCHES
Advisory Committee for the Care of Churches (*Secretary*) Mr Ian Dodd, Old Palace, The Precincts, Canterbury CT1 2EE
Tel: 01227 478390
Chairman Mrs Heather Marple (same address)

EDUCATION
Education Committee (*Director*) Revd Nigel Genders, Dioc House

Asst Director of Education (*School Improvement*) Mrs Virginia Corbyn, Dioc House
Asst Director of Education (*School Organization*) Mrs Pat Gibson, Dioc House

MINISTRY
Director of Training Revd Rob Mackintosh, Dioc House
Director of Ordinands Revd Ian Aveyard, Dioc House
Assistant Directors of Ordinands Revd Jasmine Roberts, Rectory, Knightrider St, Sandwich CT13 9ER Tel: 01304 613138; Revd Martin Burrell, Vicarage, Waterloo Rd, Cranbrook TN17 3JQ Tel: 01580 712150; Revd Anthony Everett, Christ Church Vicarage, 38 Beltinge Rd, Herne Bay CT6 5BU Tel: 01227 374906
Vocations Advisers
Revd Sara Bimson, 85 Loose Rd, Maidstone ME15 7DA Tel: 01622 679432
Revd Tim Wilson, Rectory, Great Chart TN23 3AY Tel: 01233 620371
Bishop's Officer for NSM Revd Judy Muxlow, 29 The Meadows, Biddenden, Ashford TN17 8AW
Tel: 01580 291016
email: mucat@fish.co.uk
Adviser for Women's Ministry Revd Hilary Jones, St Martin's Rectory, Horn St, Cheriton, Folkestone CT20 3JJ Tel: 01303 238509
email: hilarycjones@lycos.co.uk
Local Ministry Training Scheme Principal Dr Ivan Khovacs, Dioc House
Local Ministry Training Scheme Director of Studies Dr Wendy Dackson, Dioc House
Local Ministry Officer Revd Peter Ingrams, Dioc House
Ministry Development Officer Mr Neville Emslie, Dioc House
Youth Officer Mr Tony Washington, Dioc House
Children's Ministry Adviser Mr Ted Hurst, Dioc House
Association of Readers (*Warden*) Mrs Hilary Richter, Dioc House
(*Hon Secretary*) Mr Donald Baldwin, 11 Woodland Way, Woodnesborough, Sandwich CT13 0NG Tel: 01304 614523
email: donaldrbaldwin@supanet.com
Clergy Retirement Officer Vacancy

LITURGICAL
Chairman Vacancy
Secretary Vacancy
Advisor Revd Liz Hawkes Tel: 01227 360948

MISSION AND ECUMENICAL
Board of Mission (*Chairman*) The Bishop of Maidstone (*as above*)
Dioc Missioners Revd Richard King Tel: 01233 712598; Revd Kerry Thorpe Tel: 01843 871183

PRESS AND PUBLICATIONS
Communications Officer Vacancy
Editor of Dioc Directory Mr Mark Binns, Dioc House

DIOCESAN RECORD OFFICES

Cathedral Archives and Library, The Precincts, Canterbury CT1 2EH *Archivist* Mr Stuart Bligh *Tel:* 01227 865330 (*For parish records in the archdeaconry of Canterbury*)
Centre for Kentish Studies, County Hall, Maidstone ME14 1XQ *County Archivist* Mr Stuart Bligh *Tel:* 01622 754321 (*For parish records in the archdeaconry of Maidstone*)

CHURCH IN SOCIETY CANTERBURY AND ROCHESTER DIOCESES

Chief Executive Canon David Grimwood, Robert Runcie House, 2–3 Bedford Place, Maidstone ME16 8JB   *Tel:* 01622 755014
                                      Fax: 01622 693531
Director of Community Ministry Mrs Jane Winter
Director of Priority People Programmes Mr Adrian Speller

STEWARDSHIP

Adviser Mrs Liz Marsh, Dioc House
Asst Adviser Mrs Jenny Hunt, Dioc House

AREA DEANS
ARCHDEACONRY OF CANTERBURY

East Bridge Revd John Sweatman, The Vicarage, Queens Rd, Ash, Canterbury CT3 2BG
                                      Tel: 01304 812296
            email: ash.church@tiscali.co.uk
West Bridge Revd John Richardson, Vicarage, Cherry Garden Crescent, Wye TN25 5AS
                                      Tel: 01233 812450
            email: wyechurch@ic.ac.uk
Canterbury Canon Noelle Hall, Rectory, 13 Ersham Rd, Canterbury CT1 3AR
                                      Tel: 01227 462686
      Fax: noelle@thinker117.freeserve.co.uk

Reculver Revd Ron Hawkes, Vicarage, 25 Dence Park, Herne Bay, CT6 6BQ   *Tel:* 01227 360948
            email: reverendronald@tiscali.co.uk
Dover Revd David Ridley, St Mary's Vicarage, Taswell St, Dover CT16 1SE   *Tel:* 01304 206842
            email: davidridley@btopenworld.com
Elham Revd Hilary Jones, St Martin's Rectory, Horn St, Cheriton CT20 3JJ   *Tel:* 01303 238509
            email: revhilaryjones@btinternet.com
Ospringe Canon Tony Oehring, Vicarage, 16 Newton Rd, Faversham ME13 8DY
                                      Tel: 01795 532592
            email: anthonyoehring@aol.com
Sandwich Vacancy
Thanet Canon David Roper, The Rectory, Nelson Place, Broadstairs CT10 1HQ   *Tel:* 01843 862961
            email: roper995@btinternet.com

ARCHDEACONRY OF MAIDSTONE

Ashford Canon Sheila McLachlan, Rectory, Church Hill, Kingsnorth, Ashford TN23 3EG
                                      Tel: 01233 620433
            email: sheila.mclachlan@tesco.net
Cranbrook Canon Gill Calver, New Rectory, High St, Staplehurst TN12 0BJ   *Tel:* 01580 891258
            email: gill.calver@btinternet.com
Maidstone Vacancy
North Downs Canon Prof Robin Gill, Cornwallis Building, University of Kent at Canterbury, Canterbury CT2 7NF   *Tel:* 01622 884120
            email: R.Gill@kent.ac.uk
Romney Revd Stephen Hardy, All Saints Rectory, Park St, Lydd TN29 9AY   *Tel:* 01797 320345
            email: stephenhardy@macmail.com
Sittingbourne Canon Gilbert Spencer, Vicarage, Vicarage Rd, Minster-in-Sheppey ME12 2HE
                                      Tel: 01795 873185
            email: gilbert_spencer@hotmail.com
Tenterden Revd Jacques Desrosiers, Vicarage, Rolvenden TN17 4ND   *Tel:* 01580 241235
            email: vicarage1965@btinternet.com

DIOCESE OF CARLISLE

Founded in 1133. Cumbria, except for small areas in
the east (NEWCASTLE, BRADFORD).

Population 491,000   Area 2,477 sq m
Full-time Stipendiary Parochial Clergy 127   Benefices 126
Parishes 264   Churches 345
www.carlisle.anglican.org
Overseas link dioceses: Madras (CSI), Zululand (South Africa),
Stavanger (Norway), Northern Argentina.

BISHOP (66th)
Rt Revd Graham Dow, Rose Castle, Dalston,
Carlisle CA5 7BZ [2000]
Tel: 01697 476274
Fax: 01697 476550
email: bishop.carlisle@carlislediocese.org.uk
[Graham Carlisle:]
Bishop's Chaplain Revd Robert Saner-Haigh
email: bishop.chaplain@carlislediocese.org.uk

SUFFRAGAN BISHOP
PENRITH Rt Revd James Newcome, Holm Croft,
13 Castle Rd, Kendal LA9 7AU [2002]
Tel: 01539 727836
Fax: 01539 734380
email: bishop.penrith@carlislediocese.org.uk

HONORARY ASSISTANT BISHOPS
Rt Revd Ian Macdonald Griggs, Rookings,
Patterdale, Penrith CA11 0NP [1994]
Tel: 01768 482064
email: ian.griggs@virgin.net
Rt Revd George Lanyon Hacker, Keld House,
Milburn, Penrith CA10 1TW [1994]
Tel: 01768 361506
email: bishhack@mypostoffice.co.uk
Rt Revd Andrew Alexander Kenny Graham, Fell
End, Butterwick, Penrith CA10 2QQ [1997]
Tel: 01931 713147
Rt Revd Hewlett Thompson, Low Broomrigg,
Warcop, Appleby CA16 6PT [2000]
Tel: 01768 341281
Rt Revd Gordon Bates, Caedmon House, 2 Loyne
Park, Whittington, via Carnforth LA6 2NL [2000]
Tel: 01524 272010
Rt Revd Robert Hardy, Carleton House, Back
Lane, Langwathby, Penrith CA10 1NB [2002]
Tel: 01768 881210
Rt Revd John Richardson, The Old Rectory, Bew-
castle, Carlisle CA6 6PS [2003]   *Tel:* 01697 48389

**CATHEDRAL CHURCH OF THE HOLY
AND UNDIVIDED TRINITY**
Dean Very Revd Mark Boyling, The Deanery,
Carlisle CA3 8TZ [2004]   *Tel:* 01228 523335
Fax: 01228 547049
email: dean@carlislecathedral.org.uk

Cathedral Office 7 The Abbey, Carlisle CA3 8TZ
Tel: 01228 548151
Fax: 01228 547049
email: office@carlislecathedral.org.uk
Web: www.carlislecathedral.org.uk
Canons Residentiary
Canon David Jenkins, 1 The Abbey, Carlisle, CA3
8TZ [2004]   *Tel:* 01228 597614
Fax: 01228 815409
Canon Brian Roy McConnell, 3 The Abbey,
Carlisle CA3 8TZ [2006]   *Tel:* 01228 521834
email: canonwarden@carlislecathedral.org.uk
Vacancy, 2 The Abbey, Carlisle, CA3 8TZ [2002]
Canon Michael Alan Manley, 4 The Abbey,
Carlisle CA3 8TZ   *Tel:* 01228 542790
email: canonmissioner@carlislecathedral.org.uk

Lay Members of Chapter
Miss Jenny Bate, Solway Bungalow, Pow Hill,
Kirkbride, Wigton CA7 5LF
email: jennybate@btinternet.com
Dr Philip Herrick, Fircroft, Houghton, Carlisle
CA6 4HZ [2001]
Bursar and Chapter Clerk Mr Ian Burns, Cathedral
Office
Administrative Officer Mrs Carolyne Baines,
Cathedral Office
Cathedral Organist Mr Jeremy Suter, 6 The Abbey,
Carlisle CA3 8TZ   *Tel:* 01228 526646
Fax: 01228 547049
email: jeremysuter@hotmail.com

ARCHDEACONS
CARLISLE Vacancy, 2 The Abbey, Carlisle CA3
8TZ [2002]   *Tel:* 01228 523026
Fax: 01228 594899
email: archdeacon.north@carlislediocese.org.uk
WEST CUMBERLAND Vacancy, 50 Stainburn Rd,
Workington CA14 1SN [2004]
Tel: 01900 66190
email: archdeacon.west@carlislediocese.org.uk
WESTMORLAND AND FURNESS Ven George Howe,
Vicarage, Windermere Rd, Lindale, Grange over
Sands LA11 6LB [2000]   *Tel:* 01539 534717
Fax: 01539 535090
email: archdeacon.south@carlislediocese.org.uk

CONVOCATION (MEMBERS OF THE HOUSE OF CLERGY OF THE GENERAL SYNOD)

Proctors for Clergy
Revd Ferial Etherington
Ven George Howe
Canon Colin Randall

MEMBERS OF THE HOUSE OF LAITY OF THE GENERAL SYNOD

Miss Jennifer Bate
Mr Michael Bonner
Mr Nigel Holmes
Mr David Mills

DIOCESAN OFFICERS

Dioc Secretary Mr Derek Hurton, Church House, West Walls, Carlisle CA3 8UE   *Tel:* 01228 522573
01228 815402 (Direct Line)
Fax: 01228 815400
email: diocesan.secretary@carlislediocese.org.uk
Chancellor of Diocese Mr Geoffrey Tattersall, 2 The Woodlands, Lostock, Bolton BL6 4JD
Registrar of Diocese and Bishop's Legal Secretary
Mrs Jane Lowdon, Sintons Solicitors, The Cube, Barrack Rd, Newcastle-upon-Tyne NE4 6DB
Tel: 0191 226 7878
Fax: 0191 226 7852
email: j.lowdon@sintons.co.uk

DIOCESAN ORGANIZATIONS

Diocesan Office Church House, West Walls, Carlisle CA3 8UE   *Tel:* 01228 522573
Fax: 01228 815400
email: enquiries@carlislediocese.org.uk
Web: www.carlislediocese.org.uk

ADMINISTRATION

Dioc Synod (*Chairman, House of Clergy*) Revd Dr Peter Tiplady, Meadow Croft, Wetheral, Carlisle CA4 8JG   *Tel:* 01228 561611
email: petertiplady@mac.com
(*Chairman, House of Laity*) Mr Peter Baxter, 30 Sneckyeat Rd, Whitehaven CA28 8PE
Tel: 01946 62253
email: petrobax@lupus17.freeserve.co.uk
(*Secretary*) Mr Derek Hurton, Dioc Office
Board of Finance (*Chairman*) Mr Bob Henry, 5 The Orchard, Great Corby, Carlisle CA4 8LS
Tel: 01768 371436
email: rjhgtcorby@aol.com
(*Secretary*) Mr Derek Hurton (*as above*)
Assistant Dioc Secretary (*Finance*) Mr Neil Barrett, Dioc Office   *Tel:* 01228 815404
Assistant Dioc Secretary (*Property*) Mr Brian Cook, Dioc Office   *Tel:* 01228 815403
Finance Resources Officer Mr Geoffrey Hine, Dioc Office   *Tel:* 01228 815401
Pastoral Committee Miss Jennifer Bate, Dioc Office
Tel: 01228 815408
Designated Officer Mrs Jane Lowdon (*as above*)

CHURCHES

Advisory Committee for the Care of Churches (*Chairman*) Lord Hothfield, Drybeck Hall, Appleby in Westmorland CA16 6TF; (*Secretary*) Mr Derek Hurton, Dioc Office; (*Administrative Secretary*) Mr Brian Cook (*as above*)

EDUCATION

Board of Education, Church Centre, West Walls, Carlisle CA3 8UE   *Tel:* 01228 538086
Fax: 01228 815409
email: education@carlislediocese.org.uk
Director of Education Canon David Jenkins, Church Centre   *Tel:* 01228 815406
Senior Schools Officer Revd Bert Thomas, Church Centre   *Tel:* 0845 395 0646
RE Officer Mr Stephen Mott, Church Centre
Diocesan Youth Officer Mr Paul Wheelhouse, Church Centre
Resources Centre Mr Stephen Mott, Church Centre

MINISTRY AND TRAINING

Ministry Development Adviser Canon Amiel Osmaston, Dioc Office   *Tel:* 01228 815406
email: ministry.dev@carlislediocese.org.uk
Principal Lancashire and Cumbria Theological Partnership and Adviser for Ministry and Training Canon Tim Herbert, Dioc Office
Tel: 01228 815405
email: admin@lctp.co.uk
Adviser for Clergy Training Revd Ruth Crossley, Vicarage, Levens, Kendal LA8 8PY
Tel: 01539 560233
email: cme@carlislediocese.org.uk
Director of Ordinands Revd Robert Saner-Haigh, Rose Castle, Dalston, Carlisle CA5 7BZ
Tel: 01697 476274
email: bishop.chaplain@carlislediocese.org.uk
Adviser for Women's Ministry Canon Mary Day, Vicarage, Cross Canonby, Maryport CA15 6SJ
Tel: 01900 814192
email: vicarmary@talktalk.net

SOCIAL RESPONSIBILITY

Officer for Social Responsibility Canon Colin Laxon, Dioc Office
Industrial Mission Ven Colin Hill, 50 Stainburn Rd, Workington CA14 1SN   *Tel:* 01900 66190
email: archdeacon.west@carlislediocese.org.uk

ECUMENICAL AFFAIRS

Diocesan Ecumenical Officer Ven George Howe, Vicarage, Windermere Rd, Lindale, Grange over Sands LA11 6LB [2000]   *Tel:* 01539 534717
Fax: 01539 535090
email: archdeacon.south@carlislediocese.org.uk
Churches Together in Cumbria (*Ecumenical Development-Officer*) Revd Carole Gotham, Sedbergh United Reformed Church, Main St, Sedburgh LA10 5AB   *Tel:* 01539 622030
email: carole.marsden@urc.org

Rural Forum (*Bishop's Rural Officer*) Revd Geoffrey Watson, Vicarage, Kentmere Rd, Staveley, Kendal LA8 9PA   *Tel:* 01539 821267
email: geof_watson@talktalk.net
Rural Officer Revd Sarah Lunn, Rectory, Long Marton, Appleby in Westmorland CA16 6BN
Tel: 01768 361269
email: sarahlunn@care4free.net

EVANGELISM
Diocesan Officer Revd John Reeves, Vicarage, Irthington, Carlisle CA6 9NJ   *Tel:* 01697 741864

PARTNERSHIP IN WORLD MISSION
Officer Mrs Lynne Tembey, Holm Cultram. Vicarage, Abbeytown, Wigton CA7 4SP
Tel: 01697 361246
Fax: 01697 61506

PRESS AND PUBLICATIONS
Communications Officer Canon Richard Pratt, Dioc Office   *Tel:* 01228 521982 (Home)
email: communications@carlislediocese.org.uk
Editor of Dioc News Canon Richard Pratt, Dioc Office
Dioc Directory Mrs Jean Hardman, Dioc Office
Tel: 01228 815408

DIOCESAN ARCHIVIST
County Archivist Ms A. Rowe   *Tel:* 01228 606477

DIOCESAN RECORD OFFICES
Cumbria Record Office, The Castle, Carlisle CA3 8UR   *Tel:* 01228 607285
email: carlisle.record.office@cumbriacc.gov.uk
Cumbria Record Office, County Offices, Kendal LA9 4RQ   *Tel:* 01539 773540
email: kendal.record.office@cumbriacc.gov.uk
Cumbria Record Office & Local Studies Library, 140 Duke St, Barrow-in-Furness LA14 1XW
Tel: 01229 894363
email: barrow.record.office@cumbriacc.gov.uk
Cumbria Record Office and Local Studies Library, Scotch St, Whitehaven CA28 7BJ
Tel: 01946 852920
email:
whitehaven.record.office@cumbriacc.gov.uk

RURAL DEANS
ARCHDEACONRY OF CARLISLE
Appleby Canon Anthony Clegg, Vicarage, Appleby-in-Westmorland, Cumbria CA16 6QW
Tel: 01768 351461
email: anthony.clegg@talktalk.net
Brampton Canon Colin Randall, Holme Eden Vicarage, Warwick Bridge, Carlisle CA4 8BF
Tel: 01228 560332
email: carandall@mac.com
Carlisle Canon John Libby, St James Vicarage, Goschen Rd, Carlisle CA2 5PF   *Tel:* 01228 515639
Fax: 01228 524569
email: john.libby@btinternet.com
Penrith Canon Beth Smith, Vicarage, High Hesket, Carlisle CA4 8HU   *Tel:* 01697 473320
email: revdesmith@hotmail.com

ARCHDEACONRY OF WESTMORLAND AND FURNESS
Barrow Revd Ian Hook, St Mark's Vicarage, Rawlinson St, Barrow in Furness LA14 1BX
Tel: 01229 820405
email: ianhook@dsl.pipex.com
Furness Canon Gary Wemyss, Vicarage, Penny Bridge, Ulverston LA12 7RQ   *Tel:* 01229 861285
email: gwemyss@clara.co.uk
Kendal Revd Tim Harmer, Sunnybank, Underbarrow, Kendal, Cumbria LA8 8HG
Tel: 01539 568865
email: revtim.harmer@virgin.net
Windermere Canon Robert Coke, Vicarage, Millans Park, Ambleside LA22 9AD
Tel: 01539 433205
email: robertricia.coke@homecall.co.uk

ARCHDEACONRY OF WEST CUMBERLAND
Calder Revd John Woolcock, The Vicarage, Seascale, Cumbria CA20 1QT   *Tel:* 01946 728217
email: john.woolcock@tesco.net
Derwent Canon Bryan Rothwell, Rectory, Threlkeld, Keswick CA12 4RT
Tel: 01768 779714
email: bryan.rothwell@btinternet.com
Solway Canon Bryan Rowe, St Michael's Rectory, Dora Crescent, Workington CA14 2EZ
Tel: 01900 602311
email: bryan.rowe@dsl.pipex.com

DIOCESE OF CHELMSFORD

Founded in 1914. Essex, except for a few parishes in the north (ELY, ST EDMUNDSBURY AND IPSWICH); five East London boroughs north of the Thames; three parishes in south Cambridgeshire.

Population 2,785,000   Area 1,531 sq m
Full-time Stipendiary Parochial Clergy 365   Benefices 329
Parishes 471   Churches 608
www.chelmsford.anglican.org

Overseas link dioceses: Embu, Mbeere, Kirinyaga, Meru (Kenya); Trinidad and Tobago; Karlstad; Iasi (Romania)

BISHOP (9th)
Rt Revd John Warren Gladwin, Bishopscourt, Margaretting, Ingatestone CM4 0HD [2003]
Tel: 01277 352001
Fax: 01277 355374
email: bishopscourt@chelmsford.anglican.org
[John Chelmsford]
Bishop's Chaplain Revd Chris Newlands (*same address*)
Tel: 01277 352001
Fax: 01277 355374
email: cnewlands@chelmsford.anglican.org
Director of Communications and Bishop's Press Officer Ralph Meloy   *Tel:* 01245 294424 (Office)
07654 382674 (Pager)
email: rmeloy@chelmsford.anglican.org

AREA BISHOPS
BARKING Rt Revd David John Leader Hawkins, Barking Lodge, Verulam Ave, London E17 8ES [2003]   *Tel:* 020 8509 7377
email: b.barking@chelmsford.anglican.org
BRADWELL Rt Revd Laurence Alexander Green, Bishop's House, Orsett Rd, Horndon-on-the-Hill SS17 8NS [1993]   *Tel:* 01375 673806
Fax: 01375 674222
email: b.bradwell@chelmsford.anglican.org
COLCHESTER Rt Revd Christopher Heudebourck Morgan, 1 Fitzwalter Rd, Lexden, Colchester CO3 3SS [2001]   *Tel:* 01206 576648
Fax: 01206 763868
email: b.colchester@chelmsford.anglican.org

HONORARY ASSISTANT BISHOPS
Rt Revd Keith Newton, Richborough House, 6 Mellish Gardens, Woodford Green IG8 0BH
Tel: 020 8505 7259
email: keith@newtonfam.freeserve.co.uk
Rt Revd Charles Derek Bond, 52 Horn Brook, Saffron Walden, Essex CB11 3JW
Tel: 01799 521308
email: bondd@aol.com
Rt Revd John Martin Ball, 5 Hillview Rd, Chelmsford CM1 7RS   *Tel:* 01245 268296

CATHEDRAL CHURCH OF ST MARY THE VIRGIN, ST PETER AND ST CEDD
Dean Very Revd Peter Judd, The Dean's House, 3 Harlings Grove, Chelmsford CM1 1YQ [1997]
Tel: 01245 354318 (Home)
01245 294492 (Office)
email: dean@chelmsfordcathedral.org.uk
Cathedral Office 53 New St, Chelmsford CM1 1TY
Tel: 01245 294489
Fax: 01245 294499
Web: www.chelmsfordcathedral.org.uk

Canons Residentiary
Vice-Dean Canon Walter King, 83 Ridgewell Ave, Chelmsford CM1 2GA [2001]
Tel: 01245 267773 (Home)
01245 294493 (Office)
email: vicedean@chelmsfordcathedral.org.uk

Canon Theologian Canon Andrew Knowles, 2 Harlings Grove, Chelmsford CM1 1YQ [1998]
Tel: 01245 355041 (Home)
01245 294484 (Office)
email: theologian@chelmsfordcathedral.org.uk

Canon Precentor Canon Simon Pothen, c/o Cathedral Office [2007]
Tel: 01245 294482 (Office)
email: precentor@chelmsfordcathedral.org.uk

Hon Associate Chaplain Revd Ivor Moody, 4 Bishopscourt Gardens, Springfield, Chelmsford CM2 6AZ   *Tel:* 01245 261700 (Home)
01245 493131 (Office)
email: i.r.moody@apu.ac.uk

Hon Associate Chaplain and Bishop's Chaplain Revd Chris Newlands, Bishopscourt, Margaretting, Ingatestone CM4 0HD
Tel: 01277 352001 (Office)
email: cnewlands@chelmsford.anglican.org

Hon Associate Chaplain and Diocesan Director of Ordinands Canon Richard More, 25 Roxwell Rd, Chelmsford CM1 2LY   *Tel:* 01245 264187
email: ddo@chelmsford.anglican.org

Cathedral Administrator and Chapter Clerk Captain David Fifield, Cathedral Office
Tel: 01245 294488
email: administrator@chelmsfordcathedral.org.uk

Director of Music Mr Peter Nardone, 1 Harlings Grove, Chelmsford CM1 1YQ
Tel: 01245 262006 (Home)
01245 252429 (Office)
email: dom@chelmsfordcathedral.org.uk

Assistant Director of Music Vacancy
Tel: 01245 252429
email: adom@chelmsfordcathedral.org.uk

ARCHDEACONS
COLCHESTER Ven Annette Cooper, 63 Powers Hall End, Witham CM8 1NH [2004]
Tel: 01376 513130
Fax: 01376 500789
email: a.colchester@chelmsford.anglican.org
HARLOW Ven Peter Taylor, Glebe House, Church Lane, Sheering CM22 7NR [1996]
Tel: 01279 734524
Fax: 01279 734426
email: a.harlow@chelmsford.anglican.org
SOUTHEND Ven David Lowman, The Archdeacon's Lodge, 136 Broomfield Road, Chelmsford CM1 1RN [2001]
Tel: 01245 258257
Fax: 01245 250845
email: a.southend@chelmsford.anglican.org
WEST HAM Ven Elwin Cockett, 86 Aldersbrook Rd, Manor Park, London E12 5DH [2007]
Tel: 020 8989 8557
Fax: 020 8530 1311
email: a.westham@chelmsford.anglican.org

CONVOCATION (MEMBERS OF THE HOUSE OF CLERGY OF THE GENERAL SYNOD)
Proctors for Clergy
Ven Annette Cooper
Revd John Dunnett
Revd Brian Lewis
Revd David Parrott
Revd David Waller
Canon Martin Webster

MEMBERS OF THE HOUSE OF LAITY OF THE GENERAL SYNOD
Dr Susan Atkin
Mr Robert Hammond
Mr Philip Ivey-Ray
Mr Harry Marsh
Mr David G Llewelyn Morgan
Mr Gordon Simmonds
Mr Robin Stevens

DIOCESAN OFFICERS
Chief Executive Steven Webb, Diocesan Office, 53 New St, Chelmsford CM1 1AT
Tel: 01245 294400
Chancellor of Diocese Chancellor George Pulman QC, Diocesan Registry, 53a New St, Chelmsford CM1 1NE
Tel: 01245 259470
Registrar of Diocese and Bishop's Legal Secretary Mr Brian Hood, Diocesan Registry, 53a New St, Chelmsford CM1 1NE
Tel: 01245 259470

Legal Advisers to the Board of Finance Winckworth Sherwood, 53a New St, Chelmsford CM1 1NE
Tel: 01245 262212

DIOCESAN ORGANIZATIONS
Diocesan Office 53 New St, Chelmsford CM1 1AT
Tel: 01245 294400
Fax: 01245 294477
email: mail@chelmsford.anglican.org

ADMINISTRATION
Dioc Synod (Chairman, House of Clergy) Canon Martin D Webster, *Tel:* 01992 672115; *(Chairman, House of Laity)* Canon Dr Susan Atkin, *Tel:* 01206 854976; *(Secretary)* Steve Webb, Dioc Office *Tel:* 01245 294400
Board of Finance (Chairman) Canon John Spence OBE
(Company Secretary) Steven Webb, Dioc Office
Tel: 01245 294400
email: swebb@chelmsford.anglican.org
Synodical and Pastoral Secretary and Deputy Chief Executive Vacancy
Senior Property Manager Richard Smith, Dioc Office
Tel: 01245 294420
Designated Officer Mr Brian Hood, Dioc Registry, 53a New St, Chelmsford CM1 1NG
Tel: 01245 259470
Dioc Pastoral Committee (Chairman) Very Revd Philip Need, Deanery, Bocking CM7 5SR; *(Secretary)* Mr David Brown, Dioc Office

CHURCHES
Advisory Committee for the Care of Churches (Chairman) Dr James Bettley, The Old Vicarage, Church Rd, Malden CM9 8NP *Tel:* 01612 892450; *(Secretary)* Mrs Sandra Turner, Dioc Office
email: sturnerj@chelmsford.anglican.org
Redundant Churches Committee (Secretary) Vacancy
Ringers Association Mr Michael Bishop, 56 Edinburgh Gardens, Braintree CM7 6LH
Tel: 01376 325281

CHILD PROTECTION
Child Protection Adviser Revd Jean Halliday, Dioc Office
Tel: 01245 294457
07903 831965 (Mobile)
email: jhalliday@chelmsford.anglican.org

EDUCATION
Director of Education Canon Peter Hartley, Dioc Office
email: hartleyp@chelmsford.anglican.org
Early Years Adviser Mrs Yvonne Spence, Dioc Office
Tel: 01245 294440
email: yspence@chelmsford.anglican.org
RE Adviser Mrs Alison Seaman, Dioc Office
Tel: 01245 294440
email: aseaman@chelmsford.anglican.org

School and RE Advisers Rob Fox, Revd Lyn Hillier, Rosemary Privett Dioc Office
email: rfox@chelmsford.anglican.org
l.hillier@chelmsford.anglican.org
rprivett@chelmsford.anglican.org
Children's Work Adviser Mr Stephen Kersys, Dioc Office *email:* skersys@chelmsford.anglican.org

MISSION AND MINISTRY
Dioc Director of Ordinands and NSM Officer Canon Richard More, 25 Roxwell Rd, Chelmsford CM1 2LY *Tel:* 01245 264187
Fax: 01245 348789
email: ddo@chelmsford.anglican.org
Director of Mission and Ministry Canon Roger Matthews, Dioc Office *Tel:* 01245 294455
email: rmatthews@chelmsford.anglican.org
Lay Ministry and Education Coordinator Revd Philip Ritchie, Dioc Office *Tel:* 01245 294449
email: pritchie@chelmsford.anglican.org
Adviser for Women's Ministry Canon Ivy Crawford, Vicarage, Church St, Blackmore, Ingatestone CM4 0RN *Tel:* 01277 821464
Interfaith Adviser Vacancy

COMMUNICATIONS
Communications Director Ralph Meloy, Dioc Office *Tel:* 01245 294424
07654 382674 (Pager)
email: rmeloy@chelmsford.anglican.org

OTHER COMMITTEES
Readers' Committee Canon Pat Nappin, 7 Mavis Walk, Tollgate, Beckton, London E6 4TL
Tel: 020 7474 0222
Liturgical Committee (Chairman) Ven Elwin Cockett, 86 Aldersbrook Rd, Manor Park, London E12 5DH *Tel:* 020 8989 8557
email: a.westham@chelmsford.anglican.org

DIOCESAN RECORD OFFICE
Essex Records Office, Wharf Rd, Chelmsford CM2 6YT *Tel:* 01245 244644
email: ero.enquiry@essexcc.gov.uk

DIOCESAN HOUSE OF RETREAT
Pleshey, Chelmsford CM3 1HA (*Warden* Revd Sheila Coughtrey) *Tel:* 01245 237251
Fax: 01245 237594
email: retreathouse.pleshey@virgin.net
Web: www.retreathousepleshey.com

RURAL DEANS
ARCHDEACONRY OF WEST HAM
Barking and Dagenham Revd Kenneth Gayler, St Mark's Vicarage, 187 Rose Lane, Marks Gate, Romford RM6 5NR *Tel:* 020 8599 0414
Havering Canon John Parsons, Holy Cross Vicarage, 260 Hornchurch Rd, Hornchurch RM11 1PX *Tel:* 01708 447976
Newham Canon Ann Easter, NCRP Ltd, 170 Harold Rd, London E13 0SE *Tel:* 020 8472 2785
email: ann@renewalprogramme.freeserve.co.uk

Redbridge Revd Rosemary Enever, Vicarage, St Andrew's Rd, Ilford IG1 3PE *Tel:* 020 8554 3858
email: rosemaryenever@onetel.com
Waltham Forest Revd Paul Alan Reily, Vicarage, 2B Fairlop Rd, Leytonstone, London E11 1BL
Tel: 020 8539 6361
email: paul@reily.co.uk

ARCHDEACONRY OF HARLOW
Epping Forest Revd Geoffrey Connor, Rectory, Hartland Rd, Epping CM16 4PD
Tel: 01992 572906
email: geoffrey_connor@priest.com
Harlow Canon Tim Potter, The Vicarage, Broomfields, Hatfield Heath, Bishop Stortford CM22 7EH *Tel:* 01279 730288
email: tim.potter@btinternet.com
Ongar Canon Ivy Crawford, Vicarage, Church St, Blackmore, Ingatestone CM4 0RN
Tel: 01277 821464
email: ivycrawford@btinternet.com

ARCHDEACONRY OF SOUTHEND
Brentwood Revd Dr Ian Herbert Jorysz, The Vicarage, Wigley Bush Lane, Brentwood CM14 5QP *Tel:* 01277 212054
email: ian@jorysz.com
Basildon Revd Diane A Deer, The Rectory, Rectory Rd, Basildon SS13 2AA
Tel and Fax: 01268 556874
email: revdiane@blueyonder.co.uk
Chelmsford North Revd Carla I Hampton, The New Vicarage, 1 Glebe Meadow, Chelmsford CM3 1EX *Tel:* 01245 364081
email: carla@hamptonc.freeserve.co.uk
Chelmsford South Revd Andrew T Griffiths, 450 Beehive Lane, Chelmsford CM2 8RN
Tel: 01245 353922
email: andy.griffiths@yahoo.co.uk
Hadleigh Vacancy
Maldon and Dengie Revd Gordon Anderson, Vicarage, Burnham Rd, Southminster CM0 7ES
Tel: 01621 772300
Rochford Revd Christopher Cousins, Rectory, 36 Millview Meadows, Rochford SS4 1EF
Tel: 01702 530621
email: c4cousins@yahoo.com
Southend Revd Rick Williams, St Saviour's Vicarage, 33 Kings Rd, Westcliffe-on-Sea SS0 8LL
Tel: 01702 342920
email: stsaviourwest@aol.com
Thurrock Revd Ed W Hanson, The Rectory, School Lane, Orsett RM16 3JS *Tel:* 01375 891254
email: rector@hobnob.org.uk

ARCHDEACONRY OF COLCHESTER
Braintree Revd Philip Meader, Rectory, Shalford Rd, Rayne, Braintree CM7 6BT
Tel: 01376 320517
email: philip@revdmeader.fsnet.co.uk

Colchester Revd Ian A Hilton, The Rectory, New Town Rd, Colchester CO1 2EF
Tel: 01206 530320
email: ian.hilton@talktalk.net
Dedham and Tey Revd Colin Horseman, Rectory, Ivy Lodge Rd, Great Horkesley, Colchester CO6 4EN
Tel: 01206 241242
email: chiron@care4free.net
Dunmow and Stansted Revd Laurie Bond, Rectory, Parsonage Rd, Takeley, Bishop's Stortford CM22 6QX
Tel: 01279 870837
email: lbd.littlebury@virgin.net
Harwich Revd Andy Colebrooke, Rectory, 21 Malthouse Rd, Mistley, Manningtree CO11 1BY
Tel: 01206 392200
email: a.colebrooke@btinternet.com

Hinckford Revd John Blore, Vicarage, Parsonage St, Halstead CO9 2LD
Tel: 01787 472171
email: john@johnfblore.freeserve.co.uk
Saffron Walden and Newport Revd David R Tomlinson, St John's Vicarage, 8a Victoria Avenue, Grays RM16 2RP
Tel: 01375 372101
email: dtjtgrays@btinternet.com
St Osyth Revd Guy Douglas A Thorburn, St John's Vicarage, Valley Avenue, Great Clacton CO15 4AR
Tel: 01255 423435
*email:*revguy.thorburn@virgin.net
Witham Revd John Martin Suddards, The Rectory, 7 Chipping Dell, Witham CM8 2JX
Tel: 01376 513509
email: suddards@suddards.plus.com

DIOCESE OF CHESTER

Founded in 1541. Cheshire; Wirral; Halton, south of the Mersey; Warrington, south of the Mersey; Trafford, except for an area in the north (MANCHESTER); Stockport, except for a few parishes in the north (MANCHESTER) and in the east (DERBY); the eastern half of Tameside; a few parishes in Derbyshire; a few parishes in Manchester; a few parishes in Flintshire.

Population 1,557,000   Area 1,017 sq m
Full-time Stipendiary Parochial Clergy 231   Benefices 223
Parishes 275   Churches 370
www.chester.anglican.org
Overseas link province: Melanesia.

BISHOP (40th)
Rt Revd Dr Peter Robert Forster, Bishop's House, Abbey Square, Chester CH1 2JD [1996]
Tel: 01244 350864
Fax: 01244 314187
email: bpchester@chester.anglican.org
[Peter Cestr:]
Bishop's Chaplain Canon Christopher Burkett (*same address*)
Tel: 01244 350864

SUFFRAGAN BISHOPS
BIRKENHEAD Rt Revd (Gordon) Keith Sinclair, Bishop's Lodge, 67 Bidston Rd, Prenton CH43 6TR [2007]
Tel: 0151 652 2741
Fax: 0151 651 2330
email: bpbirkenhead@chester.anglican.org
STOCKPORT Rt Revd Robert Atwell, Bishop's Lodge, Back Lane, Dunham Town, Altrincham WA14 4SG [2008]
Tel: 0161 928 5611
Fax: 0161 929 0692
email: bpstockport@chester.anglican.org

HONORARY ASSISTANT BISHOPS
Rt Revd William Alaha Pwaisiho, Rectory, Church Lane, Gawsworth, Macclesfield, SK11 9RJ
Tel: 01260 223201
Rt Revd Colin Frederick Bazley, 121 Brackenwood Rd, Higher Bebington, Wirral CH63 2LU
Tel: 0151 608 1193
Rt Revd Geoffrey Turner, 23 Lang Lane, West Kirby, Wirral CH48 5HG   *Tel:* 0151 625 8504
Rt Revd Alan Chesters, 64 Hallfields Rd, Tarvin, Chester CH3 8ET   *Tel:* 01829 740825

CATHEDRAL CHURCH OF CHRIST AND THE BLESSED VIRGIN MARY
Dean Very Revd Professor Gordon Ferguson McPhate, Deanery, 7 Abbey St, Chester CH1 2JF [2002]
Tel: 01244 500971
email: dean@chestercathedral.com
Cathedral Office 12 Abbey Square, Chester CH1 2HU
Tel: 01244 324756
Fax: 01244 341110
email: office@chestercathedral.com
Web: www.chestercathedral.com

Vice-Dean and Canon Chancellor Canon Dr Trevor Dennis, 13 Abbey St, Chester CH1 2JF [1993]
Tel: 01244 314408
email: canon.dennis@chestercathedral.com
Canon Precentor
Canon Chris Humphries, 9 Abbey St, Chester CH1 2JF [2005]   *Tel:* 01244 500967
email: canon.humphries@chestercathedral.com
Canons Residentiary
Canon Christopher Burkett, 5 Abbey Green, Chester CH1 2JH [2000]   *Tel:* 01244 347500
email: bpchaplain@chester.anglican.org
Canon Dr Judy Hunt, 5 Abbey St, Chester CH1 2JF [2003]   *Tel:* 01244 500965
email: canon.hunt@chestercathedral.com
Chief Executive, Administrator and Chapter Clerk Mrs Annette Moor, Cathedral Office
Tel: 01244 500962
email: chief.executive@chestercathedral.com
Director of Music Mr Philip Rushforth, Cathedral Office   *Tel:* 01244 500974
email: philip.rushforth@chestercathedral.com
Surveyor of the Fabric Vacancy

ARCHDEACONS
CHESTER Ven Donald Allister, Church House, Lower Lane, Aldford, Chester CH3 6HP [2002]
Tel: 01244 681937 ext 253
Fax: 01244 620456
email: donald.allister@chester.anglican.org
MACCLESFIELD Ven Richard Gillings, 5, Robin's Lane, Bramhall, Stockport SK7 2PE [1994]
Tel: 0161 439 2254
Fax: 0161 439 0878
email: richard.gillings@chester.anglican.org

CONVOCATION (MEMBERS OF THE HOUSE OF CLERGY OF THE GENERAL SYNOD)
Proctors for Clergy
Ven Donald Allister
Canon David Felix
Canon Dr Judy Hunt
Revd Robert Munro
Revd Marc Wolverson

MEMBERS OF THE HOUSE OF LAITY OF THE GENERAL SYNOD
Prof Tony Berry
Canon Dr David Blackmore
Dr Graham Campbell
Mrs Jenny Dunlop
Mr John Freeman
Mrs Lois Haslam
Mr Kenneth Hill
Mr John Scrivener

DIOCESAN OFFICERS
Dioc Secretary Canon Dr John Mason, Church House, Lower Lane, Aldford, Chester CH3 6HP
Tel: 01244 681973 ext 249
Fax: 01244 620456
email: john.mason@chester.anglican.org
Chancellor of Diocese His Honour Judge David Turner, c/o Friars, White Friars, Chester CH1 1XS
Registrar of Diocese and Bishop's Legal Secretary Mrs Helen McFall, Friars, White Friars, Chester CH1 1XS
Tel: 01244 321066
Fax: 01244 312582
email: helen.mcfall@bclaw.co.uk

DIOCESAN ORGANIZATIONS
Diocesan Office Church House, Lower Lane, Aldford, Chester CH3 6HP   *Tel:* 01244 681973
Fax: 01244 620456
email: churchhouse@chester.anglican.org

ADMINISTRATION
Dioc Synod (Vice-President, House of Clergy) Revd Dr Jonathan Gibbs
(Vice-President, House of Laity) Canon Dr David Blackmore
(Secretary) Canon Dr John Mason, Church House
Board of Finance (Chairman) Canon Elizabeth Renshaw MBE
(Secretary) Canon Dr John Mason *(as above)*
Director of Finance Mr George Colville, Church House
Houses Committee Mr George Colville *(as above)*
Dioc Surveyor Mr Michael Cram, Church House
Pastoral Committee Canon Dr John Mason *(as above)*
Designated Officer Canon Dr John Mason *(as above)*

CHURCHES
Advisory Committee for the Care of Churches (Chairman) Canon John Briggs; *(Executive Secretary)* Mr Richard Mortimore, Church House
Redundant Churches Uses Committee Mr Richard Mortimore *(as above)*

EDUCATION
Director of Education Mr Jeff Turnbull, Church House
Children Mr David Bell, Church House
Youth Mr Mark Montgomery, Church House

MISSION AND MINISTRY
Director of Mission and Ministry Canon Dr Judy Hunt, Church House
email: judy.hunt@chester.anglican.org
Ministry Development Officer Revd Simon Chesters, Church House
email: simon.chesters@chester.anglican.org
Director of Ordinands Revd Ray Samuels, Bishop's House, Abbey Square, Chester CH1 2JD
Tel: 01244 346945
email: ray.samuels@chester.anglican.org
Parish Mission Development Officer Revd Richard Burton, Church House
email: richardburtonpmdo@yahoo.co.uk
Director of Studies for Ordinands Revd Gary O'Neill, 10 Neston Close, Helsby WA6 0FH
Tel: 01928 723327
email: gary.oneill@chester.anglican.org
Adviser in Christian Giving Mr Martin Smith, Churh House
email: martin.smith@chester.anglican.org
Rural Officer Revd Dr John Reader, Vicarage, Chelford, Macclesfield SK11 9AH
Tel: 01625 861231
email: drjohnreader@hotmail.co.uk
Officer for NSMs Canon Prof Roger Yates, 3 Racecourse Park, Wilmslow SK9 5LU
Tel: 01625 520246
Advisers for Women in Ministry Revd Anne Davis, Rectory, Church Lane, Woodchurch, Wirral CH49 7LS   *Tel:* 0151 677 5352
email: anne@revannedavis.wanadoo.co.uk
Revd Helen Chantry, Rectory, Nantwich CW5 5RQ   *Tel:* 01270 625286
Clergy Widows and Retirement Officers (Chester Archdeaconry) Revd Beth Gardner, Weston Vicarage, 225 Heath Rd South, Weston, Runcorn WA7 4LY   *Tel:* 01928 573798
(Macclesfield Archdeaconry) Revd Ian Sparks, Vicarage, 25 Wilwick Lane, Macclesfield SK11 8RS   *Tel:* 01625 424185
Director of Studies for Reader Trainees Dr James Harding, Church House
email: james.harding@chester.anglican.org
Reader Training Officers Revd Rob Green, 122 Cavendish Rd, Hazel Grove, Stockport SK7 6JH
Tel: 01625 858680
email: rob.green122@ntlworld.com
Warden of Readers Revd John Knowles, Vicarage, Wilmslow Rd, Woodford, Stockport SK7 1RH
Tel: 0161 439 2286
email: john.knowles2@virgin.net
IME 4 – 7 Officer Vacancy
Evangelism and Lay Training Officer Revd Ian Enticott, St Philip's Vicarage, Chester Rd, Kelsall, Tarporley CW6 0SA
Tel: 01829 751472
email: ian.enticott@tiscali.co.uk
CME Officer Revd David Herbert, St Andrew's Vicarage, Church St, Tarvin, Chester CH3 8EB
Tel: 01829 740354

Warden of Pastoral Workers Vacancy
Pastoral Worker Training Officer Revd Jane Stephenson, The Mount, Hobb Hill, Tilston SY14 7DU   *Tel:* 01829 250249
          email: stephenson256@btinternet.com
Senior Industrial Missioner Vacancy
Adviser in Christian Spirituality Revd Donald Brockbank, Church House

LITURGICAL

Chairman Ven Richard Gillings (*as above*)
Secretary Revd Donald Brockbank, Church House
Diocesan Worship Adviser Vacancy

MISSIONARY AND ECUMENICAL

Partners in World Mission Mr John Freeman, Stable Court, 20A Leigh Way, Weaverham, Northwich CW8 3PR   *Tel:* 01606 852872
County Ecumenical Officer and Secretary Mr Mark Thompson, 81 Forge Fields, Sandbach CW11 3RD   *Tel:* 01270 750431
          email: impress@clara.net
Dioc Ecumenical Officer Vacancy

PRESS AND PUBLICATIONS

Dioc Communications Officer Mr Stephen Regan, Church House or 07764 615069 (Mobile)
Editor of Dioc News Mr Stephen Regan (*as above*)
          email: dco@chester.anglican.org
Editor of Dioc Year Book Canon Dr John Mason (*as above*)

DIOCESAN RECORD OFFICE

Cheshire Records Office, Duke St, Chester CH1 2DN *County Archivist* Mr J. Pepler
          Tel: 01244 603391

SOCIAL RESPONSIBILITY

Director of Social Responsibility
Mrs Janice Mason, Church House
          email: janice.mason@chester.anglican.org

RURAL DEANS
ARCHDEACONRY OF CHESTER

Birkenhead Canon Ian Davenport, Oxton Vicarage, 8 Wexford Rd, Oxton, Prenton CH43 9TB   *Tel:* 0151 652 1149
Chester Revd Bob Toan, St Michael's Vicarage, 22 Plas Newton Lane, Newton, Chester CH2 1PA
          Tel: 01244 319677

Frodsham Revd Sue Wilkins, Vicarage, 6 Kirkstone Crescent, Beechwood, Runcorn WA7 3JQ
          Tel: 01928 713101
          email: suewilkins@hallwoodlep.fsnet.co.uk
Great Budworth Revd Elaine Chegwin Hall, Vicarage, Stretton, Warrington WA4 4NT
          Tel: 01925 730276
          email: petera.hall@care4free.net
Malpas Canon Leslie Thomas, Vicarage, Harthill Rd, Burwardsley, Tattenhall, Chester CH3 9NU
          Tel: 01829 771225
          email: sandstone@tesco.net
Middlewich Revd Ian Bishop, Rectory, 37 Queens St, Middlewich CW10 9AR   *Tel:* 01606 833124
          email: ian@bishopfamily.fsnet.co.uk
Wallasey Revd Frank Cain, Vicarage, 14 Albion St, Wallasey CH45 9LF   *Tel:* 0151 639 5844
Wirral North Gillian Rossiter, St John's Vicarage, 142 Birkenhead Rd, Meols, Wirral CH47 0LF
          Tel: 0151 632 1661
          email: johnsthebaptistchurch@btinternet.com
Wirral South Revd Dr Gordon Welch, 6 St James Ave, Upton, Chester CH2 1NA
          Tel: 01244 382196

ARCHDEACONRY OF MACCLESFIELD

Bowden Canon John Sutton, Vicarage, 12 Thorley Lane Timperley, Altrincham, Cheshire WA15 7AZ   *Tel:* 0161 980 4330
          email: jfsuttontimp@aol.com
Chadkirk Revd Dr Peter Jenner, The Vicarage, Church Rd, Mellor, Stockport SK6 5LX
          Tel: 0161 484 5079
          email: jennerfamily@btinternet.com
Cheadle Canon Howard Eales, All Saints Vicarage, 27 Church Rd, Cheadle Hulme, Cheadle SK8 7JL   *Tel:* 0161 485 3455
Congleton Vacancy
Knutsford Canon Prof Roger Yates, 3 Racecourse Park, Wilmslow SK9 5LU   *Tel:* 01625 520246
          email: raycandoc@yahoo.co.uk
Macclesfield Revd Taffy Davies, St James's Vicarage, Sutton, Macclesfield SK11 0DS
          Tel: 01260 252228
          email: taffy@parishpump.co.uk
Mottram Canon Stephen Wilson, Vicarage, 85 Edna St, Hyde SK14 1DR   *Tel:* 0161 367 8787
          email: hydes@fish.co.uk
Nantwich Canon Bill Baker, Vicarage, 14 Dane Bank Ave, Crewe CW2 8AA   *Tel:* 01270 569000
Stockport Canon Alan Bell, 7 Corbar Rd, Mile End, Stockport SK2 6EP   *Tel:* 0161 456 0918
          email: vicaralanbell@aol.com

DIOCESE OF CHICHESTER

Founded in 1070, formerly called Selsey (AD 681). West Sussex, except for one parish in the north (GUILDFORD); East Sussex, except for one parish in the north (ROCHESTER); one parish in Kent.

Population 1,527,000   Area 1,459 sq m
Full-time Stipendiary Parochial Clergy 282   Benefices 297
Parishes 382   Churches 512
www.diochi.org.uk
Overseas link dioceses: IDWAL (Inter-Diocesan West Africa Link) –
Ghana, Sierra Leone, Cameroon, Guinea (West Africa).

BISHOP (103rd)
Rt Revd John William Hind, The Palace, Chichester PO19 1PY [2001]   *Tel:* 01243 782161
Fax: 01243 531332
email: bishchichester@diochi.org.uk
[John Cicestr:]
Domestic Chaplain Revd Ian Gibson, The Palace (*as above*)
email: chaplainchichester@diochi.org.uk

AREA BISHOPS
HORSHAM (until Feb 2009) Rt Revd Lindsay Goodall Urwin OGS, Bishop's House, 21 Guildford Rd, Horsham RH12 1LU [1993]
Tel: 01403 211139
Fax: 01403 217349
email: bishhorsham@diochi.org.uk
Lay Chaplain Vacancy
LEWES Rt Revd Wallace Benn, Bishop's Lodge, 16a Prideaux Rd, Eastbourne BN21 2NB [1997]
Tel: 01323 648462
Fax: 01323 641514
email: bishlewes@diochi.org.uk
Chaplain Revd David Farey

HONORARY ASSISTANT BISHOPS
Rt Revd Christopher Charles Luxmoore, 42 Willowbed Drive, Chichester PO19 8JB [1991]
Tel: 01243 784680
Rt Revd Michael Eric Marshall, Upper Chelsea Rectory, 97a Cadogan Lane, London SW1X 9DU [1992]   *Tel:* 020 7235 3383
Rt Revd Michael Richard John Manktelow, 14 Little London, Chichester PO19 1NZ [1994]
Tel: 01243 531096
Rt Revd David Peter Wilcox, 4 The Court, Hoo Gardens, Willingdon, Eastbourne BN20 9AX [1995]   *Tel:* 01323 506108
Rt Revd Kenneth Barham, Rosewood, Canadia Rd, Battle TN33 0LR [2007]   *Tel:* 01424 773073

CATHEDRAL CHURCH OF THE HOLY TRINITY
Dean Very Revd Nicholas Frayling, The Deanery, Chichester PO19 1PX [2002]
Tel: 01243 812484 (Office)
01243 812494 (Home)
Fax: 01243 812499
email: dean@chichestercathedral.org.uk
Cathedral Office The Royal Chantry, Cathedral Cloisters, Chichester PO19 1PX
Tel: 01243 782595
Fax: 01243 812499
email: reception@chichestercathedral.org.uk
Precentor Canon Timothy Schofield, 4 Vicars' Close, Chichester PO19 1PT [2006]
Tel: 01243 813589
Fax: 01243 812499
email: precentor@chichestercathedral.org.uk
Chancellor Canon Dr Anthony Cane, The Residentiary, 2 Canon Lane, Chichester PO19 1PX [2007]   *Tel:* 01243 813594
Fax: 01243 812499
email: chancellor@chichestercathedral.org.uk
Treasurer Canon Peter Kefford, 12 St Martin's Square, Chichester PO19 1NR [2001]
Tel: 01243 783509
Fax: 01243 812499
email: Peter_Kefford@hotmail.com
Priest-Vicar Canon David Nason, 1 St Richard's Walk, Chichester PO19 1QA   *Tel:* 01243 775615
Fax: 01243 812499
Communar Commodore David Mowlam RN, Cathedral Office   *Tel:* 01243 812489
Fax: 01243 812499
email: communar@chichestercathedral.org.uk
Cathedral Organist and Master of the Choristers Miss Sarah Baldock, 2 St Richard's Walk, Chichester PO19 1QA   *Tel:* 01243 812486
Fax: 01243 812499
email: organist@chichestercathedral.org.uk

ARCHDEACONS
CHICHESTER Ven Douglas McKittrick, 2 Yorklands, Dyke Rd Ave, Hove BN3 6RW [2002]
Tel: 01273 505330
Fax: 01273 421041
email: archchichester@diochi.org.uk

HORSHAM Ven Roger Combes, 3 Danehurst Crescent, Horsham RH13 5HS [2003]
Tel: 01403 262710
Fax: 01403 210778
email: archhorsham@diochi.org.uk
LEWES AND HASTINGS Ven Philip Hugh Jones, 27 The Avenue, Lewes BN7 1QT [2005]
Tel: 01273 479530
Fax: 01273 476529
email: archlandh@diochi.org.uk

CONVOCATION (MEMBERS OF THE HOUSE OF CLERGY OF THE GENERAL SYNOD)
Proctors for Clergy
Canon Gavin Ashenden (elected by universities)
Canon Hugh Atherstone
Revd Ian Chandler
Revd Alastair Cutting
Revd James Houghton
Ven Douglas McKittrick
Revd Mark Payne

MEMBERS OF THE HOUSE OF LAITY OF THE GENERAL SYNOD
Mr John Ashwin
Mrs Lorna Ashworth
Mr John Booth
Mr Kevin Carey
Mrs Mary Nagel
Mr John Pope
Mr Mike Streeter
Mr Jacob Vince

DIOCESAN OFFICERS
Dioc Secretary Mr Jonathan Prichard (until end March 2009), Diocesan Church House, 211 New Church Rd, Hove BN3 4ED
Tel: 01273 421021
Fax: 01273 421041
email: diocsec@diochi.org.uk
Chancellor of Diocese Chancellor Mark Hill, Pump Court Chambers, 3 Pump Court, Temple, London EC4Y 7AJ
Registrar of Diocese and Bishop's Legal Secretary Mr John Stapleton, Thomas Eggar, The Corn Exchange, Baffins Lane, Chichester PO19 4GE
Tel: 01243 813238
Fax: 01243 775640
email: john.stapleton@thomaseggar.com

DIOCESAN ORGANIZATIONS
Diocesan Office Diocesan Church House, 211 New Church Rd, Hove BN3 4ED
Tel: 01273 421021
Fax: 01273 421041
email: admin@diochi.org.uk

ADMINISTRATION
Dioc Synod (Chairman, House of Clergy) Canon Hugh Atherstone
(Chairman, House of Laity) Dr B. Hanson
Dioc Fund and Board of Finance (Incorporated) (Chairman) Dr Clive Dilloway; *(Secretary)* Mr Jonathan Prichard *(as above)*

Finance Committee Mr Jonathan Prichard *(as above)*
Stipends Committee (Secretary) Mr Jonathan Prichard *(as above)*
Parsonages Committee (Property Director) Mr Andrew Craft, Dioc Church House
Pastoral Committee (Secretary) Mr Steven Sleight, Dioc Church House

CHURCHES
Advisory Committee for the Care of Churches (Chairman) Mr John Ebdon, c/o Dioc Church House; *(Secretary)* Mr Steven Sleight *(as above)*
email: steven.sleight@diochi.org.uk

EDUCATION AND TRAINING
Schools
Adviser (Director of Education) Mr Jeremy Taylor, Dioc Church House
email: schools@diochi.org.uk
Schools Administration Mrs Elizabeth Yates, Dioc Church House
Schools Support Mr Martin Lloyd, Dioc Church House
Children and Young People
Adviser for Work with Children and Youth Mr Alistair Campbell, Dioc Church House
Tel: 01273 425694
Youth Officer Revd Stephen Gallagher, Dioc Church House
Education and Training of Adults
Adviser Miss Joy Gilliver, Dioc Church House
Readers Board (Hon Secretary) Mrs Patricia Deane

MINISTRY
Bishop's Adviser for Ministry Canon Peter Kefford, 12 St Martin's Square, Chichester PO19 1NR
Tel: 01243 783509
Diocesan Director of Ordinands Canon Dr Philip Bourne, 6 Patcham Grange, Brighton BN1 8UR
Tel: 01273 564057
Vocations Officer Revd Moira Wickens, Kingston Buci Rectory, Shoreham-by-Sea BN43 6EB
Tel: 01273 592591
Continuing Ministerial Education Officer Canon Andrew Mayes, St Wulfran's Rectory, 43 Ainsworth Ave, Ovingdean, Brighton BN2 7BG
Tel: 01273 303633
Post-Ordination Training Canon Andrew Mayes *(as above)*
Training for the Non-Stipendiary Ministry Canon Andrew Mayes *(as above)*
Programme Director, Initial Ministerial Education 4-7: The Revd Canon Dr Anthony Cane, The Residentiary, 2 Canons Lane, Chichester, PO19 1PX
Tel: 01243 813954
email: chancellor@chichestercathedral.org.uk
Vocations Consultants
Revd David Ashton, St Richard's Rectory, 7 Priory Rd, Langney, Eastbourne BN23 7AX
Tel: 01323 761158

Chichester

35

Revd Craig Barber, St Barnabas Vicarage, 2 Crawley Lane, Pound Hill, Crawley RH10 7EB
Tel: 01293 513398
Revd Alison Bowman, 21 Fair Meadow, Rye TN31 7NL
Tel: 01797 225769
Canon Trevor Buxton, All Saints Vicarage, All Saints Lane, Sidley, Bexhill-on-Sea TN39 5HA
Tel: 01424 221071
Revd Roger Caswell, St Mary's Vicarage, 34 Fitzalan Rd, Littlehampton BN17 5ET
Tel: 01903 724410
Revd Brian Cook, Rectory, 86 Belgrave Rd, Seaford BN25 2HE
Tel: 01323 892964
Revd Alastair Cutting, Vicarage, Copthorne, Crawley RH10 3RD
Tel: 01342 712063
Revd Su Marshall, Rectory, West End, Herstmonceux, Hailsham BN27 4NY
Tel: 01323 833124
Revd Steve Daughtery, Rectory, Southover, Lewes BN7 1HT
Tel: 01273 472018
Mr John Ellis, 15 Victoria Way, East Grinstead RH19 4RX
Tel: 01342 325156
The Revd Su Marshall, The Rectory, West End, Herstmonceux, Hailsham BN27 4NY
Tel: 01323 833124
Mr Charles Merchant, Oakside, Shrub Lane, Burwash TN19 7EB
Tel: 01435 882360
Revd Lucy Murdoch, Vicarage, 39 Lydd Rd, Camber TN31 7RJ
Tel: 01797 225386
Revd Martin Onions, Vicarage, 35a Church St, Willingdon, Eastbourne BN20 9HR
Tel: 01323 502079
Mrs Jenny Peleg, 5 Piltdown Road, Brighton BN2 5LE
Tel: 01273 625338
Revd Tim Peskett, Rectory, 24 Limmer Lane, Felpham, Bognor Regis PO22 7ET
Tel: 01243 842522
Revd Paul Rampton, St Andrew's Vicarage, Steyning BN44 3YL
Tel: 01243 842522
Sister Alison Rickard, 55 Brittany Rd, St Leonards-on-Sea TN38 0RD
Tel: 01424 423367
Revd Rebecca Swyer, Rectory, 5 The Twitten, Albourne, Hassocks BN6 9DF
Tel: 01273 832129
Revd Norman Taylor, Durrington Vicarage, Bramble Lane, Durrington, Worthing BN13 3JE
Tel: 01903 693499
Revd Simon Taylor, 21 Anglesey Close, Broadfield, Crawley RH11 9HG
Tel: 01293 552287
Revd Nicholas Wetherall, Vicarage, Broad St, Cuckfield, Haywards Heath RH17 5LL
Tel: 01444 454007
Revd Christine Wilson, 12 Compton Avenue, Goring-by-Sea Worthing BN12 4UJ
Tel: 07718482378

MISSION AND RENEWAL
Adviser Revd Dr John Twisleton, Dioc Church House
Diocesan Evangelist Captain Gordon Banks, Dioc Church House
Christian Stewardship Officer Mr Ian Clark, Dioc Church House

Overseas Council (Secretary) Revd M. Payne, Vicarage, Vicarage Lane, Scaynes Hill, Haywards Heath RH17 7PB
Tel: 01444 831265

ECUMENICAL
European Ecumenical Committee (Chairman) Vacancy
Dioc Ecumenical Co-ordinator Mr Ian Chisnall
Tel: 07976 811654 (Mobile)
email: ianpchisnall@aol.com

LITURGICAL
Liturgy Consultant Revd Ian Forrester, Dioc Church House
Music Consultant Revd Ian Forrester (*as above*)

CHURCH IN SOCIETY
Adviser Revd Barry North, Dioc Church House
Association for Family Support Work, Central Office, c/o Dioc Church House

PRESS AND PUBLICATIONS
Communications Officer Revd David Guest, Dioc Church House
Tel: 01273 421021
email: media@diochi.org.uk

DIOCESAN RECORD OFFICES
East Sussex Mrs Elizabeth Hughes, *County Archivist*, The Maltings, Castle Precincts, Lewes BN7 1YT
Tel: 01273 482356
West Sussex Mr R. Childs *County Archivist*, County Records Office, County Hall, Chichester PO19 1RN
Tel: 01243 533911

RURAL DEANS
ARCHDEACONRY OF CHICHESTER
Arundel and Bognor Vacancy
Brighton Canon Neil Milmine, All Saints Vicarage, 12 Church Hill, Patcham, Brighton BN1 8YE
Tel: 01273 552157
email: neil@milmine.freeserve.co.uk
Chichester Revd Richard Hunt, Rectory, Tower House, Chichester PO19 1QN
Tel: 01243 531624
Hove Revd Phil R. Moon, 82 Holmes Ave, Hove BN3 7LD
Tel: 01273 732821
Worthing Revd Jo K. Gavigan, 56 The Boulevard, Worthing BN13 1LA
Tel: 01903 249463

ARCHDEACONRY OF HORSHAM
Cuckfield Revd Christopher Breeds, Vicarage, Wivelsfield, Haywards Heath RH17 7RD
Tel: 01444 471783
East Grinstead Canon Clive Everett-Allen, St Swithun's Vicarage, Church Lane, East Grinstead RH19 3BB
Tel: 01342 323439
email: revclive@aol.com
Horsham Revd R. C. Jackson, Vicarage, Cox Green, Rudgwick, Horsham RH12 3DD
Tel: 01403 822127
email: RJac187233@aol.com
Hurst Revd Chris J. Collison, Vicarage, Church Lane, Henfield BN5 9NY
Tel: 01273 492017

Midhurst Revd Martin Lane, The Rectory, Harting, Petersfield GU31 5QB
Tel: 01730 825234
email: martinjlane@btinternet.com

Petworth (acting) Revd Simon F. E. Newham, Vicarage, Glebe Way, Wisborough Green RH14 0DZ
Tel: 01403 700339
email: simon@fenewham.plus.com

Storrington Revd Paul Welch, Rectory, 2 London Rd, Pulborough RH20 1AP
Tel: 01798 875773
email: paul.welch@virgin.net

Westbourne Ven John J. Holliman, Vicarage, Funtingdon, Chichester PO18 9LH
Tel: 01243 575257
email: venjjh@aol.com

ARCHDEACONRY OF LEWES AND HASTINGS

Battle and Bexhill Revd David R. Frost, Vicarage, 67 Woodsgate Park, Bexhill-on-Sea TN39 4DL
Tel: 01424 211186
email: david@drfrost.worldonline.co.uk

Dallington Revd Stan Tomalin, 1 Barn Close, Hailsham, BN27 1TL
Tel: 01323 846680
email: stantomalin@googlemail.com

Eastbourne Revd Robert Lovatt, All Saints Vicarage, 1a Jevington Gardens, Eastbourne BN21 4HR
Tel: 01323 410033

Hastings Revd Chris H. Key, St Helen's Rectory, 266 Elphinstone Rd, Hastings TN34 2AG
Tel: 01424 425012
email: chriskey@st-helens-ore.freeserve.co.uk

Lewes and Seaford Revd Geoffrey Daw, The Rectory, 14 Lockitt Way, Lewes Kingston
Tel: 01273 473665
email: Geoffrey.Daw@btinternet.com

Rotherfield Revd Jeremy James, Vicarage, High St, Wadhurst TN5 6AA
Tel: 01892 782083
email: jeremy@jrjames.freeserve.co.uk

Rye Revd Hugh Mosley, St Mary's Rectory, Gungarden, Rye TN31 7HH
Tel: 01797 222430
email: hugh@rabbitwarren13.freeserve.co.uk

Uckfield Revd Phil Hodgins, Rectory, East Hoathly, Lewes BN8 6EG
Tel: 01825 840270

Re-founded in 1918. Coventry; Warwickshire, except for small areas in the north (BIRMINGHAM) and south-west (GLOUCESTER) and one parish in the south (OXFORD); an area of Solihull.

Population 783,000   Area 686 sq m
Full-time Stipendiary Parochial Clergy 104   Benefices 134
Parishes 197   Churches 241
www.coventry.anglican.org

BISHOP
Rt Revd Christopher John Cocksworth, Bishop's House, 23 Davenport Rd, Coventry CV5 6PW [2008]   *Tel:* 024 7667 2244
Fax: 024 7671 3271
email: bishcov@btconnect.com
Personal Assistant Christine Camfield (*same address*)
email: christine.camfield@btconnect.com
Secretary Mrs Maureen Prett (*same address*)

SUFFRAGAN BISHOP
WARWICK Rt Revd John Ronald Angus Stroyan, Warwick House, 139 Kenilworth Rd, Coventry CV4 7AP [2005]   *Tel:* 024 7641 2627
email: Bishop.Warwick@covcofe.org
Personal Assistant Mrs Kerry Vanston-Rumney
email: kerry.rumney@covcofe.org

ASSISTANT HONORARY BISHOP
Rt Revd David Evans, Alderminster Vicarage, Stratford-upon-Avon CV37 8PE [2008]
Tel: 01789 450 198
email: Bishop.DRJEvans@virgin.net

CATHEDRAL CHURCH OF ST MICHAEL
Dean Very Revd John Dudley Irvine, Coventry Cathedral, 1 Hill Top, Coventry CV1 5AB [2001]
Tel: 024 7652 1227
email: john.irvine@coventrycathedral.org.uk
Cathedral Offices 1 Hill Top, Coventry CV1 5AB
Tel: 024 7652 1200
Fax: 024 7652 1220
Web: www.coventrycathedral.org
Canons Residentiary and Senior Staff
Canon Precentor Canon Adrian Daffern (*same address*) [2003]   *Tel:* 024 7652 1225
email: adrian.daffern@coventrycathedral.org.uk
Canon for Mission Canon Yvonne Richmond (*same address*) [2006]   *Tel:* 024 7652 1223
Fax: 024 7652 1220
email:
yvonne.richmond@coventrycathedral.org.uk
Canon for Reconciliation Ministry Vacancy

Cathedral Administrator and Director of Finance Mrs Catherine Bartlem, Coventry Cathedral, 1 Hill Top, Coventry CV1 5AB   *Tel:* 024 7652 1226
email: catherine.bartlem@
coventrycathedral.org.uk
Director of International Ministry Revd Martin Hayward (*same address*) [2005]   *Tel:* 024 7652 1205
email: martin.hayward@coventrycathedral.org.uk
Canons Theologian
Canon Dr Christopher Lamb, Brookside Avenue, Wellesbourne, Warwick CV35 9RZ [1992]
Tel: 01789 842060
email: lamb@easynet.co.uk
Canon Tim Dakin, Church Mission Society, PO Box 1799, Oxford OX4 9BN [2001]
Tel: 0845 620 1799
Canon Professor Ben Quash, Department of Theology and Religious Studies, King's College London, Strand, London WC2R 2LS [2004]
Tel: 020 7848 2339/2073
Canon Professor Richard Farnell, Coventry University, Priory St, Coventry CV1 5FB [2006]
Tel: 024 7688 7688
Clerk to the College of Canons Mr Roger Pascall, 1 The Quadrant, Coventry CV1 2DW
Tel: 024 7663 1212
Director of Music Mr Kerry Beaumont (*same address*)   *Tel:* 024 7652 1219
email: kerry.beaumont@coventrycathedral.org.uk

ARCHDEACONS
COVENTRY Ven Ian Watson, 9 Armorial Rd, Coventry CV3 6GH [2007]
Tel: 024 7641 7750 (Home)
024 7652 1337 (Office)
email: ian.watson@covcofe.org
WARWICK Ven Michael Paget-Wilkes, 10 Northumberland Rd, Leamington Spa CV32 6HA [1990]   *Tel:* 01926 313337 (Home)
024 7652 1337 (Office)
email: michael.pagetwilkes@covcofe.org

CONVOCATION (MEMBERS OF THE HOUSE OF CLERGY OF THE GENERAL SYNOD)
Proctors for Clergy
Revd Mark Bratton
Revd Elizabeth Dyke
Revd Mark Beach

MEMBERS OF THE HOUSE OF LAITY OF THE GENERAL SYNOD
Mrs Kay Dyer
Mr Ian O' Hara
Dr David Tweedie

DIOCESAN OFFICERS
Dioc Secretary Mr Simon Lloyd, Cathedral and Diocesan Offices, 1 Hill Top, Coventry CV1 5AB   *Tel:* 024 7652 1200
Fax: 024 7652 1330
email: simon.lloyd@covcofe.org
Chancellor of Diocese Chancellor W. M. Gage, The Royal Courts of Justice, Strand, London WC2 2LL
Registrar of Diocese and Bishop's Legal Secretary Mr David Dumbleton, Rotherham & Co, 8 The Quadrant, Coventry CV1 2EL   *Tel:* 024 7622 7331

DIOCESAN ORGANIZATIONS
Diocesan Office Cathedral and Diocesan Offices, 1 Hill Top, Coventry CV1 5AB   *Tel:* 024 7652 1200
Fax: 024 7652 1330
Web: www.coventry.anglican.org

ADMINISTRATION
Dioc Synod (Chairman, House of Clergy) Revd Canon Richard Williams
(Chairman, House of Laity) Mr Graham Wright
(Secretary) Mr Simon Lloyd, Dioc Office
Board of Finance (Chairman) Canon Ian Francis, The Firs, Main St, Frankton, Rugby CV23 9NZ
Tel: 01926 632918
email: ian@frankton.org
(Secretary) Mr Simon Lloyd *(as above)*
(Asst Secretary) Mr Andrew Roberts
email: andrew.roberts@covlec.org
Systems Development Manager Mr Phil Ash
email: phil.ash@covlec.org
Financial Secretary Mr Tim Oglesby, Church House   *email:* tim.oglesby@covlec.org
Parsonages Committee Mrs Nicky Caunt, Church House   *email:* nicky.caunt@covlec.org
Trustees Mr David Dumbleton, Rotherham & Co, 8 The Quadrant, Coventry CV1 2EL
Tel: 024 7622 7331
Pastoral Committee Mr Andrew Roberts *(as above)*
Designated Officer Mr Simon Lloyd *(as above)*
Dioc Directory Editor Mr Phil Ash *(as above)*

CHURCHES
Advisory Committee for the Care of Churches Vacancy, Cathedral and Diocesan Offices
email: cov.dac@covcofe.org

EDUCATION
Dioc Director Mrs Linda Wainscot, 1 Hill Top, Coventry CV1 5AB   *Tel:* 024 7652 1200
email: linda.wainscot@covcofe.org

Religious Education and Spirituality and Schools Officer Mrs Lizzie McWhirter, 1 Hill Top, Coventry CV1 5AB   *Tel:* 024 7652 1200

MINISTRY
Director and Exec Officer Canon Roger Spiller, 1 Hill Top, Coventry CV1 5AB   *Tel:* 024 7652 1200
email: roger.spiller@covcofe.org
Dioc Adviser for Women's Ministry Revd Katrina Scott, Willenhall Vicarage, Robin Hood Rd, Coventry CV3 3AY   *Tel:* 024 7630 3266
email: krgscott@hotmail.com
Continuing Ministerial Education Adviser Revd Dr Richard Cooke, 1 Hill Top, Coventry CV1 5AB
Tel: 024 7652 1200
Readers (Hon Registrar) Mr Rupert Allen
Tel: 024 7632 5372
email: rallen893@ntlworld.com

PARISH DEVELOPMENT AND EVANGELISM
Director Vacancy, Cathedral and Diocesan Offices, 1 Hill Top, Coventry CV1 5AB
Tel: 024 7652 1200
email: roger.morris@covcofe.org

STEWARDSHIP
Dioc Adviser Mr Graham Wright, 1 Mayfield Drive, Kenilworth CV8 2SW   *Tel:* 01926 864991
email: grahampjw@aol.com

PRESS AND PUBLICATIONS
Dioc Communications Officer Revd Mervyn Roberts, Vicarage, 24 Mallory Rd, Bishops Tachbrook, Leamington Spa CV33 9QX
Tel: 01926 426922
email: mervyn.roberts@covcofe.org

DIOCESAN RECORD OFFICE
Warwickshire County Record Office, Priory Park, Cape Rd, Warwick CV34 4JS *Head of Heritage and Culture (Archives) Services* Ms Caroline Sampson
Tel: 01926 738959
Fax: 01926 738969
email: recordoffice@warwickshire.gov.uk

SOCIAL RESPONSIBILITY
Director Revd John Hall, Cathedral and Diocesan Offices, 1 Hill Top, Coventry CV1 5AB
Tel: 024 7652 1200
email: john.hall@covcofe.org

RURAL DEANS
ARCHDEACONRY OF COVENTRY
Coventry North Revd Ruth Walker, Keresley Vicarage, 34 Tamworth Rd, Coventry CV6 2EL
Tel: 024 7633 2717
email: ruth@st-thomas-keresley.org.uk
Coventry South Revd Mark Bratton, 92 De Montford Way, Coventry CV4 7DT
Tel: 024 7669 0216 (Home)
024 7652 3519 (Office)
email: m.q.bratton@warwick.ac.uk

Coventry East Revd Malcolm Tyler, Walsgrave Vicarage, 4 Faber Rd, Coventry CV2 2BG
Tel: 024 7661 5152
email: stmaryssowe@aol.com
Kenilworth Revd Richard Awre, Vicarage, 7 Elmbank Rd, Kenilworth CV8 1AL
Tel: 01926 854367 (Home)
01926 857509 (Office)
email: office@stnicholaskenilworth.org.uk
Nuneaton Revd Peter Allan, Ansley Vicarage, Birmingham Rd, Ansley, Nuneaton CV10 9PS
Tel: 024 7639 9070
email: peter@ansleychurch.org
Rugby Revd Martin Saxby, St Matthew's Vicarage, 7 Vicarage Rd, Rugby CV22 7AJ
Tel: 01788 330442
email: martinPA@stmatthews.org.uk

ARCHDEACONRY OF WARWICK
Alcester Revd David Hall, Vacancy
Fosse Revd John Burrel, The Rectory, Church Lane, Lighthorne, Warwick CV35 0AR
Tel: 01926 651279
Shipston Revd Richard Smith, Vicarage, Long Compton, Shipston-on-Stour CV36 5JH
Tel: 01608 684207
email: swarks7@tiscali.co.uk
Southam Revd John Armstrong, The Rectory, Park Lane, Southam CV47 0JA
Tel: 01926 812413
email: revarmstrong@yahoo.com
Warwick and Leamington Revd Morris Rodham, St Mary's Vicarage, 28 St Mary's Rd, Leamington Spa CV31 1JP   *Tel:* 01926 778505
email: morris@stmarysleamington.com

DIOCESE OF DERBY

Founded in 1927. Derbyshire, except for a small area in the north (CHESTER); a small area of Stockport; a few parishes in Staffordshire.

Population 1,010,000   Area 997 sq m
Full-time Stipendiary Parochial Clergy 144   Benefices 161
Parishes 252   Churches 333
www.derby.anglican.org
Overseas link of Derbyshire Churches (Baptist, Methodist, URC and Anglican):
Church of North India.

BISHOP (7th)
Rt Revd Dr Alastair Redfern, The Bishop's House, 6 King St, Duffield, Derby DE56 4EU [2005]
Tel: 01332 840132
Fax: 01332 840397
email: bishop@bishopofderby.org
[Alastair Derby]

SUFFRAGAN BISHOP
REPTON Rt Revd Humphrey Southern, Repton House, Lea, Matlock DE4 5JP [2007]
Tel: 01629 534644
Fax: 01629 534003
email: bishop@repton.free-online.co.uk

HONORARY ASSISTANT BISHOPS
Rt Revd Robert Beak OBE, Ashcroft Cottage, Butts Rd, Ashover, Chesterfield S45 0AX [1991]
Tel: 01246 590048

CATHEDRAL CHURCH OF ALL SAINTS
Dean Very Revd Dr Jeffrey Cuttell, Derby Cathedral Centre, 18–19 Iron Gate, Derby DE1 3GP [2008]
Tel: 01332 341201
Fax: 01332 203991
email: dean@derbycathedral.org
Cathedral Office Derby Cathedral Centre, 18–19 Iron Gate, Derby DE1 3GP
email: office@derbycathedral.org
Canons Residentiary
Canon Precentor Vacancy
Canon Theologian Canon Andie Brown, Vicarage, 149 Church Rd, Quarndon, Derby DE22 5JA [2003]
Tel: 01332 553424
Fax: 01332 292969
email: andie.brown@derby.anglican.org
Canon Pastor Canon Elaine Jones, 22 Kedleston Rd, Derby DE22 1GU [2004]
Tel: 01332 208995
Fax: 01332 203991
email: canon.pastor@ukonline.co.uk
Chaplains Revd Chris Hodder, 1 Peet St, Derby DE22 3RF
Tel: 01332 594172 (Home)
01332 591878 (University)
email: c.hodder@derby.ac.uk
Lay Chapter Members
Mrs Janet Love, Mrs Christine McMullen, Canon Richard Powell, Mr Mark Titterton

Senior Executive Officer and Chapter Clerk Mr David Stanbridge, Cathedral Office
email: davidstanbridgeseo@derbycathedral.org
Finance Officer Mr Peter Holdridge, Cathedral Office
email: peterh@derbycathedral.org
Visitors' Officer Vacancy, Cathedral Office
email: visitors@derbycathedral.org
Master of Music and Organist Mr Peter Gould, Cathedral Office
Tel: 01332 345848
email: pdgould@derbycathedral.org
Sub Organist Mr Tom Corfield, Cathedral Office
Tel: 01332 345848

ARCHDEACONS
CHESTERFIELD Ven David Garnett, The Vicarage, Edensor, Bakewell DE45 1PH [1996]
Tel and Fax: 01246 582130
email: davidcgarnett@yahoo.co.uk

DERBY Ven Christopher Cunliffe, Derby Church House, Full St, Derby DE1 3DR [2006]
Tel: 01332 388676 (Office)
Fax: 01332 292969
email: archderby@derby.anglican.org

CONVOCATION (MEMBERS OF THE HOUSE OF CLERGY OF THE GENERAL SYNOD)
Proctors for Clergy
Revd Dr John Davies
Canon Ian Gooding
Revd Katie Tupling

MEMBERS OF THE HOUSE OF LAITY OF THE GENERAL SYNOD
Mrs Madelaine Goddard
Mrs Christine McMullen
Mr Stephen Mitchell

DIOCESAN OFFICERS
Dioc Secretary Mr Bob Carey, Derby Church House, 1 Full St, Derby DE1 3DR
Tel: 01332 388650
Fax: 01332 292969
email: finance@derby.anglican.org
Chancellor of Diocese His Honour Judge John W. M. Bullimore, Rectory, 14 Grange Drive, Emley, Huddersfield HD8 9SF
Tel: 01924 849161

Registrar of Diocese and Bishop's Legal Secretary Mrs Nadine Waldron, Eddowes Waldron Solicitors, 12 St Peter's Churchyard, Derby DE1 1TZ   Tel: 01332 348484
email: gedward@btconnect.com

DIOCESAN ORGANIZATIONS
Diocesan Office Derby Church House, 1 Full St, Derby DE1 3DR   Tel: 01332 388650
Fax: 01332 292969
email: finance@derby.anglican.org
Web: www.derby.anglican.org

ADMINISTRATION
Dioc Synod (Chairman, House of Clergy) Revd Barry Green, Rectory, Church St, Dronfield S18 1QB   Tel: 01246 411531
email: barrie.green@dwhparish.org.uk
(Chairman, House of Laity) Mr Bill Bryant, Church House, North Church St, Bakewell DE45 1DB
Tel: 01629 815225
email: bryban@msn.com
(Secretary) Mr Bob Carey, Derby Church House
Board of Finance (Chairman) Mr Brian Dollamore, Castle House, Castle Square, Melbourne, Derby DE73 8DY
(Secretary) Mr Bob Carey (as above)
Parsonages Board Mr Jim Blackwell, Derby Church House   Tel: 01332 388650
Fax: 01332 292969
email: jim.blackwell@derby.anglican.org
Dioc Surveyors
Derby Archdeaconry Bob Spencer, Sir William Baird & Partners, St Michael's House, Queen St, Derby DE1 3DT   Tel: 01332 347203
Fax: 01332 347708
email: mail@sirwilliambaird.co.uk
Chesterfield Archdeaconry Mr G. Steel, Barlow & Associates Ltd, 7 Vernon St, Derby DE1 1FR
Tel: 01332 603000
email: gary@barlow-associates.co.uk
Pastoral Committee Mr Jim Blackwell (as above)
Designated Officer Mrs Nadine Waldron (as above)

CHURCHES
Advisory Committee for the Care of Churches (Chairman) Canon Raymond Ross, Threeways, Bridge Hill, Belper DE56 2BY   Tel: 01773 825876
email: raymondjross@talktalk.net
(Secretary) Mrs Virginia Davis, Derby Church House   Tel: 01332 388683
Fax: 01332 292969

EDUCATION
Dioc Education Office Derby Church House, 1 Full St, Derby DE1 3DR   Tel: 01332 388660
Fax: 01332 381909
email: nettarussell@ddbe.org
Director Phil Moncur
email: philmoncur@ddbe.org
Deputy Director and Schools Adviser Mrs Alison Brown   email: alisonbrown@ddbe.org

Finance Officer Mrs Lizzie Walker
Tel: 01332 388662
email: lizziewalker@ddbe.org
Children's Work Adviser Mrs Helen Proudfoot
email: helenproudfoot@ddbe.org
Youth Adviser Mr Alistair Langton
email: alistairlangton@ddbe.org
Warden, Peak Centre Champion House Revd Adrian Murray-Leslie, Champion House, Edale, Hope Valley S33 7ZA   Tel: 01433 670254
email: warden@peakcentre.org.uk

TOURISM OFFICERS
Derby North Mr Roger Harvey, Wella Cottage, 3 Main St, Newthorpe NG16 2EX
Tel: 01773 717067
Derby South Mr Les Allen, 17 South St, Littleover, Derby DE23 6BA   Tel: 01332 766642

DEVELOPING DISCIPLESHIP AND MINISTRY
CME (Clergy and Laity) Adviser Canon Andie Brown, Derby Church House
Tel: 01332 388671
email: andie.brown@tiscali.co.uk
Director of Ordinands Revd Dr John Davies, Vicarage, Church Sq, Melbourne, Derby DE73 1EN   Tel: 01332 862347
email: jhd@rdplus.net
Bishop's Convenor for NSMs and MSEs Canon Keith Orford, 27 Lums Hill Rise, Matlock DE4 3FX   Tel: 01629 55349
email: keith.orford@btinternet.com
Dean of Women Priests Revd Jackie Searle, Vicarage, 35 Church St, Littleover, Derby DE23 6GF   Tel: 01332 767802
email: j.searle80@ntlworld.com
Readers' Board (Warden) Revd Nick Watson, Rectory, 57 Rectory Lane, Breadsall, Derby DE21 5LL   Tel: 01332 831352
email: newatson@btopenworld.com
(Secretary) Vacancy
Worship Advisory Group (Chairman) Vacancy

MISSION AND UNITY
Ecumenical Officer Revd Tony Kaunhoven, Bakewell Vicarage, South Church St, Bakewell DE45 1FD   Tel: 01246 814462
email: jazzyrector@aol.com
World Development Officer Revd Christopher Harrison, Vicarage, Parwich, Ashbourne DE6 1QD   Tel: 01335 390226
email: christopher.d.harrison@btinternet.com
Dioc Mission Adviser Revd Lakshmi Jeffreys, Derby Church House   Tel: 01332 388687
email: lakshmi.jeffreys@derby.anglican.org
Bishops' Interfaith Adviser Revd Alan Fitch, Rectory, 155 Almond St, Derby DE23 6LY
Tel: 01332 766603
email: wendyalan_fitch@tiscali.co.uk

PRESS AND COMMUNICATIONS

Office Derby Church House, Full St, Derby DE1
3DR   *Tel:* 01332 388680
                                       Fax: 01332 292969
Communications Officer Contact Mrs V Alexander
(Secretary)   *Tel:* 01332 388680
        email: communications@derby.anglican.org
Editor of 'Our Diocese' Contact Mrs V Alexander
(Secretary)

DIOCESAN RECORD OFFICE

Derbyshire Record Office, County Offices,
Matlock DE4 3AG *County Archivist* Dr Margaret
O'Sullivan   *Tel:* 01629 585347
        email: record.office@derbyshire.gov.uk

SOCIAL RESPONSIBILITY

Community Action Officers
Ms Stella Collishaw, Derby Church House
                                       Tel: 01332 388685
        email: stella.collishaw@derby.anglican.org
Mrs Joy Bates, Derby Church House
                                       Tel: 01332 388686
        email: joy.bates@derby.anglican.org
Church and Society Officer Revd Richard Jordan
                                       Tel: 01332 388668
        email: richard.jordan@derby.anglican.org

RURAL DEANS
ARCHDEACONRY OF DERBY

Ashbourne Revd Christopher Harrison, Vicarage,
Parwich, Ashbourne, Derby DE6 1QD
                                       Tel: 01335 390226
        email: christopher.d.harrison@btinternet.com
Derby North Vacancy
Derby South Revd Paul Sandford, St Stephen's
Vicarage, 313 Sinfin Lane, Derby DE24 9GP
                                       Tel: 01332 760135
        email: paul.sandford@zoom.co.uk
Duffield Revd David Perkins, Christ Church
Vicarage, Bridge St, Belper DE56 1BA
                                       Tel: 01773 824974
        email: revdaveperkins@aol.com

Erewash Canon Ian Gooding, Rectory,
Stanton-by-Dale, Ilkeston DE7 4QA
                                       Tel: 0115 932 4584
                                       Fax: 0115 944 0299
        email: iangooding@zoom.co.uk
Heanor Revd Andrew C. Edmunds, Vicarage, 26
Mount Pleasant, Ripley DE5 3DX
                                       Tel: 01773 749641
        email: acedmunds@dsl.pipex.com
Longford Revd Andy Murphie, Vicarage, 28 Back
Lane, Hilton, Derby DE65 5GJ
                                       Tel: 01283 733433
        email: andymurphie@btinternet.com
Melbourne Revd Tony Luke, Rectory, Rectory
Gardens, Aston-on-Trent, Derby DE72 2AZ
                                       Tel: 01332 792658
        email: tonyluke@lineone.net
Repton Revd David Horsfall, Vicarage, Church
St, Swadlincote DE11 8LF   *Tel:* 01283 217756

ARCHDEACONRY OF CHESTERFIELD

Alfreton Revd Geoffrey Knox, Vicarage, 114
Nottingham Rd, Somercotes, Alfreton DE55 4LY
                                       Tel: 01773 602840
Bakewell and Eyam Vacancy
Bolsover and Staveley Revd Trevor Hicks,
Vicarage, Bolsover, Chesterfield S44 6HB
                                       Tel: 01246 824888
        email: trevorhicks1@aol.com
Buxton Revd John Goldsmith, Vicarage,
Monyash, Bakewell DE45 1JH
                                       Tel: 01629 812234
        email: goldsmith681@btinternet.com
Chesterfield Revd Nigel Johnson, Newbold
Rectory, St John's Rd, Chesterfield S41 8QN
                                       Tel: 01246 450374
        email: nvjohnson@tiscali.co.uk
Glossop Revd Garrie Griffiths, St Andrew's
Vicarage, 122 Hadfield Rd, Glossop SK13 2DR
                                       Tel: 01457 852431
        email: ggriffiths787@btinternet.com
Wirksworth Revd Robert Quarton, Rectory, 15
Hall Rise, Darley Dale, Matlock DE4 2HD
                                       Tel: 01629 734257
        email: robertquarton@ctlmail.co.uk

Founded in 635. Durham, except for an area in the south-west (RIPON AND LEEDS), and four parishes in the north (NEWCASTLE); Gateshead; South Tyneside; Sunderland; Hartlepool; Darlington; Stockton-on-Tees, north of the Tees.

Population 1,455,000   Area 987 sq m
Full-time Stipendiary Parochial Clergy 172   Benefices 187
Parishes 230   Churches 285
www.durham.anglican.org
Overseas link diocese: Lesotho.

BISHOP (71st)
Rt Revd Dr (Nicholas) Thomas Wright, Auckland Castle, Bishop Auckland DL14 7NR [2003]
                                        Tel: 01388 602576
                                        Fax: 01388 605264
    email: bishop.of.durham@bishopdunelm.co.uk
[Thomas Dunelm:]
Senior Chaplain, Executive Officer and Press Officer to the Bishop of Durham Canon Jon Bell *(same address)*   *email:* chaplain@bishopdunelm.co.uk

SUFFRAGAN BISHOP
JARROW Rt Revd Mark Watts Bryant, Bishop's House, Ivy Lane, Low Fell, Gateshead, NE9 6QD [2007]   *Tel:* 0191 491 0917
                            Fax: 0191 491 5116
    email: bishop.of.jarrow@durham.anglican.org

HONORARY ASSISTANT BISHOPS
Rt Revd Martyn William Jarrett, 3 North Lane, Roundhay, Leeds LS8 2QJ [2000]
(Bishop of Beverley and Provincial Episcopal Visitor)
                            Tel: 0113 265 4280
                            Fax: 0113 265 4281
email:
    bishop-of-beverley@3-north-lane.fsnet.co.uk
Rt Revd Prof Stephen Whitefield Sykes, Ingleside, Winney Hill, Durham DH1 3BE [1999]
                            Tel: 0191 384 6465
        email: S.W.Sykes@durham.ac.uk

CATHEDRAL CHURCH OF CHRIST, BLESSED MARY THE VIRGIN AND ST CUTHBERT OF DURHAM
Dean Very Revd Michael Sadgrove, The Deanery, Durham DH1 3EQ [2003]
                    Tel: 0191 386 4266 (Office)
                        0191 375 0242 (Home)
    email: canon.precentor@durhamcathedral.co.uk
Canons Residentiary
Canon Prof David Brown, 14 The College, Durham DH1 3EQ [1990]   *Tel:* 0191 386 4657
Canon Dr David Kennedy, 7 The College, Durham DH1 3EQ [2001]   *Tel:* 0191 334 5593
    email: David.Kennedy@durham.anglican.org
Canon Rosalind Brown, 6a The College, Durham DH1 3EQ [2005]   *Tel:* 0191 384 2415
    email: rosalind.brown@durhamcathedral.co.uk

Canon Dr Stephen Cherry, Carter House, Pelaw Leazes Lane, Durham DH1 1TB [2006]
                            Tel: 0191 374 6012
    email: stephen.cherry@durham.anglican.org
Ven Ian Jagger, 15 The College, Durham DH1 3EQ [2006]   *Tel:* 0191 384 7534
                            Fax: 0191 386 6915
email:
    archdeacon.of.durham@durham.anglican.org
Canon Prof Mark McIntosh (from Sep 2009), 14 The College, Durham DH1 3EQ
                            Tel: 0191 386 4657

Lay Members
Chapter Clerk Mr Paul Whittaker (Until April 2009), Chapter Office, The College, Durham DH1 3EH   *Tel:* 0191 386 4266
                            Fax: 0191 386 4267
    email: paul.whittaker@durhamcathedral.co.uk
Dr David Hunt *(Chapter Office)*
Mr Adrian Beney *(Chapter Office)*
Succentor Revd David Sudron, 3 The College, Durham DH1 3EQ   *Tel:* 0191 384 2481(Home)
                        0191 386 4266 (Office)
                        Fax: 0191 386 4267
    email: succentor@durhamcathedral.co.uk
Cathedral Organist (Lay Canon) Canon James Lancelot, 6 The College, Durham DH1 3EQ
                            Tel: 0191 386 4766
        email: organist@durhamcathedral.co.uk

ARCHDEACONS
DURHAM Ven Ian Jagger, 15 The College, Durham DH1 3EQ [2006]   *Tel:* 0191 384 7534
                            Fax: 0191 386 6915
email:
    archdeacon.of.durham@durham.anglican.org
AUCKLAND Ven Nick Barker, Vicarage, 45 Milbank Rd, Darlington DL3 9NL [2007]
                            Tel: 01325 480444
                            Fax: 01325 354027
email:
    archdeacon.of.auckland@durham.anglican.org
SUNDERLAND Ven Stuart Bain, St Nicholas Vicarage, Hedworth Lane, Boldon Colliery NE35 9JA [2002]   *Tel:* 0191 536 2300
                            Fax: 0191 519 3369
email:
archdeacon.of.sunderland@durham.anglican.org

CONVOCATION (MEMBERS OF THE HOUSE OF CLERGY OF THE GENERAL SYNOD)
Dignitaries in Convocation
The Dean of Durham
Proctors in Convocation
Canon Sheila Bamber
Revd Graeme Buttery
Revd Dr Margaret Gilley
Ven Ian Jagger

MEMBERS OF THE HOUSE OF LAITY OF THE GENERAL SYNOD
Mrs Janet Atkinson
Ms Dana Delap
Dr James Harrison
Sister Anne Williams

DIOCESAN OFFICERS
Dioc Secretary Mr Ian Boothroyd, Dioc Office, Auckland Castle, Bishop Auckland DL14 7QJ
Tel: 01388 604515
Fax: 01388 603695
email: Diocesan.Secretary@durham.anglican.org
Chancellor of Diocese The Worshipful the Revd Canon Rupert Bursell, Diocesan Registry, Messrs Smith Roddam, 56 North Bondgate, Bishop Auckland DL14 7PG   *Tel:* 01388 603073
Fax: 01388 450483
Deputy Chancellor Mr J. D. C. Harte, The Law School, Newcastle University, 21–24 Windsor Terrace, Newcastle-upon-Tyne NE1 7RU
Tel: 0191 222 7614 *or* 222 7624
Registrar of Diocese and Bishop's Legal Secretary Ms H. Monckton-Milnes, Dioc Registry (*as above*)
Deputy Registrar Mr D. Harris, Dioc Registry
Property Manager, Dioc Surveyor and Secretary to Houses Committee Mr M. Galley, Dioc Office
email: mike.galley@durham.anglican.org

DIOCESAN ORGANIZATIONS
Diocesan Office Auckland Castle, Bishop Auckland DL14 7QJ   *Tel:* 01388 604515
Fax: 01388 603695
email: dioc.sec.p.a@durham.anglican.org

ADMINISTRATION
Dioc Synod (*Chairman, House of Clergy*) Canon T. J. D. Ollier, Rectory, 10 Butts Lane, Egglescliffe, Stockton-on-Tees TS16 9BT   *Tel:* 01642 780185
(*Chairman, House of Laity*) Canon F. M. Wood, Ardenlea, 8 Butts Lane, Egglescliffe, Stockton-on-Tees TS16 9BT   *Tel:* 01642 782113
(*Secretary*) Mr Ian Boothroyd, Dioc Office
email: ian.boothroyd@durham.anglican.org
Board of Finance (*Chairman*) Dr Julian Chadwick, 31 Wearside Drive, The Sands, Durham DH1 1LE   *Tel:* 0191 384 3135
(*Secretary*) Mr Ian Boothroyd (*as above*)
Glebe Committee (*Chairman*) Dr Julian Chadwick (*as above*); (*Secretary*) Mr Ian Boothroyd (*as above*)

Houses Committee (*Chairman*) Revd A. Milne, Vicarage, Church Lane, Murton, Seaham SR7 9RD   *Tel:* 0191 526 2410
(*Secretary*) Mr M. Galley, Dioc Office
Pastoral Committee (*Chairman*) Ven Ian Jagger; (*Secretary*) Mr Paul Stringer, Dioc Office
Tel: 01388 660002 (Direct line)
email: paul.stringer@durham.anglican.org
Church Buildings Committee (*Chairman*) Mr Geoff Taylor, 14 Academy Gardens, Gainford, Darlington DL2 3EN   *Tel:* 01325 730379;
(*Secretary*) Mr Bill Heslop, Dioc Office
Tel: 01388 660001 (Direct line)
email: bill.heslop@durham.anglican.org
Redundant Churches Uses Committee (*Chairman*) Mr John Wheeler, Low Tile Close, Roman Way, Middleton St George, Darlington DL2 1DG *Tel:* 01325 332259; (*Secretary*) Mr Bill Heslop, Dioc Office (*as above*)
Designated Officer Mr Paul Stringer, Dioc Office (*as above*)
Administrative Secretary Mr Paul Stringer, Dioc Office (*as above*)
Officer Manager Mrs Mandy Blackett, Dioc Office
Tel: 01388 660010
email: mandy.blackett@durham.anglican.org

CHURCHES
Advisory Committee for the Care of Churches (*Chairman*) Very Revd Michael Sadgrove, The Deanery, Durham DH1 3EQ   *Tel:* 0191 384 7500
Fax: 0191 386 4267
email:
Michael.sadgrove@durhamcathedral.co.uk
(*Secretary*) Mr G. W. Heslop, Dioc Office (*as above*)   *Tel:* 01388 604515

EDUCATION
Director of Education Canon Sheila Bamber, Carter House, Pelaw Leazes Lane, Durham DH1 1TB
Tel: 0191 374 6009
email: Sheilab@ddemt.co.uk
Diocesan Schools Adviser Miss Lesley Richardson (*same address*)   *Tel:* 0191 374 6018
email: lesley.richardson@ddemt.co.uk
Adviser for Children's Ministry Revd Capt Paul Allinson (*same address*) *Tel:* 0191 374 6006
email: childrensadviser@durham.anglican.org
Adviser for Youth Ministry Mr Nicholas Rowark (*same address*)   *Tel:* 0191 374 6008
email: nick.rowark@durham.anglican.org

MINISTRY
Director of Ministry Canon Dr Stephen Cherry, Carter House, Pelaw Leazes Lane, Durham DH1 1TB   *Tel:* 0191 374 6012
Director of Initial Ministerial Education 4–7 Revd Rick Simpson, Rectory, Brancepeth, Durham DH7 8EL   *Tel:* 0191 380 0440
email: ricksimpson300@btinternet.com
Director of Ordinands Revd Robert Lawrance, Carter House   *Tel:* 0191 374 6015
email: ddo@durham.anglican.org

Woman *Adviser in Ministry* Canon Caroline Dick, Vicarage, 182 Sunderland Rd, South Shields NE34 6AH *Tel:* 0191 454 3804
email: carolinedick@btinternet.com
Principal of Diocesan OLM Course Canon Dr Jim Francis, Crossgate Centre, Alexandria Crescent, Durham DH1 4HF *Tel:* 0191 374 6022
email: james.francis@durham.anglican.org
Bishop's Adviser in Pastoral Care and Counselling Mrs A. Moore, Crossgate Centre (*as above*)
Tel: 0191 374 6021
email: alison.moore@durham.anglican.org
Local Ministry Officer Revd Richard Collins, Greatham House, 6 Front St, Greatham, Hartlepool TS25 2ER *Tel:* 01429 872626
email: rac@dunelm.org.uk
Lay Development Officer Vacancy, Carter House
Tel: 0191 374 6013
Local/Shared Ministry Training Officer for the Dioceses of Durham and Newcastle Revd Judy Hirst, Carter House *Tel:* 0191 374 6014
email: judy.hirst@durham.anglican.org
Pensions Officers
Revd Peter Welby, Blyth House, 9 Rhodes Terrace, Neville's Cross, Durham DH1 4JW
Tel: 0191 384 8295
Canon Keith Woodhouse, 85 Baulkham Hills, Penshaw, Houghton le Spring DH4 7RZ
Tel and Fax: 0191 584 3977
email: keith.woodhouse@durham.anglican.org
Readers' Board (*Warden*) Vacancy
Director of Reader Ministry Revd Dr M. L. Beck, Crossgate Centre, Alexandria Crescent, Durham DH1 4HF *Tel:* 0191 374 6023
(*Registrar*) Mr David Talbot, 66 Wheatall Drive, Whitburn, Sunderland SR6 7HQ
Tel: 0191 529 2265
email: talbot886@btinternet.com

LITURGICAL
Chairman Canon David Kennedy (*as above*)
Secretary Revd Dr Gareth Lloyd, 6 Ruskin Rd, Birtley, Chester-le-Street DH3 1AD
Tel: 0191 410 2115
email: Gareth@dunelm.org.uk

MISSION
Diocesan Missioner Revd Dr R. Allon-Smith, Crossgate Centre (*as above*) *Tel:* 0191 374 6025
email: rod.allon-smith@durham.anglican.org
Social Responsibility Development Officer Canon Caroline Dick, Vicarage, 182 Sunderland Rd, South Shields NE34 6AH *Tel:* 0191 454 3804
email: carolinedick@btinternet.com
DFW Adoption (*Chairman*) Ven Stuart Bain (*as above*); (*Director*) Ms Margaret Bell, Agriculture House, Stonebridge, Durham DH1 3RY
Tel: 0191 386 3719
Northumbrian Industrial Mission (*Chairman*) Mr J. G. Smith, The Durdans, Fellside Rd, Whickham, Newcastle-upon-Tyne NE16 4LA *Tel:* 0191 488 1631; (*Secretary*) Mrs Joan Smith, 64

Cornmoor Rd, Whickham, Newcastle-upon-Tyne NE16 4PY *Tel:* 0191 420 1238
Tees Valley Ministry (*Chairman*) Dr D. Hall, c/o Churches Regional Commission in the North-East, Ushaw College, Durham DH7 9RH; (*Secretary*) Mr P. Etwell (*same address*)
Tel: 0191 373 5453
Fax: 0191 373 7804
Arts and Recreation Chaplaincy (*Chairman*) Revd D. Jasper, Netherwood, 124 Old Manse Rd, Wishaw ML2 0EP; (*Secretary*) Dr A. Suggate, 56 Brookside, Witton Gilbert, Durham DH7 6RT
email: a.m.suggate@btopenworld.com

ECUMENICAL
Ecumenical Officer Vacancy

PRESS AND PUBLICATIONS
Editor of Dioc Yearbook Mr Ian Boothroyd (*as above*)
Director of Communications and Editor of Dioc News Revd Paul Judson, St Luke's Vicarage, 5 Tunstall Rd, Hartlepool TS26 8NF
Tel: 01429 293111
email: Director.of.Communications@ durham.anglican.org
Durham.Newslink@durham.anglican.org

DIOCESAN RECORD OFFICE
Archives and Special Collections, University Library (Palace Green Section), University of Durham, Palace Green, Durham DH1 3RN
Archivist Miss Margaret McCollum
Tel: 0191 334 2972
email: pg.library@durham.ac.uk
(*For diocesan records*)
County Record Office, County Hall, Durham DH1 5UL *Tel:* 0191 383 3253 (*For parochial records for the whole diocese*)

STEWARDSHIP
Stewardship Adviser Mr J. E. Roberts, Dioc Office
Tel: 01388 660000
Fax: 01388 603695
email: John.Roberts@durham.anglican.org

AREA DEANS
ARCHDEACONRY OF SUNDERLAND
Chester-le-Street Revd David Glover, 27 Wroxton, Biddick, Washington NE38 7NU
Tel: 0191 418 7911
email: htcwashington@tiscali.co.uk
Gateshead Revd Val Shedden, Heworth Vicarage, High Heworth Lane, Gateshead NE10 0PB
Tel: 0191 469 2111
email: val.shedden@durham.anglican.org
Gateshead West Revd Keith Teasdale, St Nicholas' Vicarage, Willow Ave, Dunston, Gateshead NE11 9UN *Tel:* 0191 460 0509
Fax: 0191 460 9327
email: teasdalek@hotmail.com

Houghton-le-Spring (Acting) Revd E. Wilkinson, The Vicarage, Front St. Newbottle, Houghton le Spring DH4 4EP   *Tel:* 0191 584 3244
          email: wilkinson.edward.rev@googlemail.com
Jarrow Revd Bill Braviner, St Peter's House, York Ave, Jarrow NE32 5LP   *Tel:* 0191 489 3279
          Fax: 0191 489 1925
          email: bill@braviner.com
          email: bill.braviner@durham.anglican.org
Wearmouth Vacancy

ARCHDEACONRY OF DURHAM

Durham Revd Dr Rod Allon-Smith, Crossgate Centre, Alexandria Crescent, Durham DH1 4HF
          Tel: 0191 384 4330
          email: rod.allon-smith@durham.anglican.org
Easington Revd Alan Milne, Vicarage, Church Lane, Murton, Seaham SR7 9RD
          Tel and *Fax:* 0191 526 2410
          email: alanmilne_41@hotmail.com
Hartlepool Revd Dr Michael Gilbertson, Vicarage, 34 Westbourne Rd, Hartlepool TS25 5RE
          Tel: 01429 263190
          Fax: 01429 400118
          email: michael.gilbertson@durham.anglican.org
Lanchester Revd Gary Birchall, Vicarage, Front St, Burnopfield, Newcastle-upon-Tyne NE16 6HQ
          Tel: 01207 270261
          email: gary.birchall@dsl.pipex.com

Sedgefield Revd Keith Lumsdon, St Luke's Vicarage, Church Lane, Ferryhill DL17 8LT
          Tel: 01740 651438
          email: keithlumsdon@hotmail.com

ARCHDEACONRY OF AUCKLAND

Auckland Canon Neville Vine, 4 Conway Grove, Bishop Auckland DL14 6AF
          Tel and *Fax:* 01388 604397
          email: neville.vine@btinternet.com
Barnard Castle Revd Alec Harding, Vicarage, Parsons Lonnen, Newgate, Barnard Castle DL12 8ST   *Tel:* 01833 637018
          email: alec.harding@durham.anglican.org
Darlington Revd John Dobson, Vicarage, 104 Blackwell Lane, Darlington DL3 8QQ
          Tel and *Fax:* 01325 354503
          email: john.dobson@durham.anglican.org
Stanhope Revd Vince Fenton, Rectory, 14 Hartside Close, Crook DL15 9NH
          Tel: 01388 760939
          email: vincent.fenton@durham.anglican.org
Stockton Revd David Brooke, Rectory, Church Lane, Redmarshall, Stockton-on-Tees TS21 1ES
          Tel: 01740 630810
          email: david@revd.co.uk

Founded in 1109. Cambridgeshire, except for an area in the north-west (PETERBOROUGH) and three parishes in the south (CHELMSFORD); the western quarter of Norfolk; one parish in Bedfordshire.

Population 675,000   Area 1,507 sq m
Full-time Stipendiary Parochial Clergy 128   Benefices 197
Parishes 308   Churches 334
www.ely.anglican.org
Overseas link dioceses: Vellore (Church of South India) (Ecumenical), Church of North Elbe.

BISHOP (68th)
Rt Revd Dr Anthony John Russell, The Bishop's House, Ely CB7 4DW [2000]   *Tel:* 01353 662749
Fax: 01353 669477
email: bishop@ely.anglican.org
[Anthony Ely]
Bishop's Lay Chaplain Dr Bridget Nichols (*same address and tel. no.*)
email: bridget.nichols@ely.anglican.org
Bishop's Personal Assistant Mrs Marion Howard (*same address and tel. no.*)
email: marion.howard@ely.anglican.org
Bishop's Secretary Mrs Sarah King (*same address and tel. and no.*)
email: sarah.king@ely.anglican.org

SUFFRAGAN BISHOP
HUNTINGDON Rt Revd Dr David Thomson, 14 Lynn Rd, Ely CB6 1DA [2008]   *Tel:* 01353 662137
Fax: 01353 669357
email: suffragan@ely.anglican.org
Bishop's Secretary Mrs Jane Baker (*same address, tel. no. and email*)

CATHEDRAL CHURCH OF THE HOLY AND UNDIVIDED TRINITY
Dean Very Revd Dr Michael Chandler, The Deanery, The College, Ely CB7 4DN [2003]
Tel: 01353 667735
Fax: 01353 665658
Vice Dean and Canon Pastor Canon David Pritchard, The Black Hostelry, The Precentor's House, The College, Ely CB7 4DL   *Tel:* 01353 660302
Canons Residentiary
Canon Missioner Canon Dr Alan Hargrave, The Chapter House, The College, Ely CB7 4DL [2004]
Tel: 01353 660304
Canon Precentor Canon Dr James Garrard, The Precentor's House, The College, Ely CB7 4JU [2004]   *Tel:* 01353 660335
Chapter Clerk Mrs Constance Heald, The Chapter House, The College, Ely CB7 4DL
Tel: 01353 660308
Administrator Mrs Carol Cambell, The Chapter House, The College, Ely CB7 4DL
Tel: 01353 660321

Director of Music Mr Paul Trepte, The Chapter House, The College, Ely CB7 4DL
Tel: 01353 667735

ARCHDEACONS
CAMBRIDGE Ven John Stuart Beer, St Botolph's Rectory, 1a Summerfield, Cambridge CB3 9HE [2004]   *Tel and Fax:* 01223 350424
email: archdeacon.cambridge@ely.anglican.org
HUNTINGDON AND WISBECH Ven Hugh Kyle McCurdy, 12 Boadicea Court, Chatteris, Cambs. PE16 6BN [2005]   *Tel:* 01354 692142

CONVOCATION (MEMBERS OF THE HOUSE OF CLERGY OF THE GENERAL SYNOD)
Proctors for Clergy
Ven John Beer
Canon Dr Alan Hargrave
Revd Rhiannon Jones

MEMBERS OF THE HOUSE OF LAITY OF THE GENERAL SYNOD
Dr Peter Harland
Dr Elaine Storkey

DIOCESAN OFFICERS
Dioc Secretary Dr Matthew Lavis, Bishop Woodford House, Barton Rd, Ely CB7 4DX
Tel: 01353 652701
01353 652702 (Direct Line)
Fax: 01353 652745
email: d.secretary@office.ely.anglican.org
Chancellor of Diocese The Hon Mr Justice William Gage, The Royal Courts of Justice, The Strand, London WC2 2LL
Registrar of Diocese Mr Peter Beesley, 1 The Sanctuary, London SW1P 3JT   *Tel:* 020 7222 5381

DIOCESAN ORGANIZATIONS
Diocesan Office Bishop Woodford House, Barton Rd, Ely CB7 4DX   *Tel:* 01353 652701
Fax: 01353 652745
email: jackie.cox@office.ely.anglican.org

ADMINISTRATION
Dioc Synod (*Chairman, House of Clergy*) Canon Jonathan Young, Rectory, Parsons Drive, Ellington, Huntingdon PE28 0AU
Tel: 01480 891695

(*Chairman, House of Laity*) Mr Stephen Tooke, The Haven, 21 Wisbech Rd, March PE15 8ED
Tel: 01354 652844
(*Secretary*) Dr Matthew Lavis, Dioc Office
Assistant Secretary (Pastoral) Miss Jane Logan, Dioc Office
Finance Committee (Chairman) Mr Hugh Duberly; (*Secretary*) Dr Matthew Lavis (*as above*)
Accounts Administrator Mrs Janice Sulman, Dioc Office
Dioc Surveyor Mr Stephen Layton, Dioc Office
Board of Patronage (Secretary) Miss Jane Logan, Dioc Office
Designated Officer Dr Matthew Lavis (*as above*)

CHURCHES

Advisory Committee for the Care of Churches (*Secretary*) Miss Jane Logan, Dioc Office
Archdeaconry of Ely Church Music Society (*Secretary*) Mr B. E. Eaden, 64 Green End Rd, Cambridge CB4 1RY
Tel: 01223 424363
Ely RSCM Committee (Secretary) Mrs K. M. Coulls, 74 Barton Road, Ely, Cambs. CB7 4HZ
Tel: 01353 614141

EDUCATION AND TRAINING

email: ed&t@office.ely.anglican.org
web: www.ely.anglican.org/education
Dioc Board of Education and Training (Secretary) Canon Tim Elbourne, Dioc Office
Director of Education and Training Canon Tim Elbourne (*as above*)
Children's Adviser Vacancy
Youth Officer Capt David Waters
RE Adviser (Schools) Dr Shirley Hall, Dioc Office
Schools Buildings and Finance Officer Mr David Hicks
Director of Ministerial and Adult Learning Canon Les Oglesby, Dioc Office
Ministry and Adult Learning Officer Revd Christine Worsley
Reader Ministry Contact The Bishop of Huntingdon

MINISTRY

Director of Ministry and Vocation and Diocesan Director of Ordinands Canon Vanessa Herrick, 24 Cromwell Rd, Ely CB6 1AS
Tel: 01353 662909
Fax: 01353 662056
Readers' Board (Chair) Mr Stephen Tooke, The Haven, 21 Wisbech Rd, March PE15 8ED
Tel: 01354 652844
Warden The Bishop of Huntingdon

LITURGICAL COMMITTEE

Secretary Canon Jonathan Young, Rectory, Parsons Drive, Ellington, Huntingdon PE28 0AU
Tel: 01480 891695

MISSIONARY AND ECUMENICAL

Council for Mission and Ministry (Chair) The Bishop of Huntingdon
Tel: 01353 662137

Ecumenical Officer Revd Will Adam, Rectory, 40 Church Lane, Girton CB3 0JP
Tel: 01223 276235

PRESS AND PUBLICATIONS

Bishop's Press Officer Canon Owen Spencer-Thomas, 52 Windsor Rd, Cambridge CB4 3JN
Tel: 01223 358446
Communications Officer Mrs Val Robson, Dioc Office
Editor of Dioc Directory Dr Matthew Lavis, Dioc Office

DIOCESAN RECORD OFFICES

Dioc Archivist P. M. Meadows, c/o University Library, West Rd, Cambridge CB3 9DR
Cambridge Record Office, Shire Hall, Castle Hill, Cambridge CB3 0AP *Archivist* Mrs Elizabeth Stazicker *Tel:* 01223 317281 (*For parishes in the archdeaconry of Cambridge*)
Cambridgeshire Record Office, Grammar School Walk, Huntingdon PE18 6LF *Tel:* 01480 52181 (*For parishes in the former archdeaconry of Huntingdon*)
Cambridge Record Office, Shire Hall, Cambridge (*see above*) (*For parishes in the deaneries of Ely and March*)
Norfolk Record Office, Central Library, Norwich NR2 1NJ *City and County Archivist* Dr John Alban *Tel:* 01603 22233 (*For parishes in the deaneries of Feltwell and Fincham*)
Wisbech and Fenland Museum, Museum Square, Wisbech PE13 1ES *Tel:* 01945 583817 (*For parishes in the deanery of Wisbech Lynn Marshland*)

DIOCESAN RESOURCE CENTRE

Contact Mrs R. Wright, Dioc Resource Centre, Dioc Office

SOCIAL RESPONSIBILITY

Board for Church in Society (Chairman) Canon Alan Hargrave (*see above*)
(*Secretary*) Dr Hilary Lavis, Dioc Office
Tel: 01353 652720
Committee for Family and Social Welfare (Chairman) Mr Adrian Wright, 5 Lode Ave, Waterbeach, Cambridge CB5 9PX
Tel: 01223 861846
Cambridgeshire Deaf Association (Ely Dioc Association for the Deaf) (Chairman) Mr R. Holland, 8 Romsey Terrace, Cambridge
Mothers' Union (President) Mrs Joan Cameron, 5 St Catherine's, Ely CB6 1AP
Tel: 01353 614467

RURAL AND AREA DEANS
ARCHDEACONRY OF CAMBRIDGE

Bourn Revd Cheryl Collins, St Peter's Parsonage, 70 High St, Coton CB3 7PL
Tel: 01954 210287
Cambridge North Canon Dr John Binns, Great St Mary's Vicarage, 39 Madingley Rd, Cambridge CB3 0EL
Tel: 01223 355285
Cambridge South Canon Andrew Greany, Little St Mary's Vicarage, 4 Newnham Terrace, Cambridge CB3 9EX
Tel: 01223 350733

Fordham and Quy Canon Stephen Earl, Vicarage, High St, Burwell CB5 0HB *Tel:* 01638 741262
North Stowe Revd James Blandford-Baker, St Andrew's Vicarage, Church St, Histon CB4 9EP
Tel: 01223 233456
Shelford Revd Michael Goater, Vicarage, 12 Church St, Great Shelford CB2 5EL
Tel: 01223 843654
Shingay Canon Shamus Williams, Vicarage, Church St, Guilden Morden, Royston SG8 0JP
Tel: 01763 853067

ARCHDEACONRY OF HUNTINGDON AND WISBECH
Ely Canon Fiona Brampton, Vicarage, Church Lane, Haddenham, Ely CB6 3TB
Tel: 01353 740309

Fincham and Feltwell Revd James Mather, Rectory, Downham Market PE38 9LE *Tel:* 01366 382187
Huntingdon Revd Brian Atling, Blue Cedars, Common Lane, Hemingford Abbots, Huntingdon PE28 9AW *Tel:* 01480 493975
March Canon Peter Baxandall, St Wendreda's Rectory, 21 Wimblington Rd, March PE15 9QW
Tel: 01354 53377
St Ives Revd Chris Barter, Rectory, Rectory Lane, Somersham, Huntingdon PE28 3EL
Tel: 01487 840676
St Neots Revd Annette Reed, Vicarage, 24 St James Rd, Little Paxton, Huntingdon PE19 6QW
Tel: 01480 211048
Wisbech Lynn Marshland Canon Wim Zwalf, Vicarage, Love Lane, Wisbech PE13 1HP
Tel: 01945 583559
Yaxley Canon Malcolm Griffith, Rectory, Church Causeway, Sawtry, Huntingdon PE28 5TD
Tel: 01487 830215

DIOCESE IN EUROPE

Founded 1980 by union of the Diocese of Gibraltar (founded 1842) and the (Fulham) Jurisdiction of North and Central Europe. Area, Europe, except Great Britain and Ireland; Morocco; Turkey; the Asian countries of the former Soviet Union.

Licensed Clergy 155 Churches and Congregations 295
www.europe.anglican.org

BISHOP OF GIBRALTAR IN EUROPE (3rd)
Rt Revd Dr (Douglas) Geoffrey Rowell, Bishop's Lodge, Church Rd, Worth, Crawley, W Sussex RH10 7RT [2001]   *Tel:* 01293 883051
Fax: 01293 884479
email: bishop@dioceseineurope.org.uk
Bishop's Chaplain Revd Kevin O'Brien
Bishop's Personal Assistant Mrs Margaret Gibson

SUFFRAGAN BISHOP
IN EUROPE Rt Revd David Hamid, 14 Tufton St, London SW1P 3QZ [2002]   *Tel:* 020 7898 1160
Fax: 020 7898 1166
email: david.hamid@europe.c-of-e.org.uk

HONORARY ASSISTANT BISHOPS
Rt Revd Eric Devenport, 6 Damocles Court, Pottergate, Norwich NR2 1HN [1993]
Tel: 01603 664121
email: eric@edevenport.orangehome.com
Rt Revd Richard Garrard, 26 Carol Close, Stoke Holy Cross, Norwich NR14 8NN [2001]
Tel: 01508 494165
email: garrard.r-a@btinternet.com
Rt Revd Ian Harland, White House, 11 South St, Gargrave, N. Yorks. BD23 2RT [2000]
Tel: 01756 748623
email: sue@harland1.fsnet.co.uk
Rt Revd Patrick Harris, Apartment B, Ireton House, Pavillion Gardens, The Park, Cheltenham GL50 2SP [1999]   *Tel:* 01242 231376
email: pandvharris@blueyonder.co.uk
Rt Revd Edward Holland, 37 Palfrey St, London W6 9EW [2002]   *Tel:* 020 8746 3636
email: ed.holland@btopenworld.com
Rt Revd Carlos López-Lozano, c/o IERE, Calle de Beneficencia 18, 28004 Madrid, Spain [1995]
Tel: 00 34 91 445 25 60
Fax: 00 34 91 594 45 72
email: eclesiae@arrakis.es
Rt Revd Michael Manktelow, 14 Little London, Chichester, W Sussex PO19 1NZ [1994]
Tel: 01243 531096
Rt Revd Fernando Soares, Centro Diocesano, Apartado 392, 4431–905 Vila Nova de Gaia, Portugal [1995]   *Tel:* 00 351 223 754018
Fax: 00 351 223 752016
email: bisposoares@igreja-lusitana.org

Rt Revd John Taylor, 22 Conduit Head Rd, Cambridge CB3 0EY [1998]   *Tel:* 01223 313783
email: john.taylor6529@ntlworld.com
Rt Revd Joachim Vobbe, Gregor-Mendel-Strasse 28, D-53115 Bonn, Germany [1999]
Tel: 00 49 228 23 22 85
email: ordinariat@alt-katholisch.de
Rt Revd Ambrose Weekes, Charterhouse, Charterhouse Square, London EC1M 6AN [1988]
Tel: 020 7251 4201
Rt Revd David Smith, 34 Cedar Glade, Dunnington, York YO19 5QZ [2002]   *Tel:* 01904 481225
email: david@djmhs.force9.co.uk
Rt Revd Pierre Whalon, American Cathedral, 23 Avenue George V, 75008 Paris, France [2001]
Tel: 00 33 1 53 23 84 00 (Cathedral)
Fax: 00 33 1 47 23 95 30 (Cathedral)
00 33 1 47 20 02 23 (Direct)
00 33 1 40 27 03 53 (Home)
email: office@tec-europe.org
Rt Revd Alan Chesters, 64 Hallfields Rd, Tarvin, Chester CH3 8ET [2005]   *Tel:* 01829 740825
email: alan@chesters1934.freeserve.co.uk
Very Revd David Richardson, Anglican Centre in Rome, Palazzo Doria Pamphilj, Piazza del Collegio Romano 2 Int 7, 00186 Rome, Italy [2008]
Tel: 00 39 06 678 0302
email: anglican.centre.rome@flashnet.it
Rt Revd Fritz-René Müller, Willadingweg 39, CH-3006 Bern, Switzerland [2004]
Tel: 00 41 31 351 35 30
email: bischof@christkath.ch
Rt Revd Michael Turnbull, 67 Strand St, Sandwich CT13 9HN [2003]   *Tel:* 01304 611389
email: bstmt@btopenworld.com

CATHEDRAL CHURCH OF THE HOLY TRINITY, GIBRALTAR
Dean Very Revd Dr John Paddock, The Deanery, Bomb House Lane, Gibraltar
Tel: 00 350 78377 (Deanery)
Fax: 00 350 78463
email: deangib@gibraltar.gib

PRO-CATHEDRAL OF ST PAUL, VALLETTA, MALTA
Chancellor Canon Tom Mendel, Chancellor's Lodge, St Paul's Anglican Pro-Cathedral,

Independence Square, Valletta VLT12, Malta
[2004]   *Tel:* 00 356 21 22 57 14
                   Fax: 00 356 21 22 58 67
                   email: anglican@onvol.net

PRO-CATHEDRAL OF THE HOLY TRINITY, BRUSSELS, BELGIUM
Chancellor Canon Dr Robert Innes, Pro-Cathedral of the Holy Trinity, 29 rue Capitaine Crespel, 1050 Brussels [2005]
                   Tel: 00 32 2 511 71 83 (Office)
                   Fax: 00 32 2 511 10 28
                   email: chaplain@htbrussels.com

ARCHDEACONS
THE EASTERN ARCHDEACONRY Ven Patrick Curran, Reisnerstrasse 42/7, 1030 Vienna, Austria [2002]
                   Tel: 00 43 1 718 5902 (Home)
          Tel and *Fax:* 00 43 1 714 8900 (Office)
                   Fax: 00 43 1 718 5902 (Home)
                   email: office@christchurchvienna.org
NORTH WEST EUROPE Ven John de Wit, V Hogendorpstraat 26, 3581 KE Utrecht, The Netherlands [2008]   *Tel:* 00 31 30 251 34
                   email: chaplain@holytrinityutrecht.nl
FRANCE Ven Kenneth Letts, Presbytère Anglican, 11 rue de la Buffa, 06000 Nice, France [2007]
                   Tel: 00 33 4 93 87 19 83
                   Fax: 00 33 4 93 82 25 09
                   email: kletts@mac.com
GIBRALTAR Vacancy, The Deanery, Bomb House Lane, Gibraltar   *Tel:* 00 350 78377 (Deanery)
                   00 350 75745 (Cathedral)
                   email: deangib@gibraltar.gi
ITALY AND MALTA Ven Arthur Siddall, St John's House, 92 Avenue de Chillon, CH-1820 Territet Montreux, Switzerland [2005]
                   Tel: 00 41 21 963 43 54
                   email: chaplain@stjohns-montreux.ch
GERMANY AND NORTHERN EUROPE Vacancy
SWITZERLAND Ven Arthur Siddall, St John's House, 92 Avenue de Chillon, CH-1820 Territet Montreux, Switzerland [2007]
                   Tel: 00 41 21 963 43 54
                   email: chaplain@stjohns-montreux.ch

CONVOCATION (MEMBERS OF THE HOUSE OF CLERGY OF THE GENERAL SYNOD)
Canon Jonathan Boardman
Canon Debbie Flach

MEMBERS OF THE HOUSE OF LAITY OF THE GENERAL SYNOD
Lay Canon Mrs Ann Turner
Mr Roger Fry CBE

DIOCESAN OFFICERS
Dioc Secretary Mr Adrian Mumford, Dioc Office
Assistant Dioc Secretary Mrs Jeanne French, Dioc Office

Chancellor of Diocese The Worshipful Mark Hill, 3 Pump Court, Temple, London EC4Y 7AJ (contact via Dioc Office)
Registrar of Diocese and Bishop's Legal Secretary Refer to Diocesan Office, 14 Tufton St, London SW1P 3QZ   *Tel:* 020 7898 1155
                   Fax: 020 7898 1166
          email: diocesan.office@europe.c-of-e.org.uk

DIOCESAN ORGANIZATIONS
Diocesan Office 14 Tufton St, London SW1P 3QZ
                   Tel: 020 7898 1155
                   Fax: 020 7898 1166
          email: diocesan.office@europe.c-of-e.org.uk
                   Web: www.europe.anglican.org

ADMINISTRATION
Dioc Synod (*Clerical Vice-President*) Canon Debbie Flach, 7 rue Leonard de Vinci, 59700 Marcq en Baroeul, France   *Tel* and *Fax:* 00 33 3 28 52 66 36
          email: chaplain@christchurchlille.com
(*Lay Vice-President*) Lay Canon Mrs Ann Turner, Grotesteenweg 42, 2600 Berchem, Antwerp, Belgium
          Tel and *Fax:* 00 32 3 440 25 81
                   email: ann@turner.be
(*Secretary*) Mr Adrian Mumford, Dioc Office
Board of Finance (*Chairman*) Mr Michael Hart, c/o Dioc Office; (*Secretary*) Mr Adrian Mumford, Dioc Office

CHURCHES
Faculty Committee (*Secretary*) Mr Adrian Mumford (*as above*)

MINISTRY AND TRAINING
Warden of Readers Rt Revd David Hamid, Dioc Office
Director of Ordinands Revd William Gulliford, Dioc Office
          email: william.gulliford@europe.c-of-e.org.uk
          or william.gulliford@london.anglican.org
Director of Training Revd Ulla Monberg, Borgmester Jensens Allé 9, 2th, 2100 Copenhagen Ø Denmark   *Tel:* 00 45 3526 0660
                   email: ullamonberg@msn.com

LITURGY
Enquiries to the Bishop's Chaplain

MEDITERRANEAN MISSIONS TO SEAMEN
Administrator Mr Adrian Mumford (*as above*)

PRESS AND PUBLICATIONS
Press and Communications Officer Revd Paul Needle, Dioc Office   *Tel:* 020 7898 1155 (Office)
                   Fax: 020 7898 1166 (Office)
          email: paul.needle@europe.c-of-e.org.uk
Editor of the 'European Anglican' Revd Paul Needle (*as above*)

DIOCESAN RECORD OFFICE
The Guildhall Library, Aldermanbury, London
EC2P 2EJ   *Tel:* 020 7606 3030

ARCHBISHOP'S APOKRISARIOI AND REPRESENTATIVES
To the Holy See Very Revd David Richardson, Centro Anglicano, Palazzo Doria Pamphilj, Piazza dei Collegio Romano 2, 00186 Rome, Italy
Tel: 39 06 678 0302
Fax: 39 06 678 0674
email: anglican.centre.rome@flashnet.it
To the Patriarch of Romania, and the Patriarch of Bulgaria Revd Martin Jacques, British Embassy (Bucharest), 24 Strada Jules Michelet, nr22–24 Sector 1, 70154 Bucharest   *Tel:* 00 40 21 210 2937
email: resurrectionbucharest@gmail.com
To the Archbishop of Athens and All Greece Revd Malcolm Bradshaw, British Embassy (Athens), Ploutarchou 1, 106 75 Athens
Tel and *Fax:* 00 30 210 721 4906 (Home)
email: anglican@otenet.gr

To the Patriarch of Moscow and All Russia Canon Dr Simon Stephens, British Embassy Moscow, Sofiiskaya Naberezhnaya, Moscow 109702
Tel and *Fax:* 007 495 629 0990
email: chaplain@standrewsmoscow.org
To the Patriarch of Serbia Revd Robin Fox, St Mary's Anglican Church, Visegradska 23, 11000 Belgrade, Serbia and Montenegro
Tel: 00 381 11 3232 948
email: robin.fox@sbb.co.yu

DEANERIES
The archdeaconry of Germany and Northern Europe has Deanery Synods rather than a single Archdeaconry Synod. The names and addresses of the officers are available from the Diocesan Office.

Tranferred to Exeter in 1050, formerly at Crediton in 909. Devon, except for one parish in the south-east (SALISBURY) and one parish in the west (TRURO); Plymouth; Torbay.

Population 1,121,000   Area 2,575 sq m
Full-time Stipendiary Parochial Clergy 211   Benefices 192
Parishes 496   Churches 616
www.exeter.anglican.org
Overseas link diocese: Cyprus and the Gulf; Thika (Kenya).

BISHOP (70th)
Rt Revd Michael Laurence Langrish, The Palace, Exeter EX1 1HY [2000]   *Tel:* 01392 272362
Fax: 01392 430923
email: bishop.of.exeter@exeter.anglican.org
[Michael Exon:]
Chaplain and Assistant to the Bishop Revd Dr Adrian Hough (*same address*)
email: adrian.hough@exeter.anglican.org
Personal Assistant Miss Sarah Johnson
email: sarah.johnson@exeter.anglican.org
Administrative Secretary Ms Sophie Hunt
email: sophie.hunt@exeter.anglican.org

SUFFRAGAN BISHOPS
CREDITON Rt Revd Robert John Scott Evens, 32 The Avenue, Tiverton EX16 4HW [2004]
Tel: 01884 250002
Fax: 01884 257454
email: bishop.of.crediton@exeter.anglican.org
PLYMOUTH Rt Revd John Ford, 31 Riverside Walk, Tamerton Foliot, Plymouth PL5 4AQ [2006]
Tel: 01752 769836
email: bishop.of.plymouth@exeter.anglican.org

HONORARY ASSISTANT BISHOPS
Rt Revd Andrew Burnham, Bishop's House, Dry Sandford, Abingdon OX13 6JP [2001]
Tel: 01865 390746
email: bishop.Andrew@ebbsfleet.org.uk
Rt Revd Richard Fox Cartwright, Royal Masonic Benevolent Institute, Cadogan Court, Barley Lane, Exeter EX4 1TA [1988]   *Tel:* 01392 251017
Rt Revd Ivor Colin Docker, Braemar, Bradley Rd, Bovey Tracey, Newton Abbot TQ13 9EU [1991]
Tel: 01626 832468
Rt Revd Robert David Silk, 1 Centenary Way, Torquay TQ2 7SB [2005]   *Tel:* 01803 614458
Rt Revd Richard Hawkins, 3 Westbrook Close, Whipton, Exeter EX4 8BS [2005]
Tel: 01392 462622
Rt Revd Michael Robert Westall, St Luke's Vicarage, 1 Mead Rd, Livermead, Torquay TQ2 6TE [2007]   *Tel:* 01803 605437
Rt Revd James Philip Mason, St Maurice's Rectory, 31 Wain Park, Plympton, Plymouth PL7 2HX [2006]   *Tel:* 01752 346114

CATHEDRAL CHURCH OF ST PETER
Dean Very Revd Jonathan Meyrick, The Deanery, 10 Cathedral Close, Exeter EX1 1EZ [2005]
Tel: 01392 273509
email: dean@exeter-cathedral.org.uk
Canons Residentiary
Precentor Canon Carl Turner, 6 Cathedral Close, Exeter EX1 1EZ [2001]   *Tel:* 01392 272498
email: precentor@exeter-cathedral.org.uk
Missioner Canon Mark Rylands, Rectory, 3 Spicer Rd, Exeter EX1 1SX [2002]
Tel: 01392 272450; 01392 294903
Fax: 01392 285986
email: fishing@exeter.anglican.org
Chancellor Canon Andrew Godsall, 12 Cathedral Close, Exeter EX1 1EZ [2006]   *Tel:* 01392 275756
email: andrew.godsall@exeter.anglican.org
Treasurer and Pastor Canon Tom Honey, 9 Cathedral Close, Exeter EX1 1EZ [2007]
Tel: 01392 279367
email: pastor@exeter-cathedral.org.uk
Chapter Canons Mrs Ann Barwood, Rt Revd Richard Hawkins, Mrs Hannah Foster, one vacancy
Priest Vicars Revd Alison Turner, Revd Andi Hoffbauer
Cathedral Offices 1 The Cloisters, Exeter EX1 1HS
Tel: 01392 255573
Fax: 01392 285986
email: admin@exeter-cathedral.org.uk
Web: www.exeter-cathedral.org.uk
Administrator Mr Paul Snell   *Tel:* 01392 285973
email: prs@exeter-cathedral.org.uk
Clerk to the Chapter Mr Tony Le Riche
Tel: 01392 285971
email: admin@exeter-cathedral.org.uk
Liturgy and Music Dept   *Tel:* 01392 285984
email: liturgy@exeter-cathedral.org.uk
Director of Music Mr Andrew Millington, 11 Cathedral Close, Exeter EX1 1EZ
Tel: 01392 277521
email: music@exeter-cathedral.org.uk
Cathedral Organist Mr Paul Morgan, 40 Countess Wear Rd, Exeter EX2 6LR
Tel: 01392 877623
Third Millennium Campaign Director Mrs Jill Taylor, Cathedral Campaign Office
Tel: 01392 285974
email: campaign@exeter-cathedral.org.uk

Assistant Head of Visitor Services Mrs Catherine Escott
Tel: 01392 285983
email: visitors@exeter-cathedral.org.uk

ARCHDEACONS

EXETER Ven Penny Driver, Emmanuel House, Station Rd, Ide, Exeter EX2 9RS [2006]
Tel: 01392 425577
email: archdeacon.of.exeter@exeter.anglican.org
TOTNES Ven John Rawlings, Blue Hills, Bradley Rd, Bovey Tracey, Newton Abbot TQ13 9EU [2006]
Tel: 01626 832064
Fax: 01626 834947
email: archdeacon.of.totnes@exeter.anglican.org
BARNSTAPLE Ven David Gunn-Johnson, Stage Cross, Sanders Lane, Bishop's Tawton, Barnstaple EX32 0BE [2003]
Tel: 01271 375475
Fax: 01271 377934
email:
archdeacon.of.barnstaple@exeter.anglican.org
PLYMOUTH Ven Tony Wilds, St Mark's House, 46a Cambridge Rd, Ford, Plymouth PL2 1PU [2001]
Tel: 01752 793397
Fax: 01752 774618
email:
archdeacon.of.plymouth@exeter.anglican.org

CONVOCATION (MEMBERS OF THE HOUSE OF CLERGY OF THE GENERAL SYNOD)

Proctors for Clergy
Preb Samuel Philpott
Revd Roderick Thomas
Canon Carl Turner
Ven Tony Wilds
Vacancy

MEMBERS OF THE HOUSE OF LAITY OF THE GENERAL SYNOD

Mrs Anneliese Barrell
Mrs Debra Body
Miss Emma Forward
Mr Ian Kent
Mrs Shirley-Ann Williams

Dioc Synod (*Chairman, House of Clergy*) Preb Sam Philpott, St Peter's Vicarage, 23 Wyndham Square, Plymouth PL1 5EG
Tel: 01752 222007
(*Secretary, House of Clergy*) Preb Philip Darby, Vicarage, Copperwood Close, Ashburton, Newton Abbot TQ13 7JQ
Tel: 01364 652506
(*Chairman, House of Laity*) Mr Charles Hodgson, The Smithy, East Worlington, Crediton EX17 4SY
Tel: 01884 861571
email: catherine-charles.hodgson@virgin.net
(*Secretary, House of Laity*) Mr Graham Lea, 2 Thornyville Close, Oreston, Plymouth PL9 7LE
Tel: 01752 403392
Synod Secretary Mr Mark Beedell, The Old Deanery

DIOCESAN OFFICERS

Dioc Secretary Mr Mark Beedell, The Old Deanery, The Cloisters, Exeter EX1 1HS
Tel: 01392 272686
Fax: 01392 499594
email: dsec@exeter.anglican.org
Chancellor of Diocese Hon Sir Andrew McFarlane, Royal Courts of Justice, Strand, London WC2A 2LL
Tel: 020 7947 6008
Deputy Chancellor of Diocese Mr Gregory Percy Jones, Francis Taylor Building, Inner Temple, London EC4Y 7BY
Tel: 020 7353 8415
Registrar of Diocese and Bishop's Legal Secretary Mr Martin Follett, Michelmores, Woodwater House, Pynes Hill, Exeter EX2 5WR
Tel: 01392 687421
email: mjf@michelmores.com
Deputy Registrar Mr Christopher Butcher, Michelsmores
Tel: 01392 687419
email: cnb@michelmores.com

THE DEPARTMENT FOR SUPPORT SERVICES

Director and Dioc Secretary Mr Mark Beedell (*as above*)
Asst Dioc Secretary Dr Ed Moffatt, The Old Deanery
Tel: 01392 294928
Fax: 01392 499594
email: ed.moffatt@exeter.anglican.org
Diocesan Office The Old Deanery, The Close, Exeter EX1 1HS
Tel: 01392 272686
Fax: 01392 499594
email: admin@exeter.anglican.org

ADMINISTRATION

Board of Finance (*Chairman*) Mr Michael Tagent, Challaborough Cottage, Ringmore, Kingsbridge TQ7 4HW
Tel: 01548 810520
email: michael.tagent@exeter.anglican.org
(*Secretary*) Mr Mark Beedell (*as above*)
Parsonages Committee (*Secretary*) Mr Graham Davies, The Old Deanery
Tel: 01392 294954
Fax: 01392 499594
email: graham.davies@exeter.anglican.org
Dioc Surveyors Mr Peter Stanton and Mr Mark Lewis, The Old Deanery
Tel: 01392 294952
Fax: 01392 499594
email: peter.stanton@exeter.anglican.org *or*
mark.lewis@exeter.anglican.org
Smith & Dunn, Alliance House, Cross St, Barnstaple EX31 1BA (*for Barnstaple Archdeaconry*)
Tel: 01271 327878
Fax: 01271 328288
Pastoral Committee (*Secretary*) Miss Pru Williams, The Old Deanery
Tel: 01392 294943
email: pastoral@exeter.anglican.org
Board of Patronage (*Chairman*) Mrs Shirley-Ann Williams, 2 Katherine's Lane, Ridgeway, Ottery St Mary EX11 1FB
Tel: 01404 811064
Trusts Mrs Jane Scriven, The Old Deanery
Tel: 01392 294913
email: jane.scriven@exeter.anglican.org
Designated Officer Mr Mark Beedell (*as above*)

CHILD PROTECTION

Mrs Sue Chamberlain, The Old Deanery
Tel: 01392 294912
email: sue.chamberlain@exeter.anglican.org

CHURCHES

Dioc Advisory Committee for the Care and Maintenance of Churches (Chairman) Vacancy; *(Secretary)* Miss Janet Croysdale, The Old Deanery; *Tel:* 01392 294945; *email:* dac@exeter.anglican.org
Redundant Churches Uses Committee (Secretary) Miss Pru Williams *(as above)*

COMMUNICATIONS

Communications Officer Vacancy
The Church of England, Devon (Diocesan News)
Tel: 01392 294905
07812 110636 (Mobile)
email: communications@exeter.anglican.org
Web: www.exeter.anglican.org

THE COUNCIL FOR WORK WITH CHILDREN AND YOUNG PEOPLE

Diocesan Director of Education Mrs Alyson Sheldrake, The Old Deanery, The Cloisters, Exeter EX1 1HS
Tel: 01392 294950
Fax: 01392 294966
email: dde@exeter.anglican.org
Executive Assistant Mrs Marilyn Pearce
Tel: 01392 294950
email: juliet.doswell@exeter.anglican.org
Acting Director of Education/Dioc Schools Improvement Officer Mrs Juliet Doswell
Tel: 01392 294941
email: juliet.doswell@exeter.anglican.org
Dioc Church Schools Liaison Officer Mrs Christina Mabin
Tel: 01392 294939
Dioc Consultant for SIAS, RE and Collective Worship Mrs Tricia Martin
Tel: 01392 294950
email: ress.pmartin26@btopenworld.com
Children's Work Adviser Miss Katherine Lyddon
Tel: 01392 294936
email: katherine.lyddon@exeter.anglican.org
Dioc Youth Work Adviser Martin Thompson
Tel: 01392 294932
email: martin.thompson@exeter.anglican.org
Dioc Youth Church Adviser Revd James Grier
Tel: 01392 294934
email: james.grier@exeter.anglican.org
Church Schools Surveyors Richard Power and Jason Down
Tel: 01392 294952
Fax: 01392 294967
email: school.premises@exeter.anglican.org *or* richard.power@exeter.anglican.org *or* jason.down@exeter.anglican.org
Church Schools Funding Adviser Raymond Twohig
Tel: 01392 294952
email: raymond.twohig@exeter.anglican.org

THE COUNCIL FOR WORSHIP AND MINISTRY

Director, Officer for Non-Stipendiary Ministry and Continuing Ministerial Education Canon Andrew Godsall, The Old Deanery   *Tel:* 01392 294902

Council Administrator Mrs Alyson Moore, The Old Deanery   *Tel:* 01392 294920
email: alyson.moore@exeter.anglican.org
Director of Ordinands, Adviser for Vocations and Bishop's Adviser for Women's Ministry Preb Amanda Rylands, The Palace, Exeter EX1 1HY
Tel: 01392 477702
email: ddo@exeter.anglican.org
Administrator Mrs Sandra Brown, The Palace, Exeter EX1 1HY   *Tel:* 01392 477702
email: stewardship@exeter.anglican.org
Local Stewardship Adviser, North Devon Mr Paul Mason   *Tel:* 01409 281548
email: paulgidcott@aol.com
Local Stewardship Adviser, South Devon Preb Mark Bate   *Tel:* 01392 833485
email: morleybate@freeuk.com
Board of Readers (Secretary) Mr Ronald Edinborough, The Old Deanery
Tel: 01392 294907
email: ron.edinborough@exeter.anglican.org
Adult Education Adviser Vacancy
Warden of Readers Ven David Gunn-Johnson, Stage Cross, Sanders Lane, Bishop's Tawton, Barnstaple EX32 0BE   *Tel:* 01271 375475
Fax: 01271 377934
email:
archdeacon.of.barnstaple@exeter.anglican.org
Local Ministry Teams Adviser Revd David Rudman, Rectory, Kingsnympton, Umberleigh EX37 9ST   *Tel:* 01769 580457
email: david.rudman@exeter.anglican.org
Spiritual Director Revd Viv Armstrong-MacDonnell, Strand House, Woodbury, Exeter EX5 1LZ   *Tel:* 01395 232790
email: viv.a-macdonnell@tiscali.co.uk
Mission Community Teams Adviser Revd David Rudman, Rectory, Kingsnympton, Umberleigh EX37 9ST   *Tel:* 01769 580457
email: david.rudman@exeter.anglican.org
Dioc Consultant for Worship and Music Mr Andrew Maries   *Tel:* 01884 34389
email: maries@keynotetrust.org.uk
Web: www.exeterdlc.org.uk

THE COUNCIL FOR MISSION AND UNITY

Director and Diocesan Missioner Canon Mark Rylands, The Old Deanery   *Tel:* 01392 294903
Fax: 01392 294965
email: pumpkin@exeter.anglican.org
Administrator Mrs Lindi Ching, The Old Deanery
Tel: 01392 294930
email: fishing@exeter.anglican.org
Chaplain with Deaf People Revd Catherine Carlyon, The Old Deanery
Tel: 01392 294909 (voice and text)
Fax: 01392 294965
07855 098953 (Mobile)
email: catherinecarlyon@btopenworld.com
Dioc Ecumenical Adviser Revd Simon Crittall, The Old Deanery   *Tel:* 01392 294960
email: simon.crittall@exeter.anglican.org

County Ecumenical Officer Revd Simon Taylor, 1 Albert Terrace, Princetown, Yelverton PL20 6QP
Tel: 01822 890412
email: staylor921@aol.com
Cyprus and the Gulf Link (Chairman) Mr Oliver Mayfield, Bank House, Market Square, Colyton EX24 6JS *Tel and Fax:* 01297 552942
email: oliver.colyton@tiscali.co.uk
Ministry of Healing and Deliverance Ven Mike Edson, Rectory, Abbotsham Rd, Bideford EX39 3AB *Tel:* 01237 470228
Thika Link Mrs Kate Bray (parish links), The Old Deanery *Tel:* 01392 294930
email: thika.link@exeter.anglican.org
World Development Adviser Vacancy
FRED (Fresh Expressions Devon) Canon Mark Rylands (*as above*)
Nightchurch Steve Jones, Exeter Cathedral, Exeter EX1 1HT *Tel:* 020 8144 2026
email: steve@nightchurch.org.uk

THE COUNCIL FOR CHURCH AND SOCIETY
Director Mr Martyn Goss, The Old Deanery
Tel: 01392 294924
Fax: 01392 499594
email: martyn@exeter.anglican.org
Social Responsibility Officer Miss Sally Farrant, The Old Deanery *Tel:* 01392 294918
email: sally.farrant@exeter.anglican.org
Family Life and Marriage Education Coordinator Mrs Susie Ursell, The Old Deanery
Tel: 01392 294919
email: susie.ursell@exeter.anglican.org
Rural Officer Mrs Sue Tucker, Quither Farm, Quither, Milton Abbot, Tavistock PL19 0PZ
Tel: 01822 860177 (Work)
01392 294921 (Office)
email: sue.tucker@exeter.anglican.org

MISCELLANEOUS ORGANIZATIONS
Widows and Dependants (Exeter Archdeaconry) Revd Trevor Woodbridge, 19 Malborough Rd, Exeter EX2 4TJ *Tel:* 01392 491050
(Totnes Archdeaconry) Revd Tony Meek, The Willows, Orley Rd, Ipplepen, Newton Abbot TQ12 5SA *Tel:* 01803 814370
Fax: 01803 814369
email: FrTonyMeek@aol.com
(Plymouth Archdeaconry) Preb John Richards, 24 Trewithy Drive, Crownhill, Plymouth PL6 5TY
Tel: 01752 214442
email: jfr-sjr@fish.co.uk
(Barnstaple Archdeaconry) Preb Dr Kenneth Moss, 3 Mondeville Way, Northam, Bideford EX39 1DQ

DIOCESAN RECORD OFFICE
Devon Record Office, Great Moor House, Bittern Rd, Sowton Industrial Estate, Exeter EX2 7NL
Archivist Mr John Draisey *Tel:* 01392 384253
email: devrc@devon.gov.uk

RURAL DEANS
ARCHDEACONRY OF EXETER
Aylesbeare Revd Ian Morter, Rectory, 1 Maer Lane, Exmouth EX8 2DA *Tel:* 01395 272227
email: ian.c.mortar@lineone.net
Cadbury Revd Douglas Dettmer, Rectory, Thorverton, Exeter EX5 5NR *Tel:* 01392 860332
Christianity Revd Stephen Bessent, Rectory, Alphington, Exeter EX24 8XJ *Tel:* 01392 437662
email: stephenbessent@beeb.net
Cullompton Revd Alan MacDonald, Rectory, 21a King St, Silverton, Exeter EX5 4JG
Tel: 01392 860350
email: almac01@tinyonline.co.uk
Assistant Rural Dean Revd Anna Norman-Walker, Rectory, Willand, Cullompton EX15 2RH
Tel: 01884 32509
email: anna@norman-walker.fsnet.co.uk
Honiton Preb Sue Roberts, Rectory, Rookwood Close, Honiton EX14 1BH *Tel:* 01404 42925
email: revdsue@btinternet.com
Kenn Revd Graham Mayer, Rectory, Dry Lane, Christow, Exeter EX6 7PE
Tel: 01647 252845
email: rivertide@btinternet.com
Ottery Revd Robert Wilkinson, The Rectory, Grove Rd, Whimple, Exeter EX5 2TP
Tel: 01404 822521
email: robwilkinson@lineone.net
Tiverton Revd Alan MacDonald, Rectory, 21a King St, Silverton, Exeter EX5 4JG
Tel: 01392 860350
email: almac01@tinyonline.co.uk
Assistant Rural Dean Revd Anna Norman-Walker, Rectory, Willand, Cullompton EX15 2RH
Tel: 01884 32509
email: anna@norman-walker.fsnet.co.uk

ARCHDEACONRY OF TOTNES
Moreton Revd Paul Wimsett, Vicarage, The Parade, Chudleigh, Newton Abbot TQ13 0JF
Tel: 01626 853241
email: wimsett@tesco.net
Newton Abbot and Ipplepen Revd Ian Eglin, Rectory, Paternoster Lane, Ipplepen, Newton Abbot TQ12 5RY *Tel:* 01803 812215
email: ianeglin@talktalk.net
Okehampton Revd Stephen Cook, Rectory, 1 Church Path, Okehampton EX20 1LW
Tel: 01837 659297
email: scook9673@aol.com
Torbay Revd David Witchell, Vicarage, Locarno Ave, Preston, Paignton TQ3 2DH
Tel: 01803 522872
Totnes Revd John Rowland, Vicarage, Glebelands, Buckfastleigh TQ11 0BH
Tel: 01364 644228
Woodleigh Revd Neil Barker, Vicarage, Modbury, Ivybridge PL21 0QN *Tel:* 01548 830260
email: revneil@i.am

ARCHDEACONRY OF BARNSTAPLE

Barnstaple Revd Paul Hockey, Vicarage, Fremington, Barnstaple EX31 2NX
Tel: 01271 373879
email: paul@hockey17.fslife.co.uk
Hartland Revd Andrew Richardson, Rectory, Old Market Drive, Woolsery, Bideford EX39 5QF
Tel: 01237 431571
Holsworthy Vacancy
Shirwell Revd Leslie Austin, Parsonage, 1 The Glebe, Bratton Fleming, Barnstaple EX31 4RE
Tel: 01598 710807
email: leslie@laustin4.wanadoo.co.uk
South Molton Revd Dr Andrew Jones, Rectory, Bishopsnympton, South Molton EX36 4NY
Tel: 01769 550427
email: ajctherectory@btinternet.com
Torrington Vacancy

ARCHDEACONRY OF PLYMOUTH

Ivybridge Preb David Arnott, Vicarage, Bowden Hill, Yealmpton, Plymouth PL8 2JX
Tel and *Fax:* 01752 880979
Devonport Revd Stephen Beach, Vicarage, Agaton Rd, St Budeaux, Plymouth PL5 2EW
Tel: 01752 361019
email: stephenbeach@btinternet.com
Moorside Preb Paul Hancock, Vicarage, 33 Tavistock Rd, Crownhill, Plymouth PL5 3AF
Tel: 01752 783617
email: hazelnut33@aol.com
Sutton Revd Karl Freeman, Rectory, 9 Seymour Drive, Mannamead, Plymouth PL3 5BG
Tel: 01752 248601
email: karldesk@blueyonder.co.uk
Tavistock Revd Geoff Lloyd, Rectory, Sampford Spiney, Horrabridge, Yelverton PL20 7RE
Tel: 01822 854682
email: geoff.lloyd@tiscali.co.uk

DIOCESE OF GLOUCESTER

Founded in 1541. Gloucestershire except for a few parishes in the north (WORCESTER); a few parishes in the south (BRISTOL) and one parish in the east (OXFORD); the northern third of South Gloucestershire; two parishes in Wiltshire; a small area in south-west Warwickshire; a few parishes in the southern part of Worcestershire.

Population 617,000   Area 1,140 sq m
Full-time Stipendiary Parochial Clergy 125   Benefices 126
Parishes 317   Churches 396
www.gloucester.anglican.org

BISHOP (40th)
Rt Revd Michael Francis Perham, Church House, College Green, Gloucester GL1 2LY [2004]
Tel: 01452 410022 ext. 271
Fax: 01452 308324
email: bshpglos@glosdioc.org.uk
Home address: Bishopscourt, Pitt St, Gloucester GL1 2BQ
Tel: 01452 524598
[Michael Gloucestr]
Bishop's Chaplain Revd Aidan Platten (*same address and fax no.; tel. no. as above, ext. 268*)
email: aplatten@glosdioc.org.uk
Bishop's Secretary Miss Fiona Welbourn (*same address and tel. no.*)
email: fwelbourn@glosdioc.org.uk

SUFFRAGAN BISHOP
TEWKESBURY Rt Revd John Stewart Went, Bishop's House, Staverton, Cheltenham GL51 0TW [1995]
Tel: 01242 680188
Fax: 01242 680233
email: bshptewk@star.co.uk

HONORARY ASSISTANT BISHOPS
Rt Revd Peter Vaughan, Willowbrook, Downington, Lechlade GL7 3DL [2002]
Tel: 01367 252216
Rt Revd Humphrey Taylor, 10 High St, Honeybourne, Evesham WR11 7PQ [2003]
Tel: 01386 834846
Rt Revd Jonathan Bailey, 28 Burleigh Way, Wickwar, Wotton-under-Edge GL12 8LR [2005]
Tel: 01454 294112
Rt Revd Patrick Harris, Apartment B, Ireton House, Pavilion Gardens, The Park, Cheltenham GL50 2SP [2005]
Tel: 01242 231376

CATHEDRAL CHURCH OF ST PETER AND THE HOLY AND INDIVISIBLE TRINITY
Dean Very Revd Nicholas Bury, The Deanery, 1 Miller's Green, Gloucester GL1 2BN [1997]
Tel: 01452 524167
email: thedean@gloucestercathedral.org.uk
Dean's Secretary Mrs Fiona Price, The Chapter Office, 2 College Green, Gloucester GL1 2LR
Tel: 01452 508217
email: fiona@gloucestercathedral.org.uk

Chapter Office 2 College Green, Gloucester GL1 2LR
Tel: 01452 528095
Fax: 01452 300469
Web: www.gloucestercathedral.org.uk
Canons Residentiary
Precentor Canon Neil Heavisides, 7 College Green, Gloucester GL1 2LX [1993]
Tel: 01452 523987
email: nheavisides@gloucestercathedral.org.uk
Canon Pastor Canon Celia Thomson, 3 Miller's Green, Gloucester GL1 2BN [2003]
Tel: 01452 415824
email: cthomson@gloucestercathedral.org.uk
Ven Geoffrey Sidaway, Glebe House, Church Lane, Maisemore, Gloucester GL2 8EY [2007]
Tel: 01452 528500
Fax: 01452 381528
email: archdglos@star.co.uk
Canon Dr David Hoyle, 4 College Green, Gloucester GL1 2LR [2002]
Tel: 01452 410022 ext. 231
email: dhoyle@glosdioc.org.uk
Chapter Steward Mr Mark Beckett, Chapter Office
Tel: 01452 508216
email: mbeckett@gloucestercathedral.org.uk
Director of Music Mr Adrian Partington, 7 Miller's Green, Gloucester GL1 2BN
Tel: 01452 524764
email: partington@gloucestercathedral.org.uk
Assistant Director of Music Mr Ashley Grote, 14 College Green, Gloucester GL1 2LX
Tel: 01452 526403
email: ashley@gloucestercathedral.org.uk
Music and Liturgy Administrator Mrs Helen Sims, The Chapter Office (*as above*)   *Tel:* 01452 508212
email: helen@gloucestercathedral.org.uk

ARCHDEACONS
GLOUCESTER Ven Geoffrey Sidaway, Glebe House, Church Lane, Maisemore, Gloucester GL2 8EY [2000]
Tel: 01452 528500
Fax: 01452 381528
email: archdglos@star.co.uk
CHELTENHAM Ven Hedley Ringrose, The Sanderlings, Thorncliffe Drive, Cheltenham GL51 6PY [1998]
Tel: 01242 522923
Fax: 01242 235925
email: archdchelt@star.co.uk

CONVOCATION (MEMBERS OF THE HOUSE OF CLERGY OF THE GENERAL SYNOD)
Proctors for Clergy
Revd David Primrose

MEMBERS OF THE HOUSE OF LAITY OF THE GENERAL SYNOD
Canon Nigel Chetwood
Mr William Sargison
Mr Graham Smith

DIOCESAN OFFICERS
Dioc Secretary Dr Kevin Brown, Church House, College Green, Gloucester GL1 2LY
Tel: 01452 410022 ext. 223
Fax: 01452 308324
Secretary to Dioc Secretary Ms Andrea Goodman (same address)   Tel: 01452 410022 ext. 223
email: agoodman@glosdioc.org.uk
Chancellor of Diocese Chancellor June Rodgers, 2 Harcourt Buildings, The Temple, London EC4Y 9DB
Registrar of Diocese and Bishop's Legal Secretary Mr Chris Peak, Dioc Registry, 34 Brunswick Rd, Gloucester GL1 1JW   Tel: 01452 520224
Fax: 01452 306866
email: chris.peak@madgelloyd.com

DIOCESAN ORGANIZATIONS
Diocesan Office Church House, College Green, Gloucester GL1 2LY   Tel: 01452 410022
Fax: 01452 308324
email: church.house@glosdioc.org.uk
Web: www.gloucester.anglican.org

ADMINISTRATION
Dioc Synod (Vice President, House of Clergy) Canon Dr Jeni Parsons, Rectory, Matson Lane, Matson, Gloucester GL4 6DX   Tel: 01452 522598
email: jeni@hencity.fsnet.co.uk
(Vice-President, House of Laity) Mrs Margaret Price, 33 Lambert Gardens, Shurdington, Cheltenham GL51 4SW   Tel: 01242 862683
email: margaretjprice@blueyonder.co.uk
(Secretary) Dr Kevin Brown, Church House
Board of Finance (Chairman) Revd Christopher Finlay, Coombe House, Calcot, Cheltenham GL54 3JZ   Tel: 01285 720806
email: coombehousecalcot@tiscali.co.uk
(Secretary) Dr Kevin Brown *(as above)*
Director of Finance Mr Benjamin Preece-Smith, Church House
Houses Committee (Secretary) Ms Juliet Weston, Church House
Pastoral Committee (Secretary) Dr Kevin Brown; *(as above)*
Board of Patronage (Secretary) Canon Jonathan MacKechnie-Jarvis, Church House
Designated Officer Dr Kevin Brown *(as above)*
Trust (Secretary) Canon Jonathan MacKechnie-Jarvis *(as above)*
Redundant Churches Uses Committee (Secretary) Canon Jonathan MacKechnie-Jarvis *(as above)*

Glebe Committee (Secretary) Ms Juliet Weston *(as above)*

CHURCHES
Advisory Committee for the Care of Churches (Chairman) Mr Henry Russell, Ley Mary Farmhouse, Windrush, Burford, Oxon OX18 4TS
Tel: 01451 844397
(Secretary) Canon Jonathan MacKechnie-Jarvis *(as above)*

EDUCATION
Director of Education Mrs Helena Arnold (from Jan 2009), 4 College Green, Gloucester GL1 2LR
Tel: 01452 410022 ext. 272
email: pmetcalf@glosdioc.org.uk
Adviser to Schools Mrs Shahne Vickery *(same address)*   Tel: 01452 410022 ext. 259
email: svickery@glosdioc.org.uk
Buildings and Admissions Adviser Mr Rob Stephens *(same address)*   Tel: 01452 410022 ext. 242
email: rstephens@glosdioc.org.uk
Dioc Youth Officer Mr Stephen Bullock *(same address)*   Tel: 01452 410022 ext. 245
email: sbullock@glosdioc.org.uk
Dioc Children's Officer Revd Dr Sandra Millar *(same address)*   Tel: 01452 410022 ext. 246
email: smillar@glosdioc.org.uk

MINISTRY
Director of Ministry Canon David Hoyle, 4 College Green, Gloucester GL1 2LR
Tel: 01452 410022 ext. 231
email: dhoyle@glosdioc.org.uk
Officer for Ministry Revd John Witcombe *(same address)*
Assistant Director of Ordinands Revd Catherine Williams *(as above)*   Tel: 01452 410022 ext. 241
Revd Stephen Ware *(as above)*   ext. 261
Vocations Officer Revd Catherine Williams, *(as above)*   Tel: 01452 410022
Dean of Women Clergy Canon Jane Kenchington, 7 Warren Croft, Dursley, North Nibley GL11 6EN   Tel: 01453 546509
email: janeeb.kenchington@virgin.net
NSM Officer Canon Michael Tucker, Rectory, Amberley, Stroud GL5 5JG   Tel: 01453 878515
Chaplain for Deaf and Hard of Hearing People Revd Steve Morris, The Vicarage, 27a Barnwood Avenue, Gloucester GL4 3AB   Tel: 01452 619531
email: spadework@fsmail.net
Warden of Readers Revd Stephen Ware, 4 College Green, Gloucester GL1 2LR
Tel: 01452 410022 ext. 261
email: sware@glosdioc.org.uk
West of England Ministerial Training Course (Principal) Canon Dr Michael Parsons, University of Gloucestershire, Francis Close Hall, Swindon Rd, Cheltenham GL50 4AZ
Tel and Fax: 01242 543382
email: office@wemtc.freeserve.co.uk

Local Ministry Officers Revd Grahame Humphries, Vicarage, The Square, Blockley, Moreton-in-Marsh GL56 9ES Tel: 01386 700283
Mrs Kathy Lawrence, 4 College Green, Gloucester GL1 2LR Tel: 01452 410022 ext. 263
email: klawrence@glosdioc.org.uk
Revd Brian Parfitt (same address)
Tel: 01452 410022 ext. 238
email: bparfitt@glosdioc.org.uk
Mrs Melanie Griffiths (same address)
Tel: 01452 410022 ext. 262
email: mgriffiths@glosdioc.org.uk

BISHOP'S WORSHIP, PRAYER AND SPIRITUALITY GROUP
Chairman Canon Paul Williams

PRESS AND PUBLICATIONS
Communications Officer Mrs Lucy Taylor, Church House Tel: 01452 410022 ext. 250
07811 174125 (Mobile)
email: ltaylor@glosdioc.org.uk
Editor of Dioc Directory Mrs Lucy Taylor

DIOCESAN RECORD OFFICE
Gloucestershire Records Office, Clarence Row, Gloucester GL1 3DW Dioc Archivist Ms Heather Forbes Tel: 01452 425295
email: records@gloscc.gov.uk (Office)
email: heather.forbes@gloucestershire.gov.uk

DIOCESAN RESOURCE CENTRE
Warden Mrs Carolyn Wright, 9 College Green, Gloucester GL1 2LX Tel: 01452 385217
email: glosrerc@star.co.uk

SOCIAL RESPONSIBILITY
Director of Social Responsibility Canon Adrian Slade, 38 Sydenham Villas Rd, Cheltenham GL52 6DZ Tel: 01242 253162
email: glossr@star.co.uk
Assistant Dioc Officer for Social Responsibility Mrs Fran Tolond, 1 Mickle Mead, Highnam, Gloucester GL2 8NF Tel: 01452 383441
email: glosasro@star.co.uk
County Ecumenical Officer Revd Dr Alison Evans, Elm Farm House, High St, Kings Stanley, Stonehouse GL10 3JF Tel: 01453 824034
email: malcolm.alison@btinternet.com
Accord Canon Dr Michael Tucker, Rectory, Amberley, Stroud GL5 5GJ Tel: 01453 878515
email: mike@tuckers.org.uk
Rural Adviser Mrs Barbara Bridges, 5 Churchill Place, Fairford, Glos Tel: 01452 415830
email: barbarajbridges@aol.com
Environmental Development Officer Revd Kingsley Jones, St Aldate's Vicarage, Finlay Rd, Gloucester GL4 6TN Tel: 01242 523906
email: arkj.kcj@care4free.net
Ecumenical Adviser Vacancy (contact Church House)
Tel: 01452 410022

AREA DEANS
ARCHDEACONRY OF CHELTENHAM
Campden Revd Colin Mattock, Vicarage, Stratford Rd, Honeybourne, Evesham WR11 5PP
Tel: 01386 830302
email: colin.mattock@btinternet.com
Cheltenham Canon Andrew Dow, Rectory, Thorncliffe Drive, Cheltenham GL51 1PY
Tel: 01242 701580
email: rector@stmattschelt.org.uk
Assistant Area Dean Revd Michael Garland, St Mary's Vicarage, 63 Church St, Charlton Kings, Cheltenham GL53 8AT Tel: 01242 253402
email: michael.garland50@tiscali.co.uk
Cirencester Vacancy (contact Church House)
Fairford Revd Brian Atkinson, Vicarage, Fairford GL7 4BB Tel: 01285 712467
email: Katkio1225@aol.com
Northleach Canon George Mitchell, Vicarage, Cheap St, Chedworth, Cheltenham GL54 4AA
Tel: 01285 720392
email: canongeorgemitchell@btinternet.com
Stow Revd David Francis, Rectory, Sheep St, Stow-on-the-Wold, Cheltenham GL54 1AA
Tel: 01451 830607
email: jennyfrancis@fish.co.uk
Tewkesbury and Winchcombe Revd Nikki Arthy, St Martha's, 22 Delavale Rd, Winchcombe, Cheltenham GL54 5HN Tel: 01242 603109
email: nikkiarthy@btinternet.com

ARCHDEACONRY OF GLOUCESTER
Dursley Vacancy (contact Church House)
Forest North Revd John Seaman, Vicarage, 1 Whetstones, Unlawater Lane, Newnham GL14 1BT Tel: 01594 516648
email: rj.seaman@btopenworld.com
Forest South Revd Royston Grosvenor, Tidenham Vicarage, Gloucester Rd, Tutshill, Chepstow, Monmouthshire NP16 7DH Tel: 01291 622442
email:
roystongrosvenor@tidenham42.freeserve.co.uk
Gloucester City Revd Graham Osborne, St Catharine's Vicarage, 29 Denmark Rd, Gloucester GL1 3JQ Tel and Fax: 01452 524497
email: gdosborne@bigfoot.com
Assistant Area Dean Canon Tim Newcombe, Holy Trinity Vicarage, Church Rd, Longlevens, Gloucester GL2 0AJ Tel: 01452 524129
email: tnewco@tiscali.co.uk
Gloucester North Revd Richard Mitchell, Vicarage, School Lane, Shurdington, Cheltenham GL51 4TF Tel: 01242 702911
email: richard.mitchell@talk21.com
Hawkesbury Revd David Primrose, Vicarage, 27 Castle St, Thornbury, Bristol BS35 1HQ
Tel: 01454 413209
email: primrose@blueyonder.co.uk
Stroud Revd Stephen Bowen, Vicarage, Brimscombe, Stroud GL5 2PA Tel: 01453 882204
email: sbowen6@hotmail.co.uk

Founded in 1927. The western two-thirds of Surrey south of the Thames, except for a small area in the north-east (SOUTHWARK); areas of north-east Hampshire; a few parishes in Greater London; one parish in West Sussex.

Population 964,000   Area 538 sq m
Full-time Stipendiary Parochial Clergy 162   Benefices 140
Parishes 164   Churches 217
www.cofeguildford.org.uk
Overseas link diocese: IDWAL (Inter-Diocesan West Africa Link) – Nigeria.

BISHOP (9th)
Rt Revd Christopher Hill, Willow Grange, Woking Rd, Guildford GU4 7QS [2004]
Tel: 01483 590500
Fax: 01483 590501
Bishop's Personal Assistant Mary Morris
email: mary.morris@cofeguildford.org.uk

SUFFRAGAN BISHOP
DORKING Rt Revd Ian James Brackley, Dayspring, 13 Pilgrim's Way, Guildford GU4 8AD [1996]
Tel: 01483 570829
Fax: 01483 567268
email: bishop.ian@cofeguildford.org.uk
Bishop's Personal Assistant Muriel Mulvany
email: muriel.mulvany@cofeguildford.org.uk

CATHEDRAL CHURCH OF THE HOLY SPIRIT
Dean Very Revd Victor Stock, The Deanery, 1 Cathedral Close, Guildford GU2 7TL [2002]
Tel: 01483 547861 (Office)
01483 560328 (Home)
email: dean@guildford-cathedral.org
Dean's Personal Assistant Mrs Cathy Mansell
Tel: 01483 547862 (Office)
email: cathy@guildford-cathedral.org
Cathedral Office Guildford Cathedral, Stag Hill, Guildford, Surrey GU2 7UP   *Tel:* 01483 547860
Fax: 01483 303350
email: reception@guildford-cathedral.org
Canons Residentiary
Sub-Dean and Precentor Canon Nicholas Thistlethwaite, 3 Cathedral Close, Guildford GU2 7TL [1999]   *Tel:* 01483 547865
email: precentor@guildford-cathedral.org
Canon Pastor Canon Angela Weaver, 4 Cathedral Close, Guildford GU2 7TL [2006]
Tel: 01483 547863
email: angela@guildford-cathedral.org
University Chaplain Canon Jonathan Frost, 6 Cathedral Close, Guildford GU2 7TL [2002]
Tel: 07870 277709 (Mobile)
email: j.frost@surrey.ac.uk
Cathedral Administrator Commodore Tony Lyddon RN, Cathedral Office   *Tel:* 01483 547864
email: administrator@guildford-cathedral.org

Cathedral Organist and Master of the Choristers Mrs Katherine Dienes-Williams, 5 Cathedral Close, Guildford GU2 7TL   *Tel:* 01483 547866
email: organist@guildford-cathedral.org

ARCHDEACONS
SURREY Ven Stuart Beake, Dioc House, Quarry St, Guildford GU1 3XG [2005]   *Tel:* 01483 790350
email: stuart.beake@cofeguildford.org.uk
DORKING Ven Julian Henderson, The Old Cricketers, Portsmouth Rd, Ripley, Woking, Surrey GU23 6ER [2005]   *Tel:* 01483 479300
Fax: 01483 479568
email: julian.henderson@cofeguildford.org.uk

CONVOCATION (MEMBERS OF THE HOUSE OF CLERGY OF THE GENERAL SYNOD)
Dignitaries in Convocation
The Bishop of Dorking
Proctors for Clergy
Canon John Ashe
Revd Robert Cotton
Ven Julian Henderson
Revd Jolyon Trickey

MEMBERS OF THE HOUSE OF LAITY OF THE GENERAL SYNOD
Canon Peter Bruinvels
Mr Keith Malcouronne
Anne Martin
Ms Helen Morgan

DIOCESAN OFFICERS
Dioc Secretary Mr Stephen Marriott, Diocesan House, Quarry St, Guildford GU1 3XG
Tel: 01483 571826
Fax: 01483 790333
Chancellor of Diocese Mr Andrew Jordan, 11 Fairlawn Avenue, Chiswick, London W4 5EF
Registrar of Diocese and Bishop's Legal Secretary Mr Peter Beesley, 1 The Sanctuary, London SW1P 3JT   *Tel:* 020 7222 5381
Fax: 020 7222 7502
Deputy Registrar Mr Nicholas Richens

DIOCESAN ORGANIZATIONS
Diocesan Office Diocesan House, Quarry St, Guildford GU1 3XG   *Tel:* 01483 571826
Fax: 01483 790333
email: reception.diocese@cofeguildford.org.uk

ADMINISTRATION

President The Bishop of Guildford
Dioc Synod (*Vice-President, House of Clergy*) Revd Robert Cotton, Holy Trinity Rectory, 9 Eastgate Gardens, Guildford GU1 4AZ
(*Vice-President, House of Laity*) Canon Peter Bruinvels, 14 High Meadow Close, St Paul's Rd West, Dorking RH4 2LG   *Tel:* 01306 887082
(*Secretary*) Mr Stephen Marriott, Dioc House
     email: stephen.marriott@cofeguildford.org.uk
Deputy Secretary Mr Michael Bishop, Dioc House
     email: mike.bishop@cofeguildford.org.uk
Board of Finance (*Chairman*) Mr David Smith, Dioc House; (*Secretary*) Mr Stephen Marriott (*as above*)
Accountant Mr Stephen Collyer (*as above*)
Deputy Secretary Mr Michael Bishop (*as above*)
Asst Secretaries Mr John White, Vacancy, Dioc House
Parsonages and Property Committee Mr John White (*as above*) *email:* john.white@cofeguildford.org.uk
Pastoral Committee Mr Michael Bishop (*as above*)
Designated Officer Mr Peter Beesley, 1 The Sanctuary, London SW1P 3JT   *Tel:* 020 7222 5381
                           Fax: 020 7222 7502

CHURCHES

Advisory Committee for the Care of Churches (*Chairman*) Mr Hamish Donaldson, Edgecombe, Hill Rd, Haslemere GU27 2JN; (*Secretary*) Revd Ruth Walker, Dioc House

EDUCATION

Education Centre Diocesan Education Centre, Stag Hill, Guildford GU2 7UP
                            Tel: 01483 450423
                            Fax: 01483 450424
Director of Education and Secretary Dioc Board of Education Mr Derek Holbird
     email: derek.holbird@cofeguildford.org.uk
Senior Education Officer – Children and Parish Education Mrs Heather Henderson
Assistant Children's Education Officer Mrs Alison Hendy
Youth Adviser Mr David Welch
Adviser in Adult Education Mrs Joanna Walker
Further Education Adviser Vacancy
Centre Administrator Jill Horwood
Schools' Officer Development and Personnel Vacancy
Senior Education Officer – Schools Michael Hall

MINISTRY

Director of Ministerial Training and CME Director Canon Hazel Whitehead, Dioc House
                            Tel: 01483 790307
     email: hazel.whitehead@cofeguildford.org.uk
Director of Ordinands Revd William Challis, Dioc House   *Tel:* 01483 571826
     email: william.challis@cofeguildford.org.uk
Adviser in Women's Ministry Canon Mavis Wilson, Rectory, Parsonage Way, Frimley GU16 8HZ

Guildford Diocesan Ministry Course (*Principal*) Revd John Schofield
Clerical Registry (*Registrar*) Revd Nicholas Farbridge, 55 Curling Vale, Onslow Village, Guildford GU2 5PH   *Tel:* 01483 531140
Warden of Readers Mrs Liz Lang, Rectory, Thursley Rd, Elstead GU8 6DG
                            Tel: 01252 703251
     email: lizlang@connectfree.co.uk
Senior Tutor for Pastoral Assistant's Foundation Course Revd Pauline Moyse, Dioc House
                            Tel: 01483 790321
     email: pauline.moyse@cofeguildford.org.uk
CME Tutor for Readers and Pastoral Assistants Revd Liz Boughton, Dioc House
                            Tel: 01483 790321
     email: liz.boughton@cofeguildford.org.uk
CME Tutor for Readers Revd Richard Hay
Readers' Board (*Registrar*) Dr Anthony Metcalfe, Peterstone, 15 The Mead, Ashtead KT21 2LZ
                            Tel: 01372 274162
     email: ar_metcalfe@yahoo.co.uk

MISSION, EVANGELISM AND PARISH DEVELOPMENT

Directors for Mission, Evangelism and Parish Development
Revd John Gooding, Dioc House
     email: john.gooding@cofeguildford.org.uk
Mr Tony Hennessey-Brown, Dioc House (*with specific responsibility for parish funding*)
email:
     tony.hennessey-brown@cofeguildford.org.uk
Dioc Ecumenical Officer Revd Stuart Thomas, 61 Ruxley Lane, Ewell KT19 0JG
                            Tel: 020 8393 5616
Parish Resources Officer Revd Bonnie Appleton, Dioc House
     email: bonnie.appleton@cofeguildford.org.uk
Nigeria Link Officer Revd David Minns

PRESS AND PUBLICATIONS

Director of Communications Revd Mark Rudall, Dioc House   *Tel:* 01483 790310
                           07779 654975 (Mobile)
     email: mark.rudall@cofeguildford.org.uk
Publicity Officer Mr Alan Brown (*same address*)
                            Tel: 01483 598878
     email: alan.brown@cofeguildford.org.uk
Editor of Dioc Newspaper Mrs Emma Nutbrown-Hughes (*as above*)   *Tel:* 01483 571826
     email: editorial@cofeguildford.org.uk
Editor of Dioc Directory Mrs Lynne Cowley
                            Tel: 01483 571826

DIOCESAN RECORD OFFICE

Surrey History Centre, 130 Goldsworth Rd, Woking GU2 1ND *County Archivist* Maggie Vaughan-Lewis; *Archivist* Diana Stiff
                            Tel: 01483 594594

SOCIAL RESPONSIBILITY

Director Canon Chris Rich, Dioc House
Church's Community Care Adviser Tony Oakden
email: tony.oakden@cofeguildford.org.uk

RURAL DEANS
ARCHDEACONRY OF SURREY

Aldershot Revd David Willey, Rectory, 66 Church Ave, Farnborough GU14 7AP   *Tel:* 01252 544754
Cranleigh Revd John Bundock, Vicarage, Birtley Rise, Bramley, Guildford GU5 0HZ
Tel: 01483 892109
Farnham Revd J. T. L. Still, 2 Middle Ave, Farnham GU9 8JL   *Tel:* 01252 715505
Godalming Revd J. M. Fellows, Rectory, Compton, Guildford GU3 1ED   *Tel:* 01428 810328
Guildford Revd Barbara Messham, All Saints Vicarage, 18 Vicarage Gate, Onslow Village, Guildford GU24 7QJ   *Tel:* 01483 572006
Surrey Heath Revd A. Body, Chobham Vicarage, Bagshot Rd, Chobham, Woking GU24 8BY
Tel: 01276 858197

ARCHDEACONRY OF DORKING

Dorking Revd Andrew Coe, Rectory, Dorking RH5 5DL   *Tel:* 01306 631469
email: revdandrewdj.coe@btinternet.com
Emly Revd N. J. Whitehead, Vicarage, 5 Burwood Rd, Hersham, Walton-on-Thames KT12 4AA
Tel: 01932 227445
email: thevicar@stpetershersham.com
Epsom Revd Stuart Thomas, St Francis Vicarage, 61 Ruxley Lane, Ewell KT19 0JG
Tel: 020 8393 5616
email: revstuart.thomas@btinternet.com
Leatherhead Canon Jeremy Cresswell, Vicarage, Steel's Lane, Oxshott, Leatherhead KT22 0QH
Tel: 01372 842071
email: vicar@oxshott.co.uk
Runnymede Revd T. J. Hillier, Vicarage, London St, Chertsey KT16 8AA   *Tel:* 01932 563141
email: hillier@timp33.freeserve.co.uk
Woking Revd Nick Aiken, Rectory, Aviary Rd, Pyrford GU22 8TH   *Tel:* 01932 352914
email: rector@wisleywithpyrford.org

DIOCESE OF HEREFORD

Founded *c* 676. Herefordshire; the southern half of Shropshire; a few parishes in Powys and Monmouthshire.

Population 319,000   Area 1,660 sq m
Full-time Stipendiary Parochial Clergy 82   Benefices 116
Parishes 344   Churches 422
www.hereford.anglican.org
Overseas link dioceses: Masasi and Tanga with Zanzibar,
Dar es Salaam (Tanzania), Kirchenkreis of Nurnberg.

BISHOP (104th)
Rt Revd Anthony Priddis, The Bishop's House, Hereford HR4 9BN [2004]   *Tel:* 01432 271355
Fax: 01432 373346
email: bishop@hereford.anglican.org

SUFFRAGAN BISHOP
LUDLOW Rt Revd Michael W. Hooper, Bishop's House, Corvedale Rd, Craven Arms, Shropshire SY7 9BT [2002]   *Tel* and *Fax:* 01588 673571
email: bishopofludlow@btinternet.com

CATHEDRAL CHURCH OF THE BLESSED VIRGIN MARY AND ST ETHELBERT
Dean Very Revd Michael Tavinor, The Deanery, College Cloisters, Hereford HR1 2NG [2002]
Tel: 01432 374203
email: dean@herefordcathedral.org
Cathedral Office 5 College Cloisters, Hereford HR1 2NG   *Tel:* 01432 374200
Fax: 01432 374220
email: office@herefordcathedral.org
Web: www.herefordcathedral.org
Canons Residentiary
Chancellor Canon Christopher Pullin, 2 Cathedral Close, Hereford HR1 2NG [2008]
Tel: 01432 341905
Precentor Canon Andrew Piper, 1 Cathedral Close, Hereford HR1 2NG [2003]   *Tel:* 01432 266193
email: precentor@herefordcathedral.org

Additional Members
Miss Sandra Elliott, c/o Hereford Cathedral
Mrs Rosemary Lording, 93 King's Acre Rd, Hereford HR4 0RQ
Mr Kevin Mason, The Old Rectory, Fownhope, Hereford HR1 4PS
Cathedral Administrator and Chapter Clerk Lt Col Andrew Eames, Cathedral Office
Tel: 01432 374201
email: clerk@herefordcathedral.org
Cathedral Organist Mr Geraint Bowen, 7 College Cloisters, Hereford HR1 2NG   *Tel:* 01432 374238
email: organist@herefordcathedral.org
Assistant Organist Mr Peter Dyke, 1a Cathedral Close, Hereford HR1 2NG   *Tel:* 01432 374215
email: peter.dyke@herefordcathedral.org

ARCHDEACONS
HEREFORD Ven Malcolm Colmer, Dioc Office
Tel: 01432 373316
email: archdeacon@hereford.anglican.org
LUDLOW Rt Revd Michael W. Hooper, Bishop's House, Corvedale Rd, Craven Arms, Shropshire SY7 9BT   *Tel* and *Fax:* 01588 673571
email: bishopofludlow@btinternet.com

CONVOCATION (MEMBERS OF THE HOUSE OF CLERGY OF THE GENERAL SYNOD)
Proctors for Clergy
Preb Brian Chave
Ven Malcolm Colmer
Preb Kay Garlick

MEMBERS OF THE HOUSE OF LAITY OF THE GENERAL SYNOD
Dr John Dinnen
Dr Martin Elcock
Mrs Rosemary Lording

DIOCESAN OFFICERS
Dioc Secretary Mr John Clark, Diocesan Office, The Palace, Hereford HR4 9BL
Tel: 01432 373300
Fax: 01432 352952
email: diosec@hereford.anglican.org
Chancellor of Diocese Chancellor R. Kaye, Leeds Combined Court Centre, The Court House, 1 Oxford Row, Leeds LS1 3BG   *Tel:* 0113 306 2800
Registrar of Diocese and Bishop's Legal Secretary Mr Peter Beesley, Dioc Registry, 1 The Sanctuary, Westminster, London SW1P 3JT
Tel: 020 7222 5381
Dioc Surveyors Hook Mason Partnership, 41 Widemarch St, Hereford HR4 9EA   *Tel:* 01432 352299

DIOCESAN ORGANIZATIONS
Dioc Office The Palace, Hereford HR4 9BL
Tel: 01432 373300
Fax: 01432 352952
email: diooffice@hereford.anglican.org
Bishop's Office The Palace, Hereford HR4 9BN
Tel: 01432 271355
Fax: 01432 373346

ADMINISTRATION

Dioc Synod (Chairman, House of Clergy) Preb B. Chave, Vicarage, Vowles Close, Hereford HR4 0DF *Tel:* 01432 273086
(Chairman, House of Laity) Mrs Diana George, Greenway, Walterstone, Hereford HR2 0DT
Tel: 01873 890259
(Secretary) Mr John Clark, Dioc Office
Board of Finance (Chairman) Mr Charles Hunter, Upper Grange, Bacton, Hereford HR2 0AR
Tel: 01981 240561
(Secretary) Mr John Clark *(as above)*
Financial Secretary Mr Gordon Powell, Dioc Office
Benefice Buildings Committee Mr John Clark *(as above)*
Glebe Committee Mr Stephen Challenger, Dioc Office
Board of Patronage Mr John Clark, Dioc Office
Designated Officer Mr Peter Beesley, 1 The Sanctuary, Westminster, London SW1P 3JT
Tel: 020 7222 5381
Pastoral Secretary Mr Graham Hamer, Dioc Office
Trusts Mr John Clark *(as above)*

CHURCHES

Advisory Committee for the Care of Churches (Chairman) The Archdeacon of Hereford *(as above)*
(Secretary) Mr Stephen Challenger *(as above)*

EDUCATION

Director of Education Vacancy *Tel:* 01432 373330
Fax: 01432 352952
email: education@hereford.anglican.org
Schools Adviser (Curriculum) Vacancy
Dioc Youth Officer Vacancy
Children's Adviser Mr Norris Boyland, The Cottage, Bishop Mascall Centre, Lower Galdeford, Ludlow, Shropshire SY8 1RZ
Tel: 01584 872334

BISHOP MASCALL CENTRE

Director Mrs Moira Gibbs *Tel:* 01584 873882
Fax: 01584 877945

MINISTRY AND TRAINING

Director of Ordinands Revd Mary Lou Toop, Vicarage, Minsterley, Shropshire SY5 0AA
Tel: 01743 790399
email: maryloutoop@lineone.net
Continuing Ministerial Education Officer Revd Sarah Cawdell, c/o Dioc Office
Lay Training Officer Revd Peter Massey, c/o Dioc Office
Local Ministry Officer Preb Graham Earney, Rectory, Wistanstow, Craven Arms, Shropshire SY7 8DG *Tel:* 01584 872822
Advisers for Non-Stipendiary Ministry Revd M. D. Vockins, Birchwood Lodge, Storridge, Malvern WR13 5EZ *Tel:* 01886 884366
Revd J. Edwards, 2 Madeley Wood View, Madeley, Telford TF7 5TF *Tel:* 01952 583254

Adviser on Women in Ministry Revd Jill Talbot-Ponsonby, Llan Retreat House, Twitchen, Clunbury, Craven Arms, Shropshire SY7 0HN
Tel: 01588 660417
email: jill@talbot-ponsonby.org
Readers' Association (Warden) Preb Andrew Talbot-Ponsonby, Llan Retreat House *(as above)*
Tel: 01588 660417
email: andrew@talbot-ponsonby.org
Widows and Dependants (Hereford Diocese Clerical Charity) Mr John Clark *(as above)*

WORSHIP

Chairman Canon Andrew Piper *(as above)*
Secretary Vacancy

MISSIONARY AND ECUMENICAL

Ecumenical Committee Vacancy
Council for World Partnership and Development (Chairman) Mrs Hazel Gould; *(Secretary)* Revd C. Fletcher, Rectory, Bredenbury, Bromyard, Herefordshire HR7 4TF *Tel:* 01885 482236
Evangelism Committee (Chairman) The Bishop of Ludlow

AGRICULTURE

Chaplain Revd Nick Read, Rectory, Pembridge, Hereford HR6 9EB *Tel:* 01544 388998
email: agchap@tiscali.co.uk

PRESS, PUBLICITY AND PUBLICATIONS

Dioc Communications Officer Ms Anni Holden, The Palace, Hereford HR4 9BL
Tel: 01432 373342
email: a.holden@hereford.anglican.org
Editor of Dioc Year Book Mr Graham Hamer, Dioc Office
Editor of Dioc Newspaper Mr R. Calver, The Palace *(as above)*

DIOCESAN RECORD OFFICE

Hereford Records Office, The Old Barracks, Harold St, Hereford HR1 2QX *Tel:* 01432 260750 *(For diocesan records and parish records for Hereford Archdeaconry)*
Shrewsbury Records and Research Centre, Castle Gates, Shrewsbury SY1 2AQ *Tel:* 01743 255350
Head of Records and Research Mary McKenzie *(For parish records for Ludlow Archdeaconry)*

SOCIAL RESPONSIBILITY

Social Responsibility Officer Miss Jackie Boys, The Gateway Office *(as above)* *Tel:* 01432 373311
email: j.boys@hereford.anglican.org
Council for Social Responsibility (Chairman) Mrs Caroline Bond, 25 Cartway, Bridgnorth, Shropshire WV16 4BG
(Secretary) Miss Jackie Boys *(as above)*

STEWARDSHIP

Community Partnership and Funding Officer Mrs Wendy Coombey, Dioc Office   *Tel:* 01432 373313
        email: w.coombey@hereford.anglican.org
Christian Stewardship Adviser Mrs Diana George, Greenway, Walterstone, Hereford HR2 0DT
                    Tel: 01873 890259

RURAL DEANS
ARCHDEACONRY OF HEREFORD
Abbeydore Vacancy
Bromyard Revd C. Sykes, Vicarage, 28 Church Lane, Bromyard HR7 4DZ   *Tel:* 01885 482438
Hereford City and Hereford Rural Preb P. Towner, The Vicarage, 102 Green St, Hereford HR1 2QW
                    Tel: 01432 273676
Kington and Weobley Preb S. Hollinghurst, The Rectory, Presteigne, Powys LD8 2BP
                    Tel: 01544 267777
Ledbury Revd M. D. Vockins, Birchwood Lodge, Storridge, Malvern WR13 5EZ   *Tel:* 01886 884366

Leominster Revd M. C. Cluett, Vicarage, Brookside, Caon Pyon, Hereford HR4 8NY
                    Tel: 01432 830802
Ross and Archenfield Revd E C Goddard, The Vicarage, St Weonards, Herefordshire HR2 8NN
                    Tel: 01981 580307

ARCHDEACONRY OF LUDLOW
Bridgnorth Preb A. A. Roberts, Rectory, 16 East Castle St, Bridgnorth WV16 4AL
                    Tel: 01746 767174
Clun Forest Preb R. T. Shaw, Vicarage, Clun, Craven Arms, Shropshire SY7 8JG
                    Tel: 01588 640809
Condover Revd S. Lowe, Rectory, 1 New Rd, Much Wenlock TF13 6EQ   *Tel:* 01952 727396
Ludlow Revd M. J. Stewart, The Vicarage, Bromfield, Ludlow SY8 2JP   *Tel:* 01584 856625
Pontesbury Vacancy
Telford Severn Gorge
Preb M. Kinna, Rectory, Broseley TF12 5DA
                    Tel: 01952 882647

DIOCESE OF LEICESTER

Restored in 1926. Leicestershire, except the former county of Rutland (PETERBOROUGH); one parish in Northamptonshire.

Population 924,000   Area 835 sq m
Full-time Stipendiary Parochial Clergy 118   Benefices 120
Parishes 237   Churches 321
www.leicester.anglican.org
Overseas link dioceses: Yokohama, Mount Kilimanjaro (Tanzania) and Trichy, Tanjore (India).

BISHOP (6th)
Rt Revd Timothy John Stevens, Bishop's Lodge Annexe, 12 Springfield Rd, Leicester LE2 3BD [1999]   *Tel:* 0116 270 8985
     Fax: 0116 270 3288
[Timothy Leicester]
Bishop's PA Melanie Glover
     email: Melanie.Glover@LecCofE.org
Bishop's Chaplain Revd Michael Smith (*same address*)   *Tel:* 0116 270 3390
     Fax: 0116 270 3288
     email: Mike.Smith@LecCofE.org
Executive Assistant to the Bishop Revd. Gill Jackson
     Tel: 0116 270 8985
     email: Gill.Jackson@LecCofE.org

CATHEDRAL CHURCH OF ST MARTIN
Dean Very Revd Vivienne Faull, Cathedral Centre, 21 St Martin's, Leicester LE1 5DE [2000]
     Tel: 0116 248 7456
     Fax: 0116 248 7470
     email: Viv.Faull@LecCofE.org
Cathedral Centre 21 St Martin's, Leicester LE1 5DE   *Tel:* 0116 248 7400
     Fax: 0116 248 7470
     email: LeicesterCathedral@LecCofE.org
     Web: www.cathedral.leicester.anglican.org
Canons Residentiary
Pastor Canon Michael Wilson [1988]
     Tel: 0116 248 7463
     email: Michael.Wilson@LecCofE.org
Ven Paul Hackwood [2007]   *Tel:* 0116 2487421
     email: Paul.Hackwood@LecCofE.org
Precentor Canon Dr Stephen Foster [2004]
     Tel: 0116 248 7464
     email: Stephen.Foster@LecCofE.org
Urban Canon Barry Naylor [2002]
     Tel: 0116 248 7471
     email: Barry.Naylor@LecCofE.org
Cathedral Chaplain Vacancy
Cathedral Administrator Francis Brown
     Tel: 0116 248 7559
     email: Francis.Brown@LecCofE.org
Marketing and Development Manager Ms Sarah Fuggle   *Tel:* 0116 248 7468
     email: Sarah.Fuggle@LecCofE.org

Cathedral Solicitor Mr Trevor Kirkman, Latham & Co., Charnwood House, 2 Forest Rd, Loughborough LE11 3NP   *Tel:* 01509 238822
Director of Music Mr Jonathan Gregory, Cathedral Centre   *Tel:* 0116 248 7476
     email: Jonathan.Gregory@LecCofE.org
Asst Director Master of Music Mr Simon Headley

ARCHDEACONS
LEICESTER Ven Richard Atkinson, Church House, St Martin's East, Leicester LE1 5FX [2002]
     Tel: 0116 248 7419
     Fax: 0116 253 2889
     email: Richard.Atkinson@LecCofE.org
LOUGHBOROUGH Ven Paul Hackwood, Church House, St Martin's East, Leicester LE1 5FX [2005]
     Tel: 0116 248 7421
     Fax: 0116 253 2889
     email: Paul.Hackwood@LecCofE.org

CONVOCATION (MEMBERS OF THE HOUSE OF CLERGY OF THE GENERAL SYNOD)
Dignitaries in Convocation
The Dean of Leicester
Proctors for Clergy
Ven Richard Atkinson
Revd Peter Hobson
Revd John Plant

MEMBERS OF THE HOUSE OF LAITY OF THE GENERAL SYNOD
Mr Stephen Barney
Mr John Freeman
Mr Alan Fletcher

DIOCESAN OFFICERS
Dioc Secretary Mrs Jane Easton, Church House, St Martin's East, Leicester LE1 5FX
P.A. to Dioc Secretary Mrs Jennifer Florance
     Tel: 0116 248 7426
     email: Jennifer.Florance@LecCofE.org
Chancellor of Diocese Dr James Behrens, Serle Court, 6 New Square, Lincoln's Inn, London WC2A 3QS   *Tel:* 020 7242 6105
     Fax: 020 7405 4004

Registrar of Diocese and Bishop's Legal Secretary
Mr Trevor Kirkman, Latham and Co., Charnwood
House, 2 Forest Rd, Loughborough LE11 3NP
Tel: 01509 238822
Fax: 01509 238833
email: TrevorKirkman@lathamlawyers.co.uk

DIOCESAN ORGANIZATIONS
Diocesan Office Church House, St Martin's East,
Leicester LE1 5FX   *Tel:* 0116 248 7400
Fax: 0116 253 2889
email: ChurchHouse@LecCofE.org

ADMINISTRATION
Assistant Dioc Secretary Mr Andrew Roberts,
Dioc Office   *email:* Andrew.Roberts@CovLec.org
Director of Finance Mr Tim Oglesby, Dioc Office
email: Tim.Oglesby@CovLec.org
Management Accountant Miss Caroline Berry
email: Caroline.Berry@CovLec.org
Finance Officer Mr Paul Wilson, Dioc Office
email: Paul.Wilson@CovLec.org
Accounts Officer Mrs Sue Darlow, Dioc Office
email: Sue.Darlow@LecCofE.org
Accounts Assistant Mrs Karen Issitt, Dioc Office
email: Karen.Issitt@LecCofE.org
Senior Property Manager Mrs Nicky Caunt, Dioc
Office   *email:* Nicky.Caunt@CovLec.org
Clergy Housing Officer Mrs Dinta Chauhan, Dioc
Office   *email:* Dinta.Chauhan@CovLec.org
Property Officer Miss Lesley Whitwell
email: Lesley.Whitwell@CovLec.org
I.T. Manager Mr Phil Ash, Dioc Office
email: Phil.Ash@CovLec.org
Dioc Synod (Chairman, House of Clergy) Canon
David Newman, Emmanuel Rectory, 47 Forest
Rd, Loughborough LE11 3NW
Tel: 01509 263234 (Home)
01509 261773 (Office)
email: rector@easm.co.uk
Dioc Synod (Chairman, House of Laity) Prof David
Wilson, 56 Grangefield Drive, Rothley, Leicester
LE7 7NB   *Tel:* 0116 230 3402
email: djwilson@dmu.ac.uk
Dioc Synod and Bishop's Council (Secretary) Dioc
Secretary, Dioc Office
Pastoral Committee Dioc Secretary (*as above*)
Stipends Officer Mrs Jill Benn, Dioc Office
email: Jill.Benn@CovLec.org
Board of Finance (Chairman) Mr Stephen Barney,
77 Brook St, Wymeswold, Loughborough LE12
6TT   *Tel:* 01509 881160
email: stephen@barney4747.fsnet.co.uk
Board of Finance (Secretary) Dioc Secretary (*as above*)
Finance Committee Mr Andrew Roberts (*as above*)
Property and Glebe Committee Mr Andrew Roberts
(*as above*)
Designated Officer Mrs Jane Easton (*as above*)
Director of Parish Funding and Fundraising Mr
Andrew Nutter, Dioc Office   *Tel:* 0116 248 7422
email: Andrew.Nutter@LecCofE.org

Parish Funding Director
Mrs Maxine Johnson, Brook House, Stonton Rd,
Church Langton, Market Harborough LE16 7SZ
Tel: 01858 545745
email: mjohnson@resort-solutions.co.uk
Child Protection Officer Mary Briant
Tel: 0116 248 7461
email: Mary.Briant@LecCofE.org

CHURCHES
Advisory Committee for the Care of Churches
(*Chairman*) Dr A. McWhirr, 37 Dovedale Rd,
Stoneygate, Leicester LE2 2DN *Tel:* 0116 270 3031
Adviser for the Care and Development of Church
Vacancy
Church Buildings Officer Mr Rupert Allen, Coven-
try Cathedral and Diocesan Offices, 1 Hill Top,
Coventry CV1 5AB   *Tel:* 024 7652 1200
Fax: 024 7652 1312
email: Rupert.Allen@CovLec.org

EDUCATION
Diocesan Board of Education Church House, St
Martin's East, Leicester LE1 5FX
Tel: 0116 248 7450
Fax: 0116 251 1638
Director Canon Peter D. Taylor (*same address*)
email: Peter.Taylor@LecCofE.org
Asst Director Revd Michael Asquith (*same address*)
email: Michael.Asquith@LecCofE.org
Chairman Mr D. Gwynne Jones, 19 Stanton Rd,
Sapcote LE9 6FQ
Religious Education Adviser Mrs Janet Ingram (*as*
above)   *email:* Janet.Ingram@LecCofE.org
Religious Education Administration Mrs Helen Van
Roose, Dioc Office
email: Helen.VanRoose@LecCofE.org
Schools Officer Mrs Kerry Miller (same address)
email: Kerry.Miller@LecCofE.org

INTERFAITH
Director of Interfaith Relations and of the St Philip's
Centre for Study and Engagement in a Multi Faith
Society Canon Dr Andrew Wingate, St Philip's
House, 2a Stoughton Drive North, Leicester LE5
5UB   *Tel:* 0116 273 3459
email: andrew.wingate@stphilipscentre.co.uk
Administrator Mrs Kathy Morrison (*same address*)

MINISTRY
Director of Mission and Ministry Canon Dr Mike
Harrison, Dioc Office   *Tel:* 0116 248 7417
Fax: 0116 253 2889
email: Mike.Harrison@LecCofE.org
Head of the School for Ministry Revd Dr Stuart
Burns, Dioc Office   *Tel:* 0116 248 7417
email: Stuart.Burns@LecCofE.org
Director of Youth Ministry Revd Robin Rolls
email: Robin.Rolls@LecCofE.org
Tel: 0116 248 7442
Dioc Director of Ordinands Canon Sue Field, 134
Valley Rd, Loughborough LE11 3QA
Tel: 01509 234472
email: sue.field1@tesco.net

Under 25s Children's Officer Canon Dr Mike Harrison *Tel:* 0116 248 7428
email: Mike.Harrison@LecCofE.org
Officer for Non-Stipendary Ministry Revd. Alistair Helm *Tel:* 0116 283 0603
email: alistair.helm@btinternet.com
Warden of Evangelists Revd John McGinley
Tel: 01455 442750
email: john.mcginley1@ntlworld.com
Warden of Readers Revd Simon Harvey, St Paul's House, Hamble Rd, Oadby, Leicester LE2 4NX
Tel: 0116 271 0519
email: simon@sjharvey.org.uk
Reader Training Officer Revd Amos Kasibante, 290 Victoria Park Rd, Leicester LE2 1XE
Tel: 0116 285 6493
email: ask11@leicester.ac.uk
Pastoral Assistants Adviser Canon Jane Curtis, Rectory, Church Lane, Gilmorton, Lutterworth LE17 5LU *Tel:* 01455 552119
email: jcurtis@leicester.anglican.org
Officer for NSM Revd Alistair Helm, The Vernon Wing, Aylestone Hall, Old Church St, Old Aylestone, Leicester LE2 8ND
Tel: 0116 283 0603
email: alistair.helm@btinternet.com
Director of Post-Ordination Training Revd Chris Oxley, St Anne's Vicarage, 76 Letchworth Rd, Leicester LE3 6FH *Tel:* 0116 285 8452
email: oxleycr@btopenworld.com
Director of Women's Ministry Canon Jane Curtis (*as above*)
Retired Clergy and Widows Officer Anthony Wessel Esq, The Old Forge, 16 High St, Desford, Leicester LE9 9JF *Tel:* 01455 822404
Fax: 01455 823545
email: anthony.wessel@dial.pipex.com

LITURGICAL
Chairman Canon Dr Stephen Foster, Cathedral Centre, 21 St Martin's, Leicester LE1 5DE
Tel: 0116 248 7400
email: Stephen.Foster@LecCofE.org
Secretary Revd Richard Curtis, Rectory, Church Lane, Gilmorton, Lutterworth LE17 5LU
Tel: 01455 552119
email: rcurtis@leicester.anglican.org

SOCIAL RESPONSIBILITY
Director of Social Responsibility Peter Yates, Church House, St Martin's East, Leicester LE1 5FX *Tel:* 0116 248 7404
Fax: 0116 248 7446
Fax: 01455 250833
email: Peter.Yates@LecCofE.org
Chaplain to People Affected by HIV Revd Trevor Thurston-Smith, The Lodge, Margaret Rd, Off Gwendolen Rd, Leicester LE5 5FW
Tel: 0116 273 3377
email: trevor@faithinpeople.org.uk
Rural Officer
Canon Ken Baker, Homestead, 9 The Green, Lilbourne, nr Rugby CV23 0SR
Tel: 01788 860409

email: kw.baker@btinternet.com
Environment Officer Revd Andrew Quigley, The Vicarage, 49 Ashley Way, Market Harborough, LE16 7XD *Tel:* 01858 410253
email: andrew@aquigley.wanadoo.co.uk

ECUMENICAL
Ecumenical Officer Peter Yates, Church House, St Martin's East, Leicester LE1 5FX
Tel: 0116 248 7404
Fax: 0116 248 7446
email: Peter.Yates@LecCofE.org

PRESS AND PUBLICATIONS
Communications Officer Ms Liz Jepson, Dioc Office *Tel:* 0116 248 7402
07967 388861 (Mobile)
email: Liz.Jepson@LecCofE.org
Editor of Dioc Directory Ms Liz Jepson (*as above*)
Editor of 'News and Views' Ms Liz Jepson (*as above*)

DIOCESAN RECORD OFFICE
Leicestershire Records Office, Long Street, Wigston, Leicester LE18 2AH *Tel:* 0116 257 1080
Fax: 0116 257 1120

AREA DEANS
ARCHDEACONRY OF LEICESTER
City of Leicester Canon Chris Burch, St Peter's Vicarage, Braunstone Lane, Leicester LE3 3AL *Tel:* 0116 289 3377
email: chris@burches.co.uk
Framland Revd Beverley Stark, Rectory, 23 Melton Rd, Waltham-on-the-Wolds, Melton Mowbray LE14 4AJ *Tel:* 01664 464600
email: beverley.stark@btinternet.com
Gartree I and Gartree II Canon Michael Rusk, Rectory, 31 Hill Field, Oadby, Leicester LE2 4RW
Tel: 0116 271 2135
email: m.f.rusk@leicester.anglican.org
Goscote Revd Rob Gladstone, Rothley Vicarage, 128 Hallfields Lane, Rothley, Leicester LE7 7NG
Tel: 0116 230 2241
email: rob@rgladstone.wanadoo.co.uk

ARCHDEACONRY OF LOUGHBOROUGH
Akeley East Revd Cynthia Hebden, Vicarage, 30a Brick Kiln Lane, Shepshed, Loughborough LE12 9EL *Tel:* 01509 508550 (Home)
01509 502255 (Office)
email: cynthia.hebden@btopenworld.com
North West Leicestershire Revd Brian Robertson, The Rectory, 4 Upper Packington Rd, Ashby-de-la-Zouch LE65 1EF *Tel:* 01530 414 404
email: b-robertson@sthelens@ashby.co.uk
Guthlaxton Canon Ken Baker, Homestead, 9 The Green, Lilbourne, Nr Rugby CV23 0SR
Tel: 01788 860409
email: kw.baker@btinternet.com
Sparkenhoe West Revd Tom Meyrick, Rectory, 6 The Paddock, Newbold Verdon, Leicester LE9 9NW *Tel:* 01455 824986
email: meyrick@ekit.com
Sparkenhoe East Revd John Sharpe, Rectory, Main St, Glenfield, Leicester LE3 8DG *Tel:* 0116 287 1604
email: jesharpe@leicester.anglican.org

DIOCESE OF LICHFIELD

Founded in 664, formerly Mercia (AD 656). Staffordshire, except for a few parishes in the south-east (BIRMINGHAM, DERBY); a few parishes in the south-west (HEREFORD); the northern half of Shropshire; Wolverhampton; Walsall; the northern half of Sandwell.

Population 1,995,000   Area 1,744 sq m
Full-time Stipendiary Parochial Clergy 278   Benefices 278
Parishes 421   Churches 578
www.lichfield.anglican.org
Overseas link dioceses: W. Malaysia, Kuching, Sabah (Malaysia),
Qu'Appelle (Canada), Mecklenburg.

BISHOP (98th)
Rt Revd Jonathan Gledhill, Bishop's House, 22 The Close, Lichfield WS13 7LG [2003]
Tel: 01543 306000
Fax: 01543 306009
email: bishop.lichfield@lichfield.anglican.org
Bishop's Administrator Revd Peter Walley (*same address*)
email: peter.walley@lichfield.anglican.org
Bishop's Press Officer Mr Gavin Drake, St Saviour's House, High Mount St Hednesford, Cannock WS12 4BN   *Tel:* 01543 425425
Fax: 01543 425589
07699 730404 (Pager)
ISDN (G722): 01543 871152
email: gavin.drake@lichfield.anglican.org

AREA BISHOPS
SHREWSBURY Rt Revd Alan Smith, 68 London Rd, Shrewsbury SY2 6PG [2001]   *Tel:* 01743 235867
Fax: 01743 243296
email: bishop.shrewsbury@lichfield.anglican.org
STAFFORD Rt Revd Gordon Mursell, Ash Garth, Broughton Crescent, Barlaston, Stoke-on-Trent ST12 9DD [2005]   *Tel:* 01782 373308
Fax: 01782 373705
email: bishop.stafford@lichfield.anglican.org
WOLVERHAMPTON Rt Revd Clive Gregory, 61 Richmond Rd, Merridale, Wolverhampton WV3 9JH [2007]   *Tel:* 01902 824503
Fax: 01902 824504
email:
bishop.wolverhampton@lichfield.anglican.org

CATHEDRAL CHURCH OF THE BLESSED VIRGIN MARY AND ST CHAD
Dean Very Revd Adrian Dorber, The Deanery, 16 The Close, Lichfield WS13 7LD [2005]
Tel: 01543 306250 / 306245 (Office)
01543 306294 (Home)
email: adrian.dorber@lichfield-cathedral.org
Chapter Office 19a The Close, Lichfield WS13 7LD
Tel: 01543 306100
Fax: 01543 306109
email: enquiries@lichfield-cathedral.org
Web: www.lichfield-cathedral.org

Canons Residentiary
Treasurer Ven Christopher Liley, 24 The Close, Lichfield WS13 7LD [2001]   *Tel:* 01543 306145
Fax: 01543 306147
email: chris.liley@lichfield.anglican.org
Chancellor Canon Dr Pete Wilcox, 13 The Close, Lichfield WS13 7LD [2006]
Tel: 01543 306101 (Office)
email: canon.chancellor@lichfield-cathedral.org
Precentor Canon Wealands Bell, 23 The Close, Lichfield WS13 7LD   *Tel:* 01543 306101 (Office)
email: wealands.bell@lichfield-cathedral.org
Chief Officer Mr Timothy Pain, Chapter Office, 19a The Close, Lichfield WS13 7LD
Tel: 01543 306105 (Office)
email: tim.pain@lichfield-cathedral.org
Lay Members of Chapter
Mr Peter Parsons
Mr Bernard Price
Mrs Mithra Tonking
Mrs Margaret Harding
Bursar Mr Clive Tomlinson, Chapter Office
Tel: 01543 306106
email: clive.tomlinson@lichfield-cathedral.org
Organist and Master of the Choristers Mr Philip Scriven, 11 The Close, Lichfield WS13 7LD
Tel: 01543 306200
email: philip.scriven@lichfield-cathedral.org
Visits Officer Mrs Sue Evans, Visitors' Study Centre, The Close, Lichfield WS13 7LD
Tel: 01543 306240
email: sue.evans@lichfield-cathedral.org
Communications and Marketing Officer Mrs Claire Lamplugh, Visitors' Study Centre, The Close, Lichfield WS13 7LD   *Tel:* 01543 306121
email: claire.lamplugh@lichfield-cathedral.org

ARCHDEACONS
LICHFIELD Ven Christopher Liley, 24 The Close, Lichfield WS13 7LD [2001]   *Tel:* 01543 306145
Fax: 01543 306147
email: archdeacon.lichfield@lichfield.anglican.org
SALOP Ven John Hall, Tong Vicarage, Shifnal TF11 8PW [1998]   *Tel:* 01902 372622
Fax: 01902 374021
email: john.hall@lichfield.anglican.org

STOKE-UPON-TRENT Ven Godfrey Stone, 39 The Brackens, Clayton, Newcastle-under-Lyme ST5 4JL [2002] *Tel:* 01782 663066
Fax: 01782 711165
email: archdeacon.stoke@lichfield.anglican.org
WALSALL Ven Bob Jackson, 55b Highgate Rd, Walsall WS1 3JE [2005] *Tel:* 01922 620153
Fax: 01922 445354
email: archdeacon.walsall@lichfield.anglican.org

CONVOCATION (MEMBERS OF THE HOUSE OF CLERGY OF THE GENERAL SYNOD)
Proctors for Clergy
Revd Paul Farthing
Revd Mark Thomas
Ven John Hall
Revd Maureen Hobbs
Revd Mark Ireland
Revd Richard Moy

MEMBERS OF THE HOUSE OF LAITY OF THE GENERAL SYNOD
Mr David Beswick
Mr John Clark
Mrs Wendy Kinson
Mrs Joanna Monckton
Mr William Nicholls
Dr Chik Kaw Tan
Mr John Wilson

DIOCESAN OFFICERS
Dioc Synod (Chairman, House of Clergy) Revd John Allan, Vicarage, Church Rd, Alrewas, Burton-on-Trent DE13 7BT *Tel:* 01283 790486
email: revdjohnallan@revdjohnallan.plus.com
(Chairman, House of Laity) Mrs Wendy Kinson, The Old Laundry, Maer, Newcastle-under-Lyme ST5 5EF *Tel:* 01782 680613
email: wendykinson@tiscali.co.uk
Dioc Secretary Mr David Taylor, St Mary's House, The Close, Lichfield, Staffs. WS13 7LD
Tel: 01543 306030
Fax: 01543 306039
email: info@lichfield.anglican.org
Pastoral Committee (Secretary) Revd David Wright, St Matthew's Vicarage, St George's Rd, Donnington Wood, Telford TF2 7NJ
Tel: 01952 604239
Chancellor of Diocese Judge Marten Coates, St Mary's House
Diocesan Registrar and Bishop's Legal Secretary Mr Niall Blackie, Manby Bowdler LLP, Routh House, Hall Court, Hall Park Way, Telford, Shropshire TF3 4NJ *Tel:* 01952 292129
Fax: 01952 291716
email: n.blackie@fbcmb.co.uk
Dioc Surveyors Wood, Goldstraw and Yorath, Churchill House, Regent Rd, Hanley, Stoke-on-Trent, Staffs. ST1 3RH *Tel:* 01782 208000

DIOCESAN ORGANIZATIONS
Diocesan Office, see individual addresses below

ADMINISTRATION
Chairman Mr Peter Sharpe
Team Leader Mr David Taylor, St Mary's House, The Close, Lichfield WS13 7LD *Tel:* 01543 306030
Fax: 01543 306039
Benefice Buildings and Glebe Committee (Secretary) Mr Andrew Mason, St Mary's House
Finance Director Mr Jonathan R. L. Hill, St Mary's House
Trust (Secretary) Mrs Diane Holt, St Mary's House
Designated Officer Mr Niall Blackie, St Mary's House
Parish Funding Unit Mr Neil Bradley, Mr Ian Law, St Mary's House (*as above*)
Administrator Mrs Kim Hodgkins, Ministry and Training Office *Tel:* 01543 306222
email: kim.hodgkins@lichfield.anglican.org
Dioc Director of Communications Mr Gavin Drake (*Bishop's Press Officer, as above*)
Child Protection Officer Revd Charmian Beech, Rectory, Abbots Way, Hodnet, Market Drayton TF9 3NQ *Tel:* 01630 685491
email: charmian.beech@virgin.net
Editor of Dioc Newspaper 'Spotlight' Mrs Carol Law, 19 Lincoln Croft, Shenstone, Lichfield WS14 0ND *Tel:* 01543 480308
Dioc Ecumenical Co-ordinator Miss Sue Booth, St Mary's House (*as above*)
email: unity@lichfield.anglican.org

ECUMENISM
Area Ecumenical Adviser (Black Country) Revd Simon Mansfield, St Gregory's Vicarage, 112 Long Knowle Lane, Wednesfield, Wolverhampton WV11 1JQ *Tel:* 01902 731667
email: smansfield@toucansurf.com
Area Ecumenical Adviser (Shropshire) Mrs Veronica Fletcher, 67 Derwent Drive, Priorslee, Telford TF2 9QR *Tel:* 01952 299318
Area Ecumenical Adviser (Staffordshire) Miss Sue Booth, 6 Fairoak Flats, Harrowby Drive, Newcastle-under-Lyme ST5 3JR
Tel: 01782 613855

CHURCHES
Advisory Committee for the Care of Churches (Chairman) Mr Kevin Hartley, 8 Hanbury Hill, Stourbridge DY8 1BE *Tel:* 01384 440868;
(Secretary) Mrs Katie Brown, DAC Office, Admaston Farmhouse, Admaston, Rugeley WS15 3NJ *Tel:* 01889 500304 (Office);
email: katie.brown@lichfield.anglican.org

EDUCATION
Chair of Board of Education Mrs Elaine Townsend, 2 The Old Rectory, Rectory Drive, Weston-under-Lizard, Shifnal TF11 8QG
Tel: 01952 850534
Fax: 01952 850626
email: e.townsend@wlv.ac.uk
Director of Education and Team Leader Mr Colin Hopkins, St Mary's House
email: colin.hopkins@lichfield.anglican.org

Schools Advisers Mrs Joan Furlong, 46 Gravelly Drive, Newport TF10 7QS
Tel and *Fax:* 01952 404381
email: joan.furlong@lichfield.anglican.org
Mrs Sue Blackmore, 153 Hockley Rd, Wilnecote, Tamworth B77 5EF   *Tel:* 01827 707638
email: sue.blackmore@lichfield.anglican.org
Mrs Rosemary Woodward, St Mary's House
email:
rosemary.woodward@lichfield.anglican.org
Warden of Diocesan Youth Centre Mr Arthur Hack, Dovedale House, Ilam, Ashbourne DE6 2AZ
Tel: 01335 350365
Fax: 01335 350441
email: warden@dovedale-house.org.uk
Bookings Contact – Shepherds Building (self-catering youth centre) Mrs Paula Lloyd, St Mary's House
email: paula.lloyd@lichfield.anglican.org

MISSION AND MINISTRY
Director of Ministry Development Vacancy
Director of Ordinands Revd David Newsome, St Mary's House   *Tel:* 01543 306192 (Home)
01543 306220 (Office)
email: david.newsome@lichfield.anglican.org
Vocations Dept Administrator Mrs Sue Jackson, St Mary's House   *Tel:* 01543 306220
email: sue.jackson@lichfield.anglican.org
Vocational Education Officer Revd Deborah Sheridan, 45 High Grange, Lichfield WS13 7DU
Tel: 01543 264363
email: d.sheridan@postman.org.uk
Director of Local Ministry Revd Elizabeth Jordan, St Mary's House   *Tel:* 01543 306222
email: elizabeth.jordan@lichfield.anglican.org
Ordained Local Ministry Course Leader Revd Pauline Shelton, Dray Cottage, Cheadle Rd, Draycott-in-the-Moors, Stoke-on-Trent ST11 9RQ
Tel: 01782 388834
email: pauline.shelton@lichfield.anglican.org
Adviser to Women in Ministry Revd Maureen Hobbs, Rectory, Baschurch, Shrewsbury SY4 2EB
Tel: 01939 260305
email: maureenhobbs@yahoo.co.uk
Warden of Readers Mr John Maddison, 19 Woodland Ave, Wolstanton, Newcastle-under-Lyme ST5 8AZ   *Tel:* 01782 853169
Director of Parish Mission Revd George Fisher, The Small Street Centre, 1a Small St, Walsall WS1 3PR   *Tel:* 01922 707861
email: george.fisher@lichfield.anglican.org
Bishop's Officer for Growth Ven Bob Jackson, 55b Highgate Rd, Walsall WS1 3JE
Tel: 01922 620153
email: archdeacon.walsall@lichfield.anglican.org
Diocesan Youth and Children's Adviser Mr Mark Hatcher, Hillcroft, Stoney Lane, Endon, Stoke-on-Trent ST9 9BX   *Tel:* 01782 502822
email: mark.hatcher@lichfield.anglican.org

Dioc Chaplain with Deaf People Revd John Cowburn, St Andrew's Rectory, 7 Wallshead Way, Church Aston, Newport TF10 9JG
Tel: 01952 810942
email: john.cowburn@lichfield.anglican.org
Dioc Adviser in Pastoral Care and Counselling Revd Jeff Leonardi, New Rectory, Bellamour Way, Colton, Rugeley WS14 3JW
Tel and *Fax:* 01889 570897
email: jeff.leonardi@btinternet.com
Director of Social Responsibility Vacancy
World Mission Officer Revd Dr Michael Sheard, 68 Sneyd Lane, Essington, Wolverhampton WV11 3DX   *Tel:* 01922 445844
Fax: 01922 445845
email: lichfield.wmo@btinternet.com
Black Country Urban Industrial Mission (Team Leader) Revd Olwen Smith
Office St Peter's House, Exchange St, Wolverhampton WV1 1TS   *Tel:* 01902 710407
Fax: 01902 685222
email: bcuim@nascr.net
Home Vicarage, 66 Albert Rd, Wolverhampton WV6 0AF   *Tel:* 01902 712935
Asian Missioner Revd Fiaz Samuel, 16 Bescot Drive, Pleck, Walsall WS2 9DF
Tel: 01922 631814
email: fiaz.samuel@lichfield.anglican.org
Rural Officer for Staffordshire Revd Peter Dakin, 20 Tudor Hollow, Fulford, Stoke-on-Trent ST11 9NP
Tel: 01782 397073
email: pdakin@waitrose.com
Rural Officer for Salop Revd David Baldwin, Vicarage, Tilstock, Whitchurch SY13 3JL
Tel: 01948 880552
email: revddavidbaldwin@lichfield.net
Worship and Prayer Officer Revd Jenny Hill, Church House, 25 Green Lane, Shelfield, Walsall WS4 1RN   *Tel:* 01922 692550
email: jennyhill@pawstime.co.uk
Environment Revd Paul Cawthorne, Vicarage, Eaton Constantine, Shrewsbury SY5 6RF
Tel: 01952 510333
email: paul@cawthorne52.fsnet.co.uk

DIOCESAN RECORD OFFICES
Staffordshire Record Office, Eastgate St, Stafford ST16 2LZ *Tel:* 01785 278379, *email:* staffordshire.record.office@staffordshire.gov.uk
Head of Archive Service Mrs Thea Randall *(For parishes in the archdeaconries of Lichfield and Stoke-on-Trent)*
Lichfield Record Office, The Library, The Friary, Lichfield WS13 6QG *Tel:* 01543 510720, *email:* lichfield.record.office@staffordshire.gov.uk *Archivist* Mr Andrew George *(For diocesan records and parishes within the City of Lichfield)*
Shropshire Archives, Castle Gates, Shrewsbury SY1 2AQ *Tel:* 01743 255350, *email:* archives@shropshire.gov.uk *Head of Records and Research* Dr Mary McKenzie *(For parishes in the archdeaconry of Salop)*

RURAL DEANS
ARCHDEACONRY OF LICHFIELD
Lichfield Revd John Allan, Vicarage, Church Rd, Alrewas, Burton-on-Trent DE13 7BT
Tel: 01283 790486
email: revdjohnallan@tiscali.co.uk
Penkridge Preb Ian Cook, 4 Orams Lane, Brewood, Stafford ST19 9EA   *Tel:* 01902 850960
email: prebyxkel@btopenworld.com
Rugeley Preb Michael Newman, Rugeley Rectory, 20 Church St, Rugeley WS15 2AB
Tel: 01889 582149
email: eileennewman20@aol.com
Tamworth Revd Ian Murray, 20 Melmerby, Wilnecote, Tamworth B77 4LP   *Tel:* 01827 737326
email: rockin.rev@ntlworld.com

ARCHDEACONRY OF STOKE-ON-TRENT
Alstonfield Vacancy
Cheadle Revd Steve Osbourne, The Vicarage, 8 Vicarage Crescent, Caverswall, Stoke-on-Trent ST11 9EW   *Tel:* 01782 388037
email: steve.osbourne@btopenworld.com
Eccleshall Revd Nigel Clemas, Whitmore Rectory, Snape Hall Rd, Whitmore Heath, Newcastle-under-Lyme ST5 5HZ
Tel: 01782 680258
email: nclemas@hotmail.com
Leek Revd Matthew Parker, St Edward's Vicarage, 6 Church St, Leek ST13 6AB
Tel: 01538 382515
email: matpark01@aol.com
Newcastle-under-Lyme Revd Gerald Gardiner, St Andrew's Vicarage, 50 Kingsway West, Westlands, Newcastle-under-Lyme ST5 3PU
Tel: 01782 619594
Stafford Revd Paul Thomas, St Thomas' Vicarage, Doxey, Stafford ST16 1EQ   *Tel:* 01785 258796
email: paul@wyndhamthomas.freeserve.co.uk
Stoke (*North*) Revd Rod Clark, Christchurch Vicarage, 10 Emery St, Cobridge, Stoke-on-Trent ST6 2JT   *Tel:* 01782 212639
email: revrod@tiscali.co.uk
Stoke-upon-Trent Preb David Lingwood, Stoke Rectory, 172 Smithpool Rd, Stoke-on-Trent ST4 4PP   *Tel:* 01782 747737
email: dp.lingwood@btinternet.com
Stone Revd Peter Dakin, 20 Tudor Hollow, Fulford, Stoke-on-Trent ST11 9NP
Tel: 01782 397073
email: pdakin@waitrose.com
Tutbury Revd Anthony Wood, Vicarage, 3 Church Lane, Barton-under-Needwood, Burton-on-Trent DE13 8HU   *Tel:* 01283 712359
email: tonywood@surefish.co.uk

Uttoxeter Revd Ted Whittaker, The Rectory, 12 Orchard Close, Uttoxeter ST14 7DZ
Tel: 01889 563644
email: tedwhittaker@orange.net

ARCHDEACONRY OF SALOP
Edgmond and Shifnal Revd Roger Balkwill, The Vicarage, High St, Albrighton, Wolverhampton WV7 3EQ   *Tel:* 01902 372701
email: rev@rbalkwill.freeserve.co.uk
Ellesmere Revd John Vernon, The Drift House, Lake House Mews, Grange Rd, Ellesmere SY12 9DE   *Tel:* 01691 623765
email: john.vernon@which.net
Hodnet Revd Jeremy Stagg, Vicarage, Childs Ercall, Market Drayton TF9 2DA
Tel: 01952 840229
email: jerome@fish.co.uk
Oswestry Revd David North, Rectory, Castle St, Whittington, Oswestry SY11 4DF
email: davidnorth@micro-plus-web.net
Shrewsbury Revd Chris Sims, 1 Underdale Rd, Shrewsbury SY2 5DD   *Tel:* 01743 248859
email: vicar@shrewsburyabbey.com
Telford Revd Vaughan Sweet, The Vicarage, 180 Holyhead Rd, Wellington, Telford TF1 2DW
Tel and *Fax:* 01952 254251
email: v.sweet@virgin.net
Wem and Whitchurch Revd David Baldwin, Vicarage, Tilstock, Whitchurch SY13 3JL
Tel: 01948 880552
email: revddavidbaldwin@yahoo.co.uk
Wrockwardine Preb David Chantrey, The Rectory, Wrockwardine, Telford TF6 5DD
Tel: 01952 251857
email: david.chantrey@surefish.co.uk

ARCHDEACONRY OF WALSALL
Trysull Revd Martin Inman, Vicarage, School Rd, Trysull, Wolverhampton WV5 7HR
Tel: 01902 324537
email: martininman@hotmail.co.uk
Walsall Revd Jenny Hill, Church House, 25 Green Lane, Shelfield, Walsall WS4 1RN
Tel: 01922 692550
email: jennyhill@pawstime.co.uk
Wednesbury Revd Richard Inglesby, 5 Sutton Rd, Moxley, Wednesbury WS10 8SG
Tel: 01902 653084
email: ringlesby@hotmail.com
West Bromwich Revd Margaret Smallman, Holy Trinity Vicarage, 1 Burlington Rd, West Bromwich B70 6LF   *Tel:* 0121 525 3595
email: trinity7@tiscali.co.uk

DIOCESE OF LINCOLN

Founded in 1072, formerly Dorchester (AD 886), formerly Leicester (AD 680), originally Lindine (AD 678). Lincolnshire; North East Lincolnshire; North Lincolnshire, except for an area in the west (SHEFFIELD).

Population 1,004,000   Area 2,673 sq m
Full-time Stipendiary Parochial Clergy 163   Benefices 214
Parishes 507   Churches 641
www.lincoln.anglican.org
Overseas link dioceses: RC Diocese of Brugge, Tirunelveli (CSI).

BISHOP (70th)
Rt Revd Dr John Charles Saxbee, Bishop's House, Eastgate, Lincoln LN2 1QQ [2001]
Tel: 01522 534701
Fax: 01522 511095
email: bishop.lincoln@lincoln.anglican.org
[John Lincoln]
Personal Assistant Revd Michael Silley (*same address*)

SUFFRAGAN BISHOPS
GRIMSBY Rt Revd David Douglas James Rossdale, Bishop's House, Church Lane, Irby-on-Humber, Grimsby DN37 7JR [2000]   *Tel:* 01472 371715
Fax: 01472 371716
email: bishop.grimsby@lincoln.anglican.org
GRANTHAM Rt Revd Dr Timothy William Ellis, Saxonwell Vicarage, Church St, Long Bennington, Newark NG23 5ES [2006]
Tel: 01400 283344
Fax: 01400 283321
email: bishop.grantham@lincoln.anglican.org

HONORARY ASSISTANT BISHOPS
Rt Revd Donald Snelgrove, Kingston House, 8 Park View, Barton-on-Humber DN18 6AX [1994]
Tel: 01652 634484
Rt Revd John Brown, 130 Oxford Rd, Cleethorpes DN35 0BP [1995]   .   *Tel:* 01472 698840
Rt Revd David Tustin, The Ashes, Tunnel Rd, Wrawby, Brigg DN20 8SF [2001]
Tel: 01652 655584

CATHEDRAL CHURCH OF THE BLESSED VIRGIN MARY
Dean Very Revd Philip Buckler, The Deanery, 12 Eastgate, Lincoln LN2 1QG [2007]
Tel: 01522 561611
email: dean@lincolncathedral.com
Communications Office (main switchboard)
Tel: 01522 561600
Fax: 01522 561634
Web: www.lincolncathedral.com
Canons Residentiary
Precentor Canon Gavin Kirk, The Precentory, 16 Minster Yard, Lincoln LN2 1PX [2003]
Tel: 01522 561632
email: precentor@lincolncathedral.com

Chancellor Canon Michael West, The Chancery, 11 Minster Yard, Lincoln LN2 1PJ [2003]
Tel: 01522 561633
email: chancellor@lincolncathedral.com
Subdean Canon Alan Nugent, The Subdeanery, 18 Minster Yard, Lincoln LN2 1PX [2003]
Tel: 01522 561631
email: subdean@lincolncathedral.com
Chapter Clerk and Chief Executive Mr Roy Bentham, Chapter Office, 4 Priorygate, Lincoln LN2 1PL   *Tel:* 01522 561601
Fax: 01522 561603
email: chiefexecutive@lincolncathedral.com
Director of Music and Organist and Master of the Choristers Mr Aric Prentice, Lincoln Minster School, Prior Building, Upper Lindum St, Lincoln LN2 5RW   *Tel:* 01522 551300
email: aric.prentice@church-schools.com
Assistant Director of Music and Sub-Organist Mr Charles Harrison, 2a Vicars' Court, Minster Yard, Lincoln LN2 1PT
Organist Laureate Mr Colin Walsh, Graveley Place, 12 Minster Yard, Lincoln LN2 1PJ

ARCHDEACONS
LINCOLN Vacancy   *Tel:* 01522 504050
Fax: 01522 504051
email: archdeacon.lincoln@lincoln.anglican.org
STOW and LINDSEY Ven Jane Sinclair, Sanderlings, Willingham Rd, Market Rasen, Lincoln LN8 3RE [2007]   *Tel:* 01673 849896
email:
archdeacon.stowlindsey@lincoln.anglican.org

CONVOCATION (MEMBERS OF THE HOUSE OF CLERGY OF THE GENERAL SYNOD)
Revd Christopher Lilley
Canon John A. Patrick
Canon Timothy R. Barker

MEMBERS OF THE HOUSE OF LAITY OF THE GENERAL SYNOD
Miss Rachel Beck
Miss Cynthia Bunch
Mrs Susan Slater
Mrs Carol Ticehurst

DIOCESAN OFFICERS

Chief Executive Mr Maximilian Manin, Church House, Lincoln LN2 1PU   *Tel:* 01522 504030
    Fax: 01522 504051
    email: chief.executive@lincoln.anglican.org
Chancellor of Diocese Revd Mark Bishop QC, 1 Temple Gardens, Temple, London EC4Y 9BB
Registrar of Diocese and Bishop's Legal Secretary Miss Caroline Mockford, The Diocesan Registry, Chattertons, Low Moor Rd, Doddington Rd, Lincoln LN6 3JY   *Tel:* 01522 814600
    Fax: 01522 814601
    email: caroline.mockford@chattertons.com

DIOCESAN ORGANIZATIONS

Diocesan Office The Old Palace, Lincoln LN2 1PU
    Tel: 01522 504050
    Fax: 01522 504051
    email: administrator@lincoln.anglican.org
    Web: www.lincoln.anglican.org

ADMINISTRATION

Dioc Synod (Chairman, House of Clergy) Canon J. A. Patrick   *Tel:* 01522 504050
(Chairman, House of Laity) Mr J. C. Watt
    Tel: 01522 504050
(Secretary) Mr Richard Wilkinson, Dioc Office
Diocesan Council (Chairman) Rt Revd Dr John Saxbee, Bishop of Lincoln
(Secretary) Mr Richard Wilkinson *(as above)*
Finance Executive (Chairman) Mr Hugh Drake, Dioc Office
Human Resources Mr Richard Wilkinson *(as above)*
Trusts Committee Mr Andrew Gosling
Assets (and Glebe) Committee Mr Peter Gaskell
Clergy Housing and Board Property Committee Mr Keith Nelmes
Board of Patronage Mr Richard Wilkinson *(as above)*
Designated Officer Miss Caroline Mockford, Chattertons, Low Moor Rd, Doddington Rd, Lincoln LN6 3JY   *Tel:* 01522 814600
    email: caroline.mockford@chattertons.com
Dioc Electoral Registration Officer Mrs Joy Schneider, Dioc Office

CHURCHES

Advisory Committee for the Care of Churches (Chairman) Mr Morris Felton, Dioc Office
(Acting Secretary) Mr Matthew Naylor, Dioc Office
Church Buildings Revd Neil Brunning, 11 Cavendish Drive, Lea, Gainsborough, Lincolnshire DN21 5HU   *Tel:* 01427 617938
Church Extension Committee Mr Richard Wilkinson *(as above)*
Redundant Churches Uses Committee (Secretary) Mrs Judith Crowe, Dioc Office

EDUCATION

Director of Education Mr Peter Staves, Stable Block, The Old Palace, Lincoln LN2 1PU
    Tel: 01522 504010
    email: education@lincoln.anglican.org

Dioc Board of Education (Chair) Rt Revd David Douglas James Rossdale, Bishop's House, Church Lane, Irby-on-Humber, Grimsby DN37 7JR   *Tel:* 01472 371715
    email: bishop.grimsby@lincoln.anglican.org
Church School Buildings Manager Mr Simon Hardy *(same address)*
Schools RE Adviser Mrs Paulette Bissell *(same address)*
Schools Adviser Mr David Clements *(same address)*
Technical Asst, Buildings Mr Michael Pues *(same address)*

FORMATION IN DISCIPLESHIP AND MINISTRY

Principal of the Ministry Training Course Revd David McCormick, Dioc Office
    Tel: 01522 504022
Theological Educator and Vice Principal of the Ministry Training Course Vacancy *(same address)*
Continuing Ministerial Education and Initial Continuing Ministerial Education Officer Revd Dr Mark Hocknull, Dioc Office
Diocesan Director of Ordinands and Vocations Adviser Revd Dr Jeffrey Heskins, Dioc Office
Adult Education Officer Vacancy (c/o Dioc Office)
    Tel: 01522 504020
Lay Ministry Coordinator Vacancy (c/o Dioc Office)   *Tel:* 01522 504020
Adviser on Women's Ministry Revd K. Windslow, Rectory, Vicarage Lane, Wellingore, Lincoln LN5 0JF   *Tel:* 01522 810246
    email: kathryn.windslow@btinternet.com
Ordinands' Grants Mr Peter Gaskell, Dioc Office
Warden of Readers Canon Alex Whitehead, St Mary's Rectory, Normanby Rd, Stow, Lincoln LN1 2DF   *Tel:* 01427 788251
Readers (Secretary) Mr J. Marshall, 73 Sentance Crescent, Kirton, Boston PE20 1XF
    Tel: 01205 723097
Clergy Widows Officers Canon and Mrs Michael Boughton, 45 Albion Crescent, Lincoln LN1 1EB
    Tel: 01522 569653
Clergy Retirement Officer Canon Brian Osborne, 3 Newlands Rd, Hacconby, Bourne PE10 0UT
    Tel: 01778 570818
    email: brian-ruth.osborne@tiscali.co.uk

PRESS, PUBLICITY AND PUBLICATIONS

Communications and Press Officer Mr Will Harrison, Dioc Office
Editor of Dioc Directory Mr Max Manin, Dioc Office
Editor of Crosslines and ebulletin Mr Will Harrison, Dioc Office

LITURGICAL COMMITTEE

Secretary (Acting) Revd Peter Godden, The Rectory, Hackthorn, Lincoln LN2 3PF
    Tel: 01673 860856
    email: peter@owmbygroup.co.uk

MISSION AND ECUMENICAL CONCERNS

Churches Together in all Lincolnshire Administrator, c/o Dioc Office

Lincolnshire Chaplaincy Services (Company No. 6491058)

Chair of Board Rt Revd D. D. J. Rossdale (*Bishop of Grimsby*)   *Tel:* 01472 371715

Chaplaincy Director Canon A. Vaughan, 4 Grange Close, Canwick, Lincoln LN4 2RH
     Tel: 01522 528266

Business Manager Miss A. J. McNish, Dioc Office
     Tel: 01522 504070

Industrial Chaplains

Lincoln Canon Andrew Vaughan, 4 Grange Close, Canwick, Lincoln LN4 2RH
     Tel: 01522 528266

Lincoln Revd Lynne Ward, 9 Bellwood Grange, Cherry Willingham, Lincoln LN3 4JD

North Lincs Canon Mike Cooney, 16 Neap House Rd, Gunness, Scunthorpe DN15 8TT
     Tel: 01724 784245

North East Lincs Revd Stuart Bidmead, The Rectory, 1A The Avenue, Healing, Grimsby DN41 8TT
     Tel: 01472 885602

Rural Chaplains

Chaplain for Environmental Issues and Sustainable Development Mr Terry Miller, Dioc Office
     Tel: 01522 504072

Agricultural Chaplain Canon Alan Robson, The Manse, 1 Manor Drive, Wragby, Market Rasen LN8 5SL   *Tel:* 01673 857871

Waterways Chaplain Revd Maurice Perry, Silver Birches, Stockwell Gate, Whaplode, Spalding PE12 6UE

Further and Higher Education

Lincoln University Chaplain Revd Les Acklam, 14 Nettleham Close, Lincoln LN2 1SJ
     Tel: 01522 886079

Scunthorpe Colleges Chaplain Revd Susan Walker, St Andrew's Rectory, 16 Belton Rd, Epworth, Doncaster DN9 1JL   *Tel:* 01724 282998 / 281111

Grimsby Institute Chaplain Revd Dr Michael Ward, 19 Devonshire Ave, Grimsby DN32 0BW
     Tel: 01472 311222

Grantham College and Stamford New College Mr Peter Weeks, 64 Roman Bank, Stamford PE9 2ST
     Tel: 07853 097671

Lincoln College Revd David Edgar, 1 St Giles' Avenue, Lincoln LN2 4PE   *Tel:* 01522 528199

Other Chaplains – Non Lincolnshire Chaplaincy Services

Chaplain to the Deaf Community Revd Simon Bishop, 220 Boultham Park Rd, Lincoln LN6 7SU
     Tel: 01522 787136

Youth and Children's Work Capt D. Rose CA, Dioc Office   *Tel:* 01522 504067

STEWARDSHIP AND RESOURCES

Senior Resources Consultant Mr Andrew Wright, Dioc Office

Resources Consultant Mr Keith Halliday, Dioc Office

DIOCESAN RECORD OFFICE

Lincolnshire Archives Office, St Rumbold St, Lincoln LN2 5AB   *Tel:* 01522 526204

RURAL DEANS

ARCHDEACONRY OF STOW

Isle of Axholme Canon Michael Cooney, 16 Neap House Rd, Gunness, Scunthorpe DN15 8TT
     Tel: 01724 784245
     email: mike.cooney@btinternet.com

Corringham Canon Rhys Prosser, Vicarage, 1 Westcroft Drive, Saxilby, Lincoln LN1 2PT
     Tel: 01522 702427
     email: rs.prosser@virgin.net

Lawres Revd Clive Todd, Vicarage, 14 Church Lane, Cherry Willingham, Lincoln LN3 4AB
     Tel: 01522 750356
     email: clive.todd1@btinternet.com

Manlake Canon Michael Cooney, 16 Neap House Rd, Gunness, Scunthorpe DN15 8TT
     Tel: 01724 784245
     email: michael.cooney@btinternet.com

West Wold Revd Ian Robinson, Vicarage, 3 Spa Top, Caistor, Lincoln LN7 6UH
     Tel: 01472 851339
     email: revianrobinson@tiscali.co.uk

Yarborough Canon Christopher Lilley, St Hybald's Vicarage, Vicarage Lane, Scawby, Brigg DN20 9LX   *Tel:* 01652 652725
     email: c.lilley@btinternet.com

ARCHDEACONRY OF LINDSEY

Bolingbroke Canon Peter Coates, Vicarage, Church St, Spilsby PE23 5DU   *Tel:* 01790 752526
     email: peter.coates@onetel.net

Calcewaithe and Candleshoe Revd Terry Steele, Rectory, Glebe Rise, Burgh le Marsh, Skegness PE24 5BL   *Tel:* 01754 810216
     email: father.terry@btclick.com

Grimsby and Cleethorpes Canon Peter Mullins, Rectory, 23 Littlecoates Rd, Grimsby DN34 4NG
     Tel: 01472 346986
     email: p.m.mullins@virgin.net

Haverstoe Canon Ian Shelton, Rectory, 95 High St, Waltham, Grimsby DN37 0PN   *Tel:* 01472 822172
     email: robertshelton954@hotmail.com

Horncastle Revd Alec Boyd, Rectory, Fieldside, Mareham le Fen, Boston PE22 7QU
     Tel: 01507 568215
     email: alec@ajboyd.wanadoo.co.uk

Louthesk Canon Stephen Holdaway, Rectory, 49 Westgate, Louth LN11 9YE   *Tel:* 01507 610247
     email: stephen.holdaway@btinternet.com

ARCHDEACONRY OF LINCOLN

Stamford (Formerly Aveland and, Ness with Stamford) (Acting) Rt Revd Dr Timothy William Ellis, Saxonwell Vicarage, Church St, Long Bennington, Newark NG23 5ES
     Tel: 01400 283344
     Fax: 01400 283321
     email: bishop.grantham@lincoln.anglican.org

Beltisloe Revd Andrew Hawes, Vicarage, Church Lane, Edenham, Bourne PE10 0LS
Tel: 01778 591358
email: athawes@tiscali.co.uk
Christianity Revd David Osbourne, Rectory, 2A St Helen's Avenue, Boultham, Lincoln LN6 7RA
Tel: 01522 682026
email: davidosbourne@tiscali.co.uk
Elloe East and West Canon Timothy Barker, Parsonage, 1 Halmer Gate, Spalding PE11 2DR
Tel: 01775 722772
email: tim@tjkc.co.uk
Graffoe Canon Richard Eyre, Rectory, Mill Lane, North Hykeham, Lincoln LN6 9PA
Tel: 01522 882880
email: richard.eyre3@ntlworld.com

Grantham Canon Christopher Andrews, The Rectory, 4 Church St, Grantham NG31 6RR
Tel: 01476 561342
email: chris@stwulframs.com
Holland East Revd Marc Cooper, Rectory, Rectory Close, Off Clampgate Rd, Fishtoft, Boston PE21 0RZ *Tel:* 01205 363216
email: revmarccooper@dsl.pipex.com
Holland West Vacancy
Lafford Vacancy
Loveden Revd Dr Alan Megahey, Rectory, Church End, Leadenham LN5 0PX
Tel: 01400 273987
email: rector.leadenham@btopenworld.com

DIOCESE OF LIVERPOOL

Founded in 1880. Liverpool; Sefton; Knowsley; St Helens; Wigan, except for
areas in the north (BLACKBURN) and in the east (MANCHESTER); Halton, north of
the river Mersey; Warrington, north of the river Mersey; most of West Lancashire.

Population 1,523,000   Area 389 sq m
Full-time Stipendiary Parochial Clergy 196   Benefices 176
Parishes 207   Churches 254
www.liverpool.anglican.org
Overseas link diocese: Akure (Nigeria).

BISHOP (7th)
Rt Revd James Stuart Jones, Bishop's Lodge,
Woolton Park, Woolton, Liverpool L25 6DT
[1998]   *Tel:* 0151 421 0831
[James Liverpool]
Bishop's Personal Assistant Mrs Margaret Funnell
(same address)   *Tel:* 0151 421 0831 (Office)
                                Fax: 0151 428 3055
    email: bishopslodge@liverpool.anglican.org

SUFFRAGAN BISHOP
WARRINGTON Rt Revd David Jennings, 34 Central
Ave, Eccleston Park, Prescot, Merseyside L34
2QP [2000]   *Tel:* 0151 426 1897 (Home)
                    0151 705 2140 (Office)

HONORARY ASSISTANT BISHOPS
Rt Revd Frank Sergeant, 32 Brotherton Drive,
Trinity Gardens, Salford M3 6BN [2008]
                        Tel: 0161 839 7045
Rt Revd Ian Stuart, Provost's Office, Liverpool
Hope, Hope Park, Liverpool L16 9JD [1999]
                        Tel: 0151 291 3547
Rt Revd Martyn William Jarrett (Provisional
Episcopal Visitor), 3 North Lane, Roundhay,
Leeds LS8 2QJ [2005]   *Tel:* 0113 265 4280
                              Fax: 0113 265 4281
email:
    bishop-of-beverley@3-north-lane.fsnet.co.uk

CATHEDRAL CHURCH OF CHRIST
Dean Very Revd Justin Welby, The Cathedral,
St James's Mount, Liverpool L1 7AZ [2007]
                        Tel: 0151 702 7202
                        Fax: 0151 702 7292
    email: dean@liverpoolcathedral.org.uk
Canons Residentiary
Treasurer Canon Anthony Hawley, The
Cathedral [2002]   *Tel:* 0151 702 7204
                          Fax: 0151 702 7292
    email: canon.hawley@liverpoolcathedral.org.uk
Precentor Canon Myles Davies [2008]
        Tel: 0151 702 7203 / 0151 228 5252
    email: canon.davies@liverpoolcathedral.org.uk
Canon Dr Jeremy Duff [2004]   *Tel:* 0151 702 7243
    email: jeremy.duff@liverpoolcathedral.org.uk
Residentiary: Canon Cynthia Dowdle [2008]
                        Tel: 0151 546 4266
    email: cynthia.dowdle@hotmail.com

Director of Operations Mike Eastwood, St James'
House, 20 St James' Rd, Liverpool L1 7BY
                        Tel: 0151 709 9722 /
                        0151 705 2117
    email: mike.eastwood@liverpool.anglican.org
Chapter Clerk Roger Arden, St James' House,
20 St James Rd, Liverpool L1 7BY
        Tel: 0151 709 2222/0151 705 2101
                        Fax: 0151 709 3095
    email: roger.dreg@liverpool.anglican.org
Director of Music David Poulter, The Cathedral
                        Tel: 0151 702 7240
    email: david.poulter@liverpoolcathedral.org.uk
Cathedral Organist Professor Dr Ian Tracey, The
Cathedral
    email: ian.tracey@liverpoolcathedral.org.uk

ARCHDEACONS
LIVERPOOL Ven Ricky Panter, 2a Monfa Rd,
Bootle, Merseyside L20 6BQ [2002]
                Tel and Fax: 0151 922 3758
    email: archdeaconricky@blueyonder.co.uk
WARRINGTON Ven Peter Bradley, Rectory, 1A
College Rd, Upholland, Skelmersdale WN8 0PY
[2001]   *Tel:* 01695 622936
                        Fax: 01695 625865
    email: archdeacon@peterbradley.fsnet.co.uk

CONVOCATION (MEMBERS OF THE HOUSE OF CLERGY OF THE GENERAL SYNOD)
Proctors for Clergy
Ven Peter Bradley
Canon Cynthia Dowdle
Revd Peter Spiers
Revd Timothy Stratford

MEMBERS OF THE HOUSE OF LAITY OF THE GENERAL SYNOD
Mr Paul Hancock
Mr Allan Jones
Canon Linda Jones
Christopher Pye
Canon Margaret Swinson

DIOCESAN OFFICERS
Dioc Secretary Mike Eastwood, St James' House,
20 St James Rd, Liverpool L1 7BY
                        Tel: 0151 709 9722
                        Fax: 0151 709 2885

Chancellor of Diocese Sir Mark Hedley
Registrar of Diocese and Bishop's Legal Secretary
Roger Arden, St James' House
Tel: 0151 709 2222

DIOCESAN ORGANIZATIONS

Diocesan Office St James' House, 20 St James Rd,
Liverpool L1 7BY   Tel: 0151 709 9722
Fax: 0151 709 2885
Web: www.liverpool.anglican.org

ADMINISTRATION

Dioc Synod (Chair, House of Clergy) Revd Nicholas
Anderson, The Vicarage, 1 View Rd, Rainhill,
Merseyside L35 0LE   Tel: 0151 426 4666
(Chair, House of Laity) Canon Margaret Swinson,
46 Glenmore Ave, Liverpool L18 4QF
Tel: 0151 724 3533
(Secretary) Mike Eastwood, Dioc Office
(Asst Secretary) Ultan Russell, Dioc Office
Board of Finance (Chair) David Tomkins, 7 Breeze
Rd, Birkdale, Southport PR8 2HG
Tel: 01704 562386
(Secretary) Mike Eastwood (*as above*)
Pastoral Committee (Chair) The Bishop of
Warrington; *(Secretary)* Sandra Holmes; *(Bishop's
Planning Officer)* Revd Barry Dryden, Vicarage,
20 Warren Lane, Woolston, Warrington WA1 4ES
Clergy Housing and Glebe Committee (Chair) Joy
Mills, Dioc Office; *(Surveyor)* Alan Gayner, Dioc
Office
Support Claire Evans, Dioc Office
Designated Officer Revd Barry Dryden, Dioc
Office

CHURCHES

*Advisory Committee for the Care of Churches
(Chair)* Revd Stephen Parish, 1a Fitzherbert St,
Warrington WA2 7QG   Tel: 01925 631781

EDUCATION

Chair Rt Revd David Jennings, 34 Central
Ave, Eccleston Park, Prescot L34 2QP
Director of Education Jon Richardson, Dioc Office
Asst Director Stuart Harrison, Dioc Office
Senior Diocesan Schools Adviser Revd Heather
Penman, Dioc Office
Diocesan Schools Adviser Joan Stein, Dioc Office

MINISTRY

Director of Ordinands Revd David Parry,
Vicarage, St Michael's Church Rd, Liverpool
L17 7BD   Tel: 0151 286 2422
Dean of Women's Ministries Canon Cynthia
Dowdle, Vicarage, Tithebarn Rd, Knowsley
Village, Merseyside L34 0JA   Tel: 0151 546 4266

LIFELONG LEARNING

*All Lifelong Learning departments may be contacted
via the Diocesan Office on*   Tel: 0151 705 2120
Fax: 0151 705 2215
email: lifelonglearning@liverpool.anglican.org
Director Canon Dr Jeremy Duff

Assistant Director (Education) Revd Dr David
Leslie
Assistant Director Mrs Julie Walker
Readers' Association (Warden) Mr Nick Daunt

CHURCH GROWTH AND ECUMENISM

Team Leader Linda Jones, Dioc Office
Tel: 0151 705 2109
Youth Adviser Missioner Frank Hinds
Tel: 0151 705 2147
Diocesan Missioner Phil Pawley, Dioc Office
Tel: 01744 737291
Diocesan Adviser on Liturgy and Worship Revd
Neil Kelley, Dioc Office   Tel: 0151 928 3342
email: neil.kelley@liverpool.anglican.org
Children's Work Adviser Jane Leadbetter, Dioc
Office   Tel: 0151 427 0413
Diocesan Ecumenical Adviser Revd Andrew
Edwards, Dioc Office   Tel: 01704 531615
Director of Pioneer Ministry Canon Philip Potter,
St Mark's Vicarage, 2 Stanley Bank Rd, Haydock,
St Helens WA11 0UW   Tel: 01744 23957

RESOURCES

Senior Resources Officer Revd Kath Rogers,
Dioc Office   Tel: 0151 705 2180
Resources Officer Gordon Fath
Resources/Church Urban Fund Carol Griffiths

COMMUNICATIONS

Media Manager Stuart Haynes, Dioc Office
Tel: 0151 705 2150
Communications Officer Val Hill, Dioc Office
Tel: 0151 705 2131

DIOCESAN RECORD OFFICE

For further information apply to Registrar, St James'
House, 20 St James Rd, Liverpool L1 7BY
Tel: 0151 709 9722 *or* The Lancashire Record
Office, Bow Lane, Preston PR1 8ND *Archivist*
Mr K. Hall Tel: 01772 254868

CHURCH AND SOCIETY

Tel: 0151 705 2130
Fax: 0151 705 2215
email: churchandsociety@liverpool.anglican.org
Senior Officer Ultan Russell
email: ultan.russell@liverpool.anglican.org
Disability Awareness and Vulnerable Adults Officer
Sister Ruth Reed
email: ruth.reed@liverpool.anglican.org
Racial Justice Officer Hyacinth Sweeney Dixon
email:
hyacinth.sweeney-dixon@liverpool.anglican.org
Adviser on Older People's Issues Mary Kessler
Tel: 01704 530660
email: marykessler@f2s.com
Relationship Adviser Revd Joyce Weaver
Tel: 01925 634993
Rural Issues Adviser Vacancy
Church and World Adviser Revd Julie Fleming
Tel: 0151 263 2518

Akure Link Adviser Revd Roy Doran
Tel: 01744 23601
email: revroydoran@ravenhead.fsnet.co.uk
Team Leader, Pastoral Services for the Deaf Community Revd Dr Hannah Lewis
email: hannah.lewis@liverpool.anglican.org

MERSEYSIDE AND REGION CHURCHES
ECUMENICAL ASSEMBLY
Ecumenical Development Officer Revd Ian Smith (URC), Quaker Meeting House, 22 School Lane, Liverpool L1 3BT
Tel: 0151 709 0125

MISSION IN THE ECONOMY (MitE)
Team Coordinator Revd Fran Lovett, Liverpool Cathedral, St James' Mount, Liverpool L1 7AZ
Tel: 0151 702 7208

AREA DEANS
ARCHDEACONRY OF LIVERPOOL
Bootle Revd Roger Driver, The Vicarage, 70 Merton Rd, Bootle L20 7AT
Tel: 0151 922 3316
email: rogerdriver@btinternet.com
Huyton Canon John Taylor, Vicarage, Vicarage Place, Prescot L34 1LA
Tel: 0151 426 6719
email: the-revd-john-taylor@supanet.com
Liverpool North Canon Henry Corbett, St Peter's Vicarage, Shrewsbury House, Langrove St, Liverpool L5 3PE
Tel: 0151 207 1948
email: henry-corbett@btinternet.com
Liverpool South – Childwall Canon Christopher John Crooks, Rectory, 67 Church Rd, Woolton, Liverpool L25 6DA
Tel: 0151 428 1853
email: kipcrooks@blueyonder.co.uk
Sefton Revd Collette Thornborough, St Nichola Vicarage, Nicholas Rd, Blundellsands L23 6TS
Tel: 0151 924 3551
Toxteth and Wavertree Canon Mark Stanford, Vicarage, 40 Devonshire Rd, Toxteth, Liverpool L8 3TZ
Tel: 0151 727 1248
email: mark@stphilemons.org.uk
Walton Canon Ray Bridson, St Columba's Vicarage, Pinehurst Ave, Liverpool L4 2TZ
Tel: 0151 474 7231
email: frray@blueyonder.co.uk

West Derby Revd Steve McGanity, St Andrew's Vicarage, 176 Queen's Drive, Liverpool L13 0AL
Tel: 0151 287 2887

ARCHDEACONRY OF WARRINGTON
North Meols Canon Colin Pope, Emmanuel Vicarage, 12 Allerton Rd, Southport PR9 9NJ
Tel and *Fax:* 01704 532743
email: cpope@fish.co.uk
Ormskirk Canon Gordon Greenwood, Vicarage, Church Rd, Skelmersdale WN8 8ND
Tel: 01695 722087
email: gordon757greenwood@btinternet.com
Asst Area Dean Revd Christopher Jones, Vicarage, Park Rd, Ormskirk L39 3AJ
Tel: 01695 572143
St Helens Canon Mark Cockayne, 99 Springwood Park, Haydock WA11 6XP
Tel: 01744 633104
email: markcockayne@blueyonder.co.uk
Asst Area Dean Revd Ray Doran, St John's Vicarage, Crosley Rd, Ravenhead, St Helens WA10 3ND
Tel: 01744 23601
email: revroydoran@ravenhead.fsnet.co.uk
Warrington Canon Stephen Attwater, Rectory, Station Rd, Padgate, Warrington WA2 0PD
Tel: 01925 821555
email: attwater292@btinternet.com
Widnes Canon David Gait, St John's House, Greenway Rd, Widnes WA8 6HA
Tel: 0151 424 3134
email: dave.gait@btinternet.com
Wigan Vacancy
Assistant Area Dean Revd Margaret Sherwin, St John's Vicarage, 848 Atherton Rd, Hindley Green, Wigan WN2 4SA
Tel: 01942 255833
email: revmarg@btopenworld.com
Winwick Canon Robert Lewis, Rectory, Golborne Rd, Winwick, Warrington WA2 8SZ
Tel: 01925 632760
email: the_lewises@hotmail.com

DIOCESE OF LONDON

Founded in 314. The City of London; Greater London north of the Thames, except five East London boroughs (CHELMSFORD) and an area in the north (ST ALBANS); Surrey north of the Thames; a small area of southern Hertfordshire.

Population 3,655,000   Area 277 sq m
Full-time Stipendiary Parochial Clergy 474   Benefices 406
Parishes 407   Churches 476
www.london.anglican.org
Overseas link dioceses: Niassa and Lebombo (Mozambique), Angola;
(Willesden): Hong Kong and Macao.

BISHOP (132nd)

Rt Revd and Rt Hon Richard John Carew Chartres, The Old Deanery, Dean's Court, London EC4V 5AA [1995]   *Tel:* 020 7248 6233
Fax: 020 7248 9721
email: bishop@londin.clara.co.uk
[Richard Londin:]
Personal Jurisdiction Cities of London and Westminster (*Archdeaconries of London and Charing Cross*)
Matters relating to the other Areas should be referred to the appropriate Area Bishop
Personal Assistant Janet Laws
Diary Secretary Frances Charlesworth

AREA BISHOPS

STEPNEY Rt Revd Stephen Oliver, 63 Coborn Rd, London E3 2DB [2003]   *Tel:* 020 8981 2323
Fax: 020 8981 8015
email: bishop.stepney@london.anglican.org
KENSINGTON Vacancy, Dial House, Riverside, Twickenham, Middx TW1 3DT [1996]
Tel: 020 8892 7781
Fax: 020 8891 3969
email: bishop.kensington@london.anglican.org
EDMONTON Rt Revd Peter Wheatley, 27 Thurlow Rd, London NW3 5PP [1999]   *Tel:* 020 7435 5890
Fax: 020 7435 6049
email: bishop.edmonton@london.anglican.org
WILLESDEN Rt Revd Peter Broadbent, 173 Willesden Lane, London NW6 7YN [2001]
Tel: 020 8451 0189
07957 144674 (Mobile)
Fax: 020 8451 4606
email: bishop.willesden@btinternet.com

SUFFRAGAN BISHOP

FULHAM Rt Revd John Broadhurst, 26 Canonbury Park South, London N1 2FN [1996]
Tel: 020 7354 2334
Fax: 020 7354 2335
email: bpfulham@aol.com
Assists the Diocesan in all matters not delegated to the Areas and pastoral care of parishes operating under the London Plan.

HONORARY ASSISTANT BISHOPS

Rt Revd Donald Arden, 6 Frobisher Close, Pinner HA5 1NN   *Tel:* 020 8866 6009
Fax: 020 8868 8013
email: ardendj@yahoo.co.uk
Rt Revd Edward Holland, 37 Parfrey St, London W6 9EW   *Tel:* 020 8746 3636
Rt Revd Graeme Knowles, 9 Amen Court, London EC4M 7BU   *Tel:* 020 7236 2827
Fax: 020 7332 0298
email: thedean@stpaulscathedral.org.uk
Most Revd Walter Makhulu, Cheyne House, 10 Crondace Rd, London SW6 4BB
Tel: 020 7371 9419
Rt Revd Michael Marshall, 97a Cadogan Lane, London SW1X 9DU [1984]   *Tel:* 020 7235 3383
email: bishop@holytrinitysloanesquare.co.uk
Rt Revd Preb Sandy Millar, St Mark's Vicarage, 1 Moray Rd, London N4 3LD   *Tel:* 020 7561 5462
email: sandy.millar@tollingtonteam.org.uk
Rt Revd Ambrose Weekes, Charterhouse, Charterhouse Square, London EC1M 6AN
Tel: 020 7251 4201

CATHEDRAL CHURCH OF ST PAUL

Dean Rt Revd Graeme Knowles, 9 Amen Court, London EC4M 7BU [2007]   *Tel:* 020 7236 2827
Fax: 020 7332 0298
email: thedean@stpaulscathedral.org.uk
Canons Residentiary
Canon Martin Warner, 3 Amen Court, EC4M 7BU [2003]   *Tel:* 020 7248 2559
email: martinw@stpaulscathedral.org.uk
Canon Lucy Winkett, 1 Amen Court, EC4M 7BU [2003]   *Tel:* 020 7248 1817
email: precentor@stpaulscathedral.org.uk
Canon Pastor Rt Revd Michael Colclough, 2 Amen Court, EC4M 7BU   *Tel:* 020 7236 0199
Fax: 020 7489 8579
email: pastor@stpaulscathedral.org.uk
Canon Ed Newell, 6 Amen Court, EC4M 7BU [2001]   *Tel/Fax:* 020 7248 8572
email: chancellor@stpaulscathedral.org.uk
Lay Canons Mr Peter Chapman, Chapter House, St Paul's Churchyard, EC4M 8AD
Tel: 020 7246 8370
email: peterchapman@stpaulscathedral.org.uk

Mrs Claire Foster, St Paul's Institute, 3b Amen Court, London EC4M 7BU   *Tel:* 020 7849 1011
Fax: 020 7489 1011
email: claire.foster@stpaulscathedral.org.uk
The College of Minor Canons
Sacrist Revd Laura Burgess, 7a Amen Court, EC4M 7BU [2004]   *Tel:* 020 7246 8331
email: sacrist@stpaulscathedral.org.uk
Chaplain Revd Claire Robson, 7b Amen Court, EC4M 7BU [2004]   *Tel:* 020 7246 8323
email: chaplain@stpaulscathedral.org.uk
Diaconal Succentor Revd Jason Rendell, 8a Amen Court, EC4M 7BU [2003]   *Tel:* 020 7246 8338
email: succentor@stpaulscathedral.org.uk
Headmaster of the School Mr Andrew Dobbin, St Paul's Cathedral School, New Change, London EC4M 9AD   *Tel:* 020 7248 5156
Fax: 020 7329 6568
email: admissions@spcs.london.sch.uk
Registrar Major General John Milne, Chapter House, St Paul's Churchyard, EC4M 8AD
Tel: 020 7246 8311
Fax: 020 7248 3104
email: registrar@stpaulscathedral.org.uk
Dean's Virger Mr Michael Page, 4b Amen Court, EC4M 7BU   *Tel:* 020 7246 8320
email: virgers@stpaulscathedral.org.uk
Solicitor to the Foundation at St Paul's Cathedral Mr Owen Carew-Jones, Winckworth Sherwood, The Old Deanery, EC4V 5AA   *Tel:* 020 7593 5034
Fax: 020 7248 3221
email: ocj@winckworths.co.uk
Surveyor Mr Martin Stancliffe, The Chapter House, St Paul's Churchyard, EC4M 8AD
Tel: 020 7236 4128 and 01904 644001 (York)
Director of Music Mr Andrew Carwood, 5 Amen Court, EC4M 7BU   *Tel:* 020 7651 0899
email: andrewc@stpaulscathedral.org.uk
Organist Mr Simon Johnson, 4a Amen Court, EC4M 7BU   *Tel:* 020 7236 6883
email: simon@stpaulscathedral.org.uk
Sub-Organist Mr Tim Wakerell, c/o Chapter House, St Paul's Churchyard, EC4M 8AD
Tel: 020 7236 6883
email: suborganist@stpaulscathedral.org.uk

ARCHDEACONS
LONDON Ven Peter Delaney, The Archdeacon of London's Office, The Old Deanery, Dean's Court, London EC4V 5AA [1999]   *Tel:* 020 7236 7891
Fax: 020 7248 7455
email: archdeacon.london@london.anglican.org
CHARING CROSS Ven Dr William Jacob, 15A Gower St, London WC1E 6HW [1996]
Tel: 020 7323 1992
Fax: 020 7323 4102
email: archdeacon.charingcross@london.anglican.org
HACKNEY Ven Dr Lyle Dennen, St Andrew's Vicarage, 5 St Andrew St, EC4A 3AB [1999]
Tel: 020 7353 3544
Fax: 020 7583 2750
email: archdeacon.hackney@london.anglican.org

MIDDLESEX Ven Stephan Welch, 98 Dukes Ave, London W4 2AF [2006]   *Tel:* 020 8742 8308
email:
archdeacon.middlesex@london.anglican.org
HAMPSTEAD Ven Michael Lawson, London Diocesan House, 36 Causton St, London, SW1P 4AU [1999]   *Tel:* 020 7932 1190
Fax: 020 7932 1192
email:
archdeacon.hampstead@london.anglican.org
NORTHOLT Ven Rachel Treweek, 16 Baldwyn Gardens, Acton, London W3 6HL [2006]
Tel and *Fax:* 020 8993 6415
email: archdeacon.northolt@london.anglican.org

CONVOCATION (MEMBERS OF THE HOUSE OF CLERGY OF THE GENERAL SYNOD)
Dignitaries in Convocation
The Bishop of Willesden
Revd Dr Richard Burridge
Ven William Noblett
Proctors for Clergy
Preb Philippa Boardman
Preb John Brownsell
Revd Philip Chester
Revd Jonathan Clark
Revd Stephen Coles
Revd John Cook
Preb David Houlding
Revd Rose Hudson-Wilkin
Canon Martin Warner
Revd Andrew Watson

MEMBERS OF THE HOUSE OF LAITY OF THE GENERAL SYNOD
Ms Susan Cooper
Mrs Sarah Finch
Mr Aiden Hargreaves-Smith
Mrs Mary Johnston
Mrs Elnora Mann
Mrs Rosalind O'Dowd
Mrs Alison Ruoff
Mr Clive Scowen
Mr John Ward

DIOCESAN OFFICERS
Dioc Secretary Mr Keith Robinson, London Diocesan House, 36 Causton St, London SW1P 4AU   *Tel:* 020 7932 1100
Fax: 020 7932 1114
email: keith.robinson@london.anglican.org
Chancellor of Diocese Chancellor Nigel Seed, The Old Deanery, Dean's Court, London EC4V 5AA
Tel: 020 7593 5110
Fax: 020 7248 3221
Registrar of Diocese and Bishop's Legal Secretary Mr Paul Morris (*same address*)
Official Principal of the Archdeaconry of Hackney His Honour David Smith QC, Beachcroft, Beach, Bitton, Bristol BS30 6NP

Official Principal of the Archdeaconry of Hampstead Dean Sheila Cameron, 2 Harcourt Bldgs, Temple, London EC4Y 9DB
Official Principal of the Archdeaconry of Northolt Mr Paul Morris (*as above*)

DIOCESAN ORGANIZATIONS
CHAIRMEN
London Dioc Fund (*Dioc Board of Finance*) The Bishop of London
Deputy Chairman and Treasurer Mr David Loftus
Finance Committee Ven William Jacob
Dioc Synod (*House of Clergy*) Preb David Houlding
(*House of Laity*) Mr David Loftus
Dioc Board for Schools Ven Stephan Welch

ADMINISTRATION
Diocesan Office London Diocesan House, 36 Causton St, London SW1P 4AU
Tel: 020 7932 1100
Fax: 020 7932 1112
Web: www.london.anglican.org
Director of Finance and Operations Mr John Butler
Human Resources Manager Ms Paula Bailey
Head of Property Mr Michael Bye
Synodical Secretary Mrs Monica Bolley
Communications Officer Mr Robert Hargrave
Dioc Advisory Committee (*Chair*) Ven Peter Delaney; (*Acting Secretary*) Mr Charles Smith

EDUCATION
Senior Chaplain for Higher Education Revd Stephen Williams, University Chaplaincy Office, 30B Torrington Square, London WC1E 7JL
Tel: 020 7580 9812
Fax: 020 7631 3219
email: chaplaincy@lon.ac.uk
Director, Board for Schools Mr Tom Peryer, London Dioc House
Tel: 020 7932 1161
Fax: 020 7932 1111
email: tom.peryer@london.anglican.org

MINISTRY
Vicar General to the London College of Bishops, Director of Ministry, Dioc Director of Ordinands, Dioc Warden of Readers Revd Nick Mercer, The Old Deanery, Dean's Court, London EC4V 5AA
Tel: 020 7489 4274
email: nick.mercer@london.anglican.org
Director of Professional Development Revd Neil Evans, Willesden Area Office, 268a Kenton Rd, Kenton, Harrow HA3 8DB
Tel: 020 8907 5993
email: neil.evans@london.anglican.org
Two Cities
Dean of Women's Ministry Revd Rosemary Lain-Priestley, 13d Hyde Park Mansions, Cabell St, London NW1 5BD
Tel: 020 7723 5352
email: rosemarylainpriestley@btopenworld.com
Stepney
Area Director of Training and Development Preb Andy Windross, Centre for Training and Development (Stepney Episcopal Area), St Anne's Community Hall, Hemsworth St, London N1 5LF
Tel and Fax: 020 7033 3446
email: windross@fish.co.uk
Dean of Women's Ministry Revd Irena Edgcumbe, St Anne's Vicarage, 37 Hemsworh St, London N1 5LF
Tel: 020 7729 1243
email: irena.edgcumbe@london.anglican.org
Kensington
Area Director of Training and Development Revd Lawrence Smith, St Francis Vicarage, 865 Great West Rd, Isleworth TW7 5PD
Tel: 020 8568 9098
email: lawrence.smith@london.anglican.org
Dean of Women's Ministry Revd Rosemary Hoad, St Mary's Vicarage, Osterley Rd, Isleworth TW7 4PW
Tel: 020 8560 3555
email: rosemary.hoad@dsl.pipex.com
Willesden
Area Director of Training and Development Revd Neil Evans (*as above*)
Edmonton
Area Director of Training and Development Caulene Herbert, 27 Thurlow Rd, Hampstead, London NW3 5PP
Tel: 020 7431 6827
email: caulene.herbert@london.anglican.org

MISSION
Children's Ministry Adviser Samuel Donoghue, London Dioc House
Tel: 020 7932 1255
email: sam.donoghue@london.anglican.org
Diocesan Community Ministry Adviser Jack Maple
Tel: 020 7932 1122
email: jack.maple@london.anglican.org

LITURGICAL
Chairman Rt Revd Graeme Knowles (*as above*)
Convener Revd Keith Robus, St Gabriel's Vicarage, 15 Balfour Rd, North Acton, London, W3 0DG
Tel: 020 8992 5938
email: keith@robus.demon.co.uk

PRESS AND COMMUNICATIONS
Communications Officer Mr Robert Hargrave, London Dioc House
Tel: 020 7932 1227
email: robert.hargrave@london.anglican.org
Press, media and public affairs
Tel: 020 7618 9106 (24 hours)
email: dioceseoflondon@luther.co.uk

DIOCESAN RECORD OFFICES
London Metropolitan Archive, 40 Northampton Rd, London EC1R 0HB *Head Archivist* Dr Deborah Jenkins *Tel:* 020 7332 3824 (*All parishes except City and Westminster*)
Guildhall Library, Aldermanbury, London EC2P 2EJ *Archivist* Mr S. G. H. Freeth *Tel:* 020 7606 3030, Ext 1862/3 (*City parishes*)
Westminster Archives Dept, 10 St Ann's St, London SW1P 2XR *Archivist* Mr Jerome Farrell *Tel:* 020 7798 2180 (*Westminster parishes*)

AREA DEANS

ARCHDEACONRY OF LONDON

City Revd Jeremy Crossley, Rectory, 1 St Olave's Court (off Old Jewry), London EC2V 8EX
Tel: 020 7726 4878
Fax: 020 7606 1204
email: the.rector@stml.org.uk

ARCHDEACONRY OF CHARING CROSS

Westminster (Paddington) Revd Alastair Thom, Vicarage, 19 Macroom Rd, London W9 3HY
Tel: 020 8962 0294
email: alastairthom@yahoo.co.uk
Westminster (St Margaret) Revd Philip Chester, St Matthew's House, 20 Great Peter St, London SW1P 2BU
Tel: 020 7222 3704
email: office@stmw.org
Westminster (St Marylebone) Revd Alan Moses, 7 Margaret St, London W1W 8JG
Tel: 020 7636 1788 (Office)
Fax: 020 7436 4470
email: alan@moses.org

ARCHDEACONRY OF HACKNEY

Hackney Revd Ian Harper, St Luke's Vicarage, 23 Cassland Rd, London E9 7AL
Tel: 020 8525 0950 (Home)
020 8985 2263 (Office)
email: ian@elroi.freeserve.co.uk
Islington Revd Michael Learmouth, The Rectory, 10 Thornhill Square, London N1 1BQ
Tel: 020 7607 9039
email: Michael@learmouth.fsworld.co.uk
Tower Hamlets Revd Alan Green, St John's Rectory, 30 Victoria Park Square, Bethnal Green, London E2 9PB
Tel: 020 8980 1742
email: alan.green@virgin.net

ARCHDEACONRY OF MIDDLESEX

Hammersmith and Fulham Revd Gary Piper, St Matthew's Vicarage, 2 Clancarty Rd, London SW6 3AB
Tel: 020 7731 3272
email: revgarypiper@hotmail.com
Hampton Revd Andrew Watson, St Stephen's Vicarage, 21 Cambridge Park, East Twickenham TW1 2JE
Tel: 020 8892 5258
email: andrew@st-stephens.org.uk
Hounslow Revd Derek Simpson, Rectory, 3 The Butts, Brentford TW8 8BJ
Tel: 020 8568 7442 (Office)
email: derek.simpson@parishofbrentford.org.uk
Kensington Revd Dr Mark Hargreaves, 59a Portobello Rd, London W11 3DB
Tel: 020 7229 6774
email: mark@nottinghillchurch.org.uk

Chelsea Revd Rob Gillion, St Simon Zelotes Vicarage, 34 Milner St, London SW3 2QF
Tel: 020 7589 5747
email: rob.gillion@london.anglican.org
Spelthorne Revd Rod Cosh, St Peter's Vicarage, 14 Thames Side, Staines TW18 2HA
Tel: 01784 453039 (Home)
01784 469155 (Office)
email: rod@stainesparish.com

ARCHDEACONRY OF HAMPSTEAD

Central Barnet Revd Nigel Taylor, Christ Church Vicarage, St Albans Rd, Barnet EN5 4LA
Tel: 020 8449 0942
email: nigel.taylor@london.anglican.org
West Barnet Revd John Hawkins, St John's Vicarage, Vicarage Rd, London NW4 3PX
Tel and Fax: 020 8202 8606
email: jeih.stj@tiscali.co.uk
North Camden (Hampstead) Revd Andrew Cain, 134a Abbey Rd, London NW6 4SN
Tel and Fax: 020 7624 5434
email: vicaragekilburn@btopenworld.com
South Camden (Holborn and St Pancras) Revd Andrew Meldrum, St Anne's Vicarage, 106 Highgate West Hill, London NW6 6AP
Tel and Fax: 020 8340 5190
email: javintner@aol.com
Enfield Revd John Paul, St Paul's Vicarage, Church Hill, Winchmore Hill, London N21 1JA
Tel: 020 8886 3545
email: john.paul@london.anglican.org
East Haringey Revd Luke Miller, St Mary's Vicarage, Lansdowne Rd, London N17 9XE
Tel: 020 8808 6644
email: frmiller@stmarystottenham.org
West Haringey Revd Timothy Pike, 99 Hillfield Ave, Crouch End, London N8 7DG
Tel: 020 8340 1300
email: fr.tim@holy-innocents.org.uk

ARCHDEACONRY OF NORTHOLT

Brent Revd Philip Stone, 93 College Rd, Kensal Rise, London NW10 5EU
Tel: 020 8969 4598
email: phil.stone@london.anglican.org
Ealing Revd Andrew Corsie, Perivale Rectory, Federal Rd, Greenford UB6 7AP
Tel: 020 8997 1948
email: acorsie@aol.com
Harrow Canon Richard Bartlett, Holy Trinity Vicarage, Gateway Close, Northwood, Middlesex HA6 2RP
Tel: 01923 825732
email: richard.bartlett@london.anglican.org
Hillingdon Revd Simon Evans, The Vicarage, 13 Eastcote Rd, Ruislip, Middlesex HA4 8BE
Tel: 01895 633040
email: frsimon@waitrose.com

DIOCESE OF MANCHESTER

Founded in 1847. Manchester, except for a few parishes in the south (CHESTER); Salford; Bolton; Bury; Rochdale; Oldham; the western half of Tameside; an area of Wigan; an area of Trafford; an area of Stockport; an area of southern Lancashire.

Population 1,962,000   Area 415 sq m
Full-time Stipendiary Parochial Clergy 231   Benefices 221
Parishes 281   Churches 345
www.manchester.anglican.org
Overseas link dioceses: Lahore, Namibia.

BISHOP (11th)
Rt Revd Nigel Simeon McCulloch, Bishopscourt, Bury New Rd, Manchester M7 4LE [2002]
Tel: 0161 792 2096 (Office)
Fax: 0161 792 6826
email:
bishop@bishopscourt.manchester.anglican.org
[Nigel Manchester]
Chaplain Canon Anne Hollinghurst (same address)
email:
chaplain@bishopscourt.manchester.anglican.org
Bishop's Missioner Canon Roger Hill (same address)

SUFFRAGAN BISHOPS
BOLTON Rt Revd Chris Edmonson, Bishop's Lodge, Walkden Rd, Worsley, Manchester M28 2WH [2008]
Tel: 0161 790 8289
Fax: 0161 703 9157
email: bishopchris@manchester.anglican.org
MIDDLETON Rt Revd Mark Davies, The Hollies, Manchester Rd, Rochdale OL11 3QY [2008]
Tel: 01706 358550
Fax: 01706 354851
email: bishopmark@manchester.anglican.org
HULME (Bishop for Urban Life and Faith) Rt Revd Stephen Richard Lowe, 14 Moorgate Ave, Withington, Manchester M20 1HE [1999]
Tel: 0161 445 5922
Fax: 0161 448 9687
email: lowehulme@btinternet.com

CATHEDRAL AND COLLEGIATE CHURCH OF ST MARY, ST DENYS AND ST GEORGE
Dean Very Revd Rogers Govender, Manchester Cathedral, Victoria St, Manchester M3 1SX [2006]
Tel: 0161 833 2220
email: dean@manchestercathedral.org
Cathedral Office Manchester Cathedral, Victoria St, Manchester M3 1SX
Tel: 0161 833 2220
Fax: 0161 839 6218
email: office@manchestercathedral.org
Web: www.manchestercathedral.org
Canons Residentiary
Sub-Dean Ven Andrew Ballard, 2 The Walled Garden, Ewhurst Avenue, Swinton M27 0FR
Tel: 0161 794 2401
email: archmanchester@manchester.anglican.org
Evangelist Canon Robin Gamble, 30 Rathan Rd, Withington, Manchester M20 4GH [2002]

Tel: 0161 446 1099
email: office@manchestercathedral.org
Theologian Canon Andrew Shanks, 3 Booth Clibborn Court, Park Lane, Manchester M7 4PJ [2004]
Tel: 0161 792 8820
Fax: 0161 839 6218
email: canon.shanks@manchestercathedral.org
Bishop's Chaplain Canon Anne Hollinghurst, 197a Lancaster Rd, Salford M6 8NB [2005]
Tel: 0161 788 8461
email:
chaplain@bishopscourt.manchester.anglican.org
Canon Precentor Canon Gilly Myers, Manchester Cathedral, Victoria St, Manchester M3 1SX [2008]
Tel: 0161 833 2220
Archdeacon of Manchester
Ven Andrew Ballard (Archdeacon of Manchester)
Cathedral Chaplains
Revd Peter Bellamy-Knights; Canon Adrian Rhodes
Lay Members of Chapter
Mr David Howe
Cllr Roy Walters
Mrs Jennifer Curtis
Mr Barrie Cheshire
Chapter Clerk Mr David Murray, c/o Cathedral Office (tel. ext. 229)
email: david.murray@manchestercathedral.org
Cathedral Education Officer Mrs Pam Elliott, c/o Cathedral Office (tel. ext. 236)
email: pam.elliott@manchestercathedral.org
Visitor Centre Manager Mr Peter Mellor (same address)
Tel: 0161 835 4030
email: peter.mellor@manchestercathedral.org
Cathedral Organist and Master of the Choristers Mr Christopher Stokes, c/o Cathedral Office (tel. ext. 225)
email:
christopher.stokes@manchestercathedral.org
Sub-Organist Mr Jeffrey Makinson, c/o Cathedral Office (tel. ext. 225)
email: jeffrey.makinson@manchestercathedral.org
Music Administrator Mrs Judith Parry, c/o Cathedral Office (tel. ext. 238)
email: judith.parry@manchestercathedral.org
Cathedral Administrator Mr David Murray, c/o Cathedral Office (tel. ext. 229)
email: david.murray@manchestercathedral.org

Senior Administrative Assistant: Miss Joanne Hooper, c/o Cathedral Office (tel. ext. 221)
email: joanne.hooper@manchestercathedral.org
Dean's PA Alison Galloway, c/o Cathedral Office (tel. ext. 220)
email: alison.galloway@manchestercathedral.org
Office Assistant Naomi Elliot, c/o Cathedral Office (tel. ext. 222)
email: naomi.elliott@manchestercathedral.org
Head Verger Mr Michael Scott, c/o Cathedral Office
email: michael.scott@manchestercathedral.org
Cathedral Accountant Mr John Atherton, c/o Cathedral Office
john.atherton@manchestercathedral.com

ARCHDEACONS
MANCHESTER (until 31 January 2009) Ven Andrew Ballard, 2 The Walled Garden, Ewhurst Avenue, Swinton, Manchester M27 4UX [2005]
Tel: 0161 794 2401
Fax: 0161 794 2411
email: ae.ballard@btinternet.com
ROCHDALE Ven Cherry Vann, 57 Melling Rd, Oldham OL4 1PN [2008]   *Tel:* 0161 678 1454
Fax: 0161 678 1455
email: markdavies@bigfoot.com
BOLTON Ven David Bailey, 45 Rudgwick Drive, Brandlesholme, Bury, Lancs. BL8 1YA
Tel: 0161 761 6117
Fax: 0161 763 7973
email: archdeacon.bolton@btinternet.com

CONVOCATION (MEMBERS OF THE HOUSE OF CLERGY OF THE GENERAL SYNOD)
Dignitaries in Convocation
The Bishop of Hulme
Proctors for Clergy
Ven Dr John Applegate
Canon Nicholas Feist
Revd David Griffiths
Revd Simon Killwick
Revd Dr Bill Raines
Canon Alma Servant
Revd Cherry Vann

MEMBERS OF THE HOUSE OF LAITY OF THE GENERAL SYNOD
Mr Simon Butterworth
Dr Peter Capon
Mr Alan Cooper
Mr Philip Gore
Mr Geoffrey Tattersall
Mr Roy Walker

DIOCESAN OFFICERS
Chief Executive Mr John Beck, Diocesan Church House, 90 Deansgate, Manchester M3 2GH
Tel: 0161 828 1400
Fax: 0161 828 1480
Chancellor of Diocese G. F. Tattersall, Dioc Registry, Dioc Church House

Deputy Chancellor Prof N. Doe, Dioc Registry, Dioc Church House   *Tel:* 0161 834 7545
Registrar of Diocese and Bishop's Legal Secretary Miss Jane Monks (*same address*)
Dioc Surveyor for Parsonage Houses Mr John Prichard, The Lloyd Evans Partnership, 5 The Parsonage, Manchester M3 2HS
Tel: 0161 834 6251

DIOCESAN ORGANIZATIONS
Diocesan Office Diocesan Church House, 90 Deansgate, Manchester M3 2GH
Tel: 0161 828 1400
Fax: 0161 828 1480
email: manchesterdbf@manchester.anglican.org

ADMINISTRATION
Dioc Synod (*Chairman, House of Clergy*) Ven Cherry Vann
(*Chairman, House of Laity*) Mr Phillip Blinkhorn
Board of Finance (*Chairman*) Mr Alan Cooper, 11 Ravensdale Gdns, Eccles, Manchester M30 9JD
Tel: 0161 789 1514
(*Secretary*) Miss Jane Monks; (*Head of Finance and IT*) Mrs Janet Bury, Dioc Office; (*Legal Secretary*) Miss Jane Monks, Dioc Registry, Dioc Church House   *Tel:* 0161 834 7545
Property Committee (*Property Secretary*) Mr Geoff Hutchinson, Dioc Office
Pastoral Committee Mr John Beck
Designated Officer Miss Jane Monks, Dioc Registry, Dioc Church House   *Tel:* 0161 834 7545

CHURCHES
Advisory Committee for the Care of Churches (*Chairman*) Mr Adrian Golland, Peel House, 29 Higher Dunscar, Egerton, Bolton BL7 9TE; (*DAC Secretary*) Ms Christine Hart, Dioc Office

EDUCATION
Chairman Rt Revd Mark Davies
Director of Education Mr Maurice Smith, Diocesan Church House, 90 Deansgate, Manchester M3 2GH   *Tel:* 0161 828 1400
Fax: 0161 828 1484
Education Officers
(*Buildings*) Mrs Lynn Wild (*same address*)
(*Governor Training*) Mr Wil Leeson
((*Asst Director of Education and Section 23/RE*) Mr John Wilson (*same address*)
Children's Work Revd Steve Dixon (*same address*)
Youth Work Vacancy (*same address*)
Deputy Director of Education and Training and Development Mrs Janet Cowley (*same address*)

CHURCH AND SOCIETY
Chairman The Archdeacon of Rochdale
Director and Partnership Development Officer Mr Martin Miller, Dioc Office
Training Officer (*Church and Community Engagement*) Mr Mike France, Dioc Office
Tel: 0161 828 1400
International Officer Vacancy, Dioc Office
Mission Planning Officer Ms Alison Peacock, Dioc Office

Parish Resource Officer Revd Dian Leppington, Dioc Office
Hon European Adviser Revd Dr Keith Archer, Dioc Office

DISCIPLESHIP AND MINISTRY TRAINING
Chairman Revd Canon Sarah Bullock
Director of Ministry Training and OLM Principal Revd Peter Reiss
Training Officer (CME and LD) Revd David Foster
Training Officer (Reader Training) Revd Jayne Prestwood, Dioc Office   Tel: 0161 828 1400
Dioc Director of Ordinands and OLM Officer Revd David Sharples, Bishopscourt, Bury New Rd, Manchester M4 4LE   Tel: 0161 708 9366

PRESS AND PUBLICATIONS
Director of Communications David Marshall, Dioc Office   Tel: 0161 828 1400
07836 224444 (Mobile)
email: dmarshall@manchester.anglican.org
Editor of Dioc Year Book c/o Dioc Office
Editor of Dioc Magazine Mrs Ann Mummery
email: amummery@manchester.anglican.org

DIOCESAN RECORD OFFICE
For further information apply to The Archivist, The Central Library, St Peter's Square, Manchester M2 5PD   Tel: 0161 234 1980

AREA DEANS
ARCHDEACONRY OF MANCHESTER
Ardwick Revd Ian Gomersall, St Chrysostom's Rectory, 38 Park Range, Manchester M14 5HQ
Tel: 0161 224 6971
Fax: 0161 870 6197
email: ian.gomersall@btinternet.com
Eccles Revd Ted Crofton, Rectory, 12b Westminster Rd, Eccles, Manchester M30 9EB
Tel: 0161 281 5739
email: ea_crofton@msn.com
Heaton Revd Les Ireland, St Andrew's Rectory, 27 Errwood Rd, Manchester M19 2PN
Tel: 0161 224 5877
email: LesIreland@ntlworld.com
Hulme Revd Simon Killwick, Christ Church Rectory, Monton St, Manchester M14 4LT
Tel: 0161 226 2476
email: frskillwick@tiscali.co.uk
North Manchester Revd Hilary Evans, 14 Hill Lane, Blackley, Manchester M9 8BX
Tel: 0161 740 2124
email: hilary@evanses.plus.com
Salford Revd Andy Salmon, 6 Encombe Place, Salford M3 6JF   Tel: 0161 834 2041
email: rev.andy@btinternet.com
Stretford Revd Chris Brown, St Clement's Vicarage, 24 Stretford Rd, Urmston, Manchester M41 9JZ   Tel: 0161 748 3972
email: christopher@cbrown30.fsnet.co.uk

Withington Revd Ian McVeety, St John's Vicarage, 186 Brooklands Rd, Sale M33 3PB
Tel: 0161 973 5947
email: ian@stjohnsvicarage.fsnet.co.uk

ARCHDEACONRY OF BOLTON
Bolton Revd Chris Bracegirdle, Vicarage, 2 Towncroft Lane, Heaton, Bolton BL1 5EW
Tel: 01204 840430
email: chris@bracegirdles.fsworld.co.uk
Bury Revd Stuart Millington, All Saints Vicarage, 10 Kirkburn View, Brandlesholme, Bury BL8 1DL   Tel: 0161 797 1595
email: stuart@revmillington.wanadoo.co.uk
Deane Revd Roger Cooper, St Katharine's Vicarage, Blackhorse St. Blackrod, Bolton BL6 5EN
Tel: 01204 468150
email: revrog17@hotmail.com
Farnworth Vacancy
Leigh Revd Dr Robert Buckley, Howe Bridge Rectory, Leigh Rd, Atherton M46 0PH
Tel: 01942 883359
email: revrobert@athertonparish.co.uk
Radcliffe and Prestwich Revd Chiche Hewitt, St Thomas' Vicarage, Heber St, Radcliffe, Manchester M26 2TG   Tel: 0161 723 2123
email: chich@rink-hewitt.co.uk
Rossendale Revd Susan Davies, Rectory, 539 Newchurch Rd, Rossendale BB4 9HH
Tel and Fax: 01706 219708
email: susanannedavies@aol.com
Walmsley Revd Andy Lindop, St Paul's Vicarage, Sweetloves Lane, Astley Bridge, Bolton BL1 7ET
Tel and Fax: 01204 304119
email: Andy.Lindop@tesco.net

ARCHDEACONRY OF ROCHDALE
Ashton-under-Lyne Revd Roger Farnworth, St James Vicarage, Union St, Ashton-under-Lyne OL6 9NQ   Tel: 0161 330 2777
email: rogerfarnworth@aol.com
Heywood and Middleton Revd Ian Butterworth, St Martin's Vicarage, Vicarage Rd North, Castleton OL11 2TE   Tel: 01706 632363
email: i.butterworth@tesco.net
Oldham Revd Raymond Morris, Mark's Vicarage, Perth St, Heyside, Royton, Oldham OL2 6LY
Tel: 01706 847177
email: raymondmorris80@hotmail.com
Rochdale Revd Sharon Jones, St Andrew's Vicarage, Arm Rd, Dearnley, Littleborough OL15 8NJ   Tel: 01706 378466
email: sharon@dearnleyvicarage.plus.com
Saddleworth Revd Richard Hawkins, St John's Vicarage, 1 Owen Fold, Lees, Oldham OL4 3DT
Tel: 0161 626 3630
email: richard.hawkins107@ntlworld.com
Tandle Revd Raymond Morris, St Mark's Vicarage, Perth St, Heyside, Royton, Oldham OL2 6LY   Tel: 01706 847177
email: raymondmorris80@hotmail.com

DIOCESE OF NEWCASTLE

Founded in 1882. Northumberland; Newcastle upon Tyne; North Tyneside; a small area of eastern Cumbria; four parishes in northern County Durham.

Population 778,000   Area 2,110 sq m
Full-time Stipendiary Parochial Clergy 120   Benefices 135
Parishes 172   Churches 241
www.newcastle.anglican.org
Companion link dioceses: Winchester, More (Norway), Botswana (Africa).

BISHOP (11th)
Rt Revd (John) Martin Wharton, Bishop's House, 29 Moor Rd South, Gosforth, Newcastle upon Tyne NE3 1PA [1998]   *Tel:* 0191 285 2220
email: bishop@newcastle.anglican.org
[Martin Newcastle]
Bishop's Chaplain Canon Dr Audrey A. Elkington (*same address*)

ASSISTANT BISHOP
Rt Revd Paul Richardson, (Home) Close House, St George's Close, Jesmond, Newcastle upon Tyne NE2 2TF [1998]   *Tel:* 0191 281 2556
email: p.richardson@newcastle.anglican.org
(Office) Bishop's House, 29 Moor Rd South, Gosforth, Newcastle upon Tyne NE3 1PA
Tel: 0191 285 2220

HONORARY ASSISTANT BISHOPS
Rt Revd Kenneth Edward Gill, Kingfisher Lodge, 41 Long Cram, Haddington, East Lothian EH41 4NS [1999]   *Tel:* 01620 822113
email: k.gill@newcastle.anglican.org
Rt Revd Stephen Pedley, The Blue House, Newbrough NE47 5AN   *Tel:* 01434 674238
Rt Revd John Henry Richardson, Old Rectory, Bewcastle, Carlisle, Cumbria CA6 6PS [2003]
Tel: 01697 748389

CATHEDRAL CHURCH OF ST NICHOLAS
Dean Very Revd Christopher Charles Dalliston, 26 Mitchell Ave, Jesmond, Newcastle upon Tyne NE2 3LA [2003]   *Tel:* 0191 281 6554
0191 232 1939
email: dean@stnicnewcastle.co.uk
Chapter Office St Nicholas' Cathedral, St Nicholas Churchyard, Newcastle upon Tyne NE1 1PF
Tel: 0191 232 1939
Fax: 0191 230 0735
email: office@stnicnewcastle.co.uk
Canons Residentiary
Canon Precentor Canon Peter Robert Strange, 55 Queens Terrace, Jesmond, Newcastle upon Tyne NE2 2PL [1986]   *Tel:* 0191 281 0181
0191 232 1939
email: peterstrange@stnicnewcastle.co.uk

Ven Geoffrey Vincent Miller, 80 Moorside North, Fenham, Newcastle upon Tyne NE4 9DU [1999]
Tel: 0191 273 8245
Fax: 0191 226 0286
email: g.miller@newcastle.anglican.org
Canon David John Elkington, 16 Towers Ave, Jesmond, Newcastle upon Tyne NE2 3QE [2002]
Tel: 0191 281 0714
email: djelk@tiscali.co.uk
Canon Robert Edward Gage, 2a Holly Ave, Jesmond, Newcastle upon Tyne NE2 2PY [2005]
Tel: 0191 281 4329
email: robertgage@stnicnewcastle.co.uk
Director of Music Vacancy   *Tel:* 0191 261 4505
Director of Girl's Choir Mr George Richford
Tel: 0191 232 1939
Cathedral Secretary Ms Elspeth Robertson, Cathedral Office   *Tel:* 0191 232 1939
email: office@stnicnewcastle.co.uk
Cathedral Administrator Mr Julian Haynes, Cathedral Office   *Tel:* 0191 232 1939
email: julianhaynes@stnicnewcastle.co.uk
Finance Administrator Ms Ruth Edwards, Cathedral Office   *Tel:* 0191 232 1939
email: ruthedwards@stnicnewcastle.co.uk

ARCHDEACONS
LINDISFARNE Ven Peter J. A. Robinson, 4 Acomb Close, Stobhill Manor, Morpeth NE61 2YH [2008]
Tel: 01670 503810
Fax: 01670 503 469
email: p.robinson@newcastle.anglican.org
NORTHUMBERLAND Ven Geoffrey Miller, 80 Moorside North, Fenham, Newcastle upon Tyne NE4 9DU [2005]   *Tel:* 0191 273 8245
Fax: 0191 226 0286
email: g.miller@newcastle.anglican.org

CONVOCATION (MEMBERS OF THE HOUSE OF CLERGY OF THE GENERAL SYNOD)
Proctors for Clergy
Canon Adrian Hughes
Canon Michael Webb
Revd Dr Dagmar Winter

MEMBERS OF THE HOUSE OF LAITY OF THE GENERAL SYNOD
Dr John Bull
Canon Tony Garland

DIOCESAN OFFICERS
Dioc Secretary Mr Philip Davies, Church House, St John's Terrace, North Shields NE29 6HS
Tel: 0191 270 4100
Fax: 0191 270 4101
Chancellor of Diocese The Worshipful David McClean, 6 Burnt Stones Close, Sheffield S10 5TS
Tel: 0114 230 5794
Registrar of Diocese and Bishop's Legal Secretary Mrs Jane Lowdon, Sintons Solicitors, The Cube, Barrack Rd, Newcastle upon Tyne NE4 6DB
Tel: 0191 226 7878
Fax: 0191 226 7850
email: j.lowden@sintons.co.uk

DIOCESAN ORGANIZATIONS
Diocesan Office Church House, St John's Terrace, North Shields NE29 6HS   *Tel:* 0191 270 4100
Fax: 0191 270 4101
email: church_house@newcastle.anglican.org

ADMINISTRATION
Dioc Synod (Chairman, House of Clergy) Canon Michael Webb, Vicarage, Howling Lane, Alnwick NE66 1DH   *Tel:* 01665 602184
email: michaelwebb1@hotmail.com
(Chairman, House of Laity) Dr John Bull, Gable Ends, 11 Glebe Mews, Bedlington NE22 6LJ
Tel: 07710 200416
email: John.Bull@ncl.ac.uk
(Secretary) Mr Philip Davies, Church House
Finance Board (Chairman) Mr Stephen Harper, Church House
(Secretary) Mr Philip Davies *(as above)*
Accountant Mr John Hall, Church House
Property Manager Mr Ian Beswick, Church House
Dioc Society (Trusts) Mr Philip Davies *(as above)*
Pastoral Committee Mr Nigel Foxon, Church House
Designated Officer Mrs Jane Lowdon *(as above)*

CHURCHES
Advisory Committee for the Care of Churches (Chairman) Mr Geoffrey Purves, Geoffrey Purves Partnership, 8 North Terrace, Newcastle upon Tyne NE2 4AD   *Tel:* 0191 232 0424
(Secretary) Mr Nigel Foxon *(as above)*
Redundant Churches Uses Committee Mr Philip Davies *(as above)*

EDUCATION
Director of Education Canon Margaret Nicholson, Church House
Assistant Director of Education Mr Brian Hedley, Church House
Schools Administrative Officer Mrs Vanessa Ward, Church House

MINISTRY AND TRAINING
Director of Ordinands Canon Dr Audrey A. Elkington, Bishop's House, 29 Moor Rd South, Gosforth, Newcastle upon Tyne NE3 1PA
Tel: 0191 285 2220

Continuing Ministerial Education Adviser Canon Colin Gough, Church House
Bishop's Adviser for Women's Ministry Canon Dr Audrey Elkington, Bishop's House
Development Officer for Children's Work Sandra Doore, Church House
Principal of Local Ministry Scheme and Reader Training Course Canon Richard Bryant, Church House *(as above)*
Secretary, Association of Readers Mrs Sue Hart, 73 Monkseaton Drive, Whitley Bay NE26 3DQ
Tel: 0191 2523941
Retreat House Mr Peter Dodgson *(Warden)*, Shepherds Dene, Riding Mill NE44 6AF
Tel: 01434 682212
email: shepherds_dene@newcastle.anglican.org
Sons of Clergy Society Mrs Gwenda Gofton, 4 Crossfell, Ponteland NE20 9EA
Tel: 01661 820344
Diocesan Widows Officer Mrs Marjorie Craig, 5 Springwell Meadow, Alnwick NE66 2NY
Tel: 01665 602806

LITURGICAL
Chairman Revd Christopher Clinch, St Francis Vicarage, 66 Cleveland Gardens, High Heaton, Newcastle-upon-Tyne NE7 7QH
Tel: 0191 266 1071
email: ccne1274@blueyonder.co.uk

MISSION, SOCIAL RESPONSIBILITY AND ECUMENISM
Adviser in Local Evangelism Canon David John Elkington, 16 Towers Ave, Jesmond, Newcastle upon Tyne NE2 3QE   *Tel:* 0191 281 0714
email: djelk@tiscali.co.uk
Ecumenical Officer Revd David Cant, Vicarage, Wylam, Northumberland NE41 8AT
Tel: 01661 853254
email: david@stoswin.totalserve.co.uk

PRESS, PUBLICITY AND PUBLICATIONS
Dioc Communications Officer Mrs Sue Scott, Church House
Editor of 'The New Link' Mrs Sue Scott *(as above)*
Editor of Dioc Year Book Mr Philip Davies *(as above)*

DIOCESAN RECORD OFFICE
For further information apply to Northumberland Collections Service, Queen Elizabeth II Country Park, Ashington NE63 9YF   *Tel:* 01670 528080

DIOCESAN RESOURCE CENTRE
Contact Karenza Passmore, Church House, St John's Terrace, North Shields NE29 6HS
Tel: 0191 270 4161
Fax: 0191 270 4101
email: k.passmore@resourcescentreonline.co.uk

STEWARDSHIP
Parish Giving Officer Mr Richard Gascoyne, Church House   *Tel:* 0191 270 3136
email: r.gascoyne@newcastle.anglican.org

AREA DEANS
ARCHDEACONRY OF NORTHUMBERLAND

Bedlington Revd Dr Peter Bryars, Delaval Vicarage, The Avenue, Seaton Sluice, Whitley Bay NE26 4QW *Tel:* 0191 237 1982
email: pjbryars@btinternet.com

Newcastle Central Revd Philip Cunningham, 17 Rectory Rd, Gosforth, Newcastle-upon-Tyne NE3 1XR *Tel:* 0191 285 1326
email: philipcunningham@hotmail.com

Newcastle East Revd Kevin Hunt, Walker Vicarage, Middle St, Newcastle upon Tyne NE6 4DB *Tel:* 0191 262 3666
email: kevin@hunt10.plus.com

Newcastle West Revd John R. Sinclair, The Vicarage, Newburn, Newcastle upon Tyne NE15 8LQ *Tel:* 0191 229 0522
email: johnsinclair247@aol.com

Tynemouth Canon James Robertson, St Peter's Vicarage, 6 Elmwood Rd, Whitley Bay NE25 8FX *Tel:* 0191 252 1991
email: Jim.A.Robertson@blueyonder.co.uk

ARCHDEACONRY OF LINDISFARNE

Alnwick Canon Janet Brearley, 11 Dial Place, Warkworth, Morpeth, Northumberland NE65 0UR *Tel:* 01665 711217
email: jmbrearley@stlawrence-church.org.uk

Bamburgh and Glendale Revd Brian Hurst, 2 Queen's Rd, Wooler NE71 6DR
Tel: 01668 281468
email: brianhurst1@btopenworld.com

Bellingham Revd Dr Susan Ramsaran, Rectory, Bellingham, Hexham NE48 2JS
Tel: 01434 220019
email: SMRamsaran@aol.com

Corbridge Canon Michael Nelson, Vicarage, 2 Burnside Close, Ovingham NE42 6BS
Tel: 01661 832273
email: canon.michael.nelson@care4free.net

Hexham Canon Graham Usher, Rectory, Eilansgate, Hexham NE46 3EW
Tel: 01434 603121
email: rector@hexhamabbey.org.uk

Morpeth Canon Colin R. Gough, The Vicarage, Stannington, Morpeth, Northumberland NE61 6HL *Tel:* 01670 789122
email: colingough@onetel.com

Norham Revd Martin Gillham, Vicarage, Norham, Berwick-upon-Tweed TD15 2LF
Tel: 01289 382325
email: m.gillham@virgin.net

DIOCESE OF NORWICH

Founded in 1094, formerly Thetford (AD 1070), originally Dunwich (AD 630) and Elmham (AD 673). Norfolk, except for the western quarter (ELY); an area of north-east Suffolk.

Population 854,000   Area 1,804 sq m
Full-time Stipendiary Parochial Clergy 178   Benefices 185
Parishes 570   Churches 641
Overseas link province: Papua New Guinea.

BISHOP (71st)
Rt Revd Graham Richard James, Bishop's House, Norwich NR3 1SB [1999]   *Tel:* 01603 629001
Fax: 01603 761613
email: bishop@bishopofnorwich.org
[Graham Norvic:]
Bishop's Chaplain Vacancy
Bishop's Secretary Mrs Brenda Goodson (*same address*)

SUFFRAGAN BISHOPS
THETFORD Rt Revd David Atkinson, The Red House, 53 Norwich Rd, Stoke Holy Cross, Norwich NR14 8AB [2001]   *Tel:* 01508 491014
Fax: 01508 492105
email: bishop.thetford@4frontmedia.co.uk
Bishop's Secretary Mrs Mary Brookes (*same address*)
LYNN Rt Revd James Langstaff, The Old Vicarage, Castle Acre, King's Lynn PE32 2AA [2004]
Tel: 01760 755553
Fax: 01760 755085
email: bishoplynn@norwich.anglican.org
Bishop's Secretary Mrs Avril Kee (*same address*)

HONORARY ASSISTANT BISHOPS
Rt Revd E. Devenport, 6 Damocles Court, Pottergate, Norwich NR2 1HN [2000]
Rt Revd A. C. Foottit, Ivy House, Whitwell St, Reepham NR10 4RA [2004]   *Tel:* 01603 870340
email: acfoottit@hotmail.com
Rt Revd P. J. Fox, The Vicarage, Harwood Rd, Norwich NR1 2NG [2008]   *Tel:* 01603 625678
email: peterandangiefox@yahoo.co.uk
Rt Revd R. Garrard, 26 Carol Close, Stoke Holy Cross, Norwich NR14 8NN [2003]
Tel: 01508 494165
email: garrard.r.a@btinternet.com
Rt Revd D. Leake, The Anchorage, Lower Common, East Runton, Cromer NR27 9PG [2003]
Tel: 01263 513536
Rt Revd M. Menin, 32c Bracondale, Norwich NR1 2AN [2000]   *Tel:* 01603 627987
Rt Revd D. K. Gillett, 10 Burton Close, Diss IP22 4YJ [2008]

CATHEDRAL CHURCH OF THE HOLY AND UNDIVIDED TRINITY
Dean Very Revd Graham Smith, The Deanery, The Close, Norwich NR1 4EG [2004]
Tel: 01603 218308 (Office)
email: dean@cathedral.org.uk
Cathedral Office 12 The Close, Norwich NR1 4DH
Tel: 01603 218300
Fax: 01603 766032
Web: www.cathedral.org.uk
Canons Residentiary
Canon, Pastor and Custos Canon Richard Capper, 52 The Close, Norwich NR1 4EG [2005]
Tel: 01603 665210 (Home)
01603 218331 (Office)
email: canonpastor@cathedral.org.uk
Precentor and Vice-Dean Canon Jeremy Haselock, 34 The Close, Norwich NR1 4DZ [1998]
Tel: 01603 218314 (Home)
01603 218306 (Office)
email: precentor@cathedral.org.uk *or*
jeremy@jhaselock.force9.co.uk
Canon Librarian Vacancy
Chapter Steward Mr Alan Kefford, 12 The Close, Norwich NR1 4DH
Tel: 01603 218303
email: akefford@cathedral.org.uk
Master of the Music Mr David Lowe, 12 The Close, Norwich NR1 4DH   *Tel:* 01603 626589
email: dlowe@cathedral.org.uk
Cathedral Organist Mr David Dunnett, 12 The Close, Norwich NR1 4DH   *Tel:* 01603 218315
email: organist@cathedral.org.uk
Sacrist Mr Roger Lee, 12 The Close, Norwich NR1 4DH   *Tel:* 01603 218325
email: sacrist@cathedral.org.uk

ARCHDEACONS
NORWICH Ven Jan McFarlane, 31 Bracondale, Norwich NR1 2AT (From March 2009)
LYNN Vacancy
email: archdeacon.lynn@4frontmedia.co.uk
NORFOLK Ven David Hayden, Vicarage, 8 Boulton Rd, Thorpe St Andrew, Norwich NR7 0DF [2002]
Tel and *Fax:* 01603 702477
email: archdeacon.norfolk@4frontmedia.co.uk

CONVOCATION (MEMBERS OF THE HOUSE OF CLERGY OF THE GENERAL SYNOD)
Proctors for Clergy
Canon Steven Betts
Canon Jeremy Haselock
Ven David Hayden
Ven Jan McFarlane

MEMBERS OF THE HOUSE OF LAITY OF THE GENERAL SYNOD
Mr Robin Back
Mrs Susan Johns
Dr Christopher Smith

DIOCESAN OFFICERS
Dioc Secretary Canon Richard Bowett, Diocesan House, 109 Dereham Rd, Easton, Norwich NR9 5ES   *Tel:* 01603 880853
Fax: 01603 881083
email: richard.bowett@norwich.anglican.org
Chancellor of Diocese His Honour Judge Paul Downes, 44 The Close, Norwich NR1 4EQ
Registrar of Diocese and Bishop's Legal Secretary Mr Ian Mayers, Mills and Reeve, 1 St James Court, Whitefriars, Norwich NR3 1RU
Tel: 01603 660155
Fax: 01603 633027

DIOCESAN ORGANIZATIONS
Diocesan Office Diocesan House, 109 Dereham Rd, Easton, Norwich NR9 5ES
Tel: 01603 880853
Fax: 01603 881083
email: diocesanhouse@norwich.anglican.org
Web: www.norwich.anglican.org

ADMINISTRATION
Dioc Synod (Chairman, House of Clergy) Canon S. Betts, St Margaret's Vicarage, 1 Parkside Drive, Old Catton, Norwich NR6 7DP
Tel: 01603 425615
(Chairman, House of Laity) Mr Robin Back, The Old Manse, Guestwick, Dereham NR20 5QJ
Tel: 01362 683281
(Secretary) Mr David Broom, Dioc House
Board of Finance (Chairman) Mr Geoffrey Dorling, 87 Norwich Rd, Wymondham NR18 0SH
Tel: 01953 605030
(Secretary) Canon Richard Bowett *(as above)*
Property Committee (Chairman) Mr Robin Bramall
(Secretary) Mr Ray Levett, Dioc House
Surveyor Mr Michael Marshall, Dioc House
Designated Officer Canon Richard Bowett *(as above)*
Dioc Electoral Registration Officer Canon Richard Bowett *(as above)*

DIOCESAN MISSION AND PASTORAL COMMITTEE
Chairman Vacancy
Secretary Vacancy
Redundant Churches Uses Committee (Chairman) Vacancy

(Secretary) Vacancy
Board of Patronage (Chairman) Mr David Pearson, 17 North Drive, Great Yarmouth NR30 4EW
Tel: 01493 842623
(Secretary) Mrs J. Vere, Southlands, Church Corner, North Lopham, Diss IP22 2LP
Tel: 01379 687679
Advisory Committee for the Care of Churches (Chairman) Mr Chris Brown, 18 Vicar St, Wymondham NR18 4PL
(Secretary) Mrs Jean Gosling *(as above)*
Ringers' Association Mr David McLean, 33 Milton Rd East, Lowestoft NR32 1NU
Tel: 01502 568296
Bishop's Furnishings Officer Canon P. McCrory, Dane House, The Street, Kettlestone, Fakenham NR21 0AU   *Tel:* 01328 878455

EDUCATION
Board of Education (Chairman) Mr T. Green, 11 Bluebell Rd, Eaton, Norwich NR4 7LF
Director of Education Mr Andy Mash, Dioc House
Tel: 01603 881352
email: andy.mash@norwich.anglican.org
Diocesan Project Manager Mrs Jenny Daynes, Dioc House   *Tel:* 01603 881352
email: jenny.daynes@norwich.anglican.org
The Horstead Centre (Warden) Mr Mark Heybourne, Rectory Rd, Horstead, Norwich NR12 7EP   *Tel:* 01603 737215
email: manager@horsteadcentre.org.uk
Web: www.horsteadcentre.org.uk
Youth and Children's Coordinator Mr Mark Heybourne *(as above)*

BOARD OF MINISTRY
(and Governing Board of the Ordained Local Ministry Scheme)
Board of Ministry (Chairman) Rt Revd D. Atkinson
(Lay Chairman) Mrs Maureen Bird, Abbey Bungalow, Abbey St, Bacon, Norwich NR12 0AH
Tel: 01692 651565
(Secretary) Mrs Margaret Mallett, Emmaus House, 65 The Close, Norwich NR1 4DH
Tel: 01603 729816
Bishop's Officer for Ordinands and Initial Training Canon Steven Betts, Emmaus House, 65 The Close, Norwich NR1 4DH   *Tel:* 01603 628103
Principal of Dioc Ministry Course and Vice-Principal of the Eastern Region Ministry Course Revd Sue Woan, Emmaus House, 65 The Close, Norwich NR1 4DH   *Tel:* 01603 729812
Vice-Principal of Dioc Ministry Course and Director of Studies Revd Charles Read, Emmaus House
Director of Reader Training Revd Clive Blackman, Emmaus House
Director of Continuing Ministerial Education Revd Cathy Nicholls, Emmaus House
Lay Development Co-ordinator Revd Susanna Gunner, Emmaus House *(as above)*
Dioc Officer for NSMs Revd Roger MacPhee, 8 Lawn Close, Knapton, North Walsham NR28 0SD   *Tel:* 01263 720045
email: rmacphee4@aol.com

Readers' Committee (*Chairman*) Revd Roger Key, The Vicarage, 51 The Street, Corton, Lowestoft, Suffolk NR32 5HT *Tel:* 01502 730977
email: thekeybunch@aol.com
(*Secretary*) Mr John Pountain, Brambles, Briar Lane, Swainsthorpe, Norwich NR14 8PX
Tel: 01508 470567
County Ecumenical Officer Revd Andrew Platt, 21 Homefield Paddock, Beccles NR34 9NE
Tel: 01502 717744
Bishop's Officer for Retired Clergy and Widows (*Chairman*) Canon Cedric Bradbury, 66 Grove Lane, Holt NR25 6ED *Tel:* 01263 712634
Evangelism Resources Group (*Chairman*) Ven David Hayden, 8 Boulton Rd, Thorpe St, Andrew, Norwich NR7 0DF *Tel and Fax:* 01603 661104
email: archdeacon.norwich@4frontmedia.co.uk

LITURGICAL
Liturgical Adviser Canon Jeremy Haselock, 34 The Close, Norwich NR1 4DZ *Tel:* 01603 218314
Fax: 01603 766032
Chairman of DLC Canon Richard Ames-Lewis, Rectory, 1 Vicarage Meadows, Dereham NR19 1TW *Tel:* 01362 693143

PRESS, PUBLICITY AND PUBLICATIONS
Communications Committee (*Chairman*) The Dean of Norwich (*as above*)
Communications Officer Ven J. McFarlane, Dioc House *Tel:* 07818 422395 (*Mobile*)
email: communications@norwich.anglican.org
Editor of Dioc Directory Mr G. Darley, Dioc House

DIOCESAN RECORD OFFICE
Norfolk Record Office, Archive Centre, County Hall, Martineau Lane, Norwich NR1 2DO *County Archivist* Dr John Alban *Tel:* 01603 222599
Fax: 01603 761885

SOCIAL AND COMMUNITY CONCERNS
Forum Chairman Rt Revd James Langstaff (as above)
Coordinator Revd Simon Wilson, Rectory, Guist Rd, Foulsham, Dereham NR20 5RZ
Tel: 01362 683275
email: simonwilson@norwich.anglican.org
Rural Affairs
Adviser Revd Lorna Allies, 426 Unthank Rd, Norwich NR4 7QH *Tel:* 01603 504116
email: ruraladviser@gullmeadow.com
Canon W. M. C. Bestelink, Rectory, High Road, Roydon, Diss IP22 5RD *Tel:* 01379 642180
Urban Affairs and Church Urban Fund Revd Peter Howard, St Francis Vicarage, Rider Haggard Rd, Norwich NR7 9UQ *Tel:* 01603 702799
email: plhoward@btinternet.com
Criminal Justice Revd Simon Wilson, (*as above*)
Healthcare Chaplain Revd Simon Wilson (*as above*)
Healing Ministry Rt Revd James Langstaff (*as above*)
Industrial Mission Revd C. Warner (URC Chaplain), 1b Unthank Rd, Norwich NR2 2PA
Tel: 01603 760408

Tourism Ven David Hayden (*as above*)
Major Incident Team/Emergency Planning: Revd Simon Wilson (as above)
Environmental Issues: Rt Revd Anthony Foottit, Ivy House, Whitwell St, Reepham, Norwich NR10 4RA *Tel:* 01603 870340

RURAL DEANS
ARCHDEACONRY OF NORWICH
Norwich East Revd Peter Howard, St Francis Vicarage, Rider Haggard Rd, Norwich NR7 9UQ
Tel: 01603 702799
email: plhoward@btinternet.com
Norwich North Revd John Bennett, Vicarage, 2 Wroxham Rd, Sprowston, Norwich NR7 8TZ
Tel: 01603 426492
email: vicar@sprowston.org.uk
Norwich South Revd Elsie Hutcheon, Vicarage, Russell St, Norwich NR2 4QT *Tel:* 01603 627859
email: elsie@rev.demon.co.uk

ARCHDEACONRY OF NORFOLK
Blofield Revd Michael Kingston, Rectory, 9 Lawn Crescent, Thorpe End, Norwich NR13 5BP
Tel: 01603 434778
email: mm.kingston@tiscali.co.uk
Depwade Revd Heather Potts, Rectory, Chapel Rd, Carleton Rode, Norwich NR16 1RN
Tel: 01953 789218
email: revheather@hpotts.wanadoo.co.uk
Great Yarmouth Revd Irene Knowles, 18 Royal Ave, Great Yarmouth NR30 4EB
Tel: 01493 857292
email: revmik@hotmail.co.uk
Humbleyard Revd Christopher Davies, The Vicarage, 5 Vicar St, Wymondham, NR18 0PL
Tel: 01953 602269
email: revd@christophertdavies.fsnet.co.uk
Loddon Revd Nigel Evans, Vicarage, 4 Market Place, Loddon, Norwich NR14 6EY
Tel: 01508 520251
email: nigelwevans4@btinternet.com
Lothingland Canon John Simpson, St Margaret's Rectory, 147 Hollingsworth Rd, Lowestoft NR32 4BW *Tel:* 01502 573046
email: john.simpson5@tesco.net
Redenhall Revd Anthony Billett, Rectory, 26 Mount St, Diss IP22 3QG *Tel:* 01379 642072
email: disschurch2@btconnect.com
Saint Benet at Waxham and Tunstead Revd William Hill, Grange Farm House, Yarmouth Rd, Worstead, North Walsham NR28 9LX
Tel: 01692 404917
email: revd.william.hill@btinternet.com
Thetford and Rockland Revd Michael Aisbitt, Rectory, Surrogate St, Attleborough NR17 2AW
Tel: 01953 453185
email: m_aisbitt@hotmail.com

ARCHDEACONRY OF LYNN
Breckland Canon Stuart Nairn, Rectory, Main Rd, Narborough, King's Lynn PE32 1TE
Tel: 01760 338552
email: nairn@narvalleygroup.freeserve.co.uk

Brisley and Elmham Vacancy

Burnham and Walsingham Revd Douglas Alexander, The Rectory, The Street, Reymerston, Norwich NR9 4AG   *Tel:* 01362 858377
          email: doug.alexander@btinternet.com

Dereham in Mitford Canon Richard Ames-Lewis, Rectory, Vicarage Meadows, Dereham NR19 1TW   *Tel:* 01362 693680
          email: ameslewis@btinternet.com

Heacham and Rising Revd Michael Brock, Vicarage, Shernborne Rd, Dersingham, King's Lynn PE31 6JA   *Tel:* 01485 520214
          email: mjb65@btinternet.com

Holt Revd Howard Stoker, Rectory, 11 Church St, Holt NR25 6BB   *Tel:* 01263 712048
          email: holtrectory@tiscali.co.uk

Ingworth Revd Robert Branson, Vicarage, 64 Holman Rd, Aylsham, Norwich NR11 6BZ
          Tel: 01263 733871
          email: thebransons@tiscali.co.uk

Lynn Revd Christopher Ivory, St Margaret's Vicarage, St Margaret's Place, King's Lynn PE30 5DL   *Tel:* 01553 767090
          email: vicar@stmargaretskingslynn.org.uk

Repps Revd Michael Langan, Rectory, 22a Harbord Rd, Overstrand, Cromer NR27 0PN
          Tel: 01263 759350
          email: ml@netcom.co.uk

Sparham Revd Selwyn Tillett, The Rectory, Ringland Lane, Weston Longville, Norwich NR9 5JU   *Tel:* 01603 880563
          email: selwyn@tillett.org.uk

DIOCESE OF OXFORD

Founded in 1542. Oxfordshire; Berkshire; Buckinghamshire; one parish in each of Bedfordshire, Gloucestershire, Hampshire, Hertfordshire and Warwickshire.

Population 2,170,000   Area 2,221 sq m
Full-time Stipendiary Parochial Clergy 349   Benefices 295
Parishes 622   Churches 818
www.oxford.anglican.org
Overseas link dioceses: Vaxjo (Sweden), Kimberley and Kuruman (Southern Africa).

BISHOP (42nd)
Rt Revd John Pritchard, Diocesan Church House, North Hinksey, Oxford OX2 0NB [2007]
Tel: 01865 208200 (Office)
Fax: 01865 790470
email: bishopoxon@oxford.anglican.org
Bishop's Domestic Chaplain Revd Amanda Bloor
(*same address*) Tel: 01865 208200 (Office)
Fax: 01865 790470

AREA BISHOPS
READING Rt Revd Stephen Cottrell, Bishop's House, Tidmarsh Lane, Tidmarsh, Reading RG8 8HA [2004] Tel: 0118 984 1216
Fax: 0118 984 1218
email: bishopreading@oxford.anglican.org
BUCKINGHAM Rt Revd Dr Alan Wilson, Sheridan, Grimms Hill, Gt Missenden HP16 9BG [2003]
Tel: 01494 862173
Fax: 01494 890508
email: bishopbucks@oxford.anglican.org
DORCHESTER Rt Revd Colin Fletcher, Arran House, Sandy Lane, Yarnton, Oxford OX5 1PB [2000] Tel: 01865 375541
Fax: 01865 379890
email: bishopdorchester@oxford.anglican.org

PROVINCIAL EPISCOPAL VISITOR
Rt Revd Andrew Burnham (Bishop of Ebbsfleet), Bishop's House, Dry Sandford, Abingdon OX13 6JP Tel: 01865 390746
email: bishop.andrew@ebbsfleet.org.uk

HONORARY ASSISTANT BISHOPS
Rt Revd Keith Arnold, 9 Dinglederry, Olney MK46 5ES [1997] Tel: 01234 713044
Rt Revd John Bone, 4 Grove Rd, Henley-on-Thames RG9 1DH [1997] Tel: 01491 413482
Rt Revd Dr Kenneth Cragg, 3 Goring Lodge, White House Rd, Oxford OX1 4QE [1982]
Tel: 01865 249895
Rt Revd William Down, 54 Dark Lane, Witney OX28 6LX [2001] Tel: 01993 706615
Rt Revd John Garton, 52 Clive Rd, Cowley, Oxford OX4 3EL [2006] Tel: 01865 771093
Rt Revd Ronald Gordon, 16 East St Helen St, Abingdon OX14 5EA [1991] Tel: 01235 526956

Rt Revd James Johnson, St Helena, 28 Molyneux Drive, Bodicote, Banbury OX15 4AP [2005]
Tel: 01295 255357
Rt Revd Peter Nott, 3 Valance Court, Aston Rd, Bampton OX18 2AF [1999] Tel: 01993 850688
Rt Revd Henry Richmond, 39 Hodges Court, Marlborough Rd, Oxford OX1 4NZ [1999]
Tel: 01865 790466
Rt Revd Stephen Verney, Cherry Patch, Church Rd, Blewbury, Didcot OX11 9PY [1991]
Tel: 01235 850004

CATHEDRAL CHURCH OF CHRIST
Dean Very Revd Christopher Lewis, The Deanery, Christ Church, Oxford OX1 1DP [2003]
Tel: 01865 276161
Fax: 01865 276238
Dean's Secretary Ms Rachel Perham (*same address*)
Tel: 01865 276161
email: rachel.perham@chch.ox.ac.uk
Canons Residentiary
Ven Julian Hubbard, Archdeacon's Lodging, Christ Church, Oxford OX1 1DP [2005]
Tel: 01865 276185
email: archdoxf@oxford.anglican.org
Canon Dr Marilyn Parry, Diocesan Church House, North Hinksey Lane, Oxford OX2 0NB [2001] Tel: 01865 208289
email: marilyn.parry@oxford.anglican.org
Canon Prof. Marilyn McCord Adams, Christ Church, Oxford OX1 1DP [2004] Tel: 01865 276246
email: marilyn.adams@theology.ox.ac.uk
Canon Prof. George Pattison, Priory House, Christ Church, Oxford OX1 1DP [2004]
Tel: 01865 276247
email: george.pattison@chch.ox.ac.uk
Canon Prof Sarah Foot, Christ Church, Oxford OX1 1DP [2007] Tel: 01865 286078
email: sarah.foot@chch.ox.ac.uk
Canon Prof Nigel Biggar, Christ Church, Oxford OX1 1DP [2007] Tel: 01865 276219
email: nigel.biggar@chch.ox.ac.uk
Precentor Revd John Paton, Christ Church, Oxford OX1 1DP [2003] Tel: 01865 276214
email: john.paton@chch.ox.ac.uk
Liturgy and Publicity Assistant David Bannister, Christ Church, Oxford OX1 1DP
Tel: 01865 276214
email: david.bannister@chch.ox.ac.uk

Cathedral Registrar Mr Millius Palayiwa, Christ Church, Oxford OX1 1DP   *Tel:* 01865 276155
    email: millius.palayiwa@chch.ox.ac.uk
Cathedral Secretary Miss Sally-Ann Ford, Christ Church, Oxford OX1 1DP   *Tel:* 01865 276155
    Fax: 01865 276277
    email: sally-ann.ford@chch.ox.ac.uk
Cathedral Organist Dr Stephen Darlington, Christ Church, Oxford OX1 1DP   *Tel:* 01865 276195
    email: stephen.darlington@chch.ox.ac.uk
Organist's Secretary Mrs Anthea Madden, Christ Church, Oxford OX1 1DP   *Tel:* 01865 276195
Dean's Verger Mr Edward Evans, Christ Church, Oxford OX1 1DP   *Tel:* 01865 276154
Canon's Verger Mr Jim Godfrey, Christ Church, Oxford OX1 1DP   *Tel:* 01865 276154
    email: jim.godfrey@chch.ox.ac.uk
Sacristan: Mr Matthew Power, Christ Church, Oxford OX1 1DP   *Tel:* 01865 276154
    email: matthew.power@chch.ox.ac.uk

ARCHDEACONS
OXFORD Ven Julian Hubbard, Archdeacon's Lodging, Christ Church, Oxford OX1 1DP [2005]
    Tel and *Fax:* 01865 208245
    email: archdoxf@oxford.anglican.org
BERKSHIRE Ven Norman Russell, Foxglove House, Love Lane, Donnington, Newbury RG14 2JG [1998]   *Tel:* 01635 552820
    Fax: 01635 522165
    email: archdber@oxford.anglican.org
BUCKINGHAM Ven Karen Gorham, Rectory, Stone, Aylesbury HP17 8RZ [2007]   *Tel:* 01865 208264
    email: archdbuc@oxford.anglican.org

CONVOCATION (MEMBERS OF THE HOUSE OF CLERGY OF THE GENERAL SYNOD)
Proctors for Clergy
The Bishop of Oxford
Revd Moira Astin
Revd Jonathan Baker
Revd Susan Booys
Revd John Chorlton
Canon Timothy Dakin
Revd Hugh Lee
Canon Prof Marilyn McCord Adams
Ven Norman Russell
Canon Dr Chris Sugden
Revd John Wynburne

MEMBERS OF THE HOUSE OF LAITY OF THE GENERAL SYNOD
Mr Thomas Benyon
Mr Justin Brett
Miss Prudence Dailey
Dr Philip Giddings
Mr John Hanks
Mr Brian Newey
Mr Gavin Oldham
Dr Anna Thomas-Betts

DIOCESAN OFFICERS
Dioc Secretary Mrs Rosemary Pearce, Diocesan Church House, North Hinksey Lane, Oxford OX2 0NB   *Tel:* 01865 208200
    Fax: 01865 790470
    email: diosec@oxford.anglican.org
Chancellor of Diocese Revd Dr Rupert Bursell QC, Diocesan Registry, 16 Beaumont St, Oxford OX1 2LZ   *Tel:* 01865 297200
    Fax: 01865 726274
    email: oxford@winckworths.co.uk
Registrar of Diocese and Bishop's Legal Secretary Canon John Rees (*same address*)
Registrar of the Archdeaconries Canon John Rees (*as above*)

DIOCESAN ORGANIZATIONS
Diocesan Office Diocesan Church House, North Hinksey Lane, Oxford OX2 0NB
    Tel: 01865 208200
    Fax: 01865 790470

ADMINISTRATION
Dioc Synod (*Vice-President, House of Clergy*) Revd Dr Andrew Bunch, Vicarage, Church Walk, Oxford OX2 6LY   *Tel:* 01865 510460
    email: vicar@churchwalk.eclipse.co.uk
(*Vice-President, House of Laity*) Mrs Penny Keens, 9 St Paul's Court, Stony Stratford, Milton Keynes MK11 1LJ   *Tel:* 01908 571232
    email: penny@pp.keens.plus.com
(*Secretary*) Mrs Rosemary Pearce, Dioc Church House
Board of Finance (*Chairman*) Mr Brian Newey, Chestnut Cottage, The Green South, Warborough, Wallingford OX10 7DN   *Tel:* 01865 858322
    Fax: 01865 858043
(*Secretary*) Mrs Rosemary Pearce (*as above*)
Director of Glebe and Buildings Mr Roger Harwood, Dioc Church House
    email: roger.harwood@oxford.anglican.org
Dioc Trustees (*Oxford*) *Ltd* Mrs Rosemary Pearce (*as above*)
Pastoral Committee (*Secretary*) Mrs Mary Saunders, Dioc Church House
    email: mary.saunders@oxford.anglican.org
Designated Officer Canon John Rees (*as above*)

CHURCHES
Advisory Committee for the Care of Churches (*Chairman*) Mr David Jefferson, The Vyne, Deep Field, Datchet SL3 9JS; (*Secretary*) Mrs Mary Saunders (*as above*)
Redundant Churches Uses Committee (*Secretary*) Mrs Mary Saunders (*as above*)

STEWARDSHIP, TRAINING, EVANGELISM AND MINISTRY
Director Canon Keith Lamdin, Dioc Church House   *Tel:* 01865 208251
    Fax: 01865 790470
    email: keith.lamdin@oxford.anglican.org

Parish Development Advisers
Buckingham Mr Andrew Gear, Dioc Church House   *Tel* 01865 208256
Fax: 01865 790470
email: andrew.gear@oxford.anglican.org
Oxford Revd Olivia Graham, Dioc Church House
Tel: 01865 208246
Fax: 01865 790470
email: olivia.graham@oxford.anglican.org
Berkshire Revd Janet Russell, Dioc Church House
Tel: 01865 208296
email: janet.russell@oxford.anglican.org
Children's Work Yvonne Morris, Dioc Church House   *Tel:* 01865 208255
email: yvonne.morris@oxford.anglican.org
Child Protection Officer Stephen Barber, Dioc Church House   *Tel:* 01865 208290
email: stephen.barber@oxford.anglican.org
Christian Giving and Funding Adviser Robin Brunner-Ellis, Dioc Church House
Tel: 01865 208254
email: robin.brunner-ellis@oxford.anglican.org
Director of Studies Revd Dr Keith Beech-Gruneberg, Dioc Church House
Tel: 01865 208282
email: director.of.studies@oxford.anglican.org
Training Officer and Director of LLM Training Revd Phillip Tovey, 20 Palmer Place, Abingdon, OX14 5LZ   *Tel:* 01235 527077
email: phillip.tovey@oxford.anglican.org
Youth Work Ian Macdonald, Dioc Church House
Tel: 01865 208253
email: ian.macdonald@oxford.anglican.org
Ordained Local Ministry (OLM) Principal Revd Beren Hartless   *Tel:* 01865 208258
email: beren.hartless@oxford.anglican.org
Licensed Lay Ministry (LLM) Adviser Revd Joanna Coney, 4 Rowland Close, Wolvercote, Oxford OX2 8PW   *Tel:* 01865 556456
email: joanna.coney@oxford.anglican.org
Diocesan Director of Ordinands Canon Dr Marilyn Parry, Diocesan Church House, North Hinksey Lane, Oxford OX2 0NB   *Tel:* 01865 208289
email: marilyn.parry@oxford.anglican.org
Directors of Ordinands
Oxfordshire and Berkshire Canon Christine Redgrave, Diocesan Church House, North Hinksey Lane, Oxford OX2 0NB
Tel: 01865 208291
email: christine.redgrave@oxford.anglican.org
Buckingham Revd Caroline Windley, 1 Cavalry Path, Aylesbury HP19 9RP
Tel and Fax: 01296 432921
email: caroline.windley@oxford.anglican.org
City of Oxford Canon Dr Marilyn Parry (*as above*)
Vocation Network Chair Canon Dr Marilyn Parry (contact Mrs D. Dallimore, Secretary)
Tel: 01865 208291
Accredited Lay Ministry Adviser Norman Critchell, Vicarage, Lacey Green HP27 0QX
Tel: 01844 347741
email: norman@salemproject.fsnet.co.uk

Women in Ordained Ministry Adviser Revd Antonia Cretney, 8 Elm Farm Close, Grove, Wantage OX12 9FD   *Tel:* 01235 763192

EDUCATION
Director of Education (Schools) Leslie Stephen, Dioc Church House   *Tel:* 01865 208236
email: leslie.stephen@oxford.anglican.org

MISSIONARY AND ECUMENICAL
Partnership in World Mission (Secretary) Revd Tim Naish, 307 London Rd, Headington, Oxford OX3 9EJ   *Tel:* 01865 766627
email: timnaish@ripon-cuddlesdon.ac.uk
Ecumenical Officers
Oxford Ms Tessa Kuin Lawton, Manor Croft, Church Close, Bampton OX18 2LW
Tel: 01993 850468
email: tessa.lawton@talktalk.net
Berkshire Revd Moira Astin, St James Vicarage, 23 Kingfisher Drive, Woodley, Reading RG5 3LG
Tel: 0118 954 5669
email: moira.astin@ntlworld.com
Buckingham Canon Tony Dickinson, St Francis' Vicarage, Amersham Rd, Terriers, High Wycombe HP13 5AB   *Tel:* 01494 520676
email: tony.dickinson@ukonline.co.uk
Milton Keynes Revd Chris Collinge, St James's Vicarage, 29 Bradwell Rd, Bradville, Milton Keynes MK13 7AX   *Tel:* 01908 314224
email: chriscollinge@hotmail.com

COMMUNICATIONS
Director of Communications Ms Sarah Meyrick, Dioc Church House   *Tel:* 01865 208224
Editor of Dioc Newspaper 'The Door' Miss Joanne Duckles, Dioc Church House *Tel:* 01865 208227
email: jo.duckles@oxford.anglican.org

DIOCESAN RECORD OFFICES
County Archivist, St Luke's Church, Temple Rd, Cowley, Oxford OX4 2EN   *Tel:* 01865 398200
email: archives@oxfordshire.gov.uk (*For records of the diocese, and parish records in the archdeaconry of Oxford*)
Berkshire Record Office, 9 Coley Ave, Reading RG1 6AF *Tel:* 0118 901 5132 (*For parish records in the archdeaconry of Berkshire*)
Buckinghamshire Record Office, County Hall, Aylesbury, Bucks. HP20 1UA *Tel:* 01296 382587 (*For parish records in the archdeaconry of Buckingham*)

SOCIAL RESPONSIBILITY
Social Responsibility Adviser (Secretary) Ms Alison Webster, Dioc Church House
Tel: 01865 208213
email: alison.webster@oxford.anglican.org
PACT (Parents and Children Together) Council for Social Work Mrs Jan Fishwick, 7 Southern Court, South St, Reading RG1 4QS   *Tel:* 0118 938 7600
email: pactcharity@compuserve.com
Council for the Deaf (Chairman) Mrs Jo Saunders, Dioc Church House

AREA DEANS
ARCHDEACONRY OF OXFORD

Aston and Cuddesdon Revd Sue Booys, Rectory, Manor Farm Rd, Dorchester OX10 7HZ
Tel: 01865 340007
email: rector@dorchester-abbey.org.uk
Bicester and Islip Revd Paul Hunt, Vicarage, 44 Forge Place, Fritwell, Bicester OX27 7QQ
Tel: 01869 346739
email: paul@jehu.net
Chipping Norton Revd Judy French, Vicarage, Church Lane, Charlbury OX7 3PX
Tel: 01608 810286
email: vicar@stmaryscharlbury.co.uk
Cowley Revd Bruce Gillingham, St Clement's Rectory, 58 Rectory Rd, Oxford OX4 1BW
Tel: 01865 246674
email: bruce@stclements.org.uk
Deddington Revd Ben Phillips, Vicarage, Wykham Lane, Bodicote, Banbury OX15 4BW
Tel: 01295 270174
email: revbenphillips@tiscali.co.uk
Henley Revd Graham Foulis Brown, Vicarage, Kidmore End, Reading RG4 9AY
Tel: 0118 972 3987
email: gdfb.vicarage@lineone.net
Oxford Revd Anthony Ellis, St Mary's Rectory, 19 Mill St, Kidlington OX5 2EE
Tel and *Fax:* 01865 372230
email: anthony.churchkid@talktalk.net
Witney Revd Andrew Sweeney, Cogges Priory, Church Lane, Witney OX28 3LA
Tel: 01993 702155
email: vicar@coggesparish.com
Woodstock Revd Dr Stephen M'Caw, Rectory, Fir Lane, Steeple Aston, Bicester OX25 4SF
Tel: 01869 347793
email: stephenwdean@btinternet.com

ARCHDEACONRY OF BERKSHIRE

Abingdon Revd Pam McKellen, Vicarage, Radley, Abingdon OX14 2JN   *Tel:* 01235 554739
email: p.mckellen@btinternet.com
Bracknell Canon Nick Parish, 1 Old Lands Hill, Bracknell RG12 2QX   *Tel:* 01344 641498
email: nick.parish@ntlworld.com
Bradfield Revd Peter Steele, The Vicarage, Wasing Lane, Aldermarston, RG7 4LX
Tel: 0118 9712281
email: petesteele@btinternet.com
Maidenhead Revd Dr Jeremy Hyde, 2a Belmont Park Rd, Maidenhead SL6 6HT
Tel: 01628 621651
email: jeremyrhyde@aol.com
Newbury Revd Tom Moffatt, Rectory, 17 Church Gate, Thatcham RG19 3PN   *Tel:* 01635 862616
email: tom.moffatt@ntlworld.com

Reading Canon Brian Shenton, Hamelsham, Downshire Square, Reading RG1 6NJ
Tel: 0118 956 8163
Fax: 0118 958 7041
email: stmaryshouserdg@waitrose.com
Sonning Revd David Hodgson, Rectory, 2A Norreys Ave, Wokingham RG40 1TU
Tel: 0118 979 2999
email: david@allsaintswokingham.org.uk
Vale of White Horse Revd Richard Hancock, St Andrew's Vicarage, High St, Shrivenham, Swindon SN6 8AN   *Tel:* 01793 780183
email: vicar@standrews-shrivenham.fsnet.co.uk
Wallingford Revd Edward Carter, St Peter's Vicarage, Glebe Rd, Didcot OX11 8PN
Tel: 01235 812114
email: revdedward.carter@tiscali.co.uk
Wantage Canon John Salter, Vicarage, The Cloisters, Wantage OX12 8AQ   *Tel:* 01235 762214

ARCHDEACONRY OF BUCKINGHAM

Amersham Revd John Wynburne, Rectory, Wycombe End, Beaconsfield HP9 1NB
Tel: 01494 677058
email: jwynburne@aol.com
Aylesbury, Revd Tina Stirling, Vicarage, High St, Brill, Aylesbury HP18 9ST   *Tel:* 01844 238325
email: tina.stirling@brill.uk.net
Buckingham Revd Kevin Ashby, Rectory, 39 Fishers Field, Buckingham MK18 1SF
Tel: 01280 813178
email:
areadean@buckinghamparishchurch.org.uk
Burnham Revd Allen Walker, New Vicarage, Mill St, Colnbrook, Slough SL3 0JJ   *Tel:* 01753 684181
email: mrawalker@aol.com
Claydon Revd David Hiscock, Rectory, Castle St, Marsh Gibbon, Bicester OX27 0HJ
Tel: 01869 277297
email: david@s3d.co.uk
Milton Keynes Revd Tim Norwood, 3 Daubeney Gate, Shenley Church End, Milton Keynes MK5 6EH   *Tel:* 01908 505812
email: tim.norwood@wvep.org
Mursley Revd John Waller, Rectory, 10 Pound Hill, Great Brickhill, Milton Keynes MK17 9AS
Tel: 01525 261062
email: john.waller1@virgin.net
Newport Revd Christa Pumfrey, New Rectory, 7a Northampton Rd, Lavendon, Olney MK46 4EY
Tel: 01234 240013
email: christa.cerratti@btopenworld.com
Wendover Revd Mark Dearnley, Vicarage, 34a Dobbins Lane, Wendover HP22 6DH
Tel: 01296 622230
email: areadeansofficewendover@virgin.net
Wycombe Revd David Picken, Vicarage, 6 Priory Avenue, High Wycombe HP13 6SH
Tel: 01494 525602
email: dap@dircon.co.uk

DIOCESE OF PETERBOROUGH

Founded in 1541. Northamptonshire, except for one parish in the west (LEICESTER); Rutland; Peterborough, except for an area in the south-east; one parish in Lincolnshire.

Population 828,000   Area 1,149 sq m
Full-time Stipendiary Parochial Clergy 137   Benefices 142
Parishes 348   Churches 383
www.peterborough-diocese.org.uk
Overseas link diocese: Bungoma (Kenya).

BISHOP (37th)
Rt Revd Ian Patrick Martyn Cundy, Bishop's Lodgings, The Palace, Peterborough PE1 1YA [1996]   *Tel:* 01733 562492
    Fax: 01733 890077
email: bishop@peterborough-diocese.org.uk
[Ian Petriburg:]
Bishop's Private Secretary Miss Alex Low (*same address*)
    email: alex.low@peterborough-diocese.org.uk
Bishop's Administrator and Press Officer Revd Derek Williams (*same address*)
    Tel: 01733 887014 (Office)
    01604 843881 (Home)
    077770 981172 (Mobile)
    Fax: 01733 890077 (Office)
email:
    derek.williams@peterborough-diocese.org.uk

SUFFRAGAN BISHOP
BRIXWORTH Rt Revd Frank White, 4 The Avenue, Dallington, Northampton NN5 7AN [2000]
    Tel: 01604 759423
    Fax: 01604 750925
    email: bishop.brixworth@btinternet.com
Bishop's Private Secretary Mrs Anne Pooley
    email: anne.brixworth@btinternet.com

HONORARY ASSISTANT BISHOP
Rt Revd John Robert Flack, The Vicarage, 34 Station Road, Nassington, Peterborough PE8 6QB [2003]   *Tel:* 01780 782271
    07810 714056 (Mobile)

CATHEDRAL CHURCH OF ST PETER, ST PAUL AND ST ANDREW
Dean Very Revd Charles Taylor, The Deanery, Minster Precincts, Peterborough PE1 1XS [2007]
    Tel: 01733 562780
    Fax: 01733 897874
    email: DeanPetOffice@aol.com
Precentor Canon R. Bruce Ruddock, Precentor's Lodging, 14A Minster Precincts, Peterborough PE1 1XX [2004]   *Tel:* 01733 355310
email:
    bruce.ruddock@peterborough-cathedral.org.uk

Canons Residentiary
Pastor Canon Jonathan Baker, Canonry House, Minster Precincts, Peterborough PE1 1XX [2004]
    Tel: 01733 897335 (Home)
    01733 355310 (Office)
email:
    jonathan.baker@peterborough-cathedral.org.uk
Ven David Painter (*Archdeacon of Oakham*), 7 Minster Precincts, Peterborough PE1 1XS [2000]
    Tel: 01733 891360
    Fax: 01733 554524
email:
    david.painter@peterborough-cathedral.org.uk
Lay Members of Chapter
Mr John Martin, Manor Cottage, Main St, Woodnewton, Peterborough PE8 5EB
    Tel: 01780 470298
    email: janemartin537@btinternet.com
Hon Treasurer Sir John Parsons, Old Rectory, Eydon, Daventry NN11 3QE   *Tel:* 01327 260745
    email: jparsoneydon@btopenworld.com
Mr Mike Opperman, Littleworth Mission, Main Rd, Deeping St Nicholas, Spalding, Lincs PE11 3EN   *Tel:* 01775 630497
    email: jenny@littleworthmission.com
Mrs Sally Trotman, 2 High St, Maxey, Peterborough PE6 9EB   *Tel:* 01778 344022
    email: sally_trotman@yahoo.co.uk
Chapter Administrator Elizabeth Knight, Cathedral Office, Minster Precincts, Peterborough PE1 1XS
    Tel: 01733 562780
    Fax: 01733 897874
    email: DeanPetOffice@aol.com
Director of Music Mr Andrew Reid, Cathedral Office, Minster Precincts, Peterborough PE1 1XX
    Tel: 01733 355319
email:
    andrew.reid@peterborough-cathedral.org.uk

ARCHDEACONS
NORTHAMPTON Ven Christine Allsopp, Westbrook, 11 The Drive, Northampton NN1 4RZ [2005]   *Tel:* 01604 714015
    Fax: 01604 792016
    email: archdeacon@aofn.wanadoo.co.uk
OAKHAM Ven David Painter, 7 Minster Precincts, Peterborough PE1 1XS [1999]   *Tel:* 01733 891360
    Fax: 01733 554524
    email: david.painter@
    peterborough-cathedral.org.uk

CONVOCATION (MEMBERS OF THE HOUSE OF CLERGY OF THE GENERAL SYNOD)
Proctors for Clergy
Ven Christine Allsopp
Canon David Bird
Revd Stephen Trott

MEMBERS OF THE HOUSE OF LAITY OF THE GENERAL SYNOD
Mrs Gill Morrison
Mr Andrew Presland
Mrs Anne Toms

DIOCESAN OFFICERS
Dioc Secretary Mr Richard Pestell, Diocesan Office, The Palace, Peterborough PE1 1YB
Tel: 01733 887000
Fax: 01733 555271
email: diosec@peterborough-diocese.org.uk
Deputy Dioc Secretary and Financial Controller Mr Graham Cuthbert, Dioc Office
email: depsec@peterborough-diocese.org.uk
Chancellor of Diocese Chancellor David Pittaway QC, c/o Diocesan Registrar, 4 Holywell Way, Longthorpe, Peterborough PE3 6SS
Deputy Chancellor Mr George Pulman, c/o Diocesan Registrar (*as above*)
Registrar of Diocese and Bishop's Legal Secretary Revd Raymond Hemingray, 4 Holywell Way (*as above*)
Tel and *Fax:* 01733 262523
email: rh@raymondhemingray.co.uk

DIOCESAN ORGANIZATIONS
Diocesan Office The Palace, Peterborough PE1 1YB
Tel: 01733 887000
Fax: 01733 555271
email: office@peterborough-diocese.org.uk
Web: www.peterborough-diocese.org.uk

ADMINISTRATION
Dioc Synod (Vice-President, Clergy) Canon David Bird, St Giles Vicarage, 2 Spring Gardens, Northampton NN1 1LX
Tel: 01604 634060
Fax: 01604 628623
email: david@d.bird.freeserve.co.uk
(Vice-President, Laity) Mrs Anne Toms, Epworth, Park Rd, Wellingborough NN8 4QE
Tel: 01933 275117
email: acbl@mrc-lmb.cam.ac.uk
(Secretary) Mr Richard Pestell, Dioc Office
Board of Finance (Chairman) Mr Adrian Pritchard, 7 Lonsborough Drive, Kettering NN15 7LY
Tel: 01536 410284
email: acpritchard@tiscali.co.uk
(Secretary) Mr Richard Pestell (*as above*)
Houses Committee (Chairman) Mr Michael Duerden, 21 South Rd, Oundle, Peterborough PE8 4BU
Tel: 01832 273383
Property Officer Mrs Sandra Allen, Dioc Office
Pastoral Committee Mr Richard Pestell (*as above*)
Board of Patronage Mr Richard Pestell (*as above*)

Designated Officer Revd Raymond Hemingray, 4 Holywell Way, Longthorpe, Peterborough PE3 6SS
Tel and *Fax:* 01733 262523
email: rh@raymondhemingray.co.uk

CHURCHES
Advisory Committee for the Care of Churches (Chairman) Mr Roy Atkinson, c/o DAC, Diocesan Office, The Palace, Peterborough PE1 1YB
Tel: 01733 887007
Fax: 01733 555271
email: dac@peterborough-diocese.org.uk
(Secretary) Mr Paul Middleton, Dioc Office
Redundant Churches Uses Committee (Chairman) Mr Roy Atkinson, c/o DAC, Diocesan Office, The Palace, Peterborough PE1 1YB
Tel: 01733 887007
Fax: 01733 555271
email: dac@Peterborough-diocese.org.uk
(Secretary) Mr Paul Middleton, Dioc Office

EDUCATION
Board of Education (Schools) (Director of Education (Schools) and Secretary) Dr Stephen Partridge, Bouverie Court, The Lakes, Bedford Rd, Northampton NN4 7YD
Tel: 01604 887006
Fax: 01604 887077
email: education@peterborough-diocese.org.uk
Schools Officer Revd Philip Davies, Rectory, 3 Hall Yard, King's Cliffe, Peterborough PE8 6XQ
Tel: 01780 470314
email: P.J.Davies.@tesco.net

MINISTRY
Dioc Vocations Adviser and Director of Ordinands Canon Julie Hutchinson, New Rectory, Stanwick, Wellingborough NN9 6PP
Tel: 01933 626203
email: stanwick@fish.co.uk
Coordinator of Adult Education and Training Mr Chris Peck, Bouverie Court, The Lakes, Bedford Rd, Northampton NN4 7YD
Tel: 01604 887042
Fax: 01604 887077
email: chris.peck@peterborough-diocese.org.uk
Continuing Ministerial Education Officer (CME) Revd Dr Andrew Rayment, Bouverie Court (*as above*)
Tel: 01604 887047
Fax: 01604 887077
email: andrew.rayment@peterborough-diocese.org.uk
Curates' Training Coordinator Revd Alison White, 4 The Avenue, Dallington, Northampton NN4 7AN
Tel: 01604 581400
email: alisonmarywhite@btinternet.com
NSM Officer Revd Dr Judy Craig Peck, Dreamstead, 10 Sharplands, Grendon, Northampton NN7 1JL
Tel: 01933 665965
email: Judy@peckc.fsnet.co.uk
Adviser in Women's Ministry Vacancy
Warden of Readers Canon Phillip E. Nixon, St James's Vicarage, Vicarage Rd, Northampton NN5 7AX
Tel: 01604 751164
email: phillipn@btinternet.com

Warden of Pastoral Assistants Revd Jenny Parkin, Rectory, Water Lane, Wootton, Northampton NN4 6HH   *Tel:* 01604 761891
email: parkinjen@btinternet.com
Warden of Parish Evangelists Miss Sheila Addison, Berachah, Hardwater Mill, Great Doddington, Wellingborough NN29 7TH
Tel and *Fax:* 01933 224081
email: Sheilaadd@aol.com

MISSION

Diocesan Mission Enabler Revd Miles Baker, Bouverie Court, The Lakes, Bedford Rd, Northampton NN4 7YD   *Tel:* 01604 887043
Fax: 01604 887077
email: miles.baker@peterborough-diocese.org.uk
Children's Missioner Rona Orme, Bouverie Court (*as above*)   *Tel:* 01604 887045
Fax: 01604 887077
email: rona.orme@peterborough-diocese.org.uk
Youth Officer Revd Paul Niemiec, Bouverie Court (*as above*)   *Tel:* 01604 887044
Fax: 01604 887077
*email:*paul.niemiec@peterborough-diocese.org.uk
Urban Priority Areas Link Officer and Church Urban Fund Officer Mr Roger Poolman, 13 Curtis Mews, Wellingborough NN8 5PE   *Tel:* 01933 676544
email: roger.poolman@ntlworld.com
Social Responsibility Adviser Revd Robert Hill, Bouverie Court, The Lakes, Bedford Rd, Northampton NN4 7YD   *Tel:* 01604 887046
Fax: 01604 887077
email: robert.hill@peterborough-diocese.org.uk
Ecumenical Officer Canon Giles Godber, Vicarage, 25 West St, Geddington, Kettering NN14 1BD
Tel: 01536 742200
email: gilbar@telco4u.net
Hospital Chaplaincy Adviser Canon Lesley McCormack, Barnbrook, Water Lane, Chelveston, Wellingborough NN9 6SP
Tel: 01933 492609
email: lesley.mccormack@kgh.nhs.uk
Rural Officer Vacancy

LITURGICAL

Officer Canon R. Bruce Ruddock, Precentor's Lodging, 14A Minster Precincts, Peterborough PE1 1XX   *Tel:* 01733 343389

PRESS, PUBLICITY AND PUBLICATIONS

Bishop's Press Officer Revd Derek Williams, c/o Dioc Office   *Tel:* 01733 887014 (Office)
01604 843881 (Home)
07770 981172 (Mobile)
email:
derek.williams@peterborough-diocese.org.uk
Dioc Publications and Communications Mrs Liz Hurst (c/o Dioc Office)   *Tel:* 01733 887012
Fax: 01733 555271
email:
communications@peterborough-diocese.org.uk

DIOCESAN RECORD OFFICES

Wootton Park, Northampton NN4 9BQ *County Archivist* Miss Sarah Bridges

Tel: 01604 762129
email: archivist@northamptonshire.gov.uk
(*For all parishes in Northants. and the former Soke of Peterborough*)
Leicestershire Record Office, Long St, Wigston Magna, Leicester LE18 2AH *County Archivist* Mr Carl Harrison   *Tel:* 0116 257 1080 (*For all parishes in Rutland*)

RURAL DEANS
ARCHDEACONRY OF NORTHAMPTON

Brackley Revd M. Roger H. Bellamy, Vicarage, Church Ave, Kings Sutton, Banbury OX17 3RD
Tel: 01295 811364
email: rogerbellamy@hotmail.co.uk
Brixworth Revd Clive Evans, Vicarage, 10 Hall Drive, Long Buckby, Northampton NN6 7QU
Tel: 01327 842909
email: cliver.evans@tiscali.co.uk
Daventry Revd Ann Slater, The Rectory, Church Lane, Nether Heyford, Northants NN7 3LQ
Tel: 01327 342201
email: ann.slater@btinternet.com
Northampton Revd David Wiseman, Christ Church Vicarage, 3 Christ Church Rd, Northampton NN3 2LE   *Tel:* 01604 633254
Towcester Revd Michael Burton, St Mary's Vicarage, 18 Hartwell Rd, Roade, Northampton NN7 2PT   *Tel:* 01604 862284
email: michaelburton5@aol.com
Wellingborough Revd Tony Lynett, Vicarage, 154 Midland Rd, Wellingborough NN8 1NF
Tel: 01933 227101
email: tartleknock@aol.com

ARCHDEACONRY OF OAKHAM

Barnack Canon Stephen Evans, Rectory, London Rd, Uppingham LE15 9TJ   *Tel:* 01572 823381
email: stephen@stephenjevans.wanadoo.co.uk
Corby Revd Rod Lee, St Columba's Vicarage, 157 Studfall Ave, Corby NN17 1LG
Tel: 01536 204158
email: rlee103400@aol.com
Higham Revd Grant Brockhouse, Vicarage, Wood St, Higham Ferrers, Wellingborough NN10 8DL
Tel: 01933 312433
email: grantbrockhouse@care4free.net
Kettering Revd Brian Withington, Rectory, Gate Lane, Broughton, Kettering NN14 1ND
Tel: 01536 791373
email: brian.andco@virgin.net
Oundle Canon Richard Ormston, Vicarage, 12 New St, Oundle, Peterborough PE8 4EA
Tel: 01832 273595
email: Ormston4@aol.com
Peterborough Canon Gordon J. Steele, 26 Minster Precincts, Peterborough PE1 1XZ
Tel: 01733 566265
email: gordonsteele@fish.co.uk
Rutland Canon Stephen Evans, Rectory, London Rd, Uppingham LE15 9TJ   *Tel:* 01572 823381
email: stephen@stephenjevans.wanadoo.co.uk

DIOCESE OF PORTSMOUTH

Founded in 1927. The south-eastern third of Hampshire; the Isle of Wight.

Population 736,000   Area 408 sq m
Full-time Stipendiary Parochial Clergy 95   Benefices 129
Parishes 143   Churches 174
www.portsmouth.anglican.org
Overseas link diocese: IDWAL (Inter-Diocesan West Africa Link) – Ghana, Gambia, Liberia (West Africa).

BISHOP (8th)

Rt Revd Dr Kenneth Stevenson, Bishopsgrove, 26 Osborn Rd, Fareham PO16 7DQ [1995]
Tel: 01329 280247
Fax: 01329 231538
email: bishports@portsmouth.anglican.org
[Kenneth Portsmouth]
Bishop's Chaplain Vacancy
Secretaries Ms Judy Couzens, Ms Yvonne Collins

HONORARY ASSISTANT BISHOPS

Rt Revd Michael Adie, Greenslade, Froxfield, Petersfield GU32 1EB [2005]   *Tel:* 01730 827266
Rt Revd Henry David Halsey, Bramblecross, Gully Rd, Seaview, Isle of Wight PO34 5BY [1991]
Tel: 01983 613583
Revd Dr Peter Selby, Afton Cottage, Afton Rd, Freshwater, Isle of Wight PO40 9TP [2008]
Tel: 01983 759216
Rt Revd Godfrey Ashby, 12 Jay Close, Horndean, Portsmouth PO8 9DJ [2008]   *Tel:* 023 9235 9914

CATHEDRAL CHURCH OF ST THOMAS OF CANTERBURY

Dean Very Revd David Brindley, The Deanery, 13 Pembroke Rd, Portsmouth PO1 2NS [2002]
Tel: 023 9282 4400 (Home)
email:
david.brindley@portsmouthcathedral.org.uk
023 9234 7605 (Personal Asst)
email: liz.snowball@portsmouthcathedral.org.uk
Cathedral Office Cathedral House, 63–67 St Thomas's St, Old Portsmouth PO1 2HA
Tel: 023 9282 3300
Fax: 023 9289 2964
Web: www.portsmouthcathedral.org.uk
Canons Residentiary
Canon David T. Isaac, 1 Pembroke Close, Old Portsmouth PO1 2NX [1990]
Tel: 023 9289 9654 (Office)
email: david.isaac@portsmouth.anglican.org
Pastor Canon Michael Tristram, 51 High St, Old Portsmouth PO1 2LU [2003]
Tel: 023 9273 1282 (Home)
023 9282 3300 ext. 20 (Secretary)
email:
michael.tristram@portsmouthcathedral.org.uk

Precentor Canon Nicholas Ash, 32 Woodville Drive, Pembroke Park, Old Portsmouth PO1 2TG [2003]   *Tel:* 023 9282 3300 ext 225 (Office)
Tel: 023 9242 3797 (Home)
023 9282 3300 ext. 224 (Personal Asst)
email: nick.ash@portsmouthcathedral.org.uk
University Chaplain Canon Peter Jones, 22 Silver St, Portsmouth PO5 3BW [2005]
Tel: 023 9284 3157 (University)
email: peter.jones@port.ac.uk
Cathedral Administrator, Chapter Clerk and Clerk to Cathedral Council Colonel (Rtd) Jonathan Lloyd MBE   *Tel:* 023 9289 2961
email:
jonathan.lloyd@portsmouthcathedral.org.uk
Cathedral Organist and Master of Choristers Dr David Price, Chantry House, 8 Lombard St, Old Portsmouth PO1 2HX
Tel: 023 9243 0811 (Study)
023 9289 2965 (Office)
email: david.price@portsmouthcathedral.org.uk
Cathedral Sub-Organist and Diocesan Music Adviser Marcus Wibberley, The Loft, Cathedral House, St Thomas' Street, Old Portsmouth PO1 2HA
Tel: 023 9289 2966 (Office)
Tel: 023 9289 2966
email:
marcus.wibberley@portsmouthcathedral.org.uk

ARCHDEACONS

PORTSDOWN Ven Dr Trevor Reader, 5 Brading Ave, Southsea PO4 9QJ [2006]
Tel: 023 9243 2693
Fax: 023 9229 8788
email: adportsdown@portsmouth.anglican.org
THE MEON Ven Peter Hancock, Victoria Lodge, 36 Osborn Rd, Fareham PO16 7DS [1999]
Tel: 01329 280101
Fax: 01329 281603
email: admeon@portsmouth.anglican.org
ISLE OF WIGHT Ven Caroline Baston, 5 The Boltons, Kite Hill, Wootton Bridge, Isle of Wight PO33 4PB [2006]   *Tel* and *Fax:* 01983 884432
email: adiow@portsmouth.anglican.org

CONVOCATION (MEMBERS OF THE HOUSE OF CLERGY OF THE GENERAL SYNOD)

Proctors for Clergy
Ven Peter Hancock
Canon David Isaac
Canon Bob White

MEMBERS OF THE HOUSE OF LAITY OF THE GENERAL SYNOD

Mrs Lucy Docherty
Mrs Susan Rodgers
Mrs Deborah Sutton

DIOCESAN OFFICERS

Dioc Secretary Revd Wendy Kennedy, First Floor, Peninsular House, Wharf Rd, Portsmouth PO2 8HB   *Tel:* 023 9289 9664
                                Fax: 023 9289 9651
email: wendy.kennedy@portsmouth.anglican.org
Deputy Dioc Secretary Mr Andrew R. Robinson
                                Tel: 023 9282 9664
                                Fax: 023 9289 9651
email:
        andrew.robinson@portsmouth.anglican.org
PA to Dioc and Deputy Dioc Secretaries Mrs Jane Dobbs   *Tel:* 023 9282 9664
                                Fax: 023 9289 9651
        email: jane.dobbs@portsmouth.anglican.org
Chancellor of Diocese The Worshipful C. Clark QC, Upper Croft, Goodworth, Clatford, Andover SP11 7QX   *Tel:* 01962 868161
                                Fax: 01962 867645
                email: cc@3pumpcourt.com
Deputy Chancellor His Honour Judge Keith Cutler, Woodacre, West Gomeldon, Salisbury SP4 6LS   *Tel:* 01980 611710
Registrar of Diocese and Bishop's Legal Secretary Miss Hilary Tyler, Messrs Brutton & Co., West End House, 288 West St, Fareham PO16 0AJ
                                Tel: 01329 236171
                                Fax: 01329 289915
        email: hilary.tyler@brutton.co.uk
Bishop's Council/Board of Finance/Pastoral Committee (Chairman) Rt Revd Dr Kenneth Stevenson (*as above*)
(*Secretary*) Revd Wendy Kennedy (*as above*)

DIOCESAN ORGANIZATION

Diocesan Office First Floor, Peninsular House, Wharf Rd, Portsmouth PO2 8HB   *Tel:* 023 9289 9650
                                Fax: 023 9289 9651
        email: admin@portsmouth.anglican.org
Dioc Synod (Secretary) Revd Wendy Kennedy (*as above*)
Dioc Synod (Chairman House of Clergy) Canon John Pinder, Rectory, Station Rd, Liss GU33 7AQ
                Tel: 01730 890085 (Home)
                        01730 893175 (Office)
        email: john@jrpinder.freeserve.co.uk

(*Chairman, House of Laity*) Mrs Lucy Docherty, 33 Southampton Rd, Fareham PO16 7DZ
                                Tel: 01329 233602
                        07952 780108 (Mobile)
                email: lucy@docherty1.co.uk

MISSION AND DISCIPLESHIP

Head of Department Canon David Isaac, Dioc Office   *Tel:* 023 9289 9656
                                Fax: 023 9289 9651
        email: david.isaac@portsmouth.anglican.org
Mission Resources Adviser Revd Dr Dennis Lloyd, Dioc Office   *Tel:* 023 9289 9656 (Office)
                        023 9241 2605 (Home)
        email: dennis.lloyd@portsmouth.anglican.org
Dioc Director of Ordinands Revd Robin Coutts, Vicarage, Church Lane, Hambledon, Waterlooville PO7 4RT   *Tel:* 023 9263 2717
        email: robin.coutts@portsmouth.anglican.org
Dioc Continuing Ministerial Education Officer Revd Karina Green, Vicarage, 8 Queen St, Portsmouth PO1 3HL   *Tel:* 023 9281 2215
        email: karina.green@portsmouth.anglican.org
Bishop's Adviser on Women's Ministry Vacancy
Youth and Children's Work Adviser Ben Mizen, Dioc Office   *Tel:* 023 9289 9652
        email: ben.mizen@portsmouth.anglican.org
Spirituality Adviser Revd Dr Peter Lippiett, 50 Penny St, Portsmouth PO1 2NL
                                Tel: 023 9282 6120
        email: peter.lippiett@portsmouth.anglican.org

MISSION AND EDUCATION

Director of Education, Portsmouth and Winchester Mr Tony Blackshaw, Dioc Office
                                Tel: 023 9289 9658
                                Fax: 023 9289 9651
        email: tony.blackshaw@portsmouth.anglican.org
Head of Department Mr Tony Blackshaw (*as above*)
Diocesan Further Education Adviser Mr Gareth Denby, Dioc Office
        email: gareth.denby@portsmouth.anglican.org

MISSION AND RESOURCES

Head of Department Mr Andrew R. Robinson, Dioc Office
Senior Finance Officer Miss Suzanne Baker, Dioc Office   *Tel:* 023 9289 9683
        email: suzanne.baker@portsmouth.anglican.org
Property Manager and Secretary to Property Committee Mr Christopher Flatman, Dioc Office
                                Tel: 023 9289 9661
        email: chris.flatman@portsmouth.anglican.org
Central Services Manager and Secretary to Dioc Advisory Committee Ms Sherry Sherrington, Dioc Office   *Tel:* 023 9289 9660
email:
        sherry.sherrington@portsmouth.anglican.org
Diocesan Child Protection Adviser Mr John Marshman, Dioc Office   *Tel:* 023 9289 9665
        email: john.marshman@portsmouth.anglican.org
Parish Finance Adviser Mrs Mary Makin, Dioc Office   *Tel:* 023 9289 9655
        email: mary.makin@portsmouth.anglican.org

MISSION AND SOCIETY

Head of Department and Social Responsibility Adviser Canon Nick Ralph, Dioc Office
Tel: 023 9289 9672
Fax: 023 9289 9651
email: nick.ralph@portsmouth.anglican.org
Dioc Communications Adviser Mr Neil Pugmire, Dioc Office
Tel: 023 9289 9673
Fax: 023 9289 9651
email: neil.pugmire@portsmouth.anglican.org

CHURCHES

Dioc Advisory Committee for the Care of Churches (Chairman) Very Revd David Brindley; *(Secretary)* Ms Sherry Sherrington
email:
sherry.sherrington@portsmouth.anglican.org
Redundant Churches Uses Committee (Chairman) Revd Wendy Kennedy *(as above)*; *(Secretary)* Mr Christopher Flatman

MINISTRY

Widows Officers (Mainland) The Archdeacon of Portsdown; The Archdeacon of the Meon *(Isle of Wight)*; The Archdeacon of the Isle of Wight

DIOCESAN RECORD OFFICES

Portsmouth City Records Office, 3 Museum Rd, Portsmouth PO1 2LE *Archivist* Miss Alison Drew
Tel: 023 9282 7261
email: alison.drew@portsmouth.gov.uk
(For Gosport, Fareham, Havant and Portsmouth deaneries)
Hampshire Record Office, Sussex St, Winchester SO23 8TH *County Archivist* Miss Janet Smith *Tel:* 01962 846154; *Fax:* 01962 878681; *email:* enquiries.archives@hants.gov.uk *(For Bishop's Waltham and Petersfield deaneries)*
Isle of Wight County Record Office, 26 Hillside, Newport, Isle of Wight PO30 2EB *Archivist* Mr R. Smout
Tel: 01983 823821
email: record.office @iow.gov.uk
(For the Isle of Wight deaneries)

RURAL DEANS

ARCHDEACONRY OF THE MEON

Bishop's Waltham Revd Peter Kelly, Vicarage, Church Rd, Swanmore SO32 2PA
Tel: 01489 892105
email: peter.kelly@portsmouth.anglican.org
Fareham Revd Stephen Girling, Crofton Vicarage, 40 Vicarage Lane, Stubbington, Fareham PO14 2JX
Tel: 01329 661154
email: stephengirling@f2s.com
Gosport Revd Peter Sutton, Vicarage, Victoria Square, Lee-on-the-Solent PO13 9NF
Tel: 023 9255 0269 (Home)
023 9255 6445 (Office)
email: peter.sutton4@virgin.net
Petersfield Revd Simon Weeden, Rectory, 22 Portsmouth Rd, Liphook GU30 7DJ
Tel: 01428 723119
Fax: 01428 725390
email: simon@weeden.plus.com

ARCHDEACONRY OF PORTSDOWN

Havant Revd Dr Paul Moore, Vicarage, Padnell Rd, Cowplain, Waterlooville PO8 8DZ
Tel: 023 9226 2295
email: p.h.moore@btinternet.com
Portsmouth Revd Michael Lewis, Vicarage, 26 Victoria Grove, Southsea PO5 1NE
Tel: 023 9287 3535 (Home)
023 9282 9038 (Office)

ARCHDEACONRY OF THE ISLE OF WIGHT

East Wight Revd Graham Morris, Vicarage, Maples Drive, Bonchurch, Isle of Wight PO38 1NR
Tel: 01983 853729
email: graham.morris@btinternet.com
West Wight Revd Jonathan Hall, Rectory, 69 Victoria Grove, East Cowes, Isle of Wight PO32 6DL
Tel: 01983 200107
email: jel.victoriahall@btinternet.com

DIOCESE OF RIPON AND LEEDS

Re-constituted in 1836. The central third of North Yorkshire; Leeds, except for an area in the west (BRADFORD), an area in the east (YORK) and an area in the south (WAKEFIELD); an area of south-western County Durham.

Population 812,000   Area 1,359 sq m
Full-time Stipendiary Parochial Clergy 116   Benefices 113
Parishes 166   Churches 264
www.ripon.anglican.org
Overseas link diocese: Colombo and Kurunagala (Sri Lanka).

BISHOP (12th)
Rt Revd John Richard Packer, Hollins House, Weetwood Avenue, Leeds, LS16 5NG [2000]
Tel: 01765 602045
Fax: 01765 600758
email: bishop@riponleeds-diocese.org.uk
[John Ripon and Leeds]
Bishop's Personal Assistant Mrs Janet Slater (*same address*)

SUFFRAGAN BISHOP
KNARESBOROUGH Rt Revd James Harold Bell, Thistledown, Main St, Exelby, Bedale DL8 2HD [2004]
Tel: 01677 423525
Fax: 01677 427515
email: bishop.knaresb@btinternet.com

HONORARY ASSISTANT BISHOPS
Rt Revd David Jenkins, Ashbourne, Cotherstone, Barnard Castle DL12 9PR [1994]
Tel: 01833 650804
Rt Revd Martyn Jarrett, 3 North Lane, Roundhay, Leeds LS8 2QJ [2002]
Tel: 0113 265 4280
Fax: 0113 265 4281
email:
bishop-of-beverley@3-north-lane.fsnet.co.uk

CATHEDRAL CHURCH OF ST PETER AND ST WILFRID
Dean Very Revd Keith Jukes, 17 High Saint Agnesgate, Ripon HG4 1QR [2007]
Tel: 01765 602609
email: deankeith@riponcathedral.org.uk
Cathedral Office Liberty Courthouse, Minster Rd, Ripon HG4 1QS
Tel: 01765 603462
Fax: 01765 690530
email: postmaster@riponcathedral.org.uk
Web: www.riponcathedral.org.uk
Canon Precentor: Canon Paul Greenwell, St Wildfrid's House, Minster Close, Ripon HG4 1QR
Tel: 01765 600211
email: canonpaul@riponcathedral.org
Canons Residentiary
Canon Keith Punshon, St Peter's House, Minster Close, Ripon HG4 1QR [1996]
Tel: 01765 604108
email: keithpunshon@riponcathedral.org.uk

Cathedral Administrator Lt Col Ian Horsford, Cathedral Office
email: ianhorsford@riponcathedral.org.uk
Director of Music Mr Andrew Bryden, c/o Ripon Cathedral, Ripon HG4 1QT
Tel: 01765 603496
email: andrewbryden@riponcathedral.org.uk

ARCHDEACONS
LEEDS Ven Peter Burrows, 3 West Park Grove, Leeds LS8 2HQ [2005] *Tel* and *Fax:* 0113 269 0594
email: peterb@riponleeds-diocese.org.uk
RICHMOND Ven Janet Henderson, Hoppus House, Smith Lane, Hutton Conyers, Ripon HG4 5DX [2007]
Tel: 01765 601316
email: janeth@riponleeds-diocese.org.uk

CONVOCATION (MEMBERS OF THE HOUSE OF CLERGY OF THE GENERAL SYNOD)
Proctors for Clergy
Canon Kathryn Fitzsimons
Revd Mark Sowerby

MEMBERS OF THE HOUSE OF LAITY OF THE GENERAL SYNOD
Mrs Katherine Carr
Mr Nigel Greenwood
Mrs Ruth Whitworth

DIOCESAN OFFICERS
Dioc Secretary Mr Philip Arundel, Diocesan Office, St Mary's St, Leeds LS9 7DP
Tel: 0113 200 0540
Fax: 0113 249 1129
email: philipA@riponleeds-diocese.org.uk
Chancellor of Diocese The Worshipful Simon Grenfell, St John's House, Sharow Lane, Ripon, N Yorks. HG4 5BN
email: sgrenfell@lix.compulink.co.uk
Joint Registrars of Diocese and Bishop's Legal Secretaries Mr Christopher Tunnard and Mrs Nicola Harding, Ripon and Leeds Diocesan Registry, Cathedral Chambers, 4 Kirkgate, Ripon HG4 1PA
Tel: 01765 600755
Fax: 01765 690523
email: registry@tunnardsolicitors.com
Dioc Surveyor Mr Michael Lindley, Dioc Office
email: michaell@riponleeds-diocese.org.uk

DIOCESAN ORGANIZATIONS

Diocesan Office Ripon and Leeds Diocesan Office, St Mary's St, Leeds LS9 7DP   *Tel:* 0113 200 0540
Fax: 0113 249 1129

ADMINISTRATION

Dioc Synod (Chairman, House of Clergy) Canon Anthony Shepherd, St Peter's Vicarage, 13 Beech Grove, Harrogate HG2 0ET   *Tel:* 01423 500901
email: ashepherd@onetel.net
(Chairman, House of Laity) Mrs Ann Nicholl, 17 Parkland Terrace, Leeds LS6 4PW
Tel: 0113 269 4045
email: anicholl@parkland17.freeserve.co.uk
(Secretary) Mr Philip Arundel, Dioc Office
email: philipa@riponleeds-diocese.org.uk
Board of Finance (Chairman) Mr Alastair Thompson, Woodlands Cottage, 15 Wyncroft Grove, Bramhope, Leeds LS16 9DG
Tel: 0113 267 8496
email: alastair_thompson@btopenworld.com
(Secretary) Mr Philip Arundel *(as above)*; *(Adminis trative and Deputy Secretary)* Mr Peter Mojsa, Dioc Office   *email:* peterm@riponleeds-diocese.org.uk
(Financial Secretary) Mr Norman Gardner, Dioc Office
email: Normang@riponleeds-diocese.org.uk
Parsonages Board Mr Philip Arundel *(as above)*; *(Parsonages Officer)* Mr Michael Lindley, Dioc Office
email: michaell@riponleeds-diocese.org.uk
Pastoral Committee Mr Peter Mojsa *(as above)*
Board of Patronage Mr Peter Mojsa *(as above)*
Designated Officer Mr Philip Arundel *(as above)*
Dioc Electoral Registration Officer Mr Philip Arundel *(as above)*
Widows and Dependants (Widows' Officer) Mr Philip Arundel *(as above)*

CHURCHES

Advisory Committee for the Care of Churches (Chairman) Mr C. Brown, 40 Leeds Rd, Harrogate HG4 8AY   *Tel:* 01423 567587
email: coljanbrown@virgin.net
(Secretary) Mr Peter Mojsa, Dioc Office
Church Buildings Committee Mr Peter Mojsa *(as above)*
Redundant Churches Uses Committee Mr Peter Mojsa *(as above)*

EDUCATION

Director of Education, Bradford, Ripon and Leeds Revd Clive Sedgewick, The Diocesan Education Team, Windsor House, Cornwall St, Harrogate HG1 2PW   *Tel:* 01423 817553
Fax: 01423 817051
email: clives@brleducationteam.org.uk
Schools Advisers Fiona Beevers and Eileen Bellett *(same address)*
email: fionab@brleducationteam.org.uk *and* eileenb@brleducationteam.org.uk
Buildings Advisers Helen Williams *(same address)*
email: helenw@brleducationteam.org.uk

Phillip Smith *(same address)*
email: peters@brleducationteam.org.uk
Development Education Worker Mrs Sarah Fishwick, Diocese of Ripon and Leeds Global Education Project, 233–237 Roundhay Rd, Leeds LS8 4HS   *Tel:* 0113 380 5661
email: sarah@leedsdec.org

COUNCIL FOR MISSION

Chair Revd C. J. Swift
Director of Mission Vacancy
Dioc Training Officer Mrs Liz Williams, Dioc Office   *Tel:* 0113 200 0556
email: lizw@riponleeds-diocese.org.uk
Director of Ordinands Revd Peter Clement, The Parish House, 16 Orchard Close, Sharow, Ripon HG4 5BE   *Tel:* 01765 607017
email: peterc@riponleeds-diocese.org.uk
Adviser for Women's Ministry Revd Dr Julie Nelson, Rectory, Kirklington, Bedale DL8 2NJ
Tel: 01845 567429
email: revjulie@tiscali.co.uk
Youth Work Adviser Capt Nic Sheppard, 7 Loxley Grove, Wetherby LS22 7YG   *Tel:* 01937 585440
email: nic.Sheppard@churcharmy.net
Warden of Readers Miss Ann Hemsworth, 12 Kelmscott Grove, Cross Gates, Leeds LS15 8HH
Tel: 0113 293 7494
email: ann@elancama.org.uk
Adviser for Non-Stipendiary Ministry Revd Tim Tunley, 51 St James Approach, Leeds LS14 6JJ
Tel: 0113 273 0693
email: timtunley@hotmail.com
Convenor of Advisory Group on Christian Healing Revd Tom Lusty, Sue Ryder Care, Wheatfield Hospice, Grove Rd, Leeds LS6 2AE
Tel: 0113 278 7249
email: tom.lusty@suerydercare.org
World Church Officer Ms Jose Rhodes, 21 Burn Bridge Rd, Pannal, Harrogate HG3 1PB
Ecumenical Officer Canon Jeff King, Vicarage, Church View, Thorner, Leeds LS14 3ED
Tel: 0113 289 2437
email: jeffking@thinkdifferent.co.uk
Social Responsibility Officer Revd Maureen Browell, 4 Upper Folderings, Dodworth, Barnsley S75 3EE   *Tel:* 01226 208391
email: maureenbrowell@talktalk.net
Community Chaplain for People with Learning Difficulties Canon Robert Brooke, St David's House, Waincliffe Drive, Leeds LS11 8ET
Tel: 0113 270 2829
email: bob.brooke@hotmail.co.uk
Racial Justice Officer Vacancy
Rural Ministry Officer Canon Leslie Morley, Moorstones, Ruebury Lane, Osmotherley, Northallerton DL6 2RE   *Tel:* 01609 883787
email: leslie.morley@virgin.net
Urban Ministry Officer Canon Kathryn Fitzsimons, 52 Newton Court, Leeds LS8 2PH
Tel: 0113 248 5011
email: kathrynfitzsimons@hotmail.com

LITURGICAL

Chairman Revd Clare Maclaren, St Paul's Vicarage, 58 Whinmoor Crescent, Leeds LS14 1EW *Tel:* 0113 294 0398
email: claremac@bigfoot.com
Secretary Revd Stuart Lewis, Rectory, Kirkby Overblow, Harrogate HG3 1HD
Tel: 01423 872314

COMMUNICATIONS

Communications Committee Revd John Carter, 7 Blenheim Court, Harrogate HG2 9DT
Tel: 01423 530369
Fax: 01423 538557
email: jhgcarter@aol.com
Press Officer Revd John Carter (*as above*)
Editor of 'Together' (*monthly*) Revd John Carter (*as above*)
Editor of Dioc Directory Mr Philip Arundel (*as above*)

DIOCESAN RECORD OFFICES

County Record Office, County Hall, Northallerton DL7 8DF *Senior Archivist* (*Collections*) Margaret Boustead *Tel:* 01609 777585
Leeds Archives Department, Chapeltown Rd, Sheepscar, Leeds LS7 3AP *Leeds City Archivist* Stephanie Davidson *Tel:* 0113 214 5814
Fax: 0113 214 5815

STEWARDSHIP

Stewardship Adviser Mr Paul Winstanley, Dioc Office *email:* Paulw@riponleeds-diocese.co.uk

AREA DEANS
ARCHDEACONRY OF RICHMOND

Harrogate Revd Paul Hooper, St Mark's Vicarage, Harrogate HG2 8BB *Tel:* 01423 504959
email: stmarks@hgate.btinternet.com
Richmond Revd Stan Howarth, The Rectory, 1 Appleby Close, Aldbrough St John, Richmond DL11 7TT *Tel:* 01325 374634
email: stantherevman@hotmail.com
Ripon Revd David Cleeves, Masham Vicarage, Rodney Terrace, Masham, Ripon HG4 4JA
Tel: 01765 689255
email: cleevesmasham@onetel.com
Wensley Vacancy

ARCHDEACONRY OF LEEDS

Allerton Canon Alan Taylor, Vicarage, Elford Place West, Leeds LS8 5QD *Tel:* 0113 248 6992
email: alan.taylor@leeds.gov.uk
Armley Vacancy
Headingley Revd David Calder, 2 Halcyon Hill, Leeds LS7 3PU *Tel:* 0113 269 0448
email: d.calder@talktalk.net
Whitkirk Revd Jean Sykes, Vicarage, 134 Leeds Rd, Allerton Bywater, Castleford WF10 2HB
Tel: 0113 286 9415
email: revjeansykes@googlemail.com

DIOCESE OF ROCHESTER

Founded in 604. Kent west of the Medway, except for one parish in the south-west (CHICHESTER); the Medway Towns; the London boroughs of Bromley and Bexley, except for a few parishes (SOUTHWARK); one parish in East Sussex.

Population 1,231,000   Area 542 sq m
Full-time Stipendiary Parochial Clergy 206   Benefices 190
Parishes 215   Churches 265
www.rochester.anglican.org
Overseas link diocese: Harare (Zimbabwe).

BISHOP (106th)
Rt Revd Dr Michael Nazir-Ali, Bishopscourt, Rochester ME1 1TS [1995]   *Tel:* 01634 842721
Fax: 01634 831136
[Michael Roffen:]
Chaplain Canon Tony Smith   *Tel:* 01634 814439
email: bishops.chaplain@rochester.anglican.org

SUFFRAGAN BISHOP
TONBRIDGE Rt Revd Dr Brian Castle, Bishop's Lodge, 48 St Botolph's Rd, Sevenoaks TN13 3AG [2002]   *Tel:* 01732 456070
Fax: 01732 741449
email: bishop.tonbridge@rochester.anglican.org

HONORARY ASSISTANT BISHOP
Rt Revd Michael Gear, 10 Acott Fields, Yalding, Maidstone ME18 6DQ [1999]   *Tel:* 01622 817388
email: mike.gear@rochester.anglican.org

CATHEDRAL CHURCH OF CHRIST AND THE BLESSED VIRGIN MARY
Dean Very Revd Adrian Newman, The Deanery, The Precinct, Rochester ME1 1SR [2005]
Tel: 01634 202183 (Home)
01634 843366 (Office)
email: dean@rochestercathedral.org
Chapter Office Garth House, The Precinct, Rochester ME1 1SX   *Tel:* 01634 843366
Fax: 01634 401410
Canons Residentiary
Canon Philip Hesketh, East Canonry, The Precinct, Rochester ME1 1TG [2005]
Tel: 01634 202898 (Home)
01634 810073 (Office)
email: canonpastor@rochestercathedral.org
Ven Peter Lock, The Archdeaconry, The Precinct, Rochester ME1 1TG [2000]
Tel: 01634 813533 (Home)
01634 560000 (Office)
email: archdeacon@rochestercathedral.org
Canon Neil Thompson, Easter Garth, The Precinct, Rochester ME1 1TG [2008]
Tel: 01634 405265 (Home)
01634 810063 (Office)
email: precentor@rochestercathedral.org
Canon Jean Kerr, Prebendal House, King's Orchard, The Precinct, Rochester ME1 1TG [2005]
Tel: 01634 844508 (Home)
email: jean.kerr@rochester.anglican.org

Director of Operations Dr Edwina Bell, Chapter Office   *Tel:* 810060 (Office)
email: administrator@rochestercathedral.org
Cathedral Organist and Director of Music Mr Scott Farrell, Chapter Office   *Tel:* 01634 810061
email: directorofmusic@rochestercathedral.org

ARCHDEACONS
BROMLEY AND BEXLEY Ven Paul Wright, The Archdeaconry, The Glebe, Chislehurst BR7 5PX [2004]   *Tel:* 020 8467 8743
email:
archdeacon.bromley@rochester.anglican.org
ROCHESTER Ven Peter Lock, The Archdeaconry, The Glebe, Chislehurst BR7 5PX [2004]
Tel: 01643 560000
email:
archdeacon.rochester@rochester.anglican.org
TONBRIDGE Ven Clive Mansell, 3 The Ridings, Blackhurst Lane, Tunbridge Wells TN2 4RU [2002]   *Tel:* 01892 520660
email:
archdeacon.tonbridge@rochester.anglican.org

CONVOCATION (MEMBERS OF THE HOUSE OF CLERGY OF THE GENERAL SYNOD)
Proctors for Clergy
Canon Nicholas Kerr
Revd Angus MacLeay
Ven Clive Mansell
Canon Gordon Oliver

MEMBERS OF THE HOUSE OF LAITY OF THE GENERAL SYNOD
Mr James Cheeseman
Brig Ian Dobbie
Mr Philip French
Mr Gerald O'Brien

DIOCESAN OFFICERS
Dioc Secretary and Bishop's Officer Canon Louise Gilbert, St Nicholas Church, Boley Hill, Rochester ME1 1SL   *Tel:* 01634 560000
Fax: 01634 408942
email: louise.gilbert@rochester.anglican.org
Chancellor of Diocese Mr John Gallagher, Hardwicke Building, New Square, Lincoln's Inn, London WC2A 3SB   *Tel:* 020 7242 2523

Registrar of Diocese and Bishop's Legal Secretary Mr Owen Carew-Jones, Registry Chambers, The Old Deanery, Dean's Court, London EC4V 5AA
Tel: 020 7593 5110
Fax: 020 7248 3221
email: a.harrison@winckworths.co.uk

DIOCESAN ORGANIZATIONS

Diocesan Office St Nicholas Church, Boley Hill, Rochester ME1 1SL   Tel: 01634 560000
Fax: 01634 408942
email: enquiries@rochester.anglican.org
Web: www.rochester.anglican.org

ADMINISTRATION

Assistant Secretary Mr Geoff Marsh, Dioc Office
email: geoff.marsh@rochester.anglican.org
Dioc Synod (Chairman, House of Clergy) Mrs Angela Scott, The Stead, Willow Grove, Chislehurst BR7 5BU   Tel: 020 8467 3589
(Chairman, House of Laity) Revd Ruth Oates, Vicarage, 57 New House Lane, Gravesend DA11 7HJ, Tel: 01474 740565; (Secretary) Canon Louise Gilbert, Dioc Office
Board of Finance (Chairman) Mr Graeme King, Strath Darent House, Shoreham Rd, Otford, Sevenoaks TN14 5RW Tel: 01959 522118; (Secretary) Canon Louise Gilbert (as above); (Dioc Treasurer) Mr Martyn Burt, Dioc Office
email: martyn.burt@rochester.anglican.org
Pastoral Committee Mrs Suzanne Rogers, Dioc Office
email: suzanne.rogers@rochester.anglican.org
Board of Patronage Mrs Suzanne Rogers (as above)
Designated Officer Mr Owen Carew-Jones, Registry Chambers, The Old Deanery, Dean's Court, London EC4V 5AA   Tel: 020 7593 5110
Trusts Mrs Nikki McVeagh (Legal), Vacancy (Financial), Dioc Office
email: nikki.mcveagh@rochester.anglican.org

CHURCHES

Advisory Committee for the Care of Churches (Chairman) Mr Derek Shilling, Ivy Bank, Shoreham Rd, Otford, Sevenoaks TN14 5RP   Tel: 01959 522059
(DAC Secretary) Mark Trevitt, Dioc Office
Redundant Churches Uses Committee Mr Geoff Marsh (as above)

EDUCATION

Education Office Diocesan Office
email: education@rochester.anglican.org
Board of Education (Chairman) Christopher Thornton, Kettleshill House, Underriver, Sevenoaks TN15 0RX
Secretary, Director of Education and Bishop's Officer Canon John Smith, Educ Office
Assistant Director of Education (Schools) Ms Jan Thompson, Educ Office
Assistant Director of Education (Youth Work) Mr Phil Greig, Educ Office
Assistant Director of Education (Voluntary Education) Miss Tiffany Allan, Educ Office

Assistant Director of Education (Finance) Mr John Constanti, Educ Office

MINISTRY AND TRAINING

Advisory Council for Ministry and Training (Chairman) The Bishop of Tonbridge (as above); (Secretary, Director of Ministry and Training and Bishop's Officer) Canon Gordon Oliver, Dioc Office
email: gordon.oliver@rochester.anglican.org
Director of Ordinands Canon Paul Longbottom, Vicarage, Butchers Hill, Shorne, Gravesend DA12 3EB   Tel: 01474 822239
Associate Director of Ordinands Revd Elizabeth Walker, Vicarage, Comp Lane, Platt, Sevenoaks TN15 8NR   Tel: 01732 885482
Readers' Association (Warden) Mrs Karen Senior, Dioc Office
email: readers@rochester.anglican.org
Clerical Registry, Dioc Retirement Officer and Widows Officer Revd Andrew Sangster, The Chaplain's House, Bromley College, London Rd, Bromley BR1 1PE   Tel: 020 8460 4712
email: bromcoll@aol.com
Diocesan Deaf Ministry Adviser Miss Chris Bostock, Church in Society, 2–3 Bedford Place, Maidstone ME16 8JB   Tel: 01622 755014
Evangelists (Warden) Canon Jean Kerr (as above)
Pastoral Assistants (Warden) Canon Penny Avann, 9 Ringwood Ave, Pratts Bottom, Orpington BR6 7SY   Tel: 01689 861742

WORSHIP IN MISSION

Acting Chair Revd David Graham, Rectory, Hayes St, Hayes, Bromley BR2 7LH   Tel: 020 8462 1373

MISSION, ECUMENISM AND PARISH DEVELOPMENT

Advisory Council for Mission and Unity (Chairman) The Archdeacon of Bromley and Bexley (as above)
(Secretary and Bishop's Officer for Mission and Unity) Canon Jean Kerr (as above)
(Asst Director of Mission and Unity) Vacancy
County Ecumenical Officer Revd Dr Michael Cooke, St Lawrence Vicarage, Stone St, Seal, Sevenoaks TN15 0LQ   Tel: 01732 761766
Interfaith (Chairman) Revd Malcolm Cooper, 1 Crest View, Greenhithe DA9 9QU
Tel: 01322 381213
Local Evangelism (Chairman) Canon Jean Kerr (as above)

PRESS, PUBLICITY AND COMMUNICATIONS

Advisory Council for Communications (Chairman) Vacancy
(Communications Officer) Miss Tammy Heren, Dioc Office   Tel: 01634 560000
07017 404001 (Mobile)
email: communications@rochester.anglican.org
Editor of 'Link' Newspaper Mr Bryan Harris, 57 Neal Rd, West Kingsdown, Sevenoaks TN15 6DG   Tel: 01474 852474
email: kcpress@surfaid.org

DIOCESAN RECORD OFFICES

Centre for Kentish Studies, County Hall, Maidstone ME14 1XQ *Tel:* 01622 694363; Medway Archives and Local Studies Centre, Civic Centre, Strood, Rochester ME2 4AW *Tel:* 01634 732714; Bexley Local Studies and Archive Centre, Central Library, Townley Rd, Bexleyheath DA6 7HJ *Tel:* 020 8301 1545 (*For the deaneries of Erith and Sidcup in the archdeaconry of Bromley*)

Bromley Local Studies and Archives, Central Library, High St, Bromley, Kent BR1 1EX *Tel:* 020 8460 9955 (*For the deaneries of Beckenham, Bromley and Orpington in the archdeaconry of Bromley*)

CHURCH IN SOCIETY (SOCIAL RESPONSIBILITY)

Advisory Council for Church in Society (*Chairman*) The Archdeacon of Tonbridge (*as above*)

(*Secretary, Director of Church in Society and Bishop's Officer*) Canon David Grimwood, Robert Runcie House, 2–3 Bedford Place, Maidstone ME16 8JB
Tel: 01622 755014
Fax: 01622 693531

Canterbury and Rochester Dioc Joint Council for Social Responsibility (*Senior Adviser*) Canon David Grimwood (*as above*)

Director of Workplace Ministry Revd David Helms, Robert Runcie House, 2–3 Bedford Place, Maidstone ME16 8JB
Tel: 01622 755014
Fax: 01622 693531

Rural Issues Revd Caroline Pinchbeck, Rectory, Newnham Lane, Eastling, Faversham ME13 0AS

Urban Priorities Revd John Perumbalath, St Mark's Vicarage, 123 London Rd, Northfleet, Gravesend DA11 9NH
Tel: 01474 535814
email: john.perumbalath@diocese-rochester.org

Poverty and Hope (*Director*) Mr Chris Weller, 9 Calverley Park, Tunbridge Wells TN1 2SH

STEWARDSHIP

Mr Alan Strachan, Dioc Office

AREA/RURAL DEANS

ARCHDEACONRY OF BROMLEY AND BEXLEY

Beckenham Revd Mike Porter, Vicarage, 234 Anerley Rd, London SE20 8TJ *Tel:* 020 8778 4800
email: mike.porter@diocese-rochester.org

Bromley Revd Michael Camp, Vicarage, 9 St Paul's Square, Bromley BR2 0XH
Tel: 020 8460 6275
email: michael.camp@diocese-rochester.org

Erith Revd Francis Jakeman, Vicarage, 57 Townley Rd, Bexleyheath DA6 7HY
Tel: 020 8301 5086

Orpington Revd Alan Mustoe, Vicarage, 1a Keswick Rd, Orpington BR6 0EU
Tel: 01689 824624
email: alan.mustoe@diocese-rochester.org

Sidcup Stephen Sealy, St John's Vicarage, 13 Church Avenue, Sidcup DA14 6BU
Tel: 020 8300 0383
email: stephen.sealy@diocese-rochester.org

ARCHDEACONRY OF ROCHESTER

Revd John Peal, The New Rectory, The Street, Ash, Sevenoaks TN15 7HA *Tel:* 04747 872209
email: john.peal@diocese-rochester.org

Dartford Revd Richard Arding, Vicarage, 1 Curate's Walk, Wilmington, Dartford DA2 7BJ *Tel:* 01322 220561

Gillingham Canon Alan Vousden, Vicarage, 80 Broadview Ave, Rainham, Gillingham ME8 9DE
Tel: 01634 231538
Fax: 01634 362023
email:
Alan-Vousden@rainhamvic-kent.freeserve.co.uk

Gravesend Revd Vic Lawrence, Rectory, Church Walk, Gravesend DA12 2QU *Tel:* 01474 533434
email: vic.lawrence@diocese-rochester.org

Rochester Revd Paul Kerr, Vicarage, 1 Binnacle Rd, Rochester ME1 2XR *Tel:* 01634 841183
email: stjustus.rochester@rochester.anglican.org

Strood Revd James Southward, Vicarage, Hermitage Rd, Higha, Rochester ME3 7NE
Tel: 01634 717360
email: jfsouthward@yahoo.co.uk

ARCHDEACONRY OF TONBRIDGE

Malling Revd Jim Brown, Vicarage, 2 The Grange, East Malling ME19 6AH
Tel: 01732 843282

Paddock Wood Revd Campbell Paget, Vicarage, 8 Broadoak, Brenchley, Tonbridge TN12 7NN
Tel: 01892 722140

Sevenoaks Revd Paul Francis, St Mary's Vicarage, The Glebe Field, Shoreham Lane, Riverhead, Sevenoaks TN13 3DR *Tel:* 01732 455736
email: paul.francis@diocese-rochester.org

Shoreham Revd Brenda Hurd, Rectory, Borough Green Rd, Wrotham, Sevenoaks TN15 7RA
Tel: 01732 882211
email: brenda.hurd@diocese-rochester.org

Tonbridge Revd Lionel Kevis, Vicarage, The Green, Leigh, Tonbridge TN11 8QJ
Tel: 01732 833022

Tunbridge Wells Revd Brian Senior, St Philip's Vicarage, Birken Rd, Tunbridge Wells TN2 3TE
Tel: 01892 512071

DIOCESE OF ST ALBANS

Founded in 1877. Hertfordshire, except for a small area in the south (LONDON) and one parish in the west (OXFORD); Bedfordshire, except for one parish in the north (ELY) and one parish in the west (OXFORD); an area of Greater London.

Population 1,718,000   Area 1,116 sq m
Full-time Stipendiary Parochial Clergy 241   Benefices 209
Parishes 333   Churches 406
www.stalbansdioc.org.uk
Overseas link dioceses: Jamaica, Guyana, NE Caribbean and Aruba (West Indies).

BISHOP (9th)
Vacancy (from 7 Jan 2009)   *Tel:* 01727 853305
Fax: 01727 846715
email: bishop@stalbans.anglican.org
Chaplain Capt Andrew Crooks, CA
Tel: 01727 853305
email: chaplain@stalbans.anglican.org
Secretaries Mrs Mary Handford, Mrs Lynn Bridger   *email:* bishop@stalbans.anglican.org

SUFFRAGAN BISHOPS
BEDFORD Rt Revd Richard Inwood, Bishop's Lodge, Bedford Rd, Cardington MK44 3SS [2003]
Tel: 01234 831432
Fax: 01234 831484
email: bishopbedford@stalbans.anglican.org
HERTFORD Rt Revd Christopher Richard James Foster, Hertford House, Abbey Mill Lane, St Albans AL3 4HE [2001]   *Tel:* 01727 866420
Fax: 01727 811426
email: bishophertford@stalbans.anglican.org

HONORARY ASSISTANT BISHOP
Rt Revd David John Farmbrough, St Michael Mead, 110 Village Rd, Bromham MK43 8HU [1993]   *Tel:* 01234 825042
Rt Revd Robin J. N. Smith, 7 Aysgarth Rd, Redbourn, St Albans AL3 7PJ [2002]
Tel: 01582 791964

CATHEDRAL AND ABBEY CHURCH OF SAINT ALBAN
Dean Very Revd Jeffrey John, The Deanery, Sumpter Yard, St Albans AL1 1BY [2004]
Tel: 01727 890202
Fax: 01727 890227
email: dean@stalbanscathedral.org.uk
Cathedral Office The Chapter House, Sumpter Yard, St Albans AL1 1BY   *Tel:* 01727 860780
Fax: 01727 850944
email: mail@stalbanscathedral.org.uk
Web: www.stalbanscathedral.org.uk

Canons Residentiary
Canon Stephen Lake (*Sub-Dean*), The Old Rectory, Sumpter Yard, St Albans AL1 1BY [2001]
Tel: 01727 890201
email: subdean@stalbanscathedral.org.uk
Canon Kevin Walton (*Canon Chancellor*), 2 Sumpter Yard, St Albans AL1 1BY [2008]
Tel: 01727 890242
email: canon@stalbanscathedral.org.uk
Canon Michael Sansom (*Director of Ordinands*), 4d Harpenden Rd, St Albans AL3 5AB [1988]
Tel: 01727 833777
email: ddo@stalbans.anglican.org
Canon Richard Wheeler (*Bishop's Adviser for Social Responsibility*), Holywell Close, 43 Holywell Hill, St Albans AL1 1HE [2001]   *Tel:* 01727 856753
Fax: 01727 830368
email: sro@stalbans.anglican.org
Canon Dennis Stamps (*Ministerial Development Officer*), 7 Corder Close, St Albans AL3 4NH [2002]   *Tel:* 01727 841116
email: dstamps@stalbans.anglican.org
Minor Canons
Young People Revd Darren Collins, Deanery Barn, Sumpter Yard, St Albans AL1 1BY [2007]
Tel: 01727 890206
email: mcyp@stalbanscathedral.org.uk
Liturgy Revd Anna Matthews, 1 The Deanery, Sumpter Yard, St Albans AL1 1BY [2006]
Tel: 01727 890207
email: mcl@stalbanscathedral.org.uk
Cathedral Administrator and Clerk to the Chapter Mr Justin Cross, Cathedral Office   *Tel:* 01727 890208
email: admin@stalbanscathedral.org.uk
Master of the Music Mr Andrew Lucas, 31 Abbey Mill Lane, St Albans AL3 4HA
Tel: 01727 890242
email: music@stalbanscathedral.org.uk
Assistant Master of the Music and Director of the St Albans Abbey Girls Choir Mr Tom Winpenny, 34 Orchard St, St Albans AL3 4HL
Tel: 01727 890245
email: amom@stalbanscathedral.org.uk
Cathedral Education Officer Annette Cranston, Education Centre, Sumpter Yard, St Albans AL1 1BY   *Tel:* 01727 890262
email: education@stalbanscathedral.org.uk

Cathedral Architect Mr Richard Griffiths
Archaeological Consultant Prof Martin Biddle

ARCHDEACONS
ST ALBANS Ven Jonathan Smith, 6 Sopwell Lane, St Albans AL1 1RR [2002]   *Tel:* 01727 847212
Fax: 01727 848311
email: archdstalbans@stalbans.anglican.org
BEDFORD Ven Paul Hughes, 17 Lansdowne Rd, Luton LU3 1EE [2003]   *Tel:* 01582 730722
Fax: 01582 877354
email: archdbedf@stalbans.anglican.org
HERTFORD Ven Trevor Jones, St Mary's House, Church Lane, Stapleford, Hertford SG14 3NB [1997]   *Tel:* 01992 581629
Fax: 01992 558745
email: archdhert@stalbans.anglican.org

CONVOCATION (MEMBERS OF THE HOUSE OF CLERGY OF THE GENERAL SYNOD)
Proctors for Clergy
Revd Dr Peter Ackroyd
Revd Jeremy Crocker
Revd Dr Winifred Joan Crossley
Revd Richard Hibbert
Ven Trevor Jones
Canon Stephen Lake

MEMBERS OF THE HOUSE OF LAITY OF THE GENERAL SYNOD
Mr Anthony Archer
Mr Simon Baynes
Mr Philip Lovegrove
Mr Philip McDonough
Mrs Christina Rees
Vacancy

DIOCESAN OFFICERS
Dioc Secretary Miss Susan Pope, Holywell Lodge, 41 Holywell Hill, St Albans AL1 1HE
Tel: 01727 854532
Fax: 01727 844469
email: mail@stalbans.anglican.org
Chancellor of Diocese His Honour the Worshipful Roger G. Kaye QC, Holywell Lodge, 41 Holywell Hill, St Albans AL1 1HD   *Tel:* 01727 865765
Registrar of Diocese and Bishop's Legal Secretary Mr David Cheetham (*same address*)
Surveyor Mr Alastair Woodgate, c/o 41 Holywell Hill, St Albans AL1 1HE
Tel: 01727 854516

DIOCESAN ORGANIZATIONS
Diocesan Office Holywell Lodge, 41 Holywell Hill, St Albans AL1 1HE   *Tel:* 01727 854532
Fax: 01727 844469
email: mail@stalbans.anglican.org
Web: www.stalbans.anglican.org

ADMINISTRATION
Dioc Synod (Chairman, House of Clergy) Canon Robert Sibson, Vicarage, Shortmead St, Biggleswade SG18 0AT   *Tel:* 01767 312243
Fax: 01767 600743
(Chairman, House of Laity) Mr John Wallace, 14 Church St, Leighton Buzzard LU7 7BT
(Secretary) Miss Susan Pope, Dioc Office
Board of Finance (Chairman) Vacancy
(Secretary) Miss Susan Pope (*as above*)
Financial Secretary Mr Martin Bishop, Dioc Office
Estates Secretary Mrs Michèle Manders, Dioc Office
Board of Patronage Mr Jim May, Dioc Office
Designated Officers (Joint) Mr David Cheetham and Miss Susan Pope, Dioc Office
Pastoral and Mission Committee Mr Jim May (*as above*)
Trusts Mr Nigel Benger, Dioc Office

CHURCHES
Advisory Committee for the Care of Churches (Chairman) Dr Christopher Green, Dioc Office; *(Secretary)* Mr Jim May (*as above*)

EDUCATION
Dioc Education and Resources Centre Dioc Office
Tel: 01727 854532
Fax: 01727 844469
Director of Education Mr Jon Reynolds, Education Centre (*as above*)
School Buildings Officer Mrs Julia Creasey (*as above*)
RE Adviser Mrs Jane Chipperton (*as above*)

MINISTRY
Director of Ordinands Canon Dr Michael Sansom, 4d Harpenden Rd, St Albans AL3 5AB
Tel: 01727 833777
Ministerial Development Officer Canon Dennis Stamps (*Ministerial Development Officer*), 7 Corder Close, St Albans AL3 4NH
Tel: 01727 841116
Local Ministry Officer Canon Robin Brown, Dioc Office   *Tel:* 01727 830802
Continuing Ministerial Education Officer Revd Ysmena Pentalow, Dioc Office   *Tel:* 01727 818154
Associate Director of Ordinands Revd Rebecca Totterdell, Rectory, Bockings, Walkern, Stevenage SG2 7PB   *Tel:* 01438 861322
Board of Readers' Work Mrs Margaret Tinsley, 145 The Ridgeway, St Albans AL4 9XA
Tel: 01727 859528
Mr Richard Osborn, 41 Tiverton Rd, Potters Bar EN6 5HX   *Tel:* 01707 657491
Mr Ron Upton, 65 Nunnery Lane, Luton LU3 1XB   *Tel:* 01582 596208
Youth Officer Mr David Green, Dioc Office
Children's Work Adviser, Bedfordshire Revd Ruth Pyke, Dioc Office
Hertfordshire Revd Vanessa Cato, Dioc Office

LITURGICAL
Chairman Canon Dr Michael Sansom (*as above*)

MISSIONARY AND ECUMENICAL
Ecumenical Officers
Bedfordshire Vacancy
Hertfordshire Revd Christopher Futcher, Rectory, 9 Rothamsted Ave, Harpenden AL5 2DD
Tel: 01582 712202
Board for Church and Society Mr Simon Best (*Chairman*), The Hollies, Kimpton Rd, Peters Green LU2 9QW
Council for Partnership in World Mission Revd Christopher Briggs, Lawrence Cottage, 2 Hailey Lane, Hertford SG13 7NX   *Tel:* 01992 462922
Workplace Ministry Revd Michael Shaw, 41 Holywell Hill, St Albans AL1 1HE
Tel: 01727 869461

PRESS AND PUBLICATIONS
Dioc Communications Officer Mr Arun Kataria, Dioc Office   *Tel:* 01727 818110
Fax: 01727 844469
email: comms@stalbans.anglican.org
Editor of Dioc Directory Miss Susan Pope (*as above*)
Dioc Leaflet Mrs Claudia Brown (*as above*)

DIOCESAN RECORD OFFICES
County Hall, Hertford SG13 8DE *Tel:* 01992 555105 (*For diocesan records and parish records for St Albans and Hertford archdeaconries*)
County Hall, Bedford MK42 9AP *County Archivist* Mr Kevin Ward *Tel:* 01234 63222 Ext 277 (*For parish records for Bedford archdeaconry*)

SOCIAL RESPONSIBILITY
Officer for Mission and Development Canon John Kiddle   *Tel:* 01727 851748
Social Responsibility Officer Vacancy, Dioc Office
Tel: 01727 851748

STEWARDSHIP
Stewardship Development Officer Mr Geoff Fletcher, Dioc Office   *Tel:* 01727 854532

RURAL DEANS
ARCHDEACONRY OF ST ALBANS
Aldenham Revd Geoff Buckler, The Rectory, High St, Bushey, WD23 1BD   *Tel:* 020 8950 1546
Berkhamsted Revd David Abbott, Sunnyside Vicarage, Ivy House Lane, Sunnyside, Berkhamsted HP4 2PP   *Tel:* 01442 865100
Hemel Hempstead Revd Peter Cotton, Rectory, 40 High St, Hemel Hempstead HP1 3AE
Tel: 01442 213838
Hitchin Revd Michael Roden, Church House, Churchyard, Hitchen SH5 1HP
Tel: 01462 451758
Rickmansworth Revd Gavin Collins, Christ Church Vicarage, Chorleywood Common, Rickmansworth WD3 5SG   *Tel:* 01923 282149
St Albans Revd David Ridgeway, St Stephen's Vicarage, 14 Watling Rd, St Albans AL1 2PX
Tel: 01727 862598

Watford Revd Geoffrey Warren, St Andrew's Vicarage, 18 Park Rd, Watford WD17 4DN
Tel: 01923 239265
Wheathampstead Revd Andrew Dove, The Rectory, Old Rectory Gardens, Wheathampstead, St Albans AL4 8AD   *Tel:* 01582 833144

ARCHDEACONRY OF BEDFORD
Ampthill Revd C. David Powell, 33 Putnoe Heights, Putnoe, Bedford MK41 8EB
Tel: 01234 345020
Bedford Canon Christopher Dent, St Andrew's Vicarage,1 St Edmond Rd, Bedford MK40 2NQ
Tel: 01234 354234
Biggleswade Revd William Thackray, St Andrew's Vicarage, Shortmead St, Biggleswade SG18 0AT
Tel: 01767 312243
Dunstable Canon Malcolm Grant, Vicarage, High St, Eaton Bray, Dunstable LU6 2DN
Tel: 01525 220261
Elstow Canon Nigel P. Morrell, 22 Sunderland Place, Shortstown, Bedford MK42 0FD
Tel and Fax: 01234 743202
Luton Canon Stephen Purvis, St Luke's Vicarage, High St, Leagrave, Luton LU4 9JY
Tel: 01582 572737
Sharnbrook Revd David Mason, 2a Devon Rd, Bedford MK40 3DF   *Tel:* 01234 309737
Shefford Very Revd John Morlay, Vicarage, 65 Church St, Langford, Biggleswade SG18 9QT
Tel: 01462 700248

ARCHDEACONRY OF HERTFORD
Barnet Revd Richard Watson, Rectory, 136 Church Hill Rd, East Barnet EN4 8XD
Tel: 020 8383 3840
Bishop's Stortford Revd Christopher Boulton, The Rectory, High St, Much Hadham SG10 6DA
Tel: 01279 842609
Buntingford Revd Lady Carol Kimberley, Vicarage, Great Hormead, Buntingford SG9 0NT
Tel: 01763 289258
Cheshunt Revd Carol Selby, St Clement's House, 44 Hillview Gardens, Cheshunt EN8 0PE
Tel: 01992 625098
Welwyn and Hatfield (*Joint Rural Dean*) Revd Richard E. Pyke, Rectory, 1 Fore St, Hatfield AL9 5AN   *Tel and Fax:* 01707 262072
Welwyn and Hatfield (*Joint Rural Dean*) Canon Carl Garner, Rectory, 354 Knightsfield, Welwyn Garden City AL8 7NG   *Tel:* 01707 326677
Hertford and Ware (*Joint Rural Dean*) Canon Pauline Higham, Hertford Hundred House, 1 Little Berkhamsted Lane, Little Berkhamsted Hertford SG13 8LU   *Tel:* 01707 875940
Hertford and Ware (*Joint Rural Dean*) Revd David Proud, Christ Church Vicarage, 15 Hanbury Close, Ware SG12 7BZ   *Tel:* 01920 464165
Stevenage Revd Geoffrey Tickner, Vicarage, 18 Letchmore Rd, Stevenage SG1 3JD
Tel: 01438 353229

DIOCESE OF ST EDMUNDSBURY AND IPSWICH

Founded in 1914. Suffolk, except for a small area in the
north-east (NORWICH); one parish in Essex.

Population 624,000   Area 1,439 sq m
Full-time Stipendiary Parochial Clergy 127   Benefices 131
Parishes 447   Churches 477
www.stedmundsbury.anglican.org
Overseas link dioceses: Hassalt (Belgium),
Kagera (Tanzania).

BISHOP (9th)
Rt Revd Nigel Stock, Bishop's House, 4 Park Rd,
Ipswich IP1 3ST [2007]   *Tel:* 01473 252829
    Fax: 01473 232552
email:
    bishop.nigel@stedmundsbury.anglican.org
[Nigel St Edm and Ipswich]
Bishop's Chaplain Canon Deirdre Parmenter (*same
address and telephone*)
    email: deirdre@stedmundsbury.anglican.org
Bishop's Secretary Mrs Denise Rudland (*same
address and telephone*)
    ·*email:* denise@stedmundsbury.anglican.org
Assistant Secretary Mrs Julia Venmore-Rowland
(*same address and telephone*)
    email: julia@stedmundsbury.anglican.org

SUFFRAGAN BISHOP
DUNWICH Rt Revd Clive Young, 28 Westerfield
Rd, Ipswich IP4 2UJ [1999]   *Tel:* 01473 222276
    Fax: 01473 210303
email: bishop.clive@stedmundsbury.anglican.org
Bishop's Secretary Mrs Brenda Fradd (*same address*)
    email: brendaf@stedmundsbury.anglican.org

**CATHEDRAL CHURCH OF ST JAMES,
BURY ST EDMUNDS**
Dean Very Revd Neil Collings, The Deanery,
Bury St Edmunds IP33 1RS [2006]
    Tel: 01284 754933
    email: dean@stedscathedral.co.uk
Cathedral Office Abbey House, Angel Hill, Bury St
Edmunds IP33 1LS   *Tel:* 01284 754933
    Fax: 01284 768655
    email: cathedralsecretary@stedscathedral.co.uk
Canons Residentiary
Precentor Canon Michael Hampel, 1 Abbey
Precincts, Bury St Edmunds IP33 1RS [2004]
    Tel: 01284 761982
    email: precentor@stedscathedral.co.uk
Canon Pastor Vacancy   *Tel:* 01284 701472
    email: canon.pastor@stedscathedral.co.uk/
    revpeterbarham@aol.com
Canon Theologian Canon Christopher Burdon, 3
Crown St, Bury St Edmunds IP33 1QX [2007]
    Tel: 01284 701546
    email: chris@stedmundsbury.anglican.org

Administrator Mr Keith Huddart, Cathedral
Office
    email: administrator@stedscathedral.co.uk
Visitors Officer Mrs Sarah Friswell, Cathedral
Office
    email: visitor.officer@stedscathedral.co.uk
Children's Education Officer Mrs Helen Woodroffe,
Cathedral Office
    email: discoverycentre@stedscathedral.co.uk
Director of Music Mr James Thomas, Cathedral
Office   *Tel:* 01284 756520
    email: dom@stedscathedral.co.uk
Assistant Director of Music and Arts Officer Mr
David Humphreys, Cathedral Office
    email: adom@stedscathedral.co.uk

ARCHDEACONS
SUDBURY Ven David Brierley, Sudbury Lodge,
Stanningfield Rd, Great Whelnetham, Bury St
Edmunds IP30 0TL [2006]
    Tel and Fax: 01284 386942
email:
    archdeacon.david@stedmundsbury.anglican.org
SUFFOLK Ven Geoffrey Arrand, Glebe House, The
Street, Ashfield cum Thorpe, Stowmarket
IP14 6LX [1994]   *Tel:* 01728 685497
    Fax: 01728 685969
    email: archdeacon.geoffrey@
    stedmundsbury.anglican.org

**CONVOCATION (MEMBERS OF THE
HOUSE OF CLERGY OF THE GENERAL
SYNOD)**
Proctors for Clergy
Revd Canon Jonathan Alderton-Ford
Ven Geoffrey Arrand
Revd Max Osborne

**MEMBERS OF THE HOUSE OF LAITY OF
THE GENERAL SYNOD**
Mr Tim Allen
Mrs Margaret Condick
Mr Peter Smith
Mrs Catherine Wiltshire

DIOCESAN OFFICERS

Dioc Secretary Mr Nicholas Edgell, Diocesan Office, St Nicholas Centre, 4 Cutler St, Ipswich IP1 1UQ *Tel:* 01473 298500
Fax: 01473 298501
email: dbf@stedmundsbury.anglican.org
Chancellor of Diocese The Honourable Sir Justice Blofeld, 20–32 Museum St, Ipswich IP1 1HZ
Registrar of Diocese and Bishop's Legal Secretary Mr James Hall, 20–32 Museum St, Ipswich IP1 1HZ
Tel: 01473 232300
Fax: 01473 230524
email: james-hall@birketts.co.uk

DIOCESAN ORGANIZATIONS

Diocesan Office St Nicholas Centre, 4 Cutler St, Ipswich IP1 1UQ *Tel:* 01473 298500
Fax: 01473 298501
email: dbf@stedmundsbury.anglican.org

ADMINISTRATION

Dioc Secretary Mr Nicholas Edgell, Dioc Office
Deputy Dioc Secretary Miss Nicola Andrews, Dioc Office
Dioc Synod (Chairman, House of Clergy) Revd Chris Wingfield, Rectory, Glebe Close, Sproughton, Ipswich IP8 3BQ
(Chairman, House of Laity) Mrs Barbara Rowe, The Maltings, Honey Lane, Leavenheath, Colchester CO6 4NY *Tel:* 01206 262875
(Secretary) Mr Nicholas Edgell, Dioc Office
Board of Finance (Chairman) Mrs Jane Morelli
(Diocesan Secretary and Chief Executive) Mr Nicholas Edgell *(as above)*
Assistant Secretary Miss Nicola Andrews
Pastoral and DAC Secretary Mr James Halsall
Diocesan Accountant Mrs Katy Reade
Dioc Surveyor Mr Christopher Clarke, Clarke & Simpson, Well Close Square, Framlingham IP13 9DU *Tel:* 01728 724200
Board of Patronage Mr Nicholas Edgell *(as above)*
Pastoral Committee Mr Nicholas Edgell *(as above)*
Glebe and Investment Committee Mr Nicholas Edgell *(as above)*
Parsonages Committee Mr Nicholas Edgell *(as above)*
Designated Officer Mr James Hall *(as above)*

CHURCHES

Advisory Committee for the Care of Churches (Chairman) Mr Tim Allen, Bell House, Quay St, Orford, Woodbridge IP12 2NU *Tel:* 01394 450789
(Secretary) Mr James Halsall *(as above)*
Redundant Churches Uses Committee (Chairman) The Hon Jill Ganzoni, 3 Birch Close, Woodbridge IP12 4UA *Tel:* 01394 383528
(Secretary) Mr James Halsall *(as above)*

COUNSELLING

Adviser in Pastoral Care and Counselling Canon Harry Edwards, Rectory, Marlesford, Woodbridge IP13 0AT *Tel:* 01728 746747
email: Harry@psalm23.demon.co.uk

Bishop's Adviser on Exorcism and Deliverance The Bishop of Dunwich

MINISTRY

Accredited Ministry Group (Chairman) The Bishop of Dunwich *(as above)*
Vocations Adviser Vacancy
Dioc Director of Ordinands Canon Mark Sanders, Rectory, Woodbridge Rd, Grundisburgh, Woodbridge, IP13 6UF *Tel:* 01473 735182
Dioc Director of Continuing Ministerial Education 1–4 Canon Mark Sanders *(as above)*
Continuing Ministerial Education Officer Revd Chris Burdon
Principal of Dioc Ministry Scheme Ms Christine Amjad-Ali, Abbey House, 30 Angel Hill, Bury St Edmunds IP33 1LS *Tel:* 01284 749435
email: christine@stedmundsbury.anglican.org
Vice-Principal, Dioc Ministry Scheme Revd David Herrick, Abbey House, 30 Angel Hill, Bury St Edmunds IP33 1LS *Tel:* 01284 749435
email: davidh@stedmundsbury.anglican.org
Lay Education and Training Adviser Miss Elizabeth Moore, 7 Maltings Garth, Thurston, Bury St Edmunds IP31 3PP *Tel:* 01359 233050
email: elizabeth@stedmundsbury.anglican.org
Warden of Readers Canon Lionel Simpkins, St Augustine's Vicarage, 2 Bucklesham Rd, Ipswich IP3 8TJ *Tel:* 01473 728654
Dioc Youth Adviser Mr Gavin Stone, Dioc Office
Tel and Fax: 01473 298522
email: gavin@stedmundsbury.anglican.org
Dioc Children's Officer and Educational Officer of the Cathedral Mrs Helen Woodroffe, The Discovery Centre, St Edmundsbury Cathedral, Angel Hill, Bury St Edmunds IP33 1LS
Tel and Fax: 01284 748731
email: helen@discoveryc.fsnet.co.uk
Dioc Widows Officers Revd John and Mrs Helen Elliston, 27 Wyvern Rd, Ravenswood, Ipswich IP3 9TJ *Tel:* 01473 726617
Clergy Retirement Officer Canon Cedric Catton, 60 Sexton Meadows, Bury St Edmunds IP33 2SB
Tel: 01284 749429
email: moretee@vicar1.freeserve.co.uk

SCHOOLS

Dioc Director of Education and Schools Officer Ven John Cox, Dioc Office *Tel:* 01473 298570
Dioc Schools Adviser Mrs Helen Matter, Dioc Office

LITURGICAL

Chairman The Bishop of St Edmundsbury and Ipswich
Secretary Canon David Lowe, New Vicarage, 54 Princess Rd, Felixstowe IP11 7PL
Tel: 01394 284226

MISSION AND PUBLIC AFFAIRS

Bishop's Policy and Liaison Officer Canon Graham Hedger, Dioc Office *Tel:* 01473 277042
email: graham@stedmundsbury.anglican.org
Community Affairs Adviser Mrs Kathleen Ben Rabha, Dioc Office

Agricultural Chaplain Canon Sally Fogden, Meadow Farm, Sapiston, Bury St Edmunds IP31 1RX   *Tel:* 01359 268923
          email: sallyfogden@tiscali.co.uk
Tourism Officer Revd Margaret Blackall, 6 Orchard Place, Wickham Market, Woodbridge IP13 0RU
                              Tel: 01728 747326
Bishop's Ecumenical Adviser and Inter-Faith Adviser Canon Peter Mortimer, 20 Leggart Drive, Bramford, Ipswich IP8 4ET   *Tel:* 01473 747419
          email: revpeter@fish.co.uk
Chaplain to the Deaf Community Vacancy
Parish Resources Adviser Canon Jim Pendorf, Dioc Office   *Tel:* 01473 298504
          email: jim@stedmundsbury.anglican.org

COMMUNICATIONS

Dioc Communications Director Mr Nick Clarke, Dioc Office   *Tel:* 01473 298521
                              07779 780030 (Mobile)
          email: nick@stedmundsbury.anglican.org

DIOCESAN RECORD OFFICES

77 Raingate St, Bury St Edmunds IP33 2AR *Tel:* 01284 352352 Ext 2352 (*For parish records for Sudbury and Hadleigh deaneries*)
Gatacre Rd, Ipswich IP1 2LQ *Tel:* 01473 264541 (*For parish records for Ipswich and Suffolk archdeaconries*)
The Central Library, Lowestoft NR32 1DR *Tel:* 01502 405357 (*For parish records for NE Suffolk parishes*)

SPIRITUALITY

Dioc Spiritual Director for Cursillo Revd Martin Thrower, Rectory, Harrow Green, Lawshall, Bury St Edmunds IP29 4PB   *Tel:* 01284 830855
          email: martin.thrower@btinternet.com
Lay Director for Cursillo Ms Tracey Dove, 47 St Wendred's Way, Exning, Newmarket CB8 7HJ
                              Tel: 01638 610814
          email: t.dove1@ntlworld.com

RURAL DEANS
ARCHDEACONRY OF IPSWICH

Bosmere Revd Tim Hall, Rectory, The Street, Stonham Aspal, Stowmarket IP14 6AQ
                              Tel: 01449 711409
          email: tph@tesco.net
Colneys Canon Geoffrey Grant, Rectory, Nacton, Ipswich IP10 0HY   *Tel:* 01473 659232
          email: canon@nildram.co.uk
Hadleigh Revd Michael Tillett, Rectory, Straight Rd, Polstead Heath, Colchester CO6 5BB
                              Tel: 01787 210049
          email: revtillett@aol.com
Ipswich Revd Ian Morgan, Rectory, 74 Ancaster Rd, Ipswich IP2 9AJ   *Tel:* 01473 601895
          email: ianmorgan@aol.com

Samford Revd Chris Wingfield, Rectory, Glebe Close, Sproughton, Ipswich IP8 3BQ
                              Tel: 01473 241078
          email: chris.wingfield@btinternet.com
Stowmarket Revd Barbara Bilston, Boy's Hall, Ward Green, Old Newton, Stowmarket IP14 4EY
                              Tel: 01449 781253
          email: b.b.bilston@open.ac.uk
Woodbridge Revd Pauline Stentiford, Sheepstor, The Street, Boyton, Woodbridge IP12 3LH
                              Tel: 01394 411469
          email: pauline.stentiford@btopenworld.com

ARCHDEACONRY OF SUDBURY

Clare Revd Ian Finn, Vicarage, 10 Hopton Rise, Haverhill CB9 7FS   *Tel:* 01440 708768
          email: ian.finn1@btinternet.com
Ixworth Revd Ian Hooper, Vicarage, Church Hill, Pakenham, Bury St Edmunds IP31 2LN
                              Tel: 01359 230287
          email: hooper@pakvic.freeserve.co.uk
Lavenham Revd Martin Thrower, Rectory, Harrow Green, Lawshall, Bury St Edmunds CB9 7FS   *Tel:* 01284 830855
          email: martin.thrower@btinternet.com
Mildenhall Revd Stephen Mitchell, All Saints Vicarage, The Street, Gazeley, Newmarket CB8 8RB   *Tel:* 01638 552630
          email: smitch4517@aol.com
Sudbury Revd Robin King, Vicarage, Bures CO8 5AA   *Tel:* 01787 227315
          email: robin@ricking.freeserve.co.uk
Thingoe Revd Alan Gates, The Vicarage, Church Rd, Great Barton, Bury St Edmunds IP31 2QR
                              Tel: 01284 787274
          email: alan.gates@virgin.net

ARCHDEACONRY OF SUFFOLK

Beccles and South Elmham Revd Paul Nelson, Rectory, Molls Lane, Brampton, Beccles NR34 8DB   *Tel:* 01502 575859
          email: hedgeparson@tiscali.co.uk
Halesworth Revd Paul Nelson, Rectory, Molls Lane, Brampton, Beccles NR34 8DB
                              Tel: 01502 575859
          email: hedgeparson@tiscali.co.uk
Hartismere Revd Fiona Newton, The Vicarage, 15 Noyes Avenue, Laxfield, Woodbridge IP13 8EB
                              Tel: 01986 798266
          email: fionanewton@rmplc.co.uk
Hoxne Revd Fiona Newton, The Vicarage, 15 Noyes Avenue, Laxfield, Woodbridge IP13 8EB
                              Tel: 01986 798266
          email: fionanewton@rmplc.co.uk
Loes Revd Graham Owen, Rectory, Framlingham, Woodbridge IP13 9BJ
                              Tel: 01728 621082
          email: gowen.mowen@talktalk.net
Saxmundham Revd Nigel Hartley, Vicarage, Church Walk, Aldeburgh, Saxmundham IP15 5DU   *Tel:* 01728 452223
          email: nigel.hartley@btinternet.com

Founded in 1075, formerly Sherborne (AD 705) and Ramsbury (AD 909). Wiltshire, except for the northern quarter (BRISTOL); Dorset, except for an area in the east (WINCHESTER); a small area of Hampshire; a parish in Devon.

Population 881,000   Area 2,046 sq m
Full-time Stipendiary Parochial Clergy 191   Benefices 161
Parishes 456   Churches 574
www.salisbury.anglican.org
Overseas link provinces and dioceses: Episcopal Church of the Sudan, Evreux (France).

BISHOP (77th)
Rt Revd David Stancliffe, South Canonry, 71 The Close, Salisbury SP1 2ER [1993]
Tel: 01722 334031
Fax: 01722 413112
email: dsarum@salisbury.anglican.org
[David Sarum]

AREA BISHOPS
SHERBORNE Vacancy, Sherborne Office, Little Bailie, Dullar Lane, Sturminster Marshall, Wimborne BH21 4AD   *Tel:* 01258 857659
Fax: 01258 857961
email: sherborne.office@salisbury.anglican.org
RAMSBURY Rt Revd Stephen David Conway, Ramsbury Office, Southbroom House, London Rd, Devizes SN10 1LT [2006]   *Tel:* 01380 729808
Fax: 01380 848247
email: ramsbury.office@salisbury.anglican.org

HONORARY ASSISTANT BISHOPS
Rt Revd John Kingsmill Cavell, 143 The Close, Salisbury SP1 2EY [1988]   *Tel:* 01722 334782
Rt Revd John Dudley Galtrey Kirkham, Flamstone House, Flamstone St, Bishopstone, Salisbury SP5 4BZ [2001]   *Tel:* 01722 780221

CATHEDRAL CHURCH OF THE BLESSED VIRGIN MARY
Dean Very Revd June Osborne, The Deanery, 7 The Close, Salisbury SP1 2EF [2004]
Cathedral Office 6 The Close, Salisbury SP1 2EF
Tel: 01722 555110
Fax: 01722 555155
email: thedean@salcath.co.uk
Web: www.salisburycathedral.org.uk
Canons Residentiary
Precentor Canon Jeremy Davies, Hungerford Chantry, 54 The Close, Salisbury, SP1 2EL [1985]
Tel: 01722 555179 (Home)
Office Dept of Liturgy and Music, Ladywell, 33 The Close, Salisbury, SP1 2EJ   *Tel:* 01722 555125
Fax: 01722 555117
email: precentor@salcath.co.uk
Chancellor Canon Edward Probert, 24 The Close, Salisbury SP1 2EH [2004]   *Tel:* 01722 555193

Office: The Gatehouse, 2 The Close, Salisbury SP1 2EF
Tel: 01722 555189
Fax: 01722 555109
email: chancellor@salcath.co.uk
Treasurer Canon Mark Bonney, 23 The Close, Salisbury SP1 2EH [2004]   *Tel:* 01722 555177
Office: The Gatehouse (*as above*)   *Tel:* 01722 555186
Fax: 01722 555109
email: treasurer@salcath.co.uk
Vicar of the Close Revd Charles Mitchell-Innes, 32 The Close, Salisbury SP1 2EH   *Tel:* 01722 555192
email: voc@salcath.co.uk
Chapter Clerk Brigadier Mark Elcomb, Cathedral Office (*as above*)   *Tel:* 01722 555105
Fax: 01722 555109
email: chapterclerk@salcath.co.uk
Visitors Dept Mr David Coulthard, Ladywell, 33 The Close, Salisbury SP1 2EJ   *Tel:* 01722 555120
Fax: 01722 555116
email: d.coulthard@salcath.co.uk
Education Centre Mrs Susan Hayter (*Administrator*), Wren Hall, 56c The Close, Salisbury SP1 2EL   *Tel:* 01722 555180
email: wrenhall@salcath.co.uk
Director of Music Mr David Halls, Dept of Liturgy and Music (*as above*)   *Tel:* 01722 555127
email: d.halls@salcath.co.uk

ARCHDEACONS
SHERBORNE Ven Paul Taylor, Aldhelm House, West Stafford, Dorchester DT2 8AB [2004]
Tel: 01305 269751
email: adsherborne@salisbury.anglican.org
DORSET Ven Alistair Magowan, Little Bailie, Dullar Lane, Sturminster Marshall, Wimborne BH21 4AD [2000]   *Tel:* 01258 857659
email: addorset@salisbury.anglican.org
WILTS Ven John Wraw, Southbroom House, London Rd, Devizes SN10 1LT [2004]
Tel: 01380 729808
Fax: 01380 848247
email: adwilts@salisbury.anglican.org
SARUM Ven Alan Jeans, Herbert House, 118 Lower Rd, Lower Bemerton, Salisbury SP2 9NW [2003]
Tel: 01380 729808
Fax: 01380 828247
email: adsarum@salisbury.anglican.org

CONVOCATION (MEMBERS OF THE HOUSE OF CLERGY OF THE GENERAL SYNOD)
Proctors for Clergy
Revd Maureen Allchin
Canon Mark Bonney
Canon Nigel LLoyd
Ven Alistair Magowan
Revd Christopher Strain

MEMBERS OF THE HOUSE OF LAITY OF THE GENERAL SYNOD
Mr Paul Boyd-Lee
Mr Michael Burbeck
Mr James Humphery
Mr David Jones
Mr Robert Key
Mr Hugh Privett

DIOCESAN OFFICERS
Dioc Secretary Mrs Lucinda Herklots, Church House, Crane St, Salisbury SP1 2QB
Tel: 01722 411922
Fax: 01722 411990
Chancellor of Diocese His Honour Judge Samuel Wiggs, c/o Dioc Office
Registrar of Diocese and Bishop's Legal Secretary Mr Andrew Johnson, Minster Chambers, 42–44 Castle St, Salisbury SP1 3TX
Tel: 01722 411141
Fax: 01722 411566

DIOCESAN ORGANIZATIONS
Diocesan Office Church House, Crane St, Salisbury SP1 2QB
Tel: 01722 411922
Fax: 01722 411990
email: enquiries@salisbury.anglican.org
Web: www.salisbury.anglican.org

ADMINISTRATION
Dioc Secretary Mrs Lucinda Herklots, Dioc Office
Deputy Dioc Secretaries Mr Chris Dragonetti (*Finance*) and Mr Richard Trahair (*Property*), Dioc Office
Dioc Synod (*Chairman, House of Clergy*) Canon Paul Richardson, Vicarage, Bitham Lane, Westbury BA13 3BU
Tel: 01373 822209
(*Chairman, House of Laity*) Mr Richard Southwell, Manor House, Upton Lovell, Warminster BA12 0JW
Tel: 01985 850252
(*Secretary*) Mrs Lucinda Herklots, Dioc Office
Stewardship and Resources Officer Mr Geoff Taylor, Dioc Office
Board of Finance (*Chairman*) Mr Gil Williams, Princes Farm, Ryme Intrinseca, Sherborne DT9 6JX
Tel: 01935 873580
(*Secretary*) Mrs Lucinda Herklots, Dioc Office
Diocesan Surveyor Mr John Carley, Dioc Office
Tel: 01722 411933
Pastoral Committee (*Secretary*) Mrs Christine Romano, Dioc Office
Designated Officer Mr Andrew Johnson, Minster Chambers, 42–44 Castle St, Salisbury SP1 3TX
Tel: 01722 411141

CHURCHES
Advisory Committee for the Care of Churches (*Chairman*) Cathedral Treasurer; (*Secretary*) Mrs Sue Cannings, Dioc Office
Tel: 01722 438654
Re-Use of Closed Churches Working Group and Furnishings Officer Mr Richard Trahair (*as above*)
Tel: 01722 411933
Ringers' Association Mr Anthony Lovell-Wood, 11 Brook Close, Tisbury, Salisbury
Tel: 01747 871121

EDUCATION
Director of Education Mr Chris Shepperd, Diocesan Education Centre, Devizes Rd, Salisbury SP2 9LY
Tel: 01722 428420
Fax: 01722 328010
Finance Mr Peter Kidman (*same address*)
Tel: 01722 428421
Buildings Officer Mr Simon Franklin (*same address*)
Tel: 01722 428426
Advisers for School Development Mrs Gill Hunter, Mrs Carole McCormack (*same address*)
Youth and Children's Officers Youth and Children's Ministry Team (*same address*)
Tel: 01722 428427

MINISTRY
Director of Learning for Discipleship and Ministry Canon Jane Charman, Dioc Office
Tel: 01722 411944
email: ministry@salisbury.anglican.org
Co-ordinator for Vocations and Spirituality, Revd Ian Cowley, Dioc Office
Director of Ordinands Ven Alan Jeans, Dioc Office
Co-ordinator for Learning for Discipleship Revd David Heslop, Dioc Office
Co-ordinator of Locally Deployable Ordained Ministry Revd Paul Overend, Dioc Office
Adviser for Women's Ministry Revd Vanda Rowe
Tel: 01672 851746

AREA RESOURCE TEAMS
Liturgical Canon Mark Bonney, Loders, 23 The Close, Salisbury SP1 2EH
Tel: 01722 444177
Social Responsibility (*Wilts.*) Centre for Faith and Action in Society (CeFAS), Sarum College, 19 The Close, Salisbury SP1 2EE *Tel:* 01722 424838;
(*Dorset*) (*also Ecumenical*) Mr Colin Brady, 23 Bagber Farm Cottages, Milton Rd, Milborne St Andrew, Blandford Forum DT11 0LB *Tel:* 01258 839140
Ecumenical Officer Revd Pamela Walker, Rectory, 32 Wareham Rd, Corfe Mullen, Wimborne BH21 3LE
Tel: 01202 692129
County Ecumenical Officer (*Wiltshire*) Revd Morris Munns, 101 St Mark's Ave, Salisbury SP1 3DW
Tel: 01722 328686
(*Dorset*) Mrs Val Potter, 22 Durbeville Close, Dorchester DT1 2JT
Tel: 01305 264416
Urban Priority Officer Revd Dick Saunders, St Philip's Vicarage, 41 Moores Ave, Kinson, Bournemouth BH11 8AT
Tel: 01202 581135

Officers for Rural Areas (*Ramsbury Episcopal Area*)
Revd Jim Scott, 14 Bremhill, Calne SN11 9LA
Tel: 01249 813114
(*Sherborne Episcopal Area*) (*also Dioc Environmental
Officer*) Revd Dr Jean Coates, Rectory, Main St,
Broadmayne, Dorchester CT2 8EB
Tel: 01305 852435
Interfaith Officer Dr Peter Willey, 17 Fairfield,
Upavon, Pewsey SN9 6DZ   *Tel:* 01980 630512
European Affairs Officer Canon Richard Franklin,
Holy Trinity Vicarage, 7 Glebe Close, Weymouth,
DT44 9RL   *Tel:* 01305 760354
Chaplain to Travelling People Revd Roger Redding,
Vicarage, Ebbesbourne Wake, Salisbury SP5 5JL
Tel: 01722 780408
International Development and World Mission
Canon Ian Woodward, Vicarage, West St, Bere
Regis, Wareham BH20 7HQ   *Tel:* 01929 471262

PRESS AND PUBLICATIONS
Communications Coordinator Mr Michael Ford,
Dioc Office   *Tel:* 01722 438650
email: comms@salisbury.anglican.org
Editor of 'The Sarum Link' Mrs Nicky Davies, Dioc
Office   *Tel:* 01722 438652
Editor of Dioc Directory Mrs Miriam Darke, Dioc
Office   *Tel:* 01722 411922
Editor of Dioc Handbook Dioc Secretary (*as above*)

DIOCESAN RECORD OFFICES
Diocesan Record Office and Wiltshire Parochial
Records, Wiltshire and Swindon History
Centre, Cocklebury Rd, Chippenham SN15 3QN
Tel: 01249 705500 and ask for the Duty Archivist
(*For diocesan records and parishes in the arch-
deaconries of Wiltshire and Sarum*)
Dorset History Centre, Bridport Rd, Dorchester
DT1 1RP *County Archivist* Mr Hugh Jacques
Tel: 01305 250550 (*For parishes in the County of
Dorset*)
County Record Office, 20 Southgate St, Win-
chester SO23 9EF *County Archivist* Ms Jan Smith
Tel: 01962 846154 (*For the few Salisbury diocesan
parishes situated in the County of Hampshire*)

RURAL DEANS
ARCHDEACONRY OF SHERBORNE
Dorchester Canon Karen Curnock, Vicarage, 4
Back Lane, Cerne Abbas, Dorchester DT2 7JW
Tel: 01300 341251
Lyme Bay Canon Trevor Stubbs, Rectory, 84
South St, Bridport DT6 3NW   *Tel:* 01308 422138

Sherborne Canon Henry Pearson, Rectory, Trent,
Sherborne DT9 4SL   *Tel:* 01935 851049
Weymouth Canon Richard Franklin, Holy Trinity
Vicarage, 7 Glebe Close, Weymouth DT4 9RL
Tel: 01305 760354

ARCHDEACONRY OF DORSET
Blackmore Vale Revd David Seymour, Vicarage,
Church St, Sturminster, Newton DT10 1DB
Tel: 01258 471276
Milton and Blandford Revd Simon Everett,
Vicarage, Iwerne Minster, Blandford Forum
DT11 8NF   *Tel:* 01747 811291
Poole Revd Nigel LLoyd, Rectory, 19 Springfield
Rd, Parkstone, Poole BH14 0LG
Tel: 01202 748860
Purbeck Revd John Wood, Rectory, 12 Church
Hill, Swanage BH19 1HU   *Tel:* 01929 422916
Wimborne Revd John Holbrook, Rectory, 17 King
St, Wimborne BH21 1DZ   *Tel:* 01202 882340

ARCHDEACONRY OF SARUM
Alderbury Revd Vanda Rowe, Rectory, High St,
Porton, Salisbury SP4 0LH   *Tel:* 01980 610305
Chalke Canon David Henley, Rectory, Broad
Chalke, Salisbury SP5 5DS   *Tel:* 01722 780262
Salisbury Revd David Linaker, Little Bower,
Campbell Rd, Salisbury SP1 3BG
Tel: 01722 322537
Stonehenge Canon Simon Wilkinson, Vicarage,
Church St, Amesbury, Salisbury SP4 7EU
Tel: 01980 623145

ARCHDEACONRY OF WILTS
Bradford Revd Derek Smith, Rectory, Canon
Square, Melksham SN12 6LX   *Tel:* 01225 703262
Calne Revd Thomas Woodhouse, Vicarage, Glebe
Rd, Wootton Bassett SN4 7DU
Tel: 01793 854302
Devizes Revd Sallyanne Attwater, Vicarage, The
Street, Bishop's Cannings, Devizes SN10 2LD
Tel: 01380 860650
Heytesbury Revd John Tomlinson, Rectory, 1
Bests Lane, Sutton Veny, Warminster BA12 7AU
Tel: 01985 840014
Marlborough Vacancy
Pewsey Revd Nicolas Leigh-Hunt, Vicarage, 5
Eastcourt, Burbage, Marlborough SN8 3AG
Tel: 01672 810258

DIOCESE OF SHEFFIELD

Founded in 1914. Sheffield; Rotherham; Doncaster, except for a few parishes in the south-east (SOUTHWELL AND NOTTINGHAM); an area of North Lincolnshire; an area of south-eastern Barnsley; a small area of the East Riding of Yorkshire.

Population 1,189,000   Area 576 sq m
Full-time Stipendiary Parochial Clergy 147   Benefices 152
Parishes 173   Churches 218
www.sheffield-diocese.org.uk
Overseas link dioceses: Argentina, Hattingen Witten (Germany).

BISHOP
Vacancy in See
Bishopscroft, Snaithing Lane, Sheffield S10 3LG
Tel: 0114 230 2170
Fax: 0114 263 0110
email: bishop@sheffield.anglican.org
Domestic Chaplain Revd Canon Geoffrey Harbord, Bishopscroft   Tel: 0114 230 2170
Fax: 0114 263 0110
email: geoffrey.harbord@sheffield.anglican.org

SUFFRAGAN BISHOP
DONCASTER Rt Revd Cyril Ashton, 3 Farrington Court, Wickersley, Rotherham S66 1JQ [1999]
Tel: 01709 730130
Fax: 01709 730230
email: Cyril.Ashton@virgin.net

HONORARY ASSISTANT BISHOPS
Rt Revd David Marrison Hallatt, 1 Merbeck Grove, High Green, Sheffield S35 4HE [2002]
Tel: 0114 284 4440
email: david.hallatt@sheffield.anglican.org
Rt Revd Kenneth Harold Pillar, 75 Dobcroft Rd, Millhouses, Sheffield S7 2LS [1989]
Tel: 0114 236 7902
Rt Revd Martyn William Jarrett, 3 North Lane, Roundhay, Leeds LS8 2QJ [2002]
Tel: 0113 265 4280
Fax: 0113 265 4281
email: bishop-of-beverley@
3-north-lane.fsnet.co.uk

CATHEDRAL CHURCH OF ST PETER AND ST PAUL
Dean Very Revd Peter Bradley, The Cathedral, Church St, Sheffield S1 1HA   Tel: 0114 263 6063
email: dean@sheffield-cathedral.org.uk
Cathedral Office Sheffield Cathedral, Church St, Sheffield S1 1HA   Tel: 0114 275 3434
Fax: 0114 279 7412
email: enquiries@sheffield-cathedral.org.uk
Web: www.sheffield-cathedral.org.uk
Canons Residentiary
Vice-Dean Canon Paul Shackerley, The Cathedral [2002]   Tel: 0114 263 6066
email:
paul.shackerley@sheffield-cathedral.org.uk

Precentor Canon Simon Cowling, The Cathedral [2007]   Tel: 0114 263 6065
email: precentor@sheffield-cathedral.org.uk
Dioc Director of Ordinands Canon Dr Joanne Grenfell, The Cathedral [2006]
Tel: 0114 263 6064
email: joanne.grenfell@sheffield-cathedral.org.uk
CAP Project Manager Revd Tim Renshaw, The Cathedral   Tel: 0114 263 6974
email: CBAOffice@sheffield-cathedral.org.uk
Canon Residentiary and Anglican Chaplain to the University of Sheffield Canon Will Lamb [2007]
Tel: 0114 222 8923
email: w.lamb@sheffield.ac.uk
Cathedral Administrator Vacancy
Tel: 0114 275 3434
email: bob.rabagliati@sheffield-cathedral.org.uk
Master of the Music Mr Neil Taylor, The Cathedral   Tel: 0114 263 6069
email: musicians@sheffield-cathedral.org.uk
Asst Master of Music Mr Anthony Gowing, The Cathedral   Tel: 0114 263 6070
email: musicians@sheffield-cathedral.org.uk

ARCHDEACONS
SHEFFIELD AND ROTHERHAM Ven Richard Blackburn, 34 Wilson Rd, Sheffield S11 8RN [1999]
Tel: 0114 266 6099
Fax: 0114 267 9782
email: archdeacons.office@sheffield.anglican.org
Office Diocesan Church House, 95–99 Effingham St, Rotherham S65 1BL
DONCASTER Ven Robert Fitzharris, Fairview House, 14 Armthorpe Lane, Doncaster DN2 5LZ [2001]   Tel: 01302 325787
Fax: 01302 760493
email: archdeacons.office@sheffield.anglican.org
Office Diocesan Church House (as above)

CONVOCATION (MEMBERS OF THE HOUSE OF CLERGY OF THE GENERAL SYNOD)
Proctors for Clergy
Revd Canon Simon Bessant
Revd Canon Geoffrey Harbord
Revd Matthew Porter
Revd Mike Wagstaff
Revd Lydia Wells

MEMBERS OF THE HOUSE OF LAITY OF THE GENERAL SYNOD
Dr Jacqueline Butcher
Canon Elizabeth Paver
Mr Jonathan Redden

DIOCESAN OFFICERS
Dioc Secretary Mr Malcolm Fair, Diocesan Church House, 95–99 Effingham St, Rotherham S65 1BL   *Tel:* 01709 309117
Fax: 01709 512550
email: malcolm.fair@sheffield.anglican.org
Chancellor of Diocese Worshipful David McClean, 6 Burnt Stones Close, Sheffield S10 5TS
Tel: 0114 230 5794
email: jdmc.clean@sheffield.ac.uk
Registrar of Diocese and Bishop's Legal Secretary Mr Andrew Vidler, Wake Smith and Tofields, 68 Clarkehouse Road, Sheffield S10 2LJ
Tel: 0114 266 6660
email: andrew.vidler@wake-smith.com

DIOCESAN ORGANIZATIONS
Diocesan Office Diocesan Church House, 95–99 Effingham St, Rotherham S65 1BL
Tel: 01709 309100
Fax: 01709 512550
email: reception@sheffield.anglican.org
Web: www.sheffield.anglican.org

ADMINISTRATION
Dioc Secretary Mr Malcolm Fair, Dioc Office
Tel: 01709 309117
Deputy Secretary/Finance Officer Mr Roger Pinchbeck, Dioc Office   *Tel:* 01709 309142
Property Manager Mr Paul Beckett, Dioc Office
Tel: 01709 309115
Board of Finance (Chairman) Lay Canon Sandra Newton, 50 Broomgrove Rd, Sheffield S10 2NA
Tel: 0114 266 1079
Pastoral Committee (Chairman) Rt Revd David Hallatt, 1 Merbeck Grove, High Green, Sheffield S35 4HE   *Tel:* 0114 284 4440
(Secretary) Mr Charles Jarman, Dioc Office
Tel: 01709 309150
Redundant Churches Uses Committee (Chairman) Ven Richard Blackburn *(as above)*
(Secretary) Mr Paul Beckett *(as above)*
Parsonages Committee (Chairman) Ven Robert Fitzharris *(as above)*
(Secretary) Mr Paul Beckett *(as above)*
Board of Patronages (Chairman) Prof David McClean, 6 Burnt Stones Close, Sheffield S10 5TS
Tel: 0114 230 5794
(Secretary) Mr Tony Beck, 21 Osborne Drive, Todwick, Sheffield S26 1HW   *Tel:* 01909 770 802
DAC Chairman Revd Canon Peter Ingram, The Vicarage, 80 Millhouses Lane, Sheffield S7 2HB
Tel: 0114 236 2838
DAC Secretary Mr Graham Williams, Dioc Office
01709 309 121
Administration Manager Mr Charles Jarman, Dioc Office   01709 309 150

Designated Officer Revd Canon Geoffrey Harbord, Bishopscroft, Snaithing Lane, Sheffield S10 3LG
Tel: 0114 230 2170
Fax: 0114 263 0110
email: geoffrey@bishopofsheffield.org.uk
Communications Officer The Revd Rob Marshall, Media 33, 5 Brampton Court, Brough HU15 1DZ
Tel: 0845 610 6420
email: rob@media33.co.uk

DIOCESAN SYNOD
(Chairman, House of Clergy) Canon Gordon Taylor, Vicarage, 2 Sunderland St, Tickhill, Doncaster DN11 9QJ   *Tel:* 01302 742224
(Chairman, House of Laity) Canon Elizabeth Paver, 113 Warning Tongue Lane, Bessacarr, Doncaster DN4 6TB   *Tel:* 01302 530706
(Secretary) Mr Malcolm Fair *(as above)*

CHURCHES
Advisory Committee for the Care of Churches (Chairman) Canon Peter Ingram, Holy Trinity Vicarage, 80 Millhouses Rd, Sheffield S7 2LL
Tel and Fax: 0114 236 2838
(Secretary) Mr Graham Williams, Dioc Office
Tel: 01709 309120

EDUCATION
Dioc Board of Education (Chairman) Ven Robert Fitzharris *(as above)*; *(Secretary)* Miss Heather Morris BEd Hons MSc, Dioc Office
Tel: 01709 309124
Director of Education Miss Heather Morris BEd Hons MSc, Dioc Office
RE and Worship Adviser Vacancy, Dioc Office
Tel: 01709 309125

TOURISM
Officer Vacancy

BOARD OF MINISTRY AND MISSION
Board of Ministry (Chairman) The Bishop of Doncaster; *(Secretary)* Canon Dr John Thomson, Dioc Office   *Tel:* 01709 309143
Director of Ministry Canon Dr John Thomson, Dioc Office
Director of Ordinands Canon Dr Joanne Grenfell, The Cathedral Church of St Peter and St Paul, Church St, Sheffield S1 1HA   *Tel:* 0114 275 3434
Youth Outreach Officer Vacancy
Tel: 01709 309146
Children's and Youth Officer Mrs Jennie Lambourne, Dioc Office   *Tel:* 01709 309144
Director of IME4-7 Revd Matthew Porter, St Chad's Vicarage, 9 Linden Avenue, Sheffield S8 0GA   *Tel:* 0114 274 5086
Asst POT Officers Revd Lydia Wells, The Vicarage, Kingston Rd, Intake, Doncaster DN2 6LS *(SMs)*
Tel: 01302 343 119
Revd Gary Schofield, The Vicarage, Manor Rd, Wales, Sheffield S26 5PD *(SMs)*
Tel: 01909 771 111

Revd Jan Foden, The Vicarage, Stainforth Rd, Barnby Dun, Doncaster DN3 1AA (NSM)
Tel: 01302 882 835
Discipline Development Officer Revd Alan Isaacson, The Rectory, High Bradfield, Sheffield S6 6LG
Tel: 0114 285 1225
Diocesan Missioner Co-ordinator Revd Ian Smith, St Paul's Vicarage, Wheata Rd, Sheffield S5 9FP
Tel: 0114 246 8494
Bishop's Adviser on Women in Ministry Canon Dr Joanne Grenfell, The Cathedral Church of St Peter and St Paul, Church St, Sheffield S1 1HA
Tel: 0114 275 3434
Bishop's Adviser on Parish Development Revd Richard Impey, The Vicarage, The Wheel, Ecclesfield, Sheffield S35 9BZ *Tel:* 0114 257 0002
Bishop's Adviser on Music and Worship Revd Helen Bent, The Vicarage, 61 Whitehill Lane, Brinsworth, Rotherham S60 5JR
Tel: 01709 363 850
Bishop's Adviser on Spirituality and Chaplain of Whirlow Grange Conference Centre Revd Nick Helm, Whirlow Grange Conference Centre, Ecclesall Rd South, Sheffield S11 9PZ
Tel: 0114 235 3704
Bishop's Adviser on Non-Stipendiary Ministry Vacancy
Bishop's Adviser on Church Army Ministry Vacancy
Warden of Readers Revd John Richards
Readers' Board (Secretary) Mr Stuart Carey, Corben House, 3 Station Rd, Hatfield, Doncaster DN7 6PQ *Tel:* Tel: 01302 844936
Diocesan Missioner Vacancy
Ecumenical Officer Canon Nicholas Jowett, Shirley House, 31 Psalter Lane, Sheffield S11 8YL
Tel: 0114 258 6550

PRESS AND PUBLICATIONS

Director of Communications Revd Rob Marshall, 33rpm public relations, 5 Brampton Court, Brough HU15 1DZ *Tel:* 0845 610 6420
Fax: 0870 286 3348
email: rob@media.33.co.uk
Editor of Dioc News Extra Revd Rob Marshall (*as above*)
Editor of Dioc Directory Mr Charles Jarman, Dioc Office *Tel:* 01709 309150

DIOCESAN RECORD OFFICES

Sheffield City Archives, 52 Shoreham St, Sheffield S1 4SP *Tel:* 0114 273 4756
(*For parishes in the archdeaconry of Sheffield*)
Doncaster Archives, King Edward Rd, Balby, Doncaster DN4 0NA *Tel:* 01302 859811
(*For parishes in the archdeaconry of Doncaster*)

FAITH AND JUSTICE

Board of Faith and Justice Revd Lydia Wells, Vicarage, Kingston Rd, Intake, Doncaster DN2 6LS *Tel:* 01302 343119
Secretary Vacancy *Tel:* 01709 309136
Social Responsibility Officer Vacancy

South Yorkshire Workplace Chaplaincy Capt Christopher Chesters CA, 9 The Copse, Bramley, Rotherham S66 0TP *Tel:* 0114 275 5865 (daytime)
01709 548867 (evening)
Fax: 0114 272 6767
Office South Yorkshire Workplace Chaplaincy, Cemetery Rd Baptist Church, Napier St Entrance, Sheffield S11 8HA *Tel:* 0114 275 5865
Bishop's Adviser on Black Concerns Mrs Carmen Franklin *Tel:* 0114 245 7160
Bishop's Representative for Child Protection Ms Sue Booth *Tel:* 0113 275 5266
Bishop's Rural Adviser Revd Keith Hale, Tankersley Rectory, 9 Chapel Road, Pilley, Barnsley S75 3AR *Tel:* 01226 744140
European Link Officer Ven Robert Fitzharris, (*Archdeacon of Doncaster*), Dioc Office

STEWARDSHIP

Christian Giving Director Mr Nicholas Hutton, Dioc Office *Tel:* 01709 309151

AREA DEANS
ARCHDEACONRY OF SHEFFIELD

Attercliffe Revd Steve Willett, Vicarage, 63 Sheffield Rd, Sheffield S12 4LR
Tel: 0114 248 4486
Ecclesall Canon Peter Ingram, Vicarage, 80 Millhouses Lane, Sheffield S7 2HB
Tel: 0114 236 2838
Ecclesfield Revd Martyn Snow, Vicarage, 257 Pitsmoor Rd, Sheffield S3 9AQ
Tel: 0114 272 7756
Hallam Revd Phillip Townsend, St Timothy's Vicarage, 152 Slinn St, Sheffield S10 1NZ
Tel: 0114 266 1745
Laughton Revd Jane Bolton, The Rectory, 217 Nursery Road, Dinnington, Sheffield S25 2QU
Tel: 01909 562 335
Rotherham Canon David Bliss, 51 Hallam Rd, Moorgate, Rotherham S60 3ED
Tel: 01709 364 341

ARCHDEACONRY OF DONCASTER

Adwick-le-Street Revd Mark Wigglesworth, Vicarage, Church St, Askern, Doncaster DN6 0PH *Tel:* 01302 700404
Doncaster Canon John Willett, St Wilfrid's Vicarage, Cantley Lane, Cantley, Doncaster DN4 6PA *Tel:* 01302 535133
Hickleton Revd Richard Parker, 104 Hawshaw Lane, Hoyland, Barnsley S74 0HH
Tel: 01226 749 231
Snaith and Hatfield Canon Cyril Roberts, The Orchard, Pontefract Rd, Snaith, Goole DN14 9JS
Tel: 01405 860866
Tankersley Revd Keith Hale, Tankersley Rectory, 9 Chapel Rd, Pilley, Barnsley S75 3AR
Tel: 01226 744 140
Wath Revd Nigel Elliott, Vicarage, Highthorne Rd, Kilnhurst, Mexborough S64 5UU
Tel: 01709 589674
West Doncaster Revd Brian Inston, The Vicarage, 6 Greenfield Lane, Balby, Doncaster DN4 0PY
Tel: 01302 853 278

DIOCESE OF SODOR AND MAN

Founded in 447. The Isle of Man.

Population 80,000   Area 221 sq m
Full-time Stipendiary Parochial Clergy 16   Benefices 28
Parishes 27   Churches 45
Overseas link dioceses: North Mbale (Uganda), EKD Bochum.

BISHOP
The Rt Revd Robert M. Paterson, Thie Yn Aspick, The Falls, Tromode Rd, Douglas, Isle of Man IM4 4PZ [2008]   *Tel:* 01624 622108
Fax: 01624 672890
email: bishop-sodor@mcb.net
[Robert Sodor and Man]
Domestic Chaplain Revd Geoffrey Breffitt, Kirk Patrick Vicarage, Near Peel, Isle of Man IM5 3AW   *Tel:* 01624 842637

CATHEDRAL CHURCH OF ST GERMAN, PEEL
Dean The Bishop
Canons
Canon Duncan Whitworth, St Matthew's Vicarage, Alexander Drive, Douglas, Isle of Man IM2 3QN [1996]   *Tel:* 01624 676310
Canon David Green, Vicarage, Maughold, Isle of Man IM7 1AS [2005]   *Tel:* 01624 812070
Canon Philip Frear, Vicarage, Saddle Rd, Braddan, Isle of Man IM4 4LB [2005]
Tel: 01624 675523
Canon Malcolm Convery, Vicarage, Church Rd, Onchan, Isle of Man IM3 1BF [1999]
Tel: 01624 675797
Chapter Clerk Canon Malcolm Convery (*as above*)

ARCHDEACON
ISLE OF MAN Ven Brian Smith, St George's Vicarage, 16 Devonshire Rd, Douglas, Isle of Man IM2 3RB [2005]   *Tel:* 01624 675430
email: archd-sodor@mcb.net

MANX CONVOCATION
(*Secretary*) Revd David Greenwood, St Paul's Vicarage, Walpole Drive, Ramsey, Isle of Man IM8 1NA   *Tel:* 01624 812275

CONVOCATION (MEMBERS OF THE HOUSE OF CLERGY OF THE GENERAL SYNOD)
Proctor for the Clergy
Vacancy

MEMBER OF THE HOUSE OF LAITY OF THE GENERAL SYNOD
Mrs Jacqueline Frear

DIOCESAN OFFICERS
Dioc Synod Secretary Mr Duncan Robertson
email: minsec-sodor@mcb.net
Vicar-General and Chancellor of Diocese The Worshipful Clare Faulds, 4 Finch Rd, Douglas, Isle of Man IM1 2PT   *Tel:* 01624 676868
Registrar of Diocese and Bishop's Legal Secretary Mr Jonathon D. R. Kewley, First Floor, 5 Parliament Square, Castletown, Isle of Man IM9 1LA
Tel: 01624 824665
email: castletown@manx.net
Dioc Architect Mr Guy Thompson, The Old Paint Shop, Athol St, Port St Mary, Isle of Man
Tel: 01624 835510
Fax: 01624 835521

CHURCH COMMISSIONERS FOR THE ISLE OF MAN
The Lord Bishop
The Archdeacon of Man
Mr P. Cowell
Mr W. H. Dawson
Mrs S. Ellis
Mrs J. Frear
Revd David Greenwood
Revd Michael Roberts
Revd Canon Duncan Whitworth
(*Secretary*) Mr Duncan Robertson (*as above*)

DIOCESAN ORGANIZATIONS
Diocesan Synod Office
email: minsec-sodor@mcb.net

ADMINISTRATION
Dioc Synod (*Chairman, House of Clergy*) Canon David Green, Vicarage, Maughold, Isle of Man IM7 1AS   *Tel:* 01624 812070
(*Chairman, House of Laity*) Mr Jonathan Kewley, 30 Arbory St, Castletown, Isle of Man
Tel: 01624 824734
(*Secretary*)
Board of Finance (*Chairman*) Ven Brian Smith (*as above*)
(*Secretary*) Mr Duncan Robertson, Materials Testing Laboratory, 2 North Shore Rd, Ramsey, Isle of Man IM8 3DF
Designated Officer Vacancy

CHURCHES
Advisory Committee for the Care of Churches (*Secretary*) Mr Duncan Robertson

Council of Church Music (*Secretary*) Miss Phyllis Christian, 12 Western Ave, Douglas, Isle of Man IM1 4ER　　　　　　　　*Tel:* 01624 672433

EDUCATION

Council for Education (*Chairman*) Revd Ian Davies, Vicarage, Main Rd, Crosby, Isle of Man IM4 4BH *Tel:* 01624 851378 (*Secretary*) Mrs Ruth Smart, 8 Manor Drive, Farmhill, Douglas, Isle of Man IM2 2PA　　　　　　　　*Tel:* 01624 673585
Director of Diocesan Institute Revd Peter Upton Jones, St Bridget's Rectory, Kirk Bride, Ramsey, Isle of Man IM7 4AT　　　*Tel:* 01624 880351
Bishop's Youth Officer Vacancy
Dioc Adviser for Children's Work Vacancy
Adult Education Revd Michael Roberts, Malew Vicarage, St Mark's Rd, Ballasalla, Isle of Man IM9 3EF　　　　　　　　*Tel:* 01624 822469

MINISTRY

Dioc Director of Ordinands Canon David Green (*as above*)
Council for Health and Healing (*Bishop's Adviser*) Canon David Green (*as above*)
Readers' Board (*Warden*) Revd John Gulland, Anchor House, Queen's Rd, Port St Mary, Isle of Man IM9 5ES　　　*Tel:* 01624 834548
(*Secretary*) Mr Harry Dawson, Thalloo Reagh, Cregneash, Isle of Man IM9 5PS
　　　　　　　　Tel: 01624 835770

LITURGICAL

Bishop's Adviser Canon David Green (*as above*)

MISSIONARY AND ECUMENICAL

Council for Mission (*Secretary*) Mrs Anne Kean, 14 Barrule Park, Ramsey, Isle of Man IM8 2BN
　　　　　　　　Tel: 01624 813984
Ecumenical Officer Vacancy

ACORA Officer Mr Alan Matthews, Crosh Yvor, Ballachrink Crossing, Ballasalla, Isle of Man IM9 2AD　　　　　　　　*Tel:* 01624 822432

PRESS AND PUBLICATIONS

Communications Officer Vacancy
Editor of the Dioc Newspaper Mr Duncan Robertson, Eskdale, Bowring Rd, Ramsey, Isle of Man IM8 3EN　　　　　*Tel:* 01624 817885
　　　　　email: minsec-sodor@mcb.net
Editor of Dioc Directory Bishop's Office (*as above*)

DIOCESAN RECORD OFFICE

Further information can be obtained from the Manx Museum Library, Kingswood Grove, Douglas, Isle of Man IM1 3LY *Archivist* Miss Wendy Thirkettle　　　　*Tel:* 01624 64800

SOCIAL RESPONSIBILITY

Representative Revd Cyril Rogers, Rectory, Ballaugh, Isle of Man IM7 5AQ
　　　　　　　　Tel: 01624 897873
Child Protection Adviser Mr Eric Quirk, 4 Cronk Drive, Union Mills, Isle of Man IM4 4NG
　　　　　　　　Tel: 01624 851660

STEWARDSHIP

Christian Stewardship Adviser Revd John Guilford, Strathallan Rd, Douglas, Isle of Man IM2 4PN　　　　　*Tel:* 01624 672001

RURAL DEANS

Castletown and Peel Revd Canon Peter Robinson, Arbory Vicarage, Ballabeg, Isle of Man IM9 4LG
　　　　　　　　Tel: 01624 823595
Douglas Canon Duncan Whitworth, St Matthew's Vicarage, Alexander Drive, Douglas, Isle of Man IM2 3QN　　*Tel:* 01624 676310
Ramsey Canon David Green (*as above*)

DIOCESE OF SOUTHWARK

Founded in 1905. Greater London south of the Thames, except for most of the London Boroughs of Bromley and Bexley (ROCHESTER), and a few parishes in the south-west (GUILDFORD); the eastern third of Surrey.

Population 2,495,000   Area 317 sq m
Full-time Stipendiary Parochial Clergy 324   Benefices 270
Parishes 293   Churches 365
www.southwark.anglican.org
Overseas link dioceses: Manicaland, Central Zimbabwe, Matabeleland (Zimbabwe).

BISHOP (9th)
Rt Revd Dr Thomas Frederick Butler, Bishop's House, 38 Tooting Bec Gardens, London SW16 1QZ [1998]   *Tel:* 020 8769 3256
Fax: 020 8769 4126
email: bishop.tom@southwark.anglican.org
[Thomas Southwark]
Personal Assistant and Lay Chaplain Capt Terry Drummond CA (*same address*)
email: terry.drummond@southwark.anglican.org
Bishop's Personal Secretary Ms Winsome Thomas (*same address*)
email: winsome.thomas@southwark.anglican.org
Secretary Mrs Penny Lochead (*same address*)
email: penny.lochead@southwark.anglican.org

AREA BISHOPS
CROYDON Rt Revd Nicholas Baines, St Matthew's House, 100 George St, Croydon CR0 1PE [2003]
Tel: 020 8256 9634
Fax: 020 8256 9631
email: bishop.nick@southwark.anglican.org
KINGSTON Rt Revd Dr Richard Cheetham, Kingston Episcopal Area Office, 620 Kingston Rd, Raynes Park, London SW20 8DN [2002]
Tel: 020 8545 2440
Fax; 020 8545 2441
email: bishop.richard@southwark.anglican.org
WOOLWICH Rt Revd Christopher Chessun, Dioc Office [2005]   *Tel:* 020 7939 9407

HONORARY ASSISTANT BISHOPS
Rt Revd Mark Wood, College of St Barnabas, Blackberry Lane, Lingfield RH7 6NJ [2002]
Tel: 01342 870260
Rt Revd Michael Doe, General Secretary, USPG, Anglicans in World Mission, 200 Great Dover St, London SE1 4YB [2006]   *Tel:* 0845 273 1701
Rt Revd and Rt Hon Lord Harries of Pentregarth, 41 Melville Rd, Barnes, London SW19 9RH [2006]
Tel: 020 8288 6053

CATHEDRAL AND COLLEGIATE CHURCH OF ST SAVIOUR AND ST MARY OVERIE
Dean Very Revd Colin Slee, Provost's Lodging, Bankside, London SE1 9JE [1994]
Tel: 020 7367 6731 (Office)
Fax: 020 7367 6725 (Office)
Tel and Fax: 020 7928 6414 (Home)
email: colin.slee@southwark.anglican.org
Cathedral Office Montague Chambers, London Bridge, London SE1 9DA   *Tel:* 020 7367 6700
Fax: 020 7367 6725/6730
email: cathedral@southwark.anglican.org
Canons Residentiary
Sub-Dean Canon Andrew Nunn, Cathedral Office [1999]   *Tel:* 020 7367 6727 (Office)
020 7735 8322 (Home)
email: andrew.nunn@southwark.anglican.org
Pastor Canon Bruce Saunders, Cathedral Office [2003]   *Tel:* 020 7367 6706 (Office)
020 7820 8376 (Home)
email: bruce.saunders@southwark.anglican.org
Chancellor and Theologian Canon Jane Steen, Dioc Office [2005]   *Tel:* 020 7939 9449
email: jane.steen@southwark.anglican.org
Missioner Canon Michael Hart, Dioc Office [2005]
Tel: 020 7939 9411
email: michael.hart@southwark.anglican.org
Treasurer Robert Titley, Dioc Office [2006]
Tel: 020 7939 9458
email: robert.titley@southwark.anglican.org
Succentor Revd Anna Macham, [2007] Cathedral Office
Tel: 020 7367 6705
email: anna.macham@southwark.anglican.org
Administrator Mr Matthew Knight, Cathedral Office   *Tel:* 020 7367 6726
email: matthew.knight@southwark.anglican.org
Education Officer Miss Sandra Newnham, Cathedral Office   *Tel:* 020 7367 6715
email: edcentre@southwark.anglican.org
Visitors Officer Mr David Payne, Cathedral Office
Tel: 020 7367 6734
email: david.payne@southwark.anglican.org
Cathedral Organist Mr Peter Wright, Cathedral Office   *Tel:* 020 7367 6703
email: peter.wright@southwark.anglican.org

ARCHDEACONS
CROYDON Ven Anthony Davies, St Matthew's House, 100 George St, Croydon CR0 1PE [1994]   *Tel:* 020 8256 9630
Fax: 020 8256 9631
email: tony.davies@southwark.anglican.org

LAMBETH Ven Christopher Skilton, Kingston Episcopal Area Office, 620 Kingston Rd, Raynes Park, London SW20 8DN [2003]
Tel: 020 8545 2440
Fax: 020 8545 2441
email: chris.skilton@southwark.anglican.org
LEWISHAM Ven Christine Hardman, Dioc Office [2001] *Tel:* 020 7939 9408
email:
christine.hardman@southwark.anglican.org
REIGATE Ven Daniel Kajumba, St Matthew's House (*as above*)
email: daniel.kajumba@southwark.anglican.org
SOUTHWARK Ven Michael Ipgrave, Dioc Office (*as above*) [2004] *Tel:* 020 7939 9409
email: michael.ipgrave@southwark.anglican.org
WANDSWORTH Ven Stephen Roberts, Kingston Episcopal Area Office (*as above*) [2005]
Tel: 020 8545 2440
Fax: 020 8545 2441
email: stephen.roberts@southwark.anglican.org

CONVOCATION (MEMBERS OF THE HOUSE OF CLERGY OF THE GENERAL SYNOD)

Dignitaries in Convocation
The Dean of Southwark
Proctors for Clergy
Revd Simon Butler
Revd Paul Collier
Revd Dr Giles Fraser
Ven Christine Hardman
Canon Andrew Nunn
Revd Paul Perkin
Canon Anne Stevens

MEMBERS OF THE HOUSE OF LAITY OF THE GENERAL SYNOD

Mrs April Alexander
Mr Barry Barnes
Miss Vasantha Gnanadoss
Mr Adrian Greenwood
Mr Peter Haddock
Ms Kathryn Spall
Mr Tom Sutcliffe

DIOCESAN OFFICERS

Dioc Secretary Mr Simon Parton, Diocesan Office, Trinity House, 4 Chapel Court, Borough High St, London SE1 1HW *Tel:* 020 7939 9400
Fax: 020 7939 9468
email: simon.parton@southwark.anglican.org
Deputy Dioc Secretary Mr Andrew Lane, Dioc Office (*as above*)
email: andrew.lane@southwark.anglican.org
Chancellor of Diocese The Worshipful Charles George, 2 Harcourt Buildings, Temple, London EC4Y 9DB *Tel:* 020 7353 8415

Registrar of Diocese and Bishop's Legal Secretary Mr Paul Morris, Registry Chambers, The Old Deanery, London EC4V 5AA
Tel: 020 7593 5110
Fax: 020 7248 3221

DIOCESAN ORGANIZATIONS

Diocesan Office Trinity House, 4 Chapel Court, Borough High St, London SE1 1HW
Tel: 020 7939 9400
Fax: 020 7939 9468
email: trinity@southwark.anglican.org
Web: www. southwark.anglican.org

ADMINISTRATION

Dioc Synod (Chairman, House of Clergy) Canon Graham Shaw
(Chairman, House of Laity) Mr Adrian Greenwood; *(Secretary)* Mr Simon Parton, Dioc Office
South London Church Fund and Diocesan Board of Finance (Chairman) Mr John Kempsell; *(Secretary)* Mr Simon Parton, Dioc Office
Parsonages Board (Secretary) Mr Eric Greber, Dioc Office
email: eric.greber@southwark.anglican.org
Pastoral Committee (Secretary) Mr Andrew Lane, Dioc Office
email: andrew.lane@southwark.anglican.org
Redundant Churches Uses Committee (Secretary) Mr Roger Pickett, Dioc Office
Designated Officer Mr Paul Morris, Registry Chambers, The Old Deanery, London EC4V 5AA
Tel: 020 7593 5110
Fax: 020 7248 3221

CHURCHES

Advisory Committee for the Care of Churches (Chairman) Dr Cyril Young c/o Trinity House (*as above*); *(Secretary)* Mr Andrew Lane (*as above*)

ECUMENICAL

Chair of Ecumenical Sub-Group Revd Peter Hart, Vicarage, 70 Marksbury Ave, Richmond TW9 4JF
Tel: 020 8392 1425
email: Pwhart1@aol.com

EDUCATION

Board of Education (Director) Mrs Barbara Lane, 48 Union St, London SE1 1TD
Tel: 020 7234 9200
email: barbara.lane@southwark.anglican.org

MISSION, EVANGELISM, SPIRITUAL FORMATION AND CHURCH GROWTH WORKING GROUP

Chair The Archdeacon of Southwark (*as above*)
Canon Missioner Canon Michael Hart (*as above*)
Leadership Development and Evangelism Kevin Turner, Croydon Episcopal Area Office (*as above*)
Inter Faith Relations Co-ordinator Siriol Davies
Tel: 020 7201 4854
email: sirioldavies@yahoo.co.uk

Southwark **127**

Ecumenical Projects Officer John Richardson
Tel: 01462 422502
email: john@ctslondon.org.uk
Groups Support Officer Caroline Shrieve, Dioc Office
Tel: 020 7939 9412
Fax: 020 7939 9467
email: caroline.shrieve@southwark.anglican.org

SOCIAL RESPONSIBILITY AND REGENERATION WORKING GROUP

Chair Terry Drummond CA, Bishop's House (*as above*)
Social Responsibility (Parish Development) Barry Goodwin, Croydon Episcopal Area Office (*as above*)
Community Development Adviser Sue Hutson, Woolwich Episcopal Area Office (*as above*)
Tel: 020 7939 9417
email: sue.hutson@southwark.anglican.org
Grants and Fundraising Manager Steph Blackwell, Dioc Office (*as above*)
Tel: 020 7939 9417
email: steph.blackwell@southwark.anglican.org
Regeneration Adviser Revd Tim Scott
Tel: 020 7735 4077
email: tim.scott@southwark.anglican.org
Health and Healing Adviser Canon A. N. Tredennick
Tel: 01342 843570
email: rev.nicky.hello@amserve.com
Groups Support Officer Caroline Shrieve, Dioc Office (*as above*)

CHILDREN AND YOUTH DEVELOPMENT GROUP

Chair The Archdeacon of Wandsworth, Kingston Episcopal Area Office (*as above*)
Dioc Youth Officer Dean Pusey, Woolwich Episcopal Area Office (*as above*)
Tel: 020 7939 9416
email: dean.pusey@southwark.anglican.org
Dioc Children's Officer Diane Craven, Kingston Episcopal Area Office (*as above*)
Tel: 020 8785 1980
Fax: 020 8785 1981
email: diane.craven@southwark.anglican.org
Groups Support Officer Caroline Shrieve, Dioc Office (*as above*)

OTHER OFFICERS

Dioc Safeguarding and Child Protection Adviser Jill Sandham, c/o Dioc Office
Tel: 020 7939 9400
email: jill.sandham@southwark.anglican.org
Adviser in Women's Ministry Canon Peggy Jackson
Tel: 020 8876 4816
Minority Ethnic Anglican Concerns Officer Vacancy
Tel: 020 7939 9418
Interfaith Group Chair Revd Dr Alan Gadd, 24 Holmewood Gardens, London SW2 3RS
Tel: 020 8678 8977
email: holmewood24@surefish.co.uk
Liturgical Committee Revd Dr John Thewlis (*Secretary*), Rectory, 2 Talbot Rd, Carshalton SM5 3BS
Tel: 020 8647 2366

Retirement Officer Canon Nicky Tredennick
Tel: 01342 843570
email: rev.nicky.hello@amserve.com
Rural Ministry Adviser Revd Barry Goodwin, c/o Croydon Episcopal Area Office (*as above*)
Tel: 020 8256 9637
Southwark Dioc WelCare Revd Anne-Marie Garton (*Director*), St John's Community Centre, 19 Frederick Crescent, London SW9 6XN
Tel: 020 7939 9424
email:
anne-marie.garton@southwark.anglican.org

MINISTRY AND TRAINING COMMITTEE

Canon Theologian and Director of Ministerial Education Canon Dr Jane Steen, Dioc Office
Tel: 020 7939 9449
Senior Director of Ordinands Canon Robert Titley, Dioc Office
Tel: 020 7939 9458
Director of Ordinands Revd Geoff Mason, Dioc Office
Tel: 020 7939 9473
Ordained Local Ministry Scheme Revd Judith Roberts (*Principal*), Dioc Office
Tel: 020 7939 9472
email: judith.roberts@southwark.anglican.org
Adult Education Training Adviser Revd Nigel Stone, Kingston Episcopal Area Office (*as above*)
Tel: 020 8785 1980
Reader Training Revd Anne Stevens, St Michael's Vicarage, 93 Bolingbroke Grove, London SW11 6HA
Tel: 020 7228 1990
email: anne.stevens@southwark.anglican.org
Warden of Readers Canon Andrew Nunn, Southwark Cathedral (*as above*)
Southwark Pastoral Auxiliary Training Mr Chris Chapman, Dioc Office
Tel: 020 7939 9474
email: chris.chapman@southwark.anglican.org

COMMUNICATIONS

Director of Communications and Resources and Bishop's Press Officer Wendy Robins, Dioc Office
Tel: 020 7939 9400 (Office)
email:
wendy.s.robins@southwark.anglican.org
Communications Officer Steve Harris, Dioc Office
Tel: 020 7939 9437
email: steve.harris@southwark.anglican.org

DIOCESAN RECORD OFFICES

London Metropolitan Archives, 40 Northampton Rd, London EC1R 0HB Tel: 020 7332 3820
Fax: 020 7833 9136 (*Parish records for Inner London Boroughs except Lewisham*)
Lewisham Local Studies and Archives Centre, Lewisham Library, 199–201 Lewisham High St, London SE13 6LG Tel: 020 8297 0682
Fax: 020 8297 1169 (*Parish records for East and West Lewisham deaneries*)
Bexley Local Studies and Archive Centre, Central Library, Townley Road, Bexleyheath DA6 7HJ
Tel: 020 8301 1545 (*For Parishes in the London Borough of Bexley*)

Surrey History Centre, 130 Goldsworth Rd, Woking GU21 1ND *Tel:* 01483 594594 *Fax:* 01483 594595 (*County of Surrey and Surrey London Boroughs*)
London Borough of Sutton Local Studies Centre, St Nicholas Way, Sutton SM1 1JN *Tel:* 020 8770 5000 (*London Borough of Sutton*)

STEWARDSHIP
Director of Communications and Resources Wendy Robins, Dioc Office
email:
    wendy.s.robins@southwark.anglican.org.uk
Stewardship Resources Officer Jackie Pontin, Dioc Office   *Tel:* 020 7939 9435
    email: jackie.pontin@southwark.anglican.org

AREA DEANS
ARCHDEACONRY OF SOUTHWARK
Bermondsey Revd Mark Steadman, St Philip's Vicarage, Avondale Square, London SE1 5PD
                    Tel: 020 7237 3239
        email: gonetorome@yahoo.co.uk
Camberwell Revd Toby Wright, St John's Vicarage, 10a Meeting House Lane, Peckham, London SE15 2UN   *Tel:* 020 7635 4212
Dulwich Canon Dianna Gwilliams, St Barnabas Vicarage, 38 Calton Ave, London SE21 7DG
                    Tel: 020 8693 1524
    email: dianna.gwilliams@btopenworld.com
Southwark and Newington Revd Andrew Dodd, Rectory, 57 Kennington Park Rd, London SE11 4JQ   *Tel:* 020 7735 1894
        email: rector@stmarynewington.org.uk

ARCHDEACONRY OF LAMBETH
Merton Revd David Monteith, Vicarage, 1 Trinity Rd, Wimbledon, London SW19 8QT
                    Tel: 020 8543 2838
Lambeth North Revd Penelope Rose-Casemore, Christchurch Vicarage, 39 Union Grove, London SW8 2QJ   *Tel:* 020 7622 3552
        email: penny@christchurchstjohn.com
Lambeth South Revd Simon P. Gates, Vicarage, 2 Thornton Rd, Balham, London SW12 0JU
                    Tel: 020 8671 8276
            email: sgates2207@aol.com

ARCHDEACONRY OF REIGATE
Caterham Revd Alan Middleton, Rectory, 35 Dane Rd, Warlingham CR6 9NP
                    Tel: 01883 624125
    email: alan.middleton@southwark.anglican.org
Godstone Revd Graham Paddick, St John's Vicarage, The Platt, Dormansland, Lingfield, Surrey RH7 6QU   *Tel:* 01342 832391
        email: stjohndor@btinternet.com
Reigate Revd Garth Barber, Vicarage, Woodland Way, Kingswood, Tadworth KT20 6NW
                    Tel: 01737 832164
        email: garth.barber@virgin.net

ARCHDEACONRY OF LEWISHAM
Charlton Revd Kim Hitch, St James Rectory, 62 Kidbrooke Park Rd, London SE3 0DU
                    Tel: 020 8856 3438
        email: kim@hitchoffice.org.uk
Deptford Revd Neil Nicholls, St James Vicarage, St James, New Cross, London SE14 6AD
                    Tel: 020 8691 2167
        email: revn@hotmail.co.uk
East Lewisham Revd Richard D. Bainbridge, Vicarage, 47 Handen Rd, London SE12 8NR
                    Tel: 020 8318 2363
        email: revrdb@yahoo.com
Eltham and Mottingham Revd Elaine Cranmer, St Luke's Vicarage, 107 Westmount Rd, Eltham, London SE9 1XX   *Tel:* 020 8850 3030
        email: rev.elaine@virgin.net
Plumstead Revd Harry Owen, All Saints Vicarage, 106 Herbert Rd, Plumstead, London SE18 3PU   *Tel:* 020 8854 2995
        email: h.d.owen@talk21.com
West Lewisham Revd Michael Kingston, St Bartholomew's Vicarage, 4 Westwood Hill, Sydenham, London SE26 6QR
                    Tel: 020 8778 5290
    email: michaelkingston@btinternet.com

ARCHDEACONRY OF WANDSWORTH
Battersea Revd Geoffrey Vevers, St Saviour's Vicarage, 351a Battersea Park Rd, London SW11 4LH   *Tel:* 020 7498 1642
        email: g.m.vevers@btinternet.com
Kingston Revd Kevin Scott, 5 Vicarage Close, Worcester Park KT4 7LZ
                    Tel: 020 8337 8830
        email: kevinwscott@btinternet.com
Richmond and Barnes Revd Christopher Palmer, 86 East Sheen Ave, London SW14 8AU
                    Tel: 020 8487 8208
    email: christopherpalmer@blueyonder.co.uk
Tooting Revd Kevin Parkes, 291 Burntwood Lane, London SW17 0AP   *Tel:* 020 8874 4804
        email: kevin.parkes@ukonline.co.uk
Wandsworth Revd Heinz Toller, St Paul's Vicarage, 116 Augustus Rd, London SW19 6EW
                    Tel: 020 8788 2024
    email: vicar@stpaulswimbledonpark.org.uk

ARCHDEACONRY OF CROYDON
Croydon Addington Revd Mervyn McKinney, 7 Woodland Way, West Wickham BR4 9LL
                    Tel: 020 8777 5034
        email: mervmckinney@btinternet.com
Croydon Central Revd Penny Brown, St Matthew's Vicarage, 7 Brownlow Rd, Croydon CRO 5JT
                    Tel: 020 8688 5055
    email: revpenny@st.matthews.fsnet.co.uk
Croydon North Revd Dr Ann L. Nickson, St Stephen's Vicarage, 9 Warwick Rd, Thornton Heath CR7 7NH   *Tel:* 020 8684 3820
        email: AnnNickson@aol.com

Croydon South Revd Christine Spurway, St James' Vicarage, 18 St James' Rd, Purley CR8 2DL   *Tel:* 020 8660 5436
   email: christine@christinespurway.fsnet.co.net
Sutton Revd Christopher Wheaton, Vicarage, 38 Beeches Ave, Carshalton SM5 3LW
                 Tel: 020 8647 6056
   email: good.shepherd@btinternet.com

CHAPTER OF MINISTERS IN SECULAR EMPLOYMENT
Chapter Dean for Kingston Revd Peter King, 49 Leinster Ave, East Sheen, London SW14 7JW
              Tel: 020 8876 8997

DIOCESE OF SOUTHWELL AND NOTTINGHAM

Founded in 1884. Nottinghamshire; a few parishes in South Yorkshire.

Population 1,064,000   Area 847 sq m
Full-time Stipendiary Parochial Clergy 134   Benefices 173
Parishes 263   Churches 310
www.southwell.anglican.org
Overseas link diocese: Natal (South Africa)

BISHOP (10th)
Rt Revd George Henry Cassidy, Bishop's Manor, Southwell NG25 0JR [1999]   *Tel:* 01636 812112
Fax: 01636 815401
email: bishop@southwell.anglican.org
[George Southwell]
Chaplain Canon Anthony Evans
email: chaplain@southwell.anglican.org

SUFFRAGAN BISHOP
SHERWOOD Rt Revd Anthony Porter, Dunham House, 8 Westgate, Southwell NG25 0JL [2006]
Tel: 01636 819133
Fax: 01636 819085
email: jenny@southwell.anglican.org

PROVINCIAL EPISCOPAL VISITOR
Rt Revd Martyn Jarrett, 3 North Lane, Roundhay, Leeds LS8 2QJ   *Tel:* 0113 265 4280
Fax: 0113 265 4281
email:
bishop-of-beverley@3-north-lane.fsnet.co.uk

HONORARY ASSISTANT BISHOPS
Rt Revd John Finney, Greenacre, Crow Lane, South Muskham, Newark NG23 6DZ [1998]
Tel: 01636 679791
Rt Revd Ronald Milner, 7 Crafts Way, Southwell NG25 0BL [1994]   *Tel:* 01636 816256
Rt Revd Roy Williamson, 30 Sidney Rd, Beeston, Nottingham NG9 1AN [1998]   *Tel:* 0115 925 4901

CATHEDRAL AND PARISH CHURCH OF THE BLESSED VIRGIN MARY
Dean Very Revd John Arthur Guille, The Residence, 1 Vicars' Court, Southwell NG25 0HP [2007]   *Tel:* 01636 812782
email: dean@southwellminster.org.uk
Office The Minster Office, The Minster Centre, Church St, Southwell NG25 0JP
Tel: 01636 812649/817810
Fax: 01636 817284
email: office@southwellminster.org.uk
Web: www.southwellminster.org.uk
Canons Residentiary
Canon Pastor Canon Nigel Coates, 3 Vicars' Court, Southwell NG25 0HP [2005]
Tel: 01636 817296
email: nigelcoates@southwellminster.org.uk

Precentor Canon Jacqueline D. Jones, 2 Vicars' Court, Southwell NG25 0HP [2003]
Tel: 01636 817295
email: jacquijones@southwellminster.org.uk
Cathedral Administrator Mrs Caroline Jarvis, Chapter and Finance Office, Trebeck Hall, Bishop's Drive, Southwell NG25 0JP
Tel: 01636 817285
email: administrator@southwellminster.org.uk
Rector Chori Mr Paul Hale, 4 Vicars' Court, Southwell NG25 0HP   *Tel:* 01636 812228/817297
email: paulhale@southwellminster.org.uk

ARCHDEACONS
NOTTINGHAM Ven Peter Hill, 4 Victoria Crescent, Sherwood, Nottingham NG5 4DA [2007]
Tel: 0115 985 8641 (Home)
01636 817206 (Office)
Fax: 01636 815882 (Office)
email: archdeacon-nottm@southwell.anglican.org
/peterhill@talktalk.net
NEWARK Ven Nigel Peyton, 4 The Woodwards, Newark NG24 3GG [1999]
Tel: 01636 817206 (Office)
Fax: 01636 815882 (Office)
Tel: 01636 612249 (Home)
Fax: 01636 611952 (Home)
email:
archdeacon-newark@southwell.anglican.org

CONVOCATION (MEMBERS OF THE HOUSE OF CLERGY OF THE GENERAL SYNOD)
Proctors for Clergy
Ven Nigel Peyton
Canon Prof Anthony Thiselton
Canon Tony Walker
Canon Ruth Worsley

MEMBERS OF THE HOUSE OF LAITY OF THE GENERAL SYNOD
Canon Dr Christina Baxter
Mr Nick Harding
Mr Colin Slater

DIOCESAN OFFICERS

Chief Executive Mr Nigel Spraggins, Dunham House, 8 Westgate, Southwell NG25 0JL
Tel: 01636 817204 (Office)
01636 816445 (Home)
Fax: 01636 815084
email: ce@southwell.anglican.org
Chancellor of Diocese The Worshipful Mrs Linda Mary Box, Dioc Office *Tel:* 01636 817209
Deputy Chancellor Mr Stephen Eyre
Registrar of Diocese and Bishop's Legal Secretary Mr Christopher Hodson, Dioc Office
Tel: 01636 817209
Deputy Registrar Amanda Redgate

DIOCESAN ORGANIZATIONS

Diocesan Office Dunham House, 8 Westgate, Southwell NG25 0JL *Tel:* 01636 814331
Fax: 01636 815084
email: mail@southwell.anglican.org
Web: www.southwell.anglican.org

ADMINISTRATION

Dioc Synod (Vice-president and Chair, House of Clergy) Canon Linda Church, St Mary's Rectory, Annesley Rd, Hucknall, Nottingham NG15 7DE
Tel: 0115 963 2033
email: canonlinda.church@sky.com
(Chairman, House of Laity) Vacancy
(Secretary) Chief Executive, c/o Dioc Office
Tel: 01636 817204
Director of Finance and Administration Mr David Meredith, Dioc Office *Tel:* 01636 817202
Director of Property Mr Michael Jeffrey *(as above)*
Tel: 01636 817215
Building Surveyor Mr Ian Greaves *(as above)*
Tel: 01636 817214
Director of Care of Churches and Pastoral Mr Stephen Langford, Dioc Office
Tel: 01636 817210/211
Designated Officer Mr Christopher Hodson, Dioc Office
Redundant Churches Uses Committee (Chairman) The Archdeacon of Nottingham; *(Secretary)* Mr Stephen Langford *(as above)*
Dioc Board of Patronage c/o Dioc Office

STEWARDSHIP

Director of Funding Canon Carole Park
Tel: 01636 817242
email: carolepark@southwell.anglican.org

CHURCHES

Advisory Committee for the Care of Churches (Chairman) Canon Keith Turner, Rectory, Main St, Linby, Nottingham NG15 8AE *Tel:* 0115 963 2346
email: k.h.turner@btopenworld.com
(Secretary) Mr Stephen Langford *(as above)*
Web: www.southwellchurches.nottingham.ac.uk

EDUCATION

Director of Education Revd Dr Howard Worsley, Dioc Office *Tel:* 01636 817238
01636 814504 (General Office)

RE Advisers Mrs Jane Lewis *and* Mrs Anne Lumb *(same address)* *Tel:* 01636 817236
email: jane.lewis@southwell.anglican.org /
anne.lumb@southwell.anglican.org
Youth Ministry Adviser Angela Heywood
Tel: 01636 817233
email: angela.heywood@southwell.anglican.org
Children's Ministry Adviser Mr Nick Harding *(same address)* *Tel:* 01636 817234
email: nick@southwell.anglican.org

DEPARTMENT FOR DEVELOPMENT

Diocesan Office, 8 Westgate, Southwell NG25 0JL
Director of Development Canon Alan Payne, Dioc Office, Department for Development
Tel: 01636 817216 (Office)
email: alanp@southwell.anglican.org
Diocesan Director of Ordinands and Curate Training Canon Terry Joyce, Dioc Office, Department for Development *Tel:* 01636 817212
email: tjoyce@southwell.anglican.org
Associate Director, Practical Theology Canon Dr Nigel Rooms *Tel:* 01636 817231
email: nigel.rooms@southwell.anglican.org
Associate Director, Partnerships Revd David McCoulough *Tel:* 01636 817987
email: davidmcc@southwell.anglican.org
Dean of Women's Ministry Canon Ruth Worsley, St Christopher's Vicarage, 180 Sneinton Boulevard, Sneinton, Nottingham NG2 7AE
Tel: 0115 950 5303
email: ruthworsley@aol.com
Lay Training Officer Revd Alison Cox
Tel: 01636 817985
Warden of Readers and Director of Studies Mr Christopher Perrett, Harvest Barn, Grassthorpe, Newark, Nottingham NG23 5QZ
Tel: 01636 822426
email: chris.perrett@southwell.anglican.org
Chaplain to Retired Clergy/Clergy Widows Officer Ven Garth Norman, 5 Riverside, Southwell NG25 0HA *Tel:* 01636 815209
email: gnorman@southwell.anglican.org
World Development Adviser Mrs Shelagh Baird-Smith, Dioc Office *Tel:* 01636 817988
email: shelagh@southwell.anglican.org
Bishop's Adviser on Rural Affairs Revd Derek Hollis, Dioc Office *Tel:* 01636 817229
email: rural.adviser@southwell.anglican.org
Officer for Urban Life and Mission Revd David Jones, Dioc Office *Tel:* 01636 817229
email: urban.officer@southwell.anglican.org
Associate Adviser on Rural Affairs Revd Joanna Hey *Tel:* 01777 248 143
email: jjlhay@yahoo.co.uk
Workplace Chaplain Revd Alison Maddocks
Tel: 0115 983 1553
email:
alison.maddocks@nottinghamchurches.org

Equality and Diversity Officer and Rainbow Project Leader Ms Dianne Skerritt   Tel: 0115 948 3658
                                                              01636 817229
    email: dskerritt@southwell.anglican.org
Chaplain for Sector Chaplaincies Venerable Robin Turner CB, DL   Tel: 01636 812250
    email: pr.turner@lineone.net
Dioc Tourism Officer Revd Prof Myra Shackley, 47 Eldon St, Tuxford, Newark NG22 0LG
                                              Tel: 01777 870838
    email: myra.shackley@ntu.ac.uk
Diocesan Ecumenical Officer Revd Philip Webb, Dovedale, 52 South Avenue, Chellaston, Derby DE73 6RS   Tel: 01332 705 078
    email: dovedale.revs@virgin.net
Natal Link Officer Revd Barbara Holbrook, The Rectory, 1 Eastwood Road, Kimberley, Nottingham NG16 2HX   Tel: 0115 938 3565

LITURGICAL COMMITTEE
Chairman Canon Ian Tarrant, 2 Florence Boot Close, University Park, Nottingham NG7 2QF
                                              Tel: 0115 951 3927
    email: ian.tarrant@nottingham.ac.uk

MISSION
Canon Missioner and Director of Mission Canon Mark Brown, 5 Vicars' Court, Southwell NG25 0HP   Tel: 01636 817298
    email: mark.brown@southwell.anglican.org
Diocesan Ecumenical Officer Revd David Bignell, Vicarage, Village St, Edwalton, Nottingham NG12 4AB   Tel: 0115 923 2034
    email: office@edwaltonchurch.plus.com
Dioc Tourism Officer Revd Prof Myra Shackley, 47 Eldon St, Tuxford, Newark NG22 0LG
                                              Tel: 01777 870838
    email: myra.shackley@ntu.ac.uk
Natal Link Officer Canon Graham Pigott, St Paul's House, Boundary Rd, West Bridgford, Nottingham NG2 7DB   Tel: 0115 923 3492

PRESS AND PUBLICATIONS
Director of Communications Mrs Rachel Farmer, Dioc Office   Tel: 01636 817218 (Office)
Tel and Fax: 01636 816276 (Home)
                  07712 196381 (Mobile)
    email: rachel@southwell.anglican.org
Editor of Dioc Magazine 'C' Mrs Rachel Farmer (as above)

DIOCESAN RECORD OFFICE
Nottinghamshire Archives, County House, Castle Meadow Rd, Nottingham NG1 1AG Principal Archivist Mr Mark Dorrington
                                              Tel: 0115 950 4524

SOCIAL RESPONSIBILITY
(Diocesan Director of Social Responsibility) Ms Patricia Stoat, Dioc Office   Tel: 01636 817246
    email: social.responsibility@
                  southwell.anglican.org

World Development Adviser Mrs Shelagh Baird-Smith, Dioc Office   Tel: 01636 817232
    email: shelagh@southwell.anglican.org
Diocesan Council for Family Care (Director) Mr Stuart Brook, Family Care, Warren House, Pelham Court, Pelham Rd, Nottingham NG5 1AP   Tel: 0115 960 3010
                                              Fax: 0115 960 8374
    email: admin@family-care.demon.co.uk
    Web: www.familycare-nottingham.org.uk
Bishop's Adviser on Rural Affairs Revd Derek Hollis, c/o Dioc Office   Tel: 01636 817229
Officer for Urban Life and Mission Revd David Jones, c/o Dioc Office   Tel: 01636 817229
City Commercial Chaplain Revd David McCoulough, 3 Cromdale Close, Arnold, Nottingham NG5 8DF   Tel: 0115 920 0630

AREA DEANS
ARCHDEACONRY OF NEWARK
Bassetlaw Vacancy
Mansfield Revd George Butler, St Mark's Vicarage, Nottingham Rd, Mansfield NG18 1BP
                                              Tel: 01623 655548
    email: revgib@tiscali.co.uk
Newark and Southwell Revd Tony Tucker, Vicarage, Main St, Balderton, Newark NG24 3NN   Tel: 01636 704811
                  07976 953068 (Mobile)
    email: anthony.tucker4@btopenworld.com
Canon Sue Spencer, 29 Marlock Close, Fiskerton, Newark, Nottingham NG25 0UB
                                              Tel: 01636 830 331
    email: suespencer599@btinternet.com
Newstead Revd Richard Kellett, Vicarage, Mansfield Rd, Skegby, Sutton-in-Ashfield NG17 3ED   Tel: 01623 558800
    email: richard@kellett.com

ARCHDEACONRY OF NOTTINGHAM
East Bingham Canon Jim Wellington, The Rectory, Nottingham Rd, Keyworth, Nottingham NG12 0UB   Tel: 0115 937 2017
    email: jhcwelli@btinternet.com
Gedling Revd Philip Williams, St James' Vicarage, Marshall Hill Drive, Mapperley, Nottingham NG3 6FY   Tel: 0115 960 6185
    email: phil.stjames@virgin.net
Nottingham North Revd Jerry Lepine, The Rectory, 143 Russell Drive, Nottingham NG8 2BD   Tel: 0115 928 1798
    email: jerry.lepine@btopenworld.com
Nottingham South Canon Ruth Worsley, St Christopher's Vicarage, 180 Sneinton Boulevard, Sneinton, Nottingham NG2 4GL
                                              Tel: 0115 950 5303
    email: ruthworsley@aol.com
West Bingham Revd John Bentham, 51 Chatsworth Rd, West Bridgford, Nottingham NG2 7AE   Tel: 0115 846 1054
    email: john.bentham@nottingham.ac.uk

Southwell and Nottingham   **133**

DIOCESES

Founded in 1877. Cornwall; the Isles of Scilly; one parish in Devon.

Population 527,000   Area 1,390 sq m
Full-time Stipendiary Parochial Clergy 102   Benefices 129
Parishes 222   Churches 309
www.truro.anglican.org
Overseas link diocese: Strängnas, Sweden and Umzimvubu, South Africa.

BISHOP (15th)
Rt Revd Tim Thornton, Lis Escop, Feock, Truro
TR3 6QQ [2009] (From 24 Jan 2009)
Tel: 01872 862657
Fax: 01872 862037
email: bishop@truro.anglican.org
[Timothy Truro]
Domestic Chaplain Revd Derek Carrivick,
Vicarage, Devoran, Truro TR3 6PA
Tel: 01872 863116 (Home)
01872 862657 (Office)
email: chaplain.bishop@truro.anglican.org
Bishop's Personal Assistant Mrs Lesley Rogers, Lis
Escop   *email:* lesley.r@truro.anglican.org

SUFFRAGAN BISHOP
ST GERMANS Rt Revd Royden Screech, 32 Fal-
mouth Rd, Truro TR1 2HX [2000]
Tel: 01872 273190
Fax: 01872 277883
email: bishop@stgermans.truro.anglican.org

**CATHEDRAL CHURCH OF THE BLESSED
VIRGIN MARY IN TRURO**
Dean Very Revd Dr Christopher Hardwick, The
Deanery, The Avenue, Truro TR1 1HR [2005]
Tel: 01872 272661
Cathedral Office 14 St Mary's St, Truro TR1 2AF
Tel: 01872 276782
Fax: 01872 277788
email: dean@trurocathedral.org.uk
Canons Residentiary
Precentor Canon Perran Gay, St Michael's House,
52 Daniell Rd, Truro TR1 2DA [1994]
Tel: 01872 245006
email: perran@trurocathedral.org.uk
Missioner Canon Philip Lambert, Foxhayes,
3 Knights Hill, Kenwyn, Truro TR1 3UY [2006]
Tel: 01872 245018
email: philip@trurocathedral.org.uk
Pastor Canon Peter Walker, The Vicarage, Feock,
Truro TR3 6SD [2001]   *Tel:* 01872 862534
Tel: 01872 245016
email: peter@trurocathedral.org.uk
Chapter Canons
Ven Roger Bush [2006]
Mr Robert Foulkes [2001]
Mrs Bridget Hugh-Jones [2001]

Chief Executive Mr Neil Parsons
email: chiefexecutive@trurocathedral.org.uk
Director of Music Chris Gray, Cathedral Office
email: music@trurocathedral.org.uk

ARCHDEACONS
BODMIN Ven Clive Cohen, Archdeacon's House,
Cardynham, Bodmin PL30 4BL [2000]
Tel and *Fax:* 01208 821614
email: clive@truro.anglican.org
CORNWALL Ven Roger Bush, Westwood House,
Tremorvah Crescent, Truro TR1 1NL [2006]
Tel and *Fax:* 01872 225630
email: roger@truro.anglican.org

**CONVOCATION (MEMBERS OF THE
HOUSE OF CLERGY OF THE GENERAL
SYNOD)**
Proctors for Clergy
Revd Alan Bashforth
Ven Roger Bush
Canon David Miller

**MEMBERS OF THE HOUSE OF LAITY OF
THE GENERAL SYNOD**
Mr Terence Musson
Mrs Penny Stranack
Gp Capt Paul Terrett

DIOCESAN OFFICERS
Dioc Secretary Mrs Sheri Sturgess, Diocesan
House, Kenwyn, Truro TR1 1JQ
Tel: 01872 274351
Fax: 01872 222510
email: sheri.sturgess@truro.anglican.org
Web: www.truro.anglican.org
Chancellor of Diocese The Worshipful Timothy
Briden, Lamb Chambers, Lamb Building,
Temple, London EC4Y 7AS   *Tel:* 020 7797 8300
Fax: 020 7707 8308
email: info@lambchambers.co.uk
Registrar of Diocese and Bishop's Legal Secretary Mr
Martin Follett, Truro Diocesan Registry,
MichelmoresLLP, Woodwater House, Pynes Hill,
Exeter EX2 5WR   *Tel:* 01392 687415
Fax: 01392 360563
email: mjf@michelmores.com

Dioc Surveyor and Director of Property Services Mr Matthew Williams, Dioc House, Kenwyn, Truro TR1 1JQ   *Tel:* 01872 241507
Fax: 01872 222510
email: propertyservices@truro.anglican.org

DIOCESAN ORGANIZATIONS
Diocesan Office Diocesan House, Kenwyn, Truro TR1 1JQ   *Tel:* 01872 274351
Fax: 01872 222510
email: info@truro.anglican.org

ADMINISTRATION
Dioc Synod and Bishop's Council (Secretary) Mrs Sheri Sturgess, Dioc Office
Dioc Synod (Chairman, House of Clergy) Revd David Miller, Rectory, Church Lane, Helston TR1 8PF   *Tel:* 01326 572516
(Chairman, House of Laity) Dr M. Todd
Board of Finance (Chairman) Mr D. Bishop; *(Secretary)* Mrs Sheri Sturgess *(as above)*
Parsonages Committee Mrs Sheri Sturgess *(as above)*
Pastoral Committee Mrs Sheri Sturgess *(as above)*
Glebe Committee Mrs Lyn Poole, Dioc Office
Board of Patronage Revd Paul Arthur, Rectory, 16 Trelavour Rd, St Dennis, St Austell PL26 8AH   *Tel:* 01726 822317
email: kpaularthur@googlemail.com
Designated Officer Mrs Sheri Sturgess *(as above)*

CHURCHES
Advisory Committee for the Care of Churches (Chairman) Mrs Christine Edwards, Garden Place, Camels, Veryan, Truro TR2 5PJ *Tel:* 01872 501727
(Secretary) Mrs Lyn Poole, Dioc Office
email: lyn.poole@truro.anglican.org
Truro Diocesan Guild of Ringers (President) Mr Ian Self, The Sycamores, Parc Vean, Coach Lane, Redruth TR15 2TT, *Tel:* 01209 211686; *(Gen Secretary)* Mr Robert Perry, 11 Trevaylor Close, Truro TR1 1RP, *Tel:* 01872 277117
Redundant Churches Uses Committee (Secretary) Mrs Lyn Poole *(as above)*

EDUCATION AND TRAINING
Director and Secretary of Education Mrs Sue Green, Dioc Office   *Tel:* 01872 247214
email: sue.green@truro.anglican.org
Youth Officer Miss Sarah Welply *(same address)*
email: sarah.welply@truro.anglican.org
RE Adviser Revd Sian Yates *(same address)*
email: sian.yates@truro.anglican.org
Children's Adviser Mrs Shelley Porter *(same address)*
email: shelley.porter@truro.anglican.org

MINISTRY
Director of Accredited Ministry The Bishop of St Germans *(as above)*
Director of Ministerial Training Revd Paul Arthur, Rectory, 16 Trelavour Rd, St Dennis, St Austell PL26 8AH   *Tel:* 01726 822317
email: kpaularthur@googlemail.com

Co-Directors of Ordinands The Bishop of St Germans *(as above)*; Canon Julia Wilkinson, Rectory, St Issey, Wadebridge PL27 7HJ
Tel and *Fax:* 01841 540314
email: canjulia@btinternet.com
South-west Ministry Training Course (Principal) Revd David Moss, Amory Building, University of Exeter, Rennes Drive, Exeter EX4 4RJ
Tel: 01392 264403
email: principal@swmtc.org.uk
Web: www.swmtc.org.uk
Warden of Readers Revd Paul Arthur *(as above)*
Clergy Retirement and Widows Officer Revd Owen Blatchly, 1 Rose Cottages, East Rd, Stithians, Truro TR3 7BD   *Tel:* 01209 860845

LITURGICAL
Chairman The Bishop of Truro
Secretary Canon Perran Gay *(as above)*

EVANGELISM AND UNITY
Chairman The Archdeacon of Cornwall *(as above)*
Dioc Director of Mission Canon David White, Vicarage, Carnsmerry Crescent, St Austell PL25 4NA   *Tel:* 01726 73839
Officer for Unity Canon Martin Boxall, Goonhilland Farm House, Burnthouse, Penryn TR10 9AS   *Tel:* 01872 863241
World Church Committee (Chairman) Bishop of St Germans

COUNCIL FOR SOCIAL RESPONSIBILITY
Officer Revd Andrew Yates, Dioc Office
email: andrew.yates@truro.anglican.org
FLAME Family Life Officer Vacancy
Tel: 01872 247213

PRESS AND PUBLICATIONS
Dioc Communications Officer Mr Jeremy Dowling, Penrock, Church Path, Bude EX23 8LH
Tel and *Fax:* 01288 352786
email: jeremy.dowling@truro.anglican.org
Editor of Dioc News Leaflet Mr Jeremy Dowling *(as above)*
Editor of Dioc Directory Mrs Clare Jones *(as above)*

DIOCESAN RECORDS
Diocesan Records Officer Mr Paul Brough, County Archivist, County Hall, Truro TR1 3AY
Tel: 01872 323127

STEWARDSHIP
Parish Resources Officer Revd Julie Millar, Dioc House   *Tel:* 01872 274351

RURAL DEANS
ARCHDEACONRY OF CORNWALL
St Austell Revd Paul Arthur, Rectory, 16 Trelavour Rd, St Dennis, St Austell PL26 8AH
Tel: 01726 822317
email: kpaularthur@googlemail.com
Carnmarth North Revd Martin Hogan, Vicarage, Old Vicarage Close, Stithians, Truro TR3 7DZ
Tel: 01209 860123
email: vicar@stythian.org

Carnmarth South Canon John Harris, St Gluvias Vicarage, Penryn TR10 9LQ   *Tel:* 01326 373356
Kerrier Revd David Stevens, Vicarage, Chalbury Heights, Brill, Constantine, Falmouth TR11 5UR
Tel: 01326 340259
Penwith Revd Howars Peskett, 7 North Parade, Penzance TR18 4SH   *Tel:* 01736 362913
email: howard.peskett@btinternet.com
Powder Revd Alan Bashforth, Vicarage, 6 Penwinnick Parc, St Agnes, Truro TR5 0UG
Tel: 01872 553391
email: alan@onepaw.fsnet.co.uk
Pydar Revd Christopher Malkinson, Vicarage, 46 Treverbyn Rd, Padstow PL28 8DN
Tel: 01841 533776
email: chrismalk@hotmail.com

ARCHDEACONRY OF BODMIN
East Wivelshire Revd Andrew Wilson, Rectory, Sand Lane, Calstock PL18 9QX
Tel: 01822 832518
email: andrew.wilson@virgin.net

Stratton Canon Rob Dickenson, Rectory, The Glebe, Week St Mary, Holsworthy EX22 6UY
Tel: 01288 341134
email: parsonrob@aol.com

Trigg Major Canon Geoffrey Pengelly, Vicarage, Egloskerry, Launceston PL1 8RX
Tel: 01566 785365

Trigg Minor and Bodmin Canon Sherry Bryan, Rectory, Green Briar, Coombe Lane, St Breward PL30 4LT   *Tel* and *Fax:* 01208 851829
email: sherrybryan4@aol.com

West Wivelshire Canon Tony Ingleby, The Rectory, Church St, Liskeard PL24 3AQ
Tel: 01579 342178
email: tony@ingleby100.freeserve.com

DIOCESE OF WAKEFIELD

Founded in 1888. Wakefield; Kirklees; Calderdale; Barnsley, except for an area in the south-east (SHEFFIELD); an area of Leeds; a few parishes in North Yorkshire.

Population 1,096,000   Area 557 sq m
Full-time Stipendiary Parochial Clergy 136   Benefices 150
Parishes 186   Churches 239
Overseas link diocese: Mara (Tanzania).

BISHOP (12th)
Rt Revd Stephen Platten, Bishop's Lodge, Woodthorpe Lane, Wakefield WF2 6JL [2003]
Tel: 01924 255349
Fax: 01924 250202
email: bishop@bishopofwakefield.org.uk
Bishop's Domestic Chaplain and Communications Officer Revd Matthew Bullimore, Bishops Lodge, Woodthorpe Lane, Sandal, Wakefield WF2 6JL
Tel: 01924 255349
Tel: 01924 250574 (Direct Line)
email: chaplain@bishopofwakefield.org.uk

SUFFRAGAN BISHOP
PONTEFRACT Rt Revd Anthony Robinson, Pontefract House, 181A Manygates Lane, Sandal Wakefield WF2 7DR [1998]   *Tel:* 01924 250781
Fax: 01924 240490
email: bishop.pontefract@wakefield.anglican.org

CATHEDRAL CHURCH OF ALL SAINTS
Dean Very Revd Jonathan Greener, The Deanery, 1 Cathedral Close, Margaret St, Wakefield WF1 2DP   *Tel:* 01924 239308
email:
jonathan.greener@wakefield-cathedral.org.uk
Cathedral Centre 8–10 Westmorland St, Wakefield WF1 1PJ   *Tel:* 01924 373923
Fax: 01924 215054
email: admin@wakefield-cathedral.org.uk
Web: www.wakefield-cathedral.org.uk
Administrator Dr Nigel Russell
email: nigel.russell@wakefield-cathedral.org.uk
Administrative Bursar Mrs Sue King
email: sue.king@wakefield-cathedral.org.uk
Dean's PA and Cathedral Secretary Mrs Sue Ellis
email: sue.ellis@wakefield-cathedral.org.uk
Acting Head Verger Julie Lovell
Canons Residentiary
Sub-Dean Canon Michael Rawson, 3 Cathedral Close, Margaret St, Wakefield WF1 2DP [2007]
Tel: 01924 379743
email:
michael.rawson@wakefield-cathedral.org.uk
Canon Precentor Canon John Lees, 4 Cathedral Close, Margaret St, Wakefield WF1 2DP [2006]
Tel: 01924 210008

email:
canon.precentor@wakefield-cathedral.org.uk
Rt Revd Anthony Robinson, Pontefract House, 181A Manygates Lane, Sandal, Wakefield WF2 7DR [2005]   *Tel:* 01924 250271
email: bishop.pontefract@wakefield.anglican.org
Canon Dr John Lawson, 7 Belgravia Rd, St John's, Wakefield WF1 3JP [2005]   *Tel:* 01924 380182
email: jal@bh-cc.co.uk
Canon Tony Macpherson, 14 Belgravia Rd, St John's, Wakefield WF1 3JP [2007]
email: tonymacpherson@blueyonder.co.uk
Honorary Chaplains Revd Prof Roger Grainger, Revd George Midgley, Canon Stuart Ramsden, Revd Derek Birch, Revd John Bird
Ecumenical Canons Bishop Malkaz Songulashvili (Baptist Church of Georgia) [2006], Bishop Arthur Roche (Roman Catholic Bishop of Leeds) [2006], Revd Peter Whittaker (Chair, W. Yorkshire District of Methodist Churches) [2006]
Honorary Assistant Priest Revd June Lawson
email: jlawson@mirfield.org.uk
Lay Canons
Arthur Mauya, Dr Juliet Barker, Mrs Linda Box, Mrs Angela Byram, Mr Stanley Inniss, Dr Keith Judkins, Mrs Celia Kilner, Mr Ashley Peatfield, Prof Michael Clarke
Clerk to the College of Canons Mrs Linda Box, Bank House, Burton St, Wakefield WF1 2DA
Tel: 01924 373467
Fax: 01924 366234
email: info@dixon-coles-gill.co.uk
Development Director Ms Joanne Addie
email: jo.addie@wakefield-cathedral.org.uk
Education Officer Ms Ali Bullivant
email: ali.bullivant@wakefield-cathedral.org.uk
Director of Music Mr Jonathan Bielby, Womack Cottage, Heath, Wakefield, WF1 5SN
Tel: 01924 378841
email: jlb@jbielby.freeserve.co.uk
Asst Director of Music Mr Tom Moore, Cathedral Office   *email:* tom@thomasmoore.org.uk
ARCHDEACONS
HALIFAX Ven Robert Freeman, 2 Vicarage Gardens, Rastrick, Brighouse HD6 3HD [2003]
Tel: 01484 714553
Fax: 01484 711897

email: archdeacon.halifax@wakefield.anglican.org
PONTEFRACT Ven Peter Townley, The Vicarage, Kirkthorpe, Wakefield WF1 5SZ
Tel: 01924 896387
Tel: 01924 434459 (Church House Direct Line)
Fax: 01924 364834 (Church House)
email:
archdeacon.pontefract@wakefield.anglican.org

CONVOCATION (MEMBERS OF THE HOUSE OF CLERGY OF THE GENERAL SYNOD)
Dignitaries in Convocation
The Dean of Wakefield
Proctors for Clergy
Canon Ian Gaskell
Ven Robert Freeman

MEMBERS OF THE HOUSE OF LAITY OF THE GENERAL SYNOD
Mr David Ashton
His Honour Judge John Bullimore
Mrs Mary Judkins
Dr Edmund Marshall

DIOCESAN OFFICERS
Dioc Secretary Mr Ashley Ellis, Church House, 1 South Parade, Wakefield WF1 1LP
Tel: 01924 371802
Fax: 01924 364834
email: diocesan.secretary@wakefield.anglican.org
Chancellor of Diocese Worshipful Chancellor His Honour Judge Paul Downes, Norwich Combined Court, Law Courts, Bishopgate, Norwich NR3 1UR *Tel:* 01603 728200
email: hhjudge.downes@judiciary.gsi.gov.uk
Joint Registrars of Diocese and Bishop's Legal Secretaries Mr Julian Gill and Mrs Julia Wilding, Bank House, Burton St, Wakefield WF1 2DA
Tel: 01924 373467
Fax: 01924 366234
email: info@dixon-coles-gill.com

DIOCESAN ORGANIZATIONS
Diocesan Office Church House, 1 South Parade, Wakefield WF1 1LP *Tel:* 01924 371802
Fax: 01924 364834
email: church.house@wakefield.anglican.org

ADMINISTRATION
Dioc Secretary Mr Ashley Ellis, Church House
Finance Manager and Deputy Secretary Mr Bryan Lewis, Church House
Dioc Synod (Chairman, House of Clergy) Canon Tony Macpherson, 14 Belgravia Rd, St John's, Wakefield WF1 3JP *Tel:* 01924 378360
(Chairman, House of Laity) Mrs Mary Judkins, The Old Vicarage, 3 Church Lane, East Ardsley, Wakefield WF3 2LJ *Tel:* 01924 826802
email: elephantmj@aol.com

(Secretary) Mr Ashley Ellis *(as above)*
Dioc Communications Officer Mrs Jane Bower, Church House *Tel:* 01924 371802
email: jane.bower@wakefield.anglican.org
Board of Finance (Chairman) Vacancy, Church House; *(Secretary)* Mr Ashley Ellis *(as above)*
Finance Manager Mr Bryan Lewis, Church House
Dioc Property Manager Ms Helen Price, Church House
Assistant Property Manager Mr Kevin Smith
Pastoral Committee Mr Ashley Ellis *(as above)*
Dioc Trust Mr Bryan Lewis *(as above)*
Stewardship and Resources Adviser Mr Brian Morris, Church House
Board of Patronage Mrs Julia Wilding, Bank House, Burton St, Wakefield WF1 2DA
Tel: 01924 373467
Fax: 01924 366234
email: info@dixon-coles-gill.com
Designated Officer Mrs Julia Wilding *(as above)*

CHURCHES
Advisory Committee for the Care of Churches Mrs Julia Wilding *(as above)*

EDUCATION
Director of Education Revd Canon Ian Wildey, Church House
Board of Education (Chairman) Ven Peter Townley; *(Secretary)* Revd Canon Ian Wildey
Schools Officer Mr David Barraclough, Church House
Statutory Liaison Officer Mrs Marlene Redgwick, Church House
Buildings Officer Vacancy, Church House

CHILDREN'S AND YOUTH WORK
Diocesan Children's and Youth Work Coordinator and Children's Adviser (5–13/14s) Revd Richard Burge, Church House
Adviser for Under 5s Mrs Ellie Wilson, Church House
Youth Coordinator Mrs Liz Morton, Church House

MINISTRY
Dioc Director of Ordinands Vacancy, Church House
email: sue.penfold@wakefield.anglican.org
Asst Directors of Ordinands Revd Stephen Race, St John's Vicarage, Green Rd, Dodworth, Barnsley S75 3RT *Tel:* 01226 206276
email: sprandj@yahoo.co.uk
Revd Joy Cousans, The Rectory, Church Lane, Clayton West, Huddersfield HD8 9LY
Tel: 01484 862321
email: joy@daveandjoy.plus.com
Dioc Director of Training Revd Dr John Lawson, Church House *email:* jal@bh-cc.co.uk
Warden of Readers Revd John Hellewell, Vicarage, Church Lane, Mountpellon, Halifax HX2 0EF
Tel: 01422 365027
email: john@revjhell.freeserve.co.uk

Adviser for Women's Ministry Vacancy
Vocations Officer Vacancy
Coordinator for Local Ministry Vacancy
Wakefield Ministry Scheme Officer Vacancy, Church House
Continuing Ministerial Education Officer Revd Stephen Kelly, Vicarage, Woolley, Wakefield WF4 2JU   *Tel:* 01226 382550
          email: stephen.kelly@wakefield.anglican.org
Bishop's Adviser for Pastoral Care and Counselling Revd Christine Bullimore, Rectory, 14 Grange Drive, Emley, Huddersfield HD8 9SF
          Tel: 01924 849161
          email: JCBullimor@aol.com

SOCIAL RESPONSIBILITY
Bishop's Adviser for Social Responsibility Vacancy, Church House
Development Officer Susan Parker, Church House
Family Life and Marriage Education Officers Mrs Lisa Senior *and* Mrs Liz Morton, Church House
Diocesan Rural Officer (Farming) Revd Dennis Handley, Vicarage, Ripponden, Sowerby Bridge HX6 4DF   *Tel:* 01422 822239
*email:*dennisandcatherine@ripponden.fslife.co.uk
Diocesan Rural Officer (Broader Rural Issues) Revd Hugh Baker, Vicarage, 2 Netherton Hall Gardens, Netherton, Wakefield WF4 4JA
          Tel: 01924 278384
          email: hugh.baker@tesco.net
Advisers on Urban Issues The Revd David Fletcher, 37 Hops Lane, Wheatley, Halifax HX3 5FB
          Tel: 01422 349844
          email: de.fletcher@btinternet.com
The Revd David Nicholson, The Vicarage, St John's Road, Cudworth, Barnsley S72 8DE
          Tel: 01226 710279
          email: fr_d_pp_cudworth@hotmail.com
Adviser on Disability Dr Cynthia Fox, 134 Nab Lane, Battyeford, Mirfield WF14 9QJ
          Tel: 01924 378360
          email: Cynthia@nablane.fsnet.co.uk

EVANGELISM
Canon Missioner Canon Tony Macpherson (*as above*)

OTHER OFFICERS
Bishop's Adviser for Child Protection and Child Protection Support Coordinator Mrs Jenny Price, Church House
          email: jenny.price@wakefield.anglican.org
Bishop's Adviser for Ecumenical Affairs Vacancy (*for West Yorkshire*)
Ecumenical Affairs Officer Vacancy (*for South Yorkshire*)
Chaplain Among Deaf People Revd Bob Shrine, Vicarage, 80 Carr House Rd, Shelf, Halifax HX3 5LS   *Typetalk:* 18002 01274 677693

          Fax: 01274 677693
          email: bob.shrine@ukonline.co.uk
Interfaith Relations The Revd Leslie Pinfield, The Vicarage, 17 Cross Church St, Paddock, Huddersfield HD1 4SN   *Tel:* 01484 530814
          *email:*frleslie@btopenworld.com
Retired Clergy and Widows Officers Revd John Wilkinson, 29 Pontefract Rd, Ferrybridge, Knottingley WF11 8PN   *Tel:* 01977 607250
Revd Richard Bradnum, 4 Hopton Lane, Upper Hopton, Mirfield WF14 8EL   *Tel:* 01924 493569

PRESS AND PUBLICATIONS
Dioc Year Book (*Editor*) Mr Ashley Ellis, Church House

DIOCESAN RECORD OFFICE
County Archivist Lisa Broadest, West Yorkshire Archive Service, Registry of Deeds, Newstead Rd, Wakefield WF1 2DE   *Tel:* 01924 305980
          email: wakefield@wyjs.org.uk

DIOCESAN RESOURCES CENTRE
Manager Mrs Moira Burns, Church House (Wakefield and Mirfield)
Mrs Sheila Crosby, Church House

RURAL DEANS
ARCHDEACONRY OF HALIFAX
Almondbury Revd Richard Steel, Rectory, Church Lane, Kirkheaton, Huddersfield HD5 0BH
          Tel: 01484 532410
          email: richard.steel@ntlworld.com
Brighouse and Elland Revd Michael Wood, Vicarage, 56 Bracken Rd, Brighouse HD6 2HX
          Tel: 01484 714032
          email: fr_m_wood@brighouse71.fsnet.co.uk
Calder Valley Revd James Allison, Vicarage, Brier Hey Lane, Mytholmroyd, Hebden Bridge HX7 5PJ   *Tel:* 01422 883130
          email: erringden@aol.com
Halifax Revd Stephen Bradberry, 129 Paddock Lane, Norton Tower, Halifax HX2 0NT
          Tel: 01422 358282
          email: sbradberry@tiscali.co.uk
Huddersfield Revd Martyn Crompton, Vicarage, Golcar, Huddersfield HD7 4PX *Tel:* 01484 654647
          email:
          martyncrompton@stjohnsgolcar.freeserve.co.uk
Kirkburton Revd Christine Bullimore, Rectory, 14 Grange Drive, Emley, Huddersfield HD8 9SF
          Tel: 01924 849161
          Fax: 01924 849219
          email: jcbullimor@aol.com

ARCHDEACONRY OF PONTEFRACT
Barnsley Revd Allen Briscoe, St Peter's Vicarage, 1 Osborne Mews, Doncaster Rd, Barnsley S70 1UU   *Tel:* 01226 282220
          email: abriscoe@talk21.com

Birstall Revd Dhoe Craig-Wild, 3 Vicarage Meadow, Mirfield WF14 9JL   *Tel:* 01924 505791
email: dhoecraigwild@hotmail.com
Dewsbury Revd Paul Maybury, The Vicarage, 12 Fearnley Avenue, Ossett WF5 9ET
Tel: 01924 217379
Fax: 0870 137 5994
email: paul@trinityossett.org.uk

Pontefract Revd Bob Cooper, St Giles Vicarage, 9 The Mount, Pontefract WF8 1NE
Tel: 01977 706803
email: robert.cooper@onetel.net
Wakefield Revd Patricia Maguire, St George's Vicarage, 23c Broadway, Wakefield WF2 8AA
Tel: 01924 373088
email: revmaguire@tiscali.co.uk

DIOCESE OF WINCHESTER

Founded in 676. Hampshire, except for the south-eastern quarter (PORTSMOUTH), an area in the north-east (GUILDFORD), a small area in the west (SALISBURY) and one parish in the north (OXFORD); an area of eastern Dorset; the Channel Islands.

Population 1,267,000   Area 1,216 sq m
Full-time Stipendiary Parochial Clergy 189   Benefices 195
Parishes 303   Churches 407
www.winchester.anglican.org
Overseas link provinces: Province of Uganda, Province of Myanmar, Provinces of Rwanda, Burundi and Republic of Congo (formerly Zaïre).

BISHOP (96th)
Rt Revd Michael Charles Scott-Joynt, Wolvesey, Winchester. SO23 9ND [1995]   *Tel:* 01962 854050
Fax: 01962 897088
email: michael.scott-joynt@dsl.pipex.com
[Michael Winton]
Bishop's Lay Assistant Mr Martyn Sanders (*same address*)   *Tel:* 01962 897082
email: martyn.sanders@dsl.pipex.com
Bishop's Secretary Miss Joyce Cockell (*same address*)   *Tel:* 01962 854050
email: joyce.cockell@dsl.pipex.com

SUFFRAGAN BISHOPS
SOUTHAMPTON Rt Revd Paul Butler, Bishop's Office, Ham House, The Crescent, Romsey SO51 7NG [2004]   *Tel:* 01794 516005
email: paul.butler@bpsotonoffice.clara.co.uk
BASINGSTOKE Rt Revd Trevor Willmott, Bishopswood End, 40 Kingswood Rise, Four Marks, Alton GU34 5BD [2002]   *Tel:* 01420 562925
Fax: 01420 561251
email: trevor.willmott@dial.pipex.com

HONORARY ASSISTANT BISHOPS
Rt Revd John Austin Baker, Norman Corner, 4 Mede Villas, Kingsgate Rd, Winchester SO23 9QQ [1994]   *Tel:* 01962 861388
Rt Revd Simon Hedley Burrows, 8 Quarry Rd, Winchester, SO23 0JF [1994]   *Tel:* 01962 853332
Rt Revd John Yates, 15 Abbotts Ann Rd, Harestock, Winchester SO22 6ND [1995]
Tel: 01962 882854
Rt Revd John Dennis, 7 Conifer Close, Winchester SO22 6SH [1999]   *Tel:* 01962 868881
Rt Revd Edwin Barnes, 1 Queen Elizabeth Ave, Lymington SO41 9HN [2001]   *Tel:* 01590 610133
Rt Revd Colin James, Long Meadow, 3 Back St, St Cross, Winchester SO23 9SB [2003]
Tel: 01962 868874

CATHEDRAL CHURCH OF THE HOLY TRINITY, AND OF ST PETER, ST PAUL AND OF ST SWITHUN
Dean Very Revd James Edgar Atwell, Cathedral Office, 1 The Deanery, The Close, Winchester SO23 9LS [2006]   *Tel:* 01962 857203
Fax: 01962 857264
email: the.dean@winchester-cathedral.org.uk
Cathedral Office 1 The Close, Winchester SO23 9LS   *Tel:* 01962 857200
Fax: 01962 857201
email:
cathedral.office@winchester-cathedral.org.uk
Web: www.winchester–cathedral.org.uk
Canons Residentiary
Canon Roland Riem, Cathedral Office, 1 The Close, Winchester SO23 9LS [2002]
Tel: 01962 857216
email: roland.riem@winchester-cathedral.org.uk
Canon Michael St John-Channell, 8 The Close, Winchester SO23 9LS [2006]   *Tel:* 01962 857211
email: precentor@winchester-cathedral.org.uk
Lay Canons
Receiver General and Treasurer Commodore Adrian Munns, Cathedral Office, 1 The Close, Winchester SO23 9LS   *Tel:* 01962 857206
Fax: 01962 857201
email: adrian.munns@
winchester-cathedral.org.uk
Professor Lord Raymond Plant, Cathedral Office, 1 The Close, Winchester SO23 9LS
Tel: 01962 857200
Mr John Pringle, Cathedral Office, 1 The Close, Winchester SO23 9LS   *Tel:* 01962 857200
Pastoral Assistant Revd Jacqueline Browning, Cathedral Office, 1 The Close, Winchester SO23 9LS   *Tel:* 01962 857237
email:
jackie.browning@winchester-cathedral.org.uk
Clerk at Law Mr Julian Hartwell, Martyrwell, Cheriton, Alresford SO24 0QA
Tel: 01962 841484
Fax: 01962 841554
Director of Music Mr Andrew Lumsden, Cathedral Office, 1 The Close, Winchester SO23 9LS   *Tel:* 01962 857218
email:
andrew.lumsden@winchester-cathedral.org.uk
Assistant Director of Music Mr Simon Bell, Cathedral Office, 1 The Close, Winchester SO23 9LS   *Tel:* 01962 857213
email: simon.bell@winchester-cathedral.org.uk

ARCHDEACONS

WINCHESTER Vacancy

BOURNEMOUTH Ven Adrian Harbidge, Glebe House, 22 Bellflower Way, Chandlers Ford, Eastleigh SO53 4HN [2000]
Tel and Fax: 023 8026 0955
email: adrian.harbidge@dial.pipex.com

CONVOCATION (MEMBERS OF THE HOUSE OF CLERGY OF THE GENERAL SYNOD)

Dignitaries in Convocation
The Bishop of Basingstoke
Proctors for Clergy
Revd Sarah Chapman
Ven Adrian Harbidge
Canon Michael Harley
Canon Clive Hawkins

MEMBERS OF THE HOUSE OF LAITY OF THE GENERAL SYNOD

Mr John Davies
Mr Paul Eddy
Dr Peter May
Mr Rupert Shelley
Dr Brian Walker
Channel Islands
Mrs Jane Bisson
Mr David Robilliard

DIOCESAN OFFICERS

Dioc Secretary Mr Andrew Howard, Old Alresford Place, Alresford SO24 9DH
Tel: 01962 737305
Fax: 01962 737358
email: andrew.howard@winchester.anglican.org
Chancellor of Diocese Worshipful His Honour Christopher Clark QC, c/o Dioc Office
Registrar of Diocese and Bishop's Legal Secretary Mr Peter White, 19 St Peter St, Winchester. SO23 8BU
Tel: 01962 844440
Fax: 01962 842300
email: peter.white@bllaw.co.uk

DIOCESAN ORGANIZATIONS

Diocesan Office Old Alresford Place, Alresford SO24 9DH
Tel: 01962 737300
Fax: 01962 737358
Web: www.winchester.anglican.org

ADMINISTRATION

Assistant Dioc Secretary Mrs Catherine Roberts, Old Alresford Place
Tel: 01962 737306
email: catherine.roberts@winchester.anglican.org
Director of Finance and Asst Dioc Secretary Mr Stephen Collyer, Old Alresford Place
Tel: 01962 737336
email: stephen.collyer@winchester.anglican.org
Dioc Synod (Chairman, House of Clergy) Canon Michael Harley, Vicarage, 30 Hursley Rd, Chandlers Ford, Eastleigh SO53 2FT
Tel: 023 8025 2597
email:
michaelharley@parishofchandlersford.org.uk

(Chairman, House of Laity) Mr Ian Newman, Meadow View, 15 Bowerwood Rd, Fordingbridge SP6 1BL
Tel: 01425 653269
email: griffin@innewman.co.uk
(Secretary) Mr Andrew Howard, *(as above)*
Board of Finance (Chairman) Mr Arthur Binns, Nil-Des, Ashley Lane, New Milton BH25 5AQ
Tel: 01425 611379
email: dustyakjb@aol.com
(Secretary) Mr Andrew Howard *(as above)*
Director of Property Mr Rolf Hawkins, Old Alresford Place
Tel: 01962 737330
email: rolf.hawkins@winchester.anglican.org
Pastoral Steering Group Mr Andrew Howard *(as above)*
Electoral Registration Officer Mr Andrew Howard *(as above)*
Designated Officer Canon Simon Baker, Old Alresford Place
Tel: 01962 737314
email: simon.baker@winchester.anglican.org
Editor of Dioc Directory Mr Ian Knight, Old Alresford Place
Tel: 01962 737349
email: ian.knight@winchester.anglican.org
Resource Centre (Manager) Mr Ian Knight *(as above)*

CHURCHES

Advisory Committee for the Care of Churches (Chairman) Vacancy
(Secretary) Mrs Catherine Roberts *(as above)*

EDUCATION

Director of Education Mr Tony Blackshaw
Diocese of Portsmouth, First Floor, Peninsular House, Wharf Rd, Portsmouth PO2 8HB
Tel: 023 9289 9681
email: tony.blackshaw@winchester.anglican.org

MINISTRY AND DISCIPLESHIP

Ministry and Pastoral Planning
Director of Ministry and Pastoral Planning Canon Simon Baker *(as above)*
Vocations, Recruitment and Selection Officer (including ordinands) Revd Julia Mourant
Tel: 01962 737316
email: julia.mourant@winchester.anglican.org
Ministry Training Officer (including ordinands) Revd Duncan Strathie
Tel: 01962 737314
email: duncan.strathie@winchester.anglican.org
Continuing Ministerial Development Officer Revd Norman Boakes
Tel: 01962 737314
email: norman.boakes@winchester.anglican.org
Rural Officer Revd Robert Stapleton, New Vicarage, Romsey Rd, King's Sombourne, Stockbridge SO20 6PR
Tel: 01974 388223
email: robertstapleton@hotmail.com
Director of Faith Development Revd Steve Pittis, Old Alresford Place
Tel: 01962 737322
email: pittisinc@aol.com
Director of Discipleship Mr Gordon Randall, Old Alresford Place
Tel: 01962 737232
email: gordon.randall@winchester.anglican.org

Dioceses

Children and Youth Discipleship Officer Mr Andy Saunders, Old Alresford Place *Tel:* 01962 737321
email: andy.saunders@winchester.anglican.org
Youth and Children Discipleship Officer Mr Pete Maidment *Tel:* 01962 737320
email: pete.maidment@winchester.anglican.org
Ecumenical Officer Vacancy

COMMUNICATIONS

Director of Communications Ms Abha Thakor, Old Alresford Place *Tel:* 01962 737325
email: abha.thakor@winchester.anglican.org

DIOCESAN RECORD OFFICES

Hants. Record Office, Sussex St, Winchester SO23 8TH *Archivist* Janet Smith *Tel:* 01962 846154; *email:* enquiries.archives@hants.gov.uk (*For diocesan records and parishes in Hampshire [except Southampton], Bournemouth and Christchurch*)
Southampton City Record Office, Civic Centre, Southampton SO14 7LY *Archivist* Mrs Sue Woolgar *Tel:* 023 8083 2251
email: city.archives@southampton.gov.uk (*For parishes in Southampton*)
Guernsey Island Archives, St Barnabas, Cornet St, St Peter Port, Guernsey GY1 1LF
Tel: 01481 724512
Fax: 01481 715814
email: archives@gov.gg
Jersey Archive Service, Clarence Rd, St Helier, Jersey JE2 4JY *Archivist* Linda Romeril
Tel: 01534 833300
Fax: 01534 833301
email: archives@jerseyheritagetrust.org

SAFEGUARDING AND INCLUSION

Director of Safeguarding and Inclusion Ms Jane Fisher, Old Alresford Place *Tel:* 01962 737318
email: jane.fisher@winchester.anglican.org

TOURISM

Churches and Tourism Adviser Revd Clive Parnell-Hopkinson, Rectory, Church Lane, Ellisfield, Basingstoke RG25 2QR *Tel:* 01256 381217
email: halo.cph@ukonline.co.uk

AREA DEANS
ARCHDEACONRY OF BOURNEMOUTH

Bournemouth Vacancy
Eastleigh Canon Cliff Bannister, Vicarage, Vicarage Drive, Hedge End, Southampton SO30 4DU *Tel:* 01489 782288
email: cliffbannister@tiscali.co.uk
Lyndhurst Revd Dominic Furness, The Vicarage, Lymington Rd, Milford-on-Sea, Lymington SO41 0QN *Tel:* 01590 643289
email: dominic.furness@tiscali.co.uk

Southampton Revd Gary Philbrick, The Vicarage, 357 Burgess Rd, Southampton SO16 3BD
Tel: 023 8055 4231
email: gary.philbrick@dsl.pipex.com

ARCHDEACONRY OF WINCHESTER

Basingstoke Revd Andrew Bishop, The Vicarage, Church Lane, Old Basing, Basingstoke RG24 7DJ
Tel: 01256 473762
email: as.bishop@tiscali.co.uk

RURAL DEANS
ARCHDEACONRY OF BOURNEMOUTH

Christchurch Canon Diane Webster, Vicarage, Church Corner, Burley, Ringwood BH24 4AP
Tel: 01425 402303
email: diane.mwebster@tiscali.co.uk
Romsey Revd Ron Corne, Broughton Rectory, Rectory Lane, Broughton, Stockbridge SO20 8AB
Tel: 01794 301287
email: cronandrew@aol.com

ARCHDEACONRY OF WINCHESTER

Alresford Revd Jonathan Cruickshank, Itchen Valley Rectory, Chillandham Lane, Itchen Abbas, Winchester SO21 1AS
Tel and Fax: 01962 779832
email: jcruickshank@btclick.com
Alton Vacancy
Andover Revd Jill Bentall, Old Farm Cottage, 102 Charlton Village, Andover SP10 4AN
Tel: 01264 365643
email: jill.bentall@btinternet.com
Odiham Canon Robin Ewbank, Vicarage, Church Lane, Hartley Wintney, Hook RG27 8DZ
Tel: 01252 842670
email: robin.ewbank@stjohnshw.co.uk
Whitchurch Revd Christine Dale, The Rectory, Mount Rd, Woolton Hill, Newbury RG20 9QZ
Tel: 01635 253323
email: revdc@cdsm.wanadoo.co.uk
Winchester Revd Alan Gordon, Rectory, 4 Campion Way, King's Worthy, Winchester SO23 7QP *Tel:* 01962 882166
email: alan.gordon98@ntlworld.com

CHANNEL ISLANDS

Dean of Jersey Very Revd Bob Key, The Deanery, David Place, St Helier, Jersey, CI JE2 4TE
Tel: 01534 720001
email: robert_f_key@yahoo.com
Dean of Guernsey Very Revd Paul Mellor, Deanery, Cornet St, St Peter Port, Guernsey, CI GY1 1BZ *Tel:* 01481 720036
Fax: 01481 722948
email: paul@townchurch.org.gg

DIOCESE OF WORCESTER

Founded in 679. Worcestershire, except for a few parishes in the south (GLOUCESTER) and in the north (BIRMINGHAM). Dudley; a few parishes in Wolverhampton, Sandwell and in northern Gloucestershire.

Population 821,000   Area 671 sq m
Full-time Stipendiary Parochial Clergy 131   Benefices 110
Parishes 174   Churches 282
www.cofe-worcester.org.uk
Overseas link diocese: Peru (Province of Southern Cone).

BISHOP (113th)
Rt Revd John Geoffrey Inge, The Bishop's Office, The Old Palace, Deansway, Worcester WR1 2JE [2007]   *Tel:* 01905 21897
Fax: 01905 21462
email: bishop.worcester@cofe-worcester.org.uk
[John Wigorn]

SUFFRAGAN BISHOP
DUDLEY Rt Revd David Stuart Walker, Bishop's House, Bishop's Walk, Cradley Heath B64 7RH [2000]   *Tel:* 0121 550 3407
Fax: 0121 550 7340
email: bishop.david@cofe-worcester.org.uk

HONORARY ASSISTANT BISHOPS
Rt Revd Christopher Mayfield, Harwood House, 54 Primrose Crescent, St Peter's, Worcester WR5 3HT [2002]   *Tel:* 01905 764822
Rt Revd Mark Santer, 81 Clarence Rd, Moseley, Birmingham B13 9UH [2002]   *Tel:* 0121 441 2194
Rt Revd Humphrey Taylor, 10 High St, Honeybourne, Evesham WR10 7PQ [2003]
Tel: 01386 934846

CATHEDRAL CHURCH OF CHRIST AND THE BLESSED VIRGIN MARY
Dean Very Revd Peter Gordon Atkinson, The Deanery, 10 College Green, Worcester WR1 2LH [2007]   *Tel:* 01905 27821
Chapter Office 8 College Yard, Worcester WR1 2LA   *Tel:* 01905 732900
Fax: 01905 611139
email: info@worcestercathedral.org.uk
Canons Residentiary
Vacancy
Canon Dr Alvyn Pettersen, 2 College Green, Worcester WR1 2LH [2002]   *Tel:* 01905 732900
email: AlvynPettersen@worcestercathedral.org.uk
Canon David Stanton, 15A College Green, Worcester WR1 2LH [2005]   *Tel:* 01905 732900
email: DavidStanton@worcestercathedral.org.uk
Lay Canons
Prof Michael Clarke, Chapter Office
Cathedral Steward Mr Les West, Chapter Office
Tel: 01905 732907
Master of Choristers and Cathedral Organist Mr Adrian Lucas, Chapter Office   *Tel:* 01905 732916

ARCHDEACONS
WORCESTER Ven Roger Morris, The Archdeacon's House, Walker's Lane, Whittington, Worcester WR5 2RE [2008]   *Tel:* 01905 20537 (Dioc Office)
email: jhinds@cofe-worcester.org.uk
Office The Old Palace, Deansway, Worcester WR1 2JE   *Tel:* 01905 20537
Fax: 01905 612302
DUDLEY Ven Fred Trethewey, 15 Worcester Rd, Droitwich WR9 8AA [2001]
Tel and *Fax:* 01905 773301

CONVOCATION (MEMBERS OF THE HOUSE OF CLERGY OF THE GENERAL SYNOD)
Dignitaries in Convocation
The Bishop of Dudley
Proctors for Clergy
Revd Stuart Currie
Canon Jane Fraser
Vacancy

MEMBERS OF THE HOUSE OF LAITY OF THE GENERAL SYNOD
Canon Prof Michael Clarke
Mr David Hawkins
Mr Robin Lunn

DIOCESAN OFFICERS
Dioc Secretary Mr Robert Higham, The Old Palace, Deansway, Worcester WR1 2JE
Tel: 01905 20537
Chancellor of Diocese Mr Charles Mynors, Francis Taylor Building, Inner Temple, London EC4Y 7BD   *Tel:* 020 7353 8415
Registrar of Diocese and Bishop's Legal Secretary Mr Michael Huskinson, Messrs March & Edwards, 8 Sansome Walk, Worcester WR1 1LN
Tel: 01905 723561
Fax: 01905 723812
Dioc Surveyor Mr Mark Wild, Dioc Office
Tel: 01905 20537

DIOCESAN ORGANIZATIONS
Diocesan Office The Old Palace, Deansway, Worcester WR1 2JE   *Tel:* 01905 20537
Fax: 01905 612302

ADMINISTRATION

Asst Dioc Secretary (Finance) Mr Stephen Lindner, Dioc Office
DAC Secretary (Acting) Mr John Dentith, Dioc Office
Dioc Synod (Chairman, House of Clergy) Revd Stuart W. Currie, St Stephen's Vicarage, 1 Beech Ave, Worcester WR3 8PZ   *Tel:* 01905 452169
email: sw.currie@virgin.net
(Chairman, House of Laity) Mr David Hawkins, Dioc Office
(Secretary) Mr Robert Higham, Dioc Office

RESOURCES BOARD

(Chairman) Mr Alastair Findlay; *(Secretary)* Mr Robert Higham *(as above)*
Parsonages Board (Chairman) Mr David Cariss, Dioc Office
(Secretary) Mr Stephen Lindner *(as above)*
Investment and Glebe Committee (Chairman) Mr Peter Seward *(as above)*
(Secretary) Mr Stephen Lindner *(as above)*
Glebe Agent Mr Anthony Champion, Halls, 4 Foregate St, Worcester WR1 1DB
Tel: 01905 611066
Stewardship Committee (Chairman) Mr Alan Hughes, Dioc Office
Stewardship and Resources Officer Canon Mel Smith, Dioc Office
Pastoral Committee Mr Robert Higham *(as above)*
Board of Patronage Mr Robert Higham *(as above)*
Designated Officer Mr Robert Higham *(as above)*
Diocesan Trustees Mr Michael Huskinson, Messrs March & Edwards, 8 Sansome Walk, Worcester WR1 1LN   *Tel:* 01905 723561
Fax: 01905 723812

CHURCHES

Advisory Committee for the Care of Churches (Chairman) Mr John Bailey, Dioc Office; *(Secretary)* Mr John Dentith, Dioc Office
Change Ringers Association Mr D. Andrews

EDUCATION

Board of Education (Chair) Revd Stuart W. Currie, St Stephen's Vicarage, 1 Beech Ave, Worcester WR3 8PZ   *Tel:* 01905 452169
Director of Education Revd David Morphy, Dioc Office
Tertiary Education Officer Revd David Morphy *(as above)*
Schools Improvement Officer Mr Jonathan Rendall, Dioc Office
Children's Officer Vacancy
Youth Officer Dr Sarah Brush, Dioc Office

TRAINING

Director of Development Canon Robert Jones, Dioc Office   *email:* rjones@cofe-worcester.org.uk
Dioc Director of Ordinands Ven Ron Hesketh
Convenor for Women in Ministry Revd Georgina Byrne, Rectory, St Kenelm's Rd, Romsley, Halesowen B62 0PH   *Tel:* 01562 710050

Asst Director of Development (Discipleship) Revd Stephen Winter, Dioc Office
Chaplaincy to People who are Deaf or Hard of Hearing – Chaplain Vacancy
Chaplain to MENCAP Canon Hazel Hughes, Wribbenhall Vicarage, Trimpley Lane, Bewdley DY12 1JJ   *Tel:* 01299 402196

MINISTRY

Dioc Director of Ordinands Ven Ron Hesketh *(as above)*
Convenor for Women in Ministry Revd Georgina Byrne *(as above)*
Association of Readers
Secretary Mrs E. M. Walker, 40 Vicarage Rd, Wollaston, Stourbridge DY8 4UP
Registrar Dr M. J. Robinson, 5 Park Dingle, Bewdley DY12 2JY   *Tel:* 01299 403080
email: mikejrobinson@fsmail.net

LITURGICAL

Secretary Revd D. Chaplin, Vicarage, 29 Old Coach Rd, Droitwich WR9 8BB
Tel: 01905 798929
email: doug@archy.clara.co.uk

MISSION AND UNITY

Board for Mission (Chairman) Revd Stephen G. F. Owens, Vicarage, Far Forest, Kidderminster DY14 9TT   *Tel:* 01299 266580
Mission Administrator Margaret Rutter, Dioc Office
Ecumenical Officer – Worcestershire Revd David Ryan, Vicarage, 4 Daty Croft, Home Meadow, Warndon, Worcester WR4 0JB
Tel: 01905 616109
Ecumenical Officer – Dudley Revd Barry Gilbert, Rectory, 2 Church Hill, Brierley Hill DY5 3PX
Tel: 01384 78146

PRESS AND PUBLICATIONS

Dioc Communications Officer and Bishop's Press Office Samantha Setchell, Dioc Office
Tel: 07852 302516
Editor of the Dioc Directory Mrs Alison Vincent
Editor of Dioc News Samantha Setchell

DIOCESAN RECORD OFFICES

County Archivist, Record Office, County Hall, Spetchley Rd, Worcester WR5 2NP *County Archivist* Mr R. Whittaker *Tel:* 01905 766530; *Fax:* 01905 766363 *(For diocesan records and most parish records)*
Dudley Archives and Local History Dept, Mount Pleasant St, Coseley WV14 9JR *Archivist* Mrs K. H. Atkins *Tel:* 01384 812770 *(For parish records for the deaneries of Kingswinford (formerly Himley), Dudley and Stourbridge)*

SOCIAL RESPONSIBILITY

Church Action Within Society (Chairman) Rt Revd David Walker, Bishop of Dudley
Social Responsibility Officer and Secretary Revd John Paxton

Worcestershire Industrial Mission: Team Leader Revd Phillip Jones, 7 Egremont Gardens, Worcester WR4 0QH   *Tel* and *Fax:* 01905 755037
email: phillipjones@faithatwork.org.uk
Chaplaincy to Agriculture and Rural Life Revd Robert Barlow, The White House, Ankerdine Hill, Knightwick, Worcester WR6 5PR
Tel: 07947 600627 (Mobile)
email: rbarlow@cofe-worcester.org.uk

RURAL DEANS
ARCHDEACONRY OF WORCESTER
Evesham Revd Terry M. Mason, Vicarage (formerly Lorton House), Church St, Broadway, Worcester WR12 7AE   *Tel:* 01386 852352
email: broadwayvicarage@tesco.net
Malvern Revd W. David Nichol, Holy Trinity Vicarage, 2 North Malvern Rd, Malvern WR14 4LR   *Tel:* 01684 561126
email: david@trinityandthewest.wanadoo.co.uk
Martley and Worcester West Revd David Sherwin, The Rectory, Martley, Worcester WR6 6QA
Tel: 01886 888664
Pershore Revd Matthew Baynes, Bredon Rectory, Tewkesbury, GL20 7LT   *Tel:* 01684 7772237
email: matthew@tcbaynes.fsnet.co.uk
Upton Canon Frances A. Wookey, Vicarage, 5 Westmere, Hanley Swan, Worcester WR8 0DG
Tel: 01684 310321
email: fwookey@fides.demon.co.uk

Worcester East Canon Kenneth Boyce, Rectory, St Catherine's Hill, Worcester WR5 2EA
Tel: 01905 355119
email: ken@kenboyce.fsnet.co.uk

ARCHDEACONRY OF DUDLEY
Bromsgrove Vacancy
Droitwich Revd Canon Peter Kerr, The Rectory, Ombersley, Droitwich WR9 0EW
Tel: 01905 620950
email: peter.kerr@cofe-worcester.org.uk
Dudley Canon Hilary Hanke, St Luke's Vicarage, Upper High St, Cradley Heath B64 5HX
Tel: 01384 569940
Kidderminster Revd Keith James, The Rectory, 57 Park Lane, Bewdley, Worcs. DY12 2HA
Tel: 01299 402275
email: keith.james2@btconnect.com
Kingswinford (*formerly Himley*) Revd Garth Nathaniel, 5 Leys Rd, Brockmoor, Brierley Hill, West Midlands DY5 3UR   *Tel:* 01384 263327
email: gn004d6359@blueyonder.co.uk
Stourbridge Revd Andrew Hazlewood, The Rectory, Pedmore Lane, Stourbridge, West Midlands DY9 0SW   *Tel:* 01562 887287
email: andrewhazlewood@gmail.com
Stourport Revd Louise Grace, The Rectory, Lindridge, Tenbury Wells, Worcs. WR15 8JQ
Tel: 01584 881331
email: revgrace@hotmail.co.uk

DIOCESE OF YORK

Founded in 627. York; East Riding of Yorkshire, except for an area in the south-west (SHEFFIELD); Kingston-upon-Hull; Redcar and Cleveland; Middlesbrough; the eastern half of North Yorkshire; Stockton-on-Tees, south of the Tees; an area of Leeds.

Population 1,397,000   Area 2,661 sq m
Full-time Stipendiary Parochial Clergy 217   Benefices 264
Parishes 457   Churches 607
Overseas link dioceses: Cape Town (South Africa), Mechelen-Brussels (Belgium).

ARCHBISHOP (97th)
Most Revd and Rt Hon Dr John Tucker Mugabi Sentamu, *Primate of England and Metropolitan*, Bishopthorpe Palace, Bishopthorpe, York YO23 2GE [2005]   *Tel:* 01904 707021/2
Fax: 01904 709204
email: office@archbishopofyork.org
Web: www.bishopthorpepalace.co.uk
[Sentamu Ebor]
Chaplain and Researcher Revd Dr Daphne Green
email: daphne.green@archbishopofyork.org
Domestic Chaplain Revd Brunel Hugh Grayburn James   *Tel:* 01904 772381
email: brunel.james@archbishopofyork.org
Chief of Staff Revd Michael Macnaughton
Tel: 01904 772362
email:
malcolm.macnaughton@archbishopofyork.org

SUFFRAGAN BISHOPS
SELBY Rt Revd Martin Wallace, Bishop's House, Barton-le-Street, Malton YO17 6PL [2004]
Tel: 01653 627191
Fax: 01653 627193
email: bishselby@clara.net
HULL Rt Revd Richard Frith, Hullen House, Woodfield Lane, Hessle HU13 0ES [1998]
Tel: 01482 649019
Fax: 01482 647449
email: richard@bishop.karoo.co.uk
WHITBY Rt Revd Robert Ladds, 60 West Green, Stokesley, Middlesbrough TS9 5BD [1999]
Tel: 01642 714475
Fax: 01642 714472
email: bishopofwhitby@episcopus.co.uk

PROVINCIAL EPISCOPAL VISITOR
BEVERLEY Rt Revd Martyn William Jarrett, 3 North Lane, Roundhay, Leeds LS8 2QJ [2000]
Tel: 0113 265 4280
Fax: 0113 265 4281
email:
bishop-of-beverley@3-north-lane.fsnet.co.uk

HONORARY ASSISTANT BISHOPS
Rt Revd Clifford Condor Barker, 15 Oaktree Close, Strensall, York YO3 5TR [1991]
Tel: 01904 490406

Rt Revd Michael Henshall, Brackenfield, 28 Hermitage Way, Eskdaleside, Sleights, Whitby YO22 5HG [1996]   *Tel:* 01947 811233
Rt Revd David George Galliford, 10 St Mary's Mews, Wigginton, York YO32 2SE [1995]
Tel: 01904 761489
Rt Revd Noël Jones, The Sudreys, Pickering Rd, Thornton Dale, Pickering YO18 7LH [2003]
Rt Revd David Lunn, Rivendell, 28 Southfield Rd, Wetwang, Driffield YO25 9XX [1997]
Rt Revd David Smith, 34 Cedar Glade, Dunnington, York YO19 5QZ [2002]
Tel: 01904 481225

CATHEDRAL CHURCH OF ST PETER
Dean Very Revd Keith Jones, The Deanery, York YO1 7JQ [2004]   *Tel:* 01904 623608 (Home)
01904 557202 (Office)
Fax: 01904 557204 (Office)
email: dean@yorkminster.org
Dean and Chapter Office Church House, Ogleforth, York YO1 7JN   *Tel:* 01904 557200
Fax: 01904 557201
email: reception@yorkminster.org
Pastor Vacancy
Chancellor Canon Glyn Webster, 4 Minster Yard, York YO1 7JD [1999]   *Tel:* 01904 620877 (Home)
01904 557207 (Office)
Fax: 01904 557204
email: chancellor@yorkminster.org
Theologian Canon Dr Jonathan Draper, 3 Minster Court, York YO1 7JJ [2000]
Tel: 01904 625599 (Home)
01904 557211 (Office)
email: theologian@yorkminster.org
Precentor Canon Jeremy Fletcher, 2 Minster Court, York YO1 7JJ [2002]
Tel: 01904 557205 (Office)
01904 624965 (Home)
Fax: 01904 557204
email: precentor@yorkminster.org
Chapter Steward Mr John Morris, Dean and Chapter Office   *Tel:* 01904 557212
Fax: 01904 557204
email: chapter.steward@yorkminster.org

Lay Canons
Treasurer Vacancy
Canon Maureen Loffill, Wedgwood House, Heslington, York YO10 5DP   *Tel:* 01904 430246
Fax: 01904 421481
email: maureen@maureenloffill.demon.co.uk
Canon Dr Ann Lees, Diocesan House, Aviator Court, Clifton Moor, York YO30 4WJ
Tel: 01904 699511
email: alees@yorkdiocese.org
Canon Dr Andrew Green, Juniper House, The Nookin, Husthwaite, York YO61 4PY
Tel: 07770 321564
email: andrewgreen@bpipoly.com
Chapter Clerk Mr Andrew Oates, Dean and Chapter Office   *Tel:* 01904 557210
Fax: 01904 557204
email: chapterclerk@yorkminster.org
Head Verger Mr Alex Carberry, York Minster Vestry   *Tel:* 01904 557221
email: alexc@yorkminster.org
Director of Music Mr Robert Sharpe, Dean and Chapter Office   *Tel:* 01904 557206
Fax: 01904 557204
email: roberts@yorkminster.org
Chief Accountant Mrs Sue Pace, Dean and Chapter Office   *Tel:* 01904 557213
Fax: 01904 557215
email: suep@yorkminster.org
Chamberlain and Director of Development Dr Richard Shephard, Dean and Chapter Office
Tel: 01904 557245
Fax: 01904 557246
email: richards@yorkminster.org
High Steward The Earl of Halifax, Garrowby, York YO41 1QD   *Tel:* 01759 368236
Fax: 01759 368154
email: halifax@garrowby.plus.com

ARCHDEACONS
YORK Ven Richard Seed, Holy Trinity Rectory, Micklegate, York YO1 6LE [1999]
Tel: 01904 623798
Fax: 01904 628155
email: archdeacon.of.york@yorkdiocese.org
EAST RIDING Ven David Butterfield, Brimley Lodge, 27 Molescroft Rd, Beverley HU17 7DX [2007]   *Tel and Fax:* 01482 881659
email: archdeacon.of.eastriding@yorkdiocese.org
CLEVELAND Ven Paul Ferguson, 2 Langbaurgh Rd, Hutton Rudby, Yarm TS15 0HL [2001]
Tel: 01642 706095
Fax: 01642 706097
email: archdeacon.of.cleveland@yorkdiocese.org

CONVOCATION (MEMBERS OF THE HOUSE OF CLERGY OF THE GENERAL SYNOD)
Dignitaries in Convocation
The Bishop of Beverley
Proctors for Clergy
Canon David Bailey
Revd Gillian Henwood
Canon Catherine Rowling

Ven Richard Seed
Canon Suzanne Sheriff
Canon Glyn Webster

MEMBERS OF THE HOUSE OF LAITY OF THE GENERAL SYNOD
Canon Linda Ali
Mr Martin Dales
Mrs Jennifer Reid
Mr Ian Smith
Mr Roy Thompson
Canon Stella Vernon

DIOCESAN OFFICERS
Dioc Secretary Canon Peter Warry, Diocesan House, Aviator Court, Clifton Moor, York YO30 4WJ   *Tel:* 01904 699500
Fax: 01904 699501
Chancellor of Diocese Chancellor Canon Peter Collier, 12 St Helen's Rd, Dringhouses, York YO24 1HP
Registrar of Diocese and Archbishop's Legal Secretary Mr Lionel Lennox, The Registry, Stamford House, Piccadilly, York YO1 9PP
Tel: 01904 623487
Fax: 01904 611458

DIOCESAN ORGANIZATIONS
Diocesan Office Diocesan House, Aviator Court, Clifton Moor, York YO30 4WJ   *Tel:* 01904 699500
Fax: 01904 699501
email: office@yorkdiocese.org
Web: www.dioceseofyork.org.uk

ADMINISTRATION
Dioc Synod (Chairman, House of Clergy) Canon Glyn Webster, 4 Minster Yard, York YO1 7JD
Tel: 01904 620877
email: chancellor@yorkminster.org
(Chairman, House of Laity) Canon Richard Liversedge, 1 Caledonia Park, Victoria Dock, Hull HU9 1TE   *Tel:* 01482 588357
email: r.liversedge@hulldrypool.freeserve.co.uk
(Secretary) Canon Peter Warry, Dioc Office
Assistant Dioc Secretary Ms Shirley Davies, Dioc Office
Board of Finance (Chairman) Mr Robin Clough, Dioc Office; *(Secretary)* Mr David Fletcher
Financial Secretary Mr David Fletcher, Dioc Office
Parsonages Surveyor Mr Graham Andrews, Dioc Office
Parsonages Committee Miss Kathleen Wilks, Dioc Office
Pastoral Committee Ms Shirley Davies *(as above)*
Designated Officer Canon Peter Warry, Dioc Office
Property and Trust Committee Mrs Linda Walmsley, Dioc Office
Dioc Communications Officer Dioc Office

CHURCHES
Advisory Committee for the Care of Churches (Chairman) Canon David Hodgson, The Ascension Vicarage, Penrith Rd, Berwick Hills, Middlesbrough TS3 7JR   *Tel:* 01642 244857

(*Secretary*) Mr Philip Thomas, Dioc Office
Furnishings Officer Mr David Haddon-Reece, Vicarage, Topcliffe, Thirsk YO7 3RU
Tel: 01845 577939
Redundant Churches Uses Committee Ms Shirley Davies (*as above*)

EDUCATION
Board of Education (*Director*) Canon Dr R. Ann Lees, Dioc Office
email: ann.lees@yorkdiocese.org
Asst Director of Education Mrs Viv Todd (*Educational Services and Schools Support*); Simon Quartermaine (*School Buildings Officer*)
Religious Education and Collective Worship Mrs Celia Roberts and Mrs Sue Holmes
Adviser for Children and Youth Work (East Riding) Jon Steel, 2 Appin Close, Bransholme, Hull HU7 5BB
Tel: 01482 828805
07736 378051 (Mobile)
Adviser in Children's and Youth Work (York) Revd Nigel Chapman, Vicarage, Coxwold, York YO61 4AD
Tel: 01347 868287
email: nigel.chapman@yorkdiocese.org
Web: ww.archyork.org.uk
Children's Officer (part-time) (*Cleveland*) Vacancy
Young Adults and Vocations Officer (part-time) (*Cleveland*) Revd Ashley Wilson, St Oswald's House, West Rounton, Northallerton DL6 2LW
Tel: 01609 882401

MINISTRY AND MISSION
Resources Consultant Vacancy
Director of Ordinands Canon Catherine Rowling, Rectory, Cemetery Rd, Thirsk YO7 1PR
Tel: 01845 522258
email: cathyrowling@aol.com
Officer for NSMs Revd Raymond Morris, 3 Medina Gardens, Brookfield, Middlesbrough TS5 8BN
Tel: 01642 593726
Warden of Readers Ven Paul Ferguson, 2 Langbaurgh Rd, Hutton Rudby, Yarm TS15 0HL
Tel: 01642 706095
Fax: 01642 706097
email: archdeacon.of.cleveland@yorkdiocese.org
Readers (*Secretary*) *see* Warden of Readers (*as above*)
Ecumenical Advisers
York Archdeaconry Revd Andrew Clements, Vicarage, 80 Osbaldwick Lane, York YO10 3AX
Tel: 01904 416763
email: andrew@ozmurt.freeserve.co.uk
East Riding Archdeaconry Vacancy
Cleveland Archdeaconry Revd Dr Michael Hazelton, Vicarage, Danby, Whitby YO21 2NQ
Tel: 01287 660388

LITURGICAL
York Diocesan Liturgical Group (*Chairman*) Rt Revd Richard Frith, Bishop of Hull

PRESS AND PUBLICATIONS
Archbishop's Media Adviser (*National*) Mr Arun Arora, Bishopthorpe Palace, Bishopthorpe, York YO23 2GE
Tel: 01904 707021
email: arun.arora@archbishopofyork.org
Communications Officer (*Diocese*) Dioc Office
Tel: 01904 699530
07946 748702 (Mobile)
email: comms@yorkdiocese.org
Editor of Dioc Magazine (*as above*)

DIOCESAN RECORD OFFICES
The Borthwick Institute of Historical Research, University of York, Heslington, York YO10 5DD
Acting Director and Diocesan Archivist Christopher C. Webb
Tel: 01904 321166
Web: www.york.ac.uk/inst/bihr
(*For parish records in the Archdeaconry of York*)
East Riding of Yorkshire Archive Office, County Hall, Beverley HU17 9BA *Archivist* Mr Ian Mason
Tel: 01482 392790
email: ian.mason@eastriding.gov
Web: www.eastriding.gov.uk/learning
(*For parish records in the Archdeaconry of the East Riding*)
North Yorkshire County Record Office, Malpas Rd, Northallerton DL7 8PB *Acting County Archivist* Mrs Judith A. Smeaton *Tel:* 01609 777585 (*For parish records in the Archdeaconry of Cleveland**)
*Parishes within the present county boundaries of Cleveland may, if they so wish, deposit their records in the Cleveland County Archives Dept, Exchange House, 6 Marton Rd, Middlesbrough TS1 1DB *Archivist* Mr D. Tyrell *Tel:* 01642 248321

SOCIAL RESPONSIBILITY
Secretary for Social Action Vacancy

RURAL DEANS
ARCHDEACONRY OF YORK
Derwent Revd Richard Kirkman, Rectory, York Rd, Escrick, York YO19 6EY *Tel:* 01904 728406
email: rmkquanta@onetel.net
Easingwold Revd John Harrison, Vicarage, Easingwold, York YO61 3JT *Tel:* 01347 821394
email: vicar.easingwold@hotmail.co.uk
New Ainsty Revd Peter Bristow, Vicarage, 86 High St, Boston Spa, Wetherby LS23 6EA
Tel: 01937 842454
email: peterbristow1@ntlworld.com
Selby Revd Chris Wilton, Vicarage, 2 Sir John's Lane, Sherburn in Elmet, Leeds LS25 6BJ
Tel: 01977 682122
South Wold Revd James Finnemore OGS, Rectory, Bishop Wilton, York YO42 1SA
Tel: 01759 368230
Southern Ryedale Revd Quentin Wilson, The Coach House, East Heslerton, Malton YO17 8RN
Tel: 01944 728060
York Revd Martin Baldock, Vicarage, Dringhouses, York YO24 1QG *Tel:* 01904 706120
email: parishoffice@care4free.net

ARCHDEACONRY OF THE EAST RIDING

Beverley Revd Angela Bailey, The Rectory, 31 Old Village Rd, Little Weighton Cottingham HU20 3US *Tel:* 01482 843317

Bridlington Revd Dr Peter Pike, The Vicarage, Church St, Flamborough YO15 1PE

Tel: 01262 851370

email: revpeterpike@hotmail.com

Central and North Hull Canon David Walker, St Michael's Vicarage, 214 Orchard Park Rd, Hull HU6 9BX *Tel:* 01482 803375

email: david@stmichaelsnorthhull.org.uk

Harthill Revd Mike Smith, The Vicarage, Downe St, Driffield YO25 6DX *Tel:* 01377 253394

email: mike.davica@fish.co.uk

Holderness North Revd Marjorie Hill, Rectory, Sigglesthorne, Hull HU11 5QA

Tel: 01964 533033

email: marjhill@fish.co.uk

Holderness South Revd Anthony Burdon, Vicarage, Main Rd, Thorngumbald, Hull HU12 9NA *Tel:* 01964 601381

email: tony@tonyburdon.karoo.co.uk

Howden Revd Peter Faulkner, 10 Station Rd, South Cave HU15 2AA *Tel:* 01430 423693

email: peter@faulkner.go-plus.net

Scarborough Revd Martyn Dunning, St Mary's Vicarage, 1 North Cliffe Gardens, Scarborough YO12 6PR *Tel:* 01723 371354

email: enquiries.stmaryschurch@btinternet.com

East Hull Revd Mick Fryer, St Aidan's Vicarage, 139 Southcoates Ave, Hull HU9 3HF

Tel: 01482 374403

email: mick@staidans.org.uk

West Hull Revd Allen Bagshawe, St Matthew's Vicarage, Boulevard, Hull HU3 2TA

Tel: 01482 326573

email: allen@stmatthews.karoo.co.uk

ARCHDEACONRY OF CLEVELAND

Guisborough Canon John Weetman, St Peter's Vicarage, 66 Aske Rd, Redcar TS10 2BP

Tel: 01642 490700

Helmsley Canon David Purdy, Vicarage, Kirkbymoorside, York YO6 6AZ

Tel: 01751 431452

Middlesbrough Canon Erik Wilson, St Barnabas Vicarage, 8 The Crescent, Linthorpe, Middlesbrough TS5 6SQ *Tel:* 01642 817306

email: erik.wilson@ntlworld.com

Mowbray Revd Richard Rowling, Rectory, Cemetery Rd, Thirsk YO7 1PR

Tel: 01845 523183

email: rfrowling@aol.com

Pickering Revd Paul Mothersdale, Rectory, Thornton Dale, Pickering YO18 7QW

Tel: 01751 474244

email: paulmothersdale@bigfoot.com

Stokesley Revd John Ford, Vicarage, 21 Thornton Rd, Stainton, Middlesbrough TS8 9DS

Tel: 01642 288131

email: revjohn.ford@ntlworld.com

Whitby Revd David Cook, The Vicarage, 22 Eskdaleside, Sleights, Whitby YO22 5EP

Tel: 01947 810349

National Structures

PART 2

PART 2 CONTENTS

Every effort has been made to ensure that all details are accurate at the time of going to press.

NATIONAL
STRUCTURES

THE GENERAL SYNOD OF THE CHURCH OF ENGLAND

Office

Church House, Great Smith St, London SW1P 3AZ
Tel: 020 7898 1000 *Fax:* 020 7898 1369
email: synod@c-of-e.org.uk
Web: www.cofe.anglican.org

Dates of Sessions

The following periods have been set aside for Groups of Sessions of the General Synod:

2008: 11 February – 15 February, London
4 July – 8 July, York
17 November – 19 November, London
(if necessary)
2009: 9 February –13 February, London

10 July – 14 July, York
16 November – 18 November, London (if required)
2010: 8 February – 12 February, London
9 July – 13 July, York

Composition of the General Synod

	Canterbury	York	Either	Totals
House of Bishops				
Diocesan Bishops	30	14		44
Suffragan Bishops ...	6	3		9
including the				
Bishop of Dover				
ex officio				
	36	17		53
House of Clergy				
Deans	3	2		5
Service Chaplains				
and Chaplain-				
General of				
Prisons	4			4
Elected Proctors				
and the Dean of				
Guernsey or				
Jersey	129	54		183
University Proctors ..	4	2		6
Religious				
Communities			2	2
Co-opted places				
(maximum)	3	2		5
	143	60	2	205

	Canterbury	York	Either	Totals
House of Laity				
Elected Laity	136	59		195
Religious				
Communities			2	2
Lay Armed Services .			3	3
Co-opted places			3	3
(maximum)			5	5
Ex officio (First and				
Second Church				
Estates				
Commissioners) ..			2	2
	136	59	12	207
House of				
Bishops, House of				
Clergy or House of				
Laity				
Ex officio (Dean of the				
Arches, the two				
Vicars General, the				
Third Church				
Estates				
Commissioner, the				
Chairman of the				
Pensions Board				
and six Appointed				
Members of the				
Archbishops'				
Council)			11	11
Maximum totals	317	138	21	476

The General Synod consists of the Convocations of Canterbury and York, joined together in a House of Bishops and a House of Clergy, and having added to them a House of Laity.

The House of Bishops is made up of the Upper Houses of the Convocations of Canterbury and York. It consists of the archbishops and all other diocesan bishops and the Bishop of Dover as *ex officio* members, four bishops elected by and from the suffragan bishops (and certain other bishops) of the Province of Canterbury (other than the Bishop of Dover), three bishops elected by and from the suffragan bishops (and certain other bishops) of the Province of York, and any other bishops residing in either Province who are members of the Archbishops' Council.

The House of Clergy is made up of the Lower Houses of the Convocations of Canterbury and York. It consists of clergy (other than bishops) who have been elected, appointed or chosen in accordance with Canon H 2 and the rules made under it (including deans, proctors from the dioceses and university constituencies and clerical members of religious communities) together with *ex officio* members.

The House of Laity consists of members from each diocese of the two Provinces elected by lay members of the deanery synods (or annual meetings of the chaplaincies in the case of the Diocese in Europe) or chosen by and from the lay members of religious communities, together with *ex officio* members.

Representatives of other Churches, the Church of England Youth Council, and Deaf Anglicans Together are invited to attend the Synod and under its Standing Orders enjoy speaking but not voting rights.

OFFICERS OF THE GENERAL SYNOD
Presidents
The Archbishop of Canterbury
The Archbishop of York

Prolocutor of the Lower House of the Convocation of Canterbury Ven Norman Russell

Prolocutor of the Lower House of the Convocation of York Canon Glyn Webster

Chair of the House of Laity Canon Dr Christina Baxter

Vice-Chair of the House of Laity Dr Philip Giddings

Secretary General Mr William Fittall

Clerk to the Synod Revd David Williams

Chief Legal Adviser and *Joint Registrar of the Provinces of Canterbury and York (Registrar of the General Synod)* Mr Stephen Slack

Legal Advisers Revd Judith Egar, Revd Alexander McGregor

Standing Counsel Sir Anthony Hammond

OFFICERS OF THE CONVOCATIONS
Synodical Secretary of the Convocation of Canterbury Revd Gill Dallow, New Vicarage, 22 Bosworth Rd, Barlestone, Nuneaton CV13 0EL
        email: gdallow@leicester.anglican.org

Synodal Secretary of the Convocation of York
Vacancy

NON-DIOCESAN MEMBERS
The following are non-diocesan members of General Synod:

Suffragan Bishops in Convocation
CANTERBURY
The Bishop of Dover (*ex officio*)
The Bishop of Basingstoke
The Bishop of Dorking
The Bishop of Dudley
The Bishop of Willesden
The Bishop to the Forces

YORK
The Bishop of Beverley
The Bishop of Hulme
Vacancy

Deans in Convocation
CANTERBURY
The Dean of Canterbury
The Dean of Leicester
The Dean of Southwark

YORK
The Dean of Durham
The Dean of Wakefield

Chaplain-General of Prisons and Archdeacon of Prisons Ven William Noblett

Armed Forces Synod
Ven John Green
Ven Ray Pentland
Ven Stephen Robbins
Sgt Fran Hall
Brigadier Patrick Marriott
Lt Cdr Philippa Sargent

University Representatives in Convocation
CANTERBURY
Oxford
Canon Prof Marilyn McCord Adams

Cambridge
Revd Duncan Dormor

London
Revd Dr Richard Burridge

Other Universities (Southern)
Canon Dr Gavin Ashenden

YORK
Durham and Newcastle
Revd Miranda Threlfall-Holmes

Other Universities (Northern)
Revd Dr Kevin Ward

Representatives of Religious Communities in Convocation
CANTERBURY
Sister Rosemary CHN

YORK
Revd Thomas Seville CR

Lay Representatives of Religious Communities
Sister Anita OHP
Vacancy

Ex officio **Members of the House of Laity**
Dean of the Arches
Rt Worshipful Sheila Cameron QC
Vicar-General of the Province of Canterbury
Chancellor Timothy Briden
Vicar-General of the Province of York
His Honour Thomas Coningsby
First Church Estates Commissioner Mr Andreas Whittam Smith

Second Church Estates Commissioner Sir Stuart Bell MP

Third Church Estates Commissioner Mr Timothy Walker

Chairman of the Church of England Pensions Board
Mr Allan Bridgewater

Representatives who have been appointed to the Synod under its Standing Orders with speaking but not voting rights

Ecumenical Representatives
Revd Douglas Galbraith (Church of Scotland)
Very Revd Archimandrite Ephrem Lash (Orthodox Church)
Revd Graham Maskery (United Reformed Church)
Revd Gloria David (Moravian Church)
Revd Jane Craske (Methodist Church)
Revd Prof Paul Fiddes (Baptist Union)
Revd Nezlin Sterling (Black-led Churches)
Revd Mgr Andrew Faley (Roman Catholic Church)

Church of England Youth Council Representatives
Miss Rebecca Swinson
Mr Tom Pugh
Mr Richard Whitmill

Deaf Anglicans Together Representatives
Mr Barry Higgins
Revd Vera Hunt
Mrs Hilary Sage

Appointed Members of the Archbishops' Council
Mr Andrew Britton
Prof John Craven
Mr Philip Fletcher
Mrs Katherine McPherson
Mr Mark Russell
Mrs Anne Sloman
Co-opted Members
Ven Brian Smith

House of Bishops

Chairman The Archbishop of Canterbury

Vice-Chairman The Archbishop of York

Secretary Mr Jonathan Neil-Smith
Tel: 020 7898 1373
email: jonathan.neil-smith@c-of-e.org.uk

Theological Consultant Dr Martin Davie
Tel: 020 7898 1488
email: martin.davie@c-of-e.org.uk

The House of Bishops meets separately from sessions of the General Synod three times a year, in private session. It has a special responsibility for matters relating to doctrine and liturgy under Article 7 of the Constitution of General Synod. Its agendas nevertheless range more widely, reflecting matters relating to the exercise of *episcope* in the Church.

The following committees or panels work under the umbrella of the House:

THE STANDING COMMITTEE OF THE HOUSE OF BISHOPS
Chairman Most Revd and Rt Hon John Sentamu (*Archbishop of York*)

Secretary Mr Jonathan Neil-Smith
The Standing Committee consists of the Archbishops of Canterbury and York, the two bishops

elected by the House to serve on the Archbishops' Council, one bishop appointed jointly by the Archbishops from amongst those elected by the House to serve on the Church Commissioners' Board of Governors, the member elected by the House to serve on the Business Committee, one member elected by the House, and one member appointed by the Archbishops acting jointly. Its principal role is to prepare the agendas for the House's meetings, but it also deals with other matters on the House's behalf.

THE HOUSE'S THEOLOGICAL GROUP
Chairman Rt Revd Michael Nazir-Ali (*Bishop of Rochester*)

Secretary Revd Frances Arnold
Tel: 020 7898 1372
email: frances.arnold@c-of-e.org.uk

THE HOUSE'S CONTINUING MINISTERIAL EDUCATION COMMITTEE
Chairman Rt Revd Martin Wharton (*Bishop of Newcastle*)

Secretary Mr Jonathan Neil-Smith

THE RURAL BISHOPS' PANEL
Chairman Rt Revd Anthony Priddis (*Bishop of Hereford*)

Secretary Dr Jill Hopkinson

THE URBAN BISHOPS' PANEL
Chairman Rt Revd Stephen Lowe (*Bishop of Hulme*)

Secretary Revd Dr Andrew Davey
Tel: 020 7898 1448
email: andrew.davey@c-of-e.org.uk

House of Clergy

Joint Chairmen The Prolocutors of the Convocations

Secretary Dr Colin Podmore   *Tel:* 020 7898 1385
email: colin.podmore@c-of-e.org.uk

Membership of the House of Clergy comprises the Lower House of the Convocation of Canterbury and the Lower House of the Convocation of York joined into one House.

The Standing Committee of the House of Clergy consists of the Prolocutors of the Convocations, the two persons elected by the House to serve on the Archbishops' Council, the two Pro-Prolocutors of the Convocation of Canterbury and four other persons elected by and from the Lower House of the Convocation of Canterbury, the two Deputy Prolocutors of Convocation of York and two other persons elected by and from the Convocation of York.

House of Laity

Chair Canon Dr Christina Baxter

Vice-Chair Dr Philip Giddings

Secretary Mr Nicholas Hills   *Tel:* 020 7898 1363
email: nicholas.hills@c-of-e.org.uk

The Standing Committee of the House of Laity consists of the Chair and Vice-Chair, the members of the Business and Appointments Committees elected by the House and the members of the Archbishops' Council elected by the House.

Principal Committees

THE BUSINESS COMMITTEE
Chair Revd Kay Garlick
Appointed Members
Prof John Craven
Canon Glyn Webster

Elected Members
Rt Revd Trevor Wilmott (*Bishop of Basingstoke*)
Revd Sue Booys
Ms Rosalind Fuller
Ven Alan Hawker

Mrs Sue Johns
Ven Alastair Magowan
Mr Gerry O'Brien
Secretary Revd David Williams (*Clerk to the Synod*)
Tel: 020 7898 1559
email: david.williams@c-of-e.org.uk

The Committee is responsible for organizing the business of the Synod, enabling it to fulfil its role as a legislative and deliberative body.

THE LEGISLATIVE COMMITTEE

Ex officio Members
The Archbishop of Canterbury
The Archbishop of York
The Prolocutors of the Convocations
The Chair and Vice-Chair of the House of Laity
The Dean of the Arches
The Second Church Estates Commissioner

Elected Members
Rt Revd Michael Scott-Joynt (Bishop of Winchester)
Canon David Felix
Revd Stephen Trott
Mrs April Alexander
Canon Peter Bruinvels
Ms Jacqueline Humphreys
Secretary Mr Stephen Slack   *Tel:* 020 7898 1367
email: stephen.slack@c-of-e.org.uk

THE STANDING ORDERS COMMITTEE

Chair Mr Geoffrey Tattersall QC

Ex officio Members
The Prolocutors of the Convocations
The Chair and Vice-Chair of the House of Laity

Appointed Members
Mrs Gill Ambrose
Revd Sue Booys
Ven Adrian Harbidge (*Archdeacon of Bournemouth*)
Canon Simon Killwick
Mr Clive Scowen

Secretary Mr Howard Cattermole
Tel: 020 7898 1371
email: howard.cattermole@c-of-e.org.uk

PRINCIPAL COMMISSIONS
The Clergy Discipline Commission

Chair Rt Hon Lord Justice Mummery
Deputy Chair His Honour Judge John Bullimore

Secretary Mr Howard Cattermole

Office Church House, Great Smith St, London
SW1P 3AZ   *Tel:* 020 7898 1371
Fax: 020 7898 1718/1721
email: howard.cattermole@c-of-e.org.uk

MEMBERS
Mr Niall Blackie, Ven Annette Cooper (*Archdeacon of Colchester*), Miss Vasantha Gnanadoss, Ven Alan Hawker (*Archdeacon of Malmesbury*), Rt Revd Christopher Hill (*Bishop of Guildford*), Rt Revd Michael Hill (*Bishop of Bristol*), Mr James Humphery, Mr Michael Sayers, Revd Canon Michael Webb, Revd Canon Cynthia Dowdle

The Clergy Discipline Commission is constituted under the Clergy Discipline Measure 2003. Under that Measure the Commission is required to give general advice to disciplinary tribunals, the courts of the Vicars-General, bishops and arch-bishops as to the penalties which are appropriate in particular circumstances; to issue codes of practice and general policy guidance to persons exercising functions in connection with clergy discipline; and to make annually to the General Synod through the House of Bishops a report on the exercise of its functions during the previous year.

Under the 2003 Measure the Commission is also required to compile and maintain 'provincial panels' of persons available for appointment as members of a disciplinary tribunal or a Vicar-General's Court for the purposes of dealing with cases under it and to formulate guidance for the purposes of the 2003 Measure generally and to promulgate it in a Code of Practice approved by the Dean of the Arches and the General Synod.

The Commission also monitors the exercise of discipline, highlights and encourages best practice, and builds up casework experience in disciplinary matters.

The Crown Nominations Commission

Secretary to the Commission Ms Caroline Boddington, Archbishops' Secretary for Appointments

Office The Wash House, Lambeth Palace, London
SE1 7JU   *Tel:* 020 7898 1876/7
Fax: 020 7898 1899

MEMBERS

Ex officio
The Archbishop of Canterbury
The Archbishop of York
Elected Members

Three members of the House of Clergy
Very Revd Colin Slee
Revd Canon Peter Spiers
Revd Canon Glyn Webster
Three members of the House of Laity
Mr Aiden Hargreaves-Smith
Professor Glynn Harrison
Mrs Mary Johnston

Six members of the Vacancy-in-See Committee of the diocese whose bishopric is to become, or has become, vacant

Ex officio non-voting members
Mr Paul Britton (*The Prime Minister's Appointments Secretary*)

Ms Caroline Boddington (*Archbishops' Secretary for Appointments*)

The Commission was established by the General Synod in February 1977. Its function is to consider vacancies in diocesan bishoprics in the Provinces of Canterbury and York, and candidates for appointments to them. At each meeting the Chair is taken by the Archbishop in whose Province the vacancy has arisen. The Commission agrees upon two names for nomination to the Prime Minister by the appropriate Archbishop or, in the case of the Archbishopric of Canterbury or York, by the chairman of the Commission. The names submitted are given in an order of preference voted upon by the Commission. The Prime Minister accepts the first name and reverts to the second name should the first be unable to take up the post.

The Dioceses Commission

Chairman Dr Priscilla Chadwick

Vice-Chair Ven Richard Seed (*Archdeacon of York*)

Secretary Dr Colin Podmore

Office Church House, Great Smith St, London SW1P 3AZ   *Tel:* 020 7898 1385
          email: colin.podmore@c-of-e.org.uk

MEMBERS
Revd Jonathan Alderton-Ford (St Edmundsbury and Ipswich), Prof Michael Clarke (Worcester), Mrs Lucinda Herklots, Revd Dame Sarah Mullally, Prof Hilary Russell, Mr Michael Streeter (Chichester), Rt Revd Nigel Stock (Bishop of St Edmundsbury and Ipswich), Canon Martin Warner (London).

A Dioceses Commission was set up in 1978 under the Dioceses Measure 1978. In 2008 it was replaced by a new body of the same name, established under the Dioceses, Mission and Pastoral Measure 2007. Part II of that Measure makes provision for such matters as the reorganization of diocesan boundaries, the creation and revival of suffragan sees, and the delegation of episcopal functions by diocesan bishops to suffragan and assistant bishops.

The Commission's duties are laid down by the Measure. Its primary duty is to keep under review the provincial and diocesan structure of the Church of England and in particular the size, boundaries and number of provinces; the size, boundaries and number of dioceses and their distribution between the provinces; the number and distribution of bishops and the arrangements for episcopal oversight. The Commission may make reorganization schemes either of its own volition or in response to proposals from diocesan bishops. Schemes require the approval of the diocesan synods concerned (other than in exceptional circumstances) and that of the General Synod. The Commission also gives advice on good practice regarding diocesan administration and responds to requests for advice on particular issues. It comments on proposals to change the names of episcopal sees. When a diocesan bishop proposes to fill a vacant suffragan see the Commission may require the process for creating a new see to be followed if it is not convinced that the need for a suffragan bishop has been demonstrated.

The Doctrine Commission

The functions of the Doctrine Commission are to consider and advise the House of Bishops of the General Synod upon doctrinal questions referred to it by the House as well as to make suggestions to that House as to what in its judgement are doctrinal issues of concern to the Church of England. Its last report, *Being Human,* was published in July 2003. The term of office of the previous Doctrine Commission has not been extended into the new Quinquennium and it is suggested that matters are referred to either the Faith and Order Advisory Group (*see* page 171) or the House of Bishops' Theological Group (*see* page 158).

The Fees Advisory Commission

Chair His Honour Judge Andrew Rutherford

Secretary Mr Howard Cattermole

Office Church House, Great Smith St, London
SW1P 3AZ   *Tel:* 020 7898 1371
                          Fax: 020 7898 1718/1721
email: howard.cattermole@c-of-e.org.uk

MEMBERS
Mr Timothy Allen, Mr Andrew Britton, Mr Aiden
Hargreaves-Smith, Mr Geoffrey Tattersall QC and
Mr Timothy Walker

The Fees Advisory Commission is constituted
under Part II of the Ecclesiastical Fees Measure
1986, as amended by the Church of England
(Miscellaneous Provisions) Measure 2000 and
other legislation. It makes recommendations as to
certain fees to be paid to ecclesiastical judges,
legal officers and others, and embodies those
recommendations in Orders which are laid
before the General Synod for approval. If
approved, the Orders take effect unless annulled
by either House of Parliament, and are published
as Statutory Instruments.

The Legal Advisory Commission

Chair Chancellor Rupert Bursell

Secretary Revd Judith Egar

Office Church House, Great Smith St, London
SW1P 3AZ   *Tel:* 020 7898 1722
                          Fax: 020 7898 1718/1721

MEMBERS
Ex officio
The Dean of the Arches and Auditor
The Vicar-General of Canterbury
The Vicar-General of York
The Provincial Registrar of Canterbury
The Provincial Registrar of York
The Chief Legal Adviser to the Archbishops'
Council and General Synod
Standing Counsel to the General Synod
The Official Solicitor to the Church
    Commissioners

Mr Peter Beesley, Chancellor Rupert Bursell, Mr
Owen Carew-Jones, Very Revd Nicholas
Coulton, Mrs Lesley Farrall, Canon David Felix,
Mr Ian Garden, Chancellor Charles George, Rt
Revd Christopher Hill (*Bishop of Guildford*),
Chancellor Mark Hill, Ms Jacqueline Humphreys,
Ven Trevor Jones (*Archdeacon of Hertford*), Miss

Jane Lowdon, Prof David McClean, Lord Justice
Mummery, Mr Ted Nugee, Chancellor David
Turner, Ven Richard Seed (*Archdeacon of York*)

The Legal Advisory Commission gives advice
on legal matters of general interest to the
Church which are referred to it by the Archbishops' Council and its Divisions, Boards,
Councils and Commissions, by the General Synod
and its Houses and Commissions, by the Church
Commissioners and the Church of England Pensions Board, and by diocesan clerical and lay
office holders. The Commission cannot accept
requests for advice from private individuals or
secular bodies. In addition, the Commission cannot normally give opinions on contentious matters, but it may be able to do so (depending on
the circumstances) if the facts are agreed by all
parties to the dispute, all parties join in referring
the matter to the Commission for an opinion and
it is not (and is not expected to become) the sub-
ject-matter of proceedings in the courts.
  The opinions of the Commission and its pre-
decessor, the Legal Board, on matters of general
interest are published by Church House Publishing in a loose-leaf form under the title *Legal Opinions Concerning the Church of England*. The 8th edition was published in May 2007.

The Legal Aid Commission

Chairman Mr Richard Bowman

Secretary Revd Judith Egar

Office Church House, Great Smith St, London
SW1P 3AZ   *Tel:* 020 7898 1722
                          Fax: 020 7898 1718/1721

MEMBERS
Ven Christine Allsopp (*Archdeacon of
Northampton*), Revd Moira Astin, Mr Barry
Barnes, Revd Paul Benfield, Revd Geoffrey
Harbord, Ms Jacqueline Humphreys, Rt Revd

Richard Inwood (*Bishop of Bedford*), Ven Clive
Mansell (*Archdeacon of Tonbridge*), Mrs Anne
Toms, Mr John Underwood

The Legal Aid Commission operates under the
Church of England (Legal Aid) Measure 1994,
and administers the Legal Aid Fund which was
originally set up under the Ecclesiastical Jurisdiction Measure 1963 and is continued by the 1994
Measure.
  Legal aid under the 1994 Measure may be
granted, subject to various conditions, for certain
types of proceedings before Ecclesiastical Courts

and tribunals; details of eligibility for legal aid and the Commission's procedures, together with an application form for legal aid, are obtainable from the Secretary, on request.

The Liturgical Commission

Chair Rt Revd Stephen Platten (*Bishop of Wakefield*)

Secretary Dr Colin Podmore
Tel: 020 7898 1385
email: colin.podmore@c-of-e.org.uk

National Worship Development Officer Revd Peter Moger
Tel: 020 7898 1365
email: peter.moger@c-of-e.org.uk

Office Church House, Great Smith St, London SW1P 3AZ
Tel: 020 7898 1376

MEMBERS
Rt Revd Robert Paterson (*Bishop of Sodor and Man*), Mrs Gillian Ambrose (Ely), Revd Jonathan Baker (Oxford), Revd Dr Anders Bergquist, Canon Professor Paul Bradshaw, Canon Peter Craig-Wild, Canon Dr Anne Dawtry, Ms Dana Delap (Durham), Very Revd Rogers Govender (*Dean of Manchester*), Revd Rhiannon Jones (Ely), Canon Dr David Kennedy, Canon Dr Graham Kings, Revd Timothy Lomax, Revd Timothy Stratford (Liverpool), Revd Paul Thomas, Canon Carl Turner (Exeter), Revd Gary Waddington

In response to resolutions by the Convocations in October 1954, the Archbishops of Canterbury and York appointed a standing Liturgical Commission 'to consider questions of a liturgical character submitted to them from time to time by the Archbishops of Canterbury and York and to report thereon to the Archbishops'. In 1971 the Commission became a permanent Commission of the General Synod. Its functions are:

1 to prepare forms of service at the request of the House of Bishops for submission to that House in the first instance;

2 to advise on the experimental use of forms of service and the development of liturgy;

3 to exchange information and advice on liturgical matters with other Churches both in the Anglican Communion and elsewhere;

4 to promote the development and understanding of liturgy and its use in the Church.

General Synod Publications

All General Synod publications including the *Report of Proceedings* may be obtained from Church House Bookshop. The texts of many papers are also made available on the Church of England website at www.cofe.anglican.org/about/gensynod/

THE CONVOCATIONS OF CANTERBURY AND YORK

CONSTITUTION

Each of the Convocations consists of two Houses, an Upper House and a Lower House. The Upper House consists of all the diocesan bishops in the Province, the Bishop of Dover (in the case of Convocation of Canterbury), bishops elected by and from amongst suffragan bishops of the Province, and any other bishops residing in the Province who are members of the Archbishops' Council. The Archbishop presides. The Lower House comprises clergy (other than bishops) who have been elected, appointed or chosen in accordance with Canon H 2 and the rules made under it (including deans, proctors from the dioceses and university constituencies and clerical members of religious communities) together with *ex-officio* members. The Prolocutor is the chair and spokesperson of the House.

MEMBERS OF THE CONVOCATIONS

	Canterbury	York	Either Province
Upper House			
Diocesan Bishops.....	30	14	
Suffragan Bishops....	6	3	
	36	17	
Lower House			
Deans.................	3	2	
Dean of Jersey or Guernsey...........	1		
Armed Services.......	3		
Chaplain-General of Prisons..............	1		
Elected Proctors	128	54	
University Proctors ..	4	2	
Religious			2
Co-opted Clergy......	0	0	
	140	58	2

OFFICERS

Convocation of Canterbury

President The Archbishop of Canterbury

Prolocutor of the Lower House Ven Norman Russell

Other Officers
Pro-Prolocutors:
Ven Christine Hardman
Preb David Houlding
Standing Committee of the Lower House
The Prolocutor

The Pro-Prolocutors
Revd Moira Astin
Preb Kay Garlick
Revd Peter Hobson
Revd Richard Moy
Revd Stephen Trott

Registrar Mr Stephen Slack

Synodical Secretary, Actuary and Editor of the Chronicle of Convocation
Revd Gill Dallow, 57 High St, Northwood, Middlesex HA6 1EB
Tel: 01923 827149 *or* 07801 650187
email: gdallow@btinternet.com

Ostiarius Mr Clive McCleester, Hospital of St Cross, St Cross Rd, Winchester SO23 9SD

Convocation of York
President The Archbishop of York

Prolocutor of the Lower House Canon Glyn Webster

Other Officers
Deputy Prolocutors:
Canon Judy Hunt
Canon Simon Killwick

Assessors (Standing Committee)
The Prolocutor
The Deputy Prolocutors
The Bishop of Manchester
The Bishop of Blackburn
Ven Peter Ballard
Canon Sue Penfold
Ven Nigel Peyton
Revd Peter Spiers
Revd Ruth Worsley

Registrar Mr Lionel Lennox

Registrar (Provincial Elections) Mr Stephen Slack

Synodal Secretary and Treasurer and Editor of the Journal of Convocation
Ven Alan Wolstencroft, The Bakehouse, 1 Latham Row, Horwich, Bolton BL6 6QZ
Tel and *Fax:* 01204 469985
email: alanchrisw@tiscali.co.uk

Apparitor Mr Alex Carberry, Head Verger of York Minster

ACTS AND PROCEEDINGS

For the Acts and Proceedings of the Convocations, readers are referred to *The Chronicle of the Convocation of Canterbury* and to the *York Journal of Convocation*. Back numbers are available from Wm Dawson & Sons Ltd, Cannon House, Folkestone, Kent.

THE ARCHBISHOPS' COUNCIL
(and Central Board of Finance of the Church of England)

The Archbishops' Council
Charity Registration no: 1074857
Central Board of Finance of the Church of England
Company registration no: 136413
Charity registration no: 248711

Tel: 020 7898 1000
Fax: 020 7898 1369

The Turnbull Report
In 1994, a Commission was established by the Archbishops of Canterbury and York 'to review the machinery for central policy and resource direction in the Church of England, and to make recommendations for improving its effectiveness in supporting the ministry and mission of the Church to the nation as a whole'. The following year, the Commission, chaired by the Rt Revd Michael Turnbull, the then Bishop of Durham, produced a report entitled *Working as One Body*.

The need for change
The Commission looked at the constituent parts of the central structures of the Church of England – essentially the Offices of the Archbishops of Canterbury and York, the House of Bishops, the General Synod and its Boards and Councils, the Central Board of Finance, the Church Commissioners and the Church of England Pensions Board. Its conclusion was that more coherence and coordination were needed in order to give the Church an enhanced capacity to consider policy and resource issues together.

The Archbishops' Council
Amongst the Commission's recommendations was the establishment of a new Council to provide a focus for leadership and executive responsibility and a forum for strategic thinking and planning. Within an overall vision for the Church set by the House of Bishops, the Council would propose an ordering of priorities in consultation with the House of Bishops and the General Synod and take an overview of the Church's financial needs and resources. Not all of the details of the Turnbull model were accepted, but the General Synod endorsed the main thrust and agreed to the creation of the Archbishops' Council. It came into being at the beginning of 1999 under the terms of the National Institutions Measure 1998.

Purpose and work
The objects of the Archbishops' Council under the National Institutions Measure 1998 are to '*coordinate, promote, aid and further the work and*

mission of the Church of England'. The Council seeks to do this by:

- giving a clear strategic sense of direction to the national work of the Church of England, within an overall vision set by the House of Bishops and informed by an understanding of the Church's opportunities, needs and resources;
- encouraging and resourcing the Church in parishes and dioceses;
- promoting close collaborative working between the Church's national bodies, including through the management of a number of common services (Communications, Human Resources, IT etc)
- supporting the Archbishops with their diverse ministries and responsibilities; and
- engaging confidently with Government and other bodies.

The Archbishops' Council is supported in its wide-ranging brief by the staff and members of its Divisions:

- Education
- Cathedral and Church Buildings – which includes the Council for the Care of Churches and the Cathedrals Fabric Commission for England
- Central Secretariat – which includes the Council for Christian Unity, Research and Statistics, IT and Office Services
- Finance and Central Services – which includes Financial Policy, Accounts and Internal Audit
- Communications – which includes Church House Publishing
- Human Resources
- Legal
- Ministry
- Mission and Public Affairs – which includes the Committee for Minority Ethnic Anglican Concerns and the Hospital Chaplaincies Council

The work of the Council is described in more detail in its annual report, but briefly includes the following:

- the promotion of the Church's mission and evangelism to all parts of society;
- the monitoring of Government policy where proposed legislative and other changes may bear directly on the Church of England;
- the expression of a Church of England view on social and ethical issues of importance to the nation, such as marriage and family life, penal

policy or the needs of urban and rural priority areas;

- the development of educational policy and provision of advice and support services in relation to primary, secondary and further and higher education, with particular regard to Church colleges and schools;
- the encouragement of the Church's ministry among children and young people and enabling lifelong learning within the Church;
- developing more effective and equitable financial arrangements within the Church nationally;
- proposing an annual budget for the work undertaken at Church House, funding ordination training, and grants for other purposes for approval by the General Synod;
- distributing selective stipend support and parish mission funding funded by the Church Commissioners;
- working closely with the House of Bishops, the Council has a role in developing policy over the selection, training, deployment and conditions of service of clergy and Readers, including recommending stipend levels;
- enhancing relations with other Christian Churches;
- nurturing relations with other faiths;
- encouraging the care and effective use of church buildings;
- supporting hospital chaplains and hospital chaplaincy generally;
- monitoring and making recommendations about issues with policy implications for minority ethnic groups within the Church and the wider community.

It engages on behalf of the Church with Government on a wide range of issues of concern to the Church of England and its mission to the nation.

Its programme of work for the new quinquennium, in collaboration with the Church Commissioners and the House of Bishops, is set out in GS 1607, *Into the New Quinquennium and its updates.*

MEMBERS
Joint Presidents
Most Revd and Rt Hon Dr Rowan Williams, Archbishop of Canterbury
Most Revd and Rt Hon Dr John Sentamu, Archbishop of York

Prolocutor of the Lower House of the Convocation of Canterbury
Ven Norman Russell

Prolocutor of the Lower House of the Convocation of York
Revd Canon Glyn Webster
Chair of the House of Laity
Canon Dr Christina Baxter
Vice-Chair of the House of Laity
Dr Philip Giddings
Two members elected by the House of Bishops
Rt Revd Graham Jones, Bishop of Norwich
Rt Revd Tim Stevens, Bishop of Leicester

Two members elected by the House of Clergy
Prebendary Kay Garlick
Prebendary David Houlding
Two members elected by the House of Laity
Mr Paul Boyd-Lee
Mrs Christina Rees

A Church Estates Commissioner
Mr Andreas Whittam Smith, First Church Estates Commissioner

Appointed by the Archbishops
Mr Andrew Britton, former Director, National Institute of Economic and Social Research
Professor John Craven, Vice-Chancellor, University of Portsmouth
Mr Philip Fletcher, Chairman, Water Services Regulation Authority
Mrs Katherine McPherson, business development and marketing director
Mr Mark Russell, Chief Executive, Church Army
Mrs Anne Sloman, retired Chief Political Adviser, BBC

Staff
William Fittall, *Secretary General*
Tel: 020 7898 1360
email: william.fittall@c-of-e.org.uk

Revd Janina Ainsworth, *Education/National Society*
Tel: 020 7898 1500
email: janina.ainsworth@c-of-e.org.uk

Jackie Bliss, *Finance*
Tel: 020 7898 1795
email: jackie.bliss@c-of-e.org.uk

Revd Dr Malcolm Brown, *Mission and Public Affairs*
Tel: 020 7898 1468
email: malcolm.brown@c-of-e.org.uk

Peter Crumpler, *Communications*
Tel: 020 7898 1462
email: peter.crumpler@c-of-e.org.uk

Janet Gough, *Cathedral and Church Buildings*
Tel: 020 7898 1887
email: janet.gough@c-of-e.org.uk

Declan Kelly, *Libraries, Archives and Information Services*
Tel: 020 7898 1432
email: declan.kelly@c-of-e.org.uk

Ven Christopher Lowson, *Ministry*
Tel: 020 7898 1390
email: christopher.lowson@c-of-e.org.uk

Su Morgan, *Human Resources*
Tel: 020 7898 1565
email: su.morgan@c-of-e.org.uk

Stephen Slack, *Legal Adviser*
Tel: 020 7898 0366
email: stephen.slack@c-of-e.org.uk

Revd David Williams, *Central Secretariat/Clerk to the Synod*
Tel: 020 7898 1559
email: david.williams@c-of-e.org.uk

Nicholas Hills, *Assistant Secretary*
Tel: 020 7898 1363
email: nicholas.hills@c-of-e.org.uk

Archbishops' Council: key working relationships

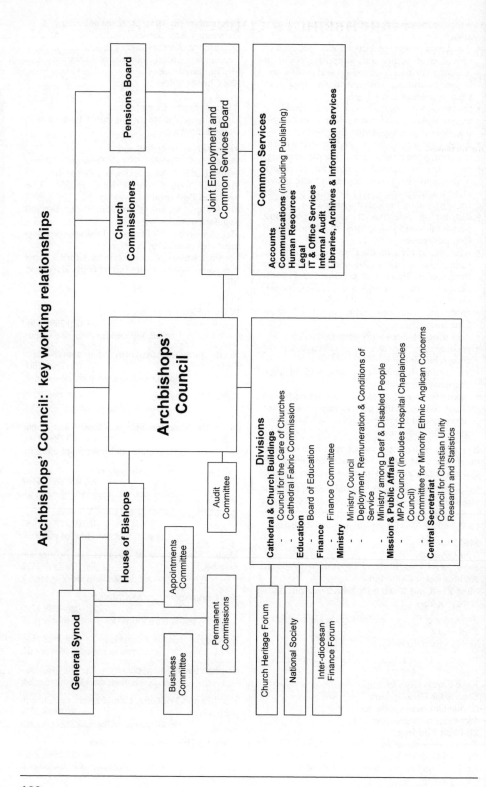

National Structures

ARCHBISHOPS' COUNCIL BUDGET

The Budget covers five areas, each of which is separately approved by the General Synod annually. These are Training for Ministry, National Church Responsibilities, grants, mission agencies pensions support and revenue costs relating to the Church's Housing Assistance for the Retired Ministry (CHARM).

There has been a welcome response to the call for increased vocations but this has presented a financial challenge. The net result has been an increase of 14.7 per cent in the budget. The budget for **National Church Responsibilities** covers all the work undertaken at Church House, Westminster. There has been a small increase of 0.9 per cent from the 2008 budget. The **Grants** budget, which mainly funds the Church of England's contributions to the Inter Anglican budget and to ecumenical bodies, increases by 4.5 per cent in 2009. This is largely due to the need to increase significantly the amount set aside for Legal Aid.

The budget for **Inter-Diocesan Support – Mission Agencies Pensions Contributions** covers payments in respect of the pension contributions of clergy employed by the mission agencies. It has been agreed that the level of expenditure will be capped at its 2004 level plus inflation. A small increase is required for 2009 despite the mission agencies employing fewer clergy. The increase is due to the higher level of pension contribution required. The final part of the budget comprises the revenue costs relating to the **Church's Housing Assistance for the Retired Ministry** (CHARM), which provides rental or mortgage assistance for retired clergy who might not otherwise be able to afford housing. The 2009 budget provides for an increase of 4.7 per cent.

The detailed budget as agreed by the General Synod in July 2008 (and set out more fully in GS 1700) is summarized in the table below. The overall picture is an increase in the apportionment of 9.1 per cent. The level of increase in apportionment has been contained by the use of reserves built up over years by the Council.

The Appointments Committee of the Church of England

Chairman Preb David Houlding

Secretary Mr Nicholas Hills   *Tel:* 020 7898 1363

Members appointed by the Archbishops' Council
Mrs Christina Rees, Ven Norman Russell, Canon Glyn Webster

Elected Members
Preb Philippa Boardman, Mrs Sarah Finch, Mr Aiden Hargreaves-Smith, Ven Richard Seed, Rt Revd Nigel Stock (*Bishop of St Edmundsbury and Ipswich*), Canon Prof Anthony Thiselton, Mrs Shirley-Ann Williams

A joint committee of the General Synod and the Archbishops' Council, the Appointments Committee is responsible for making appointments and/or recommendations on appointments to synodical and other bodies as the Archbishops, the Synod or the Archbishops' Council require. It published its guidelines for best practice in the making of such appointments in 2005 as GS Misc 802, copies of which can be obtained from its Secretary.

Audit Committee

MEMBERS
Chair Mr Anthony Hesselwood

Secretary Kim Parry

Committee Members
Two members elected by the General Synod
Mrs Jane Bisson, Mr Keith Malcouronne

One member appointed by the Archbishops' Council on the advice of the Appointments Committee
Mr John Neilson

One Finance Committee member appointed by the Appointments Committee
Mr Brian Newey

One member of the Archbishops' Council
Mr Paul Boyd-Lee

The Committee provides independent oversight of the Archbishops' Council's framework of corporate governance, risk management and internal control. It oversees the discharge of the Council's responsibilities relating to financial statements, external and internal audit and internal control systems, and reports to the Council thereon with recommendations as appropriate.

2009 Budget

	2009	
	£	£
TRAINING FOR MINISTRY (Vote 1)		
Ordination training grants – colleges	8,293,300	
Ordination training grants – courses/Ordained Local Ministry	3,921,400	
Ordained Local Ministry	214,000	
Mixed Mode	169,900	12,598,600
Financed by:		
Income	(45,000)	
Apportionment on the dioceses	(12,033,600)	
Uses of Reserves	(520,000)	(12,598,600)
NATIONAL CHURCH RESPONSIBILITIES (Vote 2)		
Central Secretariat		
(including Christian Unity/Research & Statistics)	2,014,018	
Ministry	1,516,455	
Education	861,174	
Mission & Public Affairs	1,408,517	
Cathedral and Church Buildings	1,021,482	
Finance	1,019,017	
Accounts	1,560,814	
Internal Audit	444,903	
Legal	1,232,335	
Communications	673,699	
Human Resources	668,805	
Information Technology	1,127,810	
Records	390,386	
Church House Publishing	1,208,433	
Office Services	318,383	
Accommodation	3,174,227	
Contingency	50,000	18,690,458
Financed by:		
General Income	(370,000)	
Interest on Funds	(27,350)	
Income for Services	(759,650)	
Grants	(266,393)	
Apportionment on the dioceses	(10,147,954)	
Trading Income (Publishing)	(1,175,000)	
Income from other National Church Institutions	(5,944,111)	(18,690,458)
GRANTS (Vote 3)		
Anglican Communion	421,200	
British ecumenical bodies	410,000	
Conference of European Churches	84,000	
World Council of Churches	108,000	
Church Urban Fund	203,000	
Legal aid	400,000	
Other grants and expenses	42,000	1,668,200
Financed by:		
Apportionment on the dioceses		(1,668,200)
MISSION AGENCY CLERGY PENSIONS (Vote 4)		
Expenditure		800,000
Financed by:		
Apportionment on the dioceses		(800,000)
CHARM COSTS (Vote 5)		
Expenditure		3,099,000
Financed by:		
Apportionment on the dioceses	(2,949,000)	
Reserves	(150,000)	(3,099,000)
OVERALL APPORTIONMENT		(27,598,754)

Finance Committee

MEMBERS

Chair appointed by Archbishops' Council
Mr Andrew Britton

Four members elected by the General Synod
Revd Dr Peter Ackroyd, Mr John Booth, Mr Gavin Oldham, Mr Andrew Presland

Three members elected on recommendation of the Appointments Committee
Ven Christine Hardman (*Archdeacon of Lewisham*), Rt Revd John Packer (*Bishop of Ripon and Leeds*), Revd Dr Meg Gilley (Durham)

Four members elected by the Inter-diocesan Finance Forum
Canon Alan Cooper, Mr Stephen Marriott, Mr Brian Newey, Mr Graham Smith

One member of the Archbishops' Council
Canon Dr Christina Baxter

Ex officio Dr Jonathan Spencer (*Chairman of the Church of England Pensions Board*), Mr Andreas Whittam Smith (*First Church Estates Commissioner*)

Secretary Jackie Bliss   *Tel*: 020 7898 1791
email: jackie.bliss@c-of-e.org.uk

Terms of reference

1 To advise the Archbishops' Council and the dioceses on all financial aspects of the Council's work, including its investment and trustee responsibilities, and on the overall financial needs and resources of the Church.

2 To make recommendations to the Archbishops' Council as to its annual budget and on mechanisms for monitoring and controlling the expenditure of the Council.

3 To consult with dioceses on financial matters, and to make recommendations thereon as appropriate to the Archbishops' Council and the dioceses.

4 To assess and seek to rationalize and simplify the systems for cash flow within the Church.

5 To provide a central forum for the development and promotion of Christian stewardship and fund raising.

6 To provide and coordinate research and guidance on financial, accounting and related matters.

7 To provide a channel for communicating on financial matters with Her Majesty's Government, financial regulators and other appropriate enforcement bodies, both directly and through the Churches Main Committee.

8 To work in collaboration with ecumenical partners on matters within the Committee's terms of reference.

9 To carry out such other work as may be entrusted to it by the Archbishops' Council.

CENTRAL SECRETARIAT

Under the direction of the Clerk to the Synod and Head of Central Secretariat, staff of the Central Secretariat provide the secretariat for the General Synod, its three Houses (House of Bishops, House of Clergy and House of Laity), the Archbishops' Council and the Business, Appointments and Standing Orders Committees. Members of staff of the Secretariat serve as secretaries to a number of the Synod's principal commissions and committees and also as secretaries of *ad hoc* committees and working parties as required. They also serve various other groups, such as the Churches' Funeral Group. The Clerk to the Synod acts as Secretary to the Business Committee and provides advice and assistance as necessary to synodical bodies and members of Synod.

The Central Secretariat includes the Council for Christian Unity and Research and Statistics.

Clerk to the Synod/Head of Central Secretariat
Revd David Williams   *Tel*: 020 7898 1559
email: david.williams@c-of-e.org.uk
Secretary, Council for Christian Unity
Canon Dr Paul Avis   *Tel*: 020 7898 1470
email: paul.avis@c-of-e.org.uk

Head of Research and Statistics
Revd Lynda Barley   *Tel*: 020 7898 1542
email: lynda.barley@c-of-e.org.uk

Senior Administrative Staff
Alastair Callcutt
(*Head of Synod Support*)   *Tel*: 020 7898 1374
email: alastair.callcutt@c-of-e.org.uk

Nicholas Hills
(*Secretary*: Appointments Committee, House of Laity, Standing Committee of the House of Laity; *Assistant Secretary*: Archbishops' Council)
Tel: 020 7898 1363
email: nicholas.hills@c-of-e.org.uk

Jonathan Neil-Smith
(*Secretary*: House of Bishops and Standing Committee of the House of Bishops)
Tel: 020 7898 1373
email: jonathan.neil-smith@c-of-e.org.uk

Dr Colin Podmore
(*Secretary*: House of Clergy, Standing Committee of the House of Clergy, Dioceses Commission, Liturgical Commission, Churches' Funerals Group [www.christianfunerals.org])
Tel: 020 7898 1385
email: colin.podmore@c-of-e.org.uk

Revd Pearl Luxon
(*Safeguarding Adviser – Child and Adult Protection*)
(for the Church of England and Methodist
Church)   Tel: 020 7898 1330
          email: pearl.luxon@c-of-e.org.uk
Revd Peter Moger
(*National Worship Development Officer*)
                                     Tel: 020 7898 1365
          email: peter.moger@c-of-e.org.uk
Alastair Callcutt
(*Head of Synod Support*)   Tel: 020 7898 1374
          email: alastair.callcutt@c-of-e.org.uk

Jane Melrose
(*Secretary*: House of Bishops' Inspectorate of
Theological Colleges and Courses; *Assistant
Secretary*: House of Bishops)   Tel: 020 7898 1379
          email: jane.melrose@c-of-e.org.uk
Sue Moore
(*Assistant Secretary*, Churches' Funerals Group
[www.christianfunerals.org]; *Assistant to Colin
Podmore*)   Tel: 020 7898 1376
          email: sue.moore@c-of-e.org.uk
Frances Arnold
(*Executive Officer*, House of Bishops; *Secretary*:
House of Bishops' Theological Group))
                                     Tel: 020 7898 1372
          email: frances.arnold@c-of-e.org.uk

The Council for Christian Unity

Chairman Rt Revd Christopher Hill (*Bishop of
Guildford*)

General Secretary Canon Dr Paul Avis
                                     Tel: 020 7898 1470
          email: paul.avis@c-of-e.org.uk

European Secretary Vacancy   Tel: 020 7898 1474

National Adviser (Unity-in-Mission) Revd John
Cole   Tel: 020 7898 1479
          email: john.cole@c-of-e.org.uk

Assistant Secretary Mr Francis Bassett
                                     Tel: 020 7898 1481
          email: francis.bassett@c-of-e.org.uk

Theological Secretary Dr Martin Davie
                                     Tel: 020 7898 1488
          email: martin.davie@c-of-e.org.uk

Office Church House, Great Smith St, London
SW1P 3AZ   Tel: 020 7898 1470
                                     Fax: 020 7898 1483
          Web: www.cofe.anglican.org/ccu

MEMBERS
*Three clergy and three lay members elected by the
General Synod*
Rt Revd Ian Brackley (*Bishop of Dorking*), Mr
Martin Dales, Ven George Howe, Canon Chris
Lilley, Mrs Mary Judkins, Dr Edmund Marshall
*Eight members appointed for their expertise by the
Appointments Committee, of whom at least four
should be members of General Synod*
Ven Donald Allister, Revd Will Adam, Mrs Kim
Curle, Preb David Houlding, Revd Rose Hudson-
Wilkin, Rt Revd Martyn Jarrett (*Bishop of Bever-
ley*), Mrs Margaret Swinson, Ven Joy Tetley

Consultants (attend meetings by arrangement)
Rt Revd Nicholas Baines (*Bishop of Croydon*),
Rt Revd Dr Thomas Butler (*Bishop of Southwark*),
Rt Revd and Rt Hon Richard Chartres (*Bishop of

London*), Rt Revd John Hind (*Bishop of Chichester*),
Rt Revd Dr Michael Nazir-Ali (*Bishop of Roches-
ter*), Rt Revd Dr Kenneth Stevenson (*Bishop of
Portsmouth*), Canon Jonathan Goodall (*Archbishop
of Canterbury's Chaplain and Officer for Ecu-
menism*), Canon Anthony Ball (*Archbishop of
Canterbury's Assistant Secretary for International,
Ecumenical and Anglican Communion Affairs*),
Dr David Muir (*Evangelical Alliance*)

Ecumenical representatives
Monsignor Andrew Faley (Roman Catholic
Church); Revd Sue Keegan von Allmen
(Methodist Church); Revd Richard Mortimer
(United Reformed Church); Revd Anthony
Clarke (Baptist Union); Canon Bob Fyffe
(Churches Together in Britain and Ireland);
Revd Dr David Cornick (Churches Together in
England).

The Council was established as an advisory
committee of the General Synod on 1 April 1991
to continue and develop the ecumenical work
formerly undertaken by the Board for Mission
and Unity. That Board, set up on 1 January
1972, had inherited the responsibilities of the
Missionary and Ecumenical Council of the
Church Assembly (MECCA) and the Church
of England Council on Foreign Relations
(CFR).

FUNCTIONS OF THE COUNCIL
(*Adapted from the Constitution*)
(a) To stimulate and encourage theological
    reflection in consultation with the Doctrine
    Commission and the Faith and Order
    Advisory Group and to advise the Arch-
    bishops' Council and the General Synod on
    unity issues and proposals in the light of the
    Christian understanding of God's purposes
    for the world.
(b) To advise the House of Bishops on matters
    referred to it by the House.

(c) To foster ecumenical work in the Church nationally and in the dioceses.

(d) In conjunction with the Archbishops' Council to promote unity and ecumenical concerns in the work of all the Boards, Councils, Divisions, etc.

(e) In ecumenical concerns on behalf of the Archbishops' Council to be the principal link between the General Synod and

    (i)   The Anglican Consultative Council;

    (ii) individual provinces and dioceses of the Anglican Communion and the United Churches incorporating former Anglican dioceses.

(f) On behalf of the Archbishops' Council to be the principal channel of communication between the General Synod and

    (i)   The World Council of Churches;

    (ii) The Conference of European Churches;

    (iii) Churches Together in Britain and Ireland;

    (iv) Churches Together in England;

    (v) all other Christian Churches in the British Isles and abroad.

(g) To service committees and commissions engaged in ecumenical discussions with other Churches.

THE FAITH AND ORDER ADVISORY GROUP

Chairman Rt Revd John Hind (*Bishop of Chichester*)

The Faith and Order Advisory Group consists of not more than fifteen persons appointed by the Archbishops after consultation with the Council. The Group advises the House of Bishops or the Council on matters of ecumenical or theological concern referred to it by the House of Bishops or the Council.

COMMITTEE FOR ROMAN CATHOLIC RELATIONS

Chairman Rt Revd Michael Scott-Joynt (*Bishop of Winchester*)

The Committee for Roman Catholic Relations consists of not more than fifteen persons appointed by the Archbishops after consultation with the Council. This Committee promotes relations between the Church of England and the Roman Catholic Church in this country and it

meets twice a year with the equivalent Roman Catholic body. The two bodies form the English Anglican Roman Catholic Committee.

MEISSEN COMMISSION – ANGLICAN COMMITTEE

Chairman Rt Revd Nicholas Baines (*Bishop of Croydon*)

The Meissen Commission (the Sponsoring Body for Church of England EKD Relations) was established in 1991 to oversee the implementation of the Meissen Declaration and encourage relationships with the Evangelical Church in Germany. It comprises Anglican and German committees.

CHURCH OF ENGLAND MORAVIAN CONTACT GROUP

Chairman Rt Revd David James (*Bishop of Bradford*)

The Church of England Moravian Contact Group consists of four representatives, ordained and lay, from each Church, together with ecumenical observers and staff. The Church of England representatives are appointed by the Archbishops. The Contact Group works to make real in the lives of the two Churches the commitments of the Fetter Lane Declaration overseeing the implementation of those developments that are already possible, ensuring that further consideration is given to those areas where convergence is still required and nurturing growth in communion.

ECUMENICAL INSTRUMENTS

Contact is maintained with the World Council of Churches, the Conference of European Churches, Churches Together in Britain and Ireland, and Churches Together in England, where members and staff represent the Church of England at various levels. The Council is particularly concerned with helping the Church of England to relate effectively at every level to the ecumenical instruments.

PANELS OF THE CCU

The CCU has three subsidiary panels:

Local Unity Panel
Chairman Rt Revd Nigel Stock (*Bishop of St Edmundsbury and Ipswich*)
Porvoo Panel
Chairman Rt Revd Dr Kenneth Stevenson (*Bishop of Portsmouth*)
Orthodox Relations Panel
Chairman Rt Revd and Rt Hon Richard Chartres (*Bishop of London*)

Research and Statistics

Head of Research and Statistics Revd Lynda Barley
Tel: 020 7898 1592
Fax: 020 7898 1532
email: statistics.unit@c-of-e.org.uk
Web: www.cofe.anglican.org/info/statistics
Office: Church House, Great Smith St,
London SW1P 3AZ

While the gathering of parochial statistics remains at the heart of the Research and Statistics department's work, the department has broadened the range of statistics it maintains and diversified so that it is now providing a statistical and research service to the central Church and beyond. A new series of research-based parish booklets, *Time to Listen*, has been established and the department's role as a central resource is continuing to develop within the Archbishops' Council where it forms part of the Central Secretariat.

The Research and Statistics department is responsible (through the dioceses) for the annual collection, collation and analysis of parochial finance and membership *Church Statistics*. The department is seeking to improve the efficiency of the processing of these statistics, so that more of its resources can be devoted to researching underlying trends and evaluating the merits of the statistics collected. Working closely with the Mission and Public Affairs Division, the department continues to develop the church attendance and membership statistics that are collected annually, with the aim of providing a range of statistics and research resources which will be a tool for mission. It is also developing an ongoing mechanism for monitoring diversity across the

Church. Continued efforts are being made, in conjunction with the Communications Unit, to improve and develop systems for the communication of research and statistical information within and without the Church, particularly focusing on new national survey findings concerning people's use of and attitudes towards local churches.

The department maintains a national parish database, which is being enhanced with new parish profile information and coordinated with the Geographical Information System mapping of parish boundaries. Some of the information presently held on the department's database concerns social deprivation, and the department is responsible for the coordination and, where appropriate, the mapping of census and other government statistics across the Church. The department maintains strong links with the Cathedral and Church Buildings Division regarding the use of cathedral and church buildings, with the Ministry Division in the preparation and production of *Statistics of Licensed Ministers*, and with the Church Commissioners in the development of the *Crockford* database.

The department maintains links with other denominations on statistical and research matters and reports on an annual basis local and national mission statistics to the Methodist Church. It is developing its role across the Church as a source of reliable research information regarding the place of the Church in modern society and in this it is supported by an informal professional panel of reference.

MINISTRY DIVISION

Chairman of Ministry Division Rt Revd Graham James, (*Bishop of Norwich*)   *Tel:* 01603 629001
email: bishop@bishopofnorwich.org

Director of Ministry Ven Christopher Lowson
Tel: 020 7898 1390
email: christopher.lowson@c-of-e.org.uk

Finance and Administration Revd Christopher Terry   *Tel:* 020 7898 1392
email: chris.terry@c-of-e.org.uk

Senior Selection Secretary Revd Stephen Ferns
Tel: 020 7898 1399
email: stephen.ferns@c-of-e.org.uk

Theological Education and Training Dr David Way
Tel: 020 7898 1405
email: david.way@c-of-e.org.uk

Deployment, Remuneration and Conditions of Service
Mrs Sarah Smith   *Tel:* 020 7898 1411
email: sarah.smith@c-of-e.org.uk

Adviser for Ministry of and among Deaf and Disabled People Revd Philip Maddock   *Tel:* 01543 306085
email: philip.maddock@c-of-e.org.uk

Secretary of the Central Readers' Council Dr Alan Wakely   *Tel:* 020 7898 1417
email: crcsec@hallarn.com
Web: www.readers.cofe.anglican.org

Selection Secretaries
Revd David Mann (*National Adviser for Pre-Theological Education*)   *Tel:* 020 7898 1593
email: david.mann@c-of-e.org.uk

Mr Kevin Diamond   *Tel:* 020 7898 1402
email: kevin.diamond@c-of-e.org.uk

Mrs Carys Walsh   *Tel:* 020 7898 1406
email: carys.walsh@c-of-e.org.uk

Revd Jules Cave Bergquist (*Vocations Officer*)
Tel: 020 7898 1395
email: jules.cavebergquist@c-of-e.org.uk

Revd Hilary Ison   *Tel:* 020 7898 1424
     email: hilary.ison@c-of-e.org.uk

National Continuing Ministerial Education Officer
Mr Tim Ling   *Tel:* 020 7898 1408
     email: tim.ling@c-of-e.org.uk

Grants Officer Dr Mark Hodge   *Tel:* 020 7898 1396
     email: mark.hodge@c-of-e.org.uk

National Moderator for Reader Training Revd Alec
George   *Tel:* 020 7898 1419
     email: alec.george@c-of-e.org.uk

Office Church House, Great Smith St, London
SW1P 3AZ   *Tel:* 020 7898 1412
     Fax: 020 7898 1421

MINISTRY COUNCIL
Chair Rt Revd Graham James (*Bishop of Norwich*)

Revd Prof Loveday Alexander, Mr Andrew Britton, Mrs Mary Chapman, Revd Vanessa Herrick, Mr David Mills, Rt Revd John Packer, Rt Revd John Pritchard, Very Revd Michael Sadgrove, Rt Revd Nigel Stock, Revd Mark Sowerby

The provision of a properly trained and supported ministry is critical to the Church's mission. The division brings together policy on the selection, training, deployment and remuneration of the Church of England's ministry
     The Ministry Council oversees the work of the Division. The committee meets four times a year under the chairmanship of the Bishop of Norwich (Chairman of the Division) and consists of members appointed by the House of Bishops, the Appointments Committee of the Church of England and elected by the General Synod.
     The Ministry Council is supported by panels looking after Candidates, Research Degrees, Reader Education, Quality in Formation, and Finance. In addition the work of the Deployment, Remuneration and Conditions of Service, and Ministry of and Among Deaf and Disabled People committees are represented on the Council. The Central Readers' Council continues to fulfil its role in enhancing the contribution of Readers to the overall ministry of the Church, and its secretary is a valued honorary member of the staff team.

QUALITY in FORMATION PANEL
Chair Very Revd Michael Sadgrove (*The Dean of Durham*)

Revd Prof Loveday Alexander, Revd Dr Joseph Cassidy, Dr Paula Gooder, Revd Paul Goodliff, Revd Wendy Kilworth-Mason, four vacancies
Membership of the Panel had not been determined at the time of going to press.

Terms of reference
1 To oversee the transition to a single quality framework for inspection, validation, moderation and Reader moderation and to carry out the current processes of inspection, validation, moderation and Reader moderation as required.
2 To provide training and support for reviewers involved in the current and future processes.

FINANCE PANEL
Chair Prof John Craven

Mr Tim Allen, Mr John Butler, Mr Richard Finlinson, Mrs Judith Nash

Terms of reference
The responsibility of the Finance Panel is to advise the Ministry Council on all aspects of its financial responsibility regarding the cost of ordinand training funded from Central Church Funds. Specifically:
1 To advise on policy concerning the location, establishment, inspection and financial support of theological colleges and courses;
2 to prepare and administer the Training Budget, and to advise on the financial support of candidates.

CANDIDATES PANEL
Chair Ven Jeff Watson

Rt Revd Mark Bryant, Revd Christine Bullimore, Canon Jane Curtis, Revd Dr James Gardom, Miss Caulene Herbert, Canon Will Lamb, Sister Edith Margaret CHN, Ven Stephen Roberts, Canon James Stewart, Dr Yvonne Warren, Canon Brian Watchom

Terms of reference
1 To advise sponsoring bishops on:
(1) the reduction or lengthening of candidates' training
(2) the transferral of candidates from one training institution to another
(3) the return of candidates to training after a break of more than three months
(4) the suitability of candidates for transfer of category of ministry or change of focus of ministry
(5) the suitability of ministers from other denominations to be ministers in the Church of England
(6) candidates' potential to be theological educators
2 To undertake other work in relation to recruitment and selection

RESEARCH DEGREES PANEL
Chair Canon Dr Judith Maltby

Revd Prof William Horbury, Revd Dr David Law, Revd Prof Ben Quash, Prof Andrew Wright

Terms of reference

1 To give permission to ordinands seen as potential theological educators to study for research degrees (MPhil, PhD etc) outside of Bishops' Regulations for Training as part of ore-ordination training.

2 To allocate its budget to pay for, or contribute to, the additional costs of such training.

DEPLOYMENT, REMUNERATION AND CONDITIONS OF SERVICE COMMITTEE

Chair Rt Revd John Packer (*Bishop of Ripon and Leeds*)

Mrs April Alexander, Ven Richard Blackburn, Mr Nicholas Denison, Dr Clive Dilloway, Mrs Lesley Farrall, Revd Peggy Jackson, Ven Ian Jagger, Mr David Kemp, Mrs Christine McMullen, Mrs Gill Morrison, Mr Brian Newey, Ven Nigel Peyton, Dr Susan Salt, Mrs Sarah Thewlis, Mr Timothy Walker

Terms of reference

1 To advise the House of Bishops and the Archbishops' Council on a strategy for ministry, with particular reference to the deployment, remuneration and conditions of service of those in authorized ministry, working in collaboration with dioceses, the Church Commissioners and the Church of England Pensions Board and with ecumenical partners.

2 To produce, in partnership with dioceses, a framework of national policy for stipends and other related matters, and to advise dioceses as appropriate on such matters.

3 To produce, in partnership with dioceses, a framework of national policy for the deployment of all ministerial resources, ordained and lay, available to the Church.

4 To monitor and advise in consultation with interested parties on sector and chaplaincy ministries within the total ministry of the Church.

5 To work in collaboration with the dioceses and, as far as possible, with ecumenical partners in the provision and development of continuing ministerial education for and review of accredited ministers, ordained and lay.

6 To report regularly through the Ministry Coordinating Group to the Archbishops' Council on the work of the Committee.

COMMITTEE FOR MINISTRY OF AND AMONG DEAF AND DISABLED PEOPLE

Chair Rt Revd Nicholas Reade (*Bishop of Blackburn*)

Revd Brenda Tipping (*Vice Chair*), Revd Maureen Allchin, Revd Catherine Carlyon, Mr Ken Dyson, Revd Denis Huntley, Dr Wayne Morris, Mrs Gail Robinson, Revd Bob Shrine, Mr Shaun Tindall, Revd Katie Tupling, Mrs Alison Wynne

The functions of the Committee include:

1 To monitor and advise on the progress of sector and chaplaincy ministries among deaf and disabled people within the total ministry of the Church, in consultation with those responsible for specific areas.

2 To encourage and strengthen the participation of deaf people in the life and witness of the Church, to represent the views of deaf people to the Church and of the Church to deaf people, and to support the work of the chaplains.

3 To report regularly through the Ministry Council to the Archbishops' Council on the work of the Committee.

4 To advise the Central Bodies and the dioceses on matters related to general disability issues, especially the implementation of the Disability Discrimination Act as it applies to the Church.

RECENT MINISTRY DIVISION PUBLICATIONS

Generosity and Sacrifice: the Report of the Clergy Stipends Review Group

Governance for Trustees/Governers of Theological Education and Training Institutions

Ministry in the Church of England

Preparing for Ordained Ministry: Good Practice in Assessment and Reporting on Candidates within Initial Training

Shaping the Future: New Patterns of Training for Lay and Ordained, CHP 2006

Mission and Ministry: the Churches' Validation Framework for Theological Education, 2nd edition 2003

Formation for Ministry within a Learning Church: the Structure and Funding of Ordination Training (GS 1496)

BISHOPS' REGULATIONS FOR TRAINING SELECTION

1 Candidates should be commended in the first place by someone who has pastoral responsibility for them to the Diocesan Director of Ordinands. Before being accepted for training, they are required:

(1) to have the necessary educational qualifications or show that they have the potential to benefit from a formal course of training;

(2) to satisfy medical requirements;

(3) to be sponsored by their bishop for attendance at a Bishops' Advisory Panel according to the following categories:

Ordained Ministry – Deacon (Distinctive)

Ordained Ministry – Priest

2 Where it is envisaged that a candidate will exercise a self-supporting ministry from the time of ordination, such a candidate should normally be at least 30.

EDUCATIONAL QUALIFICATIONS
Candidates are required to have the following qualifications:

1 *Under 25.* Five passes in academic subjects in GCSE, Grade C or above, one of which must be English Language, and two at 'A' level (or equivalent qualifications). The only exceptions to this rule are for candidates who are recommended to complete a formal programme of pre-theological education to prepare them for training. Bishops' Advisers will need to be assured that candidates are able to cope with and benefit from theological training.

2 *Aged 25 and over.* The academic standard is not laid down in terms of GCSE or other academic qualifications, but individuals are considered and assessed in accordance with their prior learning and experience. DDOs may ask candidates to undertake some guided reading before attending a Bishops' Advisory Panel.

TRAINING
Ministerial training has been the subject of extensive review over the last few years, leading up to the report *Formation for Ministry within a Learning Church*, which was amended and approved by General Synod in July 2003. A new points based system for ascertaining appropriate training pathways is being trialled for the academic year 2008/09. Until this is evaluated the old system will continue:

1. OLM candidates will normally train on the diocesan OLM scheme of the sponsoring diocese;
2. candidates under 30 whose sponsoring papers indicate that they will be seeking a stipendiary post at the point of ordination will normally train at a theological college;
3. candidates over 30 whose sponsoring papers indicate that they will be seeking a stipendiary post at the point of ordination (i.e. they would have been sponsored under the former stipendiary/non-stipendiary category) may train at a theological college or on a regional course;
4. candidates over 30 whose sponsoring papers indicate that they will be seeking a non-stipendiary post at the point of ordination will normally train on a regional course;
5. Bishops' Regulations on the length of training will continue to apply. These regulations (which set the former approach) are set out immediately below.
6. Exceptions to these guidelines can be reviewed by the Ministry Division's Candidates Panel.

1 *Pre-theological education.* Candidates may be required to undertake a formal programme of part-time pre-theological education normally of six to nine months' duration, approved by the Pre-Theological Education Panel, to the satisfaction of the Moderators. On completion of such a programme, candidates undertake theological training in compliance with the regulations set out below.

2 *Theological training.* Candidates should always consult their bishop or Diocesan Director of Ordinands (DDO) before applying to a theological college, course or scheme for admission. A recommendation to train for ordination from the Bishops' Advisers does not carry with it the right of acceptance by any particular theological college or course.

A candidate wishing to undertake a course of training varying from the Regulations approved by the Bishops (including study for a higher degree) should inform the DDO in order that the advice of the Ministry Division may be sought.

(1) *Candidates under 30*
(a) *Graduates in theology* (where at least half of the degree consists of theology) spend two years on a full-time course at a theological college and have to fulfil the Bishops' requirements by satisfactorily completing a course of education approved on behalf of the House of Bishops by the Theological Education and Training Committee.
(b) *Graduates in subjects other than theology* are required to spend three years on a full-time course at a theological college and have to fulfil the Bishops' requirements by satisfactorily completing a course of education approved on behalf of the House of Bishops by the Theological Education and Training Committee. Only those candidates with an upper second or first class degree may read for a degree in theology or post-graduate diploma in theology, unless the degree course is specially designed as a training course for the professional ministry, is approved by the Theological Education and Training Committee, and involves no additional expense or lengthening of the normal course of training.

Certain special courses and professional qualifications may be regarded as conferring graduate status.
(c) *Non-graduates* are required to spend three years on a full-time course at a theological college and to fulfil the Bishops' requirements by satisfactorily completing a course of education approved on behalf of the House of Bishops by the Theological Education and Training Committee.

(2) *Candidates aged 30 and over*
Candidates over 30 sponsored for the ordained ministry are required to undertake

either two years' full-time training at a theological college, or three years' part-time training on a theological course. In some instances the recommendations for training will indicate a preferred form. Candidates are required to fulfil the Bishops' requirements by satisfactorily completing a course of education approved on behalf of the House of Bishops by the Theological Education and Training Committee.

(3) *Candidates aged 50 and over*
Candidates for ordained ministry usually undertake three years' part-time training on a theological course. The exact nature of the training is decided by the sponsoring bishop.

NOTES
1 In the above regulations, where the regulation concerns training, the age refers to the candidate's age at the start of training.
2 Exceptions to the above regulations will be considered by the Candidates Panel.

GRANTS
Candidates who have been recommended for training are eligible for financial help from Church funds. Details about grants can be obtained from the Grants Officer, Ministry Division, Church House, Great Smith St, London SW1P 3AZ.

For **Theological Colleges** *and* **Regional Courses** *see also* pages 236–238.

The Central Readers' Council

Patron HRH The Duke of Edinburgh

Presidents The Archbishops of Canterbury and York

Chair Rt Revd Graham Dow (*Bishop of Carlisle*)

Vice-Chair Canon Ron Black

Secretary Dr Alan Wakely   Tel: 020 7898 1417
          email: alan.wakely@c-of-e.org.uk

Associate Secretary Jennie Macpherson
          Tel: 020 7898 1417
          email: jennie.macpherson@c-of-e.org.uk

National Moderator for Reader Education Revd Alec George   Tel: 020 7898 1414
          email: alec.george@c-of-e.org.uk

Personal Secretary Mrs Janice Milbank
          Tel: 020 7898 1416
          email: janice.milbank@c-of-e.org.uk

Editor of 'The Reader' Revd Heather Fenton
          email: reader.editor@btconnect.com

Administrative Officer Mrs Janice Milbank (*as above*)

Office Church House, Great Smith St, London SW1P 3AZ   Tel: 020 7898 1416
          Fax: 020 7898 1421
MEMBERS
The CRC Executive Committee is elected for a five-year term co-terminous with General Synod. In addition to the Chair and Vice-Chair, the Committee consists of:

Two Wardens
Revd Joanna Coney, Revd Nick Watson

Reader representatives
Mrs Christine Haines, Mrs Sue Hart, Mr Ron Edinborough, Mr Charles Flynn, Mr Andrew Lie
Co-opted member
Mrs Chrysogon Bamber

Treasurer
Mr Cliff Harris

The Central Readers' Council (CRC) works to enhance the contribution of Readers to the overall ministry of the Church, particularly to encourage the most effective integration with other forms of ministry, ordained and lay. It works in cooperation with the Ministry Division which moderates and coordinates the training of Reader candidates. CRC arranges national conferences for Readers, provides a forum for the exchange of ideas between dioceses on Reader matters and publishes a quarterly magazine, *The Reader*. The annual Summer Course at Selwyn College, Cambridge began in 1881 and is probably the longest-established Summer School held in any university.

CRC is a registered charity, which derives its income mostly from capitation grants made by diocesan Readers' boards. It has its origins in the revival of Reader ministry in the Church of England in 1866 and particularly in the Central Readers' Board, which was granted a constitution by the Archbishops in 1921. CRC today is the immediate successor to the Central Readers' Conference, under a new constitution adopted in 2002, and revised in 2007.

CRC has three representatives from each diocese, including the Warden and Secretary of Readers, and one representative from each of the Armed Forces. Any Reader appointed to a Ministry Division committee is *ex officio* a member of CRC. A non-voting observer is invited from the Deaf Readers and Pastoral

Assistants Association, the Church of Ireland, the Scottish Episcopal Church and each of the dioceses of the Church in Wales. The annual general meeting is held in March/April each year.

MISSION AND PUBLIC AFFAIRS DIVISION
Mission and Public Affairs Council

Chairman   Dr Philip Giddings

Vice-Chairs: Public Affairs Rt Revd Thomas F. Butler *(Bishop of Southwark); Mission* Rt Revd Michael Hill *(Bishop of Bristol); Hospital Chaplaincy* Rt Revd Michael Perham *(Bishop of Gloucester)*

Director Revd Dr Malcolm Brown
Tel: 020 7898 1468
email: malcolm.brown@c-of-e.org.uk

MEMBERS
The Council is constituted of:
Chair and Vice Chairs
Chair of the Committee for Minority Ethnic Anglican Concerns – Revd Rose Hudson-Wilkin
Chair of the Partnership for World Mission – Rt Revd Michael Hill *(Bishop of Bristol)*
Eleven members of the General Synod elected by the General Synod (with a minimum number of two from each House) – currently Revd Mark Bratton, Canon Tim Dakin, Mr Robert Hammond, Mr David Jones, Rt Revd Stephen Lowe, Mr Clive Scowen, Mr Ian Smith, Canon Dr Christopher Sugden, Dr Anna Thomas-Betts, Revd Andrew Watson
Four appointed members – Mrs Stella Collishaw, Canon Mrs Linda Jones, Mrs Zahida Mallard, Mr Terry Musson
Two co-opted members – Revd David Bookless, Ven Arthur Hawes

FUNCTIONS OF THE COUNCIL
The functions of the Council shall be:
(a) To advise the Archbishops' Council, the General Synod and the House of Bishops on matters within the Council's remit;
(b) To work with dioceses, relevant diocesan networks and the Church's voluntary societies on matters within its remit;
(c) To relate to and cooperate with appropriate bodies within the churches of Britain and Ireland and the ecumenical instruments of CTBI and CTE;
(d) To take lead responsibility in relating to other Churches of the Anglican Communion and the Anglican Consultative Council, its Commissions and Networks, on issues relating to the Church's mission and role in public life;
(e) To relate to government departments and voluntary bodies relevant to its work.

In discharging its functions, the MPA Council shall include within its remit the following areas:
(i) the Church's engagement with social, ethical, political, environmental issues and work for justice and peace at local, national and international levels;
(ii) mission and evangelism; the Church of England's responsibilities for world mission and development; inter faith relations; and theological and missiological reflection on them;
(iii) the Church's mission and ministry (in liaison with Ministry Division) in urban and rural areas;
(iv) the Church's responsibility to confront the reality of racism in its own life and in society;
(v) the support of minority ethnic Christians in the Church of England, and their contribution to its life and witness;
(vi) the work of Hospital Chaplaincy and the Church's relation to the Department of Health, the National Health Service and Trusts and the provision of professional training and Continuing Professional Education for Chaplains.

PARLIAMENTARY UNIT
Parliamentary Secretary Mr Richard Chapman
Tel: 020 7898 1438
email: richard.chapman@c-of-e.org.uk

Deputy Parliamentary Secretary Vacancy

COMMUNITY AND PUBLIC AFFAIRS
Home Affairs Revd Christopher Jones
Tel: 020 7898 1531
email: christopher.jones@c-of-e.org.uk

International and Development Affairs Dr Charles Reed
Tel: 020 7898 1533
email: charles.reed@c-of-e.org.uk

Marriage and Family Policy Mrs Sue Burridge
Tel: 020 7898 1535
email: sue.burridge@c-of-e.org.uk

Medical Ethics, Health and Social Care Policy Vacancy

Community and Urban Affairs Revd Dr Andrew Davey
Tel: 020 7898 1446
email: andrew.davey@c-of-e.org.uk

Adviser for Minority Ethnic Anglican Concerns Mrs
Sonia Barron   *Tel:* 020 7898 1442
                                    Fax: 020 7898 1431
               email: sonia.barron@c-of-e.org.uk

**Committee for Minority Ethnic Anglican
Concerns**
Chair Revd Rose Hudson-Wilkin

Adviser Mrs Sonia Barron

The principal tasks of the Committee are to
monitor and make recommendations about
issues which arise or which ought to arise in the
context of the work of the Archbishops' Council
and its Divisions and of the General Synod itself,
as far as they have policy implications for minority ethnic groups within the Church and the
wider community; and to assist the Bishops and
their dioceses in developing diocesan-wide strategies for combating racial bias within the Church,
encouraging them to make the problem of racism
a priority concern in their programmes and to
circulate the best analyses of racism, including
theological analyses.

MISSION
Partnership Secretary Mr Stephen Lyon
                            Tel: 020 7313 3929
              email: stephen.lyon@c-of-e.org.uk

*National Adviser for Mission Theology, Alternative
Spiritualities and New Religious Movements*
Dr Anne Richards   *Tel:* 020 7898 1444
             email: anne.richards@c-of-e.org.uk

National Adviser for Mission and Evangelism Canon
Paul Bayes   *Tel:* 020 7898 1502
               email: paul.bayes@c-of-e.org.uk

National Inter Faith Relations Adviser Revd Guy
Wilkinson   *Tel:* 020 7898 1477
             email: guy.wilkinson@c-of-e.org.uk

National Rural Officer Dr Jill Hopkinson
                           Tel: 024 7685 3073
                           Fax: 024 7669 6460
                     email: jillh@rase.org.uk

All staff are based in Church House, Westminster
with the following exceptions: the offices of
Partnership for World Mission (PWM) are at
St Andrew's House, 16 Tavistock Crescent,
London W11 1AP; the offices of the National
Rural Officer are at the Arthur Rank Centre,
Stoneleigh Park, Warwickshire CV8 2LZ. The
National Inter Faith Relations Adviser is based at
Lambeth Palace.
The Council currently has the following commit-
tees or panels. Those Committees which are
ecumenical or formally constituted with other
agencies, are described in greater detail.

Partnership for World Mission (PWM)
Chairman Rt Revd Michael Hill (*Bishop of Bristol*)

Secretary Mr Stephen Lyon   *Tel:* 020 7313 3929
              email: stephen.lyon@c-of-e.org.uk

Office St Andrew's House, 16 Tavistock Crescent,
London W11 1AP   *Tel:* 020 7313 3929

Partnership for World Mission (PWM) was set up
in 1978 as a partnership between the General
Synod and the World Mission Agencies of the
Church of England. In April 1991 it changed from
being an organization independent of General
Synod (but with synodical representation) to a
constituent committee of the appropriate sub-
ordinate body of Synod.
  PWM is governed by the PWM Panel drawing
its members from the General Synod, the full
PWM Mission Agencies, representatives of Dio-
cesan Companion Links, Associate Members and
our ecumenical partners. There are eleven full
PWM Agencies: Church Army, the Church's
Ministry among Jewish People (CMJ), Church
Mission Society (CMS), Church Pastoral Aid
Society (CPAS), Crosslinks, Intercontinental
Church Society (ICS), The Mission to Seafarers,
The Mothers' Union, South American Mission
Society (SAMS), the Society for Promoting Christian Knowledge (SPCK) and the United Society
for the Propagation of the Gospel (USPG). There
are over 20 Associate Members.
  Its main tasks are concerned with the Church
of England's role in furthering partnership in
mission within the Anglican Communion; supporting the work of Diocesan Companion Links;
and with coordinating the policies and selected
tasks of the Church of England's World Mission
Agencies. It has an advisory role in enabling
English dioceses and General Synod to see their
way more clearly towards their participation in
world mission as members of the Anglican
Communion and ecumenically.

Mission Theological Advisory Group (MTAG)
Co-Chairman (with Revd Prof John Drane) Rt
Revd Dr Brian Castle (*Bishop of Tonbridge*)

Secretary Dr Anne Richards

The ecumenical Mission Theological Advisory
Group is composed of nominees from the
Mission and Public Affairs Division of the
Archbishops' Council and the Global Mission
Network (GMN) of Churches Together in Britain
and Ireland (CTBI). It is concerned with the
theology of mission and deals with theological
issues referred to it by the participating bodies.

Presence and Engagement Task Group
Chairman Rt Revd David James (*Bishop of
Bradford*)

Secretary Canon Guy Wilkinson

Rural Strategy Group
Chair Rt Revd Michael Langrish (*Bishop of Exeter*)

Secretary Dr Jill Hopkinson
Office The Arthur Rank Centre, Stoneleigh Park,
Warwickshire CV8 2LZ   Tel: 024 7685 3073
                            Fax: 024 7641 4808

Urban Policy Consultative Group
Chairman Rt Revd Laurie Green (*Bishop of Bradwell*)
Secretary Revd Dr Andrew Davey

HOSPITAL CHAPLAINCIES COUNCIL
Chairman Rt Revd Michael Perham (*Bishop of Gloucester*)

CEO/Secretary Revd Fr Edward J. Lewis
                            Tel: 020 7898 1892
                            Mobile: 07957 529646
            email: edward.lewis@c-of-e.org.uk

Functions

(a) To consider questions of policy and practice relating to spiritual ministrations to patients and staff in medical establishments and community care programmes referred to it by the Archbishops' Council and/or the General Synod.
(b) To provide information and advice to the dioceses in their negotiations with Health Authorities and Trusts on the appointment of hospital chaplains and on other National Health Service (NHS) matters; to visit and support dioceses involved in such negotiations; and to provide similar services to hospital chaplains in their relations with NHS management.
(c) To respond promptly to enquiries from Chief Executives and Trusts regarding chaplaincy issues and the best practice for employment of Anglican clergy in the NHS.
(d) To monitor and authorize, on behalf of the Church of England, the standards and content of training provided for hospital chaplaincy in cooperation with other Churches and chaplaincy organizations.
(e) To work jointly with the Ministry Division in providing the personnel and expertise input from qualified chaplains in preparing theological students for their ministry to the sick in hospital and in the community.
(f) To monitor matters affecting spiritual ministrations in all medical establishments and community care programmes, reporting to the Archbishops' Council via the Mission

and Public Affairs Division and/or the General Synod as and when required.
(g) To act as a liaison between the Department of Health and the Church of England on all questions relating to spiritual ministrations in medical establishments and community care programmes.
(h) To contribute, in cooperation with the Community and Public Affairs team of the Mission and Public Affairs Division, to the ongoing theological reflections on contemporary medical, ethical and social issues.
(i) To exchange information and advice in matters relating to hospital chaplaincy with other Christian Churches in the British Isles and abroad.

Research Officer Mr Tim Battle   Tel: 020 7898 1893
            email: tim.battle@c-of-e.org.uk

Training and Development Facilitator and Coordinator of Electronic Communications Miss Mary
Ingledew   Tel: 020 7898 1895
            email: mary.ingledew@c-of-e.org.uk

The HCC uses its contacts to encourage, facilitate, coordinate and generally support all opportunities for learning about hospital ministry. The Joint Training Office is concerned with ensuring the provision of suitable training and study courses for Hospital Chaplains. The work is currently supported by the Church of England, the Roman Catholic Bishops' Conference of England and Wales, and the Free Churches Group.

Office Church House, Great Smith St, London
SW1P 3AZ   Tel: 020 7898 1895
                            Fax: 020 7898 1891

The Churches' Committee for Hospital Chaplaincy
In its relationships with other agencies, including the Department of Health and NHS Authorities, the Council works cooperatively with the Free Churches Group of Churches Together in England and the Roman Catholic Church in this committee, which is also a coordinating committee within Churches Together in England. The posts of Chair and Secretary of the CCHC rotate between the Churches and also act as the spokesperson and link with Churches Together in England. Further details from the Secretary.

Secretary Revd Debbie Hodge, CTE, 27
Tavistock Square, London WC1H 9HH
                            Tel: 020 7529 8136

EDUCATION DIVISION
Transforming Church and Community through Education and Learning

The Education Division staff work in three teams: Lifelong Learning; Schools Strategy; Training and Development.

THE BOARD OF EDUCATION
The Board of Education's Constitution (as laid down by General Synod) sets out three main functions: to advise the General Synod and the Archbishops' Council on all matters relating to education; to advise the dioceses similarly; to take action in the field of education (in the name of the Church of England, the Archbishops' Council and the General Synod) on such occasion as is required.

The Board of Education meets twice a year, in May and November. Panels of Board members, supplemented by a small number of non-Board members, oversee the various aspects of the work. Board and panel members receive a weekly electronic bulletin about the issues being addressed by the Education Division staff; these bulletins frequently invite guidance from Board members and from diocesan education staff who also receive the bulletins.

Chair
Rt Revd Dr Kenneth Stevenson (*Bishop of Portsmouth*)

Three members elected by the General Synod
Mrs Lorna Ashworth (Chichester), Miss Rachel Beck (Lincoln), Canon Prof Anthony Thiselton (Southwell and Nottingham)

Members appointed by General Synod
Ven Peter Ballard (Blackburn)

Four education specialists
Dr Irene Bishop, Rt Revd Michael Lewis (*Bishop of Middleton*), Mrs Marion Plant, Mrs Elizabeth Williams

Three co-opted members
Mr Leslie Stephen, Dr Rebecca Nye, Mr Mark Russell

Two National Society representatives
Rt Revd Stephen Venner (*Bishop of Dover*) (ex officio), Mrs Mary Nagel (Chichester)

Representative of the Church in Wales
Revd Edwin Counsell

Observers
Mr Derek Holbird (*Guildford Diocesan Director of Education*), Revd Dr Howard Worsley (*Southwell and Nottingham Diocesan Director of Education*), Prof Michael Wright (*Vice Chancellor, Canterbury Christ Church University*)

EDUCATION DIVISION STAFF
Chief Education Officer and Head of the Education Division Revd Janina Ainsworth
Tel: 020 7898 1500

Lifelong Learning team
National Adviser for Higher Education and Chaplaincy Revd Hugh Shilson-Thomas
Tel: 020 7898 1513
email: hugh.shilson-thomas@c-of-e.org.uk

National Further Education Adviser Mr Alan Murray
Tel: 020 7898 1517
email: alan.murray@c-of-e.org.uk

Schools Strategy team
Head of School Improvement Mr Nick McKemey
Tel: 020 7898 1490
email: nick.mckemey@c-of-e.org.uk

Head of School Development Revd David Whittington
Tel: 020 7898 1789
email: david.whittington@c-of-e.org.uk

National Schools Support Officer Mrs Liz Carter
Tel: 020 7898 1515
email: liz.carter@c-of-e.org.uk

Training and development team
National Children's Adviser Mrs Mary Hawes
Tel: 020 7898 1504
email: mary.hawes@c-of-e.org.uk

National Adviser in Lay Discipleship and Shared Ministry Miss Joanna Cox
Tel: 020 7898 1511
email: joanna.cox@c-of-e.org.uk

National Youth Adviser (Participation and Youth Work Development) Mr Peter Ball
Tel: 020 7898 1506
email: peter.ball@c-of-e.org.uk

National Youth Adviser (Training and Faith Development) Miss Yvonne Criddle   *Tel:* 020 7898 1507
email: yvonne.criddle@c-of-e.org.uk

Office Church House, Great Smith St, London SW1P 3AZ
Tel: 020 7898 1501
Fax: 020 7898 1520

LIFELONG LEARNING

Higher Education
The team aims to develop the Church's presence and witness in Higher Education by:

* monitoring developments in the higher education sector;
* working for the extension of Church contacts in, and impact on, the field of Higher Education;
* stimulating and developing the Church's practical concern in student and university affairs –

a concern both for the life of higher education institutions, their ethical, social, spiritual and religious concerns, and for the individuals who work and study in the sector;

- liaison and partnership with national bodies engaged in Higher Education, including the Department for Innovation, Universities and Skills, the Higher Education Funding Council, representative university groups, ecumenical and other faith bodies;
- helping the Church both to build up its ministry in Higher Education by means of the advisory, liaison and representative services to chaplaincy work in HE already established, and to reflect upon that ministry.

Further Education

The key role is strategic thinking and planning, to develop the Church's presence and witness within the 400 FE colleges, and the wider Learning and Skills sector.

- To engage with the Government's programme of reform of Further Education and monitor policy and developments in FE.
- To increase the Church's involvement with the FE sector through chaplaincy and college/faith partnerships in dialogue with the Learning and Skills Council.
- To help to shape the sector's understanding of spiritual and moral development, human values and ethics in students' educational experience.
- To work with ecumenical and inter-faith partners, such as the Faith and Beliefs in Further Education.

SCHOOLS STRATEGY

The work of the Schools Strategy team is undertaken in close liaison with the National Society.

The team represents the interests of the Church in relation to Government over the whole range of the ever-developing schools agenda. It interfaces with the Department for Children, Schools and Families Ofsted, the Training and Devlopment Agency for Schools, the Qualifications and Curriculum Authority, the National College for School Leadership, and represents Church of England voluntary schools on the many standing committees and working parties which these bodies generate. It liaises closely with diocesan education teams, helping them to interpret and implement government policy, and developing with them national church policies on appropriate issues. It provides advice to dioceses and schools, including a formal legal advice scheme.

School Development

The team is concerned with schools legislation as it impacts on the provision and development of church schools, on church school buildings, on governance and management, and on the

employment and support of staff in church schools. The team interfaces with the DCSF, dioceses and LAs to enable Church of England schools to grow and develop within this legislative framework. It is a 'door opener', ensuring that dioceses are aware of opportunities and that government is aware of the Church as a constructive, development-minded partner. It seeks to increase both the number and quality of Church of England schools and academies which are both distinctive and inclusive, contributing to high quality education for all young people. It has a particular concern for children in areas of deprivation, encouraging where practicable the extension of provision to offer opportunity to them.

School Improvement

The team is working to support and improve the distinctiveness and effectiveness of church schools by identifying, disseminating and sharing the best practice within the diverse national family of Anglican schools. Through Section 48 inspection it contributes to the national agenda for school improvement. It focuses not just on church schools but on all schools, having a concern for the teaching and content of Religious Education and quality of collective worship, for the National Curriculum and for the spiritual, moral, social and cultural development and wellbeing of children and young people.

Church Universities and Colleges

Nine of the universities and colleges founded by the Church of England date from the early years of a system of mass education in the nineteenth century; the other two, Canterbury Christ Church University and St Martin's College, were founded in the early 1960s. One, Whitelands, is one of the constituent colleges of Roehampton University; another, founded as St Katharine's College, is now fully part of the only ecumenical (joint C of E/RC) university in Europe, Liverpool Hope. All eleven HEIs have taught degree awarding powers: nine have university title. Although they were founded for teacher training, almost all these institutions have diversified and expanded greatly: they all still offer teacher training; many have added substantial faculties of health; all offer a diverse range of liberal arts and vocational courses; almost all have increasingly significant departments of (Anglican) theology and religious studies. A report of the Church of England Board of Education, *Mutual Expectations: the Church of England and the Church Colleges/Universities* (GS 1601) was approved by General Synod in February 2006.

TRAINING AND DEVELOPMENT

The Training and Development team supports the voluntary aspects of the Church of England's work in education and training as it relates to children, young people and adult learning and lay discipleship. By resourcing diocesan networks and supporting work in parishes and local communities, it aims to promote effective Christian nurture, discipleship and outreach and to encourage training and best practice. Much of the work at national level involves developing effective collaborations with key diocesan personnel, government, voluntary agencies, ecumenical and denominational partnerships and other divisions of the National Church Institutions. The National Youth Strategy and the National Children's Strategy are under review, through consultation with key partners, to determine priorities for the next period of work.

Work with Young People

The National Youth Advisers promote the Church's educational, spiritual and social development of young people between the ages of 11 and 25. The work encompasses those outside the Church as well as those active within it. Responding to local, regional and national needs requires regular consultation and collaborative working with the Diocesan Youth Officers' Network, and other bodies.

- Advice is provided on training opportunities and resources for both voluntary and paid youth workers. There are strong links with training providers including The Centre for Youth Ministry, University of Chester and Oasis.
- The participation of young people in the Church's life is crucial to the work and this is supported through the Church of England Youth Council, including three General Synod representatives, and the Young Adult Observer Group at General Synod's July meeting.
- The Church's work with young people also involves collaboration and partnership with Anglican voluntary societies, other Christian and secular agencies, including the DCSF and DIUS, the National Youth Agency, the National Council for Voluntary Youth Services and Churches Together in England.
- The four key elements of the National Youth Strategy – Young People and Worship, Young People as Leaders, Resourcing Youth Workers, Young People and Mission – underpin the work and are a key focus of the developmental aspects of the advisers' work. This has included 'Equipping' – Core Competencies and Learning Outcomes for Voluntary Youth Workers, which enables volunteers to work towards a Diocesan and an Archbishops'

Certificate in Youth Work, and the on-going delivery of the Youth Evangelism Fund in partnership with the National Evangelism Adviser.

Children's Work

The Key tasks of the National Children's Adviser are:

- advocacy of the place and value of children in the Church, particularly in the areas of the Church as a worshipping community and the Church as a place of learning for all;
- collaborative working with the network for Diocesan Children's Advisers;
- initiating in-service training where appropriate, in order to provide laity and clergy at all levels with the necessary resources and training to nurture the faith of children and their families;
- implementing the Church of England Children's Strategy *Sharing the Good News with Children*;
- keeping a watching brief on current government policies under the *Every Child Matters* agenda with regard to their application in the voluntary sector and among faith communities.

Lay Discipleship and Shared Ministry

The Adviser promotes and delivers consultancy, support, research and development to enhance the capacity and provision of adult Christian formation and lifelong learning in the Church. The work undertaken seeks to:

- promote the development of theological education for lay people – a current initiative is *Education for Discipleship*;
- resource new diocesan development in shared ministry, formal lay ministry and patterns of integrated training, in association with the Ministry Division;
- improve the quality of adult and lifelong learning through training the trainers, promoting partnerships, researching and disseminating good practice and developing new initiatives encouraging Christian discipleship in the Church and the world.

For a list of **Educational Chaplains** *see Crockford*. For **Church Universities and Colleges of Higher Education** *see* page 222.
See also the entries on **Chaplains in Higher and Further Education** on pages 219–220.

CATHEDRAL AND CHURCH BUILDINGS DIVISION

This area of the Archbishops' Council's responsibilities relates to the Church's concern with cathedral and church buildings and related matters.

Cathedral and Church Buildings Divisional Group

Chairman Chair of the Church Heritage Forum

Members
Chair of the Cathedrals Fabric Commission
Chair of the Church Buildings Council
4 other Members (appointed by the Appointments Committee from within the Synodical members of the CCC and CFCE)

Head of Division Mrs Janet Gough

The Division was formed in 2002 from the staff formerly serving the Cathedral Fabric Commission and the Council for the Care of Churches, and supporting the work of the Archbishops' Council in relation to cathedral and church buildings. In 2008, the Division was joined by the staff formerly serving the Advisory Board for Redundant Churches, the independent statutory adviser to the Church Commissioners on churches proposed for closure, and former Anglican churches subject to the Pastoral Measure. At the same time, the CCC and ABRC were dissolved and their functions transferred to the newly constituted Church Buildings Council. The CBC is the Church's national advisory, grant-making and educational body supporting dioceses and parishes with the care, use and development of parish churches and their contents and churchyards. Through its Statutory Advisory Committee, it also advises the Commissioners and others on churches proposed for closure and closed for regular public worship. The CFCE is the central planning body with advisory and regulatory functions relating to the fabric, contents, setting and archaeology of the Church of England's cathedrals and their precincts. The Head of Division is Secretary of the CBC and CFCE and also acts as the lead officer of the Church Heritage Forum (see below).

The Division is responsible for developing and maintaining relations between Church and State, national and local bodies on church buildings matters, and for the development of the Church's vision of how the Church of England may (in partnership with the State and local communities) best meet its responsibilities for its church buildings.

Overall the Church of England is responsible for 16,000 parish churches and 41 cathedrals that form the centres for the Church's worship and its mission in the community. These buildings and their contents represent 14 centuries of religious architecture, art and history, which have continuously developed up to the present day, and are still developing. Some 13,000 are listed buildings (including 45 per cent of all the country's Grade I buildings), while many churchyards are an important ecological resource.

The Church Buildings Council

Chairman Rt Revd Graeme Knowles (*Dean of St Paul's Cathedral*)

MEMBERS
Canon Michael Ainsworth, Mr Timothy Allen (St Edmundsbury & Ipswich), Ms Louise Bainbridge, Preb Philippa Boardman (London), Revd Stephen Brookes, Mr Oliver Caroe, Mr Quinton Carroll, Mr Mark Cazalet, Canon Alan Fell, Ms Stephanie Fischer, Mr Jonathan MacKechnie-Jarvis, Mr Neil Moat, Mrs Valerie Owen, Mrs Sarah Quail, Miss Anne Riches, Dr Hilary Taylor, Mr Roy Thompson (York), Mr Alan Thurlow, Mr Jacob Vince (Chichester), Mr Ian Wainwright, Canon Martin Webster (Chelmsford), two vacancies.

The Church Buildings Council (CBC) carries out the functions formerly of the Council for the Care of Churches (CCC) and the Advisory Board for Redundant Churches (ABRC). The CCC was formed in 1921 to coordinate the work of the Diocesan Advisory Committees for the Care of Churches, which advise diocesan chancellors on faculty applications, and clergy, churchwardens, architects and others responsible for church buildings and their contents on their care, use and development. The ABRC was formed in 1969 as the independent statutory advisor to the Church Commissioners on churches proposed for closure for regular worship and former Anglican churches subject to the Pastoral Measure.

The CBC's priority is to enable parishes to release through responsible stewardship the mission and worship potential of church buildings. We seek to encourage and assist parishes in the care and conservation, use and development of the Church's buildings including their contents and churchyards.

The CBC advises the Archbishops' Council on

all matters relating to the use, care and planning or design of places of worship, their curtilages and contents; acts on the Council's behalf in contacts with government departments and other bodies and in negotiations with professional bodies over church inspection and repair; and assists in the review or revision of legislation relating to church buildings and their contents.

The CBC, through its Statutory Advisory Committee, advises the Church Commissioners and others on the interest, quality and importance of churches and their contents, and the alteration and conversion of churches to alternative use, working closely with the central and local authorities of Church and State.

The CBC provides Diocesan Pastoral Committees with detailed reports about the architectural and historic qualities of churches likely to be closed for regular worship. It also submits specialist advice to diocesan chancellors, Diocesan Advisory Committees and parishes on proposals that are or may become the subject of faculty applications, e.g. the construction of church extensions, re-ordering schemes, the sale of church furnishings, the partial demolition of churches, the conservation of significant furnishings, and related archaeological work.

The CBC maintains contact with Diocesan Advisory Committees through regular circulation of information, by an annual meeting for Chairmen, Secretaries and other members and by visits. The membership of DACs is varied: it includes both clergy and lay, some with professional expertise in architecture, art history and archaeology, and others of no specialist knowledge but of sound judgement and experience, or representing the views of English Heritage, the local planning authority and the amenity societies. Every diocese has specialist advisers on organs, bells, clocks, archaeology, and so on.

The CBC administers funds (generously provided by charitable bodies) for the conservation of furnishings and works of art in churches, and collaborates closely with English Heritage, the Heritage Lottery Fund, National and other Lottery distributors and other grant-making bodies. Advice is available from the Council on specific conservation problems.

The CBC is not only concerned with the care and conservation of ancient buildings and their contents, but also with the development of places of worship and the encouragement of good new furnishings and works of art. It runs two web sites: www.churchcare.co.uk, generously sponsored by Ecclesiastical, which seeks to provide comprehensive advice on matters related to the use, development, care and conservation of church buildings, and www.churchart.co.uk, which gives advice on commissioning new works of art and includes details of individual artists and craftspeople.

The Council's specialist committees offer expert advice on conservation matters and administer grants from charitable foundations for the care and conservation of significant or historic furnishings and works of art in churches and churchyards. Churches in England, Scotland and Wales, of any denomination, are eligible for these grants. In addition, under an agreement reached with the Wolfson Foundation, the Council considers applications for grant aid towards fabric repairs for Grade I and Grade II* Anglican churches in England, Scotland and Wales.

FUNDING CHURCH REPAIRS AND APPLYING FOR GRANTS
Those seeking information on sources of funding for church repairs should contact the Church Buildings Council and/or the National Churches Trust (*see* Organizations section), or visit the Churchcare website (www.churchcare.co.uk).

PUBLICATIONS
The Council has an extensive list of publications on practical and technical matters relating to the care and conservation of church buildings and their contents. A complete list of titles and prices is available on request from the Council's offices. Much information is also available electronically on the Churchcare web site.

The Cathedrals Fabric Commission for England

Chairman Rt Hon Frank Field MP

Vice-Chairman Ms Jennie Page

MEMBERS
Very Revd James Atwell (*Dean of Winchester*), Miss Sarah Brown, Canon Peter Bruinvels (Guildford), Mr Richard Carr-Archer, Mr Geoffrey Clifton, Canon Jeremy Davies, Mr Peter Draper, Mr Michael Drury, Dr Richard Hall, Canon Jeremy Haselock (Norwich), Canon David Isaac (Portsmouth), Very Revd Peter Judd (*Dean of Chelmsford*), Mrs Judith Leigh, Mr John Maine, Rt Revd Stephen Platten (*Bishop of Wakefield*), Mr Nicholas Rank, Ven Jane Sinclair, Canon Peter Smith (St Edmundsbury & Ipswich), Mr Tom Sutcliffe (Southwark), Canon Dr Nicholas Thistlethwaite, Mr Paul Velluet, Lady Hilary Weir

In 1949, at the request of Deans and Chapters, the Cathedrals Advisory Committee was set up to give help and advice on places and problems affecting the fabric, furnishings, fittings and precincts of cathedrals.

In 1981, the Committee was reconstituted as a permanent Commission of the General

Synod, under the title The Cathedrals Advisory Commission for England.

In 1991, the Commission was further reconstituted as a statutory body under the Care of Cathedrals Measure and renamed The Cathedrals Fabric Commission. The Commission has regulatory powers under the Measure. Before implementing proposals affecting the cathedral, its contents or its surroundings, the Dean and Chapter require the approval of the Commission in specific cases, or of a local Fabric Advisory Committee appointed jointly by the Commission and by the Dean and Chapter. It also has advisory functions relating to the architecture, archaeology, art and history of cathedrals and their precincts.

It also publishes a series of advisory and guidance notes relating to the operation of the Measure and the Care of Cathedrals; these are available on the Church of England web site: www.cofe.anglican.org and from the Commission's offices.

Staff of the Cathedral and Church Buildings Division

Head of Division Ms Janet Gough
Tel: 020 7898 1887
email: janet.gough@c-of-e.org.uk
Deputy Head of Division Mr Stephen Bowler
Tel: 020 7898 1860
email: stephen.bowler@c-of-e.org.uk

Assistant Secretary CFCE Ms Maggie Goodall
Tel: 020 7898 1888
email: maggie.goodall@c-of-e.org.uk

Cathedrals Assistant Ms Allie Nickell
Tel: 020 7898 1862
email: allie.nickell@c-of-e.org.uk

Senior Adviser, Closed Churches Dr Jeffrey West
Tel: 020 7898 1872
email: jeffrey.west@c-of-e.org.uk

Casework Officer, Closed Churches Ms Anne McNair
Tel: 020 7898 1871
email: anne.mcnair@c-of-e.org.uk

Casework and Law Officer Mr Jonathan Goodchild
Tel: 020 7898 1883
email: jonathan.goodchild@c-of-e.org.uk

Archaeology Officer Dr Joseph Elders
Tel: 020 7898 1875
email: joseph.elders@c-of-e.org.uk

Casework Officer Mrs Jude Johncock
Tel: 020 7898 1864
email: jude.johncock@c-of-e.org.uk

Conservation Officer Mr Andrew Argyrakis
Tel: 020 7898 1885
email: andrew.argyrakis @c-of-e.org.uk

Conservation Assistant Dr David Knight
Tel: 020 7898 1886
email: david.knight@c-of-e.org.uk

Conservation Assistant Dr Pedro Gaspar
Tel: 020 7898 1889
email: pedro.gaspar@c-of-e.org.uk

Policy Officer Ms Rebecca Payne
Tel: 020 7898 1886
email: rebecca.payne@c-of-e.org.uk

Research Assistant Vacancy   *Tel:* 020 7898 1865

CHURCH HERITAGE FORUM
Chairman Rt Revd and Rt Hon Richard Chartres (*Bishop of London*)

Secretary Miss Andrea Mulkeen
email: andrea.mulkeen@c-of-e.org.uk

The Church Heritage Forum, which was established in 1997, brings together representatives of national and local church interests in matters relating to the Church's built heritage. It enables the Church to take a more proactive role in anticipating developments in the built heritage field; ensures that heritage concerns are fed into the Archbishops' Council; provides a mechanism for members to reach a view on matters of common concern; provides a point of focus for contact both within the Church and with outside bodies; promotes a wider public awareness of the Church's work in the built heritage area; and enables the exchange of information and facilitates mutual support.

Membership comprises representatives from the following: Archbishops' Council, Association of English Cathedrals, Church Commissioners' Redundant Churches Committee, Cathedrals Fabric Commission for England, Churches Conservation Trust, Church Buildings Council, and an archdeacon. A diocesan secretary and the Secretary of the Churches Legal Advisory Service (CLAS) act as assessors.

The Church Heritage Forum issued a major policy statement in 2004, *Building Faith in Our Future*, looking at the achievements carried out within church buildings and the potential fragility of these achievements, and calling for greater partnerships from public bodies of all kinds to help sustain them for the future. Discussions on this are ongoing.

FINANCIAL POLICY DEPARTMENT

Head of Financial Policy: Mr David White
Tel: 020 7898 1676
email: david.white@c-of-e.org.uk

The Financial Policy Department exists to support the Archbishops' Council and the Church Commissioners in the development of financial policy, and in the monitoring and management of its finances. It works in close partnership with dioceses as well as departments across the Archbishops' Council and commissioners, including the Common Services departments. the other national Church institutions. It consolidates, administers and monitors these two NCIs' budgets and calculates and communicates the apportionment of the Council's budget to dioceses. The latter has included supporting a recent limited review of the apportionment formula – see GS Misc 888.

The department supports the development of spending plans from the Church Commissioners' fund, including liason with their actuaries, and has responsibility for the allocation of Mission Development Fund money (currently £4.8m in 2008) between all dioceses and of the ministry support to poorer dioceses (currently £28.7m in 2008). These distributions are funded by the Church Commissioners but distributed by the Archbishops' Council (the formula having last been subject to a limited review – published as GS Misc 779 – in 2004–5).

The department's work includes providing the secretariat and administrative support for Church and Community Fund (see later separate entry) and the financial and legal aspects of the relationship with the Church Colleges. Responsibilities such as in respect of the CBF Funds (see separate entry) are currently carried out through the Central Board of Finance (whose membership is coterminous with the Archbishops' Council) but are in the process of being transferred to other bodies. At any given time the department is likely to be resourcing, or contributing to, a number of other reviews across the Archbishops' Council to improve the Church's financial arrangements and to best resource and facilitate its mission. It seeks to ensure that the General Synod (through a Financial Memorandum) is aware of the significant financial implications of proposals before decisions are taken and contributes to the development of policy on financial matters across the Church.

The department provides secretariat support for the Council's Finance Committee (which meets around five times a year) which is responsible for the management of the Council's financial business and advice and co-ordination on financial matters over the Church as a whole, the Inter-Diocesan Finance Forum (which meets twice a year and comprises three representatives of each diocese) and the Consultative Group of DBF Chairs and Diocesan Secretaries (comprising one DBF Chair and one Diocesan Secretary from each region). The Forum and the Consultative Group provide an opportunity for consultation on remuneration policy, conditions of service, pensions policy, the national Church budget and apportionment, allocations to dioceses for the support of ministry in poorer areas and other issues with a financial perspective.

The department supports the work of the Church Commissioners by supporting the work of its Assets Committee and staff level Assets Management Group. Key roles include the production of coordinated investment performance statistics and financial forecasts in respect of income and expenditure, cashflow are longer term actuarial projection.

CHRISTIAN STEWARDSHIP

National Stewardship & Resources Officer Dr John Preston
Tel: 020 7898 1540
email: john.preston@c-of-e.org.uk

Through its Christian Stewardship Committee, the Archbishops' Council affirms the principles and practice of Christian stewardship as a part of discipleship. Stewardship advisers encourage church people to respond to God's love and generosity and resource God's mission through the Church by the discovery and use of human and financial resources. This is often focused on the giving of money – regularly, tax-effectively and in proportion to income.

Initiatives are promoted, support given and ideas exchanged between the diocesan members of the Christian stewardship network. There is a particular focus on identifying, documenting and resourcing elements of good practice, so that other dioceses and parishes can benefit from what is proven to be effective. Current areas of good practice include:

- resourcing parishes to encourage giving through the appointment of a Parish Giving Officer;
- effective annual review of giving
- promoting legacy giving as part of our holistic stewardship;
- supporting parishes engaging with a capital fundraising programme.

Church people, through their giving, are rightly the providers of the largest part of the Church's income but the Committee is reviewing how it can best help the Church at all levels to seek additional income streams.

A new national web site to resource all those concerned with Christian giving, stewardship and parish finances is available at www.parishresources.org.uk. This contains a wide range of resources for treasurers, gift aid secretaries, those who preach and teach on stewardship and those who encourage giving.

Accounts Department

Chief Accountant: Mr Paul Burrage
Tel: 020 7898 1677
email: paul.burrage@c-of-e.org.uk

The Accounts Department provides accounting services principally for the Archbishops' Council, the Church Commissioners and the Church of England Pensions Board. It is responsible for financial accounting and processing, asset (property, investment and other) accounting, cash and treasury management and payroll, and provides expertise on taxation (principally property and VAT related) and other financial and accounting issues.

The finance system, which is already in place for the Archbishops' Council, is expected to be implemented for the Commissioners and the Pensions Board in 2009. This will provide for a single platform for processing and reporting, thus optimising on the centralised Accounts function. As a result, it is anticipated that the true synergies arising from the centralisation will begin to be realised during 2009.

Internal Auditing Department

Head of Internal Audit: Mr Kim Parry MIIA DipCG
Tel: 020 7898 1658
email: kim.parry@c-of-e.org.uk

The Internal Auditing Department provides internal audit services to the Church Commissioners, the Church of England Pensions Board, the Archbishops' Council and the other National Church Institutions as well as several diocesan boards of finance.

The department carries out regular departmental and process reviews in accordance with a programme agreed each year with each Audit Committee, and also investigates particular issues that might arise from time to time.

The Internal Auditing Department provides consultancy support to managers on matters of governance, risk management and internal control.

Church House Publishing

Strategic Task Group
Mr Philip Fletcher (*Chairman*), Rt Revd John Pritchard (Bishop of Oxford), Revd Mary Hawes, Mr Ian Locks, Mr Gavin Oldham, Dr David Pullinger, Canon Prof Paul Bradshaw

Functions of the Strategic Task Group
1   To advise the Director of Communications and the Head of Publishing on any matter relating to the strategic operation and development of Church House Publishing;
2   to report annually to the Archbishops' Council on its contribution to Church House Publishing's activities.

Church House Publishing (CHP) is the official publisher to the Archbishops' Council and the General Synod. In addition to publishing *Common Worship*, CHP publishes around sixty new titles each year to further the mission and enhance the reputation of the Church of England. Reference publications include *Crockford's Clerical Directory* and *The Church of England Year Book*. Both these publications are continually updated and corrections are welcome to be sent to the addresses below. For up-to-date information visit our online catalogue at www.chpublishing.co.uk

Director of Communications Peter Crumpler
Tel: 020 7898 1462
email: peter.crumpler@c-of-e.org.uk

Head of Publishing Dr Thomas Allain-Chapman
Tel: 020 7898 1450
email: thomas.allain-chapman@c-of-e.org.uk

Product Development Manager Revd Kathryn Pritchard
Tel: 020 7898 1485
email: kathryn.pritchard@c-of-e.org.uk

Commissioning Editor Tracey Messenger
Tel: 020 7898 1183
email: tracey.messenger@c-of-e.org.uk

New Media Manager Andrew Sweeney
Tel: 020 7898 1582
email: andrew.sweeney@c-of-e.org.uk

Editorial Manager Linda Foster
Tel: 020 7898 1594
email: linda.foster@c-of-e.org.uk

Production Manager Katharine Allenby
Tel: 020 7898 1452
email: katharine.allenby@c-of-e.org.uk

Marketing Manager Tracy Somorjay
Tel: 020 7898 1524
email: tracy.somorjay@c-of-e.org.uk

Sales Manager Cynthia Hamilton
Tel: 020 7898 1454
email: cynthia.hamilton@c-of-e.org.uk

Office Church House, Great Smith St, London SW1P 3AZ   *Tel:* 020 7898 1451; 020 7898 1000
Fax: 020 7898 1449
email: publishing@c-of-e.org.uk
Web: www.chpublishing.co.uk

The Church of England Year Book
email: yearbook@c-of-e.org.uk

Crockford's Clerical Directory
The Compiler, Crockford, Church House, Great Smith St, London SW1P 3AZ   *Tel:* 020 7898 1012
Fax: 020 7898 1769
email: crockford@c-of-e.org.uk

_____

Church House Bookshop was transferred to the ownership of Hymns Ancient and Modern in April 2006 and continues to trade at 31 Great Smith Street, London SW1P 3BN.
Tel: 020 7799 4064
email: bookshop@chbookshop.co.uk
Web: www.chbookshop.co.uk

Information Technology and Office Services

Head of Information Technology and Office Services
Mr John Ferguson   *Tel:* 020 7898 1666
email: john.ferguson@c-of-e.org.uk

Office Church House, Great Smith St, London SW1P 3AZ
The Information Technology department pro-

vides the IT infrastructure for the National Church Institutions, including IT systems development and integration, as well as all aspects of PC desktop and network support and training. Office Services includes reprographics, telephone and central buying facilities across the NCIs.

RECORD CENTRE

Director of Libraries, Archives and Information Services Mr Declan Kelly   *Tel:* 020 7898 1432

Address Church of England Record Centre, 15 Galleywall Rd, South Bermondsey, London SE16 3PB   *Tel:* 020 7898 1030
Fax: 020 7898 1043
email: archivist@c-of-e.org.uk
Web: www.cofe.anglican.org/about/librariesandarchives/

The Centre, which is a central service operated by the Archbishops' Council, houses the non-current

records of the Church Commissioners, the Archbishops' Council, the Church of England Pensions Board, the General Synod and the National Society, together with those of some ecumenical bodies. Its main purpose is to provide low-cost off-site storage and records management advice for the business records of the Central Church Bodies. The Centre also serves as an advisory point for queries concerning the archives of the Church of England. Enquiries are welcome; archive material can be seen at the Reading Room at Lambeth Palace Library by prior appointment.

THE LEGAL OFFICE

The Legal Office of the National Institutions of the Church of England is responsible for providing legal advice and other services to the National Church Institutions. Its principal functions are:

- responsibility for the legislative programme of the General Synod;
- giving advice to the National Church Institutions and their respective committees and staff; and
- undertaking some transactional work for the National Church Institutions, especially the Church Commissioners and the Pensions Board.

Head of the Legal Office, Legal Director to the Archbishops' Council, Registrar and Legal Adviser to the General Synod

Mr Stephen Slack   *Tel:* 020 7898 1366
email: stephen.slack@c-of-e.org.uk

Secretary Miss Judith Gracias   *Tel:* 020 7898 1367
email: judith.gracias@c-of-e.org.uk
Official Solicitor to the Church Commissioners and Deputy Head of the Legal Office Vacancy

Deputy Official Solicitor Mr Tim Crow
Tel: 020 7898 1717
email: tim.crow@c-of-e.org.uk

Standing Counsel to the General Synod Sir Anthony Hammond QC   *Tel:* 020 7898 1799
email: anthony.hammond@c-of-e.org.uk

Secretary Miss Judith Gracias   *Tel:* 020 7898 1367
                        email: judith.gracias@c-of-e.org.uk
Office Church House, Great Smith St, London,
SW1P 3AZ   *Fax:* 020 7898 1718/1721
                        email: legal@c-of-e.org.uk

DX: 148403 WESTMINSTER 5
Web: www.cofe.anglican.org/legal/about/
                        churchlawlegis/

COMMUNICATIONS OFFICE

Communication is central to the mission of the Church. The Communications Office serves the Church at every level, seeking to convey the vibrant life of the Church, and its vital role at the heart of society.

The Office serves all the National Church Institutions, General Synod and the House of Bishops, works closely with Lambeth Palace and Bishopthorpe, and supports the activities of diocesan communicators around the country.

Working to a 'mission-shaped communications' agenda, the Office seeks to ensure all its activities are mission-oriented, proactive, professional and integrated.

It works closely with all sections of the media, issuing information, assisting them in their coverage of the Church and providing a 24-hour media response service throughout the year. It also produces information to improve communications within the Church, including a monthly Communications Update available via email across the Church.

The focus for the Church's role in public discussions involving media policy, the office liaises with the BBC, commercial broadcasters, and various government bodies. It also supports the Church's role in other public affairs issues, ensuring that the Church of England's voice is heard on key issues. In addition, it presents information to Parliament and other audiences on issues of concern, such as the cost of maintaining the Church's listed buildings, embryology laws and detention without charge in terrorism cases.

A relaunched communications training programme offers a range of skills to equip the Church to communicate using the latest technologies. The full schedule and range of expert tutors can be seen at www.commstraining.cofe.anglican.org. The Office oversees development of the Church of England's popular web site, www.cofe.anglican.org, one of the first 'entry points' for information about the Church.

The Office is increasingly involved in promoting key mission opportunities such as major festivals, life's special occasions, especially weddings, and projects like Love Life Live Lent or Back to Church Sunday. and projects

The Communications Office also runs an enquiry service answering questions from the public.

Director of Communications Peter Crumpler
                        Tel: 020 7898 1462
                        email: peter.crumpler@c-of-e.org.uk

Head of Media Relations Steve Jenkins
                        Tel: 020 7898 1457
                        email: steve.jenkins@c-of-e.org.uk

Senior Media Officer Louis Henderson
                        Tel: 020 7898 1621
                        email: lou.henderson@c-of-e.org.uk

Senior Media Officer Ben Wilson *Tel:* 020 7898 1464
                        email: ben.wilson@c-of-e.org.uk

Head of Communications Development Gillian Oliver
                        Tel: 020 7898 1458
                        email: gillian.oliver@c-of-e.org.uk

Senior Communications Officer Rachel Harden
                        Tel: 020 7898 1459
                        email: rachel.harden@c-of-e.org.uk

Office Church House, Great Smith St, London
SW1P 3AZ   *Tel:* 020 7898 1000
                        Fax: 020 7222 6672
                        Web: www.cofe.anglican.org

Diocesan Communicators Panel

Chairman Rt Revd Nicholas Baines (*Bishop of Croydon*)

Executive Officer Peter Crumpler
                        Tel: 020 7898 1462
                        email: peter.crumpler@c-of-e.org.uk

Members Revd John Carter, Nick Clarke, Jeremy Dowling, Rachel Farmer, Anni Holden, Rachel Harden, Revd David Guest, Revd David Marshall, Marie Papworth

HUMAN RESOURCES DEPARTMENT

The Human Resources (HR) department delivers efficient and cost-effective HR services, including support for recruitment, in relation to the 440 staff employed by the NCIs and the 170 staff of diocesan bishops. It also contracts with the Corporation of Church House for services in relation to their 40 staff. Additionally health, safety and welfare advice and services are provided to the 200 staff employed directly by the Church Commissioners on their estates and the Pensions Board in their residential schemes.
It does this through

- developing a diverse workforce and a fair and just workplace;
- creating a high performance working environment where staff have role clarity, focus on delivery and learning, actively pursue development and where career pathways are well defined;
- establishing a 'partnership' culture between employers, staff and trade unions through effective consultation and negotiation mechanisms;
- promoting joint employer initiatives and improved cultural alignment between the NCIs;
- pursuing the optimum deployment of staff through strategic resourcing, reward and HR information systems;
- developing occupational health, safety and welfare services.

STAFF

Director of Human Resources Ms Su Morgan
Tel: 020 7898 1565
email: su.morgan@c-of-e.org.uk
HR Senior Staff
Ms Julia Hudson (*HR Manager – McClean Implementation and Bishops*)   *Tel:* 020 7898 1589
email: julia.hudson@c-of-e.org.uk
Mr Peter Cunningham (*HR Manager – Operations*)   *Tel:* 020 7898 1182
email: peter.cunningham@c-of-e.org.uk
Ms Sheila Hosangady (*HR Manager – Organizational Development*)   *Tel:* 020 7898 1751
email: sheila.hosangady@c-of-e.org.uk

Office Church House, Great Smith St, London SW1P 3AZ

THE CHURCH COMMISSIONERS FOR ENGLAND

Office Church House, Great Smith St, London SW1P 3AZ   *Tel:* 020 7898 1000
Fax: 020 7898 1131
email: commissioners.enquiry@c-of-e.org.uk

Chairman The Archbishop of Canterbury

Secretary Mr Andrew Brown   *Tel:* 020 7898 1134
email: dawn.waters@c-of-e.org.uk

Deputy Secretary Vacancy

Director of Finance for the National Church Institutions Mrs Jackie Bliss   *Tel:* 020 7898 1795
email: jackie.bliss@c-of-e.org.uk

Chief Surveyor Mr Joseph Cannon
Tel: 020 7898 1759
email: joseph.cannon@c-of-e.org.uk

Pastoral and Closed Churches Secretary Mr Paul Lewis
(Pastoral reorganization, closed churches, clergy housing and glebe)   *Tel:* 020 7898 1741
email: paul.lewis@c-of-e.org.uk

Chief Investment Officer Mr Mark Chaloner
(Commissioners' Stock Exchange portfolio; overall policy direction and ethical policy monitoring)
Tel: 020 7898 1126
email: mark.chaloner@c-of-e.org.uk

Head of Policy Unit Mr Philip James
(Commissioners' overall policy development and communications)   *Tel:* 020 7898 1671
email: philip.james@c-of-e.org.uk

Head of Financial Planning Mr David White
Tel: 020 7898 1684
email: david.white@c-of-e.org.uk

Acting Bishoprics and Cathedrals Secretary Mr Paul Lewis
(Financial and administrative support for bishops and grants towards cathedral clergy and staff)   *Tel:* 020 7898 1741

LEGAL DEPARTMENT
Official Solicitor Miss Sue Jones
Tel: 020 7898 1704
email: sue.jones@c-of-e.org.uk

Deputy Official Solicitor Mr Timothy Crow
Tel: 020 7898 1717
email: tim.crow@c-of-e.org.uk
Web: www.cofe.anglican.org/legal

MEMBERS
The Archbishops of Canterbury and York

First Church Estates Commissioner Mr Andreas Whittam Smith

Second Church Estates Commissioner Sir Stuart Bell MP

Third Church Estates Commissioner Mr Timothy Walker

Four bishops elected by the House of Bishops of the General Synod Rt Revd and Rt Hon Richard Chartres (*Bishop of London*), Rt Revd Michael Hill (*Bishop of Bristol*), Rt Revd Ian Cundy (*Bishop of Peterborough*), Rt Revd Stephen Lowe (*Bishop of Hulme*)

Two deans or provosts elected by all the deans and provosts Very Revd Robert Grimley (*Dean of Bristol*), Very Revd Christopher Hardwick (*Dean of Truro*)

Three clergy elected by the House of Clergy of the General Synod
Ven Richard Atkinson (*Archdeacon of Leicester*), Ven Clive Mansell (*Archdeacon of Tonbridge*), Revd Stephen Trott

Four lay persons elected by the House of Laity of the General Synod
Canon Peter Bruinvels, Mr Gavin Oldham, Canon Elizabeth Paver, Mrs Emma Osborne

Three persons nominated by Her Majesty the Queen Mr Richard Powers, Canon John Spence, Mr John Wythe

Three persons nominated by the Archbishops of Canterbury and of York acting jointly Mr Nicholas Sykes, Mr Peter Parker, Mr Peter Harrison QC

Three persons nominated by the Archbishops acting jointly after consultation with others including the Lord Mayors of the cities of London and York and the Vice-Chancellors of Oxford and Cambridge Revd Rachel Harrison, Sir Robert Finch, Mr Brian Carroll

Six State Office Holders The First Lord of the Treasury; the Lord President of the Council; the Secretary of State for the Home Department; the Speaker of the House of Lords; the Secretary of State for Culture, Media and Sport; and the Speaker of the House of Commons.

BROAD FUNCTIONS

The Church Commissioners' main tasks are to manage their assets, and make money available in accordance with the duties laid upon them by Acts of Parliament and Measures of the General Synod and former Church Assembly, and to discharge other administrative duties entrusted to them.

These duties include financial support for mission and ministry in parishes, particularly in areas of need and opportunity, clergy pensions for service before 1998 and other legal commitments such as those in relation to bishops and cathedrals, and the administration of the legal framework for pastoral reorganization and settling the future of churches closed for worship..

CONSTITUTION

The Church Commissioners were formed on 1 April 1948, when Queen Anne's Bounty (1704) and the Ecclesiastical Commissioners (1836) were united.

The full body of Commissioners meets once a year to consider the Report and Accounts and the allocation of available money. The management of the Commissioners' affairs is shared between the Board of Governors, the Assets Committee (which is statutory), the Bishoprics and Cathedrals Committee, the Management Advisory Committee, the Pastoral Committee, and the Redundant Churches Committee. There is also a statutory Audit Committee.

The National Institutions Measure 1998 created the Archbishops' Council, with consequential amendment to the Church Commissioners' functions and working relationships. The Measure also transferred their former function and powers as Central Stipends Authority to the Council on 1 January 1999.

Functions of the Board of Governors and the Commissioners' Committees

BOARD OF GOVERNORS

The Board is responsible for overall policy matters and there are individual committees covering policy in the following specific areas. All Commissioners are Board Members except for the six Officers of State.

ASSETS COMMITTEE

Chairman Mr Andreas Whittam Smith
Deputy Chairman Vacancy
Rt Revd Michael Hill (*Bishop of Bristol*), Ven Clive Mansell (*Archdeacon of Tonbridge*), Mr Gavin Oldham, Mr Nicholas Sykes, Mr Peter Parker, Mr Brian Carroll, Mr John Wythe, Mr Richard Powers
Secretary Mr Andrew Brown

Exclusive responsibility for managing the Commissioners' assets, for investment policy and for advising the Board on the maximum amount of money available for distribution each year. The Committee is assisted by two sub-groups working on the Commissioners' stock exchange and property portfolios.

AUDIT COMMITTEE

Chairman Canon John Spence
Mrs Emma Osborne, Mr Peter Morriss*, Mr Robert Clarke*, Mr Chris Daykin*, Sir Robert Finch, Mr Hugh Shields*
Secretary Mr Kim Parry

Responsible for all matters relating to the audit of the Commissioners' accounts and related matters.

BISHOPRICS AND CATHEDRALS COMMITTEE

Chairman Mr Timothy Walker
Deputy Chairman Vacancy

Rt Revd David Rossdale* (*Bishop of Grimsby*), Very Revd Robert Grimley (*Dean of Bristol*), Very Revd Christopher Hardwick (*Dean of Truro*), Ven Richard Atkinson (*Archdeacon of Leicester*), Mr Peter Parker, Revd Canon Jeremy Haselock*, Ms Sallie Bassham*, Rt Revd Ian Cundy (*Bishop of Peterborough*),†, Mrs Hilary Hill†
Acting Secretary Mr Paul Lewis

Responsible for the costs of episcopal administration, the provision and management of suitable housing for diocesan bishops, assisting by grants and loans with the housing of suffragan and assistant bishops, and some assistance in respect of cathedral clergy and lay staff.

MANAGEMENT ADVISORY COMMITTEE

Chairman Mr Andreas Whittam Smith
Deputy Chairman Mr Timothy Walker
Rt Revd and Rt Hon Richard Chartres (*Bishop of London*), Very Revd Christopher Hardwick (*Dean of Truro*), Ven Richard Atkinson (*Archdeacon of Leicester*), Canon Peter Bruinvels, Canon Elizabeth Paver, Sir Robert Finch
Secretary Mr Andrew Brown

Advises the Board of Governors, in particular on appointments and budgetary issues.

PASTORAL COMMITTEE

Chairman Mr Timothy Walker
Deputy Chairman Rt Revd William Ind*
Rt Revd Dr Peter Forster* (*Bishop of Chester*), Ven Rachel Treweek* (*Archdeacon of Northolt*), Revd Stephen Trott, Canon Peter Bruinvels, Ven David Gerrard, Very Revd Christopher Hardwick*, Mrs Janet Atkinson*, Revd Rachel Harrison, Mrs Christine McMullen*, Canon Elizabeth Paver
Secretary Mr Paul Lewis

Responsible for matters concerning pastoral reorganization, parsonages and glebe property.

CHURCH BUILDINGS (USES AND DISPOSAL) COMMITTEE
Chairman Mr Timothy Walker
Deputy Chairman Ven Clive Mansell (*Archdeacon of Tonbridge*)
Rt Revd Stephen Lowe (*Bishop of Hulme*), Mrs Emma Osborne, Revd Stephen Trott, Ven John Duncan*, Mr Charles Wilson*, Mr Christopher Perrett*, Revd John Swanton*, Mr Brian Carroll
Secretary Mr Paul Lewis

Responsible for the Commissioners' work relating to closed church buildings.

The Commissioners draw no income from the State.

The asterisks in the above lists indicate non-Commissioner committee members.

The dagger symbols (†) in one of the above lists indicate consultants.

EXPENDITURE IN 2007
The Commissioners' expenditure falls under two main headings:
1 Provision of non-pensions support – £72.3 million in 2007 – to the Church including parish mission and ministry support of £32.9 million which was mainly targeted towards areas of greatest financial need.
2 Payment of clergy pensions and pensions to their widows. The Church of England Pensions Board authorizes pensions, but much of the money is provided and paid by the Church Commissioners. The Commissioners are responsible for pensions earned on service before 1 January 1998 and dioceses and parishes for pensions earned after that date.

The Commissioners' expenditure in 2007 is shown in the table below*.

PASTORAL MEASURE RESPONSIBILITIES
The Commissioners are responsible for preparing schemes for pastoral reorganization based on proposals put forward by Bishops under the Pastoral Measure 2983. This includes the consideration of any representations made in response to consultation on draft schemes. Those making representations have the opportunity to address the relevant Commissioners' Committee.
The Commissioners also deal with objections to certain personage and glebe transactions.

CLOSED CHURCH BUILDINGS
The Pastoral Measure 1983 sets out the process for closing a church building which is no longer needed for public worship. The Commissioners will prepare a draft scheme to give effect to the proposals, consult locally and hear any representations received in respect of them.
The Commissioners also determine the future use of closed church buildings. Under the Pastoral Measure, dioceses are charged with the

---

MANAGEMENT OF ASSETS
The total return on the Commissioners' assets in 2007 was 9.4% and their return over the ten years to 2007 averaged 9.5% per annum (indistry benchmark 7.1% per annum).

The Commissioners' income in 2007 was: £144.6 million.

	£ million
Investments	97.0
Investment Properties	50.1
Mortgages and loans	5.9
Other interest receivable	18.5
Gross income	171.5
External management costs	(11.1)
Commissioners' management costs	(3.7)
Other property expenses	(8.7)
Interest payable	(0.6)
Income attributed to staff pension provision	(2.8)
Total income	144.6

	£ million
Parish Ministry Support	(32.9)
Bishops' stipends	(5.0)
Cathedral clergy stipends	(4.2)
Clergy pensions	(105.5)
Bishops' housing and office premises	(7.9)
Church buildings	(0.9)
Bishops' office and working costs	(12.0)
Grants to cathedrals	(2.6)
Administration of national Church functions	(2.9)
Other Church bodies' administration costs	(0.2)
Commissioners' own administration	(2.3)
Refurbishment and repairs to Commissioners' offices	(0.5)
Restructuring costs	(0.9)
Total expenditure*	(177.8)

* Includes expenditure of £33.2 million from capital for pension purposes under the provisions of the Pensions Measure 1997.

seeking of a suitable use for the buildings and reporting to the Commissioners who will then publish a draft scheme to facilitate that use and its sale for that purpose.

Buildings of high heritage value for which no suitable alternative use can be found may be vested in the Churches Conservation Trust, an independent body jointly funded by the Church and State to care for such closed church buildings.

FURTHER INFORMATION

Further information is available in the Commissioners' Annual Report and Accounts which, together with other information leaflets, is available free of charge from the Policy Unit (*see* page 191 for address) and *via* the Church of England web site at http://www.cofe.anglican.org/about/churchcommissioners/annualreport/fullreport2007.pdf. Requests for speakers to give talks about the Commissioners' work are welcome.

THE CHURCH OF ENGLAND PENSIONS BOARD

RESPONSIBILITIES
The Pensions Board was established by the Church Assembly in 1926 as the Church of England's pensions authority and to administer the pension scheme for the clergy. Subsequently it has been given wider powers, in respect of discretionary benefits and the provision of accommodation both for those retired from stipendiary ministry and for the spouses of those who have served in that ministry, and to administer pension schemes for lay employees of Church organizations.

The Board, which reports to the General Synod, is trustee of a number of pension funds and charitable funds. Whilst the Church has drawn together under the Board its central responsibilities for retirement welfare, the Board works in close cooperation both with the Archbishops' Council and with the Church Commissioners. There is also a partnership between the Board and dioceses in financial commitments towards discretionary grants and housing, and at the level of personal pastoral service through Widows Officers, archdeacons and Retirement Officers.

PENSIONS
The Board is administrator of the pension arrangements for clergy, deaconesses and licensed lay workers, and for their widows and widowers, keeping records of pensionable service and corresponding about pensions matters both with pensioners and with those not yet retired. It is corporate trustee of the Church of England Funded Pensions Scheme, which has assets of £552 million and to which contributions are currently being paid at the rate of some £59 million a year to provide for pensions and associated benefits arising from service after the end of 1997. The Church Commissioners continue to meet the cost of benefits arising from service prior to 1 January 1998.

The Clergy (Widows and Dependants) Pensions Fund was closed to new entrants after widows' pensions were introduced under the main scheme. It has assets of £26 million and provides an additional benefit to widows and other dependants of those who made contributions to it. The benefits payable are reviewed following each triennial actuarial valuation. The next valuation will be carried out as at 31 December 2006.

The Board is also corporate trustee of the

Church Workers Pension Fund, through which over 200 Church organizations make pension provision for their lay employees, and the Church Administrators Pension Fund (for staff of the National Church bodies). It is responsible for all the activities of these funds including the administration and keeping of records, payment of benefits, collection of contributions and investment of monies currently held in the funds; these now total approximately £289 million.

RETIREMENT HOUSING SCHEMES

The current retirement housing arrangements, which were designed by the Board and the Commissioners and approved by the General Synod, have been in operation since January 1983. The Commissioners lend to the Board a substantial proportion of the funds necessary to finance the scheme, subject to satisfactory terms as to interest and repayment of capital. There are two sections to the scheme; (a) a rental section of around 1,300 properties available for occupation under licence and (b) a shared ownership scheme for retiring clergy who wish to acquire an equity interest in their retirement accommodation. A value linked mortgage scheme, covering some 1,400 loans, remains in place but is closed to new loans having been replaced by the Shared Ownership scheme in April 2008. The Board has funded approximately 480 of the rental properties and some mortgage loans from its own charitable funds. Some of the properties have been received as gifts, and it continues to add to its stock further properties acquired in this way. Others have been purchased or built using monetary gifts in trust for that purpose.

SUPPORTED HOUSING AND NURSING CARE

The Board owns and manages supported housing schemes in seven locations, and one nursing home. All of these provisions were purpose-designed. The Board's charitable resources provide the capital for purchasing or building the homes and for their subsequent maintenance and operation.

Each is run by a professional resident manager who reports to the Board's Housing Manager. Fee levels are set having regard to the costs of running the scheme and increases in clergy pensions. Each resident and patient is, however, charged a fee which, with available State support, is affordable having regard to their financial resources. As the total fee income is therefore insufficient to cover the operating costs, the shortfall is met from the Board's charitable funds.

In addition, support may be given with fees payable by the Board's pensioners in privately run homes, if an individual cannot meet the full cost even with the maximum possible assistance available from the State.

THE BOARD AS A CHARITY

The care of the more elderly of its pensioners is an activity of the Board which attracts considerable regular support, voluntarily from within the Church at parochial and diocesan level, and from churchgoers and other people of goodwill everywhere. Money and other property given or bequeathed to the Board has averaged around £1 million per annum in recent years. The Pensions Board is registered as a charity. The charitable funds currently have a total net value of some £98 million (including the Board's own stake in the retirement housing scheme).

PUBLICATIONS

Your Pension Questions Answered
Information about the Pension Scheme for clergy, deaconesses and licensed lay workers, including an outline of the arrangements for paying voluntary contributions to increase retirement benefits.

Retirement Housing
Explains the assistance that the Board is able to make (with financial support from the Church Commissioners) to clergy, their spouses and widow(er)s, and also to deaconesses and licensed lay workers for their retirement housing.

Providing for Housing in Retirement
A handbook of sources of finance for the clergy to acquire property on a buy-to-let basis.

Christian Care in Retirement
Information about the Board's supported housing schemes and its nursing home.

The Church of England Pensions Board – Our Work is Caring . . .
Describes the discretionary assistance made available to its beneficiaries through the Board's charitable funds and explains how contributions may be made to support that work.

Pensions Administration for Church of England Employers
A guide to the services and schemes offered by the Board.

The Church Workers Pension Fund
An explanation of the retirement benefits available to church workers whose employers participate in the Fund.

Report and Accounts for the year 2006
Contains information about all the Board's activities during the year. Also available on our web site, www.cofe.anglican.org/about/cepb

OTHER BOARDS, COUNCILS, COMMISSIONS, ETC. OF THE CHURCH OF ENGLAND

The Advisory Board for Redundant Churches

Function transferred to the Statutory Advisory Committee of the Church Buildings Council.

The Churches Conservation Trust
(formerly the Redundant Churches Fund)

Chief Executive Mr Crispin Truman, 1 West Smithfield, London EC1A 9EE   *Tel:* 020 7213 0660
Fax: 020 7213 0678
email: central@tcct.org.uk
Web: www.visitchurches.org.uk

Director of Conservation Miss Sarah Robinson

Director of Regions Mr Colin Shearer

Director of Finance and Resources Mr Vipan Narang

Head of Development and Communications Ms Constance Barrett

BOARD OF TRUSTEES
Mr Lloyd Grossman OBE FSA (*Chairman*), Mrs Jenny Baker OBE, Ms Deborah Dance, Mr Alec Forshaw, Mr Matthew Girt, Very Revd Peter Judd, Mr Brian McHenry, Mr Nick Thompson, Ms Jane Weeks, Mr Duncan Wilson.

The Trust was set up in 1969 to preserve churches of historic, architectural or archaeological importance which had been declared redundant and so were no longer needed for pastoral use. With over 340 churches in its care, the Trust promotes public enjoyment of these churches and encourages their use as an educational and community resource. Visitors are welcome and entry to all is free. Many churches are open daily, whilst others have keyholders nearby. Trust churches host occasional services as well as concerts, exhibitions and lectures. The Trust, which is a registered charity, receives its statutory funding from the Church Commissioners (30 per cent) and the Department for Culture, Media and Sport (70 per cent).

CCLA Investment Management Limited

Registered Office 80 Cheapside, London EC2V 6DZ
Company Registration No 2183088
Authorized and regulated by the Financial Services Authority   *Tel:* 020 7489 6000
Fax: 020 7489 6128
Web: www.ccla.co.uk

Executive Directors
Chief Executive Mr Michael Quicke
email: michael.quicke@ccla.co.uk

Chief Investment Officer Mr James Bevan
email: james.bevan@ccla.co.uk
Director of Market Development Mr Andrew Robinson   *email:* andrew.robinson@ccla.co.uk
Investment Director Mr Colin Peters
email: colin.peters@ccla.co.uk

Chief Operating Officer Mr Sean Curran
email: sean.curran@ccla.co.uk

Non Executive Directors
Mr James Dawnay (*Chairman*), Mr Miles Roberts, Mr John Galbraith, Mr Richard Fitzalan Howard
Company Secretary Mrs Jacqueline Fox, Mr Rodney Dennis

CCLA Investment Management Limited (CCLA) is a specialist investment management company serving charities, churches and local authorities. It is the largest manager of charitable funds in the UK, both by the value of funds managed and the number of individual investing charities. It aims to provide good quality investment management services at reasonable cost. It is the manager, registrar and administrator of the CBF Church of England Funds, the trustee of which is CBF Funds Trustee Limited and to which CCLA is accountable. Six Funds are offered to Church of England investors: the Investment Fund, a mixed fund invested mainly in equities, the UK Equity Fund, the Global Equity Income Fund, the Fixed Interest Securities Fund, the Deposit Fund and the Property Fund. CCLA also manages several segregated charity portfolios. CCLA is owned 60 per cent by the CBF Church of England Investment Fund, 25 per cent by the COIF Charities Investment Fund (part of which is non voting)

and 15 per cent by the Local Authorities Mutual Investment Trust. CCLA is authorized and regulated by the Financial Services Authority (FSA) under the Financial Services and Markets Act 2000 (FSMA). Under the FSMA, the CBF, in its role as Trustee, is not considered to be operating the Funds 'by way of business'. In consequence, it is not required to be regulated by the FSA. Deposits taken by the CBF Church of England Deposit Fund are exempted from the FSMA by virtue of the Financial Services and Markets Act (Exemption) Order 2001.

The CBF Church of England Funds

Established under the Church Funds Investment Measure 1958, these open ended funds aim to meet most of the investment needs of a church trust and are used by diocesan boards of finance and trusts, cathedrals, diocesan boards of education, theological colleges, church schools and educational endowments, church societies, the Church Commissioners and many PCCs.

Investment Fund
The main CBF Church of England Fund for capital that can be invested for the long term. A widely spread portfolio mainly of UK and overseas equities but also including some bond and property investments. Aims to provide steady income and capital growth. Weekly share dealings.

UK Equity Fund
This Fund provides church trustees with a means of obtaining investment solely in a specialist UK equity portfolio. Weekly share dealings.

Fixed Interest Securities Fund
Invested only in UK fixed interest stocks. Intended to supplement where necessary the initial lower income yield on the Investment Fund. Recommended only for a small proportion of long term capital as it offers little protection from inflation over the longer term. Weekly share dealings.

Deposit Fund
This money Fund is for cash balances which need to be available at short notice and with minimal risk of capital loss. Accounts in the Fund obtain a rate of interest close to money market rates even on small sums. Daily deposit and withdrawal facilities. The Fund is rated AAA/VI by Fitch Ratings.

Property Fund
Invests directly in UK commercial property. Fund is intended primarily for long term investment by large church trusts. Month end share dealings but periods of notice may be imposed.

Global Equity Income Fund
This fund targets a high and growing income from a portfolio of international shares. Weekly share dealings.

Risk Warnings: The value of the Investment, UK Equity, Fixed Interest Securities and Property Funds and their income can fall as well as rise and an investor may not get back the amount invested. Past performance is no guarantee of future returns. The Funds are intended for long term investment and are not suitable for money liable to be spent in the near future. Guarantees regarding repayment of deposits in the Deposit Fund cannot be given.

Brochures and Reports and Accounts are available from CCLA Investment Management Limited at the address above and on its web site, www.ccla.co.uk

31 May 2008	Investment Fund	Fixed Interest Securities Fund	Deposit Fund	Property Fund	UK Equity Fund	Global Equity Income Fund
Value of Fund	£927 million	£71 million	£1028 million	£151 million	£137 million	£49 million
Net Asset Value per share	1176.35p	149.37p	–	145.5p	129.00p	142.35p
Income Yield %	3.54	5.88	5.61	5.03	3.60	4.19
Gross Redemption Yield %	–	5.08	–	–	–	–

The Church and Community Fund

Chairman: Ven George Howe
Secretary: Mr Kevin Norris

Formerly known as the Central Church Fund, the CCF changed its name to the Church and Community Fund (CCF) in June 2006. The CCF supports the Church of England's mission by awarding grants to community projects run by parish churches, deaneries, dioceses and other regional or national bodies.

The Archbishops' Council (registered charity number 1074857) is the trustee of the CCF but has delegated management to a CCF Committee whose members are the administrative trustees of the Fund.

CCF-funded projects should seek to take the church out into the community, bring the community into the church and strengthen the relationship between the two. The CCF trustees welcome applications that show imagination in responding to needs. They are likely to be particularly sympathetic to applications from those areas least able to raise funds themselves.

The CCF awarded a record-breaking total of £586,105 to 123 church and community projects in 2007 (2006: £548,502 to 128 projects). It also gave £300,000 as a direct grant to the Archbishops' Council in support of the national work of the Church and £20,000 to the Archbishops' Discretionary Funds.

The CCF relies on legacies and donations to increase the number of grants awarded so that more churches can reach out to their communities and respond to real local needs. Please contact the Secretary to find out more about how to make a donation, leave a legacy or apply for a grant.

The Church and Community Fund
Church House
Great Smith St
London SW1P 3AZ   *Tel:* 020 7898 1541/1767
                                         Fax: 020 7898 1558
                                  email: ccf@c-of-e.org.uk
Web: www.churchandcommunityfund.org.uk

The Corporation of the Church House

President The Archbishop of Canterbury

Chairman of Council David Webster

Treasurer Mark Cornwall-Jones

Secretary Colin Menzies   *Tel:* 020 7898 1311
             email: colin.menzies@c-of-e.org.uk

Office Church House, Great Smith St, London
SW1P 3AZ   *Tel:* 020 7898 1311
                                         Fax: 020 7898 1321

The original Church House was built in the early 1890s as the Church's memorial of Queen Victoria's Jubilee, to be the administrative headquarters of the Church of England, and was replaced by the present building to a design by Sir Herbert Baker. The foundation stone was

laid in 1937 by Queen Mary and on 10 June 1940 King George VI, accompanied by the Queen, formally opened the new House and attended the first Session of the Church Assembly in the great circular hall. The building was almost immediately requisitioned by the Government and for the rest of the war became the alternative meeting place of both Houses of Parliament; the Lords sat in the Convocation Hall and the Commons in the Hoare Memorial Hall. Oak panels in these halls commemorate this use.

By October 1946 some administrative offices of the Church Assembly returned to Church House and the Church Assembly was able to return for its Autumn Session in 1950. The building is now the headquarters of the Archbishops' Council, the Church Commissioners and the

Other Boards, Councils, Commissions, etc.   **199**

Church of England Pensions Board, as well as being the venue for the General Synod in the spring and (if it meets) in the autumn. A large-scale refurbishment carried out in 2006 has provided sufficient open-plan office space to accommodate nearly all staff of the Central Church Institutions, who moved into Church House during the early part of 2007.

Church House has also become an important national centre for conferences and meetings, the income from which contributes significantly to the maintenance costs of the building.

The business of the Corporation is vested in its Council of 9 (of whom 3 are nominated by the Appointments Committee, 2 are elected by the membership of the Corporation and 4 are co-opted by the Council).

The National Society (Church of England) for Promoting Religious Education
Leading Education with Christian Purpose

Patron Her Majesty The Queen

President The Archbishop of Canterbury

Vice Presidents The Archbishop of York and the Archbishop of Wales

Chairman of the Council Rt Revd Dr Kenneth Stevenson (*Bishop of Portsmouth*)

General Secretary Revd Janina Ainsworth

Treasurer Maurice Sharples

Deputy Secretary Vacancy

Deputy Secretary Revd David Whittington
Tel: 020 7898 1789
email: david.whittington@c-of-e.org.uk

Administration Manager Segi Yaskey
Tel: 020 7898 1497
email: segi.yaskey@c-of-e.org.uk

Administrative Assistant Lorraine Freeman
Tel: 020 7898 1499
email: lorraine.freeman@c-of-e.org.uk

Information Manager Peter Churchill
Tel: 020 7898 1518
email: peter.churchill@c-of-e.org.uk

Office Church House, Great Smith St, London SW1P 3AZ
Tel: 020 7898 1518
Fax: 020 7898 1493
email: info@natsoc.c-of-e.org.uk
Web: www.natsoc.org.uk

The Society's archives are held at the Church of England Records Centre – for further details *see* page 188.

The National Society exists 'for the promotion, encouragement and support of religious education in accordance with the principles of the Church of England'. It works in close association with the Education Division (*see* page 180) (and the Division for Education of the Church in Wales). Its status as a voluntary body enables it to take initiatives in developing new work. The Society has a particular concern for the support of Christian education and Christians in education.

Founded in 1811, the Society was chiefly responsible for setting up, in cooperation with local clergy and others, the nationwide network of Church schools in England and Wales; it was also, through the Church colleges, a pioneer in teacher education. A concern for Church schools is still at the heart of the Society's work. It provides a legal and advisory service for dioceses and schools. The Society's web site (see above) provides information and support for collective worship and Church school management, including sample contracts and application forms as well as a range of material for the guidance and encouragement of teachers and governors. The Society trains and accredits inspectors for Church schools under Section 48 of the Education Act 2005 (Statutory Inspection of Anglican Schools). The Society represents the Church of England in planning and promoting Education Sunday, an ecumenical observation that takes place every year on the ninth Sunday before Easter.

While supporting the Church's partnership with the State in statutory education, the National Society has a broader range of influence: those responsible for RE and worship in any school, lecturers and students in colleges, and clergy and lay people in diocesan and parish education can all benefit from the resources of the Society's web site, publications, courses, conferences and archives.

After nearly two centuries of close association with Church schools and colleges, the National Society has built up an impressive collection of documents in its archives. These include about 15,000 files of correspondence with schools throughout England and Wales founded in association with the National Society and many published works, including the Society's own. Access is available to *bona fide* researchers by appointment at the Church of England Record Centre.

Applications for membership and donations to The National Society from individuals, schools and other bodies wishing to support the Society's work and share its resources are welcomed.

See also the entry on Church of England schools on page 229.

THE ECCLESIASTICAL COURTS

The Ecclesiastical Courts consist of (1) the Diocesan or Consistory Courts, (2) the Provincial Courts, and for both Provinces (3) the Court of Ecclesiastical Causes Reserved and, when required, (4) a Commission of Review. In certain faculty cases an appeal lies from the Provincial Courts to the Judicial Committee of the Privy Council. The jurisdiction of the Archdeacons' Courts is now confined to the visitations of archdeacons. The Ecclesiastical Courts are in the main now regulated by the Ecclesiastical Jurisdiction Measure 1963. The Court of Faculties is the Court of the Archbishop of Canterbury through which the legatine powers transferred to the Archbishop of Canterbury by the Ecclesiastical Licences Act 1533 are exercised.

The personnel of the Diocesan Courts is given in the diocesan lists. The personnel of the Court of Faculties and of the Provincial and some of the other Courts is as follows:

THE COURT OF ARCHES
Dean of the Arches Rt Worshipful Sheila Cameron QC

Registrar Canon John Rees
16 Beaumont St, Oxford OX1 2LZ
Tel: 01865 297200
Fax: 01865 726274
email: jrees@winckworths.co.uk

THE COURT OF THE VICAR-GENERAL OF THE PROVINCE OF CANTERBURY
Vicar-General Rt Worshipful Timothy Briden

Joint Registrars
Canon John Rees (*as above*)
Mr Stephen Slack, The Legal Office, Church House, Great Smith St, London SW1P 3AZ
Tel: 020 7898 1366
Fax: 020 7898 1718/1721
email: stephen.slack@c-of-e.org.uk

THE CHANCERY COURT OF YORK
Auditor Rt Worshipful Sheila Cameron QC

Registrar Mr Lionel Lennox
The Provincial Registry, Stamford House, Piccadilly, York YO1 9PP
Tel: 01904 623487
Fax: 01904 561470
email: lpml@denisontill.com

THE COURT OF THE VICAR-GENERAL OF THE PROVINCE OF YORK
Vicar-General Vacancy

Registrar Mr Lionel Lennox (*as above*)

THE COURT OF ECCLESIASTICAL CAUSES RESERVED
Judges

Rt Revd David Hope
Rt Revd Richard Harries
Rt Revd Thomas Wright (*Bishop of Durham*)
Dame Elizabeth Butler-Sloss
Sir John Mummery
Registrar for the Province of Canterbury Canon John Rees (*as above*)
Registrar for the Province of York Mr Lionel Lennox (*as above*)

THE COURT OF FACULTIES
Master of the Faculties Rt Worshipful Sheila Cameron QC

Registrar Mr Peter Beesley
1 The Sanctuary, London SW1P 3JT
Tel: 020 7222 5381
Fax: 020 7222 7502
email: faculty.office@1Thesanctuary.com

Disciplinary Tribunals constituted under the Clergy Discipline Measure 2003

President of Tribunals Rt Hon Lord Justice Mummery
Deputy President of Tribunals His Honour Judge John Bullimore
c/o The Legal Office, Church House, Great Smith St, London SW1P 3AZ

'Legally qualified' members of the provincial panels of Canterbury and York (the same ten are appointed to each panel) from which the chair of a disciplinary tribunal will be appointed by the President of Tribunals if the President or Deputy President is not to chair the tribunal.

His Honour Judge Dr Rupert Bursell QC
Mr David Cheetham
Mr Peter Collier QC
Mr Charles George QC
His Honour Judge Simon Grenfell
Canon Raymond Hemingray
Canon Christopher Hodson
Mr Geoffrey Tattersall QC
His Honour Judge David Turner QC
His Honour Judge Samuel Wiggs

Registrar of Tribunals for the Province of Canterbury Canon John Rees (*as above*)

Registrar of Tribunals for the Province of York Mr Lionel Lennox (*as above*)
Designated Officer Mr Adrian Iles, The Legal Office, Church House, Great Smith St, London SW1P 3AZ
Appeal Panels

APPEAL PANEL CONSTITUTED UNDER SCHEDULE 4 THE PASTORAL MEASURE 1983

(Tribunals to settle compensation claims of clergy dispossessed under a Pastoral Scheme)

Chair The Dean of the Arches

Deputy Chairs
The Vicar-General of Canterbury
The Vicar-General of York

In addition to the Chair, a tribunal comprises four members of the Lower House of the relevant Province and two members of the House of Laity drawn from the following panels:

Convocation of Canterbury, Lower House
Revd Moira Astin
Preb Kay Garlick
Canon Jeremy Haselock
Revd Pete Hobson
Preb Sam Philpott
Revd Stephen Trott
Six vacancies

Convocation of York, Lower House
Revd Graeme Buttery
Canon Dr Judy Hunt
Canon Peter Mann
Canon Glyn Webster
Eight vacancies

House of Laity of the General Synod
Dr Susan Atkin
Mr Barry Barnes
Mr Martin Dales
Mrs Jennifer Dunlop
Mr Aiden Hargreaves-Smith
Ms Jacqueline Humphreys
Mrs Mary Johnston
Mrs Mary Judkins
Mr Geoffrey Tattersall QC
Mr John Ward
Two vacancies

Secretary Mr Howard Cattermole, The Legal Office, Church House, Great Smith St, London SW1P 3AZ   *Tel:* 020 7898 1371
          email: howard.cattermole@c-of-e.org.uk

APPEAL PANEL CONSTITUTED UNDER STANDING ORDER 120(d)(i)

(Tribunals to hear appeals in internal General Synod elections)

House of Bishops
Rt Revd Peter Forster (*Bishop of Chester*)
Rt Revd Graham James (*Bishop of Norwich*)

Rt Revd Michael Langrish (*Bishop of Exeter*)
Rt Revd Nigel McCulloch (*Bishop of Manchester*)
Two Vacancies

House of Clergy
Revd Johnathan Alderton-Ford
Revd Moira Astin
Ven Annette Cooper (*Archdeacon of Colchester*)
Preb Kay Garlick
Ven Alan Hawker (*Archdeacon of Malmesbury*)
Preb David Houlding
Revd Rose Hudson-Wilkin
Ven Trevor Jones (*Archdeacon of Hertford*)
Ven Alistair Magowan (*Archdeacon of Dorset*)
Ven Clive Mansell (*Archdeacon of Tonbridge*)
Two vacancies

House of Laity
Mr Anthony Archer
Mrs Janet Atkinson
Mr Martin Dales
Mrs Sarah Finch
Dr Philip Giddings
Mr John Hanks
Ms Jacqueline Humphreys
Mrs Sue Johns
Mrs Katherine McPherson
Mr Geoffrey Tattersall QC
Mr John Ward
Mrs Shirley-Ann Williams
Secretary Mr Howard Cattermole, The Legal Office, Church House, Great Smith St, London SW1P 3AZ   *Tel:* 020 7898 1371
          email: howard.cattermole@c-of-e.org.uk

APPEAL PANEL APPOINTED PURSUANT TO RULE 44(8) OF THE CHURCH REPRESENTATION RULES AS AMENDED BY THE NATIONAL INSTITUTIONS MEASURE 1998 (SCHEDULE 5, PARAGRAPH 2(c))

(Tribunals to hear appeals in elections to the House of Laity of the General Synod)

The Dean of the Arches
The Vicar-General of Canterbury
The Vicar-General of York
Mr Anthony Archer
Mr Barry Barnes
Miss Prudence Dailey
Mr Martin Dales
Mrs Sarah Finch
Mrs Sue Johns
Mr David Mills
Mrs Christina Rees
Mrs Caroline Spencer
Mr Geoffrey Tattersall QC
Dr Anna Thomas-Betts
Mrs Shirley-Ann Williams
Secretary Mr Howard Cattermole, The Legal Office, Church House, Great Smith St, London SW1P 3AZ   *Tel:* 020 7898 1371
          email: howard.cattermole@c-of-e.org.uk

APPEAL PANEL APPOINTED PURSUANT TO RULE 25(5) OF THE CLERGY REPRESENTATION RULES 1975 TO 2004
(Tribunals to hear appeals in elections to the Convocations)

The Dean of the Arches
The Vicar-General of Canterbury
The Vicar-General of York
Ven Christine Allsopp (*Archdeacon of Northampton*)
Preb Philippa Boardman
Revd Mark Bratton

Revd Simon Butler
Canon David Felix
Preb Kay Garlick
Preb David Houlding
Ven Clive Mansell (*Archdeacon of Tonbridge*)
Revd David Parrott
Revd Paul Perkin
Canon Cathy Rowling
One vacancy
Secretary Mr Howard Cattermole, The Legal Office, Church House, Great Smith St, London SW1P 3AZ   *Tel:* 020 7898 1371
email: howard.cattermole@c-of-e.org.uk

GENERAL SYNOD LEGISLATION, CONSTITUTION AND BUSINESS

Legislation passed 2003–2008 together with commencement dates

Dates in brackets are the dates of legislation coming into force. Items of legislation no longer in force are omitted.

MEASURES

Synodical Government (Amendment) Measure 2003 (1 January 2004)

Church of England (Pensions) Measure 2003 (1 May 2003)

Clergy Discipline Measure 2003 (in force 1 October 2003: sections 3, 39, 45 and 48; in force 1 June 2005: sections 44(3) and (4); in force 8 September 2005: sections 4, 5 and 21; remainder in force 1 January 2006)

Stipends (Cessation of Special Payments) Measure 2005 (1 July and 31 December 2005)

Care of Cathedrals (Amendment) Measure 2005 (in force 6 June 2005: section 19 so far as it relates to paragraph 6 of Schedule 3, section 20 and paragraph 6 of Schedule 3; in force 7 February 2006: sections 8(4)(a), 12(1), 17 (so far as it relates to paragraphs 1–8 and 12 of Schedule 1), 18 and 19 (so far as it relates to the provisions of Schedule 3 specified below) and paragraphs 1–8 and 12 of Schedule 1, Schedule 2, sub-paragraphs (b), (e), (g) and (i) of paragraph 4 of Schedule 3 and paragraph 7 of Schedule 3; remainder to come into force 1 January 2008

Church of England (Miscellaneous Provisions) Measure 2005 (1 June and 1 September 2005)

Church of England (Miscellaneous Provisions) Measure 2006 (all in force 1 October 2006 except section 1 and Schedule 1; section 1 and schedule 1 in force 1 December 2007)

Pastoral (Amendment) Measure 2006 (1 January 2007)

Dioceses, Pastoral and Mission Measure 2007 (in force 1 January 2008: sections 1, 51, 62(1)–(3), 63(1) (so far as it relates to paragraph 7(b) of Schedule 5), 63(5) and 66 and paragraph 7(b) of Schedule 5; in force 1 February 2008: sections 52, 61, 62(5), 64 and 65 (so far as it relates to the repeals in Schedule 7 coming into force on the same date), Schedules 3 and 6 and the repeals in Schedule 7 of section 1 and Schedules 1 and 5 of the Pastoral Measure 1983, section 11(e) of the Church of England (Miscellaneous Provisions) Measure 1995 and sections 2(4) and (5) of the Synodical Government (Amendment) Measure 2003; in force 31 March 2008: sections 47–50 and 63(4); in force 1 May 2008: sections 13–16, 22, 63(7) and 65 (so far as it relates to the repeals in Schedule 7 coming into force on the same date) and the repeals in Schedule 7 of sections 10–15 of the Dioceses Measure 1978, sections 8 and 10 of the Church of England (Miscellaneous Provisions) Measure 1983, section 11(2) of the Bishops (Retirement) Measure 1986, section 2 of the Clergy (Ordination) Measure 1990 and section 12 of the Church of England (Miscellaenous Provisions) Measure 1995; in force 11 June 2008: sections 23–46, 53–60, 62(4) and (6), 63(1) (so far as it is not already in force), (2) and (3) and 65 (so far as it relates to the repeals in Schedule 7 coming into force on the same date) and Schedules 4 and 5 (so far as it is not already in force) and the repeals in Schedule 7 of section 15 of the Faculty Jurisdiction Measure 1964, sections 2, 41, 45 and 87(1) of and paragraphs 1–4 of Schedule 5 to the Pastoral Measure 1983, section 20(1) of the Care of Cathedrals Measure 1990, section 31(1) of the Care of Churches and Ecclesiastical Jurisdiction Measure 1991, section 1 of the Pastoral (Amendment) Measure 1994, section 6(1) of the Care of Places of Worship Measure 1999, section 2(3) of the Synodical Government (Amendment) Measure 2003 and paragraphs 10 and 13 to Schedule 4 to the Church of England (Miscellaneous Provisions) Measure 2005; in force 1 September 2008: section 2, 3(5) and (6), 4, 5, 6((1)–(2) and (4)–(8), 7–11, 18–21, 63(6) and 65 (so far as it relates to the repeals in Schedule 7 coming into force on the same date) and the repeals in Schedule 7 of the words after "being" to "any other diocese" in rule 34(1)(c) in Schedule 3 to the Synodical Government Measure 1969, sections 1–9, 16–17 and 18(1)(a) and (2)–(4), the words "and the report of the Commission thereon" in sections 18(5) and (7) and sections 19–25 of and the Schedule to the Dioceses Measure 1978, section 6 of the Church of England (Legal Aid and Miscellaneous Provisions) Measure 1988, paragraph 18 of Schedule 3 to the Church of England (Miscellaneous Provisions) Measure 1992, paragraph 7 of Schedule 2 to the Cathedrals Measure 1999 and section 18 of the Church of England (Miscellaneous Provisions) Measure 2000; the remainder to come into force on a date or dates yet to be determined)

Church of England Marriage Measure 2008 (1 October 2008)

STATUTORY INSTRUMENTS
Church Representation Rules (Amendment) Resolution 2004 SI 2004 No. 1889 (1 August 2004, 1 January 2005 and 15 February 2005)
Clergy Discipline Rules 2005 SI 2005 No 2022 (1 January 2006)
Clergy Discipline Appeal Rules 2005 SI 2005 No 3201 (1 January 2006)
Church of England (Legal Aid) (Amendment) Rules 2006 SI 2006 No 1939 (1 August 2006)
Care of Cathedrals Rules 2006 SI 2006 No 1941 (on a date to be determined)
Parsonages Measure (Amendment) Rules 2007 SI 2007 No 862 (1 May 2007)
National Institutions of the Church of England (Transfer of Functions) Order 2007 SI 2007 No 1556 (1 January 2008)
Legal Officers (Annual Fees) Order 2008 SI 2008 No 1969 (1 January 2009)
Ecclesiastical Judges, Legal Officers and Others (Fees) Order 2008 SI 2008 No 1970 (1 January 2008)
Payments to the Churches Conservation Trust Order 2008 SI 2008 No 1968 (1 April 2009)
Parochial Fees Order 2008 (1 January 2009)

Copies of the above legislation as originally enacted may be obtained from TSO (details below) or from the Office of Public Sector Information web site: www.opsi.gov.uk/uk-church-measures. The consolidated text of the Church Representation Rules (as at 1 January 2006) is published by Church House Publishing (£7.99).

Further Details
Lists of Church of England Measures which have received the Royal Assent from 1920 onwards and of Statutory Instruments to date which are still in force are available the Legal Office web site at: www.cofe.anglican.org/about/churchlawlegis. Recently passed Measures and Rules made pursuant to Measures are sold by TSO and may be obtained from (TSO) Orders, PO Box 29, Norwich NR3 1GN (*telephone enquiries:* 0870 600 5522, *email:* customer.services@tso.co.uk *online ordering:* www.tsoshop.co.uk). TSO or the Legal Office will advise on obtaining copies of Measures that are out of print. All requests should quote as a reference the title and year of the Measure. Church of England legislation in up to date form may also be found on the UK Statute Law Database at: www.statutelaw.gov.uk.

Constitution

1 The General Synod shall consist of the Convocations of Canterbury and York joined together in a House of Bishops and a House of Clergy and having added to them a House of Laity.

2 The House of Bishops and the House of Clergy shall accordingly comprise the Upper and the Lower Houses respectively of the said Convocations, and the House of Laity shall be elected and otherwise constituted in accordance with the Church Representation Rules.

3 (1) The General Synod shall meet in sessions at least twice a year, and at such times and places as it may provide, or, in the absence of such provision, as the Joint Presidents of the Synod may direct.

(2) The General Synod shall, on the dissolution of the Convocations, itself be automatically dissolved, and shall come into being on the calling together of the new Convocations.

(3) Business pending at the dissolution of the General Synod shall not abate, but may be resumed by the new Synod at the stage reached before the dissolution, and any Boards, Commissions, Committees or other bodies of the Synod may, so far as may be appropriate and subject to any Standing Orders or any directions of the Synod or of the Archbishops of Canterbury and York, continue their proceedings during the period of the dissolution, and all things may be done by the Archbishops or any such bodies or any officers of the General Synod as may be necessary or expedient for conducting the affairs of the Synod during the period of dissolution and for making arrangements for the resumption of business by the new Synod.

(4) A member of the General Synod may continue to act during the period of the dissolution as a member of any such Board, Commission, Committee or body:

Provided that, if a member of the Synod who is an elected Proctor of the clergy or an elected member of the House of Laity does not stand for re-election or is not re-elected, this paragraph shall cease to apply to him with effect from the date on which the election of his successor is announced by the presiding officer.

4 (1) The Archbishops of Canterbury and York shall be joint Presidents of the General Synod, and they shall determine the occasions on which it is desirable that one of the Presidents shall be the chairman of a meeting of the General Synod, and shall arrange between them which of them is to take the chair on any such occasion:

Provided that one of the Presidents shall be the chairman when any motion is taken for the final approval of a provision to which Article 7 of this Constitution applies and in such other cases as may be provided in Standing Orders.

(2) The Presidents shall, after consultation with the Appointments Committee of the Church of England, appoint from among the members of the Synod a panel of no fewer than three or more than eight chairmen, who shall be chosen for their experience and ability as chairmen of meetings and may be members of any House; and it shall be the duty of one of the chairmen on the panel, in accordance with arrangements approved by the Presidents and subject to any special directions of the Presidents, to take the chair at meetings of the General Synod at which neither of the Presidents takes the chair.

[(3) Under the Synodical Government Measure the Provincial Registrars are Joint Registrars of the General Synod but since 1980 the responsibility has been exercised by the Legal Adviser to the General Synod whom each Archbishop appointed as his Joint Registrar for this purpose.]

5 (1) A motion for the final approval of any Measure or Canon shall not be deemed to be carried unless, on a division by Houses, it receives the assent of the majority of the members of each House present and voting:

Provided that by permission of the chairman and with the leave of the General Synod given in accordance with Standing Orders this requirement may be dispensed with.

(2) All other motions of the General Synod shall, subject as hereinafter provided, be determined by a majority of the members of the Synod present and voting, and the vote may be taken by a show of hands or a division:

Provided that, except in the case of a motion relating solely to the course of business or procedure, any 25 members present may demand a division by Houses and in that case the motion shall not be deemed to be carried unless, on such a division, it receives the assent of the majority of the members of each House present and voting.

(3) This Article shall be subject to any provision of this Constitution or of any Measure with respect to special majorities of the Synod or of each House thereof, and where a special majority of each House is required the vote shall be taken on a division by Houses, and where a special majority of the whole Synod is required, the motion shall, for the purposes of this Article, be one relating solely to procedure.

(4) Where a vote is to be taken on a division by Houses, it may be taken by an actual division or in such other manner as Standing Orders may provide.

6 The functions of the General Synod shall be as follows:

(a) to consider matters concerning the Church of England and to make provision in respect thereof –

(1) by Measure intended to be given, in the manner prescribed by the Church of England Assembly (Powers) Act 1919, the force and effect of an Act of Parliament, or

(2) by Canon made, promulged and executed in accordance with the like provisions and subject to the like restrictions and having the like legislative force as Canons heretofore made, promulged and executed by the Convocations of Canterbury and York, or

(3) by such order, regulation or other subordinate instrument as may be authorized by Measure or Canon, or

(4) by such Act of Synod, regulation or other instrument or proceeding as may be appropriate in cases where provision by or under a Measure or Canon is not required;

(b) to consider and express their opinion on any other matters of religious or public interest.

7 (1) A provision touching doctrinal formulae or the services or ceremonies of the Church of England or the administration of the Sacraments or sacred rites thereof shall, before it is finally approved by the General Synod, be referred to the House of Bishops, and shall be submitted for such final approval in terms proposed by the House of Bishops and not otherwise.

(2) A provision touching any of the matters aforesaid shall, if the Convocations or either of them or the House of Laity so require, be referred, in the terms proposed by the House of Bishops for final approval by the General Synod, to the two Convocations sitting separately for their provinces and to the House of Laity; and no provision so referred shall be submitted for final approval by the General Synod unless it has been approved, in the terms so proposed, by each House of the two Convocations sitting as aforesaid and by the House of Laity.

(3) The question whether such a reference is required by a Convocation shall be decided by the President and Prolocutor of the Houses of that Convocation, and the Prolocutor shall consult the Standing Committee of the Lower House of Canterbury or, as the case may be, the Assessors of the Lower House of York, and the decision of the President and Prolocutor shall be conclusive:

Provided that if, before such a decision is taken, either House of a Convocation resolves that the provision concerned shall be so referred or both Houses resolve that it shall not be so referred, the resolution or resolutions shall be a conclusive decision that the reference is or is not required by that Convocation.

(4) The question whether such a reference is required by the House of Laity shall be decided

by the Prolocutor and Pro-Prolocutor of that House who shall consult the Standing Committee of that House, and the decision of the Prolocutor and the Pro-Prolocutor shall be conclusive:

Provided that if, before such a decision is taken, the House of Laity resolves that the reference is or is not required, the resolution shall be a conclusive decision of that question.

(5) Standing Orders of the General Synod shall provide for ensuring that a provision which fails to secure approval on a reference under this Article by each of the four Houses of the Convocations or by the House of Laity of the General Synod is not proposed again in the same or a similar form until a new General Synod comes into being, except that, in the case of objection by one House of one Convocation only, provision may be made for a second reference to the Convocations and, in the case of a second objection by one House only, for reference to the Houses of Bishops and Clergy of the General Synod for approval by a two-thirds majority of the members of each House present and voting, in lieu of such approval by the four Houses aforesaid.

(6) If any question arises whether the requirements of this Article or Standing Orders made thereunder apply to any provision, or whether those requirements have been complied with, it shall be conclusively determined by the Presidents and Prolocutors of the Houses of the Convocations and the Prolocutor and Pro-Prolocutor of the House of Laity of the General Synod.

8 (1) A Measure or Canon providing for permanent changes in the Services of Baptism or Holy Communion or in the Ordinal, or a scheme for a constitutional union or a permanent and substantial change of relationship between the Church of England and another Christian body, being a body a substantial number of whose members reside in Great Britain, shall not be finally approved by the General Synod unless, at a stage determined by the Archbishops, the Measure or Canon or scheme, or the substance of the proposals embodied therein, has been approved by a majority of the dioceses at meetings of their Diocesan Synods, or, in the case of the Diocese in Europe, of the Bishop's Council and Standing Committee of that diocese.

(1a) If the Archbishops consider that this Article should apply to a scheme which affects the Church of England and another Christian body but does not fall within paragraph (1) of this Article, they may direct that this Article shall apply to that scheme, and where such a direction is given this Article shall apply accordingly.

(1b) The General Synod may by resolution provide that final approval of any such scheme as aforesaid, being a scheme specified in the resolution, shall require the assent of such special majorities of the members present and voting as may be specified in the resolution, and the resolution may specify a special majority of each

House or of the whole Synod or of both, and in the latter case the majorities may be different.

(1c) A motion for the final approval of a Measure providing for permanent changes in any such Service or in the Ordinal shall not be deemed to be carried unless it receives the assent of a majority in each House of the General Synod of not less than two-thirds of those present and voting.

(2) Any question whether this Article applies to any Measure or Canon or scheme, or whether its requirements have been complied with, shall be conclusively determined by the Archbishops, the Prolocutors of the Lower Houses of the Convocations and the Prolocutor and Pro-Prolocutor of the House of Laity of the General Synod.

9 (1) Standing Orders of the General Synod may provide for separate sittings of any of the three Houses or joint sittings of any two Houses and as to who is to take the chair at any such separate or joint sitting.

(2) The House of Laity shall elect a Chairman and Vice-Chairman of that House who shall also discharge the functions assigned by this Constitution and the Standing Orders and by or under any Measure or Canon to the Prolocutor and Pro-Prolocutor of that House.

10 (1) The General Synod shall appoint a Legislative Committee from members of all three Houses, to whom shall be referred all Measures passed by the General Synod which it is desired should be given, in accordance with the procedure prescribed by the Church of England Assembly (Powers) Act 1919, the force of an Act of Parliament; and it shall be the duty of the Legislative Committee to take such steps with respect to any such Measure as may be so prescribed.

(2) The General Synod may appoint or provide by their Standing Orders for the appointment of such Committees, Commissions and bodies (in addition to the Committees mentioned in Section 10 of the National Institutions Measure 1998), which may include persons who are not members of the Synod, and such officers as they think fit.

(3) Each House may appoint or provide by their Standing Orders for the appointment of such Committees of their members as they think fit.

11 (1) The General Synod may make, amend and revoke Standing Orders providing for any of the matters for which such provision is required or authorized by this Constitution to be made, and consistently with this Constitution, for the meetings, business and procedure of the General Synod.

(1a) Provision may be made by Standing Order that the exercise of any power of the General Synod to suspend the Standing Orders or any of them shall require the assent of such a majority of the members of the whole Synod present and voting as may be specified in the Standing Order.

(2) Each House may make, amend and revoke Standing Orders for the matter referred to in Article 10 (3) hereof and consistently with this Constitution and with any Standing Orders of the General Synod, for the separate sittings, business and procedure of that House.

(3) Subject to this Constitution and to any Standing Orders, the business and procedure at any meeting of the General Synod or any House or Houses thereof shall be regulated by the chairman of the meeting.

12 (1) References to final approval shall, in relation to a Canon or Act of Synod, be construed as referring to the final approval by the General Synod of the contents of the Canon or Act, and not to the formal promulgation thereof:

Provided that the proviso to Article 4 (1) shall apply both to the final approval and to the formal promulgation of a Canon or Act of Synod.

(2) Any question concerning the interpretation of this Constitution, other than questions for the determination of which express provision is otherwise made, shall be referred to and determined by the Archbishops of Canterbury and York.

(3) No proceedings of the General Synod or any House or Houses thereof, or any Board, Commission, Committee or body thereof, shall be invalidated by any vacancy in the membership of the body concerned or by any defect in the qualification, election or appointment of any member thereof.

13 Any functions exercisable under this Constitution by the Archbishops of Canterbury and York, whether described as such or as Presidents of the General Synod, may, during the absence abroad or incapacity through illness of one Archbishop or a vacancy in one of the Sees, be exercised by the other Archbishop alone.

General Synod Business

FEBRUARY 2008 GROUP OF SESSIONS

LEGISLATIVE BUSINESS
The Synod
Gave deemed approval that the draft Measure entitled 'Church of England (Miscellaneous Provisions) Measure' (GS 1683) be considered for revision in committee.

Promulged and executed the Canon entitled 'Amending Canon No 27 (Dioceses, Pastoral and Mission Measure 2007)' (GS 1598D).

Carried the motion on the Vacancy in See Committees Regulation 1993 (GS 1599C): 'That the Vacancy in See Committees Regulation 1993, as amended by the Vacancy in See Committees (Amendment) Regulation 2003 and as to be amended by the Vacancy in See Committees (Amendment) Regulation 2007 upon the coming into force of that Regulation, be solemnly affirmed and proclaimed an Act of Synod.'

Gave approval that the draft Measure entitled 'Church of England Pensions (Amendment) Measure'(GS 1682) be considered for revision in committee.

Amended and approved the Code of Practice under Part V of the Dioceses, Pastoral and Mission Measure 2007 (GS 1684).

Took note of a report by the Revision Committee (GS 1637–9Y) on the draft Ecclesiastical Offices (Terms of Service) Measure (GS 1637A), the draft Ecclesiastical Offices (Terms of Service) Regulations (GS 1638A) and draft Amending Canon No 29 (GS 1639A), considered the

Measure clause by clause and the Regulations and Canon paragraph by paragraph.

Debated the motion 'That the Measure entitled "Ecclesiastical Fees (Amendment) Measure" (GS 1672) be considered for revision in committee' and adjourned the debate. The voting was: *In Favour 135, Against 110, Recorded Abstentions 12.*

Took note of a report by the Revision Committee (GS 1642Y) on draft Amending Canon No 28 (GS 1642A) and considered the Canon paragraph by paragraph.

OTHER BUSINESS
The Synod
Received a Presidential Address by the Archbishop of Canterbury.

Approved revised dates for the November 2010 group of sessions.

Gave deemed approval to amendments to Standing Orders.

Debated a Private Member's Motion from Mr Thomas Benyon (Oxford) on *Casinos* (GS Misc 875A and GS Misc 875B) and carried the amended motion:

'That this Synod, gravely concerned that the total national spend on gaming has risen in each year over the past four years from £4 to £40 billion:
(a) endorse the public opposition expressed by church leaders to the introduction of regional and large casinos, and encourage local churches to participate in local

authority consultations on plans for new casino applications;

(b) declare its support for programmes of education, research and treatment undertaken with the aim of checking the growth in problem gambling, and request the Secretary of State for Culture, Media and Sport to invoke the powers granted by the Gambling Act 2005 to introduce a statutory levy on the gambling industry to fund such programmes;

(c) call upon Her Majesty's Government to monitor the addictive effects of Fixed Odds Betting Terminals and to seek an international framework for a code of conduct on internet gambling; and

(d) call upon the Mission and Public Affairs Council to report back to Synod by February 2009 on measures being taken by the churches to combat the detrimental effects of gambling in various forms.'

The voting was: *In Favour 258, Against 4, Recorded Abstentions 9.*

Debated a Private Member's Motion from Mr Timothy Cox (Blackburn) on *Bible Availability* (GS Misc 878A and GS Misc 878B) and carried the amended motion: 'That this Synod, believing in the importance of Scripture, desire that anyone entering a church building or attending a church service should have easy and unfettered access to one of the versions of the Bible referred to in the note by the House of Bishops on Versions of Scripture dated 9th October 2002 or one of the versions of the Bible that may be used by virtue of the Prayer Book (Versions of the Bible) Measure 1965 and would request all dioceses to take steps to give effect to this desire in their churches.'

Debated a Diocesan Synod Motion from the Diocese of Durham on *Eucharistic Prayer for Children* (GS Misc 876A and GS Misc 876B) and carried the amended motion: 'That this Synod request the House of Bishops to commission the expeditious preparation of Eucharistic Prayers suitable for use on occasions when a significant number of children are present or when it is otherwise pastorally appropriate to meet the needs of children present.'

Carried the amended motion on *Mental Health Issues* (GS 1678):

'That this Synod:

(a) affirm the vital necessity of improving services, in hospitals and in the community, for the support, care and treatment of people with mental health problems;

(b) welcome the acceptance by Her Majesty's Government during the passage of the Mental Health Act 2007 of amendments to

protect the liberty and interests of those subject to compulsory detention and treatment for mental disorder, and express the hope that the operation of the Act will be carefully monitored;

(c) note with concern the rising incidence of mental distress among young people;

(d) call attention to the acute needs of people with mental disorders in the criminal justice system and request effective measures to divert them, where appropriate, from prison; and

(e) welcome the recognition within mental health services of the significance of spirituality for assessment and treatment, and encourage parishes to ensure that the support and care of people with mental health problems, their carers and NHS staff is a key priority for the Church's ministry.'

The voting was: *In Favour 297, Against 0, Recorded Abstentions 3.*

Took note of the report *Anglican Communion Covenant* (GS 1679). The voting was: *In Favour 266, Against 20, Recorded Abstentions 19.*

Approved the proposals set out in the final paragraph of *Crown Appointments* (GS 1680). The voting was: *In Favour 290, Against 16, Recorded Abstentions 16.*

Debated the motion on *Crown Appointments* (GS 1680): 'That this Synod, as part of the discussions necessary to implement the proposals set out in the final paragraph of GS 1680, invite the Government to agree that Standing Orders be amended so that arrangements for the appointment of a person to preside at meetings of the Crown Nominations Commission to consider a vacancy of the Archbishopric of Canterbury be varied so that such appointment would in future be made in the same way as applies for a vacancy of the Archbishopric of York.' The motion was lost. The voting was: *In Favour 107, Against 142, Recorded Abstentions 20.*

Carried the amended motion on *Growing Together in Unity and Mission* (GS 1673):

'That this Synod, welcoming the work that has been done towards the Agreed Statement of the International Anglican–Roman Catholic Commission for Unity and Mission and endorsing its stated aim of closer collaboration in unity and mission between our two communions:

(a) note the assessment of the Agreed Statement in GS 1673 as a contribution to the further development of the text and endorse the concerns of the Faith and Order Advisory Group set out in section 4 of GS 1673;

(b) affirm that further growing together in unity and mission will depend on common witness and the exchange of spiritual gifts, as well as clarity between areas where doctrinal agreement has been achieved and areas that require further work;

(c) encourage Anglicans to implement, with Roman Catholics, the practical initiatives for bishops and people proposed in Part 2 of the Statement; and

(d) request that debates take place in Synod on all the documents listed in Appendix 2, Second Phase in *Growing Together in Unity and Mission* as the next stage in the process.'

The voting was: *In Favour 258, Against 10, Recorded Abstentions 5.*

Carried the motion on *Detention without Charge* (GS 1681):

'That this Synod, mindful both of the Christian teaching that enforcement of law should be just in process and outcome, and of the challenge that the advent of suicide attacks poses for the general public and for those who bear responsibility for protecting the public from terrorism:

(a) emphasize the importance of society maintaining a careful balance between the liberty of the individual and the needs of national security;

(b) express grave concern that an extension to the current 28-day maximum period for detention without charge of terrorist suspects would, in the absence of the most compelling arguments, disturb that balance unacceptably;

(c) while welcoming the release of most UK prisoners from Guantanamo Bay, deplore the continued holding of prisoners there without charge or due process and encourage Her Majesty's Government to continue to use all available means to press the United States administration to close the Guantanamo Bay facility and restore the full application of the rule of law; and

(d) affirm the desirability of an early review by the Government of the restrictions and other obligations that may be imposed on individuals under the Prevention of Terrorism Act 2005 and the use of undisclosed material in control order proceedings.'

The voting was: *In Favour 235, Against 2, Recorded Abstentions 7.*

JULY 2008 GROUP OF SESSIONS

LEGISLATIVE BUSINESS
The Synod
Gave deemed approval to the Legal Officers (Annual Fees) Order 2008 (GS 1696) and the Ecclesiastical Judges, Legal Officers and Others (Fees) Order 2008 (GS 1697).

Took note of a report by the Steering Committee (GS 1637Z) on the draft Ecclesiastical Offices (Terms of Service) Measure (GS 1637B), amended the Measure and gave it final approval. The voting was: *Bishops In Favour 20, Against 0, Recorded Abstentions 0; Clergy In Favour 109, Against 5, Recorded Abstentions 4; Laity In Favour 110, Against 13, Recorded Abstentions 2.*

Considered the draft Measure entitled 'Church of England Pensions (Amendment) Measure' (GS 1682A) clause by clause and gave it final approval. The voting was: *Bishops In Favour 22, Against 0, Recorded Abstentions 0; Clergy In Favour 79; Against 0, Recorded Abstentions 0; Laity In Favour 97, Against 1, Recorded Abstentions 1.*

Took note of a report by the Revision Committee (GS 1683Y) on the draft Church of England (Miscellaneous Provisions) Measure (GS 1683A) and considered the Measure clause by clause.

Gave approval that the draft Measure entitled 'Vacancies in Suffragan Sees and Other Ecclesiastical Offices Measure' (GS 1692) be considered for revision in committee.

Gave approval that the draft Measure entitled 'Crown Benefices (Parish Representatives) Measure' (GS 1693) be considered for revision in committee.

Carried the motion that the Vacancy in See Committees (Amendment) Regulation 2008 (GS 1694) be considered, amended and approved the Regulation. The Vacancy in See Committees Regulation 1993, as amended by the Vacancy in See Committees (Amendment) Regulation 2003 and the Vacancy in See Committees (Amendment) Regulation 2008, and as to be amended by the Vacancy in See Committees (Amendment) Regulation 2007 upon the coming into force of that Regulation, was solemnly affirmed and proclaimed an Act of Synod.

Approved the Payments to the Churches Conservation Trust Order 2008 (GS 1695).

Approved the Parochial Fees Order 2008 (GS 1698).

FINANCIAL BUSINESS
The Synod
Approved the Archbishops' Council's Budget for 2009 (GS 1700), approved the revised expenditure for 2008 for Training for Ministry and CHARM; and the expenditure for 2009 for Training for Ministry; National Church Responsibilities; Grants and Provisions; Inter-Diocesan Support/Mission Agencies Clergy Pension Contributions; and CHARM.

OTHER BUSINESS
The Synod
Heard addresses from Bishop Jürgen Johannes-

dotter of the Evangelical Church in Germany (EKD) and Metropolitan John of Pergamon.

Carried the motion on *The Church of the Triune God* (GS 1706):

'That this Synod:
(a) thank the International Commission for Anglican–Orthodox Theological Dialogue for the Cyprus Agreed Statement *The Church of the Triune God* and commend the Statement for study in the Church of England, where possible with members of the Orthodox Churches, and with other ecumenical partners;
(b) note the points raised in the commentary and assessment provided in the briefing paper on the Agreed Statement, produced by the Faith and Order Advisory Group; and
(c) welcome the degree of theological agreement between Anglicans and Orthodox revealed in the Agreed Statement and encourage the continuation of dialogue in those areas on which agreement has not yet been achieved.'

Took note of the Report of the Women Bishops Legislative Drafting Group (GS 1685).

Carried the amended motion on Reader Ministry (GS 1689):

'That this Synod welcome the report on Reader Ministry and, celebrating the ministry of Readers, call upon the dioceses, deaneries and parishes of the Church of England, along with the House of Bishops:
(a) to encourage the study of the report, and in particular by clergy and Readers;
(b) to consider how its recommendations and action points may be pursued nationally and in each diocesan and local situation; and
(c) in the case of dioceses, to report back to the Ministry Council of the Archbishops' Council by July 2010 on initiatives they have taken to implement one or more of the recommendations.'

The voting was: *Bishops In Favour 17, Against 2, Recorded Abstentions 6; Clergy In Favour 72, Against 27, Recorded Abstentions 16; Laity In Favour 102, Against 23, Recorded Abstentions 12.*

Debated a Private Member's Motion from Mr Roy Thompson (York) on *Church Tourism* (GS Misc 887A and GS Misc 887B) and carried the amended motion:

'That this Synod, remembering that churches are first and foremost places of prayer and faith:
(a) support the aims and objectives of the Churches Tourism Association's "Sacred Britain" strategy;
(b) call on the Archbishops' Council to

encourage each Diocese to form a Churches Tourism Group or, at least, to identify a Diocesan Tourism Officer;
(c) propose that such Groups and officers be encouraged to:
 (i) develop ecumenical church tourism networks through Churches Regional Commissions, where they exist, or similar regional bodies, to enable and facilitate strategic partnerships within Government Regions;
 (ii) work with Cathedrals and churches in their area to establish strong, sustainable, cultural and educational links to strengthen the part played by churches in the wider cultural life of the nation;
 (iii) establish and maintain regional and sub-regional contacts and dialogue with English Heritage, Churches Tourism Association, Historic Churches Preservation Trust, Churches Conservation Trust and other heritage and funding bodies; and
 (iv) seek to encourage the mission opportunities arising from church tourism to be taken in imaginative ways, and promote good practice in communicating the Christian faith appropriately to visitors to our church buildings; and
(d) ask the Archbishops' Council to report back on progress before the end of this Synod (July 2010).'

Carried the amended motion on *Climate Change and Human Security* (GS 1705):

'That this Synod, recognizing that climate change poses both an environmental and human security challenge:
(a) endorse the recommendations as set out in *Climate Change and Human Security: Challenging an Environment of Injustice*;
(b) call on the Archbishops' Council and all diocesan synods to act on this report and its conclusions with a view to developing an integrated and holistic response to climate change; and
(c) ask the Mission and Public Affairs Council to report back to this Synod by July 2010 on progress made towards developing such a response.'

The voting was: *In Favour 278, Against 5, Recorded Abstentions 6.*

Approved the appointment of Dr Jonathan Spencer as Chair of the Church of England Pensions Board from 1 January 2009 to 31 December 2013 (GS 1686).

Took note of the Annual Report of the Archbishops' Council's Audit Committee (GS 1690).

Approved the appointment of the auditors to the Archbishops' Council (GS 1704).

Took note of the Annual Report of the Archbishops' Council (GS 1701).

Took note of the report *Parochial Fees* (GS 1703) and carried the motion:

'That this Synod:
(a) request the Archbishops' Council to introduce legislation to give effect to recommendations (a)–(f) in GS 1703; and
(b) request the Deployment, Remuneration and Conditions of Service Committee to consult with relevant stakeholders on recommendations (g)–(j) in GS 1703 and to report back to this Synod.'

Carried the motion on the *Anglican/Methodist Covenant* (GS 1691):

'That this Synod:
(a) thank the members of the Joint Implementation Commission for their report *Embracing the Covenant* and for their work during the past five years;
(b) commend the report, with its recommendations, for study, action and response in the Church of England, and for discussion with members of the Methodist Church;
(c) endorse the Commission's recommendations regarding the shape of its work in the next phase; and
(d) request that Bishop's Councils consider the report and refer it for study by other appropriate bodies in the dioceses and that responses be sent to the Council for Christian Unity by 31 December 2009.'

Debated a Diocesan Synod Motion from the diocese of St Albans on *Faith, Work and Economic Life* (GS Misc 890A and GS Misc 890B) and carried the amended motion:

'That this Synod:
(a) affirm daily work be it paid or unpaid as essentially a spiritual activity;
(b) recognize the importance of Christian values within economic life;
(c) encourage bishops and clergy to give greater priority to equipping and resourcing church members through teaching, prayer, affirmation and celebration, to fulfil their vocations, ministries and mission in their places of work; and
(d) request the Mission and Public Affairs Council to:
    (i) convene a symposium on a theological understanding of work for today as outlined in sections 5.3–5.4 of GS Misc 890B; and
    (ii) compile a collection of supportive resource materials for church members as outlined in section 5.5 of GS Misc 890B.'

Carried the amended motion on the Report of the Women Bishops Legislative Drafting Group (GS1685) and the Report from the House of Bishops (GS 1685A):

'That this Synod:
(a) affirm that the wish of its majority is for women to be admitted to the episcopate;
(b) affirm its view that special arrangements be available, within the existing structures of the Church of England, for those who as a matter of theological conviction will not be able to receive the ministry of women as bishops or priests;
(c) affirm that these should be contained in a statutory national code of practice to which all concerned would be required to have regard; and
(d) instruct the legislative drafting group, in consultation with the House of Bishops, to complete its work accordingly, including preparing the first draft of a code of practice, so that the Business Committee can include first consideration of the draft legislation in the agenda for the February 2009 group of sessions.'

The voting was: *Bishops In Favour 28, Against 12, Recorded Abstentions 1; Clergy In Favour 124, Against 44, Recorded Abstentions 4; Laity In Favour 111, Against 68, Recorded Abstentions 2.*

Debated a Diocesan Synod Motion from the diocese of Guildford on *Anglican Governance* (GS Misc 891A and GS Misc 891B) and carried the motion:

'That this Synod request the House of Bishops:
(a) to prepare a report that describes and explores relationships between discussions, recommendations and decisions made by these bodies:
    the Lambeth Conference,
    the Anglican Consultative Council,
    the Primates' meeting,
    the House of Bishops of the Church of England,
    the Archbishops' Council,
    and the General Synod of the Church of England; and
(b) to promote discussion of the report to increase the understanding of the governance of the Church of England within the Anglican Communion.'

Heard a presentation on the Annual Report of the Church Commissioners from Mr Andreas Whittam Smith, First Church Estates Commissioner and Mr Timothy Walker, Third Church Estates Commissioner.

General **PART 3**

PART 3 CONTENTS

GENERAL INFORMATION

Addressing the Clergy

Since the Lambeth Conference of 1968, at which styles of address were debated, there has been a trend towards simpler forms of address. Resolution 14 stated: 'The Conference recommends that the bishops, as leaders and representatives of a servant Church, should radically examine the honours paid to them in the course of divine worship, in titles and customary address, and in style of living, while having the necessary facilities for the efficient carrying on of their work.'

Whereas formerly a bishop would have been addressed as 'My Lord' and a dean as 'Mr Dean', it has become more usual to address a bishop in speech as 'Bishop' and a dean as 'Dean'. There is, however, a correct way to address clergy on an envelope, which is normally as follows:

Archbishop of Canterbury or York	The Most Revd and Rt Hon the Lord Archbishop of
Archbishop of another Province	The Most Revd the Lord Archbishop of
Bishop of London	The Rt Revd and Rt Hon the Lord Bishop of
Diocesan/Suffragan Bishop	*Either* The Rt Revd the Lord Bishop of
	or The Rt Revd the Bishop of
Assistant/Retired Bishop	The Rt Revd J. D. Smith (*or* John Smith)
Dean	The Very Revd the Dean of
Provost	The Very Revd the Provost of
Archdeacon	The Ven the Archdeacon of
Canon	The Revd Canon J. D. Smith (*or* John or Jane Smith)
Prebendary	The Revd Prebendary J. D. Smith (*or* John or Jane Smith)
Rural Dean	No special form of address (The Revd, the Revd Canon, etc.)
Dean of Oxford/Cambridge College	No special form of address
Cleric also Professor	*Either* The Revd Professor J. D. Smith
	or Professor the Revd J. D. Smith
Canon also Professor	*Either* The Revd Canon Professor J. D. Smith
	or Professor the Revd Canon J. D. Smith
Cleric also Doctor	*Either* The Revd Dr J. D. Smith
	or The Revd J. D. Smith (degree)
Canon also Doctor	The Revd Canon J. D. Smith (degree)
Other Clergy/Priest/Deacon	The Revd J. D. Smith (*or* John or Jane Smith)

The following points should be noted particularly:

1 A diocesan or suffragan bishop has a title conferred on him by his consecration or subsequent translation, which he is entitled to hold until he resigns. He then reverts to his personal name, retaining the title 'Right Reverend'.

2 A dean, provost or archdeacon has a territorial title until he resigns. He then reverts to his personal name, and his title is 'Reverend' unless the rank of dean, provost or archdeacon emeritus has been awarded.

3 Retired archbishops properly go back to the status of a bishop but may be given as a courtesy the style of an archbishop.

4 A bishop holding office as a dean or archdeacon is addressed as The Rt Revd the Dean/Archdeacon of.

5 If a cleric's name or initials are unknown, he or she should be addressed as The Revd — Smith or the Revd Mr/Mrs/Miss/Ms Smith. It is never correct to refer to a cleric as 'The Reverend Smith' or 'Revd Smith'.

6 There is no universally accepted way of addressing an envelope to a married couple of whom both are in holy orders. We recommend the style 'The Revd A. B. and the Revd C. D. Smith'.

Archbishops of Canterbury and York

CANTERBURY

597 Augustine
604 Laurentius
619 Mellitus
624 Justus
627 Honorius
655 Deusdedit
668 Theodore
693 Beorhtweald
731 Tatwine
735 Nothelm
740 Cuthbeorht
761 Breguwine
765 Jaenbeorht
793 Æthelheard
805 Wulfred
832 Feologild
833 Ceolnoth
870 Æthelred
890 Plegmund
914 Æthelhelm
923 Wulfhelm
942 Oda
959 Ælfsige
959 Beorhthelm
960 Dunstan
c988 Athelgar
990 Sigeric Serio
995 Ælfric
1005 Ælfheath
1013 Lyfing
1020 Æthelnoth
1038 Eadsige
1051 Robert of Jumièges
1052 Stigand
1070 Lanfranc
1093 Anselm
1114 Ralph d'Escures
1123 William de Corbeil
1139 Theobald
1162 Thomas Becket
1174 Richard [of Dover]
1185 Baldwin
1193 Hubert Walter
1207 Stephen Langton
1229 Richard le Grant
1234 Edmund Rich
1245 Boniface of Savoy
1273 Robert Kilwardby
1279 John Peckham
1294 Robert Winchelsey
1313 Walter Reynolds
1328 Simon Mepeham
1333 John Stratford
1349 Thomas
    Bradwardine
1349 Simon Islip
1366 Simon Langham
1368 William Whittlesey

1375 Simon Sudbury
1381 William Courtenay
1396 Thomas Arundel[†]
1398 Roger Walden
1414 Henry Chichele
1443 John Stafford
1452 John Kemp
1454 Thomas Bourchier
1486 John Morton
1501 Henry Dean
1503 William Warham
1533 Thomas Cranmer
1556 Reginald Pole
1559 Matthew Parker
1576 Edmund Grindal
1583 John Whitgift
1604 Richard Bancroft
1611 George Abbot
1633 William Laud
1660 William Juxon
1663 Gilbert Sheldon
1678 William Sancroft
1691 John Tillotson
1695 Thomas Tenison
1716 William Wake
1737 John Potter
1747 Thomas Herring
1757 Matthew Hutton
1758 Thomas Secker
1768 Frederick
    Cornwallis
1783 John Moore
1805 Charles Manners
    Sutton
1828 William Howley
1848 John Bird Sumner
1862 Charles Thomas
    Longley
1868 Archibald Campbell
    Tait
1883 Edward White
    Benson
1896 Frederick Temple
1903 Randall Thomas
    Davidson
1928 Cosmo Gordon Lang
1942 William Temple
1945 Geoffrey Francis
    Fisher
1961 Arthur Michael
    Ramsey
1974 Frederick Donald
    Coggan
1980 Robert Alexander
    Kennedy Runcie
1991 George Leonard
    Carey
2002 Rowan Douglas
    Williams

YORK

BISHOPS

625 Paulinus
[vacancy for 30 years]
664 Ceadda
669 Wilfrith I
678 Bosa[‡]
705 John of Beverley
718 Wilfrith II

ARCHBISHOPS

c734 Ecgbeorht
767 Æthelbeorht
780 Eanbald I
796 Eanbald II
c812 Wulfsige
837 Wigmund
854 Wulfhere
900 Æthelbeald
c928 Hrothweard
931 Wulfstan I
958 Oscytel
971 Edwaldus
972 Osweald
992 Ealdwulf
1003 Wulfstan II
1023 Ælfric Puttoc
1041 Æthelric[§]
1051 Cynesige
1061 Ealdred
1070 Thomas I
1100 Gerard
1109 Thomas II
1119 Thurstan
1143 William Fitzherbert
1147 Henry Murdac[*]
1154 Roger of Pont
    l'Eveque
1191 Geoffrey Plantagenet
1215 Walter de Gray
1256 Sewal de Bovill
1258 Godfrey Ludham
1266 Walter Giffard
1279 William Wickwane
1286 John le Romeyn
1298 Henry Newark
1300 Thomas Corbridge
1306 William
    Greenfield
1317 William Melton
1342 William Zouche
1352 John Thoresby
1374 Alexander Neville
1388 Thomas Arundel
1396 Robert Waldby
1398 Richard le Scrope
1407 Henry Bowet
1426 John Kemp
1452 William Booth

1465 George Nevill
1476 Lawrence Booth
1480 Thomas Rotherham
    (or Scot)
1501 Thomas Savage
1508 Christopher
    Bainbridge
1514 Thomas Wolsey
1531 Edward Lee
1545 Robert Holgate
1555 Nicholas Heath
1561 Thomas Young
1570 Edmund Grindal
1577 Edwin Sandys
1589 John Piers
1595 Matthew Hutton
1606 Tobias Matthew
1628 George Montaigne
1629 Samuel Harsnett
1632 Richard Neile
1641 John Williams
1660 Accepted Frewen
1664 Richard Sterne
1683 John Dolben
1688 Thomas Lamplugh
1691 John Sharp
1714 William Dawes
1724 Lancelot Blackburn
1743 Thomas Herring
1747 Matthew Hutton
1757 John Gilbert
1761 Robert Hay
    Drummond
1777 William Markham
1808 Edward Venables
    Vernon Harcourt
1847 Thomas Musgrave
1860 Charles Thomas
    Longley
1863 William Thomson
1891 William Connor
    Magee
1891 William Dalrymple
    Maclagan
1909 Cosmo Gordon Lang
1929 William Temple
1942 Cyril Foster Garbett
1956 Arthur Michael
    Ramsey
1961 Frederick Donald
    Coggan
1975 Stuart Yarworth
    Blanch
1983 John Stapylton
    Habgood
1995 David Michael
    Hope
2005 John Tucker Mugabi
    Sentamu

[†] On 19 October 1399 Boniface IX annulled Arundel's translation to St Andrews and confirmed him in the see of Canterbury.
[‡] Wilfrith was restored to office in 686 and Bosa in 691.
[§] Ælfric Puttoc was restored in 1042.
[*] William Fitzherbert was restored in 1153.

Bishops in the House of Lords

The Archbishops of Canterbury and York and the Bishops of London, Durham and Winchester always have seats in the House of Lords. The twenty-one other seats are filled by diocesan bishops in order of seniority. In the case of bishops awaiting seats, the order of seniority is shown (1), (2), (3), etc.

The Bishop of Sodor and Man and the Bishop of Gibraltar in Europe are not eligible to sit in the House of Lords.

	Election as Diocesan Bishop confirmed	Translated to present See	Entered House of Lords
Canterbury (Most Revd & Rt Hon R. D. Williams)	1992*	2002	2003
York (Most Revd & Rt Hon J. T. M. Sentamu)	2002	2005	2006
London (Rt Revd & Rt Hon R. J. C. Chartres)	1995		1996
Durham (Rt Revd N. T. Wright)	2003		2003
Winchester (Rt Revd M. C. Scott-Joynt)	1995		1996
Bath and Wells (Rt Revd P. B. Price)	2002		2008
Birmingham (Rt Revd D. Urquhart)	2006		(10)
Blackburn (Rt Revd N. S. Reade)	2004		(5)
Bradford (Rt Revd D. C. James)	2002		(1)
Bristol (Rt Revd M. Hill)	2003		(3)
Carlisle (Rt Revd G. G. Dow)	2000		2008
Chelmsford (Rt Revd J. W. Gladwin)	1994	2003	1999
Chester (Rt Revd P. R. Forster)	1996		2001
Chichester (Rt Revd J. W. Hind)	2001		2008
Coventry (Rt Revd C. J. Cocksworth)	2008		(14)
Derby (Rt Revd A. L. J. Redfern)	2005		(9)
Ely (Rt Revd A. J. Russell)	2000		2007
Exeter (Rt Revd M. L. Langrish)	2000		2005
Gloucester (Rt Revd M. F. Perham)	2004		(7)
Guildford (Rt Revd C. J. Hill)	2004		(8)
Hereford (Rt Revd A. M. Priddis)	2004		(6)
Leicester (Rt Revd T. J. Stevens)	1999		2003
Lichfield (Rt Revd J. M. Gledhill)	2003		(4)
Lincoln (Rt Revd J. C. Saxbee)	2001		2008
Liverpool (Rt Revd J. S. Jones)	1998		2003
Manchester (Rt Revd N. S. McCulloch)	1992	2002	1997
Newcastle (Rt Revd J. M. Wharton)	1997		2003
Norwich (Rt Revd G. R. James)	1999		2004
Oxford (Rt Revd J. L. Pritchard)	2007		(11)
Peterborough (Rt Revd I. P. M. Cundy)	1996		2001
Portsmouth (Rt Revd K. W. Stevenson)	1995		1999
Ripon and Leeds (Rt Revd J. R. Packer)	2000		2006
Rochester (Rt Revd M. J. Nazir-Ali)	1994		1999
St Albans (Vacancy)			
St Edmundsbury and Ipswich (Rt Revd W. N. Stock)	2007		(12)
Salisbury (Rt Revd D. S. Stancliffe)	1993		1998
Sheffield (Vacancy)			
Southwark (Rt Revd T. F. Butler)	1991	1998	1997
Southwell and Nottingham (Rt Revd G. H. Cassidy)	1999		2004
Truro (Rt Revd W. Ind)	1997		(15)
Wakefield (Rt Revd S. G. Platten)	2003		(2)
Worcester (Rt Revd J. G. Inge)	2008		(13)

* As Bishop of Monmouth in the Church in Wales, the bishops of which do not have seats in the House of Lords.

Chaplains

Chaplains in Her Majesty's Services

ROYAL NAVY

Chaplains of all denominations are employed in many parts of the world, ashore and afloat in capital ships, frigates and destroyers, Royal Marine Commando Units, hospitals, Royal Naval Air Stations, HM Naval Bases and Training Establishments. Apart from conducting the customary services in their ships, units or establishments, for which all the necessary facilities are provided, chaplains find numerous opportunities for extending the work of the Church through pastoral contacts with families and dependants, as well as being 'friend and adviser of all on board'. They are given particular opportunity to teach the Christian faith to young people in Training Establishments. In-Service training for all Royal Naval Chaplains is carried out at the Armed Forces Chaplaincy Centre, Amport House, Andover, Hants. SP11 8BG. Christian Leadership Courses for all service personnel are provided at the centre during the year. The Anglican Church in the Royal Navy is served by 45 priests and is very much a part of the Church of England with the Single Service and Tri-Service Synodical structures. The Senior Anglican Chaplain in the Royal Navy is granted the ecclesiastical dignity of Archdeacon by the Archbishop of Canterbury. The Archbishop is the Ordinary for all service chaplains and grants ecclesiastical licences to all Anglican chaplains on the Active List. The Royal Navy is an Equal Opportunities employer and applications for entry from both male and female priests up to the age of 49 are always welcome. Full particulars concerning the entry of Anglican Chaplains can be obtained from the Archdeacon for the Royal Navy, Second Sea Lord and Commander in Chief, Naval Home Command, MP 1.2 Leach Building, Whale Island, Portsmouth PO2 8BY

Tel: 023 9262 5553
Fax: 023 9262 5134
email: lee.foley211@mod.uk

ARMY

There is a definite Establishment of Chaplains, Church of England, Church of Scotland, Roman Catholic, Methodist and United Board (United Reformed Church and Baptist) who serve in the Royal Army Chaplains' Department. This Establishment is governed by the strength of the Army. Chaplains of all denominations are administered by the Chaplain-General assisted by the Deputy Chaplain General at the Ministry of Defence Chaplains (Army), and through Senior Chaplains at the Headquarters of Commands/Districts at home and overseas. The Chaplain General is responsible to the 2nd Permanent Under-Secretary of State for the general well-being of the Department. The religious training of the Army is an integral part of military life. Regular periods of Religious Instruction/Discussion are provided. The Armed Forces Chaplaincy Centre is situated at Amport House, Andover. This Centre serves the double purpose of a spiritual home for all army chaplains, and as a training centre for all ranks, with different courses to develop leaders, refresh churchmen, or inform enquirers. Courses for military personnel are also held at centres overseas. *The Chaplain General* and *Archdeacon for the Army* Ven Stephen Robbins. Ministry of Defence Chaplains (Army), Trenchard Lines, Upavon, Wiltshire SN9 6BE

Tel: 01980 615804
Fax: 01980 615800

ROYAL AIR FORCE

From the foundation of the Royal Air Force, chaplains have been proud to minister to the needs of servicemen and women and their families, in peace and war. The Chaplains' Branch of the Royal Air Force offers a real challenge and a rewarding ministry to young priests who have the necessary qualities, initiative and enthusiasm. The Royal Air Force is a large body of men and women drawn from every corner of Britain and from every stratum of society. There is a continuing need for clergy to minister to these men and women and the Royal Air Force understands and supports this ministry. Chaplains are commissioned by Her Majesty the Queen to provide for the pastoral and spiritual needs of all Service personnel and their families. This care is unlimited, and extends wherever members of the Royal Air Force are called to serve. Clergy may apply for a position in either a full-time or reserve capacity. Further details concerning chaplaincy in the Royal Air Force can be obtained from: Chaplaincy Services (RAF), Valiant Block, RAF High Wycombe HP14 4UE

Tel: 01494 497595
Web: www.raf.mod.uk/chaplains
For a list of **Chaplains to Her Majesty's Services** *see Crockford.*

Forces Synodical Council

President The Archbishop of Canterbury

Senior Vice-President Rt Revd David John Conner (*Dean of Windsor, Domestic Chaplain to the Queen and the Archbishop of Canterbury's Episcopal Representative to Her Majesty's Forces*)

Lay Vice-President Lieutenant Colonel (Retired) John Peter Morrison

Secretary Paul Wright, c/o Armed Forces Chaplaincy Centre, Amport, Hants SP11 8BG

On the direction of the Secretary of State for Defence and the Archbishop of Canterbury in the 1980s, the Forces Synodical Council was first convened in 1990 in London. Since 1997 it has had thirty-six elected members, six clergy and six lay members from the Royal Navy, Army and the Royal Air Force, and nine *ex officio* members. The Council is chaired by the Bishop to HM Forces but has no fiscal or Armed Service command authority. It gives the Anglican clergy and laity of the whole Armed Services the opportun-ity to contribute to General Synod, to the Armed Services Chain of Command and to the Ministry of Defence. They can also make decisions pertin-ent to the life and ministry of the Anglican Church within the Armed Forces, and although members are not drawn exclusively from the Church of England, all ministers hold the Licence of the Archbishop of Canterbury.

Each Armed Service constitutes a separate Archdeaconry with elected representatives at chaplaincy level, forming what are known as Chaplaincy Councils and an elected Arch-deaconry Synod. The three Archdeacons (one appointed by the Archbishop of Canterbury to each of the Armed Services) chair their respective Archdeaconry Synods, are *ex officio* members of the Forces Synodical Council and were, until 2005, *ex officio* members of General Synod. Under the changes in composition of General Synod that came into force in 2005, these *ex officio* posts lapsed and the Armed Forces received a total of seven representative seats on General Synod, divided between the laity and the clergy.

Chaplains in Higher Education

The Church of England supports chaplains in uni-versities and colleges of higher education across the country including the Church Colleges and Universities. The National Adviser for Higher Education and Chaplaincy, based in the Educa-tion Division at Church House, Westminster, is the officer of the Board of Education leading on the Church's policy and ministry in higher education.

The National Adviser advises the Board on policy relating to HE; resources dioceses, universities and colleges and their chaplains, coordinates conferences, induction, and some training for HE chaplains (with ecumenical cooperation through the Churches' Higher Education Liaison Group (CHELG)), acts as con-sultant to chaplains and ecumenical chaplaincy teams, and advises enquirers considering minis-try in this sector of education. In general, organ-ized events are open to chaplains throughout Great Britain as well as to ecumenical partners and diocesan staff. The National Adviser and the Board of Education's Higher Education Panel are available to advise the government and Church at all levels when required.

A list of higher education chaplains may be found in *Crockford's Clerical Directory, 2008/2009* (pages 1214–15). Full up-to-date information is kept by the National Adviser.

The role of chaplain includes ministry to staff and students, and to institutions as a whole, their leaders and structures. Chaplains are also a point of contact for people of other faiths. The uni-versity student experience has changed dramat-ically in recent years, and the Higher Education Act 2004 has emphasized both increased access for students from non-traditional backgrounds and also increased fees for many students, to be paid back after graduation. A key focus for chap-laincy is the promotion of a new understanding of the Church's ministry in the higher education sector. This is a challenging ministry in the con-text of mission, in the face of continuing change and increasing student numbers, with all the pressures on people, finance and structures that these bring. It is increasingly carried out in a multi-faith context and is seen as bringing a major contribution to community cohesion. It requires wisdom and understanding and is certainly not restricted to recent curates.

The Board of Education's report *Pillars of the Church: supporting chaplaincy in further and higher education* (GS Misc 667, 2002) and its report to the General Synod *Aiming Higher: Higher Education and the Church's Mission* (GS 1567, 2005) are available from www.chpublishing.co.uk. Also available is *The Church of England's Higher Education Strategy: Implementing Aiming Higher*, which sets out the strategy for work over the next five years. Further enquiries may be made to: The National Adviser for Higher Education and Chaplaincy, Education Division, Church House, London SW1P 3NZ   *Tel:* 020 7898 1513
Web:
   www.cofe.anglican.org/info/education/hefe

For a list of **Educational Chaplains** *see Crockford.*
For **Church Universities and Colleges of Higher Education** *see page 222.*

GENERAL

Chaplains in Further Education

Chaplaincy to Further Education Colleges began in the 1970s and has from the beginning been ecumenical in character and funding. The Churches' National Adviser in Further Education is based at Church House, but is jointly managed and funded, in equal partnership, by the Methodist Church and the Church of England, and also works with the National Council of the National Ecumenical Agency in Further Education.

In July 2006 General Synod debated a report, *Pushing Further: from Strategy to Action*, which committed the Church to a five-year strategy and programme of action designed to develop chaplaincies in all 400 colleges and to ensure provision for spiritual and moral development of all students.

Most of the current 200 Further Education chaplaincies are organized as ecumenical teams, with a mix of ordained and lay members contributing time on a part-time and often voluntary basis to support a regular presence and activities in their local college: increasingly these teams are becoming multi-faith in organization and character. About 12 colleges support a full-time chaplain (who may have an additional role as a teacher or counsellor) and a larger and growing number fund a half-time chaplain, who also serves in a local church.

DfES, the Department for Education and Skills, published in 2006 a White Paper on FE, recognizing students' faith background as important and endorsing multi-faith chaplaincy as a means of meeting these needs. The Learning and Skills Council, the funding body for further education colleges and other further education providers, has become increasingly supportive of Further Education chaplaincy. It has funded conferences and a research study and has now published a national handbook on Further Education Chaplaincy. There are also strong partnerships and regular contact with QIA, QCA, Learn Direct, and NIACE (the National Association for Adult and Continuing Education).

Further Education Chaplaincy is concerned with providing for the spiritual and moral welfare of all students, of any faith or none. This is a vital, though challenging mission among today's young people, 43 per cent of whom are educated in further education colleges. This is more than those (40 per cent) who are in schools after the age of 16, and it includes higher proportions of young people from deprived areas, and especially, from ethnic minority backgrounds.

The National Adviser is working to implement the action programme proposed in *Pushing Further*, designed both to increase the number of colleges which support a chaplaincy and to strengthen existing chaplaincies, especially those where a single local minister is working in isolation. All who are interested in supporting or learning more about this work may order *Pushing Further*, the recently published report, or contact:

The National Further Education Adviser, Education Division, Church House, London SW1P 3NZ   *Tel:* 020 7898 1517
Web: www.cofe.anglican.org/about/education/hefe.html

Chaplains in the Prison Service

The Prison Service Chaplaincy, in partnership with the wider Church, provides chaplains for all HM Prisons in England and Wales. It works within the Prison Service and the National Offender Management Service (NOMS) in the newly created Ministry of Justice. The responsibilities of the Chaplain General and his headquarters colleagues include the giving of advice to ministers and officials about policy decisions with a religious or ethical dimension. In addition, chaplains are recruited, trained, deployed and supported in their work of providing for the religious needs of prisoners, giving opportunities for worship, formation and instruction, and offering a pastoral ministry at times of crisis and opportunity. Chaplains are also involved in enabling the observance of all faith traditions. Their ministry is always available to staff.

All prisons have an Anglican, a Roman Catholic and a Free Church chaplain, with chaplains from many different faiths; the headquarters team includes senior representatives of all three denominations, and the Muslim Adviser. The Chaplain General has responsibility for all faith traditions.

The Bishop to Prisons
Rt Revd James Jones (*Bishop of Liverpool*), Bishop's Lodge, Woolton Park, Liverpool L25 6DT
Tel: 0151 421 0831

Chaplain General
Ven William Noblett, Prison Service Chaplaincy, Room 410, Abell House, John Islip St, London SW1P 4LH   *Tel:* 020 7217 8997
Fax: 020 7217 8844
email: william.noblett@hmps.gsi.gov.uk

Anglican Advisee to HMPs
Revd Michael Kavanagh (*as above*)
Tel: 020 7217 8667
07807 509720 (Mobile)

Fax: 020 7217 8844
email: michael.kavanagh@hmps.gsi.gov.uk
For a list of **Prison Chaplains** see *Crockford*.

Chaplaincy in the National Health Service

Since the inception of the NHS, full- and part-time chaplains have been salaried members of staff. Their work in the various hospitals and healthcare institutions throughout the country furthers the mission and ministry of the Church in a secular setting. It also carries forward the Dominical command to care for the sick and dying and those who look after them.

Healthcare chaplaincy is at the cutting edge of ministry, often touching people's lives at times of great crisis and pain. The development in research techniques, the human genome project, etc. throw up new ethical challenges for chaplains, alongside other healthcare professionals. There are 422 full-time chaplains in the UK, of whom 325 are Anglican, and 3,000 part-time, of whom 1,700 are Anglican, not to mention the numerous volunteers involved to different degrees in chaplaincy (some 10,000 according to a recent survey). Together with Roman Catholic, Free Church and, increasingly, other World Faith colleagues, chaplains also minister to the 1.3 million staff employed by the NHS.

The Bishop of Gloucester (Rt Revd Michael Perham) chairs the Hospital Chaplaincies Council (HCC) and is a vice chair of the Mission and Public Affairs Division (MPA). HCC is a Council answerable through the MPA to the General Synod. HCC is the interface between the Church of England, the Department of Health and the NHS. It was created by the Church Assembly in 1951.

The Council not only holds this national overview, but is also looked to by bishops (through their advisers for Hospital Chaplaincy) and individual chief executives and NHS trusts for guidance, advice and support in all matters relating to hospital/healthcare chaplaincy. Pastoral care of chaplains is an important part of the work. The Council (in conjunction with the Free Churches Group and the Roman Catholic Bishops' Conference) also ensures the continuing professional development of new as well as serving chaplains through the work of the Joint Training Office based at Church House. Introductory training courses are delivered through Cardiff University and attract academic points upon completion. HCC has supported the development of an innovative foundation degree in chaplaincy at St Mary's University College, Twickenham.

Hospital/healthcare chaplaincy presents an opportunity to minister to patients, staff and relatives and to be a prophetic voice within a secular institution. Please remember this work and ministry in your prayers.

Further particulars may be obtained from The Revd Fr Edward J. Lewis, Chaplain to Her Majesty the Queen Chief Executive, The Hospital Chaplaincies Council, Church House, Great Smith Street, London SW1P 3NZ.
Tel: 020 7898 1895/1892
email: edward.lewis@c-of-e.org.uk
Web: www.nhs-chaplaincy-spiritualcare.org.uk

Chaplains to the Police

Apart from a handful of chaplains who are full-time or half-time with the Police, the majority of chaplains, some 425 in all, are ordinary clergy, both men and women working in parishes or local churches. They give their time and energies voluntarily to the Police through care and concern for the police officers and police staff of their area, in recognition of the value of the work done by the Police on behalf of the public. Most, but not all, chaplains are from the mainstream Christian denominations, and there are links with other faith leaders. The services of police chaplains are available to all, and not dependent on membership of a faith community. Chaplains can be contacted at local police stations, or privately by telephone or email.

The object of the National Association of Chaplains to the Police is to advance and support the work of Chaplaincy to the Police Forces of the United Kingdom by assisting the ministry of mainstream faith communities to the Police Service, and by promoting the association of Police Chaplains for mutual assistance and training.

President Baroness Harris of Richmond
Vice-President Matthew Baggott (*Chief Constable, Leicestershire Constabulary*)
National Coordinator Revd Insp Andrew Earl, The Chines, Faith St. South Kirby, Pontefract, West Yorkshire WF9 3AL   Tel: 01977 658925
National Secretary Revd Peter McConnell, St Helen's Vicarage, Drummonds Close, Longhorsley, Northumberland NE65 8UR
Tel: 01670 788218
email: mcconnellvicarage@hotmail.com
Web: www.police-chaplains.org.uk

General Information   **221**

Church Universities and Colleges of Higher Education

Bishop Grosseteste University College, Newport, Lincoln LN1 3DY　　　*Tel:* 01522 527347
Principal Professor Muriel Robinson
　　　Tel: 01522 527347 Ext 267
Chaplain Revd Carolyn James
　　　Tel: 01522 583604
　　　email: Carolyn.james@bgc.ac.uk

Canterbury Christ Church University, North Holmes Rd, Canterbury, Kent CT1 1QU
　　　Tel: 01227 767700

Vice Chancellor Professor Michael Wright
Dean of Chapel Revd Dr Jeremy Law
　　　Tel: 01227 782747
　　　email: j.law@cant.ac.uk
Chaplain Revd Sue Blade　*Tel:* 01227 782139
　　　email: sb379@cant.ac.uk
Revd Philip Hobday (Broadstairs Chaplain)
　　　Tel: 01843 609120 ext. 5138
　　　email: ph95@canterbury.ac.uk

University of Chester, Parkgate Rd, Chester CH1 4BJ　　*Tel:* 01244 375444 Ext 2305
Vice Chancellor Professor Tim Wheeler
Chaplain: Revd Ian Arch　　*Tel:* 01244 513083
　　　email: i.arch@chester.ac.uk

University of Chichester, Bishop Otter Campus, College Lane, Chichester PO19 4PE
　　　Tel: 01243 816000
Vice Chancellor Dr Robin Baker
Chaplain Revd Hadge Hughes　*Tel:* 01243 816041
　　　email: h.hughes@ucc.ac.uk

University of Gloucestershire, PO Box 220, The Park Campus, The Park, Cheltenham GL50 2QF
　　　Tel: 01242 532700
Vice Chancellor and Principal Professor Patricia Broadfoot
Chaplains Revd Tamsin Merchant
　　　Tel: 01242 532735
　　　tmerchant@glos.ac.uk

Liverpool Hope University, Hope Park, Liverpool L16 9JD　　*Tel:* 0151 291 3000
Vice Chancellor Professor Gerald Pillay
Chaplain Revd Dr Steven Shakespeare
　　　Tel: 0151 291 3547
　　　email: shakes@hope.ac.uk

Liverpool Hope is an ecumenical institution, fully Catholic and fully Anglican.

University College of St Mark and St John, Derriford Rd, Plymouth PL6 8BH
　　　Tel: 01752 636700
Principal Dr David Baker
　　　email: principal@marjon.ac.uk
Chaplain Revd Dr Gayle Rawlings
　　　Tel: 01752 636847
　　　email: chaplaincy@marjon.ac.uk

University of Cumbria, Bowerham Rd, Lancaster LA1 3JD　　*Tel:* 01524 384384
Vice Chancellor Professor Christopher Carr
Senior Chaplain Revd Mike Peatman
　　　Tel: 01524 384260
　　　email: m.peatman@ucsm.ac.uk
also at Rydal Rd, Ambleside, Cumbria LA22 8BB
　　　Tel: 01539 430300
Chaplain Revd Paul Woodcock　*Tel:* 01539 430268
　　　email: paul.woodcock@cumbria.ac.uk
also at Fusehill St, Carlisle CA1 2HH
Chaplain Revd Andrew West　*Tel:* 01228 616204
　　　email: andrew.west@ucsm.ac.uk

Whitelands College, Roehampton University, Parkstead House, Holybourne Avenue, Roehampton, London SW15 4JD
　　　Tel: 020 8392 3500
Vice Chancellor Professor Paul O'Prey
Principal Revd Dr Geoffrey Walker
　　　Tel: 020 8392 3511
Chaplain Revd Dr Daniel Eshun
　　　Tel: 020 8392 3516
　　　email: d.eshun@roehampton.ac.uk

University of Winchester, Sparkford Rd, Winchester SO22 4NR　　*Tel:* 01962 841515
Vice Chancellor Professor Joy Carter
Chaplain Revd Jonathan Watkins
　　　Tel: 01962 827246
　　　email: jonathan.watkins@winchester.ac.uk

York St John University, Lord Mayor's Walk, York YO3 7EX　　*Tel:* 01904 624624
Vice Chancellor Professor Dianne Willcocks
Chaplain Revd Jeremy Clines　*Tel:* 01904 716606
　　　email: j.clines@yorksj.ac.uk
Assistant Chaplain Mrs Sharon Lusty
　　　Tel: 01904 716607
　　　email: s.lusty@yorksj.ac.uk

Church Urban Fund

Office Church House, Great Smith St, London
SW1P 3AZ   *Tel:* 020 7898 1647
                                Fax: 020 7898 1601
                email: enquiries@cuf.org.uk
                Web: www.cuf.org.uk

Church Urban Fund (CUF) supports the Church of England in its mission to see the social, spiritual and economic renewal in England's most disadvantaged and marginalized communities. CUF support allows churches to galvanise their aspirations into actions, bringing about change at the grass roots level. Working in conjunction with dioceses and other partner organizations, CUF has developed a range of sustainable responses that take full account of the needs and requirements within these communities. CUF is also closely involved in wider debate, both inside and outside the Church, seeking to inform and influence issues of urban regeneration, working also to represent faith based social action, through initiatives such as CUF exchange. This initiative facilities the exchange of information and good practise and allows the voice of faith communities to be heard at a national level.

Set up in 1988 following the landmark report *Faith in the City*, CUF supports projects working in areas such as community development, social care, youth and education, housing and homelessness, interfaith efforts, and opening up church buildings for community use. CUF's 21st anniversary year in 2009 will see the launch of a special initiative to support its ongoing work. To date the Fund has supported nearly 6,500 projects within the poorest communities in England.

The Fund is grateful for the continuing support of individuals, parishes and dioceses who have contributed to its work, through their time, money and prayers.

Applications to CUF are made through the local diocese. The national office is happy to respond to initial enquiries and can provide details of the appropriate diocesan contact. All the information is also available on the web site.

Clergy Appointments Adviser

The adviser has been appointed by the Archbishops of Canterbury and York to assist clergy, in England and from overseas, to find suitable new appointments and to assist patrons and others responsible for making appointments to find suitable candidates. The adviser has a responsibility for beneficed and unbeneficed clergy, together with stipendiary deacons and accredited lay workers. A list of vacancies for incumbencies, team posts, assistant curates and specialized ministries is available on-line. For further information please contact: Revd John Lee, Clergy Appointments Adviser, The Wash House, Lambeth Palace, London SE1 7JU

Tel: 020 7898 1898
Fax: 020 7898 1899
email: admin.caa@c-of-e.org.uk
Web: www.cofe.anglican.org/info/caa

Conference Centres and Retreat Houses

CONFERENCE CENTRES

ASHBURNHAM PLACE	Ashburnham Place, Battle, E Sussex TN33 9NF (*Administrator:* Revd Andrew Wooding-Jones) *Tel:* 01424 892244 *Fax:* 01424 894200 *email:* bookings@ashburnham.org.uk *Web:* www.ashburnham.org.uk
HAYES CONFERENCE CENTRE	Hayes Conference Centre, Swanwick, Derbyshire DE55 1AU (*Manager:* Mr Peter Anderson) *Tel:* 01773 526000 *Fax:* 01773 540841 *email:* office@cct.org.uk *Web:* www.cct.org.uk
HIGH LEIGH CONFERENCE CENTRE	High Leigh Conference Centre, Lord St, Hoddesdon, Herts. EN11 8SG (*Manager:* Mr Ian Andrews) *Tel:* 01992 463016 *Fax:* 01992 446594 *email:* highleigh@cct.org.uk *Web:* www.cct.org.uk
LEE ABBEY	Lee Abbey Fellowship, Lynton, Devon EX35 6JJ (*Warden:* Chris Edmondson) *Tel:* 0800 389 1189 *Fax:* 01598 752619 *email:* relax@leeabbey.org.uk *Web:* www.leeabbey.org.uk

GENERAL

RETREAT HOUSES

The following is a list of diocesan conference centres and retreat houses including some run by religious communities. For details of accommodation for individual retreats *see* Religious Communities page 245, or contact the Retreat Association, The Central Hall, 256 Bermondsey St, London SE1 3JJ *Tel:* 020 7357 7736 whose journal *Retreats* is published annually in December.

BATH AND WELLS	Abbey House, Chilkwell St, Glastonbury, Som. BA6 8DH (*Retreat House*) (*Warden*: David Hill) *Tel:* 01458 831112
	Community of St Francis, Compton Durville Manor House, South Petherton TA13 5ES *Tel:* 01460 240473
BLACKBURN	Whalley Abbey, Whalley, Clitheroe, Lancs. BB7 9SS (*Warden*: Revd Christopher Sterry; *Manager:* Mr John Wilson) *Tel:* 01254 828400 *Fax:* 01254 825519
BRADFORD	Parcevall Hall, Appletreewick, Skipton, N Yorks. BD23 6DG (*Warden:* Beverley Seward) *Tel:* 01756 720213 *Fax:* 01756 720656
CARLISLE	Carlisle Diocesan Conference and Retreat Centre, Rydal Hall, Ambleside, Cumbria LA22 9LX (*General Manager:* Jonathan Green) *Tel:* 01539 432050 *Fax:* 01539 434887 *email:* bookings@rydalhall.org
CHELMSFORD	Diocesan House of Retreat, Pleshey, Chelmsford, Essex CM3 1HA (*Warden:* Revd Sheila Coughtrey) *Tel:* 01245 237251
CHESTER	Chester Diocesan Conference Centre, Foxhill, Tarvin Road, Frodsham, Cheshire WA6 6XB (*Wardens:* Mr & Mrs Ian Cameron) *Tel:* 01928 733777 *Fax:* 01928 731422 *email:* foxhillwarden@aol.com *Web:* foxhillconferences. co.uk
CHICHESTER	Monastery of the Holy Trinity, Crawley Down, Crawley, W Sussex RH10 4LH *Tel:* 01342 712074
	St Margaret's Convent, Hooke Hall, 250 High St, Uckfield, East Sussex TN22 1EN *Tel:* 01825 766808
COVENTRY	Offa House (Coventry Diocesan Retreat House), Offchurch, Leamington Spa, War. CV33 9AS *Tel:* 01926 423309
DERBY	Morley Retreat and Conference House, Church Lane, Morley, Derby DE7 6DE (*Warden:* Jeff Witts) *Tel:* 01332 831293
DURHAM	*See* entry for NEWCASTLE
ELY	Bishop Woodford House, Barton Road, Ely, Cambs. CB7 4DX *Tel:* 01353 663039
	The Community of the Resurrection, St Francis' House, Hemingford Grey, Huntingdon PE28 9BJ *Tel:* 01480 462185

GLOUCESTER	Glenfall House, Mill Lane, Charlton Kings, Cheltenham, Glos. GL54 4EP (*Warden:* Liz Palin) *Tel:* 01242 583654 *Fax:* 01242 251314
GUILDFORD	St Columba's House, Maybury Hill, Woking, Surrey GU22 8AB *Tel:* 01483 766498
	House of Bethany, 7 Nelson Rd, Southsea, Hants. PO5 2AR *Tel:* 023 9283 3498
HEREFORD	Bishop Mascall Centre, Lower Galdeford, Ludlow, Shropshire SY8 1RZ *Tel:* 01584 873882 *Fax:* 01584 877945 *email:* info@thebmc.org.uk
LEICESTER	Launde Abbey, East Norton, Leicestershire LE7 9XB (*The Warden*) *Tel:* 01572 717254 *Fax:* 01572 717454 *email:* laundeabbey@leicester.anglican.org *Web:* www.launde.org.uk
LICHFIELD	Lichfield Diocesan Retreat and Conference Centre, Shallowford House, Shallowford, Stone, Staffs. ST15 0NZ (*Warden:* David Shemilt) *Tel:* 01785 760233 *Fax:* 01785 760390
LONDON	The Royal Foundation of Saint Katharine, 2 Butcher Row, London E14 8DS (*Master:* Preb David Paton) *Tel:* 020 7790 3540 *Fax:* 020 7702 7603 *email:* enquiries@stkatharine.org.uk
NEWCASTLE/DURHAM	Shepherd's Dene, Riding Mill, Northumberland NE44 6AF (*Warden:* Mr P. Dodgson) *Tel:* 01434 682212
NORWICH	Horstead Centre, Norwich NR12 7EP (*Manager:* Mark Heybourne) *Tel:* 01603 737215 (*Office*); 01603 737674 (*Guests*)
	All Hallows Convent, Ditchingham, Bungay NR35 2DT *Tel:* 01986 892749
OXFORD	St Mary's Convent, Wantage OX12 9DJ *Tel:* 01235 760170
SALISBURY	Sarum College, 19 The Close, Salisbury SP1 2EE *Tel:* 01722 424800 *Fax:* 01722 338508 *email:* admin@sarum.ac.uk
	Society of St Francis, The Friary, Hilfield, Dorchester DT2 7BE *Tel:* 01300 342313
	St Denys Retreat Centre, Ivy House, 2 Church St, Warminster BA12 8PG *Tel:* 01985 214824
SHEFFIELD	Whirlow Grange Conference Centre, Ecclesall Road South, Sheffield, S Yorks. S11 9PZ (*General Manager:* Graham Holland) *Tel:* 0114 236 3173 (*Office*); 236 1183 (*Visitors*) *email:* info@whirlowgrange.co.uk
SOUTHWARK	Wychcroft, Bletchingley, Redhill, Surrey RH1 4NE *Tel:* 01883 743041

GENERAL

	The Community of Sisters of the Church, St Michael's Convent, 56 Ham Common, Richmond TW10 7JH *Tel:* 020 8940 8711/8948 2502
SOUTHWELL	Sacrista Prebend Retreat House, 4 Westgate, Southwell, Notts NG25 0JH *Tel:* 01636 816 833
TRURO	Epiphany House, Kenwyn, Church Rd, Truro, Cornwall TR1 3DR *Tel:* 01872 272249
WAKEFIELD	Community of the Resurrection, Mirfield, W Yorks. WF14 0BN *Tel:* 01924 494318 *Fax:* 01924 490489
	Community of St Peter, Horbury, W Yorks. WF4 6BB *Tel:* 01924 272181 *Fax:* 01924 261225
WINCHESTER	Old Alresford Place, Winchester Retreat and Conference Centre, Old Alresford, Hants. SO24 9DH (*Manager:* Isobel Chapman) *Tel:* 01962 732518 *Fax:* 01962 732593 *email:* enquiries@oldalresfordplace.co.uk
	Alton Abbey, King's Hill, Beech, Alton, Hants. GU34 4AP (*Abbot:* Rt Revd Dom Giles Hill OSB) *Tel:* 01420 562145/563575
WORCESTER	Holland House, Cropthorne, nr Pershore, Worcs. WR10 3NB (*Warden:* Ian Spenser) *Tel:* 01386 860330 *email:* laycentre@hollandhouse.org
YORK	York Diocesan Retreat and Conference Centre, Wydale Hall, Brompton-by-Sawdon, Scarborough, N Yorks. YO13 9DG (*Priest Director:* Ann Coleman) *Tel:* 01723 859270 *Fax:* 01723 859702 *email:* admin@wydale.org *Web:* www.wyedale.org
	St Oswald's Pastoral Centre, Woodlands Drive, Sleights, Whitby, N Yorks. YO21 1RY *Tel:* 01947 810496
	Sneaton Castle Centre, Whitby, N Yorks. YO21 3QN (*Centre Manager:* Linda Antill) *Tel:* 01947 600051 *Fax:* 01947 603490 *email:* sneaton@globalnet.co.uk *Web:* www.sneatoncastle.co.uk

Evangelism

The Mission and Public Affairs Division (MPA) seeks to help the Church of England to do its evangelism appropriately, courteously and clearly.

The MPA Council's report *Mission-shaped Church* has had substantial impact on the Church of England, with over 22,000 copies sold to date. The report was discussed at General Synod in February 2004 and was warmly commended to the Church; Synod is due to debate the report again in 2009. A number of follow-up volumes have also been produced by Church House Publishing, covering practical subjects such as spirituality, the rural church, children and youth as well as exploring in depth the theological questions raised by today's missional initiatives.

Mission-shaped Church encourages dioceses to build an enabling framework for new ways of being the church, alongside well-loved and traditional forms. The Dioceses, Pastoral and Mission Measure 2007 offers bishops the opportunity to make clear legal provision for new mission initiatives within the life of their dioceses. The House of Bishops has approved guidelines to identify, train and support pioneer ministers, both lay and ordained. Working alongside its partners MPA offers resource and support to dioceses as they make sense of this enabling framework in their own contexts.

Within MPA the Revd Canon Paul Bayes (National Mission and Evangelism Adviser) is responsible for encouraging and supporting the work in this area. This is done in close alliance with Fresh Expressions, the Archbishops' initiative presently led by the Revd Dr Steven Croft and funded by the Lambeth Partners. MPA also works in partnership with colleagues in other denominations, the ACC, the Mission Agencies, Churches Together in England (through its Co-ordinating Group for Evangelization), and other evangelistic agencies in this country.

The Archbishop of Canterbury's vision is of a mixed economy church, developing a spectrum of inherited and emerging forms of church and deploying these where each is most appropriate. The National Mission and Evangelism Adviser works closely with Diocesan Missioners and Advisers on Evangelism to implement this vision and to identify and share good practice across the Church.

Fresh Expressions

Fresh Expressions is an initiative of the Archbishops of Canterbury and York, supported by the Methodist Council, established in 2004 to encourage, enable and resource mission through fresh expressions of church in every diocese and district.

Archbishops' Missioner and Team Leader of Fresh Expressions Revd Dr Steven Croft, 15 Fyfield Rd, Oxford OX2 6QE   *Tel:* 01865 311838
email: contact@freshexpressions.org.uk
Web: www.freshexpressions.org.uk

Names and contact details for other team members can be found on the web site.

Faculty Office and Special Marriage Licences

The Faculty Office of the Archbishop of Canterbury, otherwise known as The Court of Faculties, exercises on behalf of the Archbishop the dispensing powers that he has by virtue of the Ecclesiastical Licences Act of 1533. These comprise the appointment of Notaries Public, the granting of degrees, and the granting of marriage licences. The right to grant a Special Licence for marriage at any convenient time or place in England or Wales is unique to the Archbishop, and this jurisdiction is sparingly exercised and good cause must always be shown why a more normal preliminary to Anglican marriage cannot be used. Marriage with any other preliminary must be solemnized between 8.00 a.m. and 6.00 p.m., and although a Special Licence could omit this requirement, that will only in practice be done in a case of serious illness.

The more common need for a Special Licence is the parties' desire to marry in a building not normally authorized for Anglican marriage, or in a parish where they cannot satisfy the residence requirements. Even in the last case cause must be shown, normally in the form of a real connection with the parish or church in question; the *Special Licence procedure is not intended to enable parties to choose a church building on aesthetic or sentimental grounds.*

More detailed guidance on the grounds that may be considered sufficient for the granting of a Special Licence may always be sought from the Faculty Office by letter or telephone.

Special arrangements may sometimes be made in a genuine emergency. In such cases the clergy or the couple concerned should first contact the Diocesan Registrar, archdeacon, or diocesan or area bishop. If unable to resolve the difficulty himself he will make arrangements for the Faculty Office to be approached.

Orders made by the Master of the Faculties prescribe from time to time fees which are to be charged for applications for Special Licences. The fee is currently £145.00.

The Faculty Office is open to telephone and personal callers between 10.00 a.m. and 4.00 p.m. Monday to Friday, except on certain days around Easter and Christmas.

Office 1 The Sanctuary, Westminster, London SW1P 3JT   *Tel:* 020 7222 5381 Ext 7162
Fax: 020 7222 7502
email: faculty.office@1Thesanctuary.com
Web: www.facultyoffice.org.uk

Hospice Movement

The word 'Hospice' was first used from the fourth century onwards when Christian orders welcomed travellers, the sick and those in need. It was first applied to the care of dying patients by Mme Jeanne Garnier who founded the Dames de Calvaire in Lyon, France in 1842. The modern hospice movement, however, with its twin emphases on medical and psychosocial intervention, dates from the founding of St Christopher's Hospice by Dame Cicely Saunders in 1967. Since 1967, 'Hospice' has become a worldwide philosophy adapting to the needs of different cultures and settings – hospital, hospice and community – and is established in six continents.

Hospice and palliative care is the active, total care of patients whose disease no longer responds to curative treatment, and for whom the goal must be the best quality of life for them and their families. Palliative medicine is now a distinct medical speciality in the UK. It focuses on controlling pain and other symptoms, easing suffering and enhancing the life that remains. It integrates the psychological and spiritual aspects of care, to enable patients to live out their lives with dignity. It also offers support to families, both during the patient's illness and their bereavement. It offers a unique combination of care in hospices and at home.

Hospice and palliative care services mostly help people with cancer although increasingly patients with other life-threatening illnesses may also be supported; this includes HIV/AIDS, motor neurone disease, heart failure, kidney disease. Hospice and palliative care is free of charge regardless of whether it is provided by a voluntary hospice, Macmillan Service, Marie Curie Cancer Care, Sue Ryder Palliative Care Centre or by an NHS service. The criteria for admission are based on medical, social and emotional need. Referral to a hospice or palliative care service (including inpatient and home care nursing services) is normally arranged by the patient's own GP or hospital doctor. Further information on hospice care in the UK and overseas, including a membership service and publications for health professionals, is available from *hospice information* (*see below*). *hospice information* is a joint venture between St Christopher's Hospice and Help the Hospices, which offers an enquiry service to the public and professionals. Publications include UK and International Directories of Hospice and Palliative Care. The UK Directory is available free of charge on receipt of a large (9" x 11") envelope with £1.48 in stamps. *hospice information*, Hospice House, 34 Britannia St, London WC1X 9JG

Tel: 0870 903 3 903 (calls charged at national rate)
Fax: 020 7278 1021
email: info@hospiceinformation.info
Web: www.hospiceinformation.info

Children's Hospices UK

Children's Hospices UK is the national charity that gives voice and support to all children's hospice services. We help children's hospices to keep improving the care and support they provide to children who are not expected to reach adulthood and their families. We raise awareness of the range of support available both within hospices and at home. We also raise funds to help children's hospices to keep providing a free service. We campaign and lobby on behalf of children's hospices, ensuring their voice is heard by government.

Children's Hospice Services
It's every parent's worst nightmare to be told their child will die before them. But for an estimated 20,000 families across the UK, this is a reality. Some of these children will die when they're very young; others will deteriorate slowly over a number of years. In most cases, full-time care falls to the parents – 24 hours a day, seven days a week. The families affected are under huge emotional, physical and financial strain.

Children's hospice services help children and their families in these situations to deal with the emotional and physical challenges they face, helping them to make the most of life. They welcome the whole family for a break in friendly, homely surroundings and provide practical help in people's own homes. They offer a diverse range of services including specialist care, 24-hour telephone support, advice and information, and bereavement support for all family members. For more information please contact:

Children's Hospices UK, First Floor, Canningford House, 38 Victoria St, Bristol BS1 6BY
Tel: 0117 989 7820
Fax: 0117 929 1999
email: info@childhospice.org.uk
Web: www.childhospice.org.uk
For details of the **Association of Hospice and Palliative Care Chaplains** *see page 000.*

Marriage: Legal Aspects

A comprehensive statement of the law and information on related matters is available from the Faculty Office of the Archbishop of Canterbury. Copies of *Anglican Marriage in England and Wales – A Guide to the Law for Clergy* were sent to incumbents and licensed clergy of the Church of England and the Church in Wales in 2000. Further copies are available by post, price £3.50, from: The Faculty Office, 1 The Sanctuary, Westminster, London SW1P 3JT

For details of **Special Marriage Licences** *see* the entry for the Faculty Office, page 227.

Press

CHURCH TIMES

Established 1863. The best-selling independent weekly newspaper, with a new, acclaimed website, reporting on the worldwide Christian Church and Anglicanism in particular. As well as its ever widening news coverage, the paper contains a full comment section on current affairs, general features, reviews of books, music and arts, a comprehensive gazette, and the biggest selection of church job advertisements. Goes to press on Wednesday; published on Friday; advertisements to be placed on Friday for the following week; price £1.10; subscription £65.

Editor Mr Paul Handley. *Office* 13–17 Long Lane, London EC1A 9PN   *Tel:* 020 7776 1060
Fax: 020 7776 1086/1017
Subscriptions: *Tel:* 01502 711171
email: editor@churchtimes.co.uk
Web: www.churchtimes.co.uk

CHURCH OF ENGLAND NEWSPAPER

A weekly newspaper which aims to provide a full, objective and lively coverage of Christian news from Britain and overseas. Contents include general features, book, music, film and art reviews, the latest clergy appointments and an ongoing focus on how the Church can improve its mission. Goes to press on Tuesday; published Friday; deadline for advertisements 2.00 pm Monday; price 90p (annual subscription UK £60.00, Eur £80, Rest of world £100; other rates on application). *Editor* C. M. Blakely. *Office* The Church of England Newspaper, Central House, 142 Central St, London EC1V 8AR
Tel: 020 7417 5800
Fax: 020 7216 6410
email: cen@churchnewspaper.com
Web: www.churchnewspaper.com

ENGLISH CHURCHMAN

Church of England newspaper (established 1843), incorporating *St James's Chronicle* 1761. Protestant and evangelical. News, various features, book reviews, correspondence and church calendar. Published fortnightly, Fridays, price 40p. *Editor* Revd Peter Ratcliff.
Tel: 020 8417 0875
email: englishchurchman@aol.com

Schools, Church of England

In January 2007 there were 4,441 Church of England primary schools (15 fewer than in 2006) and 227 Church of England secondary schools (five Church of England secondary schools closed and re-opened as academies) within the maintained system of education. 2,093 of these were voluntary aided, 2,499 voluntary controlled, 50 foundation schools, and a further five were Academies. In 2007, Church of England primary schools educated 767,320 pupils and secondary schools approximately 204,300 pupils: 18.7 per cent of primary age pupils and 6.2 per cent of secondary age pupils, an overall increase of 0.5 per cent in the number of pupils. One hundred and six of the secondary schools have sixth forms. By September 2007, three more Church of England secondary schools and seven more Academies had opened and more are planned to open in the current year towards the 'Dearing' target of 100 additional schools. The Church expects to exceed this target in due course.

All Church of England schools, although (except for Academies) revenue-funded through the Local Education Authority, retain their position as autonomous educational charities. Since the Education Act 2002, Academies (technically independent schools funded through Government grant) which have either Church of England foundations or governors appointed to represent the Church of England, are also regarded as Church of England schools within the meaning of the Diocesan Boards of Education Measure 1991 (as revised). Church of England Academies have already opened in London, Bradford, Liverpool, Salford and Southwark. A further 9 are due to open in the next two or three years and 54 more are under discussion. Many of these are being developed in partner-

GENERAL

ship with other religious groups, charities and individuals.

There are additionally in the independent sector more than 400 schools which are designated as having a Christian character. Most of these are Anglican by virtue of their foundation, and provide worship and religious teaching based on the rites, practices and doctrines of the Church of England. They are entitled to appoint heads and teachers who are actively supportive of the school's religious ethos. These include well-known public schools and grammar schools of ancient foundation, some of which are associated with cathedrals or other major churches. Figures are not available for the number of pupils in such independent schools but the total number of pupils in independent and maintained Church of England schools together can be estimated at well over a million.

Diocesan Boards of Education have responsibilities to all schools (over RE and collective worship) within the diocese and statutory duties to all maintained Church of England schools. The statutory basis for their constitution and work is the Diocesan Boards of Education Measure 1991 amended by several Education Acts in the intervening years, including most recently the School Standards and Framework Act 1998 and the Education Act 2002. The 2002 Act gave Diocesan Boards of Education the statutory duty to give advice to governing bodies that are admission authorities (i.e. those of Voluntary Aided schools) over their admission policies and imposed on such schools the requirement that they have regard to the advice they have been given. The 2006 Education and Inspections Act permits dioceses to refer school admissions policies to the Adjudicator where they feel this to be necessary. Many Diocesan Boards of Education are seeking to develop closer supportive links with independent schools affiliated to the Church of England.

The eleven Church Universities and University Colleges in England provide degree and other higher education courses for over 70,000 students. Many of them offer a wide range of courses but with a particular emphasis on education for the professions, including especially teaching and professions allied to nursing. They, with the small number of Roman Catholic colleges, train a quarter of all teachers. They have been encouraged to give particular regard to their partnership with Church schools and local dioceses. They have a strong commitment to creating access and widening participation, as part of their Christian commitment, and have a better than average record in enabling students to complete their courses.

In recent years, government legislation has created and continues to create a number of changes both in the framework within which all schools are required to operate and also in the arrangements for their administration. Such changes challenge the governors and staff of Church schools to establish clear policies which indicate how they express their understanding of their role as Church of England schools in their particular circumstances. In this task the schools are supported by the staff of the Diocesan Boards of Education and by the work of the Education Division and the National Society. A wealth of information and resources is to be found on the National Society's web site: www.natsoc.org.uk.

Guidance for the Statutory Inspection of Anglican Schools (SIAS) under section 48 of the Education Act 2005 and a related self-evaluation toolkit along with details of inspector training courses are available from the National Society and the Archbishops' Council Education Division offices, whose address is given elsewhere in the Year Book. Details of individual schools may be obtained from the Diocesan Directors of Education in the case of maintained schools and in the case of independent schools from the *Public and Preparatory Schools Year Book* (published by A & C Black).

Services Authorized and Commended

Public worship in the Church of England is a matter governed by law.

Canon B 2 provides that the General Synod may approve forms of service with or without time limit. Services thus approved are alternative to those of *The Book of Common Prayer*. The power given to General Synod under Canon B 2 derives from the Worship and Doctrine Measure 1974.

Canon B 4 provides that the convocations, the archbishops in their provinces or the bishops in their dioceses may approve forms of service for use on occasions for which *The Book of Common Prayer* or *Authorized Alternative Services* do not provide.

Canon B 5 (paragraph 2) allows discretion to any minister where no other provision has been made under Canons B 1 or B 4, to use other forms of service that are considered suitable. If questions are raised as to whether such forms of service are suitable the decision rests with the bishop.

Authorized Alternative Services are those approved by the General Synod under Canon B 1 (for fuller details *see* below).

Commended Services are those that the bishops corporately have judged to be 'suitable' either for approval under Canon B 4 or for use in the contexts envisaged in Canon B 5 (for fuller details *see* page 232).

AUTHORIZED SERVICES ALTERNATIVE TO THE BOOK OF COMMON PRAYER
As at 1 January 2009

Published in *Common Worship: Services and Prayers for the Church of England* and *Common Worship: Collects and Post Communions*

1. Calendar
2. A Service of the Word
3. Schedule of permitted variations to *The Book of Common Prayer* Orders for Morning and Evening Prayer where these occur in *Common Worship*
4. Prayers for Various Occasions
5. The Litany
6. Authorized Forms of Confession and Absolution
7. Creeds and Authorized Affirmations of Faith
8. The Lord's Prayer
9. The Order for the Celebration of Holy Communion also called The Eucharist and The Lord's Supper
10. Collects and Post Communions
11. Rules for Regulating Authorized Forms of Service
12. The Lectionary
13. Opening Canticles at Morning and Evening Prayer; Gospel Canticles; Other Canticles; A Song of Praise (Epiphany); Te Deum Laudamus

Published in *Common Worship: Christian Initiation*

14. Holy Baptism
15. Emergency Baptism
16. Holy Baptism and Confirmation
17. Seasonal Provisions and Supplementary Texts
18. Affirmation of Baptismal Faith
19. Reception into the Communion of the Church of England

Published in *Common Worship: Pastoral Services*

20. Wholeness and Healing
21. The Marriage Service with prayers and other resources
22. Thanksgiving for the Gift of a Child
23. The Funeral Service with prayers and other resources
24. Series One Solemnization of Matrimony
25. Series One Burial Services

Published in *Common Worship: Ordination Services*

26. Ordination Services

Published separately

27. Public Worship with Communion by Extension (*NB explicit permission must be obtained from the bishop for the use of this rite.*)
28. Weekday Lectionary

The above are all authorized by the General Synod for use until further resolution of the Synod.

Form of Service authorized by the Archbishops of Canterbury and York without time limit for use in their respective Provinces

A Service for Remembrance Sunday (included in *Common Worship: Times and Seasons – see* below)

COMMENDED SERVICES AND RESOURCES
As at 1 January 2009

Published in *Common Worship: Services and Prayers for the Church of England*
1   Introduction to Morning and Evening Prayer on Sunday
2   Introduction to Holy Baptism
3   Short Prefaces for the Sundays before Lent and after Trinity
4   Additional Canticles

Published in the President's Edition of *Common Worship*
5   Additional Blessings

Published in *Common Worship: Christian Initiation*
6   Rites Supporting Disciples on the Way of Christ
7   Admission of the Baptized to Communion
8   Celebration after an Initiation Service outside the Parish
9   Thanksgiving for Holy Baptism
10   A Corporate Service of Penitence
11   The Reconciliation of a Penitent

Published in *Common Worship: Pastoral Services*
12   An Order for Prayer and Dedication after a Civil Marriage
13   Thanksgiving for Marriage
14   Ministry at the Time of Death
15   Receiving the Coffin at Church before the Funeral
16   Funeral of a Child: Outline Orders and Resources
17   At Home after the Funeral
18   Memorial Services: Outline Orders and Sample Services
19   Prayers for Use with the Dying and at Funeral and Memorial Services
20   Canticles for Marriages, Funerals and Memorial Services

Published separately
21   Material contained in *New Patterns for Worship*
22   Material contained in *Common Worship: Times and Seasons*
23   Material contained in *Common Worship: Festivals*
24   *Common Worship: The Admission and Licensing of Readers*

SERVICES WHICH COMPLY WITH THE PROVISIONS OF A SERVICE OF THE WORD
(see Authorized Services, no. 2)
As at 1 January 2009

Published in *Common Worship: Services and Prayers for the Church of England*
1   An Order for Morning Prayer on Sunday
2   An Order for Evening Prayer on Sunday
3   An Order for Night Prayer (Compline)
4   An Order for Night Prayer (Compline) in Traditional Language

Published separately
5   Sample services contained in *New Patterns for Worship*
6   Services contained in *Common Worship: Daily Prayer*

PUBLICATIONS

The material is published in the following volumes:
*   *Common Worship: Services and Prayers for the Church of England*
*   *Common Worship*: President's Edition
*   *Common Worship: Collects and Post Communions*
*   *Common Worship: Christian Initiation*
*   *Common Worship: Pastoral Services*
*   *Common Worship: Daily Prayer*

- Common Worship: Times and Seasons
- Common Worship: Festivals
- Common Worship: Ordination Services (Study Edition)
- New Patterns for Worship
- Public Worship with Communion by Extension
- Common Worship: The Admission and Licensing of Readers
- annual editions of the Common Worship Lectionary

It may also be found in the Common Worship area of the Church of England web site.

VERSIONS OF THE BIBLE AND OF THE PSALMS

The following may be used in Book of Common Prayer services (with the permission of the Parochial Church Council) instead of the Authorized Version of the Bible and the Psalter in *The Book of Common Prayer*:

Revised Version
Revised Standard Version
New English Bible
The Revised Psalter
The Liturgical Psalter (The Psalms
   in a new translation for worship)

Jerusalem Bible
Good News Bible
(Today's English Version)

Any version of the Bible or Psalter not prohibited by lawful authority may be used with Alternative Services and Commended Services.

A leaflet entitled *A Brief Guide to Liturgical Copyright* deals with the procedures for local reproduction. It provides guidance on preparing local texts and information about copyright requirements. The third edition (2000) is available at £1.50 from Church House Publishing and in the *Common Worship* area of the Church of England web site.

TV and Radio

BBC LOCAL RADIO
There are thirty-nine BBC local radio stations in counties and cities throughout England. Each station is responsible for its own religious broadcasting and some have religious advisory panels. Religious programmes are often presented and produced by local clergy and lay people who observe the editorial policy of the BBC. For details of stations, contact the BBC Regions' Press Office.　　　　*Tel:* 020 7765 2795

BBC RELIGIOUS BROADCASTING DEPARTMENT
Produces a wide variety of religious broadcasts for transmission on BBC television, network radio and the World Service. It also manages an extensive web site at bbc.co.uk/religion. All BBC local radio stations and the BBC Asian Network produce their own religious programmes to cater for the particular needs of faith communities within their catchment areas. The aims of religious broadcasting are (1) to seek to reflect the worship, thought and action of the principal religious traditions represented in the UK, recognizing that those traditions are mainly, though not exclusively, Christian; (2) to seek to represent to viewers and listeners those beliefs, ideas, issues and experiences in the contemporary world which are evidently related to a religious interpretation or dimension of life; and (3) to seek also to meet the religious interests, concerns and

needs of those on the fringe of, or outside, the organized life of the religious bodies. On matters of policy the Corporation is advised by a representative Central Religious Advisory Committee which also acts as adviser to the ITC. *Head of Religion and Ethics* Michael Wakelin, BBC, PO Box 27, Oxford Rd, Manchester M60 1SJ

CENTRAL RELIGIOUS ADVISORY COUNCIL
CRAC advises the BBC and the ITC on policy matters relating to religion. Its membership is drawn from the major Christian traditions and world faiths represented in the United Kingdom. CRAC can be contacted c/o the BBC or ITC.

CHURCHES' MEDIA COUNCIL
The Churches' Media Council is an ecumenical body with charitable status. In September 2003 it succeeded and incorporated CACLB, the Churches' Advisory Council for Local Broadcasting, which was established in 1967. The Council aims to advance the Christian religion through broadcasting on radio and television and all forms of media, including the Press and the Internet. Its Council is drawn from the Church of England, Roman Catholic Church, Methodist Church, Baptist Union of Great Britain, United Reformed Church, Evangelical Alliance, Salvation Army, The Free Churches' Group, Churches

GENERAL

Together in Britain and Ireland, Churches Together in England, Church of Ireland, Churches Together in Wales, Church of Scotland, Scottish Episcopal Church and Action of Churches Together in Scotland, with representatives of the BBC, Office of Communications (Ofcom), theMediaNet (the Association of Christians in the Media), Churches' Media Trust, and Christian broadcast training organizations. *Chairman* Revd Joel Edwards *Director* Mr Andrew Graystone   *Tel:* 0845 6520027
07772 710090 (Mobile)
email: info@churchesmediacouncil.org.uk
Web: www.churchesmediacouncil.org.uk

FOUNDATION FOR CHRISTIAN COMMUNICATION LTD (CTVC)

Major producer and co-producer of television and radio programmes that look at all the ethical and religious angles on life. Certain videos available. Media training courses are held in DV and radio production as well as personal communication, such as writing press releases, interviews and preparing for interviews. Television and sound studios fitted to full broadcast standard and post-production facilities. All available for hire. New Media/Education department developing interactive production for Citizenship and RE courses. *Chief Executive Officer* Mr Nick Stuart, CTVC, 9–10 Copper Row, Tower Bridge Piazza, London SE1 2LH   *Tel:* 020 7940 8480
Fax: 020 7940 8490
email: info@ctvc.co.uk
Web: www.ctvc.co.uk

OFFICE OF COMMUNICATIONS (Ofcom)

Ofcom is the independent regulator and competition authority for the UK communications industries, with responsibilities across television, radio, telecommunications and wireless communications services. *Chairman* David Currie (Lord Currie of Marylebone) *Deputy Chairman* Philip Graf *Chief Executive* Ed Richards Ofcom, Riverside House, 2a Southwark Bridge Rd, London SE1 9HA.   *Tel:* 020 7981 3040
Textphone: 020 7981 3043
Fax: 020 7981 3333
email: contact@ofcom.org.uk
Web: www.ofcom.org.uk

INDEPENDENT TELEVISION, RELIGIOUS PROGRAMMES ON

Religious Broadcasting on Independent Television includes programmes that are carried by the entire ITV network; programmes on Channels 4 and 5; items on the breakfast service, and programmes made by individual ITV companies for their own regional audiences. Most of the ITV network religious programmes are shown on Sundays. Regional religious programmes, usually transmitted during the week, though not exclusively so, include documentary series, religious magazine programmes and short reflective slots.

Anglican Advisers to the ITV Companies:
ANGLIA TELEVISION Canon Phillip McFadyen, The Vicarage, Ranworth, Norwich NR13 6HT
      Tel: 01603 270263
CARLTON-CENTRAL Mrs Anne Gatford, c/o Ven I. Gatford, Derby Church House, Full St, Derby DE1 3DR
Rt Revd John Saxbee, Bishop's House, Eastgate, Lincoln LN2 1QQ   *Tel:* 01522 534701
      Fax: 01522 511095
CARLTON-WESTCOUNTRY Mr Jeremy Dowling, Penrock, Church Path, Bude, Cornwall EX23 8LH
      Tel: 01288 352786
CHANNEL TELEVISION Very Revd Paul Mellor, Town Church Rectory, Cornet St, St Peter Port, Guernsey GY1 1BZ   *Tel:* 01481 720036
GRAMPIAN TELEVISION Vacancy
GRANADA TELEVISION Ven Alan Wolstencroft, 2 The Walled Garden, Swinton, Manchester M27 0FR   *Tel:* 0161 794 2401
TYNE TEES TELEVISION Canon Peter Strange, St Nicholas Cathedral, Newcastle-upon-Tyne NE1 1PF   *Tel:* 0191 232 1939

SANDFORD ST MARTIN (CHURCH OF ENGLAND) TRUST

The Trust was established in 1978. From the beginning its purpose was to recognize and promote excellence in religious broadcasting, and to encourage Christian involvement in television and radio at both national and local levels. Founded through the generosity and vision of a distinguished Anglican layman, the late Sir David Wills, its origins were Anglican, but it operates ecumenically, seeking to promote high quality programmes inspired by any of the major world religions as well as all Christian traditions. The Trust's principal activity is making annual awards for outstanding achievement in religious broadcasting. For the first 25 years of its existence awards were made at Lambeth Palace for radio and for television programmes in alternate years. In 1997 the Trust inaugurated a Religious Education award for an outstanding television programme, video or CD-rom in the field of religious education, and further awards were made in 1999, 2001 and 2003. Since 2003 the awards for television and radio programmes have been made annually, and this has allowed awards ceremonies to be held both at Lambeth Palace in London and also outside London, an innovation originally made for the Religious Education awards. Hence the 2003 television awards were made in Manchester, the 2004 radio awards in Glasgow, and the 2005 television awards in Bristol. 2006 saw the Trust sponsoring the first Readers of the Radio Times Award, which was presented at the annual television awards ceremony at Lambeth Palace. In 2007 the television awards were hosted by UTV in Belfast, with radio at Lambeth. The 2008 television awards were held at Lambeth Palace and chaired by Revd Dr Colin Morris. The third Radio Times

Readers' Award was presented for programme three in the series *Extreme Pilgrim*, while the Renegade Pictures/Storylab production *The Boys from Baghdad* (for BBC TV Current Affairs for BBC 2) won the Trust's Premier Award. To mark its 30th anniversary, the Trust hosted a lecture at the Royal Institute of British Architects where the distinguished Scottish composer James Macmillan addressed the issue of 'Religion and our Contemporary Culture', chaired by Dame Joan Bakewell. *Chairman* Rt Revd Nicholas Baines, Bishop of Croydon. *Hon Secretary* Mr David Craig, Church House, Great Smith St, London SW1P 3AZ *Tel:* 020 7898 1796
Fax: 020 7898 1797
email: SandfordSMT@c-of-e.org.uk
Web: www.sandfordawards.org.uk

WORLD ASSOCIATION FOR CHRISTIAN COMMUNICATION (WACC)

WACC is an organization of corporate and personal members who wish to give high priority to Christian values in the world's communication and development needs. It is not a council or federation of churches. The majority of members are communication professionals from all walks of life. Others include partners in different communication activities, and representatives of churches and agencies. It funds communication activities that reflect regional interests, and encourages ecumenical unity among communicators. As a professional organization, WACC serves the wider ecumenical movement by offering guidance on communication policies, interpreting developments in communications worldwide, discussing the consequences that such developments have for churches and communities everywhere but especially in the Third World, and assisting the training of Christian communicators. WACC publishes *Media Action*, an on-line newsletter; *Media Development*, a quarterly journal; *Media and Gender Monitor*, a bi-annual bulletin; and occasional books, monographs and brochures. It has 1002 members in 112 countries. UK members include the Anglican Communion Office, BBC Religious Programmes Dept, The Foundation for Christian Communication, Council for World Mission, Feed the Minds, Church of England Communications Unit, Independent Television Commission, and SPCK. *Gen Secretary* Revd Randy Naylor, 357 Kennington Lane, London SE11 5QY
Tel: 020 7582 9139
Fax: 020 7735 0340
email: wacc@wacc.org.uk
Web: www.wacc.org.uk

Theological Colleges and Regional Courses

THEOLOGICAL COLLEGES

Address and Telephone Number	Diocese	Principal or Warden
Cranmer Hall (St John's College), Durham DH1 3RJ *Tel:* 0191 334 3894 *Fax:* 0191 334 3501 *email:* sj-cranmer-hall@durham.ac.uk	Durham	Revd Dr David Wilkinson (*Principal*) (*Warden*) Revd Canon Anne Dyer
College of the Resurrection, Mirfield, W Yorks. WF14 0BW *Tel:* 01924 490441 *Fax:* 01924 492738 *email:* hscott@mirfield.org.uk	Wakefield	Revd Dr Joseph Kennedy
Oak Hill Theological College, Chase Side, Southgate, London N14 4PS *Tel:* 020 8449 0467 *Fax:* 020 8441 5996 *email:* mailbox@oakhill.ac.uk	London	Revd Dr Michael Ovey
Queen's Foundation for Ecumenical Theological Education, incorporating The Queen's College, Somerset Rd, Edgbaston, Birmingham B15 2QH (Ecumenical) *Tel:* 0121 454 1527 *Fax:* 0121 454 8171 *email:* enquire@queens.ac.uk	Birmingham	Revd Dr David Hewlett
Ridley Hall, Cambridge CB3 9HG *Tel:* 01223 741080 *Fax:* 01223 741081 *email:* ridley-pa@lists.cam.ac.uk	Ely	Revd Andrew Norman
Ripon College, Cuddesdon, Oxford OX44 9EX *Tel:* 01865 874404 *Fax:* 01865 875431 *email:* enquiries@ripon-cuddesdon.ac.uk	Oxford	Revd Canon Dr Martyn Percy
St John's College, Chilwell Lane, Bramcote, Nottingham NG9 3DS *Tel:* 0115 925 1114 *Fax:* 0115 943 6438 *email:* principal@stjohns-nottm.ac.uk	Southwell	Canon Dr Christina Baxter
St Stephen's House, 16 Marston St, Oxford OX4 1JX *Tel:* 01865 613500 *Fax:* 01865 613513 *email:* enquiries@ssho.ox.ac.uk	Oxford	Revd Canon Dr Robin Ward
Trinity College, Stoke Hill, Bristol BS9 1JP *Tel:* 0117 968 2803 *Fax:* 0117 968 7470 *email:* principal@trinity-bris.ac.uk	Bristol	Revd Canon George Kovoor
Westcott House, Jesus Lane, Cambridge CB5 8BP *Tel:* 01223 741000 *Fax:* 01223 741002 *email:* general-enquiries@westcott.cam.ac.uk	Ely	Revd Martin Seeley
Wycliffe Hall, Oxford OX2 6PW *Tel:* 01865 274200 *Fax:* 01865 274215 *email:* enquiries@wycliffe.ox.ac.uk	Oxford	Revd Dr Richard Turnbull
Theological Institute of the Scottish Episcopal Church, TISEC General Synod Office, 21 Grosvenor Crescent, Edinburgh EH12 5EE *Tel:* 0131 225 6357 *Fax:* 0131 346 7247 *email:* tisec@scotland.anglican.org	Edinburgh	Revd Canon Dr Michael Fuller
St Michael's College, Llandaff, Cardiff CF5 2YJ *Tel:* 029 2056 3379 *Fax:* 029 2083 8008 *email:* ps@stmichaels.ac.uk	Llandaff	Revd Dr Peter Sedgwick

REGIONAL COURSES	
Address and Telephone Number	Principal or Director
Carlisle and Blackburn Diocesan Training Institute (CBDTI) Church House, West Walls, Carlisle, Cumbria CA3 8UE *Tel:* 01228 522573 *Fax:* 01228 815400 *email:* admin@cbdti.org.uk	Revd Canon Tim Herbert
Eastern Region Ministry Course ERMC, Wesley House, Jesus Lane, Cambridge CB5 8BJ *Tel:* 01223 741026 *Fax:* 01223 741027 *email:* mcintosh@ermc.cam.ac.uk	Revd Dr Ian McIntosh
East Midlands Ministry Training Course Room C90, School of Education, University of Nottingham, Jubilee Campus, Wollaton Rd, Nottingham NG8 1BB *Tel:* 0115 951 4854 *Fax:* 0115 951 4817 *email:* EMMTC@Nottingham.ac.uk	Dr Clive Marsh
North East Oecumenical Course Ushaw College, Durham DH7 9RH *Tel:* 0191 373 7600 *Fax:* 0191 373 7601 *email:* neocoffice@neoc.org.uk	Revd Canon Trevor Pitt
Northern Ordination Course NOC, The Mirfield Centre, Stocksbank Rd, Mirfield WF14 0BW *Tel:* 01924 481925 *Fax:* 01924 492738	Mrs Christine McMullen (*acting Principal*)
Oxford Ministry Course OMC, Ripon College, Cuddesdon, Oxford OX44 9EX *email:* omc@ripon-cuddesdon.ac.uk	Revd Gerald Hegarty (*Associate Principal*)
St Mellitus College The Crypt, St George in the East, 16 Cannon St Rd, London E1 0HB *Tel:* 020 7481 9477 *Fax:* 020 7481 8907 *email:* principal@ntmtc.org.uk	Revd Dr Graham Tomlin
South East Institute for Theological Education Ground Floor, Sun Pier House, Medway St, Chatham, Kent ME4 4HF *Tel:* 01634 846683 *Fax:* 01634 819347 *email:* administrator@seite.co.uk (*office*); principal@seite.co.uk (*Principal*)	Revd Dr Jeremy Worthen
Southern North West Course St Werburgh's Rectory, 388 Wilbraham Rd, Chorlton-cum-Hardy, Manchester M21 0UH	Vacancy
Southern Theological Education and Training Scheme 19 The Close, Salisbury, Wilts. SP1 2EE *Tel:* 01722 424820 *Fax:* 01722 424811 *email:* swheway@stets.ac.uk	Revd Canon Vernon White
South West Ministry Training Course Amory Building, University of Exeter, Rennes Drive, Exeter EX4 4RJ *Tel:* 01392 264403 *email:* pauline@swmtc.org.uk	Revd Dr David Moss
Queen's Foundation for Ecumenical Theological Education, incorporating the West Midlands Ministerial Training Course The Queen's Foundation for Ecumenical Theological Education, Somerset Rd, Edgbaston, Birmingham B15 2QH *Tel:* 0121 454 1527 *Fax:* 0121 454 8171 *email:* enquire@queens.ac.uk	Revd Canon Dr David Hewlett
West of England Ministerial Training Course University of Gloucestershire, Francis Close Hall, Swindon Rd, Cheltenham GL50 4AZ *Tel:* 01242 532884 *email:* office@wemtc.freeserve.co.uk	Revd Canon Dr Michael Parsons

ORDAINED LOCAL MINISTRY SCHEMES RECOGNIZED BY THE HOUSE OF BISHOPS

Address and Telephone Number	Principal or Director
Canterbury OLM Scheme, Diocesan House, Lady Wootton's Green, Canterbury, Kent CT1 1NQ *Tel:* 01227 459401 *Fax:* 01227 450964 *email:* crace@diocant.org	Revd Christopher Race
Carlisle OLM Scheme, Church House, West Walls, Carlisle, Cumbria CA3 8UE *Tel:* 01228 522573 *Fax:* 01228 815400 *email:* admin@cbdti.org.uk	Revd Canon Tim Herbert
Coventry OLM Scheme	Revd Oliver Simon (questions about training should be referred to The Principal, Queen's Foundation)
Durham OLM Scheme, Board of Ministries and Training, Carter House, Pelaw Leazes Lane, Durham DH1 1TB *Tel:* 0191 374 6004 *email:* james.francis@durham.anglican.org	Revd Dr James Francis
Gloucester OLM, c/o, 4 College Green, Gloucester GL1 2LR *Tel:* 01452 410022 ext. 241 *Fax:* 01452 412474 *email:* dhoyle@glosdioc.org.uk	Revd Canon Dr David Hoyle (questions about training should be referred to The Principal, WEMTC)
Guildford Diocesan Ministry Course, Diocesan House, Quarry St, Guildford GU1 3XG *Tel:* 01483 790319 *email:* john.schofield@cofeguildford.org.uk	Revd John Schofield
Hereford Local Ministry Scheme, The Cottage, Bishop Mascall Centre, Lower Galdeford, Ludlow, Shropshire SY8 1RZ *Tel:* 01584 872822 *Fax:* 01584 877945 *email:* a.holding@hereford.anglican.org	Preb Graham Earney
Lichfield OLM Scheme, Ministry and Training Office, Backcester Lane, Lichfield WS13 6JJ *Tel:* 01543 306225 *Fax:* 01543 306229 *email:* elizabeth.jordan@lichfield.anglican.org	Revd Elizabeth Jordan
Lincoln OLM Scheme, Church House, The Old Palace, Lincoln LN2 1PU *Tel:* 01522 504020 *Fax:* 01522 504051 *email:* david.mccormick@lincoln.anglican.org / matthew.naylor@lincoln.anglican.org	Revd David McCormick
Liverpool OLM Scheme, The Rectory, Church Lane, Aughton, Ormskirk, Lancs. L39 6SB *Tel* and *Fax*: 01695 423204 *email:* martin.adams@liverpool.anglican.org	Revd Martin Adams
Manchester OLM Scheme, 354 Wilbraham Rd, Manchester M21 0UX *Tel:* 0161 828 1400 *email:* preiss@manchester.anglican.org	Revd Peter Reiss
Newcastle OLM Scheme, Church House, St John's Terrace, North Shields NE29 6HS *Tel:* 0191 270 4150 *Fax:* 0191 270 4101 *email:* r.bryant@newcastle.anglican.org	Revd Canon Richard Bryant
Norwich OLM Scheme, Emmaus House, 65 The Close, Norwich NR1 4DH *Tel:* 01603 611196 *email:* suewoan@norwich.anglican.org	Miss Sue Woan
Oxford OLM Scheme, Diocesan Church House, North Hinksey, Oxford OX2 0NB *Tel:* 01865 208252 *email:* beren.hartless@oxford.anglican.org	Revd Beren Hartless
St Edmundsbury and Ipswich Diocesan Ministry Course, DMC Office, Abbey House, Angel Hill, Bury St Edmunds IP33 1LS *Tel:* 01284 749435 *email:* sheila@stedmundsbury.anglican.org	Mrs Christine Amjad-Ali
Salisbury OLM Scheme, Ministry Development Team, Church House, Crane St, Salisbury SP1 2QB *Tel:* 01722 411944 *Fax:* 01722 411990 *email:* paul.overend@salisbury.anglican.org	Revd Dr Paul Overend
Wakefield Ministry Scheme, Church House, 1 South Parade, Wakefield, W Yorks. WF1 1LP *Tel:* 01924 493569 *Fax:* 01924 364834 *email:* ministry@wakefield.anglican.org	Revd Dr John Williams/ Revd Canon Dr John Lawson

ROYAL PECULIARS, THE CHAPELS ROYAL, ETC.

 ## Westminster Abbey

Description of Arms. Azure, a cross patonce between five martlets or; on a chief or France and England quarterly on a pale, between two roses, gules, seeded and barbed proper.

COLLEGIATE CHURCH OF ST PETER
The collegiate church of St Peter in Westminster, usually called Westminster Abbey, is a Royal Peculiar, and, as such, it is extra-provincial as well as extra-diocesan and comes directly under the personal jurisdiction of Her Majesty the Queen, who is the Visitor.

Throughout medieval times it was the Abbey Church of a great Benedictine Monastery, which was in existence at Westminster before the Norman Conquest. After the dissolution of the monastery in 1540 it became increasingly a great national shrine, where famous writers, poets, statesmen and leaders in the Church and State are buried. It is the Coronation Church, and in it also take place from time to time Royal weddings and many services on great occasions of a National or Commonwealth character. Daily, the Holy Communion is celebrated and Morning and Evening Prayers are said or sung.

THE VISITOR
The Sovereign

DEAN
Very Revd Dr John Hall, The Deanery, Westminster SW1P 3PA [2006]
Tel: 020 7654 4802
Fax: 020 7654 4883
email: john.hall@westminster-abbey.org
Web: www.westminster-abbey.org

CANONS OF WESTMINSTER
Sub-Dean and Archdeacon, Steward and Chronicler, and Rector of St Margaret's Church Revd A. Robert Wright, 5 Little Cloister, SW1P 3PL [1998]
Tel: 020 7654 4805
Fax: 020 7233 2072
email: robert.wright@westminster-abbey.org

Treasurer Revd Robert P. Reiss, 1 Little Cloister, London SW1P 3PL [2005]
Tel: 020 7654 4805
Fax: 020 7233 2072
email: robert.reiss@westminster-abbey.org

Canon Theologian Revd Dr Nicholas Sagovsky, 3 Little Cloister, London SW1P 3PL [2004]
Tel: 020 7654 4805
Fax: 020 7233 2072
email: nicholas.sagovsky@westminster-abbey.org

Canon Steward Revd Dr Jane Hedges, 2 Little Cloister, London SW1P 3EL [2006]
Tel: 020 7654 4805
Fax: 020 7233 2072
email: jane.hedges@westminster-abbey.org

MINOR CANONS
Revd Graeme S. P. C. Napier (*Minor Canon and Succentor*), 4b Little Cloister SW1P 3PL [2002]
Tel: 020 7222 5152
email: graeme.napier@westminster-abbey.org

Vacancy, 7 Little Cloister, SW1P 3PL [2005]
Tel: 020 7222 5152

CHAPLAIN
Sister Judith CSC, 3b Dean's Yard, SW1P 3NY
Tel: 020 7222 5152
email: judith.csc@westminster-abbey.org

PRIEST VICARS
Revd John Pedlar
Revd Philip Chester
Revd Peter Cowell
Revd Dr Paul Bradshaw
Revd Peter McGeary
Revd Alan Boddy
Revd David Peters
Revd Gavin Williams
Revd Garry Swinton
Revd Jonathan Goodall
Revd Dominic Fenton
Revd Alasdair Coles
Revd Paul Bagott
Revd Ralph Godsall

LAY OFFICERS
Receiver General & Chapter Sir Stephen Lamport, The Chapter Office, 20 Dean's Yard, London SW1P 3PA
Tel: 020 7654 4861
Fax: 020 7654 4914
email: stephen.lamport@westminster-abbey.org
Web: www.westminster-abbey.org

Organist and Master of the Choristers Mr James O'Donnell (*same address*)
Tel: 020 7654 4854
email: music@westminster-abbey.org

Registrar Mr Stuart Holmes (*same address*)
Tel: 020 7222 5152
email: stuart.holmes@westminster-abbey.org

Press and Communications Office (*same address*)
Tel: 020 7654 4890
email: press@westminster-abbey.org

Head of Communications Mr Duncan Jeffrey (*same address*)
Tel: 020 7654 4888
Fax: 020 7654 4891
email: duncan.jeffery@westminster-abbey.org

Surveyor of the Fabric Mr John Burton, 2b Little Cloister, SW1P 3PL
Tel: 020 7222 5152
email: john.burton@westminster-abbey.org

Librarian Dr Tony Trowles, The Muniment Room and Library, Westminster Abbey, London SW1P 3PL
Tel: 020 7654 4829
email: tony.trowles@westminster-abbey.org

Keeper of the Muniments Dr Richard Mortimer (*same address*)
Tel: 020 7654 4829
email: richard.mortimer@westminster-abbey.org

Headmaster of the Choir School Mr Jonathan Milton, Dean's Yard, London SW1P 3NY
Tel: 020 7222 6151
email: jonathan.milton@westminster-abbey.org

Legal Secretary Mr Christopher Vyse, The Chapter Office, 20 Dean's Yard, London SW1P 3PA
Tel: 020 7654 4885
email: chris.vyse@westminster-abbey.org

Auditor Mr David Hunt, Smith & Williamson, 1 Riding House St, London W1A 3AS
Tel: 020 7612 9194

Windsor

Description of Arms. The shield of St George, argent a cross gules, encircled by the Garter

THE QUEEN'S FREE CHAPEL OF ST GEORGE WITHIN HER CASTLE OF WINDSOR

A ROYAL PECULIAR
Founded by Edward III in 1348 and exempt from diocesan and provincial jurisdictions, the College of St George is a self-governing secular community of priests and laymen, the first duty of which is to celebrate Divine Service daily on behalf of the Sovereign, the Royal House and the Order of the Garter. Its present Chapel was founded by Edward IV in honour of Our Lady, St George and St Edward in 1475 and, with the cloisters and buildings annexed, is vested in the Dean and Canons. In it the Eucharist, Mattins and Evensong are sung or said daily and are open to all.

The Order of the Garter has its stalls and insignia in the Quire, where Knights and Ladies Companions are installed by the Sovereign. Beneath the Quire – the scene of many Royal funerals – are vaults in which lie the bodies of six monarchs. Elsewhere in the Chapel are the tombs of four others.

The College has its own school of 400 children, where it maintains twenty-four choristerships. It also awards an organ scholarship. A house for conferences has been established under the name of St George's House.

THE VISITOR
The Sovereign

DEAN
Rt Revd David Conner, The Deanery, Windsor Castle, Windsor, Berks. SL4 1NJ [1998]
Tel: 01753 865561

CANONS
Vice-Dean and Treasurer Canon John White, 4 The Cloisters, Windsor Castle [1982]
Tel: 01753 848787

Precentor and Chaplain in the Great Park Canon John Ovenden, Chaplain's Lodge, Windsor Great Park, Windsor, Berks. [1998]
Tel: 01784 432434

Steward Canon Dr Hueston Finlay, Chapter Office, The Cloisters [2004]
Tel: 01753 848888

MINOR CANONS
Succentor Revd Michael Boag, 3 The Cloisters, Windsor Castle [2003]
Tel: 01753 848737

Chaplain to St George's School Revd Andrew Zihni, 24 The Cloisters, Windsor Castle [2006]
Tel: 01753 848888

LAY OFFICERS
Chapter Clerk Miss Charlotte Manley, Chapter Office, The Cloisters, Windsor Castle [2003]
Tel: 01753 848888

Director of Music Mr Timothy Byram-Wigfield, 5 The Cloisters, Windsor Castle [2004]
Tel: 01753 848747

Clerk of Accounts Mr Nick Grogan, Chapter Office, The Cloisters *Tel:* 01753 848720	*Virger* Mr Vaughn Wright, 22 Horseshoe Cloister, Windsor Castle *Tel:* 01753 848727

Clerk of Works Mr Ian Poole, Clerk of Works Office, The Cloisters *Tel:* 01753 848888

Headmaster, St George's School Mr Roger Jones, St George's School, Windsor Castle
Tel: 01753 865553

Archivist and Librarian Vacancy
Tel: 01753 848724

Acting Warden, St George's House Canon Dr Hueston Finlay, St George's House, Windsor Castle *Tel:* 01753 848787

Domestic Chaplains to Her Majesty the Queen

Buckingham Palace Preb William Scott
Windsor Castle The Dean of Windsor

Sandringham Revd Jonathan Riviere

Chapels Royal

The Chapel Royal is the body of Clergy, Singers and Vestry Officers appointed to serve the spiritual needs of the Sovereign – in medieval days on Progresses through the Realm as well as upon the battlefields of Europe, as at Agincourt. Its ancient foundation is first century with the British Church: its latter day choral headquarters have been at St James's Palace since 1702 along with the Court of St James. Since 1312 the Chapel Royal has been governed by the Dean who, as the Ordinary, also exercises, along with the Sub-Dean, jurisdiction over the daughter establishments of Chapels Royal at the Tower of London and at Hampton Court Palace. Members of the public are welcome to attend Sunday and weekday services as advertised.

The Chapel Royal conducts the Service of Remembrance at the Cenotaph in Whitehall, with a Forces Chaplain in company, and combines with the choral establishment of the host abbey or cathedral on the occasion of Royal Maundy, under the governance of the Lord High Almoner and Sub-Almoner. Each Member of the College of thirty-six Chaplains to Her Majesty the Queen, headed by the Clerk and Deputy Clerk of the Closet, is required by Warrant to preach in the Chapel Royal once a year, and is visibly distinguished, along with the Chapel Royal, Forces and Mohawk Chaplains, by the wearing of a royal scarlet cassock.

Dean of the Chapels Royal
The Bishop of London

Sub-Dean
Preb William Scott
Chapel Royal, St James's Palace, London SW1A 1BL

CHAPEL ROYAL AND THE QUEEN'S CHAPEL, ST JAMES'S PALACE
Priests in Ordinary
Revd Richard Bolton
Canon Paul Thomas
Revd Stephen Young

Deputy Priests
Revd Roger Hall
Revd Hugh Mead
Revd Dennis Mulliner
Revd Mark Oakley

HAMPTON COURT PALACE
Chapel Royal, Hampton Court, East Molesey, Surrey KT8 9AU *Tel:* 020 8977 2762

Chaplain
Revd Denis Mulliner

HM TOWER OF LONDON
The Chaplain's Residence, London EC3N 4AP
Tel: 020 7709 0765
(includes the Chapels Royal of St John the Evangelist and St Peter ad Vincula.)

Chaplain
Revd Roger Hall

THE ROYAL CHAPEL OF ALL SAINTS, WINDSOR GREAT PARK
This is a Private Chapel and the property of the Crown within the grounds of the Royal Lodge. Attendance is restricted to residents and employees of the Great Park.

Chaplain
Canon John Ovenden, Chaplain's Lodge, Windsor Great Park, Windsor, Berks.
Tel: 01784 432434

College of Chaplains

The position of Royal Chaplain is a very ancient one. The College of Chaplains, the members of which as such must not be confused with the Priests in Ordinary, preach according to a Rota of Waits in the Chapels Royal. The College comprises the Clerk of the Closet (who presides), the Deputy Clerk of the Closet, and thirty-six Chaplains. When a vacancy in the list of chaplains occurs, the Private Secretary to Her Majesty the Queen asks the Clerk of the Closet to suggest possible names to Her Majesty. The duties of the Clerk of the Closet include the presentation of bishops to Her Majesty when they do homage before taking possession of the revenues of their Sees; and he also examines theological books whose authors desire to present copies to Her Majesty the Queen. He preaches annually in the Chapel Royal, St James's Palace.

CLERK OF THE CLOSET
Rt Revd Christopher Hill (*Bishop of Guildford*)

DEPUTY CLERK OF THE CLOSET
Preb William Scott

CHAPLAINS TO HER MAJESTY THE QUEEN
Canon Gavin Ashenden
Preb Paul Avis
Revd Hugh Bearn
Canon Raymond Brazier
Preb David Burgess
Canon John Byrne
Canon Gillian Carver

Canon Peter Calvert
Canon Andrew Clitherow
Canon Richard Cooper
Canon Alan Craig
Canon Ann Easter
Canon Christine Farrington
Canon Roger Hill
Revd Rose Hudson-Wilkin
Canon George Kovoor
Revd Edward Lewis
Canon Bill Matthews
Canon Paul Miller
Canon George Moffat
Revd William Mowll
Ven William Noblett
Canon Brian Osborne
Canon John Ovenden
Canon Stephen Palmer
Revd Jonathan Riviere
Canon Bruce Ruddock
Canon Christopher Samuels
Canon Christopher Smith
Canon Eric Stephenson
Canon John Sykes
Preb Pippa Thorneycroft
Canon Andrew Wingate
Canon Alison Woodhouse

Extra Chaplains
Canon Anthony Caesar
Canon Eric James
Canon Gerry Murphy
Revd John Robson
Revd John Stott

Royal Almonry

The Royal Almonry dispenses the Queen's charitable gifts and is responsible for the Royal Maundy Service each year, at which Her Majesty distributes Maundy money to as many men and as many women pensioners as the years of her own age.

HIGH ALMONER
Rt Revd Nigel McCulloch (*Bishop of Manchester*)

SUB-ALMONER
Preb William Scott
Chapel Royal, St James's Palace, London SW1A 1BL

The Queen's Chapel of the Savoy

Savoy Hill, Strand, London WC2R 0DA
Tel: 020 7379 8088
email: phillipchancellor@googlemail.com

CHAPEL OF THE ROYAL VICTORIAN ORDER
The Queen's Chapel of the Savoy was built as the principal chapel of a hospital for 'pouer, nedie people' founded by King Henry VII and finished in 1512 after his death. It is a private Chapel of Her Majesty the Queen in right of her Duchy of Lancaster, and Her Majesty appoints the chap-

lain. It is, therefore, a 'free' Chapel not falling within any diocesan jurisdiction.

On the occasion of his Coronation in 1937, the late King George VI commanded that the chapel of the Savoy should become the chapel of the Royal Victorian Order, an honour in the personal gift of the Sovereign, and the Chaplain of the Queen's Chapel is ex officio Chaplain of the Order. An ante-chapel, chaplain's office and robing room were constructed in 1958 to provide additional accommodation.

A new three-manual Walker organ was presented to the Chapel by Her Majesty the Queen in 1965.

Members of the public are welcome to attend services which are held on Sundays (11 a.m.) and weekdays (except August and September) with the exception of those for special or official occasions. The Chapel has a particularly fine musical tradition with a choir of men and boys.

CHAPLAIN
Revd Peter Galloway OBE

MASTER OF MUSIC
Mr Philip Berg FRCO, ARCM

VERGER
Mr Phillip Chancellor

HONORARY WARDENS
Mr Colin Brough
Mr Randall Edwards
Dr Roy Palmer
Mr Stephen White

Royal Memorial Chapel Sandhurst

Camberley, Surrey GU15 4PQ   *Tel:* 01276 412543
                              Fax: 01276 412097
The Royal Memorial Chapel Sandhurst, the Domestic Chapel of the Royal Military Academy Sandhurst, is also the Memorial Chapel of the officers of the Army.

Built in 1879 it was considerably enlarged between 1919 and 1921 (though some work was not completed until 1937) as a memorial to all Sandhurst-trained officers who gave their lives in the First World War.

Following the Second World War, the names of all officers of the Armies of the British Commonwealth who died in that conflict were inscribed on a Roll of Honour. A page of this book is turned at the commencement of the main Sunday service.

A Book of Remembrance containing the names of all former cadets who have been killed or died whilst serving since 1947 is kept in the Chapel of Remembrance, sometimes referred to as the South Africa Chapel.

All services are open to the public; contact the Chapel Office for a pass.

CHAPLAIN
Revd Timothy A. R. Cole

ASSISTANT CHAPLAIN
Revd Duncan Macpherson (CofS)

CHOIRMASTER AND ORGANIST
Mr Peter Beaven

CONSTITUTION OF THE CHAPEL COUNCIL
Maj-Gen D. J. Rutherford-Jones (*Chairman*); Revd T. A. R. Cole (*Deputy Chairman*); Maj. E. A. James-Park (*Secretary*); Revd S. Robbins (*Chaplain-General*); Gen Sir John Waters; Maj-Gen P. Everson; Maj-Gen Sir Simon Cooper; Brig M. Owen

The Royal Foundation of St Katharine

2 Butcher Row, London E14 8DS
                    Tel: 020 7790 3540
                    Fax: 020 7702 7603
         email: enquiries@stkatharine.org.uk
           Web: www.stkatharine.org.uk
St Katharine's, founded by Queen Matilda in 1147 originally adjacent to the Tower of London, is a charitable conference and retreat house at Limehouse in East London, between the City and Canary Wharf. It serves the Church of England, other churches and charities, offering an attractive setting for day or residential group meetings, seminars or retreats. Individuals from home and overseas are also welcome to stay. There are excellent facilities with residential en suite accommodation for 44 people and a choice of 7 meeting rooms. Daily worship is held in the re-ordered chapel.

Her Majesty Queen Elizabeth II is Patron of the Foundation.

MEMBERS OF THE COURT
The Viscount Churchill (*Chairman*)
Mr Benjamin Hanbury (*Treasurer*)
Rt Revd and Rt Hon Richard Chartres (*Bishop of London*)
The Countess of Airlie
Sir Stephen Lamport
Mrs Elizabeth Marshall
Preb David Paton (*Master*)

MASTER
Preb David Paton

Deans of Peculiars

The few present-day Deans of Peculiars are the residue of some 300 such office-holders in the medieval period, when the granting of 'peculiar' status, fully or partially exempting a jurisdiction from episcopal control, was commonly employed by popes and others to advance the interests of a particular institution, or limit the power of the bishops. Unlike the Royal Peculiars, the deaneries had little in common, and the privileges and duties of the individual posts ranged from nominal to significant. Most of the special provisions were brought to an end in the nineteenth century. But each Peculiar has interesting light to throw on a phase of Anglican or national history.

Battle
Very Revd Dr John Edmondson, The Deanery, Caldbec Hill, Battle, E. Sussex TN33 0JY [2005]
Tel and *Fax:* 01424 772693

Bocking
Very Revd Philip Need, The Deanery, Bocking, Braintree, Essex CM7 5SR (Bocking, Essex) [1996]
Tel: 01376 324887
01376 553092 (Office)
email: thedeanofbocking@tiscali.co.uk
Canon David Stranack, 12 Sandy Lane, Sudbury, Suffolk CO10 7HG (Hadleigh, Suffolk) [1999]
Tel: 07729 725227

Stamford
Rt Revd Dr Timothy Ellis (*Bishop of Grantham*)

The Deans of Jersey and Guernsey
The Deans of Jersey and Guernsey are very senior members of insular society. The Dean of Jersey ranks next after the Lieutenant Governor, Bailiff and Deputy-Bailiff and is an ex officio member of the States. The Dean of Guernsey ranks third after the Lieutenant Governor and Bailiff, and though not a member of the States of Deliberation (the Island Parliament) he is a member of the States of Election (which appoints Jurats to the Royal Court). From their respective positions the Deans are expected to offer spiritual and moral leadership.

References to these offices go back to the tenth century in the case of Guernsey and 1135 in the case of Jersey; the names of the Deans of Guernsey since 1295 and almost all the Deans of Jersey since 1180 are known. Since 1495 the Dean of Jersey has been appointed by the Crown. Traditionally Rector of one of the twelve Jersey parishes, since 1875 the Dean of Jersey has always been Rector of St Helier. The Dean of Guernsey has usually been Rector of the Town Church in St Peter Port, but this has not always been the case.

The Channel Islands were formerly part of the Diocese of Coutances, Normandy, but were transferred to Winchester by Papal Bull in 1500. Their annexation to the Diocese of Winchester was confirmed by Queen Elizabeth I in 1568 (they continued to be 'annexed to' rather than being 'part of' that diocese), but, the reformation having reached the islands in an extreme Calvinist Presbyterian form, the authority of Winchester and the office of Dean were little regarded until the Restoration in 1660.

The Deans are presidents of their respective Ecclesiastical Courts and have the right to grant marriage licences, including special licences and faculties. The Guernsey Ecclesiastical Court also retains its jurisdiction in matters concerning probate of realty and issues Letters of Administration. As the Bishop's Commissaries, the Deans carry out many of the duties performed in England by suffragan bishops and archdeacons, including instituting and inducting new incumbents.

Jersey
Very Revd Robert Key, The Deanery, David Place, St Helier, Jersey JE2 4TE
Tel: 01534 720001
Fax: 01534 720001
email: robert_f_key@yahoo.com

Guernsey and Dependencies
Very Revd Paul Mellor, The Deanery, Cornet St, St Peter Port, Guernsey GY1 1BZ [2003]
Tel: 01481 720036
Fax: 01481 722948
email: paul@townchurch.org.gg

Preachers at the Inns of Court

THE TEMPLE
Master Revd Robin Griffith-Jones, The Master's House, Temple, London EC4Y 7BB
Tel: 020 7353 8559
email: master@templechurch.com

Reader Revd A. H. Mead, 11 Dungarvan Ave, London SW15 5QU
Tel: 020 8876 5833

LINCOLN'S INN
Very Revd Derek Watson, 29 The Precincts, Canterbury CT1 2EP
Tel: 01227 865238

GRAY'S INN
Revd Roger Holloway OBE, Flat 6, 2 Porchester Gardens, London W2 6JL
Tel: 020 7402 4937

RELIGIOUS COMMUNITIES

Anglican Religious Communities

The roots of the Religious Life can be traced back to the Early Church in Jerusalem, and the subsequent traditions such as the Benedictines, Franciscans, etc., were flourishing in England until the Reformation when all were suppressed.

Most Anglican Communities were founded in the nineteenth century as a result of the Oxford Movement. There are now over sixty different Communities in the British Isles and throughout the Anglican Communion. Some are very small. Some have over 80 members.

Religious Communities are formed by men and women who feel called to seek God and live out their baptismal vows in a particular way under vows. There are some 1,200 Anglican men and women living this life in the United Kingdom.

PRAYER AND WORK

Each Community has its own history and character; some follow one of the traditional Rules, and others those written by more recent founders, but all have one thing in common: their daily life based on the work of prayer and living together centred in their Daily Office and the Eucharist. The work grows from the prayer, depending on the particular Community and the gifts of its members.

Some Communities are 'enclosed'. The members do not normally go out, but remain within the convent or monastery and its grounds, seeking and serving God through silence and prayer, study and work. Other Communities share the basic life of prayer and fellowship and may also be involved in work outside the Community.

HOSPITALITY

Most Community houses offer a place where people can go for a time of Retreat, either alone or with a group, for a day, several days, or occasionally for longer periods of time. They offer a place of quiet to seek God, grow in prayer and find spiritual guidance.

THE CALLING

People who feel called to the Religious Life and who wish to apply to a Community are usually aged between 21 and 45. They normally need to be physically and psychologically robust. Academic qualifications are not essential. There is a training period of about three years before any vows are taken.

Those who are considering a vocation are advised to visit Community houses to experience their particular ethos: further information is available from the houses or general enquiries may be made to The Communities Consultative Council at the address below.

Advisory Council on the Relations of Bishops and Religious Communities

This Council, to serve the two Provinces, is responsible to the Archbishops and the House of Bishops. Its functions are (1) to advise bishops upon (a) questions arising about the charters, constitutions and rule of existing Communities, (b) the establishment of new Communities, (c) matters referred to it by a diocesan bishop; (2) to advise existing Communities or their Visitors in any matters that they refer to it; (3) to give guidance to those who wish to form Communities. The Chairman and Convenor of the Council must be a diocesan bishop appointed by the Archbishops of Canterbury and York. The Council consists of at least 13 members, 3 of whom are nominated by the bishops and 10 elected by the Communities. Up to 5 additional members may be co-opted. The present membership is: *Chairman* (vacancy); *3 members nominated by the House of Bishops* Rt Revd David Walker (*Bishop of Dudley*) *Vice Chair* Rt Revd John Pritchard (*Bishop of Oxford*), Rt Revd Humphrey Southern (*Bishop*

of Repton); *10 members elected by the Communities* Sister Anita CSC, Sister Barbara Claire CSMV, Father Colin CSWG, Brother Damian SSF, Sister Mary Julian Gough CHC, Father Peter Allan CR, Sister Rosemary CHN, Sister Mary Stephen OSB, Abbot Stuart Burns OSB, Mother Ann Verena CJGS. *Co-opted* Rt Revd Andrew Burnham (*Bishop of Ebbsfleet*), Rt Revd Dominic Walker OGS (*Bishop of Monmouth*); *ARC Representative* Sister Joyce CSF. *Roman Catholic Observer* Sister Catherine McGovern OSF.

Hon Pastoral Secretary Preb William Scott, Sub-Dean of the Chapels Royal, Marlborough Gate, St James's Palace, London SW1A 1BG
Tel: 07941 470399
email: william.scott@royal.gsx.gov.uk

Administrative Secretary Miss Jane Melrose, Central Secretariat, Church House, Great Smith St, London SW1P 3AZ   *Tel:* 020 7898 1379
email: jane.melrose@c-of-e.org.uk

Anglican Religious Communities in England

ARC is an umbrella body of all members of Anglican Religious Communities. It acts to support its members by encouraging cooperation and the exchange of ideas and experiences which are relevant to Religious Life. The ARC Committee has members elected from four constituent groups: Leaders, General Synod Representatives, Novice Guardians and Professed Religious. An annual conference is held in September. Details of Communities may be found in the *Anglican Religious Life*, published by Canterbury Press, or, in an abbreviated form, at the following Web address: http://communities.anglican.org/
Chair BrStephen CR
Contact The Secretary, Anglican Religious Communities, c/o Miss Jane Melrose, Church House, Great Smith St, London SW1P 3AZ
email: info@arcie.org.uk
Registered Charity no. 1097586

Communities for Men

BENEDICTINE COMMUNITY OF ELMORE ABBEY
Church Lane, Speen, Newbury, Berks. RG14 1SA
Tel: 01635 33080
email: elmore.abbey@virgin.net

Conventual Prior Dom Simon Jarratt OSB

Visitor Rt Revd Dominic Walker OGS (*Bishop of Monmouth*)

Founded 1914. 1926–87 Nashdom Abbey. From 1987 Elmore Abbey. Resident community 4 monks. Oblate confraternity over 300. Various pastoral works undertaken including retreats. Fine theological library.

BENEDICTINE COMMUNITY AT BURFORD
See **Mixed Communities** page 255.

COMMUNITY OF OUR LADY AND ST JOHN
Alton Abbey, Alton, Hants. GU34 4AP
Tel: 01420 562145/563575
Fax: 01420 561691

Abbot Rt Revd Dom Giles Hill OSB

Visitor Rt Revd Michael Scott-Joynt (*Bishop of Winchester*)

Founded 1884. A community of Benedictine monks which undertakes retreats. Guest accommodation for 18 people. Other work includes the manufacture of altar wafers. The Seamen's Friendly Society of St Paul is managed from the Abbey. Day conference facilities and residential groups welcome: contact the Guestmaster.

COMMUNITY OF THE GLORIOUS ASCENSION
The Priory, Lamacraft Farm, Start Point, Kingsbridge, Devon TQ7 2NG *Tel:* 01548 511474
email: ascensioncga@fsnet.com

Prior Bro Simon CGA

Visitor Rt Revd Edward Holland

Founded in 1960, the emphasis of the Community is to share the fruits of the prayer, worship and common-living through everyday work and involvement with people. This is expressed in a variety of ways reflecting the individual members.

COMMUNITY OF THE RESURRECTION
House of the Resurrection, Mirfield, W Yorks. WF14 0BN *Tel:* 01924 494318
Fax: 01924 490489
email: community@mirfield.org.uk

Superior Fr George Guiver CR *Tel:* 01924 483301

Visitor Rt Revd Graham James (*Bishop of Norwich*)

Founded 1892, it undertakes teaching (theological college), retreats, missions and missionary works.

Theological College College of the Resurrection, Mirfield, W Yorks. WF14 0BW *Tel:* 01924 481900
Fax: 01924 492738
email: registrar@mirfield.org.uk

The Mirfield Centre offers a programme of day and evening events and small conferences as well as offering a meeting place for about 50 people. *Address* Mirfield Centre, College of the Resurrection, Mirfield, W Yorks. WF14 0BW
Tel: 01924 481920
Fax: 01924 492738
email: centre@mirfield.org.uk

Retreat House St Francis House, Hemingford Grey, Huntingdon, Cambs. PE18 9BJ
Tel: 01480 462185
email: hemingford@mirfield.org.uk

COMMUNITY OF THE SERVANTS OF THE WILL OF GOD
See **Mixed Communities** page 255.

COMPANY OF MISSION PRIESTS

Secretary Canon Peter Brown CMP, The Clergy House, Sawmill Lane, Durham DH7 8NS

Tel: 0191 378 0845

email:
peterandbrian@sawmill-lane.freeserve.co.uk

Visitor The Bishop of Horsham

Warden Father Pike CMP

Founded 1940. A society of apostolic life, a dispersed community of male priests of the Anglican Communion who, wishing to consecrate themselves wholly to the Church's mission, keep themselves free from the attachments of marriage and family, and endeavour to encourage and strengthen one another by mutual prayer and fellowship, sharing the vision of St Vincent de Paul of a priesthood dedicated to service, and in association with the whole Vincentian family.

EWELL MONASTERY

Water Lane, West Malling, Kent ME19 6HH
The Anglican Cistercian Order closed in 2004.

Web: www.arnesen.co.uk

(Fr Aelred Arnesen – for information)

See **PILSDON AT MALLING COMMUNITY, Organizations** page 000.

ORATORY OF THE GOOD SHEPHERD

Provincial Secretary Revd Peter Baldwin OGS, 1 Love Lane, Brightlingsea CO7 0QQ

Web: www.ogs.net

European Provincial Revd Fr Peter Ford OGS, Vicarage, Church Rd, Warton, Preston PR4 1BD

Tel: 01206 302407

email: pford@ogs.net

Founded in 1913 at Cambridge University. The Oratory is a society of professed priests and brothers working in four provinces: Europe, Australia, North America and Southern America. Members of the Oratory are bound together by a common Rule and discipline. They do not normally live together in community but meet for Chapter and are resident regularly for an annual Oratory Retreat and for Provincial Chapter (annual) and General Chapter (triennial). Members include bishops, parish priests, lecturers and missionaries. A two year period of probation precedes profession, and after ten years of annual profession, life vows may be taken. The Rule of the Oratory requires celibacy, the daily offices, where possible daily Eucharist, and a regular account of spending and direction of life. In addition, 'Labour of the Mind' is a characteristic of the Oratory and members are expected to spend time in study. Attached to the Oratory are Companions, lay, ordained, married and single, who keep a Rule of Life and are part of the Oratory family.

THE SOCIETY OF ST FRANCIS

The Society comprises a First Order for men (Society of St Francis) and women (*see* Community of St Francis, page 249), called to the Franciscan life under the vows of poverty, chastity and obedience; a Second Order of enclosed sisters (*see* Community of St Clare, page 249); and the Third Order for ordained and lay people, pledged to the spirit of the vows (*see* Third Order, Society of St Francis, page 256).

The Brothers of the First Order, founded in 1921, live a life of community centred on prayer and engage in active work especially in the areas of the poor and underprivileged. Three Friaries in this province (at Hilfield, Glasshampton and Alnmouth) have a ministry with guests and retreatants. The other centres of work are principally within a city context from which the brothers engage in various active ministries. Some work with educational institutions, conducting retreats and with parishes continues.

There are four Provinces: Europe, Australia/New Zealand, the Pacific Islands, and the Americas.

Minister General Brother Clark Berge SSF, Little Portion Friary, PO Box 399, Mt Sinai, NY 11766/0399

Tel: (+1) 631 473 0553

email: clarke.berge@s-s-f.org

European Province

Minister Brother Samuel SSF, The Friary, Hilfield, Dorchester, Dorset DT2 7BE   *Tel:* 01300 341345

email: ministerssf@franciscans.org.uk

Web: www.franciscans.org.uk

Assistant Minister Brother Benedict SSF (Hilfield)

Bishop Protector Rt Revd Michael Perham (*Bishop of Gloucester*)

Houses
All SSF-UK houses can be emailed using [name of the house] ssf@franciscans.org.uk e.g. hilfieldssf@franciscans.org.uk
Alnmouth *Tel:* 01665 830213/830660
Fax: 01665 830580
Canterbury *Tel:* 01227 479364/477025
Doncaster *Tel:* 01302 872240
Glasshampton *Tel:* 01299 896345
Fax: 01299 896083
Hilfield *Tel:* 01300 341345
Fax: 01300 341293
Holy Island *Tel:* 01289 389216
Fax: 07092 311104
Plaistow: Divine Compassion *Tel:* 020 7476 5189
Plaistow: St Matthias' Vicarage *Tel:* 020 7511 7848
Stepney *Tel:* 020 7247 6233
Walsingham *Tel:* 01328 820762

Australia and New Zealand Province
Minister Brother Alfred BoonKong ssf. *Houses:* Brisbane (QLD), Stroud (NSW), Kirikiriroa/ Hamilton (NZ)

Pacific Islands Province
Regional Minister, Papua New Guinea Brother Lawrence Hauje ssf. Houses: Haruro, Katerada, Koki, Ukaka

Regional Minister, Solomon Islands Brother Athanasius Faifu ssf. *Houses:* Auki, Busa, Hautambu: La Verna, Hautambu: Little Portion, Honiara, Kira Kira, Kohimarama, Temotu, Vuru

Province of the Americas
Minister Brother Jude ssf. *Houses:* Long Island, San Francisco

SOCIETY OF ST JOHN THE EVANGELIST
St Edward's House, 22 Gt College St, Westminster, London SW1P 3QA

Tel: 020 7222 9234
Fax: 020 7799 2641
email: superior@ssje.org.uk
guestmaster@ssje.org.uk

Superior Revd Fr Peter Huckle ssje
Assistant Superior Brother James Simon ssje

Visitor Rt Revd Dominic Walker ogs (*Bishop of Monmouth*)

Founded 1866, for men, clerical and lay. Engaged in retreats, missions and educational work.

SOCIETY OF THE SACRED MISSION
See **Mixed Communities** page 255.

Communities for Women

BENEDICTINE COMMUNITY OF ST MARY AT THE CROSS
Convent of St Mary at the Cross, Priory Field Drive, Edgware, Middx HA8 9PZ

Tel: 020 8958 7868
Fax: 020 8958 1920
email: nuns.osb.edgware@btclick.com

Abbess Mother Mary Thérèse Zelent osb

Visitor Rt Revd Peter Wheatley (*Bishop of Edmonton*)

We are a monastic community, founded in 1866, the heart of our vocation being in prayer. The Divine Office and the Eucharist are central to our life, love finding its expression in a care for those in need. Today we welcome many people to the abbey, who find a place of peace; all are offered Benedictine hospitality and given space for rest and renewal, with the opportunity to share in the community's worship. Since our foundation we have cared for disabled people; this work, now including the care of frail elderly people, continues today in Henry Nihill House, a modern residential/nursing care home. Easily accessible from the M1 and A1, we offer an excellent day conference centre, guest accommodation for rest or retreat, and space for Quiet Days. Women are welcome to come and share in the monastic experience for up to three months alongside the Community.

BENEDICTINE COMMUNITY OF ST MARY'S ABBEY
West Malling, Kent ME19 6JX   *Tel:* 01732 843309

Abbess Sister Mary David Best osb

Visitor Rt Revd John Waine

We are a monastic community of women following the Rule of St Benedict within the grounds of a Norman foundation of the 11th century. We offer the hospitality of our guest house to those who wish to share our worship and our silence.

BENEDICTINE COMMUNITY AT BURFORD
See **Mixed Communities** page 255.

COMMUNITY OF ALL HALLOWS
All Hallows Convent, Ditchingham, Norfolk

Postal Address Bungay, Suffolk NR35 2DT
Tel: 01986 892749
Fax: 01986 895838
email: allhallowsconvent@btinternet.com

Superior Mother Elizabeth cah

Visitor Rt Revd Graham James (*Bishop of Norwich*)

Founded 1855. Augustinian Visitation Rule.

Work and Houses at Ditchingham:
The Convent (*as above*)
All Hallows House: Guests, retreats and spiritual direction   *Tel:* 01986 892840
Holy Cross House: Guests, retreats and spiritual direction   *Tel:* 01986 894092
St Mary's Lodge: Silent house for self-catering retreats   *Tel:* 01986 892731
St Gabriel's Retreat and Conference Centre: 120 residential and 120 day visitors. Ample facilities for groups wishing to come for the day and be self-contained.   *Tel:* 01986 892133 (*Bookings*)
Ditchingham Day Nursery – up to 30 children
Tel: 01986 895091

All Hallows Country Hospital (accommodates 30 patients and up to 24 day care patients)
Tel: 01986 892728

All Hallows Nursing Home: 51-bed Nursing Home (including EMI patients)
Tel: 01986 892643

All Hallows House, Rouen Rd, Norwich NR1 1QT   *Tel:* 01603 624738

Guests, retreats and spiritual direction

COMMUNITY OF ST ANDREW
8/9 Verona Court, Chiswick, London W4 2JD
Tel: 020 8987 2799

Superior Revd Mother Lillian CSA

Visitor Rt Revd Richard Chartres (*Bishop of London*)

Founded 1861. Full membership of the Community consists of professed sisters who are ordained. Present number is seven.
   The fundamental ministry is the offering of prayer and worship, evangelism and pastoral work. This is carried out through parish and diverse ministries.

COMMUNITY OF ST CLARE
St Mary's Convent, Freeland, Witney, Oxon. OX29 8AJ   *Tel:* 01993 881225
Fax: 01993 882434
email: community@oscfreeland.co.uk

Abbess Sister Paula OSC

Bishop Protector Rt Revd Michael Perham (*Bishop of Gloucester*)

Founded 1950. Second Order of Society of St Francis. Contemplative and enclosed.

COMMUNITY OF ST DENYS
St Denys Retreat Centre, 2–3 Church St, Warminster, Wilts. BA12 8PG

Contact for Sisters only Revd Sister Frances Anne CSD

Leader (Until Oct 9 2008) Canon Alan Gill (priest associate); *Deputy Leader* Mrs June Watt (oblate)

Visitor Rt Revd David Stancliffe (*Bishop of Salisbury*)

Founded 1879. Undertakes mission work in the UK, parish work, retreats, hospital chaplaincy. One sister a priest. All members (men and women) have made a commitment to live according to the evangelical counsels, and a few have made life vows.

Community House St Denys Retreat Centre, 2–3 Church St, Warminster BA12 8PG
Tel: 01985 214824
email: stdenys@ivyhouse.org

Branch
Revd Sister Frances R. Cocker CSD

Flat 7, St Nicholas Hospital, St Nicholas Rd, Salisbury SP1 2SW   *Tel:* 01722 339761

COMMUNITY OF ST FRANCIS
Founded in 1905, the sisters of the First Order of the Society of St Francis, in the European Province and in the Province of the Americas, seek to live the gospel for today through lives of prayer, study and work. Prayer, together and alone, with the Eucharist having a central place, is the heart of each house and each sister's life. Five sisters are priests, and three live the solitary life. Study nurtures each sister's spiritual life and enables and enriches ministries. Work (voluntary or salaried) includes the practical running of the houses and a wide range of ministries, presently including hospitality, prison and hospital chaplaincy, spiritual direction, leading retreats and quiet days, parish work and missions, speaking and writing, counselling, caring for the homeless, providing support for families of those with a life-threatening illness, and nursing. In all this the sisters seek to follow Christ in the footsteps of Francis and Clare of Assisi, and in the spirit of humility, love and joy.

Minister General Sister Joyce CSF, Southwark
Tel and Fax: tbc
email: ministergeneralcsf@franciscans.org.uk

Minister Provincial, European Province Sister Helen Julian CSF, Compton Durville
Tel: 01460 249348
Fax: 01460 242360
email: ministercsf@franciscans.org.uk
Web: www.franciscans.org.uk

Bishop Protector Rt Revd Michael Perham (*Bishop of Gloucester*)

Houses St Alphege Community House, 1 Pocock St, London SE1 0BJ   *Tel:* 020 8671 9401
email: southwarkcs@franciscans.org.uk

St Francis Convent, Compton Durville, South Petherton, Somerset TA13 5ES
Tel: 01460 240473/241248
Fax: 01460 242360
email: comptondurvillecsf@franciscans.org.uk

The Vicarage, 11 St Mary's Rd, Plaistow, London E13 9AE   *email:* stmaryscssf@franciscans.org.uk

St Francis House, 113 Gillott Rd, Birmingham
B16 0ET   Tel: 0121 454 8302
            email: birminghamcsf@franciscans.org.uk

St Matthew's House, 25 Kamloops Crescent,
Leicester LE1 2HX   Tel: 0116 253 9158
            email: leicestercsf@franciscans.org.uk

Minister Provincial, Province of the Americas Sister
Jean CSF, St Francis House, 3743 Cesar Chavez
St, San Francisco CA 94110, USA
                        email: csfsfo@aol.com
            Web: www.communitystfrancis.org

Bishop Protector Rt Revd Bevi Edna (Nedi) Rivera,
Suffragan Bishop, Diocese of Olympia

COMMUNITY OF ST JOHN BAPTIST
Community of St John Baptist, The Priory,
2 Spring Hill Rd, Begbroke, Kidlington, Oxon.
OX5 1RX   Tel: 01865 855320
                                 Fax: 01865 855336
                        email: csjbteam@csjb.org.uk

Superior The Leadership Team: Sr Mary Stephen
CSJB, Sr Anne CSJB, Sr Ann Verena CJGS (co-opted)

Visitor Rt Revd John Prtchard, Bishop of Oxford

Chaplain Revd Lister Tonge

Founded 1852 to honour and worship Almighty
God and to serve him in works of charity. Undertakes mission and parish work, group quiet days,
private retreats and spiritual direction.

COMMUNITY OF ST JOHN THE DIVINE
St John's House, 652 Alum Rock Rd, Birmingham, W Midlands B8 3NS   Tel: 0121 327 4174
            email: csjdivine@btinternet.com

Leaders of the Community Sister Christine CSJD
and Sister Margaret Angela CSJD

Visitor Rt Revd David Urquhart, Bishop of
Birmingham

The Community was founded in 1848. The
underpinning of our life and work is a spirituality based on St John the Apostle of Love. Today,
as we continue to welcome people to test their
vocation in the Religious Life, we have considered the challenge of change. The small core
group of the Community has become the centre
for a growing circle of Associates and Along-
siders who share much of our life. Our vision is to
be a centre of prayer within the diocese, to exercise a ministry of hospitality to individuals and
groups, to offer a ministry of spiritual accompaniment and to be open to new ways in which
God might use us here, for example building
friendships with our Muslim neighbours.

COMMUNITY OF ST LAURENCE
Convent of St Laurence, 4 Westgate, Southwell,
Nottinghamshire NG25 0JH   Tel: 01636 814800

Warden Very Revd David Leaning

Founded 1874 in Norwich and moved to Belper
in Derbyshire in 1877. Moved to Southwell in
September 2001. Accommodation for visitors is
available in the Sacrista Prebend Retreat House
next door. (See Retreat Houses page 223)).

COMMUNITY OF ST MARY THE VIRGIN
St Mary's Convent, Challow Rd, Wantage, Oxon.
OX12 9DJ   Tel: 01235 763141
            email: conventsisters@csmv.co.uk
                       guestwing@csmv.co.uk

Superior Mother Winsome CSMV

Visitor The Bishop of Oxford, Rt Revd John
Pritchard

Founded in 1848. We are called to respond to our
vocation in the spirit of the Blessed Virgin Mary:
'Behold, I am the handmaid of the Lord. Let it be
to me according to your word.' Our common life
is centred in the worship of God through the
Eucharist, the daily Office and in personal
prayer. From this all else flows. For some it
will be expressed in outgoing ministry in
neighbourhood and parish, or in living
alongside those in inner city areas. For others,
it will be expressed in spiritual direction,
preaching and retreat giving, or in creative work
in studio and press. Sisters also live and work
among the elderly at St Katharine's House, our
Care Home for elderly people in Wantage. The
Community has a share in the nurturing and
training of a small indigenous Community in
Madagascar. It was also in India and South
Africa for many years. Involvement with both
these countries remains through 'Wantage
Overseas'. Our links with South Africa are
maintained by the groups of Oblates and
Associates living there. There are also groups of
Oblates and Associates in England. At St Mary's
Convent there is a Guest Wing for those who
wish to spend time in rest, retreat and silence
within the setting of a religious community.

366 High St, Smethwick B66 3PD
                                 Tel: 0121 558 0094
            email: csmv.smethwick@btinternet.com

116 Seymour Rd, Harringay, London N8 0BG
                        Tel and Fax: 020 8348 3477
            email: wantage-os@fireflyuk.net

St Katharine's House, Ormond Rd, Wantage
OX12 8EA (Home for the Elderly.)
                                 Tel: 01235 767380
            email: sisters.stkatharines@btconnet.com

COMMUNITY OF ST PETER
St Columba's House, Maybury Hill, Woking, Surrey GU22 8AB   *Tel:* 01483 750739
email: reverendmother@stpetersconvent.co.uk
Web: stcolumbashouse.org.uk

Superior Mother Lucy Clare CSP

Visitor Rt Revd David Walker (*Bishop of Dudley*)

Founded in 1861 for mission work and nursing. The Sisters are now dispersed, but meet together at least monthly. Sister Angela and Sister Georgina Ruth have a small house in Woking and work within St Columba's House, the Sisterhood's retreat and conference centre. Reverend Mother Lucy Clare, our Ordained Sister, lives in Worcester Park and is developing links with the Korean community in that area. Sister Caroline Jane lives in Staines, is a community psychiatric nurse and also works in a local parish in Thorpe. Sister Rosamond and Sister Margaret Paul are at St Mary's Convent and Nursing Home in Chiswick.

COMMUNITY OF ST PETER, HORBURY
St Peter's Convent, Dovecote Lane, Horbury, Wakefield, W Yorks. WF4 6BD   *Tel:* 01924 272181
email: stpetersconvent@btconnect.com

Reverend Mother Mother Robina CSPH

Visitor The Bishop of Wakefield

Benedictine in spirit. Undertakes a variety of pastoral ministries and retreat work.

COMMUNITY OF THE COMPANIONS OF JESUS THE GOOD SHEPHERD
The Priory, 2 Spring Hill Rd, Begbroke, Kidlington, Oxon. OX5 1RX   *Tel:* 01865 855326

Superior Sister Ann Verena CJGS

Visitor Rt Revd Dominic Walker OGS (*Bishop of Monmouth*)

Founded 1920. Undertakes work with the elderly, lay and OLM training, quiet days and retreats, spiritual direction.

COMMUNITY OF THE GLORIOUS ASCENSION
Prasada, Quartier Subrane, 83440 Montauroux, France   *Tel and Fax:* 00 334 94 47 74 26
email: cga.prasada@orange.fr
Web: www.cgaprasada.com

The Sisters are called to unite a monastic community life with work alongside other people. At Prasada they welcome visitors who seek a peaceful environment in which to find refreshment. Guests and local English-speaking people have the opportunity to use the chapel for private prayer and to join the Sisters for Eucharist and Divine Office both on Sundays and weekdays.

COMMUNITY OF THE HOLY CROSS
Holy Cross Convent, Rempstone Hall, Ashby Rd, Rempstone, Nr Loughborough LE12 6RG
Tel: 01509 880336
Fax: 01509 881812
Web: www.holycrosschc.org.uk
email: chc.rempstone@webleicester.co.uk

Mother Superior Revd Mother Mary Luke CHC

Visitor Rt Revd Dr David Hope

Founded in 1857 for mission work but later adopted the Rule of St Benedict. All the work, centred on the daily celebration of the Divine Office and the Eucharist, is done within the Enclosure.

The Sisters contribute articles on spirituality and Christian unity to various publications and disseminate these via their web site. A variety of prayer and greeting cards are also produced by the Sisters. The Community provides for Quiet Days for individuals and groups, and there is limited residential accommodation for those wishing to make longer retreats.

COMMUNITY OF THE HOLY FAMILY
St Mary's Abbey, Swan St, West Malling, Kent ME19 6JX   *Tel:* 01732 849016

Visitor Rt Revd John Hind (*Bishop of Chichester*)

The spirit of the educational work begun by the Foundress, Mother Agnes Mason, continues in the Diocese of Chichester through the operation of the Mother Agnes Trust. The Charity has enabled the creation of an extensive educational resource centre, incorporating a substantial and growing theological library, known as 'The Magnet', at St Leonard's-on-Sea. The remaining Sister lives gratefully with the Sisters at the Abbey.

COMMUNITY OF THE HOLY NAME
Convent of the Holy Name, Morley Rd, Oakwood, Derby DE21 4QZ   *Tel:* 01332 671716
Fax: 01332 669712
email: bursarsoffice@tiscali.co.uk
web: www.chnderby.org

Superior Sr Monica Jane CHN

Visitor Rt Revd John Inge

Founded 1865. Undertakes mission and retreat work. Guests received.

Branch Houses
Holy Name House, Ambleside Rd, Keswick, Cumbria CA12 4DD   *Tel:* 01768 772998

St Peter's Vicarage, 177 Hartley Rd, Radford, Nottingham NG7 3DW   Tel: 0115 978 5101
Cottage 5, Lambeth Palace, London SE1 7JU
Tel: 020 7898 5407
64 Allexton Gardens, Welland Estate, Peterborough PE1 4UW   Tel: 01733 352077

Overseas
Lesotho Convent of the Holy Name, PO Box 22, Ficksburg 9730, RSA   Tel: 00266 22400249

Zululand Convent of the Holy Name, P/B 806, Melmoth 3835, RSA   Tel: 00273 54502892

COMMUNITY OF THE SACRED PASSION
Mother House: Convent of the Sacred Passion, 22 Buckingham Rd, Shoreham-by-Sea, W Sussex BN43 5UB   Tel: 01273 453807
email: communitysp@yahoo.co.uk
Superior Mother Philippa CSP

Visitor Rt Revd Ian Brackley (*Bishop of Dorking*)
Founded 1911. An order which combines prayer and mission work in varying forms. In England the sisters continue their life of prayer at the Mother House and a house in Clapham. Their active work is a response to the needs of the people among whom they live and so keeps developing. The Community withdrew from Tanzania in June 1991, leaving behind a community of more than ninety Tanzanian women known as the Community of St Mary. This community is still given support by CSP as is the Kwamkono Polio Hostel which was founded by CSP.

COMMUNITY OF THE SERVANTS OF THE CROSS
St Katharine's House, Ormond Rd, Wantage OX12 8EA   Tel: 01235 763535
Superior Mother Angela CSC
Visitor Rt Revd John Hind (*Bishop of Chichester*)
Warden and Chaplain Revd J. Lyon
Augustinian Rule. The sisters are now in retirement.

COMMUNITY OF THE SERVANTS OF THE WILL OF GOD
See **Mixed Communities** page 255.

COMMUNITY OF THE SISTERS OF THE CHURCH
St Michael's Convent, 56 Ham Common, Richmond, Surrey TW10 7JH
Tel: 020 8940 8711 and 020 8948 2502
Fax: 020 8948 5525
email: info@sistersofthechurch.org.uk
Web: www.sistersofthechurch.org.uk

Superior Sister Anita CSC
email: anita@sistersofthechurch.org

Visitor Rt Revd Peter Price (*Bishop of Bath and Wells*)

Founded 1870 and has a modern rule, based on the original, expressing a life rooted in prayer and worship, which flows into an active ministry through hospitality, pastoral and social justice work, spiritual direction and counselling.
Other Houses in the UK
82 Ashley Rd, St Paul's Bristol BS6 5NT
Tel: 0117 941 3268
Fax: 0117 908 6620
112 St Andrew's Rd North, St Annes-on-Sea, Lancs. FY8 2JQ   Tel: 01253 728016
10 Furness Rd, West Harrow, Middx HA2 0RL
Tel and Fax: 020 8423 3780
Well Cottage, Upper Street, Kingsdown, Nr Deal, Kent CT14 8BH   Tel: 01304 361601
Fax: 01304 360994

Novitiate
St Gabriel's, 27a Dial Hill Rd, Clevedon, North Somerset BS21 7HL   Tel and Fax: 01275 872 586

Main Houses of Overseas Provinces
Sister Linda Mary CSC, Provincial
29 Lika Drive, Kempsey, NSW 2440, Australia
Sister Marguerite Mae CSC, Provincial
St Michael's House, 1392 Hazelton Boulevard, Burlington, Ontario L7P 4V3, Canada
Sister Kathleen CSC, Provincial
Tetete ni Kolivuti, Box 510, Honiara, Solomon Islands

COMMUNITY OF THE SISTERS OF THE LOVE OF GOD
Convent of the Incarnation, Fairacres, Parker St, Oxford OX4 1TB   Tel: 01865 721301
Fax: 01865 250798
email: sisters@slg.org.uk
Guest Sister guests@slg.org.uk

Reverend Mother Sister Margaret Theresa SLG

Visitor Rt Revd Michael Lewis (*Bishop of Cyprus and the gulf*)

A contemplative community with a strong monastic tradition founded in 1906, which seeks to witness to the priority of God and to respond to the love of God – God's love for us and our love for God. We believe that we are called to live a substantial degree of withdrawal, in order to give ourselves to a spiritual work of prayer which, beginning and ending in the praise and worship of God, is essential for the peace and well-being of the world. Through offering our lives to God within the Community and through prayer and daily life together, we seek to deepen our relationship with Jesus Christ and one another. The Community has always drawn upon the spirituality of Carmel; life and prayer in silence and solitude is a very important dimension in our vocation. The Community also draws from other traditions, and our Rule is not specifically Carmelite. Another important ingredient is

General

an emphasis on the centrality of Divine Office and Eucharist together in choir, inspired partly by the Benedictine way of life.

SLG Press publishes pamphlets on spirituality and prayer.
SLG Press, Convent of the Incarnation, Fairacres, Parker St, Oxford OX4 1TB   *Tel:* 01865 241874
Fax: 01865 250798
email: editor@slgpress.co.uk
Web: www.slgpress.co.uk

ORDER OF THE HOLY PARACLETE
St Hilda's Priory, Sneaton Castle, Whitby, N Yorks. YO21 3QN   *Tel:* 01947 602079
Fax: 01947 820854
email: ohppriorywhitby@btinternet.com
Web: www.ohpwhitby.org

Superior Sister Dorothy Stella OHP

Visitor Most Revd John Sentamu

Founded in 1915 and based on the Rule of St Benedict. Main undertaking: prayer, pastoral work, retreats, conferences, missions, parish work.

Residential Conference Centre Sneaton Castle Centre, Whitby, N Yorks. YO21 3QN
Tel: 01947 600051
Fax: 01947 603490
email: sneaton@globalnet.co.uk
Web: www.sneatoncastle.co.uk
Accommodation and facilities for large and small groups for parish activities, conferences and educational courses.

Branch Houses
Beach Cliff, 14 North Promenade, Whitby, N Yorks. YO21 3JX   *Tel:* 01947 601968
St Oswald's Pastoral Centre, Woodlands Drive, Sleights, Whitby, N Yorks. YO21 1RY
Tel: 01947 810496
Fax: 01947 810759
email: ohpstos@globalnet.co.uk
9 Cranbourne St, Spring Bank, Hull HU3 1PP
Tel: 01482 586816
Fax: 01482 213114
email: ohphull@cranhull.karoo.co.uk
1A Minster Court, York YO1 7JD
Tel: 01904 620601
email: ohpyork@onetel.net.uk

Overseas
OHP Sisters Poste Restante, Piggs Peak, Swaziland   *Tel:* 00 268 4371514
email: jdean@africaonline.sz

AIDS awareness, home for abused girls and AIDS orphans.

Convent of the Holy Spirit, PO Box AH 9375, Ahinsan, Kumasi, Ashanti, Ghana
Tel: 00233 242 203 432
email: ohpjac@yahoo.com

Fostering indigenous vocations, undertaking pastoral work and eye clinic ministry.

PRIORY OF OUR LADY, WALSINGHAM
Priory of Our Lady, Walsingham, Norfolk NR22 6ED   *Tel:* 01328 820340 (Reverend Mother);
01328 820901 (Sisters and Guest Sister)

Superior Mother Mary Clare SSM
email: mothermaryclare@ssmargaret.com

Bursar Sister Alma Mary SSM
email: alma@ssmargaret.com

Visitor Rt Revd Peter Wheatley (*Bishop of Edmonton*)

Autonomous house of the Society of St Margaret. Sisters are involved in the ministry of healing and reconciliation in the Shrine, the local parishes and the wider Church. They are also available to pilgrims and visitors and work in the Sacristy, the Shrine Shop and Education Department in the Shrine. A Guest House is available. Guests are welcome for short periods of rest, relaxation and retreat. All bookings to be made through the Guest Sister.

ST SAVIOUR'S PRIORY
18 Queensbridge Rd, London E2 8NS
Tel: 020 7739 6775 (Guest bookings)
020 7739 9976 (Sisters)
email: ssmpriory@aol.com
Web: www.stsaviourspriory.org.uk

Superior Revd Sr Helen Loder SSM

Visitor Rt Revd Dominic Walker OGS (*Bishop of Monmouth*)

Autonomous convent of the Society of St Margaret, working as staff members (lay or ordained) in various parishes, dance workshops, complementary therapy, with the homeless, etc.; retreats and individual spiritual direction. The Priory has a few guest rooms and facilities for individual private retreats as well as excellent facilities for small group meetings.

SISTERS OF BETHANY
7 Nelson Rd, Southsea, Hants. PO5 2AR
Tel: 023 9283 3498
email: ssb@sistersofbethany.org.uk
Web: www.sistersofbethany.org.uk

Superior Mother Gwenyth SSB

Visitor Rt Revd Trevor Wilmott (*Bishop of Basingstoke*)

Founded 1866 for hospitality, retreat work and prayer for Christian Unity. The Sisters are available for leading quiet days and retreats, as spiritual directors, and also to give talks on prayer. People are welcome to come individually or as groups to spend time in silence and prayer. It is possible to accommodate a few residential guests, or groups of up to 24 for the day. A reference is required for guests applying to stay for the first time.

SISTERS OF CHARITY
237 Ridgeway, Plympton, Plymouth PL7 2HP
Tel: 01752 336112
email: plymptonsisters@tiscali.co.uk

Superior Revd Mother Elizabeth Mary SC

Visitor Rt Revd Robert Evens (*Bishop of Crediton*)

Founded 1869. The Rule is based on that of St Vincent de Paul. We assist as required in parish work and in intercessory prayer, and maintain a nursing home.

Branch Houses
St Vincent's Nursing Home, Plympton, Plymouth PL7 1NE
Tel: 01752 336205
Carmel, 7a Gress, Isle of Lewis HS2 0NB
Tel: 01851 820734

SOCIETY OF ALL SAINTS SISTERS OF THE POOR
All Saints Convent, St Mary's Rd, Oxford OX4 1RU
Tel: 01865 249127
Fax: 01865 726547
email: admin@socallss.co.uk
Guests' email: guestsister@socallss.co.uk

Community Leader Sister Helen Mary ASSP

Visitor Rt Revd Bill Ind

Founded in London 1851. Works of the Society: St John's Residential Home for the Elderly, St Mary's Rd, Oxford OX4 1QE
Tel: 01865 247725
Fax: 01865 247920
email: admin@st-johns-home.org

Guest House (single, twin and double accommodation available). Also conference facilities for groups of up to about 12, weekdays, daytime only. Enquiries regarding visits, private retreats and conferences welcomed. Telephone and fax numbers as shown above for All Saints' Convent.

The Society is associated with:
Helen and Douglas House; The Porch Steppin' Stone Centre; All Saints Embroidery

SOCIETY OF ST MARGARET
St Margaret's Convent, Hooke Hall, 250 High St, Uckfield RN22 1EN
Tel: 01825 766808
Fax: 01825 763474
email: motherssm@hotmail.com

Superior Sister Cynthia Clare SSM

Visitor Rt Revd John Hind (*Bishop of Chichester*)
Founded 1855 and undertakes nursing work, runs guest and retreat accommodation, also parish work. Sisters available for spiritual guidance and quiet attentions.

Branch House St Mary's Convent and Nursing Home, Burlington Lane, Chiswick, London W4 2QE (guest house for elderly ladies and nursing home for geriatric and handicapped ladies)
Tel: 020 8994 4641
Fax: 020 8995 9796

Superior Sister Jennifer Anne SSM

Visitor Rt Revd John Hind (*Bishop of Chichester*)

Has a Residential Home for elderly retired ladies; and Nursing Home for those needing full-time nursing care.

Overseas St Margaret's Convent (*semi-autonomous*), 157 St Michael's Rd, Polwatte, Colombo 3, Sri Lanka

A home for the aged, a retreat house and a children's home.

Sister Superior Sister Chandrani SSM
Tel: 00 94 11 2320692
Visitor Rt Revd Duleep de Chickera (Bishop of Colombo)
Branch House
St John's Home, 133 Galle Rd, Moratuwa, Sri Lanka.
Tel: 00 94 11 2645304

Independent Convents of the Society St Margaret
St Saviour's Priory, 18 Queensbridge Rd, London E2 8NS
Leader Sister Helen SSM
Tel: 020 7739 6775
email: ssmpriory@aol.com
Priory of Our Lady, Walsingham, Norfolk, NR22 6ED
Superior Mother Mary Clare SSM
Tel: 01328 820340
email:
mothermaryclaressm@tiscali.co.uk
St Margaret's Convent, 17 Highland Park St, Boston, MA 02119, USA
Superior Sister Carolyne SSM
Tel: 00 1 617 445 8961
Fax: 00 1 617 445 7120
email: ssmconvent@ssmbos.com

SOCIETY OF THE PRECIOUS BLOOD
Burnham Abbey, Lake End Rd, Taplow, Maidenhead, Berks. SL6 0PW   *Tel:* 01628 604080
email: burnhamabbey@btinternet.com
Web: www.burnhamabbey.org

Superior The Revd Mother SPB

Visitor Rt Revd Stephen Cottrell (*Bishop of Reading*)

Founded 1905 and based on Rule of St Augustine. Contemplative and exists for the purpose of perpetual intercession for the Church and for the world.

Overseas Independent Daughter House Priory of Our Lady Mother of Mercy, Masite, PO Box MS 7192, Maseru 100, Lesotho

Dependent House of the Overseas House St Monica's House of Prayer, 46 Green St, West End, Kimberley 8301, Cape, RSA

SOCIETY OF THE SACRED CROSS
Tymawr Convent, Lydart, Monmouth, Gwent NP25 4RN   *Tel:* 01600 860244
email: tymawrconvent@btinternet.com
Web: www.churchinwales.org.uk/tymawr

Superior Sister Mary Jean SSC

Visitor Rt Revd Dominic Walker OGS (*Bishop of Monmouth*)

Founded in 1914 at St George's, Chichester; four sisters felt called to the monastic, contemplative life, which was established in Wales in 1923. The community lives a life of prayer based on silence, solitude and learning to live together, under vows of poverty, chastity and obedience, with a modern rule, Cistercian in spirit. It is possible for women and men, married or single, to experience our life of prayer by living alongside the community for periods longer than the usual guest stay. There are facilities for retreatants and small groups. The extended community consists of companions, oblates and associates. The community is dedicated to the crucified and risen Lord as the focus of its life and the source of the power to live it. The setting in the unspoilt rural border country of Wales plays a very real part in the spirituality of the community.

SOCIETY OF THE SACRED MISSION
See **Mixed Communities** page 255.

Mixed Communities

BENEDICTINE COMMUNITY AT BURFORD
The Community of Benedictine nuns and monks is currently re-locating to a new monastery in Worcestershire. Until the new building is ready, the community is living in rented accommodation. At the time of going to press, the address and telephone number are unavailable but the email remains the same.
email: information@burfordosb.org.uk

Abbot Rt Revd Stuart Burns OSB
email: abbot@burfordosb.org.uk

Visitor Rt Revd Stephen Oliver

Burford Priory is home to a community of Benedictine nuns and monks. By a common life of prayer, manual work and study they try to create an atmosphere of stillness and silence in which the Community and its guests are enabled to be open and receptive to the presence of God.

While the recitation of the Office and celebration of the Eucharist constitute the principal work of the Community, the ministry of hospitality, the care of the grounds (which comprise a large organic kitchen garden, formal gardens and woodland), the maintenance of the historic Priory buildings, and the income-generating crafts provide a variety of manual work for the members of the Community and those guests who wish to share in it.

The Priory seeks to be a place of encounter and reconciliation. The early concern of the Community was to pray for Christian unity; and the Community enjoys links with Baptist, Lutheran, Orthodox and Roman Catholic communities. This ecumenism has broadened to include dialogue with people of other faiths, particularly those with a monastic tradition, and those who are seeking a spiritual way, either within or outside an established religious tradition.

COMMUNITY OF THE SERVANTS OF THE WILL OF GOD
Monastery of the Holy Trinity, Crawley Down, Crawley, W Sussex RH10 4LH   *Tel:* 01342 712074
email: brother.andrew@cswg.org.uk
Father Superior Revd Fr Colin CSWG
Visitor Rt Revd John Hind (*Bishop of Chichester*)
Founded 1953 for men (clerical and lay). Women are now received also. Contemplative. Retreats and conferences. The Community has also founded a charitable trust for promoting the Christian tradition of contemplative life and prayer within the Church.

SOCIETY OF ST FRANCIS, THIRD ORDER

One of the three Orders of the Society of St Francis (see also Communities for Men, page 247; Communities for Women, page 249). The Third Order is made up of women and men, lay and ordained, single and married, seeking to live out Franciscan ideals in the ordinary walks of life. There are over 2100 Tertiaries in the European Province; there are four other Provinces: Africa, the Americas, Australia and New Zealand.

Minister General Revd Dorothy Brooker TSSF, 16 Downing St, Pirimai, Napier, New Zealand
email: dmbrook@clear.net.nz

Minister Provincial Ven Richard Bird TSSF, 32 Bristol Rd, Bury St Edmunds IP33 2DL
Tel: 01284 723810
email: ministertssf@franciscans.org.uk
Web: www.tssf.org.uk

SOCIETY OF THE SACRED MISSION

Founded 1893. A religious community engaged in educational, pastoral and missionary work. The Society is divided into Provinces:

Province of Europe
Visitor The Bishop of Southwark, Rt Revd Tom Butler

Provincial Fr Jonathan Ewer SSM
The Well, Newport Rd, Willen MK15 9AA
Tel: 01908 242741
email: j_ewer@yahoo.com
Houses
St Antony's Priory, 74 Claypath, Durham DH1 1QT
Tel: 0191 384 3747
email: durham.ssm@which.net

1 Linford Lane, Milton Keynes, Bucks. MK15 9DL
Tel: 01908 663749
St Clare's Bungalow, Sneaton Castle, Whitby YO21 3QN
Tel: 01947 820361
email: ssmmbro@aol.com

Southern Province
Visitor The Archbishop of Melbourne, Most Revd Philip Freier
Provincial Fr Matthew Dowsey SSM
PO Box 149, Flemington, VIC 3031
email: ssmprov@tpg.com.au
Houses St John's Priory, 14 St John's St, Adelaide, S Australia 5000
St Michael's Priory, 75 Watsons Rd, Diggers Rest, Victoria, Australia 3427

Southern African Province
Provincial Fr Michael Lapsley SSM
SSM House, 33 Elgin Rd, Syband Park, Cape Town 7700, RSA
email: michael.lapsley@attglobal.net
SSM Priory, PO Box 1579, Maseru 100, Lesotho, Southern Africa *email:* priorssm@ilesotho.com

Organizations | **PART 4**

Classified List of Organizations Included in this Section

Animal Welfare
Anglican Society for the Welfare of Animals

Art, Architecture
Art and Christianity Enquiry
Art and Sacred Places
Christian Arts
Church Maintenance Trust
Church Monuments Society
Ecclesiological Society
Friends of Friendless Churches
Historic Churches Preservation Trust
York Glaziers' Trust

Bell-ringing
Ancient Society of College Youths
Central Council of Church Bell Ringers
Society of Royal Cumberland Youths

Bible Study
BRF
Bible Society
Lord Wharton's Charity
SASRA
Scripture Gift Mission International
Scripture Union
Vacation Term for Biblical Study

Blind People
Blind, Royal National Institute for the
Guild of Church Braillists
St John's Guild

Church Buildings
Friends of Friendless Churches
Greater Churches Group
Historic Churches Preservation Trust
Incorporated Church Building Society
Marshall's Charity
Vergers, Church of England Guild of

Church Societies – General
Additional Curates Society
Affirming Catholicism
Anglican Association
Association of English Cathedrals
Cathedral and Church Shops Association
Cathedral Libraries and Archives Association
Cathedrals Administration and Finance
    Association
Catholic Group in General Synod
Church of England Flower Arrangers
    Association
CPAS (Church Pastoral Aid Society)
Church Society
Church Union
Churches' Advertising Network
Modern Churchpeople's Union

Open Synod Group
Parish and People
Society for the Maintenance of the Faith
Society of the Faith (Inc)
Unitas – The Catholic League

Church Societies – Specific
Anglican Fellowship in Scouting and Guiding
Anglican Mainstream
Association of Diocesan Registry Clerks
    (Southern Province)
Baptismal Integrity
Christian Evidence Society
CHRISM
Church House Deaneries Group
Church of England Record Society
College of Readers
Community of Aidan and Hilda
Day One Christian Ministries
Diocesan Clergy Chairs' Forum
Ecumenical Society of the Blessed Virgin
    Mary
Forward in Faith
Foundation for Church Leadership
Guild of St Leonard
Guild of Servants of the Sanctuary
Reform
Royal Martyr Church Union
Society of King Charles the Martyr
Society of Mary
Third Province Movement

Clergy Associations
Anglo-Catholic Ordination Candidates'
    Fund
Association of Black Clergy
Association of Hospice and Palliative Care
    Chaplains
Association of Ordinands and Candidates for
    Ministry
College of Health Care Chaplains
English Clergy Association
Federation of Catholic Priests
Fellowship of Word and Spirit
Industrial Mission Association
Lesbian and Gay Clergy Consultation
Retired Clergy Association
School Chaplains' Conference
Society of Catholic Priests
Society of Ordained Scientists
Society of the Holy Cross
Unite Clergy and Faith Workers
See also **Professional Groups**

Consultancy
Christians Abroad
Grubb Institute
Living Stones

Coordinating Bodies
Church of England Evangelical Council
Churches' Funerals Group
Churches Main Committee
Ecumenical Coalition of Women Ministers
Evangelical Alliance
National Association of Diocesan Advisers for
  Women's Ministry
Religious Education Council of England and
  Wales
Universities and Colleges Christian Fellowship

Counselling
Anglican Association of Advisers in Pastoral
  Care and Counselling
Lesbian and Gay Christian Movement
Relate
True Freedom Trust

Deaf People
British Deaf Association
Deaf People, Royal Association for
National Deaf Church Conference
RNID

Defence, Disarmament, Pacifism
Anglican Pacifist Fellowship
Commonwealth War Graves Commission
Council on Christian Approaches to Defence and
  Disarmament

Diocesan Associations *see* pages 321–323

Drama
Actors' Church Union
Radius

Ecumenism
Anglican and Eastern Churches Association
Anglican–Lutheran Society
Churches' Group on Funeral Services
Churches Main Committee
Fellowship of St Alban and St Sergius
Fellowship of St Thérèse of Lisieux
International Ecumenical Fellowship
Nikaean Club
Nikaean Ecumenical Trust
Order of Christian Unity
Society of Archbishop Justus Ltd
Society of St Willibrord

Education
Archbishop's Examination in Theology
Association of Church College Trusts
Bloxham Project
Christian Education
Culham Institute
Lincoln Theological Institute
Mirfield Centre
North of England Institute for Christian
  Education
RE Today Services
Religious Education Council of England and
  Wales

Royal Alexandra and Albert School
Royal Asylum of St Ann's Society
St George's College, Jerusalem
St Hild and St Bede Trust
Scripture Union in Schools
Trinity Foundation for Christianity and Culture
United Church Schools Trust
Woodard Corporation, the (Woodard Schools)

Evangelism
Church Army
College of Evangelists

Family
CARE
Family Life and Marriage Education
  Network
Fellowship of St Nicholas
FWA (Family Welfare Association)
Mothers' Union
St Michael's Fellowship

Finance
Anglican Stewardship Association
Christian Ethical Investment Group
Ecclesiastical Insurance Office PLC
Ecumenical Council for Corporate Responsibility
Number One Trust Fund

Grant-Making Bodies
All Saints Educational Trust
Bristol Clerical Education Society
Church of England Clergy Stipend Trust
Church Pastoral Aid Society Ministers in
  Training Fund
Cleaver Ordination Candidates' Fund
Culham Educational Foundation
Elland Society Ordination Fund
Foundation of St Matthias
Hockerill Educational Foundation
Keswick Hall Charity
Newton's Trust
Ordination Candidate Funds (General)
Pilgrim Trust
Queen Victoria Clergy Fund
Revd Dr George Richards' Charity
Sarum St Michael Educational Charity
St Christopher's College Educational Trust
St Gabriel's Trust
St George's Trust
St Luke's College Foundation
St Mary's College Trust
St Peter's Saltley Trust
See also **Welfare**

Health, Healing and Medicine
Acorn Christian Healing Foundation
Association of Hospice and Palliative Care
  Chaplains
Burrswood
Cautley House
Centre for Health and Pastoral Care
Christian Healing Mission

Christian Medical Fellowship
College of Health Care Chaplains
Guild of Health
Guild of Pastoral Psychology
Guild of St Barnabas
Guild of St Raphael
Harnhill Centre of Christian Healing
Pilsdon Community
Richmond Fellowship
St Luke's Hospital for the Clergy

Inter Faith, Religions
Council of Christians and Jews
INFORM
Inter Faith Network
World Congress of Faiths

Internet
COIN: Christians on the Internet
Society of Archbishop Justus Ltd

Libraries *see pages 323–328*

Marriage
Anglican Marriage Encounter
Broken Rites
Family Life and Marriage Education Network
Relate

Ministry
CHRISM
Diaconal Association of the Church of England
Diakonia
Distinctive Diaconate
MODEM
Royal Naval Licensed Readers' Society

Ministry, Women
Ecumenical Coalition of Women Ministers
Li Tim-Oi Foundation
Society for the Ministry of Women in the Church
WATCH

Mission
Bible Society
Careforce
Christian Witness to Israel
CPAS (Church Pastoral Aid Society)
Church's Ministry Among Jewish People
Greenbelt Festivals
London City Mission
Mersey Mission to Seafarers
Mission to Seafarers, The
SASRA
Scripture Gift Mission
Scripture Union in Schools
Society for Promoting Christian Knowledge
Student Christian Movement
Trinitarian Bible Society
Universities and Colleges Christian Fellowship

Mission Overseas
Africa Inland Mission International

All Nations Christian College
Church Mission Society
Crosslinks
Feed the Minds
Highbury Centre, The
Intercontinental Church Society
Interserve
Korean Mission Partnership
Leprosy Mission
Melanesian Mission
Mid-Africa Ministry
Mozambique and Angola Anglican Association
   (MANNA)
New England Company
OMF International (UK)
Overseas Bishoprics Fund
Oxford Mission
Papua New Guinea Church Partnership
Reader Missionary Studentship Association
Selly Oak Centre for Mission Studies
South American Mission Society
Southern Africa Church Development Trust
Tearfund
USPG: Anglicans in World Mission
World Vision

Music
Archbishops' Certificate in Church Music
Choir Benevolent Fund
Choir Schools Association
Church Music Society
Gregorian Association
Guild of Church Musicians
Hymn Society of Great Britain and Ireland
Jubilate Group
Morse-Boycott Bursary Fund
Plainsong and Medieval Music Society
Royal College of Organists
Royal School of Church Music

Overseas
Christian Aid
Christians Abroad
Churches' Commission for International
   Students
Farnham Castle, International Briefing and
   Conference Centre
United Nations Association (UNA–UK)
Womenaid International
World Vision

Patronage Trusts *see pages 328–329*

Prayer, Meditation, Retreats
Archway
Association for Promoting Retreats
Confraternity of the Blessed Sacrament
Friends of Little Gidding
Guild of All Souls
Guild of St Leonard
Julian Meetings, The
Julian of Norwich, Shrine of Lady
Pilsdon at Malling Community

Organizations

Retreat Association
Sarum College
Servants of Christ the King
Society of Retreat Conductors
Women's World Day of Prayer

Professional Groups
Actors' Church Union
Anglican Association for Social Responsibility
Association of Christian Teachers
Association of Christian Writers
Association of Ordinands and Candidates for
    Ministry
Christian Arts
Christians at Work
Church House Deaneries' Group
Church Schoolmasters' and School Mistresses'
    Benevolent Institution
Deans' Conference
Deans' Vergers' Conference
Ecclesiastical Law Society
Guild of Pastoral Psychology
Homes for Retired Clergy
Industrial Mission Association
Librarians' Christian Fellowship
Amicus Clergy and Church Workers
National Association of Diocesan Advisers for
    Women's Ministry
Society of Retreat Conductors
Vergers, Church of England Guild of
See also **Clergy Associations**

Publishing, Print Media
BRF
Book Aid
Feed the Minds
Rebecca Hussey's Book Charity
Scripture Union
Society for Promoting Christian Knowledge
Trinitarian Bible Society

Renewal
Keswick Convention
Sharing of Ministries Abroad (SOMA)

Research
Arthur Rank Centre
CARE
Centre for the Study of Christianity and
    Sexuality
Christian Research
Churches' Fellowship for Psychical and
    Spiritual Studies
Culham Institute
Latimer Trust
Rural Theology Association
St George's House, Windsor
Urban Theology Unit
William Temple Foundation

Rural Affairs
Arthur Rank Centre
Rural Theology Association

Scholarship and Science
Alcuin Club
Canterbury and York Society
Christian Evidence Society
Ecclesiastical Law Society
Faith and Thought
Henry Bradshaw Society
Latimer House
Liddon Trust
National Archives, The
Philip Usher Memorial Fund
Pusey House
Society for Liturgical Study
Society for Old Testament Study
Society of Ordained Scientists
Vacation Term for Biblical Study

Social Concern
Age Concern England
Careforce
Changing Attitude
Christian Socialist Movement
Church Action with the Unemployed
Church Housing Trust
English Churches Housing Group
Lesbian and Gay Christian Movement
Livability
mediawatch–uk
Metropolitan Visiting and Relief
    Association
National Council for Social Concern
Order of Christian Unity
Pilsdon Community
St Pancras Housing
Samaritans

Training
Administry (now Matters Arising)
Anglican Marriage Encounter
Anglican Stewardship Association
Association of Church Fellowships
Bridge Pastoral Foundation
Christian Education
Christians at Work
College of Preachers
GFS Platform for Young Women
Industrial Christian Fellowship
Paradox Ministries
RE Today Services
Student Christian Movement
William Temple Foundation

Travel, Pilgrimage
Accueil, Rencontre, Communauté UK
British Isles and Eire Airport Chaplains' Network
Pilgrim Adventure
Pilgrims' Association
Walsingham, Shrine of Our Lady of

Welfare
Almshouse Association
Beauchamp Community
Bromley and Sheppard's Colleges

Organizations

Came's Charity
Church of England Soldiers', Sailors' and
    Airmen's Clubs
Church of England Soldiers', Sailors' and
    Airmen's Housing Association
Church Schoolmasters' and School Mistresses'
    Benevolent Institution
Church Welfare Association
College of St Barnabas
Community Housing and Therapy
Compassionate Friends, The
Corporation of the Sons of the Clergy
Crosse's Charity
Diocesan Institutions of Chester, Manchester,
    Liverpool and Blackburn
Elizabeth Finn Care
Family Welfare Association
Frances Ashton's Charity
Friends of the Clergy Corporation
Friends of the Elderly
Homes for Retired Clergy
House of St Barnabas in Soho
Keychange
Langley House Trust
MACA – (Mental After Care Association)
Partis College
Pyncombe Charity
Revd Dr George Richards' Charity
Rainer
St Michael's Fellowship
Samaritans
Seamen's Friendly Society of St Paul
Shaftesbury Society

Society for the Assistance of Ladies in
    Reduced Circumstances
Society for the Relief of Poor Clergymen
Society of Mary and Martha
YMCA
YWCA England and Wales

Worship
Alcuin Club
Praxis
Prayer Book Society

Youth
Accueil, Rencontre, Communauté UK
Barnardo's
Boys' Brigade
Campaigner Ministries
Children's Society
Church Lads' and Church Girls'
    Brigade
Fellowship of St Nicholas
Frontier Youth Trust
GFS Platform for Young Women
Girlguiding UK
Girls' Brigade
Lee Abbey Household Communities
Lee Abbey International Students' Club
Rainer
St Christopher's Fellowship
Scout Association
Shaftesbury Homes and 'Arethusa'
Urban Saints (formerly Crusaders)
William Temple House

ORGANIZATIONS

ORGANIZATIONS

The following list of societies and organizations with importance for the Church of England includes many that are specifically Anglican, others that are inter-denominational, and others without religious affiliation.

The inclusion of an organization is for the purposes of information and is not to be taken as implying acceptance of the objects of the organization by the Editor and Publishers of the *Year Book* or by the General Synod.

A classified list of organizations is provided in the preceding pages. **Diocesan Associations** (in support of overseas provinces and dioceses), **Libraries**, and **Patronage Trusts** are grouped together at the end of the section. *See also* Part 3 (General Information).

Accueil, Rencontre, Communaute UK (ARC UK)
ARC UK is a charity that organizes summer projects in which young people from across Europe give guided tours in their native language to visitors to churches. In so doing we seek to turn tourists into pilgrims through devotional tours in which visitors have the chance to engage, question and wonder. Our projects aim to enable churches in their ministry of welcome and education, ecumenical links and youth involvement. ARC UK is part of a network of associated organizations which organizes such projects throughout Europe. We are always interested to hear from those who might like to participate on one of our projects, or churches who might be interested in hosting a project. We are supported in our work by our Patron, the Bishop of Woolwich, the Rt Revd Christopher Chessun. *President:* Stephen Stavrou. *Secretary:* Anna Dorofeeva. *Recruitment Officer:* Christa Neudecker. *Treasurer:* Louise Lamb, Westcott House, Jesus Lane, Cambridge, CB5 8BP   *Tel:* 07528 930 966 (Mobile)
email: arc_england@yahoo.co.uk
Web: www.encounterarc.org.uk

Acorn Christian Healing Foundation
Founded originally as the Acorn Christian Healing Trust in 1983 by Bishop Morris Maddocks and his wife Anne to see the Church and nation renewed in the service of Christ the Healer, believing that every person has the right to receive the best care and attention that will enable them to grow into wholeness. Acorn offers all Christian churches a variety of teaching and training resources in Christian healing. Many of these are conducted at Whitehill Chase, Acorn's resource centre in Hampshire, where a weekly open day is held every Tuesday (except August) in conjunction with a service of healing. Quiet Days are held bi-monthly, normally on Thursdays (except in August), and include three devotional talks and a midday service with the opportunity for personal prayer and reflection. 'Deeper Healing Days' are also run bi-monthly and these are days of prayer for inner healing concluding with a communion service. The well-established Christian Listener courses range from a short introductory unit through to a twelve-session course, taught by trained tutors. There are 500 Acorn trained voluntary tutors throughout the country who teach listening skills to local church members. They in turn offer these resources in their church, home, workplace, local schools and wider community. Acorn has identified priority listening areas for rural and inner city deprived areas, a schools programme for youth, listening to Aids in Africa and reconciliation in Northern Ireland. Whitehill Chase is also available as a retreat centre and for church groups to hold meetings and conferences. Registered Charity no. 1080011. *Patron:* The Archbishop of Canterbury. *Director:* Revd Dr Russ Parker, Whitehill Chase, High St, Bordon, GU35 0AP   *Tel:* 01420 478121
Fax: 01420 478122
email: info@acornchristian.org
Web: www.acornchristian.org

Actors' Church Union
Founded 1899, members and associates serve those engaged in the performing arts through their interest, their action – often in association with other related bodies – and their prayers. Additionally, more than two hundred honorary chaplains serve all members of the profession in theatres, studios and schools at home and overseas. As well as spiritual counsel and practical advice, material help is given when possible. Through the Children's Charity, for example, funds are available for theatrical parents facing difficulties with the costs of their children's education. *President:* Rt Revd Jack Nicholls. *Senior Chaplain:* Revd Rob Gillion, St Paul's Church, Bedford St, Covent Garden, London, WC2E 9ED
Tel and Fax: 020 7240 0344
email: actors-church.union@tiscali.co.uk
Web: www.actorschurchunion.org

Additional Curates Society
Founded in 1837 to help maintain additional curates in poor and populous parishes and especially in new areas. The Society also fosters vocations to the priesthood. *General Secretary:*

Revd Darren Smith. *Chairman:* Canon J. Winston. *Vice Chair:* Rt Revd A. Robinson. *Treasurer:* Revd M. Lane, Gordon Browning House, 8 Spitfire Rd, Birmingham, B24 9PB   *Tel:* 0121 382 5533
Fax: 0121 382 6999
email: info@additionalcurates.co.uk
Web: www.additionalcurates.co.uk

Affirming Catholicism

A movement within the Church of England and the Anglican Communion, formed in 1990. 'The object of the Foundation shall be the advancement of education in the doctrines and the historical development of the Church of England and the Churches of the wider Anglican Communion, as held by those professing to stand within the catholic tradition' (extracted from the Trust Deed). Its purposes are to promote theological thinking about the contemporary implications of Catholic faith and order; to further the spiritual growth and development of clergy and laity; to organize or support lectures, conferences and seminars; to publish or support books, tracts, journals and other educational material; to provide resources for local groups meeting for purposes of study and discussion. *Chair:* Revd Jonathan Clark. *Administrator:* Lisa Martell, St Matthew's House, 20 Great Peter St, London, SW1P 2BU   *Tel:* 020 7222 5166
Fax: 020 7233 0255
email: administrator@affirmingcatholicism.org.uk
Web: www.affirmingcatholicism.org.uk

Age Concern England

Age Concern cares about all older people and believes later life should be fulfilling and enjoyable. For too many this is impossible. As the leading charitable movement in the UK concerned with ageing and older people, Age Concern finds effective ways to change that situation. Nationally, we take a lead role in campaigning, parliamentary work, policy analysis, research, specialist information and advice provision, publishing and training in the care of older people. Where possible we enable older people to solve problems themselves, providing as much or as little support as they need. Locally, Age Concern provides community-based services such as lunch clubs, day centres and home visiting. These services are made possible through the work of many thousands of volunteers. Innovative programmes promote healthier lifestyles and provide older people with opportunities to give the experience of a lifetime back to their communities. Age Concern is dependent on donations and legacies. The helpline is open seven days a week from 7 a.m. to 7 p.m. *Director General:* Mr Gordon Lishman, Astral House, 1268 London Rd, London, SW16 4ER
Tel: 020 8765 7200/0800 009966 (Helpline)
Fax: 020 8765 7211
email: ace@ace.org.uk
Web: www.ageconcern.org.uk

Aim International

(Formerly known as Africa Inland Mission)
An evangelical, interdenominational and international Mission founded in 1895. It has 900 members working in 19 countries in Africa and the adjacent islands. Aim (founded as Africa Inland Mission) is an evangelical Christian mission agency serving across Africa, and ministering to Africans living around the world. We work in partnership with the African church to reach Africa's unreached people with the good news of Jesus Christ, and to develop leaders for the fast-growing church. Aim's goal is to have Christ-centred churches amongst all African people. It has particular interest in the training of leaders and is increasing its work in urban areas, with children and responding to HIV/AIDS. *International Director:* Lanny Arenson. *UK Director:* Andrew Chard, Halifax Place, Nottingham, NG1 1QN   *Tel:* 0115 983 8120
Fax: 0115 941 7338
email: uk@aimeurope.net
Web: www.aimeurope.net

Alcuin Club

Founded in 1897 to promote the study of liturgy, the Alcuin Club has a long and proud record of publishing both works of scholarship and practical manuals. Publications include collections, tracts and a new series of liturgy guides designed to accompany Common Worship. It also publishes, in conjunction with GROW, a series of Joint Liturgical Studies which has won wide acclaim. Members pay an annual subscription and receive new titles on publication. *President:* Rt Revd Michael Perham. *Chairman:* Canon Donald Gray. *Treasurer:* Mr John Collins. *Secretary:* Mr Jack Ryding. *Editorial Secretary:* Revd Christopher Irvine, Ty Nant, 6 Parc Bach, Trefnant, LL16 4YE   *Tel:* 01745 730585
email: alcuinclub@gmail.com
Web: www.alcuinclub.org.uk

All Nations Christian College

All Nations (ANCC) came into existence in 1971 following the merger of three Bible colleges. Whilst interdenominational in character, around 20 per cent of its students are members of the Anglican Communion. The College exists to train students primarily for cross-cultural ministries. With up to 180 international students of about 30 nationalities, as well as a respected international team of tutors, the community studying and socializing life is vibrant and challenging. Students can follow a three-month, one-year or two-year Biblical and Intercultural studies course with a profound missiological emphasis. In addition to the popular Cert HE, Dip HE and BA (Hons) programmes, there is now a Certificate in the Arts and Intercultural Studies. The College also offers an intensive 10–week course in cross-cultural studies and personal development called 'en route'. There is also practical training in

church work as well as the development of technical skills helpful for work in developing countries or new cultures. At postgraduate level there are opportunities to do a PG Cert, PG Dip or MA in Contemporary Mission Studies. M Phil and Ph D are also offered. Many of the students are married, some bring children and benefit from the creche provided whilst parents attend lectures. About half of the students are from the UK, 25 per cent from continental Europe and 25 per cent from the rest of the world, a truly international mix. For details of programmes, apply to the Admissions Registrar. ANCC, Easneye, Ware, SG12 8LX   *Tel:* 01920 461243
Fax: 01920 462997
email: info@allnations.ac.uk
Web: www.allnations.ac.uk

All Saints Educational Trust

Home/EU applicants: personal scholarships for intending teachers in degree-level education and/or professional training, particularly teachers of religious education, home economics and other subjects; those studying dietetics, food and nutrition, and public health promotion. Postgraduate qualifications relevant to continuing professional development may be considered. Financial constraint must in all cases be demonstrated. Not assisted: school pupils, students of counselling, engineering, law, medicine, ordination, social work, commercial hospitality. Commonwealth applicants: scholarships for full-time, taught postgraduate study in the UK only (taught Master's programmes favoured; doctorates and PGCE programmes will not normally be funded). Corporate awards: given for imaginative new projects that will support the classroom teacher and build up the profession, preference being given to those aimed at enhancing the Church's contribution to education. Closing dates for receipt of completed applications for 2009–10: Home/EU personal scholarships and Corporate Awards: 9 March 2009; Commonwealth Scholarships: 6 April 2009; Member of the Association of Church College Trusts (see separate entry). *Clerk to the Trust:* Mr S. P. Harrow, St Katharine Cree Church, 86 Leadenhall St, London, EC3A 3DH   *Tel:* 020 7283 4485
Fax: 020 7621 9758
email: clerk@aset.org.uk
Web: www.aset.org.uk

Almshouse Association

(National Association of Almshouses)
Is concerned with the preservation and extension of over 1,750 member Almshouse Trusts. A number of major almshouses have a resident Anglican chaplain, or appoint Anglican clergy as Master or Custos of the foundation. It advises members on any matters concerning almshouses and the welfare of the elderly and aims to promote improvements in almshouses, to promote study and research into all matters affecting almshouses, and to make grants or loans to members. It also keeps under review existing and proposed legislation affecting almshouses and when necessary takes action, and encourages the provision of almshouses. *Chairman:* Mr Simon Pott. *Director:* Mr Anthony De Ritter. *Deputy Director:* Mr Trevor Hargreaves. *Assistant Director:* Mr T. P. Wild, Billingbear Lodge, Maidenhead Rd, Wokingham, RG40 5RU   *Tel:* 01344 452922
Fax: 01344 862062
email: naa@almshouses.org
Web: www.almshouses.org

Ancient Society of College Youths

Established 1637. An international bell-ringing society based in the City of London, the College Youths seeks to recruit leading ringers from any part of the world in which English style change-ringing is practised. Members are active in supporting ringing for church services throughout the world. The Society maintains a charitable fund for the maintenance of bells, fittings and towers of churches where it has a historic association. *Secretary:* Mr John N. Hughes-D'Aeth, 9 Falstaff Gardens, St Albans, AL1 2AL
Tel: 020 7760 4660/01727 863470
Fax: 020 7760 1111
email: secretary@ascy.co.uk
Web: www.ascy.org.uk

Anglican and Eastern Churches Association

Founded 1864 to promote mutual understanding of, and closer relations between, the Orthodox, Oriental and Anglican Churches. Patrons: the Archbishop of Canterbury and the Patriarch of Constantinople. Presidents: The Lord Bishop of London and Archbishop Gregorios of Thyateira and Great Britain. *Chairman:* Revd William Taylor. *General Secretary:* Ms Janet Laws, c/o The Old Deanery, Dean's Court, London, EC4V 5AA
Tel: 020 7248 6233
email: janet.laws@btopenworld.com

Anglican Association of Advisers in Pastoral Care and Counselling

Founded in 1998 to support the work of advisers already appointed; to encourage the appointment of an adviser in every diocese and to promote good practice in pastoral care and pastoral counselling through the Church of England. Full membership is open to appointed advisers, or to those who are undertaking advisers' tasks within the dioceses. Associate membership is open to those holding similar appointments in other denominations and to all who are interested in furthering the work of the Association. *Chair:* Revd Jeff Leonardi (email: jeff.leonardi@btinternet.com). *Vice-Chair:* Canon Ian Tomlinson (email: ian@raggedappleshaw.freeserve.co.uk). *Treasurer:* Canon Peter Kenney (email: sthughs church@btinternet.com). *Membership Secretary:* Mrs Sandra Grainger (email: sandragrainger@

tiscali.co.uk), 12 Pendene Rd, Leicester, LE2 3DQ *Tel:* 01889 570879 (Chair)
01264 772414 (Vice-Chair)

Anglican Fellowship in Scouting and Guiding
Founded in 1983 at the request of guiders, scouters and clergy. Its aims are to support leaders and clergy in the religious aspects of the Promise and Law and the training programme in Scouting and Guiding, and to maintain links with other Guide/Scout religious guilds and fellowships in order to foster ecumenical understanding. Individual membership is open to persons aged 18 years or over who are members of the Scout and Guide movements, or others (e.g. clergy) who are sympathetic to the aims of Guiding and Scouting. Collective membership is available for Scout Groups and Guide Units (which do not have to be church sponsored), and for Anglican churches. *Chairman:* Mrs June Davies. *Vice-Chairman:* Vacancy. *Secretary:* Miss Joan Taylor. *Treasurer:* Miss Sandra Bendall, 31 Loseley Rd, Farncombe, Godalming, GU7 3RE
Tel: 01483 428876
email: hiss2miss@yahoo.co.uk
Web: www.anglicanfellowship.org.uk

Anglican Mainstream
Anglican Mainstream is a movement of organizations, churches, dioceses and individuals within the Anglican Communion worldwide, dedicated to teaching and preserving the Scriptural truths on which the Anglican Church was founded. It seeks to nurture, support and provide a network for orthodox Anglicans throughout the Communion. It published *Repair the Tear* as a response to the Windsor Report. *Convenor:* Dr Philip Giddings. *Episcopal Adviser:* Rt Revd Graham Cray. *Executive Secretary:* Canon Dr Chris Sugden, 21 High St, Eynsham, OX29 4HE
Tel and Fax: 01865 883388
email: csugden@anglican-mainstream.net
Web: www.anglican-mainstream.net

Anglican Marriage Encounter
Anglican Marriage Encounter is a voluntary organization which offers residential and non-residential programmes for married and engaged couples to review and deepen their relationship by developing a compelling vision for their marriage, and providing the communication skills to support this. *Episcopal Adviser:* Rt Revd Michael Scott-Joynt. *Lay Executive Couple:* David and Liz Percival, 11 Lamborne Close, Sandhurst, GU47 8JL *Tel:* 01344 779658
email: mail@marriageencounter.freeserve.co.uk
Web: www.marriageencounter.org.uk

Anglican Pacifist Fellowship
Founded 1937. Members pledged to renounce war and all preparation to wage war and to work for the construction of Christian peace in the world. Quarterly newsletter 'The Anglican Peacemaker'. *Chairperson:* Mrs Mary Roe. *Hon Secretary:* Dr Tony Kempster, 11 Weavers End, Hanslope, Milton Keynes, MK19 7PA
Tel: 01908 510642
email: ajkempster@aol.com
Web: www.anglicanpeacemaker.org.uk

Anglican Society for the Welfare of Animals
Founded 1972, for the purpose of including the whole creation in the redemptive love of Christ and especially for prayer, study and action on behalf of animals. Registered Charity no. 1087270. Promotes Animal Welfare Sunday each October and offers a free information pack to all churches. *President:* Rt Revd Dominic Walker OGS. *Chairman:* Rt Revd Richard Llewellin. *Treasurer:* Mrs Jenny White, PO Box 7193, Hook, RG27 8GT *Tel and Fax:* 01252 843093
email: AngSocWelAnimals@aol.com
Web: www.aswa.org.uk

Anglican Stewardship Association
A registered charity formed to promote the ideals of responsible ownership and giving amongst Christians and the Church. The association's aim is to assist Christians at parish, deanery and diocesan level to address issues of money and wealth-handling and thus to make full use of all the latent resources of the Church so that its mission may be fully developed. *Project Director:* Wilf Crane. *General Secretary:* Carol Sims, 71 Dee Banks, Chester, CH3 5UX *Tel:* 01244 341996
Fax: 01244 400338
email: enquiries@anglican-stewardship.co.uk
Web: www.anglican-stewardship.co.uk

Anglican–Lutheran Society
Founded in 1984 to pray for the unity of the Church and especially the Anglican and Lutheran Communions; to encourage opportunities for common worship, study, friendship and witness; to encourage a wider interest in and knowledge of the Anglican and Lutheran traditions and contemporary developments within them. The Society publishes a newsletter, 'The Window', organizes conferences, lectures and other events. *Co-Presidents:* Very Revd John Arnold, Rt Revd Erik Vikstrom. *Co-Moderators:* Revd Tom Bruch, Rt Revd Dr Rupert Hoare. *Secretary:* Mrs Valerie Phillips, 15 Hampden, Kimpton, Hitchin, SG4 8QH *Tel:* 01438 832649
email: valerie_g_phillips@hotmail.com

Anglo-Catholic Ordination Candidates' Fund
Secretary: Revd J. F. H. Shead, 57 Kenworthy Rd, Braintree, CM7 1JJ *Tel:* 01376 321783/
07771 717710 (Mobile)
Fax: 01376 321783
email: j.shead@tiscali.co.uk

Archbishop's Examination in Theology
Until 2007 the Archbishop's Examination in Theology comprised the Diploma of Student in

Theology (the Lambeth Diploma) and the Degree of Master of Arts (the Lambeth MA). The Lambeth Diploma was instituted in 1905 by Archbishop Randall Davidson. It provided an opportunity for women to study theology, principally so that they could teach religious education in schools and churches. It is now open to both men and women and the means of study is by thesis. The Lambeth MA was inaugurated by Dr Runcie in 1990 in order to provide an opportunity for theological study at a more advanced level. From 2007 the Archbishop's Examination in Theology has been extended. We now offer an MPhil research degree, with the opportunity to extend to a PhD, while the Lambeth Diploma as students complete the course. The Lambeth Diploma will continue to be an option. *For more information please contact:* The Administrative Office, Archbishop's Examination in Theology, Lambeth Palace, London, SE1 7JU

Archbishops' (Canterbury, Wales and Westminster) Certificate in Church Music
See Guild of Church Musicians, page 292.

Archway
Anglican Retreat and Conference House Wardens' Association. Promotes the use of retreat and conference houses as a vital contribution to the life and development of Church and community. Is available to advise trustees/management committees and diocesan boards on issues concerning the running of retreat houses. *President:* Vacancy. *Chairperson:* Mrs Liz Palin. *Secretary:* Ms Eleanor Godber. *Treasurer:* Ms Gabrielle Watts, Holland House, Cropthorne, Pershore, WR10 3NB   *Tel:* 01386 860330
Fax: 01386 861208
email: liz@glenfallhouse.org
Web: www.archwaywardens.org.uk

Art and Christianity Enquiry (ACE)
ACE is the leading UK organisation in the field of visual arts and religion. ACE offers stimulating educational projects and publications, advice, information and skills. The ACE awards for religious art, architecture and literature are given biennially. The quarterly journal *Art and Christianity* is available by membership; complimentary copy available on request. *Director:* Laura Moffatt. *Art in Churches Officer:* Paul Bayley, All Hallows, 83 London Wall, London, EC2M 5ND
Tel and Fax: 020 7374 0600
email: enquiries@acetrust.org
Web: www.acetrust.org

Art and Sacred Places (ASP)
ASP promotes interaction between religion and art, largely by siting specially commissioned contemporary art in sacred places. It engages new audiences, by exploring the relationship between art and spirituality, encouraging debate and understanding. ASP's work is based on the conviction that art and religion share fundamental concerns and explore similar territory, albeit in significantly different ways. ASP was founded under the auspices of Bishop John Gladwin in 1999 and became a charity in 2001. Charity Registration no. 1086739. *Project Director:* Angela Peagram, Bakerswell, Meonstoke, Southampton, SO32 3NA   *Tel:* 01489 878725
Fax: 01489 878737
email: angela@artandsacredplaces.org
Web: www.artandsacredplaces.org

Arthur Rank Centre
Established 1972 as a collaborative venture between the churches, the Royal Agricultural Society of England and the Rank Foundation. The Arthur Rank Centre is now an independent Trust supported by the National Churches, the Royal Agricultural Society of England and the Rank Foundation. It is an ecumenical body and is recognized as the rural focus and resource centre for the churches nationally. It provides the secretariat for the Churches Rural Group, a representative ecumenical body which is a network of Churches Together in England. The Centre offers training for clergy recently appointed to rural areas and on multi-parish benefices. Members of staff are peripatetic and are available for consultations and conferences at local, diocesan and national levels. The Diocesan Rural Officers meet annually with the Church of England National Rural Officer, who is a member of staff at the Centre and who offers on-going advice, information and support. The Centre is also concerned with rural community issues and with farming and environmental matters. The Centre publishes the magazine *Country Way* – life and faith in rural Britain and a wide range of other resources and publications, including information on rural ministry and mission, worship, and the multi-parish benefice. Further information on the work of the Centre and the National Rural Officer will be found on the web site. *Director:* Revd Dr Gordon Gatward. *National Rural Officer to Archbishops' Council:* Dr Jill Hopkinson, Arthur Rank Centre, Stoneleigh Park, Warwickshire, CV8 2LZ
Tel: 024 7685 3060
Fax: 024 7641 4808
email: info@arthurrankcentre.org.uk
Web: www.arthurrankcentre.org.uk

Association for Promoting Retreats
Founded in 1913 to foster the growth of the spiritual life in the Anglican Communion by the practice of retreats. Welcomes as members all Christians in sympathy with this aim. Membership by subscription for individuals, parishes and retreat houses. The APR is one of the six retreat groups which form the Retreat Association (see separate entry). *Administrator:* Paddy

Lane, The Central Hall, 256 Bermondsey St, London, SE1 3UJ
Tel: 020 7357 7736
Fax: 0871 715 1917
email: apr@retreats.org.uk
Web: See 'member groups' at www.retreats.org.uk

Association of Black Clergy
Founded 1982 to bring together the minority ethnic clergy and lay ministers of the Christian Church in the United Kingdom, to provide support for all minority ethnic clergy and lay ministers, to encourage good practice and challenge racism individually, institutionally and structurally in particular in the Christian Church in the United Kingdom and to promote theological education and training that is relevant to minority ethnic Christian leadership. *Chairman:* Revd Jennifer Thomas. *Vice-Chair:* Revd Karowei Dorgu. *Facilitators (South):* Revd Yvonne Clarke, Revd Charles Lawrence. *Facilitator (North):* Very Revd Rogers Govender. *Secretary:* Revd Smitha Prasadam, Sherwood Park Vicarage, Sherwood Park Rd, Mitcham, CR4 1NJ
Tel and Fax: 020 8764 8369
email: theascension@freeuk.com

Association of Christian Teachers
ACT is a non-denominational Christian membership organization which provides professional and spiritual support to Christians engaged in pre-school, primary, middle, secondary, special, college and university education in England. ACT encourages Christians to apply their faith to their work and provides opportunities for them to share together in prayer and fellowship. ACT strives to influence policy makers, politicians, the media and the Church by speaking from a professionally well-informed standpoint with a loving, Christian voice on behalf of Christians working in education. *Chief Executive:* Mr Rupert Kaye. *Office Manager:* Mrs Carol Horne, 94A London Rd, St Albans, AL1 1NX
Tel: 01727 840298
Fax: 01727 848966
email: act@christian-teachers.org.uk
Web: www.christian-teachers.org.uk

Association of Christian Writers
A group of Christians who wish to serve God in the field of writing. Some members are professional writers, others part-time and many are beginners in different areas of writing. Three writers' days a year are held and many local groups meet regularly. Members receive a quarterly magazine, and a manuscript criticism service is available. Applicants are asked to sign a declaration of faith. *Chairman:* Brian Vincent. *Vice-Chairs:* Penny Culliford, Jan Clampett. *Company Secretary/Administrator:* Simon Baynes. *Treasurer:* Rosamund Rowe, 23 Moorend Lane, Thame, OX9 3BQ
Tel: 01844 213673
email: admin@christianwriters.org.uk
Web: www.christianwriters.org.uk

Association of Church College Trusts
In 1979 the Association of Church College Trusts was established as a loosely knit organization to facilitate an exchange of information and cooperation. It meets every six months. The Church College Trusts were formed following the closure of their respective Colleges of Education. They are autonomous, answerable only to the Charity Commission; their financial management policies are such that they are required both to sponsor present work from their income and also to ensure that their capital is maintained at a level that can finance similar levels of work in the future. In the last 29 years they have been involved in helping individual teachers, students and others, sponsoring corporate projects in part or in total, and aiding school, college and church educational activities. The individual Trusts are: All Saints Educational Trust, Culham Educational Foundation, Foundation of St Matthias, Hockerill Educational Foundation, Keswick Hall Charity, St Christopher's College Trust, St Gabriel's Trust, St Hild and St Bede Trust, St Luke's College Foundation, St Mary's College Trust, St Peter's Saltley Trust, Sarum St Michael Educational Charity (see separate entries). Please note that applications have to be made to the individual Trusts concerned and not centrally through the Association. *Secretary:* Revd Dr John Gay, Culham Institute, 15 Norham Gardens, Oxford, OX2 6PY
Tel: 01865 284885
Fax: 01865 284886
email: enquiries@culham.ac.uk
Web: www.culham.ac.uk

Association of Church Fellowships
Founded 1963. Sponsored by clergy and laity to meet a growing need in this country and overseas to encourage and enable the laity to take their full part in the life and work of the Church in open groups and in cooperation with existing groups. *National Chairman:* Revd Andrew Bullock, 34 Dudley Park Rd, Acocks Green, Birmingham, B27 6QR
Tel: 0121 706 9764

Association of Diocesan Registry Clerks
The Association was established in the Southern Province in 1999 to enable those working directly for diocesan registrars to contact one another for mutual professional support and to arrange meetings and conferences at which lectures and discussions are provided to expand knowledge of ecclesiastical law. Because of the distances involved, there is usually only one meeting a year, a day meeting alternating with a two-day residential conference. The Association is now a national one, the Clerks in the Northern Province having joined in 2004. *President:* Rt Worshipful Sheila Cameron (Dean of the Arches). *Communications Officer:* Mrs Sue Priddy, Portsmouth

Diocesan Registry, Brutton & Co. 288 West St, Fareham, PO16 0AJ
Tel: 01329 236171 DX: 40809 FAREHAM
Fax: 01329 289915
email: sue.priddy@brutton.co.uk
Web: www.brutton.co.uk

Association of English Cathedrals
Established in 1990 and authorized by the Administrative Chapters of the Anglican Cathedrals as their representative organization, the AEC deals with governmental agencies, the General Synod and its constituent bodies and the Churches' Main Committee on behalf of the English cathedrals, provided only that it cannot commit any individual cathedral chapter to a specific decision. Membership consists of one representative of each Administrative Chapter. *Chairman:* Very Revd Christopher Lewis. *Secretary:* Very Revd David Brindley. *Coordinator:* Mrs Sarah King, PO Box 53506, London, SE19 1ZL
Tel: 020 8761 5130
email: sarah.king@englishcathedrals.co.uk
Web: www.englishcathedrals.co.uk

Association of Hospice and Palliative Care Chaplains (AHPCC)
The AHPCC exists to promote good standards among Chaplains involved in the pastoral and spiritual care of people (including carers) facing death from a life threatening illness. Hospice and Palliative Care Chaplains seek to: meet spiritual and religious needs in hospice and palliative care units as a part of a multidisciplinary team that meets regularly; be proactive in assessing and addressing the complex spiritual and religious needs of patients and their families/carers that are an integral part of hospice and palliative care; discern, respect and meet the cultural, spiritual and religious needs, traditions and practices of all patients and their families/carers, including those of no faith; ensure that all spiritual and religious care is patient led and focused on the needs of the individual and their family/carers. The aims of the AHPCC are: to identify and promote good practice; to be an agent of professional development; to provide professional support and fellowship; to promote links with the constituency of palliative care; to promote links with relevant church bodies and faith communities. AHPCC offers training and support for clergy and lay people involved (whether on a full-time or part-time basis) by means of advice about appointments, induction, and training courses, keeps members up to date with current information by means of its website, and organises a three day conference/training event in May each year. St Christopher's Hospice, Sydenham, provides courses for chaplains newly appointed, and many hospices offer placements and courses which form part of pre- and post-ordination training. The AHPCC monitors professional developments within the constituency of palliative care, works to his own professional standards, and offers members support through regional groups. It works closely with the College of Health Care Chaplains, the Scottish Association of Chaplains in Healthcare, and the Chaplaincy Academic Accreditation Board to further the professionalism of healthcare chaplaincy throughout the UK. Membership fee is £30, and, in the first instance, prospective members should make contact with the membership secretary. The AHPCC is supported by 'Help the Hospices', and our link is Anne Garley at Help the Hospices, 33–44 Britannia St, London WC1X 9JG. *President:* Revd Tom Gordon. *Hon Secretary:* Revd Karen Murphy. *Treasurer:* Revd Jodie Horrocks. *Membership Secretary:* Revd Karen Murphy, Tom Gordon, Chaplain, Marie Curie Hospice, Edinburgh, EH10 7D
Tel: 0131 470 2209
email: membership@ahpcc.org.uk
Web: www.ahpcc.org.uk

Association of Ordinands and Candidates for Ministry
Founded in 1968, AOCM represents ordinands from the Church of England, Church in Wales, Episcopal Church of Scotland and Church of Ireland as well as trainee Church Army evangelists. AOCM holds regional and national conferences during the year, to which every theological college, course and OLM scheme may send a representative. These conferences allow ordinands to share fellowship, and also for information and questions to pass between AOCM and the Ministry Division. AOCM publishes an annual handbook, *Together in Training*, which is provided free of charge to all ordinands, bishops and DDOs. *Chairman:* Alan Maxwell. *Treasurer:* Ian Robinson. *Secretary:* John Allister
email: secretary@aocm.org.uk
Web: www.aocm.org.uk

Baptismal Integrity (BI)
(Formerly MORIB)
BI has four aims: to bring an end to the practice of indiscriminate infant baptism; to demonstrate that baptism is the sacrament instituted by Christ for those becoming members of the visible Church; to seek the reform of the Canons and rules of the Church of England in line with the above stated aims; to promote within the Church of England debate and review of the biblical, theological, pastoral and evangelistic aspects of Christian initiation. *President:* Rt Revd Colin Buchanan. *Chairman:* Revd David Perry. *Vice-Chairman:* Mr Roger Godin. *Secretary:* Mrs Carol Snipe. *Treasurer:* Ms Sallie Bassham, 11 Middle Garth Drive, South Cave, Brough, E Yorks HU15 2AY
Tel: 01430 421412/01823 480606
email: david.perry@baptism.org.uk
Web: www.baptism.org.uk

Barnardo's
Founded in 1866, Barnardo's is the UK's largest children's charity, whose inspiration and values

derive from the Christian faith. It runs more than 394 projects nationwide and each year helps some 115,000 youngsters and their families to overcome severe disadvantage. The charity works with children over the long term to tackle the effects of disadvantage and to help them develop into well-rounded people. Children are helped to address problems such as abuse, homelessness and poverty and to tackle the challenges of disability. Barnardo's also uses its expertise and knowledge to campaign for better care for children and their families in the community and to champion the rights of every child. The charity no longer runs orphanages and now concentrates on working with children and their families in the community. *Chair of Council:* Geoffrey Barnett. *Chief Executive:* Martin Narey, Barnardo's, Tanners Lane, Barkingside, Ilford, IG6 1QG

Tel: 020 8550 8822
Fax: 020 8551 6870
email: dorothy.howes@barnardos.org.uk
Web: www.barnardos.org.uk

Beauchamp Community
Homes for retired people, clerical or lay, either sex. Unfurnished, single and double flats available from time to time. Applicants should be aged 60 – 74. Daily Eucharist. Apply to the Chaplain. Newland, Malvern, WR13 5AX

Tel: 01684 562100

Bible Reading Fellowship
BRF is a registered charity resourcing spirituality and discipleship among adults and children. Published resources include daily Bible reading notes and books in the areas of Bible reading, discipleship, prayer and spirituality. In 2006 BRF released a web-based discipleship resource, Foundations21, offering churches and individuals a flexible approach to discipleship. Barnabas is BRF's work with children aged 3–11. Published resources include resource material for those working with children in schools and churches and colour story and activity books for young children. Barnabas training provides RE Days to help schools to explore Christianity and the Bible, INSET sessions for teachers, and training, events and activities for those working with children in churches. BRF is also involved in Messy Church, an initiative which helps churches to reach out to families on the fringe of the church. Support for churches thinking about starting a Messy Church includes practical support, creative ideas, training for leaders and a website. *Chair of Trustees:* Rt Revd Colin Fletcher, Bishop of Dorchester. *Chief Executive:* Mr Richard Fisher. *General Manager:* Mrs Karen Laister, 15 The Chambers, Vineyard, Abington, Oxfordshire OX14 3FE

Tel: 01865 319700
Fax: 01865 319701
email: enquiries@brf.org.uk
Web: www.brf.org.uk

Bible Society
Bible Society is working towards a day when the Bible's life-changing message is shaping lives and communities everywhere. We aim to show how the Bible connects with life. We make Scriptures available where there are none. And we work with the Church to help it live out the Bible's message in its daily life and witness. *Chief Executive:* James Catford. *Deputy Chief Executive:* Philip Poole. *Executive Director of England and Wales:* Ann Holt. *Executive Director of International Programme:* Ian McKay. *Services Executive:* Lesley Whelan, Stonehill Green, Westlea, Swindon, SN5 7DG

Tel: 01793 418100
Fax: 01793 418118
email: contactus@biblesociety.org.uk
Web: www.biblesociety.org.uk

Bloxham Project
Founded in 1967, charged with developing an understanding of Christian faith and values in education. Offering a spiritual, inspirational and practical resource for schools and educators, helping to develop spirituality, pastoral care, Christian leadership and ethos and values. Providing a forum for debate and the exchange of best practice. Offers consultancy services and tailor-made training, day events, regional meetings, a termly publication and some other materials. A network of schools across denominations and sectors. A resource for headteachers, leadership teams, chaplains, teaching and pastoral staff. *Chair of Trustees:* Mr David Exham. *Director:* Revd John Caperon, Ripon College, Cuddesdon, Oxford, OX44 9EY

Tel: 01865 875431
email: admin@bloxhamproject.org.uk
Web: www.bloxhamproject.org.uk

Book Aid Charitable Trust
Founded in 1988, Book Aid Charitable Trust supplies over one million handpicked new and used Christian books and Bibles to some of the poorest areas of the world each year. All these books and Bibles are donated by Christians in the UK from every denomination and background. The books are distributed mainly to Africa, Asia and the Caribbean, with smaller shipments sent to many other places. Book Aid is manned by volunteer workers and is funded by donations. Registered Charity no. 1039484. *Coordinator:* Bob Hiley, Bromley House, Kangley Bridge Rd, London, SE26 5AQ

Tel: 020 8778 2145 (Admin)
020 8778 2247 (Bookshop)
Fax: 020 8778 2265
email: office@book-aid.org
Web: www.book-aid.org

Boys' Brigade
Founded 1883 for the advancement of Christ's kingdom among boys and the promotion of habits of obedience, reverence, discipline, self-respect and all that tends towards a true

Christian manliness. *Brigade Secretary:* Steve Dickinson, Felden Lodge, Felden Lane, Hemel Hempstead, HP3 0BL   *Tel:* 01442 231681
Fax: 01442 235391
email: enquiries@boys-brigade.org.uk
Web: www.boys-brigade.org.uk

Bridge Pastoral Foundation
(formerly the Clinical Theology Association)
Founded in 1962. The core activity of the Association is seminars in pastoral care and pastoral counselling, which are directed by authorized tutors and widely available in the UK. Seminars are designed to promote self-awareness, which is needed for effective pastoral work, and to teach the theory and practice of pastoral counselling with reference to the assumptions, values and meanings of the Christian faith. Further information about Bridge Pastoral Foundation education and training may be obtained from the Administrator. *Administrator:* Angela Ryan, 8 Kingsmead Rd North, Prenton, Birkenhead, CH43 6TB
Tel: 0151 652 0429
email: admin@bridgepastoral.org.uk
Web: www.bridgepastoral.org.uk

Bristol Clerical Education Society
Grants of up to £250 to ordinands and, occasionally, to clergy undertaking CME, for specific and practical needs. *Secretary:* Mrs S. J. Clover, Drummond House, Gosditch, Ashton Keynes, SN6 6NZ   *Tel:* 01285 861199

British Deaf Association
The British Deaf Association (BDA) is the largest national organization run by deaf people, for deaf people. We represent the UK's deaf community and campaign for the official recognition of British Sign Language (BSL). Our vision is a world where deaf sign language users enjoy the same rights, responsibilities, opportunities and quality of life as everyone. Services include counselling, advocacy and youth services. BDA works with companies and organizations to make advice and information available in BSL on video or CD-ROM. We run the London Deaf Access Project and organize the annual Deaf Film and TV Festival. BDA Helpline is a national helpline giving information and advice on a range of subjects, such as the Disability Discrimination Act, welfare benefits, education and BSL; the line is open 9 a.m. to 5 p.m. Monday to Friday. *Patron:* HRH The Duke of York. *Chair:* Mr Austin Reeves. *Chief Exec:* Jeff McWhinney, 1–3 Worship St, London, EC2A 2AB
Tel: 020 7588 3520 (Voice) 020 7588 3529 (Text)
Fax: 020 7588 3527
email: helpline@bda.org.uk
Web: www.bda.org.uk

British Isles and Eire Airport Chaplains' Network
The British Isles and Eire Airport Chaplains' Network meets twice a year for a day or two-day conference and is working towards seeing airport chaplaincy established at every international or regional airport in the UK and Ireland. In 2005 there were chaplaincies at 35 airports, with others being negotiated. Of these, full-time chaplains or chaplaincy teams are at: Heathrow, Gatwick, Manchester, Luton and East Midlands. All airport chaplains are on call and are pleased to be able to assist those travelling through airports in any way. They can be contacted via the airport information desk. Some airport chaplaincies have web pages on their particular airport web sites; for a list of sites visit the address given below. (See also International Association of Civil Aviation Chaplains.) *Coordinator:* Revd Roy Monks. *General Secretary:* Vacancy, Building 34 Office 14, Nottingham E Midlands Airport, Derby, DE74 2SA
Tel: 01509 561955 01332 852990
Fax: 01332 810045
email: roy.monks@talk21.com
Web: www.aoa.org.uk/ourmem/index.asp

Broken Rites
Formed in 1983, Broken Rites is an independent association of divorced and separated wives of Anglican clergy, ministers and Church Army officers living in England, Wales, Scotland, Northern Ireland and the Republic of Ireland. It affirms the Christian ideal of lifelong marriage. It welcomes the support of everyone who is in sympathy with its aims, which are to support one another with sympathy and understanding and practical help where possible; to continue to draw the attention of the Churches to the problems of ex-wives of the clergy; and to promote a more vivid awareness among Christian people of the increasing incidence of clergy marriage breakdown and the implications for the witness of the Church and its teaching on marriage. *Hon Secretary:* Sue Atack. *Chair:* Rosemary Richards, 46 Fulmer Rd, Sheffield, S11 8UF
Tel: 0114 268 2980/01257 423893
email: chair@brokenrites.org
Web: www.brokenrites.org

Bromley and Sheppard's Colleges
Bromley College was founded in 1666 to provide houses for clergy widows and Sheppard's College in 1840 to provide houses for unmarried daughters of clergy widows who had lived with their mothers at Bromley College. Houses in both colleges have been converted into flats and widows/widowers of clergy, retired clergymen and their spouses, divorced and separated spouses of clergy or retired clergy of the Church of England, the Church in Wales, the Scottish Episcopal Church or the Church of Ireland may now be admitted. Unmarried daughters or stepdaughters of a deceased former resident may also apply. Contact the Chaplain/Clerk to the Trustees. *Clerk and Chaplain:* Revd Andrew Sangster,

Chaplain's Office, Bromley & Sheppard's Colleges, London Rd, Bromley, BR1 1PE
Tel: 020 8460 4712 (Chaplain)
020 8464 3558 (Office)
Fax: 020 8464 3558
email: bromcoll@aol.com
Web: www/bromleycollege.org

Burrswood

Burrswood is a Christian hospital and place of healing founded in 1948 by Dorothy Kerin, who received a commission from God to 'heal the sick, comfort the sorrowing and give faith to the faithless'. The Dorothy Kerin Trust is a registered charity, administered by a board of trustees and has a non-surgical hospital with 41 beds for short-term inpatient care supported by an interdisciplinary team of resident doctors, nurses, physiotherapists and counsellors; a church with resident chaplains, which is fully integrated within the hospital and has healing services open to the public twice a week; a guest/retreat house with single and twin rooms, sleeping 11; a physio- and hydrotherapy complex for inpatients and outpatients and a medical and counselling outpatient facility. Additional public facilities include a Christian bookshop and tea room onsite and a charity shop in nearby Crowborough. Profits from these trading operations go into Burrswood's 'Access to Care' bursary fund which assists financially disadvantaged patients to receive care. *Chief Executive Officer:* Dr Gareth Tuckwell . *Senior Chaplain:* Revd Christine Garrard. *Senior Physician:* Dr Paul Worthley, Groombridge, Tunbridge Wells, TN3 9PY
Tel: 01892 863637 (Enquiries)
01892 863818 (Admissions)
Fax: 01892 863623; 01892 862597 (Admissions)
email: enquiries@burrswood.org.uk
Web: www.burrswood.org.uk

Came's Charity for Clergymen's Widows

Founded to provide small annual grants to benefit clergy widows who are wanting. Apply to the Clerk. Worshipful Company of Cordwainers, Dunster Court Mincing Lane, London, EC3R 7AH
Tel: 020 7929 1121
Fax: 020 7929 1124
email: office@cordwainers.org

Campaigner Ministries

Founded 1922, Campaigner Ministries is a national youth movement working in partnership with local churches. Campaigner Ministries trains and resources local leaders, enabling them to operate an exciting and relevant relational and holistic programme of evangelism and Christian discipleship for boys and girls between 4 and 18. It is recognized by UK government education departments and is a member of the Evangelical Alliance. *Executive Director:* Mr John Radcliffe.

Resources Director: Mr Tony Etherington, 6 Eaton Court Rd Colmworth Business Park, Eaton Socon, St Neots, PE19 8ER   Tel: 01480 215622
Fax: 01480 405550
email: info@campaigners.org.uk
Web: www.campaigners.org.uk

Canterbury and York Society

Founded 1904 for the printing of bishops' registers and other ecclesiastical records. *Joint Presidents:* The Archbishops of Canterbury and York. *Chairman:* Prof J. H. Denton. *Secretary:* Dr C. Fonge. *Treasurer:* Dr R. Hayes. *Editor:* Dr P. Hoskin, Borthwick Institute, University of York Heslington, York, YO10 5DD
Web: http://www.canterburyandyork.org

CARE (Christian Action Research and Education)

CARE is a registered charity seeking to combine practical caring initiatives, at national and community level, with public policy on social and ethical issues. CARE campaigns, provides resouces, undertakes caring work and helps to bring Christian insight and experience to matters of public policy, education and practical caring initiatives, particularly on the behalf of the needy. *Chairman:* Revd Lyndon Bowring. *Chief Executive:* Mrs Nola Leach. *Director of Parliamentary Affairs:* Dr Dan Boucher. *Operations Manager:* Mr Chris Nuttall, 53 Romney St, London, SW1P 3RF
Tel: 020 7233 0455/
08453 100 244 (supporter helpline)
Fax: 020 7233 0983
email: mail@care.org.uk
Web: www.care.org.uk

Careforce

Founded in 1980 to serve churches and Christian projects by recruiting British and international volunteers aged 17 to 30 to spend a year in the UK engaged in youth and outreach ministries in local churches, serving homeless people, the elderly, those with difficult family situations, those with addiction difficulties, and those with learning difficulties or physical disability. *Director:* Revd Ian Prior, 35 Elm Rd, New Malden, KT3 3HB
Tel and Fax: 020 8942 3331
email: enquiry@careforce.co.uk
Web: www.careforce.co.uk

Cathedral and Church Shops Association

The Association provides a forum for the exchange of information, arranges an annual conference and trade fair for its members each November, sponsors meetings of shop staff in several areas of the country each spring and gives advice and assistance for the setting up and running of church shops from experienced shop managers. Membership is open to any cathedral/church/religious house which is under the sole control, or operated by a trading company for the sole benefit, of its chapter, parochial

church council or religious house. *Chairman:* Mrs Carolyne Baines. *Treasurer:* Mr Reg Steel. *Hon Secretary:* Mrs Alison Chambers. *Annual Conference and Trade Fair Organizer:* Revd Stuart M. Munns, 27 Wyedean Rise, Belmont, Hereford, HR2 7XZ
Tel: 01432 270802
email: ccsa.sec@btconnect.com
Web: www.ccsa.org.uk

Cathedral Libraries and Archives Association
The CLAA supports the work of the cathedral and capitular libraries and archives in the Anglican churches of the United Kingdom and Ireland. It seeks to advance education by the promotion, preservation and protection of those collections and provides a forum for cooperation and the exchange of information among those who care for them. *Chairman:* Very Revd Peter Atkinson. *Hon Secretary:* Mrs Gudrun Warren. *Hon Treasurer:* Mr Jo Wisdom, c/o Norwich Cathedral Library, 12 The Close, Norwich, NR1 4DH
Tel: 01603 218327
Fax: 01603 766032
email: library@cathedral.org.uk
Web: http://www.cofe.anglican.org/about/librariesandarchives/cathanddioceseslibs/

Cathedrals Administration and Finance Association (CAFA)
In 1975 cathedral administrators and treasurers began, as a body, to exchange information on all matters touching on best practice and the most effective administration of the English Anglican cathedrals. The association now enjoys a valued link with the Association of English Cathedrals for which organization it undertakes research as needed. There is an annual conference and regular regional meetings. *Chairman:* Preb John Roberts. *Admin Secretary:* Miss Jan Dawson. *Treasurer:* Mrs Caroline Robinson, Church House, Great Smith St, London, SW1P 3NZ
Tel: 020 7898 1096
email: ruth.mcilmoyle@c-of-e.org.uk

Catholic Group in General Synod
The Catholic Group consists of those on General Synod committed to the catholic, traditional and orthodox voice in the Church of England. It seeks to make a positive contribution to all debates and especially where Catholic faith and order are involved. It welcomes both the ARCIC discussions and dialogue with the Orthodox churches. The group maintains that ethical teaching which scripture and tradition have consistently upheld. It is not averse to change where contemporary church life demands it, but stands firm on a gospel that is based on God's revelation of himself as Father, Son and Holy Spirit. Members represent a variety of practice within the doctrinal framework. *Chairman:* Canon Simon Killwick. *Secretary:* Mrs Mary Nagel, Aldwick Vicarage, 25 Gossamer Lane, Bognor Regis, PO21 3AT
Tel: 01243 262049
email: nagel@aldwick.demon.co.uk

Cautley House
A Christian centre for healing and wholeness, established in 1994. An Anglican foundation which seeks to be a resource for the whole Church. Individuals or groups (up to 24) are welcome to visit for up to two weeks. Daily services are held in the chapel and staff are available for confidential listening and prayer ministry. Non-residents are invited to attend the healing services which are held twice a week. *Director:* Revd Pat Vowles, 95 Seabrook Rd, Hythe, CT21 5QY
Tel: 01303 230762
Fax: 01303 237447
email: cautleyhouse@compuserve.com
Web: www.cautleyhouse.org.uk

Central Council of Church Bell Ringers
Founded 1891. Its aims are to promote the ringing of church bells, to represent the ringing exercise to the world at large and to provide expert information and advice to ringers, church authorities and the general public on all matters relating to bells and bell-ringing. *President:* Mr Derek E. Sibson. *Hon Secretary:* Mr Ian Oram, The Cottage, School Hill, Warnham, Horsham, RH12 3QN
Tel: 01403 269 743
email: ihoram@hotmail.com
Web: www.cccbr.org.uk

Centre for the Study of Christianity and Sexuality
Launched in 1996, CSCS aims to provide a safe platform to promote objective debate within the Christian Churches on matters concerning human sexuality, with a view to developing the spiritual teaching and doctrines of such Christian Churches. CSCS is associated with the international journal *Theology and Sexuality* and publishes the quarterly *CSCS News*. It also organizes a conference each year. *Patrons and Matron:* Rt Revd John Gladwin (Bishop of Chelmsford), Revd David Gamble (Co-ordinating Secretary, Legal and Constitutional Practice, Methodist Church), Revd Roberta Rominger (Moderator, N Thames Synod of the URC). *Chair:* Canon Jane Fraser. *Secretary:* Vacancy. *Treasurer:* Mrs Daphne Cook. *Newsletter Editor:* Mr Anthony Woollard, The Campanile, Church Lane, Stoulton, Worcester WR7 4RE   *Tel:* 01905 840266/01789 762553/
Fax: 01789 400040
email: cscs@revjane.demon.co.uk
Web: www.cscs.co.uk

Changing Attitude
Working for lesbian, gay, bisexual and transgender affirmation within the Anglican Communion, Changing Attitude is a network of lesbian, gay, bisexual, transgendered and heterosexual members of the Anglican churches of the UK, founded in 1995. Local groups meet regularly in 24 dioceses to offer encouragement and support and provide educational and training resources. We have a network of contacts in over 33 dioceses

Organizations

and supporters in every English diocese. We work alongside Integrity USA and Changing Attitude organizations in Nigeria, Australia, New Zealand, Ireland and Scotland. *Director:* Revd Colin Coward. *Hon Administrator:* Brenda Harrison, 6 Norney Bridge, Mill Rd, Marston, SN10 5SF   *Tel:* 01380 724908/07770 844302/
email: info@changingattitude.org
Web: www.changingattitude.org.uk

Children's Society, The
Since 1881, when Sunday school teacher Edward Rudolph and Archbishop Archibold Tait founded The Children's Society, we have been working alongside the Church of England to reach out to those forgotten children who face danger or disadvantage in their daily lives; children who are unable to find the help or understanding they need anywhere else. Our actions are guided by Christian values and the belief that every child deserves a good childhood. Our national network of centres and projects deliver specialist services for children who need the most help. Our schools work, children's centres and mentoring programmes help more children develop the skills and confidence they need to make the most of their childhood and play a full part in their local communities. Our research and campaigning aims to influence the thinking of everyone – from the general public to politicians and decision makers – creating real change and making childhood better for all children. Together, we can make childhood better for all children in the UK. For further information on free support resources and how to get involved visit our website or call our Supporter Action Line. *Chair of Trustees:* Rt Revd T. J. Stevens, Bishop of Leicester. *Chaplain Missioner:* Revd Nigel Asbridge. *Chief Executive Officer:* Mr Bob Reitemeier, Edward Rudolf House, 69–85 Margery St, London, WC1X 0JL
Tel: 020 7841 4400 (Switchboard)
0845 300 1128 (Supporter Action Line)
Fax: 020 7841 4500
email: supporteraction@childrenssociety.org.uk
Web: www.childrenssociety.org.uk

Choir Benevolent Fund
Founded 1851. A registered Friendly Society for subscribing cathedral and collegiate lay clerks and organists. *Trustees:* The Deans of St Paul's, Westminster and Windsor. *Secretary:* Mr Roland Tatnell, Foxearth Cottage, Frittenden, Cranbrook, TN17 2AU   *Tel:* 01580 712825

Choir Schools Association
Founded 1919 to promote the welfare of cathedral, collegiate and parish church choir schools. In 1985 it set up a bursary trust to help children from low income families become choristers. *Chairman:* Mr Jonathan Milton. *Administrator:*

Mrs Susan Rees, Wolvesey, College St, Winchester, SO23 9ND   *Tel:* 01962 890530
Fax: 01962 869978
email: info@choirschools.org.uk
Web: www.choirschools.org.uk

CHRISM
(CHRistians In Secular Ministry)
Formed in 1984, CHRISM is the national association for all Christians who see their secular employment as their primary Christian ministry and for those who support that vision. CHRISM welcomes members, both lay and ordained, from all Christian denominations, encourages them to be active within their own faith communities and to champion ministry in and through secular employment. A journal is published quarterly, together with occasional papers. There is an open annual conference and also a members' reflective weekend. *Treasurer:* Susan Cooper, 28 Headstone Lane, Harrow, HA2 6HG   *Tel:* 020 8863 2094
email: scooper@hedstone.demon.co.uk
Web: www.chrism.org.uk

Christian Aid
Christian Aid is an agency of the British and Irish churches and as such is one of the largest church-related international relief and development agencies in Europe. It works largely in the developing world providing support wherever the need is greatest, irrespective of race or religion. A substantial amount of its voluntary income is received through the annual Christian Aid Week collections led by churchgoers. It funds projects in more than 50 countries, standing by poor communities whether they are digging wells or fighting the consequences of debt, unfair trade or climate change, learning to read or articulating human rights abuses, healing the wounds of war or tackling the spread of preventable illnesses. Money spent overseas is passed to local partner organizations as Christian Aid believes that poor communities are best placed to devise and run their own projects and solve their own problems. Channelling money in this way is seen as an effective and respectful way of giving poor people the means to help themselves. Prevention of the causes of poverty is better than cure, but Christian Aid remains active in emergencies, sending immediate help and capacity to cope with emergencies and disaster mitigation including food, shelter, medicine and transport when flood, famine, earthquake or war strike. The agency's charitable work includes campaigning and education work in the UK and Ireland, which accounts for up to eleven per cent of its income. This is because Christian Aid believes it must also tackle the structures and systems that keep people poor. It puts great emphasis on the involvement of individuals to address the root causes of poverty and encourage action by politicians and international institutions that will lead to their removal. *Director:* Dr Daleep Mukarji.

Chair of the Board: Rt Revd John Gladwin, Inter-Church House, 35–41 Lower Marsh, London, SE1 7RL   *Tel:* 020 7620 4444
Fax: 020 7620 0719
email: info@christian-aid.org.uk
Web: www.christian-aid.org.uk

Christian Arts
An association of artists, architects, designers, craftsmen and women all involved in the arts who are committed Christians and wish to explore and deepen the relationship between their faith and the arts. Its activities include holding exhibitions and an annual conference. An illustrated newsletter is published twice a year. Many members are available to accept commissions. Application may be made for the Christian Arts Directory of Artists. *Contact:* Paula Widdicombe, Little Morgrove, Perrymead, Bath, BA2 5AZ   *Tel and Fax:* 01225 837868
email: widdicombebutton@btinternet.com

Christian Education
(Incorporating Christian Education Publications, International Bible Reading Association, RE Today Services)
Christian Education provides advice, resources and opportunities for teaching and learning in the school, the church and the family group, carrying forward the work of the National Christian Education Council and the Christian Education Movement. *Chief Executive:* Peter Fishpool, 1020 Bristol Rd, Selly Oak, Birmingham, B29 6LB   *Tel:* 0121 472 4242
Fax: 0121 472 7575
email: enquiries@christianeducation.org.uk
Web: www.christianeducation.org.uk

Christian Ethical Investment Group
On 24th January 2008 and Extraordinary General Meeting of the Christian Ethical Investment Group was held to discuss the transfer of all its assets and activities to the Ecumenical Council for Corporate Responsibility (ECCR). The decision was ratified by the overwhelming majority of members shortly afterwards. While people are concerned as ever about individual company situations and whether investment should be maintained, the need to invest ethically is treated as a foregone assumption. The investment world is a very different place from the one in the 1980s when CEIG was among the ethical pioneers, bringing the 'Bishop of Oxford's case' to the courts and working to make ethical investment a reality. The general approach in ethical investment today is one of engagement with companies to encourage them to improve their practice: more of a focus on corporate responsibility than ethical investment per se. ECCR is in an excellent position to take this new agenda forward, and the former Executive Committee of CEIG warmly commend ECCR to anyone with a serious interest in ethical investment or corporate

responsibility. *Former Secretary:* Mr Stephen Dunham, ECCR, PO Box 500, Oxford, OX1 1ZL
Tel: 01865 245349 (Admin) 01325 580028 (Members
email: info@eccr.org.uk
Web: www.eccr.org.uk

Christian Evidence Society
Founded 1870 for the study, proclamation and defence of the Christian faith. *President:* The Archbishop of Canterbury. *Chairman:* Revd Dr Richard Burridge. *Administrator:* Canon Harry Marsh, 5 Vicarage Lane, Great Baddow, Chelmsford, CM2 8HY   *Tel:* 01245 478038
email: harry.marsh@talktalk.net
Web: www.christianevidencesociety.org.uk

Christian Healing Mission
The Christian Healing Mission is a non-residential healing centre in London, dedicated to bringing healing to individuals and encouraging healing in churches. A new link centre has been established in Milton Keynes and others are planned for the future. The CHM has four main aims: to offer a place where people may come to receive prayer for healing; to visit churches to encourage them in the healing ministry; to provide training for individuals and groups wanting to learn more about praying for the sick; and finally to offer a prayer request service whereby people can request prayer for those known to them who are sick. Although rooted in the Church of England, the CHM is keen to work with people and churches of all denominations. The Director is an Anglican priest with many years' experience of parish ministry and is also the Bishop of Kensington's Adviser for Healing. *Director:* Revd John Ryeland. *Administrator:* Clare Ingamells. *PA/Office manager:* Gillian Ryeland. *Prayer Ministry Coordinator:* Caryn Dixon, 8 Cambridge Court, 210 Shepherds Bush Rd, London, W6 7NJ
Tel: 020 7603 8118 (Office)
020 7603 0667 (Prayer Request Line)
Fax: 020 7603 5224
email: chm@healingmission.org
Web: www.healingmission.org

Christian Medical Fellowship
CMF aims (1) to unite Christian doctors and medical students in Christ, and to encourage them to deepen their faith, live like Christ, and serve him obediently, particularly through acting competently and with compassion in their medical practice; (2) to encourage Christian doctors and medical students to be witnesses for Christ among all those they meet; (3) to mobilize and support all Christian doctors, medical students and other healthcare professionals, especially members, in serving Christ throughout the world; (4) to promote Christian values, especially in bioethics and healthcare, among doctors and medical students, in the Church and in society. *General Secretary:* Mr Peter Saunders. *Director of*

Finance and Administration: Mr Giles Rawlinson, 6 Marshalsea Rd, London, SE1 1HL
Tel: 020 7234 9660
Fax: 020 7234 9661
email: info@cmf.org.uk
Web: www.cmf.org.uk

Christian Research
Christian Research works with Churches and Church leaders to help them 'turn the tide'. It identifies trends through its research programme, then interprets and publishes them in resources such as 'The Tide is Running Out', 'Religious Trends' and the UK Christian Handbook. Members receive 'Quadrant', a digest of trends in church and society. Forums and seminars help leaders apply the findings to their own context. Please ask for details. *Chairman:* Paul Sandham. *Exec Director:* Mrs Benita Hewitt, Vision Building, 4 Footscray Rd, Eltham, London, SE9 2TZ
Tel: 020 8294 1989
Fax: 020 8294 0014
email: admin@christian-research.org.uk
Web: www.ukchristianhandbook.org.uk/
www.christian-research.org.uk

Christian Socialist Movement
The Christian Socialist Movement seeks to be the Christian conscience of the Labour Party and a voice to the churches on social and political issues. We have a tradition stretching back 150 years, believing that the teachings of Jesus – justice, equality and love for one another – are inextricably linked to the foundations and continuation of the Labour Party. Our magazine *The Common Good* is published three times a year; we organize events such as hustings for the deputy leadership of the Labour Party, and have a presence at the Labour Conference, where we run fringe events. Details of membership rates are available on our web site. *Director:* Dr Andrew Bradstock. *Chair:* Rt Hon Alun Michael MP, Westminster Central Hall, Storey's Gate, London, SW1H 9NH
Tel: 020 7233 3736/
07729 323911 (Mobile)
email: info@thecsm.org.uk
Web: www.thecsm.org.uk

Christian Witness to Israel
To a people of promise – the message of Messiah. Working alongside local churches, Christian Witness to Israel has been sharing the message of Messiah with the Jewish people for over 150 years. It is a non-denominational, international and evangelical organization with workers in seven countries worldwide. We believe that the Jewish people's greatest need is to know Jesus their Messiah. In order to help meet this need, we provide appropriate literature and run an evangelistic website. We also host outreach events and provide training for Christians who wish to share the gospel with their Jewish friends, neighbours and colleagues. *General Secretary:* Mr Mike Moore, 166 Main Rd, Sundridge, Sevenoaks, TN14 6EL
Tel: 01959 565955
Fax: 01959 565966
email: hq@cwi.org.uk
Web: www.cwi.org.uk

Christians Abroad
Christians Abroad recruits skilled professionals and volunteers to serve overseas for partner Christian organizations in Britain and Ireland and overseas projects. It supplies support services to small NGOs and Christian agencies, including insurance and criminal records checks. Through 'World Service Enquiry' it gives advice and information about working in development and mission, publishes a monthly job list, an annual guide to volunteering and gives career advice through interview and on-line coaching. *Manager:* Kevin Cusack. *Finance/Admin and Recruitment:* Colin South, Room 237 Bon Marche Centre, 241–251 Ferndale Rd, London, SW9 8BJ
Tel: 0870 770 7990 (Office)
0870 770 7991 (Admin and Recruitment Consultancy)
email: recruit@cabroad.org.uk /
finance@cabroad.org.uk / wse@wse.org.uk
Web: www.cabroad.org.uk

Christians at Work
Christians at Work seeks to encourage, support and equip Christian ministry and witness in the workplace. It does this by producing resources and Bible study material; organizing conferences and seminars for local churches; and coordinating a network of around 300 workplace groups and around 200 individual members committed to the extension of Christ's kingdom in the working world. It was founded in 1942 to bring together Christians to work for the extension of Christ's kingdom in the world of business and industry; to encourage active evangelism and fellowship; to provide information, literature and other facilities; to help Christians who stand alone in their place of work and to provide a means whereby young Christians starting work may be strengthened in their faith. *National Director:* Revd Brian Allenby. *Administrator:* Miss Gail Alberts, 148 Railway Terrace, Rugby, CV21 3HN
Tel: 01788 579738
email: office@christiansatwork.org.uk
Web: www.christiansatwork.org.uk

Church Action with the Unemployed
Formed in 1981, an ecumenical organization supported by the leaders of the main Churches in Great Britain. Its objective is to help and encourage churches in their ministry with unemployed people by the promotion of Unemployment Sunday (last Sunday before Lent) and by the provision and distribution of information outlining different ways in which local churches can support and sustain unemployed people. *Chairman:*

Canon Frank Scuffham. *Contact:* Ms Catherine Smyth, 45B Blythe St, London, E2 6LN
Tel: 020 7729 9990
Fax: 020 7256 1072

Church Army

Church Army is a society of evangelists within the Anglican Communion which exists to enable people to come to a living faith in Jesus Christ. Church Army evangelists share the Christian faith through words and action and equip others to do the same. Over 350 full-time evangelists and 150 further staff are devoted to a wide range of service within five areas of focus: area evangelism, children and young people, church planting, homeless people and older people, working in Anglican churches and in projects and teams throughout the UK and Ireland. Church Army evangelists are trained at the Church Army 'Wilson Carlile College of Evangelism' in Sheffield. Evangelists-in-training undertake the Diploma in Evangelism Studies and complete vocational training specific to their calling, as approved by the Ministry Division of the Church of England. *President:* Rt Revd and Rt Hon. Lord Carey of Clifton. *Chief Secretary:* Capt Philip Johanson. *Candidates Secretary:* Capt Hugh Boorman, Marlowe House, 109 Station Rd, Sidcup, DA15 7AD
Tel: 020 8309 9991
Fax: 020 8309 3500
email: information@churcharmy.org.uk
Web: www.churcharmy.org.uk

Church House Deaneries' Group – The National Deaneries Network

The Church House Deaneries' Group – The National Deaneries Network – exists to stimulate local and national consideration of the developing role of the deanery, to encourage an informal network for the exchange of information about deanery thinking and deanery initiatives through the Deanery Forum (web: www.chdg.org.uk), and to promote the mission opportunities of deaneries. Every two years since 1988 it has held a national conference about deaneries. It has very close links with Parish and People, which resources deaneries with printed material (see separate entry and web: www.parishandpeople. org.uk). *Chairman:* Ven Colin Hill (Carlisle). *Secretary:* Mr David Maxwell (Rochester). *Treasurer:* Mr John Wilson (Lichfield), 14 Honeypot Close, Frindsbury, Rochester, ME2 3DU
Tel: 01634 722097
email: davel.maxwell@virgin.net
Web: www.chdg.org.uk

Church Housing Trust

Church Housing Trust is committed to changing the lives of homeless people, providing the help and services they would otherwise be denied. Our principal objective is to raise funds to benefit homeless people and those in housing need, and in particular those cared for by English Churches Housing Group. Church Housing Trust supports residents in over 70 projects throughout England, including hostels, move-on housing, foyers, day centres, women's refuges and mother and baby projects. Resettlement and rehabilitation are key priorities, and donations are put towards re-education and training in areas ranging from cooking to computer skills. With encouragement and preparation, homeless people are helped to regain their independence and reintegrate into the community. PO Box 50296, London, EC1P 1WF
Tel: 020 7269 1630
Fax: 020 7404 2562
email: info@cht.dircon.co.uk
Web: www.churchhousingtrust.org.uk

Church Lads' and Church Girls' Brigade

The Brigade is the Anglican Church's only uniformed youth organisation, welcoming children and young people of all faiths and none, from ages 5 years to 21 years, engaging in 'fun, faith and friendship', equipping them to cope with the demands that society places upon them. The Brigade creates a caring and safe environment in which friendships between young people, children and adults can be established; helping children and young people to grow in confidence, developing their individual skills and abilities to work together, showing concern for others and the environment, exploring their spirituality and developing moral values. Operating in four age groups: 5–7 years, 7–10 years, 10–13 years and 13–21 years, there are appropriate training and activity programmes for all leaders and members to be engaged in. *Patron:* HM The Queen. *President:* The Archbishop of Canterbury. *Governor:* Anthony Baker. *Brigade Chaplain:* Rt Revd Jack Nicholls. *Brigade Secretary:* Alan Millward, National Headquarters, Saint Martin's House, 2 Barnsley Rd, Wath-Upon-Dearne, Rotherham, South Yorkshire S63 6PY
Tel: 01709 876535
Fax: 01709 878089
email: brigadesecretary@clcgb.org.uk
Web: www.clcgb.org.uk

Church Maintenance Trust

Founded in 1996, the Trust seeks to promote the accurate and lasting repair of ecclesiastical built heritage using traditional craft skills and materials. The Trust provides academic and skills support for the Canterbury Christ Church University College BA (Hons) Built Heritage Conservation course. *Chairman:* Dr Julian W. S. Litten. *Director:* Alex MacLaren, 27 Orchard St, Canterbury, CT2 8AP
Tel and Fax: 01227 451795

Church Mission Society

CMS is committed to evangelistic mission, working to see a world transformed by the love of Jesus. As a mission community, its members seek to live a mission lifestyle, encouraging others to do the same. CMS equips people for mission service through training, sending and receiving.

CMS shares resources for mission work through fundraising, its mission education centre, and as part of mission networks such as the Faith2Share network. As an organisation, CMS operates in an increasingly decentralized, network model, from offices in Cape Coast, Nairobi, Oxford and Seoul, supporting people in mission and mission projects in some 70 countries. Its publications include YES magazine, Connect (both three times a year), Mission Update and Prayerlines (monthly), Audiomission (podcast), trax16 (youth podcast) and resources for churches, small groups and schools. Registered Charity no. 220297. *Patron:* The Archbishop of Canterbury. *Chair of Trustees:* Rt Revd Paul Butler, Bishop of Southampton. *General Secretary:* Canon Tim Dakin, Watlington Rd, Oxford, OX4 6BZ
Tel: 0845 620 1799/01865 776 400 (Switchboard)
Fax: 01865 776 375
email: info@cms-uk.org
Web: www.cms-uk.org

Church Monuments Society
Founded in 1979 to encourage the appreciation, study and conservation of monuments. The Society promotes a biennial symposium, excursions, study days, a twice-yearly newsletter and an annual refereed journal. It also offers a programme of visits to locations throughout the country, a series of occasional lectures and an opportunity for people to meet and exchange views on a subject which spans many disciplines. It is the only society to cover all periods and all types of monument, and is the sponsor of the National Ledger Stone Survey. *President:* Dr Phillip G. Lindley. *Secretary:* Dr Amy L. Harris. *Treasurer:* Dr John Brown. *Membership Secretary:* Mr Clive Easter. *Publicity:* Dr John Bromilow, c/o Society of Antiquaries of London, Burlington House, Piccadilly, London, W1J 0BE
Tel: 01752 773634 (Membership)
01837 851483 (Publicity)
Fax: 01837 851483
email: churchmonuments@aol.com
Web: www.churchmonumentssociety.org

Church Music Society
Founded 1906. The society is a leading publisher of all types of Church music, and has consistently served the Church of England by this means. An annual lecture and other events for members pursue further aims of advancing knowledge of the art and science of Church music. Although much of the society's focus is on music specifically for liturgy, CMS publications are also in world-wide use by choirs of all types for concerts, recitals and recordings. 'Te Deum Laudamus', a CD of CMS publications, is now available. Details of membership and activities are available from the Secretary. *President:* The Dean of Hereford. *Chairman:* Mr Ian Curror. *Hon Secretary:* Dr Simon Lindley. *Hon General Editor:*

Mr Richard Lyne, 17 Fulneck, Pudsey, LS28 8NT
Tel and Fax: 0113 255 6143
email: cms@simonlindley.org.uk
Web: www.church-music.org.uk

Church of England Clergy Stipend Trust
Founded 1952 to augment stipends of parochial clergy, normally through Diocesan Boards of Finance. *Chairman:* Rt Revd Dr D. G. Snelgrove, Sceptre Court, 40 Tower Hill, London, EC3N 4DX
Tel: 020 7423 8000
Fax: 020 7423 8001

Church of England Evangelical Council
Founded 1960 to (1) bring together evangelical leaders of the Church of England for mutual counsel and discussion (2) seek to reach a common mind on the issues of the day and when appropriate to reveal their findings to the Church and nation (3) encourage those societies and individuals in a position to do so to increase the evangelical contribution to the Church of England (4) assist in such work throughout the Anglican Communion. It organizes an occasional National Evangelical Anglican Congress to help further its aims. *President:* Rt Revd Wallace Benn. *Chairman:* Revd Dr Richard Turnbull. *Secretary:* Canon Michael Walters. *Treasurer:* Dr Graham Campbell, 27 Alvanley Rise, Northwich, CW9 8AY
Tel: 01606 333126
email: executive.officer@ceec.info
Web: www.ceec.info

Church of England Flower Arrangers Association
The Church of England Flower Arrangers Association (CEFAA) was founded in 1981 to help and encourage all those who tend flowers in churches and link them in fellowship and friendship. It is open to all those baptized in the Christian faith. The aims are to expand interest in church flower arranging, to use talent to enrich places of worship and to support what theology and creation try to teach. CEFAA is a voluntary charity whose constitution covers the work members do in churches, church buildings and at church events. The Association is not sponsored and is non-competitive. Registered Charity no. 514372. *President:* Revd Noel Michell. *Chairman:* Mrs Hillary Brian. *Treasurer:* Mrs Naomi Hadden. *Secretary:* Mr Laurence Fielding, 32 East Quay, Wapping Dock, Liverpool, L3 4BU
Tel: 0151 709 5116
email: cefaa@eastquay.fsnet.co.uk

Church of England Record Society
Founded in 1991 with the object of promoting interest in and knowledge of the history of the Church of England from the sixteenth century onwards, the Society publishes primary material of national significance for Church history. It aims to produce one volume each year, set against an annual subscription of £20

(individuals), and £30 (institutions). *Exec Secretary:* Miss Melanie Barber, 13 Tarleton Gardens, Forest Hill, London, SE23 3XN

Tel: 020 8699 0820
email: coers@dsl.pipex.com
Web: www.coers.org

Church of England Soldiers', Sailors' and Airmen's Clubs (1891)

A registered charity which, since its foundation in 1891, has maintained clubs at home and abroad for HM Forces and their dependants, whatever their religious denomination. The work of the association now encompasses rented housing for elderly ex-Service people or their widows/widowers. The association also helps other charities to build sheltered housing for ex-Service people, working in parallel with its sister organization, CESSA Housing Association. Donations always welcomed. *General Secretary:* Cdr Martin Marks. *Assistant Secretary:* Cdr Mike Pearce, CESSAC, 1 Shakespeare Terrace, 126 High St, Portsmouth, PO1 2RH

Tel: 023 9282 9319
Fax: 023 9282 4018
email: martin.marks@ntlbusiness.com

Church of England Soldiers', Sailors' and Airmen's Housing Association Ltd (1972)

A charitable Housing Association, registered with the Housing Corporation to provide low cost rented sheltered accommodation for elderly ex-Service people or their widows/widowers and partners of all denominations. Construction costs were provided partly by government grants, but donations are always welcome to help fund modernisation. *Chief Exec:* Cdr Martin Marks . *Housing Manager:* Cdr Mike Pearce, CESSA H. A., 1 Shakespeare Terrace, 126 High St, Portsmouth, PO1 2RH   *Tel:* 023 9282 9319
Fax: 023 9282 4018
email: mike.pearce@ntlbusiness.com
Web: www.cessaha.co.uk

Church Pastoral Aid Society Ministers in Training Fund

The Church Pastoral Aid Society administers the Ministers in Training Fund. This fund gives grants to evangelical men and women, married or single, who are facing financial hardship whilst training for ordained ministry. *Leadership and Development Adviser (Vocations):* Mrs Pauline Walden, Ministers in Training Fund, CPAS, Athena Drive, Tachbrook Park, Warwick, CV34 6NG   *Tel:* 01926 458480
Fax: 01926 458459
email: pwalden@cpas.org.uk
Web: www.cpas.org.uk

Church Schoolmasters and School Mistresses' Benevolent Institution

Founded in 1857 to provide assistance for Church of England teachers in England and Wales in times of temporary affliction or misfortune, or upon retirement or permanent disablement, and assistance towards the maintenance and education of their orphans. The CSSBI runs Glen Arun Care Home which has a strong Christian ethos and is set in a semi-rural location. The home provides residential and nursing care accomodation. It has 35 single rooms where residents can benefit from 24 hour nursing care. *Patron:* HM The Queen. *President:* The Bishop of London. *Chairman:* Miss Diana Bell. *Patient Care Manager:* Mrs Sue Green. *Company Secretary:* Mrs Marie di Cara, Glen Arun, 9 Athelstan Way, Horsham, RH13 6HA   *Tel:* 01403 253881 (Admin)
01403 255749 (Nursing Office)
Fax: 01403 254971
email: glenarun@hotmail.com

Church Society

Formed in 1950 by the amalgamation of the Church Association and National Church League, which was founded in 1835, continues to seek to maintain the evangelical and reformed faith of the Church of England, based upon the authority of Holy Scripture (see Canon A 5) and the foundational doctrines of the Thirty-nine Articles and the Book of Common Prayer. Publishes a journal, *Churchman*, and a quarterly broadsheet, *Cross+Way*. The Society publishes books, booklets and leaflets on current issues and organizes conferences and public meetings. Patronage is administered through the Church Society Trust. (See also Patronage Trusts.) *President:* The Viscount Brentford. *Chairman:* Revd George Curry. *General Secretary:* Revd David Phillips, Dean Wace House, 16 Rosslyn Rd, Watford, WD18 0NY   *Tel:* 01923 235111
Fax: 01923 800362
email: admin@churchsociety.org
Web: www.churchsociety.org

Church Union

Founded in 1859, at the time of the Oxford Movement, to promote catholic faith and order, it continues this work today by providing support and encouragement to those lay people and priests who wish to see catholic faith, order, morals and spirituality maintained and upheld, and who wish to promote catholic unity. The Union publishes books and tracts and produces an in-house magazine, the *Church Observer*. *President:* Rt Revd Edwin Barnes. *Chairman:* Mr David Morgan. *Treasurer:* Revd Richard Gomersall. *Membership:* Mrs Jenny Miller, Faith House, 7 Tufton St, London, SW1P 3QN

Tel: 020 7222 6952/01884 34563 (Membership)
Fax: 020 7976 7180
email: secretary@churchunion.co.uk /
membership@churchunion.co.uk
Web: www.churchunion.co.uk

Church Welfare Association (Incorporated)
(formerly the Church Moral Aid Association)
Founded 1851. Gives financial aid to Church projects assisting and supporting women and children in need of residential care and/or moral support. *Chairman:* Miss G. A. Reeve. *Secretary:* Mr D. J. Boddington, 15 Marina Court, Alfred St, Bow, London, E3 2BH   *Tel:* 020 8981 3341
          Web: http://cwa.awardspace.co.uk

Church's Ministry Among Jewish People
Founded 1809 as London Society for Promoting Christianity Among the Jews, to take the Christian gospel to Jewish people. *President:* Rt Revd John B. Taylor. *Chair:* Mr Ben Salter. *CEO:* Mr Robin Aldridge, Eagle Lodge, Hexgreave Hall Business Park, Farnsfield, Notts, NG22 8LS
          Tel: 01623 883960
          Fax: 01623 884295
          email: enquiries@cmj.org.uk
          Web: www.cmj.org.uk

Churches' Advertising Network
A professional group of Christians from all traditions cooperating to develop the professional use of advertising as part of the Churches' communication and outreach. CAN seeks free or low cost poster space and radio airtime from leading media owners, which it uses on behalf of the Churches. All members give their services free. Charity Registration no. 1096868. *Chair:* Mr F. Goodwin. *Secretary & Treasurer:* Revd Tony Kinch. *Asst Treasurer:* Mrs Karen Gray. *Trustee:* Revd John Carter, The Methodist Centre, 24 School St, Wolverhampton, WV1 4LF
          Tel: 01902 422100
          Fax: 01902 313301
          email: churchads@methodist.fsnet.co.uk
          Web: www.churchads.org.uk

Churches' Fellowship for Psychical and Spiritual Studies
Founded 1953 to study the psychic and spiritual and their relevance to Christian faith and life. *President:* Very Revd Alexander Wedderspoon. *Chair:* Revd Nancy Walthew. *General Secretary:* Mr Julian Drewett, The Rural Workshop, South Rd, North Somercotes, Louth, LN11 7PT
          Tel and Fax: 01507 358845
          email: gensec@churchesfellowship.co.uk
          Web: www.churchesfellowship.co.uk

Churches' Funerals Group
The Churches' Group on Funeral Services at Cemeteries and Crematoria was formed as an advisory group in 1980 by the mainstream Churches in England and Wales to co-ordinate their policies in connection with the pastoral and administrative aspects of funeral services at cemeteries and crematoria, and to represent the Churches at national level in joint discussions with public and private organizations on any matters relating to ministry at such funerals. The Group keeps in close touch with the main organizations concerned with funeral provision and bereavement counselling. To reflect its involvement in the wider aspects of all concerned with funerals and death in our society, the Group shortened its working title in 2002 to 'The Churches' Funerals Group'. Publications sponsored by the Group include *The Role of the Minister in Bereavement: Guidelines and Training Suggestions* (Church House Publishing, 1989); *Guidelines for Best Practice of Clergy at Funerals* (Church House Publishing, 1997); and two joint funeral service books (The Canterbury Press, Norwich), one for use in England (1986, 1994 and 2001), the other for use in Wales (1987). Three previous conference reports have been published: *The Role of a Minister at a Funeral* (1991), *Bereavement and Belief* (1993) and *Clergy and Cremation Today* (1995). An information leaflet entitled *Questions Commonly Asked about Funerals* (2nd edition, 2007) is also available free of charge from the Secretary. *Chairman:* Rt Revd Dr Geoffrey Rowell, Bp of Gibraltar in Europe. *Secretary:* Ms Sue Moore, Church House, Great Smith St, London, SW1P 3AZ   *Tel:* 020 7898 1376
          Fax: 020 7898 1369
          email: enquiries@christianfunerals.org
          Web: www.christianfunerals.org

Churches' Legislation Advisory Service
Founded 1941, and registered as a charity in 1966, to advance the charitable work, whether religious or otherwise, of the Churches by furthering their common interests in secular matters relating to that work, other than education; to give advice to the Churches on these matters; to conduct negotiations and take such action as may be thought fit; to act as a liaison body between the Churches and the machinery of government. *Chairman:* Rt Revd Geoge Cassidy. *Secretary:* Mr Frank Cranmer, Church House, Great Smith St, London, SW1P 3AZ   *Tel:* 020 7222 1265
          email: frank.cranmer@centrallobby.com
          Web: www.clas.org.uk

Cleaver Ordination Candidates' Fund
An academic trust to assist ordinands, clergy pursuing recognized courses of postgraduate study, and parochial clergy on approved study leave. Candidates must belong to the Catholic tradition within the Anglican Communion. Preference may be given to graduates of British universities. There is no permanent office, the Clerk of the time being working from his home address. *Clerk to the Cleaver Trustees:* Revd Dr Peter Lynn, 119 Stanford Ave, Brighton, BN1 6FA   *Tel:* 01273 553361
          email: palproof@hotmail.com

Clergy Consultation, The
(Formerly known as Lesbian and Gay Clergy Consultation)
The Clergy Consultation is a confidential support organization for lesbian, gay, bisexual or

transgender clergy, religious, ordinands and their partners. There are over 200 members, mostly Anglican, but other denominations are welcome. Day conferences are organized twice a year, usually in London, as well as some social activities. The Consultation provides mutual support and advice, offers a forum for education and discussion, and responds to the professional and pastoral needs of homosexual clergy. It invites bishops, theologians and others who work in church structures to engage in dialogue. A newsletter is sent up to four times a year to all members. The Consultation operates a policy of strict confidentiality to protect the interests of its members. Details of meetings are given only to members and those invited to participate in meetings. There is an annual membership fee and a charge is made for attendance at each meeting. Reduced rates are available for the retired, for unemployed clergy, religious and ordinands who are studying full-time. 10 Wincott St, London, SE11 4NT   *email:* clergy.consultation@virgin.net

COIN: Christians on the Internet

An interdenominational group of Christians throughout Britain and Ireland working together since 1995 to advise, help and encourage the Church in its use of the Internet. It functions both as a group of individuals able to offer their particular expertise, and also, through email, as a lively online community discussing in depth a wide variety of issues affecting Christians, including specialist lists discussing Church of England issues, and Common Worship. Further details of COIN and its activities can be found on its web site. *Chair:* Chris Wright. *Secretary:* Simon Kershaw. *Treasurer:* Revd Gordon Giles. *Membership Secretary:* Revd Alan Jesson

Tel: 01480 381471
email: secretary@coin.org.uk/
membership@coin.org.uk
Web: www.coin.org.uk

College of Evangelists

The national College of Evangelists was founded in 1999 to support and give the accreditation of the Archbishops of Canterbury and York to evangelists in the Church of England. To qualify, evangelists will be involved in active evangelistic ministry (not just training or teaching about evangelism) and will be operating nationally or regionally, beyond their diocesan boundaries. Potential candidates should contact their diocesan bishop in the first instance. *Chairman:* The Bishop of Lichfield. *Administrator:* Canon Paul Bayes, Church House, Great Smith St, London, SW1P 3NZ   *Tel:* 020 7898 1502
Fax: 020 7898 1431
email: paul.bayes@c-of-e.org.uk

College of Health Care Chaplains

Founded in 1992, the College is a multi-faith, interdenominational professional association open to all recognized health care chaplaincy staff, full-time and part-time, including voluntary and support workers, and others with an interest in health care chaplaincy. With around 960 members throughout the United Kingdom, it provides peer support, advice and fellowship for members nationally and in 12 regional branches. A focus for professional development, good practice and training, the College publishes the *Journal of Health Care Chaplaincy* (available on subscription to non-members) and issues regular newsletters. As an autonomous section of the Unite trade union, terms and conditions are negotiated for all chaplains on a national basis, and members receive professional support on employment issues. *President:* Revd Anne Aldridge. *Vice-President:* Revd Jane Shephard. *Registrar:* Revd William Sharpe, 33–37 Moreland St, London, EC1V 8HA   *Tel:* 020 7780 4053
Fax: 020 7780 4142
email: william.sharpe@unitetheunion.com
Web: www.healthcarechaplains.org.uk

College of Preachers

An ecumenical network of preachers, ordained and lay, dedicated to preaching which is faithful and fresh, biblical and relevant, and to helping one another to develop preaching skills through seminars, conferences, a journal and guided study. *Chairman:* Revd Dr Leslie Griffiths. *Director:* Mr Paul Johns. *Administrator:* Ms Morfa Jones, Chester House, Pages Lane, Muswell Hill, London, N10 1PR   *Tel:* 020 8883 7850
Fax: 020 8883 0843
email: administrator@collegeofpreachers.org.uk
Web: www.collegeofpreachers.org.uk

College of Readers

An independent membership organization providing fellowship and support for Readers of the Anglican Communion in the British Isles, especially to those Readers who subscribe to the authority of scripture, the grace of the sacraments and the traditional understanding of the ordained ministry of the bishop, priest and deacon. The College is establishing a network of local circles and chaplains, and publishes a quarterly magazine, *Blue Scarf*, which keeps all members in touch. Distance learning packages are available, as are a series of publications on aspects of Reader ministry. Regional and national meetings are organized each year. *Patron:* Rt Revd Martyn Jarrett. *Secretary:* Mr John Mitchell, 6 The Chase, Penn, High Wycombe, HP10 8BA   *Tel:* 01494 813045
email: mesnape@yahoo.co.uk
Web: www.college-of-readers.org.uk

College of St Barnabas

Set in idyllic Surrey countryside, the College is a residential community of retired Anglican clergy, including married couples and widows. Admission is also open to licensed Church Workers and Readers. There are facilities for visitors and

guests, and occasional quiet days and private retreats can also be accommodated. Residents lead active, independent lives for as long as possible. There is a Nursing Wing providing residential and full nursing care for those who need it, enabling most residents to remain members of the College for the rest of their lives. Respite care is sometimes possible here. Sheltered flats in the Cloisters all have separate sitting rooms, bedrooms and en suite facilities. There are two chapels, daily Mass and Evensong, three libraries, a well equipped common room and refectory, a snooker table and a nine-hole putting green. The College is easily accessible by road and is also next to Dormans Station on the line from London to East Grinstead. For further details or to arrange a preliminary visit, please see our website or contact the Warden. *Warden:* Revd Howard Such. *Bursar:* Paul G. F. Wilkin, The College of St Barnabas, Blackberry Lane, Lingfield, Surrey RH7 6NJ   *Tel:* 01342 870260
Fax: 01342 871672
email: warden@collegeofstbarnabas.com
Web: www.st-barnabas.org.uk

Commonwealth War Graves Commission

Founded 1917. Responsible for marking and maintaining in perpetuity the graves of those of Commonwealth Forces who fell in the 1914–18 and 1939–45 Wars and for commemorating by name on memorials those with no known grave. *President:* HRH The Duke of Kent. *Chairman:* Secretary of State for Defence in the UK. *Enquiries:* Legal Adviser and Solicitor, 2 Marlow Rd, Maidenhead, Berkshire, SL6 7DX   *Tel:* 01628 507 138
Fax: 01628 507134
email: legal@cwgc.org
Web: www.cwgc.org

Community Housing and Therapy

CHT provides group and individual psychotherapy in residential settings to clients who are experiencing mental health and emotional difficulties. The care of each client is planned through an individual Care Plan which is reviewed every three to six months. Reviews are interdisciplinary and CHT therapists with social workers and psychatrists, together with others, review progress and set goals together with the client. These goals focus on key areas in the life of each client, for example, housing needs, relationships, medication and re-training for work. *Chief Exec:* Mr John Gale. *Chief Operating Officer:* Ms Inma Vidana. *Deputy Director, Clinical Services:* Miss Beatriz Sanchez. *Senior Managers:* Mr Vasilli Magalios, Dr Alistair Black, Mr Amer Si Mohand, 24/5–6 The Coda Centre, 189 Munster Rd, London, SW6 6AW   *Tel:* 020 7381 5888/
0800 018 1261 (Freephone)
Fax: 020 7610 0608
email: co@cht.org.uk
Web: www.cht.org.uk

Community of Aidan and Hilda

A dispersed, ecumenical and international body of Christians who journey with God, and reconnect with the Spirit and the Scriptures, the saints and the streets, the seasons and the soil. The Community seeks to cradle a Christian spirituality for today which renews the Church and brings healing to fragmented people and communities. It welcomes people of all backgrounds and countries who wish to be wholly available to God the Holy Trinity, and to the way of Jesus as revealed in the Bible. In the earthing of that commitment members draw particular inspiration from Celtic saints such as Aidan and Hilda. Members follow a Way of Life based on a rhythm of prayer and study, simplicity, care for creation, and mission, seeking to weave together the separated strands of Christianity. Each shares their journey with a spiritual companion known as a Soul Friend. The work of the Community is the work of each member and can be expressed individually and corporately in many ways, such as through link houses, churches, monastic experiments, and indigenous national branches. Its mother house and spirituality centre is The Open Gate, Holy Island, Berwick-upon-Tweed, TD15 2SD. *Community Soul Friend (Episcopally endorsed visitor):* Canon Godfrey Butland. *International Guardian:* Revd Ray Simpson. *Secretary:* Naomi Ackland. *Retreat House Wardens:* Revd Graham and Dr Ruth Booth, Lindisfarne Retreat, Holy Island, Berwick-upon-Tweed, TD15 2SD
Tel: 01289 389249 (International Office)
01289 389222 (Holy Island Retreat
House Bookings)
email: admin@ca-and-h.demon.co.uk
Web: www.aidanandhilda.org

Compassionate Friends, The

A nationwide organization of bereaved parents and their families offering friendship and understanding to others similarly bereaved. Personal and group support. Quarterly newsletter, annual conferences, postal book library and a range of publications. The national helpline is open 365 days a year, 10 a.m. to 4 p.m. and 6.30 p.m. to 10.30 p.m. *Office Manager:* Michael Brown, 53 North St, Bristol, BS3 1EN
Tel: 0845 123 2304 (National Helpline)
0845 120 3785 (Admin)
Fax: 0845 120 3786
email: info@tcf.org.uk
Web: www.tcf.org.uk

Confraternity of the Blessed Sacrament

Founded 1862 to honour Jesus Christ our Lord in the Blessed Sacrament; to make mutual eucharistic intercession and to encourage eucharistic devotion. Registered Charity no. 1082897. *Superior-General:* Revd Christopher Pearson. *Secretary General:* Canon Lawson Nagel, Aldwick

Vicarage, 25 Gossamer Lane, Bognor Regis, PO21 3AT   *Tel:* 01243 262049
email: cbs@confraternity.org.uk
Web: www.confraternity.org.uk

Corporation of the Sons of the Clergy
Founded 1655. Incorporated by Royal Charter 1678. For helping clergy of the Anglican Communion in the UK and Eire and Anglican missionaries abroad providing they are sponsored by a UK-based missionary society. The Corporation can also help widows and widowers of such clergy, their separated or divorced spouses, and the children of such clergy who are dependants of any of the above. Help can also be given to unmarried daughters of pensionable age. The Corporation is also trustee for the Clergy Orphan Corporation. The Corporation of the Sons of the Clergy and the Friends of the Clergy Corporation now work together from a single office and operate a unified grant-making system with a joint application form. *President:* The Archbishop of Canterbury. *Registrar:* Mr Robert Welsford, 1 Dean Trench St, London, SW1P 3HB
Tel: 020 7799 3696
Fax: 020 7222 3468
email: enquiries@clergycharities.org.uk
Web: www.clergycharities.org.uk

Council of Christians and Jews
Founded 1942 to combat all forms of religious and racial intolerance, to promote mutual understanding and goodwill between Christians and Jews, and to foster cooperation in educational activities and in social and community service. Forty local branches in the UK. *Patron:* HM The Queen. *Presidents:* Archbishop of Canterbury; Chief Rabbi; Cardinal Archibishop of Westminster; Moderator of the Free Churches; Rabbi Tony Bayfield; Head, Reform Movement; Archbishop of Thyatira and Great Britain; Moderator of the Church of Scotland. *Chair:* Rt Revd Nigel McCulloch, Bishop of Manchester. *Chief Executive:* David Gifford MA, 1st Floor, Camelford House, 87–89 Albert Embankment, London, SE1 7TP
Tel: 020 7820 0090
Fax: 020 7820 0504
email: cjrelations@ccj.org.uk
Web: www.ccj.org.uk

Council on Christian Approaches to Defence and Disarmament
CCADD was established in 1963 by the Rt Revd Robert Stopford, then Bishop of London, to study problems relating to defence and disarmament within a Christian context. The British Group of CCADD comprises Christians of different traditions, varying vocations and specializations and political views, with a range of responsibilities, governmental and non-governmental. CCADD seeks to bring an ethical viewpoint to bear on disarmament and arms control and related issues and to this end the British Group has always stressed the importance of dialogue between official and non-official bodies. *President:* Rt Revd Richard Harries. *Chairman:* Mr Brian Wicker. *Admin Secretary:* Mrs Liza Hamilton, 5 Cubitts Meadow, Buxton, Norwich, NR10 5EF
Tel and Fax: 01603 279939
email: ccadd@lineone.net
Web: http://website.lineone.net/ccadd

CPAS (Church Pastoral Aid Society)
We long to see a Christ-centred, Bible-based, mission-focused church where leaders are clear about their call to discipleship, growing in Christ-like character, and competent to lead in a time of rapid change; where leaders discern God's direction, enable action, build teams, develop leaders, facilitate communication, and nurture people; where leaders work in teams, reflecting the diversity of ministries, and model themselves on the servant character of Jesus; where leaders help transform inherited churches, pioneer emerging churches and deliver creative residential ministry, effectively helping children, young people and adults hear and discover the good news of Jesus Christ. *President:* Rt Revd James Jones. *General Director:* Revd John Dunnett, Athena Drive, Tachbrook Park, Warwick, CV34 6NG
Tel: 01926 458458
Fax: 01926 458459
email: info@cpas.org.uk
Web: www.cpas.org.uk

Crosslinks
Founded 1922 as the Bible Churchmen's Missionary Society (BCMS). Crosslinks is an international evangelical Anglican mission agency seeking to take God's Word to God's World in creative and entrepreneurial ways. A member of the Partnership for World Mission (PWM), it works in partnership with Anglican dioceses in the developing world primarily, through the provision of mission partners and student bursaries. Mission partners work in East, North and South Africa, Europe and Asia as well as among those of other faiths in the UK. *President:* Revd Dr C. Wright. *General Secretary:* Canon Andy Lines. *Chairman:* Revd M. Payne, 251 Lewisham Way, London, SE4 1XF
Tel: 020 8691 6111
Fax: 020 8694 8023
email: info@crosslinks.org
Web: www.crosslinks.org

Culham Educational Foundation
The Trust gives mainly personal grants not exceeding £1,000 to practising Anglicans who are pursuing personal study or undertaking projects or research primarily relating to RE in schools. Normally consideration will be given only to applicants who live or work in the Diocese of Oxford or who are former members of the old college at Culham. Member of the Association of Church College Trusts (see separate entry).

Correspondent: Revd Dr John Gay, 15 Norham Gardens, Oxford, OX2 6PY   *Tel:* 01865 284885
Fax: 01865 284886
email: enquiries@culham.ac.uk
Web: www.culham.ac.uk

Culham Institute
This is a research, development and information agency working in the fields of Church schools, Church colleges, RE and collective worship. It has established a national system of networking, collaborative activity and project management. Current collaboration includes work with the Jerusalem Trust, the St Gabriel's Trust, the All Saints Trust and the National Society. It is planning to establish a national Centre for Religious Education in the City of London. The Association of Church College Trusts and RE online have their bases at Culham. *Director:* Revd Dr John Gay, 15 Norham Gardens, Oxford, OX2 6PY
Tel: 01865 284885
Fax: 01865 284886
email: enquiries@culham.ac.uk
Web: www.culham.ac.uk

Day One Christian Ministries
Incorporating The Lord's Day Observance Society (founded in 1831 to preserve Sunday as the national day of rest and to promote its observance as the Lord's Day for worship and Christian service), Day One Publications and Day One Prison Ministry. *President:* Revd Philip Hacking. *Secretary:* Mr John Roberts. *Production:* Mr Jim Holmes, Ryelands Rd, Leominster, HR6 8NZ
Tel: 01568 613740
email: sales@dayone.co.uk
Web: www.docm.org.uk / www.dayone.co.uk

Deaf People, Royal Association for
RAD promotes the welfare and interests of deaf people, working with the Deaf Community, Deaf Clubs, deaf individuals and the parents of deaf children. Most of RAD's work is in London, Essex and the south-east of England. RAD is organized around the following services: Deaf Community Development; Advice and Advocacy; Learning Disability; Mental Health; Sign Language Interpreting; Training. *Chief Executive:* Mr Tom Fenton, 18 Westside Centre, London Rd, Stanway, Colchester, CO3 8PH
Tel: 0845 688 2525/0845 688 2527 (Text)
Fax: 0845 688 2526
email: info@royaldeaf.org.uk
Web: www.royaldeaf.org.uk

Deans' Conference
The Deans' Conference is the meeting together (three times annually) of those who preside over their Cathedral Chapters to reflect upon cathedral issues of particular concern to Deans in their public and cathedral roles. *Chairman:* The Dean of Canterbury. *Treasurer:* The Dean of Exeter. *Secretary:* The Dean of Chelmsford,

Cathedral Office, New St, Chelmsford, CM1 1TY
Tel: 01245 294492   *Fax:* 01245 294499
email: dean@chelmsfordcathedral.org.uk

Deans' Vergers' Conference
Founded in 1989 to bring together Head Vergers who are employed in that capacity by a Dean and Chapter of the Church of England. The Conference enables members to communicate with one another, exchange and discuss ideas of common interest and to have regular contact with the Deans' Conference. The Head Vergers of the forty-two English cathedrals, Westminster Abbey and St George's Windsor are eligible for membership. *Chairman:* Alex Carberry . *Treasurer:* Clive McCleester . *Secretary:* Glynn Usher, Head Verger and Sub-Sacrist, Bristol Cathedral, College Green, Bristol BS1 5TJ
Tel: 0117 946 8179 (Direct)
0117 926 4879 (Cathedral Office)
Fax: 0117 925 3678
email: glynn.usher@bristol-cathedral.co.uk

Diaconal Association of the Church of England
DACE is a professional association for diaconal ministers (deacons, accredited lay workers and Church Army officers) working in the Church of England, established in 1988 to succeed the Deaconess Committee and the Anglican Accredited Lay Workers Federation. Associate membership is also open to those who support diaconal ministry, and diaconal ministers working in other provinces in the UK. DACE exists to promote the distinctive (permanent) diaconate and other diaconal ministries in the Church of England, support all nationally recognized diaconal ministers, and to consider the theological and practical implications of diaconal ministry within the total ministry of the Christian Church, in partnership with other agencies and denominations. DACE is a member of the Diakonia World Federation of Diaconal Associations and Diaconal Communities. A registered charity. *President:* Revd Ann Wren. *Secretary:* Capt Neil Thomson CA. *Treasurer:* Revd Graham Waring, 95 Ballens Rd, Lordswood, Chatham, ME5 8PA
Tel: 0870 321 3260
Fax: 07092 217679
email: secretary@dace.info
Web: www.societies.anglican.org/dace

Diakonia
Founded in 1947 to link the various European deaconess associations, it is now a 'World Federation of Diaconal Associations'. It concerns itself with the nature and task of 'Diakonia' and encourages deaconesses, deacons, and lay people doing diaconal work. It also furthers ecumenical relations between the diaconal associations in other countries. The Diaconal Association of the Church of England is a member. There is a Diakonia 'UK Liaison Group' which also includes representatives from the Methodist Diaconal

Order, the Church of Scotland Diaconate and the Deaconesses of the Presbyterian Church in Ireland. *UK Rep, Exec Cttee of World Diakonia:* Deacon Jackie Fowler, 82 Empress Road, Derby, DE23 6TE   *Tel:* 01332 361290
email: jackie.fowler@diakonia-world.org
Web: www.diakonia-world.org

Diocesan Clergy Chairs' Forum
The Forum is a voluntary group, allowing the elected chairs of the houses of clergy in each diocese to share ideas and experience, to address together various issues affecting the Church of England, to offer mutual support, and to develop principles of best practice in fulfilling this role in each diocese. Guidelines for best practice have been agreed with the House of Bishops. *Chair:* Canon Robert Cotton. *Hon. Secretary:* Revd Steve Parish, 1A Fitzherbert St, Warrington, WA2 7QG   *Tel:* 01925 631781
email: s.parish17@ntlworld.com

Diocesan Institutions of Chester, Manchester, Liverpool and Blackburn
For the relief of widows and orphans of clergymen who have officiated in their last sphere of duty in the Archdeaconries of Chester, Macclesfield, Manchester, Rochdale, Liverpool, Warrington or Blackburn. *Chair:* Canon Michael S. Finlay, Rectory, Warrington, WA1 2TL
Tel: 01925 635020
email: finlay289@btinternet.com

Distinctive Diaconate
An unofficial Church of England centre which serves to promote the diaconate as one of the historic orders of the Church's ministry with manifold potential for ministry today by sharing information about current developments through the newsletter *Distinctive Diaconate News.* It also produces *Distinctive News of Women in Ministry.* The *Mission and Ministry* report of Lambeth 1988 recommended the sharing of experiences with the diaconate within the Anglican Communion and suggested using Distinctive Diaconate. The editor was the convenor for the deacon/lay ministries group of Theological Education for the Anglican Communion. *Editor:* Revd Dr Sr Teresa CSA, St Andrew's House, 16 Tavistock Crescent, Westbourne Park, London, W11 1AP   *Tel:* 020 7221 4604
email: teresajoan@btinternet.com
Web: www.distinctive-diaconate.org.uk

Ecclesiastical Insurance Office PLC
Ecclesiastical is an independent UK-owned insurer and investment management organization that donates a significant proportion of its profits to charity. Ecclesiastical has been providing a range of personal insurances, financial advice and investment services for the Church and community for more than a century. Today they also provide specialist commercial insurances for charities, the education and care sectors, churches and historic buildings. *Chairman:* Mr Nicholas Sealy. *Group Chief Executive:* Mr Michael Tripp, Beaufort House, Brunswick Rd, Gloucester, GL1 1JZ   *Tel:* 01452 528533
Fax: 01452 423557
email: information@eigmail.com
Web: www.ecclesiastical.com

Ecclesiastical Law Society
Founded in 1987 to promote the study of ecclesiastical law, through the education of office bearers and practitioners in the ecclesiastical courts, the enlargement of knowledge of ecclesiastical law among clergy and laity of the Anglican Communion, and assistance in matters of ecclesiastical law to the General Synod, Convocations, bishops and church dignitaries. *President:* Rt Revd Dr Eric Kemp. *Chairman:* The Bishop of Guildford. *Secretary:* Mr Peter Beesley. *Deputy Secretary:* Mr Howard Dellar, 1 The Sanctuary, London, SW1P 3JT   *Tel:* 020 7222 5381
Fax: 020 7799 2781
email: info@ecclawsoc.org.uk
Web: www.ecclawsoc.org.uk

Ecclesiological Society
For those who love churches. Founded as the Cambridge Camden Society in 1839. Studies the arts, architecture and liturgy of the Christian Church by meetings, tours and publications. *President:* Donald Buttress. *Chairman of the Council:* Trevor Cooper. *Honorary Membership Secretary:* John Henman, PO Box 287, New Malden, KT3 4YT   *Tel:* 020 8942 2111/020 7021 9685
email: admin@ecclsoc.org
Web: www.ecclsoc.org

Ecumenical Coalition of Women Ministers
Sponsored by the Society for the Ministry of Women in the Church (Ecumenical), the Coalition attempts to share information among and coordinate the activities of Methodist Women's Forum, Women in Ministry Network (URC), Catholic Women's Ordination and WATCH. It normally meets only once a year and representatives of women in ministry of other Churches are invited to its meeting. It is advised by CTBI's Church Life Secretary and CTE's Secretary for Women and Social (diaconia) Concerns. It reports to the Women's Coordinating Group of CTE. *Chair:* Vacancy. *Secretary:* Ms Katrina Bradley, Church Life, Inter-Church House, 35–41 Lower Marsh, London, SE1 7SA   *Tel:* 020 7523 2132

Ecumenical Council for Corporate Responsibility
ECCR was set up in 1989 to study and research the corporate responsibility of companies and the Church, which holds investments, with special

Organizations

reference to those which are transnational corporations. ECCR is an ecumenical body with membership from many different denominations, societies, religious orders and other Church organizations. Its membership is approaching 200 corporate bodies and individuals. It has the status of a body in association with Churches Together in Britain and Ireland and it is structured as a company limited by guarantee, registered in England and Wales. *Researcher:* Suzanne Ismail. *Coordinator:* Miles Litvinoff. *Administrator:* Binia Scherrer. *Church and Membership Relations Officer:* Helen Boothroyd, PO Box 500, Oxford, OX1 1ZL

Tel: 01865 245349
email: info@eccr.org.uk
Web: www.eccr.org.uk

Ecumenical Society of the Blessed Virgin Mary

Founded in London in 1967, 'to advance the study at various levels of the place of the Blessed Virgin Mary in the Church under Christ and to promote ecumenical devotion'. Patrons: the Archbishop of Canterbury, the Archbishop of Westminster, Archbishop Gregorios of Thyateira, Revd Dr John Newton. *General Secretary:* Fr W. McLoughlin. *Hon Treasurer:* Mr F. O'Brien. *Publications Secretary:* Mr D. Carter. *Constitution Secretary:* Revd V. Cassam. *Secretary:* Mr J. P. Farrelly, 11 Belmont Rd, Wallington, SM6 8TE

Tel: 020 8647 5992
email: gensec@esbvm.org.uk /
j.farrelly.123@btinternet.com
Web: www.esbvm.org.uk

Elizabeth Finn Care

Elizabeth Finn Care is the UK's leading direct grant-giving charity dedicated specifically to helping those in poverty. These people have fallen below the poverty line and are unable to work due to a change of circumstances such as family breakdown, injury, physical or mental illness and redundancy. Elizabeth Finn also helps those who find themselves struggling to survive in retirement or who are unable to return to work, due to a long term disability or sickness, to have as normal a life as possible. Our financial grants vary from one-off payments of up to £2,000 to help deal with major costs like household repairs, to longer term support of up to £20 per week, to cover daily essentials. Elizabeth Finn offers more than financial support. Our team of caseworkers and 500 volunteers across the country work to rebuild self-esteem, restore hope and help individuals to feel a part of society again. In 2007/8 our grants totalled £3.9 million. For more information visit EFC's web site or phone the helpline. Registered charity no. 207812. *Chairman:* Richard Down. *Chief Exec:* Jonathan Welfare. *Director, Development & Communications:* Caroline Bates (acting). *Communica-*tions Manager: Rebecca Ward, 1 Derry St, London, W8 5HY

Tel: 020 7396 6700/
0800 413 220 (helpline)
Fax: 020 7396 6739
email: info@elizabethfinn.org.uk
Web: www.elizabethfinncare.org.uk

Elland Society Ordination Fund

Grants are made to applicants who are evangelical in conviction and who are in either residential or non-residential training for ordination in the Church of England. Priority is given to ordinands who are sponsored by dioceses in the Province of York or who intend to serve their title in that Province. Grants are usually to help those with unexpected or special financial needs which were not included in their main Church grant (if any). *Secretary/Treasurer:* Revd Colin Judd, 57 Grosvenor Road, Shipley, BD18 4RB

Tel: 01274 584775
email: thejudds@saltsvillage.wanadoo.co.uk
Web: www.ellandsociety.co.uk

English Churches Housing Group

Formed in 1991 by the merger of the Church Housing Association and the Baptist Housing Association and specializing in the provision of supported and older persons' housing. Based across the country with offices in Manchester, Leicester and Dartford. Manages 10,000 self-contained homes and 100 supported housing schemes with space for 2000 people. Offers a wide range of housing from general needs to sheltered schemes for elderly people and supported housing schemes for single, homeless people. *Chair:* Mrs Pam Chesters. *Chief Executive:* Mr Peter Walters, 49 Western Boulevard, Leicester, LE2 7HN

Tel: 0845 070 7071 (customers)
0151 295 6518 (customers)
email: enquiries@echg.org.uk
Web: www.echg.org.uk

English Clergy Association

Founded 1938, the Association seeks to sustain in fellowship all Clerks in Holy Orders in their vocation and ministry within the Church of England, promoting in every available way the good of English parish and cathedral life and the welfare of clergy. Related Trustees give discretionary clergy holiday grants upon application to the Hon Almoner. The Association seeks to foster the independence within the Established Church of all clergy whether in freehold office or not, and broadly supports the patronage system. Publishes twice-yearly 'Parson and Parish' magazine. Lay members may be admitted. Subscription £10 p.a. (£5 retired/ordinands). *Patron:* The Bishop of London. *Parliamentary Vice-President:* Sir Patrick Cormack MP. *Chairman:* Revd John Masding. *Deputy Chairman:* Mrs Margaret Laird. *Vice-Chairman:* Revd Jonathan Redvers Harris, The

Old School, Norton Hawkfield, Bristol, BS39 4HB   Tel: 01275 830017/01983 565953/ Fax: 01275 830017
email: benoporto-eca@yahoo.co.uk
Web: www.clergyassoc.co.uk

Evangelical Alliance

Founded in 1846 as a representative body with denominational, congregational, organizational and individual supporters, its vision is to unite evangelicals and to provide an evangelical voice in the public square. Also aims to encourage action among evangelicals leading to spiritual and social transformation in the UK. Operates in England, Northern Ireland, Scotland and Wales. *General Director:* Revd Joel Edwards. *Public Policy Director:* Dr R. David Muir. *Churches in Mission Director:* Dr Krish Kandiah. *Executive Director: Finance & Operations:* Miss Helen Calder, White-field House, 186 Kennington Park Rd, London, SE11 4BT   Tel: 020 7207 2100
Fax: 020 7210 2150
email: info@eauk.org
Web: www.eauk.org

Faith and Thought

(the operational name of the Victoria Institute or Philosophical Society of Great Britain)
Founded 1865 to enquire into the relationship between the Christian revelation and modern scientific research. Publishes *Faith and Thought new series* in succession to *The Journal of the Trans-actions of the Victoria Institute* (JTVI); from 1958 *Faith and Thought*; from 1989 *Faith&Thought Bul-letin.* Jointly with Christians in Science, since 1989 it sponsors the publication of *Science and Christian Belief.* Charity Registration no. 285871. *President:* Sir John Houghton. *Chairman:* Terence C. Mitch-ell. *Hon. Treasurer:* Revd John Buxton. *Editor & Meetings Secretary:* Reginald S. Luhman, 41 Marne Ave, Welling, DA16 2EY
Tel: 020 8303 0465/020 7352 3962/
Fax: 020 8303 0465
Web: www.faithandthought.org.uk

Family Life and Marriage Education Network

Acknowledging God's living presence both in the traditions of the Church and in all human experience, the FLAME network in the Church of England seeks to engage with the realities of fam-ily life. We seek to stimulate partnerships to address issues of family life and marriage, and co-operate with the Mothers' Union and others working ecumenically in the field. We seek to provide, share and signpost resources which provide theological reflection and practical action in relation to family life and marriage, and to that end publish material in Newsline and on the web site, as well as organizing conferences. We call on the Church of England to reaffirm family life and marriage as being at the heart of the Church's mission and ministry, and network those in the dioceses working in this field for mutual support

and stimulus. *Chair:* Revd Andrew Body. *Administrator:* Mrs Carol Davies. *Treasurer:* Mr Terry Sheppard. *Newsline Editor:* Mrs Kit MacLachlan, Flame Network, PO Box 4708, Rugby, CV21 9FL   Tel: 01788 544630
email: flamenetwork@tiscali.co.uk
Web: www.flamefamily.co.uk

Farnham Castle International Briefing and Conference Centre

Farnham Castle, the former palace of the bishops of Winchester, offers a unique and special loca-tion for church weekend retreats. Several London churches are regular visitors. The castle has 31 en suite bedrooms, including some family rooms, all with television. Facilities include two historic consecrated chapels, a wide choice of conference rooms and five acres of beautifully maintained gardens. Farnham Castle has an excellent dining room and bar. It overlooks the town of Farnham and is only seven minutes by taxi from the rail-way station. Farnham is 30 miles west of London, with good rail connections to Waterloo station (55 minutes). Special weekend rates are available for groups of over 30 adults. Please contact Teresa Clue, Events Manager, for further information. A video tour is available on the web site. *Chief Executive:* Mr James Twiss. *Director of Marketing & Client Services:* Mr Jeff Toms. *Conference Manager:* Mrs Barbara Milam. *Events Manager:* Teresa Clue, Farnham Castle, Farnham, GU9 0AG
Tel: 01252 721194
email: info@farnhamcastle.com
Web: www.farnhamcastle.com

Federation of Catholic Priests

A federation of priests in communion with the See of Canterbury who have undertaken to live in accordance with Catholic doctrine and prac-tice. It exists for mutual support in propagating, maintaining and defending such doctrine and practice and for the deepening of the spiritual life of members. *Chairman:* Revd Stephen Bould. *Sec-retary General:* Preb Brian Tubbs, Vicarage, Palace Place, Paignton, TQ3 3AQ   Tel: 01803 559059
email: fathertubbs@aol.com
Web: www.priests.org.uk

Feed the Minds

An ecumenical Christian organization, first estab-lished in 1964, that supports education in the world's poorest regions. *President:* Revd Myra Blyth. *Chair of Trustees:* Dr David Goodbourn. *Director:* Ms Josephine Carlsson, 36 Causton St, London, SW1P 4ST   Tel: 020 7592 3901/
08451 21 21 02

Fax: 020 7592 3939
email: info@feedtheminds.org
Web: www.feedtheminds.org

Fellowship of St Alban and St Sergius

Founded 1928. An unofficial body which fosters understanding and friendship between Eastern

Orthodox and Western Christians. *Presidents:* The Bishop of London and Archbishop Gregorios of Thyateira and Great Britain. *General Secretary:* Revd Stephen Platt. *Administrator:* Dr M. C. Steenberg, 1 Canterbury Rd, Oxford, OX2 6LU

Tel: 01865 552991
Fax: 01865 316700
email: gensec@sobornost.org
Web: www.sobornost.org

Fellowship of St Nicholas (FSN)

FSN uses its resources to offset the disadvantage, deprivation and abuse of children in need in Sussex. Our current services include 2 centre-based family support and day care services including mobile and outreach, UK on-line centres, youth clubs, nurseries, children's bereavement project and family support. *Chairman:* Mrs Mollie Green. *Chief Executive:* Ms Christine Unsworth, The St Nicholas Centre, 66 London Rd, St Leonards-on-Sea, TN37 6AS   *Tel:* 01424 423683/01424 855222

Fax: 01424 460446
email: enquiries@fellowshipofstnicholas.org.uk
Web: www.fsncharity.co.uk

Fellowship of St Therese of Lisieux

Founded in 1997, the centenary year of St Therese's death and in anticipation of her being proclaimed a Doctor of the Church in 1998. Its purpose is to inform members of the Church of England about her teaching and its relevance to Christians of all denominations, and to gain an entry for her in the Anglican calendar of saints. Those who would like to know more about her approach to spirituality and Christian discipleship and share in the interest of others are welcome to join the fellowship. Members commit themselves to learn more about St Therese through reading, study and prayer; pray for other members regularly; take opportunities to spread her message within our churches; meet together once a year for a time of retreat, teaching or pilgrimage; and encourage one another by contact and correspondence as appropriate. *Contact:* Revds Graeme and Sue Parfitt, Brook End, Rectory Gardens, Henbury, Bristol, BS10 7AQ

Tel: 0117 959 0293
email: suegraeme@fish.co.uk
Web: www.geocities.com/
fellowship_of_st_therese/

Fellowship of Word and Spirit

Anglican evangelical organization comprising 300 clergy and lay people committed to empowering, equipping and encouraging evangelicals through the development of thoughtful biblical theology for the 21st century using publications, conferences and a network of supportive fellowship. *Honorary President:* Rt Revd Wallace Benn. *Chairman:* Revd Simon Vibert, c/o 86 All Hallows Rd, Bispham, Blackpool, FY2 0AY

email: admin@fows.org
Web: www.fows.org

Forward in Faith

Founded in November 1992, Forward in Faith exists to support all who in conscience are unable to accept the ordination of women to the priesthood or the episcopate. It seeks an ecclesial structure which will continue the orders of bishop and priest as the Church has received them. It offers support to all who need it via a national and local network. It is governed by a council elected by the members of its National Assembly, which meets annually. Through Forward in Faith International, it collaborates with its sister organizations in Australia and North America. It publishes the monthly journal *New Directions*, the quarterly newspaper *Forward Plus*, the catechetical weekly Pew Sheet *Forward/* and the Sunday School course *Forward Teaching*. *Chairman:* The Bishop of Fulham. *Director:* Mr Stephen Parkinson, 2A The Cloisters, Gordon Square, London, WC1H 0AG   *Tel:* 020 7388 3588

Fax: 020 7387 3539
email: FiF.UK@forwardinfaith.com
Web: www.forwardinfaith.com

Foundation for Church Leadership

The Foundation aims to support, encourage and inspire church leaders and their teams as they engage with the challenges of being or becoming leaders. It is an endowed charitable trust which holds a database of training organizations and supports research into leadership. Its conferences and consultations aim to bring together church leaders, leadership training organizations, researchers and those who make leadership appointments in the churches. The Foundation encourages the development of evidence-based strategic leadership. Its activity of encouraging theological reflection leads to the production of a range of publications on leadership within the churches. *Chair:* Dame Janet Trotter. *Director:* Canon Malcolm Grundy. *Administrator:* Helen Robson, 4 Portal Rd, York, YO26 6BQ

Tel: 01904 787387/01845 578332
email: director@churchleadershipfoundation.org
Web: www.churchleadershipfoundation.org

Foundation of St Matthias

Considers applications for personal and corporate grants with preference given to higher and further education; applicants from the dioceses of Bath and Wells, Bristol and Gloucester and from former students of the college. This does not preclude applicants from elsewhere. Applications should show how the chosen subject will contribute to the advancement of the Christian religion. Examples of personal study not considered: medicine, veterinary science, engineering, law. Corporate applications should promote projects for the educational training of others and show how the Church's contribution to higher and further education will be enhanced. Closing dates for applications: 31 January, 31 May and 30 September each year. The Trust is a member of

the Association of Church College Trusts (see separate entry). *Correspondent:* Miss L. Cox, Diocesan Church House, 23 Great George St, Bristol, BS1 5QZ   *Tel:* 0117 906 0100
Fax: 0117 925 0460
Web: www.stmatthiastrust.org.uk

Frances Ashton's Charity
Supports serving or retired members of the Church of England clergy or the widows/widowers thereof who are in need. The trustees will consider almost any kind of financial hardship; so long as the applicant is a sercing or retired member of the Church of England clergy or the widow/widower thereof. There are only a few exceptions. Where the applicant has an exceptional and urgent need, the trustees will consider applications quickly and at any time. Any urgent applications should be discussed with CAF before applying. Please seek the new application form from CAF. For ordinary applications, the deadline is 1st June annually with decisions in September. *Receiver:* Charities Aid Foundation. *Senior Grants Officer:* Abigail Hiscock, Charities Aid Foundation, Kings Hill, West Malling, ME19 4TA   *Tel:* 01732 520119
Fax: 01732 520159
email: ahiscock@cafonline.org

Friends of Friendless Churches
Founded 1957 to preserve churches and chapels of architectural or historic interest. Now owns 38 redundant places of worship, half in England and half in Wales. Also administers the Cottam Will Trust, which gives grants for the introduction of works of art into ancient Gothic churches. *President:* Dr R. W. Brunskill. *Chairman:* Mr Roger Evans. *Hon Secretary:* Mr John Bowles. *Hon Director:* Mr Matthew Saunders. *Asst Director:* Mrs Caroline Carr, St Ann's Vestry Hall, 2 Church Entry, London, EC4V 5HB   *Tel:* 020 7236 3934
email: office@friendsoffriendlesschurches.org.uk
Web: www.friendsoffriendlesschurches.org.uk

Friends of Julian of Norwich
The cell of Julian of Norwich, a chapel attached to St Julian's Church, Norwich, stands on the site where the 14th-century anchoress wrote her book *Revelations of Divine Love*. The Julian Centre, beside the church, houses a small bookshop and a library of works on Julian and spirituality and welcomes visitors and pilgrims (open Monday to Saturday 10.30 a.m. to 3.30 p.m.). Large parties should book in advance (office hours as above). Accommodation is often available in the small convent beside the church. Quiet days can be arranged. Please contact the Sister in Charge, All Hallows House. The Julian Centre, Rouen Rd, Norwich, NR1 1QT
Tel: 01603 767380 (group bookings)
01603 624738 (accommodation, quiet days)
email: centre@friendsofjulian.org.uk
Web: www.friendsofjulian.org.uk

Friends of Little Gidding
Little Gidding is rightly called a 'thin place'. From the seventeenth-century Ferrar family community to T. S. Eliot's visit in 1936 and up to the present time, many have experienced the presence of God at Little Gidding. The Friends (founded in 1947) take a practical and active involvement in the care of the historic church and the old farmhouse – now a retreat centre. It co-ordinates, with the T. S. Eliot Society, an Eliot Festival in May; arranges an annual pilgrimage in July; commemorates Nicholas Ferrar's life on his feast day, 4 December; and supports the provision of accommodation and hospitality for visitors and pilgrims. *Chair:* Revd Tom Gillum. *Secretary:* Susanna Ferrar, c/o Ferrar House, Little Gidding, Huntingdon, PE28 6RJ
Tel: 01832 293383
email: info@ferrarhouse.co.uk

Friends of the Clergy Corporation
This charity gives financial and other assistance to (1) the clergy of the Anglican Communion, and (2) any widow or other dependant of such persons, who may be in financial necessity or distress, wherever they may be. Grants are made to cover many kinds of emergency including debts, bereavement or illness; also for removals, school clothing, holidays, etc. Administers the assets of the former Curates Augmentation Fund. The Friends of the Clergy Corporation and the Corporation of the Sons of the Clergy now work together from a single office and operate a unified grant-making system with a joint application form. *President:* The Bishop of London. *Secretary:* Mr Robert Welsford, 1 Dean Trench St, London, SW1P 3HB   *Tel:* 020 7799 3696
Fax: 020 7222 3468
email: enquiries@clergycharities.org.uk
Web: www.clergycharities.org.uk

Friends of the Elderly
Friends of the Elderly has been helping older people since 1905. Our vision is that all older people should retain their independence, dignity and peace of mind. We offer high quality residential and nursing care in 17 care homes, some with dementia units. We support older people to stay living in their own homes with a range of community services including welfare grants for those in financial need, day care, home support, home visiting and telephone befriending. *Patron:* HM The Queen. *Chief Executive:* Richard Furze, 40–42 Ebury St, London, SW1W 0LZ
Tel: 020 7730 8263
Fax: 020 7259 0154
email: enquiries@fote.co.uk
Web: www.fote.org.uk

Frontier Youth Trust
Founded 1964. Provides training, resources information, support and association for Christians working with disadvantaged young people

in the community, whether church-based, unattached or within the youth and community service, particularly in urban/industrial areas. *Chief Executive:* Mr Dave Wiles, Unit 208B, The Big Peg, 120 Vyse St, Birmingham, B18 6NF

Tel: 0121 687 3505
email: frontier@fyt.org.uk
Web: www.fyt.org.uk

Fulcrum

A network for evangelical clergy and laity. Launched in 2003 at the National Evangelical Anglican Congress in Blackpool, Fulcrum seeks to renew the evangelical centre by giving a voice to a nourishing, generous orthodoxy. It provides support, theological exploration and encouragement for moderate evangelical Anglicans and creates a space in which genuine debate can take place in a spirit of non-defensiveness and gracious disagreement, acknowledging that the clash of ideas can be creative and worthwhile. It has a web site with regularly updated articles from leading evangelical theologians. *Chair:* Dr Elaine Storkey. *Theological Secretary:* Canon Dr Graham Kings. *General Secretary:* Revd Simon Cawdell. *Administrator:* Revd Stephen Kuhrt, The Vicarage, Lodge Park, Claverley, WV5 7DP

Tel: 01746 710268
email: admin@fulcrum-anglican.org.uk
Web: www.fulcrum-anglican.org.uk

FWA (Family Welfare Association)

Founded 1869. Provides social work and social care services for families and individuals. Administers trust funds which give financial grants to individuals. Provides information to students through the Educational Grants Advisory Service. *Chief Executive:* Helen Dent, 501–505 Kingsland Rd, Dalston, London, E8 4AU

Tel: 020 7254 6251
Fax: 020 7249 5443
Web: www.fwa.org.uk

GFS Platform for Young Women

Established in 1875, GFS Platform works with girls and young women aged 7+. The work focuses on two specific areas, namely four community projects that work with young women between the ages of 14 and 25 who are either pregnant or who have children, and 60 parish-based youth work branches throughout England and Wales that run voluntary youth groups for girls and young women aged 7+. Main activities include reducing social exclusion and building self-esteem by providing social, formal educational and health awareness sessions and generic support in a single gender and non-judgemental environment. GFS Platform offers young women and girls the opportunity to explore their own personal and social development. This enables them to acquire new skills and knowledge, gain confidence, make informed choices and take responsibility for their own lives. *Director:* Joy Lauezzari, Unit 2 Angel Gate, 326 City Rd, London, EC1V 2PT

Tel: 020 7837 9669
Fax: 020 7837 4107
email: reception@gfsplatform.org.uk
Web: www.gfsplatform.org.uk

Girlguiding UK

Founded 1910. Open to all girls and women between 5 and 65 years regardless of race, faith or any other circumstance. Its purpose is to enable girls to mature into confident, capable and caring women determined, as individuals, to realize their potential in their career, home and personal life, and willing as citizens to contribute to their community and the wider world. Rainbows age 5–7; Brownies age 7–10; Guides age 10–14; Senior Section age 14–25; Leaders age 18 plus. *Chief Guide:* Mrs Liz Burnley. *Chief Executive:* Miss Denise King, 17/19 Buckingham Palace Rd, London, SW1W 0PT

Tel: 0800 169 5901/
020 7834 6242/
Fax: 020 7828 8317
email: join.us@girlguiding.org.uk
Web: www.girlguiding.org.uk

Girls' Brigade

An international interdenominational youth organization having as its aim 'to help girls to become followers of the Lord Jesus Christ and through self-control, reverence and sense of responsibility to find true enrichment of life'. *National Director:* Miss Ruth Gilson, PO Box 196, 129 Broadway, Didcot, OX11 8XN

Tel: 01235 510425
Fax: 01235 510429
email: gbco@girlsbrigadeew.org.uk
Web: www.girlsbrigadeew.org.uk

Greater Churches Group

The group was founded in 1991 as an informal association of non-cathedral churches which, by virtue of their great age, size, historical, architectural or ecclesiastical importance, display many of the characteristics of a cathedral, also fulfil a role which is additional to that of a normal parish church. Its aims are to provide help and mutual support in dealing with the special problems of running a 'cathedral-like' church within the organizational and financial structure of a parish church, to enhance the quality of parish worship in such churches and to promote wider recognition of the unique position and needs of churches in this category. The group also serves as a channel of communication for other organizations wishing to have contact with churches of this type. *Hon Secretary:* Mrs Patricia Wollaston, 24 Hastings Rd, Malvern, WR14 2SS

Tel: 01684 568483
email: sjandpmw@btinternet.com

Greenbelt Festivals

Organizes an annual Christian arts festival which takes place at Cheltenham racecourse. Average audience figures are around 20,000, most of whom camp for the four-day event held over the August bank holiday weekend. There are tented and indoor venues for music, seminars, theatre, film, art galleries, workshops, visual arts, resources, cafes and shops. The event is interdenominational. *Chair:* Jude Levermore. *Festival Manager:* Beki Bateson. *Development and Marketing Manager:* Paul Northup, All Hallows on the Wall, 83 London Wall, London, EC2M 5ND

Tel: 020 7374 2755 (office)
020 7874 2760 (ticket line)
Fax: 020 7374 2731
email: info@greenbelt.org
Web: www.greenbelt.org.uk

Gregorian Association

Founded 1870 to spread reliable information on Plainsong and to promote its use; to demonstrate its suitability to the English language by means of services and holding lectures and conferences; to provide expert advice and instruction on the use of Plainsong. *President:* The Archbishop of Canterbury. *General Secretary:* Mr Grey Macartney. *Director of Music:* Dr Peter Wilton, 26 The Grove, Ealing, London, W5 5LH

Tel: 020 8840 5832
Fax: 0870 055 3684
email: pjsw@beaufort.demon.co.uk
Web: www.beaufort.demon.co.uk/chant.htm

Grubb Institute

The Grubb Institute seeks to contribute to the repair, healing and transformation of the world, which we have all contributed to creating both consciously and unconsciously. It enables leaders to work with their experience of human systems, institutions and personal relations in the context of Christ's activity, using insights and concepts developed from the human sciences and Christian theology and values. It provides consultancy, action research and learning events for people of all faiths or of none, from voluntary organizations, education, health, social care, criminal justice agencies, and business. As a Christian foundation, it has worked since 1969 with leaders in churches and dioceses, religious orders and agencies worldwide. *Executive Director:* Bruce Irvine. *Senior Organizational and Institutional Analysts:* Jean Reed, Colin Quine. *Organizational Analyst:* Revd Rosy Fairhurst, The Grubb Institute, Cloudesley Street, London, N1 0HU

Tel: 020 7278 8061
Fax: 020 7278 0728
email: info@grubb.org.uk
Web: www.grubb.org.uk

Guild of All Souls

Founded 1873 as an intercessory guild, caring for the dying, the dead and the bereaved. Open to members of the Church of England and Churches in communion with her and any who share the objects of the Guild. Chantry chapel at Walsingham and at St Stephen's, Gloucester Rd, London. Patron of 41 livings of the Catholic tradition. *President:* The Bishop of Richborough. *General Secretary:* David Llewelyn Morgan. *Warden:* Louis A. Lewis. *Hon Treasurer:* Revd Paul E. Jones, St Katharine Cree Church, 86 Leadenhall St, London, EC3A 3DH

Tel: 020 7621 0098/
01371 830132
Fax: 01371 831430
Web: www.guildofallsouls.org.uk

Guild of Church Braillists

The Guild consists of a group of people who give their services to help blind readers by transcribing a variety of religious literature into Braille. Requests are welcome from individual readers for books, special services, etc. All other productions are sent to the National Library for the Blind or the Library of the RNIB. For further details contact the Secretary. *Secretary:* Mrs Mabel Owen, 321 Feltham Hill Rd, Ashford, TW15 1LP

Tel: 01727 845183

Guild of Church Musicians

Founded in 1888, but since 1961 has administered the Archbishops' Certificate in Church Music (ACert.CM) on behalf of the Archbishops of Canterbury and Westminster. This Certificate is a minimum qualification for church organists, choir trainers, cantors, choristers and leaders of instrumental groups and is fully ecumenical. The Archbishops' Award in Church Music is available for those who wish to be examined in practical skills only and the Guild's Preliminary Certificate in Church Music is aimed at young people and those starting in church music. Since 2002 the new qualification of Archbishops' Certificate in Public Worship (ACert.PW), for all who lead public worship, both clerical and lay, has been established. There is also a fellowship examination (FGCM). *General Secretary:* Mr John Ewington. *Warden:* Very Revd Dr Richard Fenwick. *President:* Dr Mary Archer. *Chairman Academic Board:* Prof Peter Aston. *Examinations Secretary:* Dr Helen Burrows, St Katharine Cree Church, 86 Leadenhall St, London, EC3A 3DH

Tel: 01883 743168
email: JohnMusicsure@orbix.co.uk
Web: www.churchmusicians.org

Guild of Health

Founded in 1904 to further the Church's Ministry of Healing through prayer, teaching, sacrament and visiting the sick, and by cooperation with Christian doctors, nurses and other members of the healing team. It publishes a quarterly magazine *Way of Life* and organizes seminars on aspects of healing which are open to all. *President:* Rt Revd John Pritchard. *Chair:* Revd Roger Hoath. *Chaplain:* Revd Christopher MacKenna.

Administrator: Ms Veronica Byrom, c/o St Marylebone Parish Church, 17 Marylebone Rd, London, NW1 5LT   *Tel:* 020 7563 1389
email: guildofhealth@stmarylebone.org
Web: www.gohealth.org.uk

Guild of Pastoral Psychology

The Guild offers a meeting ground for all interested in the relationship between religion and depth psychology, particularly the work of C. G. Jung and his followers. Depth psychology has contributed many new insights into the meaning of religion and its symbols and their relevance to everyday life. The Guild has monthly lectures in central London, a day conference in London in the spring and a three-day summer conference at Oxford. Further information and details of membership available from the Administrator. *Secretary:* Robert Macdonald, Flat 5, 75 Hatton St, London, NW8 0PL   *Tel:* 020 7724 7282
email: guild@macdonaldmedia.co.uk
Web: www.guildofpastoralpsychology.org.uk

Guild of Servants of the Sanctuary

Founded 1898 to raise the spiritual standard of Servers, to promote friendship among them and to encourage attendance at Holy Communion in addition to times of duty. *Warden:* Revd David Moore. *Secretary General:* Mr Terry Doughty, 7 Church Ave, Leicester, LE3 6AJ
Tel: 0116 262 0308
email: secretary.general@gssonline.org.uk
Web: www.gssonline.org.uk

Guild of St Barnabas

An Anglican guild for nurses and health workers, founded in 1867. Membership is open to all health care professionals, working or retired; retreats and quiet days are open events and would appeal to the broadly pastoral professions: priests, teachers, anaesthetists etc. *Guild News* is published twice a year. The annual subscription is £5. Registered Charity no. 249995. *President:* Mr Paul Willett. *Treasurer:* Mrs M. Finch. *Editor:* Mrs J. Hawthorne. *Secretary:* Mrs S. Wainman, 22 Hatfield Rd, Ipswich, IP3 9AF   *Tel:* 01473 414853

Guild of St Leonard

The Guild was founded by the Revd John Sankey. Its object is to pray for all prisoners, those on licence or probation and for all who care for them. The Guild publishes a quarterly Intercession Paper. *Warden:* Rt Revd Lloyd Rees. *Chaplain and Secretary:* Revd Peter Walker, The Chaplain's Office, HMP Ford, Arundel, BN18 0BX
Tel: 01903 663000

Guild of St Raphael

Founded 1915 to work for the restoration of the Ministry of Healing as part of the normal function of the Church, by preparing the sick for all ministries of healing, by teaching the need of repentance and faith, by making use of the Sacraments of Healing and by Intercession. *Organizing Secretary:* Mrs Hanna Hart. *Warden:* Rt Revd J. Nicholls. *Sub-Warden:* Canon Paul Nener. *Editor of 'Chrism':* Rt Revd G. Hacker, 1a Snaetell Ave, Tuebrook, Liverpool, L13 7HA
Tel: 0151 228 3193/0151 228 2023
Fax: 0151 228 3193
email: office@guildofstraphael.org.uk
Web: www.guildofstraphael.org.uk

Harnhill Centre of Christian Healing

A resource centre for the ministry of Christian Healing through counselling, prayer, quiet days, teaching courses and Christian Healing Services. The Centre provides residential accommodation. *Chairman:* Mr Barry Smith. *Chaplain/Warden:* Revd Paul Springate, Harnhill Manor, Cirencester, GL7 5PX   *Tel:* 01285 850283
Fax: 01285 850519
email: office@harnhillcentre.org.uk
Web: www.harnhillcentre.org.uk

Henry Bradshaw Society

Founded 1890 for printing liturgical texts from manuscripts and rare editions of service books, etc. For available texts, please consult the Society's web site. *Secretary:* Mr Peter Jackson, 5A Green Place, Oxford, OX1 4RF
email: peter.jackson14@btinternet.com
Web: www.henrybradshawsociety.org

Highbury Centre

Christian guesthouse on quiet private road with ample free on-street parking. Reductions for missionaries/clergy. *Manager:* Mrs S. Scalora, 20–26 Aberdeen Park, Highbury, London, N5 2BJ
Tel: 020 7226 2663
Fax: 020 7704 1853
email: enquiries@thehighburycentre.org
Web: www.thehighburycentre.org

Hockerill Educational Foundation

Personal awards are made to teachers, intending teachers and others in further or higher education, with a priority to the teaching of RE. No awards to those training for ordination, mission, social work or counselling, or to children at school. Corporate grants to support the development of religious education, particularly in the Dioceses of Chelmsford and St Albans. Applications by 31 March each year. Member of the Association of Church College Trusts (see separate entry). *Correspondent:* Mr Colin Broomfield, 16 Hagsdell Rd, Hertford, SG13 8AG
Tel: 01992 303053
Fax: 01992 425950
email: hockerill.trust@ntlworld.com

Holy Rood House, Centre for Health and Pastoral Care

Opened in 1993, the Centre is a friendly house with a residential community. The house offers a gentle and holistic approach in a Christian

environment where individuals or groups, of all ages and backgrounds, can work towards their own healing and explore their spiritual journey within an atmosphere of acceptance, love and openness. Professional counsellors and therapists, working closely with the medical profession, offer support at times of bereavement, abuse, addiction, relationship breakdown or illness, and creative arts and stress management play an important role in the healing process. Holy Rood House ministers within an awareness of justice and peace to daily or residential guests, and is also the home of the Centre for the Study of Theology and Health. *Patron:* The Archbishop of Canterbury. *Vice-Patron:* Prof Mary Grey. *Joint Exec Directors:* Revd Stanley and Revd Elizabeth Baxter. *House Manager:* Judith Bustard. *Coordinator, Centre for Study of Theology & Health:* Revd Stanley Baxter, 10 Sowerby Rd, Sowerby, Thirsk, YO7 1HX   *Tel:* 01845 522580/01845 522004
Fax: 01845 527300
email: Holyroodhouse@centrethirsk.fsnet.co.uk
Web: www.holyroodhouse.freeuk.com

Homes for Retired Clergy
See separate entries for Beauchamp Community and College of St Barnabas.

House of St Barnabas in Soho
Chief Executive: Andy Griffiths, 1 Greek St, Soho, London, W1D 4NQ   *Tel:* 020 7437 1894
Fax: 020 7434 1746
email: andy.griffiths@houseofstbarnabas.org.uk
Web: www.houseofstbarnabas.org.uk

Hymn Society of Great Britain and Ireland
Founded in 1936 to encourage study and research into hymns, both words and music; to promote good standards of hymn singing and to encourage the discerning use of hymns and songs in worship. The Society publishes a quarterly magazine and there is a three-day annual conference. Further information and details of membership from the Secretary. *Secretary:* Revd Robert A. Canham, 99 Barton Rd, Lancaster, LA1 4EN   *Tel and Fax:* 01524 66740
email: robcanham@haystacks.fsnet.co.uk
Web: www.hymnsocietygbi.org.uk

Incorporated Church Building Society
Founded 1818. The Incorporated Church Building Society offers grants towards the building of new Anglican churches. The Society is managed by the National Churches Trust. Registered Charity no. 212752. *Patron:* HM The Queen. *Chairman:* Very Revd Henry Stapleton FSA. *Chief Executive:* Andrew Edwards. *Grants Manager:* Alison Pollard, 31 Newbury St, London, EC1A 7HU
Tel: 020 7600 6090
Fax: 020 7796 2442
email: info@nationalchurchestrust.org
Web: www.nationalchurchestrust.org

Industrial Christian Fellowship
Founded 1918 as successor to the Navvy Mission (1877), and incorporating the Christian Social Union. ICF is a nationwide network which provides support for Christians who want to apply their faith in fresh and creative ways in the everyday working world. ICF aims to: bring the concerns and opportunities of the world of work to the attention of clergy and congregations so that they will be alert to the scope for prayer and Christian action; ensure that the relationship between faith, work and worship receives proper attention in Church life; promote Christian training, counselling and prayer support for members of the congregation in their working vocations; provide resources including liturgy and prayers for personal use and services related to work, and a new initiative, 'Take your minister to work'. ICF is ecumenical and has close links with other groups and agencies involved with the Church's mission to industry and commerce. Membership is open to individuals and organizations. *Chair:* Revd Carol Williams. *Secretary:* Mrs Ann Wright. *Treasurer:* Mr Geoff Hammond, PO Box 414, Horley, RH6 8WL
Tel: 01293 821322
email: wright@btinternet.com
Web: www.icf-online.org

Industrial Mission Association
The Industrial Mission Association (IMA) is a national and ecumenical association, mainly, though not exclusively, comprised of chaplains appointed to places of work throughout the UK. *Moderator:* Revd Harold Clarke. *Membership Secretary:* Revd Crispin White. *Treasurer:* Adrian Thomas. *Hon Secretary:* Revd Andy Smith. *Editor 'I M Agenda':* Stephen Hazlett, 21 Buchanan Rd, Walsall, WS4 2EW
Tel: 01922 634859 (Secretary)
020 8548 4659 (Membership Secretary)
Fax: 020 8428 3275
email: aplsmith@fish.co.uk

INFORM
Inform is an independent charity founded in 1988 with funding from the British Home Office and mainstream Churches with the aim of obtaining and making available accurate, balanced and up-to-date information about alternative spirituality and new religious movements or 'cults'. It has a large collection of data on computer and in various other forms (books, articles, cuttings, videos and cassettes), and is in touch with an international network of scholars and other specialists. People with questions or concerns about new religious movements or alternative spirituality may call the Inform information line. The line and office are open from 10 a.m. to 4.30 p.m., Mondays to Fridays. *Chairman:* Prof Eileen Barker. *Information Officer:* Amanda van Eck Duymaer van Twist. *Research Officer:* Sarah

Harvey. *Administrative Officer:* San Kim, LSE, Houghton St, London, WC2A 2AE

Tel: 020 7955 7654 (Information line)
Fax: 020 7955 7679
email: INFORM@LSE.ac.uk
Web: www.inform.ac

Inter Faith Network for the UK
Established in 1987 to encourage contact and dialogue at all levels between different faith communities in the United Kingdom. It aims to advance public knowledge and mutual understanding of the teaching, traditions and practices of the different faith communities in Britain, including an awareness of their distinctive features and of their common ground, and to promote good relations between persons of different faiths. Its member organizations include representative bodies from the Baha'i, Buddhist, Christian, Hindu, Jain, Jewish, Muslim, Sikh and Zoroastrian communities; national, regional and local inter faith bodies; and academic institutions and educational bodies concerned with inter faith issues. *Director:* Dr Harriet Crabtree. *Co-Chairs:* Rt Revd Tom Butler, Dr Nawal Prinja, 8A Lower Grosvenor Place, London, SW1W 0EN

Tel: 020 7931 7766
Fax: 020 7931 7722
email: ifnet@interfaith.org.uk
Web: www.interfaith.org.uk

Intercontinental Church Society
Founded 1823. ICS makes known the Christ of the Scriptures to people who speak English. It is a patronage society (nominating chaplains for international Anglican churches abroad), owns church buildings, and a mission agency engaged in church planting, growth and outreach to tourists, principally in Europe and around the Mediterranean; and publishes the *Directory of English-speaking Churches Abroad. President:* Viscount Brentford. *Communications Manager:* Mr David Healey, 1 Athena Drive, Tachbrook Park, Warwick, CV34 6NL

Tel: 01926 430347
Fax: 01926 888092
email: enquiries@ics-uk.org
Web: www.ics-uk.org

International Ecumenical Fellowship
IEF is a community of Christians both lay and ordained, with regional groups in Belgium, Czech Republic, France, Germany, Great Britain, Hungary, Poland, Romania, Slovak Republic and Spain. It also has individual members in various other countries. Through annual international gatherings and smaller regional groups, Christians from Catholic, Orthodox and Protestant traditions meet to worship, pray, study and enjoy fellowship together. IEF tries to strengthen the spirit of ecumenism and international friendship. IEF practises eucharistic hospitality as far as church discipline and individual conscience permit. *President of British Region:* Revd S. Armit-age. *Secretary:* Revd C. Hardiman. *Treasurer:* Mr P. Scribbins, 31 Okeley Lane, Tring, Hertfordshire, HP23 4HD

Tel: 0161 680 4793 (President)
0191 456 1643 (Secretary)
email: davidhardiman@btinternet.com
Web: www.ief.info / www.br-ief.org.uk

Interserve
(formerly BMMF International)
Founded 1852. An international and inter-denominational mission. Evangelical in its basis, it has 500 personnel serving the peoples of South and Central Asia, the Middle East and also among ethnic groups in Britain. Personnel are involved in many different ministries, all with the common aim of sharing the Good News of Jesus Christ in word and action. Those with professional training are welcomed, both long- and short-term periods of service, to fill a wide range of vacancies. *Chairman:* Hugh Bradby. *Director:* Steve Bell, 5/6 Walker Avenue, Wolverton Mills, Milton Keynes, MK12 5TW *Tel:* 01908 552700
Fax: 01908 552779
email: enquiries@isewi.org
Web: www.interserveonline.org.uk

Jubilate Group
An association of authors and musicians formed in 1974 for the purpose of publishing material for contemporary worship: *Hymns for Today's Church, Church Family Worship, Carols for Today, Carol Praise, Let's Praise/* 1 and 2, *Prayers for the People, Psalms for Today, Songs from the Psalms, The Drama-tised Bible, The Wedding Book, Hymns for the People, World Praise* 1 and 2 and *Sing Glory. Chairman:* Revd Steve James. *Secretary:* David Peacock. *Copyright Managers:* Mrs M. Williams, Mr P. Williams, 4 Thorne Park Rd, Chelston, Torquay, TQ2 6RX *Tel:* 01803 607754
Fax: 01803 605682
email: copyrightmanager@jubilate.co.uk
Web: www.jubilate.co.uk

Julian Meetings, The
A network of Christian contemplative prayer groups, begun in Britain in 1973. There are now about 400 groups in Great Britain and some in Australia, Canada, France, Ireland, Mexico, Southern Africa and the USA. Ecumenical. Magazine three times a year. *Contact:* Deidre Morris, 263 Park Lodge Lane, Wakefield, WF1 4HY *Tel:* 01924 369437
email: gb@julianmeetings.org
Web: www.julianmeetings.org

Keswick Convention
The Keswick Convention is the main event organised annually by Keswick Ministries and has been taking place since 1875. It offers something for everyone – life-changing Bible teaching, uplifting worship and great fellowship combined with the chance to relax and enjoy a

holiday in the wonderful setting of the Lake District. *Chairman:* Mr Peter Maiden. *General Director:* Mr David Bradley. *Operations Manager:* Mr Simon Overend, Keswick Convention Trust, Skiddaw St, Keswick, CA12 4BY   *Tel:* 01768 780075
Fax: 01768 775276
email: info@keswickministries.org
Web: www.keswickministries.org

Keswick Hall Trust Charity
The Trustees' spending gives priority to their own local initiatives, but they also have limited funds and give grants in response to personal or corporate applicants for research or study in religious education. Within this field, they give priority to teachers or student teachers and to work in East Anglia. Member of the Association of Church College Trusts (see separate entry). Application forms must be obtained from the Executive Secretary at the address above. *Executive Secretary:* Phil Filer, Keswick Hall Trust, PO Box 202, Wymondham, NR18 8AE
Tel: 01603 882376
Fax: 01603 882378
email: admin@keswickhalltrust.org.uk
Web: www.keswickhalltrust.org.uk

Keychange Charity
(formerly Christian Alliance)
Established 1920. Offers care, acceptance and Christian community to people in need through the provision of residential care for frail elderly people and supported accommodation for young homeless people. *Chief Exec:* David Shafik. *Operations Controller:* Barbara Barrett, 5 St George's Mews, 43 Westminster Bridge Rd, London, SE1 7JB   *Tel:* 020 7633 0533
Fax: 020 7928 1872
email: info@keychange.org.uk
Web: www.keychange.org.uk

Korean Mission Partnership
Founded in 1889 by Edward White Benson, Archbishop of Canterbury, as the Church of England Mission to Korea, the name was changed in 1993 when the Province of Korea was inaugurated. The name reflects the two-way nature of our mission today. Support goes to Korea by way of prayer, interest and funding. The Province has sent a priest from Seoul to run the Korean Chaplaincy in the Diocese of London, ministering to Korean people who live mainly in and around the Home Counties. *Presidents:* The Primate of Korea and Revd S. J. Davies. *Chairman:* Revd Luke Lee. *Hon Admin Secretary:* Revd Martin Fletcher. *Hon Treasurer:* Mr Edwin Ward, The Rectory, Rectory Rd, Tiptree, CO5 0SX
Tel: 01621 815260/01296 423133/
email: luke.gh.lee@googlemail.com
Web: www.koreanmission.org

Langley House Trust
Founded in 1958, the Langley House Trust, a national Christian charity, provides care and rehabilitation for ex-offenders (and those at risk of offending) as they work towards crime-free independence and reintegration into society. The Trust aims to help ex-offenders address their physical, emotional, mental and spiritual needs. It currently runs 15 residential projects and move-on accommodation across the UK (including a drug rehabilitation centre, women's projects and a homeless project) providing bedspaces for ex-offenders, including those who are hard to place and those who have special needs, such as mental disorders. The Trust bases its services on Christian beliefs and values but is open to men and women of any or no faith. *Chairman:* David Lane. *Chief Exec:* Steve Robinson. *Communications and Marketing Manager:* Cathy Hill. *Finance Director:* Ken Brown. *Development Director:* Colin Angus, PO Box 181, Witney, OX28 6WD
Tel: 01993 774075
Fax: 01993 772425
email: info@langleyhousetrust.org
Web: www.langleyhousetrust.org

Latimer Trust
The Latimer Trust is dedicated to providing a biblical and considered response to the issues facing today's Anglican Communion. Through a range of resources it is continuing and developing the work of Latimer House, founded in Oxford in the 1960s. *Chairman of the Council:* Revd Dr Mark Burkill. *Director of Research:* Revd Dr Gerald Bray, PO Box 26685, London, N14 4XQ
Tel: 020 8449 0467 ext. 227 020 8539 4980
email: administrator@latimertrust.org
Web: www.latimertrust.org

Lee Abbey Household Communities
There are two household communities based in Urban Priority Areas in Birmingham and Bristol. Community members live under a common rule of life and seek to be involved in their local community and church. *Contact:* Gill Arbuthnot, 101 Dorridge Rd, Dorridge, Solihull, B93 8BS
Tel: 01564 776558/0121 327 0095/

Lee Abbey International Students' Club
Founded in 1964 by the Lee Abbey Fellowship as a ministry to students of all nationalities, the Club provides long- and short-term hostel accommodation for students of all faiths or none and is served by a Christian community, which consists of young people from all over the world. Applications are invited from anyone interested in joining the community, residing as a student or staying as a holiday-maker. *Warden:* Canon Trevor Hubble, 57–67 Lexham Gardens, London, W8 6JJ   *Tel:* 020 7373 7242
Fax: 020 7244 8702
email: personnel@leeabbeylondon.com /
accommodation@leeabbeylondon.com
Web: www.leeabbeylondon.com

Organizations

Leprosy Mission, The
Founded 1874 to minister in the name of Jesus Christ to the physical, mental and spiritual needs of individuals and communities disadvantaged by leprosy; working with them to uphold human dignity and eradicate leprosy. *National Director:* Rupert Haycock, Goldhay Way, Orton Goldhay, Peterborough, PE2 5GZ   *Tel:* 01733 370505
Fax: 01733 404880
email: post@tlmew.org.uk
Web: www.leprosymission.org.uk

Lesbian and Gay Christian Movement
LGCM has four principal aims: to encourage fellowship, friendship and support among lesbian and gay Christians through prayer, study and action; to help the whole Church examine its understanding of human sexuality and to work for positive acceptance of gay relationships; to encourage members to witness to their Christian faith within the gay community and to their convictions about human sexuality within the Church; to maintain and strengthen links with other lesbian and gay Christian groups both in Britain and elsewhere. An extensive network of local groups exists and a wide range of resources are available. *Chief Executive:* Revd Richard Kirker, Oxford House, Derbyshire St, Bethnal Green, London, E2 6HG
Tel and Fax: 020 7739 1249
email: lgcm@lgcm.org.uk
Web: www.lgcm.org.uk

Li Tim-Oi Foundation
The Foundation was launched on the 50th anniversary of the priesting of the first Anglican woman, Florence Li Tim-Oi, on 25 January 1944. On the centenary of her birth on 5 May 2007 the Foundation was relaunched with the mantra: 'It takes ONE woman'. The Foundation has allocated more than £413,000 in bursaries to empower over 220 Anglican women in the Two-thirds World of the 'South' to become agents for Christian change in church and society. Requests for help, particularly from Africa, continue to outstrip available funds. Thus every donation from parishes and individuals is put to effective use. Several have chosen the Foundation to benefit in lieu of presents at birthdays, weddings, Christmas and priesting, or of funeral flowers. Bequests, especially from women in gratitude for their own priesting, are particularly welcome. *Patrons:* The Archbishop of Canterbury, the Archbishop of the Sudan, Bishop K. H. Ting and Rt Revd Dr Penny Jamieson. *Chair:* Canon Pamela Wilding MBE. *Secretary:* Canon Christopher Hall, The Knowle, Deddington, Banbury, OX15 0TB   *Tel:* 01869 338225
Fax: 0871 750 3483
email: achall@globalnet.co.uk
Web: www.ittakesonewoman.org / www.litim-oi.org

Librarians' Christian Fellowship
Constituted 1976 to provide opportunities for Christian librarians to consider issues in librarianship from a Christian standpoint, and to promote opportunities for presenting the Christian faith to people working in libraries of all kinds. *Hon Secretary:* Graham Hedges, 34 Thurlestone Ave, Ilford, IG3 9DU   *Tel:* 020 8599 1310
email: secretary@librarianscf.org.uk
Web: www.librarianscf.org.uk

Liddon Trust
See Society of the Faith (Incorporated).

Lincoln Theological Institute
Inaugurated in 1997 and now based at the University of Manchester, the Institute's primary aim is to undertake, promote and support theological enquiry into contemporary society and thereby to practise theology in the fullest sense. It focuses on postgraduate and postdoctoral research, working closely with colleagues in the Religions and Theology subject area. Core areas for research include modern ecclesiology; social, political and practical theologies; and religion in contemporary society. Its latest projects address the issues of climate change and the postcolonial. Students wishing to study under the auspices of the Institute may enrol through the University of Manchester for Master's and Doctoral degree programmes. Formal and informal enquiries from prospective students are encouraged. The Lincoln Theological Institute originated from Lincoln Theological College, founded in 1874 as an ordination training college. Since 2003 the Institute has been a fully integrated research unit within the University of Manchester.For further information please contact the Director. *Director:* Dr Peter M. Scott. *Research Associate:* Dr Stefan Skrimshire, School of Arts, Histories and Cultures, University of Manchester, Oxford Rd, Manchester, M13 9PL   *Tel:* 0161 275 3064/
0161 275 3736
email: peter.scott@manchester.ac.uk
Web: http://www.arts.manchester.ac.uk/lti

Livability
(Formerly know as the Shaftesbury Society)
Livability is a new charity, formed by the merger of the Shaftesbury Society and John Grooms. Livability creates choices for disabled people and brings life to local communities. We offer a wide range of services to around 8,000 disabled people and their families, including residential care, supported living, education and accessible holidays. We also provide community organizations with the resources, advice and confidence to transform their neighbourhoods. *Chief Executive:* Mary Bishop, 50 Scrutton St, London, EC2A 4XQ   *Tel:* 020 7452 2000
Fax: 020 7452 2001
email: info@livability.org.uk
Web: www.livability.org.uk

Living Stones
(formerly Church and Community Trust)
An independent organization that offers guidance and information to local churches concerning the more effective use of their resources – buildings, money, people – for worshipping God and serving the community. *Field Workers:* Roger Munday, Graham Ball, Quoin House, 11 East Park, Crawley, RH10 6AN
Tel and Fax: 01293 431899
email: info@living-stones.org.uk
Web: www.living-stones.org.uk

London City Mission
For over 170 years, LCM has been working with churches to bring the Christian message to the people of London. Today, in the workplace, out on the streets and in the various communities of London, nearly 400 workers and volunteers are actively seeking to bring Christian values and hope to those they meet. *Chairman:* Raymond Turner. *Chief Executive:* Revd Dr John Nicholls, Nasmith House, 175 Tower Bridge Rd, London, SE1 2AH
Tel: 020 7407 7585
Fax: 020 7403 6711
email: enquiries@lcm.org.uk
Web: www.lcm.org.uk

Lord Wharton's Charity
Founded 1696 to distribute Bibles and other religious books to children and young people of all denominations in all counties of the United Kingdom and Northern Ireland. *Clerk to the Trustees:* Mrs B. Edwards, Magnolia Cottage, Harrowbeer Lane, Yelverton, PL20 6EA
Tel and Fax: 01822 852636
email: edwards@bobbarbara7.wanadoo.co.uk

MACA (Mental After Care Association)
MACA is a leading national charity providing a wide range of quality community- and hospital-based services for people with mental health needs and their carers, including: advocacy, assertive outreach schemes, community support, employment schemes, forensic services, helplines/information, respite for carers, social clubs, supported accommodation with 24–hour care. *Chair:* Julia Ross. *Chief Executive:* Mr Gil Hitchon, 1st Floor, Lincoln House, 296–302 High Holborn, London, WC1V 7JH
Tel: 020 7061 3400
email: maca@maca.org.uk
Web: www.maca.org.uk

Marshall's Charity
Founded 1627. Makes grants for (1) building, purchasing or modernizing parsonages of the Church of England or the Church in Wales, (2) repairs to churches in Kent, Surrey and Lincolnshire. *Clerk to the Trustees:* Mr Richard Goatcher,

Marshall House, 66 Newcomen St, London, SE1 1YT
Tel: 020 7407 2979
Fax: 020 7403 3969
email: grantoffice@marshalls.org.uk
Web: www.marshalls.org.uk

Matters Arising
Matters Arising was formed by Rob Norman in 2004 to make sure that the ministry of AdMinistry was not lost to the Church in the UK. The main services offered by Matters Arising are consultancy and training, although many of the highly-regarded AdMinistry publications are still available from Matters Arising. The main focus of the work is with churches and Christian organizations and the main expertise is in the areas of management, leadership and administration. The aim with each client is to provide the help needed to maximize effectiveness, and Matters Arising works with other organizations to provide a 'one-stop' shop. *Director:* Rob Norman, 62 Farm Rd, Rowley Regis, B65 8ET
Tel: 0845 128 5177
Fax: 0845 128 5178
email: mail@mattersarising.com

mediawatch-uk
(Formerly the National Viewers' and Listeners' Association)
The association was founded in 1965 by Mrs Mary Whitehouse and her associates who felt that television was attacking and undermining Christian family life. mediawatch-uk, which is a non-denominational voluntary association, believes that violence on television contributes significantly to the increase of violence in society and should be curtailed in the public interest; that the use of swearing and blasphemy are destructive of our culture and our Christian faith and that the broadcasting authorities are failing to meet their statutory obligations by allowing the frequent use of offensive language; that sexual innuendo and explicit sex trivialize and cheapen human relationships whilst undermining marriage and family life; and that the media are indivisible and broadcasting standards are inevitably affected by the standards of film, theatre and publishing. Benefits of membership include regular newsletters and a list of media addresses to enable members to make their voices heard. After consulting members the name was changed to mediawatch-uk from 1 March 2001. *Director:* Mr John Beyer, 3 Willow House, Kennington Rd, Ashford, TN24 0NR
Tel: 01233 633936
Fax: 01233 633836
email: info@mediawatchuk.org
Web: www.mediawatchuk.org

Melanesian Mission
The Melanesian Mission was established in 1854 to buy the first 'Southern Cross' ship for Bishop Selwyn to use for mission work in the islands of Melanesia. Today the Mission supports the

Church of Melanesia (including the religious orders) through money, prayer and people – helping the church to fulfil its priorities and work through this vast and isolated region. *Chairman:* Rt Revd Michael Langrish (Bishop of Exeter). *Hon. Treasurer:* Mr Alan Waters. *Executive Officer:* David Friswell, 15 Covell Close, Bury St Edmunds, IP33 2HU   *Tel:* 01284 701988
email: mission@talktalk.net
Web: www.melanesia.anglican.org

Mersey Mission to Seafarers
Founded 1856 to 'promote the spiritual and temporal welfare of seafarers' from around the world who visit the ports of the River Mersey and the Isle of Man . *Chairman:* Sir Malcolm Thornton. *Chief Executive:* John P. Wilson, Parish Office, Christ Church Parish Centre, Alexandra Rd, Liverpool, L22 1RJ   *Tel:* 0151 9201 928/
07973 824154 (Mobile)
Fax: 0151 928 0244
email: liverangel@aol.com

Metropolitan Visiting and Relief Association
Founded 1843 for promoting the relief of destitution in London and for improving the conditions of the poor. It aims to assist the clergy of the Church of England in the Metropolitan area (1) in giving financial help in their parishes, (2) to help them in constructive social work by providing financial help for cases where permanent good results may be expected, (3) to assist clergy who cooperate with other agencies engaged in social work, and (4) to assist some married ordinands' families. Enquiries to the Grants Administrator. Family Welfare Association, 501–505 Kingsland Rd, Dalston, London, E8 4AU
Tel: 020 7249 6636
Fax: 020 7249 5443

Mid-Africa Ministry (CMS)
Mid-Africa Ministry (MAM), founded in 1921, now forms part of the Church Mission Society. See separate entry for Church Mission Society.

Mirfield Centre
Offers a meeting place for about 50 people at the College of the Resurrection. Small residential conferences are possible in the summer vacation. Day and evening events are arranged by the centre management team. *Centre Administrator:* Mrs Rachael Salmon. *Director of Adult Christian Education:* Revd June Lawson. *Centre Brother:* Father Oswin Gartside, The Mirfield Centre, College of the Resurrection, Mirfield, WF14 0BW
Tel: 01924 481920
Fax: 01924 481921
email: centre@mirfield.org.uk
Web: www.mirfield.org.uk

Mission to Seafarers, The
World mission agency which supports and links the Anglican Church's ministry to seafarers of all races and creeds in ports throughout the world. It has full-time staff and/or seafarers' centres in over 100 ports, honorary chaplains in over 120 others. In many ports it works in close cooperation with Christian societies of other denominations, and it is a member of the International Christian Maritime Association. *President:* HRH The Princess Royal. *Secretary General:* Canon Bill Christianson. *Director of Justice and Welfare:* Canon Ken Peters. *Director of Chaplaincy:* Revd Tom Heffer, St Michael Paternoster Royal, College Hill, London, EC4R 2RL   *Tel:* 020 7248 5202
Fax: 020 7248 4761
email: general@missiontoseafarers.org
Web: www.missiontoseafarers.org

MODEM
MODEM is a network/association whose mission is to lead and enable authentic dialogue between exponents of Christian leadership, management and organization, and spirituality, theology and ministry. MODEM is an ecumenical membership organization, open to all Christians irrespective of age, gender, race, culture or nationality, and welcoming dialogue with all comers of all faiths. In association with SCM-/Canterbury Press, MODEM has published three ground-breaking books, *Management and Ministry* – appreciating contemporary issues; *Leading, Managing, Ministering* – challenging questions for church and society; and *Creative Church Leadership* – on the challenge of making a difference through leadership, the latter edited by Dr John Adair and John Nelson. The fourth and latest book *How to Become a Creative Leader* was published in February 2008, and is essentially the 'how to' book following the previous three. See web site for further information and details of special introductory membership offer to include some or all of the books. *Chairman:* Revd Elizabeth Welch. *Secretary:* John Nelson. *Contact:* Peter J. Bates, Carselands, Woodmancote, Henfield, BN5 9SS   *Tel and Fax:* 01273 493172
email: info@modem-uk.org / membership@modem-uk.org
Web: www.modem-uk.org

Modern Churchpeople's Union
An Anglican society which promotes liberal theology and offers Christian debate and discussion on religious issues. It embraces the spirit of freedom and informed enquiry and seeks to involve the Christian faith in an ongoing search for truth by interpreting traditional doctrine in the light of present day understanding. It holds an annual conference on contemporary issues. Membership includes subscription to the journal *Modern Believing*. *President:* Rt Revd John Saxbee. *General Secretary:* Revd Jonathan Clatworthy, MCU Office, 9 Westward View, Liverpool, L17 7EE
Tel: 0845 345 1909/0151 726 9730/
email: office@modchurchunion.org
Web: www.modchurchunion.org

Morse-Boycott Bursary Fund
(formerly St Mary-of-the-Angels Song School Trust)
Founded in 1932 originally as a parochial Choir School but from 1935 to 1970 served the Church at large. Now provides financial assistance to the parents of boy choristers at cathedral choir schools throughout the UK. The Fund depends entirely on donations and legacies to build the capital from which bursaries can be provided to the needy. *Trustees:* Dean and Chapter of Chichester. *Administrator:* The Communar, The Royal Chantry, Cathedral Cloisters, Chichester, PO19 1PX   *Tel:* 01243 782595
Fax: 01243 812499
email: admin@chichestercathedral.org.uk
Web: www.chichestercathedral.org.uk

Mothers' Union
An Anglican organization that promotes the well-being of families worldwide. This is done through developing prayer and spiritual growth in families, studying and reflecting on family life and its place in society, and resourcing members to take practical action to improve conditions for families, both nationally and in the communities in which they live. It has over 3.6 million members in 78 countries throughout the world, and is organized locally into branches attached to a local church. It works extensively overseas throughout the Anglican Communion by supporting over 300 indigenous workers. It has a subscribers magazine *Families First* and Mothers' Union members supplement and prayer diary *Families Worldwide*, and produces numerous resources accessible through its web site. *Worldwide President:* Mrs Rosemary Kempnell. *Chief Exec:* Mr Reg Bailey, Mary Sumner House, 24 Tufton St, London, SW1P 3RB
Tel: 020 7222 5533
Fax: 020 7227 9737
email: mu@themothersunion.org
Web: www.themothersunion.org

Mozambique and Angola Anglican Association (MANNA)
Founded by 1906, MANNA was formed to support the Diocese of Lebombo in southern Mozambique; it has now developed into supporting work within both the former Portuguese Territories, which are among the poorest in the world. While two world wars and lengthy civil wars hindered the work, since peace was established in both countries the church is growing at a great rate, predominantly by indigenous clergy who need support for their work. There are now three dioceses with well over 100 clergy. Registered Charity no. 262818. *Chair:* Ven Christopher Cunliffe, Archdeacon of Derby. *General Secretary:* Mr Ian Gordon, 16 Bayle Court, The Bayle, Folkestone, CT20 1SN   *Tel:* 01303 257248
email: n_grdn@yahoo.co.uk
Web: www.newportchurches.com/Manna

National Archives, The
Records of central government and courts of law from the Norman Conquest (Domesday Book) to the recent past (for example, the Suez Campaign). Kew, Richmond-upon-Thames, TW9 4DU   *Tel:* 020 8876 3444
email: enquiry@pro.gov.uk
Web: www.nationalarchives.gov.uk

National Association of Diocesan Advisers for Women's Ministry
NADAWM is a national support network for monitoring, supporting and promoting the ministry of ordained women in the Church of England. It organizes an annual conference for diocesan representatives and provides consultancy and advice. *Chair:* Revd Vanda Rowe. *Treasurer:* Canon Sue Pinnington. *Secretary:* Revd Rosemary Lain Priestley, Rectory, High St, Porton, Salisbury, SP4 0LH   *Tel:* 01980 610305
email: rev.vandarowe@gmail.com

National Churches Trust
The National Churches Trust, launched in 2007, is the successor to the Historic Churches Preservation Trust (HCPT). The National Churches Trust aims to fund, protect and support the built heritage of 47,000 churches, chapels and meeting houses throughout the UK. It administers the Incorporated Church Building Society. The Trust offers grants mainly for structural repairs, new facilities and improved access. Registered charity no. 1119845. *Patron:* HM The Queen. *Chairman of Trustees:* Michael Hoare. *Chief Executive:* Andrew Edwards. *Grants Manager:* Alison Pollard, 31 Newbury St, London, EC1A 7HU
Tel: 020 7600 6090
Fax: 020 7796 2442
email: info@nationalchurchestrust.org
Web: www.nationalchurchestrust.org

National Council for Social Concern
(formerly the Church of England National Council for Social Aid, Church of England Temperance Society and Police Court Missionaries)
The charity (also known by the short titles 'Concern' and 'Social Concern') has promoted a wide range of activities in connection with the Church of England, but in recent years has had a particular interest in aspects of the criminal justice system and in issues arising from addictions. It works closely with the Church of England Board for Social Responsibility. Details from the Secretary. *Presidents:* The Archbishops of Canterbury and York. *Chairman:* Rt Revd Colin Docker. *Secretary:* Mr Francis Mac Namara, 3 Vinson Rd, Liss, GU33 7NE   *Tel:* 01730 300974/ 07958 425927
email: info@social-concern.org
Web: www.social-concern.org

National Deaf Church Conference
Founded in 1967 by the late Canon Tom Sutcliffe, who was himself deaf. It is the national forum for

delegates from the Deaf Church and meets twice yearly for weekend and day conferences where the spiritual and social issues facing the Church of England are discussed. The main objective is to make the general public aware that deaf Christians are not isolated worshipping communities, but part of the whole Church. *Chair:* Revd Vera Hunt. *Contact:* Ken Dyson, 27 Redriff Close, Maidenhead, SL6 4DJ *Tel and Fax:* 01628 623909
email: vera@sh-hunt.fsnet.co.uk

New England Company
A charity founded 1649. It is the senior English missionary society. *Governor:* Mr T. C. Stephenson. *Treasurer:* D. M. F. Scott. *Secretary:* Nikki Johnson, Flinders Cottage, The Street, Bolney, West Sussex RH17 5QW *Tel:* 01444 882898
email: johnsonnikki@yahoo.co.uk
Web: www.newenglandcompany.org

Newton's Trust
Established to provide assistance to widows, widowers, separated or divorced spouses and unmarried children of deceased clergy and to divorced or separated wives of clergy of the Church of England, the Church in Wales and the Scottish Episcopal Church. Applications are considered by the Trustees, and one-off cash grants are made at their discretion. The Trustees meet four times a year. *Chairman:* Ven George Frost. *Treasurer:* Mr John Allen. *Secretary:* Mr D. E. Wallington, Secretary to Newton's Trust, 1 Tudor Close, Lichfield, Staffordshire WS14 9RX
Tel: 01543 302924 (Evenings)
email: d.wallington@ntlworld.com

Nikaean Club
Founded 1925 to exercise hospitality on behalf of the Archbishop of Canterbury to Christians of non-Anglican traditions. *Chair:* Dame Rosemary Spencer. *Guestmaster:* Canon Jonathan Gough. *Hon Secretary:* Mr Christopher Austen. *Hon Treasurer:* Revd Martin Macdonald, Lambeth Palace, London, SE1 7JU *Tel:* 020 7898 1221
Fax: 020 7401 9886
email: christopher.austen@lambethpalace.org.uk

Nikaean Ecumenical Trust
Founded in 1992 and relaunched in 2002, the Trust exists to support ecumenical links between the Church of England and Christian churches overseas. It acts as the charitable wing of the Nikaean Club (see separate entry) and receives support from its members as well as from other Anglican bodies and individuals. It has also recently acquired the assets of the former Harold Buxton Trust, thanks to the generous co-operation of the SPCK. The Trust's principal activity at present is to provide grants to students from needy, non-Anglican churches overseas (particularly the Orthodox and Oriental Orthodox Churches) who wish to study at colleges in the UK which are specifically Anglican or have strong Anglican connections. As the funds are still relatively modest, donations towards the work of the Trust are welcome. *Chair:* Rt Revd Dr Geoffrey Rowell. *Hon Secretary:* Mrs Margery Roberts, 7 Nunnery Stables, St Albans, AL1 2AS *Tel:* 01727 856626

North of England Institute for Christian Education
Founded in 1981 as an ecumenical foundation managed by a board representing the educational interests of the Churches, universities and other educational institutions in the North East of England. Its primary objective is to create links, at both the theoretical and practical level, between Christian theology and education so as to contribute, mainly by research projects and publications, towards the further education of those with a responsibility for teaching the Christian faith. *Director:* Revd Prof Jeff Astley. *Secretary:* Mrs Evelyn Jackson, 18 North Bailey, Durham City, DH1 3RII
Tel: 0191 33 43331 (Director)
0191 33 43332 (Secretary)
email: Jeff.Astley@durham.ac.uk
Web: www.durham.ac.uk/neice

Number One Trust Fund
Founded 1909 for holding property and investments for the promotion of catholic practice and teaching within the Church of England, reformed by the Fidelity Trust Act 1977, and incorporated by the Charity Commissioners in 1996. One trustee is appointed by each of the Abbot of Elmore, the Superior of the Community of the Resurrection, the President of the Church Union, the President of the Society for the Maintenance of the Faith, the Master of the Guardians of the Shrine at Walsingham, the Principal of Pusey House, Oxford and the Principal of St Stephen's House, Oxford. *Chairman:* Mr T. D. Belben. *Trustees:* Revd J. P. Sheehy, Canon P. G. Cobb, Dr B. J. Hanson, Revd J. M. R. Baker, Mr D. Ll. Morgan. *Secretary and Trustee:* Canon P. E. Ursell, Ascot Priory, Priory Rd, Ascot, SL5 8RT
Tel: 01344 885157
email: secretary@numberonetrust.org.uk

OMF International (UK)
(formerly China Inland Mission)
Founded 1865 to work in partnership with East Asia's churches through evangelism, church planting, discipling, theological training and professional services. *Director for Personnel:* Mr St John Perry, Station Approach, Borough Green, Sevenoaks, TN15 8BG *Tel:* 01732 887299
Fax: 01732 887224
email: omf@omf.org.uk
Web: www.omf.org.uk

Open Synod Group
The objects of the Group are the promotion and advancement of the Christian religion. Its

particular emphasis is working through the synodical structures for the growth of unity between all the Churches and the renewal of the life and organization of the Church of England. Membership is open to all Christians but will be of particular interest to serving or one-time members of the General Synod, of any diocesan or deanery synod, and of any PCC (PCCs are also eligible for corporate membership). The Group meets during each Group of Sessions of the General Synod. It publishes a magazine twice a year. *President:* The Bishop of Ripon and Leeds. *Chairman:* Mr Tim Hind. *Secretary:* Mr Roy Thompson. *Treasurer and Membership Secretary:* Mr John Freeman. *Magazine Secretary:* Shirley-Ann Williams, May Rose Cottage, Sheriff Hutton, York, YO60 6SS   *Tel:* 01347 878644/
07779 095273 (Mobile)
email: roythompson2@btinternet.com
Web: www.opensynodgroup.org.uk

Order of Christian Unity/Christian Projects
Christians from all denominations who care about Christian values in the family, medical ethics, Christian education and the media, and run an annual Schools Bible Project for secondary schools across Britain. *Chairman:* Mrs Joanna Bogle. *Treasurer:* Mr Andrew Pollock. *Vice-Chairman:* Lady Elizabeth Benyon, PO Box 44741, London, SW1P 2XA
email: auntiejoanna@yahoo.co.uk
Web: www.christianprojects.org.uk

Ordination Candidate Funds (General)
See separate entries for Anglo-Catholic Ordination Candidates' Fund, Bristol Clerical Education Society, Church Pastoral Aid Society Ministers in Training Fund, Cleaver Ordination Candidates' Fund, Elland Society Ordination Fund, Lady Peel Legacy Trust.

Overseas Bishoprics' Fund
Founded 1841 to assist towards the endowment and maintenance of bishoprics in any part of the world and to act as trustees of episcopal endowment funds. *Chairman:* Mr John Broadley. *Secretary:* Mr Stephen Lyon. *Clerk:* Mr Paul Burrage, Church House, Great Smith St, London, SW1P 3NZ   *Tel:* 020 7803 3200
Fax: 020 7633 0185

Oxford Mission
Founded 1880. The Oxford Mission consists of two Religious Communities, the Brotherhood of St Paul and the Christa Sevika Sangha. Has houses in India and Bangladesh. Their work is pastoral, medical and educational and is carried on in the Dioceses of Kolkata and Dhaka. India: Mr Arijeet Roy (Administrator); Bangladesh: Father Francis Pande SPB and Revd Mother

Susila CSS. *General Secretary:* Mrs Mary K. Marsh, PO Box 86, Romsey, SO51 8YD
Tel and Fax: 01794 515004
email: oxfordmission@aol.com
Web: www.oxford-mission.org

Papua New Guinea Church Partnership
PNGCP is the recognized voluntary agency through which the Anglican Church of Papua New Guinea and the Church of England relate to each other. In 2007 ACPNG celebrated 30 years as an independent province in the Anglican Communion. Registered as a charity in 1960, the New Guinea Mission was founded in 1891 to give support to the then Diocese of New Guinea in prayer, by sending staff and raising money. In 1977, when the Province was inaugurated with five dioceses, the agency name was changed to Papua New Guinea Church Partnership in order to reflect the reciprocal nature of the work: giving and receiving. ACPNG continues to request people with skills and experience for governmentally approved support posts, mainly in health and administration. There are currently seven in the country, including the Bishop of Port Moresby, the Rt Revd Peter Ramsden, for whom PNGCP acts as agent. Most years see a steady trickle of 'gap year' students and medical and nursing electives travelling to PNG to gain never-to-be-forgotten experience in the poorest, most populous Pacific nation. An annual grant goes to the provincial budget, money is raised for provincially approved projects, and audited accounts are sent to the UK. *President:* Rt Revd Dr David M. Hope. *Chairman:* Revd Paul Bagott. *General Secretary:* Mrs Chris Luxton, St Mary Abbots Centre, Vicarage Gate, London, W8 4HN   *Tel:* 020 7937 4159
email: pngcpluxton@aol.com
Web: http://hometown.aol.co.uk/pngcpluxton/

Paradox Ministries
Paradox Ministries encourages Christians to understand and pray about the Israeli–Palestinian Conflict, seeing it through the eyes of both people groups involved, and taking the needs, fear and pain of both sides seriously. Its director, who was Rector of a church in the Old City of Jerusalem for a number of years, circulates a free email newsletter, speaks at seminars and encourages support of indigenous reconciliation ministry in Jerusalem. The website contains background material, advice to clergy and regular news updates, together with a blog. *Directors (Chairman):* Revd Tony Higton. *(Executive):* Mrs Patricia Higton, Rectory, 47 Castle Rising Rd, South Wootton, King's Lynn, PE30 3JA
Tel: 01553 671381
email: tony@higton.info
Web: www.prayerforpeace.org.uk

Parish and People
Parish and People was founded in 1949 and was instrumental in effecting a quiet revolution in

popularizing the parish communion. In 1963 it merged with the Keble Conference Group to spearhead movements towards team ministry, synodical government and church unity. In 1970 it was largely responsible for the formation of the ecumenical 'ONE for Christian Renewal'. Parish and People has, however, continued to promote new life in the Anglican Church, and publishes a range of stimulating material for parishes and deaneries in order to enable the growth from the grass roots up of a lively, open, people's church in which lay ministry can blossom. In 1988 it took 'Partners' under its wing, thus widening its interests to include publications on evangelism. The Deanery Resource Unit was launched in 1989, and now over 250 deaneries throughout the Church of England subscribe to its bi-annual mailing, which includes the well-established *Deanery Exchange* broadsheet, together with copies of booklets and briefings on matters of deanery concern. The Unit is working in cooperation with the Church House Deaneries Group and other bodies to bring a breath of fresh air to the 'missing link' in the Church of England's structure. We are at present working closely with them to produce a series of booklets/briefings to help deaneries and rural/area deans. Your ideas for future developments are most welcome. *Contact:* Revd Jimmy Hamilton-Brown, The Old Mill, Spetisbury, Blandford Forum, DT11 9DF
Tel: 01258 453939
email: PandPeople@tiscali.co.uk
Web: www.parishandpeople.org.uk

Partis College
Founded 1825 to provide accommodation (house) for ladies who are members of the Church of England with low incomes. The College was founded for the widows or daughters of clergymen, HM forces and other professions. Patron: The Bishop of Bath and Wells. *Chairman:* Mrs J. Pepler. *Bursar:* Mrs Jill Harman. *Asst Bursar:* Mrs A. Kemp, No. 1 Partis College, Newbridge Hill, Bath, BA1 3QD
Tel: 01225 421532 07733 363713 (Mobile)/
email: partiscoll@aol.com
Web: www.partiscollege.com

Philip Usher Memorial Fund
Founded 1948. Grants annual scholarships to Anglican priests, deacons or ordinands, preferably under 35 years of age, to study in a predominantly Orthodox country. Applications not later than 31 December for the following year. *Chairman:* Rt Revd Dr Geoffrey Rowell. *Administrator:* Janet Laws, c/o The Old Deanery, Dean's Court, London, EC4V 3AA   *Tel:* 020 7248 6233
Fax: 020 7248 9721
email: janet.laws@londin.clara.co.uk

Pilgrim Adventure
Founded in 1987, Pilgrim Adventure provides a selection of Christian Journeys inspired by the wanderings of the early Celtic saints. Hill walking, island hopping and worship in out-of-the-way places are all part of the experience. Pilgrim Adventure is Anglican-based and ecumenical in outlook. Enquiries to the Bookings Secretary. *Leader:* David Gleed. *Dep. Leader:* Paul Heppleston, South Winds, Culver Park, Tenby, SA70 7ED   *Tel:* 01834 844212
email: pilgrim.adventure@virgin.net
Web: www.pilgrim-adventure.org.uk

Pilgrim Trust
Founded 1930 by the late Edward S. Harkness of New York with a sum of £2 million. The Trustees give grants to charities or recognized public bodies concerned with specific projects within the social welfare and heritage fields. A copy of the guidelines can be downloaded from the Trust's website. Block grants are given to the Church Buildings Council and the National Churches Trust for the repair and conservation of places of worship. *Director:* Miss Georgina Nayler, Clutha House, 10 Storeys Gate, London, SW1P 3AY
Tel: 020 7222 4723
Fax: 020 7976 0461
email: georgina@thepilgrimtrust.org.uk
Web: www.thepilgrimtrust.org.uk

Pilgrims' Association
Founded in 1981, the Pilgrims' Association provides a forum in which those responsible for the care and welcome of pilgrims, visitors and tourists to our cathedrals, abbeys, churches, shrines and chapels can meet and exchange ideas and experiences. It is now also increasingly involved in bringing together those in cathedrals and churches who deliver education outside the classroom both to schools and adults. Originally a Trust, it is now a fully democratic institution governed by a Council of 15 members elected at the annual general meeting. Membership is both ecumenical and international, consisting of the great majority of Church of England cathedrals, three Roman Catholic cathedrals and several of the most visited parish churches, abbeys, priories and chapels from Anglican, Roman Catholic and Free Church denominations in England, Wales, the Republic of Ireland and Belgium. It operates mainly through an annual conference and periodic newsletters and through its web site. It is consulted regularly by government and VisitBritain on tourism and educational matters relating to cathedrals and churches. *Chairman:* Very Revd Jonathan Meyrick, Dean of Exeter. *Secretary:* Mrs Judy Davies. *Hon Treasurer:* Barry Palmer, 1 St John's Rd, Queen's Park, Chester, CH4 7AL
Tel: 01244 677991/07767 675540 (Mobile)
Fax: 01244 677991
email: judydavies10@googlemail.com
Web: www.cathedralsplus.org.uk

Pilsdon at Malling Community
The Pilsdon Community established a new community in 2004, taking over the former Ewell

Monastery site next to St Mary's Abbey, West Malling. The community is dedicated to the same ideals of the Christian Gospel as the original community in Dorset, offering community living, sustainable self-sufficient lifestyle and open hospitality. The community consists of 9 or 10 Community Members (leadership) and children, about 12 long stay residents and up to 2 visitors and wayfarers. The six acres of land and two large glasshouses are used for livestock and horticulture. The 16th-century barn chapel is used for daily offices, and the Eucharist is celebrated daily in either the barn or the Abbey chapel. Enquiries are always welcome. (See Pilsdon Community entry and website for more details.) Registered Charity no. 1123682. Company no. 6218667. *Guardian:* Revd Peter Barnett. *Treasurer:* Mr Albert Granville. *Admissions:* The Guardian. *Enquiries:* Any community member, 27 Water Lane, West Malling, ME19 6HH

Tel and Fax: 01732 870279
email: pilsdon.malling@tiscali.co.uk
Web: www.pilsdonatmalling.org.uk

Pilsdon Community

The Pilsdon Community is dedicated to the ideals of the Christian gospel in the context of community living and open hospitality. The Community at any one time will comprise six to eight community members (leadership) and their children, about 20 guests (staying from one month to several years), up to six visitors (staying one day to two weeks) and up to eight wayfarers (staying up to three days). Many of the guests have experienced a crisis in their lives (e.g. mental breakdown, alcoholism, drug addiction, marital breakdown, abuse, homelessness, prison, dropping out of college, asylum-seeking, etc.). Pilsdon provides an environment of communal living, manual work, creative opportunities (pottery, art, crafts, music, etc.), recreation, worship and pastoral care, to rebuild people's lives, self-respect, confidence and faith. Founded in 1958 by an Anglican priest, the Community occupies an Elizabethan manor house and its outbuildings and smallholding of ten acres, six miles from the sea near Lyme Regis. The community life is inspired by the monastic tradition and the Little Gidding Community built around families. The worship and spirituality is Anglican and sacramental, but ecumenical in membership, and all faiths and none as well as all races and cultures are welcome. Membership enquiries should be made to the Warden, enquiries from guests in need and visitors should be directed to Miss A. Plested, and those from volunteers to Revd Jonathan Herbert. *Warden:* Revd Jonathan Herbert. *Admissions and Visitors:* Miss A. Plested. *Administrator:* Alan Frost, Pilsdon Manor, Pilsdon, Bridport, DT6 5NZ   *Tel:* 01308 868308
Fax: 01308 868161
email: pilsdon@btconnect.com
Web: www.pilsdon.org.uk

Plainsong and Medieval Music Society

Formed 1888 to promote the study and appreciation of plainsong and medieval music, especially through performance and publications; related journal, *Plainsong and Medieval Music*. *Administrator:* Anna Burson. *Chairman:* Prof John Harper, c/o RSCM, 19 The Close, Salisbury, SP1 2EB   *Tel:* 01722 424843
Fax: 01722 424849
email: pmms@rscm.com
Web: www.plainsong.org.uk

Praxis

Founded 1990, Praxis is sponsored by the Liturgical Commission, the Alcuin Club and the Grove Group for the Renewal of Worship. Its aims are to enrich the practice and understanding of worship in the Church of England; to serve congregations and clergy in their exploration of God's call to worship; and to provide a forum in which different worshipping traditions can meet and interact. Praxis events include day meetings in London and the regions, residential conferences and national consultations. *Chair:* Canon David Kennedy. *Secretary:* Canon Michael Rawson. *Administrator:* Mrs Helen Price, c/o RSCM, 19 The Close, Salisbury, SP1 2EB
Tel: 01722 424858
email: praxis@praxisworship.org.uk
Web: www.praxisworship.org.uk

Prayer Book Society

A company limited by guarantee registered in England no. 4786973, and registered charity no. 1099295. Founded in 1975 to uphold the worship and doctrine of the Church of England as enshrined in the Book of Common Prayer. The Society has a branch in every diocese of the Church of England and affiliated branches in Ireland, Scotland and Wales. Journals are published quarterly, also a quarterly newsletter, and the Society publishes other material of a critical or educational kind, related to the Book of Common Prayer. The Society encourages the use of the Book of Common Prayer as a major element in the worshipping life of the Church of England and seeks to spread knowledge and love of the 1662 Prayer Book. *Patron:* HRH The Prince of Wales. *Chairman:* Prudence Dailey. *Administrator of Cranmer Awards:* Miss Merriel Halsall-Williams. *Head of Development:* Dr Julie Lethaby, The Studio, Copyhold Farm, Goring Heath, RG8 7RT   *Tel:* 0118 984 2582
Fax: 0118 984 5220
email: pbs.admin@pbs.org.uk
Web: www.pbs.org.uk

Pusey House, Oxford

Founded 1884 to continue the work of Dr Pusey, academic and pastoral, in Oxford. *Principal:* Revd Jonathan Baker. *Custodian of the Library:* Revd

Organizations

William Davage. *Archivist:* Revd Barry Orford, Pusey House, Oxford, OX1 3LZ
Tel: 01865 278415/01865 288024/
email: chapter@puseyhouse.org.uk
Web: www.puseyhouse.org.uk

Pyncombe Charity
Income about £10,000 p.a. applied to assist needy serving ordained clergy in financial difficulties due to illness, or occasionally other special circumstances, within the immediate family. Applications must be made through the diocesan bishop. *Secretary:* Mrs Rita Butterworth, Wingletye, Lawford, Crowcombe, Taunton, TA4 4AL
email: joeandrita@waitrose.com

Queen Victoria Clergy Fund
Founded 1897 to raise money towards the support of Church of England parochial clergy. Apart from one particular endowment, all the Fund's income is disbursed annually in block grants to dioceses specifically for the help of the clergy. Requests for assistance should be directed to the diocese. *Chairman:* Alan Cooper OBE. *Secretary:* Colin Menzies, Church House, Great Smith St, London, SW1P 3AZ
Tel: 020 7898 1311
email: colin.menzies@c-of-e.org.uk

Radius
The Religious Drama Society of Great Britain (Radius). Founded 1929 to encourage drama which throws light on the human condition. Assists and brings together those who create drama as a means of Christian understanding. Publishes a quarterly magazine, organizes workshops and play writing competitions. Publishes play scripts and has a selected list of titles for sale. *Patrons:* The Archbishop of Canterbury, Dame Judi Dench. *President:* Rt Revd Peter Firth. *Magazine/General Enquiries/Council Vice-Chair:* Margaret Hunt, 7 Lenton Rd, The Park, Nottingham, NG7 1DP
Tel: 0115 941 3922
email: office@radius.org.uk
Web: www.radius.org.uk

Rainer
(The Royal Philanthropic Society, incorporating the Rainer Foundation)
A national voluntary organization, founded in 1788, working primarily with young people at risk, through over 60 community-based projects, some in partnership with local authorities and other voluntary organizations. Particular services include leaving care projects and bail support schemes, accommodation and support to young people on release from young offender institutions or who are homeless, youth training and employment schemes. *Patron:* HRH The Prince Philip Duke of Edinburgh. *Chair:* Elizabeth

Filkin. *Chief Exec:* Mrs Joyce Moseley, Rectory Lodge, High St, Brasted, Westerham, TN16 1JF
Tel: 01959 578200
Fax: 01959 561891
email: mail@raineronline.org
Web: www.raineronline.org

RE Today Services
RE Today Services is wholly owned by the charity Christian Education, and is committed to the teaching of the major world faiths in religious education, and to an accurate and fair representation of their beliefs, values and practices in all its teaching materials. It carries forward the work of the Christian Education Movement (CEM). *Chief Executive:* Peter Fishpool. *Professional Team Director:* Pamela Draycott, 1020 Bristol Rd, Selly Oak, Birmingham, B29 6LB
Tel: 0121 472 4242
Fax: 0121 472 7575
email: retoday@retoday.org.uk
Web: www.retoday.org.uk

Reader Missionary Studentship Association
Founded 1904 to offer financial assistance to Readers training as priests for service in the Church overseas. *Chairman:* Mr G. E. Crowley. *Hon Treasurer:* Mr Ron Edinborough. *Hon Secretary:* Ms Sally Pickersgill, 39 Abbey Gardens, Canterbury, CT2 7EU
Tel: 01227 459227
email: secretary@rmsa.org.uk
Web: www.rmsa.org.uk

Rebecca Hussey's Book Charity
Established 1714 to give grants of religious and useful books to institutions in the United Kingdom. 51 Parma Crescent, London, SW11 1LT
Tel: 020 7223 4342
email: carolinej.davis@ntlworld.com

Reform
An evangelical network of clergy and laity in churches throughout the country. It came into being in 1993 and has campaigned for biblical integrity. It holds regular conferences, has over 1,600 members. It has published a number of booklets on matters relating to biblical teaching on doctrine and morality within the Church of England. *Chairman:* Revd David Banting. *Administrators:* Jonathan and Fiona Lockwood, PO Box 1183, Sheffield, S10 3YA
Tel and Fax: 0114 230 9256
email: administrator@reform.org.uk
Web: www.reform.org.uk

Relate
(formerly National Marriage Guidance Council)
Offers counselling and psychosexual therapy to those who seek advice with couple and family relationships. Relate also publishes a wide range of helpful literature available from its bookshop. There are 80 Relate Centres; to contact your nearest visit the web site. *Chief Executive:* Ms Clare Tyler. *Head of Public Policy:* Ms Jenny North,

Herbert Gray College, Little Church St, Rugby, CV21 3AP   *Tel:* 0845 456 1310
Fax: 01788 535007
email: enquiries@national.relate.org.uk
Web: www.relate.org.uk

Religious Education Council of England and Wales
The Religious Education Council of England and Wales seeks to represent the collective interests of a wide variety of organizations and communities in deepening and strengthening provision for religious education in schools and colleges. The Council was formed in 1973 and is open to national organizations which have a special interest in the teaching of religious education. The present membership of more than 45 organizations includes representation from the main Christian denominations, the world faiths, the British Humanist Association and the main educational bodies with professional RE interests. *Chair:* Prof Dr Brian Gates. *Deputy Chair:* Mr John Keast. *Treasurer:* Dr John Gay, c/o CAN, 1 London Bridge, London, SE1 9BG
Web: www.religiouseducationcouncil.org.uk

Retired Clergy Association
Founded 1927 to act as a bond of friendship in prayer and mutual help to retired clergy. Membership at 31 December 2006 was 3,400. There are local branches in Bexhill, Birmingham, Blackburn, Bournemouth, Bristol, Bury St Edmunds, Cambridge, Canterbury, Chester, Chichester, Eastbourne, East Devon, Ely, Harrogate, Henfield, Hereford, Huntingdonshire, Isle of Wight, Lancaster, Leigh-on-Sea, Ludlow, Manchester, Norwich, Oxford, Peterborough, Portsmouth (Mainland), Ripon, Rochester, Rugby, Salisbury, Scarborough and Filey, Shrewsbury, Southampton, Stockport, Wells, Weston-super-Mare, Winchester and Alresford, Worcester and York. *President:* The Bishop of Gloucester. *Chairman:* Rt Revd Richard Lewis. *Hon Secretary:* Mr John Sansom, Kiggon Cottage, St Clement, Truro, TR1 1TE
Tel: 01872 520471
email: johnandpauline@kiggoncottage.fsnet.co.uk

Retreat Association
Comprising these Christian retreat groups: Association for Promoting Retreats, Baptist Union Retreat Group, Catholic Network for Retreats and Spirituality, Methodist Retreat and Spirituality Network, Quaker Retreat Group, United Reformed Church Silence and Retreat Network. Offers information and resources about retreats to both the would-be and the seasoned retreatant, coordinates training opportunities in the field of retreat giving and spiritual direction, promotes the work of retreat houses and encourages regional activity. *Retreats*, an ecumenical journal listing retreat houses in Britain and Ireland and their programmes, is published annu-

ally (2009 edition £6.50 inc p&p). Other literature is also available; send for publications list. *Director:* Paddy Lane, The Central Hall, 256 Bermondsey St, London, SE1 3UJ
Tel: 020 7357 7736
Fax: 020 7357 7724
email: info@retreats.org.uk
Web: www.retreats.org.uk

Revd Dr George Richards' Charity
Founded 1837 to provide financial assistance to clergy of the Church of England forced to retire early owing to ill-health. Widows, widowers and dependants can also apply for assistance. *Secretary:* Dr P. D. Simmons, 98 Thomas More House, Barbican, London, EC2Y 8BU
Tel: 020 7588 5583

Richard Crosse's Charity
Provides small annuities for widows of clergymen of the Church of England. Preference given to those who, from age, ill-health, accident or infirmity, are unable to maintain themselves by their own exertions. *Clerk to Trustees:* Mr C. P. Kitto, 20 Saint John St, Lichfield, WS13 6PD
Tel: 01543 262491

Richmond Fellowship
Established in 1959, the Fellowship provides residential, supported housing, community services and employment services for people with mental health problems. It now operates more than 90 residential, supported housing, day care and employment services for people with mental health problems throughout the UK. Richmond Fellowship Training and Development Department runs an extensive programme of short courses on mental health, group work, supervision and management, which are open to those working in the care field. For further information contact Richmond Fellowship. *PA to Chief Executive:* Marise Willis, 80 Holloway Rd, London, N7 8JG
Tel: 020 7697 3300
Fax: 020 7697 3301
email: marise.willis@richmondfellowship.org.uk
Web: www.richmondfellowship.org.uk

RNID
(Formerly known as Royal National Institute for Deaf People)
RNID is the largest charity representing the 9 million deaf and hard of hearing people in the UK. It offers a range of services for deaf and hard of hearing people, and provides information and support on all aspects of deafness, hearing loss and tinnitus. As a membership charity, it aims to achieve a radically better quality of life for deaf and hard of hearing people. RNID's work involves campaigning and lobbying, providing services, training, products and equipment, and undertaking medical and technical research. It works throughout the UK. *Chairman:* Mr James

Strachan. *Chief Executive:* Dr John Low, 19–23 Featherstone St, London, EC1Y 8SL
Tel: 0808 808 0123 (Voice) 0808 808 9000 (Textphone)
email: informationline@rnid.org.uk
Web: www.rnid.org.uk

Royal Alexandra and Albert School

Founded in 1758, a voluntary-aided junior and secondary school providing boarding education for boys and girls aged 7–18 who are without one or both parents or who would benefit from boarding education because of home circumstances. Only boarding fees payable and bursaries available. Bursaries for children of clergy are available for two thirds of the fees at this state boarding school where the full fees are only £3,655 per term for full boarding. In exceptional circumstances, further bursary support can be provided. Exceptional facilities. Contact: Headmaster for further details. *Patron:* HM the Queen. *President:* HRH the Duchess of Gloucester. *Headmaster:* Paul D. Spencer Ellis. *Foundation Secretary:* Diana Bromley. *Admissions Secretary:* Sue Harrington, Gatton Park, Reigate, RH2 0TW
Tel: 01737 649000
Fax: 01737 649002
email: headmaster@gatton-park.org.uk
Web: www.gatton-park.org.uk

Royal Asylum of St Ann's Society

The Society, founded in 1702, offers grants towards the expenses of educating children, from the age of 11, at boarding or day schools. Most, but not all, of those aided are children of clergy of the Church of England; however, in the first instance clergy should approach the Corporation of the Sons of the Clergy. The Society welcomes collections, donations and legacies towards this purpose. *President:* The Dean of Westminster. *Chairman:* Mr Tom Russell. *Secretary:* Mr David Hanson, King Edward's School, Witley, Petworth Rd, Wormley, GU8 5SG

Royal College of Organists

Founded 1864, incorporated by Royal Charter 1893, 'to promote the art of organ-playing and choir training'. Holds lectures, recitals and master-classes nationwide. Examinations for certificate, Fellowship, Associateship, Licentiateship in Teaching and Diploma in Choral Directing. Membership open to all who take an interest in the work and profession of the organist and in organ music. *Patron:* HM The Queen. *President:* Peter Wright. *General Manager:* Kim Gilbert, PO Box 56357, London, SE16 7XL *Tel:* 05600 767208
email: admin@rco.org.uk
Web: www.rco.org.uk

Royal Martyr Church Union

Founded 1906: (1) Ever to cherish the sacred remembrance of Charles the First, King and Martyr, both in public worship and private devotion, and to this end to promote the restoration of his name to its proper place in the calendar of the worldwide Anglican Communion, and the observance of 30 January, the day of his martyrdom, by suitable services in the Book of Common Prayer and elsewhere. (2) To maintain the principles of faith, loyalty and liberty for which the King died – the faith of the Church, loyalty to the Crown, and the ancient liberties of the people. Holds annual commemorative eucharists in London and Edinburgh. Subscription £15.00 p.a. including *Royal Martyr Annual*. *Chairman:* Dr Barry Bracewell-Milnes. *Hon Secretary and Treasurer:* David Roberts, 7 Nunnery Stables, St Albans, AL1 2AS *Tel:* 01727 856626

Royal National Institute of Blind People (RNIB)

Royal National Institute of Blind People (RNIB) is a charity which supports blind and partially sighted people to remain independent by: giving you free advice about your eye condition, the benefits you're entitled to, and the specialist and local support that's available; providing employment services and practical help for children and their families; suggesting ideas on how you can continue to enjoy your hobbies and leisure time; recommending everyday items and gadgets to make your life easier; offering a listening ear. *President:* His Grace the Duke of Westminster. *Chairman:* Lord Low of Dalston CBE. *Chief Executive:* Lesley-Anne Alexander, 105 Judd St, London, WC1H 9NE
Tel: 0845 766 9999 (Helpline) 020 7391 2000
email: helpline@rnib.org.uk
Web: www.rnib.org.uk

Royal Naval Licensed Readers' Society

Founded 1860. Licensed Readers assist in the work of the Anglican Church amongst the men and women of the Royal Navy and their families. In ships at sea and in naval establishments ashore they work alongside Naval Chaplains in the furtherance of the Christian faith and the welfare of the Navy's people. The Society is dependent financially on voluntary contributions for the maintenance of its work. *Treasurer:* Mr Lee Foley, MP 1–2 Sir Henry Leach Building, Whale Island, Portsmouth, PO2 8BY *Tel:* 023 9262 5508
Fax: 023 9262 5134
email: lee.foley211@mod.uk

Royal School of Church Music

The Royal School of Church Music (RSCM) is the leading organization promoting and supporting church music. It is an educational charity dedicated to raising standards and promoting the best use of music in every style of Christian worship and in every denomination. It provides musical and educational resources to train, develop and inspire clergy, music leaders, musicians, singers and congregations. The RSCM runs a wide range of courses at local and national level and its *Voice for Life* programme is a training scheme for singers of all ages that can be used by individual churches and schools. A national network of volunteers runs events to meet the needs of their local areas. The RSCM also publishes music through the RSCM Press, including musical resources for *Common Worship*, and RSCM Music Direct provides a fast and efficient mail-order service for music from all publishers. Affiliated churches and schools and individual members receive *Church Music Quarterly*, a highly informative and interesting magazine for all those concerned with church music, and *Sunday by Sunday*, an essential liturgy planner aiding those who plan and lead worship to enhance it through music appropriate to the day. Appointed the official music agency for the Church of England from April 1996. *President:* The Archbishop of Canterbury. *Chairman:* Mr Mark Williams. *Director:* Mr Lindsay Gray. *Bursar:* Julia Harrison Place, 19 The Close, Salisbury, SP1 2EB

Tel: 01722 424848/01722 424841 (membership)
Fax: 01722 424849
email: enquiries@rscm.com
Web: www.rscm.com

Rural Theology Association
Founded 1981 to provide a forum for the rural churches and to focus for the Church at large the distinctive ways and needs and contributions of the rural. Its aims are to study the gospel and develop theology in a rural setting, to encourage the development of patterns of ministry and mission appropriate to the countryside today, and to discover ways of living in the countryside which embody a Christian response to the world. It publishes the journal *Rural Theology* twice yearly. *President:* Revd Prof Leslie Francis. *Chairman:* Canon Mark Rylands. *Secretary:* Revd Stephen Cope. *Treasurer:* Dr Mandy Robbins, Vicarage, 28 Park Ave, Withernsea, HU19 2JU

Tel: 01964 611426
email: secretary@rural-theology.org.uk
Web: www.rural-theology.org.uk

Samaritans
Samaritans exists to provide confidential emotional support to any person, irrespective of race, creed, age or status who is in emotional distress or at risk of suicide; and to increase public awareness of issues around suicide and depression. *Chief Exec:* Mr Dominic Rudd, The Upper Mill, Kingston Rd, Ewell, Surrey, KT17 2AF

Tel: 020 8394 8300 (admin)
08457 909090 (helpline)
Fax: 020 8394 8301
email: Admin: admin@samaritans.org /
Helpline: jo@samaritans.org
Web: www.samaritans.org

Sarum College
Sarum College is an independent ecumenical centre for learning, hospitality and spiritual growth. The College is housed in a Grade 1 listed building in Salisbury Cathedral Close and offers an extensive and varied programme of short residential and day courses, as well as academic programmes including the MA in Christian Spirituality. The College has 47 bedrooms, many en suite, including 5 newly refurbished rooms in the 17th century Wren building overlooking the Cathedral. There are a range of meeting and conference rooms, a 19th century chapel, common room/bar, and a dining room seating up to 120. On-site parking is available. Residential conferences, parish groups, training events, board meetings are all welcome, along with individual guests who may wish to enjoy our hospitality or spend time here on study leave or sabbatical. The College also houses a fine theological library of over 35,000 volumes, and Salisbury's only independent theological bookshop, both of which offer postal/mail order facilities. *Principal:* Mr Stephen Lamdin. *Director of Central Services:* Mr Mark Manterfield. *Director of Studies:* Mr Riccardo Larini. *Marketing and Communications Officer:* Christine Nielson-Craig, 19 The Close, Salisbury, SP1 2EE *Tel:* 01722 424800
Fax: 01722 338508
email: hospitality@sarum.ac.uk
Web: www.sarum.ac.uk

Sarum St Michael Educational Charity
Personal grants may be awarded for further or higher education, to those who live, work or study within the Salisbury or adjacent dioceses (also to former students of the college). Bursaries may be awarded to those who live or study within the Salisbury diocese or adjoining dioceses, who intend to train to teach RE. Grants may be made to local schools, mainly for RE and worship resources. Grants may be made to parishes within the Salisbury diocese, for work with children and young people. Corporate grants may be made, where funds permit, to certain projects within the diocese. The governors meet five times a year to consider applications: please enquire about closing dates for applications, bearing in mind that grants are not awarded retrospectively. Applications should be made on forms available from the correspondent, submitted directly by the individual. Member of the Association of Church College Trusts (see separate entry). First Floor, 27A Castle St, Salisbury, SP1 1TT *Tel:* 01722 422296
Fax: 0870 135 9943
email: ssmsarum@waitrose.com

SASRA
(The Soldiers' and Airmen's Scripture Readers Association)
Founded 1838 to present the claims of Christ to the men and women serving in the Army and later the RAF, to promote interdenominational Christian fellowship among them and to encourage individual serving Christians to witness to

their comrades. *Chairman:* Brigadier Ian Dobbie. *General Secretary:* Sqdn Ldr Colin Woodland, Havelock House, Barrack Rd, Aldershot, GU11 3NP   *Tel:* 01252 341804
Fax: 01252 350722
email: admin@sasra.org.uk
Web: www.sasra.org.uk

School Chaplains' Conference
An association for all people, ordained and lay, involved in Christian ministry in state or independent schools. *President:* Rt Revd L. Urwin. *Chairman:* Revd Dr Jan Cheeseman. *Secretary:* Revd Lindsay Collins. *Administrator:* Revd John Thackray, c/o Kings's School, Rochester, ME1 1TE   *Tel:* 01634 888555
email: treasurer@schoolchaplains.org.uk
Web: www.schoolchaplains.org.uk

Scout Association, The
Founded in 1907 to promote the development of young people in achieving their full physical, intellectual, social and spiritual potential, as individuals, as responsible citizens and as members of their local, national and international communites. Membership 475,000. Tel: 0845 300 1818 (8 a.m. to 8 p.m. Mon to Fri, 9 a.m. to 12 noon Sat) or 020 8433 7100. *Chief Scout:* Mr Peter Duncan. *Contact:* Derek Twine, Chief Executive, Gilwell Park, Bury Rd, Chingford, London, E4 7QW   *Tel:* 0845 300 1818/020 8433 7100/
Fax: 020 8433 7103
email: info.centre@scout.org.uk
Web: www.scouts.org.uk

Scripture Gift Mission
SGM creates Bible resources to help people communicate God's word to today's generation. A new, research-based range uses up-to-date Bible versions and contemporary graphics. SGM publishes materials in over 200 languages for use worldwide. *CEO:* Mr Hugh Davies. *Partnerships Director:* Mr Bryan Stonehouse. *Marketing Director:* Mr Ian Buchanan. *Financial Director:* Mr Ian Larkham. *Publications Director:* Mr David Traher, Radstock House, 5 Eccleston St, London, SW1W 9LZ   *Tel:* 020 7730 2155
Fax: 020 7730 0240
email: info@sgm.org
Web: www.sgm.org

Scripture Union
Scripture Union seeks to make the Christian faith known to children, young people and families and to support the Church through resources, Bible reading and training. SU's work in Britain includes schools work, Bible ministries, publishing, training, evangelism, holidays, missions and family ministry. Scripture Union is active in more than 100 countries. *Chief Exec/ Team Leader:* Mr Keith Civval. *Director of Theology:* Mr John Grayston. *Director of Ministry Delivery:* Mr Terry Clutterham. *Director of Ministry Promotions:* Vacancy.

Director of Ministry Support: Mr David Thorpe, 207–209 Queensway, Bletchley, Milton Keynes, MK2 2EB   *Tel:* 01908 856000
Fax: 01908 856111
email: info@scriptureunion.org.uk
Web: www.scriptureunion.org.uk

Scripture Union Schools Ministry
Works to establish, encourage and resource a voluntary Christian presence in primary and secondary schools through term-time work and holiday activities. *Head of Dept:* Mr Emlyn Williams, 207–209 Queensway, Bletchley, Milton Keynes, MK2 2EB   *Tel:* 01908 856170
Fax: 01908 856012
email: schools@scriptureunion.org.uk
Web: www.scriptureunion.org.uk

Seamen's Friendly Society of St Paul
Trust administered by Alton Abbey, able to offer financial assistance to merchant sailors. *Contact:* Rt Revd Dominican Giles Hill, Alton Abbey, Beech, Alton, GU34 4AP   *Tel:* 01420 562145/
01420 563575
Fax: 01420 561691

Selly Oak Centre for Mission Studies (SOCMS)
The Centre is sponsored by USPG Anglicans in World Mission and the Methodist Church in Britain. It is the successor to the United College of the Ascension, Selly Oak and provides training, orientation and research in global mission. SOCMS is international in nature, attracting clergy and key leaders from churches worldwide for its Masters programme in Mission and Leadership Formation in the World Church. It offers formation and training for those crossing cultures in mission, long and short term, including the Experience Exchange Programme. It invites a Scholar in Residence and two Visiting Scholars each year to pursue research in global mission, and is part of an ever growing TransContinental Training Network of centres and institutions with similar aims across the world. As part of the Queen's Foundation for Ecumenical Theological Education in Birmingham, it infuses theological education and ordination training in Britain with the global mission perspectives, possibilities and personnel. *Director:* Revd Val Ogden. *Tutor for Global Christianity and World Mission:* Revd Dr Joshva Raja. *Tutor for World Mission Education:* Revd George Wauchope. *Administrator:* Ruth Padley, The Queen's Foundation, Somerset Rd, Edgbaston, Birmingham, B15 2QH
    Tel: 0121 454 1527
Fax: 0121 454 8171
email: r.padley@queens.ac.uk
Web: www.queens.ac.uk

Servants of Christ the King
Founded 1942 by Canon Roger Lloyd of Winchester. A movement of groups or 'Companies' of Christians who seek to develop a corporate life

by praying together in silence, with disciplined discussion. They actively wait upon God to be led by the Holy Spirit, and undertake to do together any work which they are given by him to do. *Enquirers' Correspondent:* Dr Pauline Waters, Swallowfield, Wheelers Lane, Linton, Maidstone, ME17 4BN   *Tel:* 01622 743392
email: info@sck.org.uk
Web: www.sck.org.uk

Shaftesbury Homes and 'Arethusa'
Founded 1843 to house and educate homeless children in London, the charity is now the leading voluntary sector provider of residential care for children in London. In London and Suffolk the charity also provides services for young people leaving care, and supported housing for the young homeless. Personal development is promoted through venture activities at the Arethusa Venture Centre on the Medway. *Chairman:* Richard Hall. *Chief Exec:* Alison Chesney. *Director Social Work:* Chris Carey. *Director Finance:* Tony Rowell. *Manager External Relations:* Sarah Armstrong, The Chapel, Royal Victoria Patriotic Building, Trinity Rd, London, SW18 3SX
Tel: 020 8875 1555
Fax: 020 8875 1954
email: info@shaftesbury.org.uk
Web: www.shaftesbury.org.uk

Sharing of Ministries Abroad (SOMA)
Founded in 1978 to serve the renewal of the Church throughout the world, particularly in the Anglican Communion. SOMA now has eleven centres in different parts of the world. SOMA works for the transformation of individuals and churches, and the healing of communities and their lands through the renewing power of the Holy Spirit by sending and receiving teams worldwide on short-term mission within the Anglican Communion. A newsletter, *SHARING*, is published three times a year. *SOMA International Chairman:* Rt Revd Ben Kwashi. *SOMA UK National Director:* Revd Stephen Dinsmore. *SOMA UK Development Officer:* Vacancy. *SOMA UK Finance Administrator:* Vacancy, PO Box 69, Merriott, TA18 9AP   *Tel:* 01460 279737
email: info@somauk.org
Web: www.somauk.org

Social Responsibility Network, The
The Network (developed from the Anglican Association for Social Responsibility) aims to share good practice, ideas and information on a wide range of issues and provide peer support and encouragement for Christian practitioners in social responsibility. We do this by meeting together in local and regional groups, holding an annual conference on a key topic, making resources available to one another, and sharing ideas, needs and resources via our discussion e-net. Open to all Christian practitioners. *President:* The Bishop of Chelmsford. *Treasurer:* Canon

David Grimwood. *Chair:* Ultan Russell, 2–3 Bedford Place, Maidstone, ME16 8JB
Tel: 01622 755014
Fax: 01622 693531
email: wright@btinternet.com
Web: www.srnet.org.uk

Society for Liturgical Study
Founded 1978. The Society promotes liturgical study and research, and holds a conference in alternate years. Membership is interdenominational and is open to persons involved in teaching liturgy, or in research in this field, or holding official appointments with responsibility for liturgy and worship. *Secretary:* Revd Dr James Steven,, Franklin-Wilkins Building, Waterloo Bridge Wing, Waterloo Bridge, London SE1 9NH
email: james.steven@kcl.ac.uk
Web: www.studyliturgy.org.uk

Society for Old Testament Study
Founded 1917 as a society for OT scholars in Britain and Ireland. Scholars not resident in the British Isles may also become members. Two meetings to hear and discuss papers are arranged annually. The Society also publishes its annual 'Book List' and is involved in other publishing activities. It maintains links with OT scholars throughout the world, particularly the Dutch-Flemish OT Society with which it holds joint meetings every three years. Candidates for membership must be proficient in biblical Hebrew and be proposed by two existing members. *Hon Secretary:* Dr John Jarick, St Stephen's House, 16 Marston Street, Oxford, OX4 1JX
Tel: 01865 613512
Fax: 01865 613513
email: john.jarick@theology.ox.ac.uk
Web: www.sots.ac.uk

Society for Promoting Christian Knowledge
SPCK was founded in 1698 and aims to help people to understand and to grow in the Christian faith. It works to support and develop the knowledge of Christians and to interest and inform others. Throughout its history SPCK has been associated with the spread of education and informative literature in all its forms. It is an Anglican foundation but supports a diversity of Christian traditions. The Society has been involved in publishing since its foundation in 1698. SPCK publishes around 100 new titles each year. Its output includes Christian books, web sites and electronic products across a broad spectrum, from the catholic to the evangelical and from the conservative to the liberal. The range includes liturgy, theology, science and religion, biblical studies and spirituality, academic and student texts as well as stationery and books for a popular market, with resources for clergy, parishes and study groups. Another active area is the International Study Guide series, aimed particularly at those studying theology around the

world, including many for whom English is not a first language. Under the Azure imprint are books aimed to appeal to readers who are searching for faith but who might not ordinarily look to Christianity for help or guidance. SPCK has created an Assemblies web site (www.assemblies.org.uk), which provides teachers with materials for school assemblies which they can download free of charge. SPCK Diffusion aims to produce innovative materials to resource a wide audience with information in a form relevant to their interests and experience. SPCK Worldwide supports the distribution of books and educational materials for Christians overseas. It depends entirely upon donations from individuals, churches and charitable trusts. Its areas of support include theological education, funding for indigenous publishing, and primarily the provision of books and training for those in some of the poorest parts of the world. SPCK Worldwide works in partnership with Feed the Minds, with whom it has overlapping goals. *President:* The Archbishop of Canterbury. *Chairman of the Governing Body:* Rt Revd Michael Perham. *General Secretary:* Mr Simon Kingston. *Executive Administrator:* Ms Pat Phillips, 36 Causton St, London, SW1P 4ST

Tel: 020 7592 3900
Fax: 020 7592 3939
email: spck@spck.org.uk
Web: www.spck.org.uk / www.assemblies.org.uk

Society for the Assistance of Ladies in Reduced Circumstances
Founded by the late Miss Edith Smallwood in 1886. Assistance is given to ladies living alone in their own home (either owned or rented) on a low income and domiciled in the United Kingdom, irrespective of age or social status. Registered Charity no. 205798. Enquiries welcome on freephone helpline. Donations and legacies gratefully received. *Patron:* HM The Queen. *Apply:* The Secretary, Lancaster House, 25 Hornyold Rd, Malvern, WR14 1QQ   *Tel:* 01684 574645/
0800 587 4696 (freephone helpline)
Fax: 01684 577212
email: info@salrc.org.uk
Web: www.salrc.org.uk

Society for the Maintenance of the Faith
Founded in 1873, the Society presents, or shares in the presentation of, priests to over 80 benefices. As well as its work as a patronage body the Society aims to promote Catholic teaching and practice in the Church of England at large. *President:* Dr Brian Hanson. *Secretary:* Revd Paul Conrad, Christ Church Vicarage, 10 Cannon Place, London, NW3 1EJ   *Tel and Fax:* 020 7435 6784

Society for the Relief of Poor Clergy (SRPC)
Founded 1788 to aid evangelical Anglican clergy and their dependants in times of financial distress due to sickness, bereavement or other difficulties. *Secretary:* Mrs Pauline Walden, c/o CPAS, Athena Drive, Tachbrook Park, Warwick, CV34 6NG   *Tel:* 01926 458458
Fax: 01926 458459
email: srpc@cpas.org.uk
Web: www.cpas.org.uk

Society of Archbishop Justus Ltd
The Society, named after the fourth Archbishop of Canterbury, was formed in 1996 and incorporated in 1997 as a non-profit corporation in New York, USA for the purpose of using the Internet to foster and further unity among Christians, especially Anglicans. It focuses on internet information services: web and email servers that help Anglicans to be one body. Members help install, operate and maintain the computers and networks that enable online communication, and help educate the Anglican public about how best to use those computers. Directors include both Church of England and ECUSA members. The Society sponsors the Anglicans Online web site and, on behalf of the International Anglican Domain Committee, administers the anglican.org internet domain. More information is available on the web site. *Director:* Simon Sarmiento, PO Box 345, St Albans, AL1 5ZZ
email: directors@justus.anglican.org
Web: www.justus.anglican.org/soaj.html

Society of Catholic Priests
Founded in 1994, with now over 500 members, an inclusive society of priests who 'believe in one, holy, catholic and apostolic church ordaining men and women to serve as deacons, priests and bishops in the Church of God'. The objects of the Society are to promote the formation and support of priestly spirituality and catholic evangelism. *Patron:* The Archbishop of Canterbury. *Visitor General:* The Bishop of Manchester. *Rector General:* Canon Andrew Nunn. *Secretary General:* Revd Michael Skinner, St Andrew's Vicarage, 71 Anglesea Rd, Orpington, BR5 4AN
Tel and Fax: 01689 823775
email: michael.skinner@rochester.anglican.org
Web: www.scp.org.uk

Society of King Charles the Martyr
Founded 1894 to promote observance of January 30, the day of the martyrdom of King Charles I in 1649, and uphold the traditional Anglican Catholic principles for which he died. Publishes various material including the journal *Church and King. Chairman:* Mr Robin Davies, 22 Tyning Rd, Winsley, Bradford on Avon, BA15 2JJ
Tel: 01225 862965
Fax: 01225 862965 (ring first)
email: robinjbdavies@hotmail.com
Web: www.skcm.org

Society of Mary
Founded 1931 to promote devotion to Our Lady; mainly an Anglican society but welcomes

members from other churches of a Catholic tradition. *Superior General:* Rt Revd Robert Ladds. *Chaplain General:* Revd G. C. Rowlands. *Secretary:* Mrs Celia Bush, 169 Humber Doucy Lane, Ipswich, IP4 3PA

Society of Mary and Martha
An independent ecumenical charity run by a mixed lay Community providing confidential support for clergy and/or spouses, especially at times of stress, crisis, burnout or breakdown. Resources exclusively for people in ministry include the famous 12,000–mile Service weeks, Family Holiday week, and Linhay Lodges: well-appointed, self-contained accommodation for private retreats, sabbaticals, safe place, emergency bolt-hole or battery re-charge. Programme events open to everyone include retreats, reading weeks, pilgrimage, time out, MBTI, Enneagram and other resources for personal and spiritual growth. The Sheldon Centre is a beautifully converted farm with lovely views across the Teign Valley, just ten miles from the M5 and main line railway at Exeter. *Warden:* Carl Lee. *Administrator:* Sarah Horsman, Sheldon, Dunsford, Exeter, EX6 7LE   *Tel:* 01647 252752
Fax: 01647 253900
email: smm@sheldon.uk.com
Web: www.sheldon.uk.com

Society of Ordained Scientists
Founded 1987. A dispersed order for ordained scientists, men and women. Members aim to offer to God, in their ordained role, the work of science in the exploration and stewardship of creation, to express the commitment of the Church to the scientific enterprise and their concern for its impact on the world, and to support each other in their vocation. Associate membership is available to those who are not ordained but are interested in the work of the Society. *Visitor:* Rt Revd Rupert Hoare. *Secretary:* Canon Michael Soulsby. *Warden:* Revd Richard Hills, Stamford Cottage, 47 Old Rd, Mottram, Hyde, Cheshire SK14 6LW   *Tel:* 01457 763104
Web: www.thesosc.org

Society of Retreat Conductors
Founded in 1923 for the training of retreat conductors, the running of retreat houses and the conducting of retreats. *Chairman:* Revd David Sutton. *Company Secretary:* Mrs Kathryn Redington. *Superior:* Canon Howard Such, c/o St Mary Woolnoth Vestry, Lombard St, London, EC3V 9AN   *Tel:* 020 7929 0199
email: admin.src@btconnect.com

Society of Royal Cumberland Youths
Bell-ringing society founded in 1747. Its headquarters are at St Martin-in-the-Fields and the Society is responsible for ringing at a number of London churches. The society has a worldwide membership, promoting high standards among proficient change-ringers. *Master:* Mr Simon Holden. *Secretary:* Ms George Unsworth, 66 Montague Road, Cambridge, CB4 1BX
Tel: 07736 616662
email: secretary@srcy.org.uk
Web: www.srcy.org.uk

Society of St Willibrord
(The Anglican and Old Catholic Society of St Willibrord)
Founded 1908 to promote friendly relations between the Anglican and Old Catholic Churches, including the fullest use of the full Communion established between them in 1931. Membership of the society is open to members of churches in full communion with Canterbury and/or Utrecht. *Presidents:* Rt Revd Geoffrey Rowell, Bishop of Gibraltar in Europe . *Patrons:* The Archdeacons of Canterbury and Utrecht. *Hon Secretary:* Mthr Ariadne van den Hof. *Chairman:* Rt Revd J. Gledhill, Bishop of Lichfield, Y Rheithordy, Y Sgwr, Blaenau Ffestiniog, Gwynedd LL41 3UW   *Tel:* 01766 831536
email: honsecssw@gmail.com
Web: www.willibrord.org

Society of the Faith (Incorporated)
The objects of the Society are to act as an Association of Christians in communion with the See of Canterbury for mutual assistance in the work of Christ's Church and for the furtherance of charitable undertakings, especially for the popularization of the Catholic Faith. We have occupied Faith House in Westminster since 1935 and formerly ran the Faith Press and Faithcraft. We manage Faith House as a resource for the Church, promote charitable activities and hold the annual Liddon Lecture. The restricted Liddon Fund provides two or three grants per year for young Anglicans (under 25 years old) who are engaged in advanced theological study, for example for a second degree. *Principal:* Dr Julian Litten. *Vice-principal:* Canon Robert Gage. *Secretary and Treasurer:* Mrs Margery Roberts, Faith House, 7 Tufton St, London, SW1P 3QB   *Tel:* 01727 856626

Society of the Holy Cross (SSC)
Founded 1855 for priests (1100 members) 'to maintain and extend the Catholic faith and discipline and to form a special bond of union between Catholic clergy'. Provinces: European Union, Australasia, Canada, Africa, USA. *Master General:* Preb Dr David Houlding SSC. *Provincial Master:* Fr Kit Dunkeley SSC. *Registrar:* Fr Richard Arnold SSC. *Treasurer:* Fr David Lawson SSC. *Mission Director:* Fr Trevor Buxton SSC, All Hallows House, 52 Courthope Rd, London, NW3 2LD   *Tel:* 020 7267 7833/020 7263 6317/
Fax: 020 7267 6317
email: sscmaster@lineone.net

Organizations

South American Mission Society

(Incorporating the Spanish and Portuguese Church Aid Society)
Founded 1844 to make known the gospel of the Lord Jesus Christ to the people of Latin America and the Iberian Peninsula and continuing in active partnership now with the mission priorities of the Anglican churches in these regions. *International Relations Officer/Director:* Canon John Sutton. *Mission Education Officer:* Mr Robert Lunt. *Financial Secretary/Director:* Mr Philip Tadman, Allen Gardiner Cottage, Pembury Rd, Tunbridge Wells, TN2 3QU   *Tel:* 01892 538647/ 020 8787 7083/ *Fax:* 01892 525797 *email:* finsec@samsgb.org *Web:* www.samsgb.org

Southern Africa Church Development Trust

Founded 1960 to inform, encourage concern for and involvement in the Church in Southern Africa. Supports churches, community centres and schools, primary and secondary education through scholarships, clergy and lay training, and medical work. Publishes a quarterly bulletin of information and projects which is sent to all subscribers and supporters. *President:* Mr Martin Kenyon. *Director:* Dr Jack Mulder. *Chairperson:* Canon David Cook. *Hon Treasurer:* Mr Jim Wilkinson. *Secretary to the Board:* Mrs Susan Howden, 51 Heathside, Hinchley Wood, KT10 9TD   *Tel:* 020 8398 9638/020 8398 8699 *email:* jlerm2@hotmail.com *Web:* www.sacdt.org

St Christopher's College Educational Trust

Small one-off grants given to maintain or enlarge any institution or centre for religious education (Church of England) or payments towards the provision of facilities for research into theory and practice of teaching religious education, especially in young people's work. The Trustees meet in May and November. Applications to be received by mid-April and mid-October. Member of the Association of Church College Trusts (see separate entry). *Correspondent:* Mr Segi Yaskey, The National Society, Church House, Great Smith St, London, SW1P 3AZ   *Tel:* 020 7898 1497 *Fax:* 020 7898 1493 *email:* segi.yaskey@c-of-e.org.uk *Web:* www.natsoc.org.uk

St Christopher's Fellowship

St Christopher's is a charity and housing association providing care, accommodation, education, training and support to children, young people and vulnerable adults. We run children's homes, fostering services, supported housing and hostels, along with education, employment and outreach services. *Chairman:* Mr Anthony Hick-inbotham. *Chief Exec:* Mr Jonathan Farrow, 1 Putney High St, London, SW15 1SZ   *Tel:* 020 8780 7800 *Fax:* 020 8780 7801 *email:* info@stchris.org.uk *Web:* www.stchris.org.uk

St Gabriel's Trust

St Gabriel's is an Anglican teacher training foundation concerned with teacher training for school RE teachers; the Trust's main object is to further good practice in school RE. It is not able to make grants to clergy, theological students or 'Bible teachers' as such, but only to those who are actively involved in school RE; any study course must be school-related. Member of the Association of Church College Trusts (see separate entry). Owing to the overwhelming number of applications received, the Trustees have found it necessary to severely restrict funding for overseas students. Modest personal grants are made towards fees and expenses for Certificate, Diploma or MA courses, mainly to teachers studying part-time for further specialist RE qualifications while continuing with their teaching jobs. The Trust makes a few grants for higher research. The Trustees will only consider applications from experienced RE teachers with QTS studying part-time and who are committed to a long term career in RE teaching. Applicants must be able to demonstrate that their research will be of practical benefit to classroom teaching and to RE. They should apply to the Trust well before they are due to start their proposed course, explaining their financial needs and other sources of funding anticipated. The Trust is not able to assist schools as such, as its objectives are higher and further education. A way in which individual schools can benefit from the Trust is usually when one of the teaching staff receives a personal grant towards the expenses of a part-time course of study for a further specialist qualification in RE. *Correspondent:* Mr P. M. Duffell. *Asst Clerk to Trustees:* Mrs B. Duffell, Ladykirk, 32 The Ridgeway, Enfield, EN2 8QH   *Tel:* 020 8363 6474

St George's College, Jerusalem

St George's College is a unique centre of continuing education in the Anglican Communion, offering short-term courses as well as facilities for individual reflection and study. It is open to both clergy and laity. Since its founding in 1962, the College has hosted participants from 92 countries and 96 Christian traditions. Course members engage with a wide range of biblical texts in the context of the land; encounter Jewish, Christian and Muslim faith as it is exercised today; and come to appreciate anew the rich fabric of faith and spirituality that this environment offers to the pilgrim. The College is situated 500 metres north of the Damascus Gate of the Old City of Jerusalem, and set in its own grounds adjacent to the Anglican Cathedral of St George the Martyr.

Full details of courses can be obtained from the web site or the Secretary of the British Regional Committee. *Secretary of the British Regional Committee:* Revd Paul Conder, 112 Strensall Rd, Old Earswick, York, YO32 9SJ
Tel and Fax: 01904 763071
Web: www.stgeorgescollegejerusalem.org.il

St George's House, Windsor Castle
Founded 1966. A residential consultation centre within Windsor Castle, and part of the 14th-century College of St George. Apart from ecumenical clergy conferences the House also hosts a range of other consultations. Some are internally organised, while others are instigated by external groups under the guidance of House staff. The range of themes is wide but all share a concern for greater human well-being. Accommodation for up to 33 people. *Chairman, Board of Trustees and Council:* Rt Revd David J. Conner, Dean of Windsor. *Warden:* Canon Dr Hueston Finlay. *Programme Director:* Vacancy. *Clergy Course Administrator:* Ms Claire Blackburn. *Warden's Administrator:* Mrs Sue Pendry, St George's House, Windsor Castle, Windsor, Berkshire SL4 1NJ
Tel: 01753 848848/
Fax: 01753 848849
email: sue.pendry@stgeorges-windsor.org
Web: www.stgeorgeshouse.org

St George's Trust
The Trust exists to give grants to individuals to further the work of the Church of England. The Fellowship of Saint John (UK) Trust Association is the sole trustee. The funds at the Trust's disposal do not permit large grants for restoration projects, or any long-term financial support. The wide remit enables it to help a large number of individuals for sabbaticals, gap years and the like to a maximum of £500. All applications should be sent, together with a stamped addressed envelope, to the Trust with as much supporting documentation as possible. St Edward's House, 22 Great College St, London, SW1P 3QA

St Hild and St Bede Trust
The Trust's annual income is restricted to the advancement of higher and further education in the Dioceses of Durham and Newcastle, and is presently committed to supporting the North of England Institute for Christian Education, the North East Religious Learning Resources Centre, several lectureships, chaplaincies (in particular the chaplaincy in the College of St Hild and St Bede), scholarships and a Church of England aided school. Member of the Association of Church College Trusts (see separate entry). *Correspondent:* Mr W. Hurworth. *Home:* 16 Tempest Court, Wynard Park, Billingham TS22 5QF, c/o College of St Hild and St Bede, University of Durham, Durham, DH1 1SZ
Tel: 0191 334 8300/01740 644 274
email: w.hurworth@btinternet.com

St John's Guild
Founded in 1919 to assist the spiritual well-being of blind people, as well as to ease the isolation and loneliness in which some of them lived. Since that time both needs and society have changed. St John's Guild has developed to meet those changes. The Guild supports 20 Branches, which are located in different parts of the country and meet to provide worship, fellowship and friendship. An important part of the Guild's work is a residential home for the visually impaired in St Albans. Regular publications in Braille and audio are produced and widely distributed. *Warden and Chairman:* Revd Graeme Hands. *Chief Officer:* Mr Richard McEwan. *Finance Officer:* Mrs Patricia Richards, Guild Office, 8 St Raphael's Court, Avenue Rd, St Albans, AL1 3EH
Tel: 01727 864076
email: stjohnsaccounts@btconnect.com /
r.mcewan1@btinternet.com
Web: www.stjohnsguild.org

St Luke's College Foundation
The Foundation's object is the advancement of further and higher education in religious education and theology. Grants are awarded to individuals for research and taught postgraduate qualifications in these fields; and to eligible organizations for related initiatives and facilities. The Foundation does not finance buildings, or provide bursaries for institutions to administer; and it is precluded from the direct support of schools (although it supports teachers who are taking eligible studies). Member of the Association of Church College Trusts (see separate entry). *Correspondent:* Prof M. Bond, Heathayne, Colyton, EX24 6RS
Tel and Fax: 01297 552281

St Luke's Hospital for the Clergy
A surgical and medical hospital for the clergy, their spouses, widows, and dependent children, monks and nuns, deaconesses, ordinands, Church Army staff, and overseas missionaries. Over 150 leading London consultants give their services free of charge. Treatment is entirely free. The usual referral letter from a patient's doctor should be sent to the Medical Secretary at the Hospital. *President:* The Archbishop of Canterbury. *Chairman:* Mr Patrick Mitford-Slade. *Chief Executive:* Mr John Cherry, 14 Fitzroy Square, London, W1T 6AH
Tel: 020 7388 4954
Fax: 020 7383 4812
email: stluke@stlukeshospital.org.uk
Web: www.stlukeshospital.org.uk

St Mary's College Trust
The Trust's annual income is normally committed to supporting the Welsh National Centre for Religious Education, WNCRE at St Deiniol's Library, Hawarden, Flint, and the Anglican Chaplaincy at the University of Wales, Bangor.

As a result, grants to individuals and other institutions are only awarded in very exceptional circumstances. Member of the Association of Church College Trusts (see separate entry). *Correspondent and Clerk:* Mr Gwilym Jones. *Treasurer:* Revd Charles Wyndham Evans. *Joint Chairmen:* The Bishops of Bangor and St Asaph, School of Education, Univ of Wales, Eifionydd Normal Site, Holyhead Rd, Bangor, LL57 2PZ
Tel: 01248 382934 (Office) 01248 722738 (Home)
Fax: 01248 383092
email: g.t.jones@univ.bangor.ac.uk

St Michael's Fellowship
Runs four residential family assessment centres in South London working in partnership with parents to enable them to meet the needs of their child. Works with adolescent mothers, one- or two-parent families where parents may have learning disabilities, psychiatric illness, a history of abuse, domestic violence and where there are child protection concerns. Runs one supported housing scheme for vulnerable families, with self-contained flats and low support. Through Sure Start and Sure Start Plus offers community support to teenage parents and young fathers in the Borough of Lambeth. *Director:* Mrs Sue Pettigrew, 1F Gleneagle Rd, London, SW16 6AX
Tel: 020 8677 6888
Fax: 020 8677 5214
email: archangel@zetnet.co.uk
Web: www.stmichaelsfellowship.org.uk

St Pancras Housing
Founded 1924 by the Revd Basil Jellicoe, this charitable association provides housing and support for families, single people and those with special needs in nearly 4,500 flats and houses in N London and Hertfordshire. *President:* Sir Peter Barcay. *New Business Manager:* Martin Lippitt, St Richard's House, 110 Eversholt St, London, NW1 1BS
Tel: 020 7209 9287
Fax: 020 7209 9223
Web: www.sph.org.uk

St Peter's Saltley Trust
The Trust's annual income is committed to supporting, developing and evaluating locally based projects in adult theological education, church-further education partnerships and RE provision in schools. The Trust's area of benefit comprises the region covered by the Anglican Dioceses of Birmingham, Coventry, Hereford, Lichfield and Worcester. The Trust does not make grants towards capital projects (e.g., building repairs or ongoing salary costs) or to individuals for research or continuing education purposes. Member of the Association of Church College Trusts (see separate entry). *Director:* Dr Ian Jones. *Secretary and Clerk to the Trustees:* Mrs Pam Wassell. *Bursar:* Mrs Lin Brown, Grays

Court, 3 Nursery Rd, Edgbaston, Birmingham, B15 3JX
Tel: 0121 427 6800
email: director@saltleytrust.entadsl.com
Web: www.saltleytrust.org.uk

Student Christian Movement
SCM is a movement seeking to bring together students of all backgrounds to explore the Christian faith in an open-minded and non-judgemental environment. It seeks to promote a vision of Christianity that is inclusive, aware, radical and challenging. The national SCM network is made up of university links, individual members, friends and subscribers. The movement holds regular conferences and produces a variety of resources, including the journal *movement*. It is affiliated to the World Student Christian Federation. Contact: Co-ordinator. *National Coordinator:* Revd Martin Thompson. *Office Administrator:* Matt Gardner. *Links Worker:* Vacancy, 308F The Big Peg, 120 Vyse St, Hockley, Birmingham, B18 6NF
Tel: 0121 200 3355
email: scm@movement.org.uk
Web: www.movement.org.uk

Tearfund
Tearfund is an evangelical Christian relief and development charity working with the local church around the world to bring physical, emotional and spiritual transformation to people living in poverty. Responding to natural disasters and emegencies, engaging in longer-term community development and speaking out to challenge injustice, Tearfund aims to make the fullness of life promised by Christ a reality for people in need. With support from individuals and churches in the UK and Ireland, Tearfund is in active partnership with local Christians in more than 65 countries. *Chief Executive:* Mr Matthew Frost, 100 Church Rd, Teddington, TW11 8QE
Tel: 0845 355 8355
Fax: 020 8943 3594
email: enquiry@tearfund.org
Web: www.tearfund.org

Third Province Movement
The object of the Third Province Movement, which was started in November 1992, is to advocate, and eventually secure, the establishment within the Church of England of an autonomous province for all those, whatever their churchmanship, who in conscience cannot accept the ordination of women to the priesthood and other liberal developments. It also advocates a realignment on the same principle within the whole Anglican Communion. *Chairman:* Mrs Margaret Brown, Luckhurst, Mayfield, TN20 6TY
Tel: 01435 873007
email: thirdprovince@aol.com
Web: www.thirdprovince.org.uk

Trinitarian Bible Society
Founded in 1831 for the circulation of Protestant

or uncorrupted versions of the Word of God. The Society will only circulate the Authorized Version in English, and foreign language scriptures translated from the same Greek and Hebrew texts with comparable accuracy. *Office Manager:* Mr J. M. Wilson, Tyndale House, Dorset Rd, London, SW19 3NN   *Tel:* 020 8543 7857
Fax: 020 8543 6370
email: tbs@trinitarianbiblesociety.org
Web: www.trinitarianbiblesociety.org

Trinity Foundation for Christianity and Culture
TFCC is an international ecumenical institution committed to fostering community harmony through education. The Foundation's teaching programme, the TFCC Awareness Course, is designed and written by Bishop Michael Marshall and Revd Nadim Nassar to educate Christians for life in the twenty-first century. Each course module is written from a Christian viewpoint, teaching Christians about their own faith and that of their neighbours, so that they can respect the differences and live in a diverse society without fear and without compromising their faith. The Course considers Islamic and Jewish perspectives to build an awareness of 'the other' and to go deeper into the Christian faith. It is designed to be taught in churches, parish halls or any appropriate space, and is suitable for regular or occasional churchgoers, Christians outside the Church, seekers and the undecided. New courses are published each year. *President:* Rt Revd Michael Marshall. *Director:* Revd Nadim Nassar. *Chair of Trustees:* Charles Longbottom. *Chief Executive Officer:* Christopher Bunting. *Education Director:* St. John Wright, Holy Trinity Church, Sloane St, London, SW1X 9BZ
Tel: 020 7730 8830 (Office)
020 7259 0619 (Education)
Fax: 020 7730 9287
email: tfcc@tfccinternational.com
Web: www.tfccinternational.com

True Freedom Trust
An interdenominational support and teaching ministry on homosexuality and related issues, for the Church and people seeking Christian help. It believes that the Bible forbids homosexual acts. It supplies resources, speakers and organizes conferences to help the Church overcome fear and prejudice and act with understanding and love in a biblical and Christlike way. *Chairman:* Mr Stefan Cantore. *Director and Founder:* Mr Martin Hallett, PO Box 13, Prenton, Wirral, CH43 6YB
Tel: 0151 653 0773
Fax: 0151 653 7036
email: info@truefreedomtrust.co.uk
Web: www.truefreedomtrust.co.uk

Unitas – The Catholic League
Founded in 1913, its special objects are the communion of all Christians and the See of Rome, the spread of the catholic faith, the promotion of

fellowship among Catholics and the deepening of the spiritual life. It is governed by a Priest Director and an Executive of elected members. Further details from the Secretary. *Secretary:* Mr Christopher Stephenson, 293 Ordnance Rd, Enfield, EN3 6HB   *Tel:* 01992 763 893
email: nomadyane@btinternet.com
Web: www.unitas.org.uk

Unite Clergy and Faith Workers
Unite Faith Workers is the union for those who work for religious organizations as ministers, clergy and lay staff. Membership is open to all faiths and denominations. Set up in 1994, it is now part of Unite, which has more than 2 million members, following the merger of Amicus with TG&WU. Unite Faith Workers provides its members with a professional association of their own, with access to all the facilities and support of a modern union. Unite is recognized by the Church of England for staff in the National Church Institutions, and by some of the largest church-related charities, including NCH and the Children's Society. A growing number of diocesan office staff and others working for church organizations and agencies are members. Unite Faith Workers has its own Executive, and a national network of local representatives providing support for members, and belongs to the specialist Community and Non-Profit Sector within Unite, in partnership with a number of national agencies, professional associations and charities. It works to bring about fairness and dignity at work for all its members, whatever their situation, and is currently leading the campaign for modern conditions of service for those who serve as ministers. A wide range of benefits is provided for members in good standing, including legal representation and professional advice on many issues affecting work and pensions, equal opportunities, harassment and bullying at work, and much more. *Chair:* Revd Dr Gerry Barlow. *Nat'l Officer, Community & Non-profit Sector:* Rachael Maskell. *Communications:* Maureen German, Community & Non-Profit Sector, 35 King St, London, WC2E 8JG   *Tel:* 020 7420 8978
Fax: 020 7420 8999
email: maureen.german@unitetheunion.com
Web: www.unitetheunion.com

United Church Schools Trust
(Formerly Church Schools Company)
Founded as an educational charity in 1883 to create schools that offer pupils a good academic education based on Christian principles with particular reference to the Church of England. The Company's council has developed the concept of offering a broad and challenging education. To achieve this it has invested in the provision of excellent buildings and facilities including extensive ICT at each school. This ideal of strong schools embraces not just academic learning to high standards, but also the development of

skills that will be essential throughout life both at work and socially. Teamwork, leadership, an enthusiastic response to challenge and an active concern for others are all attributes which are valued. Schools at Blackpool, Guildford, Surbiton, Caterham, Ashford, Hampshire near Romsey, Hull, Lincoln and Sunderland. Clergy bursaries available. A subsidiary charity, the United Learning Trust, was founded in 2002 to manage a number of City Academies spread across the country. Thirteen Acadamies are currently open, mainly in inner city areas, with two more to be added during the academic year 2008–09. *Chairman:* Rt Revd and Rt Hon The Lord Carey of Clifton. *Chief Executive:* Sir Ewan Harper. *Deputy Chief Executive:* Charlotte Rendle-Short, Church Schools House, Titchmarsh, Kettering, NN14 3DA *Tel:* 01832 735105
Fax: 01832 734760
email: admin@church-schools.com
Web: www.ucst.org.uk

United Nations Association of Great Britain and Northern Ireland (UNA-UK)
UNA-UK is the UK's leading independent policy authority on the UN. Through the work of our staff, volunteers and members, we campaign and educate to promote the principles of the UN Charter and to support the work of the UN and its agencies. UNA-UK is a non-party political organization that maintains an ongoing dialogue with UK government ministers, parliamentarians and the media on issues relating to the UN. We promote multilateralism and adherence to international law through four policy programmes: human rights and humanitarian action; peace and security; the Millennium Development Goals and climate change; and UN reform. Education lies at the heart of our work and to this end we provide support and materials for those interested in model UN events, as well as resources for people wanting to develop their knowledge. UNA-UK is proud to be a UK-wide membership organization encompassing individuals of diverse ages, backgrounds and interests. *Executive Director:* Mr Sam Daws. *Executive Assistant:* Miss Natalie Samarasinghe, 3 Whitehall Court, London, SW1A 2EL *Tel:* 020 7766 3457/ 020 7766 3459
Fax: 020 7930 5893
email: samarasinghe@una.org.uk
Web: www.una.org.uk

Universities and Colleges Christian Fellowship
(formerly Inter-Varsity Fellowship of Evangelical Unions)
Is the coordinating body for the interdenominational evangelical student Christian Unions in Britain. Founded in 1928 by 14 university CUs, there are now groups in almost all universities, most other HE institutions and many FE colleges in Britain. The aim is to be a Christian witness in the student world, the work being based on expressing orthodox Christian belief in the contemporary scene. Christian Union staff workers support and encourage groups. The publishing arm is the Inter-Varsity Press. The academic research arms are Tyndale House and the Kirby Laing Institute for Christian Ethics in Cambridge. 38 De Montfort St, Leicester, LE1 7GP
Tel: 0116 255 1700
Fax: 0116 255 5672
email: enquiries@uccf.org.uk
Web: www.uccf.org.uk

Urban Saints
(Formerly Crusaders)
A well-established youth movement working with churches and Christians of all main denominations to show the relevance of Jesus Christ to young people between the ages of 4 and 18. The backbone of this national organization is the regular youth group, which has a mix of Bible teaching through active learning, games, outings, holidays, local and national activities. It aims to help churches with their youth outreach strategies and provides teaching resources, activity materials, an extensive Leadership Training Programme, a Leaders' magazine, short-term service opportunities, over 30 adventure holidays for young people each summer, backed up by a team of area workers and a staff team at Kestin House. There are four residential centres available to schools and youth groups. *Exec Director:* Matt Summerfield. *Operations Director:* Colin Henry. *Supporters Director:* Sharon Eason. *Activities Director:* Phil Hulks. *Volunteers Director:* Mark Arnold, Kestin House, 45 Crescent Rd, Luton, LU2 0AH *Tel:* 01582 589850
Fax: 01582 721702
email: email@urbansaints.org
Web: www.urbansaints.org /
www.crusadersreunited.org.uk

Urban Theology Unit
Ecumenical educational charity founded in 1969 to develop new insights of theology derived from the life of the city, to create a community of clergy and laity concerned to discover relevant forms of ministry and action within urban areas and to help people discover their vocation in relation to gospel calls. Academic programmes include Foundation Degree, Postgraduate Diploma/MA in Theology and new MA (Urban Theology) (York St John), and M Phil/Ph D in Contextual, Urban and Liberation Theology and M Phil/Ph D in Ministry (University of Birmingham). Other courses available in spirituality, vocation, discipleship, multi-faith ministry and urban mission. There are regular UTU publications on British Liberation Theology, urban ministry, and contextual Bible readings. *Chairperson:* Canon Mike West. *Director:* Revd Christine Jones.

Support Services Manager: Mrs Kate Thompson, 210 Abbeyfield Rd, Sheffield, S4 7AZ
Tel: 0114 243 5342
Fax: 0114 243 5356
email: office@utusheffield.org.uk
Web: www.utusheffield.org.uk

USPG: Anglicans in World Mission

Founded in 1702 as the Society for the Propagation of the Gospel in Foreign Parts (SPG), we are one of the oldest Anglican mission agencies. In 1965 we merged with the Universities' Mission to Central Africa and the Cambridge Mission to Delhi to become the United Society for the Propagation of the Gospel (USPG). The name was further changed to USPG: Anglicans in World Mission in 2007. We work in direct partnership with Anglican churches in over 50 countries. In Africa, Asia, the Middle East and Latin America we are enabling Anglican churches to reach out to poor and marginalised communities in practical and life-changing ways. This means that we are helping local churches to run schools and hospitals, build houses and wells, and provide agricultural training for substistence farmers. We also support church outreach, theological training and youth work programmes. We do not dictate what priorities our partner churches should follow, but encourage shared decision-making among equal partners. Where grants are provided, they are given on a long-term basis so that churches have a secure financial base from which to plan for the future. We run a range of mission personnel programmes, recruiting priests, teachers and medical workers and other staff in Britain and Ireland as requested by our overseas partners. We also send personnel between churches around the world. We are also able to provide volunteers, clergy and church workers from Britain and Ireland with experience of the world church by sending them on short-term placements overseas. Churches and individuals in Britain and Ireland can get involved with USPG and world mission through prayer, fundraising (including a large Project Scheme) and speakers. We produce a range of publications – our quarterly newspaper *Transmission* and *Prayer Diary* and a range of free resources for study and worship at Advent, Lent and Harvest. *President:* The Archbishop of Canterbury. *Chair:* Revd Alan Moses. *General Secretary:* Rt Revd Michael Doe, 200 Great Dover St, London, SE1 4YB
Tel: 020 7378 5678
Fax: 020 7378 5650
email: enquiries@uspg.org.uk
Web: www.uspg.org.uk

Vacation Term for Biblical Study

The Vacation Term for Biblical Study is a Summer School held each summer at St Anne's College, Oxford, primarily devoted to the study of the Bible and related subjects. The aim is to enable people of all ages, occupations and denominations to become acquainted with contemporary scholarship. Further details are available from the Secretary. *Chairman:* Dr Barbara Spensley. *Secretary:* Revd Margaret Burrow. *Treasurer:* Mr Richard Garner, 1 Thorny Rd, Douglas, Isle of Man, IM2 5EF
Tel: 01624 662173
email: margaret.burrow@mcb.net
Web: www.vtbs.org.uk

Vergers, Church of England Guild of

Founded in 1932 to promote Christian fellowship and spiritual guidance among the vergers of the cathedrals and parish churches of England. The Guild is divided into branches which meet locally every month and nationally several times throughout the year. The Guild provides a comprehensive training course which students can study from home with the help of an area tutor. The course works alongside the well-established Annual Training Conference. The Guild Diploma is awarded to successful students. Advice concerning appointments, job descriptions and contracts is available through the welfare officer. Contact can be made through the General Secretary. *General Secretary:* Miss Jeanne B. Scott, 309 Desborough Ave, High Wycombe, HP11 2TH
Tel: 01494 438335
email: jeanne@jeannescott.wanadoo.co.uk
Web: www.societies.anglican.org/guild-of-vergers

Walsingham, Shrine of Our Lady of

Founded in 1061 in response to a vision, destroyed in 1538, restored in 1922 by Revd A. Hope Patten, Vicar of Walsingham. Since 1931, when it was moved from the parish church, the Shrine has contained the image of Our Lady of Walsingham together with the Holy House, representing the house of the Annunciation and the home in Nazareth of the Holy Family. Nowadays Walsingham is England's premier place of pilgrimage. It is administered by a College of Guardians. Special facilities include accommodation for people of all ages and those with special needs, an Education Department for school visits, and retreat and conference facilities. Information is available from the Administrator. *Administrator:* Revd P. North. *Shrine Priest:* Revd P. Barnes, The College, Walsingham, NR22 6EF
Tel: 01328 820255
Fax: 01328 824206
email: pr.adm@olw-shrine.org.uk
Web: www.walsingham.org.uk

WATCH (Women and the Church)

Founded in 1996, WATCH promotes the ministry of women in the Church of England. It is based on a vision of the Church as a community of God's people where justice and equality prevail, regardless of gender. WATCH works for an inclusive church in which women will take their place alongside men at every level in the Church of England, including the episcopate. Other priorities shaping our work are to achieve honesty and openness in church appointments and better support for women in ministry, and to challenge barriers which impede the full expression of a woman's vocation and gifts. The ministry of both lay and ordained women is fostered through local diocesan WATCH branches, and members receive the magazine *Outlook*. *Chair:* Ms Christina Rees. *Secretary:* Ms Jenny Standage, St John's Church, Waterloo Rd, London, SE1 8TY

> *Tel:* 01763 848822/020 8319 3372/
> *Fax:* 01763 848774
> *email:* info@womenandthechurch.org
> *Web:* www.womenandthechurch.org

William Temple Foundation

Founded in 1947, as a research and training centre focusing on the links between theology, the economy and urban mission practice. The Foundation's current programme is to reflect theologically and strategically on the changing nature of urban space in Manchester, and the emerging patterns of church that are being created both to connect with these new spaces, and with new understandings and definitions of local civil society. The Foundation is now also engaged in primary research into the work and identity of faith-based organizations in civil society, across the UK using the concept of religious and spiritual capital. This work is currently funded by the Leverhulme Trust (2007–2010). The Foundation is working with a wide variety of partners in this research, including the Northwest Development Agency, the Manchester Centre for Public Theology and the University of Manchester. It is also working with a wide variety of community and grassroots organizations. Emerging from this research, the Foundation is contributing teaching to the University of Manchester and the Partnership of Theological Education based in Manchester. It produces several publications on its research and regularly updates its work on its web site. Luther King House, Brighton Grove, Rusholme, Manchester, M14 5JP

> *Tel:* 0161 249 2502
> *Fax:* 0161 256 1142
> *email:* temple@wtf.org.uk
> *Web:* www.wtf.org.uk

William Temple House

William Temple House is a residence for 49/50 students from overseas and the United Kingdom in full-time education. The male and female students are of all faiths and nationalities. The House is under the management of The International Students' Club (C of E) Ltd, a registered charity. Enquiries to the Warden. International Students Club (C of E) Ltd, William Temple House, 29 Trebovir Rd, London, SW5 9NQ

> *Tel:* 020 7373 6962/07958 726715 (Mobile)
> *Fax:* 020 7341 0003
> *email:* williamtemplehouse@btconnect.com
> *Web:* www.williamtemplehouse.co.uk

Women's World Day of Prayer

Founded in America in 1887 (Britain 1930–34) to unite Christian women in prayer by means of services held on the first Friday in March each year, by fostering local interdenominational prayer groups meeting throughout the year and to give financial support to Christian educational projects and Christian literature societies. *President:* Mrs Emma Wilcock. *Chairperson:* Mrs Mimi Barton. *Administrator:* Mrs Mary Judd, WWDP, Commercial Rd, Tunbridge Wells, TN1 2RR

> *Tel:* 01892 541411
> *Fax:* 01892 541745
> *email:* office@wwdp-natcomm.org
> *Web:* www.wwdp-natcomm.org

Womenaid International

A humanitarian aid and development agency run by volunteers in the UK, which provides relief and assistance to women and children suffering distress caused by war, disasters or poverty. It seeks to empower women through education, training, provision of credit, and also campaigns against violations of women's human rights. An implementing partner of the European Community Humanitarian Office (ECHO), the British Government and several UN agencies, it has provided over 30,000 tonnes of food, medical supplies and clothing to more than 1.5 million refugees in the former Yugoslavia, the Caucasus and Central Asia. Development assistance globally has ranged from building and repairing schools, supporting rescue centres for street children, repairing hospitals and providing medical equipment/supplies to micro-credit support and water/sanitation projects. *Founder:* Ms Pida Ripley, 3 Whitehall Court, London, SW1A 2EL

> *Tel:* 020 7839 1790
> *Fax:* 020 7839 2929
> *email:* admin@womenaid.org
> *Web:* www.womenaid.org

Woodard Schools

Founded by Canon Nathaniel Woodard in 1848 to promote education in the doctrines and principles of the Church of England. Woodard now runs some 23 schools and a further 16 schools are affiliated. *President:* Rt Revd Dr Anthony Russell (Bishop of Ely). *Registrar:* Mr Peter Beesley. *Finance Officer:* Mr Michael Corcoran. *Senior Provost:* Canon Brendan Clover, High St, Abbots Bromley, Rugeley, WS15 3BW

> *Tel:* 01283 840120
> *Fax:* 01283 840893
> *email:* jillshorthose@woodard.co.uk
> *Web:* www.woodard.co.uk

World Congress of Faiths

Founded in 1936 to promote mutual understanding and a spirit of fellowship between people of different religious traditions. WCF works to explain and reconcile religious conflict and the tensions between the different communities.

Conferences and lectures are arranged. The journal *Interreligious Insight* is published four times a year, jointly with the Interreligious Engagement Project and Common Ground, and has its own web site. A newsletter, *One Family*, is also published at least four times a year. *President:* Revd Marcus Braybrooke. *Chairman:* Rabbi Jacqueline Tabick. *Hon Treasurer:* Pejman Khojasteh. *Editor:* Revd Dr Alan Race. *Secretary:* Revd Feargus O'Connor, London Interfaith Centre, 125 Salusbury Rd, London, NW6 6RG

Tel: 01935 864055/020 8959 3129
Fax: 020 7604 3052
email: admin@worldfaiths.org
Web: www.worldfaiths.org

World Vision
Formed in London in 1979, World Vision UK is part of the international World Vision partnership and is a major UK relief and development agency. World Vision is at work in over 100 countries in Africa, Asia, Eastern Europe, Latin America and the Middle East. It is involved in partnering churches and other non-governmental organizations in projects which range from relief work in Africa to income generation projects in Bangladesh. *Chief Exec Officer:* Charles Badenoch. *Church Relations Manager:* Alistair Metcalfe, World Vision House, Opal Drive, Fox Milne, Milton Keynes, MK15 0ZR

Tel: 01908 841000
Fax: 01908 841001
email: church@worldvision.org.uk
Web: www.worldvision.org.uk/church

YMCA
Founded 1844 to promote the physical, intellectual and spiritual well-being of young people. *President:* The Archbishop of York. *National Secretary:* Angela Sarkis, National Council of YMCAs, 640 Forest Rd, London, E17 3DZ

Tel: 020 8520 5599
Fax: 020 8509 3190
email: national.secretary@england.ymca.org.uk
Web: www.ymca.org.uk

York Glaziers' Trust
Established 1967 by the Dean and Chapter of York and the Pilgrim Trust (1) to conserve and restore the stained glass of York Minster; (2) to conserve, restore and advise on all stained glass or glazing of historic or artistic importance, in any building whether religious or secular, public or private; (3) to establish and maintain within the City of York a stained glass workshop dedicated to the training and employment of conservators and craftsmen specializing in the preservation of glass of historic and artistic importance; and (4) to encourage public interest in the preservation of stained glass, to collaborate with educational institutions and to assist with scientific and art historical research into stained and painted glass. Advice should always be sought when considering treatment of glass of artistic or historic value. The Trust welcomes enquiries from all sources. It offers a full advisory service and will compile comprehensive condition reports. *Director:* Mr Peter M. Johnston. *Senior Conservator:* Nick Teed, 6 Deangate, York, YO1 7JB

Tel: 01904 557228
Fax: 01904 557229
email: info@yorkglaziers.org.uk
Web: www.yorkminster.org/A-Zofarticles

YWCA England & Wales
YWCA England & Wales is a force for change for women facing discrimination and inequalities of all kinds. Our principal aims are to enable young women who are experiencing particular disadvantage to identify and realize their full potential, to influence public policy in order to achieve equality and social justice for young women, and to provide opportunities for participation in a worldwide women's movement. *Presidents:* Sara Armstrong, Alison Crookes. *Chief Exec:* Ms Gill Tishler, Clarendon House, 52 Cornmarket House, Oxford, OX1 3EJ

Tel: 01865 304200
Fax: 01865 204805
email: info@ywca-gb.org.uk
Web: www.ywca-gb.org.uk

Diocesan Associations

Association of the Dioceses of Singapore and West Malaysia
Revd Ann Bucknall
20 St Margaret's Rd
Lichfield
Staffs. WS13 7RA
Tel: 01543 257382
email: bucknall20ann
@talktalk.net

Belize Church Association
Mrs Barbara Harris
Honeysuckle Cottage
19 Whittall St
Kings Sutton
Banbury
Oxon. OX17 3RD
Tel: 01295 811310
email:
b-k-harris.caye@
virgin.net

Central Tanganyika Diocesan Association
Miss S. M. Horsman
15 Woodstock Ave
Harold Park
Romford, Essex
RM3 9NF
Tel: 01708 345691
(evening)
020 7207 2156
(daytime)
email:
shorsman@
globalconnections.
co.uk

Church of Ceylon Association
Canon Bob Campbell-
Smith
Even Keel
Pillory Hill
Noss Mayo
Devon PL8 1ED
Tel: 01752 872559
email: bobandlorna@
tiscali.co.uk

Congo Church Association
Mrs Rosemary Peirce
8 Burwell Meadow
Witney
Oxford OX28 5JQ
Tel: 01993 200103
email: rosemary.peirce@
ntlworld.com

Egypt Diocesan Association
Mrs Elspeth Mackinlay
The Horseshoes
The Green
Gressenhall
Dereham
Norfolk
NR20 4DT
Tel: 01362 860302
email:
elspeth.mackinlay@
tesco.net

Fellowship of the Maple Leaf
(*Provides grants to further mutual learning between the Church in Canada and the UK*)
Canon John Williams
2 Fox Spring Rise
Edinburgh
EH10 6NE
Tel 0131 445 2983
Web:
www.mapleleaf.org.uk

Friends of the Church in India
Mrs Margaret Smith
15 Gorselands
Sedlescombe
Battle
E. Sussex
TN33 0PT
Tel: 01424 870431
email: msmith15@
tiscali.co.uk

Friends of the Diocese of Cyprus and the Gulf
Mrs Mary Banfield
Garden Corner
Old London Rd
Mickleham
Surrey RH5 6DL
Tel: 01372 373912
Fax: 01372 362770
email: mgbbmw@
aol.com

Friends of the Diocese of Iran
Mr John Clark
32 Weigall Rd
Lee
London SE12 8HE
email: john@mclark32.
freeserve.co.uk

Friends of the Diocese of Uruguay
N. J. Roberts
2 Upland Rise
Walton
Chesterfield
S40 2DD
Tel: 01246 233590
Mobile: 07896 162461
email: nick.roberts@
bcs.org
Web: www.friends-of-
the-diocese-of-
uruguay.org.uk

Guyana Diocesan Association
Mr J. R. Chee-a-tow
13E Courtleet Drive
Erith
Kent DA8 3NB
Tel: 01322 442897

Jerusalem and the Middle East Church Association
Mrs Mary Knight
1 Hart House
The Hart
Farnham
Surrey GU9 7HJ
Tel: 01252 726994
Fax: 01252 735558
email: secretary@
jmeca.eclipse.co.uk
Web:
    www.jmeca.org.uk

Kenya Church Association
Hon Secretary: Revd
Bryan Wadland
55 Copthall Rd East
Ickenham
UB10 8SE
Tel: 01895 613904
email:
    wadland@lizbryan.
        freeserve.co.uk

Lesotho Diocesan Association
Sister Jean Mary CHN
Cottage 5
Lambeth Palace
London SE1 7JU
Tel: 020 7928 5407
email: chnjmary@
    yahoo.co.uk

Mozambique and Angola Anglican Association
General Secretary:
Ian Gordon
16 Bayle Court
The Bayle
Folkestone
Kent CT20 1SN
Tel: 01303 257248
email: n_grdn@
    yahoo.co.uk

Nigeria Fellowship
Chair: Dr Anne
Phillips
33 Cliffe Road
Sheffield S6 5DR
Tel: 0114 233 8529
email: annephillips2@
    hotmail.co.uk

Province of the Indian Ocean Support Association
Hon. Secretary: Revd
Oliver Simon
The Vicarage,
St John's Ave
Rugby
Warks CV22 5HR
Tel: 01788 577331
email: oliver.simon@
rugbyteam.org.uk
Chair: Canon Hall
    Speers
The Rectory
38 Manor Rd
Barnet EN5 2JJ
Tel: 020 8449 3894
email: hall.speers@
    talk21.com
Hon. Treasurer: Revd
Hilary C. Jones
St Martin's Rectory
Horn St
Folkestone CT20 3JJ
Tel: 01303 238509
email:
    revhilaryjones@
        btinternet.com

Sierra Leone Inter-Diocesan Association
Mrs Comfort Forster
89 Grove Vale
East Dulwich
London SE22 8EN
Tel: 020 8693 3154
email: comfi@
    tiscali.co.uk

St Helena Association
Revd Patricia Ann
    Turner
The Rectory
Broughton
Skipton, North Yorks.
BD23 3AN
Tel: 01282 842332
email: ann.turner@
bradford.anglican.org

Sudan Church Association
Mrs Sara Taffinder
69 Poynders Rd
Clapham
London SW4 8PL
Tel and *Fax:*
020 8671 1974

Transvaal, Zimbabwe and Botswana Association	Mrs Liz Martin 120 Church Lane East Aldershot Hampshire GU11 3SS *Tel* and *Fax:* 01252 320108 *email:* elizmmartin@ yahoo.co.uk	**Zululand Swaziland Association**	The Zululand Swaziland Association has ceased to exist as an independent charity. The Zululand Swaziland Trusteeship has now passed to the trustees of USPG, and donations to its ongoing work can be received by cheques made payable to 'USPG', earmarked 'Zululand Swaziland Trust'. USPG: Anglicans in World Mission 200 Great Dover St London SE1 4YB
Uganda Church Association	Revd Dr Michael Hunter The Vicarage 51 Vicarage Lane Dore Sheffield S17 3GY *Tel:* 0114 236 3480 *email:* mutagwok@aol.com		
Windward Islands Diocesan Association	Mrs Mary Anderson 115 Broadfield Rd Catford London SE6 1TJ *Tel:* 020 8461 1775		

ORGANIZATIONS

Libraries

Canterbury

Cathedral Library
Cathedral House
The Precincts
Canterbury
Kent CT1 2EH

Cathedral Librarian Mr Keith M. C. O'Sullivan

Cathedral Archivist
Mrs Cressida Williams

The archives and library at Canterbury are separate departments. Information about the archives is available on the archives pages of the Cathedral web site at www.canterbury-cathedral.org/history/archives.aspx or by telephoning 01227 865330. Information about the library can be found at www.canterbury-cathedral.org/history/libraries.aspx or by telephoning 01277 865287.

Tel: 01227 865330 (Archives)
01227 865287 (Library)
Fax: 01227 865222
email: library@canterbury-cathedral.org

Library collections: 52,000 printed volumes, 15th century to present, with large collections of manuscripts and archives. The Howley-Harrison Collection (16,000 books and pamphlets) includes anti-slavery and Oxford Movement material. Also cathedral printed music, and scores of Canterbury Catch Club. Mendham Collection of Catholic and anti-Catholic writings. Two parish libraries: Elham and Preston-next-Wingham, in a Dr Bray cabinet. The collections include substantial holdings on national and local history, including the English Civil War, travel, botany, English and foreign literature.

Crowther Library

Crowther Centre for Mission
 Education
Church Mission Society
Watlington Rd
Oxford
OX4 6BZ

Librarian Miss Margaret
Acton

Tel: 01865 787552
Fax: 01865 776375
email: margaret.acton@
 cms-uk.org
Web: www.cms-uk.org/
 heritage/default.htm
Open: 0900–1700 hours
Mon–Fri
Closed public holidays.

Books can be lent by post.

30,000 volumes, 250 current
periodicals. Successor to the
Partnership House Mission
Studies Library that
incorporated the post-1945
collections of the former
Church Missionary Society and
United Society for the
Propagation of the Gospel
Stock focuses on the work of
the Church worldwide,
missiology, history of mission,
church history, African and
Asian Christianity and
interfaith relations. Also houses
CMS's pre-1945 collection
entitled the Max Warren
Collection. Reference only.

Durham

Durham Cathedral Library
The College
Durham
DH1 3EH

Librarian Dr E. D. Hunt
Assistant Librarian Miss Joan
Williams

Tel: 0191 386 2489
email: Library@
 durhamcathedral.co.uk

Open: 0900–1300; 1400–1700
hours Mon–Fri; closed for
first two full weeks in July.

Chapter Library of 40,000
printed books including 70
incunabula, 375 manuscripts
7th–16th centuries. Archival
collections include Hunter,
Sharp, Raine, Surtees, Ian
Ramsey, J. B. Lightfoot, H. H.
Henson, early music. Published
catalogues of medieval
manuscripts (1825, 1964, etc.),
printed music (1968) and
manuscript music (1986). An
online guide to the archival
collections is available at
http://flambard.dur.ac.uk/
dynaweb/cld/.Small modern
collection specializing in
history of the north-east,
church history, cathedrals
and art. Meissen Library
of theology in German of
approx. 20,000 books donated
by EKD inaugurated 1998.
Catalogue at its website
www.meissenlibrarydurham.
co.uk. Archdeacon Sharp
Library of modern theology
of approx. 10,000 books in
English. All Archdeacon Sharp
Library books and many
Chapter Library books are
included in Durham University
Library's online catalogue at
http://library.dur.ac.uk
(location 'Cathedral').

Exeter

Exeter Cathedral Library
 and Archives
Old Bishop's Palace
Diocesan House
Palace Gate
Exeter
EX1 1HX

Cathedral Librarian Peter
Thomas
Assistant Librarian Michael
Howarth
Cathedral Archivist Angela
Doughty

Tel: 01392 272894 (Library)
 01392 495954 (Archives)

20,000 items (Library); 50,000
(Archives), Manuscripts
include Exeter Book and Exon
Domesday; special collections
include cathedral manuscripts
and archives, early printed
books in medicine and science,
Cook Collection (16th–19th c.,

email: library@exeter-cathedral.org.uk
archive@exeter-cathedral.org.uk
Web: http://www.exeter-cathedral.org.uk/Admin/Library/html

Open: 1400–1700 hours Mon–Fri (Library) Mon–Wed (Archives, by appointment only). Closed on public holidays.

early linguistics), printed tracts (mainly Civil War period), Harington Collection (16th–19th c., theology, ecclesiastical history, history). Pre-2001 accessions included in online catalogue of Exeter University Library at www.ex.ac.uk/library/. Medical and scientific collections also catalogued in *Medicine and science at Exeter Cathedral Library,* compiled by Peter W. Thomas (University of Exeter Press, 2003). See also *The library and archives of Exeter Cathedral,* by L. J. Lloyd and Audrey M. Erskine, 3rd edn (Exeter 2004).

Hereford

Hereford Cathedral Library and Archives
Hereford Cathedral
Hereford
Herefordshire
HR1 2NG

Canon Chancellor and Librarian Canon Christopher Pullin
Archivist Mrs Rosalind Caird
Library and Archives Assistant Miss Kirsty Clarke
Librarian Nick Baker

Tel: 01432 374225/6
email: library@herefordcathedral.org
Web: www.herefordcathedral.org

Open: Tues and Thurs 1000–1600 hours; first Saturday of each month 1000–1300 hours. Other times by prior appointment. Closed in January for essential conservation and maintenance work.

The Library cares for the Mappa Mundi (*c.* 1300), Chained Library and All Saints' Chained Library. The collection includes 229 medieval manuscripts from the 8th to the early 16th centuries, over 3,000 pre-1801 printed books including 56 incunabula, 10,000 books published post-1800 (many borrowable) and manuscript and printed music (18th to 20th centuries). There are also 30,000 archives of the Dean and Chapter, dating from the 9th to 20th centuries. Photographic service available.

Lambeth

Lambeth Palace Library
London
SE1 7JU

Librarian and Archivist Dr Richard Palmer

Tel: 020 7898 1400
Fax: 020 7928 7932
Web: www.lambethpalacelibrary.org

Open: 1000–1700 hours Mon–Fri
Closed public holidays and ten days at Christmas and Easter.

Main library for the history of the Church of England, open for public use since 1610. 200,000 printed books, 4,700 manuscripts 9th–20th centuries. Registers and correspondence of Archbishops of Canterbury 12th–20th centuries. Records of Province of Canterbury, the Faculty Office, Lambeth Conferences, Bishops of London, and papers of churchmen, statesmen and organizations within the Church of England. Manuscripts and printed books earlier than 1850 from Sion College Library.

Pusey House

Pusey House
Oxford
OX1 3LZ

Custodian Revd William Davage
Archivist Revd Dr Barry A. Orford

80,000 volumes. A theological library specializing in patristics, Church history and liturgy. An extensive archive of

ORGANIZATIONS

Tel: 01865 278415
email: chapter@
puseyhouse.org.uk
Web:
www.puseyhouse.org.uk

Open: 0930–1230, 1400–1630
Mon–Fri; 0930–1230 Sat (by
appointment only) during
full term (weeks 0–8)
During vacation the library is
open Monday to Friday by
appointment only. The
library is closed during
August and at the beginning
of September until after the
St Giles' Fair.

Contact the Custodian for
vacation opening times

Oxford Movement and related
material.

St Deiniol's

St Deiniol's Residential
Library
Church Lane
Hawarden
Flintshire
CH5 3DF

Warden Revd Peter Francis

Tel: 01244 532350
Fax: 01244 520643
email: enquiries@
st-deiniols.com
Web:
    www.st-deiniols.org

250,000 plus volumes,
including 50,000 pamphlets.
Theology, biblical studies,
spirituality, liturgy,
19th-century ecclesiastical
and secular history, Bishop
Moorman Franciscan Library,
and all areas of the arts/
humanities. Residential
accommodation for 47 people.
Subsidized rates for clergy
and students, and bursaries
available. Financial assistance
for sabbaticals. Scholarship
grants for research and
writing for higher degrees or
publication, meeting most of the
cost of the stay at St Deiniol's.

St Paul's

The Library
St Paul's Cathedral
London
EC4M 8AE

Librarian Mr Jo Wisdom

Tel: 020 7246 8345
Fax: 020 7248 3104
email: library@
stpaulscathedral.org.uk

Re-established after the Great
Fire of 1666, the library is
strong in theology,
ecclesiastical history, and
sermons, especially of 17th and
18th centuries. Special
collections include early
printed Bibles; St Paul's Cross
sermons; 19th-century tracts.
The archive of Dean and
Chapter is deposited at
Guildhall Library,
Aldermanbury, London EC2P
2EJ.

Sarum College

Sarum College Library
19 The Close
Salisbury
Wilts.
SP1 2EE

Librarian Jennifer Monds

Tel: 01722 424803
Fax: 01722 338508
email: library@sarum.ac.uk
web: www.sarum.ac.uk

Open: 0900–1700 Mon–Fri
and some evenings during
term time

Founded 1860. 36,000 volumes
mostly on academic theology,
church history, ethics and
Christian spirituality. Rare
book collection including 274
bound volumes of mainly
20th-century tracts, sermons,
charges and letters. About 700
volumes are added each year.

Fees: £30 per annum for reading rights; £40 per annum for reading and borrowing rights; £5 per day or £10 per week for visitors

Fifty journals are taken, with back numbers available for reference use. Loan and mail order services offered. Internet, word processing facilities and Wi-Fi access available. Archive of the Christian Socialist Movement. Catalogue accessible from the library homepage at the above web address. Accommodation available. Researchers and sabbaticals welcome. Quiet space. Coffee, tea and lunches may be purchased.

Sion College

The library has closed. The older books (–1850) were transferred to Lambeth Palace Library.

The bulk of the balance of the collection is in the library of King's College, London.

Biblical studies, philosophy, Anglican theology, church history, biography and liturgy. Special collections include Sion College Port Royal Library, Industrial Christian Fellowship Library, and extensive pamphlet collections.

United Society for the Propagation of the Gospel

Bodleian Library of Commonwealth and African Studies at Rhodes House
South Parks Rd
Oxford
OX1 3RG

Archivist Miss Lucy McCann

Tel: 01865 270908
Fax: 01865 270912
email: rhodes.house.library@bodley.ox.ac.uk
Bodleian reader's ticket required – details at www.ouls.ox.ac.uk/services/admissions.

The Society's library to 1944 and archival material circa 1701–1965. Extensive collections from the 19th century, back holdings of missionary journals.

Westminster Abbey

Westminster Abbey Muniment Room and Library
London
SW1P 3PA

Librarian Dr Tony Trowles

Keeper of the Muniments Dr Richard Mortimer

Tel: 020 7654 4830
Fax: 020 7654 4827
email: library@westminster-abbey.org
Web: www.westminster-abbey.org

Open: 1000–1300, 1400–1645 hours Mon–Fri; appointments required

20,000 volumes (16th–21st centuries), in excess of 70,000 archives (monastic history 8th–16th centuries, Abbey records to present day).

York Minster

York Minster Library
Dean's Park
York
YO1 7JQ

Librarian
Mrs Deirdre Mortimer

Archivist
Peter Young

Tel: 01904 625308 (Library)
01904 611118 (Archives & MSS)
Fax: 01904 611119
email: d.mortimer@yorkminsterlibrary.org.uk
archives@yorkminster.org

130,000 volumes. Theology; church history, art, architecture and stained glass; extensive collections of pre-1801 books; manuscripts; incunables; special collections of Yorkshire history, Yorkshire topographical prints, and Yorkshire Civil War tracts; music and photographic collections; archives of Dean and Chapter from medieval times.

ORGANIZATIONS

Web: (Library catalogue)
telnet://library.york.ac.uk
(Library guide)
www.york.ac.uk/services/
library/guides/minster/
htm

Open: 0900–1700 hours
Mon–Thur; 0900–1200 Fri
Closed on public holidays

See also main Organizations section

Patronage Trusts

Church Pastoral Aid Society Patronage Trust	*Secretary* Canon John Alderman CPAS, Athena Drive Tachbrook Park Warwick CV34 6NG *Tel:* 01926 458457 *Fax:* 01926 458459 *email:* jalderman@cpas.org.uk	A Trust holding Rights of Presentation to a number of benefices. Administered by the Church Pastoral Aid Society.
Church Patronage Trust	*Secretary* Canon Roger Salisbury 12 De Walden St London W1G 8RN *Tel:* 020 7935 9811 *Fax:* 020 7436 3019 *email:* roger.salisbury@allsouls.org	A Trust holding the Rights of Presentation to a number of benefices. Evangelical tradition.
Church Society Trust	*Secretary* Revd D. Phillips Dean Wace House 16 Rosslyn Rd Watford, Herts. WD18 0NY *Tel:* 01923 235111 *Fax:* 01923 800362 *email:* admin@churchsociety.org	Patron of more than 100 livings.
Church Trust Fund Trust	*Secretary* Canon John Alderman CPAS, Athena Drive Tachbrook Park Warwick CV34 6NG *Tel:* 01926 458457 *Fax:* 01926 458459 *email:* jalderman@cpas.org.uk	A Trust holding Rights of Presentation to a number of benefices. Administered by the Church Pastoral Aid Society.
Guild of All Souls	*General Secretary* David G. Llewelyn Morgan Guild of All Souls St Katharine Cree Church 86 Leadenhall St London EC3A 3DH *Tel:* 020 7621 0098 *Fax:* 01371 831430 *Web:* www.guildofallsouls.org.uk	Patron of 41 livings of Catholic tradition.

Hulme Trustees	*Secretary* Mr Jonathan Shelmerdine, Butcher and Barlow Solicitors 31 Middlewich Rd Sandbach Cheshire CW11 1HW *Tel:* 01270 762521	A Trust holding the Rights of Presentation to a number of benefices.
Hyndman's (Miss) Trustees	*Administrative Secretary* Mrs Ann Brown 6 Angerford Ave Sheffield S8 9BG *Tel* and *Fax:* 0114 255 8522 *email:* ann.brown@hyndmans. org.uk *Web:* www.hyndmans.org.uk	Patronage Trust. Varied churchmanship.
Intercontinental Church Society	*Communications Manager* Mr David Healey 1 Athena Drive Tachbrook Park Warwick CV34 6NL *Tel:* 01926 430347 *Fax:* 01926 888092 *email:* enquiries@ics-uk.org	Manages the recruitment of clergy (especially as Patron) for many English-speaking churches abroad; evangelical.
Martyrs Memorial and Church of England Trust	*Secretary* Canon John Alderman CPAS, Athena Drive Tachbrook Park Warwick CV34 6NG *Tel:* 01926 458457 *Fax:* 01926 458459 *email:* jalderman@ cpas.org.uk	A Trust holding Rights of Presentation to a number of benefices. Administered by the Church Pastoral Aid Society.
Peache Trustees	*Secretary* Revd Kenneth Habershon Truckers Ghyll Horsham Rd, Handcross W Sussex RH17 6DT *Tel:* 01444 400274 *email:* kandmhab@btopenworld.com	A Trust holding the Rights of Presentation to a number of benefices. Evangelical tradition.
Simeon's Trustees	*Administrative Secretary* Mrs Ann Brown 6 Angerford Ave Sheffield S8 9BG *Tel:* 0114 255 8522 *email:* ann.brown@ simeons.org.uk *Web:* www.simeons.org.uk	Holds and administers the patronage of those livings in the Church of England which belong to the Trust on the principles laid down in Charles Simeon's Charge.
Society for the Maintenance of the Faith	*Secretary* Revd Paul Conrad Christ Church Vicarage 10 Cannon Place London NW3 1EJ *Tel* and *Fax:* 020 7435 6784	Administers patronage and promotes Catholic teaching and practice.

Anglican and Porvoo Communions

PART 5

PART 5   CONTENTS

THE ANGLICAN COMMUNION

The Most Revd and Rt Hon Rowan Douglas Williams, President, Archbishop of Canterbury Lambeth Palace, London SE1 7JU, UK

Office: 0207 898 1200

There are over 77 million members of the Anglican household of 38 self-governing Churches made up of about 500 dioceses, 30,000 parishes and 64,000 individual congregations in a total of 164 countries. While the Anglican Communion does not rank among the biggest groupings of Christians it is, after the Roman Catholic Church, arguably the most widespread. The Archbishop of Canterbury is the spiritual leader of Anglicans worldwide.

The Anglican Communion has developed in two stages. During the first stage, which began in the seventeenth century, Anglicanism was established by colonization in countries such as Australia, Canada, New Zealand, Southern Africa and the USA. In the early days of expansion a somewhat remote control was exercised by the Bishops of London. After the American War of Independence Samuel Seabury of Connecticut, USA, was consecrated in Scotland as the first bishop of the Anglican Communion outside the British Isles. Soon this precedent was followed by the Church in Canada and then India, Australia, New Zealand and South Africa.

The second stage began just over a century ago. During that era Anglican churches were planted all over the world as a result of the missionary work of the Churches in England, Ireland, Scotland, and Wales which were joined in this task by the Churches formed in the previous two centuries. Most of these Churches became constitutionally independent in the period following the Second World War, usually before attainment of political independence. In regions that are large, diverse, and in which the population of Anglicans is perceived as too small to support a province, a useful halfway house has been found in the development of regional councils such as the Council of the Churches of East Asia.

Anglican Churches uphold and proclaim the Catholic and Apostolic faith, based on Scripture and creeds, interpreted in the light of Christian tradition, scholarship and reason. Following the teachings of Jesus Christ, the Churches are committed to the proclamation of the good news of the gospel to the whole creation.

By baptism, in the name of the Father, Son and Holy Spirit, a person is made one with Christ and received into the Church.

Central to worship for Anglicans is the celebration of the Holy Eucharist (also called the Holy Communion, the Lord's Supper, or the Mass). In this offering of prayer and praise are recalled the life, death and resurrection of Christ, through the proclamation of the word and celebration of the sacrament.

Worship is at the very heart of Anglicanism. Its styles vary from the simple to the elaborate, from Evangelical to Catholic, from charismatic to traditional or indeed from a combination of these various traditions. *The Book of Common Prayer*, in its various revisions throughout the Communion, gives expression to the comprehensiveness found within the Church whose principles reflect, since the time of Elizabeth I, a *via media* in relation to other Christian traditions.

Other rites include Confirmation, Holy Orders, Reconciliation, Marriage and Anointing of the Sick.

Almost everywhere Anglican Churches are self-supporting. Only a small percentage of income is transferred from richer to less affluent Churches. Many of the member Churches of the Anglican Communion are to be found in the so-called developing or 'Third' world. It is estimated that 3,000 persons are added to membership each day through birth, baptism or conversion. The fastest-growing areas are in the global south.

For over 200 years there has been a process of decentralization which has led to flexibility and a capacity for indigenization and involvement in local ecumenical negotiations and projects. This leaves open the possibility of loss of identity. But to compensate for this the Anglican Communion has developed a number of institutions which have ensured cohesion and communication. The oldest and most important of these is the Lambeth Conference. The 1968 Lambeth Conference agreed to the formation of the Anglican Consultative Council which brings together clergy and lay as well as episcopal representatives once every two or three years. More recently there have been regular meetings of Primates – senior bishops and archbishops from each member Church.

The Churches of the Anglican Communion are linked by affection and common loyalty. They are in full communion with the See of Canterbury, and thus the Archbishop of Canterbury, in his person, is a unique focus of Anglican unity. He calls the once-a-decade Lambeth Conference, is Chairman of the meeting of Primates and is President of the Anglican Consultative Council.

The Secretary General of the Anglican Communion, aided by a permanent Secretariat staff, assists in servicing the Lambeth Conference and meetings of the Primates.

During recent years, in addition to local ecumenical negotiations and projects, the Anglican Communion has been engaged in international dialogues with a number of major Churches including the Roman Catholic Church, the Lutheran World Federation, the Orthodox Churches, and the World Alliance of Reformed Churches. Through the Faith and Order Commission of the World Council of Churches it has also been engaged in a multilateral dialogue process which has resulted in the publication of the Faith and Order Document *Baptism, Eucharist and Ministry*. Outstanding features within the Anglican Communion in the past 25 years are the constitution of many new autonomous provinces in Africa, Asia and Latin America and the emergence of the Anglican Consultative Council. These are both parts of a bigger process of transition and maturing whereby relationships within the Communion have progressed in becoming a family of varied but essentially equal members within the Body of Christ. The family is interdependent. There is still need for the small, the poor, the weak to receive help from the stronger and richer, because the responsibilities of the Communion and the mission of the whole family are one and interdependent in the Body of Christ.

OUR CHURCHES

The present list of member Churches or provinces, and of councils, is:

The Anglican Church in Aotearoa, New Zealand and Polynesia
The Anglican Church of Australia
The Church of Bangladesh
The Episcopal Anglican Church of Brazil
The Church of the Province of Burundi
The Anglican Church of Canada
The Church of the Province of Central Africa
The Anglican Church of the Central American Region
The Church of the Province of Congo
The Church of England
The Holy Catholic Church in Hong Kong – Hong Kong Sheng Kung Hui
The Church of the Province of the Indian Ocean
The Church of Ireland
The Anglican Communion in Japan (Nippon Sei Ko Kai)
The Episcopal Church in Jerusalem and the Middle East
The Anglican Church of Kenya
The Anglican Church in Korea

The Church of the Province of Melanesia
The Anglican Church of Mexico
The Church of the Province of Myanmar (Burma)
The Church of Nigeria
The Church of North India
The Church of Pakistan
The Anglican Church of Papua New Guinea
The Episcopal Church in the Philippines
The Church of the Province of Rwanda
The Scottish Episcopal Church
The Province of the Anglican Church in South East Asia
The Anglican Church of Southern Africa
The Anglican Church of the Southern Cone of America
The Church of South India
The Church of the Province of the Sudan
The Anglican Church of Tanzania
The Church of the Province of Uganda
The Episcopal Church (United States of America) – includes overseas dioceses in Taiwan, Haiti, Colombia, Honduras, Dominican Republic and Ecuador
The Church in Wales
The Church of the Province of West Africa
The Church in the Province of the West Indies

Extra-Provincial Dioceses and other Churches
The Anglican Church of Bermuda
The Church of Ceylon (Sri Lanka)
The Episcopal Church of Cuba
The Lusitanian Church (Portuguese Episcopal Church)
The Spanish Episcopal Reformed Church
The Anglican Church in Venezuela
The Episcopal Church of Puerto Rico
Falkland Islands

Churches in communion
The Mar Thoma Syrian Church of Malabar
The Old Catholic Churches of the Union of Utrecht
The Philippine Independent Church
The Church in China is a 'post denominational' Church whose formation included Anglicans in the Holy Catholic Church in China.
Anglicans/Episcopalians, in certain parts of the Communion, are in full communion with some Lutheran Churches.

The Lambeth Conference

It could be said that the Lambeth Conference has its origin in 1865 when, on 20 September, the Provincial Synod of the Church of Canada unanimously agreed to urge the Archbishop of Canterbury and the Convocation of his province to find a means by which the bishops consecrated within the Church of England and serving overseas could be brought together for a General Council to discuss issues facing them in North America, and elsewhere. Part of the background for this request was a serious dispute about the interpretation and authority of the Scriptures which had arisen in Southern Africa between Robert Gray, Archbishop of Cape Town, and Bishop Colenso, Bishop of Natal. Notwithstanding the opposition of a significant number of the bishops in England, Archbishop Longley invited Anglican bishops to their first Conference together at Lambeth Palace on 24 September 1867 and the three following days.

Seventy-six bishops finally accepted the invitation and the Conference was called to order and met in the Chapel of Lambeth Palace. A request to use Westminster Abbey for a service was not granted.

Of the 76 bishops attending the first Lambeth Conference the distribution was the following:

England	18 bishops
Ireland	5 bishops
Scotland	6 bishops
Colonial and Missionary	28 bishops
United States	19 bishops

It was made clear at the outset that the Conference would have no authority of itself as it was not competent to make declarations or lay down definitions on points of doctrine. But the Conference was useful in that it explored many aspects of possible inter-Anglican cooperation and by providing common counsel it inaugurated a practical way in which the unity of the faith of the Church could be maintained. The Conference did not take any effective action regarding the issues raised by Bishop Colenso but its far-reaching impact can be seen in the fact that it was the precursor of the Lambeth Conference that we know today.

In 1878 the second Lambeth Conference was convened by Archbishop Tait and 100 bishops attended. The heavy agenda included 'Modern forms of infidelity'. It marked another milestone in the growth of the relationship of diverse parts of the Anglican Communion and reinforced the value of the meeting of Anglican bishops to share their common experience.

One hundred and forty-five bishops attended the Lambeth Conference of 1888 called by Archbishop Benson. Meeting at Lambeth Palace in the Library, its agenda addressed such contemporary issues as intemperance, purity, divorce, care of immigrants, and socialism. More important for the ongoing life of the Church itself, the agenda concerned itself with the issues of ecumenism. In 1886 the House of Bishops of the Episcopal Church in the United States of America, meeting in Chicago, had devised a formula which provided a basic framework of recognition of 'authentic' Christian tradition. This formula, known as the Chicago Quadrilateral, was a statement, from the Anglican standpoint, of the essentials for a reunited Christian Church. The four main elements were as follows:

1. The Holy Scriptures of the Old and New Testaments, as 'containing all things necessary to Salvation', and as being the rule and ultimate standard of faith.
2. The Apostles' Creed, as the baptismal symbol; and the Nicene Creed, as the sufficient statement of the Christian faith.

3. The two sacraments ordained by Christ himself – Baptism and the Supper of Our Lord ministered with unfailing use of Christ's words of institution, and of the elements ordained by him.
4. The Historic Episcopate.

The 1888 Conference, taking this statement, promulgated the first of several successive versions of what has become known as the Lambeth Quadrilateral. It is this Lambeth Quadrilateral that has been one of the major contributions of the Anglican Communion to the evolving search for unity between the Churches which is at the heart of the ecumenical movement.

The 1897 Lambeth Conference was attended by 194 bishops and presided over by Archbishop Frederick Temple. There were two main matters of interest: first, the Conference warmly commended the concept of deaconesses; and, second, it asked for the establishment of a consultative committee which was to be the direct ancestor of the Anglican Consultative Council.

The Conference of 1908 with Archbishop Davidson in the chair was attended by 242 bishops and concerned itself with the issues of the Ministry of Healing, the possible revision of the Prayer Book, and the supply and training of the clergy.

The Lambeth Conference should have convened again in 1918 but this was postponed due to the outbreak of the Great War. Much had changed in the way in which many people understood the world around them when the next Conference met in 1920. This Conference, attended by 252 bishops, was dominated by the subject of Church Unity. The celebrated 'Appeal to All Christian People' which was promulgated at the 1920 Conference invited other Churches to accept episcopacy as the indispensable precondition for their unity with Anglicans. Developing from the consideration of the 1897 Conference there was also greater sympathy for a more prominent role for women in the governing and in the ministry of the Church. The 1920 Conference addressed itself to the issue of contraception and rejected its use outright.

The 1930 Conference was presided over by Archbishop Cosmo Lang, 307 bishops in attendance. It proved to be a very crowded occasion in the Lambeth Palace Library. The momentum towards Church Unity in South India found support, encouraging Anglicans in the Indian subcontinent to enter seriously into discussions related to a United Church in India.

Archbishop Geoffrey Fisher presided over two Conferences – 1948 attended by 349 bishops and 1958 attended by 310 bishops. By 1948 the Church of South India was an accomplished fact. In 1958 the proposal for a United Church of North India was welcomed. Nuclear disarmament was an issue in 1958 with the majority being in favour of disarmament, and the report on the family was a milestone with its sensitive treatment of the subject of contraception within marriage. The 1958 Conference approved the appointment of the first Anglican Executive Officer, thus assisting in the evolution both of the role of the Archbishop of Canterbury and of inter-Anglican structures. This was also the first Conference in which wives of the bishops were taken into account in the planning and organization.

The Conference of 1968, under Archbishop Ramsey, was attended by 462 bishops. With this Conference it was no longer possible to meet at Lambeth Palace and the Conference was thus convened in the Church Assembly Hall at Church House, Westminster. Preparatory papers were offered to members of the Conference written by expert consultants and some 35 committees prepared the work for the final report. The issue of the ordination of women came forward and a proposed constitution for the establishment of the Anglican Consultative Council was agreed to. With the 1968 Conference the Lambeth Conferences became the modern phenomenon that we know them to be today with more extensive preparation, more committee work, and more concern for communication both between the Churches and with the general public.

Another change of venue was to find the 1978 Conference meeting residentially in the University of Kent at Canterbury under Archbishop Coggan. Living and worshipping together gave a new community dynamic to the Conference. Again, preparatory work was a key element in the deliberations of the Conference and an important factor in this was the development of the work and role of the Anglican Consultative Council whose full Standing Committee was present for the Conference. Among the important and controversial issues on the agenda of the 1978 Conference were the ordination of women to the priesthood, the training of bishops, human rights, and the evolving inter-Anglican bodies.

In 1988, the Conference was again held at the University of Kent at Canterbury, under the chairmanship of Archbishop Runcie. The Conference began on Sunday 17 July with a great opening service at Canterbury Cathedral and concluded on Sunday 7 August with a great closing service, again in Canterbury Cathedral. The Conference resolved to set up several inter-Anglican bodies: a Commission on the Ordination of Women to the Episcopate and on the implications of such ordinations for relations between the Churches of the Anglican Communion; an Advisory Body on Prayer Book Revision; an Interfaith Committee which would offer guidelines towards establishing a common approach to people of other faiths on a Communion-wide basis; a Commission on Anglican–Oriental Orthodox relations; conversations with the World Methodist Council and the Baptist World Alliance with a view to the beginning of international dialogues with these two

traditions. The report of the Lambeth Conference 1988, *The Truth Shall Make You Free*, is published by Church House Publishing, price £8.50.

The Lambeth Conference 1998 was held in Canterbury, convened by Archbishop George Carey. Nearly 800 bishops attended. Mrs Carey led a spouses programme for over 650 women and men and there were 70 communications persons, 20 monks and nuns and a host of diocesan volunteers. This was the largest Lambeth Conference yet, as all suffragan, assistant, and auxiliary bishops were included.

Much of the energy of the Conference was centred on questions relating to the developing world Church and especially international debt. The Conference spent much time on interfaith matters as well as hearing from Cardinal Edward Cassidy from the Vatican at an Ecumenical Vespers Service.

Women who are bishops were present for the first time.

The loose attempts at discussion relating to homosexuality showed clearly that the Communion is not of one mind on this issue. A vast number of resolutions on a vast number of topics surfaced and were accepted by the Conference. These included Modern Technology and Ethics, the significance of Jerusalem for the world faiths, and the allowing of differing views on the ordination of women to the priesthood and episcopate.

The Archbishop of Canterbury, as *primus inter pares*, is president of the ACC, chairman of the Primates Meeting, and host of the Lambeth Conference. He makes pastoral visits to the provinces of the Anglican Episcopal Communion by invitation from the province concerned.

The Lambeth Conference hosted by Archbishop Williams in Canterbury in July 2008 was attended by 650 bishops. Reports and reflections can be found on the Lambeth Conference website.

Web: www.lambethconference.org

OTHER MEANS OF CONSULTATION

A second field of communication has been the Pan-Anglican Congresses. These have been held in London in 1908, in Minneapolis, USA, in 1954 and in Toronto, Canada, in 1963. Normally held at a time midway between Lambeth Conferences, the Congress, though like the Conference in having no executive authority, is distinguished from it by the presence of clerical and lay representatives from all the dioceses in the Communion.

Apart from the value of persons meeting one another, these Congresses have played a lesser role than the Lambeth Conferences and have had less influence. A significant contribution, though, to Anglican self-understanding came from the 1963 Congress. This was the concept of Mutual Responsibility and Interdependence in the Body of Christ. Unfortunately it became popularly identified solely with finance and projects, whereas it describes admirably the proper relationships within a worldwide family of autonomous Churches.

The third step in forwarding the process of inter-Anglican consultation and common action was taken in 1958, when the Lambeth Conference of that year recommended 'that a full-time Secretary of the Advisory Council on Missionary Strategy should be appointed by the Archbishop of Canterbury with the approval of the Advisory Council' and then went on to say, 'This Officer would collect and disseminate information, keep open lines of communication and make contact when necessary with responsible authority.' This official became known as the **Anglican Executive Officer**. The appointment was first held by Bishop Stephen Bayne of the United States who established the practice of travelling widely and personally meeting the Church in many parts of the world. Bishop Ralph Dean of Canada succeeded him and also acted as Episcopal Secretary to the 1968 Lambeth Conference. In 1969 he was succeeded by Bishop John Howe. The last ACC meeting was held in 2005 in Nottingham, England. The Standing Committee of the ACC and the Primates normally meet annually in the UK.

The 1968 Lambeth Conference called for the setting up of an **Anglican Consultative Council** (*see below*). The Council would come into being if two-thirds of the provinces of the Anglican Communion gave their consent. By the end of 1969 all had expressed their approval, and so the Council, asked for by the whole Anglican Communion, came into being. Canon Samuel Van Culin of the USA served as Secretary General

until retiring in 1994. Canon Peterson finished his term in 2004. The Revd Canon Kenneth Kearon from the Irish School of Ecumenics began his term in 2005.

The Lambeth Conference of 1978 requested that **Primates'** meetings should be set up to enable regular consultation between the Primates of the Anglican Communion. The first meeting took place in Ely, England, in November/December 1979. The second meeting took place in Washington DC, USA, in April/May 1981, the third was in Limuru, Kenya, in October 1983, the fourth in Toronto, Canada, in March 1986, the fifth in Larnaca, Cyprus, in April/May 1989, the sixth in Ireland in April 1991, the seventh with the ACC in Cape Town, and the eighth in Windsor, England, in 1995. The 1997 meeting was held in Jerusalem. The Primates met briefly following the Lambeth Conference 1998 in Canterbury, then again in Oporto, Portugal, in March 2000. There were meetings at the Kanuga Conference centre, North Carolina, USA, in March 2001, and at Canterbury in 2002, in Brazil in 2003, and the most recent meetings were in 2005 in Ireland and 2007 in Tanzania.

Additional work carried out by the staff of the Anglican Communion has produced significant documents and meetings, including the Windsor Commission and the subsequent Windsor Report and the Panel of Reference under the leadership of Archbishop Peter Carnley of Australia. The desk for the Listening Process as set out by Lambeth 1998 in Resolution 1.10 on sexuality began work in 2005.

The next ACC meeting is set for 2009.

The Anglican Communion Office

Secretary General Canon Kenneth Kearon
Ecumenical, Communion Affairs and Theological Studies Canon Gregory Cameron
Communications Canon James Rosenthal
Mission and Evangelism The Revd John Kafwanka
Finance and Administration Mr Andrew Franklin
Theological Education Mrs Clare Amos

Anglican Communion Office St Andrew's House, 16 Tavistock Crescent, Westbourne Park, London W11 7 1AP   *Tel:* 020 7313 3900
                                             Fax: 020 7313 3999
          email: aco@anglicancommunion.org
          Web: www.anglicancommunion.org
Warden of the Guest House Mrs Ann Quirke
          email: ann.quirke@anglicancommunion.org

The Anglican Consultative Council

MEMBERSHIP

The Archbishop of Canterbury is President and the Council chooses its own Chairman and Secretary-General, which appointment replaces the former one of Anglican Executive Officer.

Each province or member Church chooses up to three members. There are also six co-opted members, two of whom shall be women and two under 28 years of age. The resulting membership, made up of bishops, clergy and lay people,

is notable for its spread of nationalities and races.

FUNCTIONS

The Council meets every two or three years and its Standing Committee in the intervening years. Council meetings are held in different parts of the world. True to the Anglican Communion's style of working, the Council has no legislative powers. It fills a liaison role, consulting and recommending, and at times representing the Anglican Communion.

The functions of the Council are as follows:

1. To share information about developments in one or more provinces with the other parts of the Communion and to serve as needed as an instrument of common action.
2. To advise on inter-Anglican, provincial and diocesan relationships, including the division of provinces, the formation of new provinces and of regional councils and the problems of extra-provincial dioceses.
3. To develop as far as possible agreed Anglican policies in the world mission of the Church and to encourage national and regional Churches to engage together in developing and implementing such policies by sharing their resources of manpower, money and experience to the best advantage of all.
4. To keep before national and regional Churches the importance of the fullest possible Anglican collaboration with other Christian Churches.
5. To encourage and guide Anglican participation in the Ecumenical Movement and the ecumenical organizations; to cooperate with the World Council of Churches and the world confessional bodies on behalf of the Anglican Communion; and to make arrangements for the conduct of Pan-Anglican conversations with the Roman Catholic Church, the Orthodox Churches and other Churches.
6. To advise on matters arising out of national or regional Church union negotiations or conversations and on subsequent relations with united Churches.
7. To advise on problems of inter-Anglican communication and to help in the dissemination of Anglican and ecumenical information.
8. To keep in review the needs that may arise for further study and, where necessary, to promote enquiry and research.

RECORD OF MEETINGS
FIRST MEETING, LIMURU, KENYA 1971

SECOND MEETING, DUBLIN, IRELAND 1973
THIRD MEETING, TRINIDAD 1976

FOURTH MEETING LONDON, ONTARIO, CANADA 1979

FIFTH MEETING, NEWCASTLE UPON TYNE, ENGLAND 1981

SIXTH MEETING OF THE COUNCIL, BADAGRY, NIGERIA 1984

SEVENTH MEETING OF THE COUNCIL, SINGAPORE 1987

EIGHTH MEETING OF THE COUNCIL, WALES 1990

FIRST JOINT MEETING OF THE COUNCIL AND THE PRIMATES, CAPE TOWN, SOUTH AFRICA 1993

TENTH MEETING OF THE COUNCIL, PANAMA 1996

ELEVENTH MEETING OF THE COUNCIL, DUNDEE, SCOTLAND 1999

TWELFTH MEETING OF THE COUNCIL, HONG KONG 2002

THIRTEENTH MEETING OF THE COUNCIL, NOTTINGHAM, UK 2005

NEXT MEETING: KINGSTON, JAMAICA 2009

The twelfth meeting produced *For The Life of the World*; the thirteenth produced *Living Communion*, edited by Jim Rosenthal and Susan Erdey. Both were published by Morehouse Publishing.

PUBLICATIONS
The Anglican Cycle of Prayer
Anglican News and Notes
The Compass Rose Society Communiqué
The Virginia Report
The Windsor Report
Reflections from the Lambeth Conference 2008
Becoming a Global Communion: Photo Journal of Lord Carey's Ministry
Mary, Grace and Hope in Christ (ARCIC)
Church of the Triune God (Orthodox)
The Official Report of the Lambeth Conference 1998
Anglican–Lutheran Relations Report of the Anglican–Lutheran Joint Working Group (1983)
Niagara Report (1988)
Belonging Together
Clarifications on Eucharist and Ministry
The Diaconate as Ecumenical Opportunity
Sharing in the Apostolic Communion
Agros Report
Women in the Anglican Episcopate
ARCIC Agreed Statements:
Salvation and the Church (1987)
Church as Communion (1991)
Life in Christ: Morals, Communion and the Church (1994)
Gift of Authority (1999)

The Anglican Centre in Rome

The Metropolitans of the Anglican Communion endorsed the establishment of the Anglican Centre in Rome in April 1966. This followed consultations among representatives of the several Churches of the Anglican Communion on action for the furtherance of Christian Unity and the prospects for renewed fellowship and cooperation between Anglicans and Roman Catholics held out by the Second Vatican Council and by the historic visit of the Archbishop of Canterbury to Rome in March 1966. The Anglican Centre celebrated the fortieth anniversary of its foundation in 2006.

The purposes of the Centre are:

1. To provide a meeting place for clergy and seriously interested laity of the Anglican Communion, and those of other Christian denominations, particularly Roman Catholic, to come together for discussion, worship and prayer for the achievement of Christian Unity.
2. To provide a focal point for Anglican collaboration with the various agencies of the Roman Catholic Church and in particular its Council for the Promotion of Christian Unity. This collaboration was seen at its best during 2005 at the funeral of Pope John Paul II and the inauguration of Pope Benedict XVI.
3. To provide a library of Anglican history, theology and liturgy for the use of students, theologians and churchmen of all Christian denominations.
4. To give all possible help to Anglican scholars who wish to work in Rome and to aid them in meeting and working with those resident in Rome.
5. To sponsor various activities including lectures, seminars and discussion groups to elucidate Anglicanism and its relation to the thinking and practice of Roman Catholic and other theologians.
6. To provide information about the Churches of the Anglican Communion and the objectives, programmes and activities of the Anglican Centre.
7. To provide a base where the appointees of the several Anglican Churches may pursue coordinated discussions on appropriate lines of action for promoting unity, with the Roman Catholic Church and others.
8. To welcome visitors from all the churches of the Anglican Communion and to provide support for all English-speaking visitors to Rome.

The Centre publishes a magazine *CENTRO*, and organizes seminars, including the ROMESS Summer School, open to clergy and laity with a genuine interest in ecumenism. The Centre's library is open from 9 a.m. to 5 p.m. Monday to Friday, except August and public holidays.

The activities of the Centre are governed by a governing body, and a director.

Director and Archbishop of Canterbury's Representative to the Holy See Very Revd David Richardson, The Anglican Centre in Rome, Palazzo Doria Pamphilj, Piazza del Collegio Romano 2, 00186 Rome, Italy   Tel: 39 06 678 0302
Fax: 39 06 678 0674
email: (office) anglican.centre.rome@flashnet.it
(director) director.acr@flashnet.it
Web: www.anglicancentreinrome.org

Assistant to the Director Revd Sara McVane

Visiting Academic Fellow Revd Dr Bill Franklin

FRIENDS OF THE ANGLICAN CENTRE IN ROME
Founded in 1984 to enlist support both through prayer and financial assistance for the work of the Centre.

President The Archbishop of Canterbury

Chairman Rt Revd Edward Holland

Chairman, English Friends Rt Revd Edward Holland, 37 Parfrey St, London W6 9EW

Secretary Miss Virginia Johnstone, 127 Cranmer Court, Whiteheads Grove, London SW3 3HE
Tel: 020 7589 0697

ANGLICAN AND PORVOO COMMUNIONS

CHURCHES AND PROVINCES OF THE ANGLICAN COMMUNION

AUTONOMOUS CHURCHES AND PROVINCES IN COMMUNION WITH THE SEE OF CANTERBURY

Note: In the following directory section most provinces correspond to a specific country. In the postal addresses given, the name of the country is included only if some dioceses in the province are outside the country indicated by the name of the province.

Anglican Church in Aotearoa, New Zealand and Polynesia

Members 220,659

Formerly known as the Church of the Province of New Zealand, the Church covers 106,000 square miles and includes the countries of New Zealand, Fiji, Tonga, Samoa and the Cook Islands. It was established as an autonomous Church in 1857. A revised constitution adopted in 1992 reflects a commitment to bicultural development that allows freedom and responsibility to implement worship and mission in accordance with the culture and social conditions of the Maori (Tikanga Maori), European (Tikanga Pakeha) and Polynesian (Tikanga Pasefika) membership. The Church has a strong and effective Anglican Missions Board.

Primate/Archbishops Most Revd Brown Turei (*Tikanga Maori*), PO Box 568, Gisborne, New Zealand   *Tel:* 64 867 8856
Fax: 64 867 8859
email: browntmihi@xtra.co.nz

Most Revd Jabez Leslie Bryce (*Tikanga Pasefika*), PO Box 35, Suva, Fiji Islands   *Tel:* 679 330 4716
email: episcopus@connect.com.fj
Fax: 679 330 2687
Most Revd David Moxon (*Tikanga Pakeha*), PO Box 21, Hamilton 3240   *Tel:* 64 7 838 2309
Fax: 647 836 9975
email: bishop@hn-anglican.org.nz

General Secretary and *Treasurer* Mrs Jackie Pearse, PO Box 87188, Meadowbank, Auckland 1742, New Zealand   *Tel:* 64 9 521 4439
Fax: 64 9 521 4490
email: gensec@ang.org.nz/gensecpa@ang.org.nz
Web: www.anglican.org.nz

THEOLOGICAL COLLEGES
College of the Southern Cross, Private Bag 28-907, Remuera, Auckland 1541, New Zealand (serves both Anglicans and Methodists) (*Dean* Revd J. White).   *Tel:* 64 9 521 2725
Fax: 64 9 521 2420
email: stjohnscollege@auckland.ac.nz

Te Rau Kahikatea, Private Bag 28-907, Remuera, Auckland 1541, New Zealand (*Te Ahorangi/Dean* Dr J. Plane-Te Paa)

College of the Diocese of Polynesia, Private Bag 28-907, Remuera, Auckland 1136, New Zealand (*Principal* Rt Revd Dr W. Halapua)

Theology House, 30 Church Lane, Merivale, Christchurch 8001, New Zealand

Selwyn College, 560 Castle St, Dunedin, New Zealand (*Warden* Dr D. Clark)

The two last named cater for pre-ordination or post-graduate studies.

AOTEAROA

Bishop in Tai Tokerau Rt Revd Te Kitohi Wiremu Pikaahu, PO Box 25, Paihia 0247, Bay of Islands, New Zealand   *Tel:* 64 9 402 6788
Fax: 64 9 402 6663
email: tkwp@xtra.co.nz

Bishop in Te Manawa o te Wheke Rt Revd Ngarahu Katene, PO Box 146, Rotorua 3040
Tel and *Fax:* 64 7 348 4043
email: ngarahukatene@ihug.co.nz

Bishop in Tai Rawhiti Most Revd William Brown Turei, PO Box 568, Gisborne 4040, New Zealand
Tel: 64 6 867 8856
Fax: 64 6 867 8859
email: browntmihi@xtra.co.nz

Bishop in Te Upoko O Te Ika Rt Revd Muru Walters, 14 Amesbury Drive, Churton Park, Wellington 6037, New Zealand   *Tel:* 64 4 478 3549
Fax: 64 4 472 8863
email: muruwalters@xtra.co.nz

Bishop in Te Waipounamu Rt Revd John Robert Kuru Gray, PO Box 10086, Philipstown, Christchurch 8145, New Zealand
Tel: 64 3 389 1683
Fax: 64 3 389 0912
email: hawaipounamu@xtra.co.nz

AUCKLAND
Bishop Rt Revd John Campbell Paterson, PO Box 37–242, Parnell, Auckland, 151, New Zealand
Tel: 64 9 302 7202
Fax: 64 9 303 3321
Web: www.auckanglican.org.nz

CHRISTCHURCH
Bishop Rt Revd Victoria Matthews, PO Box 4438, Christchurch 8140, New Zealand
Tel: 64 3 379 5950
Fax: 64 3 379 5954
email: bishop@chch.ang.org.nz
Web: www.chch.anglican.org.nz

DUNEDIN
Bishop Rt Revd George Howard Douglas Connor, PO Box 13170, Green Island, Dunedin 9052, New Zealand
Tel: 64 3 488 0820
Fax: 64 3 488 2038
email: bishop@dn.anglican.org.nz
Web: www.dn.anglican.org.nz

NELSON
Bishop Rt Revd Richard Ellena, PO Box 100, Nelson 7140, New Zealand
Tel: 64 3 548 3124
Fax: 64 3 548 2125
email: bprichard@nelsonanglican.org.nz
Web: www.nelson.anglican.org.nz

POLYNESIA
Bishop Most Revd Jabez Leslie Bryce, Bishop's House, Box 35, Suva, Fiji
Tel: 679 330 4716
Fax: 679 330 2687
email: episcopus@connect.com.fj
Web: www.anglican.org.nz/diop.htm

Bishop for the Diocese of Polynesia in Aotearoa New Zealand Rt Revd Dr Winston Halapua, St John's College, Private Bag 28–907, Remuera, Auckland
Tel: 64 9 521 2725
Fax: 64 9 521 2420
email: loisa@stjohns.auckland.ac.nz

Bishop in Vanua Levu and Taveuni Rt Revd Apimeleki Nadoki Qiliho, Diocese of Polynesia, PO Box 29, Labasa, Fiji
Tel and *Fax:* 679 881 1420
email: minoff@connect.com.fj

Bishop in Viti Levu West Rt Revd Gabriel Mahesh Prasad Sharma, PO Box 117, Lautoka, Fiji
Tel and *Fax:* 679 666 0124
email: gabsharma@yahoo.com

WAIAPU
Bishop Rt Revd David Rice, PO Box 227, Napier 4140, New Zealand
Tel: 64 6 835 8230
Fax: 64 6 835 0680
email: bishop@waiapu.com
Web: www.waiapu.anglican.org.nz

WAIKATO
Bishop Most Revd David John Moxon, PO Box 21, Hamilton 3240, New Zealand
Tel: 64 7 857 0020
Fax: 64 7 836 9975
email: bishop@hn-ang.org.nz
Web: www.waikato.anglican.org.nz

Bishop in Taranaki Rt Revd Philip Richardson, PO Box 547, Taranaki Mail Centre, New Plymouth 4340, New Zealand
Tel: 64 6 759 1178
Fax: 64 6 759 1180
email: philip.richardson@xtra.co.nz

WELLINGTON
Bishop Rt Revd Dr Thomas John Brown, PO Box 12–046, Wellington 6144, New Zealand
Tel: 64 4 472 1057
Fax: 64 4 449 1360
email: bishoptom@paradise.net.nz
Web: www.wn.ang.org.nz

Anglican Church of Australia

Members 3,881,162 (2001)
The Church came to Australia in 1788 with the 'First Fleet', which was made up primarily of convicts and military personnel. Free settlers soon followed. A General Synod held in 1872 formed the Australian Board of Missions. The Church became fully autonomous in 1962 and in 1978 published its first prayer book. A second Anglican prayer book was published in 1995. Women were first ordained to the Diaconate in 1985 and to the Priesthood in 1992. There are 23 dioceses of which 19 ordain women as priests and chaplains. The Anglican Church of Australia is part of the Christian Conference of Asia and of the Council of the Church of East Asia. Links with Churches of New Guinea, Melanesia, and Polynesia are strong especially through the Anglican Board of Mission – Australia.

Primate of the Anglican Church of Australia Most Revd Dr Phillip John Aspinall (*Archbishop of Brisbane*)

General Secretary of the General Synod Revd Canon Bruce McAteer

Hon Treasurer Mr John McKenzie

General Synod Office Suite 2, Level 9, 51 Druitt Street, Sydney, NSW 2000   *Tel:* 61 2 8267 2700
Fax: 61 2 8267 2727
email: gsoffice@anglican.org.au
Web: www.anglican.org.au

THE ANGLICAN THEOLOGICAL COLLEGES
Moore Theological College, 1 King St, Newtown, NSW 2042 (*Principal* Revd John Woodhouse)
Fax: 61 2 9577 9988
email: info@moore.usyd.edu.au
Web: www.moore.edu.au

Nungalinya College, PO Box 40371, Casuarina, NT 0811 (*Principal* Ms Dawn Cardona)
Fax: 61 8 8927 2332
email: info@nungalinya.edu.au
Web: www.nungalinya.edu.au

Ridley College, 160 The Avenue, Parkville, VIC 3052 (*Principal* Revd Dr Peter Adam)
Fax: 61 3 9387 5099
email: registrar@ridley.unimelb.edu.au
Web: www.ridley.unimelb.edu.au

St Barnabas Theological College, 34 Lipsett Terrace, Brooklyn Park, SA 5032 (*Principal* The Ven. Dr Peter Stuart)   *Fax:* 61 8 8416 8450
email: st.barnabas@flinders.edu.au
Web: http://ehlt.flinders.edu.au/theology/information

St Francis Theological College, 233 Milton Rd, PO Box 1261, Milton QLD 4064 (*Principal* The Revd Dr Don Saines)   *Fax:* 61 7 3369 4691
email: enquiries@stfran.qld.edu.au
Web: www.stfran.qld.edu.au

St Mark's National Theological Centre, 15 Blackall St, Barton, ACT 2600 (*Director* Rt Revd Dr Tom Frame)   *Fax:* 61 2 6273 4067
email: stmarks@csu.edu.au
Web: www.stmarksntc.org.au

Trinity College Theological School, Royal Parade, Parkville, VIC 3052 (*Director* Revd Dr Andrew McGowan)   *Fax:* 61 3 9348 7460
email: tcts@trinity.unimelb.edu.au
Web: www.trinity.unimelb.edu.au/theolog

The John Wollaston Theological College, Wollaston Rd, Mt Claremont, WA 6010 (*Dean and Warden* Revd Dr Nigel Leaves)
Fax: 61 8 9286 0260
email: info@wollastoncollege.com.au
Web: www.wollastoncollege.com.au

CHURCH PAPERS
The Adelaide Church Guardian Monthly newspaper containing wide news coverage from the diocese, province and nationally. *Editorial Offices* 26 King William Road, North Adelaide, SA 5006.
email: mstenberg@adelaide.anglican.com.au

The Melbourne Anglican Large monthly diocesan newspaper contains extensive news, comment locally and from around the world; with colour pictures. *Director/Editor* The Anglican Centre, 209 Flinders Lane, Melbourne, VIC 3000.
email: editor@melbourne.anglican.com.au

Anglican Encounter Monthly newspaper of Newcastle Diocese, containing diocesan and Australian news. *Editorial Offices* PO Box 817, Newcastle, NSW 2302.
email: editor@angdon.com

Tasmanian Anglican Monthly small newspaper format, from Tasmania Diocese, containing wide comment. *Editorial Offices* PO Box 748, Hobart, TAS 7001.   *email:* editor@anglicantas.org.au

Southern Cross Large monthly newspaper of Sydney Diocese, containing diocesan, national, world news and comment, Archbishop's letter in both English and Chinese translation. Extensive use of colour. *Editorial Offices* PO Box 118, Northbridge, NSW 1560.
email: newspaper@anglicanmedia.com.au
Web: www.sydneyanglicans.net

Anglican Messenger Monthly newspaper of the Anglican Province of Western Australia, includes news from Perth, North West Australia and Bunbury. *Editorial Offices* GPO Box W2067, Perth, WA 6846.   *email:* messenger@perth.anglican.org
Web: www.anglicanmessenger.com.au

Market Place A monthly independent Anglican newspaper, includes national and international Anglican news and comment. *Editorial Offices* PO Box 335, Orange, NSW 2800.
email: market@ix.net.au

Focus Monthly newspaper based in Brisbane, containing diocesan and national news. *Editorial Offices* GPO Box 421, Brisbane, QLD 4001.
email: focus@anglicanbrisbane.org.au

All diocesan newspapers contain a letter from the Archbishop or Bishop of the Diocese. The Dioceses of Armidale, Ballarat, Bathurst, Bendigo, Canberra and Goulburn, Gippsland, Grafton, Murray, Northern Territory, Riverina, Rockhampton, Wangaratta, and Willochra also produce magazines/Bishop's newsletters, with mainly diocesan and parochial news.

PROVINCE OF NEW SOUTH WALES
Metropolitan Most Revd Dr Peter Jensen (*Archbishop of Sydney*)

ARMIDALE
Bishop Rt Revd Dr Peter Robert Brain, PO Box 198, Armidale, NSW 2350   *Tel:* 61 2 6772 4491
Fax: 61 2 6772 9261
email: diocarm@northnet.com.au
Web: www.armidaleanglicandiocese.com

BATHURST

Bishop Rt Revd Richard Hurford, PO Box 23, Bathurst, NSW 2795   *Tel:* 61 2 6331 1722
Fax: 61 2 6332 2772
email: bishop.hurford@bathurstanglican.org
Web: www.bathurstanglican.org.au

Assistant Bishop Rt Revd Peter Thomas Danaher, PO Box 619, Dubbo, NSW 2830   *Tel:* 02 6885 2670
Fax: 02 6881 6740
email: peterdanaher@bigpond.com

CANBERRA AND GOULBURN

Bishop Vacancy, GPO Box 1981, Canberra, ACT
Tel: 61 2 6248 0811
Fax: 61 2 6247 6829
Web: www.canberragoulburn.anglican.org

Assistant Bishops
Rt Revd Allan B. Ewing, PO Box 8605, Wagga Wagga, NSW 2650   *Tel:* 61 2 6926 4226
Fax: 61 2 6926 4226
email: allan.ewing@anglicancg.com.au

Rt Revd Trevor W. Edwards, 28 McBryde Crescent, Wanniassa, ACT 2903   *Tel:* 61 2 6231 7347
Fax: 61 2 6231 7500
email: trevor@stmattswanniassa.org.au

GRAFTON

Bishop Rt Revd Keith Slater, Bishopsholme, PO Box 4, Grafton, NSW 2460   *Tel:* 61 2 6642 4122
Fax: 61 2 6643 1814
email: angdiog@nor.com.au
Web: http://graftondiocese.org.au

NEWCASTLE

Bishop Rt Revd Brian George Farran, Bishop's Registry, PO Box 817, Newcastle, NSW 2300
Tel: 61 2 4926 3733
Fax: 61 2 4926 1968
email: bishop@angdon.com
Web: www.angdon.com

Assistant Bishop Vacancy   *Tel:* 02 4329 2902
Fax: 02 4329 5501
email: bishopgraeme@bigpond.com

RIVERINA

Bishop Rt Revd Douglas R. Stephens, PO Box 10, Narrandera, NSW 2700   *Tel:* 61 2 6959 1648
Fax: 61 2 6959 2903
email: rivdio@dragnet.com.au
Web: www.anglicanriverina.com

SYDNEY

Archbishop Most Revd Dr Peter Jensen (*Metropolitan of the Province of NSW*), PO Box Q190, QVB Post Office, NSW 1230
Tel: 61 2 9265 1521
Fax: 61 2 9265 1504
email: archbishop@sydney.anglican.asn.au
Web: www.sydneyanglicans.net

Assistant Bishops
Rt Revd Peter Tasker (*Bishop of Liverpool & Georges River Region*) (*same address*)   *Tel:* 61 2 9265 1530
Fax: 61 2 9265 1543
email: ptasker@sydney.anglican.asn.au
Web: www.your.sydneyanglicans.net/
senior_clergy/bishop_tasker
Rt Revd Glenn Davies (*Bishop of Northern Region*) (*same address*)   *Tel:* 61 2 9265 1533
Fax: 61 2 9265 1543
email: gdavies@sydney.anglican.asn.au
Web: www.your.sydneyanglicans.net/
senior_clergy/ bishop_davies
Rt Revd Robert Charles Forsyth (*Bishop of South Sydney*) (*same address*)   *Tel:* 61 2 9265 1501
Fax: 61 2 9265 1543
email: robforsyth@sydney.anglican.asn.au
Web: www.your.sydneyanglicans.net/
senior_clergy/bishop_forsyth
Rt Revd Alan (Al) Stewart (*Bishop of Wollongong*), 74 Church St, Wollongong, NSW 2500
Tel: 61 2 4225 2800
Fax: 61 2 4228 4296
email: astewart@wollongong.anglican.asn.au
Web: www.your.sydneyanglicans.net/
senior_clergy/bishop_stewart
Rt Revd Ivan Yin Lee (*Bishop of Western Sydney*), PO Box 1443, Parramatta, NSW 2124
Tel: 61 2 9635 3186
Fax: 61 2 9633 3636
email: ilee@westernsydney.anglican.asn.au
Web: www.your.sydneyanglicans.net/
senior_clergy/bishop_lee

PROVINCE OF QUEENSLAND

Metropolitan Most Revd Dr Phillip John Aspinall (*Primate of the Anglican Church of Australia and Archbishop of Brisbane*)

BRISBANE

Archbishop Most Revd Dr Phillip John Aspinall (*Metropolitan of the Province of Queensland and Primate of the Anglican Church of Australia*), GPO Box 421, Brisbane, QLD 4001
Tel: 61 7 3835 2222
Fax: 61 7 3832 5030
email: archbishop@anglicanbrisbane.org.au
Web: www.anglicanbrisbane.org.au

Assistant Bishops
Rt Revd Geoff Smith (*Bishop of the Southern Region*) (*same address*)   *Tel:* 61 7 3835 2213
Fax: 61 7 3831 1170

Rt Revd Jonathan Charles Holland (*Bishop of the Northern Region*) (*same address*)   *Tel:* 61 7 3835 2213
Fax: 61 7 3831 1170
email: jholland@anglicanbrisbane.org.au
Rt Revd Robert William Nolan (*Bishop of the Western Region*), Box 2600, Toowoomba, QLD 4350
Tel: 61 7 4639 1875
Fax: 61 7 4632 6882
email: rwnolan@bigpond.com

NORTH QUEENSLAND
Bishop Rt Revd William James (Bill) Ray, PO Box 1244, Townsville, QLD 4810
Tel: 61 7 4771 4175
Fax: 61 7 4721 1756
email: bishoppnq@anglicannq.org
Web: www.anglicannq.org

Assistant Bishops
Rt Revd Saibo Mabo (*Assistant Bishop and National Torres Strait Islander Bishop*), PO Box 714, Thursday Island, QLD 4875
Tel and *Fax:* 61 7 4069 1960
email: bishopti@bigpond.com
Rt Revd James Randolph Leftwich (*Assistant Bishop and National Aboriginal Bishop*), 129A Lake Street, Cairns, QLD 4878   *Tel:* 61 7 4051 1055
Fax: 61 7 4051 1033
email: bishopab@bigpond.com

THE NORTHERN TERRITORY
Bishop Rt Revd Gregory Edwin (Greg) Thompson, PO Box 2950, Darwin, NT 0801
Tel: 61 8 8941 7440
Fax: 61 8 8941 7446
email: ntdiocese@internode.on.net
Web: www.northernterritory.anglican.org

ROCKHAMPTON
Bishop Rt Revd Godfrey Charles Fryar, PO Box 6158, Central Queensland Mail Centre, Rockhampton, QLD 4702   *Tel:* 61 7 4927 3188
Fax: 61 7 4922 4562
email: bishop@anglicanrock.org.au
Web: www.anglicanrock.org.au

PROVINCE OF SOUTH AUSTRALIA
Metropolitan Most Reverend Jeffrey William Driver (*Archbishop of Adelaide*)

ADELAIDE
Archbishop Most Reverend Jeffrey William Driver (*Metropolitan of the Province of South Australia*), 26 King William Rd, N Adelaide, SA 5006
Tel: 61 8 8305 9353
Fax: 61 8 8305 9399
email: archbishop@adelaide.anglican.com.au
Web: www.adelaide.anglican.com.au

Assistant Bishop
Bishop Rt Revd Stephen Kim Pickard (*same address*)
email: spickard@adelaide.anglican.com.au

THE MURRAY
Bishop Rt Revd Ross Owen Davies, PO Box 394, Murray Bridge, SA 5253   *Tel:* 61 8 8532 2270
Fax: 61 8 8532 5760
email: registry@murray.anglican.org
Web: www.murray.anglican.org

WILLOCHRA
Bishop Rt Revd Garry Weatherill, Bishop's House, Gladstone, SA 5473   *Tel:* 61 8 8662 2249
Fax: 61 8 8662 2070
email: bishop@diowillochra.org.au
Web: www.diowillochra.org.au

PROVINCE OF VICTORIA
Metropolitan Most Revd Philip Leslie Freier (*Archbishop of Melbourne*)

BALLARAT
Bishop Rt Revd Michael George Hough, PO Box 89, Ballarat, VIC 3350   *Tel:* 61 3 5331 1183
Fax: 61 3 5333 2982
email: bpsec@ballaratanglican.org.au
Web: www.ballaratanglican.org.au/

BENDIGO
Bishop Rt Revd Andrew William Curnow, PO Box 2, Bendigo, VIC 3552   *Tel:* 61 3 5443 4711
Fax: 61 3 5441 2173
email: bishop@bendigoanglican.org.au
Web: www.bendigoanglican.org.au

GIPPSLAND
Bishop Rt Revd John Charles McIntyre, PO Box 928, Sale, VIC 3853   *Tel:* 61 3 5144 2044
Fax: 61 3 5144 7183
email: bishop@gippsanglican.org.au
Web: www.gippsanglican.org.au

MELBOURNE
Archbishop Most Revd Philip Leslie Freier (*Metropolitan of the Province of Victoria*), The Anglican Centre, 209 Flinders Lane, Melbourne, VIC 3000   *Tel:* 61 3 9653 4220
Fax: 61 3 9650 2184
email: archbishop@melbourne.anglican.com.au
Web: www.melbourne.anglican.org.au/

Assistant Bishops
Rt Revd Paul Raymond White (*Bishop of the Southern Region*) (*same address*)
Tel: 61 3 9653 4220
Fax: 61 3 9653 4268
email: pwhite@melbourne.anglican.com.au
Rt Revd Philip Huggins (*Bishop of the North-Western Region*) (*same address*)
email: phuggins@melbourne.anglican.com.au
Rt Revd Stephen Hale (*Bishop of the Eastern Region*) (*same address*)
email: shale@melbourne.anglican.com.au

WANGARATTA
Bishop Vacancy, Bishop's Lodge, PO Box 457, Wangaratta VIC 3676   *Tel:* 61 3 5721 3484
Fax: 61 3 5722 1427
email: bishop@wangaratta.anglican.org
Web: www.wangaratta.anglican.org

PROVINCE OF WESTERN AUSTRALIA

Metropolitan Most Revd Roger Adrian Herft
(*Archbishop of Perth*)

BUNBURY
Bishop Rt Revd William David Hair McCall, PO Box 15, Bunbury, WA 6231   *Tel:* 61 8 9721 2100
Fax: 61 8 9791 2300
email: bishop@bunbury.org.au
Web: www.bunbury.org.au

NORTH WEST AUSTRALIA
Bishop Rt Revd David Mulready, PO Box 171, Geraldton, WA 6531   *Tel:* 61 8 9921 7277
Fax: 61 8 9964 2220
email: bishop@anglicandnwa.org
Web: www.anglicandnwa.org

PERTH
Archbishop Most Revd Roger Adrian Herft (*Metropolitan of the Province of Western Australia*), GPO Box W2067, Perth, WA 6846
Tel: 61 8 9325 7455
Fax: 61 8 9325 6741
email: archbishop@perth.anglican.org
Web: www.perth.anglican.org

Assistant Bishops
Rt Revd Kay Goldsworthy (*same address*)
Rt Revd Tom Wilmot (*same address*)
email: twilmot@perth.anglican.org
Rt Revd Mark Gregory Burton (*same address*)
Tel: 61 8 9325 7454
Fax: 61 8 9325 6741
email: mburton@perth.anglican.org

EXTRA-PROVINCIAL DIOCESES

TASMANIA
Bishop Rt Revd John Douglas Harrower, OAM, GPO 748, Hobart, TAS 7001   *Tel:* 61 3 6223 8811
Fax: 61 3 6223 8968
email: bishop@anglicantas.org.au
Web: www.anglicantas.org.au/

DEFENCE FORCE
Bishop Rt Revd Len Eacott (*Anglican Bishop to the Australian Defence Force and Bishop Assistant to the Primate*), Department of Defence, DSG-Duntroon, ACT 2600   *Tel:* 61 2 9265 9935
Fax: 61 2 9265 9959
email: dfc@anglican.org.au
Web: www.anglican.org.au/defence

The Episcopal Anglican Church of Brazil

(Igreja Episcopal Anglicana do Brasil)

Members 106,415
The Episcopal Anglican Church of Brazil is the 19th Province of the Anglican Communion, and its work began in 1890 as a result of the missionary work of two north American missionaries in Porto Alegre: James Watson Morris and Lucien Lee Kinsolving. Autonomy from the Episcopal Church in the United States was granted in 1965. The Episcopal Church now has more than a hundred thousand baptized members and a team of more than two hundred clergy, among whom are thirty women priests. It has established communities, and educational and social institutions, in the main urban areas of Brazil. The Brazilian province comprises nine dioceses: Southern, Southwestern, Rio de Janeiro, São Paulo, Recife, Brasília, Pelotas, Curitiba and Amazon. It also has one missionary district: Missionary District West.

Primate Most Revd Mauricio José Araújo Andrade (*Bishop of Brazília*)
email: mandrade@ieab.org.br
Web: www.ieab.org.br

Provincial Secretary Revd Canon Francisco de Assis da Silva

Provincial Offices PO Box 11.510, Teresópolis, CEP 90870–970, Porto Alegre, RS
Tel and *Fax:* 55 51 3318 6200
email: assis@ieab.org.br

Provincial Treasurer Mrs Lucimara Feijó, Caixa Postal 11510, CEP 90841–970, Porto Alegre, RS
Tel and *Fax:* 55 51 3318 6200
email: feijo@ieab.org.br

CHURCH PAPER
Estandarte Cristão, a bimonthly church journal in Portuguese, published since 1893, which contains general articles and news about the life of the Church at local, national and international level. This journal is the main channel of the Communication Department of the Church. *Editorial Offices:* Caixa Postal 11510, CEP 90870–970, Porto Alegre, RS   *Tel* and *Fax:* 55 51 3318 6200
email: comunicacao@ieab.org.br

AMAZON
Bishop Rt Revd Saulo Mauricio de Barros, Av. Sezerdelo Correia, 514, Batista Campos, 66025–240, Belem, PA   *Tel* and *Fax:* 55 91 3241 9720
email: sbarros@ieab.org.br

BRASÍLIA

Bishop Most Revd Maurício José Araújo de Andrade (*Primate of the Episcopal Anglican Church of Brazil*), EQS 309/310, sala 1 – Asa Sul, Caixa Postal 093, 70359–970, Brasília, DF
Tel: 55 61 3443 4305
Fax: 55 61 3443 4337
email: mandrade@ieab.org.br
Web: www.dab.ieab.org.br

CURITIBA

Bishop Rt Revd Naudal Alves Gomes, Rua Sete de Setembro, 3927 – Centro, 80250-010 Curitiba, PR
Tel: 55 41 3232 0917
email: ngomes@ieab.org.br

PELOTAS

Bishop Rt Revd Renato da Cruz Raatz, Rua Felix da Cunha, 425 – Centro, Caixa Postal 791, 96001–970 Pelotas, RS   *Tel* and *Fax:* 55 53 3227 7120
email: rcraatz@ieab.org.br
Web: www.dap.ieab.org.br

RECIFE

Bishop Rt Revd Sebastião Armando Gameleira Soares, Rua Virgílio Mota, 70, Parnamirim, 52060–582, Recife, PE   *Tel:* 55 81 3441 6843
email: sgameleira@ieab.org.br
Web: www.dar.ieab.org.br
Suffragan Bishop Rt Revd Filadelfo Oliveira Neto (*same address*)   *email:* foliveira@ieab.org.br

RIO DE JANEIRO

Bishop Rt Revd Celso Franco de Oliveira, Rua Fonseca Guimarães, 12 Sta.Teresa, 20240–260, Rio de Janeiro, RJ   *Tel:* 55 21 2220 2148
Fax: 55 21 2252 9686
email: coliveira@ieab.org.br
Web: www.anglicana.com.br

SÃO PAULO

Bishop Rt Revd Hiroshi Ito, Rua Borges Lagoa, 172 – Vila Clementino, 04038–030 São Paulo, SP
Tel: 55 11 5549 9086/5579 9011
Fax: 55 11 5083 2619
email: hito@ieab.org.br

SOUTH WESTERN BRAZIL

Bishop Rt Revd Jubal Pereira Neves, Av. Rio Branco, 880/Sub-solo – Centro, Caixa Postal 116, 97010–970 Santa Maria, RS
Tel and *Fax:* 55 55 3221 4328
email: jneves@ieab.org.br
Web: www.swbrazil.anglican.org

SOUTHERN BRAZIL

Bishop Rt Revd Orlando Santos de Oliveira, Av. Eng. Ludolfo Boehl, 278, Teresópolis, 91720–150, Porto Alegre, RS   *Tel* and *Fax:* 55 51 318 6199
email: osoliveira@ieab.org.br
Web: www.dm.ieab.org.br

Eglise Anglicane du Burundi

(The Province of the Anglican Church of Burundi)

Members 850,000
There are at least 850,000 Anglicans out of an estimated population of just over 7 million in Burundi. An Anglican presence was established through the work of the CMS in the 1930s and grew rapidly as a result of the East African revival. The former Ruanda Mission (now CMS) set up its first mission stations at Buhiga and Matana in 1935, and Buye in 1936. Activities were mainly focused on evangelism, education and medical work. The first national bishop was consecrated in 1965 and Buye diocese was created, covering the whole country. The Church of the Province of Burundi now consists of six dioceses, and it has been an independent province within the Anglican Communion since 1992. The Church's main concerns include peace and reconciliation, repatriation of refugees and displaced people, community development, literacy and education, and HIV/AIDS. It is committed to mission and evangelism with faith in the risen Christ as Lord and Saviour. It is concerned to support theological education and training for ministry, based on the authority of Scripture.

Primate Most Revd Bernard Ntahoturi (*Archbishop of Burundi and Bishop of Matana*)

Provincial Secretary Revd Pédaçuli Birakengana, BP 2098, Bujumbura   *Tel:* 257 22 224 389
Fax: 257 22 229 129
email: peab@cbinf.com
Provincial Treasurer Vacancy

THEOLOGICAL COLLEGES
Matana Theological Institute (Provincial)
Canon Warner Memorial College, EEB Buye, BP 94 Ngozi
Kosiya Shalita Bible College, EEB Matana, DS 13, Bujumbura *or* BP 447, Bujumbura
Buhiga College, EEB Gitega, BP 23 Gitega
Makamba College, EEB Makamba, BP 96 Makamba
Bujumbura Bible College, EAB Bujumbura, BP 1300 Bujumbura

BUJUMBURA

Bishop Rt Revd Pie Ntukamazina, BP 1300, Bujumbura   *Tel:* 257 22 222 641
Fax: 257 22 227 495
email: mgrpie@cbinf.com

BUYE
Bishop Rt Revd Sixbert Macumi, BP 94, Ngozi
Tel: 257 22 302 210
Fax: 257 22 302 317
email: buyedioc@yahoo.fr

GITEGA
Bishop Rt Revd Jean Nduwayo, BP 23, Gitega
Tel: 257 22 402 247
email: eebgitega@cbinf.com

MAKAMBA
Bishop Rt Revd Martin Blaise Nyaboho, BP 96, Makamba
Tel: 257 22 508 080
Fax: 257 22 229 129
email: eabdiocmak@yahoo.fr

MATANA
Bishop Most Revd Bernard Ntahoturi (*Archbishop of Burundi*), BP 447, Bujumbura
Tel: 257 22 924 595
Fax: 257 22 229 19e;
email: ntahober@cbinf.com/
ntahober@yahoo.co.uk

MUYINGA
Bishop Rt Revd Eraste Bigirimana, BP 55, Muyinga
Tel: 257 22 306 019
Fax: 257 22 306 152
email: bigirimanaerast@yahoo.fr

The Anglican Church of Canada

Members 641,845 (2001)

The Anglican witness in Canada started in the eighteenth century with the Church Missionary Society and the United Society for the Propagation of the Gospel. The Eucharist was first celebrated in Frobisher Bay (now Iqaluit) in 1578; the first church building was St Paul's, Halifax in 1750. The Church includes a large number of the original inhabitants of Canada (Indians, Inuit, and Metis) and has been a strong advocate of their rights. A book of alternative services was published in 1985. The Church has a strong international role in crisis assistance through the Primate's World Relief and Development Fund (PWRDF).

Primate of The Anglican Church of Canada Most Revd Fred J. Hiltz, 80 Hayden St, Toronto, ON, M4Y 3G2
Tel: 1 416 924 9192
Fax: 1 416 924 0211
email: primate@national.anglican.ca
Web: www.anglican.ca

General Secretary Ven. Dr Michael F. Pollesel
email: general.secretary@national.anglican.ca

General Treasurer Mr Peter Blachford
email: pblachford@national.anglican.ca

Offices of the General Synod and of its Departments
80 Hayden St, Toronto ON, M4Y 3G2
Tel: 1 416 924 9192
Fax: 1 416 968 7983

National Indigenous Anglican Bishop Rt Revd Mark MacDonald (*same address*)
email: mmacdonald@national.anglican.ca
Web: www2.anglican.ca/im

UNIVERSITIES AND COLLEGES OF THE ANGLICAN CHURCH OF CANADA
British Columbia
Vancouver School of Theology*, 6000 Iona Dr, Vancouver, BC, V6T 1L4 (*Principal* Revd Dr Wendy Fletcher)
email: vstinfo@vst.edu

Manitoba
Henry Budd College for Ministry, Box 2518, The Pas MB, R9A IM3 (*Joint Co-ordinators* Ms Marion Jenkins and Revd Paul Sodtke)
email: hbcm@mts.net

St John's College, 92 Dysart Rd, Winnipeg, MB, R3T 2M5 (*Warden* Dr Janet Hoskins)
email: stjohns_college@umanitoba.ca

Newfoundland
Queen's College, 210 Prince Philip Dr (Q3000), St John's NF, A1B 3R6 (*Provost* Revd Dr John Mellis)
email: queens@mun.ca

Nova Scotia
Atlantic School of Theology*, 660 Francklyn St, Halifax, NS, B3H 3B5 (*Principal* Canon Dr Eric Beresford)
email: dmaclachlan@astheology.ns.ca

Nunavut
Arthur Turner Training School *Enquiries to* Diocese of the Arctic, Box 190, Yellowknife, NT X1A 2N2

Ontario
Canterbury College, 172 Patricia Rd, Windsor ON, N9B 3B9 (*Principal* Revd Dr David T. A. Symons)
email: canter@uwindsor.ca
Huron University College, 1349 Western Rd, London, ON, N6G 1H3 (*Principal* Dr Ramona Lumpkin)
email: rlumpkin@uwo.ca
Renison College, Westmount Rd N, Waterloo, ON, N2L 3G4 (*Principal* Dr John Crossley)
email: jecrossley@renison.uwaterloo.ca
Thorneloe College, Ramsey Lake Rd, Sudbury, ON, P3E 2C6 (*Provost* Revd Dr Stephen G.W. Andrews)
email: thorneprov@nickel.laurentian.ca

Trinity College, 6 Hoskin Ave, Toronto, ON, M5S 1H8 (*Dean of Divinity* Revd Canon Dr David Neelands) *email:* divinity@trinity.utoronto.ca Wycliffe College, 5 Hoskin Ave, Toronto, ON, M5S 1H7 (*Principal* Revd Dr George Sumner) *email:* wycliffe.college@utoronto.ca

Quebec
Bishop's University, PO Box 5000, Lennoxville, QC, J1M 1Z7 *email:* amontgom@ubishops.ca Montreal Diocesan Theological College, 3473 University St, Montreal, QC, H3A 2A8 (*Principal* Canon Dr John Simons)
email: diocoll@netrover.com

Saskatchewan
College of Emmanuel and St Chad, 1337 College Dr, Saskatoon, SK, S7N OW6 (*Principal* Dr Walter Deller) *email:* emmanuel.stchad@usask.ca
*Ecumenical

CHURCH PAPERS
Anglican Journal/Journal anglican Tabloid format, national church paper under management of a Board of Trustees appointed by General Synod. It circulates as an insert for a number of diocesan publications. Issued monthly except July and August. *Editorial Offices:* 80 Hayden St, Toronto, ON M4Y 3G2.
email: anglican.journal@national.anglican.ca

Ministry Matters Published three times a year by the Communication and Information Resources Dept of General Synod. Intended primarily for clergy and lay leaders. *Editorial Offices:* 80 Hayden St, Toronto, ON M4Y 3G2
email: ministry.matters@national.anglican.ca

PROVINCE OF BRITISH COLUMBIA AND YUKON
Metropolitan Most Revd Terrence O. Buckle (*Bishop of Yukon*)

BRITISH COLUMBIA
Bishop Rt Revd James A. J. Cowan, 900 Vancouver St, Victoria, BC, V8V 3V7
Tel: 1 250 386 7781
Fax: 1 250 386 4013
email: synod@bc.anglican.ca
Web: www.bc.anglican.ca

CALEDONIA
Bishop Rt Revd William J. Anderson, PO Box 278, Prince Rupert, BC, V8J 3P6 *Tel:* 1 250 624 6013
Fax: 1 250 624 4299
email: synodofc@citytel.net
Web: www.caledonia.anglican.org

CENTRAL INTERIOR, ANGLICAN PARISHES OF
Bishop Rt Vacancy, PO Box 1979, 100 Mile House, BC V0K 2E0 *Tel:* 1 250 395 1222
Fax: 1 250 395 1252
email: acpi-office@telus.net

KOOTENAY
Bishop Rt Revd John E. Privett, 1876 Richter St, Kelowna, BC, V1Y 2M9 *Tel:* 1 250 762 3306
Fax: 1 250 762 4150
email: diocese_of_kootenay@telus.net
Web: www.kootenay.anglican.ca

NEW WESTMINSTER
Bishop Rt Revd Michael C. Ingham, Suite 580, 401 West Georgia St, Vancouver, BC, V6B 5A1
Tel: 1 604 684 6306
Fax: 1 604 684 7017
email: bishop@vancouver.anglican.ca
Web: www.vancouver.anglican.ca

YUKON
Bishop Most Revd Terrence O. Buckle (*Metropolitan of the Province of British Columbia and Yukon*), PO Box 31136, Whitehorse, Yukon Y1A 5P7 *Tel:* 1 867 667 7746
Fax: 1 867 667 6125
email: synodoffice@klondiker.com
Web: http://anglican.yukon.net

PROVINCE OF CANADA
Metropolitan Most Revd A. Bruce Stavert (*Archbishop of Quebec*)

CENTRAL NEWFOUNDLAND
Bishop Rt Revd F. David Torraville, 34 Fraser Rd, Gander, NL, A1V 2E8 *Tel:* 1 709 256 2372
Fax: 1 709 256 2396
email: bishopcentral@nfld.net
Web: www.centraldiocese.org

EASTERN NEWFOUNDLAND AND LABRADOR
Bishop Rt Revd Cyrus C. J. Pitman, 19 King's Bridge Rd, St John's, NL, A1C 3K4
Tel: 1 709 576 6697
Fax: 1 709 576 7122
email: cpitman@anglicanenl.nf.net
Web: www.nfol.ca

FREDERICTON
Bishop Rt Revd Claude E.W. Miller, 115 Church St, Fredericton, NB, E3B 4C8 *Tel:* 1 506 459 1801
Fax: 1 506 460 0520
email: diocese@anglican.nb.ca
Web: www.anglican.nb.ca

MONTREAL
Bishop Rt Revd Barry B. Clarke, 1444 Union Ave, Montreal, QC, H3A 2B8 *Tel:* 1 514 843 6577
Fax: 1 514 843 3221
email: bishops.office@montreal.anglican.org
Web: www.montreal.anglican.org

NOVA SCOTIA AND PRINCE EDWARD ISLAND
Bishop Rt Revd Susan Moxley, 5732 College St, Halifax, NS, B3H 1X3   *Tel:* 1 902 420 0717
Fax: 1 902 425 0717
email: office@nspeidiocese.ca
Web: www.nspeidiocese.ca

QUEBEC
Archbishop Most Revd A. Bruce Stavert (*Metropolitan of the Province of Canada*), 31 rue des Jardins, Quebec, QC, G1R 4L6
Tel: 1 418 692 3858
Fax: 1 418 692 3876
email: synodoffice@quebec.anglican.ca
Web: www.quebec.anglican.org

Bishop Coadjutor Rt Revd Dennis Drainville (*same address*)

WESTERN NEWFOUNDLAND
Bishop Rt Revd Percy D. Coffin, 25 Main St, Corner Brook, NF, A2H 1C2   *Tel:* 1 709 639 8712
Fax: 1 709 639 1636
email: dsown@nf.aibn.ca
Web: www.westernnewfoundland.anglican.org

PROVINCE OF ONTARIO
Metropolitan Most Revd Caleb J. Lawrence (*Archbishop of Moosonee*)

ALGOMA
Bishop Rt Revd Stephen Andrews, Box 1168, Sault Ste Marie, ON, P6A 5N7   *Tel:* 1 705 256 5061
Fax: 1 705 946 1860
email: bishop@dioceseofalgoma.com
Web: www.dioceseofalgoma.com

HURON
Bishop Vacancy, 190 Queens Ave, London, ON N6A 6H7   *Tel:* 1 519 434 6893
Fax: 1 519 673 4151
email: bishops@huron.anglican.org
Web: www.diohuron.org
Suffragan Rt Revd Robert F. Bennett (*same address*)

MOOSONEE
Archbishop Most Revd Caleb J. Lawrence (*Metropolitan of the Province of Ontario*), Box 841, Schumacher, ON, P0N 1G0   *Tel:* 1 705 360 1129
Fax: 1 705 360 1120
email: dmoose@domaa.ca
Web: http://moosonee.anglican.org

NIAGARA
Bishop Rt Revd Michael A. Bird, Cathedral Place, 252 James St North, Hamilton, ON, L8R 2L3
Tel: 1 905 527 1316
Fax: 1 905 527 1281
email: bishop@niagara.anglican.ca
Web: www.niagara.anglican.ca

ONTARIO
Bishop Rt Revd George L. R. Bruce, 90 Johnson St, Kingston, ON, K7L 1X7   *Tel:* 1 613 544 4774
Fax: 1 613 547 3745
email: gbruce@ontario.anglican.ca
Web: www.ontario.anglican.ca

OTTAWA
Bishop Rt Revd John H. Chapman, 71 Bronson Ave, Ottawa, ON, K1R 6G6   *Tel:* 1 613 232 7124
Fax: 1 613 232 3955
email: c/o ann-day@ottawa.anglican.ca
Web: www.ottawa.anglican.ca

TORONTO
Bishop Rt Revd Colin R. Johnson, 135 Adelaide St East, Toronto, ON, M5C 1L8   *Tel:* 1 416 363 6121
Fax: 1 416 363 3683
email: cjohnson@toronto.anglican.ca
Web: www.toronto.anglican.ca

Area Bishops
Rt Revd Linda Nicholls (*Trent-Durham Area*), 965 Dundas St West, Suite 207, Whitby, ON, L1P 1G8
Tel: 1 905 668 1558
Fax: 1 905 688 8216
email: lnicholls@toronto.anglican.ca
Rt Revd George Elliott (*York-Simcoe Area*), 2174 King Rd, Suite 2, King City, ON, L7B 1L6
Tel: 1 905 833 8327
Fax: 1 905 833 8329
email: ysimcoe@neptune.on.ca
Rt Revd Patrick Yu (*York-Scarborough Area*), St Paul's L'Amoreaux, 3333 Finch Ave East, Scarborough, ON, M1W 2R9   *Tel:* 1 416 497 7750
Fax: 1 416 497 4103
email: officeyorkscar@bellnet.ca
Rt Revd M. Philip Poole (*York Credit Valley*), 256 Sheldon Ave, Etobicoke, ON, M8W 4X8
Tel: 1 416 503 9903
Fax: 1 416 503 8229
email: office@yorkcvalleyanglican.com

PROVINCE OF RUPERT'S LAND
Metropolitan Most Revd John R. Clarke (*Archbishop of Athabasca*)

THE ARCTIC
Bishop Rt Revd Andrew P. Atagotaaluk, Box 190, Yellowknife, NT, X1A 2N2
Tel: 1 867 873 5432
Fax: 1 867 873 8478
email: diocese@arcticnet.org
Web: www.arctic.anglican.org

Suffragan Bishops
Rt Revd Benjamin T. Arreak (*Nunavik Region*), Box 154, Kuujjuaqq, QC, J0M 1C0
Tel: 1 819 964 2324
Fax: 1 819 964 2113
email: btarreak@sympatico.ca

Rt Revd Larry D. Robertson (*Mackenzie and Kitikmeot Region*), Box 190, Yellowknife, NT, X1A 2N2   *Tel:* 1 867 873 5432
Fax: 1 867 873 8478
email: larryr@arcticnet.org

ATHABASCA

Archbishop Most Revd John R. Clarke (*Metropolitan of the Province of Rupert's Land*), Box 6868, Peace River, AB, T8S 1S6   *Tel:* 1 780 624 2767
Fax: 1 780 624 2365
email: admin@dioath.ca
Web: www.dioath.ca

BRANDON

Bishop Rt Revd James D. Njegovan, Box 21009, W.E.P.O., Brandon, MB, R7B 3W8
Tel: 1 204 727 7550
Fax: 1 204 727 4135
email: bishopbdn@mts.net/diobran@mts.net
Web: www.dioceseofbrandon.org

CALGARY

Bishop Rt Revd Derek B. E. Hoskin, 560–1207 11th Ave SW, Calgary, AB, T3C 0M5
Tel: 1 403 243 3673
Fax: 1 403 243 2182
email: synod@calgary.anglican.ca
Web: www.calgary.anglican.ca

EDMONTON

Bishop Rt Revd Jane Alexander, 10035–103 St, Edmonton, AB, T5J 0X5   *Tel:* 1 780 439 7344
Fax: 1 780 439 6549
email: bishop@edmonton.anglican.ca
Web: www.edmonton.anglican.org

KEEWATIN

Bishop Rt Revd David N. Ashdown, 915 Ottawa St, Keewatin, ON, P0X 1C0   *Tel:* 1 807 547 3353
Fax: 1 807 547 3356
email: dioceseofkeewatin@shaw.ca
Web: www.gokenora.com/~dioceseofkeewatin

Assistant Bishop Rt Revd Gordon Beardy (*same address*)

QU'APPELLE

Bishop Rt Revd Gregory K. Kerr-Wilson, 1501 College Ave, Regina, SK, S4P 1B8
Tel: 1 306 522 1608
Fax: 1 306 352 6808
email: quappelle@sasktel.net
Web: http://diocse.sasktelwebsite.net

RUPERT'S LAND

Bishop Rt Revd Donald D. Phillips, 935 Nesbitt Bay, Winnipeg, MB, R3T 1W6   *Tel:* 1 204 922 4200
Fax: 1 204 922 4219
email: general@rupertsland.ca
Web: www.rupertsland.ca

SASKATCHEWAN

Bishop Vacancy, 1308 5th Ave East, Prince Albert, SK, S6V 2H7   *Tel:* 1 306 763 2455
Fax: 1 306 764 5172
email: synod@sasktel.net
Web: www.saskatchewan.anglican.org

SASKATOON

Bishop Rt Revd Rodney Andrews, PO Box 1965, Saskatoon, SK, S7K 3S5   *Tel:* 1 306 244 5651
Fax: 1 306 933 4606
email: anglicansynod@sasktel.net
Web: www.saskatoon.anglican.org

The Church of the Province of Central Africa

Members 600,000
The province includes Botswana, Malawi, Zambia and Zimbabwe. The first Anglican missionary to Malawi was Bishop Charles Mackenzie who arrived with David Livingstone in 1861. The province was inaugurated in 1955 and has a movable bishopric. The countries forming the province are very different. Zambia and Botswana suffer the difficulties of rapid industrialization, along with underdevelopment and thinly populated areas. In Malawi 30% of the adult males are away as migrant labourers in other countries at any given time. Zimbabwe is experiencing problems of social adjustment after independence.

Archbishop of the Province Vacancy

Provincial Secretary Vacancy

Provincial Treasurer Mr R. Kanja, CPCA, PO Box 22317, Kitwe, Zambia   *Tel:* 260 351 081
260 9719 5368 (Mobile)
Fax: 267 351 668

ANGLICAN THEOLOGICAL COLLEGES
Leonard Kamungu (Anglican) Theological College, PO Box 959, Zomba. Malawi (*Dean* Revd Alinafe Kalemba)   *Tel:* 265 1 525 286
265 8 856 410 (Mobile)
National Anglican Theological College of Zimbabwe (Ecumenical Institute of Theology), 11 Thornburg Ave, Groom Bridge, Mount Pleasant, Harare, Zimbabwe
St John's Seminary, Mindolo, PO Box 20369, Kitwe, Zambia   *Tel:* 260 2 210960
email: josmers@zamnet.zm

CHURCH PAPER
Link Monthly newspaper for the Dioceses of Mashonaland and Matabeleland giving news and views of the dioceses. *Editorial Offices* Link Board of Management, PO Box UA7, Harare City.

BOTSWANA
Bishop Rt Revd Trevor Mwamba, PO Box 679, Gaborone, Botswana   *Tel:* 267 395 3779
Fax: 267 391 3015
email: angli_diocese@info.bw / musonda_mwamba@yahoo.com

CENTRAL ZAMBIA
Bishop Rt Revd Derek Gary Kamukwamba, PO Box 70172, Ndola, Zambia   *Tel:* 260 2 612 431
email: adcznla@zamnet.zm

CENTRAL ZIMBABWE
Bishop Rt Revd Ishmael Mukuwanda, PO Box 25, Gweru, Zimbabwe   *Tel:* 263 54 21 030
Fax: 263 54 21 097
email: diocent@telconet.co.zw / imukuwanda@gmail.com

EASTERN ZAMBIA
Bishop Rt Revd William Muchombo, PO Box 510154, Chipata, Zambia
Tel and Fax: 260 216 221 294
email: dioeastzm@zamnet.zm

HARARE
Bishop Vacancy, Bishops Mount Close, PO Box UA7, Harare, Zimbabwe
email: angbishophre@mango.zw

LAKE MALAWI
Bishop Vacancy (*Vicar General* Very Revd Canon Alumbeni Michael Mkoko), PO Box 30349, Lilongwe 3, Malawi   *Tel:* 265 797 858 (Office)
265 794 268 (Home)
Fax: 265 731 966
email: anglama@eomw.net

LUAPULA
Bishop Rt Revd Robert Mumbi, PO Box 710210, Mansa, Luapula, Zambia
emaill: diopula@zamtel.zm

LUSAKA
Bishop Rt Revd David Njovu, Bishop's Lodge, PO Box 30183, Lusaka, Zambia
Tel: 260 211 254 789 (Office)
260 211 252 449 (Home)
Fax: 260 1 254789
email: dnjovu@zamnet.zm

MANICALAND
Bishop Vacancy, 115 Herbert Chitepo St, Mutare, Zimbabwe   *Tel:* 263 20 64 194
Fax: 263 20 63 076
email: diomani@syscom.co.zw

MASVINGO
Bishop Rt Revd Godfrey Tawonezvi, PO Box 1421, Masvingo, Zambia   *Tel:* 263 39 362 536
email: bishopgodfreytawonezvi@gmail.com / anglicandiomsv@comone.co.zw

MATABELELAND
Bishop Rt Revd Wilson Sitshebo, PO Box 2422, Bulaweyo, Zimbabwe   *Tel:* 263 9 61 370
Fax: 263 9 68 353
email: angdiomat@telconet.co.zw / bishmat@mweb.co.zw

NORTHERN MALAWI
Bishop Rt Revd Christopher John Boyle, Box 120, Mzuzu, Malawi, Central Africa   *Tel:* 265 331 486
Fax: 265 333 805
email: bishopboyle@sdnp.org.mw

NORTHERN ZAMBIA
Bishop Rt Revd Albert Chama, PO Box 20798, Kitwe, Zambia
Tel: 260 2 223 264 (Office) / 260 2 230 082 (Home)
Fax: 260 2 224 778
email: cpca@zamnet.zm

SOUTHERN MALAWI
Bishop Rt Revd James Tengatenga, PO Box 30220, Chichiri, Blantyre, 3, Malawi   *Tel:* 265 1 641 218
Tel: 265 1 641 218
Fax: 265 1 641 235
email: angsoma@sdnp.org.mw / jatenga@sdnp.org.mw

SOUTHERN MALAWI – UPPER SHIRE
Bishop Vacancy (*Vicar General* Very Revd Brighton Vitta Malasa), Private Bag 1, Chilema, Zomba, Malawi   *Tel and Fax:* 265 1 539 514
265 9545 609 (Mobile)
email: angus@malawi.net / dionorth@zamnet.zm

The Anglican Church of the Central American Region

(Iglesia Anglicana de la Región Central de América)

Members 15,600

This province of the Anglican Communion is made up of the Dioceses of Guatemala, El Salvador, Nicaragua, Costa Rica and Panama. The Church was introduced by the Society for the Propagation of the Gospel when England administered two colonies in Central America, Belize (1783–1982) and Miskitia (1740–1894). In the later years Afro-Antillean people brought their Anglican Christianity with them. The province is multicultural and multiracial and is committed to evangelization, social outreach, and community development.

Primate Most Revd Martin de Jesus Barahona Pascacio (*Bishop of El Salvador*)

Provincial Secretary Rt Revd Hector Monterroso
(Bishop of Costa Rica)   Tel: 506 253 0790
                                        Fax: 506 253 8331
                            email: iarca@amnet.co.cr

Provincial Treasurer Mr Harold Charles, Apt R,
Balboa, Republic of Panama   Tel: 507 212 0062
                                Fax: 507 262 2097
                            email: iarcahch@sinfo.net

COSTA RICA
Bishop Rt Revd Hector Monterroso, Apt 2773, 1000
San José, Costa Rica   Tel: 506 225 0209/253 0790
                                Fax: 506 253 8331
                    email: anglicancr@racsa.co.cr

EL SALVADOR
Bishop Most Revd Martin de Jesus Barahona
Pascacio (Primate of the Anglican Church of the
Central American Region), 47 Avenida Sur, 723 Col
Flor Blanca, Apt Postal (01), 274 San Salvador,
El Salvador   Tel: 503 2223 2252
                                Fax: 503 2223 7952
                    email: anglican.sal@integra.com.sv

GUATEMALA
Bishop Rt Revd Armando Román Guerra-Soria,
Apt 58A, Avenida La Castellana 40–06,
Guatemala City, Guatemala   Tel: 502 2472 0852
                                Fax: 502 2472 0764
                    email: diocesis@terra.com.gt/
                            diocesis@infovia.com.gt

NICARAGUA
Bishop Rt Revd Sturdie Downs, Apt 1207,
Managua, Nicaragua   Tel: 505 2225 174
                                Fax: 505 2226 701
                email: episcnic@cablenet.com.ni/
                            episcnic@tmx.com.ni

PANAMA
Bishop Rt Revd Julio Murray, Box R, Balboa,
Republic of Panama
                Tel: 507 212 0062/507 262 2051
                                Fax: 507 262 2097
email: iepan@cwpanama.net/anglipan@sinfo.net
                    Web: www.episcopalpanama.org

The Church of the Province of Congo

Members 500,000
Ugandan evangelist Apolo Kivebulaya established an Anglican presence in the Democratic Republic of Congo (formerly Zaire) in 1896. The Church reached the Katanga (formerly Saba) region in 1955, but evangelization did not progress on a large scale until the 1970s. Following independence, the Church expanded and formed dioceses as part of the Province of Uganda, Burundi, Rwanda, and Boga-Zaire. The new province was inaugurated in 1992 and changed its name in 1997. On 17 September 2002 the then Archbishop Njojo and many other Congolese citizens had to flee to Uganda because of internal tribal warfare.

Archbishop Most Revd Dr Fidèle Dirokpa Balufuga (Bishop of Kinshasa)

Provincial Secretary Rt Revd Jean Molanga Botola (Assistant Bishop of Kinshasa)

Provincial Treasurer and Liaison Office in Kampala Mr Fréderick Ngadjole, PO Box 25586, Kampala, Uganda   Tel: 256 77264 7495
                    email: eac-mags@infocom.co.ug

Provincial Coordinator of Evangelism Ven Ise Somo Muhindo, PO Box 506, Bwera-Kasese, Uganda/ BP : 322, Butembo, DR Congo
                Tel: 243 998548 601 (Mobile)
                email: revd_isesomo@yahoo.fr

THEOLOGICAL COLLEGE
The Anglican Theological Seminary (Institut Supérieur Théologique Anglican, ISThA, Princi-

pal Canon Sabiti Tibafa), PO Box 25586, Kampala, Uganda   Tel: 243 99 779 1013
                    email: revdsabiti@yahoo.fr

ARU
Bishop Rt Revd Dr Georges Titre Ande, PO Box 25586 Kampala, Uganda   or c/o PO Box 226, Arua, Uganda   Tel: 243 81 039 30 71
                email: revdande@yahoo.co.uk

BOGA (formerly BOGA-ZAIRE)
Bishop Rt Revd Henri Isingoma Kahwa, PO Box 25586, Kampala, Uganda   Tel: 243 99 333 090
                email: peac_isingoma@yahoo.fr

BUKAVU
Bishop Rt Revd Sylvestre Bahati Bali-Busane, Av. Mgr Ndahura, No. Q/Nyalukemba, C/Ibanda, CAC-Bukavu, BP 2876, Bukavu, Democratic Republic of Congo / PO Box 134, Cyangugu, Rwanda   Tel: 243 99 401 3647
                email: bahati_bali@yahoo.fr

KATANGA
Bishop Rt Revd Corneille Kasima Muno, PO Box 22037, Kitwe, Zambia   Tel: 243 97 047 173
                                Fax: 243 81 475 6075
                email: kasimamuno@yahoo.fr

KINDU
Bishop Rt Revd Zacharie Masimango Katanda (Dean of the Province), BP 5, Gisenyi, Rwanda
                        Tel: 243 99 891 6258
                        243 813 286 255 (Mobile)
                    email: angkindu@yahoo.fr

KINSHASA (Missionary diocese)
Bishop Most Revd Dr Fidèle Dirokpa Balufuga (*Archbishop of the Province*), Diocèse de Kinshasa, 11 Ave. Basalakala, Quartier Immocongo Commune de Kalamu, Kinshasa 1, B.P. 16482, DR Congo   *Tel:* 243 998 611 180 (Mobile)
email: dirokpa1@hotmail.com / anglikin@yahoo.fr
Assistant Bishops
Rt Revd Jean Molanga Botola, EAC-Kinshasa, BP 16482, Kinshasa 1, DR Congo
Tel: 243 998 623 508 (Mobile)
email: molanga2k@yahoo.co.uk

Rt Revd Abiodun Olaoye (*same address*) (*Missionary in Kinsai*)   *Tel:* 243 818 995 591
email: bishopolaoyeat@yahoo.com

KISANGANI
Bishop Rt Revd Lambert Funga Botolome, Av. Bowane, N°10, Quartier des Musiciens, C/Makiso, PO Box 86, Kisangani, DR Congo *or* c/o PO Box 25586, Kampala, Uganda
Tel: 243 997 252 868 (Mobile)
email: lambertfunga@hotmail.com

NORD KIVU
Bishop Rt Vacancy, PO Box 506, Bwera-Kasese, Uganda
Assistant Bishop Rt Revd Enoch Kayeeye (*same address*)   *Tel:* 243 99 414 8579
email: email: bpkayeeye@hotmail.com

The Church of England

Baptized members 26,000,000
Covering all of England, the Isle of Man and the Channel Islands; Europe except Great Britain and Ireland; Morocco; Turkey; and the Asian countries of the former Soviet Union. The Church of England is the ancient national Church of the land. Its structures emerged from the missionary work of St Augustine, sent from Rome in AD 597, and from the work of Celtic missionaries in the north. Throughout the Middle Ages, the Church was in communion with the See of Rome, but in the sixteenth century it separated from Rome and rejected the authority of the Pope. The Church of England is the established Church, with its administration governed by a General Synod, which meets twice a year.

Hong Kong Sheng Kung Hui

(Hong Kong Anglican Church)

Members 30,000
This dynamic province was inaugurated in 1998. The history of the Church in China dates back to the mid-nineteenth century; missionaries were provided by the American Church, the Church of England, the Church of England in Canada, etc. The Province of Chung Hua Sheng Kung Hui (the Holy Catholic Church in China) was established in 1912 of which the Anglican Church in Hong Kong and Macau was an integral part. Chung Hua Sheng Kung Hui ceased to exist in the 1950s and the diocese of Hong Kong and Macau was associated to other dioceses in South East Asia under the custodianship of the Council of Churches of East Asia, until the recent establishment of the diocese as the 38th province of the Anglican Communion. It has parishes in Hong Kong and Macau, which returned to Chinese sovereignty in 1997 and 1999 respectively. It enjoys autonomy and independence as guaranteed by the Basic Law (the mini constitution governing Hong Kong, the Special Administrative Region of China).

Primate Most Revd Paul Kwong, Provincial Office, Bishop's House, 1 Lower Albert Rd, Central Hong Kong SAR   *Tel:* 852 2526 5355
Fax: 852 2521 2199
email: office1@hkskh.org
Web: www.hkskh.org

Provincial Secretary General Revd Peter Douglas Koon (*same address*)
email: peter.koon@hkskh.org

Bishop of Hong Kong Island Most Revd Paul Kwong, 25/F Wyndham Place, 40–44, Wyndham Street, Central, Hong Kong SAR
Tel: 852 2526 5366
Fax: 852 2523 3344
email: do.dhk@hkskh.org
Web: http://dhk.hkskh.org

Bishop of Eastern Kowloon Rt Revd Louis Tsui, Diocesan Office, 4/F Holy Trinity Bradbury Centre, 139 Ma Tau Chung Rd, Kowloon City, Kowloon, Hong Kong SAR   *Tel:* 852 2713 9983
Fax: 852 2711 1609
email: ekoffice@ekhkskh.org.hk
Web: ekhkskh.org.hk

Bishop of Western Kowloon Rt Revd Thomas Soo, Diocesan Office, 15F, Ultragrace Commercial Building, 5 Jordon Rd, Kowloon, Hong Kong SAR   *Tel:* 852 2783 0811
Fax: 852 2783 0799
email: hkskhdwk@netvigator.com
Web: http://dwk.hkskh.org

The Church of the Province of the Indian Ocean

Members 90,486

The Anglican mission was begun in Mauritius in 1812 by the Revd H. Shepherd, and the first Anglican church in the Seychelles was dedicated in January 1856. The growth of the church was fostered both by the Society for the Propagation of the Gospel and by the Church Missionary Society. The dioceses of Madagascar and Mauritius and Seychelles combined in 1973 to create the province, which now comprises seven dioceses.

Archbishop Most Revd Ian Gerald Ernest (*Bishop of Mauritius*)

Provincial Secretary Revd Samitiana Razafindralamo, Évêché Anglican, 12 rue Rabezavana, Ambodifilao, 101 TNR Antananarivo, Madagascar   *Tel:* 261 20 24 39162
Fax: 261 20 226 1331
email: eemtma@hotmail.com/eemdanta@dts.mg

Treasurer Mr Philip Tse Rai (*same address*)

Chancellor of the Province Mrs Hilda Yerriah, 4 rue Commerson, Beau Bassin
Tel: 230 20 80429 (Office)
230 46 75710 (Home)
email: hilda5885@hotmail.com

Dean of the Province Rt Revd Jean-Claude Andrianjafimanana (*Bishop of Mahajanga*)

THEOLOGICAL COLLEGES
St Paul's College, Ambatohararana, Merimandroso, Ambohidratrimo, Madagascar (*Warden* Revd Vincent Rakotoarisoa)

St Paul's College, Rose Hill, Mauritius (*Warden* Vacancy)

St Philip's Theological College, La Misère, Seychelles (*Diocesan Trainer* The Revd Peter Raath)

CHURCH PAPERS
Newsletters of the Province of the Indian Ocean Support Assn. *Editor* The Revd Philip Harbridge, Chaplain, Christ's College, Cambridge CB2 3BY, UK

Seychelles Diocesan Magazine A quarterly newspaper covering diocesan events and containing articles of theological and other interest.

Magazine du Diocèse de Maurice (Le Cordage) A quarterly newspaper covering diocesan events and containing articles of theological and ecumenical interest.

ANTANANARIVO
Bishop Rt Revd Samoela Jaona Ranarivelo, Évêché Anglican, Lot VK57 ter, Ambohimanoro, 101 Antananarivo, Madagascar   *Tel:* 261 20 222 0827
Fax: 261 20 226 1331
email: eemdanta@dts.mg
Assistant Bishop Rt Revd Todd MacGregor (*Tulear*) (*same address*)

ANTSIRANANA
Bishop Rt Revd Roger Chung Po Chuen, Évêché Anglican, BP 278, 4 rue Grandidier, 201 Antsiranana, Madagascar   *Tel:* 261 20 82 2 2650
email: mgrchungpo@blueline.mg

FIANARANTSOA
Bishop Rt Revd Gilbert Rateloson Rakotondravelo, Évêché Anglican Manantsara, BP 1418 Fianarantsoa, Madagascar
Tel: 261 20 75 51583
261 33 14 043 36 (Mobile)
email: eemdiofianara@yahoo.fr

MAHAJANGA
Bishop Rt Revd Jean-Claude Andrianjafimanana, BP 570, Rue de Temple Ziona, Mahajanga 401, Madagascar   *Tel:* 261 62 23611
261 32 04 55143 (Mobile)
email: andrianjajc@yahoo.fr/eemdmaha@dts.mg

MAURITIUS
Bishop Most Revd Ian Gerald Ernest (*Archbishop of the Province*), Bishop's House, Ave. Nallétamby, Phoenix, Mauritius
Tel: 230 686 5158
230 787 8131 (Mobile)
Fax: 230 697 1096
email: dioang@intnet.mu

SEYCHELLES
Bishop Rt Revd Santosh Marray, PO Box 44, Victoria, Mahé, Seychelles
Tel: 248 32 1977/32 3879
248 52 7770 (Mobile)
Fax: 248 22 4043
email: angdio@seychelles.net/
smarray@hotmail.com
Web: www.seychelles.anglican.org

TOAMASINA
Bishop Rt Revd Jean Paul Solo, Évêché Anglican, Rue James Seth, BP 531, Toamasina 501, Madagascar   *Tel:* 261 20 533 1663
261 32 04 55143 (Mobile)
Fax: 261 20 533 1689
email: eemtoam@wanadoo.mg

The Church of Ireland

Members 410,000

Tracing its origins to St Patrick and his companions in the fifth century, the Irish Church has been marked by strong missionary efforts. In 1537 the English king was declared head of the Church, but most Irish Christians maintained loyalty to Rome. The Irish Church Act of 1869 provided that the statutory union between the Churches of England and Ireland be dissolved and that the Church of Ireland should cease to be established by law. A General Synod of the Church, established in 1871 and consisting of archbishops, bishops, and representatives of the clergy and laity, has legislative and administrative power. Irish Church leaders have played a key role in the work of reconciliation in the Northern Ireland conflict.

The Primate of All Ireland and Metropolitan Most Revd Alan Edwin Thomas Harper (*Archbishop of Armagh*)

Central Office of the Church of Ireland Church of Ireland House, Church Ave, Rathmines, Dublin 6, Republic of Ireland   *Tel:* 353 1 497 8422
Fax: 353 1 497 8821
email: office@rcbdub.org

Chief Officer and Secretary, Representative Church Body Mr Denis Reardon
email: chiefofficer@rcbdub.org

Head of Synod Services and Communications Mrs Janet Maxwell   *email:* comms@rcbdub.org

THEOLOGICAL INSTITUTE
The Church of Ireland Theological College, Braemor Park, Rathgar, Dublin 14, which conducts courses in conjunction with the School of Hebrew, Biblical and Theological Studies, Trinity College, Dublin, Republic of Ireland (*Principal* Dr Maurice Elliott)   *Tel:* 353 1 492 3506
Fax: 353 1 492 3082

CHURCH PAPER
Church of Ireland Gazette (weekly) Deals with items of general interest to the Church of Ireland in a national context and also contains news from the various dioceses and parishes together with articles of a more general nature. *Editor/Editorial Offices* 3 Wallace Ave, Lisburn, Co Antrim BT27 4AA   *Tel:* 44 28 9267 5743
Fax: 44 28 9266 7580
email: gazette@ireland.anglican.org

PROVINCE OF ARMAGH
ARMAGH
Archbishop Most Revd Alan Edwin Thomas Harper (*Primate of the Church of Ireland*),

c/o Church House, 46 Abbey Street, Armagh BT61 7DZ   *Tel:* 44 28 3752 2858
Fax: 44 28 3751 0596
email: archbishop@armagh.anglican.org
Web: www.ireland.anglican.org

CATHEDRAL CHURCH OF ST PATRICK, Armagh
Dean Very Revd Patrick Rooke, The Deanery, Library House, 43 Abbey Street, Armagh BT61 7DY   *Tel:* 44 28 3752 3142 (Office)
Tel: 44 28 3751 8447 (Home)
Fax: 44 28 3752 4177
email: dean@armagh.anglican.org

CLOGHER
Bishop Rt Revd Dr Michael Geoffrey St Aubyn Jackson, The See House, Fivemiletown, Co Tyrone, BT75 0QP   *Tel and Fax:* 44 28 8952 2475
email: bishop@clogher.anglican.org

CATHEDRAL CHURCHES OF ST MACARTAN, Clogher, and ST MACARTIN, Enniskillen
Dean Very Revd Raymond Craigmile Thompson, The Deanery, 10 Augher Rd, Clogher, Co Tyrone BT76 0AD   *Tel:* 44 28 8554 9797
email: dean@clogher.anglican.org

CONNOR
Bishop Rt Revd Alan Francis Abernethy, Diocesan Office, Church of Ireland House, 61–67 Donegall Street, Belfast BT1 2QH
Tel: 44 28 9032 2268
email: bishop@connor.anglican.org

CATHEDRAL CHURCH OF ST SAVIOUR, Lisburn
Dean Very Revd John Frederick Augustus Bond, The Rectory, 49 Rectory Gardens, Broughshane, Ballymena, Co Antrim, BT42 4LF
Tel and Fax: 44 28 2586 1215
email: skerry@connor.anglican.org

CATHEDRAL CHURCH OF ST ANNE, Belfast
(Cathedral of the United Dioceses of Down and Dromore and the Diocese of Connor)
Dean Very Revd Robert Samuel James Houston McKelvey, The Deanery, 5 Deramore Drive, Belfast BT9 5JQ   *Tel:* 44 28 9066 0980 (Home)
44 28 9032 8332 (Cathedral)
Fax: 44 28 9023 8855
email: dean@belfastcathedral.org

DERRY AND RAPHOE
Bishop Rt Revd Kenneth Raymond Good, The See House, 112 Culmore Rd, Londonderry, Co Derry BT48 8JF   *Tel:* 44 28 7126 2440
Fax: 44 28 7135 2554
email: bishop@derry.anglican.org

CATHEDRAL CHURCH OF ST COLUMB, Derry
Dean Very Revd William Wright Morton, The Deanery, 30 Bishop St, Londonderry, Co Derry BT48 6PP   *Tel:* 44 28 7126 2746
email: dean@derry.anglican.org

CATHEDRAL CHURCH OF ST EUNAN, Raphoe
Dean Very Revd John Hay, The Deanery, Raphoe, Co Donegal   *Tel:* 353 74 914 5226

DOWN AND DROMORE
Bishop Rt Revd Harold Creeth Miller, The See House, 32 Knockdene Park South, Belfast BT5 7AB   *Tel:* 44 28 9023 7602
Fax: 44 28 9023 1902
email: bishop@down.anglican.org
Web: www.ireland.anglican.org

CATHEDRAL CHURCH OF THE HOLY AND UNDIVIDED TRINITY, Down
Dean Very Revd Thomas Henry Hull, Lecale Rectory, 9 Quale Road, Downpatrick, Co Down BT30 6SE   *Tel:* 44 28 4461 3101
Fax: 44 28 4461 4456

CATHEDRAL CHURCH OF CHRIST THE REDEEMER, Dromore
Dean Very Revd Stephen Harold Lowry, Dromore Cathedral Rectory, 28 Church Street, Dromore, Co Down BT25 1AA
Tel: 44 28 9269 2275 (Home)
44 28 9269 3968 (Office)
email: cathedral@dromore.anglican.org

KILMORE, ELPHIN AND ARDAGH
Bishop Rt Revd Kenneth Herbert Clarke, 48 Carrickfern, Cavan, Co Cavan, Republic of Ireland   *Tel:* 353 49 437 2759
email: bishop@kilmore.anglican.org
Web: www.ireland.anglican.org

CATHEDRAL CHURCH OF ST FETHLIMIDH, Kilmore
Dean Very Revd W. R. Ferguson, Danesfort, Cavan, Co Cavan, Republic of Ireland
Tel and *Fax:* 353 49 433 1918
email: dean@kilmore.anglican.org

CATHEDRAL CHURCH OF ST MARY THE VIRGIN AND ST JOHN THE BAPTIST, Sligo, Republic of Ireland
Dean Very Revd Arfon Williams, The Deanery, Strandhill Road, Sligo, Co Sligo, Republic of Ireland   *Tel:* 353 71 915 7993

TUAM, KILLALA AND ACHONRY
Bishop Rt Revd Dr Richard Crosbie Aitken Henderson, Bishop's House, Knockglass, Crossmolina, Co Mayo, Republic of Ireland
Tel: 353 96 31317
Fax: 353 96 31775
email: bptuam@iol.ie
Web: www.ireland.anglican.org

CATHEDRAL CHURCH OF ST MARY, Tuam
Dean Very Revd Alastair John Grimason, Deanery Place, Cong, Co Mayo, Republic of Ireland   *Tel:* 353 94 954 6017
email: deantuam@hotmail.com

CATHEDRAL CHURCH OF ST PATRICK, Killala
Dean Very Revd Susan Margaret Patterson, St

Michael's Rectory, Ballina, Co Mayo, Republic of Ireland   *Tel:* 353 96 77894
email: kilmoremoy@killala.anglican.org

PROVINCE OF DUBLIN
CASHEL, WATERFORD, LISMORE, OSSORY, FERNS AND LEIGHLIN
Bishop Rt Revd Dr Michael Andrew James Burrows, Bishop's House, Troysgate, Co Kilkenny, Republic of Ireland
Tel: 353 56 77 86633
email: ballymodanbr@eircom.net
Web: www.ireland.anglican.org

CATHEDRAL CHURCH OF ST JOHN THE BAPTIST AND ST PATRICK'S ROCK, Cashel
Dean Very Revd Philip John Knowles, The Deanery, Cashel, Co Tipperary, Republic of Ireland   *Tel:* 353 62 61232 (Home)
353 62 61944 (Office)

CATHEDRAL CHURCH OF THE BLESSED TRINITY (CHRIST CHURCH), Waterford
Dean Very Revd Trevor Rashleigh Lester, The Deanery, 41 Grange Park Rd, Waterford, Co Waterford, Republic of Ireland
Tel: 353 51 874119
email: dean@waterford.anglican.org

CATHEDRAL CHURCH OF ST CARTHAGE, Lismore
Dean Very Revd William Beare, The Deanery, The Mall, Lismore, Co Waterford, Republic of Ireland
Tel and *Fax:* 353 58 54105

CATHEDRAL CHURCH OF ST CANICE, Kilkenny
Dean Very Revd Norman Noel Lynas, The Deanery, Kilkenny, Republic of Ireland
Tel: 353 56 772 1516
Fax: 353 56 775 1817
email: dean@ossory.anglican.org

CATHEDRAL CHURCH OF ST EDAN, Ferns
Dean Very Revd Leslie David Arthur Forrest, The Deanery, Ferns, Enniscorthy, Co Wexford, Republic of Ireland   *Tel:* 353 53 936 6124
Fax: 353 53 936 6985
email: dean@ferns.anglican.org

CATHEDRAL CHURCH OF ST LASERIAN, Leighlin
Dean Very Revd Frederick John Gordon Wynne, The Deanery, Old Leighlin, Muine Bheag, Co. Carlow, Republic of Ireland

CORK, CLOYNE AND ROSS
Bishop Rt Revd William Paul Colton, The Palace, Bishop St, Cork, Co Cork, Republic of Ireland
Tel: 353 21 431 6114
email: bishop@ccrd.ie
Web: www.cork.anglican.org

CATHEDRAL CHURCH OF ST FIN BARRE, Cork
Dean Very Revd N. K. Dunne, The Deanery, 9 Dean St, Cork, Republic of Ireland
Tel: 353 21 496 4742 (Office)
email: dean@cork.anglican.org

CATHEDRAL CHURCH OF ST COLMAN, Cloyne
Dean Very Revd Alan Gordon Marley, The Deanery, Dungourney Road, Midleton, Co Cork, Republic of Ireland   *Tel:* 353 21 463 1449
email: dean@cloyne.anglican.org

CATHEDRAL CHURCH OF ST FACHTNA, Ross
Dean Very Revd Christopher Lind Peters, The Deanery, Rosscarbery, Co Cork, Republic of Ireland   *Tel:* 353 23 48166
email: peters@esatclear.ie

DUBLIN AND GLENDALOUGH
Archbishop Most Revd John Robert Winder Neill, The See House, 17 Temple Rd, Dartry, Dublin 6, Republic of Ireland   *Tel:* 353 1 497 7849
Fax: 353 1 497 6355
email: archishop@dublin.anglican.org

CATHEDRAL CHURCH OF THE HOLY TRINITY (COMMONLY CALLED CHRIST CHURCH)
Cathedral of the United Dioceses of Dublin and Glendalough, Metropolitan Cathedral of the United Provinces of Dublin and Cashel

Dean Very Revd Dermot Patrick Martin Dunne, 24 Wainsfort Monor Crescent, Terenure, Dublin 6W   *Tel:* 353 1 499 1571
353 1 677 8099 (Cathedral)
Fax: 353 1 679 8991
email: dean@dublin.anglican.org

THE NATIONAL CATHEDRAL AND COLLEGIATE CHURCH OF ST PATRICK, Dublin
(The 'National Cathedral of the Church of Ireland having a common relation to all the dioceses of Ireland')
Dean and Ordinary Very Revd Robert Brian MacCarthy, The Deanery, Upper Kevin St, Dublin 8, Republic of Ireland
Tel: 353 1 475 5449 (Home)
353 1 475 4817 (Cathedral)
353 1 453 9472 (Office)
Fax: 353 1 454 6374

LIMERICK, ARDFERT, AGHADOE, KILLALOE, KILFENORA, CLONFERT, KILMACDUAGH AND EMLY
Bishop Rt Revd Trevor Russell Williams, Rien Roe, Adare, Co Limerick, Republic of Ireland
Tel: 353 61 396 244
email: bishop@limerick.anglican.org
Web: www.ireland.anglican.org

CATHEDRAL CHURCH OF ST MARY, Limerick
Dean Very Revd John Maurice Glover Sirr, The Deanery, 7 Kilbane, Castletroy, Limerick, Republic of Ireland   *Tel* and *Fax:* 353 61 338 697
087 2541121 (Mobile)
email: dean@limerick.anglican.org

CATHEDRAL CHURCH OF ST FLANNAN, Killaloe
Dean Very Revd Stephen Ross White, The Deanery, Killaloe, Co Clare, Republic of Ireland
Tel: 353 61 376 687
email: dean@killaloe.anglican.org

CATHEDRAL CHURCH OF ST BRENDAN, Clonfert
Dean Very Revd Stephen Ross White (*as above*)

MEATH AND KILDARE
Bishop Most Revd Richard Lionel Clarke, Bishop's House, Moyglare, Maynooth, Co Kildare, Republic of Ireland   *Tel:* 353 1 628 9354
Fax: 353 1 628 9696
email: bishop@meath.anglican.org
Web: www.ireland.anglican.org/meath/
meath.html

CATHEDRAL CHURCH OF ST PATRICK, Trim
Dean of Clonmacnoise Very Revd Robert William Jones, St Patrick's Deanery, Loman St, Trim, Co Meath, Republic of Ireland   *Tel:* 353 46 943 6698

CATHEDRAL OF ST BRIGID, Kildare
Dean Very Revd John Joseph Marsden, The Deanery, Morristown, Newbridge, Co Kildare, Republic of Ireland   *Tel:* 353 45 438 158

The Anglican Communion in Japan
(Nippon Sei Ko Kai)

Members 35,000
In 1859 the American Episcopal Church sent two missionaries to Japan, followed some years later by representatives of the Church of England and the Church in Canada. The first Anglican Synod took place in 1887. The first Japanese bishops were consecrated in 1923. The Church remained oppressed during the Second World War and assumed all church leadership after the war.

Primate Most Revd Nathaniel Makoto Uematsu
(*Bishop of Hokkaido*)

Provincial Office Nippon Sei Ko Kai, 65–3 Yarai-
cho, Shinjuku-ku, Tokyo 162–0805 (Please use this address for all correspondence)
Tel: 81 3 5228 3171
Fax: 81 3 5228 3175
email: province@nskk.org
Web: www.nskk.org

General Secretary Revd John Makito Aizawa
email: general-sec.po@nskk.org

Provincial Treasurer Mr Matthias Shigeo Ozaki

THEOLOGICAL TRAINING
Central Theological College, 1–12–31 Yoga, Setagaya-ku, Tokyo 158–0097, for clergy and lay workers

Bishop Williams Theological School, Shimotachiuri-agaru, Karasuma Dori, Kamikyo-ku, Kyoto 602–8332

CHURCH NEWSPAPERS
Sei Ko Kai Shimbun Published on the twentieth of each month in Japanese. Usually eight pages, tabloid format. Subscription through the Provincial Office. Each diocese also has its own monthly paper.

NSKK News English-language newsletter. Published quarterly. Available through the Provincial Office and also on the web page of Anglican Communion.

CHUBU
Bishop Rt Revd Francis Toshiaki Mori, 28–1 Meigetsu-cho, 2-chome, Showa-ku, Nagoya 466–0034
Tel: 81 52 858 1007
Fax: 81 52 858 1008
email: office.chubu@nskk.org
Web: www.nskk.org/chubu

HOKKAIDO
Bishop Most Revd Nathaniel Makoto Uematsu (*Archbishop of the Province*), Kita 15 jo, Nishi 5-20, Kita-Ku, Sapporo 001-0015
Tel: 81 11 717 8181
Fax: 81 11 736 8377
email: hokkaido@nskk.org
Web: www.nskk.org/hokkaido

KITA KANTO
Bishop Rt Revd Zerubbabel Katsuichi Hirota, 2–172 Sakuragi-cho, Omiya-ku, Saitama-shi, 331–0852
Tel: 81 48 642 2680
Fax: 81 48 648 0358
email: kitakanto@nskk.org
Web: www.nskk.org/kitakanto

KOBE
Bishop Rt Revd Andrew Yutaka Nakamura, 5–11–1 Yamatedori, Chuo-ku, Kobe-shi 650–0011
Tel: 81 78 351 5469
Fax: 81 78 382 1095
email: aao52850@syd.odn.ne.jp
Web: www.nskk.org/kobe

KYOTO
Bishop Rt Revd Stephen Takashi Kochi, 380 Okakuencho, Shimotachiuri-agaru, Karasuma-dori, Kamikyo-ku, Kyoto 602–8011
Tel: 81 75 431 7204
Fax: 81 75 441 4238
email: nskk-kyoto@mse.biglobe.ne.jp
Web: www.nskk.org/kyoto

KYUSHU
Bishop Rt Revd Gabriel Shoji Igarashi, 2–9–22 Kusakae, Chuo-ku, Fukuoka 810–0045
Tel: 81 92 771 2050
Fax: 81 92 771 9857
email: d-kyushu@try-net.or.jp
Web: http://www1.bbiq.jp/d-kyushu

OKINAWA
Bishop Rt Revd David Shoji Tani, 3–5–5 Meada, Urasoe-shi, Okinawa 910-2102
Tel: 81 98 942 1101
Fax: 81 98 942 1102
email: office.okinawa@nskk.org
Web: www.nskk.org/okinawa

OSAKA
Bishop Rt Revd Samuel Osamu Ohnishi, 2–1–8 Matsuzaki-cho, Abeno-ku, Osaka 545–0053
Tel: 81 6 6621 2179
Fax: 81 6 6621 3097
email: office.osaka@nskk.org
Web: www.nskk.org/osaka

TOHOKU
Bishop Rt Revd John Hiromichi Kato, 2-13-15 Kokubun-cho, Aoba-ku, Sendai 980-0803
Tel: 81 22 223 2349
Fax: 81 22 223 2387
email: hayashi.tohoku@nskk.org
Web: www.nskk.org/tohoku

TOKYO
Bishop Rt Revd Peter Jintaro Ueda, 3-6-18 Shiba Koen, Minato-ku, Tokyo 105-0011
Tel: 81 3 3433 0987
Fax: 81 3 3433 8678
email: office.tko@nskk.org
Web: www.nskk.org/tokyo

YOKOHAMA
Bishop Rt Revd Laurence Yutaka Minabe, 14-57 Mitsuzawa Shimo-cho, Kanagawa-ku, Yokohama 221-0852
Tel: 81 45 321 4988
Fax: 81 45 321 4978
email: yokohama.kyouku@nskk.org
Web: anglican.jp/yokohama

The Episcopal Church in Jerusalem and the Middle East

Members 10,000
The Church comprises the dioceses of Jerusalem, Iran, Egypt, Cyprus, and the Gulf. The Jerusalem bishopric was founded in 1841 and became an archbishopric in 1957. Reorganization in January 1976 ended the archbishopric and combined the Diocese of Jordan, Lebanon and Syria with the Jerusalem bishopric after a 19-year separation. Around the same time, the new Diocese of Cyprus and the Gulf was formed and the Diocese of Egypt was revived. The Cathedral Church of St George the Martyr in Jerusalem is known for its ministry to pilgrims. St George's College, Jerusalem is in partnership with the Anglican Communion.

Anglican and Porvoo Communions

THE CENTRAL SYNOD

President-Bishop Most Revd Mouneer Hanna Anis (*Bishop in Egypt with North Africa and the Horn of Africa*)

Provincial Secretary The Revd Hanna Mansour, PO Box 3, Doha, Qatar
Tel and *Fax:* (Qatar) 974 442 4329
email: tianyoung@hotmail.com

Acting Provincial Treasurer Revd Canon William Schwartz, PO Box 87, Zamalek, Cairo 11211, Egypt
Tel: 202 738 0829
Fax: 202 735 8941
email: bishopmouneer@link.net

The Jerusalem and the Middle East Church Association acts in support of the Episcopal Church in Jerusalem and the Middle East, the Central Synod and all four dioceses. *Secretary* Mrs Vanessa Wells, 1 Hart House, The Hart, Farnham, Surrey GU9 7HA *Tel:* 01252 726994
Fax: 01252 735558
*email:*secretary@jmeca.eclipse.co.uk

CYPRUS AND THE GULF

Bishop in Rt Revd Michael Augustine Owen Lewis, PO Box 22075, Nicosia 1517, Cyprus
Tel: 357 22 671220
Fax: 357 2 22 674553
email: bishop@spidernet.com.cy
Web: www.cyprusgulf.anglican.org

EGYPT WITH NORTH AFRICA AND THE HORN OF AFRICA

Bishop in Rt Revd Mouneer Hanna Anis (*President Bishop of the Episcopal Church of Jerusalem and the Middle East*), Diocesan Office, PO Box 87, Zamalek Distribution, 11211, Cairo, Egypt
Tel: 20 2 738 0829
Fax: 20 2 735 8941
email: bishopmouneer@link.net
Web: www.dioceseofegypt.org

Suffragan Rt Revd Andrew Proud (*Horn of Africa*) (*same address*)

Assistant Bishop Rt Revd Derek Lionel Eaton (*Diocese of Egypt*) (*same address*)

IRAN

Bishop in Rt Revd Azad Marshall, St Thomas Center, Raiwind Road, PO Box 688, Lohore, Punjab, 54000, Pakistan *Tel:* 92 42 542 0452
email: bishop@saintthomascenter.org

JERUSALEM

Bishop in Rt Revd Suheil Dawani, St George's Close, PO Box 1278, Jerusalem 91 019, Israel
Tel: 972 2 627 1670
Fax: 972 2 627 3847
email: bishop@j-diocese.com
Web: www.j-diocese.org

The Anglican Church of Kenya

Members 3,500,000

Mombasa saw the arrival of Anglican missionaries in 1844, with the first African ordained to the priesthood in 1885. Mass conversions occurred as early as 1910. The first Kenyan bishops were consecrated in 1955. The Church became part of the Province of East Africa, established in 1960, but by 1970 Kenya and Tanzania were divided into separate provinces.

Primate Most Revd Benjamin M. Nzimbi (*Bishop of All Saints Cathedral Diocese*) PO Box 40502, 00100 Nairobi *Tel:* 254 2 714 755
Fax: 254 2 718 442
email: archoffice@swiftkenya.com
Web: www.ackenya.org

Provincial Secretary Rt Revd Lawrence Dena (Assistant Bishop of Mombasa)
Tel: 254 2 271 4752/3/4
Fax: 254 2 271 4750
email: ackenya@insightkenya.com/
psd@akenya.org

Provincial Treasurer Dr William Ogara, Corat Africa, PO Box 42493, 00100 Nairobi
Tel: 254 2 890 165/6
Fax: 254 2 891 900/890 481

THEOLOGICAL COLLEGES

ACK Language School and Orientation School, PO Box 47429, Nairobi *Tel:* 254 2 721893
email: c/o ackenya@insightkenya.com

ACK Guest House, PO Box 56292, Nairobi
Tel: 254 2 723200/2724780
email: ackghouse@insightkenya.com

ACK St Julian's Centre, PO Box 574, Village Market 00621 *Tel:* 254 66 76221
email: ackstjulians@swiftkenya.com

ACK Guest House Mombasa, PO Box 96170, Likoni, Mombasa
email: ackmsaghouse@swiftkenya.com

Carlile College for Theology & Business Studies, PO Box 72584, Nairobi *Tel:* 254 2 558596/253
email: Williams@insightkenya.com

St Andrews College of Theology and Development Kabare, PO Box 6, Kerugoya
Tel: 254 60 21256
email: ackstandrewskabare@swiftkenya.com

Berea Theological College, PO Box 1945, Nakuru
Tel: 254 51 51295
email: berea-tc@africaonline.co.ke

St Paul's Theological College, Kapsabet, PO Box
18, Kapsabet   *Tel:* 254 53 2053
  email: ackstpaulskapsabet@africaonline.co.ke
St Philip's Theological College Maseno, PO Box
1, Maseno   *Tel:* 254 57 51019

Bishop Hannington Institute Mombasa, PO Box
81150, Mombasa   *Tel:* 254 41 491396
  email: ackbhanning-msa@swiftmombasa.com

Provincial TEE Programme (Trinity College), PO
Box 72430, Nairobi   *Tel:* 254 2 558655/542607
  email: acktrinitycollege@swiftkenya.com

Church Commissioners for Kenya, PO Box 30422,
00100 Nairobi   *Tel:* 254 20 717106
  email: churchcom@insightkenya.com

Uzima Press, PO Box 48127, Nairobi
                      Tel: 254 20 220239/216836
                      email: uzima@nbnet.co.ke

ALL SAINTS CATHEDRAL DIOCESE
Most Revd Benjamin M. Nzimbi (*Archbishop of
Kenya*), PO Box 40502, 00100 Nairobi
                      Tel: 254 20 714 755
                      Fax: 254 20 718 442/714 750
                      email: archoffice@swiftkenya.com

BONDO
Bishop Rt Revd Johannes Otieno Angela, PO Box
240, 40601 Bondo   *Tel:* 254 57 5 20415
  email: ackbondo@swiftkenya.com

BUNGOMA
Bishop Rt Revd Eliud Wabukala, PO Box 2392,
50200 Bungoma   *Tel* and *Fax:* 254 337 30481
  email: ackbungoma@swiftkenya.com

BUTERE
Bishop Rt Revd Michael Sande, PO Box 54, 50101
Butere   *Tel:* 254 56 620 412
                           Fax: 254 56 620 038
  email: ackbutere@swiftkenya.com

ELDORET
Bishop Rt Revd Thomas Kogo, PO Box 3404,
30100 Eldoret   *Tel:* 254 53 62785
  email: ackeldoret@africaonline.co.ke

EMBU
Bishop Rt Revd Henry Tiras Nyaga Kathii, PO
Box 189, 60100 Embu   *Tel:* 254 68 30614
                           Fax: 254 68 30468
  email: ackembu@swiftkenya.com

KAJIADO
Bishop Rt Revd John Mutua Taama, PO Box 203,
01100 Kajiado   *Tel:* 254 301 21201/05
                       Fax: 254 301 21106
  email: ackajiado@swiftkenya.com

KATAKWA
Bishop Rt Revd Zakayo Iteba Epusi, PO Box 68,
50244 Amagoro   *Tel:* 254 55 54079
  email: ackatakwa@swiftkenya.com

KIRINYAGA
Bishop Rt Revd Daniel Munene Ngoru, PO Box
95, 10304 Kutus   *Tel:* 254 163 44221
                           Fax: 254 163 44 020
  email: ackirinyaga@swiftkenya.com

KITALE
Bishop Rt Revd Stephen Kewasis Nyorsok, PO
Box 4176, 30200 Kitale   *Tel:* 254 325 31631
  email: ack.ktl@africaonline.co.ke

KITUI
Bishop Rt Revd Josephat Mule, PO Box 1054,
90200 Kitui   *Tel:* 254 141 22682
                           Fax: 254 141 22119
  email: ackitui@swiftkenya.com

MACHAKOS
Bishop Rt Revd Mutie Kanuku, PO Box 282,
90100 Machakos   *Tel:* 254 145 21379
                           Fax: 254 145 20178
  email: ackmachakos@swiftkenya.com

MASENO NORTH
Bishop Rt Revd Simon M. Oketch, PO Box 416,
50100 Kakemega   *Tel* and *Fax:* 254 331 30729
  email: ackmnorth@swiftkenya.com

MASENO SOUTH
Bishop Rt Revd Francis Mwayi Abiero, PO Box
114, 40100 Kisumu   *Tel:* 254 35 21297
                           Fax: 254 35 21009
  email: ackmsouth@swiftkenya.com

MASENO WEST
Bishop Rt Revd Joseph Otieno Wasonga, PO Box
793, 40600 Siaya   *Tel:* 254 334 21483
                           Fax: 254 334 21483
  email: ackmwest@swiftkenya.com

MBEERE
Bishop Rt Revd Gideon G. Ireri, PO Box 122,
60104 Siakago   *Tel:* 254 162 21261
                           Fax: 254 162 21083
  email: ackmbeere@swiftkenya.com

MERU
Bishop Rt Revd Charles Mwendwa, PO Box 427,
60200 Meru   *Tel:* 254 164 30719
  email: ackmeru@swiftkenya.com

MOMBASA
Bishop Rt Revd Julius R. K. Kalu, PO Box 80072,
80100 Mombasa   *Tel:* 254 41 231 1105
                           Fax: 254 41 231 6361
  email: ackmsa@swiftmombasa.com

Assistant Bishop Rt Revd Lawrence Dena (*same
address*)

MOUNT KENYA CENTRAL
Bishop Rt Revd Isaac Maina Ng'ang'a, PO Box
121, 10200 Murang'a   *Tel:* 254 60 30560/30559
                      Fax: 254 60 30148
  email: ackmkcentral@wananchi.com

Assistant Bishop Rt Revd Allan Waithaka (*same address*)

MOUNT KENYA SOUTH
Bishop Rt Revd Timothy Ranji, PO Box 886, 00900 Kiambu   *Tel:* 254 66 22521/22997
Fax: 254 66 22408
email: ackmtksouth@swiftkenya.com

MOUNT KENYA WEST
Bishop Rt Revd Joseph M. Kagunda, PO Box 229, 10100 Nyeri   *Tel:* 254 61 203 2281
email: ackmtkwest@wananchi.com

MUMIAS
Bishop Rt Revd Beneah Justin Okumu Salalah, PO Box 213, 50102 Mumias   *Tel:* 254 333 41476
Fax: 254 333 41232
email: ackmumias@swiftkenya.com

NAIROBI
Bishop Rt Revd Peter Njagi Njoka, PO Box 40502, 00100 Nairobi   *Tel:* 254 2 714 755
Fax: 254 2 226 259
email: acknairobi@swiftkenya.com

NAKURU
Bishop Rt Revd Stephen Njihia Mwangi, PO Box 56, 20100 Nakuru   *Tel:* 254 37 212 155/1
Fax: 254 37 44379
email: acknkudioc@net2000ke.com

Suffragan Bishop Rt Revd Jackson Ole Sapit (*Kericho Diocese*) (*same address*)

NAMBALE
Bishop Rt Revd Josiah M. Were, PO Box 4, 50409 Nambale   *Tel:* 254 336 24040
Fax: 254 336 24040
email: acknambale@swiftkenya.com

NYAHURURU
Bishop Rt Revd Charles Gaikia Gaita, PO Box 926, 20300 Nyahururu   *Tel:* 254 365 32179
email: nyahu_dc@africaonline.co.ke

SOUTHERN NYANZA
Bishop Rt Revd James Kenneth Ochiel, PO Box 65, 40300 Homa Bay   *Tel:* 254 385 22127
Fax: 254 385 22056
email: acksnyanza@swiftkenya.com

TAITA TAVETA
Bishop Rt Revd Samson M. Mwaluda, PO Box 75, 80300 Voi   *Tel:* 254 147 30096
Fax: 254 147 30364
email: acktaita@swiftmombasa.com

THIKA
Bishop Rt Revd Gideon G. Githiga, PO Box 214, 01000 Thika   *Tel:* 254 151 21735/31654
Fax: 254 151 31544
email: ackthika@swiftkenya.com

The Anglican Church in Korea

Members 14,558

From the time when Bishop John Corfe arrived in Korea in 1890 until 1965, the Diocese of Korea has had English bishops. In 1993 the Archbishop of Canterbury installed the newly elected Primate and handed jurisdiction to him, making the Anglican Church of Korea a province of the Anglican Communion. There are four religious communities in the country as well as an Anglican university.

Primate Most Revd Solomon Jong Mo Yoon (*Bishop of Pusan*)

Provincial Offices 3 Chong-dong, Chung-ku, Seoul 100–120   *Tel:* 82 2 738 8952
Fax: 82 2 737 4210
email: abgwk@hanmail.net

Secretary-General Revd Gwang Joon Kim (*same address*)   *Tel:* 82 2 738 8952
Fax: 82 2 737 4210
email: abgwk@hanmail.net
Web: www.skh.or.kr

ANGLICAN UNIVERSITY
(*Songkonghoe Daehak*) # 1 Hand-dong, Kuro-ku, Seoul 152–140 (*President* Rt Revd Simon S. Kim)
Fax: 82 2 737 4210

CHURCH PAPER
Daehan Songgonghoesinmun This fortnightly paper of the Anglican Church of Korea is the joint concern of all three dioceses. Newspaper format. Printed in Korean. Contains regular liturgical and doctrinal features as well as local, national and international church news.   *Tel:* 82 2 736 6990
Fax: 82 2 738 1208

PUSAN
Bishop Rt Revd Solomon Jong Mo Yoon (*Archbishop of the Province*), Anglican Diocese of Pusan, 18 Daechengdong-2ga, Chung-Ku, Pusan 600–092   *Tel:* 82 51 463 5742
Fax: 82 51 463 5957
email: yoonsjm@hanmail.net

SEOUL
Bishop Most Revd Paul Keun Sang Kim, Anglican Diocese of Seoul, 3 Chong-Dong, Chung-Ku, Seoul 100–120   *Tel:* 82 2 735 6157
Fax: 82 2 723 2640
email: paulkim7@hitel.net

TAEJON
Bishop Most Revd Michael Hi Yeon Kwon, Anglican Diocese of Taejon, 87–6 Sunwha 2don, Chung-Ku, Taejon 302–823   *Tel:* 82 42 256 9987
Fax: 82 42 255 8918
email: tdio@unitel.co.kr

ANGLICAN AND PORVOO COMMUNIONS

The Church of the Province of Melanesia

Members 250,000
After 118 years of missionary association with the Church of the Province of New Zealand, the Church of the Province of Melanesia was formed in 1975. The province encompasses the Republic of Vanuatu and the Solomon Islands, both sovereign island nations in the South Pacific, and the French Trust Territory of New Caledonia.

Archbishop of the Province Vacancy, Provincial Headquarters, PO Box 19, Honiara, Solomon Islands   *Tel:* 677 26601
                                    Fax: 677 27447
        email: bishop_vunagi@solomom.com.sb

General Secretary Mr George Kiriau (*same address*)
                                    Tel: 677 20470
        email: kiriau_g@comphq.org.sb

ANGLICAN THEOLOGICAL COLLEGE
Bishop Patteson Theological College, Kohimarama, PO Box 19, Honiara, Solomon Islands (trains students up to degree standard) (*Principal* Revd Philemon Akao)   *Tel:* 677 29124
                                    Fax: 677 21098

BANKS AND TORRES
Bishop Rt Revd Nathan Tome, PO Box 19, Sola, Vanualava, Torba Province, Republic of Vanuatu
                        Tel and *Fax:* 678 38520

CENTRAL MELANESIA
Bishop Vacancy, PO Box 19, Honiara, Solomon Islands   *Tel:* 677 26101
                                    Fax: 677 21435

CENTRAL SOLOMONS
Bishop Rt Revd Charles Koete, PO Box 52, Tulagi, CIP, Solomon Islands   *Tel:* 677 32006
                                    Fax: 677 32113

HANUATO'O
Bishop Rt Revd Jonnie Kuper, PO Box 20, Kira Kira, Makira Province, Solomon Islands
                                    Tel: 677 50012
        email: dhanuatoo@solomon.com.sb

MALAITA
Bishop Rt Revd Dr Terry Michael Brown, Bishop's House, PO Box 7, Auki Malaita Province, Solomon Islands   *Tel:* 677 40125
        email: terrymalaita@yahoo.com/
                    domauki@solomon.com.sb

TEMOTU
Bishop Rt Revd David Vunagi, Bishop's House, Lata, Santa Cruz, Temotu Province, Solomon Islands   *Tel:* 677 53080

VANUATU
Bishop Rt Revd James Marvin Ligo, Bishop's House, PO Box 238, Luganville, Santo, Republic of Vanuatu   *Tel* and *Fax:* 678 37065/36631
        email: diocese_of_vanuatu@ecunet.org/
                    comdov@vanuatu.com.vu

YSABEL
Bishop Rt Revd Richard Naramana, Bishop's House, PO Box 6, Buala, Jejevo, Ysabel Province, Solomon Islands   *Tel:* 677 35124
        email: episcopal@solomon.com.sb

The Anglican Church of Mexico

Members 21,000
The Mexican Episcopal Church began with the political reform in 1857, which secured freedom of religion, separating the Roman Catholic Church from the government and politics. Some priests organized a National Church and contacted the Episcopal Church in the United States, seeking the ordination of bishops for the new church. They adopted the name 'Mexican Episcopal Church'. The Mexican Church became an autonomous province of the Anglican Communion in 1995 with the name Iglesia Anglicana de Mexico.

Archbishop Rt Revd Carlos Touché-Porter (*Bishop of Mexico*)

Provincial Secretary Revd Canon Habacuc Ramos

Huerta, Calle La Otra Banda # 40, Col. San Angel, Delegación Alvaro Obregón, 01000 México
            Tel: 52 55 5616 2490/5550 4073
                        Fax: 52 55 5616 4063
*email:*ofipam@att.net.mx / habacuc_mx@yahoo.es

Provincial Treasurer C. P. Edgar Gómez-González (*same address*)   *email:* ofipam@att.net.mx

CUERNAVACA
Bishop Rt Revd Ramiro Delgado-Vera, Calle Minerva No 1, Col. Delicias, CP 62330 Cuernavaca, Morelos, México
    Tel and *Fax:* 52 777 315 2870/322 8035 (Office)
                    52 777 322 2559 (Home)
        email: adoc@cableonline.com.mx

MEXICO

Bishop Most Revd Carlos Touché Porter (*Archbishop of the Province*), Ave San Jerónimo 117, Col. San Ángel, Delegación Álvaro Obregón, 01000 México, D.F.　　　*Tel:* 52 55 5616 3193
　　　　　　　　　　　Fax: 52 55 5616 2205
　　　　email: diomex@netvoice.com.mx

NORTHERN MEXICO

Bishop Rt Revd Marcelino Rivera Delgado, Simón Bolivar 2005 Norte, Col. Mitras Centro, CP 64460, Monterrey, NL　　　　　*Tel:* 52 81 8333 0992
　　　　　　　　　　　Fax: 52 81 8348 7362
　　email: diocesisdelnorte@prodigy.net.mx

SOUTHEASTERN MEXICO

Bishop Rt Revd Benito Juárez-Martínez, Avenida de Las Américas #73, Col. Aguacatal, 91130 Xalapa, Veracruz　　　　*Tel:* 52 228 814 6951
　　　　　　　　　　Fax: 52 228 814 4387
　　　　　email: dioste99@aol.com

WESTERN MEXICO

Bishop Rt Revd Lino Rodríguez-Amaro, Francisco Javier Gamboa #255, Col. Sector Juárez, 44100 Guadalajara, Jalisco
　　　　　　　　　　Tel: 52 33 3560 4726
　　　　　　　　　　Fax: 52 33 3616 4413
　　email: iamoccidente@prodigy.net.mx

The Church of the Province of Myanmar (Burma)

Members 63,845

Anglican chaplains and missionaries worked in Burma in the early and mid-nineteenth century. The Province of Myanmar was formed in 1970, nine years after the declaration of Buddhism as the state religion and four years after all foreign missionaries were forced to leave.

Archbishop of the Province Most Revd Stephen Than Myint Oo (*Bishop of Yangon*)

Provincial Secretary Mr Kenneth Saw, PO Box 11191, 140 Pyidaungsu Yeiktha Rd, Dagon, Yangon　　　　　　　*Tel:* 95 1 395279
　　　　　　　　　　　Fax: 95 1 395350
　　　　email: cpm.140@mptmail.net.mm

Provincial Treasurer Daw Myint Htwe Ye (*same address*)

Secretary and Treasurer, Yangon Diocesan Trust Association Daw Pin Lone Soe (*same address*)

ANGLICAN THEOLOGICAL COLLEGES
Holy Cross Theological College, 104 Inya Rd, University PO (11041), Yangon (*Principal* Dr. Simon Be Bin Htu)

Emmanuel Theological College, Mohnyin, Kachin State (*Principal* Bishop David Than Lwin)

CHURCH NEWSLETTER
The province publishes a monthly 36-page *Newsletter*. *Editor and Manager* Mr Saw Peter Aye, PO Box 11191, Bishopscourt, 140 Pyidaungsu Yeiktha Rd, Dagon, Yangon

HPA-AN

Bishop Rt Revd Saw Stylo, No (4) Block, Bishop Gone, Diocesan Office, Hpa-an, Kayin State
　　　　　　　　　　　Tel: 95 58 21696

MANDALAY

Bishop Rt Revd Noel Nay Lin, Bishopscourt, 22nd St, 'C' Rd (between 85–86 Rd), Mandalay
　　　　　　　　　　　Tel: 95 2 34110

Assistant Bishop Rt Revd Philip Aung Khin Thein (*same address*)

MYITKYINA

Bishop Rt Revd David Than Lwin, Diocesan Office, Tha Kin Nat Pe Rd, Thida Ya, Myitkyina
　　　　　　　　　　　Tel: 95 74 23104

Assistant Bishop Rt Revd Gam Dee (*same address*)

SITTWE

Bishop Rt Revd Barnabas Theaung Hawi, St John's Church, Paletwa, Southern Chin State, Via Sittwe

TOUNGOO

Bishop Rt Revd Saw (John) Wilme, Diocesan Office, Nat Shin Naung Rd, Toungoo
　　　　　　　　　Tel: 95 54 21 519 (office)
　　　　　　　　　　95 54 24216 (home)

YANGON

Bishop Most Revd Stephen Than Myint Oo (*Archbishop of the Province*), PO Box 11191, 140 Pyidaungsu-Yeiktha Rd, Dagon, Yangon
　　　　　　Tel: 95 1 395279/395350 (office)
　　　　　　　　　　95 1 381909 (home)

Assistant Bishop Vacancy

ANGLICAN AND PORVOO COMMUNIONS

The Church of Nigeria

(Anglican Communion)

Members 17,500,000
The rebirth of Christianity began with the arrival of Christian freed slaves in Nigeria in the middle of the nineteenth century. The Church Missionary Society established an evangelistic ministry, particularly in the south. The division of the Province of West Africa in 1979 formed the Province of Nigeria and the Province of West Africa. In the 1990s, nine missionary bishops consecrated themselves to evangelism in northern Nigeria. Membership growth has dictated the need for new dioceses year by year. In 1997 the Church of Nigeria was divided into three provinces to enable more effective management. In 1999 another twelve dioceses were created, and in January 2003 the Church was re-organized into ten provinces.

Primate of All Nigeria Most Revd Peter Jasper Akinola (*Archbishop of the Province of Abuja and Bishop of Abuja*)

General Secretary Ven Oluranti Odubogun, Episcopal House, PO Box 212, AD CP, Abuja
Tel: 234 9 523 6950
email: abuja@anglican.skannet.com.ng
Web: www.anglican-nig.org

Provincial Treasurer Mr J. N. Aziagba (*same address*)
email: treasurer@anglican-nig.org

THEOLOGICAL COLLEGES
Immanuel College (Ecumenical), PO Box 515, Ibadan

Trinity College (Ecumenical), Umuahia, Imo State

Vining College, Akure, Ondo State

St Francis of Assisi College, Wusasa, Zaria

Crowther College of Theology, Okene, Kogi State

Ezekiel College of Theology, Ujoelen, Ekpoma, Edo State

Please note: The Church of Nigeria is growing very fast. The compilers are aware that there are new dioceses that are not listed here, but at the time of going to press insufficient information was available to include these. Please refer to the Church of Nigeria web site for further information:
www.anglican-nig.org

PROVINCE OF ABUJA
Archbishop Most Revd Peter Jasper Akinola (*Primate of All Nigeria and Bishop of Abuja*)

ABUJA
Bishop Most Revd Peter Jasper Akinola (*Primate of All Nigeria and Archbishop of the Province of Abuja*), Archbishop's Palace, PO Box 212, ADCP, Abuja
Tel: 234 9 524 0496
email: primate@anglican-nig.org

BIDA
Bishop Rt Revd Jonah Kolo, Bishop's House, St John's Mission Compound, PO Box 14, Bida
Tel: 234 66 460 178
email: bida@anglican-nig.org

GWAGWALADA
Bishop Rt Revd Tanimu Samari Aduda, PO Box 287, Gwagwalada, F.C.T., Abuja
Tel: 234 9 882 2083
email: gwagwalada@anglican-nig.org

IDAH
Bishop Rt Revd Joseph N. Musa, Bishop's Lodge, PO Box 25, Idah, Kogi State
Tel: 234 803 385 4463 (Mobile)
email: idah@anglican-nig.org

IJUMU
Bishop Rt Revd Ezekiel Ikupolati

KAFANCHAN
Bishop Rt Revd William Diya, PO Box 29, Kafanchan, Kaduna State *Tel:* 234 61 20 634

KUBWA
Bishop Rt Revd Simon Bala, St. Andrew's Church, Opposite Julius Berger Camp, Gado Nasko Road, Phase II Site I, *Tel:* 234 9 672 4063
234 803 590 0267 (Mobile)
email: kubwa@anglican-nig.org

KUTIGI
Bishop Rt Revd Jeremiah Ndana Kolo

LAFIA
Bishop Rt Revd Miller Kangdim Maza, PO Box 560, Lafia, Nasarawa State *Tel:* 234 47 221 329

LOKOJA
Bishop Rt Revd Emmanuel Egbunu, PO Box 11, Lokoja, Kogi State *Tel:* 234 58 220 588
Fax: 234 58 221 788
email: lokoja@anglican-nig.org

MAKURDI
Bishop Rt Revd Nathaniel Inyom, Bishopscourt, PO Box 1, Makurdi, Benue State
Tel and Fax: 234 44 533 349
email: makurdi@anglican-nig.org/
makurdi@anglican.skannet.com.ng

MINNA
Bishop Rt Revd Nathaniel Yisa, PO Box 2469, Minna, Niger State *Tel:* 234 66 220 035 (Office)
234 66 220 515 (Home)

OKENE
Bishop Rt Revd Emmanuel Bayo Ajulo

OTUKPO
Bishop Rt Revd David K. Bello, St John's Cathedral, Sgt Ugbade Ave, PO Box 0360, Otukpo, Benue State   *Tel*: 234 44 663 312
    email: anglicandioceseofotukpo@yahoo.com/
                    bishopdkbello@yahoo.com

ZONKWA (Missionary diocese)
Bishop Rt Revd Duke T. Akamisoko, Bishop's Residence, PO Box 21, Zonkwa, Kaduna State 802002   *Tel*: 234 803 451 9437 (Mobile)
          email: zonkwa@anglican-nig.org

PROVINCE OF BENDEL
Archbishop Most Revd Nicholas D. Okoh (*Bishop of Asaba*)

AKOKO-EDO
Bishop Rt Revd Gabriel Akinbiyi

ASABA
Bishop Most Revd Nicholas D. Okoh (*Archbishop of the Province of Bendel*), Bishopscourt, PO Box 216, Cable Point, Asaba, Delta State
          Tel: 234 56 280 682
          email: asaba@anglican-nig.org

BENIN
Bishop Rt Revd P. O. J. Imasuen, Bishopscourt, PO Box 82, Benin City, Edo State
          Tel: 234 803 079 9560 (Mobile)
          email: petglad2002@yahoo.com

ESAN
Bishop Rt Revd Friday John Imakhai, Bishopscourt, Ujoelen, PO Box 921, Ekpoma, *email:* Edo State   *Tel*: 234 55 981 29
          email: bishopfriday@hotmail.com

IKA
Bishop Rt Revd Peter Onekpe, St John's Cathedral, PO Box 1063, Agbor, 321001 Delta State   *Tel:* 234 55 250-14
          email: ika@anglican-nig.org/bishoppeter@
                    yahoo.com

NDOKWA
Bishop Rt Revd David Obiosa

OLEH
Bishop Rt Revd Jonathan F. E. Edewor, JP, PO Box 8, Oleh, Delta State
          Tel: 234 803 549 4215 (Mobile)
          email: oleh@anglican-nig.org/angoleh2000@
                    yahoo.com

SABONGIDDA-ORA
Bishop Rt Revd John Akao, Bishopscourt, PO Box 13, Sabongidda-Ora, Edo State
          Tel: 234 57 54 049
          email: akao@cashette.com

UGHELLI
Bishop Rt Revd Vincent O. Muoghereh, Bishopscourt, Ovurodawanre, PO Box 760, Ughelli, Delta State   *Tel:* 234 53 258 307
                    234 802 302 9906 (Mobile)

WARRI
Bishop Rt Revd Christian Ideh, Bishopscourt, 17 Mabiaku Rd, GRA, PO Box 4571, Warri, Delta State   *Tel:* 234 53 255 857
          email: warri@anglican-nig.org

WESTERN IZON (Missionary diocese)
Bishop Rt Revd Edafe Emamezi, Bishopscourt, PO Box 56, Sagbama, River State
          Tel: 234 806 357 2263 (Mobile)
          email: anglizon@yahoo.co.uk

PROVINCE OF IBADAN
Archbishop Most Revd Joseph Akinfenwa (*Bishop of Ibadan*)

AJAYI CROWTHER
Bishop Rt Revd Olukemi Oduntan, Bishopscourt, Iseyin, PO Box 430, Iseyin, Oyo State
          Tel: 234 837 198 182 (Mobile)
          email: ajayicrowtherdiocese@yahoo.com

ETIKI KWARA
Bishop Rt Revd Andrew Ajayi

IBADAN
Bishop Most Revd Joseph Akinfenwa (*Archbishop of the Province of Ibadan*), PO Box 3075, Mapo, Ibadan   *Tel:* 234 2 810 1400
                    Fax: 234 2 810 1413
          email: ibadan@anglican-nig.org/
                    bishop@skannet.com

IBADAN-NORTH
Bishop Rt Revd Dr Segun Okubadejo, Bishopscourt, Moyede, PO Box 28961, Agodi, Ibadan   *Tel:* 234 2 8107 482
          email: angibn@skannet.com

IBADAN-SOUTH
Bishop Rt Revd Jacob Ademola Ajetunmobi, Bishopscourt, PO Box 166, Dugbe, Ibadan
          Tel and Fax: 234 2 231 6464
          email: ibadan-south@anglican-nig.org/
                    jacajet@skannet.com

IFE
Bishop Rt Revd Oluranti Odubogun, Bishopscourt, PO Box 312, Ile-Ife, Osun State
          Tel: 234 36 232 255
          email: stphilipscathayetoroife@yahoo.com

IFE EAST
Bishop Rt Revd Rufus Okeremi

IGBOMINA
Bishop Rt Revd Michael O. Akinyemi, Bishopscourt, Esie, PO Box 102, Oro P.A, Kwara State
          Tel: 234 31 700 0025
          email: igbomina@anglican-nig.org

ANGLICAN AND PORVOO COMMUNIONS

ILESA
Bishop Rt Revd Dr Samuel O. Sowale, Bishopscourt, Oke-Ooye, PO Box 237, Ilesa
Tel: 234 36 460 138
email: ilesha@anglican-nig.org/
bishop-solwale@yahoo.com

KWARA
Bishop Rt Revd Dr Olusegun Adeyemi, Bishopscourt, Fate Rd, PO Box 1884, Ilorin, Kwara State
Tel: 234 31 220 879
email: angkwa@skannet.com

OFFA
Bishop Rt Revd Gabriel A. Akinbiyi, PO Box 21, Offa, Kwara State
Tel: 234 31 801 011
email: offa@anglican-nig.org

OGBOMOSO (Missionary diocese)
Bishop Rt Revd Dr Matthew Osunade, Bishop's House, PO Box 1909, Ogbomoso, Osun State
Tel: 234 803 524 4606 (Mobile)
email: ogbomoso@anglican-nig.org/
maaosunade@yahoo.com

OKE-OSUN
Bishop Rt Revd Nathaniel Fasogbon, Bishopscourt, PO Box 251, Gbongan, Osun State
Tel: 234 803 356 9384 (Mobile)

OMU-ARAN
Bishop Rt Revd Philip Adeyemo, Bishop's House, Expressway, PO Box 224, Omu-Aran, Kwara State
Tel: 234 05 673 7052

OSUN
Bishop Rt Revd James Afolabi Popoola, Bishopscourt, Isale-Aro, PO Box 285, Osogbo
Tel: 234 35 240 325
234 803 356 1628 (Mobile)
email: osun@anglican-nig.org

OYO
Bishop Rt Revd Jacob Ola Fasipe, Bishopscourt, PO Box 23, Oyo
Tel: 234 38 240 225
234 803 857 2120 (Mobile)
email: oyo@anglican-nig.org

PROVINCE OF JOS
Archbishop Most Revd Emmanuel K. Mani (*Bishop of Maiduguri*)

BAUCHI
Bishop Rt Revd Musa Tula, Bishop's House, 2 Hospital Rd, PO Box 2450, Bauchi
Tel: 234 77 546 066
email: bauchi@anglican-nig.org

DAMATURU
Bishop Rt Revd Abiodun Ogunyemi, PO Box 312, Damaturu, Yobe State
Tel: 234 74 522 142
email: damaturu@anglican-nig.org

GOMBE
Bishop Rt Revd Henry C. Ndukuba, Bishopscourt, PO Box 1509, Gombe, Gombe State, 760001 Nigeria
Tel: 234 72 221 212
email: gombe@anglican-nig.org/
ndukubah@yahoo.com

JALINGO
Bishop Rt Revd Timothy Yahaya, PO Box 4, Jalingo, Taraba State 660001
Tel and Fax: 234 79 223 812
email: jalingo@anglican.skannet.com.ng

JOS
Bishop Rt Revd Benjamin A. Kwashi, Bishopscourt, PO Box 6283, Jos, 930001, Plateau State
Tel: 234 73 464 325
234 803 701 7928 (Mobile)
email: jos@anglican-nig.org

LANGTANG
Bishop Rt Revd Stanley Fube

MAIDUGURI
Bishop Most Revd Emmanuel K. Mani (*Archbishop of the Province of Jos*), Bishopscourt, Off Lagos St, GRA PO Box 1693, Maiduguri, Borno State
Tel and Fax: 234 76 234 010
234 802 374 7463 (Mobile)
email: maiduguri@anglican-nig.org

PANKSHIN
Bishop Rt Revd Olumuyiwa Ajayi, Diocesan Secretariat, PO Box 24, Pankshin, Plateau State
Tel: 234 803 344 7318 (Mobile)
email: olumijayi@yahoo.com

YOLA
Bishop Rt Revd Markus A. Ibrahim, PO Box 601, Jimeta-Yola, Adamawa State
Tel: 234 75 624 303
234 805 175 9508 (Mobile)
email: yola@anglican-nig.org/
marcusibrahim2002@yahoo.com

PROVINCE OF KADUNA
Archbishop Most Revd Josiah Idowu-Fearon (*Bishop of Kaduna*)

BARI
Bishop Rt Revd Idris Zubairu

DUTSE
Bishop Rt Revd Yusuf Ibrahim Lumu, PO Box 6, Yadi, Dutse, Jigawa State
Tel: 234 64 721 379
234 803 583 9381 (Mobile)
email: dutse@anglican-nig.org

GUSAU
Bishop Rt Revd John G. Danbinta, PO Box 64, Gusau, Zamfara State
Tel: 234 63 204 747
email: gusau@anglican-nig.org

KADUNA
Bishop Most Revd Josiah Idowu-Fearon (*Archbishop of the Province of Kaduna*), PO Box 72, Kaduna
Tel: 234 62 240 085
Fax: 234 62 244 408
email: kaduna@anglican-nig.org

KANO
Bishop Rt Revd Zakka Lalle Nyam, Bishopscourt, PO Box 362, Kano   *Tel* and *Fax:* 234 64 647 816
email: kano@anglican-nig.org

KATSINA
Bishop Rt Revd Jonathan Bamaiyi, Bishop's Lodge, PO Box 904, Katsina   *Tel:* 234 65 432 718
234 803 601 5584 (Mobile)
email: bpjonathanbamaiyi@yahoo.co.uk

KEBBI
Bishop Rt Revd Edmund E. Akanya, PO Box 701, Birnin Kebbi, Kebbi State
Tel and *Fax:* 234 68 321 179
email: kebbi@anglican-nig.org/
kebbi@anglican.skannet.com

KWOI
Bishop Rt Rvd Paul Samuel Zamani

SOKOTO
Bishop Rt Revd Augustine Omole, Bishop's Lodge, 68 Shuni Road, PO Box 3489, Sokoto
Tel: 234 60 234 639/
232 323
email: sokoto@anglican-nig.org

WUSASA
Bishop Rt Revd Ali Buba Lamido, PO Box 28, Wusasa, Zaria, Kaduna State   *Tel:* 234 69 334 594
email: wusasa@anglican.skannet.com.ng

PROVINCE OF LAGOS
Archbishop Most Revd Ephraim Adebola Ademowo (*Bishop of Lagos*)

AWORI
Bishop Rt Revd Johnson Akinwamide Atere

BADAGRY (Missionary diocese)
Bishop Rt Revd Babatunde J. Adeyemi, Bishopscourt, Kunle Gardens, Seme Road, Iyaafin Junction, PO Box 7, Badagry, Lagos State
Tel: 234 1 773 5546
234 803 306 4601 (Mobile)
email: badagry@anglican-nig.org

EGBA
Bishop Rt Revd Dr Matthew O. Owadayo, Bishopscourt, Onikolobo, PO Box 267, Ibara, Abeokuta   *Tel:* 234 39 240 933
234 803 319 2799 (Mobile)
Fax: 234 39 240 933
*email:*egba@anglican-nig.org/
mowadayo@yahoo.com

IJEBU
Bishop Rt Revd Ezekiel Awosoga, Bishopscourt, Ejinrin Rd, PO Box 112, Ijebu-Ode
Tel: 234 37 432 886
234 803 352 9600 (Mobile)
email: ijebu@anglican-nig.org/
bishop@ang-ijebudiocese.com

IJEBU NORTH
Bishop Rt Revd Solomon Kuponu, Bishopscourt, PO Box 6, Ijebu-Igbo, Ogun State
Tel: 234 803 457 8506 (Mobile)
email: dioceseofijebunorth@yahoo.com

LAGOS
Bishop Most Revd E. Adebola Ademowo (*Archbishop of the Province of Lagos*), 29 Marina, PO Box 13, Lagos   *Tel:* 234 1 263 5930
email: lagos@anglican.skannet.com.ng/
diocesan@dioceseoflagos.org

LAGOS MAINLAND
Bishop Rt Revd Adebayo Akinde, PO Box 45, Ebute-Metta, Lagos
Tel: 234 803 854 6712 (Mobile)

LAGOS WEST
Bishop Rt Revd Peter A. Adebiyi, PO Box 506, Ikeja, Lagos State   *Tel:* 234 1 493 7336/7/8
email: lagoswest@anglican-nig.org/
dioceseoflagoswest@yahoo.com

ON THE COAST
Bishop Rt Revd Joshua Ogunele, Bishopscourt, Ikoya Rd, P. M. B. 3, Ilutitun-Osooro, Ondo State
Tel: 234 805 634 5496 (*Mobile*)

REMO
Bishop Rt Revd Michael O. Fape, Bishopscourt, Ewusi St, PO Box 522, Sagamu, Ogun State
Tel: 234 37 640 598
email: remo@anglican-nig.org/
mofape@skannet.com

YEWA
Bishop Rt Revd Simeon O. M. Adebola, Bishopscourt, PO Box 484, Ilaro, Ogun State
Tel: 234 1 7924 0696
234 802 379 6166 (Mobile)

MISSIONS PROVINCE
NOMADIC MISSION
Bishop Rt Revd Simon P. Mutum, PO Box 381, Bukuru Jos, Plateau State
Tel: 234 803 623 4030 (mobile)
email: anglicannomadic@yahoo.co.uk /
angnomadic@yahoo.com

PROVINCE OF THE NIGER
Archbishop Most Revd Maxwell S. C. Anikwenwa (*Bishop of Awka*)

ABAKALIKI
Bishop Rt Revd Benson C. B. Onyeibor, All Saints' Cathedral, PO Box 112, Abakaliki, Ebonyi State   *Tel:* 234 43 220 762
234 803 501 3083 (Mobile)
email: abakaliki@anglican-nig.org

AGUATA
Bishop Rt Revd Christian Ogochukwo Efobi, Bishopscourt, PO Box 1128, Ekwulobia, Anambra State   *Tel:* 234 803 750 1077 (Mobile)
email: aguata@anglican-nig.com

ANGLICAN AND PORVOO COMMUNIONS

AWGU-ANINRI
Bishop Rt Revd Emmanuel Agwu, Bishopscourt, PO Box 305, Awgu, Enugu State
Tel: 234 803 334 9360 / 805 731 4775 (Mobile)

AWKA
Bishop Most Revd Maxwell S. C. Anikwenwa (*Archbishop of the Province of The Niger*), Bishopscourt, Ifite Rd, PO Box 130, Awka, Anambra State   *Tel*: 234 48 550 058
email: awka@anglican-nig.org/
anglawka@infoweb.com.ng

ENUGU
Bishop Rt Revd Dr Emmanuel O. Chukwuma, Bishop's House, PO Box 418, Enugu, Enugu State   *Tel*: 234 42 453 804
email: enugu@anglican-nig.org

IHIALA
Bishop Rt Revd Ralph Okafor

MBAMMILI
Bishop Rt Revd Henry Okeke

NNEWI
Bishop Rt Revd Godwin I. N. Okpala, Bishopscourt, PO Box 2630, Nnewi, Anambra State   *Tel*: 234 46 311 253/308 580
email: nnewi@anglican-nig.org/
nnewianglican@infoweb.abs.net

NSUKKA
Bishop Rt Revd Alloysius Agbo, PO Box 516, Nsukka, Enugu State
Tel: 234 804 612 5318 (Mobile)
email: nsukka@anglican-nig.org

OJI RIVER
Bishop Rt Revd Amos A. Madu, PO Box 213, Oji River, Enugu State   *Tel*: 234 42 882 219
234 803 670 4888 (Mobile)
email: ojiriver@anglican-nig.org

ON THE NIGER
Bishop Rt Revd Ken Okeke, Bishopscourt, PO Box 42, Onitsha, Anambra State
Tel: 234 46 410 337
email: niger@anglican-nig.org/
kengoziokeke@yahoo.com

PROVINCE OF NIGER DELTA
Archbishop Vacancy

ABA
Bishop Rt Revd Ugochuckwu U. Ezuoke, Bishopscourt, 70/72 St Michael's Rd, PO Box 212, Aba, Abia State   *Tel*: 234 82 308 431
email: aba@anglican-nig.org/
abanglifoserve@hotmail.com

ABA AGWA NORTH
Bishop Rt Revd John C. Ezim, Bishopscourt, PO Box 43, Aba, Abia State   *Tel*: 234 803 822 4623
email: jcezirim@yahoo.com

AHOADA
Bishop Rt Revd Clement Nathan Ekpeye, Bishopscourt, St Paul's Cathedral, PO Box 4, Ahoada East L.G.A., Rivers State
Tel: 234 803 542 2847 (Mobile)
email: ahoada@anglican-nig.org

AROCHUKWU-OHAFIA (Missionary diocese)
Bishop Rt Revd Johnson C. Onuoha, Bishopscourt, PO Box 193, Arochukwu, Abia State
Tel: 234 803 717 0234 (Mobile)
email: arooha@anglican-nig.org/
johnchiobishop@yahoo.com

CALABAR
Bishop Rt Revd Tunde Adeleye, Bishopscourt, PO Box 74, Calabar, Cross River State
Tel: 234 98 232 812
234 803 337 3120 (Mobile)
email: calabar@anglican-nig.org/
bishoptunde@yahoo.com

ETCHE
Bishop Rt Revd Okechukwu Precious Nwala, Bishopscourt, PO Box 89, Okehi, Etche Rivers State   *Tel*: 234 807 525 2842 (Mobile)
email: etchediocese@yahoo.com/
precious_model5@yahoo.com

IKWERRE
Bishop Rt Revd Blessing Enyindah, Bishopscourt, PO Box 14229, Port Harcourt, Rivers State
Tel: 234 802 321 2824 (Mobile)
email: blessingenyinday@yahoo.com

IKWUANO
Bishop Rt Revd Chigozirim Onyegbule, Bishopscourt, PO Box 5, Oloko, Ikwuano, Abia State   *Tel*: 234 803 085 9310 (Mobile)
email: ikwuano@anglican-nig.org

ISIALA NGWA
Bishop Rt Revd Owen N. Azubuike, Bishopscourt, St George's Cathedral Compound, Umuomainta Mbawsi P.M.B., Mbawsi, Abia State   *Tel*: 234 805 467 0528 (Mobile)
email: bpowenazubuike@yahoo.com

ISIALA NGWA SOUTH
Bishop Rt Revd Isaac Nwaobia, St Peter's Cathedral, PO Box 15, Owerrinta, Abia State
Tel: 234 805 787 1100
email: bishopisaacnwaobia@priest.com

ISIUKWUATO (Missionary diocese)
Bishop Rt Revd Samuel C. Chukuka, Bishop's House, PO Box 350, Ovim, Abia State
Tel: 234 803 338 6221 (Mobile)
email: isiukwuato@anglican-nig.org/
rootedword@yahoo.com

NIGER DELTA
Bishop Rt Revd Gabriel Pepple, PO Box 115, Port Harcourt, Rivers State   *Tel*: 234 84 233 308
email: nigerdelta@anglican-nig.org

NIGER DELTA NORTH
Bishop Rt Revd Ignatius Kattey, PO Box 53, Diobu, Port Harcourt, Rivers State
Tel: 234 84 231 338
email: niger-delta-north@anglican-nig.org/ nigerdeltanorth@yahoo.com

NIGER DELTA WEST
Bishop Rt Revd Adolphus Amabebe, Bishopscourt, PO Box 10, Yenagoa, Bayelsa State
Tel: 234 803 372 5982 (Mobile)
email: niger-delta-west@anglican-nig.org

NORTHERN IZON
Bishop Rt Revd Anga Fred Nyanabo

OGBAI
Bishop Rt Revd James Oruwori

OGONI (Missionary diocese)
Bishop Rt Revd Solomon S. Gberegbara, Bishopscourt, PO Box 73, Bori-Ogoni, Rivers State
Tel: 234 803 339 2545 (Mobile)
email: ogoni@anglican-nig.org/ ogoniangdiocese@yahoo.com

OKRIKA
Bishop Rt Revd Tubokosemie Abere, Bishopscourt, PO Box 11, Okrika, Rivers State
Tel: 234 84 575 003
234 803 312 5226 (Mobile)
email: dioceseofokrika@yahoo.com

UKWA
Bishop Rt Revd Samuel K. Eze, PO Box 20468, Aba, Abia State   Tel: 234 803 789 2431 (Mobile)
email: ukwa@anglican-nig.org/ kelerem53787@yahoo.com

UMUAHIA
Bishop Rt Revd Ikechi N. Nwosu, Bishopscourt, PO Box 96, Umuahia, Abia State
Tel: 234 88 220 311
234 803 549 9066 (Mobile)
email: umuahia@anglican-nig.org

UYO
Bishop Isaac Orama, Bishopscourt, PO Box 70, Uyo, Akwa Ibom State   Tel: 234 85 202 440
234 803 710 7894
email: uyo@anglican-nig.org

PROVINCE OF ONDO
Archbishop Most Revd Samuel Adedayo Abe (*Bishop of Ekiti*)

AKOKO
Bishop Rt Revd Dr O. O. Obijole, PO Box 572, Ikare-Akoko, Ondo State   Tel: 234 50 670 209
email: akoko@anglican.skannet.com.ng

AKURE
Bishop Rt Revd Michael O. Ipinmoye, Bishopscourt, PO Box 1622, Akure, Ondo State
Tel and Fax: 234 34 231 012
234 803 717 4561 (Mobile)
email: angdak@gannetcity.net/ akure@anglican-nig.org

EKITI
Bishop Most Revd Samuel A. Abe (*Archbishop the Province of Ondo*), Bishopscourt, PO Box 12, Ado-Ekiti, Ekiti State   Tel: 234 30 250 305
234 802 225 9389 (Mobile)
email: ekiti@anglican.skannet.com.ng/ ekiti@anglican-nig.org

EKITI-OKE
Bishop Rt Revd Isaac O. Olubowale, Bishopscourt, PO Box 207, Usi-Ekiti, Ekiti State
Tel: 234 803 600 9582 (Mobile)
email: ekitioke@anglican-nig.org

EKITI-WEST
Bishop Rt Revd Samuel O. Oke, Bishop's Residence, 6 Ifaki St, PO Box 477, Ijero-Ekiti
Tel: 234 803 429 2823 (Mobile)
email: ekitiwest@anglican-nig.org

KABBA
Bishop Rt Revd Samuel O. Olayanju, Bishopscourt, Obaro Way, PO Box 62, Kabba, Kogi State
Tel: 234 58 300 633
234 803 653 0180 (Mobile)

ONDO
Bishop Rt Revd George L. Lasebikan, Bishopscourt, College Rd, PO Box 265, Ondo
Tel: 234 34 610 718
234 803 472 1813 (Mobile)
email: ondo@anglican-nig.org/ angond@skannet.com

OWO
Bishop Rt Revd James A. Oladunjoye, Bishopscourt, PO Box 472, Owo, Ondo State
Tel: 234 51 241 463
email: owo@anglican-nig.org

PROVINCE OF OWERRI
Archbishop Most Revd Bennett C. I. Okoro (*Bishop of Orlu*)

EGBU
Bishop Rt Revd Prof. Emmanuel U. Iheagwam, All Saints' Cathedral, PO Box 1967, Owerri, Imo State   Tel: 234 83 231 797
234 803 491 1090 (Mobile)
email: egbu@anglican-nig.org

IDEATO
Bishop Rt Revd Caleb A. Maduomo, Bishopscourt, PO Box 2, Arondizuogu, Imo State
Tel: 234 803 745 4503 (Mobile)
email: ideato@anglican-nig.org/ bpomacal@hotmail.com

MBAISE
Bishop Rt Revd Bright J. E. Ogu, Bishopscourt, PO Box 10, Ife, Ezinihitte Mbaise, Imo State
Tel: 234 782 441 483
234 803 553 4762 (Mobile)
email: mbaise@anglican-nig.org/ bjeogu@yahoo.com

OJAHI-EGBEMA
Bishop Rt Revd Chidi Oparaojiaku

OKIGWE NORTH
Bishop Rt Revd Alfred I. S. Nwaizuzu, PO Box 156, Okigwe, Imo State
Tel: 234 806 475 8139 (Mobile)
email: okigwenorth@anglican-nig.org/
alfrednwaizuzu@yahoo.com

OKIGWE SOUTH
Bishop Rt Revd David Onuoha, Bishopscourt, Ezeoke Nsu, PO Box 235, Nsu, Ehime Mbano LGA, Imo State   *Tel:* 234 8037 454 510 (Mobile)
email: okigwe-south@anglican-nig.org/
okisouth@yahoo.com

ORLU
Bishop Most Revd Bennett C. I. Okoro (*Archbishop of the Province of Owerri*), Bishopscourt, PO Box 260, Nkwerre, Imo State   *Tel:* 234 82 440 538
234 803 671 1271 (Mobile)

OWERRI
Bishop Rt Revd Dr Cyril C. Okorocha, No. 1 Mission Crescent, PMB 1063, Owerri, Imo State
Tel: 234 83 230 784
email: owerri@anglican-nig.org/
adowe@phca.linkserve.com

ON THE LAKE
Bishop Rt Revd Chijioke Oti

The Anglican Church of Papua New Guinea

Members 166,046
Organized as a missionary diocese of Australia in 1898, the Church was part of the Australian province of Queensland until 1977. The first indigenous priest was ordained in 1914. The Anglican Church functions mostly in rural areas where mountains and rainforest provide natural barriers to travel. Some 60 per cent of the funding is raised internally; most of the balance comes from grants from Australia, New Zealand, Canada and the UK-based Papua New Guinea Church Partnership.

Archbishop Most Revd James Simon Ayong (*Bishop of Aipo Rongo*)

General Secretary Mr Charles Dalton, PO Box 673, Lae, Morobe Province   *Tel:* 675 472 4111
Fax: 675 472 1852
email: acpnggensec@global.net.pg

Provincial Registrar Mrs Winifred Kamit, PO Box 1569, Port Moresby, National Capital District
Tel: 675 321 1033
Fax: 675 321 1885
email: wkamit@gadens.com.pg

THEOLOGICAL COLLEGE
Newton Theological College, PO Box 162, Popondetta, Oro Province (*Principal* Br Justus Van Houten, SSF)   *Tel:* 675 329 7421
Fax: 675 329 7476
email: acpngntc@global.net.pg
Web: www.newtoncollege-png.org/support.htm

CHURCH PAPER
Family Magazine. Published three times a year. *Editors* Mr and Mrs Hugh Dormer, PO Box 2476, Lae, Morobe Province 411
Tel and *Fax:* 675 472 0537
email: dormer@global.net.pg

AIPO RONGO
Bishop Most Revd James Simon Ayong (*Archbishop of the Church of Papua New Guinea*), PO Box 893, Mt Hagen, Western Highlands Province   *Tel:* 675 542 1131/3727
Fax: 675 542 1181
email: acpngair@global.net.pg/
archbishopjayong@hotmail.com

Suffragan Bishops
Rt Revd Nathan Ingen (*same address*)
Rt Revd Denys Ririka, PO Box 1178, Goroka, Eastern Highlands Province

DOGURA
Bishop Rt Revd Tevita Talanoa, PO Box 19, Dogura, MBP   *Tel:* 675 641 1530
Fax: 675 641 1129

NEW GUINEA ISLANDS
Bishop Rt Revd Allan Migi, Bishop's House, PO Box 806, Kimbe   *Tel* and *Fax:* 675 9 835 120
email: acpngngi@global.net.pg/
acpngngibishop@global.net.pg

POPONDOTA
Bishop Rt Revd Joe Kopapa, Bishop's House, PO Box 26, Popondetta, Oro Province
Tel: 675 329 7194
Fax: 675 329 7476
email: acpngpop@global.net.pg
Web: http://popondota.anglican.org/

PORT MORESBY
Bishop Rt Revd Peter Ramsden, PO Box 6491, Boroko, NCD   *Tel:* 675 323 2489
Fax: 675 323 2493
email: acpngpom@global.net.pg
Web: www.portmoresby.anglican.org

The Episcopal Church in the Philippines

Members 121,000

The Philippines, having been a Spanish colony from 1521 to 1898, is a predominantly Christian and Roman Catholic country. The USA took over from Spain and continued the country's colonization in 1898. That same year, Anglican missionary work began among the indigenous populations in the north and south and among the Chinese and Caucasian groups in the central district. Three dioceses were established by 1972. The Church consecrated its first Filipino bishop in 1959 and became an autonomous province in 1990.

National Office The ECP Mission Center, 275 E Rodriguez Sr Ave, 1102 Quezon City

(Postal address) PO Box 10321, Broadway Centrum, 1112 Quezon City
Tel: 63 2 722 8478/8481
Fax: 63 2 721 1923
email: ecpnational@yahoo.com.ph
Web: www.philippines.anglican.org

Prime Bishop Most Revd Ignacio Capuyan Soliba
(same address)   *email:* isoliba@hotmail.com

Corporate Secretary Mr Victor Ananayo *(same address)*   *email:* ednpvic@hotmail.com

Administrative Assistant Rt Revd Miguel Paredes Yamoyam *(same address)*
email: miguel_yamoyam@yahoo.com.ph

National Finance Officer Mr Wayland Cabanban *(same address)*

CENTRAL PHILIPPINES
Bishop Rt Revd Dixie C. Taclobao, 281 E. Rodriguez Sr. Avenue, 1102 Quezon City
Tel: 63 2 412 8561
Fax: 63 2 724 2143
email: central@i-next.net

NORTH CENTRAL PHILIPPINES
Bishop Rt Revd Joel A. Pachao, 358 Magsaysay Ave, Baguio City 2600   *Tel:* 63 74 443 7705
email: edncp@digitelone.com

NORTHERN LUZON
Bishop Rt Revd Renato M. Abibico, Bulanao, 3800 Tabuk, Kalinga   *Tel:* 63 9921 687 1933 (Mobile)
email: reneabibico@yahoo.com

NORTHERN PHILIPPINES
Bishop Rt Revd Edward Pacyaya Malecdan, Diocesan Center, 2616 Bontoc, Mountain Province   *Tel and Fax:* 63 74 602 1026
email: ednpvic@hotmail.com

SANTIAGO
Bishop Rt Revd Alexander A. Wandag, Maharlika Highway, 3311 Divisoria Santiago City, Isabela
Tel: 63 78 682 3756
Fax: 63 78 682 1256
email: alexwandageds@yahoo.com

SOUTHERN PHILIPPINES
Bishop Rt Revd Danilo Labacanacruz Bustamante, 186 Sinsuat Ave, Rosario Heights, Cotabato City 9600   *Tel:* 63 64 421 2960
Fax: 63 64 421 1703
email: edsp_ecp@yahoo.com

The Church of the Province of Rwanda

Members 1,200,000

In just over 10,170 square miles there are more than one million Anglicans among a fast-growing population, currently eight million. The former Rwanda Mission (now CMS) established its first station at Gahini in 1925 and grew through the revival of the 1930s and 1940s, with the first Rwandan bishop appointed in 1965. Nine dioceses have up to 306 parishes and 379 clergy, organized in 96 deaconries. Like all strata of Rwandan society, the Church suffered, on many levels, through the genocide, and it is a major priority of the Church to replace clergy through training. The Church has a role as a healing ministry to the many traumatized people in Rwanda and to reconciliation, restoration, and rehabilitation. The Church has also been involved in rural development, medical work, vocational training, and education.

Archbishop Most Revd Emmanuel Mbona Kolini *(Bishop of Kigali)*

Dean of the Province Rt Revd Onesphore Rwaje *(Bishop of Byumba)*

Provincial Secretary Revd Emmanuel Gatera, BP 2487, Kigali   *Tel:* 250 514 160
Fax: 250 516 162
email: egapeer@yahoo.com

Provincial Treasurer Vacancy *(same address)*

BUTARE
Bishop Rt Revd Venuste Mutiganda, BP 225, Butare   *Tel and Fax:* 250 530 728
email: rusodilo@yahoo.fr

BYUMBA
Bishop Rt Revd Onesphore Rwaje, BP 17, Byumba   *Tel and Fax:* 250 64 242
email: eer@rwanda1.com

CYANGUGU
Bishop Rt Revd Geoffrey Rwubusisi, BP 52,
Cyangugu   *Tel* and *Fax:* 250 53 7878
            email: bishoprwubusisi@yahoo.co.uk
GAHINI
Bishop Rt Revd Alexis Bilindabagabo, BP 22,
Kigali   *Tel* and *Fax:* 250 567 422

KIBUNGO
Bishop Rt Revd Josias Sendegeya, EER Kibungo
Diocese, BP 719, Kibungo
                             Tel and *Fax:* 250 566 194
                             email: bpjosias@yahoo.fr

KIGALI
Bishop Most Revd Emmanuel M. Kolini
(*Archbishop of the Province*), BP 61, Kigali
                             Tel and *Fax:* 250 573 213
                             email: ek@terracom.rw

KIGEME
Bishop Rt Revd Augustin Mvunabandi, BP 67,
Gikongoro   *Tel:* 250 535 086 (Office)
                             250 535 088 (Secretary)
                             250 535 087 (Home)
                             email: dkigeme@rwanda1.com

SHYIRA
Bishop Rt Revd John Rucyahana Kabango, BP 26,
Ruhengeri   *Tel* and *Fax:* 250 546 449
                             email: bpjohnr@rwanda1.com

SHYOGWE
Bishop Rt Revd Jered Kalimba, BP 27, Gitarama
                             Tel: 250 562 460
                             Tel and *Fax:* 250 562 469
                             email: dsgwegit@yahoo.com

The Scottish Episcopal Church

Members 40, 816
The roots of Scottish Christianity go back to St Ninian in the fourth century and St Columba in the sixth. After the Reformation, the Episcopal Church was the established Church of Scotland. It was however replaced as the established Church by the Presbyterians at the Revolution in 1689. Penal statutes in force from 1746 to 1792 weakened the Church, although many congregations remained and the bishops maintained continuity. In 1784 in Aberdeen, the Scottish Church initiated the world-wide expansion of the Anglican Communion with the consecration of the first bishop of the American Church. There was rapid growth in the nineteenth century influenced by the Tractarian movement.

Primus Most Revd Dr Idris Jones (*Bishop of Glasgow and Galloway*)
                  email: office@glasgow.anglican.org

Secretary General Mr John Stuart, 21 Grosvenor Crescent, Edinburgh EH12 5EE
                             Tel: 0131 225 6357
                             Fax: 0131 346 7247
                  email: secgen@scotland.anglican.org
                  Web: www.scotland.anglican.org

MINISTERIAL TRAINING
The Theological Institute of the Scottish Episcopal Church, 21 Grosvenor Crescent, Edinburgh EH12 5EE   *Tel:* 0131 225 6357
                             Fax: 0131 346 7247
                  email: tisec@scotland.anglican.org

CHURCH MAGAZINE
Inspires, sixteen pages, ten issues yearly. Magazine format. Produced in-house – contact: *inspires*, 21 Grosvenor Crescent, Edinburgh, EH12 5EE   *email:* inspires@scotland.anglican.org

ABERDEEN AND ORKNEY
Bishop Rt Revd Dr Robert Gillies, Diocesan Office, 39 King's Crescent, Aberdeen AB24 3HP
                             Tel: 01224 636653
                             Fax: 01224 636186
                  email: office@aberdeen.anglican.org
                  Web: www.aberdeen.anglican.org

Dean Very Revd Dr AE Nimmo, Diocesan Office, 39 King's Crescent, Aberdeen AB24 3HP
                             Tel: 01224 636653
                  email: alexander306@btinternet.com

ST ANDREW'S CATHEDRAL, Aberdeen
Provost Very Revd Richard Kilgour
                             Tel: 01224 640119 (Office)
                  email: provost@aberdeen.anglican.org

ARGYLL AND THE ISLES
Bishop Rt Revd (Alexander) Martin Shaw, St Moluag's Diocesan Centre, Croft Avenue, Oban, Argyll, PA34 5JJ   *Tel:* 01631 570 870
                             Fax: 01631 570411
                  email: alexandermartin.shaw@virgin.net
                  Web: www.argyllandtheisles.org.uk

Dean Very Revd Norman MacCallum, Rectory, Ardconnel Terrace, Oban PA34 5DJ
                             Tel: 01631 562323

ST JOHN THE DIVINE CATHEDRAL, Oban
(The Cathedral of Argyll)
Provost Very Revd Norman MacCallum, Rectory, Ardconnel Terrace, Oban PA34 5DJ
                             Tel: 01631 562323

COLLEGIATE CHURCH OF THE HOLY SPIRIT, Cumbrae
(The Cathedral of The Isles)
Warden Helen Hamilton   *Tel:* 01475 530353
                             Fax: 01475 530204
                  email: cumbrae@island-retreats.org
                  Web: www.island-retreats.org

BRECHIN
Bishop Rt Revd Dr John Mantle, Diocesan Office. Unit 14 Prospect III, Technology Park, Gemini Crescent, Dundee DD2 1SW *Tel:* 01382 562244
email: office@brechin.anglican.org
Web: www.thedioceseofbrechin.org

Dean Very Rev Ian G Stewart (*same address*)
Fax: 01382 477 434
email: ateallach@aol.com

ST PAUL'S CATHEDRAL, Dundee
Provost Very Rev Lindsay T McKenna, Cathedral Office, Castlehill, 1 High St, Dundee DD1 1TD
Tel: 01382 224486

EDINBURGH
Bishop Rt Revd Brian Arthur Smith, Diocesan Centre, 21a Grosvenor Crescent, Edinburgh EH12 5EL *Tel:* 0131 538 7033
Fax: 0131 538 7088
email: bishop@edinburgh.anglican.org
Web: www.dioceseofedinburgh.org

Dean Very Revd Kevin Pearson (*same address*)
email: pdo@scotland.anglican.org

ST MARY'S CATHEDRAL, Edinburgh
Provost Very Revd Dr Graham John Thomson Forbes, Cathedral Office, Palmerston Place, Edinburgh EH12 5AW *Tel:* 0131 225 6293
Fax: 0131 225 3181
email: provost@cathedral.net

GLASGOW AND GALLOWAY
Bishop Most Revd Dr Idris Jones (*Primus*), Diocesan Centre, 5 St Vincent Place, Glasgow G1 2DH *Tel:* 0141 221 6911
Fax: 0141 221 7014
email: bishop@glasgow.anglican.org
Web: www.glasgow.anglican.org

Dean Very Revd Dr Gregor Duncan, St Ninian's Rectory, 32 Glencairn Drive, Glasgow G41 4PW
Tel: 0141 423 1247
email: dean@glasgow.anglican.org

ST MARY THE VIRGIN CATHEDRAL, Glasgow
Provost Very Revd Kelvin Holdsworth, St Mary's Cathedral, 300 Great Western Rd, Glasgow G4 9JB *Tel:* 0141 339 6691
Fax: 0141 334 5669
email: provost@thecathedral.org.uk

MORAY, ROSS AND CAITHNESS
Bishop Rt Revd Mark Strange, Bishop's House, St John's Rectory, Arpafeelie, North Kessock IV1 1XG *Tel:* 01463 811333
email: bishop@moray.anglican.org
Web: www.morayrossandcaithness.co.uk

Dean Very Revd Len Black, 28 Abban Street, Inverness, IV3 8HH *Tel:* 01463 233 797
email: fr.len@angelforce.co.uk

ST ANDREW'S CATHEDRAL, Inverness
Provost Very Revd Alex Gordon, 15 Ardross Street, Inverness, IV3 5NS *Tel:* 01463 233 535
email: canonalexgordon@btconnect.com

ST ANDREWS, DUNKELD AND DUNBLANE
Bishop Rt Revd David Chillingworth, Diocesan Centre, 28a Balhousie Street, Perth, PH1 5HJ
Tel: 01738 443173
Fax: 01738 443174
email: bishop@standrews.anglican.org
Web: www.standrews.anglican.org

Dean Very Revd Kenneth Rathband, 10 Rosemount Park, Blairgowrie PH10 6TZ
Tel: 01250 874 583
email: abcsaints@btinternet.com

ST NINIAN'S CATHEDRAL, Perth
Provost Very Revd Hunter Farquharson, St Ninian's Cathedral, North Methven Street, Perth PH1 5PP *Tel:* 01738 850 987
email: huntfar@gmail.com

The Province of the Anglican Church in South East Asia

Members 224,200
The Anglican Church in South East Asia was originally under the jurisdiction of the Bishop of Calcutta. The first chaplaincy was formed in West Malaysia in 1805; the first bishop was consecrated in 1855. The Diocese of Labuan, Sarawak and Singapore was formed in 1881. A separate Diocese of Singapore was formed in 1909, and in 1962 the Diocese of Jesselton, later renamed Sabah, and the Diocese of Kuching were formed from the former Diocese of Borneo. In 1970 the Diocese of West Malaysia was formed from what had been the Diocese of Malaya and Singapore.

Until the inauguration of the Church of the Province of South East Asia, the four dioceses (Kuching, Sabah, Singapore, and West Malaysia) were under the jurisdiction of the Archbishop of Canterbury. Although the province exists under certain social constraints, the Church has experienced much spiritual renewal and has sent out its own mission partners to various parts of the world, especially neighbouring Indonesia, Cambodia, Nepal, Laos, Vietnam and Myanmar.

Primate Most Revd Dr John Chew Hiang Chea (*Bishop of Singapore*)

Provincial Secretary Mr Caldwell David Joseph, No. 16, Jalan Pudu Lama, 50200 Kuala Lumpur, Malaysia
Tel: 60 3 2031 2728
Fax: 60 3 2031 3225
email: anglican@streamyx.com

Provincial Treasurer Mr Keith Chua, 35 Ford Avenue, Singapore 268714, Singapore
Tel: 65 6235 3344
Fax: 65 6736 1201

THEOLOGICAL COLLEGES
House of the Epiphany, PO Box No 347, 93704 Kuching, Sarawak, Malaysia (Warden Revd Michael Buma)

Trinity College, 490 Upper Bukit Timah Road, Singapore 678093 (interdenominational)
St Peter's Hall, residential hostel for Anglican students at Trinity College, Singapore (Warden Revd Hwa Chih)

Seminari Theoloji Malaysia (STM), Lot 3011, Taman South East, Jalan Tampin Lama, Batu 3, Seremban 70100, Negeri Sembilan, Malaysia (Principal Revd Dr Ezra Kok)

KUCHING
Bishop Rt Revd Bolly Anak Lapok, Bishop's House, PO Box 347, 93704 Kuching, Sarawak, Malaysia
Tel: 60 82 240 187
Fax: 60 82 426 488
email: bishopk@streamyx.com

SABAH
Bishop Rt Revd Albert Vun Cheong Fui, PO Box 10811, 88809 Kota Kinabalu, Sabah, Malaysia
Tel: 60 88 245 846
Fax: 60 88 245 942
email: bishopvn@streamyx.com

SINGAPORE
Bishop Most Revd Dr John Chew Hiang Chea (Primate of the Anglican Church in South East Asia), St. Andrews Village, No. 1, Francis Thomas Drive, #01–01, Singapore 359340
Tel: 65 6288 7585
Fax: 65 6288 5574
email: bpoffice@anglican.org.sg

Assistant Bishop Rt Revd Rennis Poniah, St John's and St Margaret's Church, 30 Dover Avenue, Singapore 139790, Singapore   Tel: 65 6773 9415
Fax: 65 6778 6264
email: rennis@sjsm.org.sg

WEST MALAYSIA
Bishop Rt Revd Ng Moon Hing, No. 16 Jalan Pudu Lama, 50200 Kuala Lumpur, Malaysia
Tel: 60 3 2031 2728
Fax: 60 3 2031 3225
email: anglican@streamyx.com

Assistant Bishops
Rt Revd Dr. S. Batumalai, Christ Church, No. 48, Jalan Gereja, 75000, Melaka, Malaysia
Tel: 60 6 2848804
Fax: 60 6 2848804
email: ccm1753@tm.net.my

Rt Revd Andrew Phang See Yin, Church of Our Redeemer, 306, Jalan Bagan Lebai Tahir, Bagan Ajam, 13050 Butterworth, Penang, Malaysia
Tel: 60 4 3231568
Fax: 60 4 3231568
email: christpg@streamyx.com

The Anglican Church of Southern Africa

Members 2,600,000
The province is the oldest in Africa. British Anglicans met for worship in Cape Town after 1806, with the first bishop appointed in 1847. The twenty-four dioceses of the province extend beyond the Republic of South Africa and include the Foreign and Commonwealth Office (St Helena and Tristan da Cunha), Mozambique (Lebombo and Niassa), the Republic of Namibia, the Kingdom of Lesotho, and the Kingdom of Swaziland. This Church and its leaders played a significant role in the abolition of apartheid in South Africa and in peace keeping in Mozambique and Angola. A mission diocese was inaugurated in August 2002 in Angola.

Primate Most Revd Thabo Makgoba (Archbishop of Cape Town and Metropolitan of the Anglican Church of Southern Africa)

Provincial Executive Officer Revd Canon Nangula E. Kathindi, 20 Bishopscourt Dr, Bishopscourt, Claremont, Western Cape 7708, South Africa
Tel: 27 21 763 1300
Fax: 27 21 797 1329
email: peo@anglicanchurchsa.org.za
Web: www.anglicanchurchsa.org.za

Provincial Treasurer Mr Rob S. Rogerson, PO Box 53014, Kenilworth, 7745, South Africa
Tel: 27 21 763 1300
Fax: 27 21 797 8319
email: rogerson@anglicanchurchsa.org.za

THEOLOGICAL COLLEGE
The College of the Transfiguration, PO Box 77, Grahamstown 6140   Tel: 27 46 622 3332
Fax: 27 46 622 3877
email: office@cott.co.za

ANGOLA (Missionary Diocese)
Bishop Rt Revd Andre Soares, Av. Lenini, Travessa D. Antonia Saldanha N.134, CP 10 341, Luanda, Angola   *Tel:* 244 2 395 792
Fax: 244 2 396 794
email: anglicana@ebonet.net

CAPE TOWN
Archbishop Most Revd Thabo Makgoba (*Metropolitan of Southern Africa*), 20 Bishopscourt Dr, Bishopscourt, Claremont, Cape Town 7708, Western Cape, South Africa   *Tel:* 27 21 763 1300
Fax: 27 21 797 1298/761 4193
email: archbish@anglicanchurchsa.org.za
Web: www.anglicanchurchsa.org

Bishop Suffragan
Rt Revd Garth Counsell (*Bishop of Table Bay*), PO Box 1932, Cape Town 8000   *Tel:* 27 21 465 4557
Fax: 27 21 465 1571
email: tablebay@ctdiocese.org.za

CHRIST THE KING
Bishop Rt Revd Peter John Lee, PO Box 1653, Rosettenville 2130, South Africa
Tel: 27 11 435 0097
Fax: 27 11 435 2868
email: dckpeter@corpdial.co.za

FALSE BAY
Bishop Rt Revd Merwyn Edwin Castle, PO Box 2804, Somerset West 7129, South Africa
Tel: 27 21 852 9544
Fax: 27 21 852 9430
email: bishopm@falsebaydiocese.org.za

GEORGE
Bishop Rt Revd Donald Frederick Harker, PO Box 227, George 6530, Cape Province, South Africa
Tel: 27 44 873 5680
Fax: 27 44 873 5680
email: diocese.g@pixie.co.za

GRAHAMSTOWN
Bishop Rt Revd Ebenezer St Mark Ntlali, PO Box 181, Grahamstown 6140, Cape Province, South Africa   *Tel:* 27 46 636 1996
Fax: 27 46 622 5231
email: bpgtn@intekom.co.za

HIGHVELD
Bishop Rt Revd David Albert Beetge, PO Box 563, Brakpan 1540, South Africa   *Tel:* 27 11 422 2231
Fax: 27 11 420 1336
email: dabeetge@iafrica.com

JOHANNESBURG
Bishop Rt Revd Brian Charles Germond, PO Box 1131, Johannesburg 2000, South Africa
Tel: 27 11 336 8724
Fax: 27 11 333 3053
email: bgermond@cpsajoburg.org.za

KIMBERLEY AND KURUMAN
Bishop Rt Revd Oswald Peter Patrick Swartz, PO Box 45, Kimberley 8300, South Africa
Tel: 27 53 833 2433
Fax: 27 53 831 2730
email: oppswartz@onetel.com

LEBOMBO
Bishop Rt Revd Dinis Salomâo Sengulane, CP 120, Maputo, Mozambique
Tel: 258 1 404 364/405 885
Fax: 258 1 401 093
email: bispo_sengulane@virconn.com

LESOTHO
Bishop Rt Revd Adam Andrease Mallane Taaso, PO Box 87, Maseru 100, Lesotho
Tel: 266 22 31 1974
Fax: 266 22 31 0161
email: diocese@ilesotho.com

MATLOSANE
Bishop Rt Revd Stephen Molopi Diseko, PO Box 11417, Klerksdorp 2570, South Africa
Tel: 27 18 464 2260
Fax: 27 18 462 4939
email: matlosane@lantic.net

MPUMALANGA
Bishop Rt Revd Leslie Walker, PO Box 4327, White River 1240   *Tel:* 27 13 751 1960
Fax: 27 13 751 3638
email: diompu@telkomsa.net

MTHATHA
Bishop Rt Revd Sitembele Tobela Mzamane, PO Box 25, Umtata, Transkei 5100, South Africa
Tel: 27 47 532 4450
Fax: 27 47 532 4191
email: anglicbspmthatha@intekom.co.za

NAMIBIA
Bishop Rt Revd Nathaniel Ndxuma Nakwatumbah, PO Box 57, Windhoek, Namibia
Tel: 264 61 238 920
Fax: 264 61 225 903
email: bishop@anglicanchurchnamibia.com

NATAL
Bishop Rt Revd Rubin Phillip, PO Box 47439, Greyville, 4023 South Africa   *Tel:* 27 31 309 2066
Fax: 27 31 308 9316
email: bishop@dionatal.org.za

Bishops Suffragan
Rt Revd Hummingfield Charles Nkosinathi Ndwandwe (*Suffragan Bishop of the South Episcopal Area*) (*same address*)   *Tel:* 27 33 394 1560

Rt Revd Funginkosi Mbhele (*Suffragan Bishop of the North West Episcopal Area*), PO Box 123 Escort 3310, South Africa   *Tel:* 27 36 352 2893
Fax: 27 36 352 2810
email: bishopmbhele@dionatal.org.za

ANGLICAN AND PORVOO COMMUNIONS

NIASSA
Bishop Rt Revd Mark van Koevering, CP 264, Lichinga, Niassa, Mozambique
Tel and *Fax:* 258 712 0735
email: diocese.niassa@teledata.mz

PORT ELIZABETH
Bishop Rt Revd Nceba Bethlehem Nopece, PO Box 7109, Newton Park 6055, South Africa
Tel: 27 41 365 1387
Fax: 27 41 365 2049
email: pebishop@iafrica.com

PRETORIA
Bishop Rt Revd Johannes Thomas Seoka, PO Box 1032, Pretoria 0001, South Africa
Tel: 27 12 322 2218
Fax: 27 12 322 9411
email: ptabish@dioceseofpretoria.org
Bishop Suffragan Rt Revd Mazwi Ernest Tisani, PO Box 16425, Pretoria North 0116
Tel and *Fax:* 27 12 546 6253
email: bishopmazwi@mweb.co.za

SALDANHA BAY
Bishop The Rt Revd Raphael Bernard Viburt Hess, PO Box 420, Malmesbury 7299, South Africa
Tel: 27 22 487 3885
Fax: 27 22 487 3886
email: bp.saldanhabay@wcaccess.co.za

ST HELENA
Bishop Rt Revd John William Salt, PO Box 62, Island of St Helena, South Atlantic
Tel: 290 4471
Fax: 290 4728
email: bishop@cwmail.sh

ST MARK THE EVANGELIST
Bishop Rt Revd Martin Andre Breytenbach, PO Box 643, Polokwane 0700, South Africa
Tel: 27 15 297 3297
Fax: 27 15 297 0408
email: martin@stmark.co.za

SWAZILAND
Bishop Rt Revd Meshack Boy Mabuza, Bishop's House, Muir Street, Mbabane, Swaziland
Tel: 268 404 3624
Fax: 268 404 6759
email: bishopmabuza@africaonline.co.sz

THE FREE STATE
Bishop Rt Revd (Elistan) Patrick Glover, PO Box 411, Bloemfontein, 9300, South Africa
Tel: 27 51 447 6053
Fax: 27 51 447 5874
email: bishoppatrick@dsc.co.za
Web: www.cpsa.org.za/bloemfontein

UMZIMVUBU
Bishop Rt Revd Mlibo Mteteleli Ngewu, PO Box 644, Kokstad 4700, South Africa
Tel and *Fax:* 27 39 727 4117
email: mzimvubu@futurenet.co.za

ZULULAND
Bishop Rt Revd Dino Gabriel, PO Box 147, Eshowe 3815, South Africa
Tel and *Fax:* 27 354 742 047
email: bishopdino@netactive.co.za

The Anglican Church of the Southern Cone of America

(Iglesia Anglicana del Cono Sur de América)

Members 22,490
British immigrants brought Anglicanism to South America in the nineteenth century. The South American Missionary Society continues to work effectively among indigenous peoples and today actively supports diocesan initiatives. In 1974 the Archbishop of Canterbury gave over his metro-political authority for the dioceses of the Southern Cone, and in 1981 the new province was formed. It includes Argentina, Bolivia, Chile, Northern Argentina, Paraguay, Peru and Uruguay.

Presiding Bishop Most Revd Gregory James Venables (*Bishop of Argentina*)
Web: www.anglicanos.net

Provincial Secretary Mrs Leticia Gomez, A. Gallinal 1852, Montevideo, Uruguay
email: lego@adinet.co.uy

Provincial Treasurer Mrs Margarita Cornejo, Iglesia Anglicana, Cochabamba, Bolivia
Tel and *Fax:* 591 7 226 7356
email: margarita_cornejo@hotmail.com

Executive Secretary Mrs Aída Cuenca de Fernandez, Casilla de Correo 187, CP4400, Salta, Argentina
Tel: 54 387 431 1718
Fax: 54 387 431 26
email: educris@salnet.com.ar

THEOLOGICAL EDUCATION
Planned and carried out by a Theological Education Commission which selects candidates, applies grants and sets courses of study, some of which are led by clergy of the diocese. Some students follow courses of theological training 'by extension' and others attend ecumenical seminaries.

ARGENTINA

Bishop Most Revd Gregory James Venables (*Presiding Bishop of the Province*), Rioja 2995 (1636), Olivos, Provincia de Buenos Aires, Argentina
Tel: 54 11 4342 4618
Fax: 54 11 4331 0234
email: bpgreg@ciudad.com.ar

BOLIVIA

Bishop Rt Revd Franciso Lyons, Iglesia Anglicana, Casilla 848, Cochabamba, Bolivia
Tel and *Fax:* 591 4 440 1168
email: BpFrank@sams-usa.org
Web: www.bolivia.anglican.org

CHILE

Bishop Rt Revd Héctor Zavala Muñoz, Casilla 50675, Correo Central, Santiago, Chile
Tel: 56 2 638 3009
Fax: 56 2 639 4581
email: tzavala@iach.cl
Web: www.iglesiaanglicana.cl

Assistant Bishop Rt Revd Abelino Manuel Apeleo, Casilla de Correo 26-D, Temuco, Chile
Tel and *Fax:* 56 45 910 484
email: aapeleo@iach.cl

NORTHERN ARGENTINA

Bishop Most Revd Gregory James Venables (*Bishop of Argentina*)

Assistant Bishop Rt Revd Mario Lorenzo Mariño, Casilla 19, 3636 Ingeniero Juárez, FCNGB Formosa, Argentina
Tel: 54 387 431 1718
Fax: 54 387 431 2622
email: diana.epi@salnet.com.ar

PARAGUAY

Bishop Rt Revd John Alexander Ellison, Iglesia Anglicana de Paraguay, Casilla de Correo 1124, Asunción, Paraguay
Tel: 595 21 200 933
Fax: 595 21 214 328
email: jellison@pla.net.py
Web: www.paraguay.anglican.org

Assistant Bishop Rt Revd Andrés Rodríguez (*via post box as for Bishop, or*) Calle Pte. Franco 344, Concepción, Paraguay
Tel: 595 31 42533

PERU

Bishop Rt Revd Harold William Godfrey, Calle Alcala 336, Urb. La Castellana, Santiago de Surco, Lima 33, Peru
Tel: 51 1 422 9160
Fax: 51 1 440 8540
email: wgodfrey@amauta.rcp.net.pe
Web: www.peru.anglican.org

URUGUAY

Bishop Rt Revd Miguel Tamayo, CC 6108, Montevideo, CP11000, Uruguay
Tel: 598 2 915 9627
Fax: 598 2 916 2519
email: mtamayo@netgate.com.uy
Web: www.uruguay.anglican.org

The Church of the Province of the Sudan

Members 5,000,000
The Church Missionary Society began work in 1899 in Omdurman; Christianity spread rapidly among black Africans of the southern region. Until 1974, the diocese of Sudan was part of the Jerusalem archbishopric. It reverted to the jurisdiction of the Archbishop of Canterbury until the new province, consisting of four new dioceses, was established in 1976. In 1986 the number of dioceses increased to 11 and in 1992 to 24 dioceses. The doubling of the number of dioceses by 1992 was partly due to leadership crises in the Church and partly due to church growth. Civil and religious strife and a constant flow of refugees have challenged the Church. Its heroic witness to faith in Christ continues to inspire the Anglican Communion and its people.

Archbishop and Primate Most Revd Dr Daniel Deng Bul, PO Box 110, Juba, Sudan
Tel and *Fax:* 249 811 820065
email: ecsprovince@hotmail.com
archbishopdanieldeng@yahoo.com

Provincial Secretary Revd Enock Tombe, PO Box 604, Khartoum, Sudan
Tel: 249 183 564722
email: ecsprovince@hotmail.com
Honorary Provincial Treasurer Mr Evans Sokiri (*same address*)
email: sokirik@yahoo.co.uk

THEOLOGICAL COLLEGES
Bishop Gwynne College, PO Box 110, Juba, Sudan (*Acting Principal* Revd David V. Bako)
Tel: 249 9124 54933 (Mobile)
email: davidbako7@hotmail.com

Bishop Alison Theological College, PO Box 1076, Arua, Uganda (*Principal* Dr Oliver Duku)
Tel: 254 77 685 554
email: bat_college@yahoo.com

Shokai Bible Training Institute, PO Box 65, Omdurman, 135 Khartoum, Sudan (*Principal* Revd Musa Elgadi)
Tel: 249 187 564944
email: sbti70@yahoo.com

Renk Bible School, PO Box 1532, Khartoum North, Sudan (*Acting Principal* Revd Abraham Noon Jiel)
Tel: 249 918 068 125 (Mobile)
email: joseph_atem@yahoo.com

Bishop Ngalamu Theological College, PO Box 3364, Khartoum, Sudan (*Principal* Revd Paul Issa)
email: leyeonon@hotmail.com

BOR
Bishop Rt Revd Nathaniel Garang Anyieth (*Dean of the Province*), c/o NSCC, PO Box 66168, Nairobi, Kenya   *Tel:* 254 733 855 521/855 675
email: ecs_dioceseofbor@yahoo.co.uk

CUEIBET
Bishop Rt Revd Reuben Maciir Makoi, c/o CEAS, PO Box 40870, Nairobi, Kenya   *Fax:* 254 2 570 807
email: eapo@cms-africa.org

EL-OBEID
Bishop Rt Revd Ismail Gibriel, PO Box 211, El-Obeid, Sudan   *Tel:* 249 9122 53459 (Mobile)
email: ismailabudigin2007@yahoo.com

EZO
Bishop Rt Revd John Zawo, c/o ECS Support Office, PO Box 7576, Kampala, Uganda
Tel: 256 41 343 497
email: kereborojohn@yahoo.com

IBBA
Bishop Rt Revd Wilson Elisa Kamani, c/o ECS Support Office, PO Box 7576, Kampala, Uganda
Tel and *Fax:* 256 41 343 497
email: ecs_ibbadiocese@hotmail.com

JUBA
Bishop Most Revd Dr Daniel Deng Bul (*Archbishop and Primate*), PO Box 110, Juba, Sudan
Tel: 249 811 820065
email: dioceseofjuba@yahoo.com

KADUGLI AND NUBA MOUNTAINS
Bishop Rt Revd Andudu Adam Elnail, PO Box 35, Kadugli, Sudan   *Tel:* 249 631 822898
email: bishandudu@yahoo.com

KAJO-KEJI
Bishop Rt Revd Anthony Poggo, c/o ECS Support Office, PO Box 7576, Kampala, Uganda
Tel: 256 41 343 497
email: bishopkk@gmail.com

KHARTOUM
Bishop Rt Revd Ezekiel Kondo, PO Box 65, Omdurman, 35 Khartoum, Sudan
Tel: 249 187 556931
email: ecs_bishop_Khartoum@kastanet.org

LAINYA
Bishop Rt Revd Peter Amidi, c/o ECS Support Office, PO Box 7576, Kampala, Uganda
Tel and *Fax:* 256 77 658 753
email: petamidi@yahoo.com

LUI
Bishop Rt Revd Bullen A. Dolli, PO Box 60837, Nairobi, Kenya   *Tel:* 254 2 720 037/56
Fax: 254 2 714 420
email: bishop@luidiocese.org

MALAKAL
Bishop Rt Revd Hilary Garang Aweer, PO Box 604, Khartoum, Sudan
email: ecs_malak@hotmail.com

MARIDI
Bishop Rt Revd Justin Badi Arama, ECS Support Office, PO Box 7576, Kampala, Uganda
Tel and *Fax:* 256 41 343 497
email: ecsmaridi@hotmail.com

MUNDRI
Bishop Rt Revd Bismark Monday Avokaya, c/o ECS Support Office, PO Box 7576, Kampala, Uganda   *Tel* and *Fax:* 256 41 343 497
email: ecsmundri@yahoo.com

PORT SUDAN
Bishop Rt Revd Yousif Abdalla Kuku, PO Box 278, Port Sudan, Sudan
Tel and *Fax:* 249 311 821224
email: ecsprovince@hotmail.com

REJAF
Bishop Rt Revd Michael Sokiri Lugör, PO Box 110, Juba, Sudan   *Tel:* 249 811 20 065
email: ecsdioceserejaf@yahoo.com

RENK
Bishop Rt Revd Joseph Garang Atem, PO Box 1532, Khartoum North, Sudan
Tel: 249 122 99275 (Mobile)
email: ecs_renk@hotmail.com

ROKON
Bishop Rt Revd Francis Loyo, PO Box 6702, Nairobi 00100 APO, Kenya
Tel: 254 2 568 541/539
Fax: 254 2 560 864
email: bployo@yahoo.co.uk
Web: www.rokon.anglican.org

RUMBEK
Bishop Rt Revd Alapayo Manyang Kuctiel, c/o CMS Nairobi, PO Box 56, Nakuro, Kenya
Tel: 254 37 43186
email: kuctiel@yahoo.com

TORIT
Bishop Rt Revd Bernard Oringa Abal, c/o ECS Support Office, PO Box 7576, Kampala, Uganda
Tel: 256 41 343 497
email: ecs_bishop_torit@kastanet.org

WAU
Bishop Rt Revd Henry Cuir Riak, c/o CMS Nairobi, PO Box 56, Nakuro, Kenya
Tel: 254 37 43186
email: riakcuir@yahoo.com /
wauvtc@yahoo.com

YAMBIO
Bishop Rt Revd Peter Munde Yacoub, ECS Support Office, PO Box 7576, Kampala, Uganda
Tel and *Fax:* 256 41 343 497
256 77 622 367 (Mobile)
email: yambio2002@yahoo.com

YEI
Bishop Rt Revd Hilary Luate Adeba, PO Box 588, Arua, Uganda   *Tel:* 256 756 561 175
email: hill_sherpherd@yahoo.com

YIROL
Bishop Rt Revd Benjamin Mangar Mamur, c/o St Matthew's Church, PO Box 39, Eldoret, Kenya
email: mamurmangar@yahoo.com

The Anglican Church of Tanzania

Members over 3,000,000

The Universities Mission to Central Africa and the Church Missionary Society began work in 1863 and 1876 in Zanzibar and at Mpwapwa respectively. The province was inaugurated in 1970 following the division of the Province of East Africa into the Province of Kenya and the Province of Tanzania. The 20 dioceses represent both evangelical and Anglo-Catholic Churches.

Archbishop Most Revd Dr Valentino Mokiwa (*Bishop of Dar-es-Salaam*)

Dean Rt Revd Dr Philip Baji (*Bishop of Tanga*)

Provincial Secretary Dr R. Mwita Akiri, PO Box 899, Dodoma   *Tel:* 255 26 232 4574
Fax: 255 26 232 4565
email: akiri@anglican.or.tz

Provincial Treasurer Rt Revd Hilkah Omindo Deya (*Bishop of Mara*)

Provincial Registrar Justice Augustino Ramadhani, PO Box 20522, Dar es Salaam
Tel: 255 022 211 5418
email: aslramadhani@yahoo.co.uk

THEOLOGICAL COLLEGES
St Philip's Theological College, PO Box 26, Kongwa (*Principal* Rev John Madinda)
Tel: 255 26 232 0096
email: stphilipstz@yahoo.com

St Mark's Theological College, PO Box 25017, Dar es Salaam (*Principal* Canon John Simalenga)
Tel: 255 22 286 3014
email: st-alban@kicheko.com/
jsimalenga@yahoo.com

CHURCH NEWSLETTER
ACT Forum is issued three times a year (April, August, December) in English containing diocesan, provincial and world church news. *Editor* Vacancy

CENTRAL TANGANYIKA
Bishop Rt Revd Godfrey Mdimi Mhogolo, PO Box 15, Dodoma, Tanzania   *Tel:* 255 26 232 1714
Fax: 255 26 232 4518
email: bishop@dct-tz.org/mhogolo@pnc.com.au

Assistant Bishop Rt Revd Ainea Kusenha (*same address*)   *email:* ngombe2004@kicheko.com

DAR ES SALAAM
Bishop Most Revd Dr Valentino Mokiwa (*Archbishop*), PO Box 25016, Ilala, Dar-es-Salaam   *Tel:* 255 22 286 4426
email: mokiwa_valentine@hotmail.com

KAGERA
Bishop Rt Revd Aaron Kijanjali, PO Box 18, Ngara   *Tel:* 255 28 222 3624
Fax: 255 28 222 2518
email: act-kagera@africaonline.co.tz

KONDOA
Bishop Rt Revd Yohana Zakaria Mkavu, PO Box 7, Kondoa   *Tel:* 255 26 236 0312
Fax: 255 26 236 0304/0324
email: d-kondoa@do.ucc.co.tz

LWERU
Bishop Rt Revd Jackton Yeremiah Lugumira, PO Box 12, Muleba   *Tel:* 255 713 274 085
email: act-kondoa@maf.or.tz/
jlugumira2@juno.com

MARA
Bishop Rt Revd Hilkiah Deya Omindo Deya, PO Box 131, Musoma   *Tel:* 255 28 262 2376
Fax: 255 28 262 2414
email: actmara@juasun.net

MASASI
Bishop Rt Revd Patrick Mwachiko, Private Bag, PO Masasi, Mtwara Region   *Tel:* 255 23 251 0016
Fax: 255 23 251 0351
email: actmasasi@africaonline.co.tz

MOROGORO
Bishop Rt Revd Dudley Mageni, PO Box 320, Morogoro   *Tel and Fax:* 255 23 260 4602
email: act-morogoro@africaonline.co.tz

MOUNT KILIMANJARO
Bishop Rt Revd Simon Elilekia Makundi, PO Box 1057, Arusha   *Tel:* 255 27 254 8396
Fax: 255 27 254 4187
email: dmk@habari.co.tz

MPWAPWA
Bishop Rt Revd Jacob Chimeledya, PO Box 2, Mpwapwa   *Tel:* 255 26 232 0017/0825
Fax: 255 26 232 0063
email: dmp@do.ucc.co.tz

RIFT VALLEY
Bishop Rt Revd John Lupaa, PO Box 16, Manyoni
Tel: 255 26 254 0013
Fax: 255 26 250 3014
email: act-drv@maf.or.tz

RUAHA
Bishop Rt Revd Donald Leo Mtetemela, PO Box 1028, Iringa *Tel:* 255 26 270 1211
Fax: 255 26 270 2479
email: ruaha@anglican.or.tz

RUVUMA
Bishop Rt Revd Dr Maternus Kapinga, PO Box 1357, Songea, Ruvumu *Tel:* 255 25 260 0090
Fax: 255 25 260 2987
email: mkkapinga@yahoo.com

SHINYANGA
Bishop Rt Revd Ngusa Charles Kija, PO Box 421, Shinyanga *Tel:* 255 754 347 746 (Mobile)
email: ckngusa@yahoo.com

SOUTHERN HIGHLANDS
Bishop Rt Revd John Mwela, PO Box 198, Mbeya
Tel: 255 754 266 668 (Mobile)
email: dsh-dev@atma.co.tz

SOUTH-WEST TANGANYIKA
Bishop Vacancy, PO Box 32, Njombe
Tel: 255 26 278 2010
Fax: 255 26 278 2403
email: dswt@africaonline.co.tz

TABORA
Bishop Rt Revd Sadock Makaya, PO Box 1408, Tabora *Tel:* 255 26 260 4124
Fax: 255 26 260 4899
email: smakaya1@yahoo.co.uk

TANGA
Bishop Rt Revd Dr Philip D. Baji, PO Box 35, Korogwe, Tanga *Tel:* 255 27 264 0631
Fax: 255 27 264 0568
email: bajipp@anglican.or.tz

VICTORIA NYANZA
Bishop Rt Revd Boniface Kwangu, PO Box 278, Mwanza *Tel:* 255 28 250 0627
Fax: 255 28 250 0676
email: revkahene1@yahoo.com

WESTERN TANGANYIKA
Bishop Rt Revd Dr Gerard E. Mpango, PO Box 13, Kasulu *Tel:* 255 28 281 0321
Fax: 255 28 281 0706
email: askofugm@yahoo.com

Assistant Bishops
Rt Revd Naftal Bikaka (*Lake Zone Area of Kigoma District*), PO Box 1378, Kigoma
Tel: 255 28 280 3407
email: bpwbikaka@yahoo.co.uk
Rt Revd Marko Badeleya (*Southern Zone Area of Rukwa Region in Sumbawanga*), PO Box 226, Sumbawanga *Tel:* 255 25 280 0287
email: bpbadeleya@yahoo.co.uk

ZANZIBAR
Bishop Vacancy, PO Box 5, Mkunazini, Zanzibar
Tel: 255 24 223 5348
Fax: 255 24 223 6772
email: secactznz@zanlink.com

The Church of the Province of Uganda

Members 9,200,000
After its founding in 1877 by the Church Missionary Society, the Church grew through the evangelization of Africa by Africans. The first Ugandan clergy were ordained in 1893 and the Church of Uganda, Rwanda and Burundi became an independent province in 1961. The history of the Church in Uganda has been marked by civil strife and martyrdom. In May 1980 the new Province of Burundi, Rwanda and Zaire was inaugurated; the Province of Uganda has since grown from 17 to 32 dioceses.

Archbishop of the Province Most Revd Henry Luke Orombi (*Bishop of Kampala*)

Primatial and Provincial Secretariat PO Box 14123, Kampala *Tel:* 256 41 270 218
Fax: 256 41 251 925
email: provinceuganda@yahoo.com

Provincial Secretary Canon Aaron Mwesigye Kafundizeki (*same address*)
email: ankundarev@yahoo.com
Tel: 256 772 455 129 (Mobile)

Provincial Treasurer Mr Richard Obura (*same address*) *email:* ricobura57@yahoo.com
Tel: 256 41 270 218
Fax: 256 41 251 925

Bishop in charge of continuing education for clergy in service Rt Revd David Sebuhinja (*same address*)
email: sebuhinjadavid@yahoo.co.uk

THEOLOGICAL COLLEGES
Uganda Christian University, Mukono, PO Box 4, Mukono (*Principal* Revd Prof. Stephen Noll)

Bishop Balya College, PO Box 368, Fort-Portal (*Principal* Revd Y. Kule)

Bishop Barham University College (constituent college of Uganda Christian university, Mukono), PO Box 613, Kabale (*Acting Principal* Canon Jovan Turyamureeba)
Archbishop Janani Luwum Theological College, PO Box 232, Gulu (*Principal* Revd Ayela Okot)

Mityana Theological Training College, PO Box 102, Mityana (*Principal* Revd Mukasa-Mutambuze)
Ngora Diocesan Theological College, PO Box 1, Ngora (*Principal* Revd S. Amuret)

Uganda Martyrs Seminary Namugongo, PO Box 31149, Kampala (*Principal* Canon Dr Henry Segawa)
Aduku Diocesan Theological College, PO Aduku, Lira (*Principal* Revd S. O. Obura)

Kabwohe College, PO Kabwohe, Mbarara (*Principal* Revd Y. R. Buremu)

St Paul's Theological College Ringili, PO Box 358, Arua (*Principal* Canon Dr Milton Anguyo)
Bishop Usher Wilson, Buwalasi, Mbale (*Principal* Revd Naphtah Opwata)
Uganda Bible Institute, Mbarara (*Director* Revd Amos Magezi)

Bishop McAllister College, Kyogyera (*Principal* Revd Paul Jefferees)

ANKOLE
Bishop Rt Revd George Tibeesigwa, PO Box 14, Mbarara, Ankole   *Tel:* 256 485 20290

BUKEDI
Bishop Rt Revd Nicodemus Okille, PO Box 170, Tororo   *Tel:* 256 772 542 164 (Mobile)

BUNYORO-KITARA
Bishop Rt Revd Nathan Kyamanywa, PO Box 20, Hoima   *Tel:* 256 464 40 128
256 772 648 232 (Mobile)
email: bkdioces@infocom.co.ug

BUSOGA
Bishop Rt Revd Dr Michael Kyomya, PO Box 1568, Jinja   *Tel:* 256 752 649 102 (Mobile)

CENTRAL BUGANDA
Bishop Rt Revd Jackson Matovu, PO Box 1200, Kinoni-Gomba, Mpigi
Tel: 256 772 475 640 (Mobile)
email: bishopmatovu@yahoo.com

KAMPALA
Bishop Most Revd Henry Luke Orombi (*Archbishop of Uganda*), PO Box 335, Kampala
Tel: 256 414 279 218
256 772 450 178 (Mobile)
Fax: 256 414 251 925
email: kdcou@africaonline.co.ug

Assistant Bishop Rt Revd Dr Zac Niringiye, PO Box 335, Kampala   *Tel:* 256 414 290 231
Fax: 256 414 342 601

KARAMOJA
Bishop Rt Revd Joseph Abura, PO Box 44, Moroto
Tel: 256 782 658 502

KIGEZI
Bishop Rt Revd George Katwesigye, PO Box 3, Kabale   *Tel:* 256 486 22 003
256 772 446 954 (Mobile)
Fax: 256 486 22 802
email: kigezi@infocom.co.ug

KINKIZI
Bishop Rt Revd John Ntegyereize, PO Box 77, Karuhinda, Rukungiri
Tel: 873 761 604 794/5 (Satellite)
256 772 507 163 (Mobile)
Fax: 875 761 604 796/7 (Satellite)

KITGUM
Bishop Rt Revd Benjamin Ojwang, PO Box 187, Kitgum   *Tel:* 256 772 959 924 (Mobile)
email: benojwang2004@yahoo.co.uk

KUMI
Bishop Rt Revd Thomas Edison Irigei, PO Box 18, Kumi   *Tel:* 256 772 659 460 (Mobile)
email: coukumidiocese@yahoo.com

LANGO
Bishop Rt Revd John Charles Odurkami, PO Box 6, Lira   *Tel:* 256 772 614 000 (Mobile)
email: bishoplango@yahoo.com

LUWERO
Bishop Rt Revd Evans Mukasa Kisekka, PO Box 125, Luwero   *Tel:* 256 414 610 048/070
256 772 421 220 (Mobile)
Fax: 256 414 610 132/070
email: kiromas@yahoo.co.uk

MADI / WEST NILE
Bishop Rt Revd Joel Obetia, PO Box 370, Arua
Tel: 256 752 625 414 (Mobile)
email: jobetia@ucu.ac.ug

MASINDI-KITARA
Bishop Rt Revd Stanley Ntagali, PO Box 515, Masindi   *Tel:* 256 772 618 822
email: bishopntagali@yahoo.com

MBALE
Bishop Rt Revd Patrick Gidudu, Bishop's House, PO Box 473, Mbale   *Tel:* 256 45 33 533
256 772 512 051 (Mobile)

MITYANA
Bishop Rt Revd Stephen Samuel Kaziimba, PO Box 102, Mityana   *Tel:* 256 46 2017
email: mtndiocese@hotmail.com

MUHABURA
Bishop Rt Revd Cranmer Mugisha, PO Box 22, Kisoro   *Tel:* 256 486 30 014/058
256 712 195 891 (Mobile)
Fax: 256 486 30 059

MUKONO
Bishop Rt Revd Elia Paul Luzinda Kizito, PO Box 39, Mukono   *Tel:* 256 41 290 229
256 772 603 348 (Mobile)
email: mukodise@utlonline.co.ug

NAMIREMBE
Bishop Rt Revd Samuel Balagadde Ssekkadde, PO Box 14297, Kampala   *Tel:* 256 41 271 682
256 772 500 494 (Mobile)
email: namid@infocom.co.ug

ANGLICAN AND PORVOO COMMUNIONS

NEBBI
Bishop Rt Revd Alphonse Watho-kudi, PO Box 27, Nebbi   *Tel:* 256 772 650 032 (Mobile)
email: bpalphonse@ekk.org

NORTH ANKOLE
Bishop Rt Revd John Muhanguzi, c/o PO Box 14, Rushere-Mbarara, Ankole
Tel: 256 772 369 947 (Mobile)
email: northankole@gmail.com

NORTH KARAMOJA
Bishop Rt Revd James Nasak PO Box 26, Kotido
Tel: 256 772 660 228

NORTH KIGEZI
Bishop Rt Revd Edward Muhima, PO Box 23, Rukungiri   *Tel:* 256 486 42 433
256 772 709 387 (Mobile)
email: northkigezi@infocom.co.ug

NORTH MBALE
Bishop Rt Revd Daniel Gimadu, Bishop's House, PO Box 1837, Mbale   *Fax:* 256 752 655 225
email: northmbalediocese@yahoo.com/
petgim2000@yahoo.com

NORTHERN UGANDA
Bishop Rt Revd Nelson Onono-Onweng, PO Box 232, Gulu   *Tel:* 256 772 838 193 (Mobile)
email: ononobp@yahoo.co.uk

RUWENZORI
Bishop Rt Revd Benezeri Kisembo, Bishop's House, PO Box 37, Fort Portal
Tel: 256 772 470 671 (Mobile)
email: bishop@biznas.com

SEBEI
Bishop Rt Revd Augusto Arapyona Salimo, PO Box 23, Kapchorwa   *Tel:* 256 45 51 072
256 772 550 520 (Mobile)
email: augustinesalimo@yahoo.co.uk

SOROTI
Bishop Rt Revd Charles Bernard Obaikol-Ebitu, PO Box 107, Soroti   *Tel:* 256 45 61 795
256 772 557 909 (Mobile)
email: couteddo@infocom.co.ug

SOUTH RUWENZORI
Bishop Rt Revd Jackson T. Nzerebende, PO Box 142, Kasese   *Tel:* 256 772 713 736 (Mobile)
Fax: 256 483 44 450
email: bpbende@yahoo.com

WEST ANKOLE
Bishop Rt Revd Yonah Katoneene, PO Box 140, Bushenyi   *Tel:* 256 753 377 193 (Mobile)
email: wad@westankolediocese.org

WEST BUGANDA
Bishop Rt Revd Dr Samuel Kefa Kamya, PO Box 242, Masaka   *Tel:* 256 772 413 400 (Mobile)
email: wesbug@infocom.co.ug

The Protestant Episcopal Church in the United States of America

(also known as The Episcopal Church)

Members 2,400,000
Anglicanism was brought to the New World by explorers and colonists with the first celebration of the Holy Eucharist in Jamestown, Virginia in 1607. The need for clergy in the colonies was acute and English missionaries provided temporary relief. Though the Bishop of London was responsible for maintaining the church in the colonies, there was no resident bishop for nearly two hundred years, which meant that colonists had to travel to England to be ordained; this caused difficulties when many of the colonial clergy sided with the Crown during the American Revolution. In 1784 the first American bishop (Samuel Seabury of Connecticut) was consecrated in Scotland, and three years later bishops were consecrated in England for the Dioceses of Pennsylvania and New York. In 1785 the first General Convention was held; in 1821 the Domestic and Foreign Missionary Society was formed; and in 1835, by resolution of General Convention, all members of The Episcopal Church were made members of the Missionary Society. The Episcopal Church today maintains

100 dioceses within the United States plus 10 overseas dioceses (Colombia, the Dominican Republic, Central Ecuador, Litoral Ecuador, Haiti, Honduras, Puerto Rico, Taiwan, Venezuela and the Virgin Islands), the Mission Territory of Micronesia (Guam), the Convocation of American Churches in Europe, and, together with the Anglican Church of Canada and the Church in the Province of the West Indies, is a partner in the Metropolitan Council which oversees the Episcopal Church of Cuba; it is governed by the triennial General Convention consisting of a House of Clergy and Lay Deputies, and a House of Bishops, which includes all serving diocesan, suffragan, coadjutor and assisting bishops. Between General Conventions, church affairs are managed by the Executive Council, whose members are elected in part by the two Houses and in part by the nine regional provinces. The Executive Council meets three times each year (except twice during a General Convention year). The province is a strong base of support to the Anglican Communion and has a significant crisis ministry

through Episcopal Relief and Development. Episcopalians are also very active in the areas of social justice and ecumenical and interfaith relations, and witness to their faith in all walks of national life.

Presiding Bishop and Primate Most Revd Katharine Jefferts Schori

Offices of the Episcopal Church and its departments Episcopal Church Center, 815 Second Ave, New York, NY 10017, USA *Tel:* 1 212 716 6000
Fax: 1 212 490 3298
email: pboffice@episcopalchurch.org
Web: www.episcopalchurch.org

President, House of Deputies Ms Bonnie Anderson (*same address*) *Tel:* 1 212 922 5183
Fax: 1 734 534 6043
email: banderson@episcopalchurch.org

Executive Officer of the General Convention and Secretary of the Executive Council Revd Dr Gregory Straub (*same address*) *Tel:* 1 212 922 5148
Fax: 1 212 972 9322
email: gcoffice@episcopalchurch.org

Secretary, House of Bishops Rt Revd Kenneth L. Price, The Bishop's Center, 125 East Broad St, Columbus, OH 43215, USA *Tel:* 1 614 461 8429
Fax: 1 614 461 1015
email: bishopken@aol.com

Bishop Suffragan for Chaplaincies (Armed Forces, Hospital and Prison Ministries) and Bishop in Charge of Micronesia Rt Revd George Elden Packard (*same address*) *Tel:* 1 212 716 6202
Fax: 1 212 867 1654
email: gpackard@episcopalchurch.org

Deputy to the Presiding Bishop for Ecumenical and Interfaith Relations Rt Revd C. Christopher Epting (*same address*) *Tel:* 1 212 716 6220
Fax: 1 212 682 5594
email: cepting@episcopalchurch.org

Bishop Suffragan for the Office of Pastoral Development Rt Revd F. Clayton Matthews, 2857 Trent Rd, New Bern, NC, 28562, USA
Tel: 1 252 635 5004
Fax: 1 252 635 5006
email: cmatthews@episcopalchurch.org

Treasurer Mr N. Kurt Barnes (*same address*)
Tel: 1 212 922 5296
Fax: 1 212 867 0395
email: kbarnes@episcopalchurch.org
Web: www.episcopalchurch.org

THEOLOGICAL SEMINARIES
California
Church Divinity School of the Pacific, 2451 Ridge Rd, Berkeley, CA 94709, USA (*Dean* Dr Donn F. Morgan) *Web:* www.cdsp.edu

Connecticut
Berkeley Divinity School at Yale University, 409 Prospect St, New Haven, CT 06511, USA (*Dean* Very Revd Joseph H. Britton) *Web:* http://research.yale.edu/berkeleydivinity

Illinois
Seabury-Western Theological Seminary, 2122 Sheridan Rd, Evanston, IL 60201, USA (*Dean* Very Revd Gary R. Hall) *Web:* www.seabury.edu

Massachusetts
Episcopal Divinity School, 99 Brattle St, Cambridge, MA 02138, USA (*Academic Dean* Revd Sheryl A. Kujawa-Holbrook) *Web:* www.eds.edu

New York
Bexley Hall Episcopal Seminary, 583 Sheridan Ave, Columbus, OH 43209, (*Dean* Very Revd John R. Kevern) *Web:* www.bexley.edu

The General Theological Seminary of The Episcopal Church in the United States, 175 Ninth Ave, New York, NY 10011, USA (*Dean* Very Revd Ward B. Ewing) *Web:* www.gts.edu

Pennsylvania
Trinity Episcopal School for Ministry, 311 Eleventh St, Ambridge, PA 15003, USA (*Interim Dean* Rt Revd John H. Rodgers Jr) *Web:* www.tesm.edu

Tennessee
The School of Theology, The University of the South, 735 University Ave, Sewanee, TN 37383, USA (*Dean* Very Revd William S. Stafford) *Web:* www.sewanee.edu

Texas
The Episcopal Theological Seminary of the Southwest, PO Box 2247, Austin, TX 78768, USA (*Dean* Very Revd Douglas Travis) *Web:* www.etss.edu

Virginia
The Protestant Episcopal Theological Seminary in Virginia, Seminary Post Office, 3737 Seminary Rd, Alexandria, VA 22304, USA (*Dean* Very Revd Ian Markham) *Web:* www.vts.edu

Wisconsin
Nashotah House, 2777 Mission Rd, Nashotah, WI 53058, USA (*Dean* Very Revd Robert S. Munday) *Web:* www.nashotah.edu

CHURCH PAPERS
Episcopal Life An independently edited, officially sponsored monthly newspaper published by the Episcopal Church, 815 Second Ave, New York, NY 10017, USA, upon authority of the General Convention of the Protestant Episcopal Church in the USA. Also see *episcopallife online*, our electronic news service *Web:* www.episcopalchurch.org/episcopal_life.htm

The Living Church Weekly magazine. *Editorial and Business Offices* PO Box 514036, Milwaukee, WI 53203, USA. Contains news and features about Christianity in general and the Episcopal Church in particular.

ALABAMA (Province IV)
Bishop Rt Revd Henry Nutt Parsley Jr, Carpenter House, 521 N 20th St, Birmingham, AL 35203–2611, USA   *Tel:* 1 205 715 2060
Fax: 1 205 715 2066
email: via website
Web: www.dioala.org

Bishop Suffragan Rt Revd John McKee Sloan (*same address*)

ALASKA (Province VIII)
Bishop Vacancy, 1205 Denali Way, Fairbanks, Alaska 99701–4137, USA   *Tel:* 1 907 452 3040
Fax: 1 907 456 6552
Web: www.episcopalak.org

ALBANY (Province II)
Bishop Rt Revd William H. Love, 68 South Swan St, Albany, NY 12210, USA   *Tel:* 1 518 465 4737
email: via website
Web: www.albanyepiscopaldiocese.org

ARIZONA (Province VIII)
Bishop Rt Revd Kirk Stevan Smith, 114 West Roosevelt St, Phoenix, AZ 85003–1406, USA
Tel: 1 602 254 0976
Fax: 1 602 495 6603
email: bishop@azdiocese.org
Web: www.azdiocese.org

ARKANSAS (Province VII)
Bishop Rt Revd Larry R. Benfield, PO Box 164668, Little Rock, AR 72216, USA   *Tel:* 1 501 372 2168
Fax: 1 501 372 2147
email: via website
Web: www.episcopalarkansas.org

ATLANTA (Province IV)
Bishop Rt Revd John Neil Alexander, 2744 Peachtree Rd, Atlanta, GA 30305, USA
Tel: 1 404 601 5320
Fax: 1 404 601 5330
email: bishop@episcopalatlanta.org
Web: www.episcopalatlanta.org

Assistant Bishop Rt Revd Keith B. Whitmore (*same address*)
email: bishopkeith@episcopalatlanta.org

BETHLEHEM (Province III)
Bishop Rt Revd Paul Victor Marshall, 333 Wyandotte St, Bethlehem, PA 18015, USA
Tel: 1 610 691 5655
Fax: 1 610 691 1682
email: bpoffice@diobeth.org
Web: www.diobeth.org

CALIFORNIA (Province VIII)
Bishop Rt Revd Marc Andrus, 1055 Taylor St, San Francisco, CA 94108, USA   *Tel:* 1 415 673 5015
Fax: 1 415 673 9268
email: bishopmarc@diocal.org
Web: http://episcopalbayarea.org

CENTRAL ECUADOR (Province IX)
Missionary Bishop Rt Revd Wilfrido Ramos-Orench, Centro Diocesano de la ciudad de Quito, calle Francisco Sarmiento No. 39–54 y Portete, sector el Batán, Quito, Ecuador
Tel: 593 22 456 948
Fax: 593 32 410 416
email: via website
Web: www.ecuadorepiscopal.org

CENTRAL FLORIDA (Province IV)
Bishop Rt Revd John Howe, Diocesan Office, 1017 E Robinson St, Orlando, Florida 32801, USA
Tel: 1 407 423 3567
Fax: 1 407 872 0006
email: mwalters@cfdiocese.org
Web: www.cfdiocese.org

CENTRAL GULF COAST (Province IV)
Bishop Rt Revd Philip Menzie Duncan II, Box 13330, Pensacola, Florida 32591–3330, USA
Tel: 1 850 434 7337
Fax: 1 850 434 8577
email: bishopduncan@diocgc.org
Web: www.diocgc.org

CENTRAL NEW YORK (Province II)
Bishop Rt Revd Gladstone 'Skip' Adams, 310 Montgomery St, Suite 200, Syracuse, NY 13202–2093, USA   *Tel:* 1 315 474 6596
Fax: 1 315 478 1632
email: bishop@cny.anglican.org
Web: www.cny.anglican.org

CENTRAL PENNSYLVANIA (Province III)
Bishop Rt Revd Nathan D. Baxter, PO Box 11937, Harrisburg, PA 17108, USA   *Tel:* 1 717 236 5959
Fax: 1 717 236 6448
email: via website
Web: www.diocesecpa.org

CHICAGO (Province V)
Bishop Rt Revd Jeffery Lee, 65 E Huron St, Chicago, IL 60611, USA   *Tel:* 1 312 751 4200
Fax: 1 312 787 4534
email: bishop@episcopalchicago.org
Web: www.epischicago.org

Assistant Bishop Rt Revd Victor A. Scantlebury (*same address*)   *Tel:* 1 312 751 4216
email: vscantlebury@episcopalchicago.org

COLOMBIA (Province IX)
Bishop Rt Revd Francisco J. Duque Gómez, PO Box 52964, Bogotá 2, DC Colombia
Tel: 57 1 288 3167
Fax: 57 1 288 3248
email: iec@iglesiaepiscopal.org.co
Web: www.iglesiaepiscopal.org.co

COLORADO (Province VI)
Bishop Rt Revd Robert J. O'Neill, 1300 Washington St, Denver, CO 80203, USA
Tel: 1 303 837 1173
Fax: 1 303 837 1311
email: bishoponeill@coloradodiocese.org
Web: www.coloradodiocese.org

CONNECTICUT (Province I)
Bishop Rt Revd Andrew Donnan Smith, 1335 Asylum Ave, Hartford, CT 06105–2295, USA
Tel: 1 860 233 4481
Fax: 1 860 523 1410
email: adsmith@ctdiocese.org
Web: www.ctdiocese.org

Bishops Suffragan
Rt Revd Laura Ahrens (*same address*)
email: lahrens@ctdiocese.org

Rt Revd James Elliot Curry (*same address*)
email: jcurry@ctdiocese.org

DALLAS (Province VII)
Bishop Rt Revd James Monte Stanton, 1630 North Garrett Ave, Dallas, TX 75206, USA
Tel: 1 214 826 8310
Fax: 1 214 826 5968
email: jmsdallas@episcopal-dallas.org
Web: www.episcopal-dallas.org

Suffragan Bishop Rt Revd Paul Lambert (*same address*)   *email:* plambert@episcopal-dallas.org

DELAWARE (Province III)
Bishop Rt Revd Wayne Parker Wright, 2020 North Tatnall St, Wilmington, DE 19802, USA
Tel: 1 302 656 5441
Fax: 1 302 656 7342
email: bishop@dioceseofdelaware.net
Web: www.dioceseofdelaware.net

DOMINICAN REPUBLIC (Province IX)
Bishop Rt Revd Julio Cesar Holguin, Calle Santiago No 114, Apartado 764, Santo Domingo, Dominican Republic   *Tel:* 1 809 688 7493
Fax: 1 809 686 6364
email: iglepidom@verison.net.do
Web: www.dominicanepiscopalchurch.org

EAST CAROLINA (Province IV)
Bishop Rt Revd Clifton Daniel III, PO Box 1336, Kinston, NC 28501, USA   *Tel:* 1 252 522 0885
Fax: 1 252 523 5272
email: cdaniel@diocese-eastcarolina.org
Web: www.diocese-eastcarolina.org

EAST TENNESSEE (Province IV)
Bishop Rt Revd Charles Glen von-Rosenberg, 814 Episcopal School Way, Knoxville, Tennessee 37932, USA   *Tel:* 1 865 966 2110
Fax: 1 865 966 2535
email: cgvonr@etdiocese.net
Web: www.etdiocese.net

EASTERN MICHIGAN (Province V)
Bishop Rt Revd S. Todd Ousley, Diocesan Office, 924 N Niagara St, Saginaw, Michigan 48602, USA
Tel: 1 989 752 6020
Fax: 1 989 752 6120
email: TOusley@eastmich.org
Web: www.eastmich.org

EASTERN OREGON (Province VIII)
Bishop Vacancy, PO Box 1548, The Dalles, Oregon 97058, USA   *Tel:* 1 541 298 4477
Fax: 1 541 296 0939
email: diocese@episdioeo.org
Web: www.episdioeo.org

EASTON (Province III)
Bishop Rt Revd James J. Shand, 314 North St, Easton, MD 21601, USA   *Tel:* 1 410 822 1919
Fax: 1 410 763 8259
email: bishopshand@dioceseofeaston.org
Web: www.dioceseofeaston.org

EAU CLAIRE (Province V)
Bishop Vacancy, 510 So. Farwell St, Eau Claire, WI 54701   *Tel:* 1 715 835 3331
Fax: 1 715 835 9212
email: deaconjeanne@dioceseofeauclaire.org
Web: www.dioceseofeauclaire.org

EL CAMINO REAL (Province VIII)
Bishop Rt Revd Mary Gray-Reeves, Box 1903 Monterey, CA 93942, USA   *Tel:* 1 831 394 4465
Fax: 1 831 394 7133
email: susan@edecr.org
Web: www.edecr.org

Assisting Bishop Rt Revd Sylvestre Romero (*same address*)   *email:* bishopromero@edecr.org

EUROPE, CONVOCATION OF AMERICAN CHURCHES IN
Bishop Rt Revd Pierre Welté Whalon, 23 Avenue George V, 75008 Paris, France
Tel: 33 1 53 23 84 00
Fax: 33 1 47 23 95 30
email: bishops@tec-europe.org
Web: www.tec-europe.org

FLORIDA (Province IV)
Bishop Rt Revd Samuel J. Howard, 325 Market St, Jacksonville, FL 32202, USA   *Tel:* 1 904 356 1328
Fax: 1 904 355 1934
email: jhoward@diocesefl.org
Web: www.diocesefl.org

FOND DU LAC (Province V)
Bishop Rt Revd Russell Edward Jacobus, 1047 N. Lynndale Dr., Suite 1B, Appleton, WI 54914, USA
Tel: 1 920 830 8866
Fax: 1 920 830 8761
email: diofdl@diofdl.org
Web: www.episcopalfonddulac.org

FORT WORTH (Province VII)
Bishop Rt Revd Jack Leo Iker, 2900 Alemeda Street, Fort Worth, Texas 76108, USA
Tel: 1 817 244 2885
Fax: 1 817 244 3363
email: jliker@fwepiscopal.org
Web: www.fwepiscopal.org

GEORGIA (Province IV)
Bishop Rt Revd Henry Irving Louttit Jr, 611 E Bay St, Savannah, GA 31401–1296, USA
Tel: 1 912 236 4279
Fax: 1 912 236 2007
email: diocesega@att.net
Web: www.georgia.anglican.org

HAITI (Province II)
Bishop Rt Revd Jean-Zaché Duracin, Église Épiscopale d'Haiti, Boite Postale 1309, Port-au-Prince, Haiti
Tel: 509 257 1624
Fax: 509 257 3412
email: epihaiti@hotmail.com

HAWAII (Province VIII)
Bishop Rt Revd Robert L. Fitzpatrick, Diocesan Office, 229 Queen Emma Sq, Honolulu, HI 96813, USA
Tel: 1 808 536 7776
Fax: 1 808 538 7194
email: rlfitzpatrick@episcopalhawaii.org
Web: www.episcopalhawaii.org

HONDURAS (Province IX)
Bishop Rt Revd Lloyd E. Allen, Apartado Postal 586, San Pedro Sula, Cortés 21105, Honduras
Tel: 504 556 6155/6268
Fax: 504 566 6467
email: emmanuel@anglicano.hn
Web: www.anglicano.org

IDAHO (Province VIII)
Bishop Rt Revd Brian James Thom, 1858 W. Judith Lane, Boise, ID 83705
Tel: 1 208 345 4440
Fax: 1 208 345 9735
email: carrolk@idahodiocese.org
Web: www.episcopalidaho.org

INDIANAPOLIS (Province V)
Bishop Rt Revd Catherine Elizabeth Maples Waynick, 1100 W 42nd St, Indianapolis, IN 46208, USA
Tel: 1 317 926 5454
Fax: 1 317 926 5456
email: bishop@indydio.org
Web: www.indydio.org

IOWA (Province VI)
Bishop Rt Revd Alan Scarfe, 225 37th St, Des Moines, IA 50312, USA
Tel: 1 515 277 6165
Fax: 1 515 277 0273
email: diocese@iowaepiscopal.org
Web: www.iowaepiscopal.org

KANSAS (Province VII)
Bishop Rt Revd Dean E. Wolfe, Bethany Place, 835 SW Polk St, Topeka, KS 66612–1688, USA
Tel: 1 785 235 9255
Fax: 1 785 235 2449
email: DWolfe@episcopal-ks.org
Web: www.episcopal-ks.org

KENTUCKY (Province IV)
Bishop Rt Revd Edwin Funsten Gulick Jr, 425 S Second St, Louisville, KY 40202, USA
Tel: 1 502 584 7148
Fax: 1 502 587 8123
email: TedG@episopalky.org
Web: www.episcopalky.org

LEXINGTON (Province IV)
Bishop Rt Revd Stacy Fred Sauls, PO Box 610, Lexington, KY 40586, USA
Tel: 1 859 252 6527
Fax: 1 859 231 9077
email: diolex@diolex.org
Web: www.diolex.org

LITORAL ECUADOR (Province IX)
Bishop Rt Revd Alfredo Morante, Box 0901–5250, Guayaquil-Ecuador
Tel: 593 4 443 050
Fax: 593 4 443 088
email: bishopmorante@hotmail.com/ iedl@gu.pro.ec

LONG ISLAND (Province II)
Bishop Rt Revd Orris G. Walker Jr, 36 Cathedral Ave, Garden City, NY 11530
Tel: 1 516 248 4800
Fax: 1 516 248 1349
email: owalker@dioceseli.org
Web: www.dioceselongisland.org

LOS ANGELES (Province VIII)
Bishop Rt Revd Joseph Jon Bruno, Box 512164, Los Angeles, CA 90051, USA
Tel: 1 213 482 2040
Fax: 1 213 482 0844
email: bishop@ladiocese.org
Web: www.ladiocese.org

Bishop Suffragan Rt Revd Chester L. Talton (*same address*)
email: suffragan@ladiocese.org

LOUISIANA (Province IV)
Bishop Rt Revd Charles Edward Jenkins, 205 North Fourth St, Baton Rouge, LA 70801, USA
Tel: 1 225 706 6634
Fax: 1 225 706 6653
email: atownsend@edola.org
Web: www.edola.org

MAINE (Province I)
Bishop Rt Revd Stephen T Lane, Loring House, 143 State St, Portland, ME 04101, USA
Tel: 1 207 772 1953
Fax: 1 207 773 0095
email: slane@episcopalmaine.org
Web: www.episcopalmaine.org

MARYLAND (Province III)
Bishop Rt Revd Eugene T Sutton, 4 East University
Parkway, Baltimore, MD 21218, USA
Tel: 1 410 467 1399
Fax: 1 410 554 6387
email: via website
Web: www.ang-md.org

Bishop-in-Charge Rt Revd John Leslie Rabb (*same
address*) *email:* jrabb@ang-md.org

MASSACHUSETTS (Province I)
Bishop Rt Revd M. Thomas Shaw SSJE, 138
Tremont St, Boston, MA 02111, USA
Tel: 1 617 482 4826
Fax: 1 617 482 8431
email: jdrapeau@diomass.org
Web: www.diomass.org

Bishops Suffragan
Rt Revd Roy F. (Bud) Cederholm, Jr (*same
address*) *email:* budc@diomass.org

Rt Revd Gayle E. Harris (*same address*)
email: SHP@diomass.org

MICHIGAN (Province V)
Bishop Rt Revd Wendell Nathaniel Gibbs Jr, 4800
Woodward Ave, Detroit, MI 48201, USA
Tel: 1 313 833 4436
Fax: 1 313 831 0259
email: via website
Web: www.edomi.org

MILWAUKEE (Province V)
Bishop Rt Revd Steven Andrew Miller, 804 E
Juneau Ave, Milwaukee, WI 53202–2798
Tel: 1 414 272 3028
Fax: 1 414 272 7790
email: bishop@diomil.org
Web: www.episcoplamilwaukee.org

MINNESOTA (Province VI)
Bishop Rt Revd James Louis Jelinek, 1730 Clifton
Place, Suite 201, Minneapolis, MN 55403-3242,
USA *Tel:* 1 612 871 5311
Fax: 1 612 871 0552
email: karen.o@episcopalmn.org
Web: www.episcopalmn.org

MISSISSIPPI (Province IV)
Bishop Rt Revd Duncan Montgomery Gray III,
PO Box 23107, Jackson, MS 39225–3107, USA
Tel: 1 601 948 5954
Fax: 1 601 354 3401
email: catherinejohns@dioms.org
Web: www.dioms.org

MISSOURI (Province V)
Bishop Rt Revd George Wayne Smith, 1210
Locust St, St Louis, MO 63103, USA
Tel: 1 314 231 1220
Fax: 1 314 231 3373
email: swegner@missouri.anglican.org
Web: www.diocesemo.org

MONTANA (Province VI)
Bishop Rt Revd C. Franklin Brookhart, 515 North
Park Ave, Helena, MT 59601, USA
Tel: 1 406 442 2230
Fax: 1 406 442 2238
email: cfbmt@qwestoffice.net
Web: www.montana.anglican.org

**NAVAJOLAND AREA MISSION (Province
VIII)**
Assisting Bishop Rt Revd Mark MacDonald, PO
Box 720, Farmington, NM 87499–0720, USA
Tel: 1 505 327 0326
Fax: 1 505 327 6904
email: mmacdonald@gci.net
Web: www.episcopal-navajo.org

NEBRASKA (Province VI)
Bishop Rt Revd Joe Goodwin Burnett, 109 N 18th
St, Omaha, NE 68102, USA *Tel:* 1 402 341 5373
Fax: 1 402 341 8683
email: jburnett@episcopal-ne.org
Web: www.episcopal-ne.org

NEVADA (Province VIII)
Assisting Bishop Rt Revd Dan T. Edwards, 6135
Harrison Drive, Suite 1, Las Vegas, NV 89120–
4076, USA *Tel:* 1 702 737 9190
Fax: 1 702 737 6488
email: via website
Web: www.nvdiocese.org

NEW HAMPSHIRE (Province I)
Bishop Rt Revd V. Gene Robinson, 63 Green St,
Concord, NH 03301, USA *Tel:* 1 603 224 1914
Fax: 1 603 225 7884
email: GRinNH@aol.com
Web: www.nhepiscopal.org

NEW JERSEY (Province II)
Bishop Rt Revd George E. Councell, 808 West
State Street, Trenton, NJ 08618–5326, USA
Tel: 1 609 394 5281
Fax: 1 609 394 9546
email: GCouncell@newjersey.anglican.org
Web: www.newjersey.anglican.org

NEW YORK (Province II)
Bishop Rt Revd Mark Sean Sisk, Synod House,
1047 Amsterdam Ave, Cathedral Heights, New
York, NY 10025, USA *Tel:* 1 212 316 7400
Fax: 1 212 316 7405
email: bpsisk@dioceseny.org
Web: www.dioceseny.org

Assistant Bishop Rt Revd E. Don Taylor (*same
address*) *Tel:* 1 212 932 7349
Fax: 1 212 932 7345
email: bptaylor@dioceseny.org

Suffragan Bishop Rt Revd Catherine S. Roskam,
Region Two Office, 55 Cedar St, Dobbs Ferry, NY
10522, USA *Tel:* 1 914 693 3848
Fax: 1 914 693 0407
email: bproskam@dioceseny.org

NEWARK (Province II)
Bishop Rt Revd Mark Beckwith, 31 Mulberry St,
Newark, NJ 07102, USA   *Tel:* 1 923 430 9900
Fax: 1 923 622 3503
email: mbeckwith@dioceseofnewark.org
Web: www.dioceseofnewark.org

Assistant Bishop Rt Revd Carol J. W. T. Gallagher
(*same address*)
email: cgallagher@dioceseofnewark.org

NORTH CAROLINA (Province IV)
Bishop Rt Revd Michael Bruce Curry, 200 West
Morgan St, Suite 300, Raleigh, NC 27601, USA
Tel: 1 919 834 7474
Fax: 1 919 834 7546
email: margo.acomb@episdionc.org
Web: www.episdionc.org

NORTH DAKOTA (Province VI)
Bishop Rt Revd Michael G. Smith, 3600 S. 25th St,
Fargo, ND 58104–6861, USA   *Tel:* 1 701 235 6688
Fax: 1 701 232 3077
email: RobinsNest72176@aol.com
Web: www.episcopal-nd.org

NORTHERN CALIFORNIA (Province VIII)
Bishop Rt Revd Barry L. Beisner, Box 161268,
Sacramento, CA 95816–1268   *Tel:* 1 916 442 6918
Fax: 1 916 442 6927
email: bishop@dncweb.org
Web: www.dncweb.org

NORTHERN INDIANA (Province V)
Bishop Rt Revd Edward Stuart Little II, 117 N
Lafayette Blvd, South Bend, Indiana 46601, USA
Tel: 1 574 233 6489
Fax: 1 574 287 7914
email: bishop@ednin.org/info@ednin.org
Web: www.ednin.org

NORTHERN MICHIGAN (Province V)
Bishop Vacancy, 131 E Ridge St, Marquette, MI
49855, USA   *Tel:* 1 906 228 7160
Fax: 1 906 228 7171
email: diocese@upepiscopal.org
Web: www.upepiscopal.org

NORTHWEST TEXAS (Province VII)
Bishop Rt Revd C. Wallis Ohl Jr, The Hulsey
Episcopal Center, 1802 Broadway, Lubbock, TX
79401, USA   *Tel:* 1 806 763 1370
Fax: 1 806 472 0641
email: diocese@nwt.org
Web: www.nwt.org

**NORTHWESTERN PENNSYLVANIA
(Province III)**
Bishop Rt Revd Sean W. Rowe, 145 W 6th St, Erie,
PA 16501, USA   *Tel:* 1 814 456 4203
Fax: 1 814 454 8703
email: seanrowe@dionwpa.org
Web: www.dionwpa.org

OHIO (Province V)
Bishop Rt Revd Mark Hollingsworth Jr, 2230
Euclid Ave, Cleveland, OH 44115–2499, USA
Tel: 1 216 771 4815
Fax: 1 216 623 0735
email: mh@dohio.org
Web: www.dohio.org

OKLAHOMA (Province VII)
Bishop Rt Revd Edward J. Konieczny, 924 N
Robinson, Oklahoma City, OK 73102, USA
Tel: 1 405 232 4820
Fax: 1 405 232 4912
email: pwollenberg@episcopaloklahoma.org
Web: www.episcopaloklahoma.org

OLYMPIA (Province VIII)
Bishop Rt Revd Vincent W Warner Jr, PO Box
12126, Seattle, WA 98102, USA
Tel: 1 206 325 4200
Fax: 1 206 325 4631
email: vwarner@ecww.org
Web: www.ecww.org

Bishop Suffragan Rt Revd Bavi Edna ('Nedi')
Rivera (*same address*)   *email:* nrivera@ecww.org

OREGON (Province VIII)
Bishop Vacancy, 11800 S.W. Military Lane,
Portland, OR 97219, USA   *Tel:* 1 503 636 5613
Fax: 1 503 636 5616
email: deirdres@diocese-oregon.org
Web: www.diocese-oregon.org

Assisting Bishop Rt Revd Sanford ('Sandy')
Hampton (*same address*)

PENNSYLVANIA (Province III)
Bishop Rt Revd Charles Ellsworth Bennison Jr,
240 South Fourth St, Philadelphia, PA 19106, USA
Tel: 1 215 627 6434
Fax: 1 215 627 7550
email: charlesb@diopa.org
Web: www.diopa.org

PITTSBURGH (Province III)
Bishop Vacancy, 900 Oliver Building, 535
Smithfield Street, Pittsburgh, PA 15222, USA
Tel: 1 412 281 6131
Fax: 1 412 471 5591
email: duncan@pgh.anglican.org
Web: www.pgh.anglican.org

PUERTO RICO (Province IX)
Bishop Rt Revd David Andres Alvarez, PO Box
902, St Just, PR 00978, Puerto Rico
Tel: 1 787 761 9800
Fax: 1 787 761 0320
email: obispoalvarez@spiderlink.net
Web: www.episcopalpr.org

QUINCY (Province V)
Bishop Rt Revd Keith Lynn Ackerman, 601 W.
Florence Ave, Peoria, IL 61604–1517, USA
Tel: 1 309 688 8221
Fax: 1 309 688 8229
email: bishop@dioceseofquincy.org
Web: www.dioceseofquincy.org

RHODE ISLAND (Province I)
Bishop Rt Revd Geralyn Wolf, 275 N Main St,
Providence, RI 02903–1298, USA
Tel: 1 401 274 4500
Fax: 1 401 331 9430
email: bishop@episcopalri.org
Web: www.episcopalri.org

Assisting Bishop Rt Revd David Joslin (*same
address*)   *email:* Bp.Joslin@episcopalri.org

RIO GRANDE (Province VII)
Bishop Vacancy, 4304 Carlisle Blvd NE,
Albuquerque, NM 87107–4811, USA
Tel: 1 505 881 0636
Fax: 1 505 883 9048
email: via website
Web: www.dioceserg.org

ROCHESTER (Province II)
Bishop Rt Revd Jack Marston McKelvey, 935 East
Ave, Rochester, NY 14607, USA
Tel: 1 716 473 2977
Fax: 1 716 473 3195
email: BpJackM@aol.com
Web: www.rochesterepiscopaldiocese.org

SAN DIEGO (Province VIII)
Bishop Rt Revd James R. Mathes, 2728 Sixth Ave,
San Diego, CA 92103, USA   *Tel:* 1 619 291 5947
Fax: 1 619 291 8362
email: bishopmathes@edsd.org
Web: www.sandiego.anglican.org

SAN JOAQUIN (Province VIII)
Bishop Vacant, 4159 E Dakota Ave, Fresno, CA
93726, USA   *Tel:* 1 559 244 4828
Fax: 1 559 244 4832
Web: www.diosanjoaquin.org

Interim Bishop Jerry A Lamb (*same address*)
email: jerrylamb@diosanjoaquin.org

SOUTH CAROLINA (Province IV)
Bishop Rt Revd Mark J. Lawrence, Box 20127,
Charleston, SC 29413–0127, USA
Tel: 1 843 722 4075
Fax: 1 843 723 7628
email: ljones@dioceseofsc.org
Web: www.dioceseofsc.org

SOUTH DAKOTA (Province VI)
Bishop Rt Revd Creighton L. Robertson, 500 S Main
Avenue, Sioux Falls, South Dakota 57104–6814,
USA   *Tel:* 1 605 338 9751
Fax: 1 605 336 6243
email: office.diocese@midconetwork.com
Web: www.diocesesd.org

SOUTHEAST FLORIDA (Province IV)
Bishop Rt Revd Leopold Frade, 525 NE 15 St,
Miami, FL 33132, USA   *Tel:* 1 305 373 0881
Fax: 1 305 375 8054
email: bishopfrade@aol.com
Web: www.diosef.org

SOUTHERN OHIO (Province V)
Bishop Rt Revd Thomas E. Breidenthal, 412
Sycamore St, Cincinnati, OH 45202, USA
Tel: 1 513 421 0311
Fax: 1 513 421 0315
email: bishop_breidenthal@episcopal-dso.org
Web: www.episcopal-dso.org

Suffragan Bishop Rt Revd Kenneth Price (*same
address*)   *email:* bishop_price@episcopal-dso.org

SOUTHERN VIRGINIA (Province III)
Bishop elect Rt Revd Herman 'Holly' Hollerith,
600 Talbot Hall Rd, Norfolk, VA 23505, USA
Tel: 1 757 423 8287
Fax: 1 757 440 5354
email: via website
Web: www.diosova.org

Interim Bishop Rt Revd John C. Buchanan (*same
address*)

SOUTHWEST FLORIDA (Province IV)
Bishop Rt Revd Dabney T Smith, 7313 Merchant
Ct, Sarasota, FL 34240–8437, USA
Tel: 1 941 556 0315
Fax: 1 941 556 0321
email: dsmith@episcopalswfla.org
Web: www.episcopalswfla.org

SOUTHWESTERN VIRGINIA (Province III)
Bishop Rt Revd Frank Neff Powell, PO Box 2279,
Roanoke, VA 24009–2279, USA
Tel: 1 540 342 6797
Fax: 1 540 343 9114
email: npowell@dioswva.org
Web: www.dioswva.org

SPOKANE (Province VIII)
Bishop Rt Revd James Edward Waggoner Jr, 245
E 13th Ave, Spokane, WA 99202–1114, USA
Tel: 1 509 624 3191
Fax: 1 509 747 0049
email: jimw@spokanediocese.org
Web: www.spokanediocese.org

SPRINGFIELD (Province V)
Bishop Rt Revd Peter Hess Beckwith, 821 S 2nd
St, Springfield, IL 62704–2694, USA
Tel: 1 217 525 1876
Fax: 1 217 525 1877
email: diocese@episcopalspringfield.org
Web: www.episcopalspringfield.org

TAIWAN (Province VIII)
Bishop Rt Revd David J. H. Lai, Friendship House, 7 Lane 105, Hangchow South Rd, Sec. 1, Taipei, Taiwan 10060, Republic of China
Tel: 886 2 2341 1265
Fax: 886 2 2396 2014
email: skh.tpe@msa.hinet.net
Web: www.episcopalchurch.org.tw

TENNESSEE (Province IV)
Bishop Rt Revd John C. Bauernschmidt, 50 Vantage Way, Suite 107, Nashville, TN 37228, USA
Tel: 1 615 251 3322
Fax: 1 615 251 8010
email: info@episcopaldiocese-tn.org
Web: www.episcopaldiocese-tn.org

TEXAS (Province VII)
Bishop Rt Revd Don Adger Wimberly, 1225 Texas Ave, Houston, TX 77002, USA
Tel: 1 713 520 6444
Fax: 1 713 520 5723
email: dwimberly@epicenter.org
Web: www.epicenter.org

Bishops Suffragan
Rt Revd Rayford High, Tyler Diocesan Office, 26695 S. Southwest Loop 323, Tyler, TX 75701
Tel: 1 903 579 6012
Fax: 1 903 579 6011
email: rhigh@epicenter.org

Rt Revd Dena Harrison, Austin Diocesan Office, 606 Ratervue Place, Austin, TX 78705
Tel: 1 512 478 0508
Fax: 1 512 478 5615
email: dharrison@epicenter.org

UPPER SOUTH CAROLINA (Province IV)
Bishop Rt Revd Dorsey Felix Henderson Jr, 1115 Marion St, Columbia, SC 29201, USA
Tel: 1 803 771 7800
Fax: 1 803 799 5119
email: dioceseusc@edusc.org
Web: www.edusc.org

UTAH (Province VIII)
Bishop Rt Revd Carolyn Tanner Irish, PO Box 3090, Salt Lake City, UT 84110–3090, USA
Tel: 1 801 322 4131
Fax: 1 801 322 5096
email: MNestler@episcopal-ut.org
Web: www.episcopal-ut.org

VENEZUELA (Province IX)
Bishop Rt Revd Orlando Guerrero-Torres, Apartado 49–143, Avenida Caroni 100, Colinas de Bello Monte, Caracas 1042-A, Venezuela
Tel: 58 212 753 0723
Fax: 58 212 751 3180
email: obispoguerrero@iglesianglicanavzla.org
Web: www.iglesianglicanavzla.org

VERMONT (Province I)
Bishop Rt Revd Thomas C. Ely, 5 Rock Point Road, Burlington, VT 05401–2735, USA
Tel: 1 802 863 3431
Fax: 1 802 860 1562
email: tely@dioceseofvermont.org
Web: www.dioceseofvermont.org

VIRGIN ISLANDS (Province II)
Bishop Rt Revd Ambrose Gumbs, 13 Commandant Gade, Charlotte Amalie, St Thomas, VI 00801, USA
Tel: 1 340 776 1797
Fax: 1 340 777 8485
email: bishop@episcovi.org
Web:
www.episcopaldioceseofthevirginislands.com

VIRGINIA (Province III)
Bishop Rt Revd Peter James Lee, 110 W Franklin St, Richmond, VA 23220
Tel: 1 804 643 8451
Fax: 1 804 644 6928
email: pjlee@thediocese.net
Web: www.thediocese.net

Bishop Coadjutor Rt Revd Shannon S. Johnston
(*same address*)
email: kglasco@thediocese.net

Bishop Suffragan
Rt Revd David Colin Jones, Northern Virginia Office, Goodwin House, 4800 Fillmore Avenue, Alexandria, VA 22311, USA
Tel: 1 703 824 1325
Fax: 1 703 824 1348
email: dcjones@thediocese.net

WASHINGTON (Province III)
Bishop John Bryson Chane, Episcopal Church House, Mount St Alban, Washington, DC 20016–5094, USA
Tel: 1 202 537 6555
Fax: 1 202 364 6605
email: jchane@edow.org
Web: www.edow.org

Assisting Bishop Rt Revd Barbara C. Harris (*same address*)
email: bharris@edow.org

WEST MISSOURI (Province VII)
Bishop Rt Revd Barry Robert Howe, PO Box 413227, Kansas City, MO 64141–3227, USA
Tel: 1 816 471 6161
Fax: 1 816 471 0379
email: bphowe@earthlink.net
Web: www.diowestmo.org

WEST TENNESSEE (Province IV)
Bishop Rt Revd Don Edward Johnson, 692 Poplar Ave, Memphis, TN 38105, USA
Tel: 1 901 526 0023
Fax: 1 901 526 1555
email: info@episwtn.org
Web: www.episwtn.org

WEST TEXAS (Province VII)
Bishop Rt Revd Gary R. Lillibridge, PO Box 6885, San Antonio, TX 78209, USA
Tel: 1 210 824 5387
Fax: 1 210 822 8779
email: gary.lillibridge@dwtx.org
Web: www.dwtx.org

Bishop Suffragan Rt Revd David Reed (*same address*) *email:* david.reed@dwtx.org

WEST VIRGINIA (Province III)
Bishop Rt Revd W. Michie Klusmeyer PO Box 5400, Charleston, WV 25361–0400, USA
Tel: 1 304 344 3597
Fax: 1 304 343 3295
email: mklusmeyer@wvdiocese.org
Web: www.wvdiocese.org

WESTERN KANSAS (Province VII)
Bishop Rt Revd James Marshall Adams, Jr, PO Box 2507, Salina, KS 67401–2507
Tel: 1 785 825 1626
Fax: 1 785 825 0974
email: myrnapeterson@sbcglobal.net
Web: www.westernkansas.org

WESTERN LOUISIANA (Province VII)
Bishop Rt Revd D. Bruce MacPherson, PO Box 2031, Alexandria, Louisiana 71309, USA
Tel: 1 318 422 1304
Fax: 1 318 442 8712
email: dbm3wla@aol.com
Web: www.diocesewla.org

WESTERN MASSACHUSETTS (Province I)
Bishop Rt Revd Gordon P. Scruton, 37 Chestnut St, Springfield, MA 01103, USA
Tel: 1 413 737 4786
Fax: 1 413 746 9873
email: JLewis@diocesewma.org
Web: www.diocesewma.org

WESTERN MICHIGAN (Province V)
Bishop Rt Revd Robert R. Gepert, 5220 Lovers Lane, LL100, Portage, MI 49002, USA
Tel: 1 269 381 2710
Fax: 1 269 381 7067
email: rrgsupport@edwm.org
Web: www.edwm.org/

WESTERN NEW YORK (Province II)
Bishop Rt Revd J. Michael Garrison, 1114 Delaware Ave, Buffalo, NY 14209, USA
Tel: 1 716 881 0660
Fax: 1 716 881 1724
email: jmgarrison@episcopalwny.org
Web: www.episcopalwny.org

WESTERN NORTH CAROLINA (Province IV)
Bishop Rt Revd G. Porter Taylor, 900B Centre Park Drive, Asheville, NC 28805, USA
Tel: 1 828 225 6656
Fax: 1 828 225 6657
email: bishop@diocesewnc.org
Web: www.diocesewnc.org

WYOMING (Province VI)
Bishop Rt Revd Bruce Edward Caldwell, 104 South Fourth St, Laramie, WY 82070, USA
Tel: 1 307 742 6606
Fax: 1 307 742 6782
email: bruce@wydiocese.org
Web: www.wydiocese.org

The Church in Wales

Members 78,000
The Church in Wales has been an independent province since its disestablishment and separation from the Church of England in 1920. It is practically coterminous with Wales and is the largest denomination in the country. The major policy-forming body is the Governing Body and the Church's inherited assets, including buildings, are held in trust by the Representative Body.

Archbishop Most Revd Barry Cennydd Morgan (*Bishop of Llandaff*) *Tel:* 029 2056 2400
Fax: 029 2056 8410
email: archbishop@churchinwales.org.uk

Provincial Secretary and Archbishop's Registrar Mr John Shirley, 39 Cathedral Rd, Cardiff CF11 9XF
Tel: 029 2034 8218
Fax: 029 2038 7835
email: information@churchinwales.org.uk
Web: www.churchinwales.org.uk

Archbishop's Media Officer Anna Morrell (*same address*) *Tel:* 029 2034 8208

THEOLOGICAL COLLEGE
St Michael's Theological College, 54 Cardiff Road, Llandaff, Cardiff CF5 2YJ (*Warden and Principal* Revd Peter H. Sedgwick)
Tel: 029 2056 3379
Fax: 029 2083 8008
email: info@stmichaels.ac.uk

BANGOR
Bishop Vacancy, Ty'r Esgob, Ffordd Garth Uchaf Bangor, Gwynedd LL57 2SS *Tel:* 01248 362895
Fax: 01248 372454
email: bishop.bangor@churchinwales.org.uk
Web: www.churchinwales.org.uk/bangor

CATHEDRAL CHURCH OF ST DEINIOL, Bangor, Gwynedd
Dean The Very Reverend Alun John Hawkins, The Deanery, Cathedral Precinct, Bangor LL57 1LH *Tel:* 01248 362840

LLANDAFF

Bishop Most Revd Barry Cennydd Morgan (*Archbishop of the Province*), Llys Esgob, The Cathedral Green, Llandaff, Cardiff CF5 2YE
Tel: 029 2056 2400
Fax: 029 2056 8410
email: archbishop@churchinwales.org.uk
Web: www.churchinwales.org.uk/llandaff

Assistant Bishop of Llandaff, Rt Revd David Yeoman, Llys Esgob, The Cathedral Green, Cardiff CF5 2YE   *Tel:* 029 2920 562400
email: asstbishop@churchinwales.org.uk

CATHEDRAL CHURCH OF ST PETER AND ST PAUL, Llandaff, Cardiff
Dean Very Revd John Lewis, The Deanery, The Cathedral Green, Llandaff, Cardiff CF5 2YF
Tel: 029 2056 1545

MONMOUTH

Bishop Rt Revd Dominic Walker OGS, Bishopstow, 91a Stow Hill, Newport NP20 4EA
Tel: 01633 263510
Fax: 01633 259946
email: bishop.monmouth@churchinwales.org.uk
Web: www.churchinwales.org.uk/monmouth

CATHEDRAL CHURCH OF ST WOOLOS, Newport
Dean Very Revd Dr Richard Fenwick, The Deanery, Stow Hill, Newport NP20 4ED
Tel: 01633 263338

ST ASAPH

Bishop Vacancy, Esgobty, Upper Denbigh Road, St Asaph LL17 0TW   *Tel:* 01745 583503
Fax: 01745 584301
email: bishop.stasaph@churchinwales.org.uk
Web: www.churchinwales.org.uk/asaph

CATHEDRAL CHURCH OF ST ASAPH, St Asaph, Denbighshire
Dean Very Revd Christopher Potter, The Deanery, Upper Denbigh Road, St Asaph LL17 0RL   *Tel:* 01745 583597
email: chris_potter@talk21.com

ST DAVIDS

Bishop Rt Revd J. Wyn Evans, Llys Esgob, Abergwili, Carmarthen SA31 2JG
Tel: 01267 236597
Fax: 01267 237482
email: bishop.stdavids@churchinwales.org.uk
Web: www.churchinwales.org.uk/david

CATHEDRAL CHURCH OF ST DAVID AND ST ANDREW, St Davids, Pembrokeshire
Dean Very Revd Wyn Evans, The Deanery, St Davids, Haverfordwest SA62 6RH
Tel: 01437 720202
Fax: 01437 721885

SWANSEA AND BRECON

Bishop Rt Revd John David Edward Davies, Ely Tower, Brecon LD3 9DE   *Tel:* 01874 622008
Fax: 01874 610927
email:
bishop.swansea&brecon@churchinwales.org.uk
Web: www.churchinwales.org.uk/swanbrec

CATHEDRAL CHURCH OF ST JOHN THE EVANGELIST, Brecon, Powys
Dean Very Revd Geoffrey Marshall, The Deanery, Cathedral Close, Brecon LD3 9DP
Tel: 01874 623857
email: Geoffrey@canonry.co.uk

The Church of the Province of West Africa

Members 1,200,000
Church work began in Ghana as early as 1752 and in the Gambia, Guinea, Liberia and Sierra Leone in the nineteenth century. The Province of West Africa was founded in 1951 and was divided to form the Province of Nigeria and the Province of West Africa in 1979. The Church exists in an atmosphere of civil strife and Christians remain a minority.

Archbishop and Primate of the Province of West Africa Most Revd Dr Justice Ofei Akrofi (*Bishop of Accra*)

Dean of the Province of West Africa Rt Revd Albert D. Gomez (*Bishop of Guinea*)

Episcopal Secretary of the Province of West Africa Rt Revd Matthias K. Medadues-Badohu (*Bishop of Ho*)

Provincial Secretary Revd Fr Anthony M. Eiwuley, PO Box Lt 226, Lartebiokorshie, Accra, Ghana
Tel: 233 21 257 370
233 27 720 1538 (Mobile)
email: cpwa@4u.com.gh/
morkeiwuley@gmail.com

Provincial Treasurer Mr Samuel Atuobi Twum (*same address*)   *Tel:* 233 21 506 208
233 20 201 7969 (Mobile)
email: atlantichousing@yahoo.co.uk

THEOLOGICAL COLLEGES
Ghana
Trinity College (Ecumenical), PO Box 48, Legon, Ghana

St Nicholas Anglican Theological College, PO Box A 162, Cape Coast, Ghana

Liberia
Cuttington University College, Suacoco, PO Box 10–0277, 1000 Monrovia 10, Liberia

Sierra Leone
Theological Hall and Church Training Centre, PO
Box 128, Freetown, Sierra Leone

ACCRA
Bishop Most Revd Dr Justice Ofei Akrofi,
Bishopscourt, PO Box 8, Accra, Ghana
Tel: 233 21 662 292
Fax: 233 21 668 822
email: cpwa@4u.com.gh/
bishopakrofi@yahoo.com
Web: www.anglicandioceseofaccra.com

BO
Bishop Rt Revd Dr Samuel Sao Gbonda, PO Box
21, Bo, Southern Province, Sierra Leone
Tel: 232 32 648
Fax: 232 32 605
email: bomission@justice.com

CAMEROON (Missionary Diocese)
Bishop Rt. Revd. Thomas-Babyngton Flango Dibo,
BP 15705, New Bell, Douala, Cameroon
Tel and *Fax:* 237 408 552
email: revdibo@yahoo.com

CAPE COAST
Bishop Rt Revd Daniel S. A. Allotey,
Bishopscourt, PO Box A 233, Adisadel Estates,
Cape Coast, Ghana
Tel: 233 42 32 502
Fax: 233 42 32 637
email: danallotey@priest.com

FREETOWN
Bishop Rt Revd Julius Olotu Prince Lynch,
Bishop's Court, PO Box 537, Freetown, Sierra
Leone
Tel: 232 22 251 307
232 76 620 690 (Mobile)
Fax: 232 22 251 307 (via Ghana)
email: bertajuls@yahoo.co.uk

GAMBIA
Bishop Rt Revd Dr Tilewa Johnson,
Bishopscourt, PO Box 51, Banjul, The Gambia,
West Africa
Tel: 220 228 405
220 905 227 (Mobile)
email: stilewaj@hotmail.com
Web: www.gambiadiocese.com

GUINEA
Bishop Rt Revd Albert D. Gomez, BP 187,
Conakry, Guinea
Tel: 224 451 323
email: galbertdgomez@yahoo.fr

HO
Bishop Rt Revd Matthias K. Mededues-Badohu,
Bishopslodge, PO Box MA 300, Ho, Volta
Region, Ghana
Tel: 233 91 26644/26806
233 208 162 246 (Mobile)
email: matthoda@ucomgh.com

KOFORIDUA
Bishop Rt Revd Francis B. Quashie, PO Box 980,
Koforidua, Ghana
Tel: 233 81 22 329
Fax: 233 81 22 060
email: fbquashie@yahoo.co.uk

KUMASI
Bishop Rt Revd Daniel Yinka Sarfo, Bishop's
House, PO Box 144, Kumasi, Ghana
Tel and *Fax:* 233 51 24 117
233 277 890 411 (Mobile)
email: anglicandioceseofkumasi@yahoo.com /
dysarfo2000@yahoo.co.uk

LIBERIA
Bishop Rt Revd Jonathan B. B. Hart, PO Box
10–0277, 1000 Monrovia 10, Liberia
Tel: 231 224 760
231 651 6343 (Mobile)
Fax: 231 227 519
email: jbbhart@yahoo.com /
ecldioceselib@yahoo.com
Web: www.liberia.anglican.org

SEKONDI
Bishop Rt Revd John Kwamina Otoo, PO Box 85,
Sekondi, Ghana
Tel: 233 031 4604
email: angdiocesek@yahoo.co.uk

SUNYANI
Bishop Rt Revd Thomas Ampah Brient, PO Box
23, Sunyani, Ghana
Tel: 233 61 23213
233 208 121 670 (Mobile)
Fax: 233 61 712300
email: anglicandiocesesyi@yahoo.com

TAMALE
Bishop Rt Revd Emmanuel Anyindana Arongo,
PO Box 110, Tamale, Ghana
Tel: 233 71 26639
233 277 890 878 (Mobile)
Fax: 233 71 22906
email: bishopea2000@yahoo.com

WIAWSO
Bishop Rt Revd Abraham Kobina Ackah, PO Box
4, Sefwi, Wiawso, Ghana
email: bishopackah@yahoo.com

ANGLICAN AND PORVOO COMMUNIONS

The Church in the Province of the West Indies

Members 770,000
The West Indies became a self-governing province of the worldwide Anglican Communion in
1883 because of the Church of England missions
in territories that became British colonies. It is
made up of two mainland dioceses, Belize and
Guyana, and six island dioceses including the
Bahamas and Turks and Caicos Islands, Barbados, Jamaica and the Cayman Islands, North
Eastern Caribbean and Aruba, Trinidad and
Tobago, and the Windward Islands. Great
emphasis is being placed on training personnel

for an indigenous ministry as the island locations and scattered settlements make pastoral care difficult and costly.

Archbishop of the Province Most Revd Drexel Wellington Gomez (*Bishop of The Bahamas and the Turks and Caicos Islands*) Church House, PO Box N–7107, Nassau, Bahamas
Tel: 1 242 322 3015/6/7
Fax: 1 242 322 7943
email: primate@batelnet.net.bs
Web: www.thebahamas.net/cpwi/

Administrative Assistant to the Archbishop Ven I. Ranfurly Brown (*same address*)

Provincial Secretary Mrs Elenor Lawrence, Provincial Secretariat, Bamford House, Society Hill, St John, Barbados, West Indies
Tel: 1246 423 0842/3/8
Fax: 1 246 423 0855
email: bamford@sunbeach.net

THEOLOGICAL SEMINARIES
Codrington College, St John, Barbados (*Principal* Revd Dr Ian Rock)

United Theological College of the West Indies, PO Box 136, Golding Ave, Kingston 7, Jamaica (*Anglican Warden* Revd Garth Minott)

BARBADOS
Bishop Rt Revd Dr John Walder Dunlop Holder, Mandeville House, Collymore Rock, St Michael, Barbados
Tel: 1 246 426 2761/2
Fax: 1 246 426 0871
email: jwdh@sunbeach.net
Web: www.barbados.anglican.org

BELIZE
Bishop Rt Revd Philip S. Wright, #25 Bishopsthorpe, PO Box 535, Southern Foreshore, Belize City, Belize, Central America
Tel: 501 2 73 029
Fax: 501 2 76 898
email: bzediocese@btl.net
Web: www.belize.anglican.org

GUYANA
Bishop Rt Revd Randolph Oswald George, The Diocesan Office, PO Box 10949, 49 Barrack St, Georgetown, Guyana, West Indies
Tel: 592 22 64 775
Fax: 592 22 76 091
email: dioofguy@networksgy.com

JAMAICA AND CAYMAN ISLANDS
Bishop Rt Revd Alfred C. Reid, 2 Caledonia Ave, Kingston 5, Jamaica
Tel: 1 876 920 2712
Fax: 1 876 960 1774
email: bishopja@anglicandiocese.com
Web: www.jamaica.anglican.org

Bishops Suffragan
Rt Revd Robert McLean Thompson (*Bishop of Kingston*), 3 Duke Street, Kingston, Jamaica, West Indies
Tel: 876 926 6692
Fax: 876 960 8463
email: bishop.kingston@anglicandiocese.com

Rt Revd Harold Benjamin Daniel (*Bishop of Mandeville*), Bishop's Residence, 3 Cotton Tree Road, PO Box 84, Mandeville, Jamaica, West Indies
Tel: 1 876 625 6817
Fax: 1 876 625 6819
email: hbdaniel@cwjamaica.com

Rt Revd Dr Howard Gregory (*Bishop of Montego Bay*), PO Box 346, Montego Bay, Jamaica, West Indies
Tel: 1 876 952 4963
Fax: 1 876 971 8838
email: hkagregory@hotmail.com

THE BAHAMAS AND THE TURKS AND CAICOS ISLANDS
Bishop Most Revd Drexel Wellington Gomez (*Archbishop of the West Indies*), Church House, PO Box N-7107, Nassau, Bahamas
Tel: 1 242 322 3015/6/7
Fax: 1 242 322 7943
email: primate@batelnet.bs
Web: www.thebahamas.net/cpwi/

Bishop Coadjutor Rt Revd Laish Z. Boyd (*same address*)

Bishop Suffragan Rt Revd Gilbert Arthur Thompson (*New Providence*) (*same address*)

NORTH EAST CARIBBEAN AND ARUBA
Bishop Rt Revd Leroy Errol Brooks, St Mary's Rectory, PO Box 180, The Valley, Anguilla
Tel: 1 264 497 2235
Fax: 1 264 497 8555
email: brookx@anguillanet.com

TRINIDAD AND TOBAGO
Bishop Rt Revd Calvin Wendell Bess, Hayes Court, 21 Maraval Road, Port of Spain, Trinidad, Trinidad and Tobago, West Indies
Tel: 1 868 622 7387
Fax: 1 868 628 1319
email: bessc@tstt.net.tt

WINDWARD ISLANDS
Bishop Rt Revd C. Leopold Friday, Bishop's Court, Montrose, PO Box 502, St Vincent, West Indies
Tel: 1 784 456 1895
Fax: 1 784 456 2591
email: diocesewi@vincysurf.com

Anglican and Porvoo Communions

Other Churches and Extra-Provincial Dioceses

BERMUDA
(Anglican Church of Bermuda)
This extra-provincial diocese is under the metro-political jurisdiction of the Archbishop of Canterbury.

Bishop Vacancy,   *Tel:* 1 441 292 2967
email: bishopratteray@ibl.bm

Diocesan Office Bishop's Lodge, PO Box HM 769, Hamilton HM CX, Bermuda   *Tel:* 1 441 292 6987
Fax: 1 441 292 5421
email: diocoff@ibl.bm
Web: www.anglican.bm

Archdeacon Ven Andrew Doughty, Warwick Rectory, PO Box WK 530, Warwick, WK BX, Bermuda

THE CHURCH OF CEYLON (SRI LANKA)
Members 52,500
Anglican missionaries commenced their work in Sri Lanka (Ceylon) with the coming of British colonial power in 1796. The Church of Ceylon comprises the Dioceses of Colombo (1845) and Kurunagala (1950). Prior to 1845, the Church in Ceylon was part of the diocese of Madras. The two dioceses belonged to the former Province of India, Pakistan, Burma & Ceylon. Sri Lanka is currently an extra-provincial diocese under the metropolitan authority of the Archbishop of Canterbury, and steps are now being taken for the Church of Ceylon to adopt a new constitution to replace the Provincial Constitution.

Clergy, full-time workers and the laity are trained at the Ecumenical Theological College of Lanka and the Cathedral Institute. Both dioceses are members of the National Christian Council and have cordial working relationships with the Roman Catholic Church and other major faith groups. Through a few private church schools, the dioceses are involved in primary and secondary secular education. The challenges they face include the training and the empowerment of the people of God for mission and witness in the context of poverty, ethnic conflict and a multi-faith environment. Both dioceses are part of an ecumenical journey that seeks organic union with the other older Protestant denominations.

THEOLOGICAL COLLEGE
Theological College of Lanka, Pilimatalawa, nr Kandy

COLOMBO
Bishop Rt Revd Duleep Kamil de Chickera, 368/3A Bauddhaloka Mawatha, Colombo 7
Tel: 94 1 684 810
Fax: 94 1 684 811
email: bishop@eureka.lk

Secretary Mrs Mary Thanja Pereis (*same address*)
email: diocol@eureka.lk

KURUNEGALA
Bishop Rt Revd Kumara Bandara Samuel Illangasinghe, Bishop's Office, Cathedral Close, Kurunegala   *Tel:* 94 37 22 191/94 37 222 0371
Fax: 94 37 26 806
email: bishopkg@sltnet.lk

EPISCOPAL CHURCH OF CUBA
(Iglesia Episcopal de Cuba)
Members 10,000
The Episcopal Church of Cuba is under a Metropolitan Council in matters of faith and order. Council members include the Primate of Canada, the Archbishop of the West Indies, and the Presiding Bishop of the Episcopal Church of the United States of America or a Bishop appointed by him.

Interim Diocesan Bishop Rt Revd Miguel Tamayo, Calle 6 # 273, Vedado, Ciudad de la Habana 4, C.P. 10400, Cuba   *Tel:* 537 32 11 20
Fax: 537 33 32 93
Web: www.cuba.anglican.org

THEOLOGICAL COLLEGE
Seminario Evangelico de Teologica, Aptdo. 149, Matanzas (Interdenominational, run in cooperation with the Methodist and Presbyterian Churches)

CHURCH PAPER
Heraldo Episcopal Published bimonthly. Contains diocesan, provincial and world news, homiletics, devotional and historical articles.

FALKLAND ISLANDS
In 1977 the Archbishop of Canterbury resumed episcopal jurisdiction over the Falkland Islands and South Georgia which had been relinquished in 1974 to the Church of the Southern Cone of America. In 2006 he appointed Bishop Stephen Venner, the Bishop of Dover, as his commissary, with the title Bishop for the Falkland Islands. The whole parish covers the Falkland Islands, South Georgia, and the South Sandwich Islands and British Antarctic Territory. Christ Church Cathedral is the most southerly cathedral in the world.

Bishop for the Falkland Islands Rt Revd Stephen Venner (*Bishop of Dover*), The Bishop's Office, Old Palace, The Precincts, Canterbury CT1 2EE
Tel: 01227 459382
Fax: 01227 784985
email: Bishop@bishcant.org

Rector Vacancy, The Deanery, Stanley, Falkland Islands, South Atlantic   *Tel:* 00 500 21100
Fax: 00 500 21842

Associate Minister Revd Kathy Biles (*same address*)
email: k.biles@horizon.co.fk

LUSITANIAN CHURCH
(Portuguese Episcopal Church)
Members 5,000

Founded in 1880 by a group of local Roman Catholic priests and lay people as a reaction to a number of dogmas from the first Vatican Council. The Church consisted of Roman Catholic priests who formed congregations in and around Lisbon using a translation of the 1662 English Prayer Book. Its own first Prayer Book of Common Prayer was issued in 1884. A Lusitanian bishop was consecrated in 1958 and in the early 1960s many provinces of the Anglican Communion established full communion with the Church in Portugal. Full integration occurred in 1980 when the Church became an extra-provincial diocese under the metropolitical authority of the Archbishop of Canterbury. It takes seriously its role in the emerging Europe and has a commitment to helping the poor. It has a strong mission emphasis for the many unchurched people in the country, specially by its two diaconal institutions providing services and help to children and the elderly. The Church and its leaders cooperate fully with the Diocese in Europe (Church of England) and the Convocation of American Churches in Europe, assisting in each other's congregation and being a united Anglican voice in an increasingly secular Europe. In 1998 the diocesan synod of the Lusitanian Church approved and accepted the Porvoo Declaration, expressing its desire to be involved in the life of the Porvoo Communion and to cooperate, with interchangeable ministries, with the congregations of the Porvoo Churches in Portugal.

Bishop Rt Revd Dr Fernando da Luz Soares, Secretaria Diocesana, Apartado 392, P-4431-905 Vila Nova de Gaia, Portugal *Tel:* 351 22 375 4018
Fax: 351 22 375 2016
email: centrodiocesano@igreja-lusitana.org
Web: www.igreja-lusitana.org
Treasurer Senhor António Vaz Pinto dos Santos, Tesouraria Diocesana (*same address*)

SPANISH EPISCOPAL REFORMED CHURCH
Members 5,000

Parishes: 22 self supported, plus a similar number of congregations.

The Spanish Church covers the whole country and is divided into three archdiaconates, with three archdeacons:

Archdiaconate I: Catalonia, Valencia and Balearic islands

Archdiaconate II: Andalusia and Canary islands

Archdiaconate III: Central and Northern Spain

Under the leadership of some former Roman Catholic priests, in 1868 the Spanish Reformed Episcopal Church was established in Gibraltar and was for some years under the pastoral care of the Church of Ireland. The first Bishop was appointed in 1880 and consecrated in 1894 by the Bishop of Meath along with two other Bishops, and the Church of Ireland accepted metropolitan authority. The same year the Church adopted the Mozarabic Liturgy, which was the liturgy of the early Spanish Church. The Church was fully integrated into the Anglican Communion in 1980 under the metropolitical authority of the Archbishop of Canterbury. It has a strong evangelistic and mission commitment and it is organized into departments: youth, women, ecumenism, Christian education, mission and evangelization. The Church also has a very important social programme for immigrants, which was established in many parishes by helping with clothes and food for over 10,000 people per year. The history of the Church has been one of persecution and difficulties, especially during Franco's dictatorship, but it is firm in its cooperation with the Diocese in Europe and the Convocation of American Churches in Europe for a stronger Anglican presence throughout Europe.

Bishop Rt Revd Carlos López Lozano (*Bishop of Madrid*), Spanish Reformed Episcopal Church, Calle Beneficencia 18, 28004 Madrid
Tel: 34 91 445 2560
Fax: 34 91 594 4572
email: eclesiae@arrakis.es
Web: www.iere.cjb.net

Treasurer Señor Jesus Diaz Barragan (*same address*)

Regional Councils

COUNCIL OF THE ANGLICAN PROVINCES OF AFRICA

The Council of Anglican Provinces of Africa (CAPA) was established in 1979 in Chilema, Malawi, by Anglican Primates in Africa who saw the need to form a coordinating body that would help to bring the Anglican Communion in Africa together and to articulate issues affecting the Church. The organization was set up with the following aims and objectives:

- to help the Anglican churches in Africa develop beneficial relationships between themselves and with the wider Anglican Communion;
- to provide a forum for the Church in Africa to share experiences, consult and support each other;
- to confer about common responsibilities on the African continent;
- to establish opportunities for collaboration and joint activities;

- to maintain and develop relationships between the Anglican Church in Africa, partners, other denominations, fellowships, national and regional councils.

Today CAPA works with 12 Anglican provinces in Africa and the Diocese of Egypt. These provinces include Nigeria, West Africa, Sudan, Kenya, Uganda, Tanzania, Congo, Rwanda, Burundi, Central Africa, Southern Africa and Indian Ocean.

Chairman Most Revd Ian Ernest (*Primate of Indian Ocean*)

General Secretary The Rev Canon Grace Kaiso, PO Box 10329, 00100 Nairobi, Kenya
Tel: 254 20 3873 283/700
Fax: 254 20 3870 876
email: Generalsec@capa-hq.org
Web: www.capa-hq.org

Administrative Officer Mrs Elizabeth Gichovi (*same address*) *email:* info@capa-hq.org

HIV/AIDS TB & Malaria Programme Coordinator Mr Emmanuel Olatunji (*same address*)
email: olatunji@capa-hq.org/otunuel@yahoo.com

THE COUNCIL OF THE CHURCHES OF EAST ASIA
This Council, whose history began in 1954, has gone through an evolution. With most of the dioceses forming into provinces, the Council is now a fellowship for common action. Its membership includes dioceses in the Province of South East Asia, the Church of Korea, the Philippine Episcopal Church, Hong Kong Sheng Kung Hui, the Diocese of Taiwan (which is associated with the Episcopal Church of the USA), the Province of Myanmar, Nippon Sei Ko Kai (the Holy Catholic Church in Japan), the Philippine Independent Church and the Anglican Church of Australia who are members as a national Church or province.

Chairman Most Revd Dr John Chew Hiang Chea (*Archbishop of the Province of South East Asia*) Diocese of Singapore, St. Andrew's Village, 1, Francis Thomas Drive, 01–01 Singapore 359340.
Tel: 65 6288 7585
Fax: 65 6288 5574
email: bpoffice@anglican.org.sg
anglican@streamyx.com

THE SOUTH PACIFIC ANGLICAN COUNCIL
The Council now comprises the Province of Melanesia, the Province of Papua New Guinea, and the Diocese of Polynesia.

Chairman Rt Revd Elison Pogo (*Primate of the Church of Melanesia*), Archbishop's House, PO Box 19, Honiara, Solomon Islands *Tel:* 677 26 601
Fax: 677 21 098

Secretary Rt Revd Jabez Bryce (*Bishop of Polynesia*), PO Box 35, Suva, Fiji *Tel:* 679 3304 716
Fax: 679 3302 687
email: episcopus@connect.com.fj

ANGLICAN AND PORVOO
COMMUNIONS

UNITED CHURCHES IN FULL COMMUNION

CHURCHES RESULTING FROM THE UNION OF ANGLICANS WITH CHRISTIANS OF OTHER TRADITIONS

The population of the countries of South Asia is over 1,000 million and these Churches cover the whole area. The total Christian population is around 22–3 million and Christians of many different traditions, ranging from ancient oriental to pentecostal, are to be found here. The region is undergoing rapid social, economic and political change. There is also a resurgence of some of the great world religions. Although there is a great deal of industrialization and there have been 'green revolutions' in the agricultural sector in many countries, there is still a tremendous inequality in the distribution of wealth and income. In spite of the relatively small numbers of Christians, the Churches have grown steadily and have been responsible for many initiatives in education, medical work and community development. Their influence is out of all proportion to their size. The Church of England continues to relate to these Churches mainly through its mission agencies: CMS, USPG, SPCK and Crosslinks. In addition, the Oxford Mission, the Dublin University Mission to Chota Nagpur and the Religious Communities are doing valuable work. Support in money and personnel also comes from Churches in Canada, from CMS in Australia and New Zealand, from the USA, Holland, Germany, Scandinavia, Japan and Singapore. The Churches themselves are involved in the training and sending of mission personnel both inside and outside India, including the sending of mission partners to the UK. Mission partners from the Church of England work under the authority of the local church or institution to which they have been sent. The Church of North India, the Church of South India and Mar Thoma Syrian Church of Malenkara are in full communion with each other and are members of a joint council to further and deepen their unity. Since 1988, these Churches have become full members of the Lambeth Conference and the Anglican Consultative Council. Their moderators also attend the meetings of Anglican Primates.

The Church of Bangladesh

Members 15,623
Congregations/Pastorates 72
Bangladesh was part of the State of Pakistan which was partitioned from India in 1947. After the civil war between East and West Pakistan ended in 1971, East Pakistan became Bangladesh. The Church of Bangladesh is one of the United Churches, formed by a union of Anglicans with Christians of other traditions.

Moderator Rt Revd Michael S. Baroi (*Bishop of Dhaka*)

General Secretary Mr Augustin Dipok Karmokar, St Thomas' Church, 54 Johnson Road, Dhaka – 1100
　　　　　　　Tel: 880 2 711 6546
　　　　　　　Fax: 880 2 712 1632
　　email: cbdacdio@bangla.net

Treasurer Mr Joel Mondal (*same address*)

THEOLOGICAL COLLEGE
St Andrew's Theological College, 54/1 Barobag, Mirpur 2, Dhaka – 1216, Bangladesh (*Principal* Revd Sourav Folia)　　　　*Tel:* 880 2 802 0876

DHAKA
Bishop Rt Revd Michael S. Baroi (*Bishop of Dhaka and Moderator of the Church of Bangladesh*), St Thomas's Church, 54 Johnson Rd, Dhaka – 1100
　　　　　　　Tel: 880 2 711 6546
　　　　　　　Fax: 880 2 712 1632
　　email: cbdacdio@bangla.net

KUSHTIA
Bishop Rt Revd Paul S. Sarkar, 94 N.S. Road, Thanapara, Kushtia　　*Tel* and *Fax:* 880 71 54618
　　email: cob@citechco.net

The Church of North India

Members 1,250,000
The Church was inaugurated in 1970 after many years of preparation. It includes the Anglican Church, the United Church of Northern India (Congregationalist and Presbyterian), the Methodist Church (British and Australian Conferences), the Council of Baptist Churches in Northern India, the Church of the Brethren in India, and the Disciples of Christ. Along with the Church of South India, the Church of Pakistan and the Church of Bangladesh, it is one of the four United Churches.

Moderator Most Revd Joel V. Mal (*Bishop of Chandigarh*)

Deputy Moderator The Rt Revd Purely Lyngdoh (*Bishop of North East India*)

General Secretary and Acting Treasurer Revd Dr Enos Das Pradhan, CNI Bhavan, 16 Pandit Pant Marg, New Delhi 110 001   *Tel:* 91 11 2371 6513
email: gscni@ndb.vsnl.net.in/enos@cnisynod.org
Web: www.cnisynod.org

Treasurer Revd Dr Ashish Amos (*same address*)
email: cnitr@cnisynod.org

CHURCH PAPER
The North India Church Review The official monthly magazine of the CNI. Contains articles, reports, diocesan news, world news and letters. *Editor/Editorial Office* (*same address*)

AGRA
Bishop Rt Revd S. R. Cutting, Bishop's House, 4/116-B Church Rd, Civil Lines, Agra 282 002, UP
Tel: 91 562 2851 481
Fax: 91 562 2520 074
email: doacni@sancharnet.in

AMRITSAR
Bishop Rt Revd Pradeep Kumar Samantaroy, 26 R. B. Prakash Chand Rd, Opp Police Ground, Amritsar 143 001, Punjab
Tel and Fax: 91 183 222 2910
email: bunu13@rediffmail.com
Web: www.amritsardiocese.org

ANDAMAN AND NICOBAR ISLANDS
Bishop Rt Revd Christopher Paul, Bishop's House, 21 Church Lane, Goal Ghar, Port Blair 744 101, Andaman and Nicobar Islands
Tel and Fax: 91 3192 231 362
email: cniportblair@yahoo.co.in

BARRACKPORE
Bishop Rt Revd Brojen Malakar, Bishop's Lodge, 86 Middle Rd, Barrackpore 743 101, North 24 Parganas
Tel: 91 33 2592 0147
Fax: 91 33 2593 1852

BHOPAL
Bishop Rt Revd Laxman L. Maida, Mission Compound, First Church, Ratlam 457 001, MP
Tel: 91 731 270 0232
91 98270 34737 (Mobile)
email: bhopal_diocese@rediffmail.com

CHANDIGARH
Bishop Most Revd Joel Vidyasagar Mal (*Moderator CNI*), Bishop's House, Mission Compound, Brown Rd, Ludhiana 141 001, Punjab
Tel and Fax: 91 161 222 5707
email: bishopdoc@yahoo.com/
joelvmal@yahoo.com

CHOTA NAGPUR
Bishop Rt Revd B. B. Baskey, Bishop's Lodge, PO Box 1, Church Rd, Ranchi 834 001, Jharkhand
Tel: 91 651 235 1181
Fax: 91 651 235 1184
email: rch_cndta@sancharnet.in

CUTTACK
Bishop Rt Revd Dr Samson Das, Bishop's House, Mission Rd, Cuttack 753 001, Orissa
Tel: 91 671 230 0102
email: diocese@vsnl.net

DELHI
Bishop Rt Revd Sunil Singh, Bishop's House, 1 Church Lane, Off North Ave, New Delhi 110 001
Tel: 91 11 2371 7471
email: stmartin@dels.vsnl.net.in
Web: www.delhidiocese.org

DURGAPUR
Bishop Rt Revd Probal Kanto Dutta, Bishop's House, St Michael's Church Compound, Aldrin Path, Bidhan Nagar, Dugapur 713 212
Tel: 91 343 253 6220
email: probal_dutta@yahoo.com

EASTERN HIMALAYA
Bishop Rt Revd Dr Naresh Ambala, Bishop's Lodge, PO Box 4, Darjeeling 734 101, W Bengal
Tel: 91 354 225 8183
email: bpambala@yahoo.com

GUJARAT
Bishop Rt Revd Vinodkumar Mathushellah Malaviya, Bishop's House, I.P. Mission Compound, Ellisbridge, Ahmedabad 380 006, Gujarat
Tel and Fax: 91 79 2656 1950
email: gujdio@yahoo.co.in

JABALPUR
Bishop Rt Revd Prem Chand Singh, Bishop's House, 2131 Napier Town, Jabalpur 482 001, MP
Tel: 91 761 2622 109
email: bishoppcsingh@yahoo.co.in

KOLHAPUR
Bishop Rt Revd Bathuel Ramchandra Tiwade, Bishop's House, EP School Compound, Kolhapur 416 001, MS
Tel and *Fax:* 91 231 2654 832
email: kdccni@vsnl.com

KOLKATA
Bishop Rt Revd Ashok Biwas, Bishop's House, 51 Chowringhee Rd, Calcutta 700 071, WB
Tel: 91 33 6534 7770
Fax: 91 33 2822 6340
email: samrajubh@vsnl.net

LUCKNOW
Bishop Rt Revd Anil Stephen, Bishop's House, 25/11 Mahatma Gandhi Marg, Allahabad 211 011, UP
Tel: 91 532 242 7053
Fax: 91 532 256 0713

MARATHWADA
Bishop Rt Revd M. U. Kasab, Bishop's House, E. P. School Compound, Nagala Park, Kolhapur 416 003, MS
Tel and *Fax:* 91 231 2654 832
email: revmukasab@yahoo.com

MUMBAI
Bishop Rt Revd Prakash Dinkar Patole, 19 Hazarimal Somani Marg, Fort Mumbai 400 001
Tel: 91 22 2206 0248
email: bishopbomcni@rediffmail.com

NAGPUR
Bishop Rt Rev Paul Dupare, Cathedral House, Opp. Indian Coffee House, Sadar, Nagpur 440 001, MS
Tel: 91 712 562 1737
Fax: 91 712 309 7310
email: bishop@nagpur.dot.org.in

NASIK
Bishop Rt Revd Pradip Lemuel Kamble, Bishop's House, 1 Outram Rd, Tarakpur, Ahmednagar 414 001, MS
Tel: 91 241 241 1806
Fax: 91 241 242 2314
email: bishopofnasik@rediffmail.com

NORTH EAST INDIA
Bishop Rt Revd Purely Lyngdoh (*Deputy Moderator, CNI*), Bishop's Kuti, Shillong, Meghalaya 793 001
Tel: 91 364 2223 155
Fax: 91 364 2501 178
email: bishopnei15@hotmail.com

PATNA
Bishop Rt Revd Philip Phembuar Marandih, Bishop's House, Christ Church Compound, Bhagalpur 812 001, Bihar
Tel: 91 641 2400 033/2300 714
Fax: 91 641 2400 714
email: cnipatna@rediffmail.com

PHULBANI
Bishop Rt Revd Bijay Kumar Nayak, Bishop's House, Mission Compound, Gudripori, G-udaigiri, Phulbani 762 100, Kandhamal, Orissa
Tel: 91 6842 260569
email: bp.bkn@rediffmail.com

PUNE
Bishop Rt Revd Vijay Bapurao Sathe, Pune Diocesan Council, 1 Stevely Road (General Bhagat Marg), Red Bungalow, Pune 411 001, MS
Tel: 91 20 2633 4374
email: punediocese@yahoo.co.in

RAJASTHAN
Bishop Rt Revd Collin Theodore, 2/10 CNI Social Centre, Civil Lines, Opp. Bus Stand, Jaipur Rd, Ajmer 305 001
Tel: 91 145 2420 633
Fax: 91 145 2621 627

SAMBALPUR
Bishop Rt Revd Christ Kiron Das, Mission Compound, Bolangir 767 001, Orissa
Tel and *Fax:* 91 6652 230625
email: bishop_ckdas@rediffmail.com

The Church of Pakistan

Members 800,000
One of four United Churches in the Anglican Communion, the Church of Pakistan comprises the Anglican Church of Pakistan, the dioceses of Lahore and Karachi, two conferences of the United Methodist Church, the Scottish Presbyterian Church in Pakistan, and the Pakistan Lutheran Church.

Moderator Rt Revd Dr Alexander John Malik (*Bishop of Lahore*)

Deputy Moderator Rt Revd Sadiq Daniel (*Bishop of Karachi*)

General Secretary Mr Humphrey Peters, St John's Cathedral, 1 Sir Syed Road, Peshawar
Tel: 92 91 278 916/270 812
Tel: 92 91 5270 916/5270 812
Fax: 92 91 277 499

Treasurer Mr John Wilson, 27 Liaquat Road, Civil Lines, Hyderabad
Tel: 92 221 861 187/92 222 780 221

FAISALABAD
Bishop Rt Revd John Samuel, Bishop's House, PO Box 27, Mission Rd, Gojra, Distt Toba Tek Sing
Tel: 92 46 351 4698
92 300 655 0074 (Mobile)
email: jsamuel@brain.net.pk

HYDERABAD
Bishop Rt Revd Raffique Masih, 27 Liaquat Rd, Civil Lines, Hyderabad 71000, Sind
Tel: 92 22 2780 221
Fax: 92 22 2785 879
email: hays@hyd.infolink.net.pk

KARACHI
Bishop Rt Revd Sadiq Daniel (*Deputy Moderator, COP*), Holy Trinity Cathedral, Jinnah Rd, Karachi 75530
Tel: 92 521 8112
Fax: 92 21 565 3175
email: sadiqdaniel@hotmail.com

LAHORE
Bishop Rt Revd Dr Alexander John Malik (*Moderator, COP*), Bishopsbourne, Cathedral Close, The Mall, Lahore 54000
Tel: 92 42 723 3560 (Office)
92 42 7120 766 (Home)
Fax: 92 42 722 1270/92 42 721 0121
email: bishop_Lahore@hotmail.com

MULTAN
Bishop Vacancy, 113 Qasim Rd, PO Box 204, Multan Cantt
Tel and Fax: 92 61 588 799
email: bishopmd@mul.paknet.com.pk

PESHAWAR
Bishop Rt Revd Manowar/Rumal Shah, Diocesan Centre, 1 Sir-Syed Rd, Peshawar 2500, North West Frontier Province
Tel: 92 91 5276 519
Fax: 92 91 5277 499
email: bishopdop@hotmail.com

RAIWIND
Bishop Rt Revd Samuel Azariah, 17 Warris Rd, PO Box 2319, Lahore 54000
Tel: 92 42 758 8950
Fax: 92 42 757 7255
email: sammyazariah49@yahoo.com

SIALKOT
Bishop Rt Revd Samuel Pervez, Lal Kothi, Barah Patthar, Sialkot 2, Punjab
Tel: 92 432 264 895
Fax: 92 432 264 828/92 300 8615 828
email: chs_sialkot@yahoo.com

ARABIAN GULF
Bishop for Rt Revd Azad Marshall (*Area Bishop within the Diocese of Cyprus*), PO Box 688, Lahore, Punjab 54000
Tel: 92 42 542 0452
Fax: 92 42 542 0591
email: bishop@saintthomascenter.org

The Church of South India

Members 4,000,000
The Church was inaugurated in 1947 by the union of the South India United Church (itself a union of Congregational and Presbyterian/ Reformed traditions), the southern Anglican dioceses of the Church of India, and Burma, and the Methodist Church in South India. It is one of the four United Churches in the Anglican Communion.

Moderator Most Revd Dr J. W. Gladstone (*Bishop in South Kerala*)

Deputy Moderator Rt Revd Dr A. Christopher Asir (*Bishop in Madurai-Ramnad*)

General Secretary Revd Moses Jayakumar, CSI Centre5 Whites Rd, Royapettah, Chennai 600 014, India
Tel: 91 44 2852 1566/4166 (office)
2852 3763 (home)
email: csi@vsnl.com

Honorary Treasurer Mr T. Devasahayam FCA, Tsoudury Nilayam, 2–5–211, Nakkalaguta, Hanamkonda, 506 001, Andhra Pradesh
Tel: 91 44 2852 4166 (Office)
91 870 225 2938 (Home)
Fax: 91 44 2858 4163
email: csisnd_tr@satyam.net.in

OFFICIAL MAGAZINE
CSI Life English Monthly Magazine. Contains articles, reports and news from the dioceses. *Editor:* The General Secretary CSI; *Managing Editor:* Rev.

R. Mohanraj, Director, Dept of Communication, 5 Whites Road, Royapettah, Chennai 600 014; Yearly subscription Rs.150/- (£25 in UK, $30 in USA, $ 35 in Australia, $35 in New Zealand, sent by Air Mail).

COIMBATORE
Bishop in Rt Revd Dr Manikam Dorai, Diocesan Office, 256 Race Course Rd, Coimbatore 641018, Tamil Nadu
Tel: 91 422 221 3605
Fax: 91 442 200 0400

DORNAKAL
Bishop in Rt Revd Dr B. S. Devamani, Bishop's Office S. C. RLY, Cathedral Compound, Dornakal 506 381, Warangal Dist., Andhra Pradesh
Tel: 91 8719 227 752 (Home)
227 535 (Office)
email: bishpindkl@yahoo.com

EAST KERALA
Bishop in Rt Revd Dr K. G. Daniel, Bishop's House, Melukavumattom, Kottayam 686 652, Kerala State
Tel: 4822 219 044 (Home)
91 4822 220 001 (Office)
Fax: 91 482 291 044

JAFFNA
Bishop in Rt Revd Daniel S. Thiagarajah, Bishop's office in Colombo, 36 5/2 Sinsapa Road, Colombo 6, Sri Lanka
Tel: 94 60 215 0795 (Office)
Fax: 94 11 250 5805
email: bishopthiagarajah@gmail.com

KANYAKUMARI
Bishop in Rt Revd G. Devakadasham, CSI
Diocesan Office, 71A Dennis St, Nagercoil
629 001, Tamil Nadu   *Tel:* 91 4652 231 539
Fax: 91 4652 226 560
email: csikkd@bsnl.in

KARIMNAGAR
Bishop in Rt Revd Dr P. Surya Prakash, Bishop's
House, 2–8–95 CVRN Road, PO Box 40,
Makarampura post, Karimnagar 505 001,
Andhra Pradesh   *Tel:* 91 878 22 62971
email: suryaprakash@yahoo.com/
bishopsuryaprakash@yahoo.com

KARNATAKA CENTRAL
Bishop in Rt Revd S. Vasanthkumar, Diocesan
Office, 20 Third Cross, CSI Compound,
Bangalore 560 027, Karnataka
Tel: 91 80 2222 3766/4941
email: csikcd@vsnl.com

KARNATAKA NORTH
Bishop in Rt Revd J. Prabhakara Rao, Bishop's
House, All Saints' Church Compound, Dharwad
580 008, Karnataka   *Tel:* 91 836 244 7733
Fax: 91 836 274 5461
email: bishopprabhakar@yahoo.co.in

KARNATAKA SOUTH
Bishop in Rt Revd Devaraj Bangera, Bishop's
House, Balmatta, Mangalore 575 001, Karnataka
Tel: 91 824 243 2657/242 1802
Fax: 91 824 242 1802

KRISHNA-GODAVARI
Bishop in Rt Revd Dr G. Dyvasirvadam, CSI St
Andrew's Cathedral Compound, Main Rd,
Machilipatnam 521 002, AP   *Tel:* 91 8672 220 623
email: bishopkrishna@yahoo.com

MADHYA KERALA
Bishop in Rt Revd Thomas Samuel, CSI Bishop's
House, Cathedral Rd, Kottayam 686 018, Kerala
Tel: 91 481 2566 536
Fax: 91 481 566 531
email: csimkdbishop@bsnl.in/
bishopthomassamuel@yahoo.com

MADRAS
Bishop in Rt Revd Dr V. Devasahayam, Diocesan
Office, PO Box 4914, 226 Cathedral Rd, Chennai
600 086, Tamil Nadu
Tel: 91 44 2811 3929/3933/7629
Fax: 91 44 2811 0608
Web: www.csimadrasdiocese.org

MADURAI-RAMNAD
Bishop in Rt Revd Dr A. Christopher Asir (*Deputy
Moderator, CSI*), 5 Bhulabai Desai Rd,
Chockikulam, Madurai 625 002, Tamil Nadu
Tel: 91 452 256 3196/0541
Fax: 91 452 256 0864
email: csidmr@gmail.com

MEDAK
Bishop in Vacancy
Moderator's Commissary Rt Revd Dr P. Surya
Prakash, 10–3–165 Diocesan Office, Golden
Jubilee Bhavan, Old Lancer Lane, Secunderabad
500 003, Andhra Pradesh   *Tel:* 94 40 2772 1811
Fax: 94 40 2784 4215

NANDYAL
Bishop in Rt Revd Dr P. J. Lawrence, Bishop's
House, Nandyal RS 518 502, Kurnool Dist.,
Andhra Pradesh   *Tel:* 91 8514 222 477
Fax: 91 8514 242 255
email: lawrencejoba@yahoo.com

NORTH KERALA
Bishop in Rt Revd Dr K. P. Kuruvilla, PO Box 104,
Shoranur 679 121, Kerala   *Tel:* 91 466 2222 655
Fax: 91 466 2222 545
email: csinkd@md5.vsnl.net

RAYALASEEMA
Bishop in Rt Revd Chowtipalle Bellam Moses
Frederick, Bishop's House, CSI Compound,
Gooty 515 401, Ananthapur Dist, AP
Tel: 91 8662 325 320
Fax: 91 8562 275 200

SOUTH KERALA
Bishop in Rt Revd J. W. Gladstone (*Moderator,
CSI*), Bishop's House, LMS Compound,
Trivandrum 695 033, Kerala State
Tel: 91 471 231 5490
Fax: 91 471 231 6439
email: bishopjwgladstone@yahoo.com

TIRUNELVELI
Bishop in Rt Revd Dr S. Jeyapaul David,
Bishopstowe, PO Box 118, 16, North High
Ground Rd, Tirunelveli 627 002, Tamil Nadu
Tel: 91 462 257 8744
Fax: 91 462 257 4525
email: bishop@csitirunelveli.org

TRICHY-TANJORE
Bishop in Rt Revd Dr G. Paul Vasanthakumar, PO
Box 31, 17 VOC Rd, Cantonment, Tiruchiarapalli
620 001, Tamil Nadu   *Tel:* 91 431 2771 254
Fax: 91 431 2418 485
email: csittd@rediffmail.com

THOOTHUKUDI-NAZARETH
Bishop in Charge Rt Revd J. A. D. Jebachandran,
Bishop's House, 111/32T, Polpettai Extension,
State Bank Colony, Thoothukudi 628 002, Tamil
Nadu   *Tel:* 91 461 2345 430
Fax: 91 431 2346 911
email: bishoptndone@yahoo.com

VELLORE
Bishop in Rt Revd Dr Yesurathnam William, CSI
Diocesan Office, 1/A Officer's Lane, Vellore
632 001, Tamil Nadu   *Tel:* 91 416 2232 160
Fax: 91 416 2223 835

THE HOLY CATHOLIC CHURCH IN CHINA

(Chung Hua Sheng Kung Hui)

The Chung Hua Sheng Kung Hui was an important denomination in China and its history dates back to the mid-nineteenth century. Today the CHSKU, as a separate denomination, no longer exists in the People's Republic of China, except for Hong Kong which returned to Chinese sovereignty on 1 July 1997. Under the formula 'one country – two systems' Hong Kong keeps its autonomy for 50 years, including the religious situation. The same applies to Macao which was returned by Portugal to China at the end of 1999. On the Chinese mainland the Protestant Churches, with few exceptions, have entered into a post-denominational phase under the China Christian Council. A United Church is in the process of being created and Christians of Anglican inspiration are very much a part of this process. Bishop K. H. Ting, now in his old age, has retired from active leadership of the China Christian Council.

Although the CHSKU is no longer in existence, many former Anglicans still share a strong spiritual affinity with other Anglican Churches on matters of belief and liturgical tradition. As the Chinese Protestant Church develops its own ecclesiology and forms of worship, the Anglican traditions will no doubt contribute to a richer synthesis.

The relations between the Church in China and the Churches in Britain are facilitated by the China Desk of the Global Mission Network. The latter is a commission of the Churches Together in Britain and Ireland (CTBI). It provides advice to government, churches and media, and publishes *China Study Journal*, a documentary review of Chinese religions and government policy. The China Desk is a continuation of the ecumenical China Study Project which was established in 1972 by the leading missionary societies, including Anglican organizations such as the CMS, USPG and the Archbishop's China Appeal Fund.

The Friends of the Church in China, an ecumenical association which works closely with the China Desk of CTBI, takes a more grass-roots approach in relation to Christians in China. It publishes a popular newsletter on China and organizes visits to Chinese churches. China Desk/CTBI, Bastille Court, 2 Paris Garden, London SE1 8ND. The contact is Miss Caroline Fielder, Director of China Desk (*email:* caroline-.fielder@ctbi.org.uk, *Tel:* 020 7654 7234).

Friends of the Church in China, c/o Seagulls, Pinmill, Chelmondiston, Ipswich IP9 1JN. Its Chairman is Revd John Pritchard and the Secretary is Canon Simon Brown.

ANGLICAN AND PORVOO COMMUNIONS

OTHER CHURCHES IN COMMUNION WITH THE CHURCH OF ENGLAND

Old Catholic Churches of the Union of Utrecht

The Old Catholic Churches are a family of nationally organized churches which bound themselves together in the Union of Utrecht in 1889. Most of them owe their origin to Roman Catholics who were unable to accept the decrees of the First Vatican Council in 1870 and left the communion of that Church. The Archbishopric of Utrecht, however (from which the other Old Catholic Churches derived their episcopal orders), has been independent of Rome since the eighteenth century following a complex dispute involving papal and capitular rights of nomination and accusations of Jansenism (until 1910 in the Netherlands only). The Latin Mass continued in use, though all the Old Catholic Churches now worship in the vernacular. Their rites stand within the Western tradition, with various 'Eastern' features.

By the acceptance of the Bonn Agreement on 20 and 22 January 1932, the Convocation of Canterbury established full communion with the Old Catholic Churches by means of the following resolutions:

'That this House approves of the following statements agreed on between the representatives of the Old Catholic Churches and the Churches of the Anglican Communion at a Conference held at Bonn on 2 July 1931:

1. Each Communion recognises the catholicity and independence of the other and maintains its own.
2. Each Communion agrees to admit members of the other Communion to participate in the sacraments.
3. Intercommunion does not require from either Communion the acceptance of all doctrinal opinion, sacramental devotion, or liturgical practice characteristic of the other, but implies that each believes the other to hold all the essentials of the Christian Faith.

'And this House agrees to the establishment of Intercommunion between the Church of England and the Old Catholics on these terms.'

An Anglican–Old Catholic International Coordinating Council was established in 1998.

AUSTRIA
Bishop Rt Revd Bernhard Heitz, Schottenring 17/1/3/12, A–1010 Vienna
email: bischof.heitz@altkatholiken.at
Web: www.altkatholiken.at

CROATIA
(Bishopric vacant, under the care of the Bishop of Austria) *email:* bischof.heitz@altkatholiken.at

CZECH REPUBLIC
Bishop Rt Revd Dušan Hejbal, Na Bateriich 27, CZ–16200 Prague 6 *email:* stkat@starokatolici.cz
Web: www.starokatolici.cz

FRANCE
Mission de France 15 rue de Douai, 75009 Paris, France *email:* bishof@christkath.ch
Web: www.vieux-catholique-alsace.com

GERMANY
Bishop Rt Revd Joachim Vobbe, Gregor–Mendel-Strasse 28, 53115 Bonn, Germany
email: ordinariat@alt-katholisch.de
Web: www.alt-katholisch.de

ITALY
Mission in Italy Revd Petr Zivny, Viale Caterina da Forli, 58, 1–201146, Milano, Italy
Tel: 39 2 48 70 94 43
email: altkatholischekircheitalien@guarigione-liberazione-org
Web: www.guarigione-liberazione.org

NETHERLANDS
Archbishop Most Revd Dr Joris Vercammen *(Archbishop of Utrecht and President of the International Bishops' Conference),* Kon Wilhelminalaan, 3, NL–3818 HN Amersfoort
email: buro@okkn.nl
Web: www.okkn.nl/welkom

POLAND (The Polish National Catholic Church)
Prime Bishop Most Revd Wiktor Wysoczanski, ul. Balanowa 7, PL–02–635 Warsaw
email: polskokatolicki@pnet.pl
Web: www.polskokatolicki.pl

SWEDEN AND DENMARK
(No bishop; under the care of the Bishop of Haarlem) Rt Revd Bert Wrix, Wilhelminastraat 26, NL–2011 VM Haarlem, Netherlands *email:* bvh@okkn.nl

SWITZERLAND
Bishop Rt Revd Fritz-René Müller, Willadingweg 39, CH–3006 Bern *email:* bischof@christkath.ch
Web: www.christkath.ch

Philippine Independent Church

The Philippine Independent Church is in part the result of the Philippine revolution against Spain in 1896 for religious emancipation and Filipino identity. It was formally established in 1902, declaring its independence from the Roman Catholic Church but seeking to remain loyal to the Catholic Faith. It now derives its succession from the Protestant Episcopal Church in the United States of America (and therefore from Anglican sources), with which full communion was established in September 1961. It has a membership of approximately seven million followers, 34 dioceses with 50 bishops, 600 regular church buildings and 2,000 village chapels served by about 600 priests.

Following the report of a Commission appointed by the Archbishop of Canterbury, full communion on the basis of the Bonn Agreement was established between the Church of England and the Philippine Independent Church in 1963 by the Convocations of Canterbury and York. It is in full communion with all the member Churches in the Anglican Communion.

The Philippine Independent Church is very active in its ecumenical relations. It is the most senior member in the National Council of the Churches in the Philippines, a member of the Council of Churches in East Asia, a member of the Christian Churches in Asia, and an active member of the World Council of Churches.

Supreme Bishop (*Obisbo Maximo*) Most Revd Tomas A. Millamena, 1500 Taft Avenue, Ermita, Manila, Philippines 2801.
Tel: 63 2 523 72 42
Fax: 63 2 521 39 32
email: ifiphil@hotmail.com

Mar Thoma Syrian Church of Malabar

The Christian community in South India is very ancient and is believed by its members to have been founded by the Apostle Thomas (Mar Thoma). Over the centuries contact with Christian bodies from outside India has led to the fragmentation of the original community into a number of jurisdictions. During the latter part of the nineteenth century the Christians of the West Syrian (Syrian Orthodox) tradition divided into two over the issue of the removal of non-biblical features from teaching and worship of the Church. The influence of Anglican missionaries of the Church Missionary Society who had been working in Malabar since the beginning of the nineteenth century accelerated the new stance in the Church. The larger section (which itself has subsequently divided into the Indian Orthodox and Jacobite Churches) chose closer links with Antioch and remained 'unreformed'; the smaller group, which eventually adopted the name of Mar Thoma Syrian Church of Malabar, undertook a conservative revision of its rites, removing elements (such as the invocation of saints and prayers for the dead) that were not scriptural practices but had given room for misunderstanding of the gospel. The general form of Mar Thoma worship remains eastern. Its episcopal succession derives from the Patriarchate of Antioch.

The former CIPBC (Church of India, Pakistan, Burma and Ceylon) had partial intercommunion with the Mar Thoma Church from 1937 until 1961 when a Concordat of Full Communion was established. The Mar Thoma Syrian Church of Malabar is now in full communion with the Churches of South India and North India. The union of these three churches is now known as the Communion of Churches in India (CCI), which fosters cooperation in mission, theological training, and formulations and involvement in social issues.

The Mar Thoma Church has stated its desire to preserve its eastern traditions and is not willing to merge with the two Western United Churches. A number of Anglican Provinces are in full communion with the Mar Thoma Church, the Church of England having become so in 1974.

The Malabar Independent Syrian Church of Thozhiyoor occupies a unique position in the complex history of the Church in South India. At various times in the past its bishops have consecrated bishops for both the Orthodox and Mar Thoma Churches when the episcopal succession in those churches has died out. The MISC is fully Orthodox in rite and faith. It is in communion with the Mar Thoma Church and its current practice is to extend eucharistic hospitality to Christians of other traditions. The former Metropolitan was an ecumenical participant at the 1998 Lambeth Conference.

THE MAR THOMA SYRIAN CHURCH OF MALABAR
Metropolitan Most Revd Dr Philipose Mar Chrysostom Mar Thoma, Poolatheen, Tiruvalla 689 101, Kerala, South India
Tel: 91 469 263 0313
Fax: 91 469 260 2626
email: pulathen@md3.vsnl.net.in
Sabha Secretary Revd Dr Cherian Thomas, Mar Thoma Church Headquarters, Sabha Office, SCS Campus, Tiruvalla 689 101, Kerala, South India
Tel: 91 469 263 0449
Fax: 91 469 263 0327
email: marthoma@vsnl.com

THE MALABAR INDEPENDENT SYRIAN CHURCH
Most Revd Cyril Mar Basilios, St George's Cathedral, Thozhiyoor, Thrissur Dt 680 520, Kerala, South India

Maps of the Churches and Provinces of the Anglican Communion

The maps of the Anglican Communion which follow have been supplied by Nicola Lawrence of The Mothers' Union. She will be happy to hear of any changes which need to be made.

© *The Mothers' Union 2008*

MAP 1

The Scottish Episcopal Church
1 Moray, Ross and Caithness
2 Argyll and the Isles
3 St Andrews, Dunkeld and Dunblane
4 Aberdeen and Orkney
5 Brechin
6 Glasgow and Galloway
7 Edinburgh

.... Diocesan Boundary

– – – – – Provincial Boundary

| The Isles of Scilly are included in the Diocese of Truro | The Channel Islands are annexed to the Diocese of Winchester |

ANGLICAN AND PORVOO COMMUNIONS

The Church of Ireland
Province of Armagh
 8 Derry and Raphoe
 9 Connor
10 Tuam, Killala and Achonry
11 Kilmore, Elphin and Ardagh
12 Clogher
13 Armagh
14 Down and Dromore

Province of Dublin
15 Limerick and Killaloe
16 Meath and Kildare
17 Cork, Cloyne and Ross
18 Cashel and Ossory
19 Dublin and Glendalough

The Church in Wales
20 Bangor
21 St Asaph
22 St Davids
23 Swansea and Brecon
24 Llandaff
25 Monmouth

The Church of England
Province of York
26 Carlisle
27 Newcastle
28 Durham
29 Ripon and Leeds
30 Bradford
31 Blackburn
32 York
33 Wakefield
34 Manchester
35 Liverpool
36 Chester
37 Sheffield
38 Southwell and Nottingham
39 Sodor and Man

Province of Canterbury
40 Lichfield
41 Derby
42 Lincoln
43 Hereford
44 Worcester
45 Birmingham
46 Coventry
47 Leicester
48 Peterborough
49 Ely
50 Norwich
51 St Edmundsbury and Ipswich
52 Gloucester
53 Bristol
54 Oxford
55 St Albans
56 London
57 Chelmsford
58 Truro
59 Exeter
60 Bath and Wells
61 Salisbury
62 Winchester
63 Portsmouth
64 Guildford
65 Southwark
66 Rochester
67 Chichester
68 Canterbury
Diocese in Europe

Extra-Provincial Dioceses
Bermuda
Lusitanian Church
Spanish Episcopal Reformed Church
The Church of Ceylon
Falkland Islands

MAP 2

PAPUA NEW GUINEA

The Anglican Church of Australia

Province of Western Australia
1 North West Australia
2 Perth
3 Bunbury

Province of South Australia
4 Willochra
5 Adelaide
6 The Murray

Province of Queensland
7 The Northern Territory
8 North Queensland
9 Rockhampton
10 Brisbane

Province of New South Wales
11 Riverina
12 Bathurst
13 Armidale
14 Grafton
15 Newcastle
16 Sydney
17 Canberra and Goulburn

see enlargement

Province of Victoria
18 Ballarat
19 Bendigo
20 Wangaratta
21 Melbourne
22 Gippsland

23 Tasmania *(extra-provincial)*

The Anglican Church of Papua New Guinea
24 Aipo Rongo
25 Dogura
26 New Guinea Islands
27 Popondota
28 Port Moresby

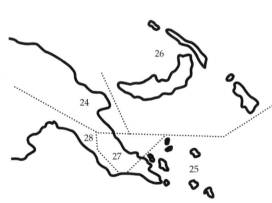

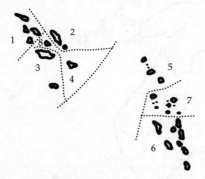

MAP 3

FIJI

16

TONGA

The Church of the Province of Melanesia
1 Ysabel
2 Malaita
3 Central Melanesia
4 Hanuato'o
5 Temotu
6 Vanuatu
7 Banks and Torres
8 Central Solomons

**The Anglican Church in Aotearoa,
New Zealand and Polynesia**
9 Auckland
10 Waikato
11 Waiapu
12 Wellington
13 Nelson
14 Christchurch
15 Dunedin
16 Polynesia

Bishopric of Aotearoa
A Hui Amorangi ki te Tai Tokerau
B Hui Amorangi ki te Manawa o te Wheke
C Hui Amorangi ki te Tairawhiti
D Hui Amorangi ki te Upoko o te Ika
E Hui Amorangi ki te Waipounamu

-------------- Bishopric of Aotearoa

The Episcopal Church in the United States of America

Province I
1 Connecticut
2 Maine
3 Massachusetts
4 New Hampshire
5 Rhode Island
6 Vermont
7 Western Massachusetts

Province II
8 Albany
9 Central New York
10 Long Island
11 New Jersey
12 New York
13 Newark
14 Rochester
15 Western New York
Haiti *(see Map 5)*
Virgin Islands *(see Map 5)*
Convocation of American Churches
    in Europe

Province III
16 Bethlehem
17 Central Pennsylvania
18 Delaware
19 Easton
20 Maryland
21 Northwestern Pennsylvania
22 Pennsylvania
23 Pittsburgh
24 Southern Virginia
25 Southwestern Virginia
26 Virginia
27 Washington
28 West Virginia

Province IV
29 Alabama
30 Atlanta
31 Central Florida
32 Central Gulf Coast
33 East Carolina

34 East Tennessee
35 Florida
36 Georgia
37 Kentucky
38 Lexington
39 Louisiana
40 Mississippi
41 North Carolina
42 South Carolina
43 Southeast Florida
44 Southwest Florida
45 Tennessee
46 Upper South Carolina
47 West Tennessee
48 Western North Carolina

Province V
49 Chicago
50 Eau Claire
51 Fond du Lac
52 Indianapolis
53 Michigan
54 Milwaukee
55 Missouri
56 Northern Indiana
57 Northern Michigan
58 Ohio
59 Quincy
60 Southern Ohio
61 Springfield
62 Western Michigan
63 Eastern Michigan

Province VI
64 Colorado
65 Iowa
66 Minnesota
67 Montana
68 Nebraska
69 North Dakota
70 South Dakota
71 Wyoming

Province VII
72 Arkansas
73 Dallas
74 Fort Worth
75 Kansas
76 Northwest Texas
77 Oklahoma
78 Rio Grande
79 Texas
80 West Missouri
81 West Texas
82 Western Kansas
83 Western Louisiana

Province VIII
84 Arizona
85 California
86 Eastern Oregon
87 El Camino Real
88 Idaho
89 Los Angeles
90 Navajoland Area Mission
91 Nevada
92 Northern California
93 Olympia
94 Oregon
95 San Diego
96 San Joaquin
97 Spokane
98 Utah
Hawaii
Alaska *(see Map 6)*
Taiwan *(see Map 14)*
Micronesia

ANGLICAN AND PORVOO
COMMUNIONS

MAP 4

see enlargement

Anglican and Porvoo Communions

MAP 5

The Church in the Province of the West Indies
32 Belize
33 Jamaica and the Cayman Islands
34 North Eastern Caribbean
   & Aruba
35 Windward Islands
36 Barbados
37 Trinidad and Tobago
38 Guyana
46 Suriname (part of the Diocese
   of Guyana)
47 Cayenne (part of the Diocese
   of Guyana)
39 Nassau and the Bahamas and
   the Turks and Caicos Islands

Province IX
2 Honduras
6 Litoral Ecuador
7 Central Ecuador
8 Colombia
9 Dominican Republic
11 Puerto Rico
12 Venezuela

The Anglican Church of Mexico
13 Western Mexico
14 Northern Mexico
15 Mexico
16 Cuernavaca
17 Southeastern Mexico

The Anglican Church of the Central American Region
1 Guatemala
3 El Salvador
4 Nicaragua
5 Panama
10 Costa Rica

The Episcopal Anglican Church of Brazil
18 Rio de Janeiro
19 Recife
20 Southern Brazil
21 São Paulo
22 Southwestern Brazil
23 Brasilia
24 Pelotas
44 Curitiba
45 Amazon
48 Missionary District of Oesle-Brasil

Anglican Church of the Southern Cone of America
25 Argentina
26 Chile
27 Northern Argentina
28 Paraguay
29 Peru
30 Uruguay
31 Bolivia

FALKLAND ISLANDS

The Episcopal Church of Cuba
(Autonomous diocese)
40 Cuba
41 Bermuda (*extra-provincial to Canterbury*)
42 Haiti (Province II ECUSA – *see Map 4*)
43 Virgin Islands (Province II ECUSA – *see Map 4*)

ANGLICAN AND PORVOO COMMUNIONS

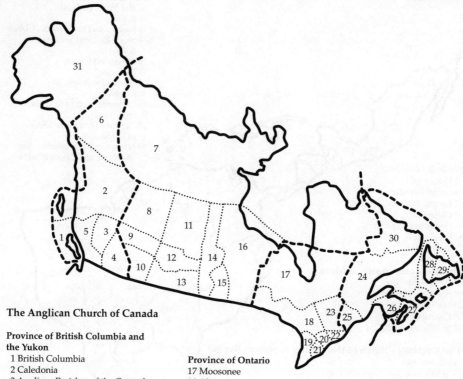

MAP 6

The Anglican Church of Canada

Province of British Columbia and the Yukon
1 British Columbia
2 Caledonia
3 Anglican Parishes of the Central Interior
4 Kootenay
5 New Westminster
6 Yukon

Province of Rupert's Land
7 The Arctic
8 Athabasca
9 Edmonton
10 Calgary
11 Saskatchewan
12 Saskatoon
13 Qu'Appelle
14 Brandon
15 Rupert's Land
16 Keewatin

Province of Ontario
17 Moosonee
18 Algoma
19 Huron
20 Toronto
21 Niagara
22 Ontario
23 Ottawa

Province of Canada
24 Quebec
25 Montreal
26 Fredericton
27 Nova Scotia and Prince Edward Island
28 Western Newfoundland
29 Central Newfoundland
30 Eastern Newfoundland and Labrador

31 Alaska *(in Province VIII of ECUSA)*

MAP 7

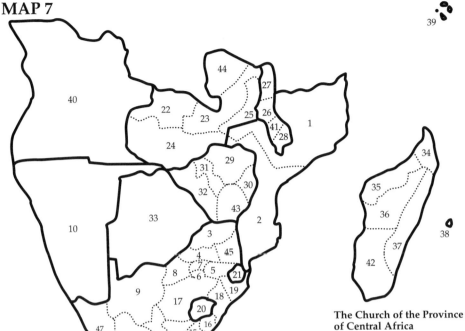

The Church of the Province of Southern Africa

1 Niassa
2 Lebombo
3 St Mark the Evangelist
4 Pretoria
5 Highveld
6 Christ the King
7 Johannesburg
8 Matlosane
9 Kimberley and Kuruman
10 Namibia
11 Cape Town
12 George
13 Port Elizabeth
14 Grahamstown

15 Mthatha
16 Umzimvubu
17 Free State
18 Natal
19 Zululand
20 Lesotho
21 Swaziland
40 Angola
45 Mpumalanga
46 False Bay
47 Saldanha Bay

St Helena

The Church of the Province of Central Africa

22 Northern Zambia
23 Central Zambia
24 Lusaka
25 Eastern Zambia
26 Lake Malawi
27 Northern Malawi
28 Southern Malawi
29 Harare
30 Manicaland
31 Central Zimbabwe
32 Matabeleland
33 Botswana
41 Upper Shire
43 Masvingo
44 Luapula

The Church of the Province of the Indian Ocean

34 Antsiranana
35 Mahajanga
36 Antananarivo
37 Toamasina
38 Mauritius
39 Seychelles
42 Fianarantsoa

ANGLICAN AND PORVOO COMMUNIONS

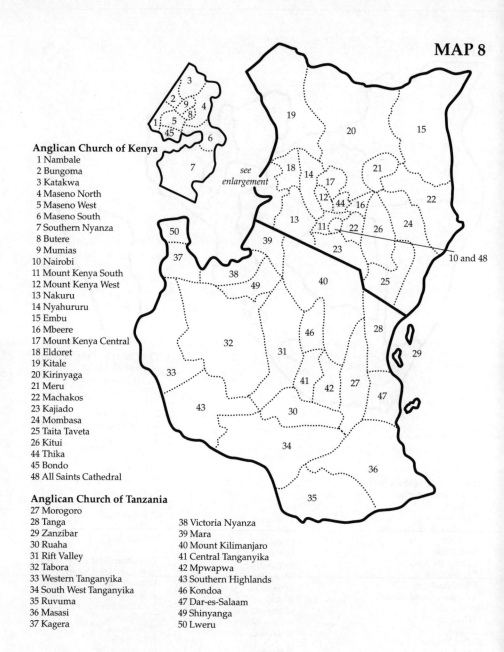

MAP 8

Anglican Church of Kenya
1 Nambale
2 Bungoma
3 Katakwa
4 Maseno North
5 Maseno West
6 Maseno South
7 Southern Nyanza
8 Butere
9 Mumias
10 Nairobi
11 Mount Kenya South
12 Mount Kenya West
13 Nakuru
14 Nyahururu
15 Embu
16 Mbeere
17 Mount Kenya Central
18 Eldoret
19 Kitale
20 Kirinyaga
21 Meru
22 Machakos
23 Kajiado
24 Mombasa
25 Taita Taveta
26 Kitui
44 Thika
45 Bondo
48 All Saints Cathedral

Anglican Church of Tanzania
27 Morogoro
28 Tanga
29 Zanzibar
30 Ruaha
31 Rift Valley
32 Tabora
33 Western Tanganyika
34 South West Tanganyika
35 Ruvuma
36 Masasi
37 Kagera

38 Victoria Nyanza
39 Mara
40 Mount Kilimanjaro
41 Central Tanganyika
42 Mpwapwa
43 Southern Highlands
46 Kondoa
47 Dar-es-Salaam
49 Shinyanga
50 Lweru

MAP 9

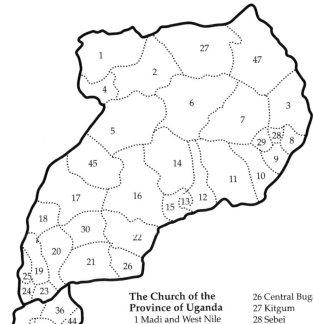

The Church of the Province of Uganda
1 Madi and West Nile
2 Northern Uganda
3 Karamoja
4 Nebbi
5 Bunyoro-Kitara
6 Lango
7 Soroti
8 North Mbale
9 Mbale
10 Bukedi
11 Busoga
12 Mukono
13 Kampala
14 Luweero
15 Namirembe
16 Mityana
17 Ruwenzori
18 South Ruwenzori
19 North Kigezi
20 West Ankole
21 Ankole
22 West Buganda
23 Kigezi
24 Muhabura
25 Kinkizi

26 Central Buganda
27 Kitgum
28 Sebei
29 Kumi
30 North Ankole
45 Masindi-Kitara
46 North Karamoja

The Church of the Province of Burundi
31 Bujumbura
32 Buye
33 Gitega
34 Matana
35 Makamba
46 Muyinga

The Church of the Province of Rwanda
36 Byumba
37 Shyira
38 Cyangugu
39 Kigeme
40 Butare
41 Shyogwe
42 Kigali
43 Kibungo
44 Gahini

MAP 10

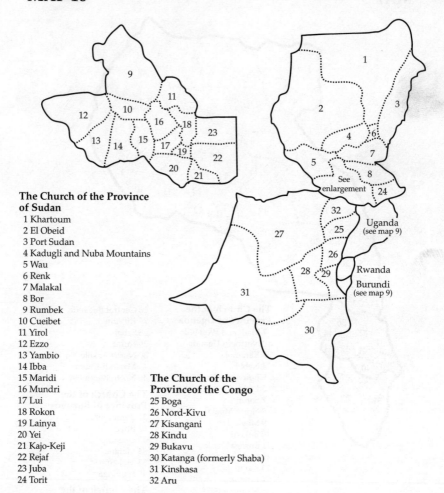

The Church of the Province of Sudan
1 Khartoum
2 El Obeid
3 Port Sudan
4 Kadugli and Nuba Mountains
5 Wau
6 Renk
7 Malakal
8 Bor
9 Rumbek
10 Cueibet
11 Yirol
12 Ezzo
13 Yambio
14 Ibba
15 Maridi
16 Mundri
17 Lui
18 Rokon
19 Lainya
20 Yei
21 Kajo-Keji
22 Rejaf
23 Juba
24 Torit

The Church of the Province of the Congo
25 Boga
26 Nord-Kivu
27 Kisangani
28 Kindu
29 Bukavu
30 Katanga (formerly Shaba)
31 Kinshasa
32 Aru

MAP 11

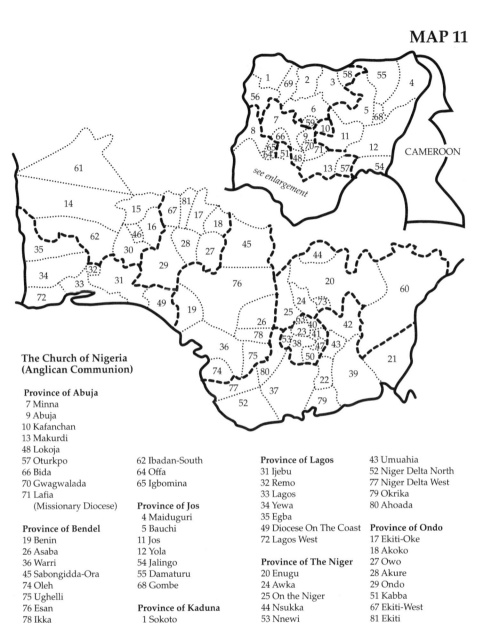

CAMEROON

see enlargement

The Church of Nigeria
(Anglican Communion)

Province of Abuja
7 Minna
9 Abuja
10 Kafanchan
13 Makurdi
48 Lokoja
57 Oturkpo
66 Bida
70 Gwagwalada
71 Lafia
   (Missionary Diocese)

Province of Bendel
19 Benin
26 Asaba
36 Warri
45 Sabongidda-Ora
74 Oleh
75 Ughelli
76 Esan
78 Ikka

Province of Ibadan
8 Kwara
14 Ibadan
15 Osun
16 Ilesa
30 Ife
46 Oke-Osun
61 Ibadan-North

62 Ibadan-South
64 Offa
65 Igbomina

Province of Jos
4 Maiduguri
5 Bauchi
11 Jos
12 Yola
54 Jalingo
55 Damaturu
68 Gombe

Province of Kaduna
1 Sokoto
2 Katsina
3 Kano
6 Kaduna
56 Kebbi
   (Missionary Diocese)
58 Dutse
   (Missionary Diocese)
59 Wusasa
69 Gusau

Province of Lagos
31 Ijebu
32 Remo
33 Lagos
34 Yewa
35 Egba
49 Diocese On The Coast
72 Lagos West

Province of The Niger
20 Enugu
24 Awka
25 On the Niger
44 Nsukka
53 Nnewi
60 Abakaliki
73 Oji River

Province of Niger Delta
21 Calabar
22 Aba
37 The Niger Delta
39 Uyo
42 Ukwa

43 Umuahia
52 Niger Delta North
77 Niger Delta West
79 Okrika
80 Ahoada

Province of Ondo
17 Ekiti-Oke
18 Akoko
27 Owo
28 Akure
29 Ondo
51 Kabba
67 Ekiti-West
81 Ekiti

Province of Owerri
23 Orlu
38 Owerri
40 Okigwe North
41 Okigwe South
47 Mbaise
50 Egbu
63 Ideato

ANGLICAN AND PORVOO
COMMUNIONS

MAP 12

The Episcopal Church in Jerusalem and the Middle East
1 Cyprus and the Gulf
2 Iran
3 Egypt
4 Jerusalem

Anglican Communion in Japan (Nippon Sei Ko Kai)
1 Hokkaido
2 Tohoku
3 Kita Kanto
4 Tokyo
5 Yokohama
6 Chubu (Mid Japan)
7 Kyoto
8 Osaka
9 Kobe
10 Kyushu
    Okinawa (*see Map 14*)

The Church of the Province of West Africa
1 The Gambia
2 Guinea
3 Liberia
4 Freetown
5 Bo
6 Tamale
7 Kumasi
8 Koforidua
9 Accra
10 Cape Coast
11 Sekondi
12 Sunyani
13 Ho
14 Wiawso
Cameroon (*see Map 11*)

Anglican and Porvoo Communions

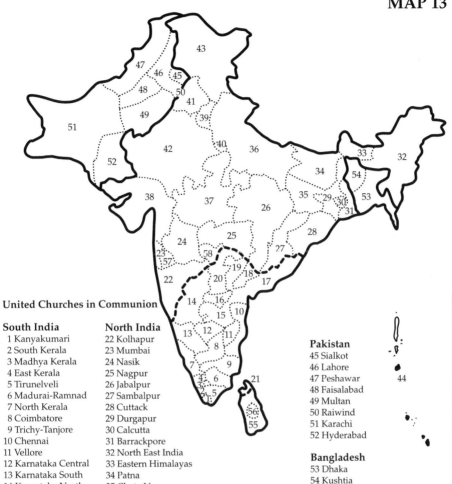

MAP 13

ANGLICAN AND PORVOO COMMUNIONS

United Churches in Communion

South India
1 Kanyakumari
2 South Kerala
3 Madhya Kerala
4 East Kerala
5 Tirunelveli
6 Madurai-Ramnad
7 North Kerala
8 Coimbatore
9 Trichy-Tanjore
10 Chennai
11 Vellore
12 Karnataka Central
13 Karnataka South
14 Karnataka North
15 Rayalaseema
16 Nandyal
17 Krishna-Godavari
18 Dornakal
19 Karimnagar
20 Medak
21 Jaffna

North India
22 Kolhapur
23 Mumbai
24 Nasik
25 Nagpur
26 Jabalpur
27 Sambalpur
28 Cuttack
29 Durgapur
30 Calcutta
31 Barrackpore
32 North East India
33 Eastern Himalayas
34 Patna
35 Chota Nagpur
36 Lucknow
37 Bhopal
38 Gujarat
39 Delhi
40 Agra
41 Chandigarh
42 Rajasthan
43 Amritsar
44 Andaman and Nicobar Islands
57 Pune
58 Marathwada

Pakistan
45 Sialkot
46 Lahore
47 Peshawar
48 Faisalabad
49 Multan
50 Raiwind
51 Karachi
52 Hyderabad

Bangladesh
53 Dhaka
54 Kushtia

The Church of Ceylon (Sri Lanka)
55 Colombo
56 Kuranegala

MAP 14

Chung Hua Sheng Kung Hui (China)

*Contact is only with the Diocese of Hong Kong
and Macao, which is under the temporary
Metropolitan Authority of the Council of the
Churches of East Asia.*

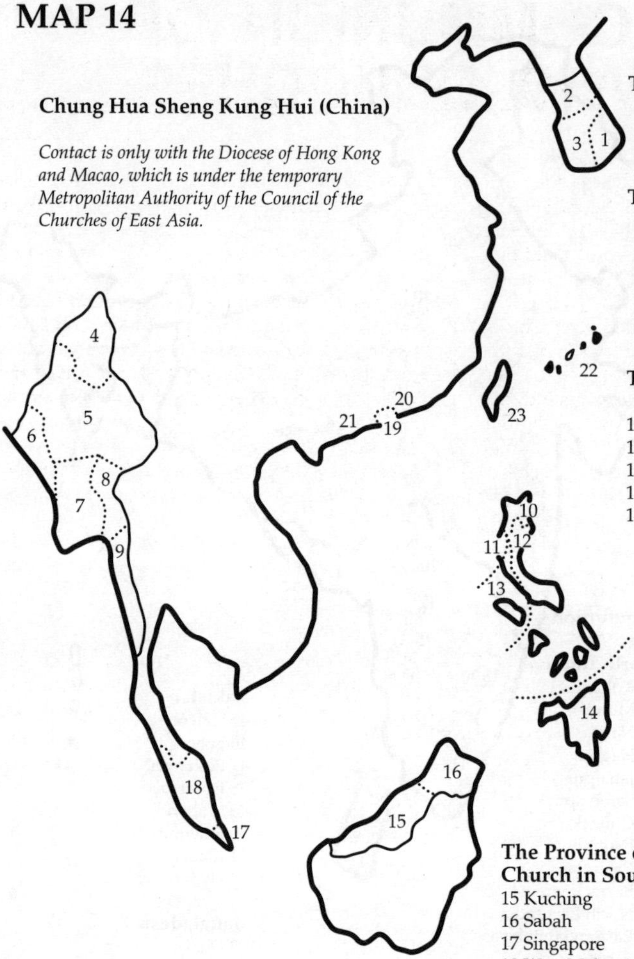

The Anglican Church of Korea
1 Pusan
2 Seoul
3 Taejon

The Province of Myanmar
4 Myitkyina
5 Mandalay
6 Sittwe
7 Yangon
8 Toungoo
9 Hpa-an

**The Episcopal Church in
the Philippines**
10 Northern Luzon
11 North Central Philippines
12 Northern Philippines
13 Central Philippines
14 Southern Philippines

**The Province of the Anglican
Church in South East Asia**
15 Kuching
16 Sabah
17 Singapore
18 West Malaysia

22 Okinawa
(Diocese in the Anglican Communion in Japan)

23 Taiwan
(Diocese in Province VIII of ECUSA)

Hong Kong Sheng Kung Hui
(Hong Kong Anglican Church)
19 Hong Kong Island
20 Eastern Kowloon
21 Western Kowloon

Anglican and Porvoo Communions

THE COMMUNION OF PORVOO CHURCHES

In October 1992 representatives of the four British and Irish Anglican Churches, the five Nordic Lutheran Churches and the three Baltic Lutheran Churches met in Finland for the fourth and final plenary session of their formal Conversations, which had commenced in 1989. They agreed *The Porvoo Common Statement*, named after Porvoo Cathedral, in which they had celebrated the Eucharist together.

The Common Statement recommended that the participating churches jointly make the Porvoo Declaration, bringing them into communion with each other. This involves common membership, a single, interchangeable ministry and structures to enable the Churches to consult each other on significant matters of faith and order, life and work. The implementation of the commitments contained in the Declaration is coordinated by the Porvoo Agreement Contact Group. The Porvoo Panel of the Church of England was established in 2000 to monitor and develop the implementation of the Porvoo commitments in dioceses and sector ministries.

In 1994 and 1995 the Declaration was approved by the four Anglican Churches, four of the Nordic Lutheran Churches and two of the Baltic Lutheran Churches. The General Synod's final approval of the Declaration in July 1995, following a reference to the diocesan synods, was by overwhelming majorities in each House. The Danish bishops announced in August 1995 that none of them was able to approve the Declaration, and the Evangelical–Lutheran Church of Latvia has not yet reached its decision. The Declaration was signed in the autumn of 1996 at services in Trondheim (Norway), Tallinn (Estonia) and Westminster Abbey.

The Nordic Lutheran Churches are the historic national Churches of their respective countries. At the Reformation, when they adhered to Lutheranism, they continued to be episcopally ordered, retaining the historic sees. In Sweden and Finland the succession of the laying on of hands at episcopal consecration was unbroken, whereas in Denmark, Norway and Iceland this was not the case. The Estonian and Latvian Lutheran Churches are similarly their countries' historic national Churches, which became Lutheran at the Reformation. Only in the northern part of Estonia was episcopacy retained, and there only until 1710, but it was restored in both Estonia and Latvia in the twentieth century, the bishops being consecrated in the historic succession. The Lithuanian Lutheran Church, which is now a small minority Church, adopted episcopacy in historic succession in 1976.

The Porvoo Agreement supersedes earlier separate agreements dating from the 1920s, 1930s and 1950s with the Churches concerned (except the Lithuanian Lutheran Church). These provided for mutual eucharistic hospitality and (with the Swedish, Finnish, Estonian and Latvian Churches) mutual participation in episcopal consecrations. Because of the Soviet occupation of the Baltic States, however, it was only in 1989 and 1992 respectively that it was possible for an Anglican bishop to participate in a Latvian and an Estonian consecration for the first time.

The Porvoo Declaration commits the signatory Churches 'to regard baptized members of all of our Churches as members of our own'. It also means that clergy ordained by bishops of the signatory Churches are placed in the same position with regard to ministry in the Church of England as those ordained by Anglican bishops overseas.

Further information can be found on the Porvoo website: www.porvoochurches.org, or is available from the European Secretary at the Council for Christian Unity at Church House, Westminster.

The Porvoo Agreement Contact Group

Co-Chairmen
Rt Revd Martin Wharton (*Bishop of Newcastle*)
email: bishop@newcastle.anglican.org
Rt Revd Dr Ragnar Persenius (*Bishop of Uppsala*)
email: ragnar.persenius@svenskakyrkan.se

Co-Secretaries
Revd Dr Matti Repo (Nordic and Baltic Churches)
email: matti.repo@evl.fi
Revd Canon Dr Charles Hill (Church of England Council for Christian Unity – *see* page 170)
email: charles.hill@c-of-e.org.uk

The Porvoo Panel
Chairman Rt Revd Dr Kenneth Stevenson
(*Bishop of Portsmouth*)

Porvoo Chaplains in England

Estonia
The Very Revd Lagle Heinla, Estonian House, 18 Chepstow Villas, London W11 2RB
Tel: 020 7229 6700

Finland
The Revd Juha Rintamaji, The Finnish Church in London, 33 Albion Street, London SE16 7JG
Tel: 020 7237 1261

Iceland
The Revd Sigurdur Arnarson, Icelandic
Embassy, 2a Hans Street, London SW1X 0JE
Tel: 020 7259 3999

Norway
The Revd Torbjørn Holt, 1 St Olav's Square,
Albion Street, London SE16 7JB
Tel: 020 7740 3900
The Revd Hallvard Mosdol (*same address*)

Sweden
The Revd Michael Persson, 6 Harcourt Street,
London W1H 2BD   *Tel:* 020 7723 5681

Churches in the Communion of Porvoo Churches

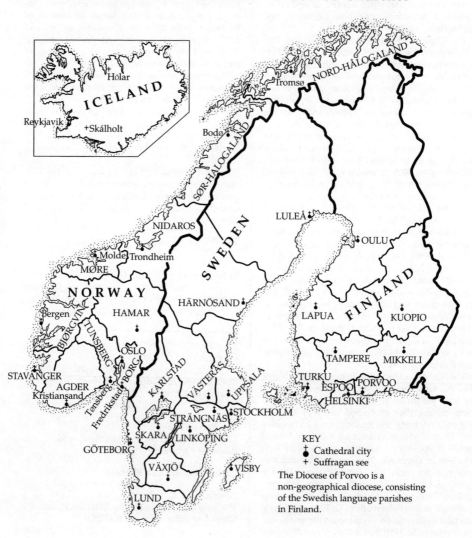

KEY
✝ Cathedral city
+ Suffragan see

The Diocese of Porvoo is a
non-geographical diocese, consisting
of the Swedish language parishes
in Finland.

NORDIC LUTHERAN CHURCHES

The Evangelical–Lutheran Church of Finland

The first bishop in the Finnish Church was St Henrik, the Apostle of Finland. According to tradition, St Henrik was an Englishman who accompanied King Erik II of Sweden on a military expedition to south-western Finland in 1155 and was martyred there the following year. From the middle of the thirteenth century until 1809 Finland was part of Sweden, and until the Reformation it formed a single diocese (Turku) in the Province of Uppsala.

In 1554 the Swedish king appointed the Finnish Lutheran Reformer Mikael Agricola (d. 1557) as Bishop of Turku, at the same time founding a second Finnish see, Viipuri (eventually transferred to Tampere). In addition to translating the New Testament and parts of the Old into Finnish, Mikael Agricola compiled the first catechism, liturgy and ritual in Finnish. He is regarded as the father of Finnish as a written language.

A wave of revivals, beginning in the eighteenth century, gave rise in the nineteenth to four mass movements. These remained within the Church of Finland and are still influential on its life today.

In 1809 Finland was annexed by Russia. As a result, the Finnish Church became entirely independent of the Church of Sweden, and from 1817 the Bishop of Turku was styled Archbishop. Finland finally gained its independence in 1917.

Today, roughly 84 per cent of Finns are members of the Evangelical–Lutheran Church of Finland, while only 4 per cent are members of other Churches. The ELCF is a 'folk church' (as is the Orthodox Church). The framework for its life is set by the Ecclesiastical Act. Amendments to this state law can only be proposed by the Synod, and Parliament can accept or reject but not amend such proposals. The Church is governed by the Synod, the Church Council and the Bishops' Conference. Although the Archbishop is only *primus inter pares* of the Finnish bishops, he is the President of the Synod and chairs both the Bishops' Conference and the Church Council.

The Church is organized in nine dioceses, one of which consists of the Swedish-speaking parishes (Porvoo). The diocese of Helsinki has recently divided into two, giving rise to the new see of Espoo.

Porvoo Agreement Contact Executive Secretary for Theology (vacant), Department for International Relations, Satamakatu 11, Box 185, FI-00161 Helsinki   *Tel:* 358 9 1802 290
Fax: 358 9 1802 230
Web: www.evl.fi/english/index.html

HELSINKI
Bishop Rt Revd Dr Eero Huovinen, Diocesan Chapter, PO Box 142, FI-00121 Helsinki
Tel: 358 9 709 25 70
Fax: 358 9 709 25 88
email: eero.huovinen@evl.fi
Web: www.helsinginhiippakunta.evl.fi/

ESPOO
Bishop Rt Revd Dr Mikko Heikka, Diocesan Chapter, PO Box 203, FI-02771 Espoo
Tel: 358 9 8050 8832
Fax: 358 9 8050 8848
email: mikko.heikka@evl.fi
Web: http://espoonhiippakunta.evl.fi/english/

KUOPIO
Bishop Rt Revd Dr Wille Riekkinen, Diocesan Chapter, PO Box 42, FI-70101 Kuopio   *Tel:* 358 17 288 8414
Fax: 358 17 288 8420
email: wille.riekkinen@evl.fi

LAPUA
Bishop Rt Revd Dr Simo Peura, Diocesan Chapter, PO Box 60, FI-62101 Lapua   *Tel:* 358 6 4339 325
Fax: 358 6 4339 320
email: simo.peura@evl.fi

MIKKELI
Bishop Rt Revd Dr Voitto Huotari, Diocesan Chapter, PO Box 122, FI-50101 Mikkeli   *Tel:* 358 15 3216011
Fax: 358 15 3216 016
email: voitto.huotari@evl.fi

OULU
Bishop Rt Revd Dr Samuel Salmi, Diocesan Chapter, PO Box 85, FI-90101 Oulu   *Tel:* 358 8 311 4654
Fax: 358 8 311 0659
email: samuel.salmi@evl.fi

PORVOO
(The Diocese of Porvoo (Borgå) is a non-geographical Swedish-language diocese.)
Bishop Rt Revd Dr Gustav Björkstrand, Diocesan Chapter, PO Box 30, FI-06101 Borgå
Tel: 358 19 529 7716
Fax: 358 19 585 705
email: gustav.björkstrand@evl.fi
Web: http://borgastift.planeetta.com

TAMPERE
Bishop Rt Revd Dr Matti Repo, Diocesan Chapter, Eteläpuisto 2C, FI-33200 Tampere
Tel: 358 3 238 1130
Fax: 358 3 238 1150
email: matti.repo@evl.fi
Web: www.tampereenhiippakunta.fi/in_english

TURKU
Archbishop of Turku and Finland Rt Revd Jukka Paarma, PO Box 60, FI-20501 Turku
Tel: 358 2 279 7031
Fax: 358 2 279 7002
email: Arkkipiispa@evl.fi

Bishop of Turku Rt Revd Dr Kari Mäkinen (*same address*)
Tel: 358 2 279 7033
Fax: 358 2 2797 001
email: kari.makinen@evl.fi

The Evangelical–Lutheran Church of Iceland

Christianity was adopted at Thingvellir by decree of the legislature in the year 1000. The ancient Icelandic sees of Skálholt and Hólar were founded in 1055 and 1106, respectively. Having previously been under the jurisdiction of Bremen and Lund, from 1153 Iceland belonged to the Province of Nidaros (Trondheim). Part of the Kingdom of Norway from 1262, Iceland eventually came under Danish rule. The Lutheran Reformation was introduced in 1541. From this time onwards until 1908 (with one exception in the late eighteenth century), Icelandic bishops were consecrated by the Bishops of Sealand (Copenhagen).

The two Icelandic sees were united in 1801, but in 1909 they were revived as suffragan sees. Iceland gained its independence from Denmark in 1918, becoming a republic in 1944.

A new Church law came into effect on 1 January 1998, granting the Church considerable autonomy from the state. The Church Assembly is the highest organ of the Church. Today, around 90 per cent of the Icelandic population are members of the Church of Iceland.

Porvoo Agreement Contact Revd Dr Sigurdur Arni Thordarson, Neskirkja, Hagatorgi, 107 Reykjavik, Iceland
Tel: 354 511 1561
email: s@biskup.is

The Church of Iceland comprises a single diocese, with two suffragan bishops in the ancient sees of Hólar and Skálholt.

Bishop of Iceland Most Revd Karl Sigurbjörnsson, Laugavegur 31, 101 Reykjavík
Tel: 354 535 1500
Fax: 354 551 3284
email: biskup@biskup.is
Web: www.kirkjan.is/?english

Bishop of Skálholt Rt Revd Sigurdur Sigurdarson, Skálholt, Biskupshús, Skálholti, 801 Selfoss
Tel: 354 486 8972
Fax: 354 486 8975
email: srsigsig@eyjar.is

Bishop of Hólar Rt Revd Jón Adalsteinn Baldvinsson, Biskupssetur, Hólar, 551 Saudárkrókur
Tel: 354 453 6300
Fax: 354 453 6301
email: jon.a.baldvinsson@kirkjan.is

Contact for ecumenical affairs Ms Steinunn A. Björnsdóttir, Ecumenical Secretary, Bishop's office, Laugavegur 31, 150 Reykjavík, Iceland
Tel: 354 535 1500
Fax: 354 551 3284
email: steinunn.bjornsdottir@biskup.is

The Church of Norway

From around AD 1000 Christianity was brought to Norway by missionaries both from the British Isles and from Germany. Central to the Christianizing of Norway was King Olav Haraldsson. After his death in 1030 he was venerated as St Olave, and his shrine in Nidaros Cathedral (Trondheim) was a centre of pilgrimage. Episcopal sees were established in Nidaros, Bergen, Oslo (by 1100), and in Stavanger (1125) and Hamar (1153). Part of the Province of Lund from 1103, Norway became a separate province when Nidaros was raised to an archiepiscopal see in 1153. In addition to the five Norwegian sees, the Province of Nidaros also included six further dioceses covering Iceland, the Faeroes, Greenland, the Shetland and Orkney Islands, the Hebrides and the Isle of Man. Under Olav IV (1380–87) Norway was united with Denmark.

The Norwegian Reformation of 1537 was imposed by the new King of Denmark, Christian III, with little evidence of popular enthusiasm. New bishops ('superintendents') were ordained to the sees of Nidaros, Bergen and Stavanger by Johannes Bugenhagen, the Superintendent of Wittenberg, in 1537, and Bugenhagen's Danish Church Order was extended to Norway in 1539. Of the pre-Reformation bishops, Bishop Hans Rev of Oslo alone accepted the Reformation, and returned to his see (to which that of Hamar had been united) as Superintendent in 1541. The diocesan structure had been retained, with four of the five historic sees, and the term 'bishop' soon replaced its Latin synonym 'superintendent', but until recent years neither Bishop Rev nor any other bishop consecrated in the historic succession of the laying on of hands participated in the consecration of future bishops. Nidaros ceased to be an archiepiscopal see.

In the eighteenth and nineteenth centuries, pietist movements became influential, but they remained within the Church of Norway, the membership of which still amounts to 86.2 per cent of the population. During the German occupation of 1940–45, the Church was a focus of resistance under the leadership of Bishop Eivind Berggrav of Oslo (1884–1959). In 1993 Rosemarie Köhn became the Church of Norway's first woman bishop, when the Norwegian government appointed her Bishop of Hamar.

The Church of Norway has an 85-member General Synod, consisting of the 80 members of the eleven diocesan councils (including the bishops), three members representing clergy, laity and lay employees, the moderators of the Sami Church Council and the Council on Ecumenical and International Relations, and three non-voting representatives of the theological faculties. Its executive is the 15-member National Council, which has a lay chairman. Related central bodies include the Bishops' Conference, the Council on Foreign Relations, the Sami Church Council and a doctrinal commission. Church legislation still requires parliamentary approval. The King of Norway remains the Church's constitutional head, and the government retains powers over the Church, exercised through the Ministry of the Church, Education and Research.

Porvoo Agreement Contact Revd Dr Stephanie Dietrich, Council on Ecumenical and International Relations, PO Box 799 – Sentrum, N-0106 Oslo   *Tel:* 47 23 08 12 74
Fax: 47 23 08 12 01
email: stephanie.dietrich@kirken.no

AGDER
Bishop Rt Revd Olav Skjevesland (*Praeses of the Bishops' Conference*), Diocesan Centre, Gyldenloves gate 9, N-4611 Kristiansand
Tel: 47 38 10 52 20
Fax: 47 38 10 51 21
email: agder.bdr@kirken.no

BJØRGVIN
Bishop Rt Revd Ole Hagesaether, Diocesan Centre, Strandgt. 198, Pb. 1960 Nordnes, 5018 Bergen   *Tel:* 47 55 30 64 70
Fax: 47 55 30 64 85
email: bjoergvin.biskop@kirken.no

BORG
Bishop Rt Revd Helga Haugland Byfuglien
Tel: 47 69 30 79 00
Fax: 47 69 30 79 01
email: borg.bdr@kirken.no

HAMAR
Bishop Rt Revd Solveig Fiske, Pb. 172, 2302 Hamar
Tel: 47 62 55 03 50
Fax: 47 62 55 03 51
email: hamar.bdr@kirken.no

MØRE
Bishop Rt Revd Odd Bondevik, Diocesan Centre, Julsundveien 13, N-6412 Molde
Tel: 47 71 25 06 70
Fax: 47 71 25 06 71
email: moere.bdr@kirken.no

NIDAROS
Bishop Rt Revd Finn Wagle, Archbishop's House, N-7013 Trondheim   *Tel:* 47 73 53 91 00
Fax: 47 73 53 91 11
email: nidaros.bdr@kirken.no

NORD-HÅLOGALAND
Bishop Rt Revd Per Oskar Kjølaas, PO Box 790, N-9258 Tromsø   *Tel:* 47 77 60 39 60/61
Fax: 47 77 60 39 70
email: nord-haalogaland.bdr@kirken.no

OSLO
Bishop Rt Revd Ole Chr. M. Kvarme, PO Box 9307, Gronland, N-0135 Oslo   *Tel:* 47 23 30 11 60
Fax: 47 23 30 11 99
email: oslo.bdr@kirken.no

SØR-HÅLOGALAND
Bishop Rt Revd Tor Berger Jørgensen, Tolder Holmersvei 11, 8003 Bodø   *Tel:* 47 75 54 85 50
Fax: 47 75 54 85 60
email: soer-haalogaland.bdr@kirken.no

STAVANGER
Bishop Rt Revd Dr Ernst Oddvar Baasland, Diocesan Centre, Domkirkeplassen 2, PO Box 629, N-4003 Stavanger   *Tel:* 47 51 84 62 70
Fax: 47 51 84 62 71
email: stavanger.bdr@kirken.no

TUNSBERG
Bishop Rt Revd Laila Riksaasen Dahl, PO Box 1253, Trudvang, N-3105 Tønsberg   *Tel:* 47 33 35 43 00
Fax: 47 33 35 43 01
email: tunsberg.bdr@kirken.no

The Church of Sweden

The first to preach the gospel in Sweden was St Ansgar (801–65), the first Archbishop of Hamburg-Bremen, but it was in the eleventh century that the systematic conversion of Sweden was begun, largely by missionaries from Eng-land. From 1104 the new Swedish dioceses formed part of the Nordic Province of Lund (which was Danish until 1658), but only until 1164, when Uppsala was raised to an archiepiscopal see. The most celebrated figure of the medieval Swedish Church is St Birgitta of Vadstena (1303–73), foundress of the Brigittine Order.

Under the Lutheran Reformers Olaus Petri (1493–1552) and his brother Laurentius (d. 1573), who became the first Lutheran archbishop in 1531, the Swedish Reformation was gradual, and moderate in character. The Augsburg Confession was adopted in 1593.

The eighteenth and nineteenth centuries saw both latitudinarian and pietist movements, and in the early twentieth century a strong high-church movement developed. Archbishop Nathan Söderblom (1866–1931), one of the leading figures of the Ecumenical Movement, used the concept of 'evangelical catholicity' to describe the Church of Sweden's position. The Conference of Bishops of the Anglican Communion adopted a resolution of altar and pulpit fellowship with the Church of Sweden in 1920. In 1997 Christina Odenberg became the Church of Sweden's first woman bishop, when she was appointed Bishop of Lund.

The Church of Sweden is governed by a General Synod with 251 members and a 15-member Central Board (chaired by the archbishop), together with the Bishops' Conference. The bishops attend the Synod, but are not members of it, although they have all the rights of members except the right to vote. They are *ex-officio* members of the Synod Committee on Church Doctrine.

A separation of Church and State was effected in the year 2000, a year which also was marked by the 1000-year celebration of Christian faith in Sweden at the well of Husaby in the Diocese of Skara.

Porvoo Agreement Contact Revd Dr Christopher Meakin, Ecumenical Officer, Church of Sweden, S-751 70 Uppsala   *Tel:* 46 18 16 96 86
Fax: 46 18 16 95 38
email: christopher.meakin@svenskakyrkan.se

Archbishop's Chaplain Revd Dr Ann-Cathrin Jarl, S-751 70 Uppsala   *Tel:* 46 18 16 96 23
Fax: 46 18 16 96 25
email: ann-cathrin.jarl@svenskakyrkan.se

(*Note: The dioceses here are arranged alphabetically. The order traditionally used in Sweden reflects the chronological seniority of the Swedish dioceses.*)

GÖTEBORG
Bishop Rt Revd Dr Carl Axel Aurelius, Stiftskansliet, Box 11937, SE-404 39 Göteborg
Tel: 46 31 771 30 00
Fax: 46 31 771 30 30
email: carlaxel.aurelius@svenskakyrkan.se

HÄRNÖSAND
Bishop Rt Revd Tony Gulbrandzén, Stiftskansliet, Box 94, SE-871 22 Härnösand   *Tel:* 46 611 254 00
Fax: 46 611 134 75
email: tony.guldbrandzen@svenskakyrkan.se

KARLSTAD
Bishop Rt Revd Esbjörn Hagberg, Stiftskansliet, Box 186, SE-651 05 Karlstad   *Tel:* 46 54 17 24 00
Fax: 46 54 17 24 70
email: esbjorn.hagberg@svenskakyrkan.se

LINKÖPING
Bishop Rt Revd Dr Martin Lind, Stiftskansliet, Box 1367, SE-581 31 Linköping
Tel: 46 13 24 26 00
Fax: 46 13 14 90 95
email: martin.lind@svenskakyrkan.se

LULEÅ
Bishop Rt Revd Hans Stiglund, Stiftskansliet, Stationsgatan 40, SE-972 32 Luleå
Tel: 46 920 26 47 00
Fax: 46 920 26 47 21
email: hans.stiglund@svenskakyrkan.se

LUND
Bishop Rt Revd Dr Antje Jackelén, Stiftskansliet, Box 32, SE-221 00 Lund   *Tel:* 46 46 35 87 00
Fax: 46 46 18 49 48
email: antje.jackelen@svenskakyrkan.se

SKARA
Bishop Rt Revd Dr Erik Aurelius, Malmgatan 14, SE-532 32 Skara   *Tel:* 46 511 262 00
Fax: 46 511 262 70
email: erik.aurelius@svenskakyrkan.se

STOCKHOLM
Bishop Rt Revd Caroline Krook, Stiftskansliet, Box 16306, SE-103 25 Stockholm
Tel: 46 8 508 940 00
Fax: 46 8 24 75 75
email: caroline.krook@svenskakyrkan.se

STRÄNGNÄS
Bishop Rt Revd Dr Hans-Erik Nordin, Stiftskansliet, Box 84, SE-645 22 Strängnäs
Tel: 46 152 234 00
Fax: 46 152 234 56
email: hans-erik.nordin@svenskakyrkan.se

UPPSALA
Archbishop Most Revd Anders Wejryd, SE-751 70 Uppsala   *Tel:* 46 18 16 95 00
Fax: 46 18 16 96 25
email: archbishop@svenskakyrkan.se

Bishop Rt Revd Dr Ragnar Persenius, Box 1314, SE-751 43 Uppsala   *Tel:* 46 18 68 07 00
Fax: 46 18 12 87 62
email: ragnar.persenius@svenskakyrkan.se

VÄSTERÅS
Bishop Rt Revd Thomas Söderberg, Stiftskansliet, V Kyrkogatan 9, SE-722 15 Västerås
Tel: 46 21 17 85 00
Fax: 46 21 12 93 10
email: thomas.soderberg@svenskakyrkan.se

VÄXJÖ

Bishop Rt Revd Dr Sven Thidevall, Box 527,
SE-351 06 Växjö

Tel: 46 470 77 38 00
Fax: 46 470 72 95 50
email: biskop.vaxjo@svenskakyrkan.se

VISBY

Bishop Rt Revd Dr Lennart Koskinen,
Stiftskansliet, Box 1334, SE-621 24 Visby

Tel: 46 498 40 49 00
Fax: 46 498 21 01 03
email: lennart.koskinen@svenskakyrkan.se

Further information about the history of the Nordic Lutheran Churches and of their relations with the Church of England can be found in Lars Österlin, *Churches of Northern Europe in Profile. A Thousand Years of Anglo-Nordic Relations* (Norwich, 1995).

ANGLICAN AND PORVOO COMMUNIONS

BALTIC LUTHERAN CHURCHES

The Estonian Evangelical–Lutheran Church

The conversion of Estonia to Christianity began at the end of the tenth century, and the first known bishop was consecrated in 1165. The mission was prosecuted by the Brethren of the Sword, an order founded in 1202 which merged with the Teutonic Order in 1237. In 1219 the Danes conquered the northern area and founded the capital Reval (Tallinn), which became an episcopal see within the Province of Lund. Further sees were established at Dorpat (Tartu) in 1224 and Hapsal (Saare-Lääne) in 1227, within the Province of Riga, the capital of Livonia, which included the southern part of modern Estonia. In some areas secular authority was in the hands of the bishops, while in others the Teutonic Order held sway. The entire area was very much under German dominance.

The Lutheran movement reached Estonia in 1523, and as early as the following year an assembly in Reval decided to adhere to the Reformation. Later in the century, however, the twin provinces of Estonia and Livonia became divided between neighbouring powers. Most of Estonia placed itself under Swedish rule in 1561, but Denmark ruled the island of Oesel (Saarema) from 1560 to 1645 and Livonia was annexed by Poland from 1561 to 1621. In Swedish Estonia, the Church was governed by a bishop and consistory, but Danish ecclesiastical law was introduced in Oesel, while Livonia came under the influence of the Counter-Reformation. Superintendents, rather than bishops, were appointed for these areas after they came under Swedish rule (in 1621 and 1645).

In 1710 both provinces came under Russian rule. In Estonia the office of bishop was replaced with that of superintendent. The consistories were chaired by laymen. In 1832 the Lutheran Churches of all three Baltic provinces were united with Russia's German-speaking Lutheran Church into a Russian Lutheran Church, with a General Consistory in St Petersburg. Each province (and – until 1890 – Reval, Oesel and Riga separately) had its own general superintendent and consistory. The University of Dorpat (Tartu), originally founded in 1632, was refounded in 1802. As the only Protestant theological faculty in the Russian Empire, it was of great importance. Throughout the period up to 1918 the clergy were German, like the ruling elite. The Moravian Church, which was active in Estonia and Livonia from 1736, enjoyed considerable influence over the Estonian peasantry, and by 1854 there were 276 Moravian prayer halls. However, the Moravian authorities blocked the development of this movement into a separate Moravian Church, and the Moravians' adherents remained within the Lutheran Church.

In 1918 Estonia and the Estonian northern part of Livonia became an independent state. The Church too became independent. It remained united, having both German and Estonian clergy and members. The office of bishop was immediately restored, the first bishop being consecrated in 1921 by the Archbishop of Uppsala and a Finnish bishop.

Estonia's independent existence lasted little more than 20 years, however. In 1940 it was occupied by the Red Army. German occupation followed, but Soviet rule was restored in 1944. Archbishop Kópp, who had remained unconsecrated because the war prevented bishops from other countries travelling to Estonia, went into exile with 70 other clergy and tens of thousands of church members. As a result of this the Estonian Evangelical–Lutheran Church Abroad was born. Of the clergy who remained, one-third were eventually deported to Siberia. Not until 1968 was it possible for an archbishop to be consecrated, although the first post-war Archbishop had already been elected in 1949.

In 1988, Estonia began to move towards independence, which was achieved in 1991. This was accompanied by a remarkable blossoming of church life. The Theological Faculty at Tartu, which had been dissolved by the Soviet authorities, was reopened. The Theological Institute of the EELC in Tallinn, which was set up after the war, also continues its work.

The Estonian Evangelical–Lutheran Church still forms one diocese, headed by an Archbishop and a Suffragan Bishop. It is governed by a General Synod, the executive organ of which is the six-member Consistory.

Porvoo Agreement Contact Very Revd Veiko Vihuri, Karja kirikla, 94201 Pärsama, Saaremaa
Tel: 372 45 73 65
email: veiko.vihuri@eelk.ee

Archbishop of Estonia Most Revd Andres Põder, Consistory of the EELC, Kirikuplats 3, 10130 Tallinn
Tel: 372 6 27 73 50
Fax: 372 6 27 73 52
email: konsistoorium@eelk.ee
Web www.eelk.ee

The Evangelical–Lutheran Church of Lithuania

Not until 1387 was an episcopal see established in Vilnius, following the baptism the previous year of Grand Duke Jogaila (whose coronation as King of Poland inaugurated a union lasting until 1795), and it was 1418 before the inhabitants of German-dominated Samogitia (covering much of present-day Lithuania) were forced to accept baptism.

A Lutheran congregation was founded in Vilnius as early as 1521, but persecution forced the Lithuanian Reformer Martin Mazvydas to flee to Königsberg. In time the Lithuanian nobility established the Reformed faith on their estates, while the numerous German merchants and craftsmen established Lutheran congregations in the towns from the 1550s. Until the early nineteenth century, the Lutheran Church continued to be a German and urban minority Church.

Sigismund Vasa (1587–1632) successfully restored Roman Catholicism as the religion of the people, and subsequent anti-Protestant policies meant that by 1775, when religious freedom was granted, just 30 Reformed and five Lutheran congregations remained (except those in Prussian-ruled Tauragé/Tauroggen).

In 1795 most of Lithuania was ceded to Russia, and Lithuania's Lutheran congregations were placed under the Consistory of Courland (now southern Latvia). Immigration of Lutheran Letts, Germans and Lithuanians from East Prussia produced new Lutheran congregations, especially in the countryside. The pastors (only nine in 1918) were all Germans.

At independence in 1918, Lithuania's population included 75,000 Lutherans, of whom roughly 30,000 were Germans, 30,000 Lithuanians and 15,000 Letts. In 1920 separate synods had to be formed for the three linguistic groups, and for much of the inter-war period tension between them paralysed the Lutheran Church. By 1939, however, there were 55 congregations with 33 pastors. To these should be added the separate Lutheran Church of the Prussian *Memelgebiet*, which Lithuania annexed in 1923. By 1939 this had 135,000 members (the majority German) in 32 parishes, served by 39 pastors.

Lithuanian Lutheranism was soon to be decimated. In 1941, following the 1940 Soviet annexation of Lithuania, most of the German population, together with a large number of Lithuanian Lutherans, emigrated to Germany. In Memelland and the Vilnius area, both reintegrated into Lithuania and thus the Soviet Union in 1945, the picture was even more stark. All but 30,000 inhabitants fled, while the pastor of the historic Lutheran church in Vilnius emigrated with his entire congregation.

A provisional Lutheran Consistory found itself responsible for 20,000 Lithuanians and Letts in Lithuania proper, together with just 15,000 Lithuanians in Klaipéda (Memelland). There were no pastors in Klaipéda and only six in the rest of the country, three of whom were soon banished to Siberia. After Stalin's death in 1953 and a first post-war synod in 1955, the structures of church life were gradually restored, but several thousand more Protestants emigrated between 1957 and 1965. At a second synod in 1970, Jonas Kalvanas, the only pastor left who had studied theology at university (he was ordained in 1940), was elected to chair the Consistory. It was with his consecration as Bishop by the Archbishop of Estonia in 1976 that his church gained the historic episcopate. He was succeeded in 1995 by his son and namesake, whose early death in 2003 left the see vacant until the consecration in June 2004 of Bishop Mindaugas Sebutis.

In 2003 the Lutheran Church had 54 congregations, with about 20,000 communicant members and twenty-four clergy.

Porvoo Agreement Contact Revd Darius Petkunas, Simonaitytes 18–21, LT-5814 Klaipéda
Tel: 370 6 220 409
email: darius.petkunas@liuteronai.lt

Bishop of the Evangelical–Lutheran Church of Lithuania Rt Revd Mindaugas Sebutis, Vokieciu 20, LT-01130 Vilnius   *Tel* and *Fax:* 370 5 212 3792
email: sabutis@times.lt
Web: www.liuteronai.lt/index_ang.html

NON-SIGNATORY CHURCHES

The Evangelical–Lutheran Church in Denmark

In August 1995 the bishops of the fifth Nordic Lutheran Church, the Evangelical–Lutheran Church in Denmark, announced that they were not able to approve the Porvoo Declaration. The Declaration's provisions therefore do not apply to that Church. At meetings held under the Porvoo Agreement, the Evangelical–Lutheran Church in Denmark is represented by observers.

However, an agreement providing for mutual eucharistic hospitality between the Anglican Churches and the Evangelical–Lutheran Church in Denmark (approved by the Churches in 1954 and 1956 respectively) remains in force.

Observer at meetings of the Porvoo Agreement Contact Group
Revd Jan Nilsson, Council on International Relations of the Evangelical–Lutheran Church in Denmark, Peter Bangs Vej 1 D, DK-2000 Frederiksberg
Tel: 45 33 11 44 88
Fax: 45 33 11 95 88
email: jn@interchurch.dk

Bishop of Copenhagen Rt Revd Erik Norman Svendsen, Nørregade 11, DK-1165 Copenhagen K
Tel: 45 33 47 65 00
Fax: 45 33 14 39 69
email: ens@km.dk
Web: www.folkekirken.dk

The Evangelical–Lutheran Church of Latvia

The Church of Latvia has not yet voted on the Porvoo Declaration.

Archbishop of Riga and Latvia Most Revd Janis Vanags, M. Pils iéla 4, LV-1050 Riga
Tel: 371 7 225406
Fax: 371 7 225436
email: konsistorija@lutheran.lv /
archbishop@lutheran.lv

Porvoo Agreement Contact Dr Sandra Gintere (*same address*) *email:* sandra.gintere@lutheran.lv

---

There are also Anglican chaplaincies in most of the countries covered by the Porvoo Agreement. These belong to the Archdeaconry of Scandinavia and Germany within the Diocese in Europe. A leaflet giving details is available from the Diocesan Office of the Diocese in Europe, *see below.*

The *Directory of English-speaking Churches Abroad* (£4.00 as at 1 May 2008) lists English-speaking churches of Anglican and many other denominations in countries where English is not the first language, and is available from Intercontinental Church Society, 1 Athena Drive, Tachbrook Park, Warwick CV34 6NL
Tel: 01926 430 347
Fax: 01926 888 092
email: enquiries@ics-uk.org
Web: www.ics-uk.org

Credit card orders accepted by telephone or on the web site.

Continental Anglican churches are listed in the *Diocesan Directory* of the Diocese of Gibraltar in Europe, available from the Diocesan Office, 14 Tufton St, Westminster, London SW1P 3QZ
Tel: 020 7976 8001
Fax: 020 7976 8002

Ecumenical **PART 6**

PART 6   CONTENTS

ECUMENICAL

The Church of England is committed to the search for the full, visible unity of the Christian Church, and to the bodies which promote this at the local, intermediate, national, European and world levels. The Council for Christian Unity advises the General Synod and the Archbishops' Council on inter-church relations and acts as the principal channel of communication between the General Synod and the churches and ecumenical bodies, at the national and international levels. The CCU engages in informal ecumenical dialogue and implements any decisions of the General Synod regarding formal conversations.

ECUMENICAL CANONS

Canon B 43 (Of Relations with Other Churches) and Canon B 44 (Of Local Ecumenical Projects) make provision for sharing in worship and ministry with other churches. Full background information is given in *The Ecumenical Relations Code of Practice* (Church House, 1989). This paper, with its supplements, is now available electronically from ccu@c-of-e.org.uk. A range of useful introductory resource papers is also available from the same address.

CHURCHES DESIGNATED UNDER THE ECUMENICAL RELATIONS MEASURE

The Church of England's legal office maintains the list of the churches that have been designated by the Archbishops of Canterbury and York as churches to which the Church of England (Ecumenical Relations) Measure, and thus Canons B 43 and B 44, apply. An up-to-date list is maintained on the Church of England web site at www.cofe.anglican.org/about/churchlawlegis/canons/suppindex.pdf, scrolling down to page 203. The following are currently listed: The Baptist Union, the Methodist Church, the Moravian Church, the Roman Catholic Church in England and Wales, the United Reformed Church, the Congregational Federation, the International Ministerial Council of Great Britain, the Lutheran Council of Great Britain, the Greek Orthodox Archdiocese of Thyateira and Great Britain (Ecumenical Patriarchate), the Council of African and Afro-Caribbean Churches, the Free Church of England, the Southam Road Evangelical Church Banbury, Member Churches of the Evangelical Church in Germany (EKD), the Assemblies of God in Great Britain and Ireland, the New Testament Church of God, the Russian Patriarchal Church of Great Britain being the Orthodox Diocese of Sourozh (Moscow Patriarchate), the Independent Methodist Churches, the Church of the Augsburg Confession of Alsace and Lorraine, the Evangelical–Lutheran Church of France, the Reformed Church of Alsace and Lorraine, the Reformed Church of France.

Churches Together in England

Churches Together in England is in association with Churches Together in Britain and Ireland. Its basis is as follows:

> Churches Together in England unites in pilgrimage those Churches in England which, acknowledging God's revelation in Christ, confess the Lord Jesus Christ as God and Saviour according to the Scriptures, and, in obedience to God's will and in the power of the Holy Spirit, commit themselves:
> – to seek a deepening of their communion with Christ and with one another in the Church, which is his body; and
> – to fulfil their mission to proclaim the Gospel by common witness and service in the world to the glory of the one God, Father, Son and Holy Spirit.

The Presidents of Churches Together in England are: The Archbishop of Canterbury, the Cardinal Archbishop of Westminster, Bishop Nathan Hovhannisian and Commissioner Elizabeth Matear, who meet together quarterly.

It has 31 Member Churches: Antiochian Orthodox Church, Baptist Union of Great Britain, Cherubim and Seraphim Council of Churches, Church of England, Church of God of Prophecy, Church of Scotland (in England), Congregational Federation, Coptic Orthodox Church, Council for African and Caribbean Churches, Council of Oriental Orthodox Christian Churches, Ichthus Christian Fellowship, Evangelische Synod Deutscher Sprache in Grossbritannien, Independent Methodist Churches, International Ministerial Council of Great Britain, Joint Council for Anglo-Caribbean Churches, Lutheran Council of Great Britain, Mar Thoma Church, Methodist Church, Moravian Church, New Testament Assembly, New Testament Church of God, Oecumenical Patriarchate (Archdiocese of Thyateira and GB), Redeemed Christian Church of God, Religious Society of Friends, Roman Catholic Church, Russian Orthodox Church, Salvation Army, Seventh Day Adventists, Transatlantic and Pacific Alliance of Churches, United Reformed Church, Wesleyan Holiness Church.

The Religious Society of Friends has membership under a clause designed for 'any Church or Association of Churches which on principle has no credal statements in its tradition'.

All substantive decisions are taken by these Member Churches.

Churches Together in England encourages its Member Churches to work together nationally, and provides various means for this purpose. There is an *Enabling Group*, which meets three times a year. Its Convenor is Revd Peter Whittaker and its Deputy Convenor Pauline Johnson. There is a *Forum* of 300 members, which meets every three years. Its Moderator is Bishop Declan Lang and its Deputy Moderator Mrs Val Potter.

There are 16 *Coordinating Groups* (*see below*).

There are also a large number of informal or as yet not formally recognized groups and networks.

Churches Together in England encourages its Member Churches to work together locally. To enable this most counties and metropolitan areas have established ecumenical councils and officers, whose task is to foster and encourage all sorts of ecumenical work locally within their areas. The main task of the two Field Officers (*see below*) is to support those working in counties and metropolitan areas.

Churches Together in England publishes an ecumenical e-news monthly, with a paper version, *CTE Digest*, available quarterly.

General Secretary Revd Dr David Cornick, Churches Together in England, 27 Tavistock Square, London WC1H 9HH   *Tel:* 020 7529 8131
Fax: 020 7529 8134
Web: www.churches-together.net

Field Officer South Revd John Bradley (*same address*)

Executive Secretary (*Free Churches*) Revd Mark Fisher (*same address*)

Finance Officer Mr Michael Wood (*same address*)

Executive Officer and Secretary of Health Care Chaplaincy Steering Committee Revd Debbie Hodge (*same address*)

Free Church Education Officer Miss Sarah Lane (*same address*)

Field Officer North & Midlands Jenny Bond (*same address*)   *Tel:* 07805 380699

Minority Ethnic Christian Affairs Secretary Bishop Joe Aldred, 269 Kingsbury Rd, Birmingham B24 8RD   *Tel:* 0121 382 3693
email: joe.aldred@cte.org.uk

COORDINATING GROUPS

GROUP FOR LOCAL UNITY
Secretary Revd John Bradley (*CTE address see above*)   *Tel:* 020 7529 8144
email: john.bradley@cte.org.uk

GROUP FOR EVANGELIZATION
Secretary Captain Jim Currin (*address see above*)
Tel: 024 7626 1895
email: jim.currin@cte.org.uk

CHURCHES JOINT EDUCATION POLICY COMMITTEE
Miss Sarah Lane (*CTE address see above*)
Tel: 020 7529 8130
email: sarah.lane@cte.org.uk

CHURCHES CRIMINAL JUSTICE FORUM
Secretary Stuart Dew, Catholic Bishops' Conference of England and Wales, 39 Eccleston Square, London SW1V 1BX   *Tel:* 020 7901 4878
email: dews@cbcew.org.uk

CHURCHES COMMITTEE FOR HOSPITAL CHAPLAINCY
Secretary Revd Debbie Hodge (*CTE address as above*)   *Tel:* 020 7529 8136
email: debbie.hodge@cte.org.uk

CHURCHES COMMUNITY WORK ALLIANCE
Secretary Nils Chittenden, St Chad's College, North Bailey, Durham DH1 3RH
Tel: 0191 374 7342
email: nilsc@ccwa.org.uk

YOUTH WORK MATTERS
Contact Carole Golden (*CTE address as above*)
Tel: 020 7529 8133
email: carole.golden@cte.org.uk

PRISON CHAPLAINCY HEADQUARTERS TEAM
Secretary Revd Alan Ogier, Prison Chaplaincy Headquarters, Room 624 Horseferry House, Dean Ryle St, London SW1P 2AW
Tel: 020 7217 8048
email: chaplaincy@prisons-chap-hq.demon.co.uk

ECUMENICAL STRATEGY GROUP FOR MINISTERIAL TRAINING
Secretary Tony Milner, Catholic Bishops' Conference of England and Wales, 39 Eccleston Square, London SW1V 1BX
email: tony.milner@dabnet.org

THEOLOGY AND UNITY GROUP
Secretary Revd Dr David Cornick (*CTE address see above*)   *Tel:* 020 7529 8133
email: david.cornick@cte.org.uk

CHURCHES RURAL GROUP
Convenor Canon Andrew Bowden, Arthur Rank Centre, The National Agricultural Centre, Stoneleigh Park, Warks. CV8 2LZ
Tel: 024 7685 3060
email: info@arthurrankcentre.org.uk

CHURCHES TOGETHER FOR FAMILIES
Secretary Sue Burridge, Church House, Great Smith St, London SW1P 3NZ
Tel: 020 7898 1000
email: sue.burridge@c-of-e.org.uk

CHURCHES TOGETHER FOR HEALING
Secretary Revd Elsie Howell, 60 Andrew Allan Rd, Rockwell Green, Wellington, Som. TA21 9DY
Tel: 01823 664529
email: revelsie@howell.freeserve.co.uk

INDEM (Group for Mission in Industry and the Economy)
Mr David Wrighton, INDEM, 34 Chalvington Rd, Chandlers Ford, Eastleigh, Hants. SO53 3DX
Tel: 023 8026 1146
email: wrcgdgshim@cs.com

SPIRITUALITY GROUP
Secretary Captain Jim Currin (*CTE address as above*)
Tel: 020 7529 8131
email: jim.currin@cte.org.uk

WOMEN'S COORDINATING GROUP
Secretary Revd Debbie Hodge (*CTE address as above*)
Tel: 020 7529 8132
email: debbie.hodge@cte.org.uk

There are also four *Agencies*:

CHURCHES' MEDIA COUNCIL
(Formerly Churches' Advisory Council for Local Broadcasting)
General Secretary Andrew Graystone, PO Box 149, Manchester M19 2AX
Tel: 0845 652 0027
email: info@churchesmediacouncil.org

CHRISTIAN ENQUIRY AGENCY
Secretary Mr Gareth Squire, 27 Tavistock Square, London WC1H 9HH
Tel: 020 7387 3659
email: enquiry@christianity.org.uk

CHRISTIAN AID
Director Dr Daleep Mukarji, PO Box 100, London SE1 7RL
Tel: 020 7620 4444
email: info@christian-aid.org

CAFOD
Director Mr Chris Bain, 2 Romero Close, Stockwell Rd, London SW9 9TY
Tel: 020 7733 7900
email: hqcafod@cafod.org.uk

The following are *Bodies in Association* with Churches Together in England: Action by Christians Against Torture, Association of Centres of Adult Theological Education, Association of Inter-Church Families, Bible Society, Christian Council on Ageing, Christian Council on Approaches to Defence and Disarmament, Christian Education, Christians Aware, Church Action on Poverty, Churches Alert to Sex Trafficking Across Europe (CHASTE), Churches Community Work Alliance (CCWA), Churches East–West Europe Relations Network (CEWERN), College of Preachers, Community of Aidan and Hilda, Corrymeela Community, Ecumenical Council for Corporate Responsibility, Ecumenical Society of the Blessed Virgin Mary, Faith in Europe, Feed the Minds, Fellowship of St Alban and St Sergius, Fellowship of Reconciliation, Focolare Movement, Housing Justice, Industrial Mission Association, International Ecumenical Fellowship, Iona Community, Irish School of Ecumenics, L'Arche, Living Stones, MODEM, Retreat Association, Society for Ecumenical Studies, Student Christian Movement, William Temple Foundation, Women's World Day of Prayer, Young Men's Christian Association, Y Care International.

For addresses, *see* page; 448 (under CTBI) or the **List of Organizations** (pages 259–320).

Intermediate County Bodies and Area Ecumenical Councils

Bedfordshire
Churches Together in Bedfordshire

Revd Ruth Bottoms
16 Verne Drive
Ampthill
Bedfordshire
MK45 2PS
Tel: 01525 420421
email: ruth.bottoms@ hotmail.co.uk

Berkshire
Churches Together in Berkshire

Mrs Honor Alleyne
CT Berkshire Office
Park URC Hall
Palmer Park Avenue
Reading
Berkshire RG6 1DN
Tel: 0118 926 1062
email: ctberks@tesco.net

Birmingham (*see also* **West Midlands**)
Birmingham Churches Together

Revd Dr Colin Marsh
All Saints House
172 Herbert Rd
Small Heath
Birmingham
B10 0PR
Tel and *Fax:*
0121 766 5522
email: office@ birminghamchurches. org.uk

ECUMENICAL

Black Country (*see also* **Staffordshire**)
Black Country Churches Engaged (BCCE)

Mr Mike Topliss
18 Selman's Hill
Bloxwich
Walsall
Staffs. WS3 3RJ
Tel: 01922 475932
email: jmtopliss@
talktalk.net

Bristol, Greater
Churches Together in Greater Bristol

Mr David Carter
6 Bampton Drive
Bristol BS16 6BJ
Tel: 0117 956 5447
email: david@
carterbristol.
eclipse.co.uk

Buckinghamshire
Churches Together in Buckinghamshire

Major David Scott
3 Criss Grove
Chalfont St Peter
Bucks SL9 9HG
Tel: 020 7367 4751
Fax: 01494 677228
email: davidscott5@
tiscali.co.uk

Cambridgeshire
Cambridgeshire Ecumenical Council

Mrs Priscilla Barlow
Silverlands, Church St
Litlington
Royston
Herts SG8 0QB
Tel: 01763 852841
email:
priscilla.barlow@
easynet.co.uk

Cheshire
Churches Together in Cheshire

Mark Thompson
81 Forge Fields
Sandbach
Cheshire
CW11 3RD
Tel: 01270 750431
email: ceo@cheshire-
churches-
together.org.uk

Cornwall
Churches Together in Cornwall

Revd Aidan Dyer
St Hilary, Higher
West Tolgus,
Redruth
Cornwall
TR15 2TP
Tel: 01209 213698
email: dyer4kernow@
hotmail.com

Coventry *See*
Warwickshire

Cumbria
Churches Together in Cumbria

Revd Carole Marsden
Sedbergh United
Reformed Church
Main Street
Sedbergh LA10 5AB
Tel: 01539 622030
email:
carole.marsden@
urc.org.uk

Derbyshire and Nottinghamshire
Churches Together in Derbyshire & Nottinghamshire

Revd Philip Webb
Dovedale
52 South Avenue
Chellaston
Derbyshire
DE73 1RS
Tel: 01332 705078
email: dovedale.revs@
virgin.net

Devon
Christians Together in Devon

Revd Simon Taylor
1 Albert Terrace
Two Bridges Road
Princetown
Devon
PL20 6QP
Tel: 01822 890412
email: staylor921@
aol.com

Dorset
Churches Together in Dorset

Mrs Val Potter
22 D'Urberville Close
Dorchester
Dorset DT1 2JT
Tel: 01305 264416
email: ctdorset@
clara.net

Durham *see* **North-East England**

Essex and London, East
Churches Together in Essex & East London CLG

Lee Batson
The Vicarage
Church Road
Boreham
Chelmsford CM3 3EG
Tel: 01245 451087
email: lbatson@
chelmsford.
anglican.org

Gloucestershire
Gloucestershire Churches Together

Revd Dr Alison
Evans
Britannia Cottage
High Street
Kings Stanley
Stonehouse
GL10 3JD
Tel: 01453 824034
email:
malcolm.alison@
btinternet.com

Guernsey
Guernsey Council of
  Churches

Mr Roy Sarre
Le Campère
Les Villets
Forest
Guernsey
Channel Islands
GY8 0HP
Tel: 01481 265004

**Hampshire and Isle of
  Wight**
Churches Together in
  Hampshire & the
  Island

Dr Paul Rolph
71 Andover Road
Winchester
SO22 6AU
Tel: 01962 862574
email: cthi@
  rolph.freeuk.com

Herefordshire
Churches Together in
  Herefordshire

Andrew Harter
Upper House
Grosmont
Abergavenny
NP7 8EP
Tel: 01981 241383
email: ctih@
  harter.co.uk

Hertfordshire
Churches Together in
  Hertfordshire

Major Gerald Peacock
83 Cromer Way
Luton
Bedfordshire LU2 7EE
Tel: 01582 492993
email:
  geraldpeacock39@
  btinternet.com

Isle of Man
Churches Together in
  Man

Mrs Mavis Matthewman
Tarnalforn
12 Ballagarey Rd
Glen Vine
Isle of Man
IM4 4EA
Tel: 01624 851693

Isle of Wight *see*
  Hampshire

Jersey
Churches Together in
  Jersey

Mr Michael J. Ruskin
Ocean View
La Route de l'Etacq
St Ouen
Jersey JE3 2FB
Tel: 01534 484366
email: oceanview@
  jerseymail.co.uk

Kent
Churches Together in
  Kent

Revd Dr Michael
  Cooke
St Lawrence
  Vicarage
Stone Street, Seal
Sevenoaks
Kent TN15 0LQ
Tel and *Fax:* 01732
  761766
email: ctk-7@
  ctkent.org.uk

Lancashire
Churches Together in
  Lancashire

Revd Steve Pearson
Email:
  frstevepearson@
  hotmail.com

Leicestershire
Churches Together in
  Leicestershire

John Downing
18 Stanley Rd
Leicester
LE2 1RE
Tel: 0116 270 8764
email: cedo@
  ctil.org.uk

Lincolnshire
Churches Together in
  All Lincolnshire

Alison McNish
  (administrator)
c/o Church House
The Old Palace
Lincoln
LN2 1PU
Tel: 01522 504070
Fax: 01652 657484
email:
  office@ctal.org.uk

London, East *see* **Essex**

London, North *see*
  North Thames

London, North Thames
Churches Together in
  NW London

Revd Bernie Collins
75 Cressex Road
High Wycombe
HP12 4PS
Tel: 01895 634280
email: Revbcollins@
  aol.com

London, South
Churches Together in
  South London

John Richardson
c/o St John's Vicarage
Secker Street
London SE1 9UF
Tel: 01462 422502
email: john@
  ctslondon.org.uk

Intermediate County Bodies

London, West
Churchlink West
London

Fr William Taylor
25 Ladbroke Grove
London W11 3PD
Tel: 020 7727 3439
email: vicar@stjohns
nottinghill.com

Manchester, Greater
Greater Manchester
Churches Together

Revd Graham
Kent
St Peter's House
Precinct Centre
Oxford Road
Manchester
M13 9GH
Tel: 0161 273 5508
Fax: 0161 272 7172
email:
sph.gmct@
man.ac.uk

Merseyside
Churches Together in
the Merseyside
Region

Revd Ian Smith
Quaker Meeting
House
22 School Lane
Liverpool L1 3BT
Tel: 0151 709 0125
email: office@
ctmr.org.uk

Milton Keynes
Milton Keynes
Churches Council

Revd Dr Mary Cotes
c/o Christian
Foundation
The Square
Aylesbury Street
Wolverton
MK12 5HX
Tel: 01908 311310
email:
missionpartnership
@tiscali.co.uk

Norfolk
Norfolk and Waveney
Churches Together

Revd Andrew Platt
21 Homefield
Paddock
Beccles
Suffolk NR34 9NE
Tel: 01502 717744
email: aplatt@
waitrose.com

North-East England
North East Christian
Churches Together
(NECCT)

Revd John Durell
4 Wearside Drive
Durham
DH1 1LE
Tel: 0191 384 1475
email: john.durell@
urc-northernsynod.
org.uk

Nottinghamshire (*see*
Derbyshire)

Oxfordshire
Churches Together in
Oxfordshire

Mr Bede Gerrard
26 Denton Close
Botley
Oxon OX2 9BW
Tel: 01865 723801
email: bjg1@
waitrose.com

Peterborough (*see*
Shire and Soke)

Shire and Soke
Churches Together in
Northamptonshire &
Peterborough

Teresa Brown
Tel: 01832 293535
email: teresabrown@
devinemusic.co.uk

Shropshire
Churches Together in
Shropshire

Mr Ged Cliffe
Fern Villa
Four Crosses
Llanymynech
Powys SY22 6PR
Tel: 01691 831374
email: gedcliffe@
tiscali.co.uk

Somerset
Somerset Churches
Together

Mr Robin Dixon
25 Claverton Rd West
Saltford
Bristol BS31 3AL
Tel and *Fax:*
01225 872903
email: sctog@
blueyonder.co.uk

Staffordshire
Churches Linked Across
Staffs & the Potteries
(CLASP) (*as* **Black
Country**)

Suffolk
Suffolk Churches
Together

Mrs Margaret
Condick
34 Rectory Lane
Kirton
Ipswich IP10 0PY
Tel: 01394 448576
email: ctsuffolk@
btopenworld.com

Surrey
Churches Together in
Surrey

Revd Susan Loveday
10 Abbey Gardens
Chertsey
Surrey KT16 8RQ
Tel: 01932 566920
email: sue.loveday.
ctsurrey@
lineone.net

Sussex
Sussex Churches

Mr Ian Chisnall
85 Hollingbury Rise
Brighton BN1 7HH
Tel: 07976 811654
(Mobile)
email: ianpchisnall@
aol.com

Swindon
Churches Together in
Swindon

Derek Collins
11 Merlin Way
Swindon SN3 5AN
Tel: 01793 523810
email: revdjc@
fish.co.uk

Telford
Telford Christian
Council

Revd David Lavender
Meeting Point House
Southwater Square
Town Centre
Telford TF3 4HS
Tel: 01952 291904
email:
davidlavender@
telfordchristian
council.co.uk

Warwickshire
Churches Together
in Coventry &
Warwickshire

Kay Dyer
6 Sycamore Close
Stratford-upon-Avon
CV37 0DZ
Tel: 01789 298299
email: ctcw@fish.co.uk

Waveney *see* **Norfolk**

Wiltshire
Wiltshire Churches
Together

Liz Overthrow
email: roy.overthrow@
btinternet.com

Worcestershire
Churches Together
in Worcestershire

Revd David Ryan
4 Daty Croft
Home Meadow
Worcester
WR4 0JB
Tel: 01905 616109
email: dpryangb@
aol.com

**Yorkshire, East
and Hull**
Kingston upon Hull &
East Yorkshire
Churches Together

Mrs Cathy Crumpton
Key Churches
Together
Methodist Central
Hall
King Edward St
Hull
HU1 3SQ
Tel: 01482 328196
email: cathy@
keyct.karoo.co.uk

**Yorkshire, North York
Moors**
Churches Together in
the North York Moors

Ann MacNamara
Calvis Hall
Thornton-le-Street
Thirsk
YO7 4AB
Tel: 01845 525430
email: nymct@
homecall.co.uk

Yorkshire, South
Churches Together in
South Yorkshire

Revd Louise Dawson
CTSY Office
Victoria Hall
Methodist Church
Norfolk St
Sheffield S1 2JB
Tel: 0114 278 8308
email: Louise@
ctsy.freeserve.co.uk

Yorkshire, Vale of York
ENVOY (Ecumenical
Network in the Vale
of York)

Nigel Currey
17 Mayfield Drive
Brayton
Selby
North Yorkshire
YO8 9JZ
Tel: 01347 838593
email: ncurrey1@
talktalk.net

Yorkshire, West
West Yorkshire
Ecumenical Council

Clive Barrett
Hinsley Hall
62 Headingley Lane
Leeds LS6 2BX
Tel: 0113 261 8053
Fax: 0113 261 8054
email: office@
wyec.co.uk

ECUMENICAL

Intermediate County Bodies

Churches Together in Britain and Ireland

Office Bastille Court, 2 Paris Garden, London
SE1 8ND   *Tel:* 020 7654 7254
Fax: 020 7654 7222
email: gensec@ctbi.org.uk
Web: www.ctbi.org.uk

Churches Together in Britain and Ireland (CTBI) is an umbrella body through which the Churches co-operate on common issues. It works closely with the other 'Churches Together' bodies, which focus separately on England, Wales, Scotland and Ireland. Together they have an important role to witness to the essential unity of the Christian movement. CTBI's core tasks are providing 'structured ecumenical space' for meeting and encounter, facilitating shared study on common issues and fostering relationships – among the Churches and between the Churches and the wider world.

Churches Together in Britain and Ireland (formerly the Council of Churches for Britain and Ireland and the direct successor of the British Council of Churches) was established by its member Churches to enable them to work together for the advancement of the Christian religion, the relief of poverty, the advancement of education and any other charitable purpose. It seeks to further these objects by providing opportunities for representatives of the Churches from the four nations to meet together and to share some of their resources in the pursuance of jointly agreed activities.

Following a review of its work, Churches Together in Britain and Ireland has become an agency serving the churches through the four National Ecumenical Instruments. As a separate charitable company, limited by guarantee, CTBI now relates to the churches, as members, through the ecumenical structures of the nations. It is now more relational and its focus is on working agreed common themes across the different work areas described below. The current themes are:

– environment/climate change
– migration and the movements of people
– culture, identity and the public space

Our principal activities and Networks are:

- Witnessing to and working towards the visible unity of the Christian Churches and providing opportunities for representatives of the Churches to meet and to plan their work together. A **Senior Representatives Forum**, attended by delegates from all member churches and bodies in association, is held in the spring of each year. A biennial event for the spiritual leaders of the Churches is also part of the new ways of working.

- Working on the Churches' behalf on issues of racial justice through the **Churches Racial Justice Network** (formerly known as CCRJ, the Churches' Commission for Racial Justice). The Racial Justice Network is a major vehicle for the Churches' engagement with the complex work of racial justice throughout Ireland, Scotland, Wales and England. Central to the work is the Racial Justice Fund, which supports a wide range of grassroots organizations. These funded groups are invited into a dynamic partnership designed to build their capacity for effective action and to provide first rate information and experience for use in education, lobbying and campaigning. **Racial Justice Sunday,** celebrated ecumenically on the second Sunday in September, gives an opportunity for vital educational work with churches and congregations and raises the media profile of the work of racial justice. Other projects include Capacity Building for Black Churches, the Bail Circle and the Peers project. The recent publication of *Migration Principles*, which in turn is building on the work of *Asylum Principles*, seeks to promote an active discussion and programme around the complex issue of migration. Working with other departments within CTBI, the Racial Justice team are taking forward Migration as a major theme.

- Through the **Global Mission Network (GMN),** seeking to serve and assist churches, agencies and the four national ecumenical instruments in our common task of participating in God's mission in the world. GMN is a key point of contact with world ecumenical mission bodies, particularly the World Council of Churches and the Council of European Churches. GMN's current projects include:

  - **Centre for Mission Accompaniment,** training Mission Accompaniers for churches and other Christian bodies negotiating change.
  - **Mission Theology Advisory Group,** offering expertise from around the four nations in Mission theology. Publications and web resources are being produced to support the ongoing work of the churches' mission in new contexts.
  - **China -** the China Desk provides a dedicated expert centre maintaining a wide range of relationships in China and undertaking research and analysis on Chinese affairs. It co-ordinates the work of the China Forum which acts as a bridge to Chinese Christians, both Catholic and Protestant, with partnership maintained through a variety of on-going projects.

- Through the **International Affairs Liaison Group,** bringing together those who work with and represent the churches in this area. The often confidential and complex nature of this work resources the work across the portfolios. An understanding and appreciation of the wider international engagement of the Churches is an important contribution to the range of work carried out at Churches Together in Britain and Ireland.
- Through the **Churches Inter Religious Network,** working with the Churches to engage effectively in relations and dialogue with other faiths in Britain and Ireland. The Network is a point of reference for the Churches which facilitates an exchange of information and experience among Christians about inter faith relations, whilst enabling critical reflection on the religiously and socially plural society of the four nations. In Scotland, it works through the Churches' Agency for Inter Faith Relations in Scotland. The Network seeks to fulfil its aims by responding to requests by the Churches on inter faith issues, monitoring inter faith relations in the four nations, nurturing links between Christians working in this field, pooling the theological resources of the Churches for ministry and witness in this area, and producing appropriate written or other material to help the Churches. In addition CTBI is a member body, on behalf of the Churches, of the Inter Faith Network for the United Kingdom, which provides a national forum for people from the main faith communities to meet, discuss and share.
- Through the **Churches International Student Network,** supporting international students by networking, education and communication among the Churches and between them, government and other agencies specializing in international students' affairs. The Network seeks to link the varied work of the many church agencies among students and supports the Churches in their response to the needs of international students. It initiated and maintains co-funding from the Foreign Office for denominational and ecumenical scholarships, administers World Council of Churches scholarships in Britain and Ireland and operates a hardship fund for international students for which it raises funding.
- Developing and publishing for the Churches **resources for study and prayer**. This includes printed and web based materials for the Week of Prayer for Christian Unity, which is observed each year from 18 to 25 January, as well as a Lent study programme.
- Through the **Church and Society Forum,** supporting and resourcing the Churches in

their work on political, social and ethical issues, paying particular attention to:

- public policy agendas of Westminster, and also Cardiff, Edinburgh, Belfast, Dublin and Brussels
- the churches' engagement with contemporary social issues
- moral/ethical issues, especially where there is a distinctive Christian contribution to be made

The Church and Society Forum takes a lead in networking those who work on church and society issues across the four nations, and in sharing and disseminating information and expertise. It represents the Churches jointly, where appropriate, to Government bodies, other agencies and elsewhere. It has one main residential meeting each year, with others as the need arises.

STAFF
Canon Robert Fyffe, *General Secretary*

Mr Stephen Cutler, *Head of Finance & Administration*
Mrs Mary Gandy, *Secretary for Church and Society*
Canon Flora Winfield, *Secretary for International Affairs*
Canon Janice Price, *Executive Secretary, Global Mission Network*
Miss Caroline Fielder, *China Desk Director*
Mrs Tessa Stawski, *Office Manager, Global Mission Network*
Andy Bruce, *Executive Secretary, Churches Racial Justice Network*
Revd Claudette Douglas, *Research and Development Officer, Churches Racial Justice Network*
Gillian Court, *Executive Secretary, Churches International Student Network*
Revd Peter Colwell, *Secretary, Church Life and Inter Faith Relations*

CTBI MEMBER CHURCHES AND BODIES OF CHURCHES
ANTIOCHIAN ORTHODOX CHURCH
Father Michael Harper, 3 West View, Newnham, Cambridge CB3 9JB   Tel: 01223 362933
email: aslanharper@clara.co.uk

BAPTIST UNION OF GREAT BRITAIN
Revd Jonathan Edwards *General Secretary*
Baptist House, 129 Broadway, Didcot OX11 8RT
Tel: 01235 517700
Fax: 01235 517715
email: info@baptist.org.uk
Web: www.baptist.org.uk

CATHOLIC BISHOPS' CONFERENCE OF ENGLAND
AND WALES
Mgr Andrew Summersgill *General Secretary*
39 Eccleston Square, London SW1V 1BX
Tel: 020 7630 8220
Fax: 020 7901 4821
email: secretariat@cbcew.org.uk
Web: www.catholic-ew.org.uk

CATHOLIC BISHOPS' CONFERENCE OF SCOTLAND
Revd Paul Conroy *General Secretary*
64 Aitken St, Airdrie ML6 6LT   *Tel:* 01236 764061
Fax: 01236 762489
email: GenSec@BpsConfScot.com
Web:
www.scmo.org/_titles/bishops_conference.htm

CHERUBIM AND SERAPHIM COUNCIL OF CHURCHES
Senior Apostle Richard Fasunloye
25 Seymour Gardens, Ilford IG1 3LN
Tel: 07957 296338
email: richardsgroup@o2.co.uk

CHURCH IN WALES
Mr John Richfield *Administrative Assistant to the
Governing Body*
39 Cathedral Rd, Cardiff CF11 9XF
Tel: 029 2034 8200
Fax: 029 2038 7835
email: johnrichfield@churchinwales.org.uk
Web: www.churchinwales.org.uk

CHURCH OF ENGLAND
Mr William Fittall *Secretary General of the General
Synod and the Archbishops' Council*
Church House, Great Smith St, London SW1P
3AZ   *Tel:* 020 7898 1000
Fax: 020 7898 1369
email: cofe.comms@c-of-e.org.uk
Web: www.cofe.anglican.org

CHURCH OF GOD OF PROPHECY
Bishop Wilton R. Powell *National Overseer*
6 Beacon Court, Birmingham Rd, Great Barr,
Birmingham B43 6NN   *Tel:* 0121 358 2231
Fax: 0121 358 8617
email: admin@cogop.org.uk
Web: www.cogop.org.uk

CHURCH OF IRELAND
Mrs Janet Maxwell *Head of Synod Services and
Communications*
Church of Ireland House, Church Avenue, Rath-
mines, Dublin 6, RoI   *Tel:* ++ 353 (0)1 4125621
Fax: ++ 353 (0)1 4978821
email: janet.maxwell@rcbdub.org
Web: www.ireland.anglican.org

CHURCH OF SCOTLAND
Very Revd Dr Finlay Macdonald
Principal Clerk's Office, 121 George St, Edinburgh
EH2 4YN   *Tel:* 0131 240 2240
Fax: 0131 240 2239
email: pracproc@cofscotland.org.uk
Web: www.churchofscotland.org.uk

CONGREGATIONAL FEDERATION
Revd Michael Heaney *General Secretary*
8 Castle Gate, Nottingham NG1 7AS
Tel: 0115 911 1460
Fax: 0115 911 1462
email: admin@congregational.org.uk
Web: www.congregational.org.uk

COPTIC ORTHODOX CHURCH
Bishop Angaelos
Coptic Orthodox Church Centre, Shephalbury
Manor, Broadhall Way, Stevenage SG2 8RH
Tel: 01438 745232
Fax: 01438 313879
email: admin@CopticCentre.com
Web: www.CopticCentre.com

COUNCIL OF AFRICAN AND CARIBBEAN CHURCHES
UK
Revd Jeri Jehu Appiah
40 Brailsford Rd, London SW2 2TE
Tel: 020 8671 7096
email: jerisdan_jehuappiah@yahoo.co.uk

COUNCIL OF ORIENTAL ORTHODOX CHURCHES
Bishop Angaelos *President*
c/o Coptic Orthodox Church Centre (*as above*)
email: admin@CopticCentre.com

GERMAN-SPEAKING CONGREGATION
Pastor Christoph Hellmich
Council for German Church Work, 35 Craven
Terrace, London W2 3EL   *Tel:* 020 7706 8589
Fax: 020 7706 2870
email: office@ev-synode.org.uk
Web: www.ev-synode.org.uk

INDEPENDENT METHODIST CHURCHES
Mr William Gabb *General Secretary*
Independent Methodist Resource Centre &
Registered Office
Fleet St, Pemberton, Wigan WN5 0DS
Tel: 01942 223526
Fax: 01942 227768
email: resourcecentre@imcgb.org.uk
Web: www.imcgb.org.uk

INTERNATIONAL MINISTERIAL COUNCIL OF GREAT
BRITAIN (IMCGB)
Rt Revd Sheila Douglas *International Moderator*
217 Langhedge Lane, London N18 2TG
Tel: 020 8345 5376
email: imcgb@aol.com
Web: www.imcgb.com

JOINT COUNCIL FOR ANGLO AND AFRICAN-
CARIBBEAN CHURCHES
Revd Esme Beswick *President*
141 Railton Rd, London SE24 0LT
Tel and Fax: 020 7737 6542

LUTHERAN COUNCIL OF GREAT BRITAIN
Revd Thomas Bruch *General Secretary*
30 Thanet St, London WC1H 9QH
Tel: 020 7554 2900
Fax: 020 7383 3081
email: enquiries@lutheran.org.uk
Web: www.lutheran.org.uk

METHODIST CHURCH
Revd David Deeks *General Secretary*
25 Marylebone Rd, London NW1 5JR
Tel: 020 7467 5143
Fax: 020 7467 5226
email: generalsecretary@methodistchurch.org.uk
Web: www.methodist.org.uk

METHODIST CHURCH IN IRELAND
Revd Donald Ker *General Secretary*
1 Fountainville Ave, Belfast BT9 6AN
Tel: 028 9032 4554
Fax: 028 9023 9467
email: secretary@irishmethodist.org
Web: www.irishmethodist.org

MORAVIAN CHURCH
Jackie Morten
Moravian Church House, 5 Muswell Hill,
London N10 3TJ
Tel: 020 8883 3409
Fax: 020 8365 3371
email: office@moravian.org.uk
Web: www.moravian.org.uk

NEW TESTAMENT ASSEMBLY
Revd Nezlin Sterling *General Secretary*
5 Woodstock Ave, London W13 9UQ
Tel: 020 8579 3841
Fax: 020 8537 9253
email: njsterlnta@aol.com

NEW TESTAMENT CHURCH OF GOD
Revd Louis R. McLeod
3 Cheyne Walk, Northampton NN1 5PT
Tel: 01604 643311
Fax: 01604 790254
email: bigmove@ntcg.org.uk
Web: www.ntcg.org.uk

OECUMENICAL PATRIARCHATE (ARCHDIOCESE OF THYATEIRA AND GREAT BRITAIN)
His Eminence Archbishop Gregorios
5 Craven Hill, London W2 3EN
Tel: 020 7723 4787
Fax: 020 7224 9301
email: thyateiragb@yahoo.com
Web: www.nostos.com/church/

PRESBYTERIAN CHURCH OF WALES
Revd Ifan Roberts *General Secretary*
Tabernacle Chapel, 81 Merthyr Road, Whit-
church, Cardiff CF14 1DD   *Tel:* 029 2062 7465
Fax: 029 2061 6188
email: swyddfa.office@ebcpcw.org.uk
Web: www.ebcpcw.org.uk

RELIGIOUS SOCIETY OF FRIENDS
Gillian Ashmore *Chief Recording Clerk*
Friends House, 173 Euston Rd, London NW1 2BJ
Tel: 020 7663 1000
Fax: 020 7663 1001
email: enquiries@quaker.org.uk
Web: www.quaker.org.uk

RUSSIAN ORTHODOX CHURCH (ECUMENICAL PATRIARCHATE)
Mrs. Gillian Crow
6 Maiden Place, London NW5 1HZ
email: gillian@crow.co.uk
Web www.exarchate-uk.org

SALVATION ARMY
Commissioner John Matear *Territorial Commander UK and RoI*
101 Newington Causeway, London SE1 6BN
Tel: 020 7367 4500
Fax: 020 7367 4728
email: info@salvationarmy.org.uk
Web: www.salvationarmy.org.uk

SCOTTISH EPISCOPAL CHURCH
Mr John Stuart *Secretary General for Synod Office*
21 Grosvenor Crescent, Edinburgh EH12 5EE
Tel: 0131 225 6357
Fax: 0131 346 7247
email: office@scotland.anglican.org
Web: www.scottishepiscopal.com

TRANS-ATLANTIC & PACIFIC ALLIANCE OF CHURCHES
Archbishop Paul Hackman *President*
281-283 Rye Lane, London SE15 4UA
Tel and Fax: 020 7639 4058
email: tapacglobal@aol.com

UNDEB YR ANNIBYNWYR CYMRAEG/UNION OF WELSH INDEPENDENTS
Revd Dr Geraint Tudor *General Secretary*
Tŷ John Penri, 5 Axis Court, Riverside Business
Park, Swansea Vale, Swansea SA7 0AJ
Tel: 01792 795888
Fax: 01792 795376
email: Undeb@annibynwyr.org
Web: www.annibynwyr.org

UNITED FREE CHURCH OF SCOTLAND
Revd John O. Fulton *General Secretary*
11 Newton Place, Glasgow G3 7PR
Tel: 0141 332 3435
Fax: 0141 333 1973
email: office@ufcos.org.uk
Web: www.ufcos.org.uk

UNITED REFORMED CHURCH
Revd Roberta Rominger *General Secretary*
86 Tavistock Place, London WC1H 9RT
Tel: 020 7916 2020
Fax: 020 7916 2021
email: urc@urc.org.uk
Web: www.urc.org.uk

ECUMENICAL

ASSOCIATE MEMBER

ROMAN CATHOLIC CHURCH OF IRELAND
Revd Aidan O'Boyle *Executive Secretary*
The Irish Episcopal Conference, Columba Centre,
Maynooth, Co Kildare, Republic of Ireland
Tel: 00 353 1 505 3020
Fax: 00 353 1 629 2360
email: ex.sec@iecon.ie

BODIES IN ASSOCIATION

ACTION BY CHRISTIANS AGAINST TORTURE
Mr Terry Newland, ACAT UK, 8 Southfield,
Saltash, Cornwall PL12 4LX   *Tel:* 01752 210389
email: uk.acat@googlemail.com
Web: www.acatuk.org.uk

ASSOCIATION OF INTER-CHURCH FAMILIES
Mr Keith Lander (*Executive Officer*), 3rd Floor,
Bastille Court, 2 Paris Garden, London SE1 8ND
Tel: 020 7654 7251
Fax: 020 7654 7222
email: info@interchurchfamilies.org.uk
Web: www.interchurchfamilies.org.uk

BIBLE SOCIETY
Revd Dr David Spriggs, 7 Frankpledge Rd, Chey-
lesmore, Coventry CV3 5GT
Tel and *Fax:* 024 7650 6320
Web: www.biblesociety.org.uk

CHRISTIAN COUNCIL ON AGEING
Mrs Christine Hodgson, 6 The Ridgeway, Market
Harborough LE16 7HQ   *Tel:* 01858 432771
email: info@ccoa.org.uk
Web: www.ccoa.org.uk

CHRISTIAN EDUCATION
Peter Fishpool (*Chief Executive*), 1020 Bristol Rd,
Selly Oak, Birmingham B29 6LB
Tel: 0121 472 4242
Fax: 0121 472 7575
email: admin@christianeducation.org.uk
Web: www.christianeducation.org.uk

CHRISTIANS AWARE
Mrs Barbara Butler, 2 Saxby St, Leicester LE2 0ND
Tel and *Fax:* 0116 254 0770
email: barbarabutler@christiansaware.co.uk
Web: www.christiansaware.co.uk

CHURCH ACTION ON POVERTY
Mr Niall Cooper (*National Coordinator*), Central
Buildings, Oldham St, Manchester M1 1JQ
Tel: 0161 236 9321
Fax: 0161 237 5359
email: info@church-poverty.org.uk
Web: www.church-poverty.org.uk

CHURCHES' ALERT TO SEX TRAFFICKING ACROSS
EUROPE
Jane J. Martin (*Trustee and In-house Counsel*), PO
Box 983, Cambridge CB3 8WY
Tel: 0845 456 9335
email: contact@chaste.org.uk
Web: www.chaste.org.uk

COLLEGE OF PREACHERS
Ms Marfa Jones (*Administrator*), Chester House,
Pages Lane, Muswell Hill, London N10 1PR
Tel: 020 8883 7850
email: administrator@collegeofpreachers.org.uk
Web: www.collegeofpreachers.org.uk

COMMUNITY OF AIDAN AND HILDA
Revd Ray Simpson (*Guardian*), Lindisfarne
Retreat, The Open Gate, Holy Island, Berwick-
upon-Tweed TD15 2SD   *Tel:* 01289 389222
email: ca-and-h@demon.co.uk
Web: www.aidanandhilda.org.uk

CORRYMEELA COMMUNITY
Corrymeela House, 8 Upper Crescent, Belfast
BT7 1NT   *Tel:* 028 9050 8080
Fax: 028 9050 8070
email: belfast@corrymeela.org /
annemcdonagh@corrymeela.org
Web: www.corrymeela.org

ECUMENICAL COUNCIL FOR CORPORATE
RESPONSIBILITY
Miles Litvinoff (*Coordinator*), PO Box 500, Oxford
OX1 1ZL   *Tel:* 020 8965 9682
email: info@eccr.org.uk
Web: www.eccr.org.uk

FAITH IN EUROPE
Dr Philip Walters (*General Secretary*), 81 Thorney
Leys, Witney OX28 5BY   *Tel:* 01993 771778
email: philip.walters@waltfam.freeserve.co.uk
Web: www.faithineurope.org.uk

FEED THE MINDS
Josephine Carlssen (*Director*), 36 Causton St,
London SW1P 4ST   *Tel:* 020 7592 3900
Fax: 020 7592 3939
email: info@feedtheminds.org.uk
Web: www.feedtheminds.org

FELLOWSHIP OF RECONCILIATION
Chris Cole (*Director*), St James' Church Centre,
Beauchamp Lane, Oxford OX4 3LF
Tel: 01865 748796
email: office@for.org.uk
Web: www.for.org.uk

FELLOWSHIP OF ST ALBAN AND ST SERGIUS
Revd Stephen Platt, 1 Canterbury Rd, Oxford
OX2 6LU   *Tel:* 01865 52991
Fax: 01865 316700
email: gensec@sobornost.org
Web: www.sobornost.org

FOCOLARE MOVEMENT
Celia Blackden, 50 Dafforne Rd, London SW17
8TZ   *Tel:* 01707 020 8767 6092
Fax: 01707 696413
email: celiablackden@yahoo.co.uk
Web: www.focolare.org.uk

HOUSING JUSTICE
Ms Alison Gelder (*Chief Executive*), 209 Old Marylebone Rd, London NW1 5QT
Tel: 020 7723 7273
Fax: 020 7723 5943
email: info@housingjustice.org.uk
Web: www.housingjustice.org.uk

INDUSTRIAL MISSION ASSOCIATION
Revd Stephen Hazlett, Northumbrian Industrial Mission, 14 The Oaks West, Sunderland SR2 8HZ
Tel: 07900 231360
Web: www.industrialmission.org.uk

INTERNATIONAL ECUMENICAL FELLOWSHIP
Jill Freston, 59 Old St, Headington, Oxford OX3 9HT
Tel: 01865 762247
email: jillfreston@tiscali.co.uk
Web: www.uk-ief.co.uk

IONA COMMUNITY
Revd Kathy Galloway (*Leader*), 4th Floor, Savoy House, 140 Sauchiehall St, Glasgow G2 3DH
Tel: 0141 332 6343
Fax: 0141 332 1090
email: admin@iona.org.uk
Web: www.iona.org.uk

IRISH SCHOOL OF ECUMENICS
Dennis Anderson (*Director*), 683 Antrim Rd, Belfast BT15 4EG *and* Bea House, Milltown Park, Dublin 6, RoI
Tel: +44 (0) 28 9077 5010
Fax: +44 (0) 28 9037 3986
email: danderso@tcd.ie
Web: www.tcd.ie/ise

L'ARCHE
Ms Lal Keenan, L'Arche Community, 15 Northwood High St, London SE27 9JU
Tel: 020 8670 6714
Fax: 020 8670 0818
email: info@larche.org.uk
Web: www.larche.org.uk

LIVING STONES
Mr Colin South (*Trust Administrator*), 22 Ebenezer Close, Witham CM8 2HX
Tel: 01376 510391
email: colinsouth@aol.com
Web: www.livingstonesonline.org.uk

MODEM
Mr John Nelson (*National Secretary and Publications Editor*), 24 Rostron Crescent, Formby L37 2ET
Tel: 01704 873973
Fax: 01704 871273
email: jrn24rcf2003@yahoo.co.uk
Web: www.modem.uk.com

RETREAT ASSOCIATION
The Central Hall, 256 Bermondsey St, London SE1 3UJ
Tel: 020 7357 7736
Fax: 020 7357 7724
email: info@retreats.org.uk
Web: www.retreats.org.uk

SOCIETY OF ECUMENICAL STUDIES
Revd Mark Woodruff (*Secretary*), 26 Daysbrook Rd, London SW2 3TD
Tel: 020 8678 8195
email: ecumenicalstudies@btinternet.com
Web: www.ecumenicalstudies.org.uk

STUDENT CHRISTIAN MOVEMENT
Mr Liam Purcell (*Coordinator*), Unit 306F, The Big Peg, 120 Vyse St, Jewellery Quarter, Birmingham B18 6NF
Tel: 0121 200 3355
email: co@movement.org.uk
Web: www.movement.org.uk

WOMEN'S WORLD DAY OF PRAYER MOVEMENT
WWDP National Office, Commercial Rd, Tunbridge Wells TN1 2RR
Tel: 01892 541411
Fax: 01892 541745
email: office@wwdp-natcomm.org
Web: www.wwdp-natcomm.org

YOUNG MEN'S CHRISTIAN ASSOCIATION (YMCA)
Ms Helen Dennis (*Policy and Parliamentary Officer*), 53 Parker St, London WC2B 5PT
Tel: 0845 873 6633
email: enquiries@ymca.org.uk
Web: www.ymca.org.uk

ECUMENICAL

Scotland, Wales and Ireland

ACTION OF CHURCHES TOGETHER IN SCOTLAND
7 Forrester Lodge, Inglewood House, Alloa FK10 2HU
Tel: 01259 216980
Fax: 01259 215964
email: ecumenical@acts-scotland.org

General Secretary Brother Stephen Smyth

Convenor of Scottish Churches Forum Revd Mary Buchanan

ACTS is the national ecumenical body for Scotland, the expression of the Churches' commitment to cooperation with one another in the service of Christ. ACTS works closely with its partners in England, Wales and Ireland. Its strategic body is the Scottish Churches' Forum, composed of representatives from the member churches. The work of ACTS is forwarded by four Networks: Church and Society, Church Life, Mission, and Faith Studies. In addition to the four core ACTS staff there are currently two part-time project funded staff: the CAIRS Interfaith Education Officer and the Scottish Churches Racial Justice Officer.

Member Churches Church of Scotland, Congregational Federation, Methodist Church, Religious Society of Friends, Roman Catholic Church, Salvation Army, Scottish Episcopal Church, United Free Church, United Reformed Church.

CYTÛN: EGLWYSI YNGHYD YNG NGHYMRU
CHURCHES TOGETHER IN WALES
58 Richmond Rd, Cardiff, South Wales CF24 3UR
Tel (main office): 029 2046 4204
Web: www.cytun.org.uk

Chief Executive Revd Aled Edwards OBE
Tel: 029 2046 4375
*email:*aled@cytun.org.uk

Office Administrator Mrs Sasha Perriam
Tel: 029 2046 4204
email: sasha@cytun.org.uk

National Assembly Policy Officer Mr Geraint Hopkins
Tel: 029 2046 4378
email: geraint@cytun.org.uk

CYTÛN shall seek to further its objects by challenging and enabling the Churches of Wales: (1) to gather together in the richness of their diversity, in a context of prayer, study and discussion, and in a parity of esteem; (2) to value and learn from each other's traditions; (3) to grow into a fuller understanding of the nature, purpose and unity of Christ's Church; (4) to face together the matters that divide them, so that they can become more fully united in faith, order, worship, ethics, pastoral care and mission; (5) to respond together to the needs of the human community, both in Wales and in other countries, through the sharing of those gifts which God provides; (6) to enter together into dialogue with other bodies and with other world religions in all appropriate matters; (7) to deepen their commitment, to share their resources and to do together whatever they can, one in love and prayer.

Member Denominations The Baptist Union of Wales, the Roman Catholic Church, the Church in Wales, the Congregational Federation, the Covenanted Baptist Churches, the German Speaking Lutheran, the Methodist Church, the Presbyterian Church of Wales, the Quakers, the Salvation Army, the Union of Welsh Independents, the United Reformed Church.

Aligned Groupings The Covenanted Churches in Wales, the Free Church Council of Wales.

CYTÛN also works in close collaboration with the Commission of the Covenanted Church in Wales and the Free Church Council of Wales.

THE IRISH COUNCIL OF CHURCHES
Inter-Church Centre, 48 Elmwood Ave, Belfast BT9 6AZ
Tel: 028 9066 3145
Fax: 028 9066 4160
email: info@irishchurches.org
Web: www.irishchurches.org

President Revd Tony Davidson

Vice-President Most Revd Richard Clarke

Hon Treasurer Mr Hilton Henry

General Secretary Mr Michael Earle

Administrator Vacancy

History From 1906 the Presbyterian and Methodist Churches had a joint committee for united efforts. In 1910 the General Assembly of the Presbyterian Church invited other evangelical Churches to set up similar joint committees with it. The Church of Ireland accepted and by 1911 the joint committee of these two Churches was in action. Following a recommendation of the 1920 Lambeth Conference, these joint committees developed in 1922 into the United Council of Christian Churches and Religious Communions in Ireland including six of the present member churches. In 1966 the United Council changed its name to the Irish Council of Churches. The Council employed its first full-time secretary in April 1972.

Aims The Irish Council of Churches is constituted by Christian Communions in Ireland willing to join in united efforts to promote the spiritual, physical, moral and social welfare of the people and the extension of the rule of Christ among all nations and over every region of life.

Member Churches (15) Antiochian Orthodox Church in Ireland, Church of Ireland, Coptic Orthodox Church, Greek Orthodox Church, Lifelink Network of Churches, Lutheran Church in Ireland, Methodist Church in Ireland, Irish District of the Moravian Church, Non-Subscribing Presbyterian Church of Ireland, Presbyterian Church in Ireland, Religious Society of Friends in Ireland, Rock of Ages Cherubim and Seraphim Church, Romanian Orthodox Church in Ireland, Russian Orthodox Church in Ireland, Salvation Army (Ireland Division).

Structure The Council consists of 77 members appointed by the member Churches, together with the Heads of the member Churches and up to ten co-opted members, the General Secretary, Treasurer and immediate Past President of the Council. There is an Annual Meeting and occasional gatherings. The member Churches appoint an Executive Committee, which meets quarterly and is responsible for the oversight of the work of the Council.

2008 The Council continues to serve both jurisdictions (Northern Ireland and the Republic of Ireland) and comprises 15 member churches (see below). It is an associate member of Churches Together in Britain and Ireland and the Conference of European Churches and has links with the World Council of Churches.

(a) It is currently re-assessing its purpose and direction in the rapidly changing contexts both sides of the border; its ecumenical witness across the island and relationships between and beyond its member churches, and its international links through its Board of Overseas Affairs.

(b) It meets quarterly with the Roman Catholic Church in Ireland through the Irish Inter-Church Committee and every 18 months as the Irish Inter-Church Meeting. The last Meeting was held in Dublin in in October 2007, taking the focus of an ecumenical study day.

(c) It is represented on the Churches Peace Education programme, which is currently being reviewed after 28 years of producing educational resources for primary/secondary schools on both sides of the border. The trustees have commissioned a research report that has been undertaken by the two main teacher training colleges in Belfast to identify a future role for the programme in the light of changing needs and government policies both sides of the border.

(d) It participates in the All-Ireland Churches Consultative Meeting on Racism, which organized a major conference for the churches on this growing issue. Further regional seminars and events are being planned.

(e) It is involved with the Inter Church Committee on Social Issues (ICCSI), which is currently applying for funds to employ a Project Officer to develop a parish-based integration programme in the Republic.

(f) It provides low interest loans to peace, reconciliation, church and community projects through the Irish Ecumenical Church Loan Fund (ECLOF).

(g) It is represented on various regional, national and CTBI bodies concerned with regional equality panels, inter-faith, international, mission, overseas aid, racial justice and TV and radio affairs, and the Week of Prayer for Christian Unity.

(h) It is currently serviced by 2.5 staff based in the Belfast office.

More information about the Council's work can be obtained from the above mentioned website which includes a downloadable version of the 2007 Annual Report.

Meissen Agreement with the Evangelical Church in Germany

The Evangelical Church in Germany (Evangelische Kirche in Deutschland – EKD) is a Communion of 23 member churches (mostly *Landeskirchen* or territorial churches). Of these, ten are Lutheran (eight of them forming the United Evangelical Lutheran Church – VELKD), one is purely Reformed, one is predominantly Reformed and twelve are United (seven forming the Evangelical Church of the Union – EKU). In many of the United churches the Lutheran tradition predominates.

In November 1988 the General Synod welcomed the Meissen Common Statement, *On the Way to Visible Unity*, which called for a closer relationship between the Church of England and the German Evangelical Churches. The Meissen Declaration, which it recommended, was approved by the General Synod in July 1990 without dissent, and solemnly affirmed and proclaimed an Act of Synod on 29 January 1991. The Meissen Declaration makes provision for the Church of England and the Evangelical Church in Germany to live in closer fellowship with one another (though not yet with interchangeable ministries) and commits them to work towards the goal of full visible unity. The member churches of the EKD have been designated as churches to which the Ecumenical Canons apply (*see* **Ecumenical Canons**).

The Meissen Commission (the Sponsoring Body for the Church of England–EKD Relations) exists to oversee and encourage relationships (*see* Council for Christian Unity). Fuller information is contained in *The German Evangelical Churches* (CCU Occasional Paper No 1 £2.95 + 35p p&p) and *Anglo-German Ecumenical Links: An Information Pack* (£1 inc. p&p). The text of the Meissen Agreement can be found in *The Meissen Agreement: Texts* (CCU Occasional Paper No 2 £2.10 inc. p&p). These are all available from the Coun-

cil for Christian Unity. Most of this material is downloadable from the CCU web site at www.cofe.anglican.org/info/ccu.

Co-Chairmen of the EKD Council Bishop Jürgen Johannesdotter (*EKD*), Rt Revd Nicholas Baines (*Church of England*)
English Co-Secretary of the Meissen Commission European Secretary, Council for Christian Unity, Church House, Great Smith St, London SW1P 3AZ   *Tel:* 020 7898 1474
German Co-Secretary of the Meissen Commission OKR Matthias Kaiser, EKD Kirchenamt, Postfach 21 02 20, D – 30402 Hannover, Germany
Tel: 00 49 511 2796 127
Fax: 00 49 511 2796 725
email: matthias.kaiser@ekd.de
Web: www.ekd.de

The Reuilly Common Statement: Relations with the French Lutheran and Reformed Churches

Encouraged by the positive reception of the Meissen and Porvoo Agreements, the Anglican Churches of Britain and Ireland engaged in dialogue with the French Reformed and Lutheran Churches, with formal conversations beginning in 1994. These Churches had signalled their desire to enter into closer fellowship with Anglican Churches on the model of the Meissen Agreement, which the Church of England had concluded with the Evangelical Church in Germany (EKD).

The relations between the Anglican and French Churches are steeped in history. Contacts go back to the Middle Ages and took on a new character through the impetus of the Reformation. In later years, at times of turbulence and persecution, churches on both sides of the Channel welcomed those persecuted for their faith.

The conversations involved four participating churches from each side: the four Anglican Churches of the British Isles (the Church of England, the Church of Ireland, the Scottish Episcopal Church and the Church in Wales) and the four French Churches of the Lutheran and Reformed traditions (the Church of the Augsburg Confession of Alsace and Lorraine, the Evangelical Lutheran Church of France, the Reformed Church of Alsace and Lorraine and the Reformed Church of France).

The Reuilly Common Statement which forms the outcome of these conversations takes its name from a community of deaconesses, committed to prayer and meditation. The Statement was approved by the General Synod of the Church of England in November 1999, and the Statement was signed by the participatory Churches in Canterbury and Paris during the summer of 2001.

In common with other ecumenical statements, the Reuilly document first sets the scene, with the history and present context of the participants, and then moves on to current theological issues: the Church as Sign, Instrument and Foretaste of the Kingdom of God; the Church as Communion (*koinonia*); Growth towards Visible Unity; Agreement in Faith and the Apostolicity of the Church and its Ministry.

The Churches declare that they have found a high degree of unity and faith, and outline three areas of future work together: common efforts in witness and service; continuing theological work, particularly on questions of oversight, authority, eucharistic ministry and formally uniting ministries; the practical consequences of the Agreement: prayer, sharing of worship, partnership, and joint ventures across a range of areas.

The implementation of the Agreement is coordinated by a Contact Group. The Anglican Co-Chairman is the Bishop of Guildford and the French Co-Chairman is Pasteur Geoffrey Goetz.

For information on current links and initiatives, contact:
The European Secretary, The Council for Christian Unity, Church House, Great Smith Street, London SW1P 3NZ

The full text of the Reuilly Declaration, together with background articles on the theological issues and the participating Churches, can be found in *Called to Witness and Service*, Church House Publishing (1999), ISBN 0 7151 5757 4.

Conference of European Churches

Moderator Revd Jean-Arnold de Clermont

Vice-President Archbishop Anastasios of Tirana and All Albania

Deputy Vice-Moderator Dean Margarethe Isberg

General Secretary Ven Colin Williams, PO Box 2100, 150 Route de Ferney, 1211 Geneva 2, Switzerland   *Tel:* 41 22 791 61 11
Fax: 41 22 791 62 27
email: cec@cec-kek.org
Web: www.cec-kek.org

Born in the era of the 'cold war' some 50 years ago, the CEC emerged into a fragmented and divided continent. Thus it was that Churches of Eastern and Western Europe felt one priority of their work to be promoting international understanding – building bridges. This the CEC has consistently tried to do, always insisting that no 'iron curtain' exists among the Churches.

The supreme governing body of the Conference is the Assembly. Here all 126 member Churches are represented. The first Assembly was in 1959 and further Assemblies were held in 1960, 1962, 1964, 1967, 1971, 1974, 1979, 1986, 1992, 1997 and 2003. The nest assembly will be held in Lyon, France, from 15–21 July 2009. It will be an opportunity to celebrate the 50th anniversary of CEC.

The CEC initiated the European Ecumenical Assembly 'Peace with Justice' held in Basel in May 1989, co-sponsored with the Council of European Bishops' Conferences (CCEE, Roman Catholic). A second European Ecumenical Assembly was held in Graz, Austria, in 1997 with the theme 'Reconciliation: Gift of God and Source of New Life'. In 2001, CEC and CCEE launched the 'Charta Oecumenica – guidelines for the growing cooperation among the Churches in Europe'. A third European Ecumenical Assembly was held in Sibiu, Romania, in 2007 with the theme 'The light of Christ shines upon all – Hope for renewal and unity in Europe'.

The 40-member Central Committee oversees the implementation of the decisions of the Assembly. A Presidium, drawn from the Central Committee, acts as the Executive Council of the Conference.

Since 1 January 1999 the European Ecumenical Commission on Church and Society (EECCS) with offices in Brussels and Strasbourg integrated with CEC, and, together with CEC's existing work, created the new Church and Society Commission of the CEC. A merger is also planned between CEC and the Brussels-based Churches' Commission for Migrants in Europe (CCME). It will be completed by 2009.

The Secretariats in Geneva, Brussels and Strasbourg ensure the continuity of the activities. There are 21.25 staff positions. These include the General Secretary and Secretaries responsible for finance and administration, communications and information, Churches in Dialogue and Church and Society.

Publications include occasional papers, and *Monitor,* a quarterly newsletter.

World Council of Churches

The Church of England has taken its full share in the international ecumenical movement since the Edinburgh Conference of 1910. In 2007 the General Synod made a grant of £108,000 to the General Budget of the World Council of Churches.

Presidium Archbishop Dr Anastasios of Tirana and All Albania (Orthodox Autocephalous Church of Albania), Mr John Taroanui Doom (Maòhi Protestant Church, French Polynesia), Revd Dr Simon Dossou (Protestant Methodist Church in Benin), Revd Dr Soritua Nababan (Protestant Christian Batak Church (HKBP), Indonesia), Revd Dr Ofelia Ortega (Presbyterian-Reformed Church in Cuba), Patriarch Abune Paulos (Ethiopian Orthodox Tewahedo Church), Revd Dr Bernice Powell Jackson (United Church of Christ, USA), Dr Mary Tanner (Church of England)

Moderator of Central Committee Revd Dr Walter Altmann (Evangelical Church of the Lutheran Confession in Brazil)
Vice-Moderators
Metropolitan Prof Dr Gennadios of Sassima (Limouris) (Ecumenical Patriarchate of Constantinople)
Revd Dr Margaretha M. Hendriks-Ririmasse (Protestant Church in the Moluccas, Indonesia)

General Secretary Revd Dr Samuel Kobia (Methodist Church in Kenya)

Office PO Box 2100, 150 route de Ferney, 1211 Geneva 2, Switzerland   *Tel:* 00 41 22 791 61 11
Fax: 00 41 22 791 03 61
Web: www.oikoumene.com
Cable: Oikoumene Geneva
email: infowcc@wcc-coe.org

The World Council of Churches was brought into formal existence by a resolution of its first Assembly at Amsterdam in 1948.

Member Churches agree to the following basis:

> The World Council of Churches is a fellowship of churches which confess the Lord Jesus Christ as God and Saviour according to the Scriptures and therefore seek to fulfil together their common calling to the glory of the one God, Father, Son and Holy Spirit.

Extract from the Constitution

The primary purpose of the fellowship of churches in the WCC is to call one another to visible unity in one faith and in one eucharistic fellowship, expressed in worship and common life in Christ, through witness and service to the world, and to advance towards that unity in order that the world may believe.

In seeking *koinonia* in faith and life, witness and service, the churches through the Council will:

1. promote the prayerful search for forgiveness and reconciliation in a spirit of mutual accountability, the development of deeper relationships through theological dialogue, and the sharing of human, spiritual and material resources with one another;
2. facilitate common witness in each place and in all places, and support each other in their work for mission and evangelism;
3. express their commitment to *diakonia* in serving human need, breaking down barriers between people, promoting one human family in justice and peace, and upholding the integrity of creation, so that all may experience the fullness of life;
4. nurture the growth of an ecumenical consciousness through processes of education and a vision of life in community rooted in each particular cultural context;
5. assist each other in their relationships to and with people of other faith communities;
6. foster renewal and growth in unity, worship, mission and service.

In order to strengthen the one ecumenical movement, the Council will:

1. nurture relations with and among churches, especially within but also beyond its membership;
2. establish and maintain relations with national councils, regional conferences of churches, organizations of Christian World Communions and other ecumenical bodies;
3. support ecumenical initiatives at regional, national and local levels;
4. facilitate the creation of networks among ecumenical organizations;
5. work towards maintaining the coherence of the one ecumenical movement in its diverse manifestations.

The World Council shall offer counsel and provide opportunity for united action in matters of common interest.

It may take action on behalf of constituent churches only in such matters as one or more of them may commit to it and only on behalf of such churches.

The World Council shall not legislate for the churches; nor shall it act for them in any manner except as indicated or as may hereafter be specified by the constituent churches.

The WCC is governed by an Assembly of Member Churches, a Central Committee, and by an Executive Committee and other subordinate bodies as may be established. Assemblies are held every six to eight years and have been as follows:

1. AMSTERDAM, 1948 – theme: 'Man's Disorder and God's Design'
2. EVANSTON, 1954 – theme: 'Christ the Hope of the World'
3. NEW DELHI, 1961– theme: 'Jesus Christ, the Light of the World'
4. UPPSALA, 1968 – theme: 'Behold, I Make All Things New'
5. NAIROBI, 1975 – theme: 'Jesus Christ Frees and Unites'
6. VANCOUVER, 1983 – theme: 'Jesus Christ the Life of the World'
7. CANBERRA, 1991– theme: 'Come, Holy Spirit – Renew the Whole Creation'
8. HARARE 1998 – theme: 'Turn to God – Rejoice in Hope'
9. PORTO ALEGRE 2006 – theme: 'God, in your grace, transform the world'

The Central Committee elected by the Ninth Assembly includes two members of the Church of England: the Rt Revd Thomas Frederick Butler, Bishop of Southwark, and Dr Mary Tanner, one of the WCC presidents.

The WCC has 348 member churches, including 38 which are associated. Almost every Church of the Anglican Communion is included, together with most of the Orthodox Churches and all the main Protestant traditions. The Roman Catholic Church is not a member but has sent official observers to all main WCC meetings since 1960. It is a full member of the Faith and Order Commission of the WCC.

Regional Conferences

ALL AFRICA CONFERENCE OF CHURCHES
General Secretary Canon Clement Janda, Waiyaki Way, PO Box 14205, Westlands, Nairobi, Kenya
email: aacc@insightkenya.com
Founded 1963.

CHRISTIAN CONFERENCE OF ASIA
General Secretary Dr Prawate Khid-arn

Central Office c/o Payap University, PO Box 183, Maung, Chiang Mai 50000, Thailand
Tel: +66-(0)53-243906 / 243907
Fax: +66-(0)53-247303
Founded 1957.

CARIBBEAN CONFERENCE OF CHURCHES
General Secretary Mr Gerard A. J. Granado, Head Office, Lot 3B Warren St, St Augustine, PO Box 876, Port of Spain, Republic of Trinidad, WI
Tel. 1 (868) 662-3064 / 1 (868) 662-9058
Fax: 1 (868) 662-1303
email: ccchq@tstt.net.tt
Web: www.ccc-caribe.org
Founded 1973.

CONFERENCE OF EUROPEAN CHURCHES
See page 453.

LATIN AMERICAN COUNCIL OF CHURCHES
(Consejo Latinoamericano de Iglesias (CLAI))

President Bishop Julio Murray Thomson, Iglesia Episcopal Diócesis de Panama *Address* Calle Culebra No. 331 – A. Ancon Balboa PO Box 0843 – 01258 Ancón Balboa – Ciudad de Panamá – Panamá
Tel: 00507–2120062
Fax: 00507–2622097
email: bpjuliomurray@hotmail.com

Interim General Secretary Revd Nilton Giese *Address* Inglaterra No. N32–113 y Mariana de Jesús, Quito, Ecuador *Postal address* PO Box 17–08–8522, Quito, Ecuador
Tel: 5932 2553996/2529933
Fax: 5932 2568373
email: nilton@claiweb.org
Web: www.claiweb..org

MIDDLE EAST COUNCIL OF CHURCHES (MECC)
HQ Address PO Box 5376, Beirut, Lebanon
Tel: +961 1 353938 / 344896
Fax: +961 1 344 894
email: mecc@cyberia.net.lb

Liaison Office PO Box 54259, 3722 Limassol, Cyprus
Tel: +357 25 584613 /586022
Fax: +357 25 586496 /584613
email. MECC-GS@spidernet.com.cy

General Secretary Mr Guirgis Saleh (*same address*)
email: guirgissaleh@cyberia.net.lb
Founded 1974. It comprises 29 member Churches from four ecclesiastical families, namely: Eastern Orthodox, Oriental Orthodox, Catholic and Evangelical (Protestant) Churches.

PACIFIC CONFERENCE OF CHURCHES
Moderator Bishop Philemon Riti

Deputy Moderator Fr. Apimeleki Qilio

General Secretary Revd Valamotu Palu (Miss), PCC Secretariat, 4 Thurston St, Suva, Fiji
Tel: 679 3311 277/3302 332
Fax: 679 3303 205
email: pacific@connect.com.fj

Who's Who   **PART 7**

Abbreviations used in the biographies

AABM ..... Archbishops' Adviser for Bishops' Ministry
ABIST .... Associate, British Institute of Surgical Technology
ABM .... Advisory Board of Ministry (now Ministry Division)
AC .... Archbishops' Council
ACA ..... Associate, Institute of Chartered Accountants
ACC .... Anglican Consultative Council
ACCM .... Advisory Council for the Church's Ministry (now Ministry Division)
ACE .... Associateship of the College of Education Member, Association of Conference Executives
ACGI ... Associate, City and Guilds of London Institute
ACIB .... Associate, Chartered Institute of Bankers (formerly AIB)
ACII .... Associate, Chartered Insurance Institute
ACIS .. Associate, Institute of Chartered Secretaries and Administrators
ACMA .. Associate, Chartered Institute of Management Accountants (formerly ACWA)
ACORA ..... Archbishops' Commission on Rural Areas
ACP .... Associate, College of Preceptors
ACS .... Additional Curates Society
ACertCM .... Archbishop of Canterbury's Certificate in Church Music
AD .... Area Dean
ADipR .... Archbishop's Diploma for Readers
AHA .... Area Health Authority
AIA .... Associate, Institute of Actuaries
AKC .... Associate, King's College London
ALA .... Associate, Library Association
ALCD .... Associate, London College of Divinity
ALCM .... Associate, London College of Music
APR .... Association for Promoting Retreats
ARC .... Anglican-Roman Catholic
ARCIC .... Anglican-Roman Catholic International Commission
ARCM .... Associate, Royal College of Music
ARCO .... Associate, Royal College of Organists
ARCO(CHM) .... Associate, Royal College of Organists with Diploma in Choir Training
ARCS .... Associate, Royal College of Science
ARMIT .... Associate, Royal Melbourne Institute of Technology
ASWA ..... Anglican Society for the Welfare of Animals
ATCL .... Associate, Trinity College of Music London
ATII .... Associate Member, Institute of Taxation
Aberd .... Aberdeen
Abp .... Archbishop
Aberw .... Aberystwyth
Acad .... Academy
AdDipEd .... Advanced Diploma in Education
Admin . Administration, Administrative, Administrator
Adn .... Archdeacon
Adnry .... Archdeaconry
Adv .... Adviser, Advisory
Agric .... Agricultural, Agriculture
Aid .... Aidan('s)
Alb .... Alban('s)
Andr .... Andrew('s), Andrews
Angl .... Anglican(s)
Ant .... Anthony('s)
Appt .... Appointment(s), appointed
Ascen .... Ascension
Assoc .... Associate, Association
Asst .... Assistant
Assur .... Assurance

Aug .... Augustine('s)
Auth .... Authority
b .... Born
B & W .... (Diocese of) Bath and Wells
BA .... Bachelor of Arts
BAGUPA .... Bishop's Advisory Group on UPAs
BBC .... British Broadcasting Corporation
BCC .... British Council of Churches (now see CCBI)
BCh or BChir Bachelor of Surgery (also see BS and ChB)
BD .... Bachelor of Divinity
BDS .... Bachelor of Dental Surgery
BEd .... Bachelor of Education
BFBS .... British and Foreign Bible Society
BLitt .... Bachelor of Letters
BM .... Board of Mission
BMU .... Board for Mission and Unity
Bmet .... Bachelor of Metallurgy
BMus .... Bachelor of Music (also see MusB or MusBac)
BNC .... Brasenose College
BPS .... British Pharmacological Society
BRF .... Bible Reading Fellowship
BS .... Bachelor of Science (also see BSc), Bachelor of Surgery (also see BCh, BChir and ChB)
BSR .... Board for Social Responsibility
BSc .... Bachelor of Science (also see BS)
BSocSc .... Bachelor of Social Science (also see BSSc)
BTh Btheol .... Bachelor of Theology (also see STB)
BVM&S . Bachelor of Veterinary Medicine and Surgery
BVSc .... Bachelor of Veterinary Science
BYFC .... British Youth for Christ
Bapt .... Baptist('s)
Barn .... Barnabas('s)
Bart .... Bartholomew('s)
Bd .... Board
Bedf .... Bedford
Bibl .... Biblical
Birm .... (Diocese of) Birmingham
Blackb .... (Diocese of) Blackburn
Boro .... Borough
Bp .... Bishop
Br .... British
Bradf .... (Diocese of) Bradford
Bris .... (Diocese of) Bristol
Bucks .... Buckingham(shire)
C .... Curate
C of E .... Church of England
C of I .... Church of Ireland
C-in-c .... Curate-in-charge
CA .... Church Army Member, Institute of Chartered Accountants of Scotland
CAB .... Citizens Advice Bureau
CAC .... Crown Appointments Commission (now Crown Nominations Commission)
CACLB .... Churches Advisory Council for Local Broadcasting (now Churches' Media Council)
CB .... Companion, Order of the Bath
CBE .... Commander, Order of the British Empire
CBF .... Central Board of Finance
CBI .... Confederation of British Industry
CCC .... Corpus Christi College, Council for the Care of Churches
CCCS Commonwealth and Continental Church Society
CCHH .... Churches Council for Health and Healing
CCLA .... Churches, Charities and Local Authorities
CCOM .... Churches' Commission on Mission
CCRJ .... Churches' Commission for Racial Justice
CCU .... Council for Christian Unity

CCYW .... Certificate in Community Youth Work
CD .... Canadian Forces Decoration, Conventional District
CDC .... Clergy Discipline Commission
CEC .... Conference of European Churches
CECC .... Church of England Committee for Communications
CEDR .... Centre for Dispute Resolution
CEEC .... Church of England Evangelical Council
CEIG .... Christian Ethical Investment Group
CEM .... Christian Education Movement
CERT TH .... Certificate in Theology
CF .... Chaplain to the Forces
CFE .... College of Further Education
CHRISM .... Christians in Secular Ministry
CJGS ...... Community of the Companions of Jesus the Good Shepherd
CLASP .. Churches Linked Across Staffs & the Potteries
CME .... Continuing Ministerial Education
CMEAC ...... Committee for Minority Ethnic Anglican Concerns
CMS ... Church Mission Society, Church Music Society
CNC .... Crown Nominations Commission
CPA .... Chartered Patent Attorney
CPAS .... Church Pastoral Aid Society
CPC ...... Certificate of Professional Competence (Road Transport)
CQSW .... Certificate of Qualification in Social Work
CR .... Community of the Resurrection (Mirfield)
CRAC ... Central Religious Advisory Committee of the BBC and ITA
CRC .... Central Readers Council
CSC .... Community of the Servants of the Cross
CSEM .... Certificate in Special Education Management
CSO .... Central Statistical Office
CSR .... Council for Social Responsibility
CSWG .... Community of the Servants of the Will of God
CTBI .... Churches Together in Britain and Ireland
CTE .... Churches Together in England
CTH .... Certificate in Theology
CTM .... Certificate in Theology for Ministry
CU .... Church Union
CUF .... Church Urban Fund
CYCW ...... Certificate in Youth and Community Work
CYFA .... Church Youth Fellowships Association
Cam .... Cambridge
Cambs .... Cambridgeshire
Can .... Canon
Cant .... (Diocese of) Canterbury
Carl .... (Diocese of) Carlisle
Cath .... Catharine('s)/Catherine('s)
Cathl .... Cathedral
Cchem .... Certified/Chartered Chemist
CdipAF . Certified Diploma in Accounting and Finance
Cen .... Centre, Center, Central
Ceng .... Chartered Engineer
Cert CT .... Certificate in Ceramic Technology
CertEd .... Certificate of Education
CertMBiol .... Certificate of Microbiology
Ch .... Christ('s), Church(es)
Chair .... Chairman, Chairwoman
Chan .... Chancellor
Chapl .... Chaplain(s), Chaplaincy(ies)
ChB .... Bachelor of Surgery (also see BCh, BChir and BS)
Ch Ch .... Christ Church
Chelmsf .... (Diocese of) Chelmsford
Ches .... (Diocese of) Chester
Chich .... (Diocese of) Chichester
Chr .... Christian(s)
Chris .... Christopher('s)
Chu .... Churchill

Cl-in-c .... Cleric-in-charge
Clem .... Clement('s)
Cllr .... Councillor/Counsellor
Cmaths .... Chartered Mathematician
Co .... Company, County(ies)
Co-ord .... Coordinator, Coordinating
Coll .... College
Colleg .... Collegiate
Com .... Community
Commn .... Commission
Commr .... Commissioner
Comp .... Comprehensive
Conf .... Confederation, Conference
Consult .... Consultant/Consultancy
Corp .... Corporation
Coun .... Council
Conv .... Convocation
Cphys ... Chartered Physicist of the Institute of Physics
Cov .... (Diocese of) Coventry
Cstat .... Chartered Statistician
Ctee .... Committee
Cuth .... Cuthbert('s)
DAC Diocesan Advisory Committee, Diploma in Adult Counselling
DBE .... Diocesan Board of Education
DBF .... Diocesan Board of Finance
DCH .... Diploma in Child Health
DCL .... Doctor of Civil Law
DCO .... Diocesan Communications Officer
DD .... Doctor of Divinity
DDO .... Diocesan Director of Ordinands
DDS .... Doctor of Dental Surgery
DHSM .... Diploma in Health Service Management
DHSS .... Department of Health and Social Security
DIC .... Diploma of Membership of Imperial College London
DL .... Deputy Lieutenant
DLC .... Diploma of Loughborough College
DMS .... Diploma in Management Studies
DN .... Diploma in Nursing
DOE .... Department of the Environment
DPA .... Diploma in Public Administration
DPS .... Diploma in Pastoral Studies
DMin .... Doctor of Ministry
DPhil .... Doctor of Philosophy (also see PhD)
DProf .... Doctor in Professional Studies
DRACSC . Deployment, Remuneration and Conditions of Service Committee
DSPT .... Diploma in Social and Pastoral Theology
DSS ... Diploma in Social Studies Department of Social Security
DSc .... Doctor of Science (also see ScD)
DTI .... Department of Trade and Industry
DTS .... Diploma in Theological Studies
DTh .... Doctor of Theology (also see ThD)
DUniv .... Doctor of the University
Dav .... David('s)
Dep .... Deputy
Dept .... Department
Devel .... Development
Dio .... Diocese
Dioc .... Diocesan
Dip .... Diploma
DipAdEd .... Diploma in Advanced Education
DipBA .... Diploma in Business Administration
DipC .... Diploma in Counselling
DipChemEng .... Diploma in Chemical Engineering
DipEd .... Diploma in Education
DipHE .... Diploma in Higher Education
DipLA .... Diploma in Liturgy and Architecture
DipLRM .... Diploma in Leadership, Renewal and Mission Studies
DipMin .... Diploma in Ministry

DipN .... Diploma in Nursing
DipPallMed .... Diploma in Palliative Medicine
DipRJ ......,................... Diploma in Retail Jewellery
DipSE .... Diploma in Special Education
DipSW .... Diploma in Social Work
DipSocSc .... Diploma in Social Sciences
DipTh .... Diploma in Theology
Dip UEM .... Diploma in Urban Estate Management
Dir .... Director
Distr .... District
Div .... Divinity, Division
Dn .... Deacon
Dny .... Deanery
Doct .... Doctrinal, Doctrine
Dom .... Domestic
Down .... Downing
Dr .... Doctor
Dss .... Deaconess
Dub .... Dublin
Dur .... (Diocese of) Durham
E .... East, Eastern
EAMTC ...... East Anglian Ministerial Training Course
ECUSA .... Episcopal Church of the United States of
America
EFAC .... Evangelical Fellowship in the Anglican
Communion
EIG . Ecclesiastical Insurance Group (now Ecclesiastical
Insurance)
EJM(RC) .... Ecclesiastical Jurisdiction Measure
(Revision Committee)
EKD .... Evangelische Kirche Deutschland
EPA .... European Patent Attorney
ERMC .... Eastern Region Ministry Course
Eccl .... Ecclesiastical
Ecum .... Ecumenical
Ed .... Editor, Editorial
Edin .... (Diocese of) Edinburgh
Edm .... Edmund('s)
Eds .... Edmundsbury
Educ .... Education
Educl .... Educational
Edw .... Edward('s)
Eliz .... Elizabeth('s)
Em .... Emmanuel('s)
Emer .... Emeritus
Eng .... Engineering
Environ .... Environmental
Engl .... English
Episc .... Episcopal Episcopalian
Eur . (Diocese of) Gibraltar in Europe Europe, European
EurIng .... European Engineer
Eur Phys .... European Physicist
Ev .... Evangelist('s), Evangelists
Evang .... Evangelical, Evangelism
Ex .... (Diocese of) Exeter
Exam .... Examining
Exec .... Executive
FAC .... Fabric Advisory Committee
FASC .... Fellow, Academy of St Cecilia
FBA .... Fellow, British Academy
FBCS .... Fellow, British Computer Society
FCA .... Fellow, Institute of Chartered Accountants
FCAA .... Fellow, Cyprus Association of Actuaries
FCCA .... Fellow, Chartered Association of Certified
Accountants (formerly FACCA)
FCEM .... Fellow, College of Emergency Medicine
FCIM .... Fellow, Chartered Institute of Marketing
(formerly FInstM)
FC INST M ... Fellow, Chartered Institute of Marketing
FCIOB .... Fellow, Chartered Institute of Building
FCIPD .... Fellow, Chartered Institute of Personnel and
Development (formerly FIPD)
FCP .... Fellow, College of Preceptors

FDSRCS .... Fellow in Dental Surgery, Royal College of
Surgeons of England
FE .... Further Education
FGMS .... Fellow, Guild of Musicians and Singers
F&GP .... Finance and General Purposes
FIA .... Fellow, Institute of Actuaries
FIBMS .... Fellow, Institute of Biomedical Sciences
FIHT .... Fellow of the Institution of Highways and
Transportation
FIMA .... Fellow, Institute of Mathematics and its
Applications
FIMgt .... Fellow, Institute of Management
FJMU .... Fellow, Liverpool John Moores University
FKC .... Fellow, King's College London
FLAME .... Family Life and Marriage Education
FOAG .... Faith and Order Advisory Group
FPMI .... Fellow, Pensions Management Institute
FRAI .... Fellow, Royal Anthropological Institute
FRAeS .... Fellow, Royal Aeronautical Society
FRAS .... Fellow, Royal Astronomical Society
FRCO .... Fellow, Royal College of Organists
FRCOG ..... Fellow, Royal College of Obstetricians and
Gynaecologists
FRCOphth . Fellow, Royal College of Ophthalmologists
FRCS .... Fellow, Royal College of Physicians and
Surgeons of England
FRCSE or FRCSEd .. Fellow, Royal College of Surgeons
of Edinburgh
FRHistS .... Fellow, Royal Historical Society
FRICS .... Fellow, Royal Institution of Chartered
Surveyors (formerly FLAS and FSI)
FRIPHH .... Fellow, Royal Institute of Public Health
and Hygiene
FRGS .... Fellow, Royal Geographical Society
FRS .... Fellow, Royal Society
FRSA .... Fellow, Royal Society of Arts
FRSC .... Fellow, Royal Society of Chemistry
(formerly FRIC)
FRSL .... Fellow, Royal Society of Literature
FRSM .... Fellow, Royal Society of Medicine
FSA .... Fellow, Society of Antiquaries
FSCA .... Fellow, Royal Society of Company and
Commercial Accountants
FTII .... Fellow, Institute of Taxation
Fell(s) .... Fellow(s), Fellowship
Fest .... Festival
Fin .... Financial
Fitzw .... Fitzwilliam
Foundn .... Foundation
Fran .... Francis(')
G&C .... Gonville and Caius
GAD .... Government Actuary's Department
GEC .... General Electric Company
GLC .... Greater London Council
GOE .... General Ordination Examination
GP .... General Practitioner
GS .... General Synod
Gabr .... Gabriel('s)
Gd .... Good
Gen .... General
Geo .... George('s)
Gib .... Gibraltar
Glas ..... (Diocese of) Glasgow and Galloway, Glasgow
Glos .... Gloucestershire
Glouc .... (Diocese of) Gloucester
Gov .... Governor
Grp .... Group
Gr .... Grammar
Greg .... Gregorian
Gt .... Great
Guildf .... (Diocese of) Guildford
H .... Holy
H&FE .... Higher and Further Education

HA	Health Authority	Lanc	Lancaster
HCC	Hospital Chaplaincies Council	Lancs	Lancashire
HDipEd	Higher Diploma in Education	Laur	Laurence('s)
HE	Higher Education	Lawr	Lawrence('s)
HM	Her (or His) Majesty('s)	Lect	Lecturer
HMP	Her Majesty's Prison(s)	Leic	(Diocese of) Leicester
HNC	Higher National Certificate	Leics	Leicestershire
HND	Higher National Diploma	Leon	Leonard('s)
HRH	Her/His Royal Highness	Legis	Legislative
Hatf	Hatfield	Lib	Librarian, Library
Hd	Head	Lic	Licence, Licensed, Licentiate
Heref	(Diocese of) Hereford	Lich	(Diocese of) Lichfield
Hertf	Hertford	Linc	(Diocese of) Lincoln
Herts	Hertfordshire	Lincs	Lincolnshire
Hist	History	Liturg	Liturgical
Ho	House	Liv	(Diocese of) Liverpool
Hon	Honorary, Honourable	Llan	(Diocese of) Llandaff
Hosp(s)	Hospital(s)	Lon	(Diocese of) London
IARCCUM	International Anglican – Roman Catholic Commission on Unity and Mission	Loughb	Loughborough
		Lt	Little
IBA	Independent Broadcasting Authority	Ltd	Limited
ICI	Imperial Chemical Industries	M	Member
ICS	Intercontinental Church Society	M&AA	Michael and All Angels
IDC	Inter-Diocesan Certificate	MA	Master of Arts
IMEC	Initial Ministerial Education Committee	MB,BS &MB,ChB	Conjoint degree of Bachelor of Medicine, Bachelor of Surgery
IOM	Isle of Man	MBC	Metropolitan (or Municipal) Borough Council
IPR	Insitute of Public Relations	MBCS	Member, British Computer Society
ITV	Independent Television	MBE	Member, Order of the British Empire
Imp	Imperial	MCIH	Corporate Member, Chartered Institute of Housing
Inc, Incorp	Incorporated		
Incumb	Incumbent	MCIJ	Member, Chartered Institute of Journalists
Ind	Industry, Industrial	MCIM	Member, Chartered Institute of Marketing (formerly MInstM)
Info	Information		
Insp	Inspector, Inspectorate	MCIPD	Member, Chartered Institute of Personnel and Development (formerly MIPD)
Inst	Institute, Institution		
Intercon	Intercontinental	MCLIP	Member, Chartered Institute of Library and Information Professionals
Internat	International		
Ips	Ipswich	MCS	Master of Christian Studies
JP	Justice of the Peace	MCSP	Member, Chartered Society of Physiotherapy
Jas	James('s)	MCST	Member, College of Speech Therapists
Jasp	Jasper('s)	MCT	Member, Association of Corporate Treasurers
Jes	Jesus	MDCT	Manager's Diploma in Ceramic Technology
Jo	John('s)	MDiv	Master of Divinity
Jos	Joseph('s)	MEd	Master of Education
Jt or jt	Joint	MIBC	Member, Institute of Business Counsellors
Jun	Junior	MICE	Member, Institution of Civil Engineers (formerly AMICE)
K	King('s)		
KA	Knight of St Andrew, Order of Barbados	MIChemE	Member, Institution of Chemical Engineers
KCVO	Knight Commander, Royal Victorian Order	MIEE	Member, Institution of Electrical Engineers (formerly AMIEE MIERE)
KHS	Knight of the Holy Sepulchre		
Kath	Katharine('s), Katherine('s)	MIMA	Member, Institute of Management Accountants
LDSRCS(Eng)	Licentiate in Dental Surgery of the Royal College of Surgeons (of England)	MIMgt	Member, Institute of Management
		MIOT	Member, Institute of Operating Theatre Technicians
LEA	Local Education Authority		
LEP	Local Ecumenical Project	MIPD	Member, Institute of Personnel and Development (now see MCIPD)
LICeram	Licenciate, Institute of Ceramics		
LLAM	Licentiate, London Academy of Music and Dramatic Art	MIPR	Member, Institute of Public Relations
		MIStructE	Member, Institute of Structural Engineers
LLB	Bachelor of Laws	MInstD	Member, Institute of Directors
LLD	Doctor of Laws	MInstGA	Member, Institute of Group Analysis
LLM	Master of Laws	MInstP	Member, Institute of Physics
LMH	Lady Margaret Hall	MLitt	Master of Letters
LNSM	Local Non-stipendiary Minister (or Ministry)	MOD	Ministry of Defence
LRAM	Licentiate, Royal Academy of Music	MOW	Movement for the Ordination of Women
LRCP	Licentiate, Royal College of Physicians	MP	Member of Parliament
LRPS	Licentiate, Royal Photographic Society	MPA	Mission and Public Affairs
LRSC	Licentiate, Royal Society of Chemistry	MPhil	Master of Philosophy
LSE	London School of Economics and Political Science	MRCGP	Member, Royal College of General Practitioners
LTCL	Licentiate, Trinity College of Music, London		
LTh	Licentiate in Theology (also see LST)	MRCS	Member, Royal College of Surgeons
LVO	Lieutenant, Royal Victorian Order	MRCVS	Member, Royal College of Veterinary Surgeons
Lab	Laboratory		
Lamp	Lampeter		

MRSC .... Member, Royal Society of Chemistry
MSc .... Master of Science
MTech .... Master of Technology
MTh or MTheol .... Master of Theology (also see STM and ThM)
MU .... Mothers' Union
Magd .... Magdalen('s)/Magdalene('s)
Man .... (Diocese of) Manchester
Man Dir .... Managing Director
Mansf .... Mansfield
Marg .... Margaret('s)
Mart .... Martin('s)
Marlboro .... Marlborough
Matt .... Matthew('s)
Mert .... Merton
Meth .... Methodist
Metrop .... Metropolitan
Mgr .... Manager
Mgt .... Management
Mich .... Michael('s), Michael and All Angels
Mil .... Military
Min .... Minister, Ministries, Ministry, Minor
Minl .... Ministerial
Miss .... Mission('s), Missionary
Missr .... Missioner
Mod .... Moderator
Movt .... Movement
Mss .... Manuscripts
Mt .... Mount
Mus .... Music
MusB or MusBac .... Bachelor of Music (also see BMus)
N .... North
NACRO .... National Association for the Care and Rehabilitation of Offenders
NAHT .... National Association of Headteachers
NCA .... National Certificate in Agriculture
NCIs .... National Church Institutions
NDA .... National Diploma in Agriculture
NDD .... National Diploma in Design
NEOC ..... North East Oecumenical Course North East Ordination Course
NHS .... National Health Service
NNEB .... National Nursery Examination Board
NSM .... Non-stipendiary Minister (or Ministry)
NSW .... New South Wales (Australia)
NT .... New Testament
NTMTC .... North Thames Ministerial Training Course
NW .... North West/Northwestern
NZ .... New Zealand
Nat .... National
Newc .... (Diocese of) Newcastle
Nic .... Nicholas('s)/Nicolas('s)
Nn .... Northern
Norf .... Norfolk
Norw .... (Diocese of) Norwich
Northn .... Northampton
Nottm .... Nottingham
Notts .... Nottinghamshire
Nuff .... Nuffield
OAM .... Order of Australia Medal
OBE .... Officer, Order of the British Empire
OCF .... Officiating Chaplain to the Forces
OGS .... Oratory of the Good Shepherd
OLM .... Ordained Local Minister (or Ministry)
ONC .... Ordinary National Certificate
OStJ ... Officer, Most Venerable Order of the Hospital of St John of Jerusalem
OT .... Old Testament
OTC .... Open Theology College
OU, Open Univ .... Open University
Ord .... Ordinand(s), Ordination
Ox .... (Diocese of) Oxford
Oxon .... Oxfordshire

P .... Patron(s), Priest
P in O .... Priest in Ordinary
P-in-c .... Priest-in-charge
PACTA .... Professional Associate, Clinical Theology Association
PCC .... Parochial Church Council
PGCE .... Postgraduate Certificate in Education
PNG .... Papua New Guinea
POT .... Post Ordination Training
PPS .... Parliamentary Private Secretary
PR .... Public Relations
PRCC .. Policy and Resources Coordinating Committee
PRO .... Public Relations Officer
PV .... Priest Vicar
PWM .... Partnership for World Mission
Par .... Parish(es)
Parl .... Parliamentary
Pastl .... Pastoral
Patr .... Patrick('s), Patronage
Pemb .... Pembroke(shire)
Perm .... Permission
Pet .... Peter('s)
Peterb .... (Diocese of) Peterborough
Peterho .... Peterhouse
PhD .... Doctor of Philosophy (also see DPhil)
Phil .... Phil(l)ip('s)
Pk .... Park
plc .... public limited company
Poly .... Polytechnic
Portsm .... (Diocese of) Portsmouth
Prchr .... Preacher
Preb .... Prebendary
Prec .... Precentor
Prep .... Preparatory
Pres .... President
Prin .... Principal
Pris .... Prison(s)
Priv .... Private
Prof .... Professor, Professorial
Prov .... Provost, Provisions
Ptnr .... Partner
Pty .... Party
pt .... part-time
QC .... Queen's Counsel
QHC .... Queen's Honorary Chaplain
Qu .... Queen('s), Queens'
R .... Rector, Royal
RAMC .... Royal Army Medical Corps
RCHME . Royal Commission on Historical Monuments of England
RAF .... Royal Air Force
RC .... Roman Catholic
RCO .... Royal College of Organists
RD .... Royal Navy Reserve Decoration, Rural Dean
RE .... Religious Education
RGN .... Registered General Nurse
RHM .... Rank Hovis McDougall
RIBA .... (Member) Royal Institute of British Architects (formerly ARIBA)
RICS .... Royal Institute of Chartered Surveyors
RM .... Registered Midwife
RMA or RMC .... Royal Military Academy (formerly College), Sandhurst
RMN .... Registered Mental Nurse
RN .... Royal Navy
RSA .... Royal Society of Arts, Republic of South Africa
RSCM .... Royal School of Church Music
RSIN .... Rural Stress Information Network
Raph .... Raphael('s)
Rdr(s) .... Reader(s)
Red .... Redundant
Relig .... Religious
Relns .... Relations

Rep(s)	Representative(s)	Ste	Sainte
Res	Residential, Residentiary	Steph	Stephen('s)
Resp	Responsibility	Stg	Standing
Resurr	Resurrection	Strg	Steering
Rev	Review	Suff	Suffragan
Revd	Reverend	Supt	Superintendent
Rich	Richard('s)	S'wark	Southwark
Ripon	Ripon and Leeds	S'well	Southwell
Roch	(Diocese of) Rochester	Syn	Synod
Rsch	Research	TCert	Teacher's Certificate

Rep(s) .... Representative(s)
Res .... Residential, Residentiary
Resp .... Responsibility
Resurr .... Resurrection
Rev .... Review
Revd .... Reverend
Rich .... Richard('s)
Ripon .... Ripon and Leeds
Roch .... (Diocese of) Rochester
Rsch .... Research
Rt .... Right
Rtd or rtd .... Retired
S .... South, Southern
S&Man .... (Diocese of) Sodor and Man
SAMS .... South American Mission Society
SAOMC .... St Albans and Oxford Ministry Course
SASRA .... Soldiers' and Airmen's Scripture Readers
                                                  Association
SBL .... Society of Biblical Literature
SCM .... State Certified Midwife, Student Christian
                                                  Movement
SDMTS .... Southern Dioceses Ministerial
                                      Training Scheme
SE .... South East Institute for Theological Education
SEITE ... South East Institute for Theological Education
SOAS .... School of Oriental and African Studies
SOSc .... Society of Ordained Scientists
SPCK ...... Society for Promoting Christian Knowledge
SPI .... Society of Practitioners of Insolvency
SRN .... State Registered Nurse
SRP .... State Registered Physiotherapist
SS .... Saints/Saints', Sidney Sussex
SSC ..... Secretarial Studies Certificate, Societas Sanctae
                          Crucis (Society of the Holy Cross)
SSF .... Society of St Francis
SSM .... Society of the Sacred Mission
SST .... Society for the Study of Theology
STB .... Bachelor of Theology (also see BTh)
STETS ... Southern Theological Education and Training
                                                  Scheme
STh .... Scholar in Theology (also see ThSchol)
STL .... Reader (or Professor) of Sacred Theology
STM ..... Master of Theology (also see MTh or MTheol
                                            and ThM)
SU .... Scripture Union
SW .... South West
Sacr .... Sacrist, Sacristan
Salis .... Salisbury
Sarum .... (Diocese of) Salisbury
Sav .... Saviour('s)
ScD .... Doctor of Science (also see DSc)
Sch(s) .... School(s)
Sec(s) .... Secretary(ies)
Secdry .... Secondary
Selw .... Selwyn
Sem .... Seminary
Sen .... Senior
Sheff .... (Diocese of) Sheffield
Shep .... Shepherd
Shrops .... Shropshire
So .... Souls, Souls'
Soc .... Social, Society
Som .... Somerset
Southn .... Southampton
Sq .... Square
St .... Saint
St Alb .... (Diocese of) St Albans
St And .... (Diocese of) St Andrews, Dunkeld and
                                                  Dunblane
St As .... (Diocese of) St Asaph
St D .... (Diocese of) St Davids
St E&I .... (Diocese of) St Edmundsbury and Ipswich

TEFL .... Teacher of English as a Foreign Language
TETC .. Theological Education and Training Committee
TM .... Team Minister (or Ministry)
TR .... Team Rector
TV .... Team Vicar, Television
Tchr .... Teacher
Tdip .... Teacher's Diploma
Tech .... Technical, Technology
Techn .... Technician
Th, Theol .... Theological
ThD .... Doctorate in Theology (also see DTh)
ThM ..... Master of Theology (also see MTh or MTheol
                                            and STM)
Thos .... Thomas('s)
Tm .... Team
Tr .... Trainer
Treas .... Treasurer('s)
Trg .... Training
Trin .... Trinity
UCCF .. Universities and Colleges Christian Fellowship
                   of Evangelical Unions (formerly IVF)
UCE .... University of Central England
UCL .... University College London
UEA .... University of East Anglia
UMIST ... University of Manchester Institute of Science
                                         and Technology
UPA .... Urban Priority Area (or Areas)
URC .... United Reformed Church
USCL .... United Society for Christian Literature
USPG .... United Society for the Propagation of the
                   Gospel (formerly SPG, UMCA, and CMD)
UWE .... University of the West of England
UWIST .... University of Wales Institute of Science
                                         and Technology
Univ .... University
V .... Vicar, Virgin('s)
VRSC .... Vocations, Recruitment and Selection
                                                  Committee
Vc .... Vice
Ven .... Venerable
Vis .... Visiting
Voc .... Vocational, Vocations
Vol .... Voluntary
W .... West, Western
w .... with
WATCH .... Women and the Church
WCC .... World Council of Churches
WEA .... Workers' Educational Association
WEMTC .. West of England Ministerial Training Course
Wadh .... Wadham
Wakef .... (Diocese of) Wakefield
Warw .... Warwickshire
Westf .... Westfield
Westmr .... Westminster
Wilf .... Wilfred('s), Wilfrid('s)
Wilts .... Wiltshire
Winch .... (Diocese of) Winchester
Wkg .... Working
Worc .... (Diocese of) Worcester
Wrdn .... Warden
YMCA .... Young Men's Christian Association

WHO'S WHO

A Directory of General Synod members, together with those suffragan bishops, deans and archdeacons who are not members of General Synod, and principal staff members of the General Synod, the Archbishops' Council, the Church Commissioners, the Pensions Board and Lambeth Palace, and Church Commissioners who are not members of General Synod. General Synod members are distinguished by the date of their membership, printed at the end of their entry, following the letters GS. Current membership of the General Synod is denoted by the lack of a closing date. The information contained here is supplied by the individuals concerned and no warranty is given as to its accuracy.

ACKROYD, Revd Dr Peter Michael, MA, MBA, MA, Dip Th, Ph D
Vicarage Church Rd Wootton Bedford MK43 9HF [ST ALBANS] *b* 1960 *educ* Nottm High Sch; Jesus Coll Cam; Insead (Fontainebleau); Edin Univ; Wycliffe Hall Ox; *CV* Intl Banking and Private Equity 1982–91; C St Jas Denton Holme, Carl 1994–97; Min Sec Proclamation Trust 1997–2000; V Wootton, Bedford from 2002; Trustee, Latimer Trust from 2005; M AC Fin Cttee from 2006; M Coun Ridley Hall from 2008
GS 2005–   *Tel:* 01234 768391
                    email: ackroyds@lineone.net

AINSWORTH, Revd Janina Helen Margaret, BEd, MA
Church House Great Smith St London SW1P 3AZ [CHIEF EDUCATION OFFICER, GENERAL SECRETARY, EDUCATION DIVISION AND NATIONAL SOCIETY] *b* 1950 *educ* Nottm High Sch for Girls; Homerton Coll Cam; Univ of Lanc; Ripon Coll Cuddesdon; *CV* Tchr-in-c RE Manor Sch Arbury Cambs 1974–75; Tchr-in-c RE Greaves Sch Lanc 1975–79; Pt Lect St Mart Coll Lanc 1979–82; Educ Liaison Worker Tameside Coun for Racial Equality 1983–84; RE Adv Man DBE 1986–98; Dioc Dir of Educ Man Dioc 1998–2006; Chief Educ Officer and Gen Sec Nat Soc from 2007   *Tel:* 020 7898 1500
                                 Fax: 020 7898 1520
        email: janina.ainsworth@c-of-e.org.uk

ALDERTON-FORD, Revd Jonathan Laurence, B Th
Church Office Christ Church Moreton Hall Symonds Rd Bury St Edmunds IP32 7EW [ST EDMUNDSBURY AND IPSWICH] *b* 1957 *educ* Denes High Sch Lowestoft; Nottm Univ; St Jo Coll Nottm; *CV* C St Faith Gaywood Norw 1985–87; C St Andr Herne Bay 1987–90; Min Ch Ch LEP Moreton Hall from 1990; host W Suffolk New Wine Network; Chair Passion Play for Bury St Edm GS 1999–
                    Tel: 01284 769956 (Home)
                          01284 725391 (Office)
                           Fax: 01284 725391
               email: minister@ccmh.org.uk

ALEXANDER, Mrs April Rosemary, BA, Cert Ed
27 Redstone Hill Redhill RH1 4AW [SOUTHWARK] *b* 1943 *educ* R Masonic Sch Rickmansworth; Open Univ; Homerton Coll Cam; *CV* Various teaching posts 1964–84; Financial Services Industry 1984–

92; Financial Services Authority (formerly Securities and Investments Bd) 1992–99; Exec Dir Occupational Pensions Regulatory Authority 1999–2005; Lay Chair Dioc Syn 1996–2006; Head of Trustee Educ, The Pensions Regulator 2005–07; Consult The Pensions Regulator and Pensions Ind 2007; M C of E Pensions Bd; M DRACSC; M GS Legis Cttee; Dep Vc-chair Pensions Bd;
GS 2000–   *Tel:* 01737 765299
                                      07867 977823
                                 Fax: 01737 768152
            email: april@abalexander.co.uk

ALI, Canon Linda, BA, MA
51 Thief Lane York YO10 3HQ [YORK] *b* 1943 *educ* Bp Anstey Gr Sch Trinidad; York Univ; *CV* Trade Marks Co-ord, Colgate Palmolive Eur 1970–89; Trade Marks Mgr, Unilever Plc UK 1989–97; Researcher/writer, Nat Archives, Lon from 2002; M York Forum for Racial Concerns; M CMEAC from 2006; M Derwent Dny Syn; M Soc Resp Coun, N Yorks
GS 2005–   *Tel:* 01904 413698
                                  07966 363721 (Mobile)
            email: linda@jj26.fsnet.co.uk

ALLAIN-CHAPMAN, Dr Thomas Joseph, BA, MA, Ph D
Church House Great Smith St London SW1P 3AZ [HEAD OF PUBLISHING, CHURCH HOUSE PUBLISHING] *b* 1969 *educ* Mount St Mary's Coll Sheff; K Coll Lon; *CV* Inglis Fell, K Coll Lon 1991–92; freelance writer and ed 1994–95; Ed, HarperCollins Relig 1995–97; Asst Commissioning Ed, Collins Educ 1997–2000, Commissioning Ed 2000, Publishing Mgr 2000–05; Head of Publishing, Church Ho Publishing from 2005   *Tel:* 020 7898 1450
                                 Fax: 020 78981449
    email: thomas.allain-chapman@c-of-e.org.uk

ALLCHIN, Revd Maureen Ann, MA, Cert Ed
4 Northfields Bulkington Devizes SN10 1SE [SALISBURY] *b* 1950 *educ* Northfields Sch Lon; Liv Univ Inst of Educ; Sussex Univ; Salis and Wells Th Coll; *CV* Tchr and Sen Mistress, Steyning Gr Sch 1979–92; C (NSM), Chich Dioc 1991–93; C Storrington, Chich 1993–95; TV Bridport Tm, Salis Dioc 1995–2005; Bp's Lic from 2005; Dioc Selector for Rdr Min 1997–2000; Staff Tutor for CM Devel 1999–2005; Bd of Min portfolio holder for CMD 2000–03, for Interim Min 2005–07; P-in-c

Canalside Benefice, Sarum 2006–08; Bp's Lic from 2008
GS 2005– Tel: 01380 828931
email: maureen@mallchin.co.uk

ALLEN, Mr Timothy Edward, MA
Bell House Quay St Orford Woodbridge IP12 2NU [ST EDMUNDSBURY AND IPSWICH] *b* 1944 *educ* Framlingham Coll;Trin Coll Cam; *CV* Bank of England 1966–86; M Haringey Coun Lon 1972–78; Sec to Securities and Investments Bd 1986–97; Sec to Bd of Fin Services Authority 1997–98; M Dioc Syn; M Bp's Coun; M DBF; M Glebe and Invest Ctee; Chair DAC; M Coun St Eds Cathl; M CNC St E and I vacancy 2006–07; M CCC 2006–08; M CBC from 2008; Chair CBC Sculpture and Furnishings Ctee; M Cathl and Ch Bldgs Div Grp; M Fees Advisory Commn; M Min Div Fin Panel; Chair Revision Cttee on draft Stipends (Cessation of Special Payments) Measure 2004; Chair Revision Cttee on draft Pastl (Amendment) Measure 2004; M Revision Cttee draft Diocs, Pastl and Mission Measure 2006; Lay Elder Par of Orford from 2001
GS 2000– Tel: 01394 450789
email: tim@bellhouseorford.com

ALLISTER, Ven Donald Spargo, MA
Church House Lower Lane Aldford Chester CH3 6HP [ARCHDEACON OF CHESTER] *b* 1952 *educ* Birkenhead Sch; Peterho Cam; Trinity Th Coll Bris; *CV* C St Geo Hyde, Ches 1976–79; C St Nic Sevenoaks, Roch 1979–83; V Ch Ch Birkenhead, Ches 1983–89; R St Mary Cheadle, Ches 1989–2002; RD Cheadle 1999–2002; Adn of Chester from 2002; M numerous dioc cttees; Chair Dioc Houses and Glebe Cttee; Chair Dioc Par Share Grp; Bp's Adv for healthcare chapl; M CCU
GS 2005– Tel: 01244 681973 (Office)
01606 882184
Fax: 01244 620456
01606 301911
email: donald.allister@chester.anglican.org

ALLSOPP, Ven Christine, B Sc
Westbrook 11 The Drive Northampton NN1 4RZ [ARCHDEACON OF NORTHAMPTON; PETERBOROUGH] *b* 1947 *educ* St Alb Girls' Gr Sch; Univ of Aston; Salis and Wells (SDMTS); *CV* C St Pet Caversham and St Marg Mapledurham 1989–94; TV Bracknell Tm Min 1994–98; TR Bourne Valley 1998–2005; RD Alderbury 1999–2005; Non-res Can Salis Cathl 2002–05; Chair Dioc Ho of Clergy 2000–04; M Bd of Min 1998–2004; Non-res Can Peterb Cathl from 2005; Chair Peterb DBE from 2005
GS 2005– Tel: 01604 714015
Fax: 01604 792016
email: archdeacon@aofn.wanadoo.co.uk

AMBROSE, Mrs Gillian Elizabeth, BA, MA, PGCE
Vicarage 1 Grantchester Rd Trumpington Cambridge CB2 9LH [ELY] *b* 1952 *educ* Salt Gr Sch Shipley; Sheff Univ; K Coll Lon; *CV* Primary Sch tchr Sheff and Cambs 1973–77; Full time parent and supply teacher 1977–86; Dioc Children's Work Adv 1986–2007; M Dioc Syn; M Bp's Coun; M Dioc Liturg Cttee; M Liturg Commn; M Stg Orders Cttee; Editor Roots Worship from 2007
GS 2000– Tel: 01223 858994
07855 513506 (Mobile)
email: gill.ambrose@ely.anglican.org

APPLEGATE, Ven John, Ph D
Southern North West Training Partnership Aiken House, University of Chester Crabb Lane, Padgate Warrington WA2 0DB [MANCHESTER] *educ* Bris Univ; Trin Coll Bris; *CV* C Collyhurst, Man 1984–87; C Broughton 1987–94; C Higher Broughton 1987–92; C St Clem w St Matthias Lower Broughton 1987–92; C St Jas w St Clem and St Matthias Broughton 1992–94; R Broughton 1994–96; TR Broughton 1996–2002; AD Salford 1997–2002; Hon Rsch Fell and p-t Lect Man Univ from 2000; Adn of Bolton 2002–08; Course Prin Southern Northwest Trg Ptnrship from 2008
GS 2002– Tel: 01925 534373
email: snwtp@chester.ac.uk

ARCHER, Mr Anthony William, LLB, ACA
Barn Cottage Little Gaddesden Berkhamsted HP4 1PH [ST ALBANS] *b* 1953 *educ* St Edw Sch Ox; Birm Univ; *CV* Mgt Consult Odgers Ray & Berndtson from 1995; M CNC 2005–07; M Appts Comm 1999–2005; M Ho of Laity Stg Cttee 1999–2005; M Panel of Chairmen 1999–2004; M Wkg Pty on Structure and Funding of Ord Trg; Coun M Wycliffe Hall from 2001; Coun M Oak Hill Th Coll 1996–2001; M ABM 1994–98; M Rev Cttee on Ch Representation Rules etc; M Eccl Law Soc
GS 1993– Tel: 01442 842397 (Home)
020 7529 1089 (Office)
07721 504125 (Mobile)
Fax: 020 7529 1005 (Office)

email: aw.archer@btinternet.com

ARMITSTEAD, Col Edward Bradley Lawrence, CBE
Pendomer House Pendomer Yeovil BA22 9PB [BATH AND WELLS] *b* 1946 *educ* Shrewsbury Sch; R Military Academy Sandhurst; Defence Services Staff Coll India; *CV* Army Officer 1967–2001, Rtd from 2001; Preacher and Tchr; M Coun SASRA; Rdr; Chair Oak Hill Th Coll Coun
GS 2000– Tel: 01935 862785
email: e.armitstead@btinternet.com

ARMSTRONG, Very Revd Christopher John, Cert Ed, B Th
The Deanery Preston New Rd Blackburn BB2 6PS [DEAN OF BLACKBURN] *b* 1947 *educ* Dunstable Gr Sch; Dur Univ; Kelham Th Coll; Nottm Univ; *CV* Tchr Dunstable 1969–72; Asst C All SS Maidstone 1975–79; Chapl Coll of St Hild & St Bede Dur 1979–85; Dom Chapl to Abp of York and DDO

1985–91; Incumb St Mart Scarboro 1991–2001; Dean of Blackburn from 2001
GS 2003–05   *Tel:* 01254 52502
01254 503090 (Office)
Fax: 01254 689666
email: dean@blackburn.anglican.org

ARRAND, Ven Geoffrey William, BD, AKC
Glebe House The Street Ashfield-cum-Thorpe Stow-market IP14 6LX [ARCHDEACON OF SUFFOLK; ST EDMUNDSBURY AND IPSWICH] *b* 1944 *educ* Scunthorpe Gr Sch; K Coll Lon; St Boniface Th Coll Warminster; *CV* C Washington 1967–70; C S Ormsby Grp 1970–73; TV Gt Grimsby TM 1973–79; TR Halesworth 1979–85; Dean of Bocking 1985–94; R Hadleigh w Layham and Shelley 1985–94; RD Hadleigh 1986–94; Hon Can St Eds Cathl from 1991; Adn of Suffolk from 1994
GS 2005–   *Tel:* 01728 685497
Fax: 01728 685969
email: archdeacon.geoffrey@
stedmundsbury.anglican.org

ASHE, Canon (Francis) John, B Met, Cert Th
Rectory Westbrook Rd Godalming GU7 1ET [GUILD-FORD] *b* 1953 *educ* Ch Hosp; Sheff Univ; Ridley Hall Cam; *CV* C Ashtead, Guild 1979–82; P-in-c St Faith Plumstead, Cape Town 1982–87; R Wisley-w-Pyrford, Guild 1987–93; V Godalming, Guild 1993–2001; RD Godalming 1996–2002; TR Godalming from 2001; M Bp's Coun; Bp's Adv BAP (Pastl) from 2002; Hon Can Guild Cathl 2003; Chair Dioc Listening Gp on Sexuality
GS 2003–   *Tel:* 01483 860594
Fax: 0871 7334357
email: fjashe@googlemail.com

ASHENDEN, Canon Dr Gavin Roy Pelham, LLB, BA, MTL, D Phil
School of Humanities Arts A 133 University of Sussex Brighton BN1 9QN [UNIVERSITIES, SOUTHERN] *b* 1954 *educ* K Sch Cant; Bris Univ; Oak Hill Coll; Heythrop Coll, Lon Univ; Sussex Univ; *CV* C St Jas Bermondsey 1980–82; TV St Ant Hamsey Green, Sanderstead, S'wark 1982–89; Univ Chapl and Lect Sussex Univ from 1989; Dir Aid to Russian Christians 1982–94; M of Coun and Vc-Chair Keston College 1982–95; M CCU 1995–2000; Dioc Adv on new relig movements; Exam Chapl to Bp of Chich; Preb of Hampstead, Chich Cathl 2003, Bursalis Preb 2005; Chapl to the Qu from 2008
GS 1995–2000, 2004–   *Tel:* 01273 877123
07879 493491 (Mobile)
Fax: 01273 678918
email: g.ashenden@sussex.ac.uk

ASHTON, Rt Revd Cyril Guy, MA
Bishop's House 3 Farrington Court Wickersley Rotherham S66 1JQ [SUFFRAGAN BISHOP OF DON-CASTER; SHEFFIELD] *b* 1942 *educ* Lanc Univ; Oak Hill Th Coll; *CV* C Blackpool St Thos 1967–70; Voc Sec CPAS 1970–74; V Lancaster St Thos 1974–91; Lanc Almshouses 1976–90; Dioc Dir of Trg

Blackb 1991–99; Hon Can Blackb Cathl 1991–99; Bp of Doncaster from 1999   *Tel:* 01709 730130
Fax: 01709 730230
email: cyril.ashton@sheffield.anglican.org

ASHTON, Mr David,
2 Manor Drive Battyeford Mirfield WF14 0ER [WAKEFIELD] *b* 1941 *educ* Warw Rd Junior Sch; Dewsbury and Batley Tech Sch; Kitson Eng Coll; *CV* Br Telecom Integrity Mgr; M GS Stg Orders Cttee; M Bp's Coun
GS 1972–   *Tel:* 01924 497996
email: david_ashton@hotmail.com

ASHWIN, Mr John Basil Edward Hamilton, MA, PGCE, FRSA
31 Wellington Rd Chichester PO19 6BB [CHICHES-TER] *b* 1937 *educ* St Olave's and St Saviour's Sch S'wark; Selwyn Coll Cam; Cam Inst of Educ; *CV* Tchr of Engl then Head of Engl Dept, Emanuel Sch SW Lon 1963–69; Head of Engl Dept then Sen Master, William Morris Sen High Sch, Waltham-stow 1969–75; Head, St Dav and St Kath Comp Sch, Hornsey 1975-81; Head, Bp Luffa Sch, Chich 1981–2000; Chair W Sussex Secdry Heads 1995–98; rtd: pt External Adv and Threshold Assessor for schools, Cam Educ Associates; Accredited Section 23 Insp; Mod Rdrs' Trg Chich Dio; Lay Chair Chich Dny Syn; Vc-Chair Govs, Univ Coll Chich; Consult for Secdry Heads
GS 2002–
Tel: 01243 786501 07939 333858 (Mobile)
email: johnashwin@tiscali.co.uk

ASHWORTH, Mrs Lorna,
28 Desmond Rd Eastbourne BN22 7LF [CHICHES-TER] *b* 1970 *CV* Elected to GS 2005
GS 2005–
email: ashko@tiscali.co.uk

ASTIN, Revd Moira Anne Elizabeth, BA, MA, Dip Min
23 Kingfisher Drive Woodley Reading RG5 3LG [OXFORD] *b* 1965 *educ* City of Lon Sch for Girls; Sir William Perkins Sch; Clare Coll Cam; Wycliffe Hall Th Coll; *CV* C Newbury 1995–99; Min Dunston Park LEP and C Thatcham from 1999; TV Thatcham 2001–05; TV Southlake St Jas Woodley from 2005; Ecum Officer Berks from 2003
GS 2000–   *Tel:* 0118 954 5669
email: moira.astin@ntlworld.com

ASTON, Archdeacon of. See RUSSELL, Ven Brian Kenneth

ASTON, Suffragan Bishop of. See WATSON, Rt Revd Andrew

ATHERSTONE, Canon (Castell) Hugh, MA, Dip Th
Vicarage 46 Sutton Rd Seaford BN25 1SH [CHICH-ESTER] *b* 1945 *educ* Maritzburg Coll; Univ of

Natal; Dur Univ; St Chad's Coll Dur; *CV* Dioc of Natal 1970–83; Chr Stewardship Adv Ely dioc and P-in-c Doddington w Benwick 1983–87; M Pastl Ctee 1984–87; M Bp's Coun 1985–87; R Frant w Eridge 1987–95; RD Rotherfield 1990–94; V Sutton w Seaford from 1995; RD Lewes and Seaford 1997–2007; Can and Preb Chich Cathl from 2002; M Coun SEITE 1993–2006; Vc-Pres Dioc Syn and Chair Ho of Clergy from 2006; M Bp's Coun from 2006
GS 2000–   *Tel and Fax:* 01323 893508
                    email: hugh@atherstoneweb.org

ATKIN, Canon Dr Susan Anne Jennifer, BA, MA, Ph D
3 St Bride Court Colchester CO4 0PQ [CHELMS-FORD] *b* 1948 *educ* Qu Eliz Girls' Gr Sch Barnet; Reading Univ; *CV* Admin Trainee Min of Defence 1973–75; Admin Asst City Univ 1975–78; Asst Registrar City Univ 1978–83; Dep Registrar City Univ 1983–86; Dep Registrar York Univ 1986–90; Planning Officer Essex Univ 1990–99; Coun and Court Officer Essex Univ 2000–02; retired 2002; M Dioc Syn from 1995; M Bp's Coun from 1998; Bp's Selector from 2002; Dioc Lay Chair from 2003; Hon Lay Can Chelms Cathl from 2006
GS 1995–   *Tel:* 01206 854976 (Home)
                    email: susan_atkin@lineone.net

ATKINSON, Rt Revd David John, B Sc, Ph D, M Litt, MA
The Red House 53 Norwich Rd Stoke Holy Cross Norwich NR14 8AB [SUFFRAGAN BISHOP OF THETFORD; NORWICH] *b* 1943 *educ* Maidstone Gr Sch; K Coll Lon; Bris Univ; Tyndale Hall; *CV* Tchr Maidstone Tech High Sch 1968–69; C St Pet Halliwell Bolton 1972–74; Sen C St Jo Harborne Birm 1974–77; Lib Latimer Ho Ox 1977–80; Chapl CCC Ox 1980–93; Fell and Lect CCC Ox 1984–93; Vis lect Wycliffe Hall Ox 1984–93; External Examiner St Jo Coll Nottm 1989–93; Can Res S'wark Cathl 1993–96; Exam Chapl 1993–96; External Examiner and ABM Mod Trin Coll Bris 1994–98; Adn of Lewisham 1996–2001; M Soc of Ordained Scientists; Bp of Thetford from 2001
                              Tel: 01508 491014
                              Fax: 01508 492105
          email: bishop.thetford@4frontmedia.co.uk

ATKINSON, Mrs Janet Mary, MA
548 Yarm Rd Eaglescliffe Stockton-on-Tees TS16 0BX [DURHAM] *b* 1932 *educ* Huyton Coll; St Anne's Coll Ox; *CV* Tchr St Leon Sch St Andr 1954–55; Hartlepool Coll FE (pt) 1979–84; pt tutor/voluntary activist WEA from 1979; JP 1984–2002; M Dioc Commn from 1990; Ch Commr 1993–99; non-Commr M Pastl Cttee from 1999; M C of E Pensions Bd 1994–97; Panel of Chairmen 1998 and 1999; M Business Cttee 1999–2001; Vc-Chair CAC Review Grp 1999–2001; Chair Care of Cathls Measure Review Grp 1999–2003; M AC Fin Cttee 2001–06; M CNC 2002–07; M Strg Cttee Pastl, Diocs and Mission Measure 2005–07; M

Election Rev Grp from 2006; M Coun Jo Snow Coll Dur Univ
GS 1985–   *Tel:* 01642 782292
          email: janet.atkinson4@btopenworld.com

ATKINSON, Very Revd Peter Gordon, MA, FRSA
The Deanery 10 College Green Worcester WR1 2LH [DEAN OF WORCESTER] *b* 1952 *educ* Maidstone Gr Sch; St Jo Coll Ox; Westcott Ho Cam; *CV* C Clapham Old Town TM 1979–83; P-in-C Tatsfield 1983–90; R H Trin Bath 1990–91; Prin Chich Th Coll 1991–94; Bursalis Preb Chich Cathl 1991–97; R Lavant 1994–97; Chan Chich Cathl 1997–2007; Dean of Worcester from 2007; Chich Th Trust from 1994; Chair Chich Dioc Eur Ecum Ctee 1997–2007; CFCE 2000–05; Chich Dioc Wrdn of Rdrs 2001–03; Master St Oswald's Hosp Worc from 2007
GS 2000–05   *Tel:* 01905 732909 (Office)
                               01905 732939 (Home)
                               Fax: 01905 732906
    email: peteratkinson@worcestercathedral.org.uk

ATKINSON, Ven Richard William Bryant, MA, OBE
46 Southernhay Rd Stoneygate Leicester LE2 3TJ [ARCHDEACON OF LEICESTER] *b* 1958 *educ* St Paul's Sch Lon; Magd Coll Cam; Cuddesdon Th Coll; *CV* C Abingdon w Shippon 1984–87; TV Sheff Manor Par 1987–91; Hon M of Staff Cuddesdon Th Coll 1987–92; TR Sheff Manor Par 1991–96; V All SS Rotherham 1996–2002; Hon Can Sheff Cathl 1998–2002; Adn of Leicester from 2002; Chair Open Syn Grp 1996–2001; M CTE and CTBI 1997–2002; Ch Commr from 2001; M Bishoprics and Cathls Cttee; M Mgt Adv Cttee; M Cen Ch Fund Cttee 1997–2002; CUF Trustee 2003–08; Dep Chair Places for People 1997–2005; Chair Braunstone New Deal for Communities Programme 2003–06; Chair St Phil Cen for Study and Engagement in Multi Faith Society; Chair Launde Abbey Mgt Cttee; M Carnegie Trust UK Enquiry into the Future of Civil Society in Britain and Ireland
GS 1991–   *Tel:* 0116 270 4441 (Home)
                              0116 248 7419 (Office)
                              07718 656229 (Mobile)
                              Fax: 0116 270 4441 (Home)
                              0116 253 2889 (Office)
          email: richard.atkinson@leccofe.org

ATWELL, Very Revd James Edgar, MA, Th M, BD
The Deanery The Close Winchester SO23 9LS [DEAN OF WINCHESTER] *b* 1946 *educ* Dauntsey's Sch; Ex Coll Ox; Harvard Univ; Cuddesdon Th Coll; *CV* C St Jo E Dulwich 1970–74; C Gt St Mary Cam 1974–77; Chapl Jes Coll Cam 1977–81; V Towcester w Easton Neston 1981–95; RD Towcester 1983–91; Prov of St Eds 1995–2000; Dean 2000–06; Dean of Winchester from 2006
                              Tel: 01962 853738 (Home)
                              01962 857205 (Office)
                              Fax: 01962 857264
    email: the.dean@winchester-cathedral.org.uk

ATWELL, Rt Revd Robert Ronald, BA (Hons),
M.Litt
*Bishop's Lodge Back Lane Dunham Town, Altrincham
Cheshire WA14 4SG* [BISHOP OF STOCKPORT] *b* 1954
educ Wanstead High Sch; St John's Coll Cam;
Westcott Ho Cam; *CV* Asst C John Keble Ch Mill
Hill 1978–81; Chapl Trinity Coll Cam 1981–87;
Benedictine Monk Burford Priory 1987–98; V Par
of St Mary-the-Virgin Primrose Hill 1998–2008;
Bp Stockport from 2008; Chair Miss and Min
Cttee Chester Dioc   *Tel:* 0161 928 5611
                            Fax: 0161 929 0692
   email: bpstockport@chester.anglican.org

**AUCKLAND, Archdeacon of. See BARKER,
Ven Nicholas John Willoughby**

AVIS, Canon Paul David Loup, BD, Ph D
Church House Great Smith St London SW1P 3AZ
[GENERAL SECRETARY, COUNCIL FOR CHRISTIAN
UNITY] *b* 1947 *educ* St Geo Monoux Gr Sch
Walthamstow; Lon Univ; Westcott Ho Th Coll;
CV C S Molton Grp 1975–80; V Stoke Canon, Pol-
timore w Huxham, Rewe w Netherexe 1980–98;
Sub Dean Ex Cathl from 1997; Dir Centre for
Study of the Christian Church from 1997–2008;
Sec CCU from 1998; Vc Chair FOAG 1994–98;
Chair Ho of Clergy Ex Dioc Syn 1996–98; ed
Ecclesiology from 2004; Canon Theologian of Ex
from 2008; Chapl to the Qu from 2008
GS 1990–95   *Tel:* 020 7898 1470
                            07974 696615 (Mobile)
                            Fax: 020 7898 1483
   email: paul.avis@c-of-e.org.uk

AYERS, Revd Paul Nicholas, MA
Vicarage Vicarage Drive Pudsey LS28 7RL [BRAD-
FORD] *b* 1961 *educ* Bradf Gr Sch; St Pet Coll Ox;
Trin Coll Bris; *CV* C St Jo Bapt Clayton 1985–88; C
St Andr Keighley 1988–91; V St Cuth Wrose 1991–
97; V St Lawr and St Paul Pudsey from 1997
GS 1995–   *Tel:* 0113 256 4197
   email: paul.ayers@tiscali.co.uk

BACK, Mr Robin Philip, AIB, FRSA
The Old Manse Church Lane Guestwick NR20 4QJ
[NORWICH] *b* 1946 *educ* Uppingham; Geneva
Univ; *CV* Standard Chartered Bank in Middle
East, India, Indonesia, Thailand and USA 1967–
88; MD Backs Electronic Publishing Ltd from
1989; Prime Wdn, Worshipful Co of Dyers of City
of Lon 2002–03; M Bp's Coun from 2003; Lay
Chair, Dioc Syn from 2003; Lay Chair, Sparham
Dny Syn 1996–2001; M DBF from 2003
GS 2005–   *Tel:* 01362 683281
                            01326 683835
   email: robin@bepl.co.uk

BAILEY, Ven David Charles, MA, M Sc, BA
Minster Vicarage Highgate Beverley HU17 0DN
[ARCHDEACON OF BOLTON] *b* 1952 *educ* Bradf Gr
Sch; Linc Coll Oxf; Nottm Univ; St Jo Coll Nottm;
CV C St Jo Worksop 1980–83; C Edgware, P-in-c

St Andr Broadfields 1983–87; V S Cave and
Ellerker w Broomfleet 1987–97; RD Howden
1991–97; Hon Can York Minster from 1998;
V Beverley Minster from 1997; Archdeacon of
Bolton from 2008
GS 2000–   *Tel:* 01482 868540
                            01482 881434
                            07944 518765 (Mobile)
                            Fax: 01482 887520
   email: baileys_bevmin@bigfoot.com

BAIN, Ven (John) Stuart, BA
*St Nicholas' Vicarage Hedworth Lane Boldon Colliery
NE35 9JA* [ARCHDEACON OF SUNDERLAND; DUR-
HAM] *b* 1955 *educ* Blaydon Sec Sch; Durham Univ;
Westcott Ho Cam; *CV* C H Trin Washington
1980–84; C St Nic Dunston 1984–86; V St Oswald
Shiney Row and St Aid Herrington 1986–92; P-in-
c St Paul Spennymoor and Whitworth 1992–97;
P-in-c St Jo Merrington 1994–97; AD Auckland
1996–2002; Hon Can Dur 1998; V St Paul Spennymoor, Whitworth and St Jo Merrington 1997–
2002; Chair DFW Adoption from 1999; Asst P St
Nic Hedworth 2002; P-in-c St Nic Hedworth from
2003; Adn of Sunderland from 2002
                            Tel: 0191 536 2300
                            Fax: 0191 519 3369
   email: Archdeacon.of.Sunderland@
                            durham.anglican.org

BAINES, Rt Revd Nicholas, BA (Hons)
53 Stanhope Road Croydon CR0 5NS [BISHOP OF
CROYDON; SOUTHWARK] *b* 1957 *educ* Holt Comp
Sch Liv; Bradf Univ; Trin Coll Bris; *CV* C St Thos
Kendal 1987–91; C H Trin Leic 1991–92; V Roth-
ley 1992–2000; RD Goscote 1995–2000; Adn of
Lambeth 2000–03; Broadcaster; Dir EIG from
2002; Bp of Croydon from 2003; Angl Co-Chair
Meissen Comm
GS 1995–2003, 2004–05
                            Tel: 020 8256 9630 (Office)
                            020 8686 1822 (Home)
                            07974 194735 (Mobile)
                            Fax: 020 8256 9631 (Office)
                            020 8649 7658 (Home)
   email: bishop.nick@southwark.anglican.org

BAKER, Revd Jonathan Mark Richard, MA,
M Phil
Pusey House Oxford OX1 3LZ [OXFORD] *b* 1966 *educ*
Merchant Taylors' Sch Northwood; St Jo Coll Ox;
St Steph Ho Th Coll; *CV* C All SS Ascot Heath
1993–96; P-in-c St Mark and H Trin Reading
1996–99; V St Mark and H Trin Reading 1999–
2002; Prin Pusey Ho, Ox from 2003
GS 2000–   *Tel:* 01865 278415
                            01865 288023
   email: jonathan.baker@stx.ox.ac.uk

BALLARD, Ven Andrew Edgar, BA
*2 The Walled Garden Ewhurst Ave Swinton Man-
chester M27 0FR* [ARCHDEACON OF MANCHESTER] *b*
1944 *educ* Rossall Sch; St Jo Coll Dur; Westcott Ho
Th Coll; *CV* Asst C St Mary Bryanston Sq and

Asst Chapl Middx Hosp Lon 1968–72; Asst C St Mary Portsea 1972–76; V St James Haslingden w St Steph Haslingden Grange 1976–82; V St Paul Walkden 1982–93; AD Farnworth 1990–98; TR Benefice of Walkden St Paul w Little Hulton St John 1993–98; P-in-c Rochdale Tm 1998–2000, TR from 2000; Hon Can Man Cathl 1998–2000; Adn of Rochdale 2000–05; Adn of Manchester from 2005
Tel: 0161 794 2401
Fax: 0161 794 2411
email: ae.ballard@btinternet.com

BALLARD, Ven Peter James, B Ed, Dip Th
Wheatfield 7 Dallas Rd Lancaster LA1 1TN [ARCH-DEACON OF LANCASTER; BLACKBURN] *b* 1955 *educ* Chadderton Gr Sch for Boys; Bede Coll Dur; Lon Univ; Sarum and Wells Th Coll; *CV* C Grantham 1987–91; Asst Chapl Grantham and Kesteven Gen Hosp 1989–91; R St Pet and St Paul Port Pirie S Australia 1991; V Ch Ch Lancaster 1991–98; RD Lancaster 1995–98; Can Res and Dioc Dir of Educ 1998–2006; Dir of Educ from 1998; Adn of Lancaster from 2006; Pro Chan Univ of Cumbria from 2007
GS 2000–
Tel: 01524 32897 (Home)
01254 503070(Office)
07970 923141 (Mobile)
Fax: 01524 66095 (Home)
01254 699963 (Office)
email: peter.ballard@blackburn.anglican.org

BAMBER, Revd Sheila Jane, BA, MA, MBA
Vicarage 8 Woodland Close Bearpark Durham DH7 7EB [DURHAM] *b* 1954 *educ* Lamp, Univ of Wales; Sheff Univ; Open Univ; Ripon Coll Cuddesdon; *CV* Various posts culminating in Housing Mgr, Endeavour Housing Assoc; C St Cuth Dur 1998–2001; TV Dur N from 2002; Dioc Dir of Educ from 2004; M Dioc Syn from 2003; M DAC from 2000; Chair Dioc Conference Planning Grp 2004–05; M Dioc Bd of Educ 2000–04; Chair Educ Adv Cttee 2003–04
GS 2005–
Tel: 0191 373 3886
0191 374 6009
07989 542565 (Mobile)
Fax: 0191 384 7529
email: sheilab@ddemt.co.uk

BARKER, Ven Nicholas John Willoughby, MA
Holy Trinity Vicarage 45 Milbank Rd Darlington DL3 9NL [ARCHDEACON OF AUCKLAND] *b* 1949 *educ* Sedbergh Sch; Oriel Coll Ox; Trin Coll Bris; *CV* C St Mary Watford 1977–80; TV St Jas and Em Didsbury 1980–86; TR St Geo Kidderminster 1986–2007; RD Kidderminster 2001–07; Adn of Auckland from 2007; Hon Can Dur Cathl from 2007
GS 2005–07
Tel: 01325 480444
07912 269 364 (Mobile)
Fax: 01325 354027
email: archdeacon.of.auckland@durham.anglican.org

BARKER, Canon Timothy Reed, MA
The Parsonage 1 Halmer Gate Spalding PE11 2DR [LINCOLN] *b* 1956 *educ* Man Gr Sch; Queen's Coll Cam; Westcott Ho; *CV* C Nantwich 1980–83; V Norton St Berteline and St Christopher 1983–88; V Runcorn All Saints 1988–94; Urban Officer Ches 1990–98; Bp of Chester's Chap 1994–98; P assoc, Ches Cath 1994–98; V Spalding St Mary and Nicholas from 1998; Rural Dean Elloe West from 2000; M Linc Cathl Chap from 2000; Can and Preb of Linc from 2003; P-in-C Spalding St Paul from 2007; M DRACS Cttee 2001–05; M CME Panel 2003–06; M Clergy Terms of Service Implementation Group 2005–07; M Marriage Law Working Party 2006; M Dioc Syn from 1999
GS 2000–05; 2008–
Tel: 01775 722772 (Office)
01775 722675 (Home)
07775 833426 (Mobile)
Fax: 01775 710273
email: tim@tjkc.co.uk

BARKING, Area Bishop of. See HAWKINS, Rt Revd David John Leader

BARLEY, Revd Lynda Mary, BA, M Sc, PGCE
Church House Great Smith Street London SW1P 3AZ [HEAD OF RESEARCH AND STATISTICS, ARCH-BISHOPS' COUNCIL] *b* 1953 *educ* Tiffin Girls' Sch Kingston-upon-Thames; York Univ; Univ Coll Lon; S'wark Ord Course; *CV* Statistician Bank of England 1976–79; Rsch Mgr Bible Soc 1979–87; Rsch Consult 1987–98; Tutor Open Univ from 1992; OFSTED and Section 23 Sch Insp 1993–2006; Ho for Duty Priest Dunsford & Doddiscombsleigh 1998–2000; Hd of Rsch & Statistics, AC, from 2000; Asst Min (NSM) Culm Valley Tm Min from 2003; Chapl S'wark Cathl from 2007; Vis Lect, K Coll Lon from 2006
Tel: 020 7898 1542
Fax: 020 7898 1532
email: lynda.barley@c-of-e.org.uk

BARNES, Mr Barry Karl,
30 Junction Rd S Croydon CR2 6RB [SOUTHWARK] *b* 1946 *educ* Selhurst Gr Sch; *CV* Solicitor; Chair Croydon YMCA Housing Assoc 1993–2000; M Legal Aid Commn from 1996; M Pastl Measure Appeals Panel from 2001; Lay Chair Croydon Cen Dny Syn from 2002; Lay Chair S'wark Forward in Faith
GS 1995–
Tel: 020 8686 5179 (Home)
020 8681 6116 (Office)
07802 150148 (Mobile)
Fax: 020 8686 9776 (Office)
email: bkb@jthirty.fsnet.co.uk

BARNEY, Mr Stephen George, B Sc, MBA
The Dower House 77 Brook St Wymeswold LE12 6TT [LEICESTER] *b* 1950 *educ* Cranfield Univ; *CV* Main Bd Dir Sketchley plc 1990–97; Chief Exec Centrica joint venture 1997–2000; rtd; Rdr; chwrdn; M Leic

Cathl Chapter, Launde Abbey Mgt Cttee, Lough-borough Transitional Coun
GS 2005–ェ*Tel:* 01509 881160
07767 320320 (Mobile)
email: stephen@barney4747@fsnet.co.uk

BARNSTAPLE, Archdeacon of. See GUNN-JOHNSON, Ven David Allan

BARRELL, Mrs Anneliese Gledhill, MCSP,
Grad Dip Phys, DSA
47 Whitleigh Ave Crownhill Plymouth PL5 3AU [EXETER] *b* 1938 *educ* Burlington Sch Lon; Prince of Wales Gen Hosp Sch of Physiotherapy, Lon; *CV* Rtd NHS physiotherapy mgr; pt lect, Plymouth Coll FE; M Dioc Coun for Work with Children and Young People, Chair of Youth and FE Cttee; Chair Devon Trefoil Guild
GS 2000–ェ*Tel:* 01752 777053
07713 147828 (Mobile)
email: annagb@blueyonder.co.uk

BASHFORTH, Revd Alan George, MA, B Th
Vicarage 6 Penwinnick Parc St Agnes TR5 0UQ [TRURO] *b* 1964 *educ* Humphrey Davy Gr Sch; Ox Univ; Ex Univ; Ripon Coll Cuddesdon; *CV* Police officer, S Yorks Police 1983–90; nursing auxiliary 1990–93; C Calstock, Truro 1996–98; C St Ives, Truro 1998–2001; V St Agnes and Mithian w. Mount Hawke from 2001; RD Powder from 2004; M Bp's Coun; M DBF; M Dioc Children and Youth Cttee; M Dioc Pastl Cttee
GS 2005–ェ*Tel:* 01872 553391
email: alan@onepaw.fsnet.co.uk

BASINGSTOKE, Suffragan Bishop of. See WILLMOTT, Rt Revd Trevor

BASSHAM, Ms Sallie, B Sc
Winshaw Barn Chapel-le-Dale Ingleton Carnforth LA6 3 AT [BRADFORD] *b* 1947 *educ* Qu Eliz Gr Sch Hexham; Salford Univ; *CV* Mathematics Lect Univ of Salford; M ABM 1996–98; M VRSC 1998–2005; M Bishoprics and Cathl Cttee from 1999; Lay Chair Bowland Dny Syn 1995–2004; M Coun St Jo Coll, Dur
GS 1995–
email: sbassham@nildram.co.uk

BASTON, Ven Caroline Jane, BSc, PGCE, Cert Theol
5 The Boltons Wootton Bridge Ryde Isle of Wight PO33 4PB [ARCHDEACON OF THE ISLE OF WIGHT; PORTSMOUTH] *b* 1956 *educ* Godolphin Sch Salis; Birm Univ; City of Birm Poly; Ripon Coll Cuddesdon; *CV* C St Chris Thornhill, Southn, Winch 1989–94; R All SS Winch w. St Andr Chilcomb w. St Pet Chesil 1995–2006; Dioc Communications Officer 1995–98; DDO 1999–2006; Adn of Isle of Wight from 2006; M Dioc Syn, Miss and Soc Forum, Bp's Coun, DAC, DBE
Tel: 01983 884432
email: adiow@portsmouth.anglican.org

BATE, Miss Jennifer Anne,
Solway Bungalow Pow Hill Kirkbride, Wigton Cumbria CA7 5LF [CARLISLE] *b* 1950 *educ* Chiswick County Gr Sch; *CV* Antique furniture dealer and restorer 1970–2002; Tourism Officer, Carl Dioc 2002–06; Dioc Pastl Sec from 2005
GS 2005–ェ*Tel:* 01228 815408 (Office)
email: jennybate@btinternet.com

BATH AND WELLS, Bishop of. See PRICE, Rt Revd Peter Bryan

BATH, Archdeacon of. See PIGGOTT, Ven Andy (Andrew John)

BAXTER, Dr Christina Ann, BA, Ph D, CBE
St John's College Chilwell Lane Bramcote Nottingham NG9 3DS [SOUTHWELL AND NOTTINGHAM] *b* 1947 *educ* Walthamstow Hall Sevenoaks; Dur Univ; Bris Univ; *CV* Hd Relig Studies John Leggott Sixth Form Coll; Dur Rsch Student and pt staff M St Jo Coll Dur; Prin St Jo Coll Nottm; M GS Stg Cttee 1985–95; Vc Chair Ho of Laity 1990–95; Chair Ho of Laity from 1995; AC and Fin Cttee
GS 1985–ェ*Tel:* 0115 922 4087 (Home)
0115 925 1114 (Office)
07990 590231 (Mobile)
Fax: 0115 943 6438
email: principal@stjohns-nottm.ac.uk

BAYNES, Mr Simon Henry Crews, BSc, C Eng, FBCS
4 Pilgrim Close St Albans AL2 2JD [ST ALBANS] *b* 1958 *educ* Orange Hill Boys' Gr Sch; Sheff Univ; *CV* Logica from 1979, Chartered Eng from 1990, Chair of Pension Trustees from 1997; Trustee, Life Academy (The Pre-Retirement Assoc) from 2007; M St Alb Dioc Syn from 2003; M St Alb DBF from 2003; M Dny Syn from 2001; M St Alb Cathl Fin Cttee 1997–2007; M Inter-Dioc Fin Forum from 2005; M Bp's Coun from 2007; Trustee Cam Univ Press Sen Staff Pension Scheme from 2008; M CNC (St Alb Vacancy-in-See) from 2008
GS 2005–ェ*Tel:* 01727 875524 (Home)
07860 828711 (Mobile)
email: simon@simonbaynes.fsnet.co.uk

BEACH, Revd Mark Howard Francis, BA, MA
The Rectory Church St Rugby CV21 3PH [COVENTRY] *b* 1904 *educ* Ellesmore Coll Shropshire; Univ of Kent; Univ of Nottm; St Stephen's Ho; *CV* C Beeston S'well 1987–90; C Hucknall 1990–93; R Gedling 1993–2001; R Netherfield 1996–2001; Bp's Chapl Wakef 2001–03; TR Rugby Cov from 2003; M Bp's Coun and Dioc Syn Cov
GS 2008–ェ*Tel:* 01788 542936 (Home)
01788 565609 (Office)
07930 577 248 (Mobile)
email: rector@rugbyteam.org.uk

BEAKE, Ven Stuart Alexander, MA
Archdeacon's House 123 Merrow Woods Guildford GU1 2LJ [ARCHDEACON OF SURREY; GUILDFORD]

b 1949 *educ* K Coll Sch Wimbledon; Em Coll Cam; Cuddesdon Coll Ox; *CV* C St Mary Hitchin 1974–79; TV St Mary Hemel Hempstead 1979–85; Dom Chapl to Bp of Southwell 1985–87; V Shottery St Andr 1987–2000; RD Fosse Dny 1992–99; DDO Cov Dioc 1995–2000; Hon Can Cov Cathl 1999–2000; Can Res and Sub-Dean Cov Cathl 2000–05; Adn of Surrey from 2005
GS 1980–85   *Tel:* 01483 790352 (Office)
                              01483 567199 (Home)
              email: stuart.beake@cofeguildford.org.uk

BECK, Miss Rachel Gillian, BA
21 Greetwell Gate Lincoln LN2 4AW [LINCOLN] *b* 1980 *educ* Wales High Sch; Bp Grosseteste Coll; *CV* Receptionist Sheff Dioc Ch Ho 1999–2000; Admin Rotherham Youth Service 2000–01; PA to Asst Dir of Educ, Rotherham 2001–02; Primary Tchr, Linc from 2005
GS 2000–   *Tel:* 01909 770802
                              07753 634477 (Mobile)
                  email: rgbeck@btinternet.com

BEDFORD, Archdeacon of. See HUGHES, Ven Paul Vernon

BEDFORD, Suffragan Bishop of.
See INWOOD, Rt Revd Richard Neil

BEER, Ven John Stuart, MA Oxon, MA Cantab
St Botolph's Rectory 1a Summerfield Cambridge CB3 9HE [ARCHDEACON OF CAMBRIDGE; ELY] *b* 1944 *educ* Roundhay Sch Leeds; Pemb Coll Ox; Westcott Ho Th Coll; *CV* C St Jo Knaresborough 1971–74; Fell and Chapl Fitzw Coll and New Hall Cam 1974–80; R Toft w Caldecote and Childerley and Harwick 1980–87; V Grantchester 1987–97; DDO, Dir of POT and Rdr Trg 1987-97; Hon Can Ely Cathl from 1989; Chair Cathl Pilgrims Assoc Conference 1986–96; M Ethics Cttee Dunn Nutrition Unit 1985–2001; Adn of Huntingdon 1997–2004; acting Adn of Wisbech 2002–04; Co-DDO and Dir POT 1997–2002; Bye-Fell Fitzw Coll from 2001; M Bp's Coun; Chair Communications Cttee; Chair Liturg Cttee; M Fin Cttee; Bps' Sen Selector from 2002; Adn of Ely 2004–07; Adn of Cambridge from 2007
GS 2003–   *Tel:* 01223 350424
                              Fax: 01223 360929
     email: archdeacon.cambridge@ely.anglican.org

BELL, Rt Revd James Harold, MA, BA, Cert Theol
Thistledown Main St Exelby Bedale DL8 2HD [SUFFRAGAN BISHOP OF KNARESBOROUGH; RIPON AND LEEDS] *b* 1950 *educ* Appleby Gr Sch; St Jo Coll Dur; Wycliffe Hall Ox; *CV* Hon C St Mich at the Northgate, Ox 1975–76; Chapl and lect BNC Ox 1976–82, Fell 1979–82; R St Mary Northolt, Lon 1982–93; Area Dean Ealing 1991–93; Adv for Min, Willesden Area 1993–97; Dir of Min and Tr, Ripon Dioc 1997–99; Res Can Ripon Cathl 1997–99; Dir of Mission Ripon Dioc 1999–2004; Hon Can Ripon Cathl 1999–2004; Bp of Knaresborough

from 2004; M Dioc Syn, DBF, DBE (ex officio), Dioc Coun for Mission, Rural Bps' Panel; Trustee NEOC; Trustee FaithCAN; Dir Meth Chapel Aid; Chair Bd of Dirs of Active Faith Communities
                              Tel: 01677 423525
                              01677 424392
                              Fax: 01677 423525
            email: bishop.knaresb@btinternet.com

BELL, Sir Stuart, MP
Church House Great Smith St London SW1P 3AZ [SECOND CHURCH ESTATES COMMISSIONER] *b* 1938 *educ* Hookergate Gr Sch Durham; Gray's Inn Lon; *CV* Barrister-at-Law; MP for Middlesbrough from 1983; PPS to Rt Hon Roy Hattersley 1983–84; Front Bench Spokesperson N Ireland 1984–87; Vc Chair Inter-Parliamentary Br Grp 1991–94; Vc Chair Br Irish Inter-Parliamentary Body 1990–92; Front Bench Spokesperson Trade and Industry 1992–97; M House of Commons Commn from 2000; Chair Fin and Services Cttee from 2000; Second Ch Estates Commr from 1997; Freeman of City of Lon from 2003; Chair Franco-Br Parliamentary Grp; Chevalier de la Legion d'Honneur 2006
GS 1997–   *Tel:* 020 7898 1623
                              Fax: 020 7898 1131

BENFIELD, Revd Paul John, LLB, B Th
St Nicholas Vicarage Highbury Ave Fleetwood FY7 7DJ [BLACKBURN] *b* 1956 *educ* Cam Gr Sch for Boys; Newc Univ; Coll of Law, Chancery Lane, Lon; Chich Th Coll; *CV* Chancery barrister 1978–86; C Shiremoor, Newc 1989–92; C Hexham, Newc 1992–93; TV All SS, St Anne, St Mich & St Thos Lewes, Chich 1993–97; R Pulborough, Chich 1997–2000; V St Nich Fleetwood, Blackb from 2000; M Legal Aid Commn from 2006
GS 2005–   *Tel:* 01253 874402
              email: benfield@btinternet.com

BENN, Rt Revd Wallace Parke, BA, Dip Th
Bishop's Lodge 16A Prideaux Rd Eastbourne BN21 2NB [AREA BISHOP OF LEWES; CHICHESTER] *b* 1947 *educ* St Andr Coll Dub; Univ Coll Dub; Univ of Lon; Trin Coll Bris; *CV* C St Mark New Ferry, Wirral 1972–76; C St Mary Cheadle 1976–82; V St Jas the Great Audley 1982–87; V St Pet Harold Wood 1987–97; pt Chapl Harold Wood Hosp 1987–96; Bp of Lewes from 1997; M Dioc Syn; M Dioc Staff Tm; Bp's Coun; M DBF; Bp w Oversight for Youth and Children's Work; Pres C of E Evang Coun; Pres Fellowship of Word and Spirit; Chair Bible by the Beach   *Tel:* 01323 648462
                              Fax: 01323 641514
                  email: lewes@clara.net

BENYON, Mr Thomas,
Rectory Farm House 2 Church St Bladon Oxon OX2O 1RS [OXFORD] *CV* Elected to GS 2005
GS 2005–

BERKSHIRE, Archdeacon of. See RUSSELL, Ven Norman Atkinson

BERRY, Professor Anthony John, B Sc, M Phil, Ph D, DIC
24 Leafield Rd Disley Stockport SK12 2JF [CHESTER]
b 1939 *educ* Bath Univ; Imp Coll Lon; Seattle Univ; Man Univ; *CV* Aerodynamicist Br Aircraft Corp 1962; Aerodynamics Engineer The Boeing Co Seattle 1965–69; Rsch Fell 1971–73, Lect 1973–86, Sen Lect 1986–95 in Mgt Devel Man Univ; Prof Sheff Hallam Univ 1995–2002; Prof emeritus 2002; M Dioc Syn; Rdr
GS 1994–   *Tel:* 01663 762393
     email: anthonyberry@btinternet.com

BESSANT, Canon Simon, B Mus, MA
All Saints Vicarage Ringinglow Rd Sheffield S11 7PQ [SHEFFIELD] *b* 1956 *educ* Francis Combe Comp Watford; Sheff Univ; St Jo Coll Nottm; *CV* C St Jo and St Jas Bootle 1981–84; C Em Holloway 1984–85, P-in-c 1985–81; Ecum Adv for Bp of Stepney 1990–91; V Ch of the Redeemer Blackburn 1991–98; RD of Blackburn 1997–98; Dioc Dir for Miss and Evang and Officer for Dioc Bd for Miss and Unity 1998–2007; Dioc Dir for CME 1–4 2002–05; V All Saints Eccleshall, Sheff from 2007; M Lon Dioc Bd of Educ 1989–91; M Blackb Dioc Bd of Min 1995–2002; M Blackb Dioc Liturg Cttee 1998–2007; Sec to Blackb Dioc, Lancs Coun of Mosques Dialogue Grp 1998–2007; initiator and M Churches Together in Lancs Inter-Faith Forum 1999–2007, Chair 1999–2003; initiator and M Lancs Inter-Faith Forum 2000–2007, Chair 2001–03; GS rep on NEOC Bd 2001–05; M MPA Coun 2003–05; M Presence and Engagement Strg Grp 2004–05; M Follow-up Grp, Strg Cttee and Rev Cttee, Rev of Diocs Pastl and Miss Measure 2004–06; Chair Wkg Party creating code of practice on Miss Initiatives under Diocs, Pastl and Miss Measure from 2006; M Bradf Chs for Dialogue and Diversity Adv Grp from 2006; M AC 2006–07; M C of E Appts Cttee 2006–07; Hon Can Blackb Cath 2006–07; Can Emer Blackb Cath from 2006
GS 2001–07, 2008–   *Tel:* 0114 236 0084
        07957 211319 (Mobile)
        email: simon.bessant@
        eccleshall.parishchurch.org.uk

BESWICK, Mr David Terence,
6 Sheriffs Way Eccleshall Stafford ST21 6BQ [LICHFIELD] *b* 1933 *educ* Tarporley C of E Sch; Chwdn, St Helen Tarporley 1972–77; chwdn, H Trin Eccleshall 1984–2003, lay chair PCC 2003–04; lay chair Eccleshall Dny Syn from 2003; M Lich Dioc Syn from 2002, Pastl Cttee from 2004
GS 2005–   *Tel:* 01785 850622
        Fax: 01785 851249

BETTS, Revd Canon Steven James, B Sc, Cert Th
Emmaus House 65 The Close Norwich NR1 4DH [NORWICH] *b* 1964 *educ* Nottm Bluecoat Gr Sch;

York Univ; Cuddesdon Th Coll; *CV* C Bearsted w Thurnham 1990–94; Chapl to Bp of Norw 1994–97; V Old Catton Norw 1997–2005; RD Norw N 2001–05; M Dioc Commn from 2001; Chair Dioc Ho of Clergy from 2003; M Bp's Coun from 2003; M DBF Exec from 2003; Bp's Officer for Ord and Initial Trg from 2005
GS 2000–   *Tel:* 01603 628103 (Office)
     email: steven.betts@norwich.anglican.org

BEVERLEY, Bishop of. See JARRETT, Rt Revd Martyn William

BIRD, Canon David Ronald, BA, L Th
St Giles Vicarage Spring Gardens Northampton NN1 1LX [PETERBOROUGH] *b* 1955 *educ* K Edw VI Gr Sch Nuneaton; York Univ; Westhill Coll Birm; St Jo Coll Nottm; *CV* Youth Worker All So Clubhouse Lon 1977–80; Com Centre Warden Nottm City Coun 1980–83; C Kinson TM 1986–90; R Thrapston 1990–97; RD Higham 1994–97; V St Giles Northn from 1997; M Bp's Coun from 1994; Chair CPAS 1996–2001; Hon Can Peterb Cathl from 2001; Chair Ho of Clergy, Peterb Dioc from 2003
GS 1995–   *Tel:* 01604 634060 (Home)
        01604 628623 (Office)
        Fax: 01604 628623
        email: drbird@talktalk.net

BIRKENHEAD, Suffragan Bishop of. See SINCLAIR, Rt Revd (Gordon) Keith

BIRMINGHAM, Archdeacon of. See OSBORNE, Ven Hayward John

BIRMINGHAM, Bishop of. See URQUHART, Rt Revd David Andrew

BIRMINGHAM, Dean of. See WILKES, Very Revd Robert Anthony

BISSON, Mrs Jane Victoria, FSI, ACIS, MSc
Glenhaven La Rocque Grouville Jersey JE3 9BB [WINCHESTER [CHANNEL ISLANDS]] *b* 1949 *educ* Blancheland Coll; *CV* Legal Trustees (Jersey) Ltd 1988–91; Integro Trust Co 1991–94; Fin Services Commn 1994; Royal Bank of Scotland Internat 1994–2000; Mourant Internat Fin Admin, Legal and Risk Dept from 2005; Regional Mgr KYCOS Ltd, Jersey and Guernsey; M AC Audit Cttee; M Dioc Syn
GS 1995–   *Tel:* 01534 853162
        07797 750896 (Mobile)
     email: jane_bisson@hotmail.com

BLACKBURN, Ven Richard Finn, BA, MA
34 Wilson Rd Botanical Gardens Sheffield S11 8RN [ARCHDEACON OF SHEFFIELD AND ROTHERHAM] *b* 1952 *educ* Aysgarth Sch; Eastbourne Coll; St Jo Coll Dur; Hull Univ; Westcott Ho Th Coll; *CV* NatWest Bank 1976–81; C St Dunstan and All SS Stepney 1983–87; P-in-c St Jo Bapt Isleworth

1987–92; V St Mark Mosborough w Em Water-
thorpe 1992–99; RD Attercliffe 1996–99; Hon Can
Sheff Cathl 1998–99; Can Res Sheff Cathl 1999–
2005; M Pensions Bd from 2004, Vc-Chair from
2006; Adn of Sheff and Rotherham from 1999
GS 2000–05   *Tel:* 0114 266 6009 (Home)
                    01709 309110 (Office)
                    07714 329638 (Mobile)
                    Fax: 01709 309107 (Office)
email: archdeacons.office@sheffield.anglican.org

**BLACKBURN, Archdeacon of. See HAWLEY,
Ven John Andrew**

**BLACKBURN, Bishop of. See READE, Rt Revd
Nicholas Stewart**

**BLACKBURN, Dean of. See ARMSTRONG,
Very Revd Christopher John**

BLACKMORE, Canon Dr David Richard, MA, D
Phil, MRSC
Coniston Newton Lane Chester CH2 2HJ [CHESTER]
b 1938 *educ* Whitgift Sch S Croydon; CCC Ox; *CV*
Rsch Assoc UMIST 1962–64; Sen Prin Rsch Scien-
tist Shell Rsch, Thornton 1984–97; Rdr; Lay Chair
Dioc Syn; Lay Can Chester Cathl from 2003
GS 1980–   *Tel:* 01244 323494
          email: blackmore@virtual-chester.com

BLISS, Mrs Jackie (Jacqueline) Charmaine, BA,
ACA
Church House Great Smith St London SW1P 3AZ
[DIRECTOR OF FINANCIAL POLICY, NATIONAL
CHURCH INSTITUTIONS] *b* 1963 *educ* Westcliff High
Sch (Gr) for Girls; Univ of Wales, Cardiff;
CV Fin Dir/Company Sec, Maplin Electronics plc
1988–99; Dir of Fin and Admin, Coram Family
(Thomas Coram Foundn) 1999–2003; Non-exec
Dir, Pensions Trust 2001–06; Non-exec Dir, Dept
of Agriculture and Rural Devel (N Ireland) 2004–
06; Non-exec Dir, Southend Univ Hosp NHS
Foundn Trust 2005–06; Hon Treas, Foundling
Museum from 2005; Dir of Fin Policy for NCIs
from 2006   *Tel:* 020 7898 1000
          email: jackie.bliss@c-of-e.org.uk

BOARDMAN, Revd Jonathan Thomas, MA
Via del Babuino 153 00187 Rome Italy [EUROPE] *b*
1963 *educ* Bolton Sch; Magd Coll Ox; Magd Coll
Cam; Westcott Ho; *CV* C St Mary W Derby, Liv
1990–93; Prec St Alb Abbey 1993–96; TR Catford
and Downham, S'wark 1996–99; RD E Lewisham
1998–99; Chapl All SS Rome from 1999; Sen tutor,
Angl Cen Rome from 2001; M S'wark Dioc Syn
and Bp's Coun 1996–99; M Eur Dioc Syn and Bp's
Coun 2004–07; Area Dean Italy and Malta from
2007; Can Dioc Cath Chapter from 2007
GS 2005–   *Tel:* +39 06 3600 1881
          +39 349 655 8844 (Mobile)
          Fax: +39 06 3600 1881
          email: office@allsaintsrome.org

BOARDMAN, Preb Philippa Jane, MA
Vicarage St Stephen's Rd London E3 5JL [LONDON] *b*
1963 *educ* Haberdashers' Aske's Sch for Girls; Jes
Coll Cam; Ridley Hall Th Coll; *CV* C St Mary and
St Steph Walthamstow 1990–93; Asst Pr St Mary
of Eton Hackney Wick 1993–96; P-in-c St Paul w
St Mark Old Ford 1996–2003, V from 2003; Preb St
Paul's Cathl from 2002
GS 1994–   *Tel and Fax:* 020 8980 9020

BODDINGTON, Ms Caroline Elizabeth, MA
(Oxon), MCIPD
The Wash House Lambeth Palace London SE1 7JU
[ARCHBISHOPS' SECRETARY FOR APPOINTMENTS] *b*
1964 *educ* Malvern Girls' Coll; Keble Coll Ox; *CV*
BG Grp 1986–2003: HR Strategy and Devel Mgr
1997–99, Hd of Learning and Devel 2000, Hd of
HR Operations 2001–03; Abps' Sec for Appts
from 2004   *Tel:* 020 7898 1876
          020 7898 1877
          Fax: 020 7898 1899
          email: caroline.boddington@c-of-e.org.uk

**BODMIN, Archdeacon of. See COHEN,
Ven Clive Ronald Franklin**

BODY, Mrs Debra Jane, CTABRSM
*Linden Lea Bushley 2 Church St Bladon Oxon OX20
1RS* [EXETER] *b* 1966 *educ* Hayesfield Sch, Bath;
Newton Park; Bath Coll of HE; *CV* Under-
writer/claims assessor, Royal Insurance 1988–92;
music tchr from 1995; M PCC; M dny syn, dioc
syn
GS 2005–   *Tel:* 01684 275 963
          email: timanddebbody@phonecoop.coop

**BOLTON, Archdeacon of. See BAILEY, Ven
David Charles**

**BOLTON, Suffragan Bishop of. See GILLETT,
Rt Revd David Keith**

BONNER, Mr Michael, FCA
1 Fell View Branthwaite Workington CA14 4SY
[CARLISLE] *b* 1945 *educ* Carlisle Gr Sch; *CV* Rtd
2005; Commissioned Lay Min Carl Dio from
2003; Non-Exec Dir N Cumbria Acute Hosps
NHS Trust from 2007
GS 2000–   *Tel:* 01900 605536
          email: bonner@ireneandmichael.wanadoo.co.uk

BONNEY, Canon Mark Philip John, MA, PGCE
Loders 23 The Close Salisbury SP1 2EH [SALISBURY]
b 1957 *educ* Northgate Gr Sch Ipswich; St Cath
Coll Cam; St Steph Ho Th Coll; *CV* C St Pet
Stockton-on-Tees 1985–88; Chapl St Alb Abbey
1988–90; Prec St Alb Abbey 1990–92; V Eaton
Bray w Edlesborough 1992–96; R Gt Berkham-
sted 1996–2004; M Bp's Coun 1997–2003; GS Rep
RSCM Coun 1998–2001 and from 2006; Chaplain
to GS 2001–07; M Westcott Ho Coun 2002–05; M

Liturg Commn 2002–07; RD Berkhamsted 2002–04; Can Treas Salis Cathl from 2004
GS 1995–   *Tel:* 01722 555186 (Office)
01722 322172 (Home)
07811 466517 (Mobile)
email: treasurer@salcath.co.uk

BOOTH, Mr John David Sebastian, MA
Simon's Lee Amberley West Sussex BN18 9NR [CHICHESTER] *b* 1958 *educ* Huish's Gr Sch Taunton; Mert Coll Ox; *CV* Vc Pres Merrill Lynch 1983–86; Sen Vc Pres Prudential Bache 1988–93; Man Dir Bankers Trust Internat 1993–96; Chair Luther Pendragon Ltd from 1992; Maintel Holdings PLC from 1996; Integrated Asset Mgt PLC from 1998; Exec Chair Link Asset and Securities Co; M AC Fin Cttee; M CAC; M DBF; M Dioc Syn; Chair Pensions Measure Review Cttee from 2001; Guardian Nat Shrine of Our Lady of Walsingham; M Chancellor's Forum, Univ of the Arts Lon; M Coun St Steph Ho, Ox; Gov Pusey Ho, Ox
GS 1999–   *Tel:* 01798 831344
020 7663 4305
07767 474343 (Mobile)
Fax: 020 7851 6621
email: j@johnbooth.com

BOOYS, Revd Canon Sue (Susan) Elizabeth, BA, Cert Th, PGCE, MA
Rectory Manor Farm Rd Dorchester-on-Thames Wallingford OX10 7HZ [OXFORD] *b* 1956 *educ* Harrow County Girls' Sch; Bristol Univ; Ox Min Course; Heythrop, Lon Univ; *CV* C Kidlington Tm Ox 1995–99; TV Dorchester Tm Ox from 1999, TR from 2005; M Bp's Coun; M GS Business Cttee; Gov Ripon Coll Cuddesdon from 2006; AD Aston and Cuddesdon from 2007
GS 2002–   *Tel:* 01865 340007
07815 609602 (Mobile)
Fax: 01865 341192
email: rector@dorchester-abbey.org.uk

BOURNEMOUTH, Archdeacon of.
See HARBIDGE, Ven Adrian Guy

BOWER, Mrs (Helen) Janet, MA, CQSW
Stone Croft Lothersdale Keighley BD20 8EE [BRADFORD] *b* 1948 *educ* Bradf Girls' Gr Sch; Leeds Poly; Bradf and Ilkley Community Coll; *CV* Various social svcs social work appts 1966–85; Sen Caseworker Barnardos 1985–98; Parent Partnership Officer 1998–2000; Lay M Tribunal Service from 1994; Family Support Worker Tuberous Sclerosis Assoc 2001–05; Family Fund Trust Adv from 1977; M Disability Benefit Tribunal from 1992; Archdeaconry rep on Bp's Coun; M Bradf, Ripon & Leeds and Wakef Dioc Disability Stakeholders Grp; M Bradf Dioc Disability Task Grp
GS 2000-   *Tel:* 01535 633747
email: bower@zetnet.co.uk

BOYD-LEE, Mr Paul Winston Michael, BA, Dip Th
Manor Barn Horsington Templecombe BA8 0ET

[SALISBURY] *b* 1941 *educ* Brighton Coll; Open Univ; Ex Univ; *CV* Theatre Mgr Rank Organization 1963–66; Credit Controller Internat Factors Ltd 1966–72; Dir Bible Truth Publishers from 1972; a Dir of Ch Army from 1999; M Ch Army Investment and Remuneration Cttees; M AC from 2005; M Audit Cttee from 2006; M Ethical Investment Adv Gp
GS 1991–   *Tel:* 01963 371137
07710 604777 (Mobile)
email: paulbl@classicfm.net

BOYLING, Very Revd Mark Christopher, MA
The Deanery Carlisle CA3 8TZ [DEAN OF CARLISLE] *b* 1952 *educ* K Jas Gr Sch Almondbury, W Yorks; Keble Coll Ox; Cuddesdon Th Coll; *CV* C St Mark Northwood, Kirkby 1977–79, TV 1979–85; Chapl to Bp of Liv 1985–89; V St Pet Formby, Liv 1989–94; Can Res and Prec Liv Cathl 1994–2004; Dean of Carlisle from 2004   *Tel:* 01228 523335
Fax: 01228 547049
email: dean@carlislecathedral.org.uk

BRACKLEY, Rt Revd Ian James, MA
Dayspring 13 Pilgrims Way Guildford GU4 8AD [SUFFRAGAN BISHOP OF DORKING; GUILDFORD] *b* 1947 *educ* Westcliff High Sch; Keble Coll Ox; Cuddesdon Th Coll; *CV* C St Mary Magd w St Fran Lockleaze Bris 1971–74; Asst Chapl Bryanston Sch 1974–77; Chapl 1977–80; V St Mary E Preston Chich 1980–88; RD Arundel and Bognor 1982–87; TR St Wilf Haywards Heath 1988–96; RD Cuckfield 1989–95; Bp of Dorking from 1996; M Ho of Bps CME Cttee from 2001; M Bd of Ch Army 2002; M CCU 2006; Chair Bd of Govs of STETS 1999
GS 1990–95, 2001, 2005   *Tel:* 01483 570829
Fax: 01483 567268
email: bishop.ian@cofeguildford.org.uk

**BRADFORD, Archdeacon of. See LEE,
Ven David John**

**BRADFORD, Bishop of. See JAMES, Rt Revd
David Charles**

**BRADFORD, Dean of. See ISON, Very Revd
David John**

BRADLEY, Ven Peter David Douglas, B Th
Rectory 1A College Rd Up Holland Skelmersdale WN8 0PY [ARCHDEACON OF WARRINGTON; LIVERPOOL] *b* 1949 *educ* Brookfield Comp Sch; Nottm Univ; Ian Ramsey Coll; Linc Th Coll; *CV* C Up Holland 1979–83; V H Spirit Dovecot 1983–94; Sec Dioc Bd of Min 1983–88; Sec Grp for Urban Min and Leadership 1984–88; Asst Dir In-Service Trg 1988–89; Dir CME from 1989; TR St Tho Up Holland from 1994; M BM Mission at Home Cttee; M Dioc Bd of Min; Hon Can Liv Cathl from 2000; Adn of Warrington from 2001/2
GS 1990–   *Tel:* 01695 622936
Fax: 01695 625865
email: archdeacon@peterbradley.fsnet.co.uk

BRADLEY, Very Revd Peter Edward, MA, FRSA
Sheffield Cathedral Church St Sheffield S1 1HA
[DEAN OF SHEFFIELD] *b* 1964 *educ* R Belfast
Academical Inst; Trin Hall Cam; Ripon Coll
Cuddesdon; *CV* C St Mich & All A w St Edm
Northampton 1988–90; Chapl Gonville & Caius
Coll Cam 1990–95; TV St Mich Abingdon 1995–
98; TV All SS High Wycombe 1998–2003, TR 2003;
Dean of Sheffield from 2003; Fell Coll of Prchrs,
Washington DC from 2006   *Tel:* 0114 275 3434
                                            0114 263 6063
                                    Fax: 0114 279 7412
        email: dean@sheffield-cathedral.org.uk

**BRADWELL, Area Bishop of. See GREEN,
Rt Revd Laurie (Laurence Alexander)**

BRATTON, Revd Mark Quinn, BA, Dip Law, BA,
MA
*92 De Montfort Way Cannon Park Coventry CV4
7DT* [COVENTRY] *b* 1962 *educ* Millfield Sch, Street;
Univ Coll Lon; Ox Univ; City Univ; K Coll Lon;
Wycliffe Hall Ox; *CV* C St Jo w. St Jas W Ealing
1994–98; Legal Adv, Dept of Health 1989–91; Rsch
Asst, Law Commn 1988–89; Sen Chapl, Warwick
Univ from 1998; AD Cov S from 2002; M CCU
1996–2001; M Cov Dioc Forum for Min; M Cov
Dioc Spirituality Grp; M Coun MPA from 2005
GS 2005–   *Tel:* 024 7669 0216 (Home)
                            024 7652 8158 (Office)
                            07824 540978 (Mobile)
        email: m.q.bratton@warwick.ac.uk

BRETT, Mr Justin Edward, MA, PGCE
1 Chesterfield Rd Newbury RG14 7QB [OXFORD] *b*
1971 *educ* Cheltenham Coll; Ex Coll Ox; *CV*
Teacher; elected to GS 2005
GS 2005–   *Tel:* 07876 746074
        email: justin.brett@yahoo.co.uk

BRIDEN, Rt Worshipful Timothy John, MA, LLB
*Lamb Chambers Lamb Building Temple London EC4Y
7AS* [VICAR-GENERAL OF CANTERBURY] *b* 1951 *educ*
Ipswich Sch; Downing Coll Cam; *CV* Chancellor
of Dioc of B&W from 1993; Chancellor of Dioc of
Truro from 1998; Vicar-General of Canterbury
from 2005; M Legal Adv Commn
GS 2005–   *Tel:* 020 7797 8300
                            Fax: 020 7797 8308
        email: info@lambchambers.co.uk

BRIDGEWATER, Mr Allan, LVO, CBE, ACII, FCIPD,
CCMI, FRSA
Linquenda 447 Unthank Rd Norwich NR4 7QN [EX-
OFFICIO, CHAIRMAN, CHURCH OF ENGLAND PEN-
SIONS BOARD] *b* 1936 *CV* Dir Norw Union Grp
1985–97, Chief Exec 1989–97; Chair Swiss GB
1998–2007; Vc-Chair Trustees HRH Duke of Edin
Commonwealth Study Conf 1993–2007; Dir
Riggs Bank Europe 1991–2005; Chair C of E Pen-
sions Bd from 1998
GS 1998–
                                    Fax: 01603 455120

BRIERLEY, Ven David James, BA Hons
*Sudbury Lodge Stanningfield Rd Great Whelnetham
Bury St Edmunds IP30 0TL* [ARCHDEACON OF SUD-
BURY; ST EDMUNDSBURY AND IPSWICH] *b* 1953 *educ*
Fearns Co Secdry; Bacup and Rawtenstall Gr Sch;
Bristol Univ; Oak Hill Th Coll; *CV* C St Mary Bal-
derstone, Rochdale, Manch 1977–80; TV Eccles
1980–85; Manch Dioc Ecum Officer 1981–88; V
Harwood 1985–95; Chair Decade of Evang,
Manch 1991–99; V and RD Walmsley 1995–2002;
Dioc Missr, Bradf 2002–06; Res Can Bradf 2002–
04; Adn of Sudbury from 2006
                        Tel and Fax: 01284 386942
                        email: archdeacon.david@
                        stedmundsbury.anglican.org

BRINDLEY, Very Revd David Charles, BD, M Th,
M Phil, AKC
The Deanery 13 Pembroke Rd Portsmouth PO1 2NS
[DEAN OF PORTSMOUTH] *b* 1953 *educ* Wednesfield
Gr Sch; K Coll Lon; *CV* C Epping, Chelms 1976–
79; Lect, Coll of St Paul and St Mary, Cheltenham
1979–82; V Quorn and Dir of Clergy Trg, Leic
1982–86; Prin W of Eng Minl Trg Course 1987–94;
TR Warwick 1994–2002; Dean of Portsm from
2002; Chair Portsm DAC from 2003; Sec and Treas
Assoc of Engl Cathls from 2005
GS 1985–87, 2004–   *Tel:* 023 9282 4400 (Home)
                            023 9234 7605 (Office)
                            Fax: 023 9229 5480
                        email: david.brindley@
                        portsmouthcathedral.org.uk

**BRISTOL, Archdeacon of. See McCLURE,
Ven Tim (Timothy Elston)**

**BRISTOL, Bishop of. See HILL, Rt Revd
Michael Arthur**

**BRISTOL, Dean of. See GRIMLEY, Very Revd
Robert William**

BRITTON, Mr Andrew James Christie, BA, MSc
*2 Shabden Park High Rd, Chipstead Coulsden, Surrey
CR5 3SF* [ARCHBISHOPS' COUNCIL] *b* 1940 *educ* R
Gr Sch, Newc-upon-Tyne; Oriel Coll Ox; Lon Sch
of Economics; *CV* Economist HM Treasury 1968–
82; Dir Nat Institute of Economic and Social
Research 1982–95; Exec Sec Ch's Enquiry into
Unemployment and the Future of Work 1995–97;
Chair S'wark Dioc Bd of Fin 2000–2007; Chair
Abps' Coun Fin Cttee from 2007
GS 2007–   *Tel:* 01737 553 678

**BRIXWORTH, Suffragan Bishop of.
See WHITE, Rt Revd Frank (Francis)**

BROADBENT, Rt Revd Pete (Peter Alan), MA
173 Willesden Lane Brondesbury London NW6 7YN
[AREA BISHOP OF WILLESDEN; LONDON] *b* 1952 *educ*
Merchant Taylors Sch Northwood; Jes Coll Cam;
St Jo Coll Nottm; *CV* C St Nic Dur City 1977–80; C
Em Holloway 1980–83; Chapl to N Lon Poly and

Hon C St Mary Islington 1983–89; Bp's Chapl for Miss in Stepney 1980–89; Councillor and Chair of Planning Lon Boro of Islington 1982–89; V Trin St Mich Harrow 1989–95; AD Harrow 1994; Adn of Northolt 1995–2001; Bp of Willesden from 2001; M Dioc Commn 1989–92; M Panel of Chairmen GS 1990–92; M C of E Evang Coun 1984-95, from 2006; Chair Vacancy-in-See Cttee Regulation Wkg Pty 1991–93; M GS Stg Orders Cttee 1991–95; M Appts Sub-Cttee 1992–95; M CBF 1991–98; M GS Stg Cttee 1992–98; Chair GS Business Sub-Cttee 1996–98; Chair Elections Review Grp 1996–2000; Chair Lon Dioc Bd for Schs 1996–2006; Tm Leader Spring Harvest Leadership Tm; Chair Business Cttee 1999–2000; M AC 1999–2000; M City Parochial Foundn 1999–2003; M Urban Bps Panel from 2001; Trustee CUF from 2002; Chair Coun St Jo Coll Nottm from 2002; Pres W Lon YMCA from 2004; Chair Standards Cttee, Lon Boro Harrow from 2006

GS 1985–2001; 2004–   *Tel:* 020 8451 0189
                            07957 144674 (Mobile)
                            Fax: 020 8451 4606
email: bishop.willesden@btinternet.com

BROADHURST, Rt Revd John Charles, S Th, AKC, DD
26 Canonbury Park South London N1 2FN [SUFFRAGAN BISHOP OF FULHAM; LONDON] *b* 1942 *educ* Owen's Sch Lon; K Coll Lon; St Boniface Th Coll Warminster; *CV* C St Mich-at-Bowes 1966–70; P-in-c St Aug Wembley Pk 1970–75; V 1975–85; M Stg Cttee Ho of Clergy 1981–88; AD Brent 1982–85; AD Haringey E 1986–92; M Panel of Chairmen 1981–84; M Coun Corp of Ch Ho 1980–90; TR Wood Green 1985–96; Bp of Fulham from 1996; M GS Stg Cttee 1988–96; Pro-Prolocutor Conv of Cant 1990–96; Chair Dioc Ho of Clergy 1986–96; M Legal Aid Commn 1991–96; M Fees Adv Commn 1991–96; Delegate WCC Canberra 1991; M ACC from 1991; M CTE; Delegate CEC Prague 1992; Nat Chair Forward in Faith
GS 1973–96   *Tel:* 020 7354 2334
                            Fax: 020 7354 2335
email: bpfulham@aol.com

BROMLEY AND BEXLEY, Archdeacon of. See WRIGHT, Ven Paul

BROOKFIELD, Mr Joseph Adam, BA, MSc
30 Alexandra St Preston PR1 4BL [BLACKBURN] *b* 1978 *educ* Bootham Sch York; Lanc Univ; Ox Media and Bus Sch; Bath Univ; *CV* Intern, United Nations Info Cen 2002; freelance rsch, Immigration Adv Service 2003–04; vol rsch asst, Choices Team, Refugee Action 2003–04; M Blackb Dioc Youth Cttee; admin asst Manch Salford Housing Market Renewal Pathfinder from 2004
GS 2004–2005; 2005–   *Tel:* 01772 889442
email: j.brookfield@yahoo.co.uk

BROWN, Mr Andrew Charles, B Sc, FRICS
Church House Great Smith St London SW1P 3AZ [SECRETARY, CHURCH COMMISSIONERS] *b* 1957 *educ* Ashmole Comp Sch; S Bank Poly; *CV* Healey & Baker 1981–84; St Quintin 1984–94; Dep Sec and Chief Surveyor Ch Commrs 1994–2003, Sec from 2003; M Fin and Invest Cttee, Lionheart from 2007; Dir William Leech (Foundn) and William Leech (Invest) from 2007   *Tel:* 020 7898 1785
                            Fax: 020 7898 1131
email: andrew.brown@c-of-e.org.uk

BROWN, Revd Dr Malcolm Arthur, MA, PhD, FHEA
Church House Great Smith St London SW1P 3AZ [DIRECTOR, MISSION AND PUBLIC AFFAIRS DIVISION, ARCHBISHOPS' COUNCIL] *b* 1954 *educ* Eltham Coll; Oriel Coll Ox; Man Univ; Westcott Ho Cam; *CV* C Riverhead w. Dunton Green, Roch 1979–83; TV and Ind Missioner, Southn City Centre, Winch 1983–91; Exec Sec William Temple Foundn 1991–2000; Hon C St Paul Heaton Moor, Man 1993–2000; Prin EAMTC 2000–05; Prin ERMC 2005–07; Dir MPA from 2007; M BSR Ind and Economic Affairs Cttee 1987–91; M BSR Soc, Economic and Ind Affairs Cttee 1997–2002; Th Consult Rev of Diocs, Pastl and Related Measures 2001–04; M Min Div Th Educ and Trg Cttee; M Min Div Fin Panel 2006–07
                            Tel: 020 7898 1468
email: malcolm.brown@c-of-e.org.uk

BROWNSELL, Prebendary John Kenneth, MA
All Saints' Vicarage Powis Gardens London W11 1JG [LONDON] *b* 1948 *educ* Ashby de la Zouche Gr Sch; Hertf Coll Ox; Cuddesdon Th Coll; *CV* C All SS w St Columba Notting Hill 1973–74; C Notting Hill 1974–76; TV 1976–82; V from 1982; AD Kensington 1984–92; Preb St Paul's Cathl from 1992; Dir of Ords Kensington Area Lon dio; Commissary for Bp of Windward Islands; M Initiation Services Revision Cttee; M Nat Coun Forward in Faith
GS 1995–   *Tel:* 020 7727 5919
email: jkb@allsaintsnottinghill.co.uk

BRUINVELS, Canon Peter Nigel Edward, LLB, FRSA, FCIM, MCIJ, MCIPR
14 High Meadow Close St Paul's Rd West Dorking RH4 2LG [GUILDFORD] *b* 1950 *educ* St Jo Sch Leatherhead; Lon Univ; Inns of Court Sch of Law; *CV* MP Leic E 1983–87; Party Candidate The Wrekin 1997; Prin Peter Bruinvels Associates, Media Mgt and Public Affairs Consults; M Dioc Syn and Dorking Dny Syn from 1974; Freeman of City of Lon 1980; M Dios Commn 1991–96; M Legislative Cttee 1991–96 and from 2000; News Broadcaster, Political Commentator and Freelance Journalist; Ch Commr from 1992, Pastl Cttee from 1993, Mgt Adv Cttee from 1999; Ofsted and Section 48 SIAS RE Sch Insp from 1994; M DSS Child Support and Soc Security Appeals Tribunal 1994–99; Man Ed Bruinvels News & Media, Press and Broadcasting Agents; M Dioc Bd of Educ from 1994; M GS Bd of Educ 1996–2006; Co-opted M Surrey LEA 1997–2007; Gov Univ of York St Jo 1999–2007; Dir Ch Army and Chair Remuneration Cttee 1999–

2004; Independent Lay Chair NHS Complaints Tribunal 1999–2004; M Clergy Discipline Review Grp from 1999; Chair Surrey Schs Organization Cttee 2000–07; Court Member Univ of Sussex 2000–08; M Dearing Implementation Grp from 2001; County Field Officer (Surrey) Royal Br Legion from 2002; Dir E Elmbridge and Mid Surrey Primary Care Trust 2002–07; Lay Can Guildf Cathl from 2002; Vc-Pres and Chair Ho of Laity, Dioc Syn from 2003; Guild CNC from 2003; M SE War Pensions Cttee from 2003; Chair Surrey Joint Services Charities Cttee from 2004; Chair Guildf Dioc Bd of Educ 2005–08; Hon Sec Surrey County Appeals Cttee form 2002; M Guildf Coll of Cans from 2002; M Cathls Fabric Commn for Eng from 2006; M Guildf Cathl Coun from 2006; Gov Whitelands Coll (Roehampton Univ) from 2007
GS 1985–   *Tel:* 01306 887082 (Home)
                                  01372 386500 (Office)
                                07721 411688 (Mobile)
                                     Fax: 0870 133 1756
                                           01372 375843
email: canonpeterbruinvels@talk21.com / pba@supanet.com (Office)

BRYANT, Rt Revd Mark Watts, BA
Bishop's House 25 Ivy Lane Gateshead NE9 6QD [SUFFRAGAN BISHOP OF JARROW; DURHAM] *b* 1949 *educ* St Jo Sch Leatherhead; St Jo Coll Dur; Cuddesdon Th Coll; *CV* C Addlestone 1975–79; C St Jo Studley, Trowbridge 1979–83, V 1983–88; Chapl Trowbridge CFE 1979–83; DDO and Dir Vocations and Tr, Cov 1988–96; Hon Can Cov Cathl 1993–2001; TR Cov Caludon 1996–2001; AD Cov E 1999–2001; Adn of Coventry 2001–07; Can Res Cov Cathl 2006–07; Bp of Jarrow from 2007
GS 1998–   *Tel:* 0191 491 0917
                                     Fax: 0191 491 5116
email: bishop.of.jarrow@durham.anglican.org

BUCKINGHAM, Archdeacon of.
See GORHAM, Ven Karen Marisa

BUCKINGHAM, Area Bishop of. See WILSON, Rt Revd Alan Thomas Lawrence

BUCKLER, Very Revd Philip John Warr, MA
The Deanery 12 Eastgate Lincoln LN2 1QG [DEAN OF LINCOLN] *b* 1949 *educ* Highgate Sch; St Pet Coll Ox; Cuddesdon Coll; *CV* C St Pet Bushey Heath 1972–75; Chapl Trin Coll Cam 1975–81; Sacr and Min Can St Paul's Cathl 1981–86; V Hampstead 1987–99; AD N Camden 1993–98; Can Res St Paul's Cathl 1999–2007, Treas 2000–07; Dean of Lincoln from 2007   *Tel:* 01522 561611
                                     Fax: 01522 561603
email: dean@lincolncathedral.com

BULL, Dr John W, B Sc, Ph D, D Sc, Eur Ing, C Eng, FIHT, FIStructE, FIWSC, FICE
Gable Ends 11 Glebe Mews Bedlington NE22 6LJ [NEWCASTLE] *b* 1944 *educ* Farnborough Gr Sch; Ches Coll of Educ; Univ Coll Cardiff; *CV* Tchr

ILEA 1966–68; Engineer/Chartered Engineer Dur Co Coun 1974–79; Lect in Structural Engineering Newc Univ 1979–2002, sen lect from 2002; Author and Ed of Engineering textbooks; M Dioc Syn from 1988; M Bp's Coun from 1988; Vc Pres Dioc Syn 1994–2006; Chair Dioc Bd of Educ 1991–97; Lay Chair Bedlington Dny Syn 1990–97; Dioc Bd of Educ from 2004
GS 1995–   *Tel:* 0191 222 7924 (Office)
                                         0191 222 6418
                                07710 200416 (Mobile)
                                     Fax: 0191 222 5322
                                           01670 821019
                         email: John.Bull@newcastle.ac.uk

BULLIMORE, His Honour Judge John Wallace MacGregor, LLB
14 Grange Drive Emley Huddersfield HD8 9SF [WAKEFIELD] *b* 1945 *educ* Qu Eliz Gr Sch Wakefield; Bris Univ; *CV* Circuit Judge from 1991; Chan Dioc of Derby from 1980; Chan Dioc of Blackb from 1990; Rdr from 1968; M Bp's Coun
GS 1970–   *Tel:* 01924 849161
                                     Fax: 01924 849219
                        email: johnwbullimore@tiscali.co.uk

BUNCH, Miss Cynthia Fairfax, MSc, Cert HE, Adv Cert Ed, Dip CLD, CRK, LRAM
22 Low Church Rd Middle Rasen Market Rasen LN8 3TY [LINCOLN] *b* 1937 *educ* Brentwood C H Sch; St Osyth's Coll Clacton; Univ E Anglia; Nottm Univ; Hull Univ; St Mich Ho, Ox; *CV* Primary and secdry teaching posts 1959–75; Primary and Middle Schs Sec (Eng & Wales), Scripture Union 1975–80; Headtchr Necton CE VA First Sch, Norfolk 1981–91; Parish Educ Officer and Children's Work Adv, Linc Dioc 1991–98; rtd
GS 2005–   *Tel:* 01673 844661
                        email: cynbunch@globalnet.co.uk

BURNHAM, Rt Revd Andrew, MA, ARCO (CHM)
Bishop's House Dry Sandford Abingdon OX13 6JP [BISHOP OF EBBSFLEET, PROVINCIAL EPISCOPAL VISITOR, CANTERBURY; HONORARY ASSISTANT BISHOP, BATH AND WELLS, EXETER, LICHFIELD, OXFORD, WORCESTER] *b* 1948 *educ* S'well Minster Gr Sch; New Coll Ox; St Steph Ho Th Coll; *CV* Schoolmaster 1972–78; freelance conductor and music tchr 1978–85; NSM Clifton TM Nottm 1983–85; C Beeston 1985–87; V St Jo Ev Carrington 1987–94; Vc Princ St Steph Ho 1995–2000; Bp of Ebbsfleet from 2000; M Stg Cttee Eucharistic Prayers 1995; M Stg Cttee Calendar and Lectionary 1996; M Liturg Commn 1996–2000, Consultant from 2001; GS Rep NTMTC Coun 1996–2000; M Stg Cttee Amending Canon 22 1998; M Stg Cttee Pastl Rites 1998; M Anglican-Methodist Formal Conversations from 1998; Hon Asst Bp of B & W, Ex, Lich, Ox, Worc
GS 1990–2000   *Tel:* 01865 390746
                                     Fax: 01865 390611
                        email: bishop.andrew@ebbsfleet.org.uk

BURNLEY, Suffragan Bishop of.
See GODDARD, Rt Revd John William

BURRAGE, Mr Paul, BSc, FCA
Church House Great Smith St London SW1P 3AZ
[DIRECTOR OF FINANCE AND RESOURCES (ACTING),
NATIONAL CHURCH INSTITUTIONS] *b* 1952 *educ*
Reading Sch; Sir William Borlase's Sch; Newcastle Univ; *CV* Fin Man to Fin Dir in various internat Freight Forwarding Companies 1979–91; Fin Dir Heating Oil and Petroleum Distributor 1991–92; Consult, Dir of Fin and Resources British Red Cross 1993–2004; Head of Fin Refugee Coun 2005–05; Chief Accountant NCIs 2005–07; (Acting) Dir of Fin Accounting NCIs from 2008
Tel: 020 7898 1677
Fax: 020 7898 1770
email: paul.burrage@c-of-e.org.uk

BURRIDGE, Revd Prof Richard Alan, MA, Ph D,
PGCE, Dip Th, FKC
King's College London Strand London WC2R 2LS
[UNIVERSITIES, LONDON] *b* 1955 *educ* Bris Cathl Sch; Univ Coll Ox; Nottm Univ; St Jo Coll Nottm; *CV* Classics Master and Ho Tutor Sevenoaks Sch 1978–82; C SS Pet and Paul Bromley 1985–87; Chapl and pt Lect in Depts of Th and Classics & Ancient History Univ of Ex 1987–94; Dean of K Coll Lon from 1994; M Academic Bd NTMTC from 1994; Chair Chr Evidence Soc from 1994; Chair Eric Symes Abbott Memorial Fund from 1994; M Studiorum Novi Testamenti Societas from 1995; M SST from 1995; M SBL from 1995; ABM External Moderator to SW Min Tr Course 1995–99; Chair Min Div Educ Validatory Panel 1998–2004; M Min Div TETC 1998–2004; M CECC; Commr to Bp of High Veld from 1996; GS Rep PIM Consultation to Province of W Africa 1997; Adv and Writer for Nat Millennium Experience Co and Greenwich Dome 1998–99; M Vote 1 Min Div Wkg Party 1999–2000; M Review Grp on Structure and Funding of Ordination Tr 2000–03; FKC 2002; Chair Bp of S'wark's Theol Grp from 2004; rep Abp of Cant and Angl Communion at Second World Congress for Pastl Care of Catholic Foreign Students, Rome, Dec 2005; Prof of Bibl Interpretation at K Coll Lon from 2008
GS 1994–
Tel: 020 7848 2333
Fax: 020 7848 2344
email: richard.burridge@kcl.ac.uk

BURROWS, Mr Gerald David, B Sc, M Sc, T Cert
3 Hall Rd Fulwood Preston PR2 9QD [BLACKBURN]
b 1942 *educ* Wellington Gr Sch; Univ Coll of N Wales, Bangor; *CV* Scientific Officer Rutherford High Energy Lab 1967–69; Lect Grimsby Coll of Tech 1969–71; Sen Lect Blackb Coll from 1971
GS 1990–
Tel: 01772 719159
email: gerald.burrows@talk21.com

BURROWS, Ven Peter, B Th
Archdeacon's Lodge 3 West Park Grove Roundhay Leeds LS8 2HQ [ARCHDEACON OF LEEDS; RIPON

AND LEEDS] *b* 1955 *educ* Spondon Ho Sec Sch; Derby Coll of FE; Sarum and Wells Th Coll; *CV* C Baildon 1983–87; R Broughton Astley 1993–93; P-in-c Stoney Stanton w Croft 1993–95; TR Broughton Astley and Croft w Stoney Stanton 1995–2000; RD Guthlaxton I 1994–2000; DDO and Par Development Officer 1996–2000; M Dioc Syn; M Vacancy-in-See Cttee; M DAC; Coord Dioc Tm Forum; M Bp's Coun; Hon Can Leic Cathl; Dep Dir Min from 2002; Dir Min 2003–05; Adn Leeds from 2005
GS 2000–05
Tel: 0113 269 0594
email: peterb@riponleeds-diocese.org.uk

BURY, Very Revd Nicholas Ayles Stillingfleet,
MA
The Deanery 1 Miller's Green Gloucester GL1 2BN
[DEAN OF GLOUCESTER] *b* 1943 *educ* K Sch Cant; Qu Coll Cam; Cuddesdon Th Coll; *CV* C Liv Par Ch 1968–71; Chapl Ch Ch Ox 1971–75; V St Mary Shephall Stevenage 1975–84; V St Pet-in-Thanet 1984–97; RD Thanet 1993–97; Dean of Gloucester from 1997
GS 1990–96, 2000–05
Tel: 01452 524167
01452 508217
Fax: 01452 300469
email: thedean@gloucestercathedral.org.uk

BUSH, Ven Roger Charles, BA
Westwood House Tremorvah Crescent Truro TR1 1NL
[ARCHDEACON OF CORNWALL; TRURO] *b* 1956 *educ* Fakenham Gr Sch; K Coll Lon; Coll of the Resurr, Mirfield; *CV* C Newbold, Derby 1986–90; TV Parish of the Resurr, Leic 1990–94; TR Redruth w. Lanner & Treleigh, Truro 1994–2004; Can Chan, Truro Cathl 2004–06; Adn of Cornwall from 2006
GS 2004–
Tel: 01872 225630
01872 274351
email: rogerbush56@hotmail.com

BUTCHER, Dr Jackie (Jacqueline Anne), MA,
M Sc, Ph D
10 Vernon Rd Totley Rise Sheffield S17 3QE [SHEFFIELD] *b* 1965 *educ* Wootton Upper Sch; Newnham Coll Cam; Sussex Univ; Leic Univ; *CV* Rsch Associate 1992–95; full-time mother 1995–2000; pt Kindergarten Asst from 2000; M Dioc Faith and Justice Cttee; Bp's Adv in World Development Issues
GS 2000–
Tel: 0114 262 1293
email: ja_butcher@yahoo.co.uk

BUTLER, Rt Revd Paul Roger, BA (Hons) Nottm;
BA (Hons), Cert Theol Ox
Ham House The Crescent Romsey SO51 7NG [SUFFRAGAN BISHOP OF SOUTHAMPTON; WINCHESTER] *b* 1955 *educ* Kingston Gr Sch; Nottm Univ; Wycliffe Hall Ox; *CV* Travelling Sec UCCF 1978–80; C All SS w. H Trin Wandsworth 1983–87; Inner Lon Evangelist SU 1987–92; Dep Hd of Missions SU 1992–94; NSM St Paul E Ham 1987–94; P-in-c St Mary w. St Steph Walthamstow and St Luke Walthamstow1994–97; P-in-c St Gabr Walthamstow 1997; TR Parish of Walthamstow 1997–2004;

Area Dean Waltham Forest 2000–04; Can St Paul's Cathl Byumba, Rwanda from 2001; Bp of Southampton from 2004; M Chelms Dioc Syn 1997–2000, 2003–04; M Mid Africa Ministry Coun 1988–99, 2000–01; Trustee World Mission Assoc 2002 -05; Trustee Friends of Byumba from 2003; Trustee Five Talents UK from 2005; Trustee Forest YMCA 1994–2004; Pres Southn YMCA from 2004; Trustee Damaris from 2007; Chair CMS from 2008   *Tel:* 01794 516005
email: paul.butler@bpsotonoffice.clara.co.uk

BUTLER, Canon Simon, BSc, DTS, MA
Rectory 1 Addington Rd Sanderstead South Croydon CR2 8RE [SOUTHWARK] *b* 1964 *educ* Bournemouth Sch; UEA; Britannia R Naval Coll; St Jo Coll Nottm; *CV* C Chandler's Ford, Winch 1992–94; C St Jos Worker Northolt, Lon 1994–97; V Immanuel and St Andr Streatham, S'wark 1997–2004; AD Streatham 2002–04; P-in-c and acting TR Sanderstead TM, S'wark from 2004, TR from 2006; M S'wark Dioc Liturg Cttee
GS 2005–   *Tel:* 020 8657 1366
email: rector@sanderstead-parish.org.uk

BUTLER, Rt Revd Thomas Frederick, M Sc, Ph D, LLD, D Sc, DD, FKC
Bishop's House 38 Tooting Bec Gardens London SW16 1QZ [BISHOP OF SOUTHWARK] *b* 1940 *educ* K Edw's Sch Five Ways Birm; Univ Leeds; Mirfield Th Coll; *CV* Asst C St Aug Wisbech 1964–66; Asst C St Sav Folkestone 1966–67; Lect and Chapl Univ Zambia 1967–73; Chapl Univ Kent 1973–80; Six Preacher Cant Cathl 1980–84; Adn of Northolt 1980–85; Bp of Willesden 1985–91; Bp of Leic 1991–98; Bp of S'wark from 1998; Chair BM 1995–2001; Chair BSR from 2001; Vc-Chair MPA Div, AC from 2003
GS 1991–   *Tel:* 020 8769 3256
                                  Fax: 020 8769 4126
email: bishop.tom@southwark.anglican.org

BUTTERFIELD, Ven David John, B Mus, Dip Th, DPS
Brimley Lodge 27 Molescroft Rd Beverley HU17 7DX [ARCHDEACON OF THE EAST RIDING; YORK] *b* 1952 *educ* Belle Vue Boys Gr Sch Bradf; R Holloway Coll Lon Univ; St Jo Coll Nottm; *CV* C Ch Ch Southport 1977–81; Min St Thos CD Aldridge 1981–91; V St Mich Lilleshall w. St Mary Sheriff-hales 1991–2002; V St Mich Lilleshall w. St Jo Muxton and St Mary Sheriffhales 2002–07; M BM 1995–96; RD Edgmond 1997–98; RD Edgmond and Shifnal 1999–2006; M Bp's Coun (Lich) 1994–2006; Chair Dioc Syn Ho of Clergy 2003–06; Adn of E Riding from 2007
GS 1990–2005   *Tel and Fax:* 01482 881659
email: archdeacon.of.eastriding@yorkdiocese.org

BUTTERY, Revd Graeme, BA, MA
St Oswald's Clergy House Brougham Terrace Hartle-pool TS24 8EY [DURHAM] *b* 1962 *educ* Dame Allan's Boys Sch Newc; York Univ; Newc Univ;

St Steph Ho Th Coll; *CV* C Peterlee 1988–91; C Sunderland, TM 1991–92; TV Sunderland, TM 1992–94; V St Lawr the Martyr Horsley Hill 1994–2005; V St Oswald Hartlepool from 2005
GS 1995–   *Tel:* 01429 273201

CALVER, Revd Canon Gill, B Sc
New Rectory High St Staplehurst TN12 0BJ [CANTERBURY] *b* 1947 *educ* Sydenham High Sch; Q Eliz Coll, Univ of Lon; *CV* Elected to GS 2005
GS 2005–   *Tel and Fax:* 01580 891258
                    email: gill.calver@btinternet.com

CAMBRIDGE, Archdeacon of. See BEER, Ven John Stuart

CAMERON, Rt Worshipful Dr Sheila Morag Clark, CBE, QC, DCL, MA, LLM
Bayleaves Bepton Midhurst GU29 9RB [DEAN OF THE ARCHES AND AUDITOR] *b* 1934 *educ* Com-monweal Lodge Sch Purley; St Hugh's Coll Ox; Univ of Cardiff; *CV* Barrister-at-Law; Official Prin Adnry of Hampstead 1968–86; Chan Chelms Dioc 1969–2001; Chan Lon Dioc 1992–2001; Chair Eccl Judges Assoc 1997–2004; M Legal Adv Commn from 1975; M Marriage Commn 1975–78; Chair Abps' Grp on the Episcopate 1986–90; Boundary Commr for England 1989–96; Vic-Gen Province of Cant 1983–2005; Recorder of Crown Court 1985–99; M Coun on Tribunals 1986–90
GS 1983–   *Tel:* 020 7828 0770
                                  01730 813971
              Fax: 020 7828 0770 01730 716300

CAMPBELL, Dr (John) Graham, Ph D, B Sc, FCA
18 Eaglesfield Hartford Northwich CW8 1NQ [CHES-TER] *b* 1942 *educ* Man Gr Sch; *CV* Birm Univ Rsch Chemist ICI 1966–71; Student Accountant Worth & Co 1971–74; Audit Sen Spicer & Pegler 1974–76; Accountant then Commercial Mgr Br Nuclear Fuels plc 1976–2003; M Bp's Coun from 1998; M Dioc Fin and Cen Services Cttee from 1997; M Foxhill Dioc Conf Cen Coun from 1998; M C of E Pensions Bd from 2004; Treas C of E Evang Coun from 2005
GS 2000–   *Tel:* 01606 75849
              email: graham.campbell@tesco.net

CAMPION-SPALL, Ms Kathryn May, BA
153 Sturton St Cambridge CB1 2QH [SOUTHWARK] *b* 1979 *educ* Sir Roger Manwood's Sch Sandwich; K Sch Cant; York Univ; *CV* Trg and Devel Co-ord, Lon Inst Students' Union 2002–04; Day provision Mgr, L'Arche, Lambeth 2004–05; Chaplaincy Asst, Imp Coll Lon from 2005; Ord Westcott Ho from 2007
GS 2005–   *Tel:* 07960 588015 (Mobile)
                    email: kat.spall@btinternet.com

CANTERBURY, Archbishop of. See WILLIAMS, Most Revd and Rt Hon Rowan Douglas

CANTERBURY, Archdeacon of. See WATSON, Ven Sheila Anne

CANTERBURY, Dean of. See WILLIS, Very Revd Robert Andrew

CAPON, Dr Peter Charles, B Sc, Ph D
137 Birchfields Rd Manchester M14 6PJ [MANCHES-TER] *b* 1944 *educ* Kimbolton Sch; Southn Univ; Cam Univ; Man Univ; *CV* Sen Lect in Computer Science Man Univ 1976–2004; rtd; Rdr at H Trin Rusholme, Manch from 1991
GS 1995–   *Tel:* 0161 225 5970
                     email: peter.capon@cs.man.ac.uk

CAREY, Mr Kevin, MA
112A High St Hurstpierpoint BN6 9PX [CHICHES-TER] *b* 1951 *educ* Downing Coll Cam; Harvard Univ; K Coll Lon; *CV* Founder Dir, humanITy from 1997; Chair Ofcom Com Radio Fund; Adv DCFS/UFI; Vc-Chair and Chair Audit Cttee, RNIB; official UK rep, DGInfoSoc; Dir jesus4u; lic Rdr from 2004
GS 2005–   *Tel:* 01273 835113 (Home)
                                        01273 834321 (Work)
                     email: humanity@atlas.co.uk

CARLISLE, Archdeacon of. (NOT APPOINTED AT TIME OF GOING TO PRESS)

CARLISLE, Bishop of. See DOW, Rt Revd (Geoffrey) Graham

CARLISLE, Dean of. See BOYLING, Very Revd Mark Christopher

CARR, Mrs Katherine Mary, BA, PGCE
Old Post Office Marrick Richmond DL11 7LQ [RIPON AND LEEDS] *b* 1932 *educ* Richmond High Sch for Girls; Westf Coll Lon; Lon Univ Inst of Educ; *CV* Asst Mistress Burghley Primary Sch Lon 1953–55; Asst Mistress Parliament Hill Comp Sch 1955–59; Lect Darlington Coll of Educ 1959–60, 1969–72; Dep Hd Sedgefield Comp Sch 1972–80; Hd Woodham Comp Sch Newton Aycliffe 1980–90; Rtd; JP; M Dioc Syn; Lay Chair Richmond Dny Syn; M Bp's Coun; Talking Newspaper; Life Pres Richmondshire Concert Soc
GS 1995–
                     email: katherinecarr@btinternet.com

CASSIDY, Rt Revd George Henry, B Sc, M Phil
Bishop's Manor Southwell NG25 0JR [BISHOP OF SOUTHWELL AND NOTTINGHAM] *b* 1942 *educ* Belfast High Sch; Qu Univ Belfast; Univ Coll Lon; Oak Hill Th Coll; *CV* C Ch Ch Clifton Bris 1972–75; V St Edyth Sea Mills Bris 1975–82; V St Paul Portman Sq Lon 1982–87; Adn of Lon and Can Res St Paul's Cathl 1987–99; Bp of S'well and Nottm from 1999; entered Ho of Lords 2003
GS 1995–   *Tel:* 01636 812112
                                        Fax: 01636 815401
                     email: bishop@southwell.anglican.org

CASTLE, Rt Revd Dr Brian Colin, BA, MA, Ph D
Bishop's Lodge 48 St Botolph's Road Sevenoaks TN13 3AG [SUFFRAGAN BISHOP OF TONBRIDGE; ROCHES-TER] *b* 1949 *educ* Wilson's Gr Sch, Camberwell; Univ Coll London; Cuddesdon Coll Ox; Univ of Birm; *CV* Asst C St Nic Sutton 1977; Asst C St Pet Limpsfield, S'wark 1977–81; P-in-c Chingola, Chililabombwe and Solwezi, N Zambia 1981–4; Vis Lect Ecum Inst, Bossey, Switzerland 1984–5; V N Petherton and Northmoor Green 1985–92; Vc Prin and Dir of Pastl Studies Ripon Coll Cuddesdon 1992–2001; Hon Can Roch Cathl and Bp of Tonbridge from 2002; Abps' Adv for Alternative Spiritualities and New Relig Movts; Co-chair Miss Thel Adv Grp   *Tel:* 01732 456070
                                        Fax: 01732 741449
        email: bishop.tonbridge@rochester.anglican.org

CHALONER, Mr Mark Daniel Dawson, MA
Church House Great Smith St London SW1P 3AZ [CHIEF INVESTMENT OFFICER, CHURCH COMMIS-SIONERS] *b* 1961 *educ* K Sch Roch; Jes Coll Cam; *CV* On staff of Ch Commrs from 1988; Chief Investment Officer, Ch Commrs from 2000
                                        Tel: 020 7898 1126
                                        Fax: 020 7898 1111
                     email: mark.chaloner@c-of-e.org.uk

CHANDLER, Revd Ian Nigel, BD, AKC, CMTh
St Richard's Vicarage 8 Queens Rd Haywards Heath RH16 1EB [CHICHESTER] *b* 1965 *educ* Bishopsgarth Sch Stockton-on-Tees; Stockton Sixth Form Coll; K Coll Lon; Chich Th Coll; *CV* C All SS Hove 1992–96; Dom Chapl to Bp of Chich 1996–2000; V St Rich Haywards Heath from 2000; RD Cuckfield from 2004; M Dioc Syn from 2000; M Dioc Fin Cttee from 2004
GS 2005–   *Tel:* 01444 413621
                     email: ianchandler@hotmail.com

CHANDLER, Very Revd Dr Michael John, Dip Th, S Th, Ph D
The Deanery Ely CB7 4DN [DEAN OF ELY] *b* 1945 *educ* K Coll Lond; Brasted Place Coll: Linc Th Coll; *CV* C St Dunstan, Cant 1972–75; C St Jo Bapt Margate 1975–78; V Newington 1978–88; RD Sittingbourne 1984–88; R St Steph Hackington 1988–95; RD Cant 1994–95; Can Treas Cant Cathl 1995–2003; Dean of Ely from 2003   *Tel:* 01353 667735
                                        Fax: 01353 665658
             email: dean@cathedral.ely.anglican.org

CHAPMAN, Revd Sarah Jean, Dip COT, GME
Bitterne Park Vicarage 7 Thorold Rd Southampton SO18 1HZ [WINCHESTER] *b* 1955 *educ* Cheltenham Ladies' Coll; Lon Coll of Occupational Therapy; SDMTS; *CV* C (NSM) Rogate w. Terwick and Trotton w. Chithurst, Chich 1989–94; C (NSM) Easebourne, Chich 1994–96; Dioc Lic to Officiate, Portsm 1996–97; NSM St Phil Cosham; V St Mary Magd Sheet, Portsm 1997–2002; V Bitterne Park, Winch from 2002; M Winch Dioc Healing and

Wholeness Cttee 2003–05; Bp's Exam Chapl from 2003; M VRSC from 2006
GS 2003–05; 2005–   Tel: 023 8055 1560
                        email: revsarah@sargil.co.uk

CHARING CROSS, Archdeacon of. See JACOB, Ven William Mungo

CHARTRES, Rt Revd and Rt Hon Richard John Carew, DD, FSA
The Old Deanery Dean's Court London EC4V 5AA [BISHOP OF LONDON] *b* 1947 *educ* Hertf Gr Sch; Trin Coll Cam; Cuddesdon Th Coll; Linc Th Coll; *CV* C St Andr Bedford 1973–75; Bp's Dom Chapl 1975–80; Chapl to Abp of Cant 1980–84; P-in-c St Steph w St Jo Westmr 1984–85; V 1986–92; DDO 1985–92; Prof Div Gresham Coll 1986–92; Six Preacher Cant Cathl 1991–96; Bp of Stepney 1992–95; Bp of Lon from 1995; Dean of HM Chapels Royal and PC 1996; Chair Ch Heritage Forum; Ch Commrs from 1999; M Centr Cttee CEC; M Jt Liaison Grp between CEC and Coun of Eur Catholic Bps' Confs
GS 1995–   Tel: 020 7248 6233
                             Fax: 020 7248 9721
                 email: bishop@londin.clara.co.uk

CHAVE, Preb Brian Philip, BA (OU)
The Vicarage Vowles Close Hereford HR4 0DF [HEREFORD] *b* 1951 *educ* Winslade Sch Ex; Seale-Hayne Agric Coll Devon; Trinity Coll Bris; *CV* C Cullompton w Kentisbeare and Blackborough, Ex 1984–87; TV Oakmoor Tm Min, Ex 1987–93; C for Agric, Heref 1993–96; Comms Officer and Bp's Staff Officer (Dom Chapl), Heref 1997–2001; TV W Heref Tm Min from 2001; Vc Pres Heref Dioc Syn and Chair Ho of C; M Bp's Coun; M Dioc Policy and Resources Cttee; Chair Bd of Govs Whitecross High Sch, Heref
GS 2008–   Tel: 01432 273086 (Office)
                 email: brianchave@btinternet.com

CHEESEMAN, Mr James Reginald,
25 Lambarde Drive Sevenoaks TN13 3HX [ROCHESTER] *b* 1934 *educ* Sevenoaks Sch; Coll of St Mark and St Jo; *CV* Supply Staff Kent Educ Cttee 1954–55; Asst Tchr Midfield Prim Sch 1957–68; Dep Hdmaster Edgebury Prim Sch 1968–69; Chair Ho of Laity Roch Dioc Syn 1976–79; M GS Bd of Educ 1981–91; Hdmaster Pet Hills' Sch Rotherhithe 1969–97; Co-Chair Sevenoaks Dny Syn 1976–96; Sec Sevenoaks Dny Syn; Trustee Guild of All So; Treas Qu Victoria Clergy Fund from 1991; Lay Chair Forward In Faith Roch; Chair Dioc Bd of Patronage; Sec Kent Cricket Bd
GS 1975–   Tel: 01732 455718
                 email: jim@cheeseman7.freeserve.co.uk

CHEETHAM, Rt Revd Dr Richard Ian, MA, PGCE, Cert Theol, Ph D
Kingston Episcopal Area Office 620 Kingston Rd Raynes Park SW20 8DN [AREA BISHOP OF KINGSTON; SOUTHWARK] *b* 1955 *educ* Kingston Gr Sch;

CCC Ox; Ripon Coll Cuddesdon; K Coll Lon; *CV* C H Cross Fenham 1987–90; V St Aug of Cant Limbury, Luton 1990–99; RD Luton 1995–98; Adn of St Alb 1999–2002; Bp of Kingston from 2002
                             Tel: 020 8545 2440
                             Fax: 020 8545 2441
          email: bishop.richard@southwark.anglican.org

CHELMSFORD, Bishop of. See GLADWIN, Rt Revd John Warren

CHELMSFORD, Dean of. See JUDD, Very Revd Peter Somerset Margesson

CHELTENHAM, Archdeacon of. See RINGROSE, Ven Hedley Sidney

CHESSUN, Rt Revd Christopher Thomas James, MA
37 South Rd Forest Hill London SE23 2UJ [AREA BISHOP OF WOOLWICH; SOUTHWARK] *b* 1956 *educ* Hampton Gr Sch; Univ Coll Ox; Westcott Ho Cam; *CV* Asst C St Mich and AA Sandhurst 1983–87; Sen C St Mary Portsea 1987–99; Chapl and Min Can St Paul's Cathl 1989–93; R Stepney, St Dunstan and All SS 1993–2001; AD Tower Hamlets 1997–2001; Adn of Northolt from 2001; M Dioc Syn 2001–05; Bp of Woolwich from 2005
                     Tel: 020 7939 9407 (Office)
                          020 8699 7771 (Home)
                          Fax: 020 8699 7949
                     email: bishop.christopher@
                          southwark.anglican.org

CHESTER, Revd Philip Anthony Edwin, LLB, Dip Th
St Matthew's House 20 Great Peter St London SW1P 2BU [LONDON] *b* 1955 *educ* Calday Grange; Birm Univ; St Jo Coll Dur; *CV* Asst P St Chad Shrewsbury 1980–85; Asst P St Martin-in-the-Fields Lon 1985–88; Chapl K Coll Lon 1988–95; PV Westmr Abbey from 1990; V St Matt Westmr from 1995
GS 2005–   Tel: 020 7222 3704
                             Fax: 020 7233 0255
                          email: office@stmw.org

CHESTER, Archdeacon of. See ALLISTER, Ven Donald Spargo

CHESTER, Bishop of. See FORSTER, Rt Revd Peter Robert

CHESTER, Dean of. See McPHATE, Very Revd Prof Gordon Ferguson

CHESTERFIELD, Archdeacon of. See GARNETT, Ven David Christopher

CHETWOOD, Canon Nigel John, B Sc
23 Wigeon Lane Tewkesbury GL20 7RS [GLOUCESTER] *b* 1939 *educ* Oswestry Gr Sch; Man Univ; *CV* Rdr; Fell Glos Univ Foundation from 1990; M Gov Body Trin Coll 1990-95; M CPAS Coun 1991–96 and from 2003; Glouc Dioc Lay Chair 1990–97,

2000–03; M Bp's Coun 1990–2003, 2006–; M MPA Coun 2003–06; M Tewkesbury LSP 2004–05; Lay Chair Tewkesbury & Winchcombe Dny 2005–08; M Coun WEMTC from 2006; Lay Can from 2008
GS 1985–   *Tel:* 01684 292473
           07811 896561 (Mobile)
           email: nigel@chetwood.net

CHICHESTER, Archdeacon of.
See McKITTRICK, Ven Douglas Henry

CHICHESTER, Bishop of. See HIND, Rt Revd John William

CHICHESTER, Dean of. See FRAYLING, Very Revd Nicholas Arthur

CHORLTON, Revd John Samuel Woodard, BSc, Cert Theol
St George's House Long Furlong Drive Britwell Slough SL2 2LX [OXFORD] *b* 1945 *educ* Leiston Gr Sch Suffolk; Newc Univ; Wycliffe Hall Ox; *CV* Glaciological rsch associate, Newc Univ 1967–68; maths tchr, Blaydon Comp Sch 1968–73; Hd of Maths, Castle Manor Upper Sch, Haverhill 1973–78; Dep Hd, Angl Sch Jerusalem 1979–82, Headmaster 1982–92; C St Aldate Ox 1992–95, Assoc P 1995–2004; AD Ox 1999–2004; V St Geo Britwell, Slough from 2008
GS 2005–   *Tel:* 01753 554684
           07709 873831
           Fax: 01753 554684
           email: jsw@chorlton.org

CLARK, Revd Jonathan Dunnett, BA, M Litt, MA
St Mary's Rectory Stoke Newington Church St London N16 9ES [LONDON] *educ* Ex Univ; Bris Univ; Southn Univ; Trin Coll Bris; *CV* C Stanwix, Carl 1988–92; Chapl Bris Univ 1992–93; Dir of Studies S Diocs Minl Tr Scheme 1994–97; Chapl Univ of N Lon 1997–2002; Chapl Lon Metrop Univ 2002–03; AD Islington 1999–2003; R St Mary Stoke Newington from 2003; P-in-c Brownswood Park from 2004
GS 2005–   *Tel:* 020 7254 6072
           07968 845698 (Mobile)
           Fax: 020 7923 4135
           email: rectorofstokey@btinternet.com

CLARK, Mr John Guthrie,
12 Ash Drive Haughton Stafford ST18 9EU [LICHFIELD] *b* 1938 *educ* Slough Gr Sch; Wrekin Coll; Ches Dio Tr Coll; *CV* Tchr Dawley Sec Mod Sch 1960–65; Phoenix Comp Sch 1965–67; Hd of RE, Wobaston Sec Mod Sch 1967–68; Hd of Religious, Social and Moral Educ, Aelfgar Comp Sch 1968–86 and Hagley Pk Comp Sch Rugeley 1986–93; M Dioc Pastl Cttee, Bp's Coun and Bd of Educ; Local Min Consult; Rdr
GS 1970–   *Tel:* 01785 780689

CLARKE, Very Revd John Martin, MA, BD
The Dean's Lodgings 25 The Liberty Wells BA5 2SZ [DEAN OF WELLS; BATH AND WELLS] *b* 1952 *educ* W Buckland Sch; Hertf Coll Ox; New Coll Edin; Edin Th Coll; *CV* C Ascen Kenton, Newc 1976–79; Prec St Ninian's Cathl, Perth 1979–82; Info Officer and Communications Adv to GS of Scottish Episcopal Ch 1982–87; Philip Usher Memorial Sch, Greece 1987–88; V St Mary Battersea 1989–96; Prin Ripon Coll Cuddesdon 1997–2004; Dean of Wells from 2004   *Tel:* 01749 670278
           email: dean@wellscathedral.uk.net

CLARKE, Canon Prof Michael Gilbert, CBE, BA, MA, DL
Millington House 15 Lansdowne Crescent Worcester WR3 8JE [WORCESTER] *b* 1944 *educ* Qu Eliz Gr Sch Wakef; Sussex Univ; *CV* Lect in Politics Edin Univ 1969–75; Dep Dir Policy Planning Lothian Regional Coun 1975–81; Dir Local Government Tr Bd 1981–90; Chief Exec Local Government Mgt Bd 1990–93; Hd of Sch of Public Policy Birm Univ 1993–98; Pro-Vc Chan Birm Univ from 1998, Vc-Prin 2003–08; Lay Can and Chapter Member Worc Cathl from 2001; Gov Qu Foundn, Birm from 2000; M Diocs Commn from 2008
GS 1990–93, 1995–   *Tel:* 01905 617634
           Fax: 01905 29502

CLEVELAND, Archdeacon of.
See FERGUSON, Ven Paul John

COCKETT, Ven Elwin Wesley, BA
86 Aldersbrook Rd Manor Park London E12 5DH [ARCHDEACON OF WEST HAM; CHELMSFORD] *b* 1959 *educ* St Paul's Cathl Choir Sch; Forest Sch, Snaresbrook; Aston Trg Scheme; Oak Hill Coll; *CV* C St Chad, Chadwell Heath 1991–94; C-in-c St Paul, Harold Hill 1994–95, P-in-c 1995–97, V 1997–2000; TR Billericay and Little Burstead TM 2000–07; RD Basildon 2004–07; Adn of West Ham from 2007; Club Chapl West Ham United Football Club from 1992   *Tel:* 020 8989 8557
           Fax: 020 8530 1311
           email: a.westham@chelmsford.anglican.org

COCKSWORTH, Rt Revd Dr Christopher John, BA (Hons), PhD
Bishop's House 23 Davenport Rd Coventry CV5 6PW [BISHOP OF COVENTRY] *b* 1959 *educ* Forest Sch for boys, Horsham; Univ of Man; Didsbury Sch of Educ; St John's Coll, Nottm; *CV* Asst C Ch Ch Epsom 1988–92; Chapl Royal Holloway Univ of Lon 1992–96; Dir S Theol Educ and Training Scheme 1996–2001; Prin Ridley Hall Cam 2001–08; Bp Cov from 2008   *Tel:* 024 7667 2244
           Fax: 024 2671 3271
           email: bishcov@btconnect.com

COHEN, Ven Clive Ronald Franklin, ACIB
Archdeacon's House Cardinham Bodmin PL30 4BL [ARCHDEACON OF BODMIN; TRURO] *b* 1946 *educ* Tonbridge Sch; Sarum and Wells Th Coll; *CV* C

Esher 1981–85; R Winterslow 1985–2000; RD Alderbury 1989–93; Non Res Can and Preb Sarum Cathl 1992–2000; Adn of Bodmin from 2000
Tel and Fax: 01208 821614
email: clive@truro.anglican.org

COLCHESTER, Archdeacon of. See COOPER, Ven Annette Joy

COLCHESTER, Area Bishop of. See MORGAN, Rt Revd Christopher Heudebourck

COLES, Revd Stephen Richard, MA, BA
The Cardinal's Hat 25 Romilly Rd Finsbury Park London N4 2QY [LONDON] *b* 1949 *educ* Latymer Upper Sch Hammersmith; Univ Coll Ox; Trin Hall Cam; Leeds Univ; Coll of the Resurrection, Mirfield; *CV* C St Mary Stoke Newington 1981–84; Chapl K Coll Cam 1984–89; V St Thos Finsbury Park from 1989; Chair Br Federation Against Sexually Transmitted Infections from 2002
GS 2000–
Tel: 020 7359 5741
email: cardinal.jeoffry@btconnect.com

COLLIER, Revd Paul Edward, BA, PGCE
5 Wickham Rd London SE4 1PF [SOUTHWARK] *b* 1963 *educ* Haileybury Coll; Mert Coll Ox; S'wark Ord Course; *CV* Solicitor Pritchard Joyce and Hinds 1991–94; C St Jo Ev Dulwich 1994–97; P-in-c St Hugh Charterhouse, Bermondsey 1997–2002; M CNC from 2002; Chapl, Goldsmiths Coll, Univ of Lon from 2003
GS 2000–
Tel: 020 8692 1821
email: p.collier@gold.ac.uk

COLLINGS, Very Revd Neil, BD, AKC
The Deanery Bury St Edmunds IP33 1RL [DEAN OF ST EDMUNDSBURY] *b* 1946 *educ* Torquay Gr Sch; K Coll Lon; St Aug, Cant; *CV* C Littleham-cum-Exmouth 1970–72, TV 1972–74; Chapl Westmr Abbey 1974–79; R St Nic Hereford 1979–86; DDO and Dir of POT, Heref dioc 1979–86; Chair St Alb DAC 1987–99; R St Nic Harpenden 1986–99; Can Res and Treas Ex Cathl 1999–2006; Dean of St Edmundsbury from 2006
Tel: 01284 748722
Fax: 01284 768655
email: dean@stedscathedral.co.uk

COLMER, Ven Malcolm John, M Sc, BA, SO SC
Diocesan Office The Palace Hereford HR4 9BL [ARCHDEACON OF HEREFORD] *b* 1945 *educ* R Gr Sch Guildf; Sussex Univ; Nottm Univ; St Jo Coll Nottm; *CV* C St Jo Egham 1973–76; C Chadwell St Mary 1976–79; V S Malling, Lewes 1979–85; V St Mary w St Steph Hornsey Rise 1985–87; TR Hornsey Rise Whitehall Park Tm 1987–96; AD Islington 1990–95; Adn of Middx 1996–2005; Adn of Hereford from 2005; M Soc of Ordained Scientists from 1998
GS 2000–05; 2005–
Tel: 01432 373316
Fax: 01432 352952
email: archdeacon@hereford.anglican.org

COMBES, Ven Roger Matthew, LLB
3 Danehurst Crescent Horsham RH13 5HS [ARCHDEACON OF HORSHAM; CHICHESTER] *b* 1947 *educ* Sherborne Sch; K Coll Lon; Ridley Hall Th Coll; *CV* C St Paul Onslow Sq Lon 1974–77; C H Trin Brompton Lon 1976–77; C H Sepulchre Cam 1977–86; R St Matt St Leonards-on-Sea 1986–2003; M Bp's Coun from 1998; RD Hastings 1998–2002; Adn of Horsham from 2003
GS 1995–2005
Tel: 01403 262710
Fax: 01403 210778
email: archhorsham@diochi.org.uk

CONDICK, Mrs Margaret, B Sc, Cert Ed
34 Rectory Lane Kirton Ipswich IP10 0PY [ST EDMUNDSBURY AND IPSWICH] *b* 1944 *educ* Sutton High Sch GPDST; Manch Univ; *CV* Tchr of Physics, Stockport 1967–70; pt tchr of maths, Suffolk 1985–97; Communications Officer, Chs Together in Suffolk 1998–2000; County Ecum Officer for Suffolk from 2000
GS 2003–
Tel: 01394 448576
email: margaret.condick@btopenworld.com

CONNER, Rt Revd David John, MA
The Deanery Windsor Castle Windsor SL4 1NJ [DEAN OF WINDSOR] *b* 1947 *educ* Ex Coll Ox; St Steph Ho Th Coll; *CV* Hon C Summertown Ox 1971–76; Asst Chapl St Edw Sch Ox 1971–73; Chapl 1973–80; TV Wolvercote w Summertown 1976–80; Chapl Win Coll 1980–87; V Gt St Mary w St Mich Cam 1987–94; RD Cam 1989–94; Bp of Lynn 1994–98; Dean of Windsor from 1998; Bp to HM Forces from 2001
Tel: 01753 865561
Fax: 01753 819002
email: david.conner@stgeorges-windsor.org

CONWAY, Rt Revd Stephen David, MA, MA, PGCE
Bishop's Croft Winterbourne Earls Salisbury SP4 6HJ [AREA BISHOP OF RAMSBURY; SALISBURY] *b* 1957 *educ* Abp Tenison's Gr Sch Lon; Keble Coll Ox; Selw Coll Cam; Westcott Ho; *CV* C St Mary Heworth 1986–89; C St Mich and AA Bishopwearmouth 1989–90; DDO 1989–94; Hon C St Marg Dur 1990–94; P-in-c then V St Mary Cockerton 1994–98; Sen Chapl to Bp of Dur and Dioc Communications Officer 1998–2002; Adn of Dur and Can Res Dur Cathl 2002–06; Area Bp of Ramsbury from 2006; M Bps' Insp of Th Colls and Courses from 1997; Trustee Affirming Catholicism; Trustee Mental Health Matters from 2003, Chair from 2004; Chair Dioc Learning, Discipleship and Min Coun from 2006; Trustee Affirming Catholicism 2001–08, Vc-Pres from 2008
GS 1995–2000
Tel: 01380 729808
Fax: 01380 738096
email: sramsbury@salisbury.anglican.org

COOK, Revd John Richard Millward, BA
Vicarage 43 Park Walk London SW10 0AU [LONDON] *b* 1961 *educ* Repton Sch; St Jo Coll Dur;

Wycliffe Hall Th Coll; *CV* C St Thos Brampton 1985–89; C St Pet Farnboro 1989–92; C and Dir of Tr All So Langham Place Lon 1992–98; V St Jo w St Andr Chelsea from 1998; M CCU 1996–99; M VRSC from 1999; M CEEC from 1999; Hon Chapl Worshipful Company of Tylers and Bricklayers from 1999; M Crosslinks Gen Coun from 2001; CEEC Exec from 2002; M Coun Wycliffe Hall Ox from 2006
GS 1995–   *Tel and Fax:* 020 7352 1675
     email: johnrmcook@fish.co.uk

COOPER, Mr Alan, OBE, B Ed
11 Ravensdale Gardens Eccles Manchester M30 9JD [MANCHESTER] *b* 1927 *educ* St Andr Sch Eccles; Didsbury Coll of Educ; Liv Univ; *CV* Headmaster; Councillor Eccles Boro Coun 1958–73; M Ch Assembly 1965–70; Mayor of Eccles 1970–71; Councillor Salford 1975–79; Lay Chair Eccles Dny Syn; Chair DBF; M Bp's Coun; Dep Vc Chair AC Fin Cttee; Ch Commr 1988–2004; JP; Lay Can Manch Cathl
GS 1970–   *Tel:* 0161 789 1514
   email: thecooperhouse2@ntlworld.com

COOPER, Ven Annette Joy, BA, CQSW, Dip RS
63 Powers Hall End Witham CM8 1NH [ARCHDEACON OF COLCHESTER; CHELMSFORD] *b* 1953 *educ* Lilley and Stone Newark Girls High Sch; Open Univ; Lon Univ Extra-mural Dept; S'wark Ord Course; *CV* Local Auth Social Worker; Asst Chapl Tunbridge Wells Health Auth 1988–91; NSM Dn St Pet Pembury 1988; Chapl Bassetlaw Hosp and Community Services NHS Trust 1991– 96; Chapl to Center Parcs Sherwood Village 1996– 99; Chapl to S'well Dioc MU 1996–99; P-in-c Edwinstowe 1996–2004; AD Worksop 1999–2004; Hon Can S'well Minster 2002–04; M Dioc Bd of Educ 1994–97; M Bp's Coun from 1999; Vc-Pres/ Chair Dioc Ho of Clergy 2001–04; M GS Panel of Chairmen 2003–04; 2005–; M Discipline Commn from 2003; Adn of Colchester from 2004
GS 2000–2004; 2005–   *Tel:* 01376 513130
              Fax: 01376 500789
email: a.colchester@chelmsford.anglican.org

COOPER, Ms Susan Margaret, B Sc, FIA, DPS, FCAA
28 Headstone Lane Harrow HA2 6HG [LONDON] *b* 1947 *educ* Harrow Weald Co Gr Sch; Univ Coll of Wales Aberystwyth; Birm Univ; *CV* Legal and Gen Assurance Soc 1969–80; Corporate Business Actuary BUPA 1980–90; Consultant Actuary 1992–2002; Consulting Actuary, GAD from 2002; Rdr St Jo Bapt Pinner from 1995; M Strg Cttee for Draft Stipends (Cessation of Special Payments) Measure 2003–04; M Br Regional Cttee St Geo Coll Jerusalem from 2003; Hon Sec CHRISM from 2006; M Strg Ctee for Draft C of E Pensions (Amendment) Measure 2007–08
GS 2000–   *Tel:* 020 8863 2094 (Home)
             020 7211 2626 (Office)
               Fax: 08700 516752
   email: scooper@hedstone.demon.co.uk

CORNWALL, Archdeacon of. See BUSH, Ven Roger Charles

COTTON, Canon Robert Lloyd, MA, Dip Th
Holy Trinity Rectory 9 Eastgate Gardens Guildford GU1 4AZ [GUILDFORD] *b* 1958 *educ* Uppingham; Merton Coll Ox; Westcott Ho Cam; *CV* C St Mary Bromley 1983-85; C Bisley & W End 1987–89; P-in-c St Paul E Molesey 1989–96; Prin Guildf Dioc Min Course 1989–96; R H Trin & St Mary Guildf from 1996; Chair Ho of Clergy from 2004; Can Dioc of Highveld, S Africa from 2006
GS 2004–   *Tel:* 01483 575489
   email: rector@holytrinityguildford.org.uk

COTTRELL, Rt Revd Stephen Geoffrey, BA
Bishop's House Tidmarsh Lane Tidmarsh Reading RG8 8HA [AREA BISHOP OF READING; OXFORD] *b* 1958 *educ* Belfairs High Sch for Boys; Poly of Central Lon; St Steph Ho; *CV* C Ch Ch & St Paul Forest Hill, S'wark 1984–88; P-in-c St Wilf Parklands, Chich and Asst Dir of Pastl Studies, Chich Th Coll 1988–93; Dioc Missr, Wakef 1993–98; Springboard Missr 1998–2001; Can Pastor Peterb Cathl 2001–04; Bp of Reading from 2004
              Tel: 0118 984 1216
              Fax: 0118 984 1218
email: bishopreading@oxford.anglican.org

COVENTRY, Archdeacon of. See WATSON, Ven Ian

COVENTRY, Bishop of. See COCKSWORTH, Rt Revd Christopher John

COVENTRY, Dean of. See IRVINE, Very Revd John Dudley

COX, Cllr Timothy Daniel, HND (Computing), B Sc (Computing, Lancs), CCNA 1–3
16 Convent Crescent Blackpool FY3 7QF [BLACKBURN] *b* 1980 *educ* Poynton High Sch; Montgomery High Sch Blackpool; Blackpool Sixth Form Coll; Man Metropolitan Univ; Blackpool and Fylde Coll; Lancaster Univ; UCLAN; *CV* Costing draughtsman 2001–04; Blackpool Unitary Authority Cllr from 2007; Co Ditr Blackpool Coastal Housing from 2007; Vc-Chair SACRE from 2007; Vc-Chair Business, Culture and Communities Overview and Scrutiny Cttee from 2007; Religious Diversity Champion Blackpool Coun from 2008; Database Support (Lancs County Coun) from 2008; Officer and Battalion Treas Boys' Brigade; Literacy Gov Anchorsholme Primary Sch 2004–07; Gov Bispham Endowed C of E Primary Sch from 2007; Gov Montgomery Language Coll from 2007; Lay Communion Asst; Co Dir and Charity Trustee; M Bp's Coun
GS 2000–   *Tel:* 01253 535000
                0161 397007
            07747 794903 (Mobile)
               email: tim@asmine.com

CRASKE, Revd Dr Jane Valerie, BA, BA, PhD
16 Kingswood Gardens Leeds LS8 2BT [ECUMENICAL
REPRESENTATIVE (METHODIST CHURCH)] *b* 1965
educ Longdean Comp Sch, Hemel Hempstead;
UEA; Leeds Univ; Dur Univ; Wesley Study Cen,
Dur; *CV* Sec Sch tchr, Hatton Sch, Hatton,
Derbys 1987–90; Min, Lon Mission (W Lon) Cir-
cuit 1995–98; Min, Man (Withington) Circuit
1998–2002; Tutor, Hartley Victoria Meth Coll,
Man 1998–2007; Superintendent Min, Leeds NE
Circuit from 2007; Chair Meth Ch Faith and
Order Cttee
GS 2007–   *Tel:* 0113 266 2066
                     email: jvcraske@btconnect.com

CRAVEN, Prof John Anthony George, MA Cantab,
Hon D Sc
Fyning Cross Rogate Petersfield GU31 5EF
[APPOINTED MEMBER, ARCHBISHOPS' COUNCIL] *b*
1949 *educ* Pinner Gr Sch; K Coll Cam; Kennedy
Memorial Scholar, Massachusetts Inst of Tech; *CV*
Univ of Kent (Cant) Lect in Mathematical Eco-
nomics 1971, Sen Lect 1976; Reader in Economics
1980, Prof of Economics 1986; elected Dean of
Social Sciences 1987, re-elected 1990; Pro Vc-
Chan 1991, Dep Vc-Chan 1993; Vc-Chan Univ of
Ports from 1997; 1977–96 in Cant Dioc, at various
times M and Treas Eastry PCC, M Dny and Dioc
Syns, M CUF Dioc Cttee, Chair St Mart Trust for
Homeless in Deal and Dover; in Ports Dioc,
Foundn Gov St Luke's C of E Vol Aided Sch from
2002, Chair from 2003; M Ports Cathl Coun from
2003; Lay Can Ports Cathl from 2006; Gov S Kent
Coll of FE 1991–96; Gov Highbury Coll of FE
1997–2002
GS 2006–   *Tel:* 01730 821392 (Home)
                              023 9284 3190 (Office)
                              Fax: 023 9284 3400
                     email: john.craven@port.ac.uk

**CRAVEN, Archdeacon of. See SLATER, Ven
Paul John**

CRAY, Rt Revd Graham Alan, BA
*Bishop's House Pett Lane Charing Ashford TN27
0DL* [SUFFRAGAN BISHOP OF MAIDSTONE; CANTER-
BURY] *b* 1947 *educ* Trinity Sch of John Whitgift,
Croydon; Leeds Univ; St Jo Coll Nottm; *CV* C St
Mark Gillingham, Roch 1971–75; N Co-ord Ch
Pastl Aid Soc 1975–78; V St Mich-le-Belfrey
1978–92; Prin Ridley Hall Cam 1992–2000; Six
Prchr of Cant Cathl 1997–2002; Bp of Maidstone
from 2001; M Dioc Abp's Coun; Chair Dioc
Local Min and Trg Coun; Chair Dioc Bd of Rdrs;
Chair Dioc BM; M Coun South East Inst for Theol
Educ
GS 1985–92   *Tel:* 01233 712950
                                    Fax: 01233 713543
                     email: bishop@bishmaid.org

**CREDITON, Suffragan Bishop of. See EVENS,
Rt Revd Robert John Scott**

CROCKER, Revd Jeremy Robert, MBA, MCIM,
M Th
The Abbey Rectory Church End Elstow MK42 9XT
[ST ALBANS] *b* 1967 *educ* Dane Court Gr Sch
Broadstairs; South Bank Univ; Heythrop Coll
Lon; Westcott Ho Cam; *CV* C H Trin Stevenage
1997–2000; V St Jo S Hatfield 2000–04; TR Elstow
from 2004
GS 2001–   *Tel and Fax:* 01234 261477
                     email: Jeremy.Crocker@tesco.net

**CROYDON, Archdeacon of. See DAVIES,
Ven Tony (Vincent Anthony)**

**CROYDON, Area Bishop of. See BAINES,
Rt Revd Nicholas**

CRUMPLER, Mr Peter George, FCIPR, Dip Cam
Church House Great Smith St London SW1P 3AZ
[DIRECTOR OF COMMUNICATIONS FOR THE CHURCH
OF ENGLAND] *b* 1956 *educ* Chiswick Sch, Lon;
Harlow Coll; *CV* Communications posts within
British Gas plc 1982–91; Internat Public Affairs
Mgr, British Gas plc 1991–97; Hd of External
Affairs Internat, BG plc 1997–2000; Hd of Com-
munications, BG Group plc 2000–01; Communi-
cations Officer, St Alb Dioc 2001–04; Dir of Com-
munications for C of E from 2004; Admitted as
Rdr, St Alb dioc 2008   *Tel:* 020 7898 1462
                                    Fax: 020 7222 6672
                     email: peter.crumpler@c-of-e.org.uk

**CUMBERLAND, Archdeacon of West.
See HILL, Ven Colin**

CUNDY, Rt Revd Ian Patrick Martyn, MA
Bishop's Lodging The Palace Peterborough PE1 1YA
[BISHOP OF PETERBOROUGH] *b* 1945 *educ* Monkton
Combe Sch; Trin Coll Cam; Tyndale Hall Th Coll;
CV C Ch Ch New Malden 1969–73; Tutor Oak
Hill Th Coll 1973–77; TR Mortlake w E Sheen
1978–83; Warden Cranmer Hall St Jo Coll Dur
1983–92; Bp of Lewes 1992–96; Bp of Peterb from
1996; Chair CCU 1998–2008; Pres St Jo Coll Dur
1999–2008; Bd of Govs, Ch Commrs from 2004;
Co-Chair Joint Implementation Commission
(Angl-Meth Covenant) from 2003
GS 1996–   *Tel:* 01733 562492
                                    Fax: 01733 890077
            email: bishop@peterborough-diocese.org.uk

CUNLIFFE, Ven Dr Christopher John, MA, D Phil,
MA, A R Hist S
Derby Church House Full St Derby DE1 3DR
[ARCHDEACON OF DERBY] *b* 1955 *educ* Charter-
house; Ch Ch Ox; Trin Coll Cam; Westcott Ho
Cam; *CV* C Chesterfield Par Ch 1983–85; Chapl
and Jun Rsch Fell, Linc Coll Ox 1985–89; Chapl
City Univ and Guildhall Sch of Music and Drama
1989–91; Selection Sec and Voc Officer, Adv Bd of
Min 1991–96; Bp of Lon's Adv for Ord Min 1996–
2003; Clerk, All SS Educ Trust 2004; Chapl to Bp
of Bradwell 2004–06; Adn of Derby from 2006;

Chair Derby Dioc Communications Cttee; Vc-Chair Derby Coun for Soc Resp; Can Res Derby Cathl 2006–08 *Tel:* 01332 388676
Fax: 01332 292969
email: archderby@derby.anglican.org

CURLE, Mrs Kim, BSc Econ, PGCE, CThM
89 Kings Drive Bishopston Bristol BS7 8JQ [BRISTOL] *b* 1961 *educ* Rainham Mark Gr Sch; LSE; Inst of Educ, Lon Univ; St Jo Coll Nottm; *CV* Tchr, Invicta Gr Sch for Girls, Maidstone 1984–89; tchr, Sandford Engl Com Sch, Addis Ababa, Ethiopia 1990–92; Miss Ptnr, CMS teaching at Bp Kivengere Girls' Sch, SW Uganda 1993–96; Evangelist and schools worker, Lon City Miss, Peckham Chr Cen 1996–99; tchr, Atherley Sch, Southn 1999–2000; tchr, St Anne's Convent Sch, Southn 2000–03; Team Evangelist, Bishopston and St Andr from 2004; M Bris City Dny Uganda Link Cttee; M CCU
GS 2005– *Tel:* 0117 942 9693
Fax: 0117 942 9695
email: kim.curle@btopenworld.com

CURRAN, Ven Patrick Martin Stanley, BA, B Th
British Embassy Jauresgasse 12 Vienna 1030 Austria [ARCHDEACON OF THE EASTERN ARCHDEACONRY; EUROPE] *b* 1956 *educ* Ostsee Gymnasium, Timmendorfer Strand, Germany; Univ of K Coll Halifax, Nova Scotia, Canada; Southampton Univ; Chich Th Coll; *CV* C Heavitree with Ex St Paul Ex 1984–87; Bp's Chapl to Students, Bradf 1987–93; Chapl Bonn with Cologne, Eur 1993–2000; Can Malta Cathl 2000; Chapl Ch Ch Vienna from 2000; Adn of the Eastern Archdeaconry from 2002 *Tel:* 00 43 1 7148900
00 43 1 7185902
Fax: 00 43 1 7148900
email: office@christchurchvienna.org

CURRIE, Revd Stuart William, MA, PGCE
St Stephen's Vicarage 1 Beech Avenue Worcester WR3 8PZ [WORCESTER] *b* 1953 *educ* Boteler Gr Sch, Warrington; Hertford Coll Ox; Univ Coll Dur; Fitzwilliam Coll Cam; Westcott Ho; *CV* C Ch Ch Reading 1985–89; V in Banbury TM 1989–94; V Barbourne St Stephen from 1994; Chair Worc Dioc Ho of Clergy; Chair Worc DBE
GS 2008– *Tel:* 01905 452169
email: sw.currie@virgin.net

CUTTELL, Very Revd Jeffrey Charles B Sc, PhD
Derby Cathedral Centre, 18–19 Iron Gate, Derby DE1 3GP [DEAN OF DERBY] *b* 59 *edu* Trin Coll Bris; *CV* C Normanton 1987–91; V 1991–95; Producer Relig Progr BBC Radio Stoke 1995– 97; Presenter Relig Progr BBC 1997–99; CF (TA) 1997–2006; R Astbury and Smallwood *Ches* 1999–2008; RD Congleton 2004–08; Assoc Lect Th Univ of Wales (Cardiff) 2001–06; Tutor St Mich Coll Llan 2001–06; Dean of Derby from 2008.
Tel: 01332 341201
Fax: 01332 203991
email: dean@derbycathedral.org

CUTTING, Revd Alastair Murray, B Ed, MA, L Th, DPS
St John's Vicarage Church Rd Copthorne Crawley RH10 3RD [CHICHESTER] *b* 1960 *educ* Geo Watson's Coll Edin; Lushington Sch Ooty, S India; Watford Boy's Gr Sch; Westhill Coll Birm; Heythrop Coll Lon; St Jo Coll Nottm; *CV* C All SS Woodlands, Sheff 1987–88; C Wadsley, Sheff 1989–91; Chapl to Nave and Town Cen, Uxbridge, Lon 1991–96; V Copthorne, Chich from 1996; M Bp's Coun; Asst RD E Grinstead
GS 2005– *Tel:* 01342 712063
07736 676106 (Mobile)
Fax: 01342 712063
email: acutting@mac.com

DAILEY, Miss Prudence Mary Prior, MA
15 Northfield Rd Headington Oxford OX3 9EW [OXFORD] *b* 1965 *educ* Simon Langton Gr Sch for Girls Cant; K Sch Cant; Mert Coll Ox; *CV* NHS Gen Mgt Trainee and various admin posts in NIIS 1988–97; Ox City Coun 1992–96; Sen Business Systems Analyst, Toys 'R' Us from 1998; Chair Prayer Book Soc
GS 2000– *Tel:* 01865 766023
07730 516620 (Mobile)
email: prudence.dailey@tiscali.co.uk

DAKIN, Canon Timothy John, BA, MTh
3 Highgrove Place Ruscombe Reading RG10 9LF [OXFORD] *b* 1958 *educ* Priory Sch Shrewsbury; St Mary's Sch Nairobi; Henley Sixth Form Coll; St Mark's and St Jo Coll Plymouth; Ch Ch Ox; Carlile Coll Nairobi; *CV* Prin Carlile Coll, Nairobi 1993–2000; Gen Sec CMS from 2000; Can Theol Cov Cathl from 2001; M MPA Coun; M PWM Panel
GS 2005– *Tel:* 0118 934 3909
email: timdakin@freenet.co.uk

DALES, Mr Martin Paul,
Priory Cottage Old Malton YO17 7HB [YORK] *b* 1955 *educ* St Dunstan's Coll; Bretton Hall; Open Univ; *CV* Dep Hd, Housemaster and Dir of Music various schs 1976–94; Freelance musician, tchr and composer from 1994; Organist and Choirmaster from 1976, St Edw the Confessor York from 1998; freelance broadcaster from 1976, BBC Radio York from 1994; music publisher from 1981; Media Relations Officer RSCM NE Yorks Area (Sec 2000–02); media and PR Adv various: Coun Malton Town Coun 1989–99, 2003– (Mayor 1991–92, 1996–97); Vc Chair Amotherby Sch Govs; M Dioc Syn from 1995; M Coun for Min and Trg 1998–2000; M Abp's Coun; M Revision Cttee Draft Amending Canon No 22; M Appts Cttee; M Ho of Laity Stg Cttee; M CCU; M CMEAC; M CTE Forum and CTBI Assembly; past Chair Chs Together in S Ryedale; M EKD Delegation 2005
GS 1995– *Tel:* 01653 600990
07764 985009 (Mobile)
Fax: 08707 064748
email: mpd@martindales.me.uk

DALLISTON, Very Revd Christopher Charles, MA
The Deanery 26 Mitchell Avenue Newcastle upon Tyne NE2 3LA [DEAN OF NEWCASTLE] *b* 1956 *educ* Diss Gr Sch; Peterhouse Cam; St Steph Ho Ox; *CV* C St Andr Halsead w H Trin and Greenstead Green 1984–87; Dom Chapl to Bp of Chelms 1987–91; V St Edm Forest Gate, Chelms 1991–95; V St Botolp w St Chris Boston 1995–2003; Dean of Newcastle from 2003   *Tel:* 0191 281 6554
0191 232 1939
email: dean@stnicnewcastle.co.uk

DALLOW, Revd Gillian Margaret, BA, M Ed, PGCE, CEM
57 The High St Northwood Middlesex HA6 1EB [SYNODICAL SECRETARY, CONVOCATION OF CANTERBURY] *b* 1945 *educ* Cathays High Sch Cardiff; Univ of N Wales Bangor; Bris Univ; Oak Hill Th Coll; W of Eng Univ; *CV* Tchr Mill St Sec Mod Sch Pontypridd 1968–70; Hd of RE Heref High Sch for Girls 1970–73; Hd of RE and Student Counselling Heref Sixth Form Coll 1973–74; Scripture Union Schs Worker S West and Wales 1974–79; Hd of RE Colston's Girls Sch Bris 1979–85; Dioc Educ Adv B & W 1985–91; Dir Tr Lon Bible Coll 1991–98; Adv for Children's Min and P-in-c St Giles Barlestone from 1999; Dioc Dir Under 25s Trg from 2002; Synodical Sec, Conv of Cant from 2006; M C of E Evang Coun from 2006; Sec Eggs (Evangs on GS) from 2009
GS 2000–05   *Tel:* 01923 827149
07801 650187 (Mobile)
email: gdallow@btinternet.com

DAVIES, Revd Dr John Harverd, MA, M Phil, PhD
Vicarage Church Square Melbourne DE73 8JH [DERBY] *b* 1957 *educ* Brentwood Sch; Keble Coll Ox; Corpus Christi Coll Cam; Lancaster Univ; Westcott Ho; *CV* C Liv Par Ch 1984–87; C Peterb Par Ch and Minor Can Peterb Cathl 1987–90; V St Marg Anfield, Liv 1990–94; Chapl, Fell and Dir of Studies in Theol, Keble Coll Ox 1994–99; V Melbourne and DDO Derby Dioc from 1999; M Derby Dioc Bd for Min; M Dioc Syn; M GS Theol Educ and Trg Cttee from 2006
GS 2005–   *Tel:* 01332 862347
email: jhd@rdplus.net

DAVIES, Mr John,
Vicarage Cottages Baughurst Rd Ramsdell Tadley RG26 5SH [WINCHESTER] *CV* Elected to GS 2005
GS 2005–

DAVIES, Rt Revd Mark, BA, Cert PS
The Hollies Manchester Rd Rochdale OL11 3QY [BISHOP OF MIDDLETON; MANCHESTER DIOCESE] *b* 1962 *educ* Hanley High Sch; Stoke-on-Trent Sixth Form Coll; Univ Coll of Ripon and York St Jo; Mirfield Th Coll; *CV* C St Mary Barnsley 1989–92; P-in-c St Paul Old Town Barnsley 1992–95; R Hemsworth from 1995; Asst DDO from 1998; RD Pontefract from 2000; Hon Can Wakef Cathl

2002–06; Adn of Rochdale 2006–08; Bp of Middleton from 2008
GS 2000–06   *Tel:* 01706 358550
Fax: 01706 354851
email: bishopmark@manchester.anglican.org

DAVIES, Ven Tony (Vincent Anthony), FRSA
St Matthew's House 100 George St Croydon CR0 1PJ [ARCHDEACON OF CROYDON; SOUTHWARK] *b* 1946 *educ* Green Lane Sec Mod Sch Leic; Brasted Th Coll; St Mich Coll Llan; *CV* C St Jas Owton Manor Hartlepool 1973–76; C St Faith Wandsworth 1976–78, V 1978–81; V St Jo Walworth 1981–93; RD S'wark and Newington 1988–93; Adn of Croydon from 1994   *Tel:* 020 8688 2943 (Home)
020 8256 9630 (Office)
Fax: 020 8256 9631
email: tony.davies@southwark.anglican.org

DE WIT, Ven John, MA
Van Hogendorpstraat 26 Utrecht The Netherlands 3581 KE [ARCHDEACON OF NORTH WEST EUROPE] *b* 1947 *educ* The Leys Sch Cam; Oriel Coll Ox; Clare Coll Cam; Westcott Ho Cam; *CV* Asst C Quinton Birm 1978–81; TV St Michael Solihull 1981–85; V All Saints Kings Heath Birm 1985–94; Area Dean Moseley Birm 1991–94; P-in-C Hampton-in-Arden Birm 1994–2004; Chap Holy Trin Utrecht from 2004; Sec Birm Dioc Liturg Cttee 1981–87; M Birm DAC 1988–2004   *Tel:* 00 31 30 251 34 24

DELANEY, Ven Peter Anthony, AKC, MBE
The Archdeacon of London The Old Deanery, Dean's Court London EC4V 5AA [ARCHDEACON OF LONDON] *b* 1939 *educ* Hendon Gr Sch; Hornsey Coll of Art; K Coll Lon; St Boniface Coll Warminster; *CV* C St Marylebone 1966–70; Chapl Univ Ch of Ch the K 1970–74; Res Can and Prec S'wark Cathl 1974–77; V All Hallows by the Tower 1977–2004; Can of Nicosia and Sr Commissary Dioc of Cyprus and the Gulf from 1984; Preb St Paul's Cathl 1995–99; V St Katharine Cree 1997–2000; R St Steph Walbrook from 2002; Adn of Lon from 1999; M DAC from 1980, Chair from 2004; M Dioc Syn from 1995
GS 1985–90   *Tel:* 020 7236 7891
Fax: 020 7248 7455
email: archdeacon.london@london.anglican.org

DELAP, Ms Dana Lrske, BA, MA, Dip SW
9 Wanless Terrace Durham DH1 1RU [DURHAM] *b* 1965 *educ* Lancaster Girls' Gr Sch; St Jo Coll Dur; *CV* Pastl Asst St Pet Monkwearmouth 1997–99; Dioc Devel Officer for Common Worship 1998–2001; M Dioc Liturg Cttee; Liturg Commn from 2001; substitute Chapl HMP Low Newton
GS 2000–   *Tel:* 0191 384 3854
07952 096789 (Mobile)
email: Dana@delap.org.uk

DENNEN, Ven Dr Lyle, LLB, MA, Ph D
St Andrew's Vicarage 5 St Andrew Street London EC4A 3AB [ARCHDEACON OF HACKNEY; LONDON] *b*

1942 *educ* Harvard Univ; Trin Coll Cam; Cuddesdon Th Coll; *CV* C St Ann S Lambeth 1972–75; C St Mary Richmond 1975–78; P-in-c St Jo Kennington 1978–79, V 1979–99; RD Brixton 1990–99; Hon Can S'wark Cathl from 1999; Adn of Hackney from 1999; V St Andr Holborn from 1999

Tel: 020 7353 3544
Fax: 020 7583 2750
email: archdeacon.hackney@london.anglican.org

DERBY, Archdeacon of. See CUNLIFFE, Ven Dr Christopher John

DERBY, Bishop of. See REDFERN, Rt Revd Dr Alastair Llewellyn John

DERBY, Dean of. See CUTTELL, Very Revd Jeffrey

DESMOND ALBAN SSF, Brother, BSc, Akc, PGCE
The Friary of St Francis Alnmouth Alnwick NE66 3NJ [RELIGIOUS COMMUNITIES (LAITY)] *b* 1964 *educ* The Wavell Sch; Farnborough 6th Form Coll; Kings Coll Lon; Univ of Ex; *CV* SSF from 1993; SSF Provincial Sec (Eur Province) from 2002
GS 2008–
Tel: 01665 830213
Fax: 01665 830580
email: desmondalbanssf@franciscans.org.uk

DINNEN, Dr John Sheridan, MB, BS, B Sc, AKC, FRC Path
Minstercote Much Birch Hereford HR2 8HT [HEREFORD] *b* 1947 *educ* Portora Royal Sch; K Coll Lon; *CV* Consult pathologist, Hereford; M Heref Dioc Syn, Bp's Coun, Coun for World Partnership and Devel, Dioc Ecum Cttee, Chs Together in Herefordshire; Chair Vacancy-in-see Cttee, Heref Chr Aid Cttee, Heref Fair Trade Strg Cttee; pt fair trader with Traidcraft
GS 2005–
Tel: 01981 540730
07855 444995 (Mobile)
email: john@dinnen.plus.com

DOE, Rt Revd Michael David, BA, LLD (Hon)
USPG: Anglicans in World Mission 200 Great Dover St London SE1 4YB [GENERAL SECRETARY, USPG: ANGLICANS IN WORLD MISSION; HONORARY ASSISTANT BISHOP OF SOUTHWARK] *b* 1947 *educ* Brockenhurst Gr Sch; Dur Univ; Ripon Hall Th Coll; *CV* C St Pet St Helier 1972–76, Hon C 1976–81; Youth Sec BCC 1976–81; V Blackbird Leys LEP Ox 1981–89; RD Cowley 1987–89; Soc Resp Adv Portsm 1989–94; Can Res Portsm Cathl 1989–94; Bp of Swindon 1994–2004; Convenor CTE 1999–2003; Gen Sec USPG from 2004
GS 1990–94, 2000–04
Tel: 020 7378 5661
020 7378 5678
Fax: 020 7378 5650
email: michaeld@uspg.org.uk

DONCASTER, Archdeacon of.
See FITZHARRIS, Ven Robert Aidan

DONCASTER, Suffragan Bishop of.
See ASHTON, Rt Revd Cyril Guy

DORBER, Very Revd Adrian John, BA, M Th
The Deanery 16 The Close Lichfield WS13 7LD [DEAN OF LICHFIELD] *b* 1952 *educ* St Jo Coll, Dur Univ; K Coll Lon; Westcott Ho Cam; *CV* C Easthampstead, Bracknell, Ox 1979–85; Dny Youth Officer 1982–85; P-in-c St Barn Emmer Green 1985–88; Chapl Portsm Poly 1988–92, Lect 1991–97, Sen Chapl, Public Orator Portsm Univ 1992–97; Hon Chapl Portsm Cathl 1992–97; P-in-c Brancepeth, Dur 1997–2001; Dir Min and Trg 1997–2005; Hon Can Dur Cathl 1997–2005; Dean of Lichfield from 2005; M Dioc Syn and Bp's Coun; Gov Staffordshire Univ; M Ch Leaders' Oversight Grp, W Midlands Regional Trg Partnership; Chair Lich Local Min Scheme Governing Body
Tel: 01543 306294 (Home)
01543 306250 (Office)
Fax: 01543 306251
email: adrian.dorber@lichfield-cathedral.org

DORCHESTER, Area Bishop of.
See FLETCHER, Rt Revd Colin William

DORKING, Archdeacon of. See HENDERSON, Ven Julian Tudor

DORKING, Suffragan Bishop of.
See BRACKLEY, Rt Revd Ian James

DORMOR, Revd Duncan James, MA, MSc, BA
St John's College Cambridge CB2 1TP [UNIVERSITIES, CAMBRIDGE] *b* 1967 *educ* Sherborne Sch; Magd Coll Ox; Lon Sch of Hygiene and Tropical Medicine; Ripon Coll Cuddesdon; *CV* C Wolverhampton Cen Par, Lich 1995–98; Chapl, St Jo Coll Cam 1998–2002, Dean and Fell from 2002; affiliated lect, Faculty of Div, Cam Univ from 2004; M Coun of Westcott Ho
GS 2005–
Tel: 01223 338633
email: djd28@cam.ac.uk

DORSET, Archdeacon of. See MAGOWAN, Ven Alistair James

DOVER, Suffragan Bishop of. See VENNER, Rt Revd Stephen Squires

DOW, Canon Andrew John Morrison, MA (Oxon)
The Rectory Thorncliffe Drive Cheltenham GL51 6PY [GLOUCESTER] *b* 1946 *educ* St Alb Sch; Univ Coll Ox; Oak Hill Theo Coll; *CV* C St Luke's Watford 1971–74; P-in-c St Saviour's Chadderton 1974–78; V St Paul's Leamington Spa 1978–88; V St John the Baptist Knowle 1988–97; V Ch Ch Clifton 1997–2004; R and Area Dean Cheltenham from 2004; Chair Patronage Bd of Ch Pastl Aid Soc
GS 1995–97, 2008–
Tel: 01242 701580
email: andrewdow@blueyonder.com

DOW, Rt Revd (Geoffrey) Graham, MA, M Sc, M Phil, DPS
Rose Castle Dalston Carlisle CA5 7BZ [BISHOP OF CARLISLE] *b* 1942 *educ* St Geo Sch Harpenden; St Alb Sch; Qu Coll Ox; Nottm Univ; Birm Univ;

Clifton Th Coll; *CV* C St Pet and St Paul Tonbridge 1967–72; Chapl St Jo Coll Ox 1972–75; Lect in Chr Doct St Jo Coll Nottm 1975–81; V H Trin Cov 1981–92; Can Th Cov Cathl 1988–92; Bp of Willesden 1992–2000; Bp of Carlisle from 2000
GS 1999–					*Tel:* 01697 476274
					Fax: 01697 476550
email: bishop.carlisle@carlislediocese.org.uk

DOWDLE, Canon Cynthia,
Vicarage Tithebarn Rd Knowsley Village Prescot L34 0JA [LIVERPOOL] *b* 1948 *educ* Cranmer Hall; *CV* C All Hallows Allerton 1990–94; TR Halewood 1994–2000; V Knowsley from 2000; Dean of Women's Min from 2001; Chair, Partners in Miss from 2000
GS 2004–					*Tel:* 0151 546 4266
			email: cynthiadowdle@hotmail.com

DOWN, Ven Philip Roy, MA, M Th, ARMIT, CCPE
The Old Rectory The Street Pluckley Ashford TN27 0QT [ARCHDEACON OF MAIDSTONE; CANTERBURY] *b* 1953 *educ* Lakeside and Watsonia High Sch, Victoria, Australia; R Melbourne Inst of Tech; Melbourne Coll of Div; Hull Univ; *CV* Parish P Brighton, Victoria (Uniting Ch in Australia) 1982–86; Scunthorpe Circuit (Br Meth Conf) 1986–89; C St Mary and St Jas Gt Grimsby, Linc 1989–91, TV 1991–95; R St Steph Cant 1995–2002; AD Cant 1999–2002; Adn of Maidstone from 2002; M DAC; M Dioc Property and Pastl Cttees; Chair Dioc Bd of Min and Trg, Archbp's Coun, Dioc Syn
GS 2005–					*Tel:* 01233 840291
					Fax: 01233 840759
			email: pdown@archdeacmaid.org

DRIVER, Ven Penny (Penelope May), M Ed, Cert Ed, MA Adult Ed
Emmanuel House Station Rd Ide Exeter EX2 9RS [ARCHDEACON OF EXETER] *b* 1952 *educ* All SS Coll Tottenham; Nn Ord Course; Man Univ; *CV* Dioc Youth Adv Newc 1986–88; C St Geo Cullercoats 1987–88; Dioc Youth Chapl Ripon from 1988–96; Min Can Ripon Cathl from 1996; Dioc Adv for Women's Min from 1991; Asst DDO 1996–98; DDO 1998–2006; Hon Can 1998–2006; M CNC from 2003; Adn of Exeter from 2006
GS 1995–2006			*Tel and Fax:* 01392 425577
email: archdeacon.of.exeter@exeter.anglican.org

DUDLEY, Archdeacon of. See TRETHEWEY, Ven Frederick Martyn

DUDLEY, Suffragan Bishop of. See WALKER, Rt Revd David Stuart

DUNLOP, Mrs Jennifer Mary, LLB
180a Dowson Rd Hyde SK14 5BW [CHESTER] *b* 1951 *educ* Woking Gr Sch for Girls; Hull Univ; *CV* Solicitor Dukinfield 1975–81; M Dioc Syn from

1988; Family Solicitor in Salford from 1995; Lay Chair Mottram Dny Syn 1990–2000
GS 2000–					*Tel:* 0161 368 2149
			email: jennydunlop2004@yahoo.co.uk

DUNNETT, Revd John Frederick, MA, MSc, BA, CQSW
39 Crescent Rd Warley Brentwood Essex CM14 5JR [CHELMSFORD] *b* 1958 *educ* K Edw Sch Edgbaston; Sidney Sussex Coll Cam; Worc Coll Ox; Trin Coll Bris; *CV* Rsch Asst and Press Officer to Bp of B&W 1987–88; C Kirkheaton Par Ch 1988–93; V St Luke Cranham Park 1993–2006; Gen Dir CPAS from 2006
GS 2005–					*Tel:* 01277 221419
			email: jd@johndunnett.co.uk

DUNWICH, Suffragan Bishop of. See YOUNG, Rt Revd Clive

DURHAM, Archdeacon of. See JAGGER, Ven Ian

DURHAM, Bishop of. See WRIGHT, Rt Revd (Nicholas) Thomas

DURHAM, Dean of. See SADGROVE, Very Revd Michael

DYER, Mrs Kay, BA, Cert Ed
6 Sycamore Close Stratford-upon-Avon CV37 0DZ [COVENTRY] *b* 1949 *educ* Blakedown High Sch Leamington Spa; Open Univ; Wolverhampton Univ; *CV* County Ecum Officer, Cov and Warw from 2004; OU tutor from 2003; Chair Cov Dioc Youth Initiative 1997–2001; Children's Work Co-ord, St Andrew Shottery, Stratford-upon-Avon from 2005
GS 2005–					*Tel:* 01789 298299
			email: kay.dyer@ntlworld.com

DYKE, Revd Elizabeth Muriel, B Sc, PGCE, Dip HE
11 Critchley Drive Dunchurch Rugby CV22 6PJ [COVENTRY] *b* 1955 *educ* Harrogate High Sch; Dur Univ; St Mart Coll Lanc; Oak Hill Th Coll; *CV* C St Andr High Wycombe 1994–95; C Bledlow Ridge, Bradenham, Radnage & W Wycombe 1995–97; TV Bedworth 1997–2002; V Dunchurch w. Thurlaston from 2002; Dir of Rdr Initial Trg 2002–08
GS 2004–					*Tel:* 01788 810274
			email: elizabeth.dyke@surefish.co.uk

EAST RIDING, Archdeacon of. See BUTTERFIELD, Ven David John

EASTERN ARCHDEACONRY (Europe). See CURRAN, Ven Patrick Martin Stanley

EBBSFLEET, Bishop of. See BURNHAM, Rt Revd Andrew

EDDY, Mr Paul Anthony, FRSA, MCIOJ
38 Farm Rd Chilwell Nottingham NG9 5BZ [WIN-CHESTER] *b* 1967 *educ* Bedminster Down Comp Sch, Bris; *CV* PA to Solicitors, Bris 1984–88; PR consult and journalist from 1988; M Bournemouth Dny Syn; M PCC of St Paul, Throop; M Winch Dioc Syn
GS 2005–   *Tel and Fax:* 0115 922 4805
                  email: paul@pauleddy.org

EDMONDSON, Rt Revd Christopher Paul, BA, Dip Th, MA, MBII
Bishop's Lodge Walkden Rd Worsley Manchester M28 2WH [BISHOP OF BOLTON] *b* 1950 *educ* Blandford Gr Sch Dorset; Univ of Durham; Cranmer Hall, St John's Coll Dur; *CV* C Kirkheaton Par Ch 1973–79; V Ovenden St George 1979–86; Bp's Adv on Evang 1981–86; Dioc Officer for Evang and P-in-C Bampton, Carl 1986–92; V Shrimpley St Peter, Bradf 1992–2002; Warden Lee Abbey 2002–08; Bp of Bolton from 2008; Bp's Coun Carl 1989–1992; Chair Bradf Dioc Pastl Cttee 1994–2002; Dir SNWTP from 2002; M Bp's Coun Man from 2008   *Tel:* 0161 790 8289
                  Fax: 0161 703 9157
email: bishopchris@manchester.anglican.org

EDMONDSON, Very Revd Dr John James William, BA, Cert Th, MA, PhD
The Deanery Caldbec Hill Battle TN33 0JY [DEAN OF BATTLE] *b* 1955 *educ* Strode's Sch, Egham; Dur Univ; Cranmer Hall, Dur; *CV* C Gee Cross, Ches 1983–86; C St Paul Camberley, Guildf 1986–88; TV 1988–90; Chapl Elmhurst Ballet Sch, Camberley 1986–90; V Foxton w. Gumley and Laughton and Lubenham, Leic 1990–94; R St Mark Bexhill, Chich 1994–2005; Chich Dioc Vocations Adv 1998–2002; Asst DDO, Chich 2002–05; Dean of Battle, V Battle, Chich from 2005; P-in-c Sedlescombe and Whatlington, Chich 2005–07
                  Tel and Fax: 01424 772693

EDMONTON, Area Bishop of.
See WHEATLEY, Rt Revd Peter William

ELCOCK, Dr Martin, BA, MB, Ch B
The Cottage 3 Digbeth Lane Claverley Wolverhampton WV5 7BP [HEREFORD] *b* 1963 *educ* Oldbury Wells Comp Sch Bridgnorth; Bris Univ; Man Univ; *CV* GP; Chair Good Shepherd Trust (homelessness and social inclusion charity in W Midlands/Derbys); primary sch gov
GS 2000–   *Tel:* 01746 710423
                  07971 784639 (Mobile)

ELLIS, Rt Revd Tim (Timothy William), D Phil, AKC
Saxonwell Rectory Church St Long Bennington Newark NG23 5ES [SUFFRAGAN BISHOP OF GRANTHAM; LINCOLN] *b* 1953 *educ* City Sch Sheff; K Coll Lon; York Univ; St Aug Cant; *CV* C St Jo Old Trafford 1976–80; V St Tho Pendleton 1980–

87; Chapl Salford Coll of Tech 1980–87; V St Leon Norwood, Sheff 1987–2001; P-in-c St Hilda Shiregreen, Sheff 1994–97; Adn of Stow and Lindsey 2001–2006; Vc Chair CCC; FAC York Min, Sheff Cathl, Linc Cathl; Bp of Grantham from 2006
                  Tel: 01400 283344
                  Fax: 01400 283321
email: bishop.grantham@lincoln.anglican.org

ELY, Bishop of. See RUSSELL, Rt Revd Anthony John

ELY, Dean of. See CHANDLER, Very Revd Dr Michael John

EUROPE, Archdeacon in North-West. See VAN LEEUWEN, Ven Dirk Willem

EUROPE, Bishop of Gibraltar in. See ROWELL, Rt Revd (Douglas) Geoffrey

EUROPE, Suffragan Bishop in. See HAMID, Rt Revd David

EVENS, Rt Revd Robert John Scott, ACIB, Dip Th
32 The Avenue Tiverton EX16 4HW [SUFFRAGAN BISHOP OF CREDITON; EXETER] *b* 1947 *educ* Maidstone Gr Sch; Trin Coll Bris; *CV* C St Simon Southsea 1977–79; C St Mary Portchester 1979–83; V St Jo Bapt Locks Heath 1983–96; RD Fareham 1993–96; Adn of Bath 1996–2004; Chair Som Chs Together 1996–2000; Suff Bp of Crediton from 2004; Chair Coun for Worship and Min from 2004; Chair Devon Chs Together from 2007
GS 1994–95, 2000–04   *Tel:* 01884 250002
                  Fax: 01884 257454
email: bishop.of.crediton@exeter.anglican.org

EXETER, Archdeacon of. See DRIVER, Ven Penny (Penelope May)

EXETER, Bishop of. See LANGRISH, Rt Revd Michael Laurence

EXETER, Dean of. See MEYRICK, Very Revd (Cyril) Jonathan

FALEY, Revd Monsignor Andrew James,
Catholic Bishops' Conference of England and Wales 39 Eccleston Square London SW1V 1BX [ECUMENICAL REPRESENTATIVE (ROMAN CATHOLIC CHURCH)] *b* 1954
GS 2007–   *Tel:* 020 7901 4811
                  Fax: 020 7901 4821
email: andrew.faley@cbcew.org.uk

FARRELL, Mr (Michael Geoffrey) Shaun,
Dip MAN, FCMI, Lic CIPD
Church House Great Smith St London SW1P 3PS [SECRETARY AND CHIEF EXECUTIVE TO THE CHURCH OF ENGLAND PENSIONS BOARD] *b* 1950 *educ* Gillingham Gr Sch; Open Univ; *CV* On staff of Ch Commrs 1969–98; Commercial Property Mgr 1991–94; Stipends and Allocations Sec 1994–98;

Fin Sec AC 1999–2004; Sec and Chief Exec C of E Pensions Bd from 2004 *Tel:* 020 7898 1800 *Fax:* 020 7898 1801 *email:* shaun.farrell@cepb.c-of-e.org.uk

FARTHING, Revd Paul Andrew, BA, STM, Dip Min
Vicarage Rangemore St Burton-on-Trent DE14 2ED [LICHFIELD] *b* 1958 *educ* Wilsons Gr Sch Camberwell; Vanier Coll Montreal; McGill Univ Montreal; Montreal Dioc Th Coll; *CV* C St Phil Montreal W 1983–85; R St Jo Divine Verdun 1985–96; R St Jo Ev Montreal 1996–99; V St Aidan and St Paul and P-in-c St Modwen Burton-on-Trent from 1999; M Gen Syn Angl Ch of Canada 1989–95; M Doct and Worship Cttee Angl Ch of Canada 1989–92; M Lichf Dioc Syn from 2000; M DBF from 2000
GS 2000– *Tel:* 01283 544054 *email:* p.farthing@ukonline.co.uk

FAULL, Very Revd Vivienne Frances, MA, BA, MBA
21 St Martin's Leicester LE1 5DE [DEAN OF LEICESTER] *b* 1955 *educ* Qu Sch Ches; St Hilda's Coll Ox; Nottm Univ; Open Univ Business Sch; St Jo Coll Nottm; *CV* Dss St Matt and St Jas Mossley Hill 1982–85; Chapl Clare Coll Cam 1985–90; Chapl Glouc Cathl 1990–94; Can Pastor Cov Cathl 1994–2000; Vc Prov Cov Cath 1995–2000; Prov of Leic 2000–02; Dean of Leic from 2002
GS 1987–90, 2004– *Tel:* 0116 248 7456 (Office) 0116 270 1630 (Home) *Fax:* 0116 2487470 *email:* viv.faull@LecCofE.org

FEIST, Canon Nicholas James, L Th
Middleton Rectory Mellalieu St Middleton Manchester M24 5DN [MANCHESTER] *b* 1945 *educ* Merchant Taylors Sch; Lon Coll of Law; St Jo Coll Nottm; *CV* Solicitor; C St Jas and Em Didsbury 1976–80; V St Thos Friarmere 1980–88; R St Leon Middleton 1988–94; TR Middleton and Thornham from 1994; Hon Can Man Cathl from 1998; AD Heywood and Middleton 1999–2007; M Dioc Syn; M Bp's Coun; Dioc Fin Cttee; GS Legal Aid Commn from 2001
GS 2000– *Tel and Fax:* 0161 643 2693 *email:* nickjfeist@ntlworld.com

FELIX, Revd David Rhys, LLB, Cert Th
Vicarage Daresbury Warrington WA4 4AE [CHESTER] *b* 1955 *educ* Calday Grange County Gr Sch; Univ of Wales; Ripon Coll, Cuddesdon; *CV* C St Barn Bromborough 1986–89; V St Andr Grange, Runcorn 1989–99; Chapl Halton Gen Hosp 1995–99; P-in-c H Trin Runcorn 1996–99; RD Frodsham 1998–99; Ind Missr, Halton 1998–99; V All SS Daresbury from 1999; Sen Ind Missr Chester Dio 2000–08; M Dioc Adv Bd for Min 1988–90; M Dioc Adoption Services Cttee 1990–92; Dny Ord Chapl 1990–96; M Dioc Pastl Grp 1994–95; M Dioc Syn from 1994; Dir DBF and M Bp's Coun from 1995; M Dioc Bd of Educ and Schs Cttee 1997–2003; M

Archidiaconal Pastl Cttee 1992–94 and from 1998; M Eccl Law Soc from 1987 and of Gen Cttee from 2002; M Dioc Cttee for Miss and Unity 2001–08; Hon Can Ches Cathl 2006
GS 2002– *Tel:* 01925 740348 07778 859935 (Mobile) *email:* david.felix@btinternet.com

FERGUSON, Mr John William,
Church House Great Smith St London SW1P 3AZ [HEAD OF INFORMATION TECHNOLOGY AND OFFICE SERVICES, ARCHBISHOPS' COUNCIL] *b* 1947 *educ* Jo Watson's Sch Edin; *CV* Computer Services Mgr Matthew Hall Grp 1981; Computer Services Mgr Ch Commrs from 1981; Computer and Office Services Mgr from 1994; Hd of Information Technology and Office Services AC from 1998
Tel: 020 7898 1666 *email:* john.ferguson@c-of-e.org.uk

FERGUSON, Ven Paul John, MA, FRCO (CHM), PGCE
48 Langbaurgh Road Hutton Rudby Yarm TS15 0HL [ARCHDEACON OF CLEVELAND; YORK] *b* 1955 *educ* Birkenhead Sch; New Coll Ox; Westmr Coll Ox; K Coll Cam; Westcott Ho Th Coll; *CV* C St Mary Chester 1985–88; Chapl and Sacr Westmr Abbey 1988–92; Prec Westmr Abbey 1992–95; Prec and Res Can York Minster 1995–2001; Adn of Cleveland from 2001; Wrdn of Rdrs from 2004; Sec Ho Bps' Th Grp 1992–2001 *Tel:* 01642 706095 07770 592746 (Mobile) *email:* archdeacon.of.cleveland@yorkdiocese.org

FIDDES, Revd Prof Paul, MA, D Phil, DD
Regent's Park College Pusey St Oxford OX1 2LB [ECUMENICAL REPRESENTATIVE] *b* 1947 *educ* St Pet Coll, Ox; Regent's Park Coll, Ox; *CV* Principal, Regent's Park Coll, Ox; Prof of Systematic Theol, Ox Univ; Min of Bapt Union of Gt Britain
GS 2005– *Tel:* 01865 288134 *Fax:* 01865 288121 *email:* paul.fiddes@regents.ox.ac.uk

FINCH, Alderman Robert Gerard, JP
1 Silk Street London EC2Y 8HQ [CHURCH COMMISSIONER] *b* 1944 *educ* Felsted Sch Essex; Coll of Law; *CV* Linklaters from 1969: Asst Solicitor 1969–73, Partner from 1974, Hd of Real Estate 1997–99; Ch Commr from 2000; Sheriff of the City of Lon 1999–2000; Lord Mayor of Lon 2003–04; Master City of Lon Solicitors Co 2000–01; M FRICS (Hon); Trustee Morden Coll; Dir IFSL; Gov Christ's Hosp, K Edw School and Coll of Law; M Coun St Paul's Cathl; Deputy Lieutenant City of Lon 2003; Asst on Court of Worshipful Company of Innholders from 2000; Liveryman of Chartered Surveyors *Tel:* 020 7456 2000 *Fax:* 020 7456 2222

FINCH, Mrs Sarah Rosemary Ann, BA
97 Englefield Rd Canonbury London N1 3LJ [LONDON] *b* 1945 *educ* Godolphin Sch Sarum; Dur

Univ; Ox Univ; *CV* Ed Barrie and Jenkins 1972–75; Trustee BFBS 1978–2005; Chair Exec Cttee BFBS 1991–94; Freelance Non-Fiction Ed from 1986; Gov Sir John Cass's Foundn Primary Sch (C of E) from 1996; M CEEC from 2000; Coun M Latimer Trust from 2003; M Revision Ctee, Common Worship Ordinal; elected M Appts Ctee from 2005; Coun M Oak Hill Theol Coll from 2006; M Angl Mainstream Strg Cttee from 2006; Trustee Latimer Trust from 2007
GS 2000–   *Tel:* 020 7226 2803
                       Fax: 020 7704 2257
    email: sarahrafinch@yahoo.co.uk

FITTALL, Mr William Robert, MA
Church House Great Smith St London SW1P 3AZ [SECRETARY GENERAL OF THE GENERAL SYNOD AND THE ARCHBISHOPS' COUNCIL] *b* 1953 *educ* Dover Gr Sch; Ch Ch Ox; *CV* Home Office 1975–80; Ecole Nat d'Administration Paris 1980–81; Home Office 1981–91; Prin Private Sec to N Ireland Sec 1992–93; Home Office 1993–95; Under Sec and Chief of Assessments Staff, Cabinet Office 1995–97; Dir Crime Reduction and Com Programmes, Home Office 1997–2000; Assoc Political Dir, N Ireland Office 2000–02; Sec Gen GS and AC from 2002   *Tel:* 020 7898 1360
                07738 883712 (Mobile)
                Fax: 020 7898 1369
    email: william.fittall@c-of-e.org.uk

FITZHARRIS, Ven Robert Aidan, BDS
Fairview House 14 Armthorpe Lane Doncaster DN2 5LZ [ARCHDEACON OF DONCASTER; SHEFFIELD] *b* 1946 *educ* St Anselm's Coll Birkenhead; Sheff Univ; Linc Th Coll; *CV* Gen Dental Practitioner 1971–87; pt Clinical Asst Dept Child Dental Health Univ of Sheff 1976–84; Asst C Dinnington St Leonard 1989–1992; V St Pet Bentley 1992–2001; AD Adwick 1995–2001; Hon Can Sheff Cathl from 1998; Substitute Chapl HMP Moorland 1992–2001; Hon Asst Chapl Doncaster R Infirmary from 1995; Eur Link Person from 1997; Adn of Doncaster from 2001; M Bp's Coun from 1995; M Dioc Parsonages Cttee from 1992, Chair from 2001; M Dioc Bd of Educ, Chair from 2001; Chair Dioc Strategy Grp 1999–2001; Surrogate from 2000; Chair Wildwood Project (Bentley) Ltd 1999–2004; Chair Doncaster Cancer Detection Trust from 2003; Chair Doncaster Minster Devel Appeal 2005–07; M Sheff Univ Rsch Ethics Cttee from 2004; Chair Doncaster Re-Furnish Ltd from 2007; M Sheff Univ HR Mgt Cttee from 2006; Chair Together for Regeneration from 2005; Hon Freeman Metrop Boro of Doncaster from 2008
            Tel: 01709 309110 (Office)
                01302 325787 (Home)
                07767 355357 (Mobile)
            Fax: 01709 309107 (Office)
                01302 760493 (Home)

email: archdeacons.office@sheffield.anglican.org

FITZSIMONS, Canon Kathryn Anne, Cert Th, Cert Ed
52 Newton Court Oakwood Leeds LS8 2PH [RIPON AND LEEDS] *b* 1957 *educ* Richmond Sch; Bedford Coll of HE; NEOC; *CV* NSM C St Jo Bilton, Harrogate 1990–2002; Soc Resp Officer 1992–99; Dioc Urban Officer from 1999; Hon Can Ripon Cathl from 2004; Pres Diaconal Assoc of the C of E from 2003; Officer, Mission Resourcing Team; M DBF
GS 2004–   *Tel:* 0113 248 5011
    email: kathrynfitzsimons@hotmail.com

FLACH, Canon Deborah Mary, Dip HE, Dip Counselling
63 Rue de Boissy 60340 St Leu d'Esserent France [EUROPE] *b* 1954 *educ* Beckenham Convent Sch; Trin Coll Bris; Salis and Wells Th Coll; *CV* C St Pet Chantilly, France 1994–96; C H Trin Maisons-Laffitte, France 1996–2004, Asst Chapl 2004–07; M Dioc Syn from 1994; Asst Dir of Ordinands (France) from 1997; P-in-c Ch Ch, Lille (Eur) from 2007
GS 2005–   *Tel:* +33 3 4456 7608 (Home)
   +33 3 2852 6636 (Lille) +33 684985126 (Mobile)
          email: debbieflach@gmail.com

FLETCHER, Rt Revd Colin William, MA, OBE
Arran House Sandy Lane Yarnton Oxford OX5 1PB [AREA BISHOP OF DORCHESTER; OXFORD] *b* 1950 *educ* Marlboro Coll; Tr Coll Ox; Wycliffe Hall Th Coll; *CV* C St Pet Shipley 1975–79; Tutor Wycliffe Hall and C St Andr Ox 1979–84; V H Tr Margate 1984–93; RD Thanet 1989–93; Dom Chapl to Abp of Cant 1993–2000; Canon Dallas Cathl 1993–2000; Bp of Dorchester from 2000
                Tel: 01865 208218
                Fax: 01865 849003
    email: bishopdorchester@oxford.anglican.org

FLETCHER, Mr Philip John, CBE, MA
20 Calais St Camberwell London SE5 9LP [APPOINTED MEMBER, ARCHBISHOPS' COUNCIL] *b* 1946 *educ* Marlborough Coll; Trin Coll Ox; *CV* Dir Gen Cities and Countryside Dept of Environment to 1996; Receiver, Metropolitan Police District 1996–2000; Dir Gen Water Services (OFWAT) 2000–06; Chair OFWAT from 2006
GS 2007–   *Tel:* 0121 625 1350
    email: philip.fletcher@ofwat.gsi.gov.uk

FORD, Rt Revd John Frank, MA
31 Riverside Walk Tamerton Foliot Plymouth PL5 4AQ [SUFFRAGAN BISHOP OF PLYMOUTH; EXETER] *b* 1952 *educ* Chich Th Coll; *CV* C Ch Ch Forest Hill 1979–82; V St Aug Lee 1982–91; V Lower Beeding 1991–94; Dom Chapl to Bp of Horsham 1991–94; Dioc Missr from 1994; Can and Preb Chich Cathl from 1997; Prec of Chich Cathl from 2000; Bp of Plymouth from 2005
GS 1999–2005   *Tel:* 01752 769836
   email: bishop.of.plymouth@exeter.anglican.org

FORSTER, Rt Revd Dr Peter Robert, MA, BD, Ph D
Bishop's House Abbey Square Chester CH1 2JD
[BISHOP OF CHESTER] *b* 1950 *educ* Tudor Grange Gr
Sch Solihull; Merton Coll Ox; Edin Univ; Edin Th
Coll; *CV* C St Matt and St Jas Mossley Hill Liv
1980–82; Sen Tutor St Jo Coll Dur 1983–91; V
Beverley Minster 1991–96; Bp of Ches from 1996;
Ch Commr 1999–2004
GS 1985–91,1996–   *Tel:* 01244 350864
                          Fax: 01244 314187
email: bpchester@chester.anglican.org

FORWARD, Miss Emma Joy, BA
24 Whitchurch Ave Exeter EX2 5NT [EXETER] *b* 1984
educ St Pet C of E High Sch Ex; St Hugh's Coll Ox;
CV Trainee tchr from 2005; full time tchr from
2006
GS 2005–   *Tel:* 01392 251617
                       email: emmaforward@yahoo.co.uk

FOSTER, Rt Revd Christopher Richard James,
BA, MA (ECON), MA
Hertford House Abbey Mill Lane St Albans AL3 4HE
[SUFFRAGAN BISHOP OF HERTFORD, ST ALBANS] *b*
1953 *educ* R Gr Sch Guildf; Dur Univ; Manch
Univ; Trinity Hall Cam, Wescott Ho Cam; *CV*
Lect in Economics Univ of Dur 1976–77; Asst C
Tettenhall Regis TM Wolverhampton 1980–82;
Chapl Wadham Col Ox and Asst P St Mary w St
Cross and St Pet in the East Ox 1982–86; V Ch Ch
Southgate 1986–94; CME Dir Edmonton Area
1988–94; Sub Dean and Res Can St Alb1994–2001;
Bp of Hertford from 2001   *Tel:* 01727 866420
                              Fax: 01727 811426
email: bishophertford@stalbans.anglican.org

FRANCE, Archdeacon of. See LETTS,
Ven Kenneth John

FRASER, Revd Dr Giles,
45 St John's Avenue Putney London SW15 6AL
[SOUTHWARK] *CV* M GS from 2000
GS 2000–

FRASER, Canon Jane Alicia, BA, CQSW
*The Campanile Church Lane Stoulton Worcester WR7
4RE* [WORCESTER] *b* 1944 *educ* N Lon Collegiate
Sch; Man Univ; Birm Univ; Glouc Sch for Min;
CV Various social work posts 1966–90; Projects
Officer, Brook Publications 1980–2000; freelance
trg and consult 1990–2005; Faith Adv, Independ-
ent Adv Grp of Teenage Pregnancy Unit 2000–05;
Chair CSCS (Cen for Study of Christianity and
Sexuality)
GS 2005–   *Tel:* 01905 840266
                      email: ministry@revjane.demon.co.uk

FRAYLING, Very Revd Nicholas Arthur, BA,
Hon LLD, FJMU
The Deanery Canon Lane Chichester PO19 1PX
[DEAN OF CHICHESTER] *b* 1944 *educ* Repton; Ex
Univ; Cuddesdon; *CV* Mgt trg retail trade 1962–
64; prison welfare 1964–66 and part-time 1966–

71; C St Jo Peckham 1971–74; V All SS Tooting
Graveney 1974–83; Can Res and Prec Liv Cathl
1983–87; R Liv 1987–2002; Dean of Chich from
2002; Chair S'wark DAC 1980–83; M Liv Dioc Syn
and Bishop's Coun   *Tel:* 01243 812485 (Office)
                      01243 812494 (Home)
                      Fax: 01243 812499
email: dean@chichestercathedral.org.uk

FREAR, Mrs Jacqueline, T Cert
*Kirk Braddan Vicarage Saddle Rd Braddan Isle of
Man IM4 4LB* [SODOR AND MAN] *b* 1942 *educ*
Annecy Convent Seaford; St Gabr Coll Lon; *CV*
Teaching posts in Beds, Wilts and Avon
GS 2000–   *Tel:* 01624 675523

FREEMAN, Mr John, BA, Ad Dip Ed Mgt, DMS,
Cert Ed, JP
The Smiths' House 99 High St Barwell LE9 8DS
[LEICESTER] *b* 1947 *educ* Hinckley Gr Sch; Open
Univ; De Montfort Univ, Garnett Coll; Birm Coll
of Food; *CV* Lect South Fields Coll Leic 1972–82;
Dir Faculty of Arts, N Herts Coll 1982–99; Ptnr,
The Grove Tavern, Lon 1999–2003; Mgt Consult,
Leic Univ from 2005
GS 2005–   *Tel:* 01455 842548
                      email: j.freeman5@btinternet.com

FREEMAN, Mr John Jeremy Collier, Eur Ing, DLC,
B Sc, MIChemE, C ENG
*Stable Court 20a Leigh Way Weaverham Northwich
CW8 3PR* [CHESTER] *b* 1937 *educ* Embley Park Sch;
Loughb Univ; *CV* Graduate Chemical Engineer
ICI 1961–94 inc Asst to Gen Mgr Magadi Soda
Co, Kenya 1975–77; Rtd 1994, now very active in
vol sector; M Local Agenda 21 Forum; Par Coun
from 1980; Sch Gov from 1980; M Dioc Fin and
Central Services Cttee from 1994; M Exec Chs
Together in Cheshire from 1995; Treas Ch Action
on Poverty from 2004; Chairman Dioc PWM
Cttee; M Dioc CSR Cttee; Chr Aid activist; Sec
Dioc Justice and Devel Educ Grp; M Bp's Coun;
M Dioc Syn; Dioc World Devel Adv; M Core Grp
Angl World Devel Advs; Treas Open Syn Grp;
Companion of the Melanesian Brotherhood
GS 2000–   *Tel:* 01606 852872
                      Fax: 01606 854140
email: jjcfreeman@tiscali.co.uk

FREEMAN, Ven Robert John, B Sc, MA
2 Vicarage Gardens Rastrick Brighouse HD6 3HD
[ARCHDEACON OF HALIFAX; WAKEFIELD] *b* 1952
educ Cambs High Sch; St Jo Coll Dur; Fitzw Coll
Cam; Ridley Hall Cam; *CV* C St Jo Blackpool
1977–81; TV St Winifred Chigwell 1981–85; V Ch
of the Martyrs Leic 1985–99; RD Christianity S
(Leic) 1994–98; Hon Can Leic 1994–2003; Nat
Evang Adv, AC from 1999; Chair rejesus.co.uk
from 2000; Chair Agenda and Support Cttee of
Grp for Evangelisation (CTE) 2000–03; Sec Miss,
Evang and Renewal in Eng Cttee, Bd of Mission,
AC 1999–2003; Dir Just Fairtrade Ltd 2000–03;
Adn of Halifax from 2003; M Chs Regional

Commn for Yorkshire and Humberside 2004; Chair Chr Enquiry Agency from 2006; Trustee Simeon and Hindman's from 2007
GS 1997–99, 2008–   *Tel:* 01484 714553
07980 751902 (Mobile)
Fax: 01484 711897
email: archdeacon.halifax@
wakefield.anglican.org

FRENCH, Mr Philip Colin, MA, MIET, CPhys, MInstP
Arden Five Oak Green Rd Five Oak Green Tonbridge TN12 6TJ [ROCHESTER] *b* 1960 *educ* R Gr Sch Newc; Br Sch Brussels; Churchill Coll Cam; *CV* Rsch Asst, Univ Coll Lon 1984–87; Overseas Career Service Officer, Br Coun 1987–96; (First Sec (Educ & Science), Calcutta 1988–91); Sen Consult, Hewlett-Packard Ltd 1996–99; Tech Dir, Software.com, later Openwave Systems Inc 1999–2003; Hd of Information & Communications Technology, HM Prison Service 2003–08; Chief Info Officer Nat Offender Mgt Service from 2008; Gov F Peckham Primary Sch; M Bp's Coun, Roch Dioc
GS 1985–88, 2005–   *Tel:* 01892 838713 (Home)
020 7217 6486 (Office)
07952 273253 (Mobile)
email: philip.c.french@btinternet.com

FRENCH, Revd Peter Robert, MA, BA (Hons)
67 Cherry Orchard Rd Handsworth Wood Birmingham B20 2LD [BIRMINGHAM] *b* 1965 *educ* Duston Upper Sch, Northn; Man Univ; Queens Birm; *CV* C St George's Unsworth Bury 1990–93; V Christ the King Bury 1993–98; V St Andrew's Handsworth Birm 1998–2006; Schs Support Officer, Birm Dioc from 2006
GS 2003–05, 2008–   *Tel:* 0121 426 0418
email: p.french@birmingham.anglican.org

FRITH, Rt Revd Richard Michael Cokayne, MA
Hullen House Woodfield Lane Hessle HU13 0ES [SUFFRAGAN BISHOP OF HULL; YORK] *b* 1949 *educ* Marlboro Coll; Fitzw Coll Cam; St Jo Coll Nottm; *CV* C Mortlake w E Sheen 1974–78; TV Thamesmead 1978–83; TR Keynsham 1983–92; Adn of Taunton 1992–98; Bp of Hull from 1998
GS 1995–98   *Tel:* 01482 649019
Fax: 01482 647449
email: richard@bishop.karoo.co.uk

FRY, Dr Roger Gordon, BD, AKC, D Litt, FRSA, CBE
Avda Pio XII 92 28036 Madrid Spain [EUROPE] *b* 1943 *educ* Portsm Gr Sch; Lon Univ; *CV* Chair, Coun of Br Independent Schs in the Eur Com from 1996; Chair Coun of Br Internat Schs from 1996; Chair, King's Grp; Dir Independent Schs Coun
GS 1990–95; 2005–   *Tel:* +34 91 3598800
Fax: +34 91 3592767
email: roger.fry@kingsgroup.org

FULHAM, Suffragan Bishop of.
See BROADHURST, Rt Revd John Charles

FULLARTON, Mr Derek, FRSA
Lambeth Palace London SE1 7JU [PATRONAGE SECRETARY TO THE ARCHBISHOP OF CANTERBURY] *b* 1952 *educ* Camphill Sch Paisley; Glasgow Univ; *CV* On staff of Ch Commrs from 1974; on secondment as Private Sec to the Sec-General of GS 1985–89; M Engl Cttee, Friends of Angl Cen in Rome from 1990; Sec Palace Trustees Wells 1992–99; Sec Lambeth Palace Library Trustees 1996–2006; Admin Sec Lambeth Palace 1999–2006; Dir Lambeth Projects (2000) Ltd; Abp's Patronage Sec from 2006
Tel: 020 7898 1252
07771 811681 (Mobile)
Fax: 020 7261 9836
email: derek.fullarton@lambethpalace.org.uk

GARLAND, Canon Tony (Anthony), JP, BSc
46 Abbots Way North Shields NE29 8LX [NEWCASTLE] *b* 1942 *educ* S Shields Gr-Tech Sch; Univ Coll Lon; *CV* Health Service Mgr 1963–93; Chief Exec Chs Acting Together, N Tyneside 1996–2003; Lay Can Newc Cathl 2002; Vol Projects Adv, Newc Dioc 2003–07
GS 2003–   *Tel:* 0191 296 5358
email: tgarland@talk21.com

GARLICK, Preb Kay (Kathleen Beatrice), BA, Cert Ed
Rectory Birch Lodge Much Birch HR2 8HT [HEREFORD] *b* 1949 *educ* Prendergast Gr Sch Catford; Leeds Univ; Birm Univ; Glouc Sch of Min; *CV* Hon C Much Birch w Lt Birch, Much Dewchurch etc 1990–2003; Ecum Chapl Heref Sixth Form Coll 1996–2002; P-in-c Parishes of the Wormelow Hundred from 2003; Rector from 2006; M AC from 2006; Chair GS Business Cttee from 2006
GS 1995–   *Tel:* 01981 540666
email: kaygarlick@hotmail.com

GARNETT, Ven David Christopher, BA, MA
The Vicarage Edensor Bakewell Derbys DE45 1PH [ARCHDEACON OF CHESTERFIELD; DERBY] *b* 1945 *educ* Giggleswick Sch; Nottm Univ; Fitzw Coll Cam; Westcott Ho Th Coll; *CV* C Cottingham 1969–72; Chapl, Fell and Tutor Selw Coll Cam 1972–77; Pastl Adv Newnham Coll Cam 1972–77; R Patterdale 1977–80; DDO Carlisle 1977–80; V Heald Green 1980–87; Chapl St Ann's Hospice 1980–87; R Christleton 1987–92; TR Ellesmere Port 1992–96; Adn of Chesterfield from 1996; Chair Bp's Th Adv Grp 1987–93; Chair Assoc of Ch Fells 1987–92; V Edensor and Beeley from 2007
GS 1990–96, 2000–05   *Tel:* 01246 582130
email: davidcgarnett@yahoo.co.uk

GARRARD, Revd Dr James Richard, BA, MA, D Phil
Vicarage Commons Lane Balderstone Blackburn BB2 7LL [BLACKBURN] *b* 1965 *educ* St Dunstan's Coll; Dur Univ; Leeds Univ; Keble Coll Ox; Westcott

Ho Cam; *CV* C Elland 1994–98; TV Brighouse and Clifton 1998–2001; P-in-c St Leon Balderstone and Dioc Wdn of Rdrs from 2001; M Dioc Syn from 2003; M Coun Coll of Resurrection, Mirfield from 2006
GS 2005– *Tel:* 01254 812232
email: james@balderstonevicarage.co.uk

GERMANY AND NORTHERN EUROPE, Archdeacon of. (NOT APPOINTED AT TIME OF GOING TO PRESS)

GIBRALTAR, Archdeacon of. See DE WITT, Ven John

GIBRALTAR IN EUROPE, Bishop of.
See ROWELL, Rt Revd (Douglas) Geoffrey

GIBRALTAR, Dean of. See PADDOCK, Very Revd John

GIDDINGS, Dr Philip James, MA, D Phil
5 Clifton Park Rd Caversham Reading RG4 7PD [OXFORD] *b* 1946 *educ* Sir Thos Rich's Sch Glouc; Worc and Nuff Colls Ox; *CV* Lect in Public Admin Ex Univ 1970-72; Hd, Sch of Politics and Intl Relations, Reading Univ; Rdr; M Dioc Syn from 1974; M Bp's Coun 1979–2006; Lay Vc Pres Dioc Syn 1989–2000; M BSR 1991–96, Exec Cttee 1992–96; M CAC 1992–97; M GS Panel of Chairmen 1995–96; Vc Chair GS Ho of Laity 1995–2000, 2005–; M AC from 1999; Chair Ch and World Div AC 1999–2002; M Crown Appts Commn Review Grp 1999–2001; Elected M AC from 2000; Chair Coun of MPA from 2003; Convenor, Angl Mainstream UK from 2003
GS 1985– *Tel:* 0118 954 3892 (Home)
0118 378 8207 (Office)
Fax: 0118 975 3833
email: P.J.Giddings@reading.ac.uk

GILLEY, Revd Dr Margaret (Meg) Mary, MTheol, PhD
Vicarage 76 Fairfield Rd Stockton-on-Tees TS19 7BP [DURHAM] *b* 1954 *educ* Nelson Gr Sch; St And Univ; Dur Univ; NEOC; *CV* Primary Care Devel rsch, Sunderland Health Commn 1991–94; Programmes Mgr, Sunderland Health Auth 1994–96; Locality Dir, Co Durham Health Auth 1996–98; Chief Exec, Darlington Primary Care Grp 1998–2000; C St Jo Birtley 2000–03; V St Mark Stockton & St Jo Elton from 2003; M AC Fin Cttee
GS 2005– *Tel:* 01642 586179
07752 432366 (Mobile)
email: meg.gilley@durham.anglican.org

GILLINGS, Ven Richard John, BA
5 Robins Lane Bramhall Stockpot SK7 2PE [ARCHDEACON OF MACCLESFIELD; CHESTER] *b* 1945 *educ* Sale Co Gr Sch; St Chad's Coll Dur; Linc Th Coll; *CV* C St Geo Altrincham 1970–75; P-in-c St Thos Stockport 1975–77; R St Thos Stockport 1977–83 and P-in-c St Pet Stockport 1978–83; R Priory Tm Par Birkenhead 1983–93; RD Birkenhead 1985–93;

Hon Can Ches Cathl 1992–94; V St Mich Bramhall 1993–2005; Adn of Macclesfield from 1994
GS 1980–2005 *Tel:* 0161 439 2254
Fax: 0161 439 0878
email: richard.gillings@chester.anglican.org

GLADWIN, Rt Revd John Warren, MA, Dip Th
Bishopscourt Margaretting Ingatestone CM4 0HD [BISHOP OF CHELMSFORD] *b* 1942 *educ* Hertford Gr Sch; Chu Coll Cam; St Jo Coll Dur; *CV* C St Jo Bapt Kirkheaton 1967–71; Tutor St Jo Coll Dur 1971–77; Dir of Shaftesbury Project 1977–82; Sec to GS BSR 1982–88; Preb of St Paul's Cathl 1984–88; Prov of Sheff 1988–94; Bp of Guildf 1994–2003; Bp of Chelmsf from 2003
GS 1990– *Tel:* 01277 352001
Fax: 01277 355374
email: bishopscourt@chelmsford.anglican.org

GLEDHILL, Rt Revd Jonathan Michael, BA, MA, BCTS, D Univ (Keele)
Bishop's House 22 The Close Lichfield WS13 7LG [BISHOP OF LICHFIELD] *b* 1949 *educ* Strode's Sch Egham; Keele Univ; Bris Univ; Trin Coll Bris; *CV* C All SS Marple 1975–78; P-in-c St Geo Folkestone 1978–83; V St Mary Bredin Cant 1983–96; Tutor/Lect Cant Sch of Min 1983–94; Tutor/Lect SE Inst for Th Educ 1994–96; RD Cant 1988–94; Hon Can Cant Cathl 1992–96; Bp of Southn 1996–2003; M Meissen Commn 1993–96; Chair Angl Old Catholic Internat Consultative Coun from 1998; Chair Nat Coll of Evangelists from 1998; Bp of Lichfield from 2003
GS 1995–96, 2003– *Tel:* 01543 306000
Fax: 01543 306009
email: bishop.lichfield@lichfield.anglican.org

GLOUCESTER, Archdeacon of. See SIDAWAY, Ven Geoffrey Harold

GLOUCESTER, Bishop of. See PERHAM, Rt Revd Michael Francis

GLOUCESTER, Dean of. See BURY, Very Revd Nicholas Ayles Stillingfleet

GNANADOSS, Miss Vasantha Berla Kirubaibai, B Sc
242 Links Rd London SW17 9ER [SOUTHWARK] *b* 1951 *educ* Portsm Gr Sch; Birkbeck Coll Lon; *CV* Commissioner's Secretariat, Metropolitan Police Service
GS 1990– *Tel:* 020 8769 3515
020 7230 5017
07803 590610 (Mobile)
email: vasanthi.gnanadoss@met.police.uk

GODDARD, Rt Revd John William, BA
Dean House 449 Padiham Rd Burnley BB12 6TE [SUFFRAGAN BISHOP OF BURNLEY; BLACKBURN] *b* 1947 *educ* St Chad's Coll Dur Univ; *CV* C S Bank 1970–74; C Cayton w Eastfield 1974–75; V Ascen Middlesbrough 1975–82; RD Middlesbrough

1981–87; V All SS Middlesbrough 1982–88; Can and Preb York Minster 1987–88; Can Emer York from 1988; Vc Prin Edin Th Coll 1988–92; TR Ribbleton 1992–2000; Bp of Burnley from 2000 GS 2008– *Tel:* 01282 470360
07779 786114 (Mobile)
Fax: 01282 470361
email: bishop.burnley@ntlworld.com

GODDARD, Mrs Madelaine, BSc, SRD
35 Princes Drive Littleover Derby DE23 6DX
[DERBY] *b* 1944 *educ* Lewis Sch for Girls; Lon Univ; *CV* Sen Dietitian, Bethnal Green 1967–69; District Dietitian, N Gwent HMC 1969–77; pt tchr, Derby High Sch from 1986; Dioc Pres MU; Tax Commr GS 2003– *Tel:* 01332 348077
07817 043257 (Mobile)
email: goddard35@btinternet.com

GODDARD, Mrs Vivienne, BA, PGCE
Dean House 449 Padiham Rd Burnley BB12 6TE
[BLACKBURN] *b* 1948 *educ* Roch Girls' Gr Sch, Dur Univ; *CV* Bp's Officer for OLM 1996–2007 GS 2000– *Tel:* 01282 470360
07779 786141 (Mobile)
Fax: 01282 470361
email: vivienne.goddard@ntlworld.com

GOLDSMITH, Mr Peter James, FCIH
29 Great Smith St London SW1P 3PS [HOUSING MANAGER, CHURCH OF ENGLAND PENSIONS BOARD] *b* 1958 *educ* Romford Tech High Sch; Anglia Poly Univ; *CV* Area Dir and other posts, Shaftesbury Housing from 1993; Service Delivery Mgr and other posts, Homes in Havering 2005–07; Housing Mgr, C of E Pensions Bd from 2007; Bd M (vol), S Essex Homes from 2007
Tel: 020 7898 1800
Fax: 020 7898 1801
email: peter.goldsmith@c-of-e.org.uk

GOODER, Dr Paula Ruth, MA, D Phil
61 Linden Rd Bournville Birmingham B30 1JT
[BIRMINGHAM] *b* 1969 *educ* Fallowfield C of E H Sch, Loreto Sixth Form Coll, Manch; Worc Coll Ox; Qu Coll Ox; *CV* Tutor in Biblical Studies, Ripon Coll Cuddesdon 1995–2001; Tutor in NT Studies, Qu Foundn from 2001 GS 2005– *Tel:* 0121 744 0260
email: prgooder@gmail.com

GOODING, Canon Ian Eric, B Com, BSc, LTh, Dip PS, C Eng
Rectory Stanhope St Stanton-by-Dale Ilkeston Derbyshire DE7 4QA [DERBY] *b* 1942 *educ* Nottm H Sch; Leeds Univ; St Jo Coll Nottm; *CV* Devel/Production Engineer Turner & Newhall 1965–67, PA to Works Dir 1967–68, Systems Analyst 1968–70; Rdr, Manch Dioc 1968–70; C Wandsworth S'wark 1973–75; C with charge of All SS Wandsworth 1975–77; R Stanton-by-Dale w. Dale Abbey, Derby from 1977, R Risley, Derby from 1994; sen industrial chapl from 1977; RD Erewash from

1997; Hon Can Derby Cathl from 2002; M DBF and Exec Coun DBF; M Bp's Coun; M Derbyshire Ecum Industrial Cttee; Chair Trustees Chr Broadcasting Coun from 1988; Bd M Erewash Local Strategic Ptnrship from 2004; M C of E Pensions Bd from 2006; Chair Stanton-by-Dale Par Coun from 2007 GS 2005– *Tel:* 0115 932 4584
07974 370330 (Mobile)
Fax: 0115 932 4584
email: iangooding@zoom.co.uk

GORE, Mr Philip, BA, MIMgt, FRSA
12 Ellesmere Rd Morris Green Bolton BL3 3JT
[MANCHESTER] *b* 1957 *educ* Smithills Gr Sch Bolton; Hull Univ; *CV* Chair Philip Gore (Bolton) Ltd from 1981; Dir Silverwood Forestry Ltd from 1991; pt Tutor and Lect; M Bp's Coun; DBF, Dioc Fin Cttee; M Dioc Bd of Min; M Dioc Bd of Patronage; M Ch Soc Trust; Lay Chair Deane Dny Syn from 1990; M Coun Ch Soc; JP GS 1985– *Tel:* 01204 63798 (Home)
01204 62126 (Office)
Fax: 01204 659750
email: philipgore@compuserve.com

GORHAM, Ven Karen Marisa, BA
Rectory Stone Aylesbury HP17 8RZ [ARCHDEACON OF BUCKINGHAM; OXFORD] *b* 1964 *educ* Mayflower Sch, Billericay; Trin Th Coll Bris; *CV* C Northallerton w Kirby Sigston 1995–99; P-in-c St Paul Maidstone, Asst DDO and RD Maidstone 1999–2007; Hon Can Cant 2006–07; Adn of Buckingham from 2007 GS 2003–07 *Tel:* 01865 208264
01865 208266
email: archdbuc@oxford.anglican.org

GOUGH, Janet Frances MA, ACA
Church House, Great Smith Street, London SW1P 3AZ [DIRECTOR OF CATHEDRALS AND CHURCH BUILDINGS DIVISION, ARCHBISHOPS' COUNCIL] *b* 1961 married to Jim Lloyd *educ* St Margaret's Sch Bushey; Haileybury; Emmanuel Coll, Cam; *CV* Art for Offices 1984; KPMG-ACA 1985–89; Charterhouse Bank 1989–91; Sotheby's 1999–2000; Phoenix Trust 2000–01; V & A and Architectural Tours 2003–08; Trustee Churches Conservation Trust 1998–2005; Trustee Fulham Palace Trust from 1997 *Tel:* 020 7898 1887
email: janet.gough@c-of-e.org.uk

GOVENDER, Very Revd Rogers Morgan, BTh, Dip Th
Manchester Cathedral Cathedral Yard, Victoria St Manchester M3 1SX [DEAN OF MANCHESTER] *b* 1960 *educ* Glenover High Sch, Durban, S Africa; Univ of Natal (Pietermaritzburg), S Africa; St Paul's Coll, Grahamstown, S Africa; *CV* C Ch Ch Overport, S Africa 1985–87; R St Mary Greyville, Durban, S Africa 1988–92; R St Matt Hayfields, Pietermaritzburg, S Africa 1993–99; Adn of Pietermaritzburg 1997–99; R St Thos Berea, Durban 1999–2000; P-in-c Ch Ch Didsbury, Man

2001–05; P-in-c St Chris Withington, Man 2003–05; AD Withington 2003–05; Dean of Man from 2006; M Dioc Syn; M Bp's Coun; M AC CMEAC from 2006; M AC Liturg Commn from 2006; Chair Dioc Pastl Cttee
GS 2008–   *Tel:* 0161 833 2220
                                      0161 792 2801 (Home)
                                      07983 978346 (Mobile)
                                      Fax: 0161 839 6218
email: dean@manchestercathedral.com

GRANTHAM, Suffragan Bishop of. See ELLIS, Rt Revd Dr Tim (Timothy William)

GRAY, Ven Martin Clifford, Dip Chem Eng
Holly Tree House Whitwell Rd Sparham NR9 5PN [ARCHDEACON OF LYNN; NORWICH] *b* 1944 *educ* Trin Gr Sch Wood Green; W Ham Coll of Tech; Westcott Ho Th Coll; *CV* C St Faith Kings Lynn 1980–84; V Sheringham 1984–94; TR St Marg Lowestoft 1994–99; Adn of Lynn from 1999
                              Tel and Fax: 01362 688032
email: archdeacon.lynn@4frontmedia.co.uk

GREEN, Ven John, QHC, BCS
RN Chaplaincy Service MP 1.2 Leach Building Whale Island Portsmouth PO2 8BY [CHAPLAIN OF THE FLEET AND ARCHDEACON FOR THE ROYAL NAVY; ARMED FORCES SYNOD] *b* 1953 *educ* SW Ham County Tech Sch; Hendon Coll of Science and Tech; NE Lon Poly; Linc Th Coll; *CV* Project Eng, Thorn Lighting 1974–77, Sen Eng 1977–80; C St Mich and All Angels, Watford 1983–86; C St Steph w. St Julian, St Alb 1986–91; Chapl RN from 1991; Chapl of the Fleet and Adn for RN from Mar 2006; Hon Can Portsmouth Cath from 2006
GS 2005–   *Tel:* 023 9262 5055
                                      Fax: 023 9262 5134
email: john.green107@mod.uk

GREEN, Rt Revd Laurie (Laurence Alexander), BD, AKC, STM, D Min
Bishop's House Orsett Rd Horndon-on-the-Hill SS17 8NS [AREA BISHOP OF BRADWELL; CHELMSFORD] *b* 1945 *educ* East Ham Gr Sch; K Coll Lon; New York State Univ; New York Th Seminary; St Aug Coll Cant; *CV* C St Mark Kingstanding Birm 1970–73; V St Chad Erdington 1973–83; Prin Aston Tr Scheme 1983–89; Hon C H Trin Birchfield 1984–89; TR All SS Poplar Lon 1989–93; Bp of Bradwell from 1993   *Tel:* 01375 673806
                                      Fax: 01375 674222
email: b.bradwell@chelmsford.anglican.org

GREENER, Very Revd Jonathan Desmond Francis, MA
The Deanery 1 Cathedral Close Margaret St, Wakefield WF1 2DP [DEAN OF WAKEFIELD] *b* 1961 *educ* Reigate Gr Sch; Trin Coll Cam; Coll of Resurrection Mirfield; *CV* C H Trin w St Matt, Southwark 1991–94; Dom Chapl to Bp of Truro 1994–96; V Ch of Good Shepherd, Brighton 1996–2003;

Adn of Pontefract 2003–07; Dean Wakefield from 2007
GS 2003–07   *Tel:* 01924 239308 (Home)
                                      01924 373923 (Office)
                                      Fax: 01924 215054
email: jonathan.greener@wakefield-cathedral.org.uk

GREENWOOD, Mr Adrian Douglas Crispin, MA, MCIH
91 Lynton Rd Bermondsey London SE1 5QT [SOUTHWARK] *b* 1951 *educ* Judd Sch Tonbridge; Jes Coll Cam; Coll of Law Lon; *CV* Chwrdn St James Bermondsey 1983–92, 1995–2004; Lay Chair St James Bermondsey from 1982; Chief Exec Gateway Housing Assoc (formerly Bethnal Green and Victoria Park Housing Assoc Ltd) from 1992; Trustee Salmon Youth Centre Bermondsey from 2000; Trustee Isle of Dogs Community Foundation from 1998; M Dioc Syn from 1994, Lay Chair from 2006; M Tower Hamlets Local Strategic Ptnrship from 2002; Lay Chair Bermondsey Dny Syn from 2004;
GS 2000–   *Tel:* 020 7237 6920
email: amgreenwood@tiscali.co.uk

GREENWOOD, Mr Nigel Desmond, M Phil, M Ed, C CHEM, FRSC, FIBMS, FRIPH
47 Broomfield Adel Leeds LS16 7AD [RIPON AND LEEDS] *b* 1944 *educ* Leeds Gr Sch; Leeds Univ; Leic Univ; *CV* Posts in Public Health Services and FE Leeds Public Health Dept 1962–68; Tobacco Rsch Coun 1968–69; United Leeds Hosps 1969–74; Wigston CFE 1974–77; Keighley Tech Coll 1978–80; Airedale and Wharfedale Coll 1981–95; Educ and Trg Consult 1995–99; Co-ord One City Projects from 1999; Chair Dioc Bd of Educ; Convenor W Yorks F.E. Chapl Gp; Gov Yorks Min Course
GS 1990–   *Tel:* 0113 261 1438
                                      07940 587618 (Mobile)

email: greenwoodnd@aol.com

GREGORY, Rt Revd Clive Malcolm, BA, MA
61 Richmond Rd Wolverhampton WV3 9JH [AREA BISHOP OF WOLVERHAMPTON; LICHFIELD] *b* 1961 *educ* Sevenoaks Sch; Lanc Univ; Qu Coll Cam; Westcott Ho Cam; *CV* C St Jo Bapt Margate 1988–92; Sen Chapl Univ of Warwick 1992–98; TR Coventry East 1998–2007; Hon MA, Univ of Warwick 1999; Assoc DDO Coventry 2001–07; Area Bp of Wolverhampton from 2007   *Tel:* 01902 824503
                                      Fax: 01902 824504
email: bishop.wolverhampton@lichfield.anglican.org

GRIFFITHS, Revd David Bruce, BA, MA, Cert Ed
Ainsworth Vicarage Ainsworth Hall Rd Ainsworth Bolton BL2 5RY [MANCHESTER] *b* 1944 *educ* Birkenhead Sch; Brighton Coll of Ed; Sussex Univ; Hull Univ; Linc Th Coll; *CV* Farm Apprentice J Bibby and Sons 1962–63; Tchr Birkenhead Sec Sch 1966–67; Com Ldr Ox Cyrenian Com 1968–69;

Tutor Youth and Com Work YMCA Nat Coll 1969–76; Tr Tutor Play and Recreation Work Islington 1976–80; C All SS Springfield Chelmsf 1982–84; TV St Cath Horwich 1984–92; C Ch Ch Heaton 1992–2002; M Dioc Syn, Bd of Min and CME Cttee, Pastl Cttee 1989–92; Rdr and OLM Tr Tutor 1990–92 and from 1998; Tr Incumbent from 1992; M Dioc Tr Forum from 1999; Par Priest Ch Ch Ainsworth from 2002; Ecum Min Devel Adv for MB Bury from 2002; Ecum Officer Adnry of Bolton from 2006
GS 2000–   *Tel and Fax:* 01204 398567
       email: d.griffiths007@btinternet.com

GRIMLEY, Very Revd Robert William, MA, Hon D Litt
The Deanery 20 Charlotte St Bristol BS1 5PZ [DEAN OF BRISTOL] *b* 1943 *educ* Derby Sch; Ch Coll Cam; Wadham Coll Ox; Ripon Hall Th Coll; *CV* C Radlett 1968–72; Chapl K Edw Sch Birm 1972–84; V St Geo Edgbaston 1984–97; Exam Chapl to Bp of Birm 1988 97; Vc Chair Dioc Pastl Cttee 1996–97; Dean of Bris from 1997; Bps' Inspector of Th Colls from 1998; M Ch Commrs' Bishoprics and Cathls Cttee from 2005; Trustee Bp's Palace, Wells 2005–06; Ch Commr from 2007
               Tel: 0117 926 2443 (Home)
       0117 946 8176 / 0117 926 4879 (Office)
                    Fax: 0117 925 3678
       email: dean@bristol.anglican.org

GRIMSBY, Suffragan Bishop of. See ROSSDALE, Rt Revd David Douglas James

GUERNSEY, Dean of. See MELLOR, Very Revd (Kenneth) Paul

GUILDFORD, Bishop of. See HILL, Rt Revd Christopher John

GUILDFORD, Dean of. See STOCK, Very Revd Victor Andrew

GUILLE, Very Revd John Arthur, MA, B Th, Cert Ed
The Residence Vicars Court Southwell NG25 0HP [DEAN OF SOUTHWELL; SOUTHWELL AND NOTTINGHAM] *b* 1949 *educ* Guernsey Gr Sch; Ch Ch Coll Cant; Southn Univ; Sarum and Wells Th Coll; *CV* C Chandlers Ford 1976–80; P-in-c St Jo Bournemouth 1980–83; P-in-c St Mich Bournemouth 1983–84; V St Jo w St Mich Bournemouth 1984–89; R St Andre de la Pommeraye Guernsey 1989–99; Vc Dean Guernsey 1996–99; Adn of Basingstoke 1999–2000; Can Res Win Cathl from 1999; Adn of Win 2000–07; M Dioc Syn from 1977; M Guernsey LEA 1990–98; Chair N Area Pastl Cttee from 1999; Chair Trustees Old Alresford Place Retreat and Conf Cen from 1999; Vc Chair Dioc Bd of Educ from 2000; Vc-Dean Win Cathl 2006–07; Dean of S'well from 2007
GS 1990–2000   *Tel:* 01636 817282
       email: dean@southwellminster.org.uk

GUNN-JOHNSON, Ven David Allan, S Th, MA
Stage Cross Sanders Lane Bishop's Tawton Barnstaple EX32 0BE [ARCHDEACON OF BARNSTAPLE; EXETER] *b* 1949 *educ* Stratton Gr Sch Biggleswade; St Steph Ho Ox; *CV* C St Matt Oxhey, St Albans 1981–84; C Cheshunt, St Albans 1984–88; TR Colyton, Exeter 1988–2003; RD Honiton 1990–96; Preb Ex Cathl 1999–2003; M Dioc Coun for Worship and Min; Convenor Child Protection Team; Adn of Barnstaple from 2003; Dioc Wrdn of Rdrs from 2004
               Tel: 01271 375475
                    Fax: 01271 377934
       email: archdeacon.of.barnstaple@
                    exeter.anglican.org

HACKNEY, Archdeacon of. See DENNEN, Ven Lyle

HACKWOOD, Ven Paul, B Sc Dip Theol, MBA
The Archdeaconry 21 Church Rd Glenfield LE3 8DP [ARCHDEACON OF LOUGHBOROUGH; LEICESTER] *b* 1961 *educ* Darlaston Comp Sch; Bradf Coll; Huddersfield Univ; Birm Univ; Bradf Sch of Mgt; Qu Coll Birm; *CV* C All SS Horton Bradf 1989–93; C St Oswald Chapel Green 1991–93; Soc Resp Adv St Alb Dioc 1993–97; V St Marg Thornbury Bradf 1997–2005; Adn Loughborough from 2005; Trustee CUF, M Funding Cttee from 2004; M W Yorks Police Auth 2003–05   *Tel:* 0116 248 7421
                    0116 231 1632
                    Fax: 0116 253 2889
       email: paul.hackwood@leccofe.org

HADDOCK, Mr Peter,
43 Woodland Way Morden SM4 4DS [SOUTHWARK] *CV* Elected to GS 2005
GS 2005–

HALIFAX, Archdeacon of. See FREEMAN, Ven Robert John

HALL, Sergeant Frances Mary,
SNCO A1 Ops Air Command RAF High Wycombe HP14 4UE [REPRESENTATIVE, ARMED FORCES SYNOD] *b* 1970 *educ* Whitecross High Sch Heref; Heref Sixth Form Coll; *CV* HM Forces from 1992; M RAF Adny Syn from 1999, Sec 2003–05; M Forces Synodical Coun from 2003, Asst Sec from 2004; Sec Armed Forces Syn from 2005
GS 2005–   *Tel:* 01270 610415 (Home)
                    01494 495230 (Office)
                    Fax: 01494 496830
       email: fran.hall865@mod.uk

HALL, Ven John Barrie,
Tong Vicarage Shifnal TF11 8PW [ARCHDEACON OF SALOP; LICHFIELD] *b* 1941 *educ* Sarum and Wells Th Coll; *CV* C St Edw Cheddleton 1984–88; V Rocester 1988–94; V Rocester and Croxden w Hollington 1994–98; RD Uttoxeter 1991–98; Adn of Salop and V Tong from 1998; Vc-Chair DBF; M DAC; Chair Dioc Pastl Cttee; M Ch Buildings Cttee; M Benefice Buildings Cttee; M Dioc Trust; Chair Lich Dioc Red Chs Uses Cttee; Chair

Shrops Hist Chs Trust; Chair Dioc Child Protection Grp; Pres Telford Chr Coun
GS 2002–   *Tel:* 01902 372622
                             Fax: 01902 374021
email: archdeacon.salop@lichfield.anglican.org

HALL, Canon John Michael, BA Hons, MA
The Vicarage Main St Warton Lancs LA5 9PG
[BLACKBURN] *b* 1962 *educ* St Michael's CE High Sch Chorley; Runshaw Sixth Form Coll Leyland; Leeds Univ; Lanc Univ; Mirfield Theol Coll; *CV* V Fleetwood, St David and St Peter
GS 2000–05, 2008–   *Tel:* 01524 732946
          email: johnbloem@aol.com

HALL, Very Revd John Robert, BA, FRSA, hon DD
The Deanery Westminster Abbey London SW1P 3PA
[DEAN OF WESTMINSTER] *b* 1949 *educ* St Dunstan's Coll Catford; St Chad's Coll Dur; Cuddesdon Th Coll; *CV* Head of RE Malet Lambert High Sch Hull 1971–73; C St Jo Divine Kennington 1975–78; P-in-c All SS S Wimbledon 1978–84; V St Pet Streatham 1984–92; Exam Chapl to Bp of S'wark 1988–92; M GS Bd of Educ 1991–92; Chair FCP 1990–93; Dioc Dir of Educ Blackb 1992–98; Fell Woodard Corp from 1992; M Gov Body, St Mart's Coll Lanc 1992–98; Hon Can Blackb Cathl 1992–94 and 1998–2000; Res Can Blackb Cathl 1994–98; Can Emer from 2000; M Nat Soc Coun 1997–98; Trustee St Gabr's Trust 1998–2006; M Gov Body Cant Ch Ch Univ Coll 1999–2006; Trustee Urban Learning Found 1999–2002; M Gen Teaching Coun 2000–04; Gen Sec Bd of Educ and Nat Soc 1998–2002; CEO, Educ Division and Gen Sec Nat Soc 2003–06; Hon Asst C St Alban S Norwood 2003–06; Gov St Dunstan's Coll from 2003; Chair of Govs Westmr Sch from 2006; Hon Fell Cant Ch Ch Univ; Dean of Westmr from 2006
GS 1984–92   *Tel:* 020 7654 4801
                  07973 418859 (Mobile)
                    Fax: 020 7654 4883
email: john.hall@westminster-abbey.org

HAM, Archdeacon of West. See COCKETT, Ven Elwin Wesley

HAMID, Rt Revd David, B Sc, M Div, DD
14 Tufton St London SW1P 3QZ [SUFFRAGAN BISHOP IN EUROPE] *b* 1955 *educ* Nelson High Sch, Burlington, Canada; McMaster Univ Canada; Univ of Trin Coll, Toronto, Canada; *CV* C St Chris Burlington Canada 1981–83; R St Jo Burlington Canada 1983–87; Miss Co-ord for Latin America/Caribbean, GS of Angl Ch of Canada 1987–96; Dir of Ecum Affairs and Studies, Angl Ch of Canada 1996–2002; Suff Bp in Europe from 2002; ex officio M FOAG (C of E) 1996–2002; Co-Sec ARCIC 1996–2002; Co-Sec Angl-Orthodox Theol Dialogue 1996–2002; Co-Sec Angl-Lutheran Internat Wkg Grp 1999–2002; Co-Sec Angl-RC Commn on Unity and Miss 2001–02; Co-Sec Angl-Baptist Internat Conversations 1999–2002; Co-Sec Angl-Old Catholic Internat Co-ord Coun 1998–2002; Co-Sec Angl-Oriental Orthodox Dialogue 2001–

02; Sec Inter-Angl Theol and Doct Commn 2001–02; Sec Inter-Angl Stg Cttee on Ecum Relns 2000–02; Consult to Jt Wkg Grp of WCC and RC Church 2000–06; Consult to Angl-RC Commn on Unity and Miss from 2002; M Angl-Old Catholic Internat Co-ord Coun from 2005; dep Chair Porvoo Panel; Abp of Cant's Link Bp for Common Word Process   *Tel:* 020 7898 1160
                  07801 449113 (Mobile)
                    Fax: 020 7898 1166
          email: david.hamid@c-of-e.org.uk

HAMMOND, Sir Anthony Hilgrove, KCB, QC, MA, LLM
The White Cottage Blackheath Guildford GU4 8RB
[STANDING COUNSEL TO THE GENERAL SYNOD] *b* 1940 *educ* Malvern Coll; Em Coll Cam; *CV* Solicitor GLC 1965–68; Legal Asst Home Office 1968; Sen Legal Asst 1970; Asst Legal Adv 1974; Prin Asst Legal Adv 1980; Legal Adv and Dep Under-Sec of State and Legal Adv Nn Ireland Office 1988; Solicitor and Dir Gen Legal Services DTI 1992; Treasury Solicitor HM Procurator Gen and Hd of Government Legal Service 1997–2000; Stg Counsel to the GS from 2000; M Legal Adv Commn   *Tel:* 01483 892607
                  01726 833156 (Home)
                  020 7898 1799 (Office)
                  Fax: 01483 890667
                  01726 833156

HAMMOND, Mr Robert Ian, BA, MA, FRSA
22 South Primrose Hill Chelmsford CM1 2RG
[CHELMSFORD] *b* 1966 *educ* Hylands Sch Chelmsf; Open Univ; Heythrop Coll, Lon Univ; *CV* NatWest Bank 1985–87; HM Customs and Excise Exec Officer 1987–91; Higher Exec Officer 1991–96; Sen Exec Officer 1996–2001, Prin from 2001; HM Revenue and Customs from 2005; Chelms Dioc Syn from 1996; M Bp's Coun from 2003; M Chelms Cathl Coun from 2003; M MPA Coun from 2006; M Dioc Bd of Patr from 2007; M Dioc Pastl Ctee from 2007; M C of E (Eccl Fees) Measure: Steering Ctee from 2008
GS 2000–   *Tel:* 01245 269105
                  07711 672308 (Mobile)
        email: rihammond@tiscali.co.uk

HAMPSTEAD, Archdeacon of. See LAWSON, Ven Michael Charles

HANCOCK, Ven Peter, MA, BA
Victoria Lodge 36 Osborn Rd Fareham PO16 7DS
[ARCHDEACON OF THE MEON; PORTSMOUTH] *b* 1955 *educ* Price's Sch Fareham; Selw Coll Cam; Oak Hill Th Coll; *CV* C Ch Ch Portsdown 1980–83; C Radipole and Melcombe Regis TM 1983–87; V St Wilf Cowplain 1987–99; RD Havant 1993–98; Hon Can Portsm Cathl 1997–99; Adn of The Meon from 1999; Acting Warden of Rdrs 1999–2001; Acting RD Gosport 2002–03; Dir of Mission 1999–2006; M Bp's Coun; M DAC; M Dioc Parsonage and Property Cttee; Chair Chs Together for Deaf

People in Hants; Chair Miss and Discipleship Forum; Chair CPAS Trustees
GS 2005–   Tel: 01329 280101
                                  Fax: 01329 281603
                  email: admeon@portsmouth.anglican.org

HANCOCK, Mr Paul, BDS, MSc, Dip HSM, MHSM, FRSH
Mamre 3 Arncliffe Drive Burtonwood Warrington WA5 4NB [LIVERPOOL] *b* 1946 *educ* K Edw VI Sch Lich; Man Univ; *CV* Gen dental practitioner 1968–74; Com Dental Officer 1974; Sen Dental Officer 1974–93; Asst District Dental Officer 1993–97; Asst Dir Dental Services 1997–99; Asst Clinical Dir Dental Services from 1999; M Liv Dioc Syn 1997–2003; M Bd of Miss and Unity 1998–2003; Lay Swanwick Conference Cttee Sec and Treas 1998–2003; Par Treas from 2004; M Dny Syn from 2005; M Dioc Syn from 2008
GS 2005–   Tel: 01925 292559
                                  Fax: 01925 295988
                    email: hancockpa1@aol.com

HANKS, Mr John Martin, BA, LLM
50 Thames St Oxford OX1 1SU [OXFORD] *b* 1957 *educ* Henry Fanshawe Sch Dronfield; St Chad's Coll Dur; Selw Coll Cam; Cardiff Law Sch; *CV* Chartered Accountant; Treas Pusey Ho Ox from 1987; Bursar Ascot Priory from 1995; Trustee Eng Clergy Assoc Benefit Fund from 1995; Trustee Soc for the Maintenance of the Faith from 1998; Treas Number One Trust from 2006; Sec Keston Coll from 2006
GS 2000–   Tel: 01865 438572
                    email: john@hanksox.com

HARBIDGE, Ven Adrian Guy, BA, LLM
Glebe House 22 Bellflower Way Chandler's Ford Eastleigh SO53 4HN [ARCHDEACON OF BOURNEMOUTH; WINCHESTER] *b* 1948 *educ* Marling Sch Stroud; St Jo Coll Dur; Cuddesdon Th Coll; *CV* C Romsey 1975–80; V St Andr Bournemouth 1980–86; V Chandler's Ford 1986–99; RD Eastleigh 1993–98; Adn of Win 1999–2000; Adn of Bournemouth from 2000; Can Tororo Cathl, Bukedi Dioc, Uganda 1999
GS 1999–   Tel and Fax: 023 8026 0955
                email: adrian.harbidge@dial.pipex.com

HARBORD, Canon (Paul) Geoffrey, MA
4 Clarke Drive Sheffield S10 2NS [SHEFFIELD] *b* 1956 *educ* Thornbridge Gr Sch Sheff; Keble Coll Ox; Chich Th Coll; *CV* C Rawmarsh w Parkgate 1983–86; C St Geo Doncaster 1986–90; P-in-c St Edm Sprotbrough 1990–95; V Masbrough 1995–2003; JP from 1999; M Legal Aid Commn; M DAC; M Dioc Worship and Liturg Cttee; Dom Chapl to Bp of Sheff from 2003; M Coun Coll of Resurrection, Mirfield; M CDC 2003–06; Hon Can Sheff Cathl 2007
GS 2000–   Tel: 0114 266 1932
                                  0114 230 2170
                                  Fax: 0114 263 0110
              email: geoffrey@bishopofsheffield.org.uk

HARDING, Mr Nick (Nicholas) Andrew, B Ed
8 Belmont Close Mansfield Woodhouse NG19 9GD [SOUTHWELL AND NOTTINGHAM] *b* 1964 *educ* St Philip's RC Coll Birm; Ex Univ; *CV* Primary sch tchr 1985–88; Dir ICIS Trust 1989–94; Educ Officer, S'well Minster 1995–2002; S'well Dioc Children's Officer from 2002; M AC TRICS (children's work trg); M GS Bd of Educ Children's Panel; M Dioc Liturg Cttee, Bd of Educ, Lay Min Grp; magistrate
GS 2005–   Tel: 01623 622272
                                  07778 922438 (Mobile)
                                  Fax: 01623 622272
                email: nick@southwell.anglican.org

HARDMAN, Ven Christine Elizabeth, B Sc (Econ), M Th
129A Honor Oak Park Forest Hill London SE23 3LD [ARCHDEACON OF LEWISHAM; SOUTHWARK] *b* 1951 *educ* Qu Eliz Girls' Gr Sch Barnet; City of Lon Poly; Westmr Coll Ox; St Alb Dioc Minl Trg Scheme; *CV* Dss St Jo Bapt Markyate 1984–87; C 1987–88; Course Dir St Alb Minl Trg Scheme 1988–96; V H Trin Stevenage from 1996; RD Stevenage from 1999; Adn of Lewisham from 2001; M Dioc Syn; M Bp's Coun
GS 1998–2001, 2004–   Tel: 020 8699 8207 (Home)
                                  020 7939 9400 (Office)
                                  Fax: 020 7939 9465
                    email: christine.hardman@
                         southwark.anglican.org

HARDWICK, Very Revd Dr Christopher George, MA, Ph D, ACIB
The Deanery The Avenue Truro TR1 1HR [DEAN OF TRURO] *b* 1957 *educ* K Edw VI Sch Lich; Open Univ; Birm Univ; Cuddesdon Ox; *CV* C Worc SE Tm 1992–95; pt Chapl St Rich Hospice Worc and RNIB New Coll Worc 1992–95; R Ripple, Earls Croome w. Hill Croome & Strensham 1995–2005; RD Upton 1997–2005; R Upton-upon-Severn 2000–2005; Worc Dioc Trg Incumbent 2000–03; Chair Worc Dioc Ho of Clergy 2002–05; Hon Can Worc Cathl 2003–05; Dean of Truro from 2005; M Ch Commrs Pastl Cttee from 2002–07; GS Proctor in Conv 2004–05; M SST from 2001; Ch Commr from 2007; M Ch Commn Bishoprics and Cathls Cttee from 2007
                                  Tel: 01872 245006
                                  01872 276782
                                  Fax: 01872 277788
                email: dean@trurocathedral.org.uk

HARGRAVE, Canon Alan Lewis, B Sc, Ph D
Powcher's Hall The College Ely CB7 4DL [ELY] *b* 1950 *educ* Tadcaster Gr Sch; Birm Univ; Ridley Hall Th Coll; *CV* Miss Partner N Argentina 1977–80; Vc Pres and Commercial Dir San Miguel SA 1978–80; Hon Lect Food Science Leeds Univ 1980–81; Miss Partner Peru and Bolivia 1981–87; pt Sen Lect Industrial Microbiology Univ of La Paz 1981–83; M Exec Coun and Syn Angl Province of S Cone of America 1982–86; Dir Angl Ch in Bolivia 1983–87; C H Trin Cam 1989–93; M Dioc Syn from 1992; P-in-c H Cross Cam 1993, V

1994–2004; Dioc UPA Link Officer 1993–2001; Set up Primary Sch Pastl Studies Unit Cam Theol Federation 1996; Bp's Inspector of Th Colls from 1998; Vc-Pres Friends of Leper Chapel 1999–2004; Dir Barnwell Urban Trg Project with Cam Theol Federation 2001–2004; Spiritual Dir of Ely Cursillo 2002–05; Can Missioner Ely Cathl from 2004; Chair Ely Dioc Bd for Ch in Soc from 2004
GS 2000–   Tel: 01353 660304
email: alan.hargrave@cathedral.ely.anglican.org

HARGREAVES-SMITH, Mr Aiden Richard, MA, LLM, FRSA
23 Battlebridge Court Wharfdale Rd London N1 9UA [LONDON] *b* 1968 *educ* Batley Gr Sch; Man Univ; Europeenne de Formation Professionnelle, Paris; Univ of Westminster; Man Metropolitan Univ; Coll of Law; *CV* Civil Service 1992–95; Tutor St Anselm Hall 1991–93, Sen Tutor 1993–98, M SCR from 1991; Trainee Solicitor Winckworth and Pemberton 1998–2000; Solicitor Winckworth Sherwood from 2000, Partner from 2007; Assoc Fell, Soc for Advanced Legal Studies from 1998; M Eccl Law Soc from 2002, M Gen Cttee from 2005; M Soc for the Maintenance of the Faith from 2002; M Coun Qu Victoria Clergy Fund from 2003; Gov Pusey Ho, Ox from 2003; M Charity Law Assoc; M Sen Appts Review Grp; Assoc M Ecum Coun for Corporate Responsibility from 2005; M C of E Appts Cttee from 2005; M Fees Adv Commn (appt by Pres of Law Soc) from 2005; M Stg Cttee Ho of Laity; M CNC; M C of E delegation to Third Eur Ecum Assembly; M Pastl Measure Appeals Panel
GS 2000–   Tel and Fax: 020 7833 9182 (Home)
email: arhs1@tiscali.co.uk

HARLAND, Dr Peter John, BA, PhD, MA
1 Malvern Rd Cherry Hinton Cambridge CB1 9LD [ELY] *b* 1967 *educ* St Olave's Gr Sch Orpington; St Jo Coll Dur Univ; *CV* Admin Officer, Ch Commrs 1992–94; Admin Officer, Southn Univ 1994–96; Admin Officer, Cam Univ from 1997
GS 2005–   Tel: 01223 243525

HARLEY, Canon Michael, AKC, Cert Ed, S Th, M Phil
Vicarage 30 Hursley Rd Chandlers Ford SO53 2FT [WINCHESTER] *b* 1950 *educ* Qu Eliz Gr Sch Crediton; K Coll Lon; Ch Ch Coll Cant; St Aug Coll Cant; Lambeth; Univ of Kent at Cant; *CV* C St William Walderslade, Roch 1975–78; C-in-charge St Barn Weeke, Winch 1978–81; V Pear Tree, Southn 1981–86; V Hurstbourne Tarrant 1986–99; V Chandler's Ford from 1999; Winch Dioc Rural Officer 1991–97; RD Andover 1994–99; Chair Winch Dioc Ho of Clergy from 2005; STETS tutor 2003–06
GS 2005–   Tel: 023 8025 2597
email: michaelharley@
parishofchandlersford.org.uk

HARLOW, Archdeacon of. See TAYLOR, Ven Peter Flint

HARRISON, Prof Glynn, MD, FRCPsych
2 Harley Place Clifton Bristol BS8 3JT [BRISTOL] *b* 1949 *educ* Havelock Sch Grimsby; Dundee Univ; *CV* Consult psychiatrist, Nottm 1982–94; Foundation Chair of Com Mental Health, Nottm Univ 1994–97; Norah Cooke Hurle Prof of Mental Health, Bris Univ from 1997; Hon Consult Psychiatrist, AWP Trust, Bath from 1997; Pres Internat Federation of Psychiatric Epidemiology from 2007; M CNC from 2007
GS 2005–   Tel: 0117 970 6430
email: g.harrison@blueyonder.co.uk

HARRISON, Dr Jamie (James Herbert), MB, BS, MRCGP, MA
5 Dunelm Court South St Durham DH1 4QX [DURHAM] *b* 1953 *educ* Stockport Gr Sch; Magd Coll Ox; K Coll Hosp Medical Sch Lon; *CV* GP Durham City from 1990; M Coun St Jo Coll Dur; Rdr
GS 1995–   Tel: 0191 384 8643
                                     Fax: 0191 386 5934
email: dunelm5@btinternet.com

HARRISON, Revd Rachel Elizabeth, Dip Th&Min, NNEB
Vicarage 9 Blenheim Terrace Coatham Redcar TS10 1QP [CHURCH COMMISSIONER] *b* 1953 *educ* Northn Sch for Girls; Northn Coll of FE; NEOC; *CV* M GS 1995–2000; Ch Commr Pastl Cttee and Bd of Govs from 1999; NVQ Trainer/Assessor in Childcare, Cleveland Youth Assoc 1998–2001; C Skelton w Upleatham Cleveland 2001–04; P-in-c New Marske and Wilton from 2004, V from 2006; Industrial Chapl Tees Valley Min, York from 2004; Sub-Wrdn of Rdrs, Guisborough Dny, York Dioc
GS 1995–2000   Tel: 01642 482870 (Home)
                         01642 484833 (Office)
email: rachelhere@hotmail.com

HARTLEY, Revd Dr John Peter, BA, PhD
Eccleshill Vicarage 2 Fagley Lane Bradford BD2 3NS [BRADFORD] *b* 1956 *educ* Man Gr Sch; Leeds Univ; Cranmer Hall, St Jo Dur Univ; *CV* C St Mary Osterley, Lon 1985–88; C St Pet Bexleyheath, Roch 1988–91; P-in-c Hanford, Stoke-on-Trent and Faith in the City (Potteries) Officer 1991–2000; V Eccleshill from 2000
GS 2004–   Tel: 01274 636403
email: vicar@stluke-eccleshill.org.uk

HASELOCK, Canon Jeremy Matthew, BA, B Phil, MA, FSA. Hon FGCM
34 The Close Norwich NR1 4DZ [NORWICH] *b* 1951 *educ* St Nic Gr Sch Northwood; York Univ; York Cen for Medieval Studies; St Steph Ho Th Coll; *CV* C St Gabr Pimlico 1983–86; C St Jas Paddington 1986–88; Dom Chapl to Bp of Chich 1988–91; V Boxgrove 1991–98; Dioc Liturg Adv Chich 1991–98; Preb of Fittleworth and Canon Chich Cathl 1994-2000, Can Emeritus 2000; Can Res and Prec Norw Cathl from 1998, Vc-Dean from 2005; M Liturg Commn 1996–2006; M Initiation Rites Revision Cttee; M Wholeness and Healing Revision Cttee; M Steering Cttee Eucha-

ristic Rites Revision; M Steering Cttee Eucharistic Prayers Revision; Chair Steering Cttee Extended Communion; M Design Sub-Cttee Common Worship; M Liturg Publ Grp; Chair Times and Seasons Grp; M Cathls Measure Revision Cttee; M Cathls Fabric Commn from 2003; M Rules Cttee (Care of Cathls Measure) 2005–06; M Cathls and Ch Buildings Div Grp from 2006; M Ch Commrs Bishoprics and Cathls Cttee from 2006
GS 1995–
Tel: 01603 619169 (Home)
01603 218314 (Office)
07711 698996 (Mobile)
Fax: 01603 766032 (Office)
email: precentor@cathedral.org.uk

HASLAM, Mrs (Agnes) Lois, Dip Ad Ed, Cert Ed
3 Poplar Close Gatley Cheadle SK8 4LU [CHESTER] *b* 1938 *educ* Whalley Range High Sch Man; Man Univ; Totley Hall Coll of Educ; *CV* Tchr St Marg C of E Secdry Sch Man 1959–60; tchr Cheadle Adult Educ Cen 1961–70, 1972–75, Prin 1975–84; tchr Gatley Playgroup 1970–72; Stockport Boro Co ord for Adult Basic Educ 1984–95; retd 1995; M Stockport Dny Syn; Dioc Selector for Ordinands; M Melanesian Wkg Grp; past M Dioc Bd of Educ, Adult Educ and Lay Trg, Cathls Meas 1999 Transitional Coun, Round Tables Future of Educ and Trg; nat Bp's Selector for 4 years
GS 2005–
Tel and Fax: 0161 428 2164

HAWKER, Ven Alan Fort, BA, Dip Th, PACTA
Church Paddock Church Lane Kington Langley Chippenham SN15 5NR [ARCHDEACON OF MALMESBURY; BRISTOL] *b* 1944 *educ* Buckhurst Hill Co High Sch; Hull Univ; Clifton Th Coll; *CV* C St Leon Bootle 1968–71; C-in-c Em Fazakerley 1971–73; V St Paul Goose Green 1973–81; TR S Crawley, TM 1981–98; Preb of Bury and Can Chich Cathl 1991–98; RD E Grinstead 1994–98; M CBF; Adn of Swindon 1998–99; Adn of Malmesbury from 1999; M Team and Grp Min Revision Cttee 1993; Chair Wkg Grp on Clergy Discipline and Reform of Eccl Courts 1994–2002; M GS Stg Cttee 1995–98; M GS Policy Cttee 1995–98; M CBF Budget Cttee 1995–98; M DBF; M Bp's Coun; M GS Business Cttee from 2000; M GS Legislative Cttee 2000–05; M CDC from 2003; M Accountability & Transparency Wkg Grp 2004–05; Chair Amending Canon 28 Revision Cttee from 2007; M Glos Univ Coun from 2000, Vc-Chair from 2005–08
GS 1990–
Tel: 01249 750085
Fax: 01249 750086
email: alan.hawker@bristol5.gotadsl.co.uk

HAWKINS, Revd Canon Clive, MA, Dip Th, DHSM
Eastrop Rectory 2A Wallis Rd Basingstoke RG21 3DW [WINCHESTER] *b* 1953 *educ* Simon Langton Gr Sch for Boys, Cant; St Pet Coll Ox; Trin Th Coll Bris; *CV* C Ch Ch Winch 1982–86; R St Mary Eastrop, Basingstoke from 1986; AD Basingstoke 2000–08; M Bp's Coun, Dioc Stg Cttee, Dioc Syn, N Area Team 2000–08, N Area Pastl Cttee 2000–

08; M Strg Cttee Eccl Offices (Terms of Service) Measure
GS 2005–
Tel: 01256 830021 (Home)
01256 464249 (Church)
Fax: 01256 330305
email: clive.hawkins@ stmarys-basingstoke.org.uk

HAWKINS, Rt Revd David John Leader, B Th, L Th, ALCD
Barking Lodge Verulam Ave Walthamstow London E17 8ES [AREA BISHOP OF BARKING; CHELMSFORD] *b* 1949 *educ* Wrekin Coll Shrops; Nottm Univ; Lon Coll of Div; St Jo Coll Nottm; *CV* C St Andr Bebington 1973–76; Wrdn Bida Bible Trg Cen, Nigeria 1976–82; Can Emer Kaduna, Nigeria 1982; P-in-c St Matt with St Luke Ox 1983–86; V St Geo Leeds 1986–99, TR 1999–2002; Exec Trustee, St Geo's Crypt 1986–2002; Chair Dioc Communications Cttee, Ripon and Leeds 1998–2002; Chapl Yorks Country Cricket Club 1986–2002; Chair of Trustees Leeds Faith in Schs 1993–2002; Dir Ashlar Ho 1986–2002; Area Bp of Barking from 2003; Dioc Hd Bp Miss and Par Devel from 2004; Dioc Hd Bp Youth from 2004; Apb's Hd Bp on Black Majority Ch from 2006; Pres Bardsey Bird and Field Observatory from 2007; Chair Lon Global Day of Prayer 2007
Tel: 020 8509 7377
Fax: 020 8521 4097
email: b.barking@chelmsford.anglican.org

HAWKINS, Mr David Nicholas,
Manor House Barn Fladbury Pershore WR10 2QN [WORCESTER] *b* 1939 *educ* Clifton Coll Bris; *CV* Dir Elgar Foundn 1973; Founder and Dir annual Farncombe Lectures, 1991; Trustee CPRE; M Worc DAC 1992; Vc-Chair Friends of Pershore Abbey 2002; Chair Worc Dioc Ho of Laity 2003; Vc-Pres Worc Dioc Syn
GS 2005–
Tel: 01386 860518
Fax: 01386 860801
email: d.hawkins459@btinternet.com

HAWLEY, Ven John Andrew, BD, AKC, Cert Theol
19 Clarence Park Blackburn BB2 7FA [ARCHDEACON OF BLACKBURN] *b* 1950 *educ* Ecclesfield Gr Sch; K Coll Lon; Wycliffe Hall Th Coll; *CV* C H Trin Hull 1974–77; C Bradf Cathl 1977–80; V All SS Woodlands, Doncaster 1980–91; TR Dewsbury 1991–2002; Chair Mission Doncaster 1985–2001; M Bp's Coun 1985–91; Vc Chair Wakef Dioc BMU 1991–96; M Action Partners Coun 1992–99; Chair Wakef Dioc Communications Grp 1996–2002; Chair Wakef Dioc Red Chs Uses Cttee 1999–2002; Chair Wakef Dioc Ho of Clergy 2000–02; M Pastl Measure Review Grp from 2001; M Misc Provisions Measure Revision Grp from 2000; Adn of Blackburn from 2002
GS 1996–2002
Tel: 01254 262571 01254 503074 (Secretary)
07980 945035 (Mobile)
Fax: 01254 263394
email: archdeacon.blackburn@milestonenet.co.uk

HAYDEN, Ven David Frank, Dip Th, BD
8 Boulton Rd Thorpe St Andrew Norwich NR7 0DF
[ARCHDEACON OF NORFOLK; NORWICH] *b* 1947 *educ*
Langley Sch Norwich; Tyndale Hall Bris; *CV* C St
Matt Silverhill, Chich 1971–75; C Galleywood
Common, Chelms 1975–79; R Redgrave cum
Botesdale with Rickinghall, St E & I 1979–1984;
RD Hartismere 1981–84; P-in-c Gresham, Norw
1984–98; V Cromer, Norw 1984–2002; pt hosp
chapl 1984–2000; RD Repps 1995–2002; Hon Can
Norw Cathl 1996–2002; Adn of Norfolk from
2002; M Bp's Coun; M DAC; Bp's Staff Rep
Church and Tourism and New Ways of Being
Church; Fresh Expressions; Creative Use of Ch
Buildings   *Tel and Fax:* 01603 702477
email: archdeacon.norfolk@4frontmedia.co.uk

HENDERSON, Ven Janet, BA, RGN
*Hoppus House Smith Lane, Hutton Conyers Ripon
HG4 5DX* [ARCHDEACON OF RICHMOND; RIPON
AND LEEDS] *b* 1957 *educ* Ardwyn Gr Sch, Aberw;
Dur Univ; Addenbrooke's Sch of Nursing, Cam;
Cranmer Hall Dur; *CV* C SS Pet and Paul Wis-
bech 1988–90; Par Deacon, Bestwood TM Nottm
1990–93; Lect, St Jo Coll Nottm 1993–97; Lect,
Cam Theol Federation 1997–2001; P-in-c St Patr
Nuthall and Dean of Women's Min, S'well and
Nottm Dioc 2001–07; Adn of Richmond and Res
Can Ripon Cathl from 2007   *Tel:* 01765 601316
email: janeth@riponleeds-diocese.org.uk

HENDERSON, Ven Julian Tudor, MA
*The Old Cricketers Portsmouth Rd Ripley Woking
GU23 6ER* [ARCHDEACON OF DORKING; GUILD-
FORD] *b* 1954 *educ* Radley Coll; Keble Coll Ox;
Ridley Hall Cam; *CV* C St Mary Islington 1979–
83; V Em and St Mary in the Castle, Hastings
1983–92; V H Trin Claygate 1992–2005; RD
1996–2001; Chair Dioc Evangelical Fellowship
1997–2001; Hon Can Guild Cathl 2002; Tutor Dioc
Min Course from 2003; Adn of Dorking from
2005
GS 2004–   *Tel:* 01483 479300 (Office)
                          01483 479568 (Home)
email: julian.henderson@cofeguildford.org.uk

HENWOOD, Revd Gill (Gillian Kathleen), MA
*Nunthorpe Vicarage Church Lane Nunthorpe
Middlesbrough TS7 0PD* [YORK] *b* 1956 *educ* N Lon
Collegiate Sch; Harrow Sch of Photography; Carl
and Blackb Dioc Trg Inst; *CV* C (NSM) St Jas
Whitechapel and St Eadmer Admarsh-in-
Bleasdale 1997–2000; NSM Fellside Team 2000–
01; Blackb Dioc Rural Chapl, Tourism Officer and
Chapl to Myerscough Coll 2000–03; Assoc P St Jas
Piccadilly 2003–04; V St Mary Virgin Nunthorpe
from 2004; Blackb Dioc Work and Economic
Affairs Cttee 2001–03; Blackb Dioc Rural Affairs
Grp 2000–03
GS 2005–   *Tel:* 01642 316570
         email: gillhenwood@hotmail.com

HERBERT, Rt Revd Christopher William, BA, M
Phil, PhD, PGCE, FRSA, Hon D Litt
*Abbey Gate House Abbey Mill Lane St Albans AL3
4HD* [BISHOP OF ST ALBANS] *b* 1944 *educ* Mon-
mouth Sch; St D Univ Coll Lamp; Wells Th Coll;
Bris Univ; Leic Univ; *CV* C Tupsley and School-
master Bp's Sch Heref 1967–71; Adv in Relig
Educ Heref 1971–76; Dir of Educ Heref 1976–81;
V Bourne 1981–90; Dir of POT Guildf 1983–90;
Adn of Dorking 1990–95; Bp of St Alb from 1995
GS 1995–   *Tel:* 01727 853305
                             Fax: 01727 846715
    email: bishop@stalbans.anglican.org

**HEREFORD, Archdeacon of. See COLMER,
Ven Malcolm John**

**HEREFORD, Bishop of. See PRIDDIS, Rt Revd
Anthony Martin**

**HEREFORD, Dean of. See TAVINOR,
Very Revd Michael Edward**

**HERTFORD, Archdeacon of. See JONES,
Ven Trevor Pryce**

**HERTFORD, Suffragan Bishop of.
See FOSTER, Rt Revd Christopher Richard
James**

HESKETT, Mr Robert William, B Sc, FRICS
5 Strand London WC2N 5AF [CHURCH COMMIS-
SIONER] *b* 1953 *educ* St Edw Sch Ox; Univ of S
Bank; *CV* With Land Securities plc from 1978,
currently Portfolio Dir for Lon; Dep ChairAssets
Cttee and Chair Property Grp; Ch Commr from
1998   *Tel:* 020 7024 3857
                              Fax: 020 7024 3770
    email: robert.heskett@landsecurities.com

HIBBERT, Revd Richard Charles, BA
*Christ Church Vicarage 115 Denmark St Bedford
MK40 3TJ* [ST ALBANS] *b* 1962 *educ* Merchant Tay-
lors' Sch Northwood; Trin Coll Bris; *CV* C St
Mary Luton 1996–2000; V Ch Ch Bedford from
2000; asst RD Bedford from 2004; M CEEC from
2006
GS 2005–   *Tel and Fax:* 01234 359342
    email: vicar@christchurchbedford.org.uk

HILL, Rt Revd Christopher John, BD, AKC, M Th
Willow Grange Woking Rd Guildford GU4 7QS
[BISHOP OF GUILDFORD] *b* 1945 *educ* Sebright Sch
Worcs; K Coll Lon; *CV* C Tividale Lich 1969–73; C
Codsall 1973–74; Abp's Asst Chapl on Foreign
Relations 1974–81; Abp's Sec for Ecum Affairs
1981–89; Angl Sec ARCIC I and II 1974–91; Hon
Can Cant Cathl 1982–89; Chapl to HM The Queen
1987–96; Can Res and Prec St Paul's Cathl 1989–
96; M C of E-German Chs Conversations 1987–89;
C of E Nordic-Baltic Conversations 1989–93; Vc
Chair Eccl Law Soc 1993–2002, Chair from 2002;

Chair Cathl Precs Conf 1994–96; Co-Chair C of E-French Protestant Conversations 1993–98; M Legal Adv Cttee from 1991; Co-Chair Lon Soc Jews and Chrs 1991–96; M CCU 1991–96, Chair from 2008; Bp of Stafford 1996–2004; M FOAG 1997–2008, Vc Chair from 1998; Co-Chair Meissen Th Conversations from 1998; Vc-Chair Ho of Bps' Wkg Pty on Women in the Episcopate 2000–04; M Wkg Pty on Review of Bps' legal costs, Fees Adv Commn 2003; M Liturg Commn 2003–05; M Ordinal Revision Grp from 2004; M CDC from 2004; Chair Wkg Pty on Women Bps 2005–06; M Ho of Bps Theol Grp from 2005; Clerk of the Closet from 2005; Bp of Guildford from 2004; Chair CCU from 2008; Chair Bps' Eur Grp from 2008
GS 2000–   *Tel:* 01483 590500
Fax: 01483 590501
email: bishop.christopher@cofeguildford.org.uk

HILL, Mr Kenneth John,
36 Daisybank Drive Congleton CW12 1LX [CHESTER] *b* 1938 *educ* Ellergreen High Sch Liv; *CV* Retired
GS 2005–   *Tel:* 01260 279791
email: kjgah@btopenworld.com

HILL, Rt Revd Michael Arthur,
Wethered House 11 The Avenue Clifton Bristol BS8 3HG [BISHOP OF BRISTOL] *b* 1949 *educ* Wilmslow Gr Sch; NW Cheshire CFE; Man Coll of Commerce; Ridley Hall Cam; Fitzw Coll Cam; *CV* C St Mary Magd Addiscombe 1977–80; C St Paul Slough 1980–83; P-in-c St Leon Chesham Bois 1983–90, R 1990–92; RD Amersham 1989–92; Adn of Berks 1992–98; Bp of Buckingham 1998–2003; Bp of Bristol from 2003
GS 1995–98, 2003–   *Tel:* 0117 973 0222
07808 290908 (Mobile)
Fax: 0117 923 9670
email: bishop@bristoldiocese.org

HILL, Ven Peter, BSc, MTh
4 Victoria Crescent Sherwood Nottingham NG5 4DA [ARCHDEACON OF NOTTINGHAM; SOUTHWELL AND NOTTINGHAM] *b* 1905 *educ* Man Univ; Nottm Univ; Wycliffe Hall, Ox; *CV* C Porchester, S'well 1983–86; V Huthwaite 1986–95; P-in-c Calverton 1995–2004; RD S'well 1997–2001; Dioc Chief Exec 2004–07; Hon Can S'well Minster from 2001; Adn of Nottingham from 2007
Tel: 01636 816445 (Home)
01636 817206 (Office)
Fax: 01636 815882 (Office)
email: archdeacon-nottm@southwell.anglican.org

HIND, Rt Revd John William, BA
The Palace Chichester PO19 1PY [BISHOP OF CHICHESTER] *b* 1945 *educ* Watford Gr Sch; Leeds Univ; Cuddesdon Th Coll; *CV* Asst Master Leeds Modern Sch 1966–69; Asst Lect K Alfred's Coll Win 1969–70; C Catford, Southend and Down-

ham 1972–76; V Ch Ch Forest Hill 1976–82; P-in-c St Paul Forest Hill 1981–82; Prin Chich Th Coll 1982–91; Bursalis Preb Chich Cathl 1982–91; Bp of Horsham 1991–93; Chair FOAG from 1991; Bp of Gib in Eur 1993–2001; Bp of Chich from 2001; Consult to CCU; M Ho of Bps Th Grp; M Faith and Order Commn of WCC; M Inter Angl Stg Commn on Ecum Relns from 2000
GS 1993–   *Tel:* 01243 782161
Fax: 01243 531332
email: bishchichester@diochi.org.uk

HIND, Mr Timothy Charles, MA, FCII
Plowman's Corner The Square Westbury-sub-Mendip Wells BA5 1HJ [BATH AND WELLS] *b* 1950 *educ* Watford Boys Gr Sch; St Jo Coll Cam; *CV* Various posts at Sun Life (now AXA) from 1972; IT Process and Compliance Mgr, AXA UK; Chartered Insurer; M Bp's Coun; Chair Dioc Vacancy-in-See Cttee 1996–98; M Dioc Bd of Educ 1995–97; M Bd of Educ (Schs and Colls) 1995–97; M C of E Pensions Bd 1996–; M C of E Pensions Bd Investment and Fin Cttee 1996–97; M ABM 1998; M DRACSC 1999–2008; Lay Vc-Chair Dioc Syn from 1999; Lay Chair Axbridge Dny Syn 1984–91; M Dioc Bd of Patr 1986–94; Vc-Chair Bd of Govs Kings of Wessex Com Sch 1996–99; Churchwarden St Jo Bapt Axbridge 2001–05; Sec OSG 2001–04; Chair OSG from 2004
GS 1995–2000, 2001–   *Tel:* 01749 870356 (Home)
07977 917434 (Mobile, Office)
07977 580374 (Mobile)
email: tim@hind.org.uk

HOBBS, Revd Maureen Patricia, BSc, Dip Bus Admin, CTM
Rectory Baschurch Shrewsbury SY4 2EB [LICHFIELD] *b* 1954 *educ* Wanstead High Sc Lon; Surrey Univ; Warwick Univ; Westcott Ho Cam; *CV* Asst linguist specialist, GCHQ 1976–78; recruitment and mgt consult 1978–95; C St Chad w. St Mary, Shrewsbury 1997–2001; R Baschurch and Weston Lullingfield w. Hordley from 2001; Dioc Adv for Women in Min from 2003
GS 2005–   *Tel:* 01939 260305
07812 805371 (Mobile)
email: hobbsmaureen@yahoo.co.uk

HOBSON, Revd (Anthony) Peter, BA
17 Westcotes Drive Leicester LE3 0QT [LEICESTER] *b* 1953 *educ* K Sch, Macclesfield; St Jo Coll Cam; St Jo Nottm; *CV* C Ch Ch Brunswick, Man 1977–82; R St Bride Old Trafford, Man 1982–92; TR Hackney Marsh, Lon 1992–2000; V The Martyrs, Leic from 2000; M Leic Dioc Bp's Coun 2000–06; Chair Par Share Grants Panel 2001–06; Dir dioc 'Shaped by God' project from 2006
GS 1985–90, 2005–   *Tel:* 0116 254 5643
0116 254 6162
07810 023659 (Mobile)
email: petehobson@mac.com

HOLMES, Mr Nigel Craven, BA
Woodside Great Corby Carlisle CA4 8LL [CARLISLE]
b 1945 *educ* Rossall Sch Fleetwood; Dur Univ; *CV*
Joined BBC Radio 1968; BBC Radio Producer
1970–97; M CECC 1986–95; M CACLB 1993–2004;
M BM 1996–2001; Rdr; Chair Ed Cttee CRC 1997–
2007; Chairman Ho of Laity Dioc Syn 1997–2003;
M Religion in Broadcasting Grp 2000–08; M Rev
Body, Rdr Min 2006–08
GS 1985–   *Tel:* 01228 560617
       email: nigel@gtcorby.plus.com

HOLT, Canon Douglas Robert, MA (Oxon), MA
(Cantab), MA (Lon), PGCE
9 Leigh Rd Clifton Bristol BS8 2DA [BRISTOL] *b* 1949
educ Coleraine Academical Institution; Ox Univ;
Cam Univ; Lon Univ; Ridley Hall Th Coll; *CV* C
St Barn Cam 1982–84, P-in-c 1984–85, V 1985–91;
V St Mary Ealing 1991–98; Dir Miss and Min Dev,
Bris from 1998
GS 2005–   *Tel:* 0117 906 0100 (Office)
                 0117 973 7427 (Home)
                 Fax: 0117 925 0460
    email: douglas.holt@bristoldiocese.org

HOOPER, Rt Revd Michael Wrenford, BA
Bishop's House Corvedale Rd Craven Arms SY7 9BT
[SUFFRAGAN BISHOP AND ARCHDEACON OF LUD-
LOW; HEREFORD] *b* 1941 *educ* Crypt Sch Glouc; St
D Coll Lamp; St Steph Ho Th Coll; *CV* C St Mary
Bridgnorth 1966–70; V Minsterley and R Hab-
berley 1970–81; R Leominster 1981–85; TR
Leominster 1985–97; RD Leominster 1981–97;
Adn of Heref 1997–2002; Can Res Heref Cathl
1997–2002; Bp and Adn of Ludlow from 2002
GS 1993–2002   *Tel and Fax:* 01588 673571
    email: bishopofludlow@btinternet.com

**HORSHAM, Archdeacon of. See COMBES,
Ven Roger Matthew**

**HORSHAM, Area Bishop of. See URWIN,
Rt Revd Lindsay Goodall**

HOUGHTON, Revd James Robert, AKC, Cert Ed
*St Michael's Vicarage 15 Long Acre Close Eastbourne
BN21 1UF* [CHICHESTER] *b* 1944 *educ* Highgate
Sch; K Coll Lon; St Luke's, Ex; *CV* C St Chad E
Herrington, Sunderland, Dur 1968–70; Asst
Youth Chapl, Bris 1970–72; C St Lawr Heavitree,
Ex 1973–78; Mgr Yiewsley and W Drayton Com
Cen and Hon C St Mart W Drayton, Lon 1978–80;
Chapl and Head of Relig Studies Grey Coat
Hosp, Westmr, Lon 1980–88; Chapl and Head of
Relig Studies Stonar Sch, Melksham, Salis 1988–
96; Chapl and Head of Relig Studies Sch of St
Mary and St Anne, Abbots Bromley, Lich 1996–
99; R Buxted and Hadlow Down, Chich 1999–
2002; V St Mich and All Angels, Eastbourne,
Chich from 2002
GS 2005–   *Tel:* 01323 645740
    email: fatherjamie@btopenworld.com

HOULDING, Preb David Nigel Christopher,
AKC, DD(hc)
*All Hallows' House 52 Courthope Rd London NW3
2LD* [LONDON] *b* 1953 *educ* K Sch Cant; K Coll
Lon; St Aug Coll Cant; *CV* Lay Chapl Chr Medical Coll Vellore, S India 1976–77; C All SS Hillingdon 1977–81; C St Alb Holborn w St Pet Saffron Hill 1981–85; V St Steph w All Hallows
Hampstead from 1985; Preb St Paul's Cath from
2004; Pro-Prolocutor Conv of Cant form 1998;
Chair Dioc Ho of Clergy and Vc-Chair Dioc Syn
from 2000; AD of N Camden 2001–03; Master SSC
from 1997; M Dioc Syn from 1991; M Bp's Coun
from 1997; M Edmonton Coun; M Dioc Liturg
Grp; M Coun ACS; M Coun of St Steph Ho, Ox
from 2001; Ldr, Cath Grp in GS 2000 07; M Adv
Panel for Vocations 1997–2002; M Weekday Lectionary and Rules to Order the Service Revision
Cttees 1999; M CCRJ 2000–01; M GS Appts Cttee
from 2001; M CAC Perry Review Strg Grp 2002–
03; M Conv Wkg Grp on Clergy Code of Practice
2000–03; M Clergy Employment Review Grp
2003–05 and Follow-up Grp from 2005; M Meth
Cov Impl Grp from 2003; Chair C of E Appts
Cttee from 2004, reappointed 2006; M AC 2004–
05, re-elected 2007; M CCU from 2006; M strg
ctee, Clergy Terms of Service
GS 1995–   *Tel:* 020 7267 7833
                020 7267 6317(Office)
                07710 403294 (Mobile)
          Fax: 020 7267 6317 (Office)
       email: fr.houlding@lineone.net

HOWE, Ven George Alexander, BA
*Vicarage Windermere Rd Lindale-in-Cartmel Grange-
over-Sands LA11 6LB* [ARCHDEACON OF WESTMOR-
LAND AND FURNESS; CARLISLE] *b* 1952 *educ* Liv Inst
High Sch; St Jo Coll Dur; Westcott Ho Th Coll; *CV*
C St Cuth Peterlee 1975–79; C St Mary Norton-
on-Tees 1979–81; V Hart w Elwick Hall 1981–85;
R Sedgefield 1985–91; RD Sedgefield 1988–91; V
H Trin Kendal 1991–2000; RD Kendal 1994–99;
Dioc Ecum Officer; Adn of Westmorland and
Furness from 2000; Chair Ch and Com Fund from
2007
GS 2001–   *Tel:* 01539 534717
          Fax: 01539 535090
   email: archdeacon.south@carlislediocese.org.uk

HUBBARD, Ven Julian Richard Hawes,
MA (Cantab, Oxon)
*Archdeacon's Lodging Christ Church Oxford OX1
1DP* [ARCHDEACON OF OXFORD] *b* 1955 *educ* K Edw
VI Gr Sch Chelms; Em Coll Cam; Wycliffe Hall
Ox; *CV* C St Dionis Parsons Green Lon 1981–84;
Chapl Jesus Coll Ox 1984–89; Tutor Wycliffe Hall
Ox 1984–89; Selection Sec ACCM 1989–91; Sen
Selection Sec ABM 1991–93; V St Thos on the
Bourne Guildf 1993–99; RD Farnham 1996–99;
Guildf Dioc FE Officer 1993–97; Dir Minl Trg
Guildf Dioc 1999–2005; Res Can Guildf Cathl

1999–2005; Adn Oxf and Res Can Ch Ch from 2005
Tel: 01865 208245
01865 276185
Fax: 01865 276185
email: archdoxf@oxford.anglican.org

HUDSON-WILKIN, Revd Rose Josephine,
B Phil Ed
Vicarage Livermere Rd London E8 4EZ [LONDON] *b*
1961 *educ* Montego Bay High Sch for Girls,
Jamaica; Birm Univ; Queens Th Coll Birm; *CV* C
St Matt, Wolverhampton 1991–95; Assoc Priest
Ch of Good Shepherd, W Bromwich 1995–98;
Dioc Officer for Black Angl Concerns 1995–98; V
H Trin Dalston and All SS Haggerston from 1998;
Chair CMEAC; Bp's Senior Selector
GS 1995–98; 2003–
Tel: 020 7254 5062
07882 459289 (Mobile)
Fax: 020 7249 7028
email: revdrose@aol.com

HUGHES, Canon Adrian John, BA
*St George's Vicarage Beverley Gardens Cullercoats
North Shields NE30 4NS* [NEWCASTLE] *b* 1957 *educ*
Geo Dixon Gr Sch; Newc Univ; Dur Univ; Cran-
mer Hall Dur; *CV* C Shard End, Birm 1983–86; TV
Solihull, Birm 1986–90; TV Glendale Grp, Newc
1990–94; V Belford & Lucker, Newc from 1994;
AD Bamburgh & Glendale from 1997; Asst DDO
1998–2006; V Cullercoats, Newc from 2006
GS 2005–
Tel: 0191 252 1817
email: revajh@btinternet.com

HUGHES, Canon John Patrick, Dip Th, Dip LRM
*St John's Vicarage 99 Wentworth Rd Harborne Bir-
mingham B17 9ST* [BIRMINGHAM] *b* 1941 *educ* K
Sch Roch; Oak Hill Th Coll; *CV* C St Andr Chorleywood 1967–71; C St Steph E Twickenham
1971–76; TV St Andr High Wycombe 1977–91;
Chapl Wycombe Hosp 1977–83; V St Jo Harborne
from 1992
GS 2005–
Tel: 0121 428 2093
07961 022087 (Mobile)
email: jphughes@stjohns-church.co.uk

HUGHES, Ven Paul Vernon, Dip UEM,
Cert Theol Oxon
17 Lansdowne Rd Luton LU3 1EE [ARCHDEACON OF
BEDFORD; ST ALBANS] *b* 1953 *educ* Pocklington Sch,
E Yorks; Poly Cen Lon; Ripon Coll Cuddesdon;
CV Res Property Surveyor, Chestertons 1974–79;
C Chipping Barnet w Arkley 1982–86; TV Dun-
stable Tm Min 1986–93; V Boxmoor 1993–2003;
RD Hemel Hempstead 1996–2003; Adn of Bed-
ford from 2003; M DBF Cttees, DAC, Dioc Pastl
and Miss Cttee, Closed Chs Uses Cttee, Com-
munications Adv Grp, Bd for Ch and Soc, New
Devel Areas, Bp's Staff, Bp's Staff Deployment
Grp
Tel: 01582 730722
Fax: 01582 877354
email: archdbedf@stalbans.anglican.org

**HULL, Suffragan Bishop of. See FRITH,
Rt Revd Richard Michael Cokayne**

**HULME, Suffragan Bishop of. See LOWE,
Rt Revd Stephen Richard**

HUMPHERY, Mr James Hambrook,
Pound Cottage Middle Woodford Salisbury SP4 6NR
[SALISBURY] *b* 1954 *CV* Mgr The Hill Drug Scheme
Britain-Nepal Medical Trust 1973–75; M DBF
1991–2003, Vc-Chair 2000-03; Lawyer from 1981,
specialist in employment law; CEDR accredited
mediator; Chair Revision Cttee on Ch Representation Rules 1998; Syn Gov Amendment Measure
2000; GS Panel of Chairmen from 2001; M CDC
from 2004; Chair Dioc Ho of Laity from 2003
GS 1993–
Tel: 023 8032 1000
email: humphery@onetel.com

HUMPHREYS, Ms Jacqueline Louise, MA, LLM
St John's Chambers 101 Victoria St Bristol BS1 6PU
[BRISTOL] *b* 1970 *educ* Churchill Comp Sch; Worc
Coll Ox; Inns of Court Sch of Law; Cardiff Univ;
CV Barrister from 1994; M Family Law Bar Assoc
from 1998; M Eccles Law Soc from 1999; M Legis
Cttee from 2000; M Legal Adv Commn from
2000; M Rules Cttee from 2004, M Legal Aid Cttee
from 2006
GS 2000–
Tel: 0117 921 3456
Fax: 0117 929 4821
email: jacqueline.humphreys@
stjohnschambers.co.uk

HUNT, Canon Dr Judy (Judith Mary), BVSC, MA,
Ph D, Dip C, MRCVS, FRSM
5 Abbey St Chester CH1 2JF [CHESTER] *b* 1957 *educ*
Bolton Sch; Bris Univ Veterinary Sch; R Veterinary Coll Lon Univ, Fitzw Coll Cam; Chester Coll;
Ridley Hall Th Coll; *CV* Par Dn St Pet Heswall
1991–94, C 1994–95; P-in-c St Mary Tilston w St
Edith Shocklach 1995–2003; Malpas Dny Officer
for Min Amongst Children and Young People
1995–98; Adv for Women in Min 1996–2000; Dny
Subwarden of Rdrs 1998–2001; Archdny Vocations Officer (Asst DDO) 1999–2003; M Dioc Cttee
for Min, Educ and Tr; M Rural Min Grp; Min
Reviewer; Dioc Dir of Min 2003–06; Dioc Dir of
Miss and Min from 2006; Res Can Chester from
2003; M nat CME and Devel Panel 2003–06; M
CDC 2004–07
GS 2000–
Tel: 01244 346893
01244 681973
Fax: 01244 346893
01244 620456
email: hunt@chestercathedral.com / judy.hunt@
chester.anglican.org

HUNT, Revd Vera Susan Henrietta, SDMTC, MBE
54 Highway Avenue Maidenhead Berks SL6 5AQ
[REPRESENTATIVE, DEAF ANGLICANS TOGETHER] *b*
1933 *educ* Oak Lodge Residential Sch; Salis and
Wells Th Coll; *CV* Pres and Cttee M Deaf Anglicans Together
GS 2005–
Fax: 01628 623909
email: vera.hunt@yahoo.co.uk

HUNTINGDON AND WISBECH, Archdeacon of. See McCURDY, Ven Hugh Kyle

HUNTINGDON, Suffragan Bishop of. See THOMSON, Rt Revd David

HYDON, Veronica Weldon BA, PGCE
Vicarage, 35A Shrigley Rd, Bollington, Macclesfield SK10 5RD [CHELMSFORD] *b* 1952 *edu* Ch Hosp Hertf; N Lon Poly; Maria Grey Coll of Educ; Aston Tr Scheme; Westcott Ho Th Coll; *CV* Marine cargo insurance broker at Lloyds' 1975–88; C All SS Poplar 1991–95; P-in-c Roxwell and Dioc Lay Devel Officer 1995–2000; V Em Forest Gate w St Pet Upton Cross 2000–03; Wdn of Ords Newham, Barking and Dagenham; Locl Adv for Rdrs; Co-convenor Years 1–4 POT; Assoc V Ch Ch with Holy Cross Timperley 2003–07; V Bollington (St Oswald Bollingtion with Holy Trinity Kerridge) from 2007
GS 2000–03   *Tel:* 1: 01625 573162
                    email: vhydon@hotmail.com

INGE, Rt Revd Dr John Geoffrey, B Sc, PGCE, MA, Ph D
Bishop's Office Worcester Diocesan Office The Old Palace Deansway Worcester WR1 2JE [BISHOP OF WORCESTER] *b* 1955 *educ* Kent Coll Cant; Dur Univ; Keble Coll Ox; Coll of the Resurrection Mirfield; *CV* Asst Chapl Lancing Coll 1984–86; Jun Chapl Harrow Sch 1986–89, Sen Chap 1989–90; V Wallsend St Luke, Newc 1990–96; Res Can Ely Cathl 1996–2003, Vice Dean 1999–2003; Bp of Huntingdon 2003–07; M Coun Ridley Hall from 2004; Trustee, Common Purpose from 2005; Bp of Worcester from 2007   *Tel:* 01905 21397
                    Fax: 01905 21462
email: bishop.worcester@cofe-worcester.org.uk

INWOOD, Rt Revd Richard Neil, MA, B Sc, BA
Bishop's Lodge Bedford Rd Cardington Bedford MK44 3SS [BISHOP OF BEDFORD; ST ALBANS] *b* 1946 *educ* Burton-on-Trent Gr Sch; Univ Coll Ox; St Jo Coll Nottm; *CV* C Ch Ch Fulwood Sheff 1974–78; C (Dir of Pastoring) All So Langham Place 1978–81; V St Luke Bath 1981–89; R Yeovil w Kingston Pitney 1989–95; Preb Wells Cathl 1990–95; Ch Commr 1991–95; Hon Treas Simeon's Trustees/Hyndman Trust 1986–2003; Adn of Halifax 1995–2003; Chair Coun St Jo Coll Nottm 1998–2002; Bp of Bedford from 2003; Cen Chapl MU from 2004
GS 1985–95,1997–2000   *Tel:* 01234 831432
                    Fax: 01234 831484
email: bishopbedford@stalbans.anglican.org

IPGRAVE, Ven Dr Michael Geoffrey, PhD, MA
Trinity House 4 Chapel Court Borough High St London SE1 1HW [ARCHDEACON OF SOUTHWARK] *b* 1958 *educ* Magd Coll Sch, Brackley; Oriel Coll Ox; St Chad's Coll Dur; SOAS, Lon Univ; Ripon Coll Cuddesdon; *CV* Dn 1982; P 1983 (Peterb); C All SS Oakham w. Hambleton and Egleton, and Braunston w. Brooke, Peterb 1982–85; Asst P The Resurrection, Chiba, Yokohama, Japan 1985–87; TV The Ascension, Leic 1987–90; TV The Holy Spirit, Leic 1990–94; P-in-c St Mary de Castro, Leic 1994–95; TR The Holy Spirit, Leic 1995–99; Dioc Adv on Inter Faith Relns 1990–99; Bp's Chapl 1990–99; Hon Asst P The Presentation, Leic 1999–2004; Hon Can Leic Cathl 1994–2004; Inter Faith Relns Adv, AC 1999–2004; Sec Chs Commn on Inter Faith Relns 1999–2004; Adn of Southwark from 2004   *Tel:* 020 7939 9409
                    020 7928 4866
                    Fax: 020 7939 9465
email: michael.ipgrave@southwark.anglican.org

IRELAND, Revd Mark Campbell, M Theol, MA
35 Crescent Rd Wellington Telford TF1 3DW [LICHFIELD] *b* 1960 *educ* Bromsgrove High Sch; Oban High Sch; St Jo Sch Marlborough; St Andr Univ; Wycliffe Hall Ox; Cliff Coll, Sheff Univ; *CV* Tchr, Murree Chr Sch, Pakistan 1981–82; C St Gabriel Blackb 1984–87; C Lancaster Priory 1987–89; Chapl HM Prison, Lancaster 1987–89; V Baxenden, Accrington 1989–97; Dioc Missr, Lich 1998–2007; TV St Matt Walsall 1998–2007; Tm Leader, Miss Div, Lich Dioc 2002–06; M Bp's Coun 2000–03; V All SS Wellington w. St Cath Eyton from 2007
GS 1995–98; 2005–   *Tel:* 01952 641251 (Home)
                    01952 248554 (Office)
email: vicar@allsaints-wellington.org

IRVINE, Very Revd John Dudley, BA, MA
The Deanery 11 Priory Row Coventry CV1 5EX [DEAN OF COVENTRY] *b* 1949 *educ* Haileybury Coll; Sussex Univ; Ox Univ; Wycliffe Hall Th Coll; *CV* C H Trin Brompton 1981–85; V St Barn Kensington 1985–2001; Dean of Cov from 2001
                    Tel: 024 7663 1448
                    024 7652 1200
                    Fax: 024 7652 1220
email: john.irvine@coventrycathedral.org.uk

ISAAC, Canon David Thomas, BA
1st Floor Peninsular House Wharf Rd Portsmouth PO2 8HB [PORTSMOUTH] *b* 1943 *educ* Rhondda Gr Sch; Univ Coll of Wales, Aberw; Cuddesdon Th Coll; *CV* C Llandaff Cathl 1967–71; C St Mary Swansea 1971–73; Prov Youth Chapl Ch in Wales 1973–77; V Pontardawe 1977–79; Ripon Dioc Youth Officer 1979–83; Nat Youth Officer GS Bd of Educ 1983–90; Res Can and Dir of Educ Portsm from 1990; Chair St Chris Educnl Trust from 1998; Res Can and Hd of Miss and Discipleship, Portsm from 2006
GS 1995–   *Tel:* 023 9289 9654
email: david.isaac@portsmouth.anglican.org

ISLE OF MAN, Archdeacon of. See SMITH, Ven Brian

ISLE OF WIGHT, Archdeacon of the. See BASTON, Ven Caroline Jane

ISON, Very Revd David John, BA, PhD, DPS
The Deanery 1 Cathedral Close Bradford BD1 4EG
[DEAN OF BRADFORD] *b* 1954 *educ* Brentwood Sch;
Leic Univ; Nottm Univ; K Coll Lon; St Jo Coll
Nottm; *CV* C St Nic w. St Luke Deptford, S'wark
1979–85; Tutor, Ch Army Trg Coll 1985–88; V St
Phil Potters Green, Cov 1988–93; Dioc Officer for
CME, Ex 1993–2005; Res Can Ex 1995–2005; Dean
of Bradf from 2005 GS 1990–93
                                    Tel: 01274 777720
                                          01274 777727
                                    Fax: 01274 777730
            email: dean@bradford.anglican.org

ITALY AND MALTA, Archdeacon of.
See SIDDALL, Ven Arthur

JACKSON, Ven Robert William, MA (Cantab),
MA (Econ), Dip Th, DPS
55B Highgate Rd Walsall WS1 3JE [ARCHDEACON
OF WALSALL; LICHFIELD] *b* 1949 *educ* High Storrs
Gr Sch Sheff; K Coll Cam; Manch Univ; St Jo Coll
Nottm; *CV* Govt Economic Adv 1972–78; C Ch
Ch Fulwood, Sheff 1981–84; V St Mark Greno-
side, Sheff 1984–92; V St Mary Scarborough, York
1992–2001; Springboard Missr 2001–04; Adn of
Walsall from 2004   *Tel:* 01922 620153
email: archdeacon.walsall@lichfield.anglican.org

JACOB, Ven William Mungo, LLB, MA, Ph D
15a Gower Street London WC1E 6HW [ARCH-
DEACON OF CHARING CROSS; LONDON] *b* 1944 *educ*
K Edw VII Sch King's Lynn; Hull Univ; Linacre
Coll Ox; Edin Univ; Ex Univ; St Steph Ho Th Coll;
CV C Wymondham 1970–73; Asst Chapl Ex Univ
1973–75; Dir of Pastl Studies Sarum and Wells Th
Coll 1975–80; Vc-Prin 1977–80; Sec Cttee for Th
Educ ACCM 1980–86; Warden Linc Th Coll 1986–
96; Adn at The Old Deanery 1996–2000; Adn of
Charing Cross from 1996; R St Giles-in-the-Fields
from 2000
GS 1999–2000   *Tel:* 020 7636 4646 (Home)
                          020 7323 1992 (Office)
                    Fax: 020 7323 4102 (Office)
            email: archdeacon.charingcross@
                          london.anglican.org

JAGGER, Ven Ian, MA, MA
15 The College Durham DH1 3EQ [ARCHDEACON OF
DURHAM] *b* 1955 *educ* Huddersfield New Coll; K
Coll Cam; St Jo Coll Dur; *CV* C St Mary Virgin
Twickenham Lon 1982–85; P-in-c Willen, Milton
Keynes Ox 1985–87; TV Willen, Stantonbury LEP
1987–94; Chapl Willen Hospice 1985–94; Dir Mil-
ton Keynes Chr Trg Scheme 1986–94; TR Fareham
H Trin Portsm 1994–98; Ecum Officer Portsm Dio
1994–96; RD Fareham 1996–98; Can Res Portsm
Cathl and Dioc Missr 1998–2001; Adn of Auck-
land 2001–06; Adn of Durham and Can Res Dur
Cathl from 2006
GS 2002–   *Tel:* 0191 384 7534
                       Fax: 0191 386 6915
            email: archdeacon.of.durham@
                          durham.anglican.org

JAGO, Mr Derek, ONC
21 Clarence Gdns Bishop Auckland DL14 7RB [DUR-
HAM] *b* 1949 *educ* Willington Sec Sch; Bp Auckland Coll; New Coll Dur; Gateshead Coll; *CV* Rdr
to pars of Witton Park, Etherley and Escomb from
1999; pt Broadcaster; LibDem District Coun Wear
Valley; M Auckland Dny Syn
GS 1998–   *Tel and Fax:* 01388 458358
            email: Derek_Jago@btclick.com

JAMES, Rt Revd David Charles, B Sc, BA, Ph D
Bishopscroft Ashwell Rd Heaton Bradford BD9 4AU
[BISHOP OF BRADFORD] *b* 1945 *educ* Nottm High
Sch; Ex Univ; Nottm Univ; St Jo Coll Nottm; *CV*
C Ch Ch Portswood 1973–76; C Goring-by-Sea
1976–78; Chapl UEA Norw 1978–82; V Ecclesfield
1982–90; RD Ecclesfield 1987–90; V Ch Ch Ports-
wood 1990–98; Hon Can Win Cathl 1998; Bp of
Pontefract 1998–2002; Bp of Bradford from 2002
GS 1985–90, 2000, 2002–   *Tel:* 01274 545414
                            Fax: 01274 544831
            email: bishop@bradford.anglican.org

JAMES, Rt Revd Graham Richard, BA
Bishop's House Norwich NR3 1SB [BISHOP OF NOR-
WICH] *b* 1951 *educ* Northampton Gr Sch; Lanc
Univ; Cuddesdon Th Coll; *CV* C Christ Carpenter
Peterb 1975–78; C Digswell 1978–82; TR Digswell
1982–83; Selection Sec and Sec for CME ACCM
1983–85; Sen Selection Sec 1985–87; Chapl to Abp
of Cant 1987–93; Bp of St Germans 1993–99; Bp of
Norw from 1999; M Bd of Countryside Agency
2001–06; Chair Rural Bps Panel 2001–06; Chair
CRAC, BBC and Ofcom from 2004; M AC from
2006; Chair Min Div from 2006
GS 1995–   *Tel:* 01603 629001
                       Fax: 01603 761613
            email: bishop@bishopofnorwich.org

JAMES, Mr Philip John, B SocSc
Church House Great Smith St London SW1P 3AZ
[HEAD OF POLICY UNIT, CHURCH COMMISSIONERS]
b 1967 *educ* Bris Gr Sch; Birm Univ; *CV* On staff of
Ch Commrs from 1988; Hd of Policy Unit from
1999   *Tel:* 020 7898 1671
            email: philip.james@c-of-e.org.uk

JARRETT, Rt Revd Martyn William, BD, AKC,
M Phil
3 North Lane Roundhay Leeds LS8 2QJ [BISHOP OF
BEVERLEY; PROVINCIAL EPISCOPAL VISITOR: YORK] *b*
1944 *educ* Cotham Gr Sch Bris; K Coll Lon; St Boniface Th Coll Warminster; Hull Univ; *CV* C St Geo
East Bristol 1968–70; C Swindon New Town
1970–74; P-in-c St Jos the Worker Northolt 1974–
76, V 1976–81; V St And Uxbridge 1981–85; Selection Sec ACCM 1985–88; Sen Selection Sec
ACCM 1989–91; V Our Lady and All SS Chesterfield 1991–94; Bp of Burnley 1994–2000; Bp of
Beverley from 2000; Asst Bp Dur from 2000; Asst
Bp Ripon and Leeds from 2000; Asst Bp Sheff
from 2000; Asst Bp S'well and Nottm from 2000;
Asst Bp Man from 2001; Asst Bp Wakef from

2001; Asst Bp Bradf from 2002; Asst Bp Liv from 2003; M Chs Commn for Inter-Faith Rels 2000–05; M CCU from 2001; Patr Coll of Rdrs from 2003; M Urban Bps' Panel from 1998; Chair Revision Cttee on Lectionary 2004; M Revision Ctte on Canon 28 2008
GS 2000–   *Tel:* 0113 265 4280
                            Fax: 0113 265 4281
            email: bishop-of-beverley@3–north-
                              lane.fsnet.co.uk

JARROW, Suffragan Bishop of. See BRYANT, Rt Revd Mark Watts

JEANS, Ven Alan Paul, B Th, MIAS, MIBC, MA
Herbert House 118 Lower Rd Salisbury SP2 9NW [ARCHDEACON OF SARUM; SALISBURY] *b* 1958 *educ* Bournemouth Sch; Dorset Inst of HE; Southn Univ; Sarum and Wells Th Coll; Univ Wales Lamp; *CV* C Parkstone Team 1989–93; P-in-c Bp Cannings, All Cannings and Etchilhampton 1993–98; Dioc Adv for Par Develt 1998–2005; M DAC; Adn of Sarum from 2003; Asst DDO from 2005; RD Alderbury 2005–07; DDO from 2007
GS 2000–05   *Tel:* 01722 336290 (Home)
                    01380 729808 (Office)
                    Fax: 01380 738096
        email: adsarum@salisbury.anglican.org

JENNINGS, Rt Revd David Willfred Michael, AKC
34 Central Ave Eccleston Park Prescot L34 2QP [SUF-FRAGAN BISHOP OF WARRINGTON; LIVERPOOL] *b* 1944 *educ* Radley Coll; K Coll Lon; St Boniface Coll Warminster; *CV* C Walton Liv 1967–69; C Ch Ch Win 1969–73; V Hythe 1973–80; V St Edw Romford 1980–92; RD Havering 1985–92; Hon Can Chelmsf Cathl 1987–92; Adn of Southend 1992–2000; Bp of Warrington from 2000
GS 1997–2000   *Tel:* 0151 426 1897 (Home)
                    0151 705 2140 (Office)
                    Fax: 0151 493 2479 (Home)
                    0151 709 2885 (Office)
        email: bishopofwarrington@
                              liverpool.anglican.org

JEPSON, Dr Rachel Margaret Elizabeth, B Ed, MA, PhD, TEFL, FIMA
56a Upland Rd Selly Park Birmingham B29 7JS [BIRMINGHAM] *b* 1967 *educ* Edgbaston CE Coll for Girls; Univ Coll of St Mart Lanc; Univ of Glos w Trin Coll Bris; St Jo Coll Dur; *CV* Tchr Grove Sch Handsworth 1993–98; Res Tutor St Jo Coll Dur 1998–2002; M Dioc Bd of Educ to 2006; GS Rep, CTE Forum and CTBI Assembly; Appt M Revision Cttee Care of Cathls Measure; Appt M Additional Collects Revision Cttee; M Birm Dioc Bp's Coun; M Birm Stg Adv Coun for Relig Educ; Tchr, Rookery Sch, Handsworth from 2007
GS 2000–   *Tel:* 0121 472 2064
                    07759 858734 (Mobile)
                    Fax: 0121 472 2064
        email: rachel.jepson@tiscali.co.uk

JERSEY, Dean of. See KEY, Very Revd Robert Frederick

JOHN, Very Revd Jeffrey Philip Hywel, MA, D Phil
The Deanery Sumpter Yard St Albans AL1 1BY [DEAN OF ST ALBANS] *b* 1953 *educ* Tonyrefail Gr Sch; Hertf Coll Ox; BNC Ox; Magd Coll Ox; St Steph Ho; *CV* C St Aug Penarth 1978–80; Asst Chapl Magd Coll Ox 1980–82; Chapl and lect BNC Ox 1982–84; Fell and Dean of Divinity Magd Coll Ox 1984–91; V H Trin Eltham 1991–97; Dir of Trg S'wark Dioc and Can Theol and Chanc S'wark Cathl 1997–2004; M GS Stg Cttee 1996–2000; M GS Appts Cttee 1995–2000; M S'wark Dioc Syn, Bp's Coun 1997–2004; Dean of St Alb from 2004   *Tel:* 01727 890202
                    Fax: 01727 890227
        email: dean@stalbanscathedral.org.uk

JOHNS, Mrs Sue (Susan Margaret), HNC, M Phil
103 Greenways Eaton Norwich NR4 6PD [NOR-WICH] *b* 1955 *educ* Thorpe Gr Sch; Norw City Coll; Leeds Univ; *CV* Analytical Chemist, Public Analyst's Lab 1973–80; Housewife and Mother; Food Scientist MAFF CSL Food Science Lab Norw 1991–98; Joint Food Safety and Standards Grp 1998–2000; Food Standards Agency from 2000, currently Priv Sec to Chair
GS 1990–   *Tel and Fax:* 01603 455029 (Home)
                    email: sue1326@hotmail.com

JOHNSTON, Mrs Mary Geraldine, BA, AKC, MCIPD
56 Fairlawn Grove Chiswick London W4 5EH [LON-DON] *b* 1939 *educ* Barking Abbey Sch; K Coll Lon; *CV* Personnel Dept ICI 1961–66; Personnel Admin and Employee Relations Singer Co New York 1966–68; American Express New York 1968–70; Asst Personnel Mgr and Staff Devel Mgr Guinness Overseas 1970–80; M Lon and S'wark Dioc Jt Prisons and Penal Concerns Grp; M Coun Corp of Ch Ho; Trustee of Affirming Catholicism; Convenor of Affirming Catholics in Synod; M CNC
GS 1995–   *Tel:* 020 8995 6427
        email: marygjohnston@btinternet.com

JONES, Mr David Arthur,
Vicarage Loders Bridport DT6 3SA [SALISBURY] *b* 1936 *educ* Abingdon; RMA Sandhurst; RAF & Army Command & Staff Coll; *CV* Army officer 1959–85 (Colonel); Assoc Dir Oxfam 1985–93; Assoc Dir Internat Alert 1994–97; vol Cov Dio rep for CUF and Dioc Devel Fund; retired; Insp of Th Colls; Lyme Bay Dny Info Officer; M MPA Coun of AC from 2006; PCC Sec, Powerstock
GS 1995–2001; 2003–   *Tel:* 01308 425419
                        Fax: 01308 422921
        email: david@nerissajmes.plus.com

JONES, Mr (James) Allan,
30 Pimbo Rd Kings Moss St Helens WA11 8RD
[LIVERPOOL] *b* 1950 *educ* Cen Secondary Boys' Sch
St Helens; St Helens Coll of Tech; *CV* Production
Control Clerk 1966–84; Navigator for Emergency
Doctor Service 1987–98; Rtd; M Liv Dioc Bd of
Educ 1991–94 and from 2003; Vc-Chairman Liv
Branch Prayer Book Soc 1991–95; Dioc Lay Co-
ord Forward in Faith 1993–2003; M Dioc BSR and
Exec Cttee 1998–2003; M Dioc Regional Issues
Sector Cttee 1998–2003; M Dioc Schs Cttee 2000–
03; M CCC 2001–06; M Dioc Schs and RE Exec
Cttee from 2003; Sch Gov (C of E VC primary)
from 2003, Chair from 2007; M DBF and Fin Cttee
from 2004; M Liv DAC from 2004; M Dioc Sup-
porting Local Chs Forum 2004–05; M Merseyside
Change Up Rural Issues Task Grp 2005–08; M
Rainford Par Coun (Conservative) from 2007
GS 1990–   *Tel:* 01744 893367
                                  07715 254692 (Mobile)

JONES, Rt Revd James Stuart, BA, PGCE, DD
Bishop's Lodge Woolton Park Liverpool L25 6DT
[BISHOP OF LIVERPOOL] *b* 1948 *educ* Duke of York's
Military Sch Dover; Ex Univ; Wycliffe Hall Th
Coll; *CV* C Ch Ch Clifton 1982–90; V Em S Croy-
don 1990–94; Bp of Hull 1994–98; Bp of Liv from
1998
GS 1995–   *Tel:* 0151 421 0831
                                  Fax: 0151 428 3055
   email: bishopslodge@liverpool.anglican.org

JONES, Very Revd Keith Brynmor, MA
The Deanery York YO1 7JQ [DEAN OF YORK] *b* 1944
educ Ludlow Gr Sch; Selw Coll Cam; Cuddesdon
Th Coll; *CV* C Limpsfield w Titsey 1969–72;
Dean's V St Alb Abbey 1972–76; P-in-c St Mich
Borehamwood 1976–79; TV 1979–82; V St Mary le
Tower Ipswich 1982–96; RD Ipswich 1993–95;
Dean of Ex 1996–2004; Dean of York from 2004
GS 1999–2005
   Tel: 01904 557202 (Office) 01904 623608 (Home)
             email: dean@yorkminster.org

JONES, Canon Mrs Linda Mary, BA, Cert Ed,
A Dip R
Vicarage Park Rd Ormskirk L39 3AJ [LIVERPOOL] *b*
1951 *educ* Shelburne Sch; All SS Coll Lon; Open
Univ; *CV* Project Asst Thos Coram Rsch Unit Inst
of Educ Lon 1974–83; Asst Dir of Pre-Admission
Tr for Rdrs 1994–2001; M CCU Engl-Angl RC
Cttee; Educ Selector Min Div; M VRSC Candi-
dates Panel; Chair Dioc BMU 1996–2001; M Bp's
Coun; Sen Officer Dioc Ch Growth and Ecum
Team from 2001; lay M Liv Cathl Chapter from
2004; Educ Adv Min Div
GS 2000–   *Tel:* 0151 705 2109 (Office)
                                  01695 572515 (Home)
   email: linda.jones@liverpool.anglican.org

JONES, Ven Philip Hugh, Dip Chr Theol & Min,
Solicitor
27 The Avenue Lewes BN7 1QT [ARCHDEACON OF
LEWES AND HASTINGS; CHICHESTER] *b* 1951 *educ*

Leys Sch Cam; Chich Theol Coll; *CV* C St Mary V
Horsham 1994–97; V H Innocents Southwater
1997–2005; RD Horsham 2002–05; Adn of Lewes
& Hastings from 2005   *Tel:* 01273 479530
                                  Fax: 01273 476529
            email: archlandh@diochi.org.uk

JONES, Revd Rhiannon Elizabeth, BA, MA, MA
*Rectory 2 Apthorpe St Fulbourn Cambridge CB21
5EY* [ELY] *b* 1972 *educ* Ox High Sch; Ex Univ; Lon
Sch of Theol; Ridley Hall, Cam; *CV* Co0ord of
Jubilee Cen, Cam 1995–98; C Huntingdon Team
Min 2000–04; R Fulbourn, Great Wilbraham, Lit-
tle Wilbraham and Six Mile Bottom from 2004; M
Ely Bp's Coun from 2005; M Lit Com from 2006
GS 2005–   *Tel:* 01223 880337
   email: rhiannon.jones@ely.anglican.org

JONES, Ven Trevor Pryce, B Ed, B Th, LL M, Cert Ed,
ACP
*Glebe House St Mary's Lane Hertingfordbury Hert-
ford SG11 2LE* [ARCHDEACON OF HERTFORD; ST
ALBAN'S] *b* 1948 *educ* Dial Stone Sch Stockport; St
Luke's Coll Ex; Southn Univ; Sarum and Wells Th
Coll; Univ of Wales, Cardiff Law Sch; St Jo Coll
Dur; *CV* C St Geo Glouc 1976–79; Warden Bp
Mascall Centre Ludlow and M Heref Dioc Educ
Tm 1979–84; DCO 1981–96; Sec Heref-Nurnberg
Eur Ecum Partnership 1982–87; M Bp's Coun
1987–87; M Dioc Ecum Cttee 1985–87, Chair
1996–97; TR Heref S Wye TM 1984–97; OCF 1985–
97; Preb Heref Cathl 1993–97; M Dioc Pastl/Minl
Cttee 1996–97; Adn of Hertford from 1997; Hon
Can St Alb Cathl 1997; Chair St Alb and Ox Min
Course 1998–2007; Chair Reach out Projects Mgt
Coun from 1998; Bp's Selector 2001–08; Chair
Rural Strategy Grp from 2001; Vc-Chair ERMC
from 2004; Chair Hockerill Educ Foundn 2005; M
Legal Adv Commn 2006
GS 2000–05; 2005–   *Tel:* 01992 581629
                                  Fax: 01992 558745
   email: archdhert@stalbans.anglican.org

JUDD, Very Revd Peter Somerset Margesson,
MA
*The Dean's House 3 Harlings Grove Waterloo Lane
Chelmsford CM1 1YQ* [DEAN OF CHELMSFORD] *b*
1949 *educ* Charterhouse Sch; Trin Hall Cam;
Cuddesdon Th Coll; *CV* C St Phil w St Steph Sal-
ford 1974–76; Chapl Clare Coll Cam 1976–81; Act-
ing Dean Clare Coll 1980–81; TV Burnham w
Dropmore, Hitcham and Taplow 1981–88; V St
Mary V Iffley 1988–97; RD Cowley 1995–97; R
and Prov of Chelmsf from 1997, Dean from 2000
GS 2003–05   *Tel:* 01245 354318 (Home)
                                  01245 294492 (Office)
                                  07740 456844 (Mobile)
                                  Fax: 01245 294499
   email: dean@chelmsfordcathedral.org.uk

JUDKINS, Mrs Mary, BA, PGCE, MA
*Old Vicarage 3 Church Lane East Ardsley Wakefield
WF3 2LJ* [WAKEFIELD] *b* 1951 *educ* Leominster Gr

Sch; Bris Univ; St Mary's Coll Cheltenham; Open Univ; *CV* Tchr in Bris and E Grinstead 1984–94; Supply Tchr; Homemaker/Mother; Lay Chair Dioc Syn; GS Rep SAMS 1995–2005; M CCU; M CMEAC 2000–05; delegate WCC 9th Assembly 2006; vol co-ord N Kirklees Chr Faith Cen, Dewsbury Minster from 2005
GS 1995–   *Tel:* 01924 826802
       email: elephantmj@aol.com

JUKES, Very Revd Keith Michael, BA
17 High St Agnesgate Ripon HG4 1QR [DEAN OF RIPON; RIPON AND LEEDS] *b* 1954 *educ* Leeds Univ; Linc Th Coll; *CV* C H Trin Wordsley, Lich 1978–81; C Wolverhampton 1981–83; C-in-c Stoneydelph St Martin CD 1983–90; TR Glascote and Stoneydelph 1990–91; RD Tamworth 1990–91; TR Cannock and V Hatherton 1991–97; Preb Lich Cathl 1996–97; P-in-c Selby Abbey, York 1997-99; V 1999–2007; Dean of Ripon from 2007
                Tel: 01765 602609
                   01765 603462
          07890 956004 (Mobile)
            Fax: 01765 602609
email: dean@keithjukes.orangehome.co.uk

KAJUMBA, Ven Daniel Steven Kimbugwe, BA, HND, Dip Th, Dip IMBM, LAMDA
84 Higher Drive Purley CR8 2HJ [ARCHDEACON OF REIGATE; SOUTHWARK] *b* 1952 *educ* Christian Life Coll; Bournemouth Univ; Open Univ; S'wark Ord Course; Lond Univ; *CV* C St Alb Goldington 1985–87; pt Chapl Bedford Prison; Uganda 1987-98: Man Dir Transocean; Gen Man Rio Holdings Internat; Kingdom of Buganda Sec Gen, Cabinet Min PR, Functions and Protocol, Min Foreign Affairs; TV St Fran Horley 1999–2001; Adn of Reigate from 2001; M Dioc Syn; M Bp's Coun; M Business Cttee; M Fin Cttee; M Exec and Glebe Cttee; M Stipends and Budget Cttee; M Parsonages and Property Maintenance Cttee; M Fairer Shares Cttee; M Sites/Advisory and Red Churches Uses Cttee; M CMEAC; M Croydon Area Coun   *Tel:* 020 8660 9276 (Home)
           020 8681 5496 (Work)
        07949 594460 (Mobile)
        Fax: 020 8660 9276 (Home)
          020 8686 2074 (Work)
email: daniel.kajumba@southwark.anglican.org

KEARON, Canon Kenneth Arthur, BA, MA, M Phil, DD
Anglican Communion Office St Andrew's House 16 Tavistock Crescent London W11 1AP [SECRETARY GENERAL, ANGLICAN COMMUNION] *b* 1953 *educ* Mountjoy Sch Dub; Trin Coll Dub; Cam Univ; Irish Sch of Ecumenics; *CV* Dn 1981; P 1982; C All SS Raheny and St Jo Coolock, Dioc of Dublin and Glendalough 1981–84; Dean of Residence Trin Coll Dub 1984–91; R Tullow, Dub 1991–99; Dir Irish Sch of Ecumenics 1999–2004; M Chapter of Ch Ch Cathl, Dub from 1995, Chan 2002–04; Sec Gen Angl Communion from 2005; Hon Can St

Paul's Cathl Lon, St Geo Cathl Jerusalem, Ch Ch Cathl Cant   *Tel:* 020 7313 3905
             Fax: 020 7313 3999
email: kenneth.kearon@anglicancommunion.org

KELLY, Mr Declan Gerard, MSc, BSc, MCLIP
Church House Great Smith St London SW1P 3AZ [DIRECTOR OF LIBRARIES, ARCHIVES AND INFORMATION SERVICES, ARCHBISHOPS' COUNCIL] *b* 1960 *educ* St Hugh's Coll Nottm; Qu Mary Coll Lon; Sheffield Univ; *CV* Rsch Centre Mgr, BBC World Service 1993–97; Intake and Acquisitions Mgr, BBC Archives 1997–99, Rsch Services Mgr 2000-03, Output Services Mgr 2003–05; Dir of Libraries, Archives and Information Services, AC from 2005   *Tel:* 020 7898 1432
       email: declan.kelly@c-of-e.org.uk

KENSINGTON, Area Bishop of. (NOT APPOINTED AT TIME OF GOING TO PRESS)

KENT, Mr Ian David,
Brightmanshayes Petrockstowe Okehampton EX20 3EY [EXETER] *b* 1980 *educ* Gt Torrington Sch; Plymouth Coll of Art and Design; *CV* Printer from 1996; M Dioc Syn from 2000
GS 2000–   *Tel and Fax:* 01409 281281
email: ian.kent@brightmanshayes.freeserve.co.uk

KERR, Canon Nicholas Ian, MA, Cert Theol
Vicarage 64 Day's Lane Sidcup DA15 8JR [ROCHESTER] *b* 1946 *educ* Dulwich Coll; Emm Coll Cam; Westcott Ho Cam; *CV* C St Mary V Merton Park 1977–80; C St Marg Rainham 1980–84; V St Edmund K M Dartford and pt Chapl, Joyce Green Hosp Dartford 1984–90; V Holy Redeemer Lamorbey from 1990; RD Sidcup 1998–2003; Chair Roch Dioc Ho of Clergy 2000–06
GS 2005–   *Tel:* 020 8300 1508
           020 8302 5356 (Office)
        07885 619595 (Mobile)
       email: nicholaskerr@btinternet.com

KEY, Very Revd Robert Frederick, BA, DPS, FSA
The Deanery David Place St Helier Jersey JE2 4TE [DEAN OF JERSEY; WINCHESTER] *b* 1952 *educ* Alleyn's Sch Dulwich; Bris Univ; Oak Hill Th Coll; *CV* C St Ebbe Ox 1976–80; Min St Patr Wallington 1980–85; V Eynsham and Cassington 1985–91; V St Andr Ox 1991–2001; M Coun Wycliffe Hall from 1985; M Coll of Evangelists; Gen Dir CPAS 2001–05; Dean of Jersey from 2005; Lay Can Salis Cathl from 2008
GS 1995–2005   *Tel:* 01534 720001
       email: robert_f_key@yahoo.com

KEY, Mr Simon Robert, MA, Cert Ed
4 Old St Salisbury SP2 8JL [SALISBURY] *b* 1945 *educ* Salis Cathl Sch; Sherborne Sch; Clare Coll Cam; *CV* Master, Loretto Sch Edin 1967–69; Harrow Sch 1969–83; Min for Local Government and Inner Cities 1990–92, for Nat Heritage 1992–93, for Transport 1993–94; Shadow Min for Defence

1997–99, for Internat Devel 1999–2001, for Science 2003–05; M Defence Select Cttee; MP for Salis from 1983; M Salis Dioc Syn from 2003; M Coun of Salis Cathl from 2002; M Eccl Cttee of Parliament from 2005

GS 2005–   *Tel:* 01722 326699
01722 323050
Fax: 01722 326699
01722 327080
email: rob@robertkey.com

KILLWICK, Canon Simon David Andrew, BD, AKC, Cert Th
Christ Church Rectory Monton St Moss Side Manchester M14 4GP [MANCHESTER] *b* 1956 *educ* Westmr Sch; K Coll Lon; St Steph Ho Th Coll; *CV* C St Mark Worsley 1981–84; TV St Mary Ellenbrook 1984–97; P-in-c Ch Ch Moss Side from 1997, R from 2006; Exam Chapl to Bp of Man 2002–07; Hon Can Manch from 2004; AD Hulme from 2007

GS 1998–   *Tel:* 0161 226 2176
email: frskillwick@btinternet.com

KINGSTON, Area Bishop of. See CHEETHAM, Rt Revd Richard Ian

KINSON, Mrs Wendy Elizabeth, BA
The Old Laundry Maer Newcastle ST5 5EF [LICHFIELD] *b* 1953 *educ* Bp Blackhall Sch Ex; Sussex Univ; *CV* CAB Adv from 1993; Child care worker from 2000; Chair Dioc Syn Ho of Laity from 2003

GS 1995–   *Tel:* 01782 680613

KNARESBOROUGH, Suffragan Bishop of. See BELL, Rt Revd James Harold

KNOWLES, Rt Revd Graeme Paul, AKC
The Deanery 9 Amen Court London EC4M 7BU [DEAN OF ST PAUL'S; LONDON] *b* 1951 *educ* Dunstable Gr Sch; K Coll Lon; St Aug Coll Cant; *CV* C St Peter-in-Thanet 1974–79; C and Prec Leeds Par Ch 1979–81; Chapl Prec Portsm Cathl 1981–87; V Leigh Park 1987–93; RD Havant 1990–93; Adn of Portsm 1993–99; Dean of Carl 1999–2003; M CCC 1995–2001, Vc-Chair 1996–2001; Chair CCC from 2003; Bp of Sodor and Man 2003–07; Dean of St Paul's from 2007; Chair CCC 2003–08; Chair CBC from 2008

GS 1995–98, 2003–07   *Tel:* 020 7236 2827
Fax: 020 7332 0298
email: thedean@stpaulscathedral.org.uk

LADDS, Rt Revd Robert Sidney, SSC, B Ed, LRSC, FCS
60 West Green Stokesley Middlesbrough TS9 5BD [SUFFRAGAN BISHOP OF WHITBY; YORK] *b* 1941 *educ* Swanley Sch; NW Kent Coll; Ch Ch Coll Cant Lon Univ; Cant Sch of Min; *CV* C St Leon Hythe 1980–83; R St Jo Bapt Bretherton 1983–91; Chapl Bp Rawsthorne Sch 1983–86; Bp's Chapl for Min 1986–90; Bp of Blackb Audit Officer 1990–91; R

Preston 1991–97; Hon Can Blackb Cathl 1993–97; Adn of Lanc 1997–99; Commr of Bp of Taejon to Province of York 1998–2000; Bp of Whitby from 1999; Superior-Gen Soc of Mary from 2000; Vc Pres Korean Miss Partnership from 2000; Chairman Dioc Bd of Educ 2003–08   *Tel:* 01642 714475
01642 714476
Fax: 01642 714472
email: bishopofwhitby@episcopus.co.uk

LAKE, Canon Stephen David, B Th
Old Rectory Sumpter Yard St Albans AL1 1BY [ST ALBANS] *b* 1963 *educ* Homefield Sch; Chich Th Coll; *CV* C Sherborne w. Castleton & Lillington 1988–92; P-in-c St Aldhelm Branksome 1992–96, V 1996–2001; RD Poole 2000–01; Can Res and Sub Dean Cathl and Abbey Ch of St Alb from 2001; Chair Dioc Liturg Cttee; Chair Easter Monday Pilgrimage Cttee

GS 2004–   *Tel:* 01727 890201
07900 988646 (Mobile)
email: subdean@stalbanscathedral.org.uk

LAMBETH, Archdeacon of. See SKILTON, Ven Christopher John

LANCASTER, Archdeacon of. See BALLARD, Ven Peter James

LANCASTER, Suffragan Bishop of. See PEARSON, Rt Revd Geoffrey Seagrave

LANGHAM, Revd Paul Jonathan, BA, Dip Th, BA, M Th
Lonsdale Church Rd Combe Down Bath BA2 5JJ [BATH AND WELLS] *b* 1960 *educ* Q E Sch Kirkby Lonsdale; Ex Univ; Cam Univ; Ridley Hall Cam; *CV* C All SS Bath Weston w. N Stoke, B&W 1987–91; Chapl and Fell, St Cath Coll Cam 1991–96; V Combe Down w. Monkton Combe & S Stoke, B&W from 1996; dep RD Bath Dny; M Bp's Liturg Grp; M Dioc Syn; M Adnry Pastl Cttee

GS 2005–   *Tel:* 01225 835835
email: vicar@htcd.org

LANGRISH, Rt Revd Michael Laurence, B Soc Sc, BA, MA, Hon DD (Birm), Hon DD (Ex)
The Palace Exeter EX1 1HY [BISHOP OF EXETER] *b* 1946 *educ* K Edw Sch Southn; Birm Univ; Fitzw Coll Cam; Ridley Hall Th Coll; *CV* C Stratford-upon-Avon 1973–76; Chapl Rugby Sch 1976–81; V Offchurch and DDO 1981–87; Exam Chapl to Bp of Cov 1982–89; Chair ACCM Vocations Cttee 1984–91; TR Rugby 1987–93; Chair Ho of Clergy Dioc Syn 1988–93; Hon Can Cov Cathl 1990–93; Bp of Birkenhead 1993–2000; M BAGUPA 1996–98; M Urban Bps' Panel 1996–2000; M BSR Community and Urban Affairs Cttee 1998–2001; Bp of Exeter from 2000; Chair Rural Affairs Cttee, M BM 2001–06; M Ch Commrs Bishoprics and Cathls Cttee 2002–06; Chair Melanesian Mission from 2002; M Bd of Chr Aid from 2003; Chair Toyne Follow-up Grp 2004–06; M Ho of Lords

WHO'S WHO

from 2005; Chair Diocs Pastl and Miss Measure Grp 2006–08; Chair Rural Strategy Grp from 2006 GS 1985–93, 1999–   *Tel:* 01392 272362
Fax: 01392 430923
email: sarah.johnson@exeter.anglican.org

LANGSTAFF, Rt Revd James Henry, MA (Oxon), BA (Nottm)
The Old Vicarage Castle Acre King's Lynn PE32 2AA [SUFFRAGAN BISHOP OF LYNN; NORWICH] *b* 1956 *educ* Cheltenham Coll; Ox Univ; Nottm Univ; St Jo Coll Nottm; *CV* C St Pet Farnborough, Guildf 1981–86, P-in-c 1985–86; P-in-c St Matt Duddeston & St Clem Nechells, Birm 1986, V 1987–96; RD Birm City 1995–96; Chapl to Bp of Birm 1996–2000; R H Trin Sutton Coldfield, Birm 2000–04; Area Dean of Sutton Coldfield 2002–04; Bp of Lynn from 2004; Chair Flagship Housing Grp from 2006; M E of England Regional Assembly from 2007   *Tel:* 01760 755553
07989 330582 (Mobile)
email: bishoplynn@norwich.anglican.org

LASH, Very Revd Archimandrite Ephrem, MA, STB
217 Clarendon Rd Whalley Range Manchester M16 0AY [ECUMENICAL REPRESENTATIVE (ORTHODOX CHURCHES)] *b* 1930 *educ* Downside Sch; St Jo Coll Ox; Seminaire St Sulpice, Paris; *CV* Lect in Bibl and Patristic Studies Univ of Newc 1978–84; rtd GS 1995–2001; 2005–   *Tel:* 0161 881 5774
email: ephrem@chorlton.com

LAWSON, Ven Michael Charles, BA
London Diocesan House 36 Causton St London SW1P 4AU [ARCHDEACON OF HAMPSTEAD; LONDON] *b* 1952 *educ* Hove Gr Sch; Guildhall Sch of Music; Sussex Univ; Ecoles d'Art Americaines, Conservatoire de Musique Fontainebleu, France; Trin Coll Bris; *CV* C St Mary Horsham; 1978–81; Dir of Pastoring All So Langham Place 1981–86; V Ch Ch Bromley 1987–99; Adn of Hampstead from 1999; Dir and Trustee Langham Arts Trust from 1987; Coun and Exec M CEEC from 1996; Gov Highgate Sch from 1999; M Angl Mainstream Strg Grp from 2005; M Oak Hill Coll Coun from 1999; Chair Pipe Village Trust from 2007; Documentary Producer, High Definition Ltd from 2006   *Tel:* 020 7932 1190
Fax: 020 7932 1192
email: archdeacon.hampstead@
london.anglican.org

LEATHARD, Prof Helen Louise, B Sc, Ph D, F B Pharmacol S, MA
29 Coronation Way Lancaster LA1 2TQ [BLACKBURN] *b* 1947 *educ* Kirkby Stephen Gr Sch Westmorland; Chelsea Coll Lon; K Coll Hosp Medical Sch; St Mart Coll Lancaster; *CV* Rsch Fell K Coll Hosp Medical Sch 1974–76; Lect in Pharmacology; Charing Cross and Westmr Medical Sch 1977–92; Sen Lect in Physiology St Martin's Coll

Lanc 1992–94; Rdr in Pharmacology and Human Physiology Univ of Cumbria 1994–2001; Prof of Healing Science and Pharmacology from 2001; M Dioc Syn; Guild of St Raph Coun; M Order of St Luke from 2003; Consult Cen for Study of Theol and Health; M Tunstall Dny Syn; Rdr; M B Pharmacol S from 1973, Fell from 2006, Educ Subcttee from 2001, Clinical Pharmacology Section Cttee from 2004, Educ and Trg Ctee from 2006; M Physiological Soc from 1992
GS 2000–   *Tel:* 01524 849495 (Home)
01524 384384 ext. 2502 (Work)
email: h.leathard@ucsm.ac.uk

LEE, Ven David John, B Sc, MA, PhD, Dip Theol, Dip Miss Studies
14 Park Cliffe Rd Undercliffe Bradford BD2 4NS [ARCHDEACON OF BRADFORD] *b* 1946 *educ* Wolverhampton Gr Sch; Bris Univ; All Nations Chr Coll; Lon Univ; Cam Univ; Birm Univ; Ridley Hall, Cam; *CV* Sch Master, Lesotho 1967–68; Sch Master, Walsall 1968–77; C St Marg Putney, S'wark 1977–80; Lect in NT and Theol, Bp Tucker Coll Uganda 1980–86; Lect in Biblical Studies and Missiology, Selly Oak Colls, Tutor Crowther Hall, Selly Oak 1986–91; R Middleton and Wishaw 1991–96; Dir for Miss and Res Can Birm Cathl 1996–2004; Adn of Bradford from 2004; sometime involvement with Angl Ch Planting Initiatives, Nat Coun for Chr Unity (Local Unity Panel), Grace Houses, Birm (internat student work), Chaplaincy Plus, Birm (work-based chaplaincy and mission), Samuel White Charities, Middleton (almshouse trust); Bradf Chs for Dialogue and Diversity (miss educ); Gov Imm C of E Com Coll, Idle, Bradf
GS 2005   *Tel:* 01274 200698
07711 671351 (Mobile)
Fax: 01274 200698
email: david.lee@bradford.anglican.org

LEE, Revd John, B Sc, M Sc, MInstGA
The Wash House Lambeth Palace London SE1 7JU [CLERGY APPOINTMENTS ADVISER] *b* 1947 *educ* St Dunstan's Coll Catford; Univ Coll Swansea; Inst of Grp Analysis Lon; Ripon Hall Th Coll; *CV* Experimental Officer R Australian Navy Rsch Laboratory Sydney 1971–73; pt Nursing Auxiliary Chu Hosp Ox 1973–75; C Cockett 1975–78; P-in-c St Teilo Cockett 1976–78; Pr/Counsellor St Botoloph Aldgate 1978–84; Hon Psychotherapist Dept of Psychological Medicine St Bart's Hosp Lon 1980–86; Course Consultant St Alb Minl Tr Scheme 1980–85; P-in-c Chiddingstone w Chiddingstone Causeway 1984–89; R 1989–98; Tutor in Individual and Grp Psychotherapy Dept of Psychological Medicine St Bart's Medical Sch 1987–92; Staff Consult Richmond Fell 1989–98; Psychotherapist and Grp Analyst in private practice 1987–98; Clergy Appointments Adv from 1998   *Tel:* 020 7898 1898
Fax: 020 7898 1899
email: admin.caa@c-of-e.org.uk

LEE, Revd (John Charles) Hugh Mellanby, MA, M Tech, FRSA
12 Walton St Oxford OX1 2HG [OXFORD] *b* 1944 *educ* Marlboro Coll; Trin Hall Cam; Brunel Univ; Ox NSM Course; *CV* Operational Rsch Scientist Nat Coal Bd 1966–76; Coal Supply Tm Leader Internat Energy Agency 1976–84; Dep Hd of Economics Br Coal 1984–91; Dir Coal and Electricity Consulting WEFA Energy 1992–95; NSM Amersham-on-the-Hill 1981–88; NSM St Aldate Ox 1988–93; NSM Wheatley 1993–95; pt Work and Economic Life Missr Berks, Bucks and Oxon 1995–2002; NSM House for Duty P-in-c, St Mich at the North Gate, Ox and City R from 2002; pt Consult Energy Economist from 1995; Treas and Trustee Chs Media Trust 1994–2001; Dir Equigas and Equipower from 1998, Chair from 2003; Moderator CHRISM 1998–2001; married Anne Mellanby 1967; children Kate born 1971, Alexander born 1973; founding trustee Ox Industrial Chapl from 1998; M DRACSC from 2004–06
GS 2000–   *Tel:* 01865 316245
                                            07879 426625 (Mobile)
                                            Fax: 01865 316245
                           email: hugh.lee@btinternet.com

LEEDS, Archdeacon of. See BURROWS, Ven Peter

LEICESTER, Archdeacon of. See ATKINSON, Ven Richard William Bryant

LEICESTER, Bishop of. See STEVENS, Rt Revd Timothy John

LEICESTER, Dean of. See FAULL, Very Revd Vivienne Frances

LENNOX, Mr Lionel Patrick Madill, LLB
Provincial and Diocesan Registry Stamford House Piccadilly York YO1 9PP [REGISTRAR OF PROVINCE AND DIOCESE OF YORK; REGISTRAR OF CONVOCATION OF YORK; REGISTRAR OF TRIBUNALS FOR PROVINCE OF YORK] *educ* St Jo Sch Leatherhead; Birm Univ; Leeds Metropolitan Univ; *CV* Solicitor from 1973; In private practice 1973–80; Asst Legal Adv GS 1981–87; Sec Abp of Cant's Grp on Affinity 1982–84; Sec Bp of Lon's Grp on Blasphemy 1981–87; Sec Legal Adv Commn 1986–89; Registrar Province and Dioc York, Legal Secretary to the Archbp of York, Registrar York Conv and Eccl Notary from 1987 and Ptnr Denison Till (York) Solicitors from 1987; M Legal Adv Commn from 1987; Notary Public from 1992; M Eccll Rule Cttee from 1992; Trustee Yorks Hist Chs Trust; Trustee St Leon Hospice York; City of York Under Sheriff 2006–07; Pres Yorkshire Law Soc 2007–08
                                            Tel: 01904 623487
                                            01904 611411
                                            Fax: 01904 561470

LEROY, Mr Peter John, MA, PGCE
8 Brook Cottage Lower Barton Corston Bath BA2 9BA [BATH AND WELLS] *b* 1944 *educ* Monkton Combe Sch; Qu Coll Cam; *CV* History tchr and Housemaster Radley Coll 1967-84; Hdmaster Monkton Combe Jun Sch and Relig Studies tchr 1984–94; Vc-Chair Incorp Assoc of Prep Schs 1993–94; Sec Studylink EFAC Internat Tr Partnership 1995–2002; M Bd of Educ 1997–2005; M Dioc Bd of Educ from 1997; Sch Gov; Scripture Union Bd and Coun 1997–2006; Chair Trustees, Open the Book from 2007; Rdr from 1997
GS 1975–85, 1995–   *Tel:* 01225 873023
                                    email: panda@leroy.com

LETTS, Ven Kenneth John, BA, Dip Ed
11 rue de la Buffa 06000 Nice France [ARCHDEACON OF FRANCE; EUROPE] *b* 1942 *educ* Coll of Resurr Mirfield; *CV* C St Steph Mt Waverley (Australia) 1971–74; Chapl Melbourne C of E Gr Sch 1974–81; P-in-c Albert Park 1981–94; Sen Chapl St Mich Sch 1982–94; Chapl Nice w Vence from 1994; Can Gib Cathl from 2004; Adn of France from 2007
                                    Tel: 00 33 4 93 87 19 83
                                    Fax: 00 33 4 93 82 25 09
                                    email: anglican@free.fr

LEWES AND HASTINGS, Archdeacon of. See JONES, Ven Philip Hugh

LEWES, Area Bishop of. See BENN, Rt Revd Wallace Parke

LEWIS, Revd Brian,
Little Ilford Rectory 124 Church Rd Manor Park London E12 6HA [CHELMSFORD] *CV* Re-elected to GS 2005
GS 2005–   *Tel:*

LEWIS, Very Revd Christopher Andrew, BA, Ph D
The Deanery Christ Church Oxford OX1 1DP [DEAN OF CHRIST CHURCH, OXFORD] *b* 1944 *educ* Marlboro Coll; Bris Univ; CCC Cam; Westcott Ho Th Coll; Episc Th Sch Cam Mass; *CV* Royal Navy 1961–66; C Barnard Castle 1973–76; Tutor Ripon Coll Cuddesdon 1976–81; Dir Ox Inst for Ch and Soc 1976–79; P-in-c Aston Rowant and Crowell 1978–81; Vc Prin Ripon Coll Cuddesdon 1981–82; V Spalding 1982–87; Can Res Cant Cathl 1987–94; Dir Minl Tr Cant dio 1989–94; Dean of St Alb 1994–2003; Chair Inspections Wkg Pty, Ho of Bp's Cttee for Min 1996–2003; TETC 1996–2003; Chair Assoc of Engl Cathls from 2000; Dean Ch Ch Ox from 2003
GS 1985–88, 1995–2005   *Tel:* 01865 276161
                                Fax: 01865 276238
                       email: rachel.perham@chch.ox.ac.uk

LEWIS, Revd Edward John, JP, BA, B Ed, MA, FRSA, M Inst D
Church House Great Smith St London SW1P 3AZ [CHIEF EXECUTIVE AND DIRECTOR OF TRAINING, HOSPITAL CHAPLAINCIES COUNCIL] *b* 1958 *educ* Penlan Sch Swansea; Univ of Wales; Chich Th Col; Univ of Surrey; *CV* C Llangiwg 1983–85; Sen C Morriston and Asst Chapl Morriston Hosp 1985–87; V Tregaron, Strata Florida and Ystrad-

meurig and Chapl Tregaron Hosp 1987–89; Sen Chapl Walsall Hosps NHS Trust, Walsall Com Trust and District Chapl Walsall HA 1989–2000; Asst RD Walsall 1995–2000; Sec and Dir Tr HCC from 2000; Visiting Lect, St Mary's Univ Coll Twickenham from 2003; Chair City of Westmr Magistrates' Trg Ctee from 2007; Chaplain to HMQ from 2008   *Tel:* 020 7898 1892
07957 529646 (Mobile)
Fax: 020 7898 1891
email: edward.lewis@c-of-e.org.uk

LEWIS, Mr Paul, BA, Postgrad Dip (Environmental Planning)
Church House Great Smith St London SW1P 3AZ [PASTORAL AND CLOSED CHURCHES SECRETARY, CHURCH COMMISSIONERS] *b* 1952 *educ* Cantonian High Sch, Cardiff; Liv Univ; *CV* Asst Planner Chorley Borough Coun 1974–85; Appeals Officer Monmouth Borough Coun 1985–91; Asst Borough Planning Officer Hastings Borough Coun 1991–95, Borough Planning Officer/Chief Planner 1995–2004; Pastl and Closed Chs Sec Ch Commrs from 2004   *Tel:* 020 7898 1741
07894 930474 (Mobile)
Fax: 020 7898 1873
email: paul.lewis@c-of-e.org.uk

LEWISHAM, Archdeacon of. See HARDMAN, Ven Christine Elizabeth

LICHFIELD, Archdeacon of. See LILEY, Ven Christopher Frank

LICHFIELD, Bishop of. See GLEDHILL, Rt Revd Jonathan Michael

LICHFIELD, Dean of. See DORBER, Very Revd Adrian John

LILEY, Ven Christopher Frank, B Ed
24 The Close Lichfield WS13 7LD [ARCHDEACON OF LICHFIELD] *b* 1947 *educ* Bp Lonsdale Coll of Educ, Derby; Linc Th Coll; *CV* C Kingswinford 1974–79; TV Ch Ch Stafford 1979–84; V Norton, Letchworth 1984–96; RD Hitchin 1990–96; P-in-c St Alkmund Shrewsbury 1996–2001; V St Chad w St Mary Shrewsbury 1996–2001; Adn of Lich from 2001; Chair Bd of Min to 2002   *Tel:* 01543 306145
01543 306146
Fax: 01543 306147
email: archdeacon.lichfield@lichfield.anglican.org

LILLEY, Canon Christopher Howard, Dip CM, FTII
St Hybald's Vicarage Vicarage Lane Scawby Brigg DN20 9LX [LINCOLN] *b* 1951 *educ* K Sch Grantham; St Jo Coll Nottm; *CV* Hon C Skegness and Winthorpe 1985–93; C Gt Limber w Brocklesby 1993–96; P-in-c Middle Rasen Grp 1996–97; R Middle Rasen Grp 1997–2002; V Scawby with Redbourne and Hibaldstow and P-in-c Waddingham, Snitterby and Bishop Norton from 2002; RD Yarborough from 2002; M Bp's Coun

from 2001; Dioc Ecum Officer from 2001; Ch Commr 1997–98; M AC Fin Cttee 1999–2001 and 2004–07; M Ch Commrs Bishoprics and Cathls Cttee 1999–2006; P-in-c Kirton w. Lindsey and Grayingham from 2006; M CCU from 2007 GS 1996–   *Tel:* 01652 652725
email: c.lilley@btinternet.com

LINCOLN, Archdeacon of. (NOT APPOINTED AT TIME OF GOING TO PRESS**)**

LINCOLN, Bishop of. See SAXBEE, Rt Revd John Charles

LINCOLN, Dean of. See BUCKLER, Very Revd Philip John Warr

LINDISFARNE, Archdeacon of. See ROBINSON, Ven Peter John Alan

LINDSEY, Archdeacon of Stow and. See SINCLAIR, Ven Jane Elizabeth Margaret

LIVERPOOL, Archdeacon of. See PANTER, Ven Ricky (Richard) James Graham

LIVERPOOL, Bishop of. See JONES, Rt Revd James Stuart

LIVERPOOL, Dean of. See WELBY, Very Revd Justin Portal

LIVESEY, Mr Timothy Peter Nicholas, BA
Lambeth Palace London SE1 7JU [ARCHBISHOP OF CANTERBURY'S SECRETARY FOR PUBLIC AFFAIRS] *b* 1959 *educ* Stonyhurst Coll; New Coll Ox; *CV* 2nd Lieut, R Irish Rangers 1977–78; Asst Registrar and Dep Sec UMDS, Guy's and St Thos Hosps 1984–87; Foreign and Commonwealth Office 1987–2006; First Sec (Aid), Lagos 1989–93; Hd, Press and Public Affairs, Paris 1996–2000; Asst Press Sec, 10 Downing St 2000–02; on secondment as Princ Adv for Public Affairs to Cardinal Abp of Westmr 2002–04; Asst Dir, Information and Strategy, FCO 2004–06; Abp of Cant's Sec for Public Affairs from 2006   *Tel:* 020 7898 1200
Fax: 020 7898 1210
email: mary.whitticase@lambethpalace.org.uk

LLOYD, Revd Jonathan Wilford, B Sc, MA, Dip Applied Social Studies, CQSW
Rectory Richmond Place Bath BA1 5PZ [BATH AND WELLS] *b* 1956 *educ* Lancing Coll; Surrey Univ; City of Lon Poly; Goldsmiths Coll Lon Univ; North Lon Poly; S'wark Ord Course; *CV* PA to Bp of Namibia-in-Exile 1975–78; Rsch IDAF 1978–80; Com Wkr Lewisham 1980–81; Soc Wkr Lon Boro of S'wark 1982–84; Family Soc Wkr and Practice Tchr, Newham FWA 1984–86; Prin Soc Wkr St Chris Hospice Lond 1986–91; Help the Hospices Intl Fell (Sloan Kettering Meml Hosp, New York) 1991; Peace Monitor Kwa Zulu Natal (EMPSA) 1993; hon C St Bart Sydenham 1990–93, hon P-in-

c 1993–94; Dir of Soc Resp, S'wark dioc 1991–95; M Lambeth Millennium Gp 1996–99; Priest V S'wark Cathl 1991–97; Chair Lond and S'wark Diocs Prisons and Criminal Justice Gp 1992–96; Bp's Officer for Ch and Society, S'wark 1995–97; M S'wark Dioc Miss Team 1995–97; M Bd of Dirs S Lon Industrial Miss 1991–95; S'wark Dioc Eur Link Officer 1991–97; Univ Chapl and Ecum Chaplaincy Team Leader, Univ of Bath 1997–2004; M Dioc Bd of Ed 1998–2003; Trustee Dorothy Ho Hospice Care 1998–2001; Chair Conf of Eur Univ Chapls 1998–2002; P-in-c Charlcombe w. Bath St Steph from 2004; Co-Vc-Chair B & W Dioc Coun for Miss 2004–06; Non-Exec Dir R United Hosp Bath NHS Trust 2002–08; Chair B & W Dioc Soc Resp Grp from 2004; M Bp's Coun from 2008
GS 1995–97, 2005–
Tel: 01225 466114 (Home) 01225 420946 (Office)
email: jlloyduk@btinternet.com

LLOYD, Canon Nigel James Clifford, B Th, S Th
19 Springfield Rd Parkstone Poole BH14 0LG [SALISBURY] b 1951 educ Lancing Coll; Nottm Univ; Linc Th Coll; CV C Sherborne Abbey 1981–84; R Lytchett Matravers 1984–92; TR Lower Parkstone from 1992; Area Ecum Officer 1994–99; Dioc Ecum Officer 1999–2001; Asst RD Poole 2000–01, RD from 2001; non-res Can and Preb of Salis Cathl from 2002; M CCU 2001–05; M Bp's Coun 2000–05
GS 2000–
Tel: 01202 748860 (Home)
01202 749085 (Office)
07940 348776 (Mobile)
email: nigel.lloyd@dsl.pipex.com

LOCK, Ven Peter Harcourt D'Arcy, AKC
The Archdeaconry King's Orchard Rochester ME1 1TG [ARCHDEACON OF ROCHESTER] b 1944 educ Kingston Gr Sch; K Coll Lon; St Boniface Warminster; CV C St Jo Bapt Meopham 1968–72; C St Matt Wigmore w All SS Hempstead 1972–73; C Parish of S Gillingham 1973–77; R All SS Hartley 1977–83; R Fawkham and Hartley 1983–84; V H Trin Dartford 1984–93; Hon Can Roch Cathl from 1990; V St Pet and St Paul Bromley 1993–2000; RD Bromley 1996–2000; Adn Roch from 2000; M Bp's Coun from 1994; Chair Dioc Ho of Clergy 1996–2000; M Revision Cttee Eucharistic Prayers 1994; M Wkg Party on Marriage in Church after Divorce 1997–98; Can Res Roch Cathl from 2000
GS 1980–2000
Tel: 01634 560000 (Office)
01634 813533 (Home)
Fax: 01634 408942
email: archdeacon.rochester@rochester.anglican.org

LONDON (ST PAUL'S), Dean of. See KNOWLES, Rt Revd Graeme Paul

LONDON, Archdeacon of. See DELANEY, Ven Peter Anthony

LONDON, Bishop of. See CHARTRES, Rt Revd and Rt Hon Richard John Carew

LONDON, Hon. Assistant Bishop of. See MARSHALL, Rt Revd Michael Eric

LORDING, Mrs Rosemary Kathleen, BA
93 Kings Acre Rd Hereford HR4 0RQ [HEREFORD] b 1947 educ Eliz Newcomen Sch, Lon; Mid Essex Tech Coll, Chelms; Herefordshire Coll of Tech; CV Catering mgt 1968–73; Personnel and trg mgr, retail 1988–96; Gen Mgr, Three Counties Trg 1996–99; Trg and Devel Mgr, Herefordshire Primary Care Trust 1999–2001; voluntary worker; M Bp's Coun, Dioc Policy and Resources Cttee, DBF Revenue Cttee; additional M Heref Cathl Chapter
GS 2004–
Tel: 01432 340050
email: rk.lording@virgin.net

LOUGHBOROUGH, Archdeacon of. See HACKWOOD, Ven Paul

LOVEGROVE, Mr Philip Albert, LLB, LLM, OBE
177 Pixmore Way Letchworth Garden City SG6 1QT [ST ALBANS] b 1937 educ Pet Symonds Sch Win; K Coll Lon; CV Investment Banker and Fin Consult from 1962; M Ch Assembly 1965–70; Ch Commr 1983–98; Chair St Alb DBF 1970–2004; M Bp's Coun 1970–2004; M GS Stg Cttee 1980–85 and 1990–98; Lay Can St Alb Cathl 1998–2004
GS 1977–
Tel: 01462 481880 (Home)
020 7448 4754 (Office)
07767 458097 (Mobile)
Fax: 020 7448 4765 (Office)
email: philip.lovegrove@fiskeplc.com

LOWE, Rt Revd Stephen Richard, B Sc
14 Moorgate Ave Withington Manchester M20 1HE [SUFFRAGAN BISHOP OF HULME; MANCHESTER] b 1944 educ Leeds Gr Sch; Reading Sch; Lon Univ; Ripon Hall Th Coll; CV C St Mich Angl/Meth Ch Gospel Lane Birm 1968–72; P-in-c Woodgate Valley CD 1972–75; TR E Ham 1975–88; Chelmsf Dioc Urban Officer 1986–88; Hon Can Chelmsf Cathl from 1985; Adn of Sheff 1988–99; Bp of Hulme from 1999; Ch Commr 1992–99, M Bishoprics and Cathls Cttee 1991–2008, Dep Chair from 2002, M Bd of Govs 1994–99, 2001–; Trustee CUF 1991–97, Chair Grants Cttee from 1993; M BAGUPA 1993-96; M CTBI 1991–96; M CBF Exec 1993–96; M GS Staff Cttee 1991–96; M Abps' Commn on Organisation of C of E 1994–95; Chair Dioc Social Resp Cttee 1995–99; Chair Dioc Faith in the City Cttee; M Engl Nat Forum of BBC 1994–96; M Westcott Ho Coun and N Ord Course Coun 1999–2006; M Ho of Bps, Urban Bps' Panel from 2000, Chair from 2006; M Ho of Bps Stg Cttee 2003–06; M Abps' Commn on Urban Life and Faith 2003–06; Bp for Urban Life and Faith from 2006; Special Adv Cen Salford URG from 2008; M Red Chs Cttee from 2008
GS 1990–99, 2000–
Tel: 0161 445 5922
Fax: 0161 448 9687
email: lowehulme@btinternet.com

LOWMAN, Ven David Walter, BD, AKC
The Archdeacon's Lodge 136 Broomfield Road Chelmsford CM1 1RN [ARCHDEACON OF SOUTHEND; CHELMSFORD] *b* 1948 *educ* Crewkerne Gr Sch; K Coll Lon; St Aug Coll Cant; *CV* Civil Servant 1966–70; C Notting Hill TM 1975–78; C St Aug w St Jo Kilburn 1978–81; Selection Sec and Voc Adv ACCM 1981–86; TR Wickford and Runwell 1986–93; DDO, Lay Min Adv and NSM Officer 1993–2001; Hon Can Chelmsf Cathl from 1993; M Dioc Syn from 1986; Chair N Thames Min Tr Course 2008; Vc Chair St Mellitus Coll 2008; Gov Brentwood Sch; Sen Selector, Bps' Selection Confs; M Marriage Law Reform Group
GS 1995–2005   *Tel:* 01245 258257
                               Fax: 01245 250845
email: a.southend@chelmsford.anglican.org

LOWSON, Ven Christopher, M Th, STM, LLM, AKC
Church House Great Smith St London SW1P 3AZ [DIRECTOR OF MINISTRY, ARCHBISHOPS' COUNCIL] *b* 1953 *educ* Newc Cathl Sch; Consett Gr Sch; K Coll Lon; St Aug Coll Cant; Pacific Sch of Religion Berkeley California (WCC Scholar); Heythrop Coll Lon; Cardiff Law Sch; *CV* C St Mary Richmond 1977–82; P-in-c H Trin Eltham 1982–83, V 1983–91; Chapl Avery Hill Coll 1982–85; Chapl Thames Poly 1985–91; V Petersfield and R Buriton 1991–99; RD Petersfield 1995–99; Vis Lect Portsm Univ from 1998; Adn of Portsm Jan-Nov 1999; Adn of Portsdown 1999–2006; Chair Bd of Min; Bp of Portsm's Adv to Hosp Chaplaincy; Dioc Rep on Inter-Diocesan Fin Forum 1999–2006; Dir of Min, AC from 2006
GS 2000–05   *Tel:* 020 7898 1390
                          07957 657312 (Mobile)
                           Fax: 020 7898 1421
email: christopher.lowson@c-of-e.org.uk

LUDLOW, Archdeacon of. See HOOPER, Rt Revd Michael Wrenford

LUDLOW, Suffragan Bishop of. See HOOPER, Rt Revd Michael Wrenford

LUMUTENGA, Mrs Naomi Elizabeth, BA, Dip Ed, MA
25 Wilberforce Rd Coxheath Maidstone ME17 4HD [CANTERBURY] *b* 1959 *educ* Tororo Girls Sec Sch Uganda; Makerere Univ Kampala; Univ of London IOE; *CV* Sec Sch Tchr 1981–83; Accountant Uganda 1983–87; Sen Accountant Uganda 1987–89; Tchr and Hd of Year Maidstone Gr Sch from 1991; Learning Mgr MGS from 2007; GS rep CMS Bd of Trustees; GS rep URC
GS 1999–   *Tel:* 01622 746930
                                01622 752101
                                07969 429170
email: Lumut2@talk21.com

LUNN, Councillor Robin Christopher, BA
Little Hambledon 10 Malthouse Crescent Inkberrow WR7 4EF [WORCESTER] *b* 1968 *educ* Ditcham Park Sch; Univ of Kent; *CV* Business Devel Mgr from 2005; County Councillor for Redditch N from 2005
GS 2004–   *Tel:* 01386 792073
                          07785 305849 (Mobile)
                           Fax: 01386 791531
email: rlunn@worcestershire.gov.uk

LYNAS, Revd Stephen Brian, B Th, MBE, PGCE
Bishops' Office The Palace Wells Somerset BA5 2PD [BATH AND WELLS] *b* 1952 *educ* Borden Gr Sch, Kent; St Jo Coll Nottm; Trin Hall Cam; *CV* C Penn, Lich 1978–81; Relig Progr Org BBC Radio Stoke-on-Trent 1981–84; C Hanley 1981–82; C Edensor 1982–84; Relig Progr Producer BBC Bris 1985–88; Relig Progr Sen Producer BBC S and W Eng 1988–91; Hd Relig Progr TV South 1991–92; Com and Relig Affairs Ed Westcountry TV from 1992; Abps' Officer for Millennium 1996–2001; P Resources Adv, B&W Dioc 2001–07; Sen Chapl and Adv to Bps of B & W and Taunton from 2007
GS 2005–   *Tel:* 01749 672341
                               Fax: 01749 679355
email: chaplain@bathwells.anglican.org

LYNN, Archdeacon of. See GRAY, Ven Martin Clifford

LYNN, Suffragan Bishop of. See LANGSTAFF, Rt Revd James Henry

MACCLESFIELD, Archdeacon of. See GILLINGS, Ven Richard John

MacLEAY, Revd Angus Murdo, MA, M Phil
Rectory Rectory Lane Sevenoaks TN13 1JA [ROCHESTER] *b* 1959 *educ* The Vyne Basingstoke; Qu Mary's Sixth Form Coll Basingstoke; Univ Coll Ox; Wycliffe Hall Ox; *CV* C H Trin Platt, Man 1988–92; V St Jo Houghton w. St Pet Kingmoor, Carl 1992–2001; R St Nich Sevenoaks from 2001; M Angl-Meth Formal Conversations 1998–2001; M Dioc Syn
GS 1995–2001; 2005–   *Tel:* 01732 740340
                               Fax: 01732 742810
email: office@stnicholas-sevenoaks.org

MAGOWAN, Ven Alistair James, B Sc, Dip HE, M Th (Oxon)
Little Bailie Dullar Lane Sturminster Marshall Wimborne BH21 4AD [ARCHDEACON OF DORSET; SALISBURY] *b* 1955 *educ* K Sch Worc; Leeds Univ; Trin Coll Bris; Westmr Coll Ox; *CV* C St Jo Bapt Owlerton 1981–84; C St Nic Dur 1984–89; Chapl St Aid Coll Dur 1984–89; V St Jo Bapt Egham 1989–2000; RD Runnymede 1993–2000; Chair Guidf Dioc Bd of Educ 1996–2000; Adn of Dorset from 2000; Chair Salis DBE from 2004
GS 1995–2000, 2004–   *Tel:* 01258 859110
                               Fax: 01258 859118
email: addorset@salisbury.anglican.org

MAIDSTONE, Archdeacon of. See DOWN, Ven Philip Roy

MAIDSTONE, Suffragan Bishop of. See CRAY, Rt Revd Graham Alan

MALCOURONNE, Mr Keith Robert, MA, FCA, CF
20 Riverside Rd Staines TW18 2LE [GUILDFORD] b 1959 educ Sutton Manor Gr Sch; New Coll Ox; CV Chair Insight Management & Systems Consultants Ltd from 2005; Dir Globus Energy plc from 2007; Fin Dir The Specialist Washing Company Ltd from 2007; Managing ptnr, Bolton Colby Chartered Accountants 1993–2005; Fin ptnr BC technologies LLP from 2000; Man Dir Heathrow Corporate Consulting Ltd from 2005; Dir and Chair Bd Fin and Audit Ctee, World Vision UK; Chartered Accountant, corporate financier and bus consult from 1983; Nat Chair of Crusaders 1991–97; Chair Berega Relief Equipment and Devel Trust from 2001; Treas Ox Cen for Miss Studies; Vc-Chair AC Audit Cttee from 2006; Chair Fin and Audit Ctee Urban Saints; M Guildf Dioc Bp's Coun and DBF exec, Dioc Audit Cttee; Lay Chair Runnymede Dny
GS 2005–   Tel: 01784 455501
                             07990 511905 (Mobile)
                    email: keith@bc-group.co.uk

MALLARD, Mrs Zahida, Dip Mgt Studies
17 The Crescent Crossflatts Bingley BD16 2EU [BRADFORD] b 1968 educ Westborough High Sch Dewsbury; Dewsbury and Batley Tech and Art Coll; Wulfrun Coll Wolverhampton; Wolverhampton Poly; Bradf Univ; CV Welfare Rights Officer from 1992; Welfare Rights Manager from 2000; M DBE; M Dioc Bd for Ch in Society; Dioc Link Person to CMEAC; M MPA Coun; M Bradf Com Legal Services Advice Partnership Bd; Common Purpose Graduate
GS 2000–   Tel: 01274 562640 (Home)
                             01274 435174 (Office)
                             07931 761202 (Mobile)
                    email: zahidamallard@yahoo.co.uk

MALMESBURY, Archdeacon of. See HAWKER, Ven Alan Fort

MAN, Archdeacon of. See SMITH, Ven Brian

MANCHESTER, Archdeacon of.
See BALLARD, Ven Andrew Edgar

MANCHESTER, Bishop of. See McCULLOCH, Rt Revd Nigel Simeon

MANCHESTER, Dean of. See GOVENDER, Very Revd Rogers Morgan

MANN, Mrs Elnora, BA, MA
188 Yeading Lane Hayes UB4 9AU [LONDON] b 1950 CV Elected to GS 2005
GS 2005–   Tel: 020 8845 9541
                             07973 857207 (Mobile)
                    email: elnoramann@aol.com

MANSELL, Ven Clive Neville Ross, LLB, Dip HE
3 The Ridings Blackhurst Lane Tunbridge Wells TN2 4RU [ARCHDEACON OF TONBRIDGE; ROCHESTER] b 1953 educ City of Lon Sch; Leic Univ; Coll of Law; Trin Coll Bris; CV Solicitor (no longer practising); C Gt Malvern Priory 1982–85; Min Can Ripon Cathl 1985–89; R Kirklington w Burneston, Wath and Pickhill 1989–2002; AD Wensley 1998–2002; Archdeacon of Tonbridge from 2002; M Revision Cttee on the Draft Churchwardens Measure from 1996; M Legal Aid Commn from 1996; Ch Commr from 1997; M Revision Cttee on Draft Amending Canon No 22; M Revision Cttee on Draft C of E (Misc Provisions) Measure and Draft Amending Canon No 23; Chair Strg Cttee C of E Pensions (Amendment) Measure; M Dioc Bd of Educ; M Dioc Bd of Patronage; M Dioc Rural Adv Grp; Chair Ch in Society; M Bp's Coun; M Eccl Law Soc; Dep Prolocutor N Province/Prov of York 2001–02; M Appeal Panel for Internal Syn Elections and Elections of Convocations; M GS Panel of Chairmen; M Nat Adns Forum; Chair of Adns on GS; M Ch Commissioners' Assets Cttee, Red Chs Cttee; M Strg Cttee, Common Worship Ordinal; Simeon's Trustee
GS 1995–   Tel: 01892 520660
                    email: archdeacon.tonbridge@
                             rochester.anglican.org

MARRIOTT, Brigadier Patrick Claude, PSC, HCSC, CBE
79 Arior Drive Northwood Middlesex HA6 3LG [REPRESENTATIVE, ARMED FORCES SYNOD] b 1958 educ Gresham's Sch, Holt; CV Military service in Germany, UK inc N Ireland, Canada, Israel, Egypt, Bosnia, Kosovo, Norway, USA, Hong Kong, Oman, Kuwait, Iraq; Commanding Officer The Queen's Royal Lancers 1998–2000; Chief of Staff HQ 1 (UK) Armoured Division (invasion of Iraq); Commander 7th Armoured Brigade from 2005
GS 2005–   Tel: 0049 5051 962726
                    email: marriottpckh@hotmail.com

MARSH, Canon Harry (Henry Arthur),
5 Vicarage Lane Great Baddow Chelmsford CM2 8HY [CHELMSFORD] b 1943 educ Wirral Gr Sch; CV Inspector of Taxes 1961–2001; M Pensions Bd and Audit Ctee; M Bp's Coun; M DBF; M Chelms Cathl Coun; Vc-Chair Friends of Chelms Cathl; Trustee of CPAS and its Pension Fund
GS 1994–   Tel: 01245 478038
                    email: harry.marsh@ntlworld.com

MARSHALL, Dr Edmund Ian, MA, Ph D
37 Roundwood Lane Harpenden Herts AL5 3BP [WAKEFIELD] b 1940 educ Humberstone Foundn Sch Clee; Magd Coll Ox; Liv Univ; CV Univ Lect Liv and Hull 1962–66; Mathematician in Industry 1967–71; MP Goole 1971–83; Lect in Management Science Bradf Univ 1984–2000; Vc-Pres Meth Conf 1992–93; M Dioc Syn from 1996; M Bp's Coun 1997–2007; M Dioc Pastl Cttee 1998–2007;

Bp's Adv for Ecum Affairs Wakef 1998–2007; Chair Wakef Cathl Com Cttee 2000–07; Rdr 1994–2007; M Wakef Cathl Chap 2003–07; M CCU from 2006; Chair Rev Ctee for Diocs Pastl and Miss Measure 2006; Reader St Alb Dioc from 2008
GS 2000–   *Tel:* 01582 461236
     email: edmund.marshall@btinternet.com

MARTIN, Mrs (Bridget Elizabeth) Anne, B Ed, M Mus, M Phil, LTCL
8 Woodberry Close Chiddingfold GU8 4SF [GUILDFORD] *b* 1949 *educ* Whyteleafe Gr Sch; Homerton Coll Cam; Lon Univ Inst of Educ; Surrey Univ; Trin Coll of Music; *CV* Primary sch music specialist in state (inc ch schs) and private sectors in Suffolk, Cambs and Germany 1972–79; lect in music, Basford Hall FE Coll Nottm 1982–84; head of music, St Ives Prep Sch, Haslemere 1988–96; rsch Renaissance music Surrey Univ 1996–98; music tchr, Tormead Sch Guildf 1998–2001; head of music, St Teresa's Prep Sch 2001–04; presently working as specialist recorder tchr in state and private sectors; arranger, writer, adjudicator and conductor; M Godalming Dny Syn and Guildf DBE from 2006; long serving M of ch choir; involved with Chr Aid locally for 20 yrs
GS 2005–   *Tel:* 01428 683854
     email: be_anne_martin@hotmail.com

MAURICE, Rt Revd Peter David, BA, Dip Th
The Palace Wells BA5 2SU [SUFFRAGAN BISHOP OF TAUNTON; BATH AND WELLS] *b* 1951 *educ* Purley Gr Sch; St Chad's Coll Dur; Mirfield Th Coll; Westmr Coll Ox; *CV* C St Paul Wimbledon Park 1975–79; TV All SS East Sheen 1979–85; V H Trin Rotherhithe 1985–96; RD Bermondsey 1991–96; V All SS Tooting 1996–2003; Adn of Wells 2003–06; Bp of Taunton from 2006   *Tel:* 01749 672341
     Fax: 01749 679355
    email: bishop.taunton@bathwells.anglican.org

MAY, Dr Peter George Robin, MRCS, LRCP, MRCGP
41 Westridge Rd Southampton SO17 2HP [WINCHESTER] *b* 1945 *educ* R Free Hosp Medical Sch; *CV* Ho Officer Northallerton Hosp 1973–74; Staff Worker UCCF 1974–77; Senior Ho Officer Southn Gen Hosp 1977–79; GP Shirley Health Centre Southn from 1980; M BM 1991–2002; Medical Columnist C of E Newspaper 1997–2001; Chair UCCF Trust Bd from 2003
GS 1985-   *Tel:* 023 8055 8931
     Fax: 023 8078 3156
    email: may@ukgateway.net

McCLURE, Ven Tim (Timothy Elston), BA
10 Great Brockeridge Bristol BS9 3TY [ARCHDEACON OF BRISTOL] *b* 1946 *educ* Kingston Gr Sch; St Jo Coll Dur; Ridley Hall Th Coll; *CV* C Kirkheaton 1970–73; Marketing Mgr Agrofax L.I.P. Ltd 1973–74; C St Ambrose Chorlton-on-Medlock 1974–79; TR Whitworth Man and Presiding Chapl 1979–82; Chapl Man Poly 1974–82; Gen Sec SCM 1982–

92; Dir Chs Coun for Ind and Social Resp 1992–99; Lord Mayor's Chapl Bris 1996–99; Hon Can Bris Cathl from 1992; Adn of Bris from 1999; Chair Traidcraft plc 1990–97; Chair Chr Conf Trust 1998–2003; Chair Social Enterprise Works from 2000   *Tel:* 0117 962 2438 (Home)
     0117 962 1433 (Office)
     07725 047318 (Mobile)
     Fax: 0117 962 9438
    email: tim.mcclure@bristoldiocese.org

McCULLOCH, Rt Revd Nigel Simeon, MA; Hon DCL
Bishopscourt Bury New Rd Manchester M7 4LE [BISHOP OF MANCHESTER] *b* 1942 *educ* Liv Coll; Selw Coll Cam; Cuddesdon Th Coll; *CV* C Ellesmere Port 1966–70; Chapl Ch Coll Cam 1970–73; Dir of Th Studies Ch Coll Cam 1970–75; Dioc Missr Norw Dioc 1973–78; R SS Thos & Edm Sarum 1978–86; Adn of Sarum 1979–86; Chair ABM Finance Cttee 1987–92; Bp of Taunton 1986–92; Bp of Wakef 1992–2002; Chair Dec of Evang Stg Grp 1989–98; Chair Communications Cttee 1993–98; Lord High Almoner from 1997; Chair BM Miss, Evang and Renewal Cttee 1998–99; Chair Statistics Rev Grp 1998–2000; Chair Sandford St Mart Trust and Relig in Broadcasting Grp from 1999; Bp of Manchester from 2002; M Ho of Lords Cttees on BBC and Communications from 2005; Chair Coun of Chr and Jews from 2007; Chair Women in the Episcopate Legislation Grp from 2006
GS 1990–   *Tel:* 0161 792 2096 (Office)
     Fax: 0161 792 6826
     email: bishop@
bishopscourt.manchester.anglican.org

McCURDY, Ven Hugh Kyle,
12 Boadicea Court Chatteris PE16 6BN [ARCHDEACON OF HUNTINGDON AND WISBECH; ELY] *b* 1958 *educ* Geo Abbot Sch Guild; Portsm Poly; Cardiff Univ; Trin Coll Bris; *CV* C St Jo Egham 1985–88; C St Jo Woking 1988–91; V St Andr Histon 1991–2005; P-in-c St Andr Impington 1998–2005; RD N Stowe 1994–2005; Adn of Huntingdon and Wisbech from 2005; M DAC, Pastl Cttee, Bp's Coun; M Coun Ridley Hall Th Coll; M CPAS Coun of Reference
     Tel: 01354 692142
    email: archdeacon.handw@ely.anglican.org

McDONOUGH, Canon Philip Michael James, B Sc
28 Washbrook Close Barton-le-Clay MK45 4LF [ST ALBANS] *b* 1939 *educ* Wandsworth Tech Coll Lon; Imp Coll Lon; *CV* Asst Chapl Luton and Dunstable Hosp 1996–2004; Rdr from 1985; Sec St Alb Dioc Rdrs Assoc 1995–2004; M CRC Exec 1999–2004; M AC Min Div VRSC 2000–05; M C of E Hosp Chapl Coun, Coun St Alb Cathl from 2001; Lay Chair Ampthill Dny Syn from 2002; Hon Can St Alb Cathl from 2002; Associate Sec CRC 2004–

05; Trustee Br Red Cross Soc Staff Pension Fund from 2006
GS 2000–
    Tel: 01582 881772
    07759 444879 (Mobile)
email: canonpmcdonough@btinternet.com

McFARLANE, Ven Janet (Jan) Elizabeth,
B Med Sci, BA, Dip Min Std
(From March 09) 31 Bracondale Norwich NR1 2AT
[ARCHDEACON OF NORWICH] *b* 1964 *educ* Blythe Bridge High Sch Stoke-on-Trent; Sheff Univ; Dur Univ; Cranmer Hall Dur; *CV* Speech therapist 1987–90; C Stafford TM, Lich 1993–96; Chapl and Min Can, Ely Cathl 1996–99; Norw Dioc Communications Officer 1999–2009; Chapl to Bp of Norw 2001-09; M Bp's Coun, Dioc Syn, Dioc Communications Cttee; Adn Norwich from 2009; Dioc Dir of Communications from 2009
GS 2005–
    Tel: 07818 422395
email: (from Mar 09) archdeacon.norwich@norwich.anglican.org

McKITTRICK, Ven Douglas Henry,
2 Yorklands Dyke Rd Avenue Hove BN3 6RW [ARCHDEACON OF CHICHESTER] *b* 1953 *educ* John Marley Comp Sch, Newcastle-upon-Tyne; St Steph Ho Ox; *CV* C St Paul Deptford, S'wark 1977–80; C St Jo Tuebrook, Liv 1980–81; TV St Steph Grove St, Liv 1981–89; V St Agnes Toxteth Pk, Liv 1989–97; V St Pet with Chapel Royal Brighton, Chich from 1997; RD of Brighton from 1998; Can and Preb of Chich Cathl from 1998; Archdeacon of Chichester from 2002; M DAC, Bd of Educ, DBF, Pastl Cttee, Parsonages Cttee; Bp's Adv Hosp Chaplaincy; Coun M Additional Curates Soc 2005; M Hosp Chapl Coun 2006; Bp's Adv on Ecumenism
GS 2004–
    Tel: 01273 505330 (Home)
    01273 421021 (Office)
    Fax: 01273 421041
email: archchichester@diochi.org.uk

McMULLEN, Mrs Christine Elizabeth, BA,
Dip Ad Ed, MA
Farm Cottage Montpelier Place Buxton SK17 7EJ [DERBY] *b* 1943 *educ* Homelands Sch Derby; R Holloway Coll Lon; Nott Univ; Derby Univ; *CV* Rdr from 1986; Dir of Pastl Studies Nn Ord Course from 1994, Vc-Prin from 2005; Lay Chair Buxton Dny from 2005; M DRACS from 2000; Lay M Derby Cathl Chapter from 2000; M Ch Commrs Pastl Cttee from 2001
GS 1990–
    Tel: 01298 73997
    0161 249 2511
email: christine@thenoc.org.uk

McPHATE, Very Revd Prof Gordon Ferguson,
BA, MA, M Th, M Sc, MB, Ch B, MD, FRCP
The Deanery 7 Abbey St Chester CH1 2JF [DEAN OF CHESTER] *b* 1950 *educ* Perth Gr Sch; Cam Univ; Aberd Univ; Edin Univ; Surrey Univ; Westcott Ho Cam; *CV* Lect in Physiology, Guy's Hosp Lon 1979–84; Hon C Sanderstead, S'wark 1978–80;

Hon PV and Sacrist, S'wark Cathl 1980–86; Registrar in Chemical Pathology, Guildf Hosps 1984–86; Lect and Sen Lect in Pathology, Univ of St Andr 1986–2002; Hon Angl Chapl, Univ of St Andr 1986–2002; Consult Chemical Pathologist, Fife Hosps 1993–2002; Dean of Chester from 2002; Vis Prof of Theol, Univ of Chester from 2003
GS 2004–05
    Tel: 01244 500971
email: dean@chestercathedral.com

McPHERSON, Mrs Katherine, MBA, BA
59 Mycenae Rd London SE3 7SE [APPOINTED MEMBER, ARCHBISHOPS' COUNCIL] *b* 1964 *educ* P. L. Meth Girls' Sch Singapore; Temasek Jun Coll Singapore; Nat Univ of Singapore; Univ of Kent; *CV* Exec Consult, Ernst and Young Singapore 1987–92; Sen Mgr, Ernst and Young Lon 1992–95; Lon Hd of Sales and Marketing (Media & Resources), Ernst and Young 1996–98; Nat Hd of Sales and Marketing (Telecoms, Media & Entertainment), Ernst and Young 1998–99; Project Dir (secondment), BBC Mar Nov 1999; Managing Consult, Cap Gemini Ernst and Young 1999–2001; Operations Dir, YMCA Lambeth, Lewisham and S'wark 2001–2002; Dir Business Devel and Marketing, EMEA, White and Case 2002–04; Apptd M AC from 2003; Head of Bus Devel, Corporate Div, Herbert Smith 2004–05; Head of Bus Devel, Europe, Herbert Smith 2005–07; Consult Cornerstone PDC from 2007
GS 2003–
    Tel: 020 8858 1856 (Home)
    07984 046149 (Mobile)
email: mcpherson.katherine@gmail.com

MELLOR, Very Revd (Kenneth) Paul, BA, MA
The Deanery Cornet St St Peter Port Guernsey GY1 1BZ [DEAN OF GUERNSEY; WINCHESTER] *b* 1949 *educ* Ashfield Sch, Kirkby-in-Ashfield; Southn Univ; Leeds Univ; Mirfield Th Coll; Cuddesdon Th Coll; *CV* C St Mary V Cottingham 1973–76; C All SS Ascot 1976–80; V St Mary Magd Tilehurst 1980–85; V Menheniot 1985–94; RD E Wivelshire 1990–94; Hon Can Truro Cathl 1990–94; Chair Dioc Bd of Miss and Unity 1990–95; CFCE 1996–2000; Can Treas Truro Cathl 1994–2003; Dean of Guernsey from 2003
GS 1994–2003; 2005–
    Tel: 01481 720036
    07720 506863 (Mobile)
    Fax: 01481 722948
email: paul@townchurch.org.gg

MENZIES, Mr Colin Douglas Livingstone, MA,
FRSA
Church House Great Smith St London SW1P 3AZ [SECRETARY, CORPORATION OF THE CHURCH HOUSE] *b* 1944 *educ* Glenalmond Coll; Keble Coll Ox; *CV* Christian Salvesen plc Edin 1971–84; RICS Edin 1984–86; City admin and recruitment 1986–90; Sec to Corp of Ch Ho from 1990; Treas Corp of Sons of the Clergy from 2005
    Tel: 020 7898 1310
    Fax: 020 7898 1321
email: colin.menzies@c-of-e.org.uk

MEON, Archdeacon of The. See HANCOCK, Ven Peter

MEYRICK, Very Revd (Cyril) Jonathan, MA (Oxon)
The Deanery 10 Cathedral Close Exeter EX1 1EZ [DEAN OF EXETER] *b* 1952 *educ* Lancing Coll; St Jo Coll Ox; Salis & Well Th Coll; *CV* C Bicester, Ox 1976–78; Bp's Chapl, Ox 1978–81; OT tutor, Codrington Coll, Barbados 1981–84; TV Burnham Team, Ox 1984–90; TR Tisbury, Salis 1990–98; RD Chalke, Sarum 1997–98; Res Can Roch 1998–2005; acting Dean of Roch 2002–04; Dean of Exeter from 2005; Chair Coun for Miss & Unity from 2005 *Tel:* 01392 273509
01392 431266
Fax: 01392 285986
email: dean@exeter-cathedral.org.uk

MIDDLESEX, Archdeacon of. See WELCH, Ven Stephan John

**MIDDLETON, Suffragan Bishop of.
See DAVIES, Rt Revd Mark**

MILLER, Canon David George, MA, BD
St Michael's Rectory Church Lane Helston TR13 8PF [TRURO] *b* 1954 *educ* Chr Hosp Horsham; Oriel Coll Ox; Ripon Coll Cuddesdon; *CV* C Henfield, Shermanbury & Woodmancote, Chich 1981–84; C St Paul Monk Bretton, Barnsley, Wakef 1984–87; V St Jo Rastrick, Wakef 1987–93; TR Helston & Wendron, Truro from 1993; Chapl Helston Com Hosp 1995–2007; M Dioc Exec and Bd of Finance, Dioc Spirituality Grp; Chair Ho of Clergy 2004; Hon Can Truro Cathl 2006
GS 2004– *Tel:* 01326 572516
email: millerourrectory@tiscali.co.uk

MILLER, Ven Geoff (Geoffrey Vincent), B Ed, MA
80 Moorside North Fenham Newcastle-upon-Tyne NE4 9DU [ARCHDEACON OF NORTHUMBERLAND; NEWCASTLE] *b* 1956 *educ* Sharston High Sch, Manch; Dur Univ; St Jo Coll Nottm; Newc Univ; *CV* C Jarrow 1983–86; TV St Aidan Billingham 1986–92; Dioc Urban Devel Officer 1991–99; Com Chapl Stockton-on-Tees 1992–94; P-in-c St Cuth Darlington 1994–96, V 1996–99; Dioc Urban Officer and Res Can Newc Cathl 1999–2005; Adn of Northumberland from 2005; M DAC; M Dioc Pastl Cttee; M Fin, Pastl, Parsonages, Priorities & Planning cttees and Strat Dev Gp of Bp's Coun; M Dioc Child Protection Cttee; M Shepherd's Dene, Sons of Clergy, Ch Inst, Hosp of God at Greatham, Lord Crewe Trust; Chair Br Cttee of French Protestant Industrial Miss
Tel: 0191 273 8245
Fax: 0191 226 0286
email: g.miller@newcastle.anglican.org

MILLS, Mr David John, MBE
51 Greenways Over Kellet Carnforth LA6 1DE [CARLISLE] *b* 1937 *CV* Senior Probation Officer (Rtd); Rdr; Bp's Selector Min Div; M Dioc Bd of Educ
GS 1985– *Tel:* 01524 732194

MITCHELL, Mr Steve (Stephen Andrew), MA, BA, Dip I M
7 Tarnside Fold Glossop SK13 6ND [DERBY] *b* 1948 *educ* Grove Sec Sch St Leonards on Sea; Willows Sec Sch Marple; Tameside Coll of FE; Man Poly; Open Univ; Dioc Rdr trg; N Cornhill Tr Course; Cliff Coll; *CV* Lay Pastor Whitfield Par Glossop from 1996; Greater Man Police Officer 1968–95; M CTBI; M CTE; Dioc Vocations Adv; M Bp's Coun; M Dioc Bd of Educ; M Dioc Rdrs Bd; M Dioc Coun for Devel of Discipleship and Ministry; M Dioc Evang Fell; Lay Chair Glossop Dny Syn; Rdr from 1990
GS 2000– *Tel and Fax:* 01457 861097
email: steve@glossop.org

MONCKTON, Mrs Joanna Mary,
Horsebrook Hall Brewood Stafford ST19 9LP [LICHFIELD] *b* 1941 *educ* Oxton Ho Sch Kenton Ex; *CV* High Sheriff of Staffordshire 1995–96; Dir Penk (Holdings) Ltd and Penk Ltd; Farm Partner; Housewife; Chairman Lichf Branch Prayer Book Soc 1982–2001; Shannon Trust rep for HMYOI Brinsford
GS 1990– *Tel:* 01902 850288

MOON, Mr Richard James, FRSA, MIoD
Chestnut Barn Parsonage Lane Chilcompton Radstock Bath BA3 4JZ [BATH AND WELLS] *b* 1950 *educ* Somervale, Midsomer Norton; Bris Poly; *CV* Eng apprentice, EMI Electronics Ltd 1966–71; Production Eng/Mgr, EMI/Thorn EMI Electronics 1971–89; Operations Dir, Thorn EMI Electronics 1989–92; Man Dir, Thorn Automation 1992–94; Man Dir, Thorn EMI Electronics, Sensors Grp 1994–97; Man Dir, Racal Radio Ltd 1997–98; Chief Exec, Racal Defence Electronics Ltd 1998–99; Chief Exec, Thales PLC 2000–02; Dir, IFCO Systems NV 2003–04; Dir, Netia SA 2003–06; Chair, Vivista Holdings Ltd 2003–05; Chair Acal Plc from 2004; Chair t+Medical Ltd from 2004; Chair Oxford BioSignals Ltd from 2003; Chair Securistyle Holdings Ltd 2004–06; Chair SRT Plc from 2005; Chair Kylmar Holdings Ltd from 2006; M Midsomer Norton Dny; Vc-Chair Chilcompton w. Downside PCC; Chair Planit Holdings Ltd from 2006
GS 2005– *Tel and Fax:* 01761 232490
email: richard.moon@synbus.co.uk

MORGAN, Rt Revd Christopher Heudebourck, Dip Th, BA, M Th
1 Fitzwalter Rd Lexden Colchester CO3 3SS [AREA BISHOP OF COLCHESTER; CHELMSFORD] *b* 1947 *educ* City of Bath Boys Sch; Lanc Univ; Heythrop Coll Lon; Kelham Th Coll; *CV* C Birstall 1973–76; Asst Chap Brussels 1976–80; P-in-c Redditch St Geo 1980–81; TV Redditch, The Ridge 1981–85; V Sonning 1985–96; Prin Berks Chr Tr Scheme 1985–89; Dir Pastl Studies St Alb and Ox Min Course 1992–95; Glouc Dioc Officer for Min 1996–2001; Dioc Can Res Glouc Cathl 1996–2001; Bp of Colchester from 2001 *Tel:* 01206 576648
Fax: 01206 763868
email: b.colchester@chelmsford.anglican.org

MORGAN, Mr David Geoffrey Llewelyn,
25 Newbiggen St Thaxted CM6 2QS [CHELMSFORD]
b 1935 *educ* St Jo Sch Leatherhead; *CV* Rtd Solicitor; Company Dir; Chair Dioc Bd of Patr; M Dioc Fin Cttee from 1988; Trustee Victoria Clergy Fund from 1989; Chair Nat CU Coun from 1998; Gen Sec Guild of All Souls from 2003
GS 1990–   *Tel:* 01371 830132
                       Fax: 01371 831430

MORGAN, Mrs Helen, BA
13 Broadwater Close Woking GU21 5TW [GUILD-FORD] *b* 1942 *educ* Harrow Co Gr Sch for Girls; St Aidan's Coll Dur; *CV* Tchr Spennymoor Gr Tech Sch 1964–66; Sec to Chair of Hosp Recognition Cttee R Coll of Obstetricians and Gynaecologists 1967–70; Asst to Rsch Grants Officer and Contracts Officer Imp Coll Lon 1970–71; Homemaker since 1971; Classroom helper 1977–2000; Sch Gov 1985–2002, Chair of Govs Personnel Cttee 1990–2000; Pastl Asst 1988–2000; Dny Lay Chair 1993–2002; M Dny Syn from 1991; M Dioc Coun for Social Resp 1991–97; Fundraising Co-ord Par Miss 1994–2000; M Dioc Syn from 1997; MU Dioc Trustee from 2000
GS 2000–   *Tel:* 01932 346454
      email: helen@rihm.freeserve.co.uk

MORGAN, Mrs Susan Deirdre, BA (Hons),
Chartered FCIPD, MHSM, FRSA
Church House Great Smith St London SW1P 3AZ [DIRECTOR OF HUMAN RESOURCES, ARCHBISHOPS' COUNCIL] *b* 1956 *educ* The Dame Alice Harpur Sch Bedford; N Lon Poly; *CV* Dir of Personnel Essex and Herts Health Services 1991–94; Dir Human Resources and Commercial Services Princess Alexandra Hosp NHS Trust Harlow 1994–97; Employers' rep on the Employment Tribunals for Engl and Wales from 1992; Personnel Dir CBF 1997–98; Dir of Human Resources to AC from 1998, serving all of the Nat Church Insts; M Race Panel of Employment Tribunals from 2002; Chair Staff Cttee, Chelmsf Dioc from 2005   *Tel:* 020 7898 1565
      email: su.morgan@c-of-e.org.uk

MORRIS, Ven Roger Anthony Brett, BSc (Hons),
ARCS, MA (Cantab)
The Archdeacon's House Walkers Lane Whittington Worcester WR5 2RE [ARCHDEACON OF WORCESTER] *b* 1968 *educ* Chipping Sodbury Sch; Filton Tech Coll; Imperial Coll Lon; Trin Coll Cam; Ridley Hall Cam; *CV* Asst C of Northleach, W Hampnett and Farmington, Cold Aston, W Notgrove and Turkdean 1993–96; R of Sevenhampton w Charlton Abbotts, Hawling and Whittington, Dowdeswell w Andoversford, The Shiptons and Salperton, and Withington 1996–2003; Dir Par Devel and Evang, Cov 2003–08; Adn of Worc from 2008
      email: rmorris@cofe-worcester.org.uk

MORRISON, Mrs Gill (Gillian Barbara), SRN,
SCM, ONC, RNT
Rectory Rectory Rd Rushden NN10 0HA [PETER-BOROUGH] *b* 1946 *educ* Malvern Ho Sch and Kendrick Girls' Sch, Reading; *CV* Nurse trg, Hammersmith Hosp Lon and Heatherwood, Ascot 1963–68; midwifery trg Bris and Maidenhead 1968–69; St Mary's Paddington 1970–75; Qu Eliz Coll Lon, nurse teacher's diploma 1975–77; Tutor, St Mary's Paddington 1977–81; Sen Nurse Tutor, St Bart's Hosp 1981–83; clergy wife and homemaker from 1983; youth and adult JP, inner Lon and Northants from 1990, appraisal and trg cttee from 1998; sch gov from 1997; eclectics conf admin 1999–2005; patr trustee for CPAS from 2000
GS 2005–   *Tel:* 01933 312554
   email: morrison@barryandgill.freeserve.co.uk

MOY, Revd Richard John, MA, MA, ADMT
21 St Jude's Rd Wolverhampton WV6 0FB [LICHFIELD] *b* 1978 *educ* Caterham Sch; St Cath Coll Cam; Trin Coll Bris; *CV* C St Pet Collegiate Ch, Wolverhampton and Pioneer Min for Wolverhampton from 2007
GS 2005–   *Tel:* 01902 653942
            07894 230304 (Mobile)
      email: notintheratrace@yahoo.co.uk

MUNRO, Revd Dr Robert Speight, B Sc, BA, Dip
Ap Th, PGCE, D Min
Rectory 1 Depleach Rd Cheadle SK8 1DZ [CHESTER] *b* 1963 *educ* William Hulme's Gr Sch Man; Bris Univ; All Souls Coll Lon; Man Univ; Oak Hill Th Coll; Refrmd Th Sem US; *CV* C St Jo Bapt Hartford 1993–97; R St Wilf Davenham 1997–2003; R St Mary Cheadle from 2003; M Bp's Coun
GS 2005–   *Tel:* 0161 428 3440
                   0161 428 8050
           Fax: 0161 428 3440
                   0161 428 8050
      email: rob@munro.org.uk

MURSELL, Rt Revd (Alfred) Gordon, MA, BD,
ARCM, DD
Ash Garth Broughton Crescent Barlaston Stoke-on-Trent ST12 9DD [AREA BISHOP OF STAFFORD; LICHFIELD] *b* 1949 *educ* Ardingly Coll; Pontifical Inst of Sacred Mus Rome; BNC Ox; Cuddesdon Th Coll; *CV* C St Mary Walton Liv 1973–77; V St Jo E Dulwich 1977–87; Tutor in Spirituality Sarum and Wells Th Coll 1987–91; TR Stafford 1991–99; Provost of Birm from 1999; Dean of Birm 2002–05; Bp of Stafford from 2005   *Tel:* 01782 373308
                 07906 490032 (Mobile)
                   Fax: 01782 373705
   email: bishop.stafford@lichfield.anglican.org

MUSSON, Mr Terence Robert, HND
Alpenrose 20 Polsham Park Paignton TQ3 2AD [TRURO] *b* 1940 *educ* Grantham Boys Central Sch;

Caythorpe Coll; *CV* Self-Employed Farmer from 1962; Company Chairman 1981–90
GS 1995–   *Tel*: 01803 558430
                                          07810 311487 (Mobile)
             email: alpenrose@blueyonder.co.uk

NAGEL, Mrs Mary Philippa, B Ed
Aldwick Vicarage 25 Gossamer Lane Bognor Regis PO21 3AT [CHICHESTER] *b* 1954 *educ* Worthing High Sch; Lon Univ; *CV* Section 23 Insp of Schs until 2005
GS 1990–   *Tel*: 01243 262049
             email: nagel@aldwick.demon.co.uk

NAZIR-ALI, Rt Revd Michael James, BA, B Litt, M Litt, Th D, DH Litt, DD, Hon DD, Hon D Litt
Bishopscourt Rochester ME1 1TS [BISHOP OF ROCHESTER] *b* 1949 *educ* St Paul's Sch Karachi; St Patr Coll Karachi; Karachi Univ; Fitzw Coll Cam; St Edm Hall Ox; ACT NSW; Ridley Hall Th Coll; *CV* Tutorial Supervisor Th Cam Univ 1974–76; C H Sepulchre and All SS Cam 1974–76; Tutor then Sen Tutor Karachi Th Coll 1976–81; Provost of Lahore Cathl 1981–84; Bp of Raiwind 1984–86; Asst to Abp of Cant and Dir in Residence Ox Cen for Miss Studies 1986–89; Co-ord of Studies and Ed Lambeth Conf 1988; Hon C St Giles and SS Phil and Jas w St Marg Ox 1986–89; Gen Sec CMS 1989–94; Asst Bp S'wark 1989–94; Can Th Leic 1992–94; Sec Abp's Commn on Communion and Women in the Episcopate 1988–98; M Bd of Chr Aid 1988–97; M CTBI 1991–95; M ARCIC II from 1991; M BM 1991–2001, Chair Miss Th Adv Grp 1992–2001; Bp of Roch from 1994; Chair Ho of Bps' Theol Grp from 2004; Theol Consult to Crown Appts Review Grp; Vis Prof of Th and Rel Studies Univ of Greenwich from 1996; M HFEA and Chair Ethics and Law Cttee 1998–2003; Chair Trin Coll Bris Coun; Fell St Edm Hall Ox; Fell Fitzwilliam Coll Cam; Select Prchr Cam Univ and Ox Univ; Qu Lect Belfast Univ; Selw Lect St Jo Coll Auckland; Sadleir Lect Wycliffe Coll Toronto; Henry Martyn Lect Cam Univ; Scott Holland Lect Ox; Chavasse Lect Wycliffe,Ox; M AC 2000–05; M Ho of Bps' Stg Cttee 2000–05; Chair Ho of Bps' Working Party on Women in the Episcopate 2001–04; M IARCCUM from 2001; Paul Harris Rotary Fell 2005
GS 1994–   *Tel*: 01634 842721
                                          Fax: 01634 831136
      email: bishops.secretary@rochester.anglican.org

NEIL-SMITH, Mr (Noel) Jonathan, MA
Church House Great Smith St London SW1P 3AZ [ADMINISTRATIVE SECRETARY, CENTRAL SECRETARIAT] *b* 1959 *educ* Marlboro Coll; St Jo Coll Cam; *CV* On staff of Ch Commrs from 1981; Bishoprics Officer 1994–96; Seconded to GS from 1997; Asst Sec Ho of Bps 1997–98; Sec Ho of Bps from 1998; Hon Lay Can Guildf Cathl from 2002   *Tel*: 020 7898 1373
                                          Fax: 020 7898 1369
      email: jonathan.neil-smith@c-of-e.org.uk

NEWARK, Archdeacon of. See PEYTON, Ven Nigel

NEWCASTLE, Assistant Bishop of. See RICHARDSON, Rt Revd Paul

NEWCASTLE, Bishop of. See WHARTON, Rt Revd (John) Martin

NEWCASTLE, Dean of. See DALLISTON, Very Revd Christopher Charles

NEWCOME, Rt Revd James William Scobie, MA, FRSA
Holm Croft 13 Castle Rd Kendal LA9 7AU [SUFFRAGAN BISHOP OF PENRITH; CARLISLE] *b* 1953 *educ* Marlboro Coll; Trin Coll Ox; Selw Coll Cam; Ridley Hall Th Coll; *CV* C All SS Leavesden 1978–82; Min Bar Hill LEP Ely 1982–94; Tutor Ridley Hall Cam 1983–88; V Dry Drayton 1990–94; RD N Stowe 1993–94; DDO Ches 1994–2000; Res Can Ches Cathl 1994–2002; Dioc Dir of Min 1996–2002; Suff Bp of Penrith from 2002; Chairman Dioc Bd of Min and Trg; Pres Chs Together in Cumbria; CCU Local Unity Panel; CPAS Coun of Reference
GS 2000–02   *Tel*: 01539 727836
                                          Fax: 01539 734380
      email: bishop.penrith@carlislediocese.org.uk

NEWEY, Mr (Sidney) Brian, MA
Chestnut Cottage The Green South Warborough OX10 7DN [OXFORD] *b* 1937 *educ* Burton-upon-Trent Gr Sch; Worc Coll Ox; *CV* With Br Rail from 1960, Gen Mgr W Region 1984–87; Dir Regional Railways 1987–90; Asst to Chief Exec Br Rail 1990–93; Consult in transport 1993–96; rtd; M AC Fin Cttee; Chair Ox DBF and assoc cttees
GS 2005–   *Tel*: 01865 858322
                                          Fax: 01865 858043

NEWMAN, Very Revd Adrian, B Sc, Dip Th, M Phil
The Deanery Priors Gate House Rochester ME1 1SR [DEAN OF ROCHESTER] *b* 1958 *educ* Rickmansworth Comp Sch; Bris Univ; Trin Coll Bris; *CV* C St Mark Forest Gate 1985–89; V Hillsborough and Wadsley Bridge, Sheff 1989–96; R St Mart in the Bull Ring, Birm 1996–2004; Dean of Roch from 2005   *Tel*: 01634 843366
                                          01634 202183
                                          07916 238269 (Mobile)

      email: dean@rochestercathedral.org.uk

NEWTON, Rt Revd Keith, BD, AKC, PGCE
Richborough House 6 Mellish Gardens Woodford Green IG8 0BH [SUFFRAGAN BISHOP OF RICHBOROUGH; PROVINCIAL EPISCOPAL VISITOR, CANTERBURY] *b* 1952 *educ* Alsop High Sch Liv; Lon Univ; K Coll, Ch Ch Coll Cant; St Aug Coll Cant; *CV* C St Mary Gt Ilford 1975–78; V St Matt Wimbledon TM 1978–85; R St Paul Blantyre, S Malawi 1985–86; Dean of Blantyre 1986–91; P-in-c H Nativity

Knowle 1991–93, V 1993–2002; P-in-c All Hallows Easton 1997–2002; Bp of Richborough from 2002
Tel: 020 8505 7259
07976 585891 (Mobile)
Fax: 020 8504 3349
email: pev@btinternet.com

NICHOLLS, Mr William Charles, I Eng, MCIPD, MIET
2 Grotto Lane Tettenhall Wolverhampton WV6 9LP [LICHFIELD] *b* 1945 *educ* Wednesfield C of E Sch; Wulfrun Coll; Wolverhampton Univ; *CV* Apprentice 1961–66; projects engr 1966–73; Trg and Devel Mgr 1973–84; Trg Adv 1984–88; Dir, Educ and Trg Devel 1988–2008; M Dioc Bd of Min; M Dioc Bd of Fin; Lay Chair of Dny; Rdr; Co-ord of Evang and Outreach; Dir Re-Entry; Chair New Park Village Activity Network; Chair Bilston SP Projects Gp
GS 2005–
Tel: 01902 759262
07831 109216 (Mobile)
email: w.c.n@talktalk.net

NOBLETT, Ven William Alexander, B Th, M Th
Room 410 Abell House John Islip St London SW1P 4LH [CHAPLAIN GENERAL OF HM PRISONS] *b* 1953 *educ* High Sch Dub; Southn Univ; Ox Univ; Sarum and Wells Th Coll; *CV* C Sholing, Win 1978–80; Incumbent Ardamine, Kiltennel & Glascarrig 1980–82; Chapl RAF 1982–84; V St Thos Middlesbrough 1984–87; Dep Chapl HMP Wakefield 1987–89, Chapl 1989–92; Chapl HMP Norwich 1992–97; Chapl HMP Full Sutton 1997–2001; Chapl Gen HM Prisons from 2001; Can York Min from 2001; Chapl to the Queen 2005
GS 2001–
Tel: 020 7217 8997
020 7217 8201
Fax: 020 7217 8980
020 7217 8844
email: william.noblett@hmps.gsi.gov.uk

NORFOLK, Archdeacon of. See HAYDEN, Ven David Frank

NORTH-WEST EUROPE, Archdeacon in. See VAN LEEUWEN, Ven Dirk Willem

NORTHAMPTON, Archdeacon of. See ALLSOPP, Ven Christine

NORTHOLT, Archdeacon of. See TREWEEK, Ven Rachel

NORTHUMBERLAND, Archdeacon of. See MILLER, Ven Geoff (Geoffrey Vincent)

NORWICH, Archdeacon of. See McFARLANE, Ven Janet Elizabeth

NORWICH, Bishop of. See JAMES, Rt Revd Graham Richard

NORWICH, Dean of. See SMITH, Very Revd Graham Charles Morell

NOTTINGHAM, Archdeacon of. See HILL, Ven Peter

NUNN, Canon Andrew Peter, BA, BA
Southwark Cathedral London Bridge London SE1 9DA [SOUTHWARK] *b* 1957 *educ* Guthlaxton Upper Sch Wigston, Leic; Leic Poly; Leeds Univ; Coll of Resurr Mirfield; *CV* C St Jas Manston, Ripon 1983–87; C Leeds Richmond Hill 1987–91, V 1991–95; Chapl Agnes Stewart C of E High Sch, Leeds 1987–91; Personal Asst to Bp of S'wark 1995–99; Sub-Dean, Prec and Can Res S'wark Cathl from 1999; Wrdn of Rdrs, S'wark; Chair Dioc Liturg Cttee; Bp's Selector; M Dioc Syn; M S'wark Min and Trg Cttee
GS 2005–
Tel: 020 7367 6727
Fax: 020 7367 6725
email: andrew.nunn@southwark.anglican.org

O'BRIEN, Mr Gerald Michael, B Sc, DMS
Chestnuts 14 Oakhill Rd Sevenoaks Kent TN13 1NP [ROCHESTER] *b* 1948 *educ* Dulwich Coll; Bris Univ; *CV* Promotions Sec, ICS 1994–97; Dir of Communications, Crosslinks 1997–2002; M CEEC 1988–92, from 1996; M CPAS Coun 1999–2004
GS 1980–85, 1987–
Tel: 01732 453894
07711 938517 (Mobile)
email: gmobrien@btinternet.com

O'DOWD, Mrs Rosalind Kate, BA
93 Uxbridge Rd Hanworth TW13 5EH [LONDON] *b* 1978 *educ* Alton Convent; Peter Symonds Coll, Liv Univ; *CV* Marketing Asst, Sanford 2001–04; Marketing Exec, 3M 2004–07; Chs Audience Mgr Tearfund from 2008; M CCU 2000–05; M CTE Enabling Grp from 2000; M CTE Forum Plng Grp from 2005; M CTE Ducamus youth leadership project 2003–05; M Bus Cttee from 2005
GS 2000–05; 2005–
Tel: 020 8893 8558
07803 001646 (Mobile)
email: rosalind.odowd@yahoo.com

O'HARA, Mr Ian Daniel, MBPsS, MITOL
38 Lole Close Longford Coventry CV6 6PR [COVENTRY] *b* 1963 *educ* K Henry VIII Sch Cov; *CV* Recruitment and Trg Mgr, Choices Video 1995–2004; Hd of Learning and Devel, Courts Furnishers 2004–05; Learning and Devel Consult, Roadchef from 2005; Chair Cov Dioc Forward in Faith; M organizing cttee, annual Ebbsfleet children's and young people's eucharistic festival; M Bp's Coun
GS 2005–
Tel: 024 7636 7957
07745 784439 (Mobile)
email: ianoh1@tiscali.co.uk

OAKHAM, Archdeacon of. See PAINTER, Ven David Scott

OLDHAM, Mr Gavin David Redvers, MA (Cantab) *Ashfield House St Leonards Tring HP23 6NP* [OXFORD; CHURCH COMMISSIONER] *b* 1949 *educ* Eton; Trin Coll Cam; *CV* Wedd Durlacher Mordaunt 1975–86, Partner 1984–86; Secretariat Barclays De Zoete Wedd (BZW) 1984–88; Chief Exec Barclayshare Ltd 1986–89, Chair 1989–90; Chair/Chief Exec The Share Cen Ltd from 1990; Chief Exec Share plc from 2000; Chair The Share Foundn from 2005; Ch Commr from 1999; M Fin Cttee AC from 2001; M Ethical Investment Adv Grp from 1999
GS 1995–   *Tel:* 01494 758348 (Home)
01296 439100 (Office)
07767 337696 (Mobile)
Fax: 01296 414410
email: bravo@btinternet.com

OLIVER, Rt Revd Stephen John, AKC
63 Coborn Rd London E3 2DB [AREA BISHOP OF STEPNEY; LONDON] *b* 1948 *educ* Man Central Gr Sch; K Coll Lon Univ; St Aug Coll Cant; *CV* C Clifton Team Min, S'well 1971–75; P-in-c Ch Ch Newark S'well 1975–79; R St Mary Plumtree S'well 1979–85; Sen Producer, BBC 1985–87, Chief Producer 1987–91; R Leeds, Ripon 1991–97; Res Can St Paul's Cathl, Lon 1997–2003; M Liturg Commn 1991–2001; Bp of Stepney from 2003
Tel: 020 8981 2323
Fax: 020 8981 8015
email: bishop.stepney@london.anglican.org

OLIVER, Canon Thomas Gordon, L Th, B Th, Dip Ad Ed
18 Kings Ave Rochester Kent ME1 3DS [ROCHESTER] *b* 1948 *educ* Whinney Hill Sec Mod Sch Dur; Dur Johnson Gr Tech Sch; Lon Coll of Div; St Jo Coll Nottm; *CV* C St Jo the Divine Thorpe Edge 1972–76; C St Mark Woodthorpe 1976–80; V All SS Huthwaite 1980–85; Dir Pastl Studies St Jo Coll Nottm 1985–94; Dioc Dir of Tr 1994–99; Bp's Officer for Min and Trg from 1999
GS 1995–   *Tel:* 01634 560000 (Office)
01634 841232 (Home)
Fax: 01634 408942
email: gordon.oliver@rochester.anglican.org

OSBORNE, Mrs Emma Charlotte, MA
Lawn Farm Milton Lilbourne Pewsey SN9 5LQ [CHURCH COMMISSIONER] *b* 1964 *educ* Redland High Sch, Bris; Ch Ch Ox; *CV* County NatWest 1985–89; Lloyds Investment Mgrs 1989–91; Credit Suisse/CSFB 1991–97; Investment Mgr, Chubb Insurance from 1997   *Tel:* 01672 563459
020 7956 5362
email: emma.osborne@lawnfarm.co.uk

OSBORNE, Ven Hayward John, MA, PGCE
Birmingham Diocesan Office 175 Harborne Park Rd Birmingham B17 0BH [ARCHDEACON OF BIRMINGHAM] *b* 1948 *educ* Sevenoaks Sch; New Coll Ox; Westcott Ho Th Coll; *CV* C St Pet and St Paul Bromley 1973–77; C Halesowen 1977–80, TV

1980–83; TR St Barnabas Worc 1983–88; V St Mary Moseley 1988–2001; AD Moseley 1994–2001; Hon Can Birm Cathl from 2000; Adn of Birm from 2001
GS 1998–   *Tel:* 0121 426 0441 (Office)
email: hs.osborne@btinternet.com

OSBORNE, Very Revd June, BA (Econ) Hons, M Phil, Cert Theol, DL
The Deanery 7 The Close Salisbury SP12EF [DEAN OF SALISBURY] *b* 1953 *educ* Whalley Range Gr Sch, Manch; Manch Univ; Birm Univ; St Jo Coll Nottm; Wycliffe Hall Ox; *CV* C St Mart-in-the-Bullring and Chapl, Birm Children's Hosp 1980–84; St Mark Old Ford 1984–89; St Paul w. St Steph and St Mark Old Ford 1989–95; Can Treas Salis Cathl 1995–2004; Dean of Salis from 2004; M Bd of Soc Resp 1985–90; M Stg Cttee GS 1990–95; Sen Insp of Theol Educ 1994–2004; Chair DAC 2003–07; Deputy Lieut of Wilts from 2006
GS 1985–95; 2004–05   *Tel:* 01722 555110
Fax: 01722 555155
email: thedean@salcath.co.uk

OSBORNE, Revd Malcolm Eric (Max), DipTHm
All Saints Vicarage 32 Warrington St Newmarket CB8 8BA [ST EDMUNDSBURY AND IPSWICH] *b* 1964 *educ* St John's Nottm; *CV* P Cavendish Com Ch 1996–98; Min-in-Charge Triangle Ch Ipswich 1999–2002; Deanery Adv for Social Responsibility 1999–2002; St Lawrence Preacher 1999–2002; V All Saints Newmarket from 2002
GS 2003–5, 2008–   *Tel:* 01638 662514
email: max9@btopenworld.com

OXFORD (CHRIST CHURCH), Dean of.
See LEWIS, Very Revd Christopher Andrew

OXFORD, Archdeacon of. See HUBBARD,
Ven Julian Richard Hawes

OXFORD, Bishop of. See PRITCHARD,
Rt Revd John Lawrence

PACKER, Rt Revd John Richard, MA
Hollin House Weetwood Avenue Leeds LS16 5NG [BISHOP OF RIPON AND LEEDS] *b* 1946 *educ* Man Gr Sch; Keble Coll Ox; Ripon Hall Th Coll; *CV* C St Pet St Helier 1970–73; Dir Pastl Studies Ripon Hall 1973–75 and Ripon Coll Cuddesdon 1975–77; Chapl St Nic Abingdon 1973–77; V Wath upon Dearne w Adwick upon Dearne 1977–86; RD Wath 1983–86; R Sheff Manor 1986–91; RD Attercliffe 1990–1991; Adn of W Cumberland 1991–96; P-in-c Bridekirk 1995–96; Bp of Warrington 1996–2000; Bp of Ripon and Leeds from 2000
GS 1985–91, 1992–96, 2000–
Tel: 01765 602045 (Office)
01765 604148 (Home)
Fax: 01765 600758
email: bishop.riponleeds@virgin.net

PADDOCK, Very Revd John Allan Barnes MA, PhD
The Deanery, Bomb House Lane, Gibraltar [DEAN OF GIBRALTAR] *b* 51 *edu* Liv Univ; Ox Univ; Man Univ; Glas Univ; St Steph Hous Ox; *CV* C Matson Glouc 1980–82; Asst Chapl Madrid 1982–83; Chapl R Gr Sch Lanc 1983–86; Hon C Blackb Ch Ch w St Matt 1983–86; Chapl RAF 1986–91; Offg Chapl RAF 1992–94; Chapl St Olave's Gr Sch Orpington 1991–94; Chapl R Russell Sch Croydon 1997–2000; Hon C Bickley 1997–1000; V Folkestone St Pet 2000–03; Hon Min Can Cant Cathl 2001–03; V Glouc St Geo w Whaddon 2003–08; Dean of Gibraltar from 2008.   *Tel:* 00 350 78377
Fax: 00 350 78463
email: deangib@gibraltar.gib

PAGET-WILKES, Ven Michael Jocelyn James, ALCD, NDA
10 Northumberland Rd Leamington Spa CV32 6HA [ARCHDEACON OF WARWICK; COVENTRY] *b* 1941 *educ* Dean Close Sch Cheltenham; Harper Adams Agric Coll; Lon Coll of Div; *CV* C All SS Wandsworth 1969–74; V St Jas Hatcham 1974–82; V St Matt Rugby 1982–90; Adn of Warwick from 1990 GS 2000–   *Tel:* 01926 313337 (Home)
024 7652 1200 (Office)
Fax: 01926 313337 (Home)
024 7652 1330 (Office)
email: michael.pagetwilkes@covcofe.org

PAINTER, Ven David Scott, MA, LTCL, Cert Ed
7 Minster Precincts Peterborough PE1 1XS [ARCHDEACON OF OAKHAM; PETERBOROUGH] *b* 1944 *educ* Qu Eliz Sch Crediton; Trin Coll of Music; Worc Coll Ox; Cuddesdon Th Coll; *CV* C St Andr Plymouth 1970–73; C All SS Marg St 1973–76; Dom Chapl to Abp of Cant and DDO 1976–80; V Roehampton 1980–91; RD Wandsworth 1985–90; Can Res and Treas S'wark Cathl and DDO 1991–2000; Adn of Oakham and Can Res Peterb Cathl from 2000, Vc-Dean 2004–05; M Panel of Bps' Selectors from 1997
GS 2000–05   *Tel:* 01733 891360
Fax: 01733 554524
email: david.painter@peterborough-cathedral.org.uk

PALMER, Dr Richard John, BA, Ph D, RMSA, MCLIP, FSA
Lambeth Palace Library London SE1 7JU [LIBRARIAN AND ARCHIVIST, LAMBETH PALACE LIBRARY] *b* 1949 *educ* Canton High Sch Cardiff; Univ of Kent; *CV* Asst Lib Lon Boro Hounslow 1970–73; Rsch Asst Royal Commn on Historical Mss 1976–80; Post-Doctoral Rsch Fell Wellcome Inst 1980–83; Curator Western Mss, Wellcome Inst for the History of Medicine and Hon Lect in History of Medicine at UCL 1983–91; Librarian and Archivist Lambeth Palace Library from 1991
Tel: 020 7898 1400
Fax: 020 7928 7932
email: richard.palmer@c-of-e.org.uk

PANTER, Ven Ricky (Richard) James Graham, Cert Ed, GOE
2a Monfa Rd Bootle L20 6BQ [ARCHDEACON OF LIVERPOOL] *b* 1948 *educ* Monkton Combe Sch Bath; Worc Coll of Educ; Oak Hill Th Coll; *CV* RE tchr, Chatham Tech High Sch for Boys 1970–71; primary tchr, Boscombe C of E Primary 1971–73; C H Trin Rusholme, Man 1976–80; Asst V St Cyprian w Ch Ch Toxteth 1980–85; V St Andr Clubmoor 1985–96; V St Jo and St Jas Orrell Hey, Bootle from 1996; AD Bootle 1999–2002; Archdeacon of Liverpool from 2002; M Dioc BMU Ecumenism Cttee 1985–90; M Dioc Pastl Cttee 1991–96   *Tel:* 0151 922 3758 (Home)
0151 705 2154 (Office)
Fax: 0151 922 3758
email: archdeaconricky@blueyonder.co.uk

PARKER, Mr Peter William, TD, MA, FIA
1 Turner Drive London NW11 6TX [CHURCH COMMISSIONER] *b* 1933 *educ* Win Coll: New Coll Ox; *CV* Ptnr, Phillips & Drew 1962–85; Vc-Pres, Inst of Actuaries 1988–91; M Abps' Rev of Bps' Needs and Resources 1999–2002; M C of E Pensions Bd from 2003; M Assets Cttee from 2003; M Bishoprics & Cathls Cttee from 2004; Ch Commr and M Bd of Govs from 2003   *Tel:* 020 8458 2646
Fax: 020 8455 8498

PARROTT, Canon David Wesley, BA, LLM
5 Poole Rd Hornchurch RM11 3AS [CHELMSFORD] *b* 1958 *educ* Hastings Sec Modern Sch for Boys; Cardiff Law Sch; Oak Hill Th Coll; *CV* C Thundersley 1984–86; C Rainham 1986–89; R Heydon, Gt Chishill, Little Chishill, Chishill Elmdon w. Wenden Lofts and Strethall 1989–96; TR Rayleigh 1996–2004; CME Adv, Chelms Dioc from 2004; Educ Adv, Eccl Law Soc from 2005; Hon Can Chelms Cathl from 2007
GS 2005–   *Tel:* 01708 464591
email: dwparrott@chelmsford.anglican.org

PARRY, Mr Kim, BA, MIIA, Dip CG
Church House Great Smith St London SW1P 3AZ [HEAD OF INTERNAL AUDIT FOR THE NATIONAL CHURCH INSTITUTIONS] *b* 1955 *educ* Penlan Sch Swansea; Univ of Keele; *CV* Civil Servant from 1979; Hd of Internal Audit from 2000
Tel: 020 7898 1658
Fax: 020 7898 1637
email: kim.parry@c-of-e.org.uk

PATERSON, Rt Revd Robert Mar Eskine, BA, MA, DipTh
Thie Yn Aspick 4 The Falls Tromode Rd, Douglas Isle of Man, IM4 4P2 [BISHOP OF SODOR AND MAN] *b* 1949 *educ* King Henry VIII Sch, Cov; St John's Coll Dur Univ; Cranmer Hall Dur; *CV* C Harpurhey Man 1972–73; C Sketty Swansea 1973–78; R Llangattock and Llangynidr 1978–83; V Ga Balfa Cardiff 1983–94; TR Cowbridge, Llandaff 1994–2000; Prin Officer Ch in Wales Coun for Miss and Min 2000–06; Chapl and Researcher to Abp of

York 2006–08; Bp Sodor and Man from 2008; Vc Chair Liturg Commn; Vc Chair Theol Educ for the Angl Communion   *Tel:* 01624 622108
email: bishop-sodor@iommail.com

PAVER, Canon Elizabeth Caroline, FRSA
113 Warning Tongue Lane Bessacar Doncaster DN4 6TB [SHEFFIELD] *b* 1944 *educ* Doncaster Girls High Sch; St Mary's Coll Cheltenham; *CV* In Primary Educ 28 years; Hdtchr Crags Rd Nurs/Inf Sch 1976–80; Hdtchr Askern Nurs/Inf Sch Littlemoor 1980–86; Hdtchr Intake Nursery and First Sch Doncaster from 1986; M Nat Coun NAHT from 1991; Centenary Nat Pres 1997–97; NAHT Appointee to Gen Teaching Coun from 2000; past M Panel of Chairmen GS; Lay Chair Dioc Syn; M Bp's Coun; M Dioc Bd of Educ Tr Cttee; apptd M AC 1999–2002; Lay Can Sheff Cathl from 2000; Ch Commr from 2004
GS 1991–   *Tel:* 01302 530706
Fax: 01302 360811
email: ecp@intake.doncaster.sch.uk

PAYNE, Canon Mark James Townsend, BA
Vicarage Vicarage Lane Scaynes Hill RH17 7PB [CHICHESTER] *b* 1969 *educ* Heref Cathl Sch; Dur Univ; Ridley Hall; *CV* C St Marg Angmering 1995–99; Dioc Evangelist 1999–2004; Adv for work with children and young people 2001–04; P-in-c St Aug Scaynes Hill and Dioc World Miss Officer from 2004; M Dioc Overseas Coun; M Inter-dioc W Africa Link; Sec Dioc Overseas Coun; Preb of Colworth from 2008; M C of E Angl Communion Panel from 2008
GS 2005–   *Tel:* 01444 831265
07880 728800 (Mobile)
email: markjtpayne@tesco.net

PEARSON, Rt Revd Geoffrey Seagrave, BA
Shireshead Vicarage Whinney Brow Forton Preston PR3 0AE [SUFFRAGAN BISHOP OF LANCASTER; BLACKBURN] *b* 1951 *educ* St Jo Coll Dur; Cranmer Hall Dur; *CV* C Kirkheaton, Wakef 1974–77; C-in-c Redeemer, Blackb 1977–82, V 1982–85; Asst Home Sec GS Bd for Miss and Unity 1985–89; Hon C Forty Hill, Lon 1985–89; Exec Sec BCC Evang Cttee 1986–89; V Roby, Liv 1989–2006; AD Huyton 2002–06; Hon Can Liv Cathl 2003–06; Bp of Lancaster from 2006   *Tel:* 01524 799900
07809 618385 (Mobile)
Fax: 01524 799901
email: bishoplancaster@btconnect.com

PENRITH, Suffragan Bishop of. See NEWCOME, Rt Revd James William Scobie

PENTLAND, Ven Raymond Jackson, QHC, BA, MTh
Chaplaincy Services (RAF) HQ AIR CMD, Royal Air Force High Wycombe HP14 4UE [ARCHDEACON FOR THE ROYAL AIR FORCE] *b* 1957 *educ* Cowdenknowes High Sch Greenock; William Booth Memorial Coll; Open Univ; Ox Univ; St Jo Coll Nottm; *CV* C St Jude Mapperley, S'well 1988–90; Chapl RAF 1990–2005; Command Chapl 2005–06; Archdeacon for the RAF from 2006; Hon Can and Preb Linc Cathl from 2006
GS 2005–   *Tel:* 01494 496800
email: ray.pentland929@mod.uk

PERHAM, Rt Revd Michael Francis, MA, FRSCM, Hon DPhil
Church House College Green Gloucester GL1 2LY [BISHOP OF GLOUCESTER] *b* 1947 *educ* Hardye's Sch Dorchester; Keble Coll Ox; Cuddesdon Th Coll; *CV* C St Mary Addington 1976–81; Chapl to Bp of Win 1981–84; TR Oakdale, Poole 1984–92; Can Res and Prec Norw Cathl 1992–98; Vc Dean 1995–98; Prov of Derby 1998–2000; Dean of Derby 2000–04; M Liturg Commn 1986–2001; M Cathls Fabric Commn 1996–2001; M AC 1999–2004; Chair GS Business Cttee 2001–04; Bp of Gloucester from 2004; Chair SPCK from 2003; Bp Protector Soc of St Francis from 2005; Chair Hosp Chapl Coun from 2007; Vc-Chair MPA Coun from 2007; Author
GS 1989–92, 1993–   *Tel:* 01452 410022 ext. 271
01452 524598
Fax: 01452 308324
email: bshpglos@glosdioc.org.uk

PERKIN, Revd Paul John Stanley, MA, Cert Ed, Cert Th
7 Elsynge Rd London SW18 2HW [SOUTHWARK] *b* 1950 *educ* Leys Sch Cam; Ch Ch Ox; K Coll Lon; Wycliffe Hall Th Coll; *CV* C St Mark Gillingham 1980–84; C H Trin Brompton 1984–87; Chapl Brompton Hosp 1984–87; V St Mark Battersea Rise from 1987; P-in-c St Pet and St Paul Battersea from 2000
GS 2000–   *Tel:* 020 7223 6188 (Office)
020 7326 9412 (Direct)
Fax: 020 7326 9429
email: paul.perkin@stmarks-battersea.org.uk

PETERBOROUGH, Bishop of. See CUNDY, Rt Revd Ian Patrick Martyn

PETERBOROUGH, Dean of. See TAYLOR, Very Revd Charles William

PEYTON, Ven Nigel, MA, BD, STM
4 The Woodwards Balderton Newark NG24 3GG [ARCHDEACON OF NEWARK; SOUTHWELL AND NOTTINGHAM] *b* 1951 *educ* Latymer Upper Sch Lon; Edin Univ; Edin Th Coll; Union Th Seminary New York; Lanc Univ; *CV* Chapl St Paul's Cathl Dundee 1976–82; P-in-c All So Invergowrie 1979–85; V All SS Nottm 1985–91; P-in-c H Trin Lambley 1991–99; Dioc Min Devel Adv 1991–99; Adn of Newark from 1999; JP 1987; Bps' Vocational Adv; M Bp's Coun; Chair Dioc Bd of Min and Pastl Cttee 2000–03; M Min Div DRACSC; M

Legal Aid Commn 2001–06; M Provincial Panel, Clergy Discipline Commn; Dir EIG from 2005
GS 1995–   *Tel:* 01636 612249 (Home)
                        01636 817206 (Office)
                        07917 690576 (Mobile)
                   email: archdeacon-newark@
                        southwell.anglican.org

PHILPOTT, Preb Sam (Samuel),
St Peter's Vicarage 23 Wyndham Square Plymouth PL1 5EG [EXETER] *b* 1941 *educ* R Naval Hosp Sch Holbrook; Kelham Th Coll; *CV* C St Mark Swindon 1965–70; C St Martin Torquay 1970–73; TV All SS Exmouth 1973–76; V Shaldon 1976–78; P-in-c St Pet Plymouth 1978–80, V from 1980; RD Plymouth Devonport 1985–91 and 1995–2001; Preb of Ex Cathl from 1991; Acting P-in-c St Thomas N Keyham from 1997, P-in-c from 1999; Chair Dioc Ho of Clergy from 2000; M Bp's Coun; M Dioc Bd of Educ, portfolio holder for church school buildings; M Dioc Budget Assess Grp; M DBF Stg Cttee; M Dioc Vacancy-in-See Cttee; M Bp of Plymouth's Adv Grp for Plymouth city; Chair Ship Hostel Plymouth; M Drake Foundn Plymouth; M Plymouth Policing Adv Bd; Dir and Vc-Chair Millfields Comm Economic Devel Trust Plymouth; M Plymouth Scrutiny Panel for Children's Services; Bp of Ebbsfleet's Coun of Priests and Episcopal V Plymouth; M Nat Coun and Exec Cttee Forward in Faith; Regional Dn Tamar, Forward in Faith
GS 1990–   *Tel and Fax:* 01752 222007
                   email: frphilpott@aol.com

PIGGOTT, Ven Andy (Andrew John), B Sc (Econ), Dip Th, PGCE
56 Grange Rd Saltford Bristol BS31 3AG [ARCHDEACON OF BATH; BATH AND WELLS] *b* 1951 *educ* Thornes Ho Gr Sch Wakef; Holly Lodge Gr Sch Smethwick; Q Mary Coll Lon; Nottm Univ; St Jo Coll Nottm; *CV* C St Phil w. St Jas Dorridge, Birm 1986–89; TV St Chad Kidderminster w. St Geo Team, Worc 1989–94; V St Lawr Biddulph, Lich 1994–99; CPAS Min & Vocations Adv 1999–2001, acting Gen Dir 2000–01, Patr Sec 2001–05; Adn of Bath from 2005   *Tel:* 01225 873609
                              Fax: 01225 874610
     email: adbath@bathwells.anglican.org

PLATTEN, Rt Revd Stephen George, B Ed, Dip Theol, BD, D Litt
Bishop's Lodge Woodthorpe Lane Wakefield WF2 6JL [BISHOP OF WAKEFIELD] *b* 1947 *educ* Stationers' Company's Sch; Lon Univ Inst of Educ; Trin Coll Ox; Cuddesdon Th Coll; *CV* C Headington 1975–78; Chapl and Tutor Linc Th Coll 1978–82; DDO and Minl Tr and Can Res Portsm Cathl 1982–89; Sec for Ecum Affairs to Abp of Cant 1990–95; Dean of Norw 1995–2003; Bp of Wakefield from 2003; Chair SCM Cant Press from 2001; Chair Liturg Commn from 2005
GS 1997–   *Tel:* 01924 255349
                        Fax: 01924 250202
   email: bishop@bishopofwakefield.org.uk

PLYMOUTH, Archdeacon of. See WILDS, Ven Anthony Ronald

PLYMOUTH, Suffragan Bishop of. See FORD, Rt Revd John Frank

PODMORE, Dr Colin John, MA, D Phil, F R Hist S
Church House Great Smith St London SW1P 3AZ [ADMINISTRATIVE SECRETARY, CENTRAL SECRETARIAT] *b* 1960 *educ* Bodmin Gr Sch; Bodmin Sch; Keble Coll Ox; Selw Coll Cam; *CV* Tchr St Mich C of E High Sch Chorley 1983–85; Asst Sec BMU, CCU 1988–97; Dep Sec CCU 1998–99; Sec IFCG 1988–91; Co-Sec Meissen Commn 1991–99; Co-Sec Porvoo Contact Grp 1996–99; Cen Secretariat from 1999; Sec Liturg Publ Grp 1999–2002; Sec CAC Rev Grp 1999–2001; Sec Sen Appts Rev Grp 2005–07; Sec Ho of Clergy; Sec Diocs Commn; Sec Liturg Commn; Trustee Nikaean Ecum Trust, Cleaver Trust   *Tel:* 020 7898 1385
              email: colin.podmore@c-of-e.org.uk

PONTEFRACT, Archdeacon of. See TOWNLEY, Ven Peter Kenneth

PONTEFRACT, Suffragan Bishop of. See ROBINSON, Rt Revd Anthony William

POPE, Mr John Henry William,
6 Hawthylands Rd Hailsham BN27 1EU [CHICHESTER] *b* 1945 *educ* Roan Sch for Boys; Woolwich Poly; *CV* Rtd Customs Officer; Chair of Govs Park Mead C P Sch 1986–90; M Bp's Coun from 1992; M Dioc Miss and Renewal Team from 1995; M Stg Cttee Nat Coun of Church Union from 1995; Dioc Bd Patr from 1996; Inter-Dioc Fin Forum from 2001
GS 1997–   *Tel:* 01323 841613

PORTER, Rt Revd Anthony, MA (Oxon), MA (Cantab)
Dunham House 8 Westgate Southwell NG25 0JL [SUFFRAGAN BISHOP OF SHERWOOD; SOUTHWELL AND NOTTINGHAM] *b* 1952 *educ* Aire Boro Gr Sch; Don Valley High Sch; Gravesend Sch for Boys; Hertford Coll Ox; Ridley Hall Cam; *CV* C Edgware, Lon 1977–80; C St Mary Haughton, Manch 1980–83; P-in-c Ch Ch Bacup 1983–87, V 1987–91; R Rusholme 1991–2006; Bp of Sherwood from 2006; M Dioc Syn, Bp's Coun   *Tel:* 01636 819133
                                   Fax: 01636 819085
   email: bishopsherwood@southwell.anglican.org

PORTER, Revd Matthew James, BA, B Th, MA
9 Linden Ave Woodseats Sheffield S8 0GA [SHEFFIELD] *b* 1969 *educ* Oundle Sch; Nottm Univ; Ox Univ; Sheff Univ; Wycliffe Hall Ox; *CV* C Ch Ch Dore, Sheff 1996–99, Assoc V 1999–2000; V St Chad Woodseats, Sheff from 2000; Dir of IME 4–7, Sheff Dioc from 2005; M Sheff Dioc Bd of Min from 2005; M Dioc Syn; Bp's Adv for clergy selection
GS 2005–   *Tel:* 0114 274 5086
                        07985 645844
              email: matt@stchads.org

PORTSDOWN, Archdeacon of. See READER, Ven Dr Trevor Alan John

PORTSMOUTH, Bishop of. See STEVENSON, Rt Revd Kenneth William

PORTSMOUTH, Dean of. See BRINDLEY, Very Revd David Charles

PRESLAND, Mr Andrew Roy, B Sc
58 Harborough Rd Rushden NN10 0LP [PETERBOR-OUGH] *b* 1966 *educ* Rushden Boys' Sch; Leic Univ; *CV* Asst Statistician, DOE 1989–95; Statistician DOE, later DETR 1995–99; Sen Lib Clerk (Statistics), Ho of Commons Lib (secondment) 1999–2001; Statistician, Office of Dep Prime Min (local govt finance) 2001–06, DCLG from 2006 (strategy and performance); Lay Chair, Higham Dny Syn; M Bp's Coun from 2006; M AC Fin Cttee from 2006
GS 2003–   *Tel:* 01933 316927
email: andrewpresland@
harboroughroad58.freeserve.co.uk

PRESTON, Dr John Philip Harry, BSc, PHD
Church House Great Smith St London SW1P 3AZ [NATIONAL STEWARDSHIP AND RESOURCES OFFICER, ARCHBISHOPS' COUNCIL] *b* 1965 *educ* Lakes Sch; Exeter Sch; Lancs Univ; *CV* Marketing Mgr Proctor and Gamble 1989–2000; Grp Marketing Dir S Staffordshire Grp 2000–02; Marketing, Sales and NPD Mgr, Freshway Foods 2002–05; Nat Stewardwhip and Resources Officer from 2005; Non-exec Dir Send the Light Ltd 2001–2008   *Tel:* 020 7898 1540
email: john.preston@c-of-e.org.uk

PRICE, Rt Revd Peter Bryan, Cert Ed, DPS
The Palace Wells BA5 2PD [BISHOP OF BATH AND WELLS] *b* 1944 *educ* Glastonbury Sch Morden; Redland Coll of Educ Bris; Oak Hill Th Coll; Heythrop Coll Lon; *CV* Asst Tchr Ashton Park Sch Bris 1966–70; Sen Tutor Lindley Lodge Young People's Cen 1970; Head of RE Cordeaux High Sch Louth 1970–72; Com Chapl and C Ch Ch Portsdown 1974–78; Chapl Scargill Ho 1978–80; V St Mary Magd Addiscombe 1980–88; Can Chan S'wark Cathl 1988–91; Gen Sec USPG 1992–97; M Miss Agencies Wkg Grp 1992–93; M Angl Commn on Miss 1993–96; Bp of Kingston 1997–2002; M BM; M PWM; M Ch Commn on Miss; M Miss Th Adv Grp; M Gov Body SPCK; Chair S'wark Dioc Bd of Educ; Chair The Manna Soc 1997–2001; Bp of Bath and Wells from 2002
GS 2002–   *Tel:* 01749 672341
Fax: 01749 679355
email: bishop@bathwells.anglican.org

PRIDDIS, Rt Revd Anthony Martin, MA, Dip Th, FCEM
The Bishop's House Hereford HR4 9BN [BISHOP OF HEREFORD] *b* 1948 *educ* Watford Gr Sch; CCC

Cam; New Coll Ox; Cuddesdon Th Coll; *CV* C New Addington 1972–75; Chapl Ch Ch Ox 1975–80; TV St Jo High Wycombe 1980–86; P-in-c Amersham 1986–90, R 1990–96; RD Amersham 1992–96; Hon Can Ch Ch Ox from 1995; Bp of Warwick 1996–2004; Trustee Cov Relate 2001–03; Trustee FLAME Network 2001–06, Co-Chair 2003–06; Lay M Bd Coll of Emergency Medicine from 2002; Child Protection Liaison Grp from 2002; W Midlands Cultural Consortium 2002–05; Bp of Hereford from 2004; Trustee Eveson Charitable Trust from 2004; Hon Fell Coll of Emergency Medicine from 2004; Chair Rural Bps' Panel from 2006
GS 2004–   *Tel:* 01432 271355
Fax: 01432 373346
email: bishop@hereford.anglican.org

PRIMROSE, Revd David Edward Snodgrass, MA, B Th, M Phil, CQSW
Vicarage 27 Castle St Thornbury Bristol BS35 1HQ [GLOUCESTER] *b* 1955 *educ* Fettes Coll Edin; St Jo Coll Cam; Univ of Wales, Cardiff; Ex Univ; Trin Coll Bris; *CV* Probation Officer 1978–82; Miss Ptnr CMS 1983–89; C Gloucester 1992–95; V Shurdington 1996–2003; V Thornbury and Oldbury-on-Severn with Shepperdine from 2003; M Bp's Coun
GS 2005–   *Tel:* 01454 413209
email: primrose@blueyonder.co.uk

PRITCHARD, Rt Revd John Lawrence, MA, M Litt
Diocesan Church House North Hinksey Lane Oxford OX2 0NB [BISHOP OF OXFORD] *b* 1948 *educ* Arnold Sch Blackpool; St Pet Coll Ox; Ridley Hall Th Coll; St Jo Coll Dur; *CV* C St Mart-in-the-Bull-Ring Birm 1972–76; Dioc Youth Officer B and W 1976–79; P-in-c St Geo Wilton 1980–88; Dir Pastl Studies Cranmer Hall, St Jo Coll Dur 1989–93; Warden Cranmer Hall 1993–96; Adn of Cant and Can Res Cant Cathl 1996–2001; Bp of Jarrow 2002–07; Bp of Oxford from 2007
GS 1999–2002, 2007–   *Tel:* 01865 208222 (Office)
Fax: 01865 790470
email: bishopoxon@oxford.anglican.org

PRIVETT, Mr (John) Hugh Charles, MA
The Manor House Marston Magna Yeovil BA22 8DW [SALISBURY] *b* 1939 *CV* Solicitor; Chairman DBF 1989–2000
GS 2000–   *Tel:* 01935 850294
email: jhcp@talktalk.net

PWAISIHO, Rt Revd William Alaha, OBE, SECONDARY CERT, Dip Th
Rectory Church Lane Gawsworth Macclesfield SK11 9RJ [HONORARY ASSISTANT BISHOP OF CHESTER] *b* 1948 *educ* Alangaula Sch, Pawa and Selwyn Coll, Bp Patteson Theol Centre Kohimarama, Honiara, all in Solomon Islands; *CV* Chapl to Abp of Melanesia 1976–77; C Kohimarama Par Auckland NZ 1977–78; Chapl/Tutor Bp Patteson Theol Cen

Kohimarama 1978–79; Dean St Barn Cathl Honiara 1980–81; Bp of Malaita Solomon Islands 1981–89; Gen Sec Melanesian DM 1990–95; Industrial Mgr and Chapl to Kumagai Gumi Ltd, Solomon Islands 1995–96; Asst Bp and C in Sale from 1997; Asst Bp and R Gawsworth from 1999; M Dioc Syn; M Ho Bps Dioc Minority Ethnic Cttee; Melanesian Miss Engl Cttee; M ChsTogether UK Pacific Forum; first missionary Bp from Melanesia to UK since 1849; first Pacific islander to hold office of Rector in UK and to be appointed Chapl to High Sheriff; awarded OBE 2004; M Cheshire Constabulary Ethnic Minority Independent Adv Grp; Hon Chapl to Crimebeat Eng and Wales; M Rotary Club of Macclesfield
GS 1997–   *Tel and Fax:* 01260 223201
email: bishop.gawsworth@virgin.net

PYE, Mr Christopher Charles, BA, M Sc
140 Hinckley Rd St Helens WA11 9JY [LIVERPOOL] *b* 1946 *educ* Grange Park Sch St Helens; Open Univ; Manchester Univ; *CV* Technologist in Glass Industry from 1963; Occupational Hygiene Mgr; Lay Chair St Helens Dny Syn from 1986; Lay Chair Dioc Syn 1991–2003; Rdr
GS 1985–90, 1992–   *Tel:* 01744 609506
email: chrispye@blueyonder.co.uk

RAINES, Revd William Guy, MSc, BA
197 Old Hall Lane Manchester M14 6HJ [MANCHESTER] *b* 1946 *educ* The American Sch in Lon; Univ of Lon Bedford Coll; Univ of Ox; The Ecum Inst Bossey, Switzerland; Ripon Coll Cuddesdon; *CV* Asst C St Martin W Drayton, Lon 1981–84; Asst C St Luke Charlton, S'wark 1984–87; Univ Chapl W Lon Chapl Tm 1987–94; R Birch w Fallowfield from 1994; Chapl to Rdrs and Lay Assts, Man Adnry
GS 2008–   *Tel:* 0161 224 1310
0774 337 3617 (Mobile)
email: wraines@btinternet.com

RAMSBURY, Area Bishop of. See CONWAY, Rt Revd Stephen David

RANDALL, Revd Colin, BD, B Ed, M Th
Vicarage Warwick Bridge Carlisle CA4 8RF [CARLISLE] *b* 1957 *educ* Rednock Sch Dursley; Coll of St Paul & St Mary Cheltenham; Trin Coll Bris; *CV* C St Jas Denton Holme, Carl 1984–87; C to RD of Brampton, Carl 1987–90; R Hanborough and Freeland, Ox 1990–99; P-in-c Croglin, Holme Eden and Wetheral with Warwick from 1999; M Adny Pastl Cttee and Adny Parsonage Bd from 2000; RD Brampton from 2005
GS 2005–   *Tel:* 01228 560332
email: colinrandall@mac.com

RANDALL, Preb Colin Michael Sebastian, BSc
Rectory 72 High St Wellington TA21 8RF [BATH AND WELLS] *b* 1950 *educ* Bedford Sch; Aston Univ; Qu Coll Birm; *CV* C St Mich Tonge w. Alkrington, Man 1975–78; C All SS Elton, Man 1978–82; P-in-c, then V H Trin Bridgwater 1982–90; V Bp's Hull, Taunton 1990–2000; pt chapl St Marg Hospice 1990–2000; TR Wellington and district TM from 2000; M Dioc Pastl Cttee 1989–2004; M Dioc Coun for Min 2004–08; M Dioc Syn from 1985; appt Preb Wells Cathl 2005; Chair Dioc Ho of Clergy from 2008
GS 2005–   *Tel:* 01823 662248
email: colinms.randall@virgin.net

RAWLINGS, Ven John Edmund Frank, AKC
Blue Hills Bradley Rd Bovey Tracey Newton Abbot TQ13 9EU [ARCHDEACON OF TOTNES; EXETER] *b* 1947 *educ* Godalming Gr Sch; K Coll Lon; St Aug Coll Cant; *CV* C Rainham 1970–73; C Tattenham Corner w. Burgh Heath 1973–76; Chapl RN 1976–92; V Tavistock w. Gulworthy 1992–2006; RD Tavistock 1997–2002; Preb of Ex 1999–2006; Adn of Totnes and Min Devel Trg Officer from 2006; Chapl to Melanesian Brotherhood Companions from 2006   *Tel:* 01626 832064
Fax: 01626 834947
email: archdeacon.of.totnes@exeter.anglican.org

RAYFIELD, Rt Revd Dr Lee Stephen, B Sc (Hons), PhD, CTM
Mark House Field Rise Swindon SN1 4HP [SUFFRAGAN BISHOP OF SWINDON; BRISTOL] *b* 1955 *educ* Thos Bennett Comp Sch, Crawley; Crawley Coll of Tech; Southn Univ; St Mary's Hosp Medical Sch, Lon Univ; Ridley Hall, Cam; *CV* C All SS w. St Andr Woodford Wells, Chelmsf 1993–97; P-in-c St Pet w. St Mark Hosp Ch Furze Platt, Ox 1997–2004, V 2004–05; AD Maidenhead & Windsor, Ox 2000–05; Bp of Swindon from 2005; M UK Gene Therapy Adv Cttee from 2000; M Soc of Ordained Scientists from 1995; M Fell of Par Evang from 1995; Coun M Evang Alliance from 2007; M Ho of Bps CME Cttee from 2007; M Ethical Investment Adv Grp from 2007   *Tel:* 01793 538654
Fax: 01793 525181
email: bishop.swindon@bristoldiocese.org

READE, Rt Revd Nicholas Stewart, BA, Dip Th
Bishop's House Ribchester Rd Blackburn BB1 9EF [BISHOP OF BLACKBURN] *b* 1946 *educ* Eliz Coll Guernsey; Leeds Univ; Coll of the Resurrection, Mirfield; *CV* C St Chad Coseley 1973–75; C-in-c H Cross Bilbrook and C Codsall 1975–78; V St Pet Upper Gornal and Chapl Burton Rd Hosp Dudley 1978–82; V Mayfield 1982–88; RD Dallington 1982–88; V and RD Eastbourne 1988–97; Chair Dioc Liturg Cttee 1989–97; Can and Preb Chich Cathl from 1990; Pres Eastbourne Police Court Miss from 1994; Adn of Lewes and Hastings 1997–2004; Chair Dioc Bd of Patr 1992–97; Vc-Pres Dioc Syn and Chair Ho of Clergy 1997–2000; M Dioceses Commn from 2000; Pres Crowhurst Chr Healing Cen from 2001; Bp of Blackburn from 2004; M Ho of Bps Healing Min Strg Grp from 2004; Patron Rosemarie Cancer Foundn from 2005; Patron SELRAP from 2006; Patron

Dorian House Children's Hospice from 2006; Chair Ctee for Min of and among Deaf and Disabled People from 2008; M SAG(E) from 2008
GS 1995–2000, 2002–   *Tel:* 01254 248234
Fax: 01254 246668
email: bishop@bishopofblackburn.org.uk

READER, Ven Dr Trevor Alan John, B Sc, M Sc, Ph D, SOSc
5 Brading Ave Southsea PO4 9QJ [ARCHDEACON OF PORTSDOWN; PORTSMOUTH] *b* 1946 *educ* Haverfordwest Gr Sch; Portsm Poly; S Diocs Min Trg Scheme, Salis & Wells Th Coll; *CV* Rsch Asst biological sciences Ports Poly 1968–72, Sen Lect 1972–86; C St Mary, Alverstoke 1986–89; P-in-c, then V St Mary, Hook w Warsash 1989–98; P-in-c Blendworth, H Trin w Chalton St Mich & All Angels w Idsworth St Hubert and Ports Dioc Dir of NSM 1998–2003; Adn of Isle of Wight 2003–06; Adn of Portsdown from 2006; Chair Dioc Bd of Educ; M DAC for Care of Chs; M Dioc Parsonages and Property Cttee; Bp's Liaison Officer for Prisons 2003–06; Bp's Adv to Hosp Chapl from 2006   *Tel:* 023 9243 2693
07737 180384 (Mobile)
Fax: 023 9229 8788
email: adportsdown@portsmouth.anglican.org

READING, Area Bishop of. See COTTRELL, Rt Revd Stephen Geoffrey

REDDEN, Mr Jonathan Francis, MB, BS, FRCS
Tofield House Carr Lane Wadworth Doncaster DN11 9AR [SHEFFIELD] *b* 1947 *educ* Loughb Gr Sch; St Bart Hosp Medical Coll Lon Univ; *CV* Senr Registrar Edin 1977–81; Lect Orthopaedic Surgery Wellington Medical Sch New Zealand; Consult Orthopaedic Surgeon Doncaster R Infirmary from 1981
GS 1989–   *Tel:* 01302 853829

REDFERN, Rt Revd Dr Alastair Llewellyn John, MA, MA, Ph D
The Bishop's House 6 King St Duffield Belper DE56 4EU [BISHOP OF DERBY] *b* 1948 *educ* Bicester Sch; Ch Ch Ox; Trin Coll Cam; Westcott Ho Th Coll; Bris Univ; *CV* C Tettenhall 1976–79; Lect in Ch Hist, Dir of Pastl Studies and Vc-Prin Cuddesdon Th Coll 1979–87; C All SS Cuddesdon 1983–87; Can Res Bris Cathl 1987–97; Can Theologian and Dir of Tr 1987–97; Mod of Par Resource Tm 1995–97; M ABM Initial Minl Educ Cttee; Mod Abps Dip for Rdrs; Bp of Grantham 1997–2005; Dean of Stamford 1998–2005; Chair Fin Panel, Min Div; M Theol, Educ and Trg Cttee; M Bp's Cttee for Min; M Bp's CME Cttee; M Legal Aid Commn; Bp of Derby from 2005; M Ho of Bps Th Gp
GS 2005–   *Tel:* 01332 840132
Fax: 01332 840397
email: bishop@bishopofderby.org

REED, Ven John Peter Cyril, BD, AKC, Cert Th (Oxon)
4 Westerkirk Gate Staplegrove Taunton TA2 6BQ [ARCHDEACON OF TAUNTON; BATH & WELLS] *b* 1951 *educ* Monkton Combe Sch; K Coll Lon; Cuddesdon Th Coll; *CV* Asst C Croydon Par Ch 1979–82; Prec St Alb 1982–86; R Timsbury and Priston 1986–93; Chapl for Rural Affairs Bath Adnry 1987–93; TR Ilminster and District TM 1993–99; Adn Taunton from 1999; Dioc Warden of Rdrs   *Tel:* 01823 323838
Fax: 01823 325420
email: adtaunton@bathwells.anglican.org

REES, Mrs Christina (Henking Muller), BA, MA, FRSA
Churchfield Pudding Lane Barley Royston SG8 8JX [ST ALBANS] *b* 1953 *educ* Hampton Day Sch; Pomona Coll; Wheaton Graduate Sch; K Coll Lon; *CV* Researcher IBA 1980; Asst Public Relns Officer The Children's Society 1985–87; Writer from 1980; Broadcaster from 1990; M CAC 1995; M Strg Cttee and Initiation Services Revision Cttee 1996–98; M CECC 1996–98; M ABM 1996–98; Chair WATCH from 1996; Trustee, Li Tim-Oi Foundn from 1997; Elected M AC 1999–2000; Trustee, Chr Evidence Soc 2000–05; M Theol Educ and Trg Cttee 2000–05; GS rep, Bd Govs Ripon Coll Cuddesdon from 2000; co-opted Bd Govs Tr Coll Bris 2000–05; M CMEAC 1999–2004; Dir Churchfield Trust; M CRAC; Dip in Coaching (Coaching Futures/OCR); elected M AC from 2005; Trustee Chr Assoc of Business Execs
GS 1990–   *Tel:* 01763 848472
01763 848822
Fax: 01763 848774
email: christina@mediamaxima.com

REES, Canon (Vivian) John (Howard), MA, LLB, M Phil
16 Beaumont St Oxford OX1 2LZ [JOINT REGISTRAR, PROVINCE OF CANTERBURY] *b* 1951 *educ* Skinners' Sch Tunbridge Wells; Southn Univ; Ox Univ; Leeds Univ; Wycliffe Hall Th Coll; *CV* Solicitor and Eccl Notary (Admitted 1975); C Moor Allerton TM 1979–82; Chapl and Tutor Sierra Leone Th Hall, Freetown 1983–86; Ptnr Winckworth Sherwood Solicitors from 1986; Treas Eccl Law Soc from 1995; Jt Registrar Ox Dioc from 1998; Jt Registrar Prov of Cant from 2000; Legal Adv ACC from 1998; Vc-Chair Legal Adv Commn from 2001; Provincial Can Cant Cathl from 2001; Registrar, Clergy Discipline Tribunals Prov of Cant from 2006
GS 1995–2000   *Tel:* 01865 865875 (Home)
01865 297200 (Office)
07973 327417 (Mobile)
Fax: 01865 726274
email: vjhrees@btinternet.com / jrees@winckworths.co.uk

REID, Mrs Jennifer, BA
*Healam 9 Poplars Rd Linthorpe Middlesbrough TS5
6RL* [YORK] *b* 1943 *CV* University lecturer, rtd
GS 2000– *Tel:* 01642 823127 (Home)
01642 782095 (Office)
email: jennyreid@ntlworld.com

**REIGATE, Archdeacon of. See KAJUMBA,
Ven Daniel Steven Kimbugwe**

**REPTON, Suffragan Bishop of.
See SOUTHERN, Rt Revd Humphrey Ivo John**

RICHARDSON, Rt Revd Paul, MA
*Close House St George's Close Jesmond Newcastle-
upon-Tyne NE2 2TF* [ASSISTANT BISHOP OF NEW-
CASTLE] *b* 1947 *educ* Keswick Sch; Queen's Coll
Ox; Harvard Divinity Sch; Cuddesdon Th Coll;
CV Asst C St Jo Earlsfield, S'wark 1972–75; Asst
Chapl Oslo Norway 1975–77; P-in-c Nambaiyufa
PNG 1977–79; Lect Newton Th Coll PNG 1979–
80, Prin 1981–85, Dean Port Moresby Cathl PNG
1985–86; Bp of Aipo Rongo PNG 1987–95; Bp of
Wangaratta Australia 1995–97; Asst Bp of Newc
from 1998; Inter Angl Doctrinal and Th Commn
from 2001 *Tel:* 0191 285 2220 (Office)
0191 281 2556 (Home)
07973 771378 (Mobile)
Fax: 0191 284 6933
email: ulpha@gotadsl.co.uk

**RICHBOROUGH, Bishop of. See NEWTON, Rt
Revd Keith**

**RICHMOND, Archdeacon of. See
HENDERSON, Ven Janet**

RINGROSE, Ven Hedley Sidney, BA
*The Sanderlings Thorncliffe Drive Cheltenham GL51
6PY* [ARCHDEACON OF CHELTENHAM; GLOUCES-
TER] *b* 1942 *educ* W Oxfordshire Coll; Open Univ;
Sarum Th Coll; *CV* C Bishopston 1968–71; C
Easthampstead 1971–75; V St Geo Glouc w
Whaddon 1975–88; RD Glouc City 1983–88; V
Cirencester w Watermoor 1988–98; RD Ciren-
cester 1989–97; Hon Can Glouc Cathl 1986–98;
Chair Dioc Bd of Patr 1990–98; Chair Dioc Ho of
Clergy 1994–98; Adn of Chelt from 1998;
Reserved Can Glouc Cathl from 1998; Chair Dioc
Bd of Educ from 1998; Trustee Glenfall Ho from
1998; Trustee St Matthias Trust from 1998, Chair
from 2005; Trustee Sylvanus Lysons Trust from
2000
GS 1990–2005 *Tel:* 01242 522923
Fax: 01242 235925
email: archdchelt@star.co.uk

**RIPON AND LEEDS, Bishop of. See PACKER,
Rt Revd John Richard**

**RIPON, Dean of. See JUKES, Very Revd Keith
Michael**

ROBBINS, Ven Stephen, BD, AKC
*MoD Chaps (A) Trenchard Lines Upavon Pewsey
SN9 6BE* [ARCHDEACON FOR THE ARMY] *b* 1953
educ Jarrow Gr Sch; K Coll Lon; St Aug Coll Cant;
CV C St Andr Tudhoe Grange, Dur 1976–80; C-in-
c St Ninian Harlow Green, Dur 1980 84, V 1984–
87; R Army Chapls' Dept from 1987; Dir Trg
MOD Chapls (Army) and Adn for the Army from
2004; Dep Chapl Gen 2007–08; Chapl Gen from
2008
GS 2004– *Tel:* 01980 615801
07747 100993 (Mobile)
Fax: 01980 615800
email: armychaplains@armymail.mod.uk

ROBERTS, Canon (John) Mark Arnott, AKC,
PGCE
Rectory Knightrider St Sandwich CT13 9ER [CAN-
TERBURY] *b* 1954 *educ* Caterham Sch; K Coll Lon
Univ; Ch Ch Coll Cant; Chich Th Coll; *CV* C St
Mary V, Ashford, Kent 1977–82; V and R St
Mary's Bay, St Mary in the Marsh, Ivychurch
1982–91; R Sandwich from 1991; P-in-C Worth
from 2004; Area Dean of Sandwich 2000–06; M
Dioc Syn; M Abp's Coun; Chairman Dioc Pastl
Grp; M Dioc Liturg Grp; Hon Can Cant Cathl
from 2003; Chair Dioc Syn Ho of Clergy from
2006
GS 2003– *Tel:* 01304 613138
email: revdmarkroberts@supanet.com

ROBERTS, Canon Dr Paul John, BA, Ph D, PGCE
12 Belgrave Rd Bristol BS8 2AB [BRISTOL] *b* 1960
educ Olchfa Comp Sch Swansea; Man Univ; Man
Poly; St Jo Coll Nottm; *CV* C St Marg Burnage
1985–88; Tutor in Worship and Doct Trin Coll Bris
1988–2000; V St Sav w St Mary Cotham and St
Paul Clifton from 2000; M Dioc Syn; M Liturg
Commn 2001–06; Chair Praxis 2001–06; Hon Can
Bris Cathl 2006
GS 2000– *Tel:* 0117 377 1086
email: paul.roberts@bristol.anglican.org

ROBERTS, Ven Stephen John, BD, MTh
2 Alma Rd Wandsworth London SW18 1AB [ARCH-
DEACON OF WANDSWORTH; SOUTHWARK] *b* 1958
educ Newcastle-under-Lyme High Sch; K Coll
Lon; Westcott Ho Cam; Heythrop Coll Lon; *CV* C
St Mary Riverhead w. St Jo Dunton Green, Roch
1983–86; C St Martin-in-the-Fields, S'wark 1986–
89; V St Geo Camberwell and Wrdn Trin Coll
Centre, S'wark 1989–2000; Sen DDO and Can
Res, S'wark Cathl 2000–05; Adn of Wandsworth
from 2005 *Tel:* 020 8874 8567 (Home)
020 8785 1985 (Work)
Fax: 020 8785 1981
email: stephen.roberts@southwark.anglican.org

ROBILLIARD, Mr David John,
Le Petit Gree Torteval Guernsey GY8 0RD [WIN-
CHESTER (CHANNEL ISLANDS)] *b* 1952 *educ* Guern-
sey Gr Sch for Boys; *CV* Clearing and Internat

Banking 1969–82; HM Dep Greffier 1982–87; Prin Asst Chief Exec Guernsey Civil Service 1987–94; Hd of Constitutional Affairs States of Guernsey 1994–2007; Prin Officer States Assembly and Constitution Ctee from 2008; M Dioc Stg Cttee; Treas Guernsey Dny Syn; chwdn of Torteval
GS 1998– Tel: 01481 264344 (Home)
01481 717027 (Office)
07781 164344 (Mobile)
Fax: 01481 264543 (Home)
01481 713884 (Office)
email: villula@cwgsy.net

ROBINSON, Rt Revd Anthony William, Cert Ed
Pontefract House 181a Manygates Lane Wakefield WF2 7DR [SUFFRAGAN BISHOP OF PONTEFRACT; WAKEFIELD] *b* 1956 *educ* Bedf Modern Sch; Bedf Coll of HE; Sarum and Wells Th Coll; *CV* C St Paul Tottenham 1982–85; TV Resurr Leic 1985–89, TR 1989–97; RD Christianity N 1992–97; Hon Can Leic Cathl from 1994; M CBF 1995–97; M CMEAC 1996–97; Adn of Pontefract 1997–2003; Bishop of Pontefract from 2002
GS 1995–97, 2000–02 Tel: 01924 250781
Fax: 01924 240490
email: bishop.pontefract@wakefield.anglican.org

ROBINSON, Ven Peter John Alan MA PhD
4 Acomb Close, Morpeth NE61 2YH [ARCHDEACON OF LINDISFARNE] *b* 61 *edu* St Jo Col Cam; St Jo Coll Dur; Cranmer Hall Dur; *CV* C N Shields 1995–99; PC Byker St Martin 1999–2008; PC Byker St Mich w St Lawr 2001–08; Hon Can Newc Cathl 2007–08; Archdeacon of Lindisfarne from 2008
Tel: 01670 503810
Fax: 01670 510469
email: p.robinson@newcastle.anglican.org

ROCHDALE, Archdeacon of. See VANN,
Cherry Elizabeth

ROCHESTER, Archdeacon of. See LOCK,
Ven Peter Harcourt D'Arcy

ROCHESTER, Bishop of. See NAZIR-ALI,
Rt Revd Michael James

ROCHESTER, Dean of. See NEWMAN,
Very Revd Adrian

RODGERS, Mrs Sue (Susan Elizabeth),
13 Rowlands Ave Waterlooville PO7 7RT [PORT-SMOUTH] *b* 1954 *educ* Haywards Heath Sec Sch; *CV* WRNS 1971–79; Night Staff St Mary's Hosp Portsm; Bereavement Cllr; Co-ord Bereavement Grp; Par Asst/Administrator St Wilf Cowplain until 2001; Lay Can Portsm Cath from 2009
GS 2000– Tel: 023 9225 3091
07974 570414 (Mobile)
Fax: 023 9223 3367
email: Sue@Rodgersuk.com

ROSEMARY CHN, Sister, MA, MA, Dip Pastl Th (APU)
Convent of the Holy Name Morley Rd Oakwood Derby DE21 4QZ [RELIGIOUS COMMUNITIES (SOUTH)] *b* 1944 *educ* Barr's Hill Sch Cov; Newnham Coll Cam; St Mary's Coll Dur Univ; Westcott Ho Cam; *CV* Various teaching posts, 1967–76; Community of the Holy Name from 1976; Dn 1998; P 1999 (Derby Dioc); C St Osmund, Derby 1998–2001; Perm to officiate, Derby and S'well Diocs from 2001
GS 2003– Tel: 0115 978 5101
email: rosemarychn@yahoo.co.uk

ROSSDALE, Rt Revd David Douglas James,
MA, M Sc
Bishop's House Church Lane Irby-on-Humber Grimsby DN37 7JR [SUFFRAGAN BISHOP OF GRIMSBY; LINCOLN] *b* 1953 *educ* St Jo Sch Leatherhead; K Coll Lon; Westmr Coll Ox; Roehampton Inst; Chich Th Coll; *CV* C St Laur Upminster 1981–86; V St Luke Moulsham 1986–90; V H Trin Cookham 1990–2000; AD Maidenhead 1994–2000; Hon Can Ch Ch Ox 1999–2000; Bp of Grimsby from 2000; Hon Can and Preb Lincoln from 2000
Tel: 01472 371715
Fax: 01472 371716
email: rossdale@btinternet.com

ROWELL, Rt Revd (Douglas) Geoffrey, MA, Ph D, D Phil, DD, Hon DD
Bishop's Lodge Worth Crawley RH10 7RT [BISHOP OF GIBRALTAR IN EUROPE] *b* 1943 *educ* Eggar's Gr Sch Alton; Win Coll; CCC Cam; Cuddesdon Th Coll; *CV* Asst Chapl and Hastings Rashdall Student New Coll Ox 1968–72; Hon C St Andr Headington 1968–72; Fell, Chapl and Tutor in Th Keble Coll Ox 1972–94, Emer Fell from 1994; Univ Lect in Th 1977–94; M Liturg Commn 1980–90; Gov Pusey Ho Ox from 1979, Pres from 1995; M Gov Body SPCK 1984–94 and from 1997; Hon Dir Abp's Exam in Th 1986–2001; Can and Preb Chich Cathl 1981–2001; M Angl-Oriental Orthodox Internat Forum from 1985, Angl Co-Chair from 1996; Conservator Mirfield Cert in Pastl Th 1987–93; M Coun Mgt St Steph Ho Th Coll from 1988, Chairman from 2004; M Doct Commn 1990–95, Consult 1996–99, M 1999–2004; Bp of Basingstoke 1994–2001; C of E Rep on CTBI 1995–2001; Vis Prof Univ Coll Chich (Sch of Religion and Theol) 1996–2003; Chair Chs Funerals Grp from 1997; M Inter Angl Stg Commn on Ecum Relns from 2000, Vc-Chairman from 2003; Hon Can Win Cathl 2000–2001; Ho Bps Theol Grp from 1999; M Clergy Discipline (Theol and Liturg) Wkg Pty 2000–03; M Ho of Bps' Wkg Pty on Women in the Episcopate 2000–04; Bp of Gib in Eur from 2001
GS 2001– Tel: 01293 883051
Fax: 01293 884479
email: bishop@dioceseineurope.org.uk

ROWLING, Canon Catherine, B Ed, PG Dip (HE), MA
Rectory Cemetery Rd Thirsk YO7 1PR [YORK] *b* 1955 *educ* Adelphi Ho Gr Sch Salford; Preston Sixth Form Coll; Man Poly; Dur Univ; Westcott Ho and NEOC; *CV* Dss and Dn Great Ayton 1986–89; Chapl Teesside Poly/Univ 1989–96; non-res Can York from 2001; Dn of Women's Min 1996–2008; Co-DDO from 1996, DDO from 2005; Dir of Rdr Studies from 2002
GS 2005–   *Tel and Fax:* 01845 522258
                                 email: cathyrowling@dunelm.org

RUOFF, Mrs Alison Laura, SRN, SCM, DN
The White House 75 Crossbrook St Cheshunt EN8 8LU [LONDON] *b* 1942 *educ* Sutton Coldfield Girls High Sch; Nightingale Sch of Nursing, St Thos Hosp; Br Hosp for Mothers and Babies; Nursing Inst Worc; RCN; *CV* VSO India 1961–62; Night Sister St Thos Hosp 1966–67; Asst Dir of Nursing Internat Grenfell Assoc Newfoundland 1968–70; Admin Sister St Thos Hosp Grp 1970–72; Nursing Officer/Sen Nursing Officer Univ Coll Hosp 1972–74; Housewife and mother; JP 1979–2003; M Dioc Bp's Coun; CEEC Exec; Lay Chair Lon DEF; M UK Coun Girl Crusaders' Union; speaker and broadcaster
GS 1995–   *Tel:* 01992 623113
                                 07956 569323 (Mobile)
                          email: alison_ruoff@hotmail.com

RUSSELL, Rt Revd Anthony John, D Phil, FRAg.s
The Bishop's House Ely CB7 4DW [BISHOP OF ELY] *b* 1943 *educ* Uppingham Sch; St Chad's Coll Dur; Trin Coll Ox; Cuddesdon Th Coll; *CV* C Hilborough Grp of Parishes 1970–73; V of Preston-on-Stour, Atherstone-on-Stour and Whitchurch 1973–88; Chapl Arthur Rank Cen (Nat Agric Cen) 1973–82; Dir Arthur Rank Cen 1983–88; Can Th Cov Cathl 1977–88; Chapl to HM Queen 1988–; Exam Chapl to Bp of Hereford 1983–88; M BMU 1986–88; Bp of Dorchester from 1988; Bp of Ely from 2000; Vc-Pres R Agric Soc of England from 1991, Pres 2005–06; Commr Rural Devel Commn 1991–99; Pres Woodard Corp from 2003; Fell R Agricultural Soc from 2008
GS 1980–88, 2000–   *Tel:* 01353 662749
                                   Fax: 01353 669477
                             email: bishop@ely.anglican.org

RUSSELL, Ven Brian Kenneth, MA, PhD
26 George Rd Edgbarton Birmingham B15 1PJ [ARCHDEACON OF ASTON; BIRMINGHAM] *b* 1950 *educ* Bris Gr Sch; Trin Hall Cam; Birm Univ; Cuddesdon Ox; *CV* C St Matt Redhill 1976–79; P-in-c St Jo Kirk Merrington, Dur and Dir of Studies NEOC 1979–83; Dir of Studies and Lect in Chr Doct, Linc Theol Coll 1983–86; Sec Cttee for Theol Educ and Selection Sec, ACCM/ABM 1986–93; Bp's Dir for Min, Birm Dioc 1993–2005; sch gov; Hon Can Birm Cathl from 1999; M Vol and Continuing Educ Cttee, GS Bd of Educ 1994–99; Bp's Sen Selector from 1998; Bp's Sen Insp for Theol

Colls and Courses from 2001; M Bps' Inspections Wkg Pty from 2003; Bp's Exam Chapl, Birm from 1996; Chair Birm Dioc Ministries Forum from 2005; Gov Q Foundn for Theol Educ, Birm from 1994; Adn of Aston from 2005
                                     Tel: 0121 426 0428
                                          0121 454 5525
                                   Fax: 0121 428 1114
                    email: b.russell@birmingham.anglican.org

RUSSELL, Mr Mark Kenneth, LLB
Church Army Marlowe House 109 Station Rd Sidcup DA15 7AD [APPOINTED MEMBER, ARCHBISHOPS' COUNCIL] *b* 1974 *educ* Portadown Coll; Q Univ Belfast; *CV* Project exec, W. D. Irwin & Sons Ltd, Portadown 1995–97; youth pastor, High St Meth Ch, Lurgan 1997–2000; youth min, Ch Ch Chorleywood 2000–06; Chief Exec Ch Army from 2006; appt M AC from 2005; M Bd of Educ from 2006; M Coll of Evs from 2008
                                     Tel: 020 8309 3505
                                   Fax: 020 8309 3500
                        email: m.russell@churcharmy.org.uk

RUSSELL, Ven Norman Atkinson, MA, BD
Foxglove House Love Lane Donnington Newbury RG14 2JG [ARCHDEACON OF BERKSHIRE; OXFORD] *b* 1943 *educ* R Belfast Academical Inst; Chu Coll Cam; Lon Coll of Div; *CV* C Ch Ch w Em Clifton 1970–74; C Ch Ch Trent Park Enfield 1974–77; R Harwell w Chilton 1977–84; P-in-c Gerrards Cross 1984–88; P-in-c Fulmer 1985–88; R Gerrards Cross and Fulmer 1988–98; Hon Can Ch Ch Ox 1995–98; RD Amersham 1996–98; Adn of Berks from 1998; Prolocutor Lower Ho Conv of Cant from 2005; M Abp's Coun from 2005; M Appts Cttee from 2006; M Ch Heritage Forum from 2006; Vc-Chair Ecum Coun for Corporate Resp 1999–2002; M Clergy Terms of Service Implementation Grp 2005–07
GS 2002–   *Tel:* 01635 552820
                                 07776 180991 (Mobile)
                                   Fax: 01635 522165
                          email: archdber@oxford.anglican.org

SADGROVE, Very Revd Michael, MA, FRSA
The Deanery Durham DH1 3EQ [DEAN OF DURHAM] *b* 1950 *educ* Univ Coll Sch Lon; Ball Coll Ox; Trin Coll Bris; *CV* Lic to Offic Ox dio 1975–76; Lect OT Sarum & Wells Th Coll 1977–82; Vc-Prin 1980–82; V Alnwick 1982–87; Can Res, Prec and Vc-Provost Cov Cathl 1987–95; Provost of Sheff 1995–2000, Dean 2000–03; Bps' Sen Insp of Th Colls and Courses; Dean of Durham from 2003; Chair Ho of Bps Inspections Wkg Party; M Min Coun; M TETC; Chair Dur Dioc Adv Cttee; Chair Dur Univ Ethics Adv Cttee; M Dur Univ Coun; Visitor St Chad's Coll Dur; Chair Quality in Formation Panel
GS 2003–   *Tel:* 0191 384 7500
                                   Fax: 0191 386 4267
                   email: michael.sadgrove@durhamcathedral.co.uk

SAGE, Mrs Hilary Charlotte,
32 Nathans Rd North Wembley HA0 3RX [REPRE-
SENTATIVE, DEAF ANGLICANS TOGETHER] *b* 1944
educ Thomasson Memorial Sch; *CV* M Cttee Deaf
Anglicans Together
GS 2005–   *Fax:* 020 8904 0494
        email: hilary.sage@btinternet.com

**SALISBURY, Bishop of. See STANCLIFFE,
Rt Revd David Staffurth**

**SALISBURY, Dean of. See OSBORNE,
Very Revd June**

**SALOP, Archdeacon of. See HALL, Ven John
Barrie**

**SARGENT, Lieutenant Commander Philippa
Mary,** MA, PGCert
*31 Launceston Close Priddy's Hard Gosport PO12
4GE* [REPRESENTATIVE, ARMED FORCES SYNOD] *b*
1968 *educ* Bennett Memorial Sch for Girls; Ox
Univ; Portsm Univ; *CV* Naval Officer from 1991
GS 2005–   *Tel:* 023 9258 3080
        email: philippa.sargent@virgin.net

SARGISON, Mr Bill (Ralph William), MIPD
*18 Montgomery Rd Up Hatherley Cheltenham GL51
3LB* [GLOUCESTER] *b* 1941 *educ* S'well Min Gr Sch;
Qu Eliz Gr Sch Wakef; Qu Coll Guiana; *CV*
YMCA Youth Worker Worc 1960–64; YMCA Res
Worker Northn 1964–68; YMCA Gen Sec Birm
1968–76; YMCA Exec Sec Cheltenham 1976–84;
YMCA Regional Dir 1984–94; YMCA Nat Dir
1994–2000; Rtd; Chair Dioc Ho of Laity and Bp's
Coun
GS 2000–   *Tel and Fax:* 01242 694301
        email: billsargison@yahoo.co.uk

**SARUM, Archdeacon of. See JEANS, Ven Alan
Paul**

SAXBEE, Rt Revd John Charles, BA, Ph D
Bishop's House Eastgate Lincoln LN2 1QQ [BISHOP
OF LINCOLN] *b* 1946 *educ* Cotham Gr Sch Bris; Bris
Univ; Dur Univ; St Jo Coll Dur; *CV* C Em w St
Paul Plymouth 1972–76; V St Phil Weston Mill
1976–81; TV Cen Ex 1981–87; Dir SW Minl Tr
Course 1981–92; Preb of Ex Cathl 1988–92; Adn of
Ludlow 1992–2002; Warden of Rdrs 1992–2002;
Bp of Ludlow 1994–2002; Bp of Lincoln from
2001; Pres Modern Churchpeople's Union from
1997; Relig Adv to Carlton TV 1997–2006; M Coll
of Evang from 1999; M Pastl and Dioc Measures
Rev Grp; M Bps' Cttee for Min; M Insp Wkg Pty
1999–2007
GS 1985–94, 2000–   *Tel:* 01522 534701
                                  Fax: 01522 511095
        email: bishop.lincoln@lincoln.anglican.org

SCOTT-JOYNT, Rt Revd Michael Charles, MA
Wolvesey Winchester SO23 9ND [BISHOP OF WIN-
CHESTER] *b* 1943 *educ* Bradfield Coll; K Coll Cam;

Cuddesdon Th Coll; *CV* C Cuddesdon 1967–70;
Tutor Cuddesdon Th Coll 1967–72; TV Newbury
1972–75; R Bicester 1975–81; Can Res St Alb
Cathl, DDO and POT 1982–87; Bp of Stafford
1987–95; Bp of Win from 1995; M Legislative
Cttee; Visitor Alton Abbey
GS 1993–   *Tel:* 01962 854050
                                  Fax: 01962 897088
    email: michael.scott-joynt@dsl.pipex.com

SCOWEN, Mr Clive Richard, LLB
69 Brooke Ave Harrow HA2 0ND [LONDON] *b* 1958
educ John Lyon Sch Harrow; Bris Univ; Inns of
Court Sch of Law; *CV* Called to bar (Inner Tem-
ple) 1981; law reporter, Incorporated Coun of
Law Reporting 1983–90; Dep Ed Weekly Law
Reports 1990–2000; Joint Ed, Law Reports Con-
solidated Index from 2000; Man Ed, Weekly Law
Reports 2006–07; Ed Law Reports and Weekly
Law Reports from 2008; Councillor, Lon Boro of
Harrow 1990–2002; Rdr from 1991; M Bris Univ
Court from 1980; Dir Glencoe Trust Ltd; Trustee,
Charles Gardner Meml Fund; Trustee, Maseno
Project Trust; M MPA Coun; M GS Stg Orders
Cttee; M Lon Dioc Bp's Coun; Dir Lon Dioc Fund;
M Willesden Area Coun; M Bp of Lon's Miss
Fund Bd; M Harrow Dny Stg Cttee
GS 2005–   *Tel:* 020 8422 1329
                          07771 780805 (Mobile)
        email: clivescowen@onetel.com

SCREECH, Rt Revd Royden, BD, AKC
32 Falmouth Rd Truro TR1 2HX [SUFFRAGAN
BISHOP OF ST GERMANS; TRURO] *b* 1953 *educ*
Cotham Gr Sch Bris; K Coll Lon; St Aug Coll
Cant; *CV* C St Cath Hatcham 1976–80; V St Ant
Nunhead 1980–87; P-in-c St Silas Nunhead 1983–
87; RD Camberwell 1983–87; V St Edw New Add-
ington 1987–94; ABM Selection Sec and LNSM
Co-ord 1994–96; Sen Selection Sec ABM 1997–98;
Sen Selection Sec Min Div 1999–2000; Staff M Min
Div; Sec to VRSC; Bp of St Germans from 2000
                                  Tel: 01872 273190
                                  Fax: 01872 277883
    email: bishop@stgermans.truro.anglican.org

SCRIVENER, Mr John Rupert, MA
*The Old Royal Oak Oak Bank Lane Hoole Village
Chester CH2 4ER* [CHESTER] *b* 1951 *educ* Cranleigh
Sch; Sussex Univ; Liv Univ; *CV* Ed 'Faith and
Worship' review of Prayer Book Soc from 2003;
lect in Continuing Educ (Eng Literature), Liv
Univ from 1997
GS 2005–   *Tel:* 01244 300389
        email: john@johnscrivener.fsnet.co.uk

SEED, Ven Richard Murray Crosland, MA
Holy Trinity Rectory 81 Micklegate York YO1 6LE
[ARCHDEACON OF YORK] *b* 1949 *educ* St Phil Sch
Burley-in-Wharfedale; Leeds Univ; Edin Th Coll;
CV C Ch Ch Skipton 1972–75; C Baildon 1975–77;
TV Kidlington Ox 1977–80; V Boston Spa 1980–
99; Adn of York from 1999; Chairman Martin Ho

Children's Hospice; Chairman Dioc Pastl Cttee and Dioc Red Chs Users Cttee
GS 2000–   *Tel:* 01904 623798
                                   Fax: 01904 628155
email: archdeacon.of.york@yorkdiocese.org

SELBY, Suffragan Bishop of. See WALLACE, Rt Revd Martin William

SENTAMU, Most Revd and Rt Hon Dr John Tucker Mugabi, LLB, MA, Ph D, LLD (Hon), DD (Hon), FRSA, Privy Counsellor
Bishopthorpe Palace Bishopthorpe York YO23 2GE [ARCHBISHOP OF YORK] *b* 1949 *educ* Makerere Univ Kampala; Selw Coll Cam; Ridley Hall Th Coll; *CV* Asst Chapl Selw Coll Cam 1979; Chapl HM Remand Cen Latchmere Ho 1979–82; C St Andr Ham 1979–82; C St Paul Herne Hill 1982–83; P-in-c H Trin Tulse Hill; Par Priest St Matthias 1983–84; V H Trin and St Matthias Tulse Hill 1984–96; P-in-c St Sav Brixton 1987–89; Bp of Stepney 1996–2002; M NACRO Young Offenders Cttee 1986–95; M Abp's Adv Grp on UPAs 1986–92; M ABM Coun from 1985; M Stg Cttee GS Ho of Clergy 1985–96; M GS Stg Cttee 1988–96; M GS Policy Cttee 1990–96; Chair Dioc Ho of Clergy 1992–96; M Decade of Evang Strg Grp and Springboard Exec 1991–96; M Turnbull Proposals Strg Grp; M Strg Grp Women (Priests) Ordination Measure; Pro-Prolocutor Conv of Cant 1990–94; Chair CMEAC 1990–99; Prolocutor Conv of Cant 1994–96; M The Stephen Lawrence Judicial Inquiry 1997–99; Pres and Chair Lon Marriage Guidance Coun from 2000; Chair Damilola Taylor Murder Review 2002; Fell Univ Coll Ch Ch Cant; Fell Qu Mary Coll Univ of Lon; Hon Dr OU; D Phil (Hon) Univ of Glos; DD (Hon) Univ of Birm; Chair ECI NDC 2002–04; Chair NHS Sickle Cell and Thalassaemia Screening Programme from 2001; Bp of Birmingham 2002–05; Midlander of the Year 2003; Vc-Chair Commn on Urban Life and Faith; Pres Youth for Christ, Eng and Nat YMCA; Abp of York from 2005; LLD (Hon), Univ of Leic 2005; Hon Fell Selw Coll Cam; Chan York St Jo Univ; Freeman City of Lon 2000; DD (Hon) Univ of Hull 2007; DL (Hon) Univ of Sheff 2007; Yorkshire Man of the Year 2007; Speaker of the Year 2007; Master Bencher (Hon) Gray's Inn 2007; Freeman City of Montego Bay 2007; Chan Univ of Cumbria from 2007; Hon Dr Birm City Univ 2008; DD (Hon) Univ of Cam 2008
GS 1985–96; 2002–   *Tel:* 01904 707021
                                   Fax: 01904 709204
email: office@archbishopofyork.org

SERVANT, Canon Alma Joan, BA
Rectory Royce Rd Hulme Manchester M15 5FQ [MANCHESTER] *b* 1951 *educ* W Leeds Girls' High Sch; Nottm Univ; N Lon Poly; Westcott Ho Cam; *CV* C All Hallows Ordsall, S'well 1985–88; Chapl Man Metropolitan Univ 1988–96; P-in-c St Thos

Heaton Norris, Man 1996–2000; P-in-c Ascen Hulme, Man from 2000, R from 2005
GS 2005–   *Tel:* 0161 226 5568

SEVILLE, Revd Thomas Christopher John,
House of the Resurrection Mirfield WF14 0BN [RELIGIOUS COMMUNITIES IN CONVOCATION, NORTH] *CV* Elected to GS 2005
GS 2005–

SHEFFIELD AND ROTHERHAM, Archdeacon of. See BLACKBURN, Ven Richard Finn

SHEFFIELD, Bishop of. (NOT APPOINTED AT TIME OF GOING TO PRESS)

SHEFFIELD, Dean of. See BRADLEY, Very Revd Peter Edward ⸱

SHELLEY, Mr Rupert Harry, BSc
135 Kingston Rd Oxford OX2 6RW [WINCHESTER] *b* 1978 *educ* Marlborough Coll; Bris Univ; *CV* Army Officer 2000–04; Asst Min (Youth) St Mary Eastrop, Basingstoke
GS 2005–   *Tel:* 01256 464249
                                   email: rupertshelley@hotmail.com

SHERBORNE, Archdeacon of. See TAYLOR, Ven Paul Stanley

SHERBORNE, Area Bishop of. (NOT APPOINTED AT TIME OF GOING TO PRESS)

SHERIFF, Canon Suzanne, BA
78 Station Rd Tadcaster LS24 9JR [YORK] *b* 1963 *educ* Dorchester Gr Sch for Girls; Trin Coll Bris; *CV* Par Dn St Nich Hull 1987–91; Par Dn/C St Aidan Hull 1991–96; TV Marfleet 1996–2000; TR Marfleet 2000–07; M York Dioc Syn; M Coll of Cans York Minster from 2001; V Tadcaster and Newton Kyme from 2007
GS 2005–   *Tel:* 01937 833394
                                   email: sue.sheriff@virgin.net

SHERWOOD, Suffragan Bishop of. See PORTER, Rt Revd Anthony

SHREWSBURY, Area Bishop of. See SMITH, Rt Revd Alan Gregory Clayton

SIDAWAY, Ven Geoffrey Harold,
Glebe House Church Lane Maisemore Gloucester GL2 8EY [ARCHDEACON OF GLOUCESTER] *b* 1942 *educ* Kelham Th Coll; *CV* C Beighton 1966–70; C All SS Chesterfield 1970–72; V St Bart Derby 1972–77; V St Mart Maidstone 1977–86; V Bearsted and Thurnham 1986–2000; RD Sutton 1992–2000; Hon Can Cant Cathl 1994–2000; Commr for Bp of Kinkizzi Uganda from 1995; Adn of Glos from

2000; Reserved Can Glos Cathl from 2000, Res Can from 2007
GS 1995–2000, 2005–07

Tel: 01452 528500
Fax: 01452 381528
email: archdglos@star.co.uk

SIDDALL, Ven Arthur, MA, LTh, DMS, PGCEA, MCMI
St John's House 92 Avenue de Chillon 1820 Territet Switzerland [ARCHDEACON OF ITALY, MALTA AND SWITZERLAND; EUROPE] *b* 1943 *educ* Liv Blue Coat Gr Sch; Univ of Lancaster; Univ of Surrey; Blackb Coll; St Jo Hall; *CV* C H Trin Formby, Liv 1967–70; C All SS Childwall, Liv 1970–72; Miss Ptnr CMS, Ch Ch Chittagong, Bangladesh 1972–77; V St Paul Clitheroe, Blackb 1977–82; V St Gabr Blackb 1982–90; Dep Gen Sec Miss to Seafarers 1990–93; Vis Lect St Mary's Univ Coll Roehampton Inst 1993–96; V Chipping w. Whitewell, Blackb and Dioc Rural Officer 1996–2004; Chapl Ch Ch Naples and UKNSU, JFC, NATO, Naples from 2004; Adn of Italy and Malta from 2005; Chair Adnry Syn 2007; Mointeux, St John, Switzerland and Adn Switzerland, Chair Adnry Syn

Tel: 0041 021 963 4354
Fax: 0041 021 963 4391
email: chaplain@stjohns-montreux.ch

SIMMONDS, Mr Gordon Robert William, B Sc, M Sc, F ERG S
2A Castle Drive Rayleigh S56 7HT [CHELMSFORD] *b* 1940 *educ* Worthing High Sch; Univ Coll Lon; Cranfield Inst; *CV* Rsrch Eng Motor Industry Rsch Assoc 1965–66; Prin Rsch Eng Ford Motor Co 1966–86; Co-ord R & D Educ and Tr Ford Motor Co Ltd 1986–96; Rtd 1997; M Dioc Budget Cttee; M Bp's Coun; M Finance Cttee
GS 2000–

Tel and Fax: 01268 745825
email: gordon.simmonds@talktalk.net

SINCLAIR, Rt Revd (Gordon) Keith, MA, BA
Bishop's Lodge 67 Bidston Rd Prenton CH43 6TR [SUFFRAGAN BISHOP OF BIRKENHEAD; CHESTER] *b* 1952 *educ* Trin Sch Croydon; Ch Ch Ox; Cranmer Hall Dur; *CV* C Ch Ch Summerfield 1984–88; pt Chapl, Children's Hosp Birm; V SS Pet & Paul Aston juxta Birm 1988–2001; AD Aston 2000–01; V H Trin Cov 2001–06; Bp of Birkenhead from 2007; M Bp's Coun and Dioc Syn, Ches; Trustee/Chair Ches DBE; Gov Bp's High Sch Ches; Trustee Historic Cheshire Chs Preservation Trust; Trustee Chs Together in Merseyside

Tel: 0151 652 2741
Fax: 0151 651 2330
email: bpbirkenhead@chester.anglican.org

SINCLAIR, Ven Jane Elizabeth Margaret, MA, BA
Sanderlings Willingham Rd Market Rasen LN8 3RE [ARCHDEACON OF STOW AND LINDSEY; LINCOLN] *b* 1956 *educ* Westonbirt Sch Tetbury; St Hugh's Coll Ox; Nottm Univ; St Jo Coll Nottm; *CV* Dss St Paul w St Jo Herne Hill and St Sav Ruskin Park 1983–86; Lect in Liturg and Chapl St Jo Coll Nottm

1986–93; Can Res and Prec Sheff Cathl 1993–2003; M Liturg Commn 1986–2001; M Cathl Fabric Commn for Eng from 2001; V Rotherham Minster (All SS) 2003–07; Adn of Stow and Lindsey from 2007
GS 1995–2007

Tel: 01673 849896
07809 521995 (Mobile)
email: archdeacon.stowlindsey@lincoln.anglican.org

SKILTON, Ven Christopher John, MA, Cert Theol, MA (Miss & Min)
7 Hoadly Rd London SW16 1AE [ARCHDEACON OF LAMBETH; SOUTHWARK] *b* 1955 *educ* Latymer Upper Sch Hammersmith; Magd Coll Cam; Wycliffe Hall Ox; *CV* C St Mary Ealing 1980–84; C Newborough w Leigh St Jo Wimborne 1984–88; TV St Paul Gt Baddow 1988–95; TR Sanderstead 1995–2003; RD Croydon S 2000–03; Adn of Lambeth from 2004

Tel: 020 8545 2440 (Office)
020 8769 4384 (Home)
07903 704506 (Mobile)
Fax: 020 8545 2441 (Office)
email: chris.skilton@southwark.anglican.org

SLACK, Mr Stephen, MA
Church House Great Smith Street London SW1P 3AZ [REGISTRAR AND CHIEF LEGAL ADVISER TO THE GENERAL SYNOD, JOINT REGISTRAR OF THE PROVINCES OF CANTERBURY AND YORK, AND CHIEF LEGAL ADVISER TO THE ARCHBISHOPS' COUNCIL] *b* 1954 *educ* Aylesbury Gr Sch; Ch Ch Ox; *CV* Solicitor in private practice 1979–84; Sen Lawyer Charity Commn Liv 1984–89; Hd Legal Section Charity Commn Taunton 1989–2001; Hd Legal Office and Chief Legal Adv to AC and GS from 2001, Registrar GS, Jt Registrar Provinces Cant and York, M Legal Adv Commn from 2001

Tel: 020 7898 1366
Fax: 020 7898 1718
020 7898 1721
email: stephen.slack@c-of-e.org.uk

SLATER, Mr Colin Stuart, MBE
11 Muriel Rd Beeston Nottingham NG9 2HH [SOUTHWELL AND NOTTINGHAM] *b* 1934 *educ* Belle Vue Gr Sch Bradf; *CV* Chief PRO Notts Co Coun 1969–87, Severn Trent Water 1987–89, Notts Co Cricket Club 1989–95; Chair BBC Radio Nottm Adv Coun 1975–79; former Chair Soc of Co PROs and IPR Local Govt Grp; M Coun Inst of PR 1986–90; JP 1977–2004; Chair Nottingham Magistrates 2003 and 2004; Chair Notts Courts Bd 2005–07; Chair Notts-Derbys Courts Bd from 2007; PR Consult and freelance broadcaster from 1995; M Bp's Coun, Fin Cttee; Vc-Chair Chr Stewardship Cttee of AC from 1999; M Coun St Jo (Nottm) Coll from 2006 and its Stg Ctee from 2008
GS 1990–

Tel: 0115 925 7532
07919 008788 (Mobile)
Fax: 0115 925 7532
email: colinslater@mac.com

SLATER, Ven Paul John, MA, BA
Woodlands Netherghyll Lane Cononley Keighley BD20 8PB [ARCHDEACON OF CRAVEN; BRADFORD] *b* 1958 *educ* Bradf Gr Sch; Corpus Christi Ox; St Jo Coll Dur; *CV* C St Andr Keighley 1984–88; P-in-c St Jo Cullingworth 1988–93; Dir Lay Trg Foundn Course 1988–93; PA to Bp of Bradf 1993–95; Wrdn of Rdrs 1992–96; R St Mich Haworth 1995–2001; Bp's Officer for Min from 2001; Adn of Craven from 2005   *Tel and Fax:* 01535 635113
email: paulj.slater@dial.pipex.com

SLATER, Mrs Susan Gay, Cert Ed, DGA
3 Church St Spalding PE11 2PB [LINCOLN] *b* 1944 *educ* Ox High Sch; Homerton Coll Cam; *CV* Admin trainee/Higher Exec Officer, DHSS 1967–74; domestic admin and voluntary work 1974–94; PA to Nat Dir Leprosy Mission England and Wales 1994–2005; rtd 2005; Gen Adv S Holland CAB; M Linc Dioc HR Cttee; Sec Elloe W Dny Syn; M Ch & Com Fund Cttee; M S Holland Fairtrade Campaign Crp
GS 2005–   *Tel:* 01775 768286
email: sueslater@d-lweb.net

SLATER, Canon Dr Terence Richard, BA, PhD, FRGS
5 Windermere Rd Moseley Birmingham B13 9JP [BIRMINGHAM] *b* 1946 *educ* Shooters Hill Sch Woolwich; Hull Univ; Univ Coll Lon; *CV* Lect in geography, Birm Univ 1971–92, Sen Lect 1992–95, Rdr in historical geography from 1995; M Bp's Coun from 1992; Lay Chair Birm Dioc Syn 1995–2004; Trustee Birm Dioc 1995–2004; M Dioc Fin, Investments and Properties Cttee from 2001; Hon Lay Can Birm Cathl from 2005; Chair Birm Cathl Fabric Cttee from 2006
GS 2005–   *Tel:* 0121 414 5534 (Office)
Fax: 0121 414 5528
email: t.r.slater@bham.ac.uk

SLEE, Very Revd Colin Bruce, OBE, FKC, BD, AKC
Provost's Lodging London SE1 9JE [DEAN OF SOUTHWARK] *b* 1945 *educ* Ealing Gr Sch; K Coll Lon; St Aug Coll Cant; *CV* C St Fran Heartsease Norw 1970-73; C Gt St Mary Cam 1973–76; Chapl Girton Coll Cam 1973–76; Chapl and Tutor K Coll Lon 1976–82; Sub Dean and Can Res St Alb 1982–94; Provost of S'wark from 1994, Dean from 2000
GS 1995–   *Tel:* 020 7928 6414 (Home)
020 7367 6731 (Office)
07831 627090 (Mobile)
Fax: 020 7928 6414 (Home)
020 7367 6725 (Office)
email: Colin.Slee@dswark.org.uk (Office)
/ SleeBanks@aol.com (Home)

SLOMAN, Mrs Anne, BA, OBE
All Saints Cottage Bale Rd Sharrington NR24 2PF [APPOINTED MEMBER, ARCHBISHOPS' COUNCIL] *b* 1944 *educ* Farlington, Horsham; St Hilda's Coll Ox; *CV* BBC journalist 1967-2003; ed five gen election programmes 1974–92; asst ed Today Pro-gramme 1981–82; ed Special Current Affairs 1983–93; dep hd weekly TV and radio programmes 1994–96; M Coun RIIA 1992–2002; BBC's Chief Political Adv 1996–2003; OBE 2004; M McLean Wkg Pty, Clergy Terms of Service from 2003; M C of E Broadcasting Grp from 2004; M Communications Panel from 2004; Trustee Norfolk Com Foundn from 2005; Vc-Chair Norfolk Com Foundn from 2006; Co-ord Ch Buildings Campaign from 2006
Tel: 01263 862291 (Norfolk)
020 77402 0576 (London)
07717 772174 (Mobile)
Fax: 01263 862291 (Home)
email: annesloman@hotmail.com

SMITH, Rt Revd Alan Gregory Clayton, BA, MA, PhD
Athlone House 68 London Rd Shrewsbury SY2 6PG [AREA BISHOP OF SHREWSBURY; LICHFIELD] *b* 1957 *educ* Trowbridge High Sch for Boys; Birm Univ; Wycliffe Hall Th Coll; Univ of Wales, Bangor; *CV* C St Lawr Pudsey 1981–82, w St Paul 82–84; Chapl Lee Abbey 1984–90; Dioc Missr and Exec Sec Lichf Dioc BMU 1990–97; TV St Matt Walsall 1990–97; Adn of Stoke-upon-Trent 1997–2001; Bp of Shrewsbury from 2001; Chair Shrops Strategic Ptnrship; M Rural Bps Panel from 2006
GS 1999–2001   *Tel:* 01743 235867
Fax: 01743 243296
email: bishop.shrewsbury@lichfield.anglican.org

SMITH, Ven Brian, MTh (Oxon), Cert Th
St George's Vicarage 16 Devonshire Rd Douglas IM2 3RB [ARCHDEACON OF THE ISLE OF MAN; SODOR AND MAN] *b* 1944 *educ* Preston Gr Sch, Barton Peveril Gr Sch, Eastleigh; Westmr Coll Ox; Salis & Wells Th Coll; *CV* C St Thos w. St Oswald Pennywell, Sunderland, Dur 1974–77; Chapl RAF 1977–95; V St Jo Keswick, Carl 1995–2005; P-in-c St Bridget Bridekirk, Carl 2002–04; RD Derwent 1997–2005; Hon Can Carl Cath 1999–2005; Adn of Isle of Man and V St Geo Douglas from 2005; M GS, Dioc Syn, Chair DAC, IOM Ch Commrs, DBF, Soc Resp Cttee, Legislative Cttee, Vacancy-in-see Cttee, Communications Cttee from 2005; Trustee K William's Coll IOM   *Tel:* 01624 675430
email: arch-sodor@mcb.net

SMITH, Dr Christopher Graham, BSc, PhD, DIC, Grad Cert Ed
35 Cantley Lane Cringleford Norwich NR4 6TA [NORWICH] *b* 1944 *educ* Tiffin Sch; Univ of Wales, Swansea; Imp Coll Lon; *CV* Killam Memorial Post-doctoral Fell, Univ of Alberta, Canada 1968–70; Lect and Hd of Arts and Sciences Dept, Norw City Coll 1971–97; rtd 1997; CAB volunteer adv
GS 2005–   *Tel:* 01603 453010
07742 727080 (Mobile)

email: chris-g-smith@tiscali.co.uk

SMITH, Mr Christopher John Addison, BA, FCA
Lambeth Palace London SE1 7JU [CHIEF OF STAFF, LAMBETH PALACE] *b* 1949 *educ* St Pet Sch York; Univ of E Anglia; *CV* Price Waterhouse 1970–93, various trainee and mgmt posts 1970–89, Human Resources Ptnr 1989–93; Gen Sec Dioc of Lon 1993–99; Gen Mgr C. Hoare & Co. Bankers 1999–2003; M CBF, Exec, Staff Cttee, AC Fin Cttee 1995–2000; Chief of Staff, Lambeth Palace from 2003
GS 1995–2000   *Tel:* 020 7898 1200
        email: chris.smith@lambethpalace.org.uk

SMITH, Very Revd Graham Charles Morell, BA
The Deanery The Close Norwich NR1 4 EG [DEAN OF NORWICH] *b* 1947 *educ* Whitgift Sch Croydon; Dur Univ; Westcott Ho Cam; *CV* C All SS Tooting Graveney, S'wark 1976–80; TV Thamesmead Ecum Par, S'wark 1980–87; TR Kidlington w. Hampton Poyle, Ox 1987–97; R Leeds 1997–2004; Dean of Norwich from 2004   *Tel:* 01603 218302
                                         Fax: 01603 766032
        email: dean@cathedral.org.uk

SMITH, Mr Graham William, BSc, DMS, MIEE, MCMI
20 Parklands Wotton-under-Edge GL12 7LT [GLOUCESTER] *b* 1943 *educ* Mundella Gr Sch; Aston Univ; *CV* Principal Eng, Project Management Dept, Nat Power plc until 1992; Bursar and Clerk to Govs, Katharine Lady Berkeley's Sch 1993–96; rtd 1996; M Bp's Coun; M Dioc Syn; M IDFF; M Abp's Coun Fin Cttee
GS 2005–   *Tel:* 01453 842618
        email: smithgra@supanet.com

SMITH, Mr Ian Rodney, B Ed, MCMI
c/o 6 Seapark Lane Holywood Co Down BT18 0LA [YORK] *b* 1948 *educ* Hyde Co Gr Sch Ches; Dur Univ; *CV* Tchr Fitzharry's Sch Abingdon 1970–71; Tchr Convent High Sch Stockport 1971–74; Personnel Mgt Eagle Star Insurance Co 1974–82; Personnel Mgt NEM Insurance Co 1982–84; CMS Area Co-ord Ripon and Leeds and York Dios from 1984, N Co-ord 1998–2002, N Tm Leader from 2003; Rdr; Hon Dioc Adviser in Evang from 1990; M BM 1990–2000; M PWM Panel 1996–2006; M CECC 1996–98; M CCU 2000–06; M M&PAC from 2006; Dir and CEO of Miss, CMS Ireland from 2007
GS 1990–   *Tel:* 028 9078 2154
        email: ianrsmith@dunelm.org.uk

SMITH, Ven Jonathan Peter,
6 Sopwell Lane St Albans Herts AL1 1RR [ARCHDEACON OF ST ALBANS] *b* 1955 *educ* Ipswich Sch; King's Coll London; Queen's Coll Cam; Westcott Ho Cam; *CV* Asst C All Saints' Gosforth 1980–82; Asst C Waltham Abbey 1982–85; Chapl The City Univ 1985–88; R Harrold and Carlton w Chellington 1988–97; V St John's Harpenden 1997–2008; Rural Dean Wheathampstead 1999–2008; Adn St Alb from 2008   *Tel:* 01727 818121
                                         Fax: 01727 848311
        email: archdstalbans@stalbans.anglican.org

SMITH, Mr Peter Reg, FRICS
Lusaka House Great Glemham Saxmundham IP17 2DH [ST EDMUNDSBURY AND IPSWICH] *b* 1946 *educ* K Edw VI Sch Southn; Coll of Estate Mgt; *CV* M Coun USPG from 1991; Chair Dioc Overseas Miss Grp 1997–2004; Chair Dioc Ho of Laity 1997–2000; M Bd of Miss 2001–03; M Bp's Coun and Pastl Cttee; M Vacancy-in-See Cttee; M Revision Cttee, Common Worship Ordinal; M Revision Cttee, Pastl (Amendment) Measure; M CFCE from 2006; Lay Can St Eds Cathl from 2005; M dioc Red Chs Uses Cttee
GS 1993–   *Tel:* 01728 663466
                                07790 596502 (Mobile)
                                     Fax: 01728 663466
        email: happyhackers@usa.net

SODOR AND MAN, Bishop of.
See PATERSON, Rt Revd Robert Mar Eskine

SOUTHAMPTON, Suffragan Bishop of.
See BUTLER, Rt Revd Paul Roger

SOUTHEND, Archdeacon of. See LOWMAN, Ven David Walter

SOUTHERN, Rt Revd Humphrey Ivo John, MA
Repton House Church St, Lea Matlock DE4 5JP [SUFFRAGAN BISHOP OF REPTON; DERBY] *b* 1960 *educ* Harrow Sch; Ch Ch Ox; Ripon Coll Cuddesdon; *CV* C St Marg Rainham, Roch 1986–89; C Walton-on-the-Hill, Liv 1989–92; V Hale, TR Hale w. Badshot Lea, Guild 1992–99; Guild Dioc Ecum Officer 1993–99; TR Tisbury, TR Nadder Valley Tm Min, Sarum 1999–2007; Hon Can Salis Cathl 2006–07; Bp of Repton from 2007; M Guild Dioc Syn 1992–99; M Sarum Dioc Syn 2000–07; Chair Ho of Clergy, Sarum Dioc Syn 2004–07; M Sarum Dioc Pastl Cttee 2000–07; Chair Derby Dioc Pastl Cttee from 2007   *Tel:* 01629 534644
                                     Fax: 01629 534003
        email: bishop@repton.free-online.co.uk

SOUTHWARK, Archdeacon of. See IPGRAVE, Ven Dr Michael Geoffrey

SOUTHWARK, Bishop of. See BUTLER, Rt Revd Thomas Frederick

SOUTHWARK, Dean of. See SLEE, Very Revd Colin Bruce

SOUTHWELL AND NOTTINGHAM, Bishop of. See CASSIDY, Rt Revd George Henry

SOUTHWELL AND NOTTINGHAM, Dean of. See GUILLE, Very Revd John Arthur

SOWERBY, Revd Mark Crispin Rake, BD, AKC, MA
St Wilfrid's Rectory 51B Kent Rd Harrogate HG1 2EU [RIPON AND LEEDS] *b* 1963 *educ* Barnard Cas-

tle Sch; St Aidan & St Jo Fisher's United Sixth Form Harrogate; K Coll Lon; Lanc Univ, Coll of Resurrection, Mirfield; *CV* C Knaresborough 1987–90; C St Cuth Darwen w. St Steph Tockholes 1990–92; V St Mary Magd Accrington 1992–97; Chapl St Christopher's CE Hich Schl Accrington 1992–97; Chapl Accrington Victoria Hosp 1992–97; Asst DDO Blackb 1993–96; M Blackburn Dioc Syn; Selection Sec/Vocations Officer ABM/Min Div of AC 1997–2001; Sec Vocations Adv Sub-Cttee (ABM) then Voc Panel (Min Div); Staff M VRSC and Candidates Cttee/Panel 1997–2001; V St Wilf Harrogate 2001–04, TR from 2004; M Ripon Dioc Syn; Asst DDO Ripon from 2005; Dio Minl Rev Adv from 2008; M Mirfield/NOC Jt Monitoring Body; Bp's Insp of Colls and Courses; M Coun Coll of Ressurrection, Mirfield; Frere Trustee (Mirfield); M VRSC 2006–07; M Min Coun from 2008
GS 2005–   *Tel:* 01423 503259
                 07778 451145 (Mobile)
       email: MCRSowerby@aol.com

SPENCER, Mrs Caroline Sarah, BA, PGCE
Little Eggarton Godmersham Canterbury CT4 7DY [CANTERBURY] *b* 1953 *educ* Wycombe Abbey Sch; St Hilda's Coll Ox; Lon Univ Inst of Educ; *CV* Asst Tchr Hist Sydenham High Sch 1976–80; pt Tutor Westmr Tutors Ltd 1981–84; Mother and Vol Worker for Ch and Com from 1980; M Abp's Coun; Gov Cant Ch Ch Univ; Chair Dioc Ho of Laity; Lay Member, Chapter of Cant Cathl
GS 1995–   *Tel:* 01227 731170
                 07947 045025 (Mobile)
                     Fax: 01227 731170
    email: c.spencer@canterbury.ac.uk

SPIERS, Canon Peter Hendry, BA, Cert Th
St Luke's Vicarage 71 Liverpool Rd Crosby Liverpool L23 5SE [LIVERPOOL] *b* 1961 *educ* Liv Coll; St Jo Coll Dur; Ridley Hall Th Coll; *CV* C St Luke Princess Drive 1986–90; TV St Pet Everton 1990–95; V St Geo Everton 1995–2005; P-in-c St Luke Crosby from 2005
GS 2000–   *Tel:* 0151 924 1737
   email: pete@spiersfamily.eclipse.co.uk

ST ALBANS, Archdeacon of. See SMITH, Ven Jonathan Peter

ST ALBANS, Bishop of. See HERBERT, Rt Revd Christopher William

ST ALBANS, Dean of. See JOHN, Very Revd Jeffrey Philip Hywel

ST EDMUNDSBURY AND IPSWICH, Bishop of. See STOCK, Rt Revd (William) Nigel

ST EDMUNDSBURY, Dean of. See COLLINGS, Very Revd Neil

ST GERMANS, Suffragan Bishop of. See SCREECH, Rt Revd Royden

ST PAUL'S, Dean of. See KNOWLES, Rt Revd Graeme Paul

STAFFORD, Area Bishop of. See MURSELL, Rt Revd (Alfred) Gordon

STANCLIFFE, Rt Revd Dr David Staffurth, MA, DD, D Litt, FRSCM
South Canonry 71 The Close Salisbury SP1 2ER [BISHOP OF SALISBURY] *b* 1942 *educ* Westmr Sch; Trin Coll Ox; Cuddesdon Th Coll; *CV* C St Bart Armley, Leeds 1967–70; Chapl Clifton Coll Bris 1970–77; Can Res of Portsm, DDO and Dioc Lay Min Adv 1977–82; Prov of Portsm 1982–93; Bp of Salisbury from 1993; M Liturg Commn 1986–2005, Chair 1993–2005; Pres Affirming Catholicism; Vc-Pres RSCM
GS 1985–   *Tel:* 01722 334031
                     Fax: 01722 413112
   email: dsarum@salisbury.anglican.org

STEPNEY, Area Bishop of. See OLIVER, Rt Revd Stephen John

STERLING, Revd Nezlin Jemima, BA, Cert Th, SRN, RMN
5 Woodstock Ave Ealing London W13 9UQ [ECUMENICAL REPRESENTATIVE (BLACK MAJORITY CHURCHES AND THE NEW TESTAMENT ASSEMBLY)] *b* 1942 *educ* Secondary Schs in Jamaica; Westmr Univ; Univ of Wales Lamp; *CV* Dir of Nursing Mental Health 1989–95; Internat Exec Sec NT Assembly from 1994, Gen Sec NT Assembly England from 1998; Trustee African and Caribbean Evang Alliance; Company Sec NT Assembly from 2005; Course Dir NT Assembly Inst of Theo and Christian Counselling; Trustee CTBI from 2008; pt Mgt Consult; pt Lect Univ of Wales Lampeter
GS 1999–   *Tel:* 020 8579 3841
                 07970 547528 (Mobile)
                     Fax: 020 8537 9253
      email: NJSterlNTA@aol.com

STEVENS, Canon Anne, BA, MA, MTh
93 Bolingbroke Grove London SW11 6HA [SOUTHWARK] *b* 1961 *CV* Elected to GS 2005
GS 2005–   *Tel:* 020 7228 1990
    email: anne.stevens@southwark.anglican.org

STEVENS, Mr Robin Michael, B Sc
3 Aldeburgh Way Chelmsford CM1 7PB [CHELMSFORD] *b* 1945 *educ* Chigwell Sch; Birm Univ; *CV* Eng Marconi Communication Systems 1967–79; eng Thames Television 1979–91; Nat Stewardship Officer, AC 1992–2005; Chelmsford Borough councillor from 2005; C of E Pensions Bd trustee from 1998; Rdr from 1990
GS 2005–   *Tel:* 01245 268042
       email: rms@ukgateway.net

STEVENS, Rt Revd Timothy John, MA, DCL, DLitt
Bishop's Lodge 10 Springfield Rd Leicester LE2 3BD

[BISHOP OF LEICESTER] *b* 1946 *educ* Chigwell Sch; Selw Coll Cam; Ripon Coll Cuddesdon; *CV* C E Ham TM 1976–79; TV St Alb Upton Park 1979–80; TR Canvey Island 1980–88; Bp of Chelmsf's Urban Officer 1988–91; Adn of West Ham 1991–95; Bp of Dunwich 1995–99; Bp of Leic from 1999 GS 1987–95, 1999–
Tel: 0116 270 8985
07860 692258
Fax: 0116 270 3288
email: bishop.tim@leccofe.org

STEVENSON, Rt Revd Dr Kenneth William,
MA, Ph D, DD, LLD, F R Hist S
Bishopsgrove 26 Osborn Rd Fareham PO16 7DQ [BISHOP OF PORTSMOUTH] *b* 1949 *educ* Edin Academy; Edin Univ; Southn Univ; Man Univ; Sarum and Wells Th Coll; *CV* C Grantham 1973–76; Lect Boston Par Ch 1976–80; pt Lect Linc Th Coll 1975–80; Chapl and Lect Man Univ 1980–86; TV Whitworth Man 1980–82, TR 1982–86; Vis Prof Univ of Notre Dame Indiana 1983; ABM Selector 1982–92; R H Trin w St Mary Guildf 1986–95; M Liturg Comm 1986–96; M FOAG 1991–96; Bp of Portsm from 1995; Chair Anglo-Nordic-Baltic Th Conf from 1997; M Doct Commn 1996–2003; Vc-Chair Porvoo Panel 1999–2005, Chair from 2005; Chair C of E Bd of Educ and Nat Soc from 2003; apptd M AC 2003–05
GS 1995–
Tel: 01329 280247
Fax: 01329 231538
email: bishports@portsmouth.anglican.org

STOCK, Very Revd Victor Andrew, OAM, AKC, FRSA
The Deanery 1 Cathedral Close Guildford GU2 7TL [DEAN OF GUILDFORD] *b* 1944 *educ* Christopher Wren Sch; K Coll Lon; St Boniface Coll Warminster; *CV* C Pinner, Lon 1969–73; Res Chapl Lon Univ 1973–79; R Friern Barnet 1979–86; R St Mary-le-Bow, City of Lon 1986–2002; Dean of Guildford from 2002
GS 1980–86
Tel: 01483 560328 (Home)
01483 547862 (Office)
Fax: 01483 303350
email: dean@guildford-cathedral.org

STOCK, Rt Revd (William) Nigel, BA, Dip Theol
Bishop's House 4 Park Rd Ipswich IP1 3ST [BISHOP OF ST EDMUNDSBURY AND IPSWICH] *b* 1950 *educ* Dur Sch; Dur Univ; Ripon Coll Cuddesdon; *CV* C St Pet Stockton 1976–79; P-in-c St Pet Taraka, PNG 1979–84; V St Mark Shiremoor 1985–91; TR N Shields 1991–98; RD Tynemouth 1992–98; Hon Can Newc Cathl 1997–98; Res Can Dur Cathl 1998–2000; Bp of Stockport 2000–07; Bp of St E & I from 2007; M Ho of Bps CME Cttee from 2002; M Appts Cttee of C of E from 2003; Chair Local Unity Panel (CCU) from 2007; M Min Coun from 2008; M Dioc Commn from 2008
GS 2003–
Tel: 01473 252829
Fax: 01473 232552

STOCKPORT, Suffragan Bishop of.
See ATWELL, Rt Revd Robert Ronald

STOKE-UPON-TRENT, Archdeacon of.
See STONE, Ven Godfrey Owen

STONE, Ven Godfrey Owen, MA, PGCE, Dip LRM
39 The Brackens Clayton Newcastle-under-Lyme ST5 4JL [ARCHDEACON OF STOKE-UPON-TRENT; LICHFIELD] *b* 1949 *educ* St Bart Gr Sch Newbury; Ex Coll Ox; Wycliffe Hall Ox; *CV* C Rushden with Newton Bromswold, Peterb 1981–87; Dir of Pastl Studies, Wycliffe Hall Ox 1987–92; TR Bucknall Tm Min, Lich 1992–2002; RD Stoke-upon-Trent 1998–2002; Adn of Stoke-upon-Trent from 2002
Tel: 01782 663066
07786 447115
Fax: 01782 711165
email: archdeacon.stoke@lichfield.anglican.org

STORKEY, Dr Elaine, BA, MA, DD, Ph D (Hon)
The Old School High St Coton Cambridgeshire CB23 7PL [ELY] *educ* Ossett Gr Sch; Univ Coll of Wales Abth; McMaster Univ Ontario; York Univ; *CV* Tutor in Philosophy Man Coll Ox 1967–68; Rsch Fell in Sociology Stirling Univ 1968–69; Tutor Open Univ 1976–80; Vis Lect Calvin Coll USA 1980–81; Covenant Coll USA 1981–82; Lect in Philosophy Oak Hill Th Coll 1982–87; Lect in Faculty of Social Science Open Univ 1987–91; Dir Inst for Contemporary Christianity 1992–98; Vis Lect in Theol K Coll Lon 1996–2001; Ext Mod Birkbeck Coll Lon from 1998; Scriptwriter for BBC OU; Assoc Ed 'Third Way' from 1984; Broadcaster BBC from 1987; M ACORA 1988–90; M Crown Appts Commn 1990; Vc-Pres UCCF 1987–93; M Abps' Commn on Cathl 1992–94; M Lausanne Wkg Pty on Th 1992–97; M CRAC 1993–98; Examiner Sociology of Religion Lon Univ from 1993; Trustee C of E Newspaper from 1994; Vc-Pres Cheltenham and Glouc Coll of HE from 1994; M Forum for the Future 1995–98; M Orthodox-Evang Dialogue WCC from 1996; New Coll Scholar Univ of NSW Sydney 1997; Pres Tear Fund from 1997; M Wkg Pty on Chr-Jewish Relns from 1998; Lambeth DD 1998; M John Ray Inst from 1999; Sen Rsch Fell Wycliffe Hall, Ox 2003–07; M CNC 2002–07; Visiting Prof Messiah Coll, Pennsylvania, USA summer 2005; Chair Fulcrum from 2006; columnist for Swedish newspaper 'Dagen' from 2006; Chair Ch Army Ord and Commn Review Gp 2007–08; Examiner Univ of Wales 2008
GS 1987–
Tel: 01954 212381
07969 354673 (Mobile)
email: elaine@storkey.com

STOW AND LINDSEY, Archdeacon of.
See SINCLAIR, Ven Jane Elizabeth Margaret

STRAIN, Revd Christopher Malcolm, LLB, Solicitor, Cert Theol
St Luke's Vicarage 2 Birchwood Rd Parkstone Poole BH14 9NP [SALISBURY] *b* 1956 *educ* Aldwickbury

Prep Sch; Bedford Sch; Southn Univ; Guildf Coll of Law; Wycliffe Hall; *CV* C St Jo w. Em Werrington, Peterb 1986–89; C-in-charge St Steph Broadwater, Worthing, Chich 1989–1994; TV Hampreston and Stapehill, Wimborne, Salis 1994–2000; V St Luke Parkstone from 2000; Sch gov; Chapl to Scouts, Poole
GS 2005– *Tel:* 01202 741030
email: cmstrain@tiscali.co.uk

STRANACK, Mrs Penny (Penelope Jane), BA, PGCE
8 Sunwine Place Exmouth Devon EX8 2SE [TRURO] *b* 1939 *educ* Frensham Heights Sch; Leeds Univ; Bris Univ; *CV* Sec Ho of Laity, Dioc Syn; M Coun of Br Funeral Services; M Chs Funerals Grp; M Dioc Parsonages Bd
GS 2000– *Tel:* 01395 225638
email: rnstranack@yahoo.co.uk

STRATFORD, Revd Timothy Richard, B Sc
Rectory Old Hall Lane Kirkby L32 5TH [LIVERPOOL] *b* 1961 *educ* Knowsley Hey Comp Sch; York Univ; Wycliffe Hall Th Coll; *CV* C Mossley Hill 1986–89; C St Helens St Helen 1989–91; Chapl to Bp of Liv 1991–94; V Gd Shep W Derby 1994–2003; TR Kirkby and TV St Chad Kirkby from 2003; M Liturg Commn from 2006
GS 2000– *Tel:* 0151 547 2155
078855 734914 (Mobile)
Fax: 08701 673589
email: tim.stratford@btinternet.com

STREETER, Mr Michael Grainger, IPFA, FCCA
16 Portsmouth Wood Close Lindfield Haywards Heath RH16 2DQ [CHICHESTER] *b* 1942 *educ* St Jo Coll, Southsea; Trin Coll Bris; *CV* Sec/Treas Mid Sussex Water Co 1982–87; Man Dir Mid Sussex/ W Kent Water Co 1987–92; Administy acting Chief Exec 1993–94; chwdn All SS Lindfield 1997–2002; Trust Dir, The 40s Trust; M Chich Dioc miss and renewal team 1998–2005; Growing Healthy Chs co-ord; M dioc Bp's Coun, Pastl Cttee; lay chair Cuckfield Dny
GS 2005– *Tel:* 01444 414516
07906 647547 (Mobile)
email: mike@mstreeter.me.uk

STROYAN, Rt Revd John Ronald Angus, M Theol, MA
Warwick House 139 Kenilworth Rd Coventry CV4 7AP [SUFFRAGAN BISHOP OF WARWICK; COVENTRY] *b* 1955 *educ* Harrow Sch; St Andr Univ; Q Coll Birm; Ecum Inst, Bossey, Switzerland; Univ of Wales; *CV* C St Pet Hillfields, Cov E Tm 1983–87; V St Matt w. St Chad Smethwick, Birm 1987–94; V Bloxham, Milcombe & S Newington, Ox 1994–2005; AD Deddington, Ox 2002–05; Bp of Warwick from 2005; Pres Com of the Cross of Nails UK from 2007
Tel: 024 7641 2627
Fax: 024 7641 5254
email: bishop.warwick@CovCofE.org

STUART, Rt Revd Ian Campbell, MA, BA, Cert Ed, Dip Ed Admin
Pro Vice-Chancellor's Office Liverpool Hope University Hope Park Taggart Avenue Liverpool L16 9JD [ASSISTANT BISHOP, LIVERPOOL] *educ* New England Univ (NSW); Melbourne Univ; St Barn Coll of Min, Townsville; *CV* Australia 85–99; Asst Bp and Bp Administrator N Queensland 1992–99; Chapl Liv Hope 1999–2001; Asst Bp Liv from 1999; Provost Hope Park 2001–05; Asst Vc-Chan Liv Hope Univ from 2005
Tel: 0151 291 3547
Fax: 0151 291 3669
email: Stuarti@hope.ac.uk

SUDBURY, Archdeacon of. See BRIERLEY, Ven David James

SUFFOLK, Archdeacon of. See ARRAND, Ven Geoffrey William

SUGDEN, Canon Dr Christopher Michael Neville, MA, M Phil, PhD
36 North Hinksey Village Oxford OX2 0NA [OXFORD] *b* 1948 *educ* K Sch Roch; St Pet Coll Ox; Nottm Univ; Westmr Coll Ox; St Jo Coll Nottm; *CV* C St Geo Leeds 1974–77; relig programmes producer, BBC Radio Leeds 1977; Asst Presbyter St Jo Bangalore, Ch of S India 1978–83; Asst Dir Assoc for Theol Educ by Extension, India 1978–83; Registrar and Dir of Academic Affairs, Ox Cen for Miss Studies 1983–2001; Exec Dir OCMS 2001–04; Exec Sec Angl Mainstream Internat from 2004; M MPA Coun from 2006; Can St Luke's Cathl, Jos, Nigeria from 2001
GS 2005– *Tel:* 01865 883388
Fax: 01865 517722
email: csugden@anglican-mainstream.net

SULLIVAN, Ven Nicola Ann, BTh, SRN, RM
6 The Liberty Wells BA5 2SU [ARCHDEACON OF WELLS; BATH AND WELLS] *b* 1958 *educ* Ips Convent of Jesus and Mary; Mills Gr Sch, Framlingham; St Bart's Hosp; Bris Maternity Hosp; Wycliffe Hall Ox; *CV* C St Anne Earlham, Norw 1995–99; Assoc V Bath Abbey 1999–2002; Subdean Wells Cathl 2003–07; Bp's Chapl and Pastl Asst 2002–07; Adn of Wells and Res Can Wells Cathl from 2007; M Norw Dioc Syn 1997–99; M B & W Dioc Syn, Bp's Coun, DBF
Tel: 01749 685147
Fax: 01749 679755
email: adwells@bathwells.anglican.org

SUNDERLAND, Archdeacon of. See BAIN, Ven (John) Stuart

SURREY, Archdeacon of. See BEAKE, Ven Stuart Alexander

SUTCH, Ven (Christopher) David, AKC, TD
St Andrew's Chaplaincy, Oficina 1 Edf Jupiter, Avda Nuestro Padre Jesus Cautivo 74 Los Boliches Fuengirola 29640 [ARCHDEACON OF GIBRALTAR] *b* 1947 *educ* St John's Sch Leatherhead; King's Coll Lon;

St Augustine's Theo Coll Cant; *CV* C Hartcliffe 1970–75; T V Dorcan 1975–79; V Alveston 1979–89; V Cainscross w Selsley 1999–2007; Chapl Costa Del Sol (East) 2007–08; Adn Gibraltar from 2008
Tel: 0034 952 580 600
Fax: 0034 952 472 140
email: frdavid@standrews-cofe-spain.com

SUTCLIFFE, Mr Tom (James Thomas), MA
12 Polworth Rd Streatham London SW16 2EU [SOUTHWARK] *b* 1943 *educ* Prebendal Sch Chich; Hurstpierpoint Coll; Magd Coll Ox; *CV* Engl tchr Purcell Sch 1964–65; Countertenor lay-clerk Westmr Cathl 1966–70; Mgr Musica Reservata 1966–69; performer with Schola Polyphonica, Pro Cantione Antiqua, Concentus Musicus, Vienna and Darmstadt Opera 1966–70; Advertisement Mgr and Ed 'Music and Musicians' magazine 1968–73; Sub-ed, opera critic, dep arts ed, dep obits ed 'Guardian' 1973–96; Opera Critic 'Evening Standard' 1996–2002; Leverhulme Fell 1991, 2005; Hon Fell Rose Bruford Coll from 2006; M Exec Cttee Affirming Catholicism 1996–2002; Chair Music Section of Critics' Circle from 1999; dramaturg in Brussels, Vienna from 1998; M Cathls Fabric Commn for Eng from 2002
GS 1990–
Tel: 020 8677 5849
07815 101314 (Mobile)
Fax: 020 8677 7939
email: tomsutcliffe@email.msn.com

SUTTON, Mrs Debbie (Deborah Margaret), BSc, PG Dip Dietetics
2 Taswell Rd Southsea PO5 2RG [PORTSMOUTH] *b* 1957 *educ* Walthamstow Hall, Sevenoaks; Chelsea Coll, Lon Univ; *CV* Dietitian, Portsm Hosps NHS Trust 1981–98; renal rsch dietitian from 1999
GS 2005–
Tel: 023 9275 6926
email: deb2tas@hotmail.com

SWINDON, Suffragan Bishop of.
See RAYFIELD, Rt Revd Dr Lee Stephen

SWINSON, Mrs Margaret Anne, MA, ACA, CTA
46 Glenmore Ave Liverpool L18 4QF [LIVERPOOL] *b* 1957 *educ* Alice Ottley Sch Worc; Liv Univ; *CV* Accountant (Tax Specialist); GS Stg Cttee 1991–97; M BSR 1990–95; Chair Race and Com Relns Cttee 1990–95; Trustee CUF 1987–97; M CTBI; C of E Delegate to WCC Canberra 1991; M CBF 1996–98; M Bd of Miss 2001–03; M CCU from 2006; Mod CTBI from 2006
GS 1985–
Tel and Fax: 0151 724 3533
email: maggie@swinsonfamily.net

SWITZERLAND, Archdeacon in.
See SIDDALL, Ven Arthur

SYKES, Mr John Nicholas, MA
Tower Place West London EC3R 5BU [CHURCH COMMISSIONER] *b* 1959 *educ* Bradford Gr Sch; Jes Coll Ox; *CV* Investment Consult; Baillie, Gifford & Co Ltd 1980–84; Baring Asset Mgt 1984–97; Sen Consult William M Mercer Investment from 1997; Ch Commr from 2001; M Assets Cttee and Securities Grp
Tel and Fax: 020 7178 3268
email: nick.sykes@mercer.com

SYKES, Rt Revd Stephen Whitefield, MA, Hon DD (Zurich)
Ingleside Whinney Hill Durham DH1 3BE [HONORARY ASSISTANT BISHOP, DURHAM] *b* 1939 *educ* Bris Gr Sch; Monkton Combe Sch; St Jo Coll Cam; Harvard Univ; Ripon Hall Th Coll; *CV* Asst Lect Div Cam Univ 1964–68; Fell and Dean St Jo Coll Cam 1964–74; Lect 1968–74; Van Mildert Prof Dur Univ 1974–85; Can Res Dur Cathl 1974–85; Regius Prof Div Cam Univ 1985–90; Bp of Ely 1990–99; Prin St Jo Coll Dur 1999–2006; Prof Theol Dur Univ; Asst Bp Dur; Chair Doct Commn 1997–2005
GS 1990–99
Tel: 0191 384 6465
Fax: 0191 375 0637

TAN, Dr Chik Kaw, B Pharm, MSc, PhD, MRPharmS
12 Montfort Place Westlands Newcastle-under-Lyme ST5 2HE [LICHFIELD] *b* 1956 *educ* Anglo-Chinese Sch, Ipoh, Malaysia; Bath Univ; Aston Univ; Keele Univ; *CV* Pres Bath Univ Chr Union 1979–80; Adv Bris Chinese Chr Fellowship 1981–86; Prayer Grp leader, Newcastle-under-Lyme OMF Prayer Grp 1986–95; M OMF Internat 1996–2002; Assoc Pastor, Surabaya (Indonesia) Internat Chr Fellowship 2001–02; M Preaching Tm, St Jas Audley from 2002; Sen Lect Keele Univ from 2005; M Newc Dny Syn; M Lich Dioc Syn; M N Staffs Local Rsch Ethics Cttee
GS 2005–
Fax: 01782 583326 (Work)
email: ck11x@yahoo.ie

TATTERSALL, Mr Geoffrey Frank, MA, QC
2 The Woodlands Lostock Bolton BL6 4JD [MANCHESTER] *b* 1947 *educ* Man Gr Sch; Ch Ch Ox; *CV* Barrister; Called to Bar Lincoln's Inn 1970; Bencher 1997; In practice Nn Circuit from 1970; Recorder Crown Court from 1989; QC from 1992; Called to Bar NSW 1992; SC from 1995; Judge of Appeal IOM from 1997; Deputy High Court Judge from 2003; Lay Chair Bolton Dny Syn 1993–2002; Chair Ho of Laity Dioc Syn 1994–2003; M Fees Adv Commn from 1995; M Strg Cttee Clergy Discipline Measure from 1996; M Bp's Coun; M DBF and Trust and Fin Cttee till 2004; Chair Stg Orders Cttee GS from 1999; Chan of Carl Dioc from 2003; Hon Lay Can Manch Cathl 2003; Chan Manch Dioc from 2004; Dep V-Gen S & Man 2004–08; External Reviewer of decisions of Dir of Fair Access from 2005; Chair Disciplinary Tribunals, Clergy Discipline Measure from 2006; Chair Revision Cttee, draft C of E Marriage Measure 2006–07; Chair Revision Cttee, draft Eccl Officer (Terms of Service) Measure 2007–08; Par Clerk St George-in-the-East
GS 1995–
Tel: 01204 846265
Fax: 01204 849863
email: gftqc@hotmail.co.uk

TAUNTON, Archdeacon of. See REED, Ven John Peter Cyril

TAUNTON, Suffragan Bishop of. See MAURICE, Rt Revd Peter David

TAVINOR, Very Revd Michael Edward, MA, M Mus, ARCO, PGCE
The Deanery College Cloisters Cathedral Close Hereford HR1 2NG [DEAN OF HEREFORD] *b* 1953 *educ* Bishopshalt Sch Hillingdon, Middx; Univ Coll Dur; Em Coll Cam; K Coll Lon; Ripon Coll Cuddesdon; *CV* C St Pet Ealing Lon 1982–85; Prec, Sacrist and Min Can Ely Cathl 1985–90; P-in-c Stuntney Ely 1987–90; V Tewkesbury with Walton Cardiff Glouc 1990–2002; V Twyning Glos 1999–2002; Hon Can Glouc Cathl 1997–2002; Dean of Hereford from 2002; M Dioc Syn from 2002; Pres Ch Music Soc 2005; Hon Fell Guild of Ch Musicians from 2006   *Tel:* 01432 374203
Fax: 01432 374220
email: dean@herefordcathedral.org

TAYLOR, Very Revd Charles William, BA, MA, FGCM
The Deanery Minster Precincts Peterborough PE1 1XS [DEAN OF PETERBOROUGH] *b* 1953 *educ* St Paul's Cathl Choir Sch; Marlborough Coll; Selwyn Coll Cam; Cuddesdon Coll Ox; Ch Divinity Sch of Pacific, Graduate Theol Union, Berkeley, Calif USA; *CV* C Cen Wolverhampton TM 1976–79; Chapl Westmr Abbey (Minor Can) 1979–84; V Stanmore w. Oliver's Battery, Winch 1984–90; R N Stoneham & Bassett, Southn 1990–95; Can Res and Prec, Lich Cathl 1995–2007; Dean of Peterb from 2007; M Lich Dioc Liturg Cttee 1976–79; M Winch Dioc Liturg Cttee 1984–95; Chair Lich Dioc Worship Team 1995–2006; M Cathls Liturg and Music Cttee 1996–2007; Gov   *Tel:* 01733 562780
email: charles.taylor@peterborough-cathedral.org.uk

TAYLOR, Preb Mrs Diana Mary,
Volis Farm Hestercombe Kingston St Mary Taunton TA2 8HS [BATH AND WELLS] *b* 1945 *educ* Scunthorpe Gr Sch; Harper Adams Agric Coll; *CV* Farmer; M BM Rural Affairs Ctee from 1993, Vc-Chair from 1998; Bp's Visitor 1995–2000; M Gov Body SW Min Tr Course 1996–2000; Chair Dioc Ho of Laity from 1999; M Bp's Coun; M MPA Rural Strategy Grp from 2006; Lay Can Wells Cath from 2006; C of E M of Governing Body and Trustee Arthur Rank Cen, Stoneleigh from 2008; Life Trustee Pyncombe Clergy Charity GS 1993–   *Tel:* 01823 451545
email: diana.taylor0@farmersweekly.net

TAYLOR, Ven Peter Flint, MA, BD
Glebe House Church Lane Sheering Bishop's Stortford CM22 7NR [ARCHDEACON OF HARLOW; CHELMSFORD] *b* 1944 *educ* Clifton Coll Bris; Qu Coll Cam; Lon Univ; Lon Coll of Div; *CV* C St Aug

Highbury New Park 1970–73; C St Andr Plymouth 1973–77; V Ironville, Derby 1977–83; P-in-c Riddings 1982–83; R Rayleigh 1983–96; pt Chapl HM Young Offenders Inst and Prison Bullwood Hall 1985–90; RD Rochford 1989–96; Adn of Harlow from 1996; M Dioc Syn; M DBF; M Family Purse Revision Cttee and Sub Cttee; Adns' Nat Forum   *Tel:* 01279 734524
Fax: 01279 734426
email: a.harlow@chelmsford.anglican.org

TAYLOR, Ven Paul Stanley, B Ed, M Th
Aldhelm House Rectory Lane West Stafford Dorchester DT2 8AB [ARCHDEACON OF SHERBORNE; SALISBURY] *b* 1953 *educ* Lodge Farm Co Sec Sch; Redditch Co High Sch; Westmr Coll Ox; Westcott Ho Cam; *CV* C St Steph Bush Hill Park 1984–88; V St Andr Southgate 1988–97; Asst Dir POT 1987–94, Dir 1994–2000, 2002–04; V St Mary & Ch Ch Hendon 1997–2004; AD W Barnet 2000–04; Assoc Tutor NTMTC 2001–04; Adn of Sherborne from 2004   *Tel:* 01305 269074
07796 691203 (Mobile)
Fax: 01305 269074
email: adsherborne@salisbury.anglican.org

TERRETT, Group Captain Paul Everard, OBE, LLB
Idle Cottage Sharptor Liskeard PL14 5AT [TRURO] *b* 1934 *educ* Cotham Gr Sch; Bris Univ; *CV* Dny lay Chair from 1996; Can Emer Truro Cathl; Chair Truro DBF 2003–06, Vc-Chair from 2006; M Bp's Coun, DBF, Patr, Pastl and Glebe Ctees GS 2005–   *Tel:* 01579 362741
email: terretts@sharptor.co.uk

TETLEY, Ven Dr Joy Dawn, BA, Cert Ed, MA, Ph D, FRSA
23 Cripley Rd Oxford OX2 OAH [ARCHDEACON EMERITUS] *b* 1946 *educ* St Mary's Coll Dur; Leeds Univ; St Hugh's Coll Ox; Dur Univ; NW Ord Course; *CV* Dss Bentley Sheff 1977–79; Dss St Aid Buttershaw 1979–80; Dss Dur Cath 1980–83; Lect Trin Coll Bris 1983–86; Dss Chipping Sodbury and Old Sodbury 1983–86; Dn Roch Cathl 1987–89; Hon Can Roch Cathl 1990–93; Assoc Dir POT 1987–88; Dir POT 1988–93; Hon Par Dn H Family Gravesend w Ifield 1989–93; Prin E Anglian Minl Tr Course 1993–99; Adn of Worc and Can Res Worc Cathl 1999–2008; Adn Emer from 2008 GS 2001–08   *Tel:* 01865 250209
email: briantetley@btinternet.com

TEWKESBURY, Suffragan Bishop of. See WENT, Rt Revd John Stewart

THETFORD, Suffragan Bishop of. See ATKINSON, Rt Revd David John

THISELTON, Canon Prof Anthony Charles, BD, M Th, Ph D, DD, DD
Southview Lodge 390 High Rd Chilwell Nottingham NG9 5EG [SOUTHWELL AND NOTTINGHAM] *b* 1937

educ City of Lon Sch; K Coll Lon; Sheff Univ; Oak Hill Th Coll; *CV* C H Trin Sydenham 1960–63; Tutor Tyndale Hall Bris 1963–67, Sen Tutor 1967–70; Lect Bibl Studies Sheff Univ 1970–79, Sen Lect 1979–85; Prof Calvin Coll Grand Rapids 1982–83; Prin St Jo Coll Nottm 1985–88; Special Lect Nottm Univ 1986–88; Prin St Jo Coll and Cranmer Hall Dur 1988–92; Hon Prof Th Dur Univ 1992; Prof Chr Th Nottm Univ and Hd of Th Dept 1992–2000, Em Prof Chr Th in Res from 2001; re-appointed Prof of Chr Th from 2006; Can Th Leic Cathl from 1994; M HFEA 1995–98; M Doct Commn 1976–91 and 1996–2004; Pres Soc for Study of Th 1998–2000; M Th Educ Tr Cttee 1999–2005; Can Th Southwell Min and Assoc Min St Mary Attenborough from 2000; Clergy Discipline (Doct) Grp 2000–04; M Crown Appts Commn 2001–07; M Ho of Bps' Wkg Pty on Women in the Episcopate 2001–05; Exam Chapl to Bp of S'well from 2002; Rsch Prof Chr Th, Univ Ches 2003–08; Ed Bd Intern Journal Systematic Theol from 2000; M Task Grp, Theol Educ for the Angl Communion 2004–08; M Appts Cttee from 2005; M Bd of Educ from 2006
GS 1995–   *Tel:* 0115 917 6391 (Home)
                                          0115 917 6392
                            Fax: 0115 917 6392 (Home)
                      email: thiselton@ntlworld.com

THOMAS, Revd Mark Wilson, BA, MA
25 The Crescent Town Walls Shrewsbury SY1 1TH [LICHFIELD] *b* 1951 *educ* Sherborne Sch; Dur Univ; Hull Univ; Ripon Coll Cuddesdon; *CV* Asst C Chapelthorpe Wakef 1978–81; Asst C Seaford Chich 1981–84; V St Mary's Gomersal Wakef 1984–92; TR Almondbury Wakef 1992–2001; RD Almondbury 1993–2001; Hon Can Wakef 1999–2001; V Shrewsbury, St Chad w St Mary and St Alkmund from 2001; Lich Dioc Min Reviewer
GS 2008–   *Tel and Fax:* 01743 343761
                      email: markthomas51@hotmail.co.uk

THOMAS, Revd Rod (Roderick Charles Howell), B Sc, Cert Th
St Matthew's Vicarage 3 Sherford Rd Elburton Plymouth PL9 8DQ [EXETER] *b* 1954 *educ* Ealing Gr Sch for Boys; LSE; Wycliffe Hall Th Coll ; *CV* Dir Employment Affairs CBI 1987–91; C St Paul Stonehouse Plymouth 1993–95; C St Andr Plymouth 1995–99; P-in-c St Matt Elburton 1999–2005, V from 2005; Chair Reform; M BM 2001–03; M Wkg Pty on Sen Ch Appts from 2005; M CPAS Coun of Reference from 2005
GS 2000–   *Tel:* 01752 402771
                      email: roderick.t@tiscali.co.uk

THOMAS-BETTS, Dr Anna, MA, Ph D, MBE
68 Halkingcroft Langley Slough SL3 7AY [OXFORD] *b* 1941 *educ* Christava Mahilalayam, Alwaye, S India; Madras Chr Coll, Madras Univ; Keele Univ; *CV* Lect in Physics Madras Chr Coll 1960–62; Post-Doctoral Rsch Asst Imp Coll Lon 1966–74; Lect in Geophysics Imp Coll Lon 1974–92, Sen

Lect from 1992; Coll Tutor from 1998; M CCU 1991–96; M CBF 1996–99; M BSR 2000–02; M MPA from 2003; M Gov Body of Ripon Coll Cuddesdon from 2006; Chair Independent Monitoring Bd, Colnbrook Immigration Removal Cen from 2004; Chair Forum of Chairs of Independent Monitoring Bds at Immigration Removal Cen from 2007
GS 1990–   *Tel:* 01753 822013 (Home)
                                    020 7594 6430 (Office)
                      email: a.thomas-bts@ic.ac.uk

THOMPSON, Mr Roy, AIBD
May Rose Cottage Sheriff Hutton York YO60 6SS [YORK] *b* 1937 *educ* High Storrs Gr Sch Sheff; Sheff Coll of Art; Guildf Sch of Art; *CV* Construction Marketing Consult, CBC; Sec, Open Syn Grp; CRC YH Culture Task Grp; Trustee Chs Tourism Assoc
GS 2000–   *Tel:* 01347 878644
                                    07779 095273 (Mobile)
                      email: roythompson2@btinternet.com

THOMSON, Canon Celia Stephana Margaret,
MA
3 Miller's Green Gloucester GL1 2BN [GLOUCESTER] *b* 1955 *educ* St Swithun's Winch 1967–71; Ox Univ; Salisbury and Wells Theol Coll; *CV* C St Barnabas Southfields, S'wark 1991–95; V Ch Ch W Wimbledon, S'wark 1995–2003; Tutor in Ethics, SEITE 1995–2000; Vocations Adv Lambeth Adnry 1995–2000; Bp's Adv from 2007; Can Pastor Glouc Cath from 2003
GS 2008–   *Tel:* 01452 415824
                      email: cthomson@gloucestercathedral.org.uk

THOMSON, Rt Revd David, MA, D Phil, FRSA, FSA, FRHistS
14 Lynn Road Ely CB6 1DA [SUFFRAGAN BISHOP OF HUNTINGDON] *b* 1952 *educ* K Edw VII Sch Sheffield; Keble Coll Ox; Selwyn Coll Cam; Westcott Ho Cam; *CV* C Maltby 1981–84; TV Banbury 1984–94; TR Cockermouth 1994–2002; Chair Dioc Children and Young People's Cttee; Bp's Adv for Healthcare Chapl, Team and Grp Mins and Deliverance Min; Archdeacon of Carlisle and Can Res Carl Cathl 2002–08; Bp Huntingdon from 2008; Hon Can Ely Cathl from 2008   *Tel:* 01353 662137
                                    07771 864550 (Mobile)
                                    Fax: 01353 669357
                      email: bishop.huntingdon@ely.anglican.org

THORNTON, Rt Revd Tim (Timothy) Martin,
BA, MA
Lis Escop Feock Truro TR3 6QQ [BISHOP OF TRURO] *b* 1957 *educ* Devonport High Sch for Boys; Southn Univ; St Steph Ho Ox; K Coll Lond; *CV* C Todmorden 1980–82; P-in-c Walsden 1982–85; Lect Univ of Wales (Cardiff) 1985–87; Chapl 1985–86; Sen Chapl 1986–87; Bp's Chapl Wakef 1987–91; DDO Wakef 1988–91; Bp's Chapl Lon 1991–94; Dep P in O 1992–2001; Prin N Thames Minl Tr Course 1994–98; V Kensington St Mary Abbots w

S Geo, Gov St Mary Abbots C of E Primary Sch, Chair Campden Charities 1998–2001; AD Kensington 2000–01; K Coll Theol Trustee; Area Bp of Sherborne 2001–08; Trustee BRF; Bp Truro from 2009   *Tel:* 01872 862657
Fax: 01872 862037
email: tim.thornton@talk21.com

TICEHURST, Mrs Carol Ann,
57 Silver St Coningsby Lincoln LN4 4SG [LINCOLN] *b* 1938 *CV* Medical Sec; hdmaster's PA; Pres R Br Legion Lincs Women's Section and caseworker from 1998; M GS Catholic Grp; M Forward in Faith
GS 1995–   *Tel:* 01526 342076
email: caticehurst@tiscali.co.uk

TILLEY, Mrs Margaret Rose, B Sc, M Sc, Dip Th, C ENG, C MATHS, CITP, MBCS, MCMI, MIMA
8 Preston Malthouse Faversham ME13 8EZ [CANTERBURY] *b* 1944 *educ* Grey Coat Hosp Westmr; Lon Univ; City Univ; Ch Ch Coll Cant; *CV* Lect in FE for 26 years including Hd of Sch of Business Studies Brighton Coll of Tech 1986–95; Adv for Bp of Lon 1995–2004; M Dioc Abp's Coun; Rdr from 1976; Chair Coll of Rdrs; M Nat Assembly of Victim Support
GS 2000–   *Tel:* 01795 530090
email: avimar@madasafish.com

TILLOTSON, Revd Simon Christopher, BA, MA
The Vicarage Church St Whitstable CT5 1PG [CANTERBURY] *b* 1967 *educ* Eton Coll; Westfield Coll Lon Univ; Trinity Coll Cam; Univ of Wales; Ridley Hall Cam; *CV* C St Andrew's Paddock Wook 1994–98; Senior C St Peter and St Paul's Ormskirk 1998–2000; V St Peter and St Paul's Aylesford 2000–07; TV All Saints and St Peters Whitstable from 2007; Par Cllr Aylesford 2002–03; Chapl to Mayor of Tonbridge and Malling 2004–05; Chair Almshouses Cttee Aylesford 2000–07; Chair Brassey Trust (Com Hall) 2000–07; Sch Gov Com Coll Whitstable from 2007; M Roch Dioc Syn 2003–07; M Bp's Coun Roch 2003–07; M Cant Dioc Syn from 2007
GS 2007–   *Tel:* 01227 272308
email: tillotsons@googlemail.com

TOMS, Mrs Anne Christine Bloomer, MA, D Phil
Epworth Park Rd Wellingborough NN8 4QE [PETERBOROUGH] *b* 1945 *educ* Rotherham High Sch for Girls; Cam Univ; Ox Univ; *CV* Scientific staff, Medical Rsch Coun 1974–2002; pt M Northants Probation Bd 2002–08; Chair Daylight Cen Fellowship; various roles in vol and com sector in Northants from 2002; Chair Peterb Dioc Syn from 2003; M DBF, Houses Cttee
GS 2005–   *Tel:* 01933 275117
email: acb.toms@btinternet.com

TONBRIDGE, Archdeacon of. See MANSELL, Ven Clive Neville Ross

TONBRIDGE, Suffragan Bishop of. See CASTLE, Rt Revd Dr Brian Colin

TOTNES, Archdeacon of. See RAWLINGS, Ven John Edmund Frank

TOWNLEY, Ven Peter Kenneth, BA, DSPT
The Vicarage Kirkthorpe Wakefield WF1 5SZ [ARCHDEACON OF PONTEFRACT] *b* 1955 *educ* Moston Brook High Sch Man; Sheff Univ; Man Univ; Ridley Hall Th Coll; *CV* C Ch Ch Ashton-under-Lyne 1980–83; P-in-c St Hugh's CD Oldham 1983–88; R All SS Stretford 1988–96; V St Mary-le-Tower Ipswich 1996–2008; M Meissen Commn 1991–2001; RD of Ipswich from 2001; Hon Can from 2003; M Porvoo Panel from 2003; M Inter-dioc Fin Forum; Adn Pontefract from 2008
GS 1992–95, 2000–08   *Tel:* 01924 434459 (Office)
01924 896327 (Home)
Fax: 01924 364834 (Office)
01924 896327 (Home)
email: archdeacon.pontefract@
wakefield.anglican.org

TRETHEWEY, Ven Frederick Martyn, BA, Dip Th, S Th
15 Worcester Rd Droitwich WR9 8AA [ARCHDEACON OF DUDLEY; WORCESTER] *b* 1949 *educ* St Austell Gr Sch; Lon Univ; Oak Hill Th Coll; *CV* C Tollington Pk St Mark w St Anne 1978–82; C Whitehall Pk St Andr Hornsey Lane 1982–87; TV Hornsey Rise Whitehall Pk Tm 1987–88; V Brockmoor, Lich 1988–93; V Brockmoor, Worc 1993–2001; Chapl Russells Hall Hosp Dudley 1988–94; Chapl Dudley Grp of Hosps NHS Trust 1994–2001; RD Himley 1996–2001; Hon Can Worc Cathl 1999–2001; Adn Dudley from 2001; Rep Dudley Com Ptnrship 2001–05; Chair Black Country Chs Engaged Enabling Grp 2003–05
Tel and Fax: 01905 773301
email: ftrethewey@cofe-worcester.org.uk

TREWEEK (nee Montgomery), Ven Rachel, BA, BTh
16 Baldwyn Gardens Acton London W3 6HL [ARCHDEACON OF NORTHOLT; LONDON] *b* 1963 *educ* Broxbourne Sch; Reading Univ; Wycliffe Hall Ox; *CV* Paediatric Speech and Language Therapist, Gospel Oak Health Cen, Hampstead Health Auth 1985–87; Speech and Language Therapist, Child Devel Team, Hampstead Health Auth 1987–89; Clinical Mgr for Paediatric Speech and Language Therapists in Health Cens, Bloomsbury, Hampstead & Islington Health Auths 1989–91; C St Geo Tufnell Park, Lon 1994–97, Assoc V 1997–99; V St Jas the Less Bethnal Green, Lon 1999–2006; Adn of Northolt from 2006; CME Officer, Stepney Area, Lon Dioc 1999–2001; Bp's Visitor, Stepney Area 2004–06
Tel: 020 8993 6415
email: archdeacon.northolt@london.anglican.org

TRICKEY, Revd (Christopher) Jolyon, MA, BA
Busbridge Rectory Brighton Rd Godalming GU7 1XA
[GUILDFORD] *b* 1957 *educ* Dean Close Cheltenham;
Jesus Coll Cam; Trin Coll Bris; *CV* C St Leon
Chesham Bois, Ox 1990–94; R St Jo Bapt Bus-
bridge from 1994, Busbridge and Hambledon
from 1997
GS 2005–   *Tel:* 01483 418820
                            01483 421267
                            07725 942424 (Mobile)
                            Fax: 01483 421267
email: rev_j_trickey@yahoo.co.uk

TROTT, Revd Stephen, BA, MA, LLM, FRSA
*Rectory 41 Humfrey Lane Boughton Northampton
NN2 8RQ* [PETERBOROUGH] *b* 1957 *educ* Bp Vesey's
Gr Sch Sutton Coldfield; Hull Univ; Fitzw Coll
Cam; Cardiff Univ; Westcott Ho Th Coll (Cam
Federation of Th Colls); *CV* C Hessle 1984–87; C
St Alb Hull 1987–88; R Pitsford w Boughton from
1988; Sec CME 1988–93; Vis Chapl Northants Gr
Sch from 1991, Gov and Dir from 2001; Surrogate
for Marriage Licences from 2001; M Legis Cttee
1995–2000, from 2005; M Legal Adv Commn
1996–2006; M CCBI and CTE 1996–99; M Revi-
sion Cttee on Calendar, Lectionary and Collects
1996; Ch Commr and M Pastl Cttee from 1997,
Red Chs Cttee 1999–2001, from 2004; Bd of Govs
from 1999; M DRACSC 1999–2001; M Revision
Cttee on Clergy Discipline Measure 1999–2000;
GS Rep on Gov Body of SAOMC 2001–06; C of E
Delegate to Conf of Eur Chs, Trondheim, 2003;
FRSA 1986; M Eccl Law Soc from 1988; M Dioc
Syn from 1990; M Vacancy-in-See Cttee from
1995; Clerical Vc-Pres Dioc Syn and Chair Dioc
Ho of Clergy 2000–03; M Peterb Cathl Coun
2001–04; M Pastl (Amendment) Measure Revi-
sion Cttee from 2004; M Follow-up Grp, Review
of Diocs, Pastl & Related Measures from 2004; M
Panel of Reference, Angl Communion from 2005;
M Strg Cttee Diocs Pastl and Miss Measure 2005–
06; M Legis Cttee from 2005; Stg Cttee, Conv of
Cant from 2006
GS 1995–   *Tel:* 01604 845655
                            07712 863000 (Mobile)
                            Fax: 0870 130 5526
email: revstrott@sky.com

**TRURO, Bishop of. See THORNTON, Rt Revd
Tim Martin**

**TRURO, Dean of. See HARDWICK, Very Revd
Dr Christopher George**

TUPLING, Revd Katie (Catherine Louise),
B Theol, ODMTG
*Vicarage Church Bank Hathersage, Hope Valley S32
1AJ* [DERBY] *b* 1974 *educ* St Mary Redcliffe and
Temple Sch Bris; Westhill Coll Birm; Wycliffe Hall
Ox; *CV* Vol Chr Youth Worker, Bris 1992–93; Ch
Com and Youth Worker, Birm 1997–98; Co-ord,
After Sch Clubs, Birm 1997–98; Playleader, After
Sch Club, Birm 1998–2001; C St Pet Belper 2003–

07; P-in-c Hathersage, P-in-c Bamford w. Derwent from 2007, P-in-c Grindleford from 2008
GS 2005–   *Tel:* 01433 650215
email: revtup@tup-house.freeserve.co.uk

TURNER, Canon Carl Francis, BA, M Th
6 Cathedral Close Exeter EX1 2EZ [EXETER] *b* 1960
educ David Lister High Sch, Hull; St Chad's Coll,
Dur Univ; Westmr Coll, Ox Univ; St Steph Ho,
Ox; *CV* Lic Lay Worker, All SS Cathl, Milwaukee,
USA 1981–83; C St Marg Leigh-on Sea, Chelmsf
1985–88; C St Thos of Cant, Brentwood, Chelmsf
1988–90; p-t Chapl, Highwood and St Faith's
Hosps, Brentwood 1988–90; TV Plaistow Tm
Min, Chelmsf 1990–94, P-in-c (acting R) 1995–96;
TR Par of Divine Compassion, Plaistow & N
Canning Town, Chelmsf 1996–2001; Can res and
Prec Ex Cathl from 2001; M Dioc Coun for Wor-
ship and Min; Chair Dioc Liturg Grp
GS 2005–   *Tel:* 01392 285976 (Office)
                            01392 272498 (Home)
                            Fax: 01392 285986
email: precentor@exeter-cathedral.org.uk

TURNER, Mrs (Thelma) Ann, B Sc
Grote Steenweg 47/42 2600 Berchem Belgium
[EUROPE] *b* 1948 *educ* Wintringham Gr Sch,
Grimsby; Univ of Kent at Cant; *CV* Hd of Science,
Upminster Comp Sch 1972–78; Scientific Engl
trainer 1985–91; written communication trainer
from 1991; M Adnry of NW Eur Stg Cttee; Vc-
Chair Ho of Laity, Dioc in Eur; M Dioc Com-
munications Cttee, Dioc OLM Wkg Party, Dioc
PIM Consultation, Bp's Coun
GS 2005–

                            email: ann@turner.be

TWEEDIE, Dr David Gilbert, MB, BS, FRCA
Castle Hill Lower Fulbrook Warwick CV35 8AS
[COVENTRY] *b* 1937 *educ* Birkenhead; Westminster
Medical Sch, Lon Univ; *CV* Consult Anaesthetist,
Warwick Hosp 1968–2002, now rtd; M Cov Dioc
Syn; M Bp's Coun; M Cov DBF; M Dioc Pastl
Cttee; Chair Dioc Forum for Par Devel and Evang
GS 2003–   *Tel:* 01926 624686
                            07774 839230 (Mobile)
email: david@tweedie.info

URQUHART, Rt Revd David Andrew, BA
Bishop's Croft Harborne Birmingham B17 0BG
[BISHOP OF BIRMINGHAM] *b* 1952 *educ* Rugby Sch;
Ealing Business Sch; Wycliffe Hall Th Coll; *CV* C
St Nic Hull 1984-87; TV Drypool Hull 1987–92; V
H Trin Cov 1992–2000; Bp of Birkenhead 2000–06;
Chair CMS Trustees 1994–2007; Prelate of Order
of St Mich and St Geo from 2005; Abp of Cant's
Episcopal Link with China from 2006; Bp of Birm
from 2006
GS 2006–   *Tel:* 0121 427 1163
email: bishop@birmingham.anglican.org

URWIN, Rt Revd Lindsay Goodall, OGS, MA
21 Guildford Rd Horsham RH12 1LU [AREA BISHOP
OF HORSHAM; CHICHESTER] *b* 1956 *educ* Camber-

well Gr Sch Victoria, Australia; Cuddesdon Th Coll; Heythrop Coll Lon Univ; *CV* C St Pet Walworth 1980–83; V St Faith Red Post Hill 1983–88; Dioc Missr Chich 1988–93; OGS from 1990; Bp of Horsham from 1993; M Springboard Exec from 1995; Nat Chair CU 1995–99; UK Provincial OGS 1996–2005; M Abps' Coll of Ev from 1999; Chair Dioc Bd of Educ 1999–2006; MA (Heythrop) 2003; Provost Woodard Corp of Schs, S Region from 2006; Guardian of Shrine of Our Lady of Walsingham from 2006; Pres Sch Chapls Conf from 2007   *Tel:* 01403 211139
Fax: 01403 217349
email: bishhorsham@diochi.org.uk

VANN, Ven Cherry Elizabeth, GRSM, ARCM, Dip Relig Studies, Cert in Counselling, Br Sign Lang Level 3
57 Melling Rd Oldham OL4 1PN [ARCHDEACON OF ROCHDALE; MANCHESTER] *b* 1958 *educ* Lutterworth Upper Sch; R Coll of Music; Westcott Ho; *CV* C St Mich, Flixton 1989–92; Chapl Bolton Coll of HE and FE and C Bolton Par Ch 1992–98; Chapl among Deaf People and TV E Farnworth and Kearsley 1998–2004; TR E. Farnworth & Kearsley from 2004; Bp's Adv in Women's Min from 2004; AD Farnworth from 2005; Hon Can Man Cathl 2007; Adn Rochdale from 2008
GS 2003–   *Tel:* 0161 678 1454
07803 139274 (Mobile)
email: CVannSkye@aol.com

VENNER, Rt Revd Stephen Squires, BA, MA, DD
The Bishop's Office Old Palace Canterbury CT1 2EE [BISHOP OF DOVER; CANTERBURY] *b* 1944 *educ* Hardye's Sch Dorchester; Birm Univ; Linacre Coll Ox; Lon Inst of Educ; St Steph Ho Th Coll; *CV* C St Pet Streatham 1968–71; Hon C St Marg Streatham Hill 1971–72; V St Pet Clapham and Bp's Chapl to Overseas Students 1974–76; V St Jo Trowbridge 1976–82; V H Trin Weymouth 1982–94; M Dorset LEA 1982–94; Chair Dioc Bd of Educ Sarum 1989–94; RD Weymouth 1988–94; Non-Res Can Sarum Cathl 1989–94; Chair Ho of Clergy Dioc Syn 1993–94; M GS Bd of Educ from 1985, Chair VCE Cttee from 1997; Bp of Middleton 1994–99; Chair Dioc Bd of Educ 1994–99; Bp of Dover (Bp in Cant) from 1999; Co-Chair C of E/Moravian Contact Grp 1994–99; Pres Woodard Corp 1999–2002; Vc-Chair Gov Ch Ch Univ Coll Cant 2000–05; Vc-Chair C of E Bd of Educ from 2001; Chapl to Lord Warden of the Cinque Ports from 2004; Chair of Govs (Pro-Chan) Cant Ch Ch Univ from 2005; Bp for the Falklands from 2006
GS 1985–94, 2000–   *Tel:* 01227 464537 (Home)
01227 459382 (Office)
07980 743628 (Mobile)
Fax: 01227 784985 (Office)
email: bishop@bishcant.org

VERNON, Canon Stella Lilian, T Dip
6 St Stephen's Close Willerby Hull HU10 6DG [YORK] *b* 1940 *educ* S Park High Sch Linc; Leic

Dom Science Coll; *CV* Rdr from 1980; Dioc Pres MU 1984–2000; Provincial Pres MU York 2001–06; M Dioc Syn; M DBF; Hon Lay Canon Emeritus York Minster; M Archbp's Coun, Soc Resp Coun; C of E rep, Women's World Day of Prayer Nat Cttee
GS 2000–   *Tel:* 01482 659787

VINCE, Mr Jacob Peter, MA, DBA, MRICS
3 High St Horam Heathfield TN21 0EJ [CHICHESTER] *b* 1960 *educ* Latymer Upper Sch; Univ of Wales; City Univ; *CV* Dir and Charterer Surveyor from 1996; M Bp's Coun; M Ch Buildings Coun
GS 2005–   *Tel:* 01453 812623
01825 765066
Fax: 01825 762475
email: jvince@caxtons.com / jacob.vince@tiscali.co.uk

WAKEFIELD, Bishop of. See PLATTEN, Rt Revd Stephen George

WAKEFIELD, Dean of. See GREENER, Very Revd Jonathan

WALKER, Canon Anthony (Tony) Charles St John, MA
St Saviour's Vicarage 31 Richmond Rd Retford DN22 6SJ [SOUTHWELL AND NOTTINGHAM] *b* 1955 *educ* Brentwood Sch; Tr Coll Ox; Wycliffe Hall Ox; *CV* C Bradf Cathl 1981–84; C St Ann w. Em Nottm 1984–88; V St Saviour Retford 1988–2001; P-in-c St Swithun E Retford 2001; TR Retford from 2002; AD Retford from 2000; Hon Can S'well Minster from 2004; M Dioc Syn, Cathl Coun, Bp's Coun
GS 2004–   *Tel and Fax:* 01777 703800
email: tony@tonywalker.f9.co.uk

WALKER, Dr Brian, Ph D, MA, BA (Hons), BSc (Hons), C.Eng, FCMI, FIET, MIoF (Cert)
Hope Cottage Micheldever Winchester SO21 3DG [WINCHESTER] *b* 1944 *educ* Southfield Sch, Ox; Univ of Winch; Univ of Southn; Open Univ; *CV* Dir Fundraising Naomi Ho Children's Hospice from 1992, Vc-P from 1997; Dir Customer Services Southern Electric 1993–94; Regional Mgr Southern Electric PLC 1996–96; Customer Service and Operations Dir MBP Utility Services 1996–97; Sen Devel Mgr Sabre Power 1998–99; Consult Cohort Ltd, Sierra Leone 2001–04; Exec Dir Religions for Peace (UK) from 2004; M Newc Ptnrship Panel; M Overseas Ch Panel; M Eur Ptnrship Panel; M Dioc Ecum Panel
GS 2008–   *Tel:* 01962 774221
email: hopeis@btinternet.com

WALKER, Rt Revd David Stuart, MA, FRSA
Bishop's House Bishops Walk Cradley Heath B64 7RH [SUFFRAGAN BISHOP OF DUDLEY; WORCESTER] *b* 1957 *educ* Man Gr Sch; K Coll Cam; Qu Th Coll Birm; *CV* C Handsworth 1983–86; TV Maltby 1986–91; Ind Chapl Maltby 1986–91; V Bramley and Ravenfield 1991–95; TR Bramley and

Ravenfield w Hooton Roberts and Braithwell 1995–2000; Hon Can Sheff Cathl 2000; Bp of Dudley from 2000; M Adv Coun on Relns of Bps and Relig Coms from 2002; Sec W Midlands Regional Bps' Grp from 2003; Chair Housing Justice from 2003; Chair Housing Justice 2003–07; Sec W Midlands Regional Bps Grp 2003–08; Chair Housing Assoc Charitable Trust from 2004; M Bps' Urban Panel from 2004; M NPIA Independent Adv Panel from 2005; M C of E Pensions Bd from 2006; M CMEAC from 2006; M CUF from 2008
GS 2005–   *Tel:* 0121 550 3407
         Fax: 0121 550 7340
email: bishop.david@cofe-worcester.org.uk

WALKER, Mr Roy Edward, BA, M Ed, PGCE
22 Freckleton Drive Bury BL8 2JA [MANCHESTER] *b* 1943 *educ* Firth Pk Gr Sch Sheff; Ex Univ; Lon Univ; Man Univ; Bradf Univ; *CV* Sen Lect Bolton Inst HE 1972–2000; Lect City Coll Man 2001–03; Coun Stockport MBC 1973–81; Coun Bury MBC from 1982 (Mayor 1997–98); M Greater Man Police Auth
GS 2000–   *Tel:* 0161 764 8809
email: Roy@edwardwalker.freeserve.co.uk

WALKER, Mr Timothy Edward Hanson, CB, MA, D Phil, D Sc (Hon), FIET, FRSA
Church House Great Smith St London SW1P 3AZ [THIRD CHURCH ESTATES COMMISSIONER] *b* 1945 *educ* Tonbridge Sch; Brasenose Coll Ox; *CV* Dir Gen Immigration, Home Office 1995–98; Dep Chair HM Customs and Excise, 1998–2000; Dir Gen Health and Safety Exec 2000–05; Third Ch Estates Commr from 2006; Chair Ch Commrs Bishoprics and Caths, Pastl and Closed Chs Ctees; Non Exec Dir Lon Strategic Health Auth from 2006; Trustee Prostate Cancer Charity from 2006; Chair Accountancy and Actuarial Discipline Bd from 2008; Dir Fin Reporting Coun from 2008; Trustee De Morgan Foundn
         Tel: 020 7898 1624
email: timothy.walker@c-of-e.org.uk

WALLACE, Rt Revd Martin William, BD, AKC
Bishop's House Barton-le-Street Malton YO17 6PL [SUFFRAGAN BISHOP OF SELBY; YORK] *b* 1948 *educ* Varndean Gr Sch for Boys Brighton; Tauntons Sch Southn; K Coll Lon; St Aug Coll Cant; *CV* C Attercliffe Sheff 1971–74; C New Malden 1974–77; V St Mark Forest Gate 1977–93; Chapl Forest Gate Hosp 1977–80; RD Newham 1982–91; P-in-c Em Forest Gate 1985–89; P-in-c All SS Forest Gate 1991–93; Dioc Urban Officer 1991–93; Hon Can Chelmsf Cathl 1989–97; P-in-c St Thos Bradwell and St Lawr 1993–97; Ind Chapl Maldon and Dengie 1993–97; Adn of Colchester 1997–2003; Suff Bp of Selby from 2003   *Tel:* 01653 627191
         Fax: 01653 627193
email: bishselby@clara.net

WALLER, Revd David Arthur,
St Saviour's Vicarage 210 Markhouse Rd London E17 8EP [CHELMSFORD] *b* 1961 *educ* Leeds Univ; *CV* C Aldwick, Chich 1991–95; pt Chapl Bognor Regis War Memorial Hosp 1994–95; TV Crawley 1995–2000; V St Saviour Walthamstow from 2000; M Dioc Bd of Educ from 2000; Asst AD Waltham Forest from 2004
GS 2005–   *Tel:* 020 8520 2036
email: d.a.waller@btinternet.com

WALSALL, Archdeacon of. See JACKSON, Ven Robert William

WANDSWORTH, Archdeacon of. See ROBERTS, Ven Stephen John

WARD, Mr John Selwyn, LLB
Flat 7 18 Holmdale Rd London NW6 1BN [LONDON] *b* 1971 *educ* Abbey Gate Coll Ches; Bris Univ; Katholieke Universiteit Leuven; Coll of Law, Ches; *CV* Solicitor; trainee solicitor, S J Berwin, Lon 1994–96; Stagiaire, Directorate Gen for Competition, Eur Commn 1996–97; asst solicitor, S J Berwin, Brussels 1997; Sen Legal Adv, Office of Fair Trading 1997–2003; Sen Legal Adv, DEFRA 2003–07; M PCC Emm Ch W Hampstead from 1999; M N Camden Dny Syn from 2002; Convener GS Human Sexuality Grp from 2006; Legal Sec to the Advocate Gen for Scotland from 2007
GS 2005–   *Tel:* 07734 080573 (Mobile)
email: jward.anglican@zen.co.uk

WARD, Revd Dr Kevin, MA, Ph D
School of Theology & Religious Studies University of Leeds Leeds LS2 9JT [UNIVERSITIES, NORTHERN] *b* 1947 *educ* Pudsey Gr Sch; Edin Univ; Trin Coll Cam; Bp Tucker Th Coll, Mukono, Uganda; *CV* CMS Miss Ptnr (Tutor Bp Tucker Th Coll, Ch of Uganda) 1975–91; Tutor Qu Coll Birm 1991; Par Min Halifax, Wakef Dio 1991–95; Sen Lect in African Studies, Sch of Th and Relig Studies, Leeds Univ from 1995; NSM St Mich Headingley, Ripon Dio; M Ripon Dioc Wkg Grp in Human Sexuality; Trustee CMS
GS 2003–05; 2005   *Tel:* 0113 343 3641
email: trskw@leeds.ac.uk

WARNER, Mr David Hugh, Dip Ed, GOE
41 Ox Lane Harpenden AL5 4HF [ST ALBANS] *b* 1932 *educ* St Jo Sch Leatherhead; St Mark and St Jo Coll Chelsea; Cam Inst of Educ; St Alb Min Tr Scheme; *CV* Dep Head St Nic Harpenden C of E JMI Sch 1964–71; Head Wigginton C of E JMI Sch 1972–73; Head St Helen's Wheathampstead C of E JMI Sch 1974–93; Rtd
GS 1995–   *Tel and Fax:* 01582 762379
email: dhwarner@tiscali.co.uk

WARNER, Canon Martin Clive, BA, MA, PhD
3 Amen Court London EC4M 7BU [LONDON] *b* 1958 *educ* K Sch Roch; Maidstone Gr Sch; St Chad's

Coll Dur; St Steph Ho; *CV* C St Pet Plymouth 1984–88; TV Resurr Leic 1988–93; P Admin Shrine of Our Lady of Walsingham 1993–2002; Can Pastor, St Paul's Cathl from 2003; Treasurer, St Paul's Cathl from 2008
GS 2005–   *Tel:* 020 7248 2559
     email: treasurer@stpaulscathedral.org.uk

WARRINGTON, Archdeacon of.
See BRADLEY, Ven Peter David Douglas

WARRINGTON, Suffragan Bishop of.
See JENNINGS, Rt Revd David Willfred Michael

WARWICK, Archdeacon of. See PAGET-WILKES, Ven Michael Jocelyn James

WARWICK, Suffragan Bishop of.
See STROYAN, Rt Revd John Ronald Angus

WATSON, Rt Revd Andrew John, MA
16 Coleshill St Sutton Coldfield B72 1SH [SUFFRAGAN BISHOP OF ASTON] *b* 1961 *educ* Win Coll; CCC Cam; Ridley Hall Th Coll; *CV* C St Pet Ipsley 1987–90; C St Jo and St Pet Notting Hill 1990–95; V St Steph E Twickenham 1995–2008; M Bp's Coun; M MPA Coun from 2006; AD Hampton 2003–08; Suffragan Bishop of Aston from 2008
GS 2000–   *Tel:* 0121 426 0448
     Fax: 0121 428 1114
email: bishopofaston@birmingham.anglican.org

WATSON, Ven Ian Leslie Stewart, CTH, GOE
9 Armorial Rd Coventry CV3 6GH [ARCHDEACON OF COVENTRY] *b* 1950 *educ* Nottm High Sch; Britannia R Naval Coll; Army Staff Coll; Joint Warfare Coll; Wycliffe Hall Ox; *CV* C St Andrew Plymouth w St George w St Paul Stonehouse 1981–85; TV Ipsley, Meth Min Matchborough 1985–89; V Woodley 1989–92; TR Woodley 1992–95; Chapl Amsterdam, Helloo and Dan Helder 1995–2001; DDO Benelux 1997–2001; Chief Exec Intercontinental Ch Soc 2001–07; Can Gib Cathl 2001–07 (Emer from 2007); Adn Cov from 2007; Adv on Deliverance Min (Worc) 1987–89; M Meth Syn 1985–89; M Bp's Coun (Eur) 2001–07; M Dioc Syn (Cov) from 2007   *Tel:* 024 7652 1337 (Office)
     024 7641 7750 (Home)
     07714 214790 (Mobile)
     Fax: 024 7652 1330
     email: ian.watson@covcofe.org

WATSON, Ven Sheila Anne, MA, M Phil
29 The Precincts Canterbury CT1 2EP [ARCHDEACON OF CANTERBURY] *b* 1953 *educ* Ayr Acad; St And Univ; Corpus Christi Coll Ox; Coates Hall Th Coll Edin; *CV* Dss St Sav Bridge of Allan and St Jo Alloa, St And 1979–80; Dss St Mary Monkseaton Newc 1980–84; Officer for Miss and Min Kensington Episc Area Lon 1984–87; Hon C St Luke and Ch Ch Chelsea Lon 1987–96; Selection

Sec ABM 1992–93, Senior Selection Sec 1993–96; Adv in CME Salis 1997–2002; Dioc Dir of Min Salis 1998–2002; Hon Can Salis 2000; Adn of Buckingham 2002–07; Adn of Canterbury from 2007   *Tel:* 01227 865238
     Fax: 01227 785209
email: archdeacon@canterbury-cathedral.org

WEBB, Canon Michael John, MA
The Vicarage Howling Lane Alnwick NE66 1DH [NEWCASTLE] *b* 1949 *educ* Eastbourne Coll; Linc Coll Ox; Linc Th Coll; *CV* C Tring 1972–75; C Chipping Barnet 1975–82; Chapl Barnet Gen Hosp 1975–82; P-in-c St Pet Arkley 1978–82; TV Cullercoats St Hilda Marden 1982–89; V H Cross Newc 1989–97; Dir Continuing Rdr Educ 1994–98; MU Chapl 1996–2002; V St Gabr Heaton 1997–2006; RD Newc E 1997–2004; V Alnwick from 2006; past Chair Dioc Children's Cttee; M Dioc Bd of Min and Tr to 1998; M Bp's Coun; Hon Can Newc Cathl from 2002; Chair Ho of Clergy Dioc Syn from 2003; M CDC from 2007
GS 2000–   *Tel:* 01665 602184
     email: michaeljwebb1@btinternet.com

WEBSTER, Canon Glyn Hamilton, SRN
4 Minster Yard York YO1 7JD [YORK] *b* 1951 *educ* Darwen Sec Tech (Gr) Sch; St Jo Coll Dur; *CV* C All SS Huntington York 1977–81; V St Luke Ev York and Sen Chapl York District Hosp 1981–92; Sen Chapl York Health Services NHS Trust 1992–99; Can and Preb York Minster 1994–99; RD York 1997–2004; Can Res and Treas York Minster from 1999; Can Pastor from 2000; Prolocutor of York from 2000; M AC from 2000; Chair Dioc Ho of Clergy; Chan York Minster from 2004; Assoc DDO from 2005; M GS Business Cttee from 2005; M Hosp Chapl Coun from 2005
GS 1995–   *Tel:* 01904 620877 (Home)
     01904 557207 (Office)
     Fax: 01904 557204
     email: chancellor@yorkminster.org

WEBSTER, Canon Martin Duncan, BSc, Dip Th
Rectory Highbridge St Waltham Abbey EN9 1DG [CHELMSFORD] *b* 1952 *educ* Durn Falls Sec Modern Sch; Abbs Cross Tech High Sch; Nottm Univ; Linc Th Coll; *CV* C St Pet and St Mich Thundersley, Chelmsf 1978–81; TV Canvey Island 1981–86; V All SS and St Giles Nazeing 1986–99; AD Harlow 1989–99; NSM Officer 1995–99; TR Waltham Abbey from 1999
GS 2005–   *Tel:* 01992 762115
     email: martin-webster@rectory1952.demon.co.uk

WELBY, Very Revd Justin Portal, MA, BA
Liverpool Cathedral St James' Mount Liverpool L1 7BR [DEAN OF LIVERPOOL] *b* 1956 *educ* Eton Coll; Trin Coll Cam; St Jo Coll Dur; Cranmer Hall; *CV* Mgr Project Finance, Soc Nationale Elf Aquitaine, Paris 1978–83; Treas Elf UK plc, Lon 1983–84; Grp Treas Enterprise Oil plc, Lon 1984–89; C All SS Chilvers Coton and St Mary V, Astley, Nuneaton,

Cov 1992–95; R St Jas Southam and St Mich & All Angels Ufton, Cov 1995–2002; Dir of Internat Min and Res Can Cov Cathl 2002–05; Sub-Dean and Can for Reconciliation Min, Cov Cathl 2005–07; P-in-c H Trin Cov 2007; Dean of Liv from 2007
Tel: 0151 709 6271
Fax: 0151 702 7292
email: dean@liverpoolcathedral.org.uk

WELCH, Ven Stephan John, BA, DipTheol, MTh
98 Dukes Ave Chiswick London W4 2AF [ARCH-DEACON OF MIDDLESEX; LONDON] *b* 1950 *educ* Luton Gr Sch; Luton Sixth Form Coll; Hull Univ; Birm Univ; Heythrop Coll, Lon Univ; Qu Coll Birm; *CV* C Ch Ch Waltham Cross, St Alb 1977–80; P-in-c and V St Mary Reculver & St Bart Herne Bay, Cant 1980–92; V St Mary Hurley & St Jas the Less Stubbings, Ox 1992–2000; V St Pet Hammersmith, Lon 2000–06; AD Hammersmith and Fulham 2001–06; Adn of Middlesex from 2006; Chair Lon Dioc Bd for Schs; M DAC, DBF, Bp's Coun
Tel: 020 8742 8308
07780 704059 (Mobile)
email: archdeacon.middlesex@london.anglican.org

WELLS, Archdeacon of. See SULLIVAN, Ven Nicola Ann

WELLS, Dean of. See CLARKE, Very Revd John Martin

WENT, Rt Revd John Stewart, MA
Bishop's House Church Rd Staverton Cheltenham GL51 0TW [SUFFRAGAN BISHOP OF TEWKESBURY; GLOUCESTER] *b* 1944 *educ* Colchester R Gr Sch; Cam Univ; Oak Hill Th Coll; *CV* C Em Northwood 1969–75; V H Trin Margate 1975–83; Vc Prin Wycliffe Hall Ox 1983–89; Adn of Surrey 1989–96; Bp of Tewkesbury from 1996
GS 1990–95
Tel: 01242 680188
Fax: 01242 680233
email: bshptewk@star.co.uk

WEST CUMBERLAND, Archdeacon of.
(NOT APPOINTED AT TIME OF GOING TO PRESS)

WEST HAM, Archdeacon of. See COCKETT, Ven Elwin Wesley

WESTMINSTER, Dean of. See HALL, Very Revd John Robert

WESTMORLAND AND FURNESS, Archdeacon of. See HOWE, Ven George Alexander

WHARTON, Rt Revd (John) Martin, MA
Bishop's House 29 Moor Rd South Newcastle-upon-Tyne NE3 1PA [BISHOP OF NEWCASTLE] *b* 1944 *educ* Ulverston Gr Sch; Dur Univ; Linacre Coll Ox; Ripon Hall Th Coll; *CV* C St Pet Birm 1972–75; C

St Jo Bapt Croydon 1975–77; Dir of Pastl Studies Ripon Coll Cuddesdon 1977–83; Exec Sec Bd of Min and Tr Bradf Dio 1983–91; Can Res Bradf Cathl and Bp's Officer for Min and Tr 1992; Bp of Kingston-upon-Thames 1992–97; Bp of Newc from 1997
GS 1998–
Tel: 0191 285 2220
Fax: 0191 284 6933
email: bishop@newcastle.anglican.org

WHEATLEY, Rt Revd Peter William, MA
27 Thurlow Rd London NW3 5PP [AREA BISHOP OF EDMONTON; LONDON] *b* 1947 *educ* Ipswich Sch; Qu Coll Ox; Pemb Coll Cam; Mirfield Th Coll; Ripon Hall Th Coll; *CV* C All SS Fulham 1973–78; V H Cross, Cromer St, St Pancras 1978–82; V St Jas W Hampstead, P-in-c St Mary w All So Kilburn 1982–95; Chair Chr Concern for S Africa 1992–95; Dir POT Edmonton Area 1985–95; M BSR Internat Affairs Cttee 1981–96; Adn of Hampstead 1995–99; Bp of Edmonton from 1999
GS 1975–95
Tel: 020 7435 5890
Fax: 020 7435 6049
email: bishop.edmonton@london.anglican.org

WHITBY, Suffragan Bishop of. See LADDS, Rt Revd Robert Sidney

WHITE, Mr David Peter, B Sc, FCMA
Church House Great Smith St London SW1P 3AZ [HEAD OF FINANCIAL POLICY AND PLANNING, ARCHBISHOPS' COUNCIL AND CHURCH COMMISSIONERS] *b* 1966 *educ* Dartford Gr Sch; LSE; *CV* On staff of Church Commissioners since 1990, Head of Fin Planning, Ch Crs 2002–07, Head of Fin Policy and Planning, AC and Ch Crs from 2007.
Tel: 020 7898 1684
Fax: 020 7898 1131
email: david.white@c-of-e.org.uk

WHITE, Rt Revd Frank (Francis), B Sc, Dip Th
4 The Avenue Dallington Northampton NN5 7AN [SUFFRAGAN BISHOP OF BRIXWORTH; PETERBOROUGH] *b* 1949 *educ* St Cuth Gr Sch Newc; Consett Tech Coll; UWIST Cardiff; Univ Coll Cardiff; St Jo Coll Nottm; *CV* Dir Youth Action York 1971–73; Detached Youth Worker Man Catacombs Trust 1973–77; C St Nic Dur 1980–84; C St Mary and St Cuth Chester-le-Street 1984–87; Chapl to Dur HA Hosps 1987–89; V St Jo Ev Birtley 1989–97; RD Chester-le-Street 1993–97; Hon Can Dur Cathl 1997–2002; Adn of Sunderland 1997–2002; Bp of Brixworth from 2002; Hon Can Peterb Cathl from 2002
GS 1987–2000
Tel: 01604 759423
Fax: 01604 750925
email: bishop.brixworth@btinternet.com

WHITE, Canon Bob (Robert Charles), MA, Cert Th
St Mary's Vicarage Fratton Rd Portsmouth PO1 5PA [PORTSMOUTH] *b* 1961 *educ* Portsmouth Gr Sch; Mansfield Coll Ox; St Steph Ho Ox; *CV* C St Jo Forton 1985–88; C St Mark North End with

special responsibility for St Fran Hilsea 1988–92; V St Clare Warren Park 1992–2000; V St Fran Leigh Park 1994–2000; RD Havant 1998–2000; V St Mary Portsea from 2000; M Bp's Coun; Dioc Adv on Urban Ministry; CUF Link Officer GS 1995–2000, 2004–   *Tel:* 023 9282 2687
email: revrcwhite@aol.com

WHITTAM SMITH, Mr Andreas, MA, CBE
154 Campden Hill Rd London W8 7AS [FIRST CHURCH ESTATES COMMISSIONER] *b* 1937 *educ* Birkenhead Sch; Keble Coll Ox; *CV* Founder & Ed 'The Independent' 1986–94; Dir Independent News and Media (UK); Pres Br Bd of Film Classification 1997–2002; Chair Fin Ombudsman Service Ltd 1999–2003; Chair The Children's Mutual; Vc-Pres Nat Coun for One-Parent Families; Chair Ch Commrs Assets Cttee; M Ch Commrs Bd of Govs; M AC from 2002
GS 2002–   *Tel:* 020 7221 8354
email: andreasws@yahoo.co.uk

WHITWORTH, Mrs Ruth,
Green End Melmerby Ripon HG4 5HL [RIPON AND LEEDS] *b* 1952
GS 1990–99; 2005–   *Tel:* 01765 640922

WIGHT, Archdeacon of the Isle of.
See BASTON, Ven Caroline Jane

WILDS, Ven Anthony Ronald, BA
St Mark's House 46A Cambridge Rd Ford Plymouth PL2 1PU [ARCHDEACON OF PLYMOUTH; EXETER] *b* 1943 *educ* Yeovil Gr Sch; Hatfield Coll; Univ of Dur; Bp's Coll Cheshunt; *CV* Asst C Newport Pagnell 1966–72; P-in-c Chipili, Zambia 1972–75; V Chandler's Ford 1975–85; V Andover 1985–97; R Solihull 1997–2001; Adn of Plymouth from 2001
GS 1993–95, 2005–   *Tel:* 01752 793397
07748 167437 (Mobile)
Fax: 01752 793397
email: archdeacon.of.plymouth@
exeter.anglican.org

WILKES, Very Revd Robert Anthony, MA
The Cathedral Colmore Row Birmingham B3 2QB [DEAN OF BIRMINGHAM] *b* 1948 *educ* Pocklington Sch, York; Trin Coll Ox; Wycliffe Hall Ox; *CV* C St Oswald Netherton, Liv 1974–77, V 1977–81; Chapl/Press Officer to Bp of Liv 1981–85; CMS Miss Ptnr, Raiwind Dioc, Pakistan 1985–86; CMS Regional Dir Middle East and Pakistan 1987–98; P-in-c then TR Mossley Hill, Liv 1998–2006; Hon Can Liv 2003–06; Chair Merseyside Coun of Faiths 2005–06; Chair Lifelong Learning, Liv 2001–05; Dean of Birm from 2006; M Birm Dioc Syn and Bp's Coun; Chair Believing in Birm; M Presence and Engagement Task Grp
Tel: 0121 262 1840
Fax: 0121 262 1860
email: dean@birminghamcathedral.com

WILLESDEN, Area Bishop of.
See BROADBENT, Rt Revd Pete (Peter Alan)

WILLIAMS, Sister Anne,
Good Shepherd Clergy House Forest Rd Ford Estate Sunderland SR4 0DX [DURHAM] *b* 1946 *educ* A J Dawson Gr Sch Wellfield; Wilson Carlile Coll of Evang; *CV* Civil Servant 1964–70; Fin Office Admin 1971–93; Communications/PR Support for Third World charity 1993–96; Dep Bursar Dur High Sch for Girls 1996–2002; Vc-Chairman Forward in Faith from 1994; Ch Army Ev in trg from 2003
GS 1990–   *Tel:* 01142 753621 (Home)
07715 178654 (Mobile)
email: sranneca@aol.com

WILLIAMS, Mr Tony (Anthony) James, B Sc, ARCS, FPMI
29 Great Smith St London SW1P 3PS [PENSIONS MANAGER, CHURCH OF ENGLAND PENSIONS BOARD] *b* 1953 *educ* Grove Park Gr Sch Wrexham; Imp Coll Lon Univ; *CV* Post Office 1975–89; Dep Pensions Mgr, C of E Pensions Bd 1989–2003, Pensions Mgr from 2003   *Tel:* 020 7898 1839
Fax: 020 7898 1801
email: tony.williams@c-of-e.org.uk

WILLIAMS, Revd David Michael, MA, Dip LIB, FSA, FRSA
Church House Great Smith St London SW1P 3AZ [CLERK TO THE GENERAL SYNOD AND HEAD OF CENTRAL SECRETARIAT, ARCHBISHOPS' COUNCIL] *b* 1950 *educ* Glyn Gr Sch Ewell; Ex Univ; Lon Univ; *CV* Employed at CCC 1972–73 and 1974–87; Dep Sec CCC 1982–87; Employed by CBF from 1987; Dep Sec CBF 1991–94; Sec CBF 1994–98; Clerk to GS and Dir Central Services, AC 1999–2002; Clerk to GS and Head of Central Secretariat, AC from 2002; JP   *Tel:* 020 7898 1559
Fax: 020 7898 1369
email: david.williams@c-of-e.org.uk

WILLIAMS, Most Revd and Rt Hon Rowan Douglas, MA, D Phil, DD, FBA
Lambeth Palace London SE1 7JU [ARCHBISHOP OF CANTERBURY] *b* 1950 *educ* Dynevor Sec Sch; Ch Coll Cam; Wadham Coll Ox; Coll of Resurrection Mirfield; *CV* Tutor, Westcott Ho Cam 1977–80; Hon C St Geo Chesterton, Ely 1980–83; Lect in Div, Cam 1980–86; Dean and Chapl, Clare Coll Cam 1984–86; Can Theologian, Leic Cathl 1981–92; Can Res, Ch Ch Ox 1986–92; Lady Margaret Prof of Div, Ox 1986–92; Bp of Monmouth 1992–2002; Abp of Wales 2000–02; Abp of Canterbury from 2002
GS 2002–   *Tel:* 020 7898 1200
Fax: 020 7898 1281

WILLIAMS, Mrs Shirley-Ann, LRAM, LLAM, Hon FLAM, Cert Th
2 Katherine's Lane Ridgeway Ottery St Mary EX11 1FB [EXETER] *educ* Barr's Hill Sch Cov; Leeds

Univ; Ex Univ; *CV* Freelance Tutor and Examiner in Speech and Drama, Public Speaking and Communication Skills; Tutor, Coll of Preachers; Broadcaster; M GS Appts Cttee; M GS Ho of Laity Stg Cttee; Chair Dioc Bd of Patr; M Bp's Dioc Coun; M Dioc Syn; M Dioc Coun for Worship and Ministry; M Dioc Liturg Grp; M Dioc Coun for Work with Children and Young People; Lay Chair Ottery Dny Syn; Vc Pres Dioc Syn and Chair Dioc Ho of Laity 1982–2003; Dir/Exec Trustee Rural Com Coun of Devon 1990–2005; MU Trustee, Ex Dioc, rep, Com Coun of Devon; Chair Nat Wkg Pty Ecum Decade of Chs in Solidarity w Women 1995–98; Chair Ch Working for Women Grp 1999–2003; M Review of Diocs, Pastl and Related Measures; M CTE and CTBI; Ed Open Syn Grp magazine
GS 1985–   *Tel and Fax:* 01404 811064
email: shanwill@tinyonline.co.uk

WILLIS, Very Revd Robert Andrew, BA
The Deanery The Precincts Canterbury CT1 2EP [DEAN OF CANTERBURY] *b* 1947 *educ* Kingswood Gr Sch; Warw Univ; Worc Coll Ox; Cuddesdon Th Coll; *CV* C St Chad Shrewsbury 1972–75; V Choral Sarum Cathl 1975–78; TR Tisbury and RD Chalke 1978–89; V Sherborne 1987–92; RD Sherborne 1991–92; Dean of Heref 1992–2001; Dean of Cant from 2001; M PWM Cttee 1990–2001; M Cathls Fabric Commn from 1993; M Liturg Commn 1994–98; Chair Deans' Conf from 1999
GS 1985–92, 1994–   *Tel:* 01227 762862
Fax: 01227 865250
email: dean@canterbury-cathedral.org

WILLMOTT, Rt Revd Trevor, MA, Dip Theol
Bishopswood End 40 Kingswood Rise Four Marks Alton GU34 5BD [SUFFRAGAN BISHOP OF BASINGSTOKE; WINCHESTER] *b* 1950 *educ* Plymouth Coll; St Pet Coll Ox; Fitzw Coll Cam; Westcott Ho Th Coll; *CV* C St Geo Norton 1974–77; Asst Chapl Oslo w Trondheim 1978–79; Chapl Naples w Capri, Bari and Sorrento 1979–83; R Ecton and Wdn Peterb Dioc Retreat Ho 1983–89; DDO and Dir of POT 1986–97; Can Res and Prec Peterb Cathl 1989–97; Adn of Dur and Can Res Dur Cathl 1997–2002; Suff Bp of Basingstoke from 2002; M GS Business Sub-cttee from 2005; M Ho of Bps Stg Cttee from 2005; Trustee Foundn for Chr Leadership; M Rural Bps Panel from 2004; Patr Cross Borders YMCA from 2005; Vc-Chair Hampshire and Isle of Wight Com Foundn; Trustee St Michael's Coll, Llandaff; Visitor to the Sisters of Bethany
GS 2000–   *Tel:* 01420 562925
Fax: 01420 561251
email: trevor.willmott@dial.pipex.com

WILSON, Rt Revd Alan Thomas Lawrence, MA, D Phil
Sheridan Grimms Hill Great Missenden HP16 9BG [AREA BISHOP OF BUCKINGHAM; OXFORD] *b* 1955 *educ* St Jo Coll Cam; Ball Col Ox; Wycliffe Hall Ox; *CV* Hon C Eynsham, Ox 1979–81, C 1981–82; C Caversham and Mapledurham 1982–89; V St Jo Caversham 1989–92; R Sandhurst 1992–2003; RD Sonning 1998–2003; Area Bp of Buckingham from 2003
     Tel: 01494 862173
07525 655756 (Mobile)
Fax: 01494 890508
email: bishopbucks@oxford.anglican.org / alan.wilson49@btopenworld.com

WILSON, Mr John,
49 Oakhurst Lichfield WS14 9AL [LICHFIELD] *CV* With Charity Support Services, supporting charity and voluntary sector
GS 2005–   *Tel:* 01543 268678
Fax: 01543 411685
email: charity.services@btclick.com

WILSON-RUDD, Miss Fay (Felicity),
3 Old School Place North Grove Wells BA5 2TD [BATH AND WELLS] *b* 1941 *educ* Filton High Sch; *CV* Asst Stewardship Adv St Alb Dio 1981–84; Resources Adv B & W 1984–2001; pt Chapl Co-ord Somerset NHS Ptnrship and Soc Care Trust from 1999
GS 1993–   *Tel and Fax:* 01749 677286 (Home)
07712 581903 (Mobile)
email: faywilsonrudd@msn.com

WILTS, Archdeacon of. See WRAW, Ven John Michael

WILTSHIRE, Mrs Catherine Lesley, BA, MA, PGCE, NPQH, Dip Th
Lake House North Rd Southwold IP18 6BH [ST EDMUNDSBURY AND IPSWICH] *b* 1958 *educ* Sir Jo Leman High Sch, Beccles; Kent Univ; Ch Ch Coll Cant; UEA; *CV* Hd of RE, Aylesham Secdry Sch, Dover 1980–85; RSA Courses Co-ord, Geoffrey Chaucer Sch, Cant 1985–88; Hd of Humanities, Thurleston High Sch, Ips 1988–90; sen tchr, Benjamin Britten High Schl, Lowestoft 1990–96; Dep Hd, Bungay High Sch from 1996; acting Hd Tchr, Orwell High Sch, Felixstowe 2004
GS 2005–   *Tel:* 01502 724051 (Home)

WINCHESTER, Archdeacon of. (NOT APPOINTED AT TIME OF GOING TO PRESS)

WINCHESTER, Bishop of. See SCOTT-JOYNT, Rt Revd Michael Charles

WINCHESTER, Dean of. See ATWELL, Very Revd James Edgar

WINDSOR, Dean of. See CONNER, Rt Revd David John

WINSTANLEY, Rt Revd Alan Leslie, B Th
Vicarage Preston Rd Whittle-le-Woods Chorley PR6 7PS [HONORARY ASSISTANT BISHOP OF BLACKBURN] *b* 1949 *educ* Leigh Boys' Gr Sch, Lancs; St Jo

Coll Nottm; *CV* C St Andr Livesey, Blackb 1972–75; C St Mary Gt Sankey Liv 1975–78; V Penketh Liv 1978–81; SAMS Miss Lima, Peru 1982–85, Arequipa 1986–87; Bp of Peru and Bolivia 1988–93; V Eastham and Hon Asst Bp of Chester 1994–2003; V St Jo Ev, Whittle-le-Woods and Hon Asst Bp of Blackburn from 2003

Tel and Fax: 01257 241291
email: bpalan.winstanley@ic24.net

WINTER, Revd Dr Dagmar, Dr Theol
Vicarage Kirkwhelpington Newcastle upon Tyne NE19 2RT [NEWCASTLE] *b* 1963 *educ* Gesamtschule Oberursel; Erlangen Univ; Aberd Univ; Heidelberg Univ; Herborn Th Coll; *CV* C St Mark Bromley 1996–99; Assoc V and Dny Trg Officer Hexham Abbey 1999–2006; P-in-c Kirkwhelpington, Kirkharle, Kirkheaton and Cambo and Dioc Officer for Rural Affairs from 2006
GS 2005– *Tel:*

WISBECH, Archdeacon of, [NOT APPOINTED AT TIME OF GOING TO PRESS],

WOLVERHAMPTON, Area Bishop of.
See GREGORY, Rt Revd Clive Malcolm

WOLVERSON, Revd Marc Ali Morad, BA, Dip Min
Vicarage 85 Buxton Rd High Lane Stockport SK6 8DS [CHESTER] *b* 1968 *educ* St Louis Country Day Sch, USA; Loyola Univ, USA; Kansas Univ, USA; Ripon Coll Cuddesdon; *CV* C St Mary Nantwich 1996–99; Asst R and sch Chapl, St Luke's Episcopal Ch and Sch, Baton Rouge, Louisiana 1999–2000; Assoc V St Mich and All Angels Bramhall 2000–04; V St Thos High Lane from 2004; M Ches Dioc Syn; Dioc Spiritual Dir, Cursillo
GS 2005– *Tel:* 01663 762627
email: frmarc@onetel.com

WOOLWICH, Area Bishop of. See CHESSUN, Rt Revd Christopher Thomas James

WORCESTER, Archdeacon of.
See MORRIS, Ven Roger Anthony Brett

WORCESTER, Bishop of. See INGE, Rt Revd Dr John Geoffrey

WORCESTER, Dean of. See ATKINSON, Very Revd Peter Gordon

WORSLEY, Revd Ruth Elizabeth, BA, MA, LTh
St Stephen's Vicarage 18 Russell Rd Forest Fields Nottingham NG7 6HB [SOUTHWELL AND NOTTINGHAM] *b* 1962 *educ* Bp Wand C of E Comp, Sunbury-on-Thames; Man Univ; St Jo Coll Nottm; *CV* Trainee nurse 1985–87; Spouse Chapl, St Jo Coll Nottm 1993–95; C St Steph w. St Paul Hyson Green and Forest Fields 1996–2001, P-in-c

from 2001; Bp's Insp of Colls and Courses; M Urban Congress dioc wkg pty
GS 2004– *Tel:* 0115 978 7473
0115 924 9700
email: ruthworsley@aol.com

WRAW, Ven John Michael, BA
Southbroom House London Rd Devizes SN10 1LT [ARCHDEACON OF WILTS; SALISBURY] *b* 1959 *educ* K Sch Chester; Lincoln Coll Ox; Fitzwilliam Coll Cam; Ridley Hall Cam; *CV* C St Pet Bromyard, Heref 1985–88; TV Sheff Manor Team 1988–92; V Clifton St Jas, Sheff 1992–2001; P-in-c Wickersley St Alb, Sheff 2001–04; Adn of Wilts from 2004
Tel: 01380 729808
Fax: 01380 738096
email: adwilts@salisbury.anglican.org

WRIGHT, Rt Revd Dr (Nicholas) Thomas, MA, D Phil, DD
Auckland Castle Bishop Auckland DL14 7NR [BISHOP OF DURHAM] *b* 1948 *educ* Sedbergh; Ex Coll Ox; Wycliffe Hall; *CV* Jun Rsch Fell, Merton Coll Ox, College Tutor in theol, Jun Chapl, acting Lect in theol 1975–78; Fell and Chapl, Downing Coll Cam and Coll Tutor in theol 1978–81; Asst Prof of NT Language and Literature, McGill Univ Montreal and Hon Prof, Montreal Dioc Theol Coll 1981–86; Lect in NT Studies, Ox Univ and Fell, Tutor and Chapl, Worcester Coll Ox 1986–93; Dean of Lichfield 1994–99; Can Westminster and SPCK Rsch Fell 2000–03; Bp of Durham from 2003
GS 2003– *Tel:* 01388 602576
Fax: 01388 605264
email: bishop@bishopdunelm.co.uk

WRIGHT, Ven Paul, BD, M Th, AKC
The Archdeaconry The Glebe Chislehurst BR7 5PX [ARCHDEACON OF BROMLEY AND BEXLEY; ROCHESTER] *b* 1954 *educ* Crayford Sch; K Coll Lon; Heythrop Coll Lon; Ripon Coll, Cuddesdon; *CV* C St Geo Beckenham, Roch 1979–83; C St Mary w St Matthias & St Jo, S'wark 1983–85; Chapl Ch Sch Richmond, S'wark 1983–85; V St Aug Gillingham, Roch 1985–90; R St Paulinus Crayford, Roch 1990–99; RD Erith 1993–97; Hon Can Roch Cathl 1998–2003; V St Jo Evang Sidcup, Roch 1999–2003; Adn of Bromley and Bexley from 2003; M Bp's Coun; M Dioc Bd of Patr; M Eccl Law Soc; Bp's Insp of Theol Colls; Chair Adv Bd for Miss and Unity *Tel:* 020 8467 8743
07985 902601 (Mobile)
Fax: 020 8467 8743
email: archdeacon.bromley@
rochester.anglican.org

WYNNE, Mrs Alison,
88 Balcarres Rd Leyland PR25 3ED [BLACKBURN] *b* 1961 *educ* Pleckgate High Sch, Blackb; *CV* Wages clerk, MOD 1979–83; Computer Programmer, MOD 1983–86; Computer Applications Programmer, Lancs Constabulary 1986–87; IT

Systems Programmer, Lancs Constabulary 1987–89; Chr outreach worker from 2001
GS 2005– *Tel:* 01772 454209
07719 727527 (Mobile)
email: alison@wynne.org.uk

WYTHE, Mr John Michael, BSc, FRICS
Woodpeckers Ashwood Rd Woking GU22 7JN [CHURCH COMMISSIONER] *b* 1956 *educ* Woking Gr Sch for Boys; Reading Univ; *CV* Dir Prudential Property Investment Mgrs; Hd of Life and Internat Funds; Ch Commr from 2007; M Assets Cttee *Tel:* 020 7548 6574
email: john.wythe@prupim.com

YEOMAN, Revd Ruth Jane, MA, BSc, MSc
Vicarage 12 Fairfax Gardens Menston Ilkley LS29 6ET [BRADFORD] *b* 1960 *educ* Nottm Bluecoat Sch; Sheff Univ; Ripon Coll Cuddesdon; *CV* C St Pet and St Paul Coleshill w. Maxstoke, Birm 1991–95; Asst P St Phil and St Jas Hodge Hill and Adv for Children's Work, Birm Dioc 1995–2000; Houseleader, L'Arch Lambeth Com 2001–02; V St Jo Divine Menston w. Woodhead from 2003
GS 2005– *Tel:* 01943 877739
07752 912646 (Mobile)
email: ruthjyeoman@hotmail.com

YORK, Archbishop of. See SENTAMU, Most Revd and Rt Hon Dr John Tucker Mugabi

YORK, Archdeacon of. See SEED, Ven Richard Murray Crosland

YORK, Dean of. See JONES, Very Revd Keith Brynmor

YOUNG, Rt Revd Clive, BA
28 Westerfield Rd Ipswich IP4 2UJ [SUFFRAGAN BISHOP OF DUNWICH; ST EDMUNDSBURY AND IPSWICH] *b* 1948 *educ* K Edw VI Gr Sch Chelmsf; Dur Univ; Ridley Hall Cam; *CV* C Neasden cum Kingsbury 1972–75; C St Paul Hammersmith 1975–79; P-in-c St Paul w St Steph Old Ford 1979–82; V 1982–92; AD Tower Hamlets 1988–92; Adn of Hackney 1992–99; V St Andr Holborn 1992–99; Bp of Dunwich from 1999 *Tel:* 01473 222276
Fax: 01473 210303
email: bishop.clive@stedmundsbury.anglican.org

INDEX

Index

Who does Christ's work in the Holy Land today?

Bible*Lands* is a Christian agency serving the poor, vulnerable and disadvantaged in the lands of the Bible – regardless of their faith or nationality.

Our vision is to enable and resource local Christian partners working in the areas of **education, health** and **community development**.

For further information, resources or to invite a guest speaker, please contact us on:

01494 897950
www.biblelands.org.uk

SHARPEN
YOUR FOCUS

Ministerial development is a life-long process. At Spurgeon's College you can sharpen your skills and refocus your energy. Our unique MTh in Preaching, in conjunction with the College of Preachers, will help improve your existing skills, assist you to reflect on your ministry and engage with current trends.

For details of our postgraduate courses visit **www.spurgeons.ac.uk**

SPURGEON'S COLLEGE
PREPARING CHRISTIANS
FOR MISSION AND MINISTRY

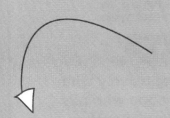
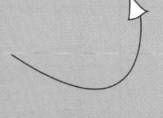

The Church and Community Fund

The CCF exists to support the mission of the Church of England. We awarded over £580,000 to church and community projects in 2007.

- We welcome imaginative applications from projects which meet needs and build bridges between the Church and the community.
- We also fund some central functions of the Church such as training for ministry.

We need your help to extend our mission.

- Your gift could help to employ a local youth worker, renovate an old church hall for use as a community centre, provide hot meals for the homeless in a church room and much more!
- Please contact us today to find out how to make a donation or legacy.
- Please do also contact us to find out if we can help your project.

The Church and Community Fund, Church House,
Great Smith St, London SW1P 3AZ;
020 7898 1767; ccf@c-of-e.org.uk.
Our web address: www.churchandcommunityfund.org.uk

The CCF is an excepted charity under the trusteeship of the Central Board of Finance of the Church of England, whose registered charity number is 248711.

Church and Community Fund, previously called the Central Church Fund (name changed in June 2006).

587

Youth for Christ

taking good news relevantly to every young person in britain

British Youth for Christ (YFC) is a national Christian charity that was founded by Billy Graham in 1946. Working with over 300,000 young people each month, we draw along side teens from every background and culture in Britain. Our staff and local volunteers specialise in working with unchurched youth: communicating and demonstrating the Christian faith.

Local Centres

Through 68 Local Centres we tackle the real issues facing youth today, such as: family breakdown, binge drinking, bullying and self-worth. We run drop-in youth clubs, school lessons, social-action projects and detached youth work on the streets.

Mission Teams

Our unique approach to mission is to reach *youth with youth.* Through our year-out programme we teach young people how to use their individual gifts to share their faith with their peers, placing volunteers in teams around Britain.

Marginalised, Socially Excluded Youth

Through 'Reflex' our prison ministry, we invest in young people on the fringe of society, building their self-esteem with accredited training and skills. We also work with marginalised 'at risk' young people. YFC's 'Urban Skillz' community workshops teach music production, DJ-ing, MC-ing, and Rapping - challenging negative social trends.

Resources

YFC serves local churches and schools by providing all the necessary resources and support for effective Christian youth work - from evangelism through to discipleship. YFC's school resources; 'the Crux' and 'exploRE', communicate Christianity in an engaging and relevant way, allowing unchurched young people to discover the Christian faith.

Youth for Christ, Coombswood Way, Halesowen, West Midlands, B62 8BH
t: 0121 502 9620
e: yfc@yfc.co.uk
Visit us online at: www.yfc.co.uk

British Youth for Christ Registered Charity 263446, SC039297

Youth for Christ
taking good news relevantly to every young person in britain

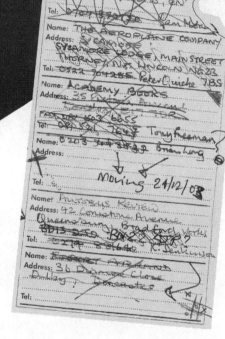